ENCYCLOPEDIA OF
WORLD WRITERS
1800 TO THE PRESENT

ENCYCLOPEDIA OF WORLD WRITERS 1800 TO THE PRESENT

Marie Josephine Diamond

GENERAL EDITOR
Department of Comparative English
Rutgers University

Maria DiBattista

ADVISER TO THE FIRST EDITION
Department of English
Princeton University

Julian Wolfreys

ADVISER TO THE FIRST EDITION
Department of English
Loughborough University

Facts On File
An Infobase Learning Company

Encyclopedia of World Writers, 1800 to the Present

Facts On File, Inc.
An Imprint of Infobase Learning
132 West 31st Street
New York NY 10001

Library of Congress Cataloging-in-Publication Data

Diamond, Marie Josephine.
  Encyclopedia of world writers, 1800 to the present / Marie Josephine Diamond.
      p. cm.
  Includes bibliographical references and index.
  ISBN 978-0-8160-8204-9 (alk. paper)
  1. Authors—20th century—Bio-bibliography—Dictionaries. 2. Authors—19th century—
Bio-bibliography—Dictionaries. I. Title.
  PN451.D525 2011
  809'. 04—dc22
  [B]   2010038158

Facts On File books are available at special discounts when purchased in bulk quantities for businesses, associations, institutions, or sales promotions. Please call our Special Sales Department in New York at (212) 967-8800 or (800) 322-8755.

You can find Facts On File on the World Wide Web at http://www.infobaselearning.com.

Excerpts included herewith have been reprinted by permission of the copyright holders; the author has made every effort to contact copyright holders. The publishers will be glad to rectify, in future editions, any errors or omissions brought to their notice.

Text design by Rachel L. Berlin
Composition by Publication Services, Inc.
Cover printed by Yurchak Printing, Inc., Landisville, Pa.
Book printed and bound by Yurchak Printing, Inc., Landisville, Pa.
Date printed: July 2011
Printed in the United States of America

10 9 8 7 6 5 4 3 2 1

This book is printed on acid-free paper.

CONTENTS

PREFACE

The *Encyclopedia of World Writers, 1800 to the Present* is an engaging survey of the changing map of world literature during the past 200 years, covering the world outside Great Britain, Ireland, and the United States. (British writers are covered in the *Encyclopedia of British Writers, 1800 to Present,* Facts On File, 2009.) Our survey begins at the turn of the 19th century, a time of great change in Europe, catalyzed by the French Revolution of 1789 and the expansion of colonialism.

Literature in the 19th century, especially the dissemination of the novel, reflects the profound social, economic, and political changes that were taking place throughout Europe. By the end of the century, when colonialism had changed the map of the world through occupation and trade, Western literary movements and forms had deeply affected the ancient and traditional literatures of Asia and the Middle East and the post-Conquest literatures of South America and had marginalized the oral traditions of African and indigenous peoples.

The entries of the 19th century include the well-known European figures who have dominated the Western canon; lesser-known European writers who, for many reasons, have been rediscovered; and Asian, Latin American, and African writers or storytellers celebrated in their own cultures but often unfamiliar to the American reader. Entries include descriptions of major European literary movements, such as ROMANTICISM, REALISM, and SYMBOLISM, and their deployment and transformation, especially toward the end of the century, in the very different cultural contexts of Asia, Africa, the Middle East, and Latin America. These entries also show both the continuation and transformation of traditional genres and the growing importance of the novel in the context of modernization.

The entries of the 20th and 21st centuries include avant-garde, modernist, social realist, postmodernist, postcolonial, and minority writers (among others), responding to the dramatic changes of the last 100 years. These include profound social upheavals and technological transformations, such as the Russian Revolution of 1917, world wars, fascism, nuclear threats, genocide, independence and women's movements, terrorism, the Internet revolution, and economic globalization. Particularly after World War II, national independence movements and changing patterns of migration created new literatures and genres, challenging the established European canon and reviving cultural traditions. Similarly, since the 1970s and 1980s, new spaces have opened up in the study of world literature, particularly for works by marginalized women and indigenous writers. With the creation of the European Union and the collapse of the Soviet Union, European literature itself has been reconfigured by new expressions of national identity, from the Balkans among other places, and by new immigrant and multicultural literatures, particularly from western and southern Europe. The world has changed dramatically, and writers have responded to those changes, a shift reflected in the encyclopedia's newest entries.

Directed to young scholars in high school and colleges, the entries encourage students to investigate further writers who, for the most part, have lived lives of passionate engagement with their craft and with the compelling, often disturbing, historical events of their time. They include biographical information, descriptions of major works, cross-referencing, and suggestions for further reading and research. Most of the works mentioned have been translated into English. Where practical, titles are also provided in the original language. (Given the vast number of languages and alphabets involved, this is not always feasible or useful.) Definitions of traditions

and movements from a wide variety of literatures make it possible for the American student to situate writers within the context of their literary cultures. A general bibliography suggests wider vistas for exploration.

This encyclopedia opens up worlds. It reveals how literature has been and continues to be not only a source of aesthetic pleasure and self-knowledge but also a means of responding to tyranny and injustice, to the alienation or suppression of identity, and to the loss of marginalized or indigenous cultures. For many writers in the last century, literature has been more than a quest for pleasure, success, or escape from the everyday. It has often been a matter of life and death.

We hope that for young researchers coming of age in the 21st century, a time of dramatic change on an international scale, the encyclopedia will be many things: an introduction to literary traditions from a wide diversity of cultures, an introduction to aesthetic experience and exploration in the global context, and an introduction to the extraordinary writers who have lived through and responded in their works to the social and political challenges of the past two centuries.

NOTE TO THE NEW EDITION

It has become clear over the last decade that national borders are being redefined, and, for diverse economic and political reasons, migrations across borders and between continents have increased. Consequently, the concept of stable "national" literatures has changed, and it is frequently difficult to situate writers in a single national context. In fact, the diasporic or exiled writer with two or more languages and identities has become a common phenomenon in the contemporary literary landscape. Thus, the study of literature in a world context has become increasingly relevant.

With the changing landscape of world literatures in mind, this second edition of the *Encyclopedia of World Writers, 1800 to the Present* has been significantly supplemented and updated to improve its effectiveness for American students of literature. Not only have a number of Western European writers been added, particularly those who now appear more frequently in the high school and college curricula, but we also have included more writers from Eastern Europe and the Balkans, many of whom have gained reputations over the last decade since the emergence and redefini-

tion of national literatures following the disintegration of the former Soviet Union. Also, from the proliferation of new writers from Latin America, Canada, Africa, the Caribbean, Asia, the Middle East, and Australasia, we have selected the most significant in terms of their influence and positive critical reception, although we have had to exclude those who are still unavailable in translation to the English-speaking reader.

Another significant improvement in this edition is the expansion of critical analyses of representative texts by major authors. The analyses provide students and all readers with clear and succinct examples of how to situate an author's writing in relation to his or her life and literary history as well as how to read and evaluate specific linguistic characteristics and innovations.

We hope that the improvements and additions to the new edition of the *Encyclopedia of World Writers, 1800 to the Present* will open up more exciting new worlds for exploration.

—Marie Josephine Diamond
General Editor

INTRODUCTION

World literature is as diverse as it is vast. From the turn of the 19th century to the present, different cultures and national literatures have followed unique and specific forms of development and change. However, it is possible to discern some major trends and patterns to suggest a way for American readers in particular to orient themselves among the more than 500 writers, literatures, and literary movements presented here.

The mapping of the world has undergone many transformations since the beginning of the 19th century, and it continues to be revised at an accelerated rate. This volume begins with literatures at the turn of the 19th century, a time of great change. The French Revolution of 1789 marked a watershed in Europe. Subsequently, many countries of the world were affected by both the ideals of the European Enlightenment and the expansion of colonialism.

In the modern age, beginning with the colonization of the Americas, countries of Western Europe—Spain, Portugal, France, the Netherlands, and England—have been the dominant colonial nations. They have exported their languages and cultures throughout the Americas, Africa, Asia, and the Pacific through conquest and occupation or, as in the case of China and Japan in the latter half of the 19th century, through trade wars and the imposition of trade agreements. During the last 200 years, there have been very few, if any, nations that have not been affected in one way or another by the cultures and values of Western Europe and, especially since World War II (1939–45), of the United States. With the breakdown of European colonialism after 1945, the liberation from Western influences has been a rallying cry for contemporary literary movements in many parts of the world. The map of the world in the 21st century has already begun to present a different, as yet undefined, literary landscape.

THE NINETEENTH CENTURY

In Europe, the values of the Enlightenment—freedom, scientific progress, the importance of the individual—expressed the needs of the rising middle class and the growing capitalist economy. These ideas challenged the principles of inherited power and the rule of an aristocratic and ecclesiastical elite traditionally dependent on ownership and exploitation of the land. They found political expression in the French Revolution of 1789. The Revolution was greeted as a new dawn by writers, musicians, and artists throughout Europe and by oppressed peoples, including many women.

However, as the Revolution turned into the Terror and was followed by the dictatorial reign of Napoléon—who extended French dominion through much of Europe, and led an incursion into Russia and a venture into Egypt—many writers and artists lost faith in the future of the revolutionary ideal.

COLONIAL ENCOUNTERS

Colonialism flourished in the 19th century through a combination of new ideas and political projects. The confidence of Europeans in the superiority of their civilization reached its height as scientific discoveries produced new technologies and industrialization promised ever-expanding markets. It seemed an obvious good to impose European values on the rest of the world. Yet at the same time science was undermining religious faith, and people became aware of what was lost when cities and factories obliterated the old ways of life. Slaves, women, and the colonized discovered that people's rights as promised by the French Revolution did not apply to them. Although Haiti (Saint-Domingue) won its independence from France in 1802, slavery continued in the French Caribbean until 1848, and France and England continued to fight for domination over India, Africa, and the Caribbean. Nevertheless, Enlightenment ideals continued to both support and challenge the colonial enterprise of trade and conquest.

Latin America

Financed by kings and queens vying for power and national prestige, European colonialism from the 16th century on had justified itself in the name of Christianity and civilization. Encountering people with predominantly oral cultures and animist beliefs, the first colonists of what now constitutes Latin America imposed their religion and assimilated or suppressed local cultural forms and languages, which they considered to be inferior. In the 19th century, colonialism in Latin America produced a unique pattern of cultural development. By that time, most countries were controlled by powerful elites who fought for their independence from Spain and Portugal. The longing for freedom was expressed in literature. Fernandez de Lizardi (1776–1827), Mexico's first novelist, for example, satirized corrupt colonial officials and contributed to the movement for independence. Andrés Bello (1781–1865) of Venezuela argued that Latin America would be independent only when it had freed itself from forms of government modeled on those of Europe. On the other hand, Domingo F. Sarmiento (1811–88) of Argentina wished to eradicate traces of both Native and Spanish cultures and replace them with northern European economic and cultural models. By the end of the century, most of Latin America had undergone rapid modernization with varying consequences and had produced varied, often cosmopolitan, literatures.

Africa

When Europe colonized Africa, it encountered hundreds of different languages and diverse traditions. The north and northwest had long been influenced by Islamic and Arabic written culture, and East Africa, open to trade with Indonesia and India, had a rich multicultural history. Most of this vast continent had a rich oral tradition that included epics, legends, proverbs, genealogies, and praise poetry. When colonial schools were set up to produce local administrators and impose Western cultures, African languages were marginalized, but oral genres, many of which were then written down, continued to modify and contest imported European literary forms and ideas.

South Asia

European confrontations with ancient civilizations and literatures in Asia are complex in a different way. The establishment of the East India Company by the English, which took place in 1600, was the beginning of the colonization of India and the imposition of British cultural institutions. Until 1835, when English became the common language of instruction, Sanskrit, Arabic, and Persian were the dominant official languages. The British gave their preference to the Sanskrit tradition, with its

Indo-European associations, and to Hindu culture, whose caste system approximated their own class system. Sanskrit epics, such as the *Ramayana* and the *Mahabarata,* as well as Hindu spiritual texts, were translated by and also influenced many 19th-century European writers. However, the dozens of languages and cultures of the Indian subcontinent and Sri Lanka withstood assimilation and continued their own traditional forms of epic, drama, and lyrical and devotional poetry.

The introduction of English instruction coincided with the widespread dissemination of printing, and English literature and European literary forms were introduced to the subcontinent and a new reading public. With English as the official language, works in languages such as Urdu, Tamil, Bengali, Telegu, and Kannada were translated into English, giving South Asians easier access to each other's literatures. The European novel gave new direction to South Asian literature, but it also was transformed and enriched by South Asian traditions of the epic and mythology as well as by specific cultural dynamics. RABINDRANATH TAGORE, the great Bengali nationalist, was awarded the Nobel Prize in literature in 1913.

East Asia

Beginning with the Opium War (1840–42), China was exposed to Western influences when it was forcefully brought into the orbit of European financial interests. Western and Japanese incursions—including the sacking of Beijing in 1860, the Sino-Japanese War (1894–95), and the Boxer Rebellion (1900–01)—contributed to a critique of Chinese conservatism, Confucianism, and the power of the scholarly literati. In 1911, a thousand years of imperial rule came to an end with the establishment of the republic. May 4, 1919, became famous for a new realist literary movement (*see* REALISM) that broke with the past and turned toward the West for inspiration. The language of the common people, as opposed to the scholarly language of the imperial bureaucrats, was increasingly used as the language of literature, and, under the influence of countless translations from

European writers, particularly French, English, and Russian, the novel became popular. Such writers as HU SHI and LU XUN turned away from traditional forms and looked to Western novels for inspiration and renewal.

Japan is famous for its distinctive forms of poetry, such as the complex linked forms of the *renga,* which developed into the haiku, and its indigenous forms of drama, such as the No and Kabuki. It also has a long narrative tradition and its own forms of the novel, the most famous of which is probably the classic *Tale of Genji* (ca. A.D. 1000) by Lady Murasaki. Japan did not open up to the West until it was forced to by the United States and Commodore Perry's warships in 1853. This event had a profound effect on Japanese literature. Japanese translations of European and Russian novels appeared and influenced new expressions of the Japanese novel, as in the works of NATSUME SŌSEKI. [Chinese, Japanese, Korean, and Vietnamese personal names are rendered in traditional East Asian order, with surnames followed by given names.]

The Middle East

Middle Eastern literature—Arabic, Persian, and Turkish—was dominated from its pre-Islamic beginnings by poetry, written by both men and women. With the spread of Islam, the Qur'an became a literary and aesthetic model for Muslim writers. In the 19th century, Europeans began to look to the Middle East for literary inspiration: French and English translations of *The Thousand and One Nights,* a collection of stories from Persia with Indian influences, had a profound impact on the Western imagination.

At the same time, the growing imperial powers of Europe undermined the declining Ottoman Empire, which finally collapsed after World War I, and introduced to the Middle East Western liberal values such as equal rights and freedom of trade and travel, as well as new genres such as the novel. Modern and secular ideas were contentious from the beginning: European aesthetics and progressive ideas threatened traditional and national literary forms and were associated with political domination.

Australasia

An Aboriginal culture had existed in Australia for at least 50,000 years before the arrival of the Europeans. It included songs, myths, and stories, which were orally transmitted. White settlement of Australia began in 1788 with the establishment of penal colonies by the British. Nineteenth-century Australian literature, produced both by convicts and free settlers, followed English models while exploring new experiences of life in the bush and outback. At the same time, Aboriginal culture was threatened with extinction. It was not until 1901, when Australia won its independence, that a strong national literature emerged.

The first British missionary arrived in New Zealand in 1801, and the colony was formalized in 1841. The Treaty of Waitangi (1840) established an uneasy peace between the indigenous Maoris and the colonizers, but the oral language and culture of the Aboriginal people inevitably declined. British models dominated 19th-century New Zealand literature.

EUROPEAN ROMANTICISM AND ITS DISCONTENTS

The literary movement that best expresses the aspirations, contradictions, and disappointments of the turn of the 19th century is romanticism. Romanticism began in Germany with writers such as GOETHE, SCHILLER, and HÖLDERLIN. It was influenced by Jean-Jacques Rousseau, the critic of the inequities of civilization, in his fiction and essays and by Immanuel Kant's ideas about the beautiful and sublime. His *Critique of Judgment* (1790) had a profound effect on romantic aesthetics. The German mystical and idealistic tradition competed with the more rational and scientific ideals of French thinkers and influenced writers throughout Europe. GERMAINE DE STAËL, the Swiss/French intellectual and writer who introduced German literature and philosophy into France at the beginning of the 19th century, held

that a nation's literature is reflective of its forms of government and its historical moment. Literature thus provides insight into national identity.

Because classical ideals were embedded in oppressive cultural institutions, romantic writers often turned to the myths and oral traditions of the Middle Ages, perpetuated in the folktales of the people, for inspiration and a redefinition of nationhood. Oral traditions seemed to offer a social cohesion missing in a society that was fragmented by revolution and strife. Folktales by German writers such as BENEDIKTE NAUBERT and the brothers GRIMM were very popular. At the same time, the romantic love of freedom inspired subjugated nations, such as Greece, which was long dominated by the Turks, to struggle for liberation and to revive their ancient cultural heritage. In both Germany and France, the theater of such dramatists as Schiller and HUGO threw off classical constraints and advocated passion and rebellion in the name of social justice.

Inspired by Enlightenment ideals of freedom, most romantic writers were critical of imperialism and slavery, but they were also fascinated by the exotic, especially the culture of the Orient. Even before the French Revolution, romantic writers, such as Goethe, were interested in the spiritual literature of India. After the Revolution, the development of romanticism coincided with a new phase of colonial expansion in the Middle East and North Africa. The Orient, often geographically vague and exoticized, came to represent the possibility of passion and escape from an increasingly utilitarian and secular world dominated by the pursuit of money and power. It provided not only luxury goods and cheap labor but also, in varying forms, a vision of sensuous fulfillment and respite from the pursuit of profits. Parallel to romantic exoticism was the romantic interest in nature as a source of inspiration. Many elements of the romantic movement were to reappear at the end of the century in countries outside Europe, including China and Latin America, as evidenced by the works of the Brazilian ANTONIO GONÇALVES

DIAS, who wrote about nativist issues, that is, the relation between indigenous peoples and the land.

A major theme of romantic writers, for example BALZAC and STENDHAL, is the struggle for survival of the sensibilities of the artist in a new world of industrialization, material values, and the brutal struggle for success. The defeat of romantic ideals, which sought refuge in an idealized imagination, is often embodied in the novel. The fate of the romantic hero who refuses the material values of the new bourgeois world is often suicide or madness.

THE NOVEL

Just as colonialism was facilitated in the 19th century by rapid advances in technology, engineering, and industrialization, improvements in printing techniques permitted cheaper and easier publication of books. At the same time, the growth of the urban population and extension of education and literacy provided a growing readership. The serialized novel, one of the great innovations of 19th-century European literature, established this literary form, variously defined by movements such as realism and NATURALISM, as the dominant genre. It became the place for discussion of every important social issue. Filled with energy and movement, novels by Stendhal, Balzac, FLAUBERT, and ZOLA place an individual within the social maelstrom and follow his or her development or destruction. The effects of modern Western values are also tragically explored in the Russian novels of DOSTOYEVSKY and TOLSTOY, both affected by and resistant to Westernization, who develop an alternative to modernity through their different syntheses of their own culture and interpretations of Christianity.

The novel was one of the major exports of Western culture to other parts of the world. Its effects were felt, especially toward the end of the 19th century, in China, Japan, India, and the Middle East.

DECADENCE

By the late 19th century, the long advance of European modernity was accelerated by developments in technology and capital-driven imperialism. By 1914, the reach of Western civilization throughout the world was unprecedented. Although 19th-century colonialism had reached its heights in terms of appropriated land and affected cultures, the system at home was under pressure, and its crisis is evident in European literature. The great Scandinavian dramatists IBSEN and STRINDBERG explored the dilemmas of capitalist entrepreneurs and the tensions of bourgeois marriage. Symbolist poets (see SYMBOLISM) tried to lose themselves in an alternate linguistic world distilled of the dross of the everyday. The decadents (see DECADENCE) luxuriated in their disaffection with the bourgeoisie and espoused the artificiality of the aesthetic and technology. Misogyny and masculine symbols of power were glorified in the theories of FUTURISM.

Misogyny and racism flourished at the end of the 19th century in Europe, bringing to a crisis a process implicit in 19th-century social practice and ideology. Colonialism, of course, depended on racist beliefs in the superiority of white European civilization. The bourgeois family similarly supported a dichotomy between the pure domestic wife and mother and an inferior woman—working class or prostitute—identified with the fulfillment of base needs. There was no legitimate place in this schema for the woman writer.

If the expansion of education brought more literacy to Europeans and missionaries exported literacy to far reaches of the world, the institutions of literature were still owned and controlled by the male upper and middle classes. Literature was not considered an appropriate calling for a woman. It was common for women writers in the late 18th and early 19th centuries to disguise their identities in order to be published. Benedikte Naubert was successful in Germany when she published anonymously and was neglected when her female identity was revealed. GEORGE SAND was the pseudonym of the woman born Aurore Dupin. Still, women writers made a major mark on 19th-century literature, even though their contributions were not always recognized or acknowledged. With the crisis of the bourgeois family structure at the end of the century, there was a flurry of defiant women writers, such as COLETTE, who disregarded conventions and claimed their freedom.

However, the outbreak of World War I in 1914 severely challenged the hopes of the bourgeoisie for progress and enlightenment, and the Russian Revolution of 1917 signified the cataclysmic beginnings of a new era.

THE TWENTIETH CENTURY

Twentieth-century literature began in disillusion. Capitalism and the bourgeois family were in crisis, and an optimistic faith in progress through rationality and science was tested by the horrors of war. The avant-garde movements of DADA and surrealism, which emerged in the wake of World War I, rejected bourgeois civilization as repressive and exploitative and gave value to the world of the unconscious and dreams, as explored by SIGMUND FREUD. The war years and the 1920s also saw the emergence of MODERNISM.

The modernist movement in Europe, while celebrating the autonomous sphere of the aesthetic, had an acute sense that "the center does not hold." It sought carefully wrought and experimental forms with which to respond to what many writers saw as the chaos and cultural decline of the modern age. In their skepticism about civilization, modernists such as W. B. Yeats turned toward myth and the unconscious.

Although European modernism and the playful and iconoclastic surrealism may have expressed a crisis of Western civilization, both seemed out of touch with the social and economic lives of ordinary people, especially after the collapse of the stock market in 1929, a catastrophe felt throughout the world. The avant-garde movements that lamented the alienation of modern urban life were countered by a very different attitude to the future.

TOTALITARIANISM AND THE SECOND WORLD WAR

Revolutionary writers rejected the past and looked toward the liberation of the peasants and working classes with renewed hope. The 1920s in Russia, for example, saw a flowering of creativity among experimental poets and filmmakers. However, this euphoria was not to last. The lyrical poets VLADIMIR MAYAKOVSKY and SERGEY YESENIN, for example, frustrated by political imperatives, committed suicide. The 1930s saw the growth of fascism in Germany and Spain and the hardening of oppression in communist Russia. Both fascism and the communist SOCIALIST REALISM, the official aesthetic, condemned experimentation and modernist literature and art as decadent.

The totalitarian regimes of Japanese militarism, fascism, and communism targeted writers whom they considered decadent or enemies of the people. Writing against the grain of oppressive political authority became, in the 20th century, a dangerous activity. The Korean writer YUN TONGJU, who spoke for Korean independence, was arrested by the Japanese in 1943 and died in prison. Jewish intellectuals and dissident writers were exterminated by the German fascists. Books that were considered dangerous were burned. For protesting against fascism, THOMAS MANN and HERMANN HESSE lost their German citizenship. Many others lost their lives, including FEDERICO GARCÍA LORCA, one of Spain's most highly revered poets. RAFAEL ALBERTI, the Spanish surrealist poet, had to go into exile in Argentina after the victory of fascist general Francisco Franco.

Writers who lived during and after World War II had to confront the reality that modern civilization and technology had produced destruction and cruelty on an unprecedented scale. The Holocaust, in which millions of Jews and other civilians were exterminated; the mass destruction of cities; and the nuclear devastation visited on Hiroshima and Nagasaki seemed to defy the very possibilities of language. The critic Theodor Adorno (1903–69) suggested that after the Holocaust, lyric poetry might be impossible. However, the horrors of the

Holocaust produced extraordinary poems and testimonials in the work of such writers as PRIMO LEVI, NELLY SACHS, and ELIE WIESEL. With the establishment of the state of Israel in 1948, a new literature in Hebrew came into being. Opposition to Fascist oppression also inspired an existential literature of engagement exemplified by the writings of JEAN-PAUL SARTRE, SIMONE DE BEAUVOIR, and ALBERT CAMUS. The unspeakable suffering of the war, along with the stark reality of the cold war between the United States and the Soviet Union, created the climate for the THEATER OF THE ABSURD of the 1950s.

The Soviet empire that emerged from World War II suppressed the national literatures of the countries under its sway and, particularly during the Stalinist era, imprisoned and killed its dissident writers. Among many others, VARLAM SHALAMOV, ANDREI AMALRIK, and ALEKSANDR SOLZHENITSYN were imprisoned; OSIP MANDELSTAM died during imprisonment; and ISAAC BABEL was summarily executed. Similarly in China, during the Cultural Revolution, such writers as DING LING and HU FENG (1903–85), who resisted the restrictions of socialist realism, were imprisoned.

Throughout these periods of repression, writers have been remarkably resilient. Some, like the exiled novelist VLADIMIR NABOKOV, reinvented themselves in exile. Surviving imprisonment, illness, and forced exile, Solzhenitsyn returned to acclaim in Russia after the fall of the Soviet Union. Paris, after the war, became a particular magnet for exiled writers from Russia, Central Europe, Latin America, and Greece. At the same time, writers who remained in the Soviet Union used their creative resources to develop a genre of dissident literature, samizdat, which was often distributed underground at great risk and depended on humor, irony, obliqueness, and allegory. Literary movements affirming freedom and national identity emerged—as in Poland, Hungary, and Czechoslovakia—surreptitiously to challenge both socialist realism and Soviet domination.

THE AFTERMATH OF COLONIALISM

One of the more inspiring effects of the postwar years was the end of colonialism and the emergence of cultures, albeit changed, that colonialism had tried to destroy or assimilate. The NEGRITUDE movement, for example, united French-speaking African and Caribbean writers in an effort to forge a new self-expression from the colonial language they had learned in French schools and universities and the language they spoke at home. This produced the extraordinary writings of LÉOPOLD SENGHOR, BIRAGO DIOP, and AIMÉ CÉSAIRE, among others, and revitalized a sense of African identity. Similarly, the independence of India in 1947 had a profound effect on definitions of Indian identity and catalyzed a resurgence of regional writers.

Postcolonialism and national independence movements produced new authors throughout Africa and the Caribbean, including the Nigerian WOLE SOYINKA, the South Africans NADINE GORDIMER and J. M. COETZEE, the Saint Lucian DEREK WALCOTT, and the Trinidadian V. S. NAIPAUL, all of whom have won the Nobel Prize in literature. CHINUA ACHEBE wrote what has been called the first Nigerian novel, *Things Fall Apart* (1958), and NGŨGĨ WA THIONG'O was actively involved in African communal theater and encourages Africans to write in their native languages. Caribbean writers have explored their African, Indian, Chinese, Middle Eastern, and European identities to construct a new "creole" West Indian literature. In North Africa and the Middle East, in particular, the aftermath of postcolonialism has produced literatures of trauma and violence, as in the struggles for independence in Algeria, Egypt, and Lebanon and the wars surrounding the establishment of the nation of Israel and the displacements and migrations of Palestinians.

In South America, new national identities have been forged through the emergence of suppressed voices of formerly colonized, indigenous peoples and slaves and through resistance to economic neocolonialism, particularly by the United

States. Therefore, testimonial literature—a form of resistance autobiography—has emerged as a new genre, which became internationally known through the *testimonio* of RIGOBERTA MENCHÚ, the indigenous Guatemalan of the Quiche Maya ethnic group who won the Nobel Peace Prize in 1992. Because of threats to the environment and the survival of indigenous peoples and languages, ecological themes play an important part in the new Latin American literary consciousness.

The independence and partition of India in 1947 had a profound effect on definitions of Indian identity and catalyzed a resurgence of Indian writers negotiating between traditional Indian genres and forms, especially the novel, imported from the West. Movements of political emancipation also produced new literatures. For example, inspired by the writings of B. R. Ambedkar, who called for the end of the caste system, and by African Americans demanding their freedom from oppression, Indian untouchables adopted the name dalits and created political organizations and a new consciousness expressed through poetry, autobiography, essays, and short fiction. Dalit literature has developed further since the 1970s, and since the 1990s the voices of untouchable women, such as BAMA, have also begun to emerge. At the same time, emigration and exile have produced a powerful South Asian diasporic literature that has transformed the literature of countries throughout the world.

Countries belonging to the Commonwealth of Nations—such as Canada, Australia, and New Zealand—have also been transformed by the collapse of colonialism. Native American and Aboriginal movements emerged during the 1970s and have produced their own literary expressions, drawing on Aboriginal cultures shattered by colonial domination. In the case of Canada, a French tradition calling for independence generated its own literature, and Native Canadians affirmed their specific cultural identity. Australia, New Zealand, and Canada have changed

demographically with significant immigration from Asia and south Asia and, since the collapse of the Soviet Union, from southern and eastern Europe, especially the Balkan countries.

Even within Europe, up until World War II, marginalized cultures such as Breton, Provençal, Welsh, Irish, and Scottish Gaelic were disappearing because, within a centralized educational system, only the dominant, official language was encouraged. Increasingly, these cultures have resisted such internal colonization, and their languages are now included in the curriculum of some schools. This trend has continued under the aegis of the institution of the European Union. In Canada, the revival of the Québécois identity and the emergence of major authors writing in French as a response to the dominant Anglophone culture have been other remarkable examples of renewed cultural self-determination.

Postcolonialism also has produced a strong immigrant and diasporic literature. For economic and political reasons, South Asians, Indonesians, Africans, Turks, and Caribbeans have established themselves in the West and have produced a new definition of what constitutes, for example, English, French, German, or Dutch literature.

WOMEN WRITERS

Feminist movements in America and Europe since the 1970s have had an equally transformative effect on world literature. They have revealed the difficulties of women writers in the past who, for the most part, had no legal or civil rights and were not supposed to participate in public life or have their work published. They have also brought to light works that had once been influential (when published anonymously or with male pseudonyms) but were later excluded from the literary canon. They have questioned the conventional notions of what is considered literary—the priority given to poetry, drama, and the realistic novel—and have given value to "inferior" forms of expression, such as letters, memoirs, and diaries, often pejoratively described as "women's literature."

Above all, the women's movement has inspired women writers throughout the world. Even in cultures that have hardened against the engagement of women in public life, as in some nations of North Africa and the Middle East, women writers such as ASSIA DJEBAR from Algeria and NAWAL SAADAWI from Egypt have changed the political and literary map. Confronting very different social and economic conditions, women in Latin America, Africa, and South Asia are engaging in the complex issues of liberation, modernization, and their roles in traditional patriarchal, religious communities.

Many women writers have been recipients of the Nobel Prize. Swedish novelist SELMA LAGERLÖF became the first woman to receive the Nobel Prize in 1909. Chilean poet GABRIELA MISTRAL became the first Latin American woman to receive the prize in 1945. Over the last few decades, more women writers from all parts of the world have been prizewinners, a political acknowledgment on the part of the Nobel Committee of their increasing cultural significance.

LITERATURE AFTER THE COLLAPSE OF THE SOVIET UNION

The collapse of the Soviet Union has transformed the map of European literature. In the affirmation of independence, writers have reexamined their lives under Communist rule and redefined national identities and their new relations with Western Europe and the European Union. For example, the 2009 Nobel Prize in literature was awarded to HERTA MÜLLER, a Romanian-born German who describes her life under communism and the landscape of the dispossessed. This process has been marked by the emergence of extraordinary poetry, fiction, and drama, especially by Balkan writers, also touched by violent conflicts in the name of national identity following the breakup of Yugoslavia. At the same time, former Muslim satellites of the Soviet Union have increasingly looked to the Middle East in their assertion of religious identity. Immigration to

Western Europe from every country in the world by people escaping poverty or persecution has changed Europe's demographics, producing new genres of literature. An example is the collaborative memoir, in which an established writer or editor records oral accounts of refugees or survivors of abuse.

EFFECTS OF GLOBALIZATION

Despite revivals of national identities, the technological revolution of the Internet and the globalization of markets pose the threat of cultural homogenization. At the same time, the Internet has provided an alternative publishing sphere for writers, especially poets, often excluded from the market-driven agenda of international publishing. Increasing poverty and political crises in many areas of the world have created new patterns of emigration. As a result, it is increasingly difficult to define world writers in terms of a fixed national identity. Many have hybrid and fluid identities, and the subject of much literature in a globalized context addresses issues concerned with the loss of a sense of home and the transnational experience of displacement. In contrast to these postmodern crises of identity and cultural fluidity, there has been a resurgence of religious fundamentalism critical of literature considered blasphemous, immoral, or disrespectful of fixed religious beliefs and customs. The persecution of writers and artists by religious institutions for blasphemy or obscenity has had a long history. States and churches have often codified what should and should not be read and punished transgressions. Since the 1980s, writers considered offensive by Muslim clerics have increasingly been targeted for blasphemy. In 1986, for example, a fatwa was pronounced on SALMAN RUSHDIE.

THE TWENTY-FIRST CENTURY

During the first decade of the 21st century, writers have been challenged by crises on a global scale, including concerns about the environment. The attack on the World Trade Center in New

York City on September 11, 2001, and the consequent wars in the Middle East have led to increased censorship. Civil wars and poverty have accelerated migrations. The industrialization of China and India has created powerful economies, which in turn have created new writers and readers. Literature has had to stretch its boundaries to address the disequilibrium of the new cultural, religious, economic, and political landscapes. Thus, writers have been increasingly sensitive to the voices of the disempowered and the experiences of trauma and terror, generating new forms of expression both to reveal and understand the conditions of the contemporary world. In this global context, it has become especially important to learn foreign languages and to encourage translations of world writers, not only the most accessible but poets, dramatists, and essayists engaged in the experiences and complexities of expression in today's rapidly changing and challenged cultures.

—M. Josephine Diamond
New York City, May 2010

Authors'
Time Line

Dates	Author
1749–1842	Goethe, Johann Wolfgang von
1756–1819	Naubert, Benedikte
1759–1805	Schiller, Friedrich
1764–1842	Fischer, Caroline Auguste
1765–1820	Nguyen Du
1766–1826	Karamzin, Nikolai
1766–1877	Staël, Germaine de
1767–1830	Constant de Rebecque, Benjamin
1768–1848	Chateaubriand, François-René de
1770–1843	Hölderlin, Friedrich
1776–1820	Ho Xuan Huong
1776–1822	Hoffmann, E. T. A.
1777–1828	Duras, Claire de
1778–1827	Foscolo, Ugo
1783–1842	Stendhal
1785–1859	Arnim, Bettina von
1785–1863	Grimm, Jacob and Wilhelm
1785–1873	Manzoni, Alessandro
1786–1859	Desbordes-Valmore, Marceline
1790–1869	Lamartine, Alphonse de
1797–1856	Heine, Heinrich
1797–1863	Vigny, Alfred-Victor de
1797–1869	Ghālib, Mirzā Asadullāh Khān

Dates	Author
1798–1837	Leopardi, Giacomo
1798–1855	Mickiewicz, Adam Bernard
1799–1837	Pushkin, Aleksandr
1799–1850	Balzac, Honoré de
1802–1885	Hugo, Victor
1804–1876	Sand, George
1805–1875	Andersen, Hans Christian
1807–1893	Pavlova, Karolina
1808–1842	Espronceda y Delgado, José de
1808–1852	Gogol, Nikolay
1808–1855	Nerval, Gérard de
1808–1889	Barbey d'Aurevilly, Jules-Amédée
1810–1857	Musset, Alfred de
1811–1872	Gautier, Théophile
1812–1870	Herzen, Aleksandr
1812–1891	Goncharov, Ivan
1813–1837	Büchner, Georg
1814–1841	Lermontov, Mikhail
1818–1883	Turgenev, Ivan
1819–1898	Fontane, Theodor
1821–1867	Baudelaire, Charles
1821–1880	Flaubert, Gustave
1821–1881	Fyodor Dostoyevsky
1822–1896	Goncourt, Edmond
1823–1864	Gonçalves Dias, Antônio

Dates	Author	Dates	Author
1828–1889	Chernyshevsky, Nikolai	1862–1946	Hauptmann, Gerhardt
1828–1906	Ibsen, Henrik	1862–1949	Maeterlinck, Maurice
1828–1910	Tolstoy, Leo	1863–1920	Ansky, S.
1829–1877	Alencar, José Martiniano de	1863–1933	Cavafy, Constantine P.
1830–1870	Goncourt, Jules	1863–1938	D'Annunzio, Gabriele
1832–1910	Bjørnson, Bjørnstjerne	1864–1925	Rosas, Oscar
1836–1870	Bécquer, Gustavo Alfonso	1864–1936	Unamuno y Jugo, Miguel de
1837–1885	Castro, Rosalía	1867–1900	Nobre, António
1838–1889	Villiers de L'Isle-Adam,	1867–1902	Masaoka Shiki
	Auguste de	1867–1916	Darío, Rubén
1838–1894	Cattopadhyay, Bankim-Chandra	1867–1916	Natsume Sōseki
1839–1908	Machado de Assis, Joachim	1867–1922	Lawson, Henry
	Maria	1867–1928	Blasco Ibáñez, Vicente
1840–1902	Zola, Émile	1867–1936	Pirandello, Luigi
1840–1922	Verga, Giovanni	1868–1933	George, Stefan
1842–1891	Quental, Antero Tarquínio de	1868–1936	Gorky, Maxim
1842–1898	Mallarmé, Stéphane	1868–1955	Claudel, Paul
1843–1920	Pérez Galdós, Benito	1869–1945	Lasker-Schüler, Else
1844–1900	Nietzsche, Friedrich	1869–1948	Gandhi, Mohandas K.
1845–1900	Queiroz, José Maria Eça de	1869–1951	Gide, André
1846–1870	Lautreamont, Comte de	1870–1953	Bunin, Ivan
	(Isidore-Lucien Ducasse)	1871–1922	Proust, Marcel
1846–1916	Sienkiewicz, Henryk	1871–1945	Valéry, Paul
1848–1907	Huysmans, Joris-Karl	1871–1950	Mann, Heinrich
1849–1912	Strindberg, August	1872–1896	Higuchi Ichiyō
1850–1893	Maupassant, Guy de	1872–1956	Baroja y Nessi, Pío
1851–1896	Verlaine, Paul	1873–1907	Jarry, Alfred
1851–1921	Pardo Bazán, Emilia	1873–1924	Bryusov, Valery Yakovlevich
1852–1915	Peretz, Isaac Leib	1873–1954	Colette
1853–1900	Solovyov, Vladimir Sergeyevich	1874–1929	Hofmannstahl, Hugo von
1854–1891	Rimbaud, Arthur	1874–1947	Machado y Ruiz, Manuel
1856–1939	Freud, Sigmund	1875–1926	Rilke, Rainer Maria
1857–1909	Liu E	1875–1939	Machado, Antonio
1858–1940	Lagerlöf, Selma	1875–1955	Mann, Thomas
1859–1916	Akhmatova, Anna	1876–1938	Chatterji, Sarat Chandra
1859–1916	Aleichem, Shalom	1876–1944	Marinetti, Filippo
1859–1952	Hamsun, Knut	1877–1938	Iqbāl, Muhammad
1860–1904	Chekhov, Anton	1877–1962	Hesse, Hermann
1860–1943	Roberts, Charles	1878–1942	Yosano Akiko
1861–1913	Johnson, Pauline	1878–1957	Döblin, Alfred
1861–1928	Svevo, Italo	1879–1944	Han Yongun
1861–1941	Tagore, Rabindranath	1879–1949	Naidu, Sarojini
1862–1922	Mori Ōgai	1880–1918	Apollinaire, Guillaume

Dates	Author	Dates	Author
1880–1934	Bely, Andrei	1892–1923	Södergran, Edith
1880–1936	Premchand, Munshi	1892–1927	Akutagawa Ryūnosuke
1880–1942	Musil, Robert von	1892–1938	Storni, Alfonsina
1880–1967	Arghezi, Tudor	1892–1938	Vallejo, César
1881–1936	Lu Xun (Lu Hsün)	1892–1941	Tsvetaeva, Marina
1881–1958	Jiménez, Juan Ramón	1892–1942	Schulz, Bruno
1882–1944	Giraudoux, Jean	1892–1975	Andrić, Ivo
1882–1949	Undset, Sigrid	1893–1930	Mayakovsky, Vladimir
1883–1923	Hašek, Jaroslav	1893–1980	Collymore, Frank A.
1883–1924	Kafka, Franz	1893–1984	Guillén, Jorge
1883–1955	Ortega y Gasset, José	1894–1940	Babel, Isaac
1883–1956	Takamura Kotaro	1894–1953	Tuwim, Julian
1883–1957	Kazantsakis, Nikos	1894–1961	Céline, Louis-Ferdinand
1883–1971	Shiga Naoya	1895–1925	Yesenin, Sergey Aleksandrovich
1884–1937	Zamyatin, Yevgeny	1895–1952	Éluard, Paul
1885–1962	Dinesen, Isak	1895–1974	Pagnol, Marcel
1886–1921	Gumilev, Nikolai	1895–1976	Satyanarayana, Visvanatha
1886–1942	Hagiwara Sakutarō	1895–1998	Jünger, Ernst
1886–1951	Broch, Hermann	1896–1948	Artaud, Antonin
1886–1956	Benn, Gottfried	1896–1957	Lampedusa, Giuseppe di
1886–1965	Tanizaki Jun'ichirō	1896–1963	Tzara, Tristan
1886–1978	Madariaga, Salvador de	1896–1966	Breton, André
1886–1980	Kokoschka, Oskar	1896–1981	Montale. Eugenio
1887–1914	Trakl, Georg	1897–1962	Bataille, Georges
1887–1966	Arp, Hans	1897–1982	Aragon, Louis
1887–1975	Perse, Saint-Jean	1898–1936	García Lorca, Federico
1888–1923	Mansfield, Katherine	1898–1956	Brecht, Bertolt
1888–1935	Pessoa, Fernando	1898–1970	Remarque, Erich Maria
1888–1970	Agnon, Shmuel Yosef	1899–1950	Langgässer, Elisabeth
1888–1970	Ungaretti, Giuseppe	1899–1960	Shute, Nevil
1889–1957	Mistral, Gabriela	1899–1966	Lao She
1889–1963	Cocteau, Jean	1899–1972	Kawabata Yasunari
1889–1965	Alberti, Rafael	1899–1977	Nabokov, Vladimir
1889–1975	Gunnarsson, Gunnar	1899–1984	Michaux, Henri
1890–1960	Pasternak, Boris	1899–1986	Borges, Jorge Luis
1890–1979	Rhys, Jean	1899–1988	Ponge, Francis
1891–1938	Mandelstam, Osip	1900–1944	Saint-Exupéry, Antoine de
1891–1940	Bulgakov, Mikhail	1900–1971	Seferis, George
1891–1958	Becher, Johannes Robert	1900–1987	Freyre, Gilberto de Mello
1891–1962	Hu Shih	1900–1999	Bing Xin (Ping Hsin)
1891–1967	Ehrenburg, Ilya	1900–1999	Sarraute, Nathalie
1891–1970	Sachs, Nellie	1901–1956	Fadeyev, Aleksandr Aleksandrovich
1891–1974	Lagerkvist, Pär		

Dates	Author	Dates	Author
1901–1968	Quasimodo, Salvatore	1909–1973	Brasch, Charles Orwell
1901–1974	Kaschnitz, Marie-Luise	1909–1994	Onetti, Juan Carlos
1901–1976	Malraux, André	1910–1983	Sri Sri
1901–1986	Seifert, Jaroslav	1910–1986	Genet, Jean
1901–1988	Ausländer, Rose	1910–1987	Anouilh, Jean
1901–1989	James, C. L. R.	1910–2003	Queiróz, Raquel de
1901–1990	Leiris, Michel	1911–1991	Frisch, Max
1902–1963	Hikmet, Nazim	1911–1996	Elytis, Odysseus
1902–1974	Torres Bodet, Jaime	1911–2001	Curnow, Allen
1902–1975	Levi, Carlo	1911–2002	Rinser, Luise
1902–1983	Stead, Christina	1911–2004	Milosz, Czeslaw
1902–1989	Guillén, Nicolás	1911–2006	Mahfouz, Naguib
1903–1937	Rabéarivelo, Jean-Joseph	1912–1980	White, Patrick
1903–1951	Hayashi Fumiko	1912–1984	Faiz, Faiz Ahmed
1903–1976	Queneau, Raymond	1912–1994	Ionesco, Eugène
1903–1981	Huchel, Peter	1912–2001	Amado, Jorge
1903–1982	Sargeson, Frank	1913–1960	Camus, Albert
1903–1987	Yourcenar, Marguerite	1913–1995	Davies, Robertson
1903–1988	Paton, Alan	1913–2005	Simon, Claude
1903–1989	Simenon, Georges	1913–2008	Césaire, Aimé
1904–1936	Ostrovsky, Nikolai	1914–1950	Kanik, Orhan Veli
1904–1969	Gombrowicz, Witold	1914–1980	Gary, Romain
1904–1973	Neruda, Pablo	1914–1984	Cortázar, Julio
1904–1980	Carpentier, Alejo	1914–1987	Abbas, K.A.
1904–1986	Ding Ling	1914–1996	Duras, Marguerite
1904–1991	Singer, Isaac Bashevis	1914–1998	Paz, Octavio
1904–2005	Ba Jin	1914–2008	Dağlarka, Fazil Hüsnü
1905–1980	Sartre, Jean-Paul		
1905–1984	Sholokhov, Mikhail	1915–1986	Allfrey, Phyllis
1905–1986	Enchi Fumiko	1915–1991	Chugtai, Ismat
1905–1993	Feng Zhi (Feng Chih)	1915–2000	Wright, Judith
1905–1994	Canetti, Elias	1915–2001	Hwang Sun-won
1905–2004	Anand, Mulk Raj	1915–2001	So Chŏng-ju
1906–1989	Beckett, Samuel	1916–1978	Pak Mogwol
1906–1989	Diop, Birago	1916–1985	Tian Jian
1906–2001	Narayan, R. K.	1916–1991	Ginzburg, Natalia
1906–2001	Senghor, Léopold Sédar	1916–2000	Bassani, Giorgio
1907–1972	Eich, Günter	1916–2000	Hébert, Anne
1907–1982	Shalamov, Varlam	1916–2002	Cela, Camilo José
1907–1988	Char, René	1917–1945	Yun Tongju
1907–1990	Moravia, Alberto	1917–1985	Böll, Heinrich
1908–1950	Pavese, Cesare	1918–1985	Morante, Elsa
1908–1986	Beauvoir, Simone de	1918–1998	Dudintsev, Vladimir

Dates	Author	Dates	Author
1918–2008	Solzhenitsyn, Aleksandr	1925–	Jaccottet, Philippe
1918–	Haasse, Hella	1926–1973	Bachmann, Ingeborg
1919–1987	Levi, Primo	1926–1987	Laurence Margaret
1919–2006	Bennett, Louise	1926–	Dépestre, René
1919–	Abrahams, Peter	1926–	Devi, Mahasweta
1920–1970	Celan, Paul	1926–	Fo, Dario
1920–1977	Lispector, Clarice	1927–1960	Diop, David
1920–1993	Noonuccal, Oodgeroo	1927–1991	Idris, Yūsuf
1920–2004	Rin Ishigaki	1927–2007	Hyder, Qurratulain
1920–	Memmi, Albert	1927–	Grass, Günter
1921–1988	Fried, Erich	1927–	Jhabvala, Ruth Prawer
1921–1990	Dürrenmatt, Friedrich	1927–	Lamming, George
1921–1996	Habibi, Emile	1928–1953	Capécia, Mayotte
1921–	Aichinger, Ilse	1928–1996	Miron, Gaston
1921–	Harris, Wilson	1928–	Fuentes, Carlos
1921–	Okara, Gabriel	1928–	García Márquez, Gabriel
1921–	Sereny, Gitta	1928–	Wiesel, Elie
1922–1975	Pasolini, Pier Paolo	1928–	Yu Guanzhong (Yü Kwang-chung)
1922–1979	Neto, António Agostinho		
1922–1991	Popa, Vasko	1929–1981	Bâ, Mariama
1922–2003	Höllerer, Walter	1929–1989	Yacine, Kateb
1922–2008	Robbe-Grillet, Alain	1929–1995	Müller, Heiner
1922–2010	Burkart, Erika	1929–1999	Munonye, John
1922–2010	Saramago, José	1929–2005	Cabrera Infante, Guillermo
1923–1985	Calvino, Italo	1929–2009	Saleh, Tayyib
1923–1998	Kabbani, Nizar	1929–	Enzensberger, Hans Magnus
1923–2007	Mala'ika, Nazek al-	1929–	Kertész, Imre
1923–2007	Sembène, Ousmane	1929–	Kundera, Milan
1923–	Bonnefoy, Yves	1929–	Kunert, Günter
1923–	Gordimer, Nadine	1929–	Maillet, Antonine
1923–	Kemal, Yaşar	1929–	Wolf, Christa
1923–	Szimborska, Wislawa	1930–1986	Pagis, Dan
1924–1993	Abe Kōbō	1930–1996	Rifaat, Alifa
1924–1997	Donoso, José	1930–2006	Fallaci, Oriana
1924–2000	Amichai, Yehuda	1930–2006	Kunene, Mazisi
1924–2004	Frame, Janet	1930–2007	Ōba Minako
1924–	Skvorecky, Jozef	1930–	Achebe, Chinua
1925–1970	Mishima Yukio	1930–	Adonis
1925–1974	Castellanos, Rosario	1930–	Brathwaite, Edward Kamau
1925–1985	La Guma, Alex	1930–	Hayashi Kyoko
1925–2004	Astley, Thea	1930–	Mrożek, Slawomir
1925–2006	Toer, Pramoedya Ananta	1930–	Ogot, Grace
1925–	Gomringer, Eugen	1930–	Walcott, Derek

WRITERS COVERED, BY GEOGRAPHICAL AREA

AFRICA

Abrahams, Peter
Achebe, Chinua
Aidoo, Ama Ata
Anyidoho, Kofi
Bá, Mariama
Breytenbach, Breyten
Brink, André
Busia, Abena
Coetzee, J. M.
Cronin, Jeremy
De Kok, Ingrid
Diop, Birago
Diop, David
Emecheta, Buchi
Farah, Nuruddin
Gordimer, Nadine
Head, Bessie
Kunene, Mazisi
La Guma, Alex
Laing, B. Kojo
Malange, Nise
Munonye, John
Ndebele. Njabulo, S.
Neto, António Agostinho
Ngũgĩ wa Thiong'o

Nkosi, Lewis
Nortje, Arthur
Nwapa, Flora
Ogot, Grace
Okara, Gabriel
p'Bitek, Okot
Paton, Alan
Rabéarivelo, Jean-Joseph
Saleh, Tayyib
Sembène, Ousmane
Senghor, Léopold Sédar
Serote, Mongane Wally
Soyinka, Wole
Wicomb, Zoë
Yacine, Kateb

THE AMERICAS

Canada

Atwood, Margaret
Davies, Robertson
Hébert, Anne
Ipellie, Alootook
Johnson, Pauline
Kogawa, Joy
Laurence, Margaret
Maillet, Antonine

Miron, Gaston
Mootoo, Shani
Munro, Alice
Nichol, bp
Ondaatje, Michael
Richler, Mordecai
Roberts, Charles
Shields, Carol

The Caribbean

Allfrey, Phyllis
Bennett, Louise
Braschi, Giannina
Brathwaite, Edward Kamau
Capécia, Mayotte
Césaire, Aimé
Chamoiseau, Patrick
Cliff, Michelle
Collymore, Frank A.
Condé, Maryse
Dépestre, René
Espinet, Ramabai
Goodison, Lorna
Guillén, Nicolás
Harris, Wilson
James, C. L. R.
Kincaid, Jamaica
Laird, Christopher
Lamming, George
Meeks, Brian
Naipaul, V. S.
Perse, Saint-Jean
Rhys, Jean
Schwarz-Bart, Simone
Walcott, Derek

Latin America

Alencar, José Martiniano de
Allende, Isabel
Amado, Jorge de
Arenas, Reinaldo
Bolaño, Roberto
Borges, Jorge Luis
Cabrera Infante, Guillermo

Carpentier, Alejo
Castellanos, Rosario
Cortázar, Julio
Darío, Rubén
Donoso, José
Ferré, Rosario
Fraire, Isabel
Freyre, Gilberto de Mello
Fuentes, Carlos
García Márquez, Gabriel
Gonçalves Dias, Antônio
Lispector, Clarice
Machado de Assis, Joachim Maria
Menchú, Rigoberta
Mistral, Gabriela
Neruda, Pablo
Onetti, Juan Carlos
Paz, Octavio
Queirós, Raquel de
Rosas, Oscar
Storni, Alfonsina
Torres Bodet, Jaime
Vallejo, César
Vargas Llosa, Mario
Yáñez, Mirta

ASIA

China

Ba Jin
Bei Dao
Bing Xin
Chen Yuan-tsung
Ding Ling
Feng Zhi
Gao Xingjian
Huang Chunming (Huang Ch'un-ming)
Hu Shi
Lao She
Liu E
Lu Xun
Mo Yan
Tian Jian
Yu Guangzhong

Japan
Abe Kōbō
Akutagawa Ryūnosuke
Enchi Fumiko
Hagiwara Sakutarō
Hayashi Fumikō
Hayashi Kyōko
Higuchi Ichiyō
Ishigaki Rin
Kawabata Yasunari
Kurahashi Yumiko
Masaoka Shiki
Mishima Yukio
Mori Ōgai
Murakami Haruki
Natsume Sōseki
Oba Minako
Ōe Kenzaburō
Shiga Naoya
Takamura Kotarō
Tanikawa Shuntaro
Tanizaki Jun'ichirō
Tsushima Yukō
Yamada Eimi
Yosano Akiko

Korea
Han Yongun
Hwang Sun-won
Hwang Tonggyu
Pak Mogwol
So Chông-ju
Yun Tongju

South Asia
Abbas, K. A.
Adiga, Aravind
Anand, Mulk Raj
Bama
Bhatt, Sujata
Cattopadhyay, Bankim-Chandra
Chatterjee, Upamanyu
Chatterji, Sarat Chandra
Chugtai, Ismat
Desai, Anita

Devi, Mahasweta
Dhasal, Namdeo
Faiz, Faiz Ahmed
Gandhi, Mohandas K.
Ghālib, Mirza Asadullah Khan
Ghosh, Amitav
Gunesekara, Ramesh
Hyder, Qurratulain
Iqbal, Muhammad
Jhabvala, Ruth Prawer
Karnad, Girish
Mehta, Gita
Mistry, Rohinton
Naidu, Sarojini
Narayan, R. K.
Premchand, Munshi
Roy, Arundhati
Rushdie, Salman
Satyanarayana, Visvanatha
Seth, Vikram
Souza, Eunice de
Sri Sri
Suleri, Sara
Tagore, Rabindranath

Southeast Asia and the Pacific
Dhammachoti, Ussiri
Hayslip, Le Ly
Ho Xuan Huong
Kauraka Kauraka
Lim, Shirley Geok-Lin
Nguyen Du
San Juan, Epifanio
Toer, Pramoedya Ananta
Yathay Pin

AUSTRALIA AND NEW ZEALAND
Astley, Thea
Brasch, Charles Orwell
Carey, Peter
Curnow, Allen
Flanagan, Richard
Frame, Janet

Hasluck, Nicholas
Keneally, Thomas
Lawson, Henry
Malouf, David
Mansfield, Katherine
Sargeson, Frank
Stead, Christina
White, Patrick
Wright, Judith

EUROPE

Eastern and Central Europe

Albahari, David
Ansky, S.
Arghezi, Tudor
Canetti, Elias
Esterházy, Péter
Gombrowicz, Witold
Hašek, Jaroslav
Havel, Václav
Kertesz, Imre
Kiš, Danilo
Kundera, Milan
Mickiewicz, Adam
Milosz, Czeslaw
Mroźek, Slawomir
Peretz, Isaac Leib
Popa, Vasko
Seifert, Jaroslav
Shulz, Bruno
Sienkiewicz, Henryk
Singer, Isaac Bashevis
Škvorecký, Jozef
Szimborska, Wislawa
Tuwim, Julian
Wiesel, Elie
Zagajewski, Adam

French-Speaking Europe

Anouilh, Jean
Apollinaire, Guillaume
Aragon, Louis
Artaud, Antonin
Balzac, Honoré de

Barbey d'Aurevilly, Jules-Amédée
Bataille, Georges
Baudelaire, Charles
Beauvoir, Simone de
Beckett, Samuel
Bonnefoy, Yves
Breton, André
Camus, Albert
Céline, Louis-Ferdinand
Char, René
Chateaubriand, François-René de
Cixous, Hélène
Claudel, Paul
Cocteau, Jean
Colette
Constant, Benjamin
Desbordes-Valmore, Marceline
Duras, Claire de
Duras, Marguerite
Éluard, Paul
Flaubert, Gustave
Gary, Romain
Gautier, Théophile
Genet, Jean
Gide, André
Giraudoux, Jean
Goncourt brothers, Edmond and Jules
Houellebecq, Michel
Hugo, Victor
Huysmans, Joris-Karl
Ionesco, Eugène
Jaccottet, Philippe
Jarry, Alfred
Lamartine, Alphonse de
Lautreamont, Comte de (Isidore-Lucien Ducasse)
Le Clézio J. M. G.
Leiris, Michel
Maeterlinck, Maurice
Mallarmé, Stéphane
Malraux, André
Maupassant, Guy de
Mauriac, François
Michaux, Henri
Musset, Alfred de
Nerval, Gérard de

Mann, Thomas
Maron, Monika
Müller, Heiner
Müller, Herta
Musil, Robert von
Nietzsche, Friedrich
Nooteboom, Cees
Remarque, Erich Maria
Rilke, Rainer Maria
Rinser, Luise
Sachs, Nellie Leonie
Schiller, Friedrich
Sebald, W. G.
Sereny, Gitta
Södergran, Edith
Strindberg, August
Trakl, Georg
Undset, Sigrid
Wolf, Christa

Greece, Turkey, and the Balkans

Andrić, Ivo
Cavafy, Constantine P.
Dağlarka, Fazil Hüsnü
Elytis, Odysseus
Hikmet, Nazim
Kanik, Orhan Veli
Kazantsakis, Nikos
Seferis, George
Vassilikos, Vassilis

Italy

Bassani, Giorgio
Calvino, Italo
D'Annunzio, Gabriele
Eco, Umberto
Fallaci, Oriana
Fo, Dario
Foscolo, Ugo
Ginzburg, Natalia
Lampedusa, Giuseppe di
Leopardi, Giacomo
Levi, Carlo
Levi, Primo
Manzoni, Alessandro

Marinetti, Filippo
Montale, Eugenio
Morante, Elsa
Moravia, Alberto
Pasolini, Pier Paolo
Pavese, Cesare
Pirandello, Luigi
Quasimodo, Salvatore
Svevo, Italo
Tabucchi, Antoni
Ungaretti, Giuseppe
Verga, Giovanni

Russia

Akhmadulina, Izabella
Akhmatova, Anna
Amalrik, Andrey
Babel, Isaac
Bely, Andrei
Bryusov, Valery Yakovlevich
Bulgakov, Mikhail
Bunin, Ivan
Chekhov, Anton
Chernyshevsky, Nikolay
Dostoyevsky, Fyodor
Dudintsev, Vladimir
Ehrenburg, Ilya
Fadeyev, Aleksandr Aleksandrovich
Gogol, Nikolai
Goncharov, Ivan
Gorky, Maxim
Gumilev, Nikolai
Herzen, Aleksandr
Karamzin, Nikolai
Lermontov, Mikhail
Mandelstam, Osip
Mayakovsky, Vladimir
Nabokov, Vladimir
Ostrovsky, Nikolai
Pasternak, Boris
Pavlova, Karolina
Pushkin, Aleksandr
Shalamov, Varlam
Sholokhov, Mikhail
Solovyov, Vladimir Sergeyevich

Solzhenitsyn, Aleksandr
Tolstoy, Leo
Tsvetaeva, Marina
Turgenev, Ivan
Voinovich, Vladimir
Yesenin, Sergey
Yevtushenko, Yevgeny
Zamyatin, Yevgeny

Spain and Portugal

Alberti, Rafael
Arrabal, Fernando
Baroja y Nessi, Pío
Bécquer, Gustavo Alfonso
Blasco Ibáñez, Vicente
Castro, Rosalía
Cela, Camilo José
Espronceda y Delgado, José de
García Lorca, Federico
Guillén, Jorge
Jiménez, Juan Ramón
Machado y Ruiz, Antonio
Machado y Ruiz, Manuel
Madariaga, Salvador de
Nobre, António
Ortega y Gasset, José
Pardo Bazán, Emilia
Pérez Galdós, Benito
Pessoa, Fernando
Queiroz, José Maria Eça de
Quental, Antero Tarquínio de
Saramago, José

Unamuno y Jugo, Miguel de

THE MIDDLE EAST

Adonis
Agnon, Samuel Joseph
Aleichem, Shalom
Amichai, Yehuda
Appelfeld, Aharon
Bitton, Erez
Darwish, Mahmud
Djebar, Assia
Grossman, David
Habibi, Emile
Hosseini, Khaled
Idris, Yūsuf
Jayyusi, Salma al-Khadra al-
Kabbani, Nizar
Kemal, Yaşar
Mahfouz, Naguib
Malaika, Nazik al-
Memmi, Albert
Oz, Amos
Pagis, Dan
Pamuk, Orhan
Ravikovitch, Dahlia
Rifaat, Alifa
Saadawi, Nawal
Sammam, Ghada

A

Abbas, K(hawaja) A(hmad) (1914–1987)
novelist, short story writer, screenwriter
Khawaja Ahmad Abbas was born in Panipat, India, into a privileged, upper-middle-class family. After graduating from the University of Aligarh, Abbas became a journalist and went on to write novels and screenplays. While studying law, Abbas founded a fledgling newspaper called *Aligarh Opinion*. He was also a major Hindi movie director and screenwriter. Throughout his career, Abbas used films because of their accessibility to the uneducated and poor to promote his views on social castes and class conflicts. Abbas was also one of the founders and a member of the Indian People's Theatre Association (IPTA), which produced two of his plays.

Like many other writers, Abbas was concerned with national politics and wrote from a marxist, sociopolitical perspective. This attitude was fostered and grew under the influence of Sri Aurobindo (1872–1950) and MOHANDAS GANDHI (1869–1948). Some of Abbas's most famous English works are *Tomorrow Is Ours: A Novel of the India of Today* (1943) and *Inquilab: A Novel of the Indian Revolution* (1955). These novels are good examples of Abbas's treatment of the oppressed as they struggle against social and political systems such as untouchability, fascism, and imperialism.

His screenplay for the classic Hindi movie *Awara* (Vagabond, 1952) is perhaps one of Indian cinema's most lyrical and compelling compositions on the irrepressible human spirit against the shadow of colonial capitalism.

In 1951, Abbas established his own film production company. His movie *Pardesi* (Foreigner) was selected for screening at the 1958 Cannes Film Festival in France. In 1968, Abbas was awarded the Padma Shri in recognition of his contribution to Indian literature.

Another Work by K. A. Abbas
The World Is My Village: A Novel with an Index. Columbia, Mo.: South Asia Books, 1984.

Abe Kimifusa
See ABE KŌBŌ.

Abe Kōbō (Abe Kimifusa) (1924–1993)
novelist, short story writer, playwright
Abe Kōbō was born in Tokyo to Abe Asakichi and Yorimi. He moved to Manchuria with his family in 1925 but returned to Tokyo to finish high school. In 1943, he entered the medical department of Tokyo Imperial University, graduating in 1948.

Abe's first work was reflective of his experiences in Manchuria. In *On the Sign at the End of the Road* (1948), an opium addict relates his story of flight and imprisonment in Manchuria at the end of World War II. The narration is conveyed through a series of notebooks that the protagonist kept during the war as he mused over the nature of his native country and the loss of his home.

Abe's writing quickly became more surrealistic. The novel *The Crime of S. Karma* (1951) portrays a man who wakes up one morning to find that he has lost his identity. When he arrives at work, he finds that his business card has stolen his identity and, with the help of his fountain pen, wristwatch, and glasses, is making a play for his secretary. Like many of Abe's stories, *The Crime of S. Karma* combines logic and fantasy. The story won the Akutagawa Prize for new writers.

In the 1950s, Abe joined the Japanese Communist Party (JCP) and wrote for publications associated with the party. However, by the late 1950s, Abe was writing articles critical of the JCP's restrictive policies, which earned his expulsion in 1962.

During this period, Abe also began writing science fiction stories. As a genre, science fiction was new to Japan, but Abe broke open the field with his novel *Inter Ice Age 4,* serialized in the journal *Sekai* from 1958 to 1959. In the story, the scientist Katsumi uses a computer to predict the future and discovers that a future race of gilled underwater dwellers has condemned him because he cannot adapt to the changes that are in store for society.

Abe's most acclaimed writing was published in the 1960s: *The Woman in the Dunes* (1962), *The Face of Another* (1964), and *The Ruined Map* (1967). All three novels explore the theme of alienated protagonists who must overcome or accept change. For example, in *The Face of Another,* the protagonist's face has been disfigured, so he creates a latex mask to hide his scars. However, with the mask, he assumes a new identity, and the mask eventually forms its own identity and threatens to take over the wearer. *The Ruined Map* follows suit with a detective who searches for a missing husband and, during the process, becomes jealous of

the freedom the escaped husband has found. The most well known of the three novels, *The Woman in the Dunes,* portrays the kidnapping of a man who collects insects as a hobby. Held captive in a dwelling at the foot of the sand dunes, he must come to term with his new life.

In the next decade, Abe founded an experimental theater troupe called the Abe Kōbō Studio. For nine years, he directed plays, adapted a number of his stories, and wrote several plays for the troupe. Notably, one of these adaptations—*Friends* (1967)—has been translated into several languages and performed internationally. It tells the story of a man whose life is invaded by a family who adopts him, moves into his apartment, and takes over his life.

Following the disbanding of the troupe in 1979, Abe wrote only three major novels: *Secret Rendezvous* (1977), *The Ark Sakura* (1984), and *Kangaroo Notebook* (1991). Unlike his earlier stories, these novels were not greeted with acclaim because they are difficult to interpret. For example, in *Secret Rendezvous,* a man searches for his missing wife in a hospital. During his investigation, he meets a man with a horse's body as well as a cavalcade of other strange characters. The reader is bombarded not only with bizarre visual images but also with a cacophony of sound imagery.

Abe died of heart failure while writing his final novel, *The Flying Man,* which was published posthumously in 1993.

Critical Analysis

Kōbō Abe made his international reputation with his 1962 novel *Suna no onna* (literally, *Sand Woman,* or more commonly *The Woman in the Dunes*). Abe's novels were favorably compared to those of FRANZ KAFKA, as they explored similar themes about the inherent meaninglessness or absurdity of human action in the face of an infinite, uncaring universe. Critic J. Thomas Rimes writes, "Abe uses every emotion, from pride and fear to sexual desire and despair, to force his protagonist, and so his reader, into an acute self-awareness of the absurdity of human condition."

In *The Woman in the Dunes*, Abe focuses on Niki Jumpei, a teacher and amateur etymologist who, on a research trip during a holiday, finds himself through a series of unfortunate circumstances in a shack at the bottom of a vast sand pit, where lives an enigmatic woman who every night shovels away the slowly advancing sand dunes from her home. Held against his will in the pit, Jumpei transforms into a modern Sisyphus, doomed to shovel out an endless avalanche of sand in order to protect himself and the village from burial by the massive dunes that surround it. In a Kafkaesque twist, Jumpei's life begins to mirror that of the insects he studies, continuously moving sand from one pile to another in order to stave off the inevitable death. "The village," Abe writes, "resembling the cross section of a beehive, lay sprawled over the dunes. Or rather the dunes lay sprawled over the village." Abe's visual description of the village prepares the reader for the central thematic thrust of the novel, which is articulated by Jumpei when, early on in the novel, he asks the woman, "Are you shovelling to survive, or surviving to shovel?" Are our actions truly intended for a quality, or a quantity, of life?

Abe was also a renowned playwright, best known internationally for his 1967 one-act play *The Man Who Turned into a Stick*, described by one critic as "a play that isn't easily understood, and many people believe that that is exactly how he wanted it." Like his contemporaries SAMUEL BECKETT and Harold Pinter, Abe explored themes of solitude and alienation in his plays, producing powerful images. *The Man Who Turned into a Stick* focuses on a literal stick that falls from the sky and is discovered by Hippie Girl and Hippie Boy who consider its origins, only to learn that the stick is alive. Abe confronts his audience with an obviously absurd scenario in order to explore the meaning of life and death as an essential aspect of the human condition. In the final moments of the play, a character advances toward the audience and says, "Look—there's a whole forest of sticks around you . . . All those sticks. You may never be judged, but at least you don't have to worry about being punished." This pronouncement is merely, he claims, "the simple truth, the truth as I see it."

Other Works by Abe Kōbō

Beyond the Curve. Translated by Juliet Winters Carpenter. New York: Kodansha International, 1991.
The Box Man. Translated by E. Dale Saunders. New York: Knopf, 1974.
Three Plays. Translated by Donald Keene. New York: Columbia University Press, 1993.

Works about Abe Kōbō

Currie, William. *Metaphors of Alienation: The Fiction of Abe, Beckett and Kafka*. Ann Arbor, Mich.: University Microfilms, 1973.
Yamanouchi, Hisaki. "Abe Kōbō and Ōe Kenzaburō: The Search for Identity in Contemporary Japanese Literature." In *Modern Japan: Aspects of History, Literature and Society*. Edited by W. G. Beasley. Berkeley: University of California Press, 1975.

Aboriginal movement

Aboriginal people have inhabited Australia for between 40,000 and 100,000 years. Prior to English settlement in 1788, Aboriginal people had minimal contact with other peoples. Their culture was very diverse, with more than 200 different languages spoken, but they shared a commonality of territoriality, kinship, family structures, the Dreamtime, spirituality, and ceremonies. The Dreamtime and dream songs of the Aborigines reveal their sense of sacred interrelation with the land and all other living creatures. They also explain the group's spiritual life and history and are the traditional source of their music, painting, and storytelling. Dreamtime connects the past, present, and future in a sacred spiritual reality.

A well-known musical form is the corroboree, a singing of life stories, rich in rhyme, rhythm, repetition, and poetry. This is part of a translation of a corroboree called *Moonbone:* "Now the moon is changing, having cast away his bone/ Gradually he grows larger, taking on new bone and flesh."

Rock paintings and engravings also show the richness of the imagination in Aboriginal culture. Sacred rituals include singing, music, dance, and performance.

After colonization, European settlers appropriated Aboriginal lands and, through conquest and policies of forced assimilation (children were stolen from their parents and placed in European families), almost wiped out Aboriginal culture. However, beginning in 1938, an Aboriginal movement emerged that began to demand civil rights. This movement, influenced by the American Civil Rights movement, became stronger in the 1960s and again in the 1990s when Aborigines won some land rights and an apology from the Australian government for past abuses.

Aboriginal storytelling and poetry is very strongly influenced by traditional oral narratives. The storyteller Pauline McLeod, for example, has revived and created dream songs for a modern Aboriginal audience that had largely forgotten them. The following few lines of a typical modern poem, by Stephen Clayton, express the Aboriginal loss of a connectedness to nature:

> I am born of the land, my soul is the sun
> Nature is my mother,
> I am Mother Nature's son
> The wind is my spirit, running wild,
>   running free
> Water is my mirror, reflecting visions in me
> I am like a great river that slowly runs dry
> Polluted and abused, I am the River
>   slowly—I die with . . . .

Anthropologists such as Robert Louis Nathan and Kingsley Palmer have revealed Aboriginal culture to the rest of the world, but it was not until the 1960s that the world heard the voice of the Aborigines speaking for themselves about their lives. Monica Clare's *Karobran: The Story of an Aboriginal Girl* (1978) is the first novel ever written by an Aboriginal woman. It was completed, edited, and published by Jack Horner because Monica Clare died in 1973 before she could finish the book. *Karobran* means "togetherness." The book is a moving autobiographical novel about Isabelle, an Aboriginal girl who was removed from her family and ill-treated as a domestic servant.

Several other Aboriginal writers followed Monica Clare. Hyllus Maris (1934–1986) wrote *Women of the Sun* in the early 1950s, but the book was not published until 1985. It is a collection of stories of the lives of strong Aboriginal women who looked to the ancestors for guidance. Jack Davis (1917–2000), a noted poet and playwright, belonged to the Nyoongarah people of southwest Australia and later became the editor of the Aboriginal Publications Foundation. His first play, *Kullark* (1982), was popular as a documentary on the history of the Aboriginals in western Australia. He also wrote *The Dreamers* (1982) and *No Sugar* (1986), both known for their depth and closeness to the reality of the Aboriginal experience. *No Sugar* was voted the best stage play of the year by the Australian Writers Guild.

OODEGEROO NOONUCCAL, commonly known as Kath Walker, started writing in the 1950s. Her poems were about the struggles of the Aboriginal people and their demands for land rights and education. Noonuccal combined social issues with literature, thus revealing her depth of experience and a unique skill with the English language. She is one of Australia's greatest poets. Faith Bandler (1920–   ) wrote *Wacvie* (1977), in which she retraces her father's history as a forced worker on a sugar plantation in Queensland. Writers such as Noonuccal and Bandler also built political coalitions to lobby for positive changes for the Aborigines.

Holding up the Sky: Aboriginal Women Speak (1999) is a collection of powerful stories by Aboriginal women. They talk about issues concerning displacement from their homelands, forced removal from families, physical abuse, and lost identities. Collections like this one and *Writing Us Mob: New Indigenous Voices* (2000) are of great value because these are the voices of the Aborigines.

B. Wongar's *The Track to Bralgu* (1977) is a collection of 12 short stories that portray the barrenness of the once fertile land of the Aborigines and the exploitation by the white world of all the Aborigines' resources.

Several writers of mixed origin emerged to tell the stories of the Aboriginal experience because the government considered them to be Aborigines. One such writer is Sally Morgan (1951–), who wrote *My Place* (1987), an autobiography tracing the lives of her ancestors of the Nyoongal people of southwest Australia. Morgan captures their struggles to be educated and find jobs to sustain their families. She emphasizes the importance of the family roots that kept her family together. She also talks about the deep Aboriginal spirituality that believes in the spirits of the ancestors protecting future generations.

Today, there are institutions that specifically promote Aboriginal art and literature, such as the Aboriginal Center in Perth, the Aboriginal Publications Foundation, the Australian Institute of Aboriginal and Torres Strait Islander Studies in Canberra, and the Aboriginal Arts Board of the Australian Arts Council.

The Aboriginal literary movement emerged from autobiographies and life experiences. Memoirs written by women are often referred to as "herstories." They reveal a strong sense of the writers' connection with the land and the spirit world. Herstories are self-presentations, an expression of the self as part of others, even across generations. They were also a means of resisting government control. Aboriginal writings are seen by some scholars as political acts in themselves, as the writers fight against the oblivion imposed on Aborigines by the white culture to identify, recognize, and recapture some of the social, spiritual, and literary elements of the Aboriginal past.

Works about the Aboriginal Movement

Brock, Peggy, ed. *Women, Rites and Sites: Aboriginal Women's Cultural Knowledge*. Boston: Allen and Unwin, 1900.
Clayton, Stephen. "I Am-Aborigine." Available online at www.dreamtime.auz.net/StoryAbor.htm.
Heiss, Anita, ed. *Anthology of Australian Aboriginal Literature*. Montreal: McGill University Press, 2008.
Nathan, Robert Louis. *The Dreamtime*. Woodstock, N.Y.: Overlook Press, 1975.
Simms, Norman. *Silence and Invisibility: A Study of the New Literature from the Pacific*. Washington, D.C.: Three Continents Press, 1986.

Abrahams, Peter Henry (Peter Graham)
(1919–) *novelist, short story writer, journalist*

When Peter Abrahams was five years old, his father, an Ethiopian, died. Abrahams was sent to live with relatives in Johannesburg, South Africa, far from his mixed-race mother. Although he returned three years later, the family's desperate financial situation forced young Abrahams to go to work for a metal worker. This nine-year-old boy was to grow up to become one of South Africa's best-known writers.

When Abrahams was still a young man, an office worker took him under her wing and read Shakespeare to him, awakening a lifelong love of learning. Throughout many years of menial employment, Abrahams held fast to his educational dreams, going to school when he could. At one point, Abrahams even tried to start a school for poor, black, and colored South Africans, one where native languages could be spoken.

When Abrahams was 20, he took a job as a stoker on a freighter bound for England. Abrahams wrote regularly, publishing his first books during World War II: a collection of short stories, *Dark Testament* (1942), and a novel, *Song of the City* (1945), which begins to examine the costs of urbanization for black South Africans, a theme he took up again more successfully two years later in *Mine Boy*. His growing professional reputation made it possible for him to return to South Africa in 1952, when he took a job as a reporter for *The London Observer*.

His work as a journalist, including employment as a scriptwriter for the BBC, provided the opportunity to write creatively. Of Abrahams's eight novels, the two that have most solidified his reputation are *Mine Boy* (1946) and *Wild Conquest* (1951). Both novels deal with the great movements of peoples within South Africa during its several centuries of settlement and development. *Wild Conquest* focuses on the Great Trek of the Boers in the 19th century. These descendants of Dutch settlers spread north from Cape Province in search of a religious and secular paradise. They inevitably encountered indigenous peoples, including the Matabeles, who challenged the Boers' sense of mission. Because the descendants of the Boers were to set the foundation for the next century's apartheid laws, Abrahams's focus on these interactions combines historical perspective with contemporary focus. This type of novelistic approach made him something of a literary spokesperson for the developing antiapartheid movement in the 1950s and 1960s. *Mine Boy* follows a migration of a different sort: the economic movement of people in search of jobs in mines and in urban areas. Such economic migrations led to the dissolution of families and the creation of company- and industry-controlled living areas. Although this novel calls for a multiracial coexistence as the only possible future for South Africa, the story ends with the deaths of many characters who embraced this noble goal.

Critical reception of Abrahams's many essays, novels, and autobiographical writings has been mixed, in part because of the contradictory messages of novels such as *Mine Boy*. However, his fusion of a European narrative style with a focus on African themes and tendencies made Abrahams one of the first voices from South Africa to question the divisiveness of apartheid from the perspective of a person of color.

Other Works by Peter Abrahams

The Black Experience in the 20th Century: An Autobiography and Meditation. Bloomington: Indiana University Press, 2001.

A Night of Their Own. New York: Knopf, 1965.

The View from Coyaba. London: Faber and Faber, 1985.

A Wreath for Udomo. London: Faber and Faber, 1956.

Works about Peter Abrahams

Lindfors, Bernth. "Exile and Aesthetic Distance: Geographical Influences on Political Commitment in the Works of Peter Abrahams." *International Fiction Review* 13 (Summer 1986).

Wade, Michael. *Peter Abrahams*. London: Evans Bros., 1972.

———. "Peter Abrahams at 70." *Southern African Review of Books* (June/July 1989). Available online. URL: http://www.uni-ulm.de/~rturrell/antho4html/Wade.html.

Achebe, Chinua (1930–) *novelist*

Albert Chinualumogu Achebe (ah CHAY bay) was born in Ogidi, eastern Nigeria, when Nigeria was a British colony. His father, Isaiah Okafor Achebe, was raised according to the traditions of the Ibgo people but converted to Christianity and became a church teacher. His mother, Janet Achebe, told him traditional folktales as he was growing up. Achebe learned to respect the old ways even as his country was adopting new ones.

After studying at University College in Ibadan, Achebe received a B.A. from London University in 1953. He became a producer and eventually a director for the Nigerian Broadcasting Company. In 1961, he married Christie Chinwe Okoli, with whom he had four children. After establishing his reputation as a writer, he left broadcasting in 1966. When civil war broke out the following year—eastern Nigeria, the Igbo homeland, attempted to secede from the Nigerian federation as a new country called Biafra—he traveled abroad to promote the Biafran cause. *Beware, Soul Brother* (1971) describes his war experiences, including his family's narrow escape when their apartment was hit by a bomb. In 1976, he became professor of English at the University of Nigeria. A serious car accident in 1990 left him paralyzed from the waist down. In June 2007, Achebe won the Man Booker

International Prize for fiction. The $120,000 prize is awarded for a body of work. Achebe is currently the David and Marianna Fisher University Professor and professor of Africana studies at Brown University in Providence, Rhode Island.

In *Home and Exile* (1988), Achebe writes that he decided to become a writer after reading Joyce Cary's *Mr. Johnson.* Critics praised the book's realistic portrayal of Africa, but Achebe thought its Nigerian hero was "an embarrassing nitwit." He decided that "the story we had to tell could not be told for us by anyone else, no matter how gifted and well-intentioned." His novels tell the story of Nigeria "from the inside," from Igbo resistance to British colonization through the coup that established the commander of the Nigerian army, General Ironisi, as head of state in 1966.

Critical Analysis

Achebe's first novel, *Things Fall Apart* (1958), tells the story of Okonwo, a great man among his people but someone who cannot adapt to the changes brought by colonization. Achebe does not idealize the old ways, but he presents them as worthy of respect. However, as Okonkwo's son Obierika tells him, "He [the white man] has put a knife on the things that held us together, and we have fallen apart." Okonkwo's refusal to adapt leads him to violence and ultimately to destruction. As Achebe explained in a 2000 interview in *Atlantic,* "With the coming of the British, Igbo land as a whole was incorporated . . . with a whole lot of other people with whom the Igbo people had not had direct contact before. . . . You had to learn a totally new reality, and accommodate yourself to the demands of this new reality, which is the state called Nigeria."

Things Fall Apart established Achebe as "the founding father of modern African literature," according to Harvard philosopher K. Anthony Appiah. Achebe was the first novelist to present colonization from an African point of view. He also introduced what he calls a "new English," using Igbo proverbs and pidgin English to express the African oral tradition in English. As

editor of the journal *Okike,* which he founded in 1971, Achebe continues to promote new African writing.

The most influential of his works, *Things Fall Apart* has been translated into more than 50 languages. In the *Atlantic* interview, Achebe explains its appeal: "There are many, many ways in which people are deprived or subjected to all kinds of victimization—it doesn't have to be colonization. Once you allow yourself to identify with the people in a story, then you might begin to see yourself in that story."

At the beginning of Achebe's second novel, *No Longer at Ease* (1960), Okonkwo's grandson Obi is on trial for accepting bribes. Obi is one of the educated elite to whom the British plan to turn over the government when Nigeria becomes independent. "Like his grandfather, Obi was another victim of cultural conflict," notes Bernth Lindfors. "Obi had been weaned away from traditional values but had not fully assimilated Western ideals; having no firm moral convictions, he was confused by his predicament and fell." Torn between tradition and modern ways, Obi—and his generation—are "no longer at ease."

Arrow of God (1964) is set in the 1920s. Enzelu, chief priest of the patron god of his Igbo village, finds himself caught in a conflict between his people and British colonial administrators, who want to make him village chieftain. Gerald Moore, in *Seven African Writers,* notes that "As in Achebe's other novels, it is the strong-willed man of tradition who cannot adapt, and who is crushed by virtues in the war between the new, more worldly order, and the old conservative values of an isolated society."

The narrator of Achebe's fourth novel, *A Man of the People,* is involved in a fictional coup that foreshadows the actual coup the occurred the year the novel was published. Odili, a schoolteacher, at first supports M. A. Nanga, a villager who has become minister of culture, but runs against him when he realizes that Nanga abuses his power. Although set in the fictional Republic of Kangan, the satire has obvious parallels to present-day Nigeria. The novel reflects the conviction Achebe expressed in *The Trouble with Nigeria* (1983): "Hopeless as it may seem today, Nigeria is not absolutely beyond redemption. Critical, yes, but not entirely hopeless. Nigerians are what they are only because their leaders are *not* what *they* should be."

In 1979, Achebe received the Order of the Federal Republic for his contributions to African literature. "I would be quite satisfied if my novels (especially the ones I set in the past) did no more than teach my readers that their past—with all its imperfections—was not one long night of savagery from which the first Europeans acting on God's behalf delivered them," he reflected in *Morning Yet on Creation Day* (1975). Today, he is recognized as the first African to adapt the conventions of the European novel successfully and is Africa's most widely translated writer.

Another Work by Chinua Achebe

The Education of a British-Protected Child: Essays. New York: Knopf, 2009.

Works about Chinua Achebe

Ezenwa-Ohaeto. *Chinua Achebe: A Biography.* Bloomington: Indiana University Press, 1997.

Innes, C. L. *Chinua Achebe.* New York: Cambridge University Press, 1992.

Lindfors, Bernth. *Conversations with Chinua Achebe.* Jackson: University Press of Mississippi, 1997.

———. *Early Achebe.* Trenton, N.J.: Africa World Press, Inc., 2009.

Moore, Gerald. *Seven African Writers.* New York: Oxford University Press, 1960.

acmeism

Acmeism (a term derived from the Greek word meaning "perfection") was a Russian poetic movement established in St. Petersburg in 1913. In a sense, acmeism was a reactionary movement that opposed the mystical elements of SYMBOLISM. The poets NIKOLAI GUMILEV, Sergey Gorodetsky (1884–1967), ANNA AKHMATOVA, and OSIP MAN-DELSTAM were the leaders of the movement and regularly contributed to *Apollon,* the main literary journal of acmeism. According to the acmeists, poetry should contain concrete ideas about culture and human experience rather than abstract and, often, solipsistic notions that are found in symbolist poetry. At the same time, however, the acmeists incorporated the symbolist emphasis on the role of mythical and religious figures in poetry. The mythical figures found in acmeist poetry stressed continuity of history and culture.

The movement lasted until the early 1920s and eventually disintegrated with the advent of SOCIALIST REALISM. The role of the acmeists, however, is enormous in terms of their influence on the later generations of poets and writers. The acmeists attempted to provide verse with significance that extended the bounds of social and political reality. Their revolution was of a linguistic kind. The acmeists treated the individual as a being of cosmic significance rather than a dispossessed creature, tethered to a landscape grown ungovernably hostile.

A Work about Acmeism

Doherty, Justin. *The Acmeist Movement in Russian Poetry: Culture and the Word.* New York: Oxford University Press, 1997.

Adiga, Aravind (1974–   ) *novelist, journalist*

Indian-born writer Aravind Adiga came to literary prominence when his critically acclaimed first novel, *The White Tiger* (2008), received the 2008 Man Booker Prize. Born in Chennai (Madras), India, on October 23, 1974, he was raised in Mangalore in the state of Karnataka, attending St. Aloysius High School. In 1990, Adiga emigrated to Sydney, Australia. He then relocated to New York City, attending Columbia University, graduating second in his class with a B.A. in English literature in 1997. Adiga attended Magdalen College, Oxford, where he received a master's degree. Beginning in 2000, Adiga worked as a journalist for the *Financial Times* covering Wall Street and returned to India in 2003 as a correspondent for

Time magazine, writing chiefly about business, politics, and arts.

A novel written as a series of letters from Balram Halwai, a newly rich chauffeur, to Wen Jiabao, the Chinese premier, *The White Tiger* presents a grimly sardonic picture of the seamy, striving underclass of contemporary India. In telling his life story in his self-serving way, Balram applies the triumphalist rhetoric associated with the modernization of India to the brutal institutionalized impoverishment from which he charts his ascent. The chief conceit of the novel divides India into haves and have-nots, "the Darkness" and "the Light." "In the old days there were 1,000 castes," Adiga writes. "These days, there are just two castes: Men with Big Bellies, and Men with Small Bellies." The son of a rickshaw driver who dies of tuberculosis, Balram emerges from a corrupt, hardscrabble existence where the "sewage glistens" and the teacher in the local school bullies and lies to his students. A visiting inspector gives Balram the name the White Tiger, the rarest of the rare, the only boy in a classroom of emaciated dullards to identify the photograph of a corrupt politician. This marks Balram's ambition, and as he manages to secure a position in Delhi he continues to mark the great division of modern Indian society.

> With their tinted windows up, the cars of the rich go like dark eggs down the roads of Delhi. Every now and then, an egg will crack open— a woman's hand, dazzling with gold bangles, stretches out of an open window, flings an empty mineral water bottle onto the road—and then the window goes up, and the egg is resealed.

Balram contrasts this picture with Old Delhi in a manner that amounts to a social critique:

> Go to Old Delhi . . . and look at the way they keep chickens there in the market. Hundreds of pale hens and brightly coloured roosters, stuffed tightly into wire-mesh cages . . . They see the organs of their brothers lying around them. They know they're next. Yet they do not rebel. They do not try to get out of the coop. The very same thing is done with human beings in this country.

Balram turns out to be as much sociopath as social critic. Reminscent of Patricia Highsmith's Tom Ripley, Adiga's protagonist murders his employer and steals a large sum of cash with which he launches a taxi service in Bangalore, catering to a new class of technology workers.

"As a parable of the new India, then, Balram's tale has a distinctly macabre twist," as Akash Kapur noted in the *New York Times*. "He is not (or not only) an entrepreneur but a roguish criminal with a remarkable capacity for self-justification. Likewise, the background against which he operates is not just a resurgent economy and nation but a landscape of corruption, inequality and poverty." In accepting the Man Booker Prize, Adiga remarked that *The White Tiger* was an "attempt to catch the voice of the men you meet as you travel through India—the voice of the colossal underclass." He dedicated it to "the people of New Delhi where I lived and where I wrote this book."

With the success of *The White Tiger*, Adiga has subsequently published a number of editorials, book reviews, and a linked series of short stories entitled *Between the Assassinations* (2008). Written prior to *The White Tiger*, these stories mine a similar terrain to that of *The White Tiger*, describing economic, religious, and ethnic tensions in the southern Indian city of Kittur. The title refers to the period between the assassination of Indira Gandhi in 1984 and that of her son Rajiv in 1991 and signals Adiga's abiding interest in linking the small stories of peddlers and their like to the broad currents of Indian political life.

Given the success (and similar themes) of the 2009 motion picture *Slumdog Millionaire*, there has been growing interest in turning *The White Tiger* into a film. Adiga's second novel, *Last Man in the Tower*, is expected to be published in 2011. Unlike his first novel, which was set in New Delhi, Adiga's second book is set in Mumbai, where the author currently resides.

A Work about Aravind Adiga

Merritt Moseley. "Ordinary Novels." In *Sewanee Review* 118, no. 1 (winter 2010): 154–160.

Adonis (Ali Ahmad Sa'id; Adunis)
   (1930–) *poet, critic*

Adonis is one of the fathers of modernism in Arabic literature and is its leading proponent of avant-garde verse. *Songs of Mihyar the Damascene* (1960) is his most important book of poems, combining his concern for history and politics with his demand for a new kind of poetic language and a radically experimental poetic form. *The Static and the Dynamic in Arabic Culture* is one of his many books of cultural theory and literary criticism that earned a key, if controversial, place on the Arabic bookshelf. In it, Adonis describes cycles of change and stagnation in the history of Arabic culture, defining moments of MODERNISM as those times when creative new ways of looking at the world emerge and challenge habitual ways. These breakthroughs, themselves, gradually become habitual and inhibit creativity until the next moment breaks with tradition. In other volumes of theory, such as *The Time of Poetry* (1972), *The Shock of Modernity* (1978), and a massive work entitled simply *The Book* (1995), Adonis continues his philosophical task of clearing away what he sees as stagnant Arabic literary traditions and calling for an embrace of modernism.

Adonis is a proponent of intellectual poetry, opposing the traditional connection of Arabic poetics to musicality and *tarab,* the state of being entranced by a poem, typically a goal of Arabic poetry. "A Grave for New York" is a long, important political poem that cites Walt Whitman as an influence and also demonstrates the influence on Adonis of SYMBOLISM and surrealism, and a cryptic, almost mystical use of language. So contrary are many of his poetic methods to Arabic expectations that his readership tends to be small, though refined. Adonis's literary criticism, on the other hand, has had considerable weight in the world of Arabic literature, through his books as well as his founding and editorship of two literary magazines, *Shi'r* (Poetry) with poet Yusuf al-Khal (1957), and *Mawaqif* (Stances) (1968).

Born in the Syrian mountains and educated in Syria, Adonis moved to Beirut and took Lebanese citizenship. Influenced in his belief in the importance of myth and symbol by Anton Sa'ada, founder of the Syrian Nationalist Socialist Party, Adonis changed his name to that of a figure from ancient Syrian myth. He has taught at the Sorbonne and other European and American universities and is translated most extensively in French. His wife of many years, Khalida Sa'id, is an important literary critic. In 2007, Adonis was awarded the Bjørnson Prize by the Norwegian Academy of Literature and Freedom of Expression.

Other Works by Adonis

The Blood of Adonis. Translated by Samuel Hazo. Pittsburgh, Pa.: University of Pittsburgh Press, 1971.

Introduction to Arabic Poetics. Translated by Catherine Cobham. Austin: University of Texas Press, 1991.

The Pages of Day and Night. Translated by Samuel Hazo. Evanston, Ill.: Marlboro Press/Northwestern University Press, 1994.

Shatz, Adam. "An Arab Poet Who Dares to Differ." *New York Times,* July 13, 2002.

Victims of a Map: A Bilingual Anthology of Arabic Poetry by Samih al-Qasim, Adonis, and Mahmud Darwish. Translated by Abdullah al-Udhari. London: Al-Saqi Books, 1984.

Adunis

See ADONIS.

Agnon, Samuel Joseph (Shmuel Yosef Czaczkes) (1888–1970) *novelist, short story writer*

Samuel Joseph Agnon was born Shmuel Yosef Czaczkes in the Jewish town of Buczacz, in the Austro-Hungarian Empire (now Poland). Agnon began writing at eight years old in both Hebrew and Yiddish and published his first poems in a newspaper at age 15. Though he did not attend school, he was educated by both his father, a fur trader with rabbinical training, and his mother, who taught him German literature. In 1907, he left home for Palestine (now Israel), where he changed his surname from Czaczkes to Agnon. He remained there his entire life, with the exception of 11 years spent in Germany from 1913 to 1924.

His folk-epic *The Bridal Canopy* (1931), an allegory on the decline of the Jewish religious life in Poland, is considered a classic in modern Hebrew literature. The plot chronicles the travels and the inner religious turmoil of a Hasidic Jew who seeks a dowry for his daughters in early 19th-century Europe. Agnon's greatest novel, however, is *The Day Before Yesterday* (1945), which is set in the period of the second aliyah, the wave of Jewish emigration to Palestine between 1907 and 1913. The novel is considered a cornerstone of modern Hebrew literature.

Nearly all of Agnon's symbolic and folkloric writing is set in Palestine. Many of his stories are influenced by the Jewish emigration to Palestine, Jewish assimilation into Western culture, and the contrasts between a traditional Jewish life and a modern Jewish life.

Agnon secured his place as one of the central figures of modern world literature for bringing the conflicts of Jewish culture to life. He won the Nobel Prize for literature in 1965 and is widely considered the greatest writer of modern fiction in Hebrew.

Other Works by Shmuel Yosef Agnon

Days of Awe. New York: Schocken Books, 1995.
Only Yesterday. Princeton, N.J.: Princeton University Press, 2002.
Shira. New York: Syracuse University Press, 1996.
A Simple Story. New York: Syracuse University Press, 1999.

A Work about Shmuel Yosef Agnon

Shaked, Gershon. *Shmuel Yosef Agnon: A Revolutionary Traditionalist.* Translated by Jeffrey M. Green. New York: New York University Press, 1989.

Aichinger, Ilse (1921–) *poet, short story writer, novelist*

Ilse Aichinger was born in Vienna, Austria. Her father, Leopold, was a Jewish doctor, and her mother, Berta Kremer, was a gentile teacher. Aichinger grew up in Vienna and Linz, graduating from high school in 1939. The Nazis prevented her from attending medical school because of her Jewish heritage. During World War II, many of her relatives were killed in concentration camps. Aichinger became fiercely antifascist, a trait that would characterize her postwar writing.

Following the war, Aichinger enrolled in medical school in Vienna. She quit after five semesters to devote herself full time to a writing career. In 1948, she worked as a reader for Fischer Publishing Company and wrote *Die Größere Hoffnung* (*The Greater Hope,* 1948), a novel about a Viennese girl who sympathizes with her Jewish friends after the Nazi takeover of Austria. The following year, Aichinger cofounded the Hochschule für Gestaltung (Academy for Arts and Designs) in Ulm, West Germany. She married poet GÜNTER EICH in 1953. The couple occasionally attended the annual meetings of the German writers' association, GRUPPE 47.

Aichinger wrote numerous short stories, radio plays, and poems in the second half of the 20th century. Influenced by the Holocaust, Aichinger's writings often take the perspective of the victims of German-Austrian society. Literary scholar James Alldridge explains that "her appeal is to a humanity deep within each of us, addressed in a language unadorned by flourishes and unadorned by experiments in usage." Aichinger won numerous German and Austrian awards, including the Georg Trakl Prize for Poetry and the Literature Prize of the Bavarian Academy of Fine Arts.

Other Works by Ilse Aichinger

The Bound Man and Other Stories. Translated by Eric Mosbacher. New York: Noonday Press, 1956.
Herod's Children. Translated by Cornelia Schaeffer. New York: Atheneum, 1963.

A Work about Ilse Aichinger

Alldridge, James C. *Ilse Aichinger*. Chester Springs, Pa.: Dufour Editions, 1969.

Aidoo, Christina Ama Ata (1942–   )

short story writer, novelist, poet, dramatist

Ghana gained its independence from Britain in 1957 when Christina Ama Ata Aidoo was 15; thus, in a sense, Aidoo came of age at the same time as her country. Her very name, with its combination of Christian and indigenous elements (she dropped her Christian name in the early 1970s), speaks to Aidoo's lifelong passion for exploring the fusion of elements that makes her people unique. Aidoo's works speak to the synthesis of traditional and Christian beliefs inherent in Ghana. Her family has a tradition of resistance to oppression, including a grandfather who was killed by the British. Aidoo is descended from the Fante, a group that was particularly active in their resistance to the British during the colonial period in Ghana. The Fante are part of a larger group of people, the Akan, whose traditionalist values are explored—and questioned—in many of her texts.

At an early age, Aidoo won a short-story competition sponsored by a prestigious publisher. This led her to have confidence in herself as a voice for her people, but especially as a voice for women of color in Ghana and throughout the world. Because very few women in developing countries have easy access to educational opportunities, Aidoo has often written from the perspective of one who has succeeded against the odds. She voices the belief that education can lead to an awareness of a culture's limitations. In short-story collections such as *No Sweetness Here* (1970), poems such as those collected in *An Angry Letter in January and Other Poems* (1992), and in novels such as *Our Sister Killjoy* (1977), Aidoo voices a fierce resistance to gender subjugation—the oppression of women—and class domination. Her essay, "To Be a Woman," published in 1980, bemoans the traditional Akan degradation of women. As such,

Aidoo challenges both the vestiges of the British colonial presence and the ingrained attitudes of Africans.

Aidoo was Ghana's minister of education for a brief time in the early 1980s, until her controversial views led to her removal from office. She now lives primarily in Zimbabwe and the United States, where she has had a series of academic appointments. Aidoo is a regular speaker at African literary gatherings throughout the United States and the world, where she continues to influence those interested in issues of gender, race, and class.

Another Work by Ama Ata Aidoo

Someone Talking to Sometime. Harare, Zimbabwe: College Press, 1985.

A Work about Ama Ata Aidoo

Nasta, Susheila, ed. *Motherlands: Black Women's Writing from Africa.* New Brunswick, N.J.: Rutgers University Press, 1992.

Akhmadulina, Izabella Akhatovna

(1937–2010) *poet*

Izabella Akhmadulina was born in Moscow, Russia. She graduated from high school in 1954 and began her literary career working for a small newspaper *Metrostroevets*. In 1955, Akhmadulina began her studies at the prestigious Gorky Institute of Literature and published her first poem. During her studies, she was briefly expelled from the university for the apolitical focus of her verse. She was allowed to return only when Pavel Antokolsky, a respected Russian writer (1896–1978), intervened on her behalf. In 1958, she married the poet YEVGENY YEVTUSHENKO, but they were later divorced.

Akhmadulina is often associated with the "New Wave" of Russian poets that emerged after Stalin's death. The New Wave poets often focused on themes outside the political agenda of SOCIALIST REALISM. Akhmadulina, in particular, addressed the craft of poetry in her verse, often exploring metapoetics as a subject in itself. Akhmadulina considered MARINA TSVETAEVA and ANNA AKHMATOVA to be the greatest influences on her own work.

With the publication of her first poetry collection, *Strings* (1962), Akhmadulina established her position among the major contemporary poets of Russia. Her careful attention to the poetic form and diction made her enormously popular with both the Russian public and critics. During Akhmadulina's prolific career, she published eight books of verse: *Chills* (1968), *Music Lessons* (1969), *Poems* (1975), *Candle* (1977), *Dreams of Georgia* (1977), *The Secret: New Poems* (1983), *The Garden* (1987), *Poems* (1987), and *Selected Works* (1988). Virtually all of these books were critically acclaimed and celebrated for their lyrical beauty and impressive poetic form. These lines from "Autumn" are an example:

> *Not working, not breathing,*
> *the beehive sweetens and dies.*
> *The autumn deepens, the soul*
> *ripens and grows round . . .*

As Sonia I. Ketchian points out, "Akhmadulina's poetry has been lauded for forcefulness of expression and masterful execution of form, in its finesse and sentient approach to her subject and its underlying surroundings, the product of Izabella Akhmadulina's pen bears the unmistakable signature of a woman."

Akhmadulina was elected a member of the American Academy of Arts and Literature in 1977, but at home she often faced government criticism, and she was not permitted to publish any works between 1977 and 1983. This government mandate, however, was completely reversed by 1989, when Akhmadulina was awarded the State Prize in Literature—the highest prize for literature in the Soviet Union. Her work is continuously acclaimed both in Russia and abroad. In 2004, Akhmadulina was awarded the State Prize of the Russian Federation for literature.

Works by Izabella Akhmadulina

Fever & Other New Poems. With an introduction by Yevgeny Yevtushenko. Translated by Geoffrey Dutton and Igor Mezhakoff-Koriakin. New York: William Morrow, 1969.

The Garden: New and Selected Poetry and Prose. Translated by F. D. Reeve. New York: Henry Holt, 1990.

A Work about Izabella Akhmadulina

Ketchian, Sonia I. *The Poetic Craft of Bella Akhmadulina*. University Park: Pennsylvania State University Press, 1993.

Akhmatova, Anna (Anna Andreyevna Gorenko) (1889–1965) *poet*

Anna Akhmatova was born in a small town near Odessa, Russia, into a family of minor nobility. Her father, Andrey Gorenko, was a retired navy engineer, and her mother, Inna Gorenko, was in charge of the family affairs. The Akhmatovs moved to Zarskoye Selo, the birthplace of ALEKSANDR PUSHKIN, when Anna was one year old. Akhmatova began writing poetry when she was 11. While in school, Akhmatova was an academically average student, more concerned with writing poetry than studying. Her father disapproved of her writing and told her that it brought shame to the family's name. From then on, Anna Gorenko signed her work as Anna Akhmatova. Akhmatova was an intense reader, and she particularly loved the poetry of Aleksandr Pushkin.

In 1907, Akhmatova began to study law at the university in Kiev. In 1910, she married the poet NIKOLAI GUMILEV, whom she had known since her school days. These years of intense work and passionate personal relationships produced two collections of lyrical poems, *Evening* (1912) and *Chiotki* (1914), notable for their striking images and skillful use of rhyme and meter. In all her work, Akhmatova cared more about the craft of poetry and its personal implications than about social issues. Both volumes received favorable reviews from the critics. During this time, Akhmatova adhered to ACMEISM, a poetic movement that opposed SYMBOLISM and emphasized clarity of expression and concrete imagery. Along with Gumilev, Akhmatova became the leading figure of this movement.

In 1918, Akhmatova divorced Gumilev, but his political difficulties (he was executed in 1921 for alleged involvement in an anti-Soviet plot) affected her standing with the authorities, who were already uncomfortable with her poetic preoccupation with love and religion. Between 1923 and 1940, none of her work was published in book form, although a few poems were published in journals. She worked as an assistant librarian at the Agricultural Institute and lived in poverty. In the 1930s, she faced personal tragedy when her son and her second husband were arrested for espionage. They were released only after personal intervention by Stalin. Her lyric cycle *Requiem* was composed during this period; inspired by her grief over her son's absence, the poems memorialize the suffering of the entire Russian people under Stalin. They were not published in Russia until 1989, but Akhmatova developed an enormous underground following in Russia, as well as a large audience abroad. During World War II, when Germany invaded Russia and laid siege to Leningrad, Akhmatova was enlisted to help boost public morale with radio addresses and readings.

Akhmatova refused to conform to the standards of SOCIALIST REALISM, and for this she was ostracized by many in the Soviet Writers' Union. She criticized the Stalinist regime and paid dearly for her honesty when, in 1946, she was publicly humiliated and expelled from the Writers' Union. In addition, in 1949, her son was sent to Siberia as a political prisoner, remaining there until 1956. Even after Stalin's death in 1953, Akhmatova continued to be criticized by government officials because her work supposedly did not address the needs and reality of the Soviet people. In spite of these adversities, however, Akhmatova became one of Russia's most famous poets. Small volumes of her poems

and translations and her critical essays on Pushkin began to be issued in Russia after 1958.

Akhmatova did not break with the rich tradition of Russian poetry but rather enriched it. She also introduced Russian readers to a larger world with her translations of such great poets as VICTOR HUGO, RABINDRANATH TAGORE, and GIACOMO LEOPARDI. Today, she is one of the most widely read and quoted poets in Russia. In addition to its extraordinary lyrical beauty, Akhmatova's poetry is associated with personal freedom, the expression of emotions, and political liberty.

During her lifetime Akhmatova received a number of awards, particularly from European countries, including the Etna-Taormina literary prize from the Italian government in 1964 and an honorary doctorate from Oxford University in 1965. She established a reputation as a "Russian Sappho" in many countries.

Other Works by Anna Akhmatova
Kunitz, Stanley, ed. *Poems of Akhmatova: Izbrannye Stikhi.* Translated by Max Hayward. Boston: Houghton Mifflin, 1997.

Meyer, Ronald, ed. *My Half-century: Selected Prose.* Evanston, Ill.: Northwestern University Press, 1997.

Reeder, Roberta, ed. *The Complete Poems of Anna Akhmatova.* Translated by Judith Hemschemeyer. Tucson, Ariz.: Zephyr Press, 1998.

Works about Anna Akhmatova
Dalos, Gyorgy. *The Guest from the Future: Anna Akhmatova and Isaiah Berlin.* Translated by Antony Wood. New York: Farrar, Straus & Giroux, 1999.

Reeder, Roberta. *Anna Akhmatova: Poet and Prophet.* New York: Picador, 1995.

Akutagawa Ryūnosuke (1892–1927)
short story writer, poet, essayist

Akutagawa Ryūnosuke was born in Tokyo to Niihara Toshizō and Fuku. Shortly after his birth, his mother went insane, so Akutagawa was adopted by his uncle, Akutagawa Dōshō. He was an excellent student and took lessons in English and Chinese in addition to doing his regular schoolwork. In 1913, he entered the English department of Tokyo Imperial University. After graduating in 1916, he took up teaching at a naval school in Yokosuka and soon married Tsukamoto Fumiko. Three years later, he resigned to write stories full-time for the *Osaka Mainichi Newspaper*. In 1921, the newspaper sent him to China as a correspondent; however, health problems prevented him from writing any articles until he had returned home. At the age of 35, he committed suicide by drinking poison.

While still at university, Akutagawa began publishing short stories in a school literary magazine called *Shinshichō* (New tides) and he published a short story collection called *Rashōmon* (1915), set in medieval Kyoto. In 1916, the respected novelist Natsume Sōseki promoted his story "The Nose" for publication. The short story achieved widespread popularity, establishing Akutagawa as a writer. "The Nose" draws on the classical stories of *Tales of Times Now Past* (ca. 1107) for its main character, a priest who is troubled by a long, dangling nose. Akutagawa's best-known work, "Hell Screen" (1918), portrays the madness of an artist inspired to depict hell's burning fires. Toward the end of his short life, Akutagawa's style shifted sharply from well-plotted historical tales. In works such as "A Fool's Life" (1927), he wrote stories that were more confessional in style, set in the modern period, and narrated in the first person.

Akutagawa is known as a master craftsman. He commonly drew on traditional stories for his tales, in part to provide a believable setting for his fantastic subject matter. In all, he wrote about 150 stories in a variety of styles and diction with strikingly evocative precision. He achieved international renown as one of the earliest Japanese authors to be translated into European languages.

Other Works by Akutagawa Ryūnosuke

The Essential Akutagawa. Edited by Seiji Lippit. New York: Marsilio, 1999.

Tales Grotesque and Curious. Translated by Glen W. Shaw. Tokyo: Hokuseido, 1948.

A Work about Akutagawa Ryūnosuke

Yu, Beongsheon. *Akutagawa: An Introduction*. Detroit, Mich.: Wayne State University Press, 1972.

Albahari, David (1948–) *novelist, short story writer, translator*

David Albahari was born in the Serbian city of Peć, but his formative years were spent in Zemun, an ancient town that is today part of the Serbian capital of Belgrade. Albahari moved to Canada in 1993, and his literary opus can be divided into two periods: the time before moving to Canada and the time after, starting with the novel *Snow Man* in 1995. The works of the first period (1973–93) reflect Albahari's interest in postmodernist experimentation, while those of the second, while still experimenting with new forms, express his focus on exile and the interplay of history and identity.

Albahari has published 10 collections of short stories, a dozen novels, and three books of essays. His works have been translated into 16 languages, and six books, including *Leeches*, have been translated into English. Albahari published the first collection of short stories, *Family Time*, in 1973. He became known to a wider audience in 1982 with *Description of Death*, which won the Ivo Andrić Award for the best short story collection of the year. The novel *Bait* (*Mamac*) received the NIN Award in 1997, the Balkanica Award in 1998, and the Brücke Berlin Prize in 2006.

Preferring the rootlessness of Canadian exile to the political pressures of Serbia, Albahari left home at the beginning of the turbulent '90s, after the breakup of former Yugoslavia and the ensuing ethnic conflicts. In spite of his endeavors, however, he could not avoid the politicization of his life and works during the war in former Yugoslavia. Albahari, who is Jewish, became the chair of the Federation of Jewish Communes of Yugoslavia in 1991 and worked on the evacuation of the Jewish population from Sarajevo.

Since his emigration, Serbian history has developed into a prominent theme in Albahari's writing, as has the concept of exile. Still, he has never abandoned his early interest in dreams, secrets, and surprises emerging from a seemingly dull everyday life, where the most prominent character is My Wife, the author's second self who readily responds to his thoughts and visions.

Albahari's crucial theme remains the family: "If you understand what is going on inside the family, you will understand what is going on in the world. Patterns repeat themselves, only the scales are different." The reader approaches historical reality through the protagonists' subjective impressions that are presented in individual memories and life experiences. Albahari's use of his autobiographical emigrant experience is best seen in *Bait*, where his mother's life story is narrated by three voices: the mother's (recorded on tape), the son's, and the voice of a Canadian friend who represents the author's new homeland. The novel *Götz and Meyer* (1998) focuses on two SS officers, guilty of murdering Jews, among other people, during World War II. Although the narrator tells the story in cold and detached tones in order to prevent the reader from identifying with the protagonists, he remains incapable of keeping a critical, unemotional attitude and is shattered by the confrontation with the past.

As the editor of several literary magazines, small presses, and book-length anthologies, Albahari introduced American postmodernist writing into Serbian literature. His translations exerted a major influence on the writers of his generation. Albahari translated such modern writers as VLADIMIR NABOKOV, John Updike, Sam Shepard, Thomas Pynchon, Saul Bellow, MARGARET ATWOOD, and many others.

Albahari is known for his interest in countercultures and fringe phenomena, from rock' n' roll to the classic Chinese divination text, *I Ching*. In the late '80s, he initiated the first formal petition to legalize marijuana in Yugoslavia.

Today, Albahari lives with his family in Calgary, Alberta, Canada. He continues to write and publish in the Serbian language.

Other Works by David Albahari

Words Are Something Else. Translated by Ellen Elias-Bursać. Evanston, Ill.: Northwestern University Press, 1996.

Tsing. Translated by David Albahari. Evanston, Ill.: Northwestern University Press, 1997.

Alberti, Rafael (1902–1999) *poet*

Rafael Alberti was born in Puerto de Santa María near the Mediterranean city of Cadíz, Spain. After moving with his family to Madrid when he was 15, he began to study painting and had his first show in 1922. Soon afterward, he contracted tuberculosis and left Madrid for Sierra de Guadarrama to recover. It was then that he began writing poetry, and within several years, he published his first collection, *Landlocked Sailor* (1925), a group of folkloric poems that won that year's National Prize for Literature.

With the publication of other poetry collections, including *Passion and Form* (1927) and *Concerning the Angels* (1928), which differ from his earlier work in their more anguished and emotional themes, Alberti's reputation as a poet grew. He was considered part of the Generation of 1927, a group of surrealist Spanish poets influenced by the language and imagery used by the 17th-century Spanish poet, Luis de Góngora.

Like many other surrealist writers and artists, Alberti became much more political in the 1930s, first joining the Communist Party, then being expelled from it, and finally fighting on behalf of the republic when the Spanish civil war broke out in 1936. Being on the losing side, he was forced to flee Spain in 1939, settling in Argentina, where he wrote poetry, painted, and worked for a publishing house. During his exile, Alberti continued to publish, including two collections, *Between the Carnation and the Sword* (1941) and *On Painting* (1945), the latter of which reflects his love of that medium, and an autobiography, *The Lost Grove* (1942). Far from his native Spain, he experienced loss, as seen in his poignant 1952 poem, "The Coming Back of an Assassinated Poet," translated by poet Mark Strand, in which the speaker mourns the death of his dear friend García Lorca: "You come back to me older and sadder in the drowsy / light of a quiet dream in March."

In 1961 Alberti moved to Italy, and after the death in 1975 of Franco, dictator of Spain, he finally returned to Spain, where he lived from 1977 until his death. His later poems, in *The Eight Names of Picasso* (1970), reflect his long friendship with the Spanish artist Pablo Picasso. Alberti is considered one of Spain's greatest 20th-century poets.

Another Work by Rafael Alberti

The Owl's Insomnia: Poems Selected and Translated by Mark Strand. New York: Athenaeum, 1973.

A Work about Rafael Alberti

Nantell, Judith. *Rafael Alberti's Poetry of the Thirties: The Poet's Public Voice.* Athens: University of Georgia Press, 1986.

Alcayaga, Lucila Godoy

See Mistral, Gabriela.

Aleichem, Shalom (Sholem Rabinowitz) (1859–1916) *novelist, short story writer, playwright*

Shalom Aleichem was born in Pereyaslavl in the Poltava area of what is now Ukraine. His father was a religious scholar and wealthy man, but the family fell on hard times when Aleichem was 12. His mother died of cholera soon after. At this time, Jews in western Russia faced the increasing threat of pogroms (organized persecution or massacres). Throughout these difficult times, Aleichem attended a traditional cheder, an elementary Jewish school in which children are taught to read the Torah and other books in Hebrew. His father encouraged him to write and, when his family again achieved stability, he sought additional schooling at the Russian district school.

As a young man, Aleichem joined the army and then worked as a government rabbi for three years.

He began his writing career in the 1880s, rejecting his mother tongue, Yiddish (considered, in that place and time, an inappropriate language for literature), to write in Hebrew and Russian. He published his first short stories under his pen name in 1883 at age 20.

When Aleichem turned to writing in Yiddish, "for the fun of it," he said, he described the impoverishment and oppression of Russian Jews with surprising, yet appropriate, humor. These stories are set in eastern Europe and in New York in the late 19th and early 20th centuries. Aleichem's themes are apparent most notably in *Fiddler on the Roof* (1964), the popular musical based on his stories in *Tevye the Dairyman,* (1918). Humor, combined with insight, have led many to compare Aleichem with the American writer and humorist Mark Twain.

A combination of the pogroms of 1905 and World War I convinced Aleichem and his family to abandon their home and relocate in the United States, where he attempted to establish himself as a playwright. He helped found, through his plays, the Yiddish theater in New York City.

Today, Shalom Aleichem is recognized as having been one of the greatest Yiddish writers. His five novels, many plays, and some 300 short stories illustrate universal themes of wisdom, humiliation, pride, and humor that find their voice in the poverty of the Jews of his era. His tales have touched generations of readers around the world. Known as the "bard of the poor," he said, "Life is a dream for the wise, a game for the fool, a comedy for the rich, a tragedy for the poor" ("Putting Sholom Aleichem on a Belated Pedestal," The *New York Times,* January 5, 2002).

Other Works by Shalom Aleichem

Letters to Menakhem. New Haven, Conn.: Yale University Press, 2002.

Nineteen to the Dozen. Syracuse, N.Y.: Syracuse University Press, 2002.

Tevye the Dairyman. New York: Random House, 1988.

A Work about Shalom Aleichem

Samuel, Maurice. *The World of Shalom Aleichem.*
New York: Dramatists Play Series, 1948.

Alencar, José Martiniano de
(1829–1877) *novelist*

José Martiniano de Alencar was born on May 1 in Mecejana in the state of Ceará in Brazil. He came from a well-to-do family of the northeastern region of Brazil, and he pursued his higher education in Rio de Janeiro and São Paulo. After completing his studies, he moved to Rio de Janeiro in 1850 to begin his career as a lawyer and a journalist. In 1856, he rose to literary fame through his critiques of the sentimental poetry of a famous Brazilian author, Domingos José Gonçalves de Magalhães. That same year, Alencar published his first novel, *Five Minutes,* which came out as a serial in a daily newspaper.

Alencar also wrote plays, biographies, political analyses, and journalistic works, but he is best known as a novelist. He was one of the earliest novelists in Brazil, and his goal was to create novels that were unique to Brazil's situation as a newly independent nation and that could represent the Brazilian national identity. He wrote historical novels and novels about modern Brazilian life in urban and rural areas, but his most famous works are three novels whose main characters are indigenous Brazilians: *O Guarani* (*The Guaraní Indian,* 1857), *Iracema* (1865), and *Ubirajara* (1874). Alencar's image of Brazil's identity as a new nation was based on the mix of cultures between native Brazilians and Portuguese colonialists. Alencar's representation of miscegenation between Indians and white Portuguese colonialists as the root of the Brazilian race predicts the theories of an important Brazilian author of the 20th century, GILBERTO FREYRE, who defined Brazil as a racial democracy. For Alencar, it was this mix that made Brazil's cultural identity unique. He valorizes the noble Indian characters in his romantic novels, and his work is considered part of the INDIANIST

movement in Brazilian literature. Because he was the only novelist from that movement (all of the other Indianist writers were poets), and because he was one of the earliest Brazilian novelists, his work is especially important in the history of Brazilian literature.

In addition to being a novelist, Alencar had a long career in public affairs, which influenced his social ideals and his writing. Following his success as a lawyer and a journalist, Alencar was a deputy in the legislature and then minister of justice from 1868 to 1870. He ran for the senate in 1869 and received the highest number of votes. However, Pedro II, the emperor, had the constitutional privilege to select from three finalists, and he chose a different candidate because Alencar had previously criticized him. In spite of this disappointment, Alencar participated in public affairs throughout his life, in addition to his career as a journalist and later as a university professor. He was considered one of the greatest orators of his day. Alencar died on December 12, 1877, of tuberculosis.

Another Work by José de Alencar

Senhora: Profile of a Woman. Translated by Catarina Feldmann Edinger. Austin: University of Texas Press, 1994.

Works about José de Alencar

Haberly, David. *Three Sad Races: Racial Identity and National Consciousness in Brazilian Literature.* New York: Cambridge University Press, 1983.

Schwarz, Roberto. "The Importing of the Novel to Brazil and its Contradictions in the Work of Alencar." In *Misplaced Ideas: Essays on Brazilian Culture.* New York: Verso, 1992.

Treece, David. *Exiles, Allies, Rebels: Brazil's Indianist Movement, Indigenist Politics, and the Imperial Nation-State.* Westport, Conn.: Greenwood Press, 2000.

Alepoudelis, Odysseus
See ELYTIS, ODYSSEUS.

Allende, Isabel (1942–) novelist

Born in Lima, Peru, Allende is the daughter of Chilean diplomat Tomas Allende and Francisca Llona Barros. Her parents divorced when Allende was two, and she, her mother, and two brothers moved in with her mother's parents in Santiago, Chile. It was while living with her grandparents, spending many hours in their library, that Allende developed her passion for the written word. Her grandparents were the inspiration behind the characters Clara del Valle and Esteban Trueba in *The House of the Spirits* (1982).

Allende began her career working for the United Nations but soon found herself drawn to journalism. She wrote for the women's magazine *Paula* and also edited *Mampato*, a children's magazine. During this time she also experimented with writing short stories for children and producing plays. She finally turned to novel writing, which allowed a free range of expression. In 1962, she married Miguel Frias, an engineer, with whom she had two children, Paula and Nicolas. In 1973 her uncle, President Salvador Allende, was assassinated, and she and her family were moved to Venezuela for safety. The assassination had a profound effect on her: "I think I have divided my life [into] before that day and after that day," she told *Publishers Weekly*. "In that moment, I realized that everything was possible, that violence was a dimension that was always around you." While in Venezuela, Allende learned that her grandfather was dying in Chile, and, unable to go to him, she wrote him a letter that evolved into her first novel, *The House of the Spirits* (1982).

Set in an unnamed South American country, the novel traces the experiences of four generations of the del Valle–Trueba family through 75 years of social change and politics in the 20th century. The novel employs MAGIC REALISM (a literary technique that allows fantasy and magic to intrude on otherwise realistic depictions of settings or characters) to tell a story of power relations and passion. It became an international best-seller and inspired a 1994 American film version starring Jeremy Irons and Meryl Streep.

Allende's next novel, *Of Love and Shadows* (1984), also set in an unnamed South American country (one that clearly resembles Chile in the 1970s), treats topics that are prominent in all Allende's novels: love, politics, violence, death, and strong women. Her third novel, *Eva Luna* (1989), is a first-person narrative by a heroine who tells stories first to save her own life and then to find love and fortune. Written after her divorce from Frias, the novel mirrors aspects of Allende's life.

In 1988, Allende married American lawyer William Gordon and moved to California. Her new home did not distract her from writing about Latin America, and her next work, *The Stories of Eva Luna* (1990), is a collection of 23 short stories that contain many of the characters first introduced in the novel *Eva Luna*. Allende followed this with *The Infinite Plan* (1991), a novel inspired by the life of her second husband.

Although all of Allende's novels draw deeply on personal experience and historical events, none of her works is more poignant than *Paula* (1995). Written in a Madrid hospital at the bedside of her dying daughter, this autobiographical work is a "collage of memories," tracing Allende's life, profession, and beliefs. The book ends on the day of Paula's death at Allende's home in California.

Allende found it difficult to contemplate writing again after the wrenching work of *Paula*; yet, by 1998, she had come back joyously into print with *Aphrodite: A Memoir of the Senses*, a memoir that celebrates the connections between eroticism and food and includes more than 100 recipes. Her subsequent novels, *Daughter of Fortune* (1999) and *Portrait in Sepia* (2001), reflect their creator's journey, telling sweeping stories set both in Chile and in California, involving characters first encountered in *The House of the Spirits*.

Inés of My Soul (2006) is a swashbuckling tale of the conquistadors who swept into Chile from Peru in the 16th century and conquered that unknown land. The novel is based on fact and populated with historical figures such as Francisco Pizarro and others from the history of Chile—Pedro Valdivia, Francisco de Aguirre, and Rodrigo de

Quiroga, among others. The most surprising historical figure in the novel is the heroine, Doña Inés Suárez, a woman who on her own followed her first husband to the New World. When she found out that he was dead, she became a conquistadora, traveling with her lover Valdivia as he conquered the lands south of Peru. In 2008, Allende published a memoir, *The Sum of Our Days.* Her next novel, *The Island Beneath the Sea* (2010) tells the story of Zarité, a nine-year-old girl sold as a slave in 18th-century Santo Domingo.

Allende's books, all of which are written in Spanish, have been translated into 27 different languages. She has received numerous literary prizes, including the Panorama Literio Award (Chile) in 1983, Author of the Year and Book of the Year Awards (Germany) in 1984, Colima Award for Best Novel (Mexico) in 1985, Mulheres Best Foreign Novel Award (Portugal) in 1987, *Library Journal*'s Best Book Award (United States) in 1988, Bancarella Literature Award (Italy) in 1993. Allende is one of the most widely read Latin American authors in the world.

Critical Analysis

Allende's first novel, *The House of the Spirits,* has often been favorably compared to GABRIEL GARCÍA MÁRQUEZ's *One Hundred Years of Solitude.* Indeed, it has the same epic scope, the magic, the lush and steamy prose, and the mixture of laughter and tragedy.

Allende's novel tells the story of the Trueba family through four generations, from the late 19th through the middle of the 20th century, amid the turmoil of a fictional South American country. Everyone in the novel is larger than life, from the exquisite Rosa, who has green hair and "seemed to be made of a different material from the rest of the human race," to Esteban Trueba, whose temper is monumental, to Clara, who chooses not to speak for nine years and moves tables and saltcellars with her mind, to the twins Jaime—who did not like anyone "to breathe too close to him, shake his hand, ask him personal questions, ask to borrow books, or write him letters" and who would give

his clothes away to the poor—and Nicolás, who "was as pretty as a girl" and "blindingly intelligent."

Allende's style reflects the epic scope and size of her characters and her story. Of one character's wedding she tells us:

The wedding culminated in a spectacular party, with five hundred guests in evening dress who invaded the big house on the corner, enlivened by an orchestra of hired musicians, with a scandalous number of whole steers grilled with herbs, fresh seafood, Baltic caviar, Norwegian salmon, birds stuffed with truffles, a torrent of exotic liquors, a flood of champagne, and an extravagance of desserts: ladyfingers, millefeuilles, éclairs, sugar cookies, huge glass goblets of glazed fruits, Argentine strawberries, Brazilian coconuts, Chilean papayas, Cuban pineapple, and other delicacies impossible to remember, all arrayed on a long table that ran the length of the garden terminating in a colossal three-story wedding cake . . . a replica of the Acropolis crowned with a cloud of meringue . . . .

The novel has three distinct narrative voices. One, who is clearly a character in the story, claims to be reconstructing events from Clara's extensive notebooks; one is an omniscient narrator who can see the future and describe the past in detail; and the third is Esteban himself, at the age of 90, chastened by his rage, shrunken by his sins. This narrative strategy gives the tale a sense of both immediacy and tragic inevitability.

The House of the Spirits is a tour de force. As one reviewer put it, the novel is "Nothing short of astonishing . . . In *The House of the Spirits* Isabel Allende has indeed shown us the relationships between past and present, family and nation, city and country, spiritual and political values. She has done so with enormous imagination, sensitivity, and compassion."

Another Work by Isabel Allende
Zorro. New York: HarperCollins, 2005.

A Work about Isabel Allende

Rojas, Sonia Riguelme, and Edna Aguirre Rehbeim, eds. *Critical Approaches to Isabel Allende's Novels.* New York: Peter Lang, 1991.

Allfrey, Phyllis (1915–1986) *novelist, poet, politician, journalist*

Phyllis Allfrey was born in Dominica, West Indies, to Francis Byam Berkeley Shand, former crown attorney of Dominica, and Elfreda Nicholls, daughter of Doctor H. A. A. Nicholls (later Sir Henry Alford Nicholls). She was educated by tutors and started writing poems, short plays, and short stories at a young age, publishing her first short story in *Tiger Tim's Weekly* at age 13.

Many years passed before Allfrey published her first collection of poems, *Palm and Oak I* (1950), which foreshadows one of Allfrey's self-expressed themes, her ancestry's "tropical and Nordic strains." Having her poem, "While the young sleep," win second prize in the Society of Women Writers and Journalists' 1953 contest and hearing a literary agent's encouragement prompted Allfrey to finish her first novel, *The Orchid House* (1953). The novel's antichurch sentiment and its focus on a white family's decreasing powers rather than black empowerment distinguishes it from preceding West Indian literature.

Subsequent political involvement with the Dominica Labour Party, which she cofounded to assist the island's tropical-fruit workers, diverted Allfrey's attention from literary work. After the West Indies Federation (a political organization of Caribbean islands) dissolved in 1962, Allfrey worked as the editor for *The Dominica Herald,* an opposition newspaper, and the *Star,* a weekly newspaper that encouraged local writers, while writing poems, short stories, political essays, and editorials. As Elaine Campbell writes in a 1986 essay in *Fifty Caribbean Writers,* republications and critical examinations of Allfrey's works might enable her to "enjoy an overdue appreciation of her role as one of the few West Indian women to participate in the early growth of West Indian literature."

Other Works by Phyllis Allfrey

Contrasts. Bridgetown, Barbados: Advocate Press, 1955.
Palm and Oak II. Roseau, Dominica, West Indies: Star Printery, 1974.

Works about Phyllis Allfrey

Paravisini-Gerbert, Lizabeth. "Jean Rhys and Phyllis Shand Allfrey: The Story of a Friendship." *Jean Rhys Review* 9, nos. 1–2 (1998): 1–24.
———. *Phyllis Shand Allfrey: A Caribbean Life.* New Brunswick, N.J.: Rutgers University Press, 1996.

al-Malaika, Nazik

See MALAIKA, NAZIK AL-.

al-Sa'dawi, Nawal

See SAADAWI, NAWAL.

Amado, Jorge (1912–2001) *novelist*

Born in 1912 in Bahia, the northeastern province of Brazil, Jorge Amado was educated in Salvador and Rio de Janeiro. He began to work as a journalist for a local paper at 15, and he was 19 when his first novel, *O país do Carnaval* (*Land of Carnival,* 1931), was published. It has never been translated into English. *Jubiabá* (1935) is a picaresque novel about the childhood and youth of a black hero, set in the slums of a Brazilian city. *Sea of Death* (1936) examines the lives of the mulatto families who run small transport boats out of Salvador. *Captains of the Sands* (1937), the most commercially successful of all his novels, describes the daily existence of a band of homeless children led by a white boy.

By 1936 Amado had joined the Communist Party and had been arrested for his participation in a attempted coup backed by the Kremlin. As a result of his political activities, he spent much of the 1940s in exile in Paris and Prague. When he settled in Brazil again in 1952, he adopted a softer tone in his work, employing rich sensuality and a sometimes outrageous humor, but his novels still focus on the difficulties faced by the poor and by Brazilians of color. Two of the many novels of this later period are *Gabriela, cravo e canela* (*Gabriela, Clove and Cinnamon*, 1958) and *Dona Flor and Her Two Husbands: A Moral and Amorous Tale* (1966). Both of these were adapted for Brazilian TV, and he became in his lifetime the most famous of all Brazilian writers.

Brazilians took pride in Amado's international reputation. He was awarded France's Legion of Honor and Portugal's Camoens Prize and was a perpetual nominee for the Nobel Prize, though he never won. His death in Salvador in August 2001 was an occasion for national mourning.

Other Works by Jorge Amado

Dona Flor and Her Two Husbands: A Moral and Amorous Tale. Translated by Harriet De Onis. New York: Avon, 1998.
Gabriela, Clove and Cinnamon. Translated by William Grossman. New York: Bard Books, 1998.
Showdown. Translated by Gregory Rabassa. New York: Bantam Books, 1989.
The War of the Saints. Translated by Gregory Rabassa. New York: Bantam Books, 1995.

Works about Jorge Amado

Brower, Keith H., Earl E. Fitz, and Enrique Martínez-Vidal, eds. *Jorge Amado: New Critical Essays.* New York: Routledge, 2001.
Chamberlain, Bobby J. *Jorge Amado.* Boston: Twayne, 1990.

Amalrik, Andrey (1936–1980) *publicist, dramatist*

Andrey Amalrik, a playwright who had achieved modest success, caused an enormous scandal for the government of the Soviet Union when his essay, *Will the Soviet Union Survive to 1984?* (1969) was published in the West. Andrey Amalrik was sentenced to three years of hard labor on charges of "parasitism." On the day of his release, the Soviet officials added another three years to his sentence. The extended sentence caused an

uproar around the world, and Amalrik went on a hunger strike for 117 days. In light of the protests, Amalrik's sentence was reduced to two years of exile in Siberia.

Will the Soviet Union Survive to 1984? painted a realistic and gloomy picture of Soviet reality. Amalrik recognized that the Soviet government's policies encouraged in the Soviet people a perverted psychology of mediocrity, in which the main goal was not to stand out from one's peers. He predicted that the Soviet Union would fall as a result of a great war with China and a massive revolt by different ethnic groups within Russia. Many of his predictions were realized when the Soviet Union finally collapsed in 1991.

On his release from exile, Amalrik emigrated to Western Europe in 1976, settling in Spain, where he died in a car accident in 1980. His other work of great importance, *Involuntary Journey to Siberia* (1971), describes the hardships that he faced in the Soviet labor camp for political prisoners.

Andrey Amalrik was one of the first Soviet dissidents to be seen on U.S. television when an interview he and his colleagues Vladimir Bukowsky and Pyotr Yakir gave to a correspondent was broadcast in July 1970. He is remembered today as one of the dissidents who exposed the dark side of the Soviet system to people around the world.

Other Works by Andrey Amalrik

Nose! Nose? No-Se and Other Plays. New York: Harcourt Brace, 1973.
Notes of a Revolutionary. Translated by Guy Daniels. New York: Knopf, 1982.

Amichai, Yehuda (1924–2000) *poet, novelist, short story writer, playwright*

Yehuda Amichai, one of Israel's most widely esteemed poets in modern Hebrew, was born in Wurzburg, Germany, into a religiously observant family. By the time he and his family emigrated to Palestine (now Israel) in 1935, Amichai was able to read Hebrew fluently. He settled in Jerusalem but left to fight with the Jewish brigade of the

British army in World War II. When he returned, he joined the elite Palmach unit to fight with the Israeli defense forces in the 1948 Arab–Israeli war. He also attended Hebrew University, where he studied literature and biblical studies and trained as a teacher.

Amichai is best known for his revolutionary style that helped create modern Israeli poetry. He evoked contemporary images—tanks, airplanes, and fuel—and used an accessible, nontraditional voice—charged with puns, idioms, and colloquialisms—that was new to Hebrew verse in the 1950s.

With his first volume of poetry, *Now and in Other Days* (1955), Amichai began to establish himself as a leading contemporary Hebrew poet and national treasure. His poems are now recited at weddings and funerals and by schoolchildren. He has published volumes of poetry, novels, a book of short stories, and a number of plays that have been produced in Israel. His poetry has been translated into more than 30 languages, including Chinese and Arabic, and, in 1982, Amichai received the prestigious Israel Prize for poetry.

Other Works by Yehuda Amichai

Amen. New York: Harper & Row, 1977.
Even a Fist Was Once an Open Palm with Fingers. New York: Harper Perennial, 1991.
Songs of Jerusalem and Myself. New York: Harper & Row, 1973.

Works about Yehuda Amichai

Abramson, Glenda. *The Writing of Yehuda Amichai: A Thematic Approach.* Albany: State University of New York Press, July 1989.
Cohen, Joseph. *Voices of Israel: Essays on and Interviews with Yehuda Amichai, A.B. Yehoshua, T. Carmi, Aharon Appelfeld, and Amos Oz.* Albany: State University of New York Press, 1990.

Anand, Mulk Raj (1905–2004) *novelist, short story writer, essayist*

Mulk Raj Anand was born in Peshawar, in what is now Pakistan. Educated in Lahore, Pakistan, and

in London, Anand's fiction has been influenced by the literary traditions of both countries. Anand first began writing while in England as a book critic for T. S. Eliot's *Criterion.* After spending a number of years in England, he returned to India in 1945.

Anand used the structural techniques of the Western novel to write about India's social issues. He is often compared to R. K. NARAYAN, but Anand is different because of his choice of subject, which was the poor communities of rural India. His decision to write in English about people who could not read the language is the basis of much criticism against him. Anand claims, however, that he had to write in English because of practical necessity. Punjabi and Hindustani (his mother tongues) publishers would not accept his books because of their "unpopular" themes; English language publishers were far more supportive.

His novels *Untouchable* (1935) and *Coolie* (1936) represent the struggles of the poor and underprivileged in British India. *Coolie* explores the life of an indentured laborer, Munoo, as he must travel across northern India to keep a job. *Untouchable* approaches the national problem of "untouchability" as it is revealed in a day in the life of an 18-year-old man, Bakha. Symbolically, the characters' growth in these narratives catalogues humanity's struggle against social abuse and represents the underprivileged state of an oppressed nation, such as India under British colonialism.

Untouchable leads up to a moment in Bakha's life when class and caste barriers cease to matter. This occurs when Bakha climbs up a tree to listen to GANDHI's speech. Slowly gathering courage to enter the crowd, his fears of touching other people evaporate. As the novel progresses, Bakha finds that he must decide between Christianity and following Gandhi if he is to be free from social injustices. It becomes clear, however, that these choices do not offer Bakha any real escape from the evils of his own life. Either option would only negate the specificity of Bakha's struggles. Through Bakha, Anand tries to show that untouchability is not just a problem of casteism in India but a global problem whenever a powerful force seeks to oppress a weaker one.

Along with MUNSHI PREMCHAND, Anand was involved in forming DALIT literature, a genre addressed exclusively to the oppressed sections of Indian society. Because he wrote exclusively in English, his unwavering focus on the downtrodden helped bring their social issues into the international literary world for the first time in Indian literary history. In 1971, Anand was awarded India's National Academy of Letters Award for his novel *Morning Face* (1968).

Other Works by Mulk Raj Anand

The Road. New Delhi: Sterling Publishers, 1974.
Two Leaves and a Bud. New York: Liberty Press, 1954.

Works about Mulk Raj Anand

Cowasjee, Saros. *So Many Freedoms: A Study of the Major Fiction of Mulk Raj Anand.* Delhi: Oxford University Press, 1977.
Dhawan, R. K. *The Novels of Mulk Raj Anand.* New York: Prestige Books, 1992.

Andersen, Hans Christian (1805–1875)
fiction writer, poet, dramatist

It is believed that Hans Christian Andersen was born near Odense, Denmark. His father, Hans Andersen, was a poor shoemaker, and there is no record of his mother's name or occupation. Despite poverty and harsh living conditions, Andersen's father devoted much of his time to his son: He made him a wooden theater and other toys and read to him every evening. The time Andersen spent with his paternal grandmother also provided some of his most important childhood experiences, including going with her to Greyfriars Hospital, an asylum for the elderly, where she worked as a gardener. Andersen listened to the traditional stories of Denmark told by the old women in the spinning rooms of the hospital.

Andersen was as apt and studious a student as he was a voracious reader. Although his family could not afford books, Andersen borrowed them from the people in his neighborhood. He was fascinated by theater, reading Shakespeare and Danish dramatists. In 1819, he left Odense for Copenhagen in hopes of becoming an actor. He held various minor acting jobs at the Royal Theater, performing as a ballet dancer and a singer in an opera choir. He was dismissed by the management after three years. His years as an actor were not a complete failure: He attended the theater every night, acquired a knowledge of drama, and was befriended by several important figures of the Danish cultural community. He began writing plays, and his talent was recognized by Jonas Collin, a senior civil servant in the Danish government, who arranged a grammar-school scholarship for Andersen. At age 17, Andersen was placed in a class with 10-year-old students. He studied hard and passed his final exams in 1828.

Andersen began his literary career as a poet. Between 1827 and 1828, he published minor poems in newspapers and periodicals and won public favor. By 1832, he had produced two collections of poems, written lyrics for two operas, and created adaptations of two French plays for the Danish stage. In 1831, he traveled to Germany, where he established contacts with some of the leading figures of the romantic movement (*see* ROMANTICISM). In 1833, he received a grant from the Danish government that allowed him to travel throughout Europe.

Andersen wrote three novels between 1835 and 1837: *The Improvisator* (1835), *O.T.* (1836), and *Only a Fiddler* (1837). Surprisingly, Andersen's works were better received in Germany and France than they were in Denmark. Although his novels were popular, he achieved his status as a great figure of world literature by writing his famous fairy tales, the first volume of which was published in 1835. Written at the height of the romantic movement, Andersen's fairy tales were praised throughout Europe. He was treated as an equal by VICTOR HUGO and ALEXANDRE DUMAS. In Germany, the reading public raved over Andersen's latest works, and publishing companies engaged in bidding wars over the rights to them. In 1844, Andersen finally received recognition in Denmark: He was personally invited to be the guest of King Christian VIII. In 1845, he visited England, where his works were enormously popular. He made numerous acquaintances, including a lifelong friendship with Charles Dickens.

During the late 1840s, Andersen wrote some of his best fairy tales, including "The Nightingale," "The Ugly Duckling," "The Snow Queen," and "The Story of a Mother." In his tales, Andersen often celebrated the common people, whom he portrayed as ingenious, diligent, and brave. The fantastic element accentuated emotion and imagination, qualities cherished by romanticism. In conjunction with his work on the fairy tales, Andersen also wrote numerous travel books and plays.

By the time of his death in 1875, Andersen was considered a national monument. He enjoyed personal visits from the king, numerous public awards, and appreciative letters from readers throughout the world. His fairy tales are as popular today as they were during his lifetime, and they have been translated into virtually every major language. As one obituary remarked, Andersen had known how "to strike chords that reverberated in every human breast."

Another Work by Hans Christian Andersen

Hans Christian Andersen: The Complete Fairy Tales and Stories. Translated by Erik Christian Haugaard. New York: Anchor, 1983.

Works about Hans Christian Andersen

Lederer, Wolfgang. *The Kiss of the Snow Queen: Hans Christian Andersen and Man's Redemption by Woman.* Berkeley: University of California Press, 1990.

Wullschlager, Jackie. *Hans Christian Andersen: The Life of a Storyteller.* New York: Knopf, 2001.

Andrézel, Pierre

See DINESEN, ISAK.

Andrić, Ivo (1892–1975) *novelist, poet short story writer*

Ivo Andrić was born in Dolac, near Travnik, Bosnia and Herzevovinia, to a family of artisans. As a college student, he worked to help achieve unity and independence for the South Slavic peoples by joining Mlada Bosnia (Young Bosnia), a revolutionary nationalist student organization. During World War I, Andrić was arrested and spent three years in prison, where he read the works of Sören Kierkegaard and FYODOR DOSTOYEVSKY. After his release, Andrić held a number of diplomatic posts for the Yugoslav government. He was the ambassador in Berlin when World War II broke out, narrowly escaping when the city was bombed by German planes.

In the shadow of war, Andrić wrote the historical series for which he received the Nobel Prize in literature in 1961. Commonly referred to as the Bosnian Trilogy, *The Bridge on the Drina* (1945; translated 1959), *Bosnian Story* (1945; translated 1959), and *Woman from Sarajevo* (1945; translated 1965), examine life in a country where multiple nationalities and religions meet and often clash. Influenced by both the war and a Kierkegaardian sense of isolation and pessimism, Andrić wrote primarily about the misery of man and his struggle to maintain his existence. *The Bridge on the Drina,* Andrić's most famous work, for example, tells the history of Bosnia from 1516, when the bridge was first built, to 1914, when it was partially destroyed in World War I. The bridge is Andrić's metaphor for sorrow born out of struggle, particularly that between Christians and Muslims. Although the bridge was originally built to connect the eastern and western sides of the Ottoman Empire, in actuality it both united and divided people along cultural, religious, and generational lines. As the novel shows, it was Andrić's hope, like the original purpose of a bridge, that people would someday live in peace.

After World War II, Andrić continued to write short stories, essays, and travel memoirs about Bosnia. He wrote continuously until his death in Belgrade on March 13, 1975.

Another Work by Ivo Andrić

The Day of the Consuls. Translated by Celia Hawkesworth. New York: Defour Editions, 1993.

A Work about Ivo Andrić

Vucinich, Wayne, ed. *Ivo Andrić Revisited: The Bridge Still Stands*. Berkeley Calif.: UC Regents, 1996.

Anouilh, Jean (1910–1987) *playwright*

Jean Anouilh, one of the most popular French dramatists of the post-World War II era, was born on June 23 in Bordeaux, France. Anouilh began writing plays at age 12. He briefly studied law at the Sorbonne while writing comic scenes for the cinema and working as a copywriter. In 1929 he collaborated with Jean Aurenche on his first play, *Humulus the Mute,* and by age 25 dedicated himself to a career as a writer. His best-known plays are *Antigone* (1944) and *Becket* (1959), both of which explore the individual's resistance to state oppression.

Anouilh's works, ranging from serious drama to absurdist farce, are too diverse to be considered a part of any one literary movement, but he was influenced by both SARTRE's existentialism and the plays of Jouvet, COCTEAU, GIRAUDOUX, and Molière. He often blended choreography and music into his plots, and used the theater itself as the setting of his plays; yet, beneath the farce and spectacle, the tone was almost always serious and pessimistic.

Anouilh titled the collections of his plays with adjectives that described their dominant tone. The "black" plays, such as *Eurydice* (1941) and *Antigone* (1944), are his tragedies and realistic pieces. The "pink" pieces are dominated by fantasy and include *Thieves' Carnival* (1938; translated 1952) and *Time Remembered* (1939; translated 1955). The "brilliant" pieces, such as *Ring Round the Moon* (1947; translated 1950), *Colombe* (1951; translated 1952), and *The Rehearsal* (1950; translated 1961), are a blending of both "pink" and "black" plays set among the aristocracy. There are only four "jarring" or "grating" plays, black plays with bitter humor: *Ardele* (1949; translated 1959), *The Waltz of the Toreadors* (1952; translated 1956), *Ornifle* (1955; translated 1970), and *Poor Bitos,* or *The Masked Dinner* (1956;

translated 1963). His "costumed" or "history" plays, including *The Lark* (1953; translated 1955), about Joan of Arc, and the Tony Award–winning *Becket* (1959; translated 1962), were especially popular in the United States.

In 1936, Anouilh began to collaborate on screenplays, directed two films, and wrote ballets. In the 1980s, he directed productions of several plays, both his own works and those of other authors. He died in Switzerland on October 3, 1987.

Other Works by Jean Anouilh

The Collected Plays. London: Methuen, 1966.
Ornifle. Translated by Lucienne Hill. New York: Hill and Wang, 1970.

A Work about Jean Anouilh

Falb, Lewis W. *Jean Anouilh*. New York: F. Unger, 1977.

S. Ansky (Shloyme–Zanvl ben Aaron Hacohen Rappoport (1863–1920) *poet, playwright, ethnographer*

Born in 1863 in Chashniki, Belarus, a city renowned as a center for traditional rabbinic Judaism, S. (Saul) Ansky was first inspired by the works of the Haskalah, or Jewish enlightenment movement. Ansky rejected Judaism at the age of 15, embracing the secular and radical principles of socialism. His status as a political subversive made him an enemy of his family, his culture, and the state, and for many years he lived in hiding.

After working on a commune and as a tutor in the Pale of Settlement—a territory set aside for the Russian Jewish population that today comprises Poland, Latvia, Lithuania, Ukraine, and his home country Belarus—Rappoport subsequently worked for three years as an itinerant miner in Russia. In 1890 he narrowly escaped arrest and found work and support in the literary and intellectual circles of Saint Petersburg, as well as in its Jewish community. His experiences as a miner provided Rappoport with the material for a seminal series of articles entitled "Sketches on Folk Literature" that he wrote in 1890. For this series, Rappoport would first use the pseudonym S. A. An-Ski, later modifying his name to S. Ansky.

In 1892, Russian authorities tracked Ansky down and forced him to leave Saint Petersburg. Before his return to the city 13 years later in 1905, he lived in Paris and in Switzerland, where he worked as a secretary to the Russian philosopher and revolutionary Piotr Lavrov and helped found the Russian Social Revolutionary Party in 1901. Upon his return, Ansky was deeply affected by the carnage that resulted from the 1905 Russian Revolution, in particular the anti-Semitic pogroms carried out against members of the Jewish Labour Bund, a Russian socialist political party. Ansky joined the Bund Party soon after and composed "Di Shvu'e," or "The Oath," the anthem that is still performed by party members and at Jewish socialist meetings around the world.

From 1905 to 1910, Ansky immersed himself in the collective effort of preserving Jewish folk culture in Russia; he worked for the Jewish Literary Society as well as the Russian-Jewish monthly *Evreiski Mir* (Jewish World). Ansky also toured the Pale of Settlement, lecturing on Jewish folklore and Yiddish literature. In 1908, Ansky and several other members of the Saint Petersburg Jewish community formed the Jewish Ethnographic Expedition. The objective of the Expedition was to collect, preserve, and analyze historical and ethnographic materials related to the lives of Jews in Russia and Poland. From 1911 to 1914, Ansky and the other members of the Expedition collected 2,000 photographs, 1,800 folktales, and over 1,000 melodies and songs, among many other important artifacts. This journey, which was interrupted by the outbreak of World War I, had a profound effect on Ansky, who subsequently devoted the remainder of his life to the conservation of Jewish artifacts.

Ansky's best-known work is representative of this particular devotion. His play *The Dybbuk, or Between Two Worlds*, written from 1912 to 1919 and first performed in 1920, is the result of this intensive period of amassing folklore and melodies. Originally called *Tsvishn Tsvey Veltn* and first written in Yiddish, *The Dybbuk* is considered by most to be a seminal work in the history of Jewish theater. The four-act drama concerns Khonnon, a brilliant Talmudic scholar, who falls in love with Leah, the daughter of a merchant, who loves Khonnon, but is forced by her father to marry another man. Khonnon dies of heartbreak, but Leah is possessed by Khonnon's soul in the form of a Dybbuk, a dislocated spirit as described in Jewish folklore who attaches itself to a living person in order to fulfill a function it was unable to carry out in life. In spirit form, Khonnon is able to possess Leah forever. Before the Dybbuk is finally exorcised, Leah faces the choice between an unfulfilling marriage and a supernatural union with the spirit of her lover.

After the Russian Revolution of 1917, Ansky moved to Vilna, Lithuania, to continue his work preserving Jewish culture. During this time, he also founded the Vilna Historic-Ethnographic Society. After World War I, he moved to Warsaw, where he died at the age of 56 from complications of pneumonia resulting from his years of hard labor as a miner. Today, S. Ansky is considered one of the great builders of modern Jewish culture.

Another Work by S. Ansky
The Enemy at His Pleasure: A Journey Through the Jewish Pale of Settlement During World War I. Translated by Joachim Neugroschel. New York: Macmillan, 2003.

Works about S. Ansky
Beizer, Mikhail. *The Jews of St. Petersburg.* Translated by Michael Sherbourne. Philadelphia: Jewish Publication Society, 1989.
Sherman, Joseph. *Writers in Yiddish.* Detroit: Thomson Gale, 2007.

Antschel, Paul
See CELAN, PAUL.

Anyidoho, Kofi (1947–   ) poet

Anyidoho was born at Wheta, a small town on the Keta lagoon in the Volta region of Ghana. His mother, Abla Adidi Anyidoho, was a composer and cantor of traditional poetry, as was his uncle, Kodzovi Anyidoho, who was responsible for the poet's early education. The region's rich poetic tradition became an important resource for Anyidoho's work. Anyidoho trained as a teacher at Accra Teacher Training College, where he began to submit poetry for publication. He graduated with honors in 1977 from the University of Ghana with a degree in English and linguistics. He then left for the United States to study at Indiana University for an M.A. in folklore and later received a Ph.D. in comparative literature from the University of Texas at Austin. His experiences in America provided material for *A Harvest of Our Dreams with Elegy for the Revolution* (1984), a collection of poems written as a series of letters home.

Although America may have served as subject matter for a series of poems, Anyidoho's work always seems to turn home. He uses the oral tradition of the Ewe people in many of his poems. He retranslates English to fit the cadences and rhythms of the Ewe people and uses many of the images and idioms of traditional Ewe poetry in his own verse. He draws on traditional poetic genres such as the funeral dirge and the halo, the song of abuse. He also uses the spiritual imagery of invocation, a calling upon the spirits. Yet, his poetry is aware of the fractures and challenges caused by globalization. "Slums of Our Earth" (1983) includes the lines:

> The darkness of the slums
> is the shadow side of
> proud structures on Wall Street

Anyidoho is committed to writing in both English and Ewe. He has won many awards: His first collection of poems, *Earthchild, with Brain Surgery* (1985), won the Valco Fund Literary Award for Poetry in 1976 while still in manuscript, the BBC Poetry Award for "Arts in Africa" in 1981, and the Poet of the Year in Ghana in 1984.

Other Works by Kofi Anyidoho

Ancestral Logic and Caribbean Blues. Trenton, N.J.: Africa World Press, 1993.

Elegy for the Revolution. New York: Greenfield Review Press, 1978.

Fontomfrom: Contemporary Ghanaian Literature, Theatre and Film. Edited by Kofi Anyidoho and James Gibbs. Amsterdam: Editions Rodopi B.V., 2000.

Apollinaire, Guillaume (Wilhelm Apollinaris de Kostrowitski) (1880–1918) poet

Guillaume Apollinaire was a major figure in early 20th-century French avant-garde literary movements. He was one of the innovators of the THEATER OF THE ABSURD, and, as a critic, with his publication of *The Cubist Painters* (1913), established cubism as an artistic movement. He is best known, however, for his poetry.

Most of Apollinaire's personal history remains unknown. He was most likely born in Rome, the illegitimate son of the Swiss-Italian aristocrat Francesco Flugi d'Aspermont and Angelica de Kostrowitzky, a notoriously rebellious and adventurous Polish girl. He was raised by his mother, a heavy gambler, and they resided at various times in Italy, in Monaco, on the French Riviera, and in Paris.

A highly intelligent child, Apollinaire managed to pursue a solid education at the Collège Saint-Charles in Monaco and later at schools in Cannes and Nice by assuming the identity of a Russian prince. In 1900, he moved to Paris where he took a position working in a bank and became friends with artists such as Pablo Picasso and André Derain, playwright ALFRED JARRY, and painter Marie Laurencin, who was also his lover. He traveled to Germany in 1921, which was where he received his introduction to two of his major influences: German romantic poetry and the torments of unrequited love.

Bold, forward-thinking, and often controversial, Apollinaire began his career as a writer by editing a number of reviews and publishing both satirical and semipornographic texts. He quickly gained a reputation as a dangerous foreigner and a thief, and in 1911, he was imprisoned for a week under suspicion of having stolen the Mona Lisa (it was missing, but Apollinaire was not involved). As a poet, Apollinaire began his career with the publication of a collection called *L'enchanteur pourrissant* (*The Rotting Magician*, 1909). The poems depict a vision of Merlin the Enchanter who, entombed by love, creates a new world of poetry from the depths of his suffering. The work was illustrated by André Derain.

It was not until the publication of Apollinaire's second collection, however, that he began to gain true critical notice as a promising young poet.

Critical Analysis

Alcools (1913) was a breakthrough work in form and content, combining elements of classical verse with modern imagery. The poems were transcriptions of overheard street conversations and were often devoid of punctuation. The poem "Zone," for instance, which opens the collection, focuses on a period of time in the life of a tormented poet as he wanders through the streets, lamenting the recent loss of his mistress.

The beginnings of the cubist movement had a profound effect on Apollinaire. In *The Cubist Painters,* a collection of essays, Apollinaire explores cubism as a theoretical concept and as a psychological phenomenon. However, he was not one to hold to any school of thought for long. Shortly after the publication of his work on the cubists, he deserted cubism altogether for orphism, a movement which he created and described, as quoted by William Bohn, as "the art of painting new structures out of elements that have not been borrowed from the visual sphere but have been created entirely by the artist himself, and have been endowed by him with the fullness of reality."

When World War I broke out in 1915, Apollinaire enlisted in the army. A wound he sustained left him in fragile health. Nonetheless, he kept writing. *The Poet Assassinated* (1916), written from his hospital bed, is a novella in the form of a tribute to the life of the fictional great poet Croniamantal, from his birth to his life as a poet and ultimately his death at the hands of an angry mob.

Apollinaire's one play, *Les mamelles de Tirésias* (The Breasts of Tiresias), was staged in 1917. Apollinaire subtitled the work "Drame surréaliste" (surrealist drama)—thus laying ground for yet another avant-garde movement, surrealism. The play combines the playwright's own sexual obsessions with a satirical exploitation of Greek legend. It also focuses, in a farcical manner, on the low birthrate in France during the late 19th and early 20th centuries. It tells the story of Thérèse, a discontented housewife who decides to give up being a woman. She lets her breasts (red and blue balloons) float out over the audience and becomes Tiresias, named for the Greek seer who, in the legend, was granted the opportunity to experience life as a woman. In 1947, the play was made into an opera by Francis Poulenc.

For several years beginning in 1913, Apollinaire worked on a collection of experimental poems that form visual images on the page. The result, *Calligrammes,* was published in 1918, shortly before the poet's death.

After a series of well-known and often high-profile affairs, Apollinaire married Jaqueline Kolb in 1918. He succumbed to influenza that same year, dying on November 9 in Paris.

Other Works by Guillaume Apollinaire
Calligrammes: Poems of Peace and War (1913–1916). Translated by Anne Hyde Greet. Berkeley: University of California Press, 1991.
Les onze mille vierges (The eleven thousand virgins) and *Les Mémoires d'un jeune Don Juan* (Memoirs of a young Don Juan). In *Flesh Unlimited.* Translated by Alexis Lykiard. London: Creation, 2000.

The Poet Assassinated. Translated by Matthew Josephson. Cambridge, Mass.: Exact Change, 2000.

Selected Writings of Guillaume Apollinaire. Translated by Roger Shattuck. New York: Norton, 1971.

A Work about Guillaume Apollinaire

Bohn, Willard. *Apollinaire and the International Avant-Garde.* Albany: State University of New York Press, 1997.

Appelfeld, Aharon (1932–) *novelist, essayist, short story writer*

Aharon Appelfeld was born in Czernowitz, Romania (now Chernivtsi, Ukraine). When he was eight, his mother was killed by the Nazis, and his father was sent to a Nazi work camp. Appelfeld himself was deported to a concentration camp but managed to escape and spent the next three years hiding and wandering in the nearby forests and villages of the Ukraine on his own. In a 1998 interview with the *New York Times* he said, "I lived with marginal people during the war—prostitutes, horse thieves, witches, fortune tellers. They gave me my real education."

Eventually, Appelfeld became a kitchen boy in the Russian army. He found his way to refugee camps in Yugoslavia and Italy and, in 1948, at age 16, went to the new state of Israel. It was there, at age 28, that he reunited with his father and began to teach at a kibbutz.

Much of Appelfeld's writing explores themes of the Holocaust. Yet, he says, "Mainly, I write Jewish stories, but I don't accept the label Holocaust writer. Of all my books, perhaps one-third are on the Holocaust period, one-third on Israel, and one-third on Jewish life in general." In his highly acclaimed novels, such as *Badenheim 1939* (1979), Appelfeld rejects literalism and instead uses abstract symbolism—creating dreamlike scenes—and fable to examine the inner workings of his characters. In both *Badenheim,* and another novel, *To the Land of Cattails* (1987), he employs an almost hallucinatory sense of the Holocaust that is evident in much of his work.

Two of Appelfeld's recent works include *All Whom I Have Loved* (2007) and *Blooms of Darkness* (2010). *All Whom I Have Loved* is the story of a young boy growing up in Bucharest before World War II. *Blooms of Darkness* tells the story of an 11-year-old boy in occupied Ukraine during World War II. When the Jews are rounded up for deportation, his mother must leave him with her childhood friend, Mariana, now a prostitute.

Appelfeld is one of Israel's preeminent novelists, largely due to his literary style of exploring the Holocaust and his ability to bring the enormous dimensions of the Holocaust to a human scale. His works have received critical and popular acclaim. He has served as professor of Hebrew Literature at Ben-Gurion University and has held visiting professorships at Boston University, Brandeis, and Yale. He has been a visiting scholar at Oxford and Harvard. Among his many awards and honors are the Bialik Prize, the Harold U. Ribelow Prize, and the Israel Prize. In 2005, Appelfeld was awarded the Nelly Sachs Prize for outstanding literary contributions to the promotion of understanding between peoples.

Other Works by Aharon Appelfeld

The Age of Wonders. Boston: Godine, 1990.

Katerina. New York: Norton, 1992.

The Story of a Life: A Memoir. New York: Shocken, 2006.

To the Land of Reeds. New York: Grove Atlantic Monthly Press, 1994.

TZILI: The Story of a Life. New York: Grove Press, 1996.

A Work about Aharon Appelfeld

Cohen, Joseph. *Voices of Israel: Essays on and Interviews with Yehuda Amichai, A.B. Yehoshua, T. Carmi, Aharon Applefeld, and Amos Oz.* Albany: State University of New York Press, 1990.

Aragon, Louis (1897–1982) *poet, novelist, essayist*

Louis Aragon was born in Paris. He studied medicine at the University of Paris and served as an auxiliary doctor in World War I. During this time, he met the poet ANDRÉ BRETON, who introduced him to surrealism and DADA.

In 1919, Aragon, Breton, and fellow writer and activist Philippe Soupault (1897–1990) founded the literary review *Littérature*. Aragon wrote his first collection of poems, *Feu de joie* (1920), to echo the dadaist desire to destroy traditional institutions and values. He also published *Anicet; ou, le panorama* (1921), a novel that parodies Picasso's success through the career of its cynical hero, Bleu; *Le libertinage* (1924), a surrealist short-story collection; *Le mouvement perpetual* (*Perpetual Movement*, 1925), a novel; and *Le paysan de Paris* (*The Paris Peasant*, 1926), in which the city's parks and cafés are the setting for a series of intense encounters.

Aragon broke from Breton and Soupault in 1931 and joined the Communist Party. He visited the Soviet Union and returned to France to write "The Red Front," a poem influenced by the Russian poet VLADIMIR MAYAKOVSKY that calls for revolution in France. In the 1930s and 1940s, Aragon advocated SOCIALIST REALISM in his works.

During World War II, Aragon was taken prisoner but managed to escape to the Unoccupied Zone. When the Nazis occupied France, he became a key figure in the resistance. *Le crève-coeur* (1941) was one of five poetry collections Aragon wrote, detailing the Nazi occupation of France. His poetry took on a nationalistic sentiment, and he helped form a network of writers for the Resistance journals.

After the liberation, Aragon attempted a new form of novel that was almost journalistic in style. He also edited a French literary magazine and served as a member of the French Communist Party. In 1957, he was awarded the Lenin Peace Prize. He began to express a dislike for socialist realism and in 1968 attacked the Soviet Union for its intervention in Czechoslovakia. His later works include criticism and several autobiographical poems and novels. He died in Paris on December 24, 1982.

Other Works by Louis Aragon

The Adventures of Telemachus. Translated by Renee Riese Hubert and Judd D. Hubert. Cambridge, Mass.: Exact Change, 1997.

Le Con d'Irène. In *Flesh Unlimited.* Translated by Alexis Lykiard. London: Creation, 2000.

Paris Peasant. Translated by Simon W. Taylor. Cambridge, Mass.: Exact Change, 1995.

Works about Louis Aragon

Adereth, Max. *Elsa Triolet and Louis Aragon: An Introduction to Their Interwoven Lives and Works.* Lewiston, N.Y.: Edwin Mellen Press, 1994.

Becker, Lucille F. *Louis Aragon.* Boston: Twayne, 1971.

Arenas, Reinaldo (1943–1990) *novelist, poet, essayist, short story writer, playwright*

Reinaldo Arenas was born in Holguín, Cuba, to Oneida Fuentes Rodríguez and Antonio Arenas Machín. Because of his family's impoverished condition, Arenas received virtually no formal education and had little access to books, but his active imagination drove him to begin writing at an early age. After joining Fidel Castro's revolutionary army at age 15 and serving for a short time, he completed a degree in agricultural accounting.

Published when he was 21, Arenas's first book, *Singing from the Well,* (the first of a series of autobiographical novels) brought him some recognition, but because relatively few copies were printed, it remained unknown outside of Cuba. As Arenas began to speak out in his writings against Castro's regime and about his own homosexuality, his books were increasingly censored and suppressed in Cuba. He was, however, able to publish some works overseas, including *The Ill-Fated Peregrinations of Fray Servando,* which first appeared in a French translation in 1968. A first-person account of the title character's fantastic travels through Europe and the Americas, the novel may represent Arenas's best-known and most widely read book. Here and elsewhere, Arenas writes about homosexuality, as well as the more encompassing issue of the individual's right to self-determination and self-expression. After escaping Cuba and establishing residence in the United States, Arenas went on to publish an extensive amount of fiction, drama, poetry, and criticism. Among the works he wrote in exile are *The Color of Summer* (1993) and *The Assault* (1994), both part of his fictional autobiography and published posthumously.

Arenas was and continues to be a controversial but much celebrated author in Latin America and the rest of the world. His confrontation of issues related to sexuality and societal stereotypes and his vivid depiction of life under the Castro regime set him apart as one of the most important Cuban writers of the 20th century. Terminally ill with AIDS, he committed suicide on December 7, 1990.

Another Work by Reinaldo Arenas

Before Night Falls. Translated by Dolores M. Koch. New York: Viking, 1993.

A Work about Reinaldo Arenas

Soto, Francisco. *Reinaldo Arenas.* Boston: Twayne, 1998.

Arghezi, Tudor (Ion N. Theodorescu)
(1880–1967) *poet, novelist, nonfiction writer*

Tudor Arghezi was born in Bucharest, Romania. He took the pseudonym Arghezi because of its similarity to Argesis, the ancient name of the river Arges, of which he was very fond. As a teenager, Arghezi was rebellious and was often involved in political youth movements. He turned to writing as a focus for his ideas and began to publish in 1896, signing his works as Ion Theo. In his early 20s, Arghezi began to travel abroad, spending four years in the Cernica Monastery and a brief period at a monastery in Paris, where he converted to Catholicism. He ultimately moved to Geneva, where he wrote poetry, much of which was influenced by religion and Arghezi's own thoughts on the nature of life and death.

In 1912, Arghezi returned to Romania, where he published pamphlets and lyrics, many of which aggressively advocated the neutrality of Romania. For this, Arghezi was imprisoned, along with 11 other writers and journalists, and spent from 1918 to 1920 at Vacaresti Penitentiary.

Arghezi's first volume of poetry, *Cuvinte potrivite (Arranged Words),* was published in 1927. This work gained him celebrity status among the Romanian people. He continued to publish other volumes, including *Flowers of Mould* (1931), inspired by his years in prison, *Notebook for the Night* (1935), and *Choirs* (1939). The artistic novelty of these collections shocked readers. Arghezi did not conform to any preexisting poetic formulas. Instead, his writing showed a restlessness, and a bold and innovative combination of often crude, forceful language, and a traditional reliance on folklore and mythology. Mainly religious in theme, Arghezi focused on life, love, humanity, death, and the nature of God.

In 1931, the same year in which Arghezi published *Flowers of Mould,* he turned his attention to writing poetry and prose for children. *Cartea cu jucarii* (1931) was the first of several of his works for children that are still used in Romanian schools today. Between 1931 and 1967, Arghezi was at his most prolific, writing, in addition to the children's works, the poetry collections *Notebook for the Night* and *Choirs,* and three novels: *Mother's Love and Filial Devotion* (1934), *Cimitrul Buna-Vestire* (1936), and *Lina* (1942), which was actually an extended poem in prose form.

Alongside his work as a writer, Arghesi also managed the Romanian newspaper, *Bilete de Papagal.* Because of the sarcastic and often satirical political pamphlets it published, Arghezi once again came under police scrutiny. The paper was ultimately confiscated, and he was imprisoned for a year in Bucharest.

After his release from prison, Arghezi was considered to be rehabilitated. Under the Communist regime, he was awarded numerous prizes for his work, was elected as a member of the Romanian Academy, and twice was celebrated as the National Poet of Romania. He began to collaborate with political officials, writing poetry that supported the goals of the regime. He was buried in the garden of his house, which is managed today as a museum in his honor.

Other Works by Tudor Arghezi

Poems: Tudor Arghezi. Translated by Andrei Bantas. Bucharest: Minerva Publishing House, 1983.

Selected Poems of Tudor Arghezi. Translated by Michael Impey and Brian Swann. Princeton, N.J.: Princeton University Press, 1976.

Arnim, Bettina von (Catarina Elisabetha Ludovica Magdalena Brentano, Bettine) (1785–1859) *poet, fiction writer*

Bettina von Arnim was one of 20 children fathered by the wealthy Italian merchant Peter Anton Brentano. She was the seventh child of her mother, Maximiliane von La Roche. Bettina was born in the German city of Frankfurt am Main. Her early influences included her grandmother Sophie von La Roche and brother Clemens Brentano, both well-known writers. Like her grandmother and mother, Bettina developed a friendship with JOHANN WOLFGANG VON GOETHE. In 1811, Bettina married Clemens's friend, Ludwig Achim von Arnim, an editor of folk song collections. Although she published a few songs for her husband's company, Bettina did not work full time as a writer until after Achim's death in 1831.

Bettina's first book, *Goethe's Briefwechsel mit einem Kinde* (*Goethe's Correspondence with a Child,* 1835), was based on her correspondence with Goethe and his mother. Arnim edited these letters and poems to provide a fictionalized description of events, dreams, and thoughts. Although controversial for its erotic content, the book was a literary success. Arnim used her correspondence with two friends and a brother to produce three more books exploring the topics of love and friendship.

Arnim's other writings include musical compositions and fairy tales that she wrote with her daughters. As a widow, she was actively involved in the political causes of opposing censorship and governmental abuse. Arnim also used her works to promote social reforms to help the poor and the sick. Her biographers Arthur Helps and Elizabeth Jane Howard explain that Arnim "had a talent for social satire" and was "a penetrating observer" of life in early 19th-century Europe.

Other Works by Bettina von Arnim

Goethe's Correspondence with a Child. Boston: Tichner and Fields, 1859.

The Life of High Countess Gritta von Ratsinourhouse. Gisela von Arnim Grimm, coauthor. Translated by Lisa Ohm. Lincoln: University of Nebraska Press, 1999.

A Work about Bettina von Arnim

Helps, Arthur, and Elizabeth Jane Howard. *Bettina: A Portrait.* London: Chatto and Windus, 1957.

Arp, Hans (Jean Arp) (1887–1966) *poet*

Hans Arp was born in Strasbourg, Alsace. Now part of France, Alsace belonged to Germany at the time of Arp's birth. His father, Pierre-Guillaume Arp, operated a cigar and cigarette factory. Arp's mother, Josephine, was French, and the family sympathized politically with France. Arp grew up speaking German, French, and the Alsatian dialect. His childhood daydreams translated into an early literary creativity. Arp published his first poem, written in Alsatian, at age 15. Two years later, he published three more poems.

Although a gifted poet, Arp would achieve his greatest fame as a painter and sculptor. He studied art in Strasbourg, Weimar, and Paris. After moving to Switzerland, Arp produced abstract painting and in 1916 helped found the DADA movement in art. In 1921, he married the artist Sophie Taeuber. Five years later, he changed his name from Hans to Jean.

Arp published his first collection of poetry, written in German, in 1920. His poems gained a wider audience in 1948 when a New York firm published his collection *On My Way: Poetry and Essays, 1912–1947*. Arp's early verse was conventional but amusing and inventive. In the 1940s and 1950s, his poems were written as a series of dreamlike word associations and had more emotional depth. The historian Hermann Boeschenstein explains that Arp was a pioneer in "freeing the word from the task of relating to and disclosing the meaning of outer and inner realities. Language as such is advanced to the central position in poetry and forms its theme."

Other Works by Hans Arp

The Isms of Art. 1925. Authorized Reprint Edition. New York: Arno Press, 1968.

Jean, Marcel, ed. *Arp on Arp: Poems, Essays, Memories.* Translated by Joachim Neugroschel. New York: Viking Press, 1972.

A Work about Hans Arp

Last, Rex W. *German Dadaist Literature: Kurt Schwitters, Hugo Ball, Hans Arp.* Boston: Twayne, 1973.

Arp, Jean
See ARP, HANS.

Arrabal, Fernando (1937–) *playwright, novelist*

Fernando Arrabal was born in Melilla, Spanish Morocco. His childhood was extremely traumatic. In the Spanish civil war his father was an officer in the liberal republican army, and his mother was a fascist sympathizer. At the end of the war, she betrayed his father to the authorities, and he was condemned to death. The violent loss of his father, combined with Arrabal's knowledge of his mother's betrayal, permanently scarred him.

When Arrabal was four years old, his family moved to Spain, where he attended school.

As a young boy, he would entertain himself by constructing puppet theaters and putting on plays. These experiences play an important role in some of his later works. Arrabal was also fascinated by Charlie Chaplin movies; later in life, he used slapstick and the stylized acting techniques of Chaplin in the context of his Panic Theater movement.

Unable to find attractive career opportunities in Franco's Spain, Arrabal moved to Paris to pursue his career as a playwright. Around the same time he arrived in Paris, he discovered he had tuberculosis. Nevertheless, he persisted in working arduously at his writing and, in 1958, his efforts paid off when a Paris publisher gave him a lifetime contract.

The Labyrinth (1956), one of Arrabal's early plays, reflects the depressing and daunting quality of his early life. It resembles to some degree the dark fantasies of FRANZ KAFKA. A nightmarish play, it portrays the horrors of the modern world as a sort of absurd hell. As Arrabal developed as a writer, he persisted in his use of absurdity. In his later plays, however, the effect was more often black humor rather than terror or angst.

In the 1960s, Arrabal emerged as one of the central writers of the THEATER OF THE ABSURD, a movement pioneered by such writers as ANTONIN ARTAUD and SAMUEL BECKETT. The movement had many subcategories of playwrights who shared a common use of absurd elements as a method to revitalize the stolid conventions of traditional Western theater.

Arrabal's particular subcategory was a style of theater he called Panic Theater. The Greek god of surprise and confusion, Pan, for whom the movement was named, brings both pleasure and terror when he appears. It is important to remember that the scope of Panic Theater extends beyond the simple definition of fear that we normally associate with panic.

In 2005, Arrabal was named to France's Légion d'honneur. In 2007, he was awarded an honorary doctorate by the Aristotle University of Thessaloniki, Greece.

Critical Analysis

Arrabal's play *The Architect and the Emperor of Assyria* (1965) is an example of the height of Panic Theater. The play begins when the emperor of Assyria's plane crashes on a desert island and he is the only one who survives. He finds on this island an architect who is not quite human. He is a supernatural creature who is able to control night and day and the seasons. The emperor nevertheless is unimpressed and begins to try to educate the architect in the manners of bourgeois society. The two men fall into a sadomasochistic relationship that involves acting out plays in which they assume opposite roles, such as a pair of fiancés, mother and son, a nun and her confessor, and a doctor and his patient. As the play progresses, the two actors switch roles, behave like each other, and act out scenes by themselves playing two people. It becomes obvious that they are each other's double and part of the same mind.

The use of games and ritualized behavior to structure the action of the play in lieu of a plot is one of Arrabal's major innovations. In addition, the absurd sequence of events creates confusion and incomprehensibility that embodies one of the main aspects of Panic Theater. Arrabal believed that to be accurate to life, art must be confusing and filled with chance or absurdity. *The Architect and the Emperor of Assyria* can be seen as a psychological drama that, perhaps, takes place within a single mind, a kind of dream projected onto the stage.

In the late 1960s, after being censored and arrested in Spain, Arrabal began to become more political in his drama. He wrote a series of plays that he called Guerrilla Theater, many of which were meant to be performed impromptu on the street. *And They Put Handcuffs on the Flowers* (1969), the culmination of this period in Arrabal's work, is performed in a theater; however, the actors sit with the audience, and the staging is highly unconventional. Arrabal continues to use many of the methods of Panic Theater, but now his purpose was to convey a public, political message.

Arrabal is primarily a dramatist, but he has also had success in a number of other genres. His novel *The Tower Struck by Lightning* (1988) is a semiautobiographical work structured entirely around the game of chess, at which Arrabal is an expert. He has made several films, including a film for children, *Pacific Fantasy* (1981), starring Mickey Rooney. He has also exhibited his dreamlike paintings. Although under the Franco regime his plays were banned in Spain, in 1986 King Juan Carlos of Spain awarded him the Medalla d'Oro de las Bellas Artes. His other awards include France's Prix du Centre National du Livre. Arrabal lives and works in Paris. In a review of the La Mama (New York) production of *The Architect and the Emperor of Assyria*, Clive Barnes wrote: "Mr. Arrabal, with his perceptions, absurdities, loves and understanding, is a playwright to be honored, treasured and understood. In this play he is saying something about the isolation, the solitariness and the need of 20th-century man that, so far, as I can see, no other playwright has quite gotten on stage before."

Other Works by Fernando Arrabal

Baal Babylon. Translated by Richard Howard. New York: Grove, 1961.
Selected Plays: Guernica; The Labyrinth; The Tricycle; Picnic on the Battlefield; And They Put Handcuffs on the Flowers; The Architect and the Emperor of Assyria; Garden of Delights. New York: Grove Press, 1986.

A Work about Fernando Arrabal

Donahue, Thomas John. *The Theater of Fernando Arrabal: A Garden of Earthly Delights.* New York: New York University Press, 1980.

Artaud, Antonin (1896–1948) *poet, dramatist*

Antonin Artaud was born in Marseille, France. In 1920, he moved to Paris to become an actor. His work, both on stage and as a writer, was influential to the development of experimental theater. In particular, he visualized a new form of theater, both for stage and screen, known as the Theater of Cruelty, in which traditional forms of representation would be cast aside in favor of new actions and spectacles and in which language would be all but abandoned in a carefully choreographed new creation. His efforts to produce his visions, however, failed, not so much as a result of a lack of vision but because he spent most of his life destitute, addicted to numerous drugs, and hampered by both physical and mental illness. His book *The Theatre and Its Double* (1938; translated 1958), however, was later used as the basis for much of the ensemble-theater movement as well as for identifying characteristics that would be linked to the THEATER OF THE ABSURD.

A prime example of this type of work was his play *The Cenci* (1935), which was produced at the Théâtre Alfred Jarry, a theater cofounded by Artaud himself. An illustration of the Theater of Cruelty, it was performed without a traditionally constructed set and featured minimal spoken dialogue, relying instead on movement, gestures, and incoherent sounds. The goal of this form of art was to force the audience to confront a "primal self" devoid of the trappings of civilization.

A pioneer, Artaud first began to publish his texts, complete with detailed instruction on lighting, violent gestures, and a noisy cacophony of sound in place of music, in 1924, almost 40 years before Andy Warhol introduced the trend of multimedia spectacle. He initially aligned himself with the SURREALISTS, but he was expelled from their group in 1926 because he was unwilling to follow the movement's mission. Finding himself with few artistic allies, he focused his creative energies on writing essays and poetry, as well as taking small roles in mainstream films, something he felt was degrading to him as an artist.

In 1936 and 1937, Artaud traveled to Mexico (where he studied the rituals of the Tarahumaras Indians), Belgium, and Ireland (where he became increasingly disillusioned with the social restrictions placed on creative artists). He suffered a mental breakdown that involved episodes of violent behavior and hallucinations. On his return from Ireland, Artaud was placed in a psychiatric hospital. Institutionalized from 1937 to 1946, he was subjected to various experimental forms of therapy, including 51 electric shock treatments, coma-inducing insulin therapy, and periods of starvation. As a result, his health declined rapidly.

The final two years of Artaud's life, after his release from the asylum, were unquestionably his most productive. He sought desperately to give voice to his vision. His final work was *To Have Done With The Judgment Of God* (1947), a radio script in which Artaud sought revenge against those who had kept him in the asylum. Billed as vicious, obscene, anti-American and anti-Catholic, the script did not air until 30 years after Artaud's death; it was eventually banned. In the script itself, the United States is presented as a baby factory and war machine. Death rituals are depicted, and excrement is revered as symbolic of life and mortality. Questions about reality are answered with more questions, leading to the final scene in which God takes the stage as a dissected organ on an autopsy table.

Artaud died of cancer, shortly after suffering the disappointment of having his radio broadcast banned, but he left behind a legacy that would influence many generations of artists. As recently as 1982, the punk musical group Bauhaus recorded a song in tribute to the genius of Antonin Artaud.

Another Work by Antonin Artaud

Artaud on Theatre. Edited by Claude Schumacher. London: Methuen Drama, 1991.

Works about Antonin Artaud

Bermel, Albert. *Artaud's Theatre of Cruelty*. New York: Taplinger, 1977.
Plunka, Gene A., ed. *Antonin Artaud and the Modern Theatre*. Cranbury, N.J.: Associated University Presses, 1994.

Astley, Thea (1925–2004) *novelist*

Thea Astley was born in Brisbane, Australia. Almost all of her novels are set in south Queensland. She studied for 12 years in the University of Queensland, graduated with an arts degree, and has taught in several schools and institutions in Queensland, New South Wales, and Sydney. Astley won several prizes for her works, including the Miles Franklin Award on three occasions. She published several novels, some short stories, and edited an anthology of short stories in 1971.

Astley's writings are marked by a unique blend of comedic wit and biting sarcasm. Her novels reflect her constant struggle to come to terms with Queensland society and with Catholicism. Her characters come from a variety of backgrounds, and her settings are usually small towns. Astley believed that the closely knit community of a small town allowed her to express the depths of her characters fully. Her novel *Reaching Tin River* (1980), for example, is set in a rural town whose economic life is centered on the sugar industry.

The most intriguing aspect of Astley's novels is her point of view. She often chose to write from the perspective of the misfits or outsiders of a society. In *A Boat Load of Home Folk* (1968), Astley told of the inability of a group of elderly Australians to cope with the strange environment of a tropical island, revealing their inadequacies. In another novel, *The Slow Natives* (1965), she examined relationships between the elders and the young in the Leverson. She exposes the estrangement between generations and laments the way the aged are marginalized and neglected within the community. This novel won both a Miles Franklin Award and a Moomba Festival prize and is considered to be one of Astley's best novels for the way it finds the depths in shallow, constricted lives.

Astley's poetic prose explores the depth of experience and emotions of her flawed characters. She mixes her chastisement and mockery with humor, as in her depiction of Paul Vesper in *The Acolyte.* This penchant for injecting humor in her narrative makes a deeper impact on her readers.

Other Works by Thea Astley

A Descant for Gossips. St. Lucia: University of Queensland Press, 1986.
Girl With A Monkey. New York: Viking Press, 1987.
Hunting the Wild Pineapple. New York: Penguin USA. 1982.
An Item from the Late News. New York: Viking Press, 1984.
It's Raining in Mango: Pictures from a Family Album. New York: Penguin USA, 1988.
A Kindness Cup. New York: Penguin USA, 1989.
The Well Dressed Explorer. New York: Penguin USA, 1988.

A Work about Thea Astley

Matthews, Brian. "Life in the Eye of the Hurricane: The Novels of Thea Astley." *Southern Review* 5 (1973): 148–173.

Atwood, Margaret (1939–) *novelist, poet*

Margaret Atwood was born in Ottawa, Ontario, to Carl Atwood, an entomologist, and Margaret Killam, a nutritionist. She spent her childhood accompanying her father on his researches in the wilderness of Quebec. Graduating from the University of Toronto with a B.A. in 1961, she received an M.A. from Radcliffe in 1962 and did some graduate work at Harvard University, beginning a thesis on Gothic fiction.

Atwood's first published work, *Double Persephone* (1961), was a book of poetry exploring the mythological figure Persephone. Her most important collection of verse, *The Circle Game* (1966) uses Gothic imagery to explore issues of gender; for example, the first poem, "This Is a Photograph of Me," is narrated by a dead woman: "The photograph was taken / the day after I drowned." Atwood's first novel, *Edible Woman* (1969) is a darkly comic tale of a woman who fears marriage and stops eating.

Her most celebrated novel, *The Handmaid's Tale* (1985), is set in a horrifying future society, Gilead, where women are condemned to illiteracy and servitude. The novel purports to be the recorded narration of Offred, a servant: "Where the edges are we aren't sure, they vary, according to the attacks and counterattacks; but this is the centre, where nothing moves. The Republic of Gilead, said Aunt Lydia, knows no bounds. Gilead is within you." Critic Sandra Tomc sees the novel as a critique not merely of male oppression but also of United States domination over Canada: "In the nightmare future she imagines, women have succumbed to a totalizing patriarchy. Appropriately, given Atwood's conflation of feminism and nationalism, Canada, in some analogous gesture, has succumbed to its totalizing southern neighbor."

The Robber Bride (1993), focuses on the demonic Zenia's haunting of her three friends, robbing them of their money and men, and has dark Gothic undertones: "Zenia, with her dark hair sleeked down by the rain, wet and shivering, standing on the back step as she had done once before, long ago. Zenia, who had been dead for five years." *Alias Grace* (1996) continues Atwood's exploration of gender and power, based on the story of Grace Marks, a servant accused of murdering her master in 1843. Her novel *Blind Assassin* (2000) contains three interconnected stories, beginning with a woman, Iris Griffin, telling of her sister's death in 1945. It won the Booker Prize. Fellow Canadian writer ALICE MUNRO comments: "It's easy to appreciate the grand array of Margaret Atwood's work—the novels, the stories, the poems, in all their power and grace and variety. This work in itself has opened up the gates for a recognition of Canadian writing all over the world."

In recent years, Atwood has published *Oryx and Crake* (2003) and *The Year of the Flood* (2009), dystopic novels that contain many of the same characters. Both novels focus on a society destroyed by technology and commercialization. Atwood also published *The Penelopiad* (2005), a retelling of the story of Penelope, wife of Odysseus. In 2010, Atwood shared the $1 million Dan David Prize with the Indian author AMITAV GHOSH at Tel Aviv University.

Other Works by Margaret Atwood

Cat's Eye. New York: Doubleday, 1989.
Power Politics. New York: Harper & Row, 1973.
Year of the Flood. New York: Nan A. Talese, 2009.

Works about Margaret Atwood

Cooke, Nathalie. *Margaret Atwood: A Biography.* Toronto: ECW Press, 1998.
Howells, Carol Ann. *The Cambridge Companion to Margaret Atwood.* Cambridge: Cambridge University Press, 2006.

Ausländer, Rose (Rosalie Scherzer) (1901–1988) *poet*

Rose Ausländer was born in Czernowitz, Austria-Hungary, a city now situated in Ukraine. Her father Sigmund Scherzer, a former rabbinical student, ensured that the family practiced traditional Jewish customs and rituals. As part of her upbringing, she learned both Hebrew and Yiddish and later attended the University of Czernowitz where she studied literature, EXPRESSIONISM, and philosophy. After her father died in 1920, she emigrated to the United States in 1921 to relieve some of the financial strain on her mother, Etie Scherzer, and was joined by another student from the university, Ignaz Ausländer, whom she married in 1923. The couple divorced after three years, and she moved back to Czernowitz in 1931.

Rose Ausländer started writing poetry in German while in the United States. After returning to Czernowitz, she published her first book-length collection of poetry, *Der Regenbogen* (*The Rainbow*, 1939). Although it received positive reviews, the Nazis prevented the book from achieving a wide circulation because Ausländer was Jewish. During World War II, Ausländer and her mother avoided Nazi death camps by hiding in a cellar. Ausländer composed poetry to cope with the traumatic situation. During this time, she met PAUL CELAN, a poet who would influence Ausländer's works after 1957.

Following World War II, Ausländer published 12 volumes of poetry while living in West

Germany and the United States. Her best poems describe her personal experiences in Czernowitz and the fear and suffering of the Holocaust. As the literary scholar Kathrin Bower writes, "Ausländer's poems evidence a dialogue of remembrance and mourning at once historical and redemptive." Ausländer thus became a voice for a shattered generation of German Jews.

Another Work by Rose Ausländer

Selected Poems of Rose Ausländer. Translated by Ewald Osers. London: London Magazine Editors, 1977.

A Work about Rose Ausländer

Bower, Kathrin M. *Ethics and Remembrance in the Poetry of Nelly Sachs and Rose Ausländer*. Rochester, N.Y.: Camden House, 2000.

꧁꧂

Ba Jin (Pa Chin; Li Feigan) (1904–2005)
novelist

Li Feigan was born on November 25 in Chengdu and received a private education. He studied English at Chengdu Foreign Languages School, participating in antifeudal activity and studying Russian writers and anarchist philosophers. He adopted a pen name from syllables of the Chinese names of Russian anarchists Mikhail Bakunin (1814–76) and Pyotr Kropotkin (1842–1921).

After moving to France in 1927, Ba Jin wrote autobiographical essays and articles on anarchism, as well as his first novel, *Destruction* (1929), about the life of a young anarchist, Du Daxin. He produced many works, mostly political in nature, with clear-cut moral lessons. His subjects were frequently the Chinese gentry class or intellectuals. In 1931, he published his best-known work, *Family,* a sentimental melodrama of several generations living in one compound. The novel chronicled a family's rise and fall and charted the fate of feudalism after the May Fourth Movement (1919 student demonstrations against the weak Chinese concessions of the imperialist Versailles Treaty). *Family* became part of Ba Jin's Torrent Trilogy, which included *Spring* (1938) and *Autumn* (1940).

The three-year period between 1931 and 1933 brought a novella companion to *Destruction* called *New Life,* as well as two novels about mining life, *The Antimony Miners* and *The Sprouts.* In 1935, Ba Jin also completed the *Trilogy of Love,* which followed the revolutionary activities of a group of intellectuals.

Ba Jin was active in many aspects of literary and political life. He published two manifestos on behalf of and with other Chinese artists and writers, including Lu Xun, for freedom of speech and against imperialism. He actively urged a united front against Japanese aggression during the Sino-Japanese War and continued his literary output with the novelettes *The Garden of Repose* (1944), *Ward No. 4* (1946), and *Cold Nights* (1946). As a Korean War correspondent, he wrote two books about the battlefields, *Living Amongst Heroes* (1953) and *Defenders of Peace* (1954).

Ba Jin earned many awards and distinctions, including France's Legion of Honor. He has an honorary doctorate from the Chinese University of Hong Kong and was one of China's most prominent writers.

Other Works by Ba Jin
"My *J'accuse* Against This Moribund System: Notes on a Crumbling Landlord Clan of Western Sichuan." In Helmut Martin and Jeffrey Kinkley, eds.,

Modern Chinese Writers: Self-Portrayals. Armonk, N.Y.: M. E. Sharpe, 1992.

Random Thoughts. Translated by Geremie Barmé. San Francisco: China Books & Periodicals, 1984.

Selected Works of Ba Jin. Beijing: Foreign Language Press, 1988.

Ward Four: A Novel of Wartime China. Translated by Haili Kong and Howard Goldblatt. San Francisco: China Books & Periodicals, 2001.

Bâ, Mariama (1929–1981) *novelist, essayist, activist*

Mariama Bâ was born into a prominent family in Dakar, Senegal. At a time when only Europeans maintained political positions in Senegal, Bâ's father became the first Senegalese minister of health. Her maternal grandparents raised her in the Muslim tradition. Against her grandparents' wishes, she graduated from the Teacher's College in 1947 and taught for 12 years. Bâ was married to Obèye Diop, a member of Parliament, with whom she had nine children. After they divorced, she remained single, becoming an advocate for women in Senegal.

Bâ's first novel, *So Long a Letter* (1979), was an international success that illuminated the complex lives of African women. Although the critics have mostly viewed the novel as a criticism of polygamy, exposing the inequalities between men and women, it addresses multiple women's issues. The story centers on two educated women who had happy, loving marriages until their husbands took second wives. Each woman responds in her own way: One stays and one leaves. The book reveals the limited choices for women and also presents the strong bonds and support systems between women. Writing in letter format, Bâ gives the reader an intimate look at a woman's internal reflections. This novel received the Noma Award for Publishing in Africa in 1980.

Bâ died prior to the publishing of her second novel, *Scarlet Song* (1981), which tackles the difficulties of interracial marriage. Today, she is considered one of the most important French West African feminists.

Works about Mariama Bâ

Cham, Mbye B. "Contemporary Society and the Female Imagination: A Study of the Novels of Mariama Bâ." *African Literature Today* 15 (1987): 89–101.

d'Almeida, Irene Assiba. "The Concept of Choice in Mariama Bâ's Fiction." In Carole Boyce Davies and Anne Adams Graves, eds., *Nagambika: Studies of Women in African Literature.* Trenton, N.J.: Africa World Press, 1986.

Edson, Laurie. "Mariama Bâ and the Politics of the Family." *Studies in Twentieth Century Literature* 17.1 (1993): 13–25.

Babel, Isaac (1894–1940) *short story writer, novelist, dramatist*

Isaac Emmanuelovich Babel was born in Odessa, Russia, into a Jewish family. Emmanuel Babel, his father, was a sales representative for an agricultural firm. At the time, Odessa had the largest Jewish population in Russia, and Babel grew up in the city's Jewish ghetto, Moldavanka. He was constantly faced with anti-Semitism from teachers and peers, a fact that played a substantial role in his development as a writer.

Babel's father was a domineering patriarch who forced young Isaac to practice violin for hours every day and sent him, when he was 11, to study business in Kiev, where he stayed until 1914. Although Babel excelled in all areas as a student, literature was his only passion.

Babel began his career as a writer while studying at Kiev, often drawing upon his experience growing up in the Jewish ghetto. His first published story, "Old Shloyme" (1913), explores anti-Semitism directly; in the story, a Jewish family faces a choice between renouncing their religion and losing their home.

In 1914, Babel moved to St. Petersburg to pursue writing professionally. He had difficulty publishing his material until a meeting with MAXIM GORKY in 1916. Gorky assisted Babel with the publication of two stories in the prestigious literary journal *Letopis*.

Babel supported the Bolshevik cause during the Russian Revolution. Like many other Jews in Russia faced with persecution, Babel was intrigued by the Bolshevik promises of freedom and equality for all. Between 1917 and 1919, Babel served in the Red Army. His most famous collection of stories, *Red Cavalry* (1926), reflects his experiences during the war. The work raises issues of violence, anti-Semitism, and political ideology, as well as the themes of friendship, love, and compassion. The success of *Red Cavalry* firmly established Babel as one of the leading writers in Russia.

In 1929, Babel left Russia and traveled throughout Europe, visiting France, Italy, Belgium, and Germany. When he returned to Russia, he became skeptical of the Communists. During the same period, he began writing drama, completing his most notable play, *Sunset,* in 1928. Set in Odessa in 1913, the play explores the social interactions of the Jewish ghetto. In the play, the reader notices a duality that persistently appears throughout Babel's works: He embraces his Jewishness and at the same time intellectually opposes Judaism. The play was criticized by the authorities for its lack of socialist themes.

During the 1930s, Babel was repeatedly criticized by the government. Arrested in 1939, Babel was executed in 1940 after a 20-minute trial for allegedly spying for France and Austria. The charges were false, as the records, released in 1954, confirm.

Babel made an enormous contribution to Russian literature, emerging as one of the first writers to discuss openly and positively the cultural and social position of the Jews in Russia. As Natalie Babel, his wife, later pointed out, "His life centered on writing, and it can be said without exaggeration that he sacrificed everything to his art, including his relationship with his family, his liberty, and finally even his life."

Other Works by Isaac Babel

Babel, Natalie, ed. *The Collected Stories of Isaac Babel.* Translated by Peter Constantine. New York: Norton, 2002.

The Complete Works of Isaac Babel. Translated by Peter Constantine. New York: Norton, 2001.

Works about Isaac Babel

Bloom, Harold, ed. *Isaac Babel: Modern Critical Views.* Broomall, Pa.: Chelsea House, 1987.
Ehre, Milton. *Isaac Babel.* Boston: Twayne, 1986.

Bachmann, Ingeborg (1926–1973) *poet, novelist, dramatist*

A daughter of a teacher, Ingeborg Bachmann was born in Klagenfurt, Austria. She grew up in a disturbing political atmosphere, as Nazi Germany was gaining control of Austria, and at the age of 12 she watched Nazi troops march into her town. Bachmann studied philosophy at the universities of Innsburg, Graz, and Vienna; she completed a dissertation on Ludwig Wittgenstein under the direction of the famous philosopher Martin Heidegger in 1950.

Bachmann began her career as a professional writer in the early 1950s, writing radio plays. In 1953, Bachmann published her first collection of poetry, *The Deferred Time.* The collection was critically praised and received the prestigious GRUPPE 47 award. In 1953 she spent a year in the United States as a visiting scholar at Harvard University, and she later moved to Italy, where she wrote a number of political articles for Austrian and German newspapers. In 1959, Bachmann was appointed to the newly created position as chair of poetics at the University of Frankfurt, where she lectured on philosophy and literature.

Her poetry is influenced by many sources, including CLASSICISM, surrealism, and the avant-garde movement. The somber tone of her poetry lyrically and precisely describes the anguish of a personal experience. Bachmann's dark, powerful, and complex imagery is thematically juxtaposed against simple individual emotions such as love, guilt, and failed aspirations. Her use of imagery is exemplified by these lines from "In the Storm of Roses": "Wherever we turn in the storm of roses,/the night is lit up by thorns. . . ." Unlike her prose, which is often read as social and feminist fiction, her poetry centers on deeply personal observations.

In 1961, Bachmann published her highly influential autobiographical work, *The Thirtieth Year,* which was awarded the Berlin Critics Prize and the Georg Büchner Prize in 1964. Her first published novel, *Malina* (1971), deals with a number of feminist issues. Malina, the protagonist of the novel, has a relationship with Ivan, a younger man of Hungarian descent. The relationship becomes psychologically complex as Malina has recurrent nightmares of her father as a Nazi who kills her in a gas chamber, nightmares that seem to contribute to the deterioration of her relationship with Ivan. *Malina* also confronts the theme of national memory and national identity in postwar Europe. The issues of ego and alter ego and with the subtle influence of the memory of genocide create a powerful combination. The novel was highly praised and remains an excellent representative work of German POSTMODERNISM.

Just before her death, Bachmann visited Auschwitz in Poland and gave a series of readings. She died under mysterious circumstances in a fire in her apartment. Bachmann was awarded numerous prizes, including the Austrian Medal of Honor, the highest prize in literature an Austrian citizen can receive from the government. Her works continue to be of great social and literary importance.

Other Works by Ingeborg Bachmann

The Book of Franza and Requiem for Fanny Goldman. Translated by Peter Filkins. Evanston, Ill.: Northwestern University Press, 1999.

Selected Prose and Drama. New York: Continuum, 1998.

Songs in Flight: The Collected Poems of Ingeborg Bachmann. Translated by Peter Filkins (bilingual edition). New York: Marsilio Publications, 1995.

Three Radio Plays. Translated by Lilian Friedberg. Riverside, Calif.: Ariadne Press, 1999.

A Work about Ingeborg Bachmann

Redwitz, Eckenbert. *The Image of the Woman in the Works of Ingeborg Bachmann.* New York: Peter Lang, 1993.

Balzac, Honoré de (1799–1850) *novelist*

Honoré de Balzac, one of the creators of REALISM in literature, was born in Tours, France, to a middle-class family. Originally from Paris, the family had moved to Tours during the French Revolution because of their royalist opinions. In 1814, however, they were able to return to Paris. Balzac, neglected by his mother, spent his early years in boarding schools. After graduating from the Collège de Vendôme he went on to the Sorbonne, where he read the works of the mystical philosophers Jakob Böhme (1575–1624) and Emanuel Swedenborg (1688–1772) and was particularly interested in Franz Anton Mesmer's lectures on animal magnetism. These influences are detectable in his early fiction. After graduation, he began to work in a law office. When, in 1819, his family was forced by financial setbacks to move to the small town of Villeparisis, Balzac decided that he would return to Paris alone and embark on a career as a writer.

Balzac rented a shabby room in Paris, a room he later described in the novel *Le peau de chagrin* (*The Wild Ass's Skin,* 1831), and began what would become a habit of late night writing and excessive consumption of caffeine. In his lifetime, he wrote more than 100 novels, mostly between the hours of midnight and six in the morning, always on blue paper and by candlelight, while drinking large quantities of thick Turkish coffee. By 1822 Balzac, using a variety of pseudonyms, had written several plays and novels, all of which were ignored. Undaunted, he continued to write.

A compulsive spender, Balzac had a difficult time staying ahead of his creditors. He attempted to run a publishing company and also bought a printing house. Both of these endeavors left him with large debts that would stay with him throughout his life. Destitute at 29, he accepted an invitation to stay at the home of Général de Pommereul in Fougères in Brittany, where he worked on his novel *Le dernier chouan, ou la Bretagne en 1800* (1829), a historical work that he eventually published under his own name. Finally, with this work, Balzac began to gain some recognition and popularity, although not enough to release him from debt.

In 1833, Balzac developed the idea of collecting all of his previously written novels under one name and linking them together as a series of works which, when taken as a whole, would encompass all the customs, atmosphere, and habits of French society. This idea eventually led to the collection of more than 2,000 characters appearing in 90 novels and novellas. The works were eventually collected under the title *La comédie humaine,* or *The Human Comedy,* a name Balzac borrowed from Dante's *The Divine Comedy.*

Critical Analysis

Included in *La comédie humaine* were well-known works such as *Le père Goriot* (*Father Goriot,* 1834–35), *Les paysans* (*The Peasants,* 1844), and *Illusions perdues* (*Lost Illusions,* 1837–43). The settings for these works include all levels of society in Paris and the provinces. The characters include a mix of old aristocracy and new money, set alongside middle-class tradespeople and professionals, servants, young intellectuals, and criminals. Some of the characters, such as Eugène de Rastignac, the poor provincial man who comes to Paris with big dreams and makes good on them through gambling, affairs, and connections with the nobility, recur throughout the works. Balzac inserted himself in his works as well, alluding to incidents and adventures in which he participated side by side with his characters who grew to exist not only on paper but in his imagination outside of his novels as if they were actual acquaintances. It is said that Balzac once interrupted a conversation in which a friend of his was telling him about his sister's ill health by saying, "That's all very well, but let's get back to reality: to whom are we going to marry Eugénie Grandet?"

During the height of his productivity, Balzac was known to spend anywhere from 14 to 16 hours a day writing. He would eat a large meal each evening, sleep for a few hours, and then wake at midnight to continue writing. There are reports that once he consumed 100 oysters and 12 lamb chops in a single meal. His few free hours were spent having amorous affairs and pursuing the joy of life. One of his affairs was with Eveline Hanska, a wealthy Polish woman who had been among his friends for 15 years. He based several of his female characters on her, such as Mme. Hulot in *La cousine Bette* (*Cousin Bette,* 1846). She was married throughout most of their acquaintance, but after her husband passed away in 1841, Balzac spent increasing amounts of time in her company. Already in poor health, he eventually married her and brought her back to Paris in the spring of 1850, only five months before his death in August, when his excesses got the better of him and he died, reportedly of caffeine poisoning.

Other Works by Honoré de Balzac

The Girl with the Golden Eyes. Translated by Carol Cosman. New York: Carroll and Graf, 1998.
The Unknown Masterpiece; and, Gambara. Translated by Richard Howard. New York: New York Review of Books, 2001.

Works about Honoré de Balzac

Graham, Robb. *Balzac: A Biography.* New York: Norton, 1994.
Kanes, Martin. *Pere Goriot: Anatomy of a Troubled World.* Boston: Twayne, 1993.
Kanes, Martin, ed. *Critical Essays on Honoré de Balzac.* Boston: G. K. Hall, 1990.

Bama (Faustina Mary Fatima Rani)
(1958–) *novelist, activist*

Bama is the pseudonym of a South Indian writer, a Tamil Dalit woman from a Roman Catholic family who has made a great impact upon Indian literature by giving voice to a people who are traditionally viewed as "untouchables" in the rigid caste system. Indeed, in India's caste system Dalit people are considered to be so lowly as to have no caste at all and are restricted to menial labor and scavenging. They comprise as much as 20 percent of the overall population, are generally deprived of educational opportunities, and are frequently the victims of caste-based crime. Furthermore, as a woman, Bama has been discriminated against because of her sex and so comes to speak for a segment of Indian society that has never had a voice. She also has been instrumental as an activist for dalit rights as well as a leading voice for dalit literature.

Bama was born in 1958 in Puthupatti, a village in the Virudunagar district of Tamil Nadu in southern India. Her ancestors worked as laborers for their landlords. Her grandfather had converted to Christianity, and her father, who was in the Indian army, was very particular about his children's education. According to Bama, "If he had not joined the army, we would never have had the regular income for education. Education also gave us freedom to get away from the clutches of the landlords and lead our own lives." Bama attended a convent school, acquiring a solid educational background and cultivating a strong religious faith while preparing for college. Her brother, Raj Gautaman, also a writer and advocate for dalit literature, introduced her to the world of books. "During my childhood," Bama said, "it was the books he used to bring home from the library or elsewhere that I first read. Thus I was exposed to Tamil writers like [S.] Mani, [Indira] Parthsarthy, Jayakantan, Akhilan." In college, she read works in English and a few other Indian languages, especially the works of Kahlil Gibran and RABINDRANATH TAGORE. At this time she also began writing poetry or lyrical prose, as she has described it. After college, Bama became a teacher in a Catholic school, working with very poor girls.

In her autobiography, *Karukku* (1992), Bama describes this period: "I worked there for five years. All the children who attended that school were from poor families. About three-fourths of them were from Dalit families. I liked teaching them. . . . But when I observed some of the atrocities that were going on, I would be ablaze with fury." Bama was outraged at the way the nuns treated the Dalit children, ostensibly running a boarding school for the benefit of destitute children but in reality reinforcing the notion of caste and teaching the children that it was their fate to accept their status on the lowest rung of Indian society.

Although conflicted by the hypocrisy and cruelty she saw in the behavior of the nuns and priests, Bama still felt a strong religious calling. At the age of 26, she took vows to become a nun with the hope of being a different kind of nun, one who might break with the bonds of caste and further the cause of the Dalit: "I felt that at the seminary I would be able to carry forward my work with the poor."

Karukku relates the story of Bama's seven years in the religious order culminating in her departure after coming to the grim realization that the Roman Catholic Church is as "casteist" (or caste-bound) and as discriminatory as the world she had left behind. All its talk of ". . . serving the poorest of the poor was mere cant and hypocrisy. Until I actually entered the convent," she writes, "I truly did not understand their approach nor any of their procedures. It was only after my sojourn with them that I understood the lack of humanity in their piety."

When *Karukku* was published, it changed not only the way Dalit literature was perceived in the literary circles of Tamil Nadu but also how it was viewed in Indian society as a whole. Lakshmi Holmström's English translation of *Karukku* (2001) won the Crossword Award in India and established Bama as a distinctive and important voice in Indian literature. Bama wrote her second work, the novel *Sangati*, in 1994. If her autobiography was about the realization of the Dalit condition, then *Sangati* explores the ways in which that consciousness might sound and think. It conveys in a stream-of-consciousness manner the mentality of a Dalit who constantly questions her caste status. Realizing that leaving her community is no escape, she has to come to terms with her identity as an educated, economically independent woman living alone. In an interview, Bama was asked about her marital status and she replied, "I am a single woman and you can imagine how difficult it is to lead a single woman's life in a village in Tamil Nadu. It is not easy. There are all kinds of myths surrounding you."

Bama also published a collection of short stories, *Kisumbukkaran* (1996), reaffirming her status as an important south Indian writer. She continues to write and teach and has published a book on intercaste rivalries in Tamil Nadu, *Vanmam Vendetta* (2003).

Critical Analysis

As Bama's English translator Lakshmi Holmström has observed, *Karukku* means palmyra leaves, which are shaped like double-edged swords, representing the author's incisive self-examination and the wounding power of a a society that is openly oppressive while professing to be democratic. *Karukku* was the first Dalit autobiography to appear in Tamil, and its power derives from Bama's sensitivity to the cultural implications of her own personal and spiritual crisis. Its genesis derives from a morning in 1992 when Bama left the Catholic seminary where she had resided for many years—never to return again. She soon met with severe impoverishment, as well as either apathy or scorn from her community. Having little or no idea what to do with herself, unemployed, condemned by her culture and the church she had abandoned, she began working on her life story. "I began writing," Bama has said, "to stop myself from taking my own life. *Karukku* came out naturally. It was more of an outpouring of all my experiences in life than a literary act."

Karukku presents the arc of the narrator's spiritual development as a Catholic and a dalit. The narrative is written in colloquial language. Rather than using deliberately literary or lyrical language, Bama invites the reader into her own voice and vision. As one reviewer noted, *Karukku* says "to English-educated readers an entirely different sensibility, a startlingly honest reality." That reality of ordinary Dalit life was one that had not previously found expression in Indian literature or history. "The story told in *Karukku* was not my story alone," Bama has said. "It was the depiction of a collective trauma—of my community—whose length cannot be measured in time." In telling her life story, Bama has tried to record a reminder of the atrocities and abuse sustained by her people over vast periods of time. Through *Karukku*, the Dalit community found a place in mainstream Tamil history and Indian culture as a whole.

A Work about Bama

Bhagvan, Manu, and Anne Feldhaus. *Speaking Truth to Power: Religion, Caste and the Subaltern Question in India.* New York: Oxford University Press, 2010.

Barbey d'Aurevilly, Jules-Amédée
(1808–1889) *novelist*

Jules-Amédée Barbey d'Aurevilly was born in Saint-Sauveur-le-Vicomte on November 2 into an aristocratic family, was well educated, and was accustomed to privilege. In 1833, he moved to Paris, where he had numerous love affairs and led the unprincipled life of a "dandy," supporting his activities through journalism. In 1841, he converted to strict Catholicism and eventually became, as would be apparent in his novels, a strong Christian moralist.

Barbey d'Aurevilly wrote numerous works of criticism and articles, but it was his novels that brought him acclaim. He was influenced by BALZAC and greatly admired BAUDELAIRE. As well as harshly criticizing NATURALISM, his novels and stories are notable for their highly moralistic but sadistic portrayals of the struggles and tragedies associated with life in the provinces of France.

Barbey d'Aurevilly is perhaps best known for his work *Les Diaboliques* (1874; *The Diabolic Ones*, 1925), a collection of six stories, all having some basis in fact and all carrying a similar satanic motif. This shocking work achieved great success both critically and popularly. He died in Paris, 15 years after its publication, at the age of 81.

Another Work by Jules Barbey d'Aurevilly

Dandyism. Translated by Douglas Ainsley. New York: PAJ Publications, 1988.

Works about Jules Barbey d'Aurevilly

Chartier, Armand B. *Barbey d'Aurevilly.* Boston: Twayne, 1977.
Eisenberg, Davina L. *The Figure of the Dandy in Barbey D'Aurevilly's "Le Bonheur Dans Le Crime".* New York: Peter Lang, 1996.

Baroja y Nessi, Pío (1872–1956) *novelist*

Pío Baroja y Nessi was born in San Sebastian, Spain. His father was a mining engineer, and the family moved frequently during his childhood, relocating from town to town, following his father's professional career. Baroja y Nessi studied to be a doctor, and when he graduated from school, he began a medical practice in the town of Cestona in northern Spain. The medical profession did not suit him. His practice was a disaster; after a short time, he gave it up and moved to Madrid, a cosmopolitan city, where he ran a bakery that was owned by his aunt.

It was at this time that he began to publish his novels. He was successful as an author and quickly gave up the management of the bakery to write full time.

Baroja y Nessi was a member of the GENERATION OF 1898. He shared with the other writers of the Generation of '98 a strong sense of Spanish nationalism and a need to reform society. However, Baroja y Nessi was particularly individualistic. As a youth, he had briefly been an anarchist but found even this ideology too constraining. Because of an aversion to any societal structure that limited his freedom, he never married. This individualism was the main theme of his novels.

In his trilogy *The Struggle for Life* (1903–04), Baroja y Nessi depicts the slums of Madrid and a collection of characters who, by living outside the norms of society, manage to achieve personal freedom. Though the books are distinctly melancholy and terse, written in what critics call Baroja y Nessi's gray style, they are optimistic in that some of the characters do achieve a degree of freedom by opposing society. In later novels, such as *The Tree of Knowledge* (1911), Baroja y Nessi depicts the same scenario but in a more pessimistic manner. At the end, the protagonist is unable to realize his goal of personal freedom and is crushed by society.

Baroja y Nessi was a formal innovator. He did not believe in the "closed" novel, the standard model of the 19th century, because he felt its carefully planned plot, structure, and resolution of every conflict did not accurately reflect reality. Instead he wrote in a style of apparent aimlessness. For example, he creates scenes in which suspense is carefully built but never resolved. His stark tone and innovative structure had a great effect on many 20th-century writers, most notably Ernest Hemingway.

Baroja y Nessi is one of the greatest Spanish novelists of the early 20th century. His work, along with that of the other members of the Generation of '98, revitalized Spanish literature. His influence on later Spanish writers is widespread, but it can be particularly seen in the works of CAMILO JOSÉ CELA. His innovative style, as well as his theme of the struggle of the individual in modern society, has secured his place among other great writers of world literature.

Another Work by Pío Baroja y Nessi

The Restlessness of Shanti Andia and Other Writings. Translated by Anthony Corrigan. Ann Arbor: University of Michigan Press, 1959.

A Work about Pío Baroja y Nessi

Patt, Beatrice P. *Pío Baroja y Nessi.* Boston: Twayne, 1971.

Bassani, Giorgio (1916–2000) *novelist, short story writer, poet, scriptwriter, essayist, editor*

Giorgio Bassani was born on March 4, 1916, in Bologna, Italy, to Jewish upper-class parents. His early years were spent in public school in the northern Italian town of Ferrara, where his family had strong roots in the community. These years were quiet and could be perceived as idyllic, but events were taking place that would rock the foundation of Italian society—and the world—and profoundly affect the course of Bassani's life.

Bassani was barely 10 years old when Benito Mussolini became prime minister, then dictator of Italy, and a fascist police state was imposed. It is difficult to imagine what this must have meant to a young Jewish boy; however, Bassani has so clearly evoked in his fiction the thoughts and experiences of young boys such as himself that readers can feel almost as if they were there. In evocative language that survives even in translation, Bassani builds a world of school, friendship, family, and community that is richly detailed.

In 1936, when Bassani was 20 and enrolled in his second year at the University of Bologna, Mussolini cemented Italian ties to Germany by declaring the Rome-Berlin Axis. While at university, Bassani forged friendships that he would keep throughout his life. He studied under art historian Roberto Longhi and was influenced by the antifascist ideals, namely the triumph of individual liberties in the face of suppression, of the philosopher Benedetto Croce. It was in this environment that Bassani formed the principal values that he would keep throughout his life. By the time he graduated in 1939, Bassani was involved in the antifascist movement and committed to fighting against the political agenda of the fascist regime. Also in 1939, Germany attacked Poland, which prompted Great Britain and France to declare war on the Axis. Italy enacted new laws in keeping with the Axis's anti-Semitic stances of persecution and intolerance for the Jews, with laws designed to limit the Jewish populations's opportunities and personal liberties. Bassani's first job after graduating was teaching the Jewish children of Ferrara because they were no longer admitted to the public schools.

In 1940, Bassani published *Una città di pianura (A City of the Plain)* under the pseudonym Giacomo Marchi, using his Catholic grandmother's surname to avoid the recently enacted ban on Jewish publication. In 1942, Bassani helped found the Partito d'Azione (Action Party), which would become a leader among political Resistance parties, and in May of 1943 he was arrested on charges of antifascist acts. He was released in July of that same year after Mussolini was ousted from power. Bassani promptly married his sweetheart, Valeria Sinigallia, and set out for Rome, but was forced into hiding there because of the uneasy political climate.

As Italy sorted out its post–World War II politics and formed a republican state, Bassani continued his interrupted literary career. He published various important articles in periodicals and newspapers, as well as poetry and novels. He became the editor of an international literary journal, *Botteghe Oscure,* where he was responsible for recognizing and developing fresh young talent.

In 1956, Bassani published his award-winning book of stories, *Cinque storie ferraresi (Five Stories of Ferrara),* which began an exploration of the town of Bassani's childhood, Ferrara, and the interaction of its Jewish and Christian citizens. Bassani continued this exploration in what is arguably his most widely recognized work, *Il giardino dei Finzi-Contini (The Garden of the Finzi-Continis,* 1962). These works and several others set in Ferrara and its surrounding countryside were collected into *Il romanzo di Ferrara* (1974).

Throughout the remainder of his life, Bassani would continue to set his novels and literary works in Ferrara and indulged in his love of rewriting his previously published work. He died in Rome in the year 2000 after a long life and a well-respected literary career.

Critical Analysis

In 1943, 183 Jewish residents of Bassani's hometown of Ferrara were deported to concentration camps in Germany. This event was one of many that together and individually scar the history of the town of Ferrara. That such events affected Bassani is beyond question, but in his fiction he chose to focus not on the events themselves but instead on the various roles individuals played in the community.

Bassani returned to two themes again and again in these works. The first theme is the marginalization of those deemed outsiders by the society in which they live, especially Italian Jews. He also explored the deeper meaning that can be brought to the fore when people face difficult and divisive elements within their own community.

The literature written in support of the Fascist Party and the propaganda the party produced showed a distorted picture of history and society to make a point. In contrast to this manipulation of reality, Bassani sought to find the truth of living history inside himself. This was a view of history Bassani had learned in his university days under Roberto Longhi, and through this expression of art, the writer allowed his readers to see in mundane life both the commonality of everyday existence and the larger themes of liberty and truth. Giorgio Bassani said in *Vengeance of the Victim*, "It is impossible to imagine life without death, and it is impossible to imagine art, which is the opposite of truth, without truth."

Bassani was the recipient of several prestigious Italian awards for literature, and the film adaptation of *Il giardino dei Finzi-Contini* received the Academy Award for Best Foreign Language Film in 1971. Bassani's novels have been widely studied, and *Il giardino dei Finzi-Contini* in particular lends itself to analysis of themes such as death, sexual awakening, withdrawal from society, and the rise and fall of a Jewish community in Italy. Bassani is a master at creating detailed fictional worlds without seeming to tell the reader how those worlds should be interpreted. By doing so he inspires the reader to personally engage with his challenging texts.

Other Works by Giorgio Bassani

Behind the Door. New York: Harcourt Brace Jovanovich, 1972.

Le storie Ferraresi. Turin, Italy: Giulio Einaudi Editore, 1960.
The Heron. New York: Harcourt, Brace & World, 1970.

Works about Giorgio Bassani

Radcliff-Umstead, Douglas. *The Exile into Eternity.* London and Toronto: Associated University Presses, 1987.
Schneider, Marilyn. *Vengeance of the Victim.* Minneapolis: University of Minnesota Press, 1986.

Bastida, Gustavo Adolfo Dominguez
See Béquer, Gustavo Adolfo.

Bataille, Georges (1897–1962) *novelist, essayist*

Often called the "metaphysician of evil" because of his interests in sex, death, and the obscene, Georges Bataille was born in Billon, Puy-de-Dôme, France. His childhood was difficult because his mother repeatedly attempted suicide, and his father, whom Bataille dearly loved, became both blind and paralyzed as a result of syphilis before he died.

Bataille converted to Catholicism just prior to World War I and served in the army from 1916 to 1917. Troubled by poor health throughout his life as well as by recurring periods of depression, he was discharged from the army as a result of tuberculosis. He joined a seminary, thinking of becoming a priest, and spent time with a Benedictine congregation, but he soon experienced a profound loss of faith. He continued his education at the École des Chartres, writing his thesis in 1922 on 13th-century verse.

Bataille aligned himself early on with surrealism, but he considered himself to be the "enemy from within." André Breton officially excommunicated Bataille from the movement. After a period of psychoanalysis, Bataille began to write. He founded several journals and was the first to publish innovative thinkers such as Barthes, Foucault, and Derrida.

Bataille rejected the traditional, believing that all artistic and intellectual pursuits should ultimately focus on the violent annihilation of the rational individual. His work was greatly influenced by both FRIEDRICH NIETZSCHE and Gilles de Rais, a 15th-century serial killer. All of Bataille's writings deal with violence and sexuality. His best known erotic works are *The Story of the Eye* (1928), *Blue of Noon* (1945), and *The Abbot C.* (1950). Bataille believed pornography was a means of understanding the relation between life and death. *The Story of the Eye,* which he wrote under the pseudonym Lord Auch, for example, is the story of a young couple who test the boundaries of sexual taboos, escalating to extreme playing out of sexual fantasies. The novel quickly gained and still maintains a cult status decades after Bataille's death in Paris on July 8, 1962.

Other Works by Georges Bataille

Eroticism: Death and Sensuality. Translated by Mary Dalwood. San Francisco: City Lights Books, 1991.
The Unfinished System of Nonknowledge. Translated by Michelle Kendall and Stuart Kendall. Minneapolis: University of Minnesota Press, 2001.

Works about Georges Bataille

Champagne, Roland A. *Georges Bataille.* Boston: Twayne, 1998.
Surya, Michel. *Georges Bataille: An Intellectual Biography.* Translated by Krysztof Kijalkowski and Michael Richardson. New York: Verso, 2002.

Baudelaire, Charles (1821–1867) *poet, critic*

Considered one of the greatest 19th-century French poets, Charles-Pierre Baudelaire was born on April 9, 1821. He was the son of Joseph-François Baudelaire and Caroline Archimbaut Dufays. His father had been an ordained priest who left the ministry during the French Revolution to work as a tutor for the Duke of Choiseul-Praslin's children. During this time, he met a number of influential people and amassed a small financial fortune. A modestly talented poet and painter, he taught his son an early appreciation for art.

Considered by many to be a revolutionary even in his own time, Baudelaire was often given to depression and cynicism. His father died when Baudelaire was only six years old. For a short time, he received a great deal of attention from both his mother and his nurse, Mariette, until his mother's remarriage, this time to a man much closer to her own age, Major Jacques Aupick. Aupick was an intelligent and self-disciplined man who served as a military general, an ambassador, and ultimately as a senator. Baudelaire's relationship with his stepfather was not a good one, although he did not reveal his dislike of the man until later in life, at which point he attributed much of his depression and dual personalities to his mother's remarriage.

In 1833, the family moved to Lyons, and Aupick enrolled Baudelaire in a strict military boarding school. The influence of the education and discipline he received there had a great impact on his outlook on life; it also increased his dislike for his stepfather. He continued his education at Louis-le-Grand, a respected French high school in Paris. His growing behavior problems led to his expulsion in 1839. It was at this point that he announced his decision to become a writer. To appease his family, he also agreed to study law at the École de Droit, but his attention was never focused on his studies. He led a bohemian life, going deeply into debt and becoming an increasingly radical thinker. During these years, he also made his first contacts in the literary world and discovered the use of hashish and opium.

In 1841, hoping to encourage him to change his way of life, Baudelaire's parents sent him by boat on a trip to India. Throughout the voyage, he remained depressed and sullen; therefore, when the ship was forced to stop for repairs after a terrible storm, he decided to return to France. Although he did not enjoy the journey, it did have a strong influence on his writing by giving him a unique perspective on the world that few other writers of his time could claim. On his return, he collected a large inheritance that allowed him to immerse himself in art and literature, paying particular attention to the satanic-based and horror literature that was popular at the time. However, in only two years, he had spent almost half of his money. He was placed by his family under a legal guardianship and was forced to live on a controlled income for the duration of his life.

A series of amorous affairs provided much of the impetus for Baudelaire's erotic poetry. The Martinican Jeanne Duval, whom Baudelaire met in 1842, held perhaps the greatest influence. Her exotic black hair provided the erotic imagery for his poem "La chevelure" ("The Head of Hair"). A dark-haired, dark-skinned beauty, she was referred to quite derogatorily by Baudelaire's mother as the "Black Venus." Marie Daubrun, an actress and his mistress from 1855 to 1860, as well as Apollonie Sabatier, who presided over a salon for artists and writers, were also the objects of Baudelaire's poetic and as well as romantic attentions.

In 1845, Baudelaire's depression caused him to unsuccessfully attempt suicide. Soon after, he published *La fanfarlo* (1847), an autobiographical novella that anticipated his experimentation with prose poetry. In 1848, French workers against social injustice minimally involved him in the revolution: He fired a few shots through the barricades and worked on radical political publications.

Baudelaire turned to literary and art criticism, for which he became well respected. His admiration for Delacroix and Constantin Guys influenced his own modern aesthetics. He translated Edgar Allan Poe's works into French, publishing five volumes of these translations from 1856 to 1865. He became greatly influenced by the dark melancholic brooding nature of Poe's works and began to incorporate the ideas into his own writing. He was particularly interested in the transformation of life in the modern city.

Critical Analysis

The first edition of Baudelaire's collected poems, *Les fleurs du mal* (*Flowers of Evil*) was published in 1857. Focusing on erotic, satanic and often lesbian themes, the work was not well received by the public. Scathing reviews of the work published in literary journals had a profoundly negative effect on Baudelaire's writing career, and both he and the publisher were ultimately prosecuted and heavily fined for offending public morality. Six poems from the collection were expressly banned as too radical for public consumption.

Baudelaire became more depressed as a result of this seeming failure and, after the death of his stepfather, he returned in 1859 to live once again with his mother. He wrote 35 new poems for the second edition of *Les fleurs du mal* (1861), including one of his best-known poems, "Le voyage," first published in 1857. He also published a book of essays on the use of drugs, *Les paradis artificiels* (*Artificial Paradises*, 1860). He had often used opium and hashish as a means of inspiring creativity. He began to become convinced, however, of the dangers inherent in this habit.

Baudelaire's life, however, was plagued by tragedies. He was financially unable to assist his publisher, who had been jailed for debt from the first edition of Baudelaire's poems, and he learned that his mistress Jeanne Duval had been living with another man. He also began to experience severe headaches and suffered from nightmares, most probably as a result of syphilis, which caused him to think he was becoming insane. He moved to Brussels in 1863, hoping to find a new publisher, but his health steadily declined until a series of strokes left him partially paralyzed. He returned once again to Paris, where he died in his mother's arms on August 31, 1867.

Baudelaire's works, including his critical essays *Curiositiés esthétiques* (*Aesthetic Curiosities*, 1868) and his collections of prose poems *Les petits poèmes en prose* (*Little Prose Poems*, 1868) and *L'art romantique* (*Romantic Art*, 1869) were major influences on the symbolist and modernist movements (*see* MODERNISM). Through his use of irony and his depiction of the scenes of modern life, he transformed poetic language, and his criticism founded an aesthetics of modernism.

Another Work by Charles Baudelaire

Baudelaire: Poems. Translated by Laurence Lerner. London: J. M. Dent, 1999.

Works about Charles Baudelaire

Benjamin, Walter. *Charles Baudelaire: A Lyric Poet in the Era of High Capitalism.* Translated by Harry Zohn. London: New Left Books, 1973.

Hyslop, Lois Boe. *Charles Baudelaire Revisited.* New York: Twayne Publishers, 1992.

Richardson, Joanna. *Baudelaire.* New York: St. Martin's Press, 1994.

Beauchamp, Katherine Mansfield

See MANSFIELD, KATHERINE.

Beauvoir, Simone de (Simone Lucie-Ernestine-Marie-Bertrand de Beauvoir)

(1908–1986) *novelist, essayist*

Simone de Beauvoir was born in Paris, France, on January 9, 1908. A leading feminist and existentialist (*see* EXISTENTIALISM), her works bear a clear resemblance to those of her lifelong friend, mentor, colleague, and lover JEAN-PAUL SARTRE. Best known for her two-volume work *The Second Sex* (1949), a work in which de Beauvoir calls for the abolition of the myth of the "eternal feminine," she is considered by many scholars working in the field of cultural studies to be the primary voice for early feminist studies. This work quickly became a classic among feminist theorists and scholars and is considered to be the founding text of gender studies.

De Beauvoir's life history is well known, largely as a result of the publication of numerous autobiographical works such as *Memoirs of a Dutiful Daughter* (1958), *The Prime of Life* (1960), *Force of Circumstance* (1963), and *All Said and Done* (1972). In these texts, she also documents the life of Sartre, ALBERT CAMUS, and other influential philosophers, novelists, and intellectuals from the 1930s to the 1970s.

Educated first at private schools and then at the Sorbonne, where she received a degree in philosophy and first became acquainted with Sartre, de Beauvoir pursued a career as a teacher after receiving her degree. She left this occupation to become a full-time writer in 1943, the same year that she published her first novel, *She Came to Stay* (1943), which explores existential themes by examining the ways in which a relationship between two people is destroyed as a result of a guest, a young girl, who stays for an extended period of time in a young couple's home. Although purportedly fictional, this work was based largely on de Beauvoir's own relationship with Sartre and Olga Kosakiewicz, a former student, who came to stay with them in occupied Paris during the war. Her presence created many difficulties for Sartre and de Beauvoir within their own relationship, but it gave de Beauvoir much inspiration in her work.

Critical Analysis

Although intellectual and existential issues are a concern of all de Beauvoir's works, she is best known for her application of existentialism to an understanding of the oppression of women. In *The Second Sex* she makes known her firm belief that an individual's choices must be made on the basis of equality between the male and female, not on the basis of any essential differentiation between the sexes. The importance of choice—free will—is also a prevalent theme in many of de Beauvoir's other works. Her *Ethics of Ambiguity* (1947) is devoted largely to the study of individual choices and the resultant anxieties associated with the ramifications of those choices, an underlying theme of existentialism.

In addition to feminist issues and free will, de Beauvoir was also interested in the theme of aging. She first covers this topic in *A Very Easy Death* (1964), in which she addresses the issue of her own mother's death. She returns to this theme again in *Old Age* (1970), a work that details the indifference and lack of respect that the elderly receive from society.

Political activism is another theme in de Beauvoir's writings, particularly those works written after World War II when she and Sartre both worked on a leftist journal. She published two novels, *The Blood of Others* (1945), exploring the life of members of the wartime resistance to the Nazi occupation, as well as *The Mandarins* (1954), which describes the struggles faced by middle-class intellectuals as they attempt to enter into the sphere of political activism. Her political views tended increasingly toward the left, and by the 1950s, she was defending communism and criticizing U.S. and Western European capitalism regularly in her works. This attitude becomes even clearer after de Beauvoir visited the United States and, on returning to France, published her observations. Her *America Day by Day* (1948) is a critique of the social problems caused by capitalism in the United States. While there, she also fell in love with fellow writer Nelson Algren, complicating her existing love affair with Sartre. Elements of *The Mandarins* reflect this new development in her life.

De Beauvoir's final years were marked by Sartre's death and her attempts to write about the nature of their relationship, the end result of which she eventually published in *Adieux: A Farewell to Sartre* (1981). It was her desire to remain as honest and true as possible in her examination of their life together. To the critics and to members of Sartre's family, however, it seemed as if she was attacking the late philosopher.

De Beauvoir passed away on April 14, 1986. After her death, several additional works were published, including *Letters to Sartre* (1990), *Journal of a Resistance Fighter* (1990), and, in 1997, her passionate *Letters to Algren*. Most important, *The Second Sex* is still considered a primary text for feminist studies.

Other Works by Simone de Beauvoir

All Men Are Mortal. Translated by Euan Cameron. London: Virago, 1995.
When Things of the Spirit Come First: Five Early Tales. Translated by Patrick O'Brian. New York: Pantheon Books, 1982.

Works about Simone de Beauvoir

Bair, Deidre. *Simone de Beauvoir. A Biography.* New York: Touchstone, 2002.

Bauer, Nancy. *Simone de Beauvoir, Philosophy and Feminism.* New York: Columbia University Press, 2001.
Moi, Toril. *Simone de Beauvoir: The Making of an Intellectual Woman.* New York: Oxford University Press, 2009.
Pilardi, Jo-Ann. *Simone de Beauvoir Writing the Self: Philosophy Becomes Autobiography.* Westport, Conn.: Praeger, 1999.
Scholz, Sally. *On de Beauvoir.* Belmont, Calif.: Wadsworth/Thomson Learning, 2000.
Simons, Margaret A. *Beauvoir and "The Second Sex": Feminism, Race and the Origins of Existentialism.* Boston: Lanham, Rowman and Littlefield Publishers, 1999.

Becher, Johannes Robert (1891–1958)
poet, novelist

Johannes Robert Becher was born into an upper-middle-class Catholic family in Munich, Germany. His father was a high-ranking Bavarian judge. Although Becher studied philosophy and medicine, he favored poetry as the creative outlet for his political views. His early poems were radical and rooted in EXPRESSIONISM. He published his first collection of verse in 1914. During World War I, Becher refused to join the German military and became a pacifist. He joined the left-wing Spartacus League in 1918 and the German Communist Party in 1919.

Becher emerged as a leader among German communists and radical writers in the 1920s. The literary historian Adolf D. Klarmann noted that, at this time, Becher wrote revolutionary poetry that "literally bursts and scatters the traditional shackles of sentence, logic, and grammatical structure." Becher served as a deputy to the Reichstag (German legislature) in 1925 and became head of the League of Proletarian–Revolutionary Writers in 1928. His book of poetry *Der Leichnam auf dem Thron* (*The Corpse on the Throne*, 1925) and his novel *Levisite oder der einzig gerechte Krieg* (*The Only Just War*, 1926) led to accusations of treason against the German government. The rise of the Nazis to power in 1933 made Germany too dangerous for left-wing writers like Becher. He fled the country and eventually settled in Moscow.

After the defeat of Nazi Germany in 1945, Becher moved to Communist East Berlin. He soon became president of the East German Academy of Arts. He won several awards for his works, including the Lenin Peace Prize in 1952. Becher's poem "Auferstanden aus Ruinen" ("Risen from the Ruins", 1949) was used as the text for his country's national anthem. In 1954, Becher was appointed cultural minister of East Germany. His support for modernist authors, such as BERTOLT BRECHT, created tension with his government, which officially favored SOCIALIST REALISM. Becher's efforts to promote cooperation with noncommunist German intellectuals earned him a reprimand from his party. He had already lost much of his political power when he died in 1958.

Another Work by Johannes Robert Becher

Farewell. Translated by Joan Becker. Berlin: Seven Seas Publishers, 1970.

A Work about Johannes Robert Becher

Haase, Horst. *Johannes R. Becher, Leben and Werk.* West Berlin: Das Europäische Buch, 1981.

Beckett, Samuel (1906–1989) *playwright, novelist, poet*

Samuel Beckett was born on April 13, 1906, in Dublin, Ireland. He was educated at Earlsfort House in Dublin and later in Enniskillen at Portora Royal School, the alma mater of writer Oscar Wilde. Although Beckett came from an Anglo-Irish Protestant family, he wrote most of his work in French. He received a degree from Trinity College in Dublin in Romance languages. During this time, he also began to enjoy the vibrant theater scene that was emerging in a postindependence Ireland. He was particularly influenced by the plays of J. M. Synge, the arrival of American silent movies, and the vaudeville antics of performers such as Charlie Chaplin and Buster Keaton, which he would later incorporate into his plays.

After graduation, Beckett spent two years, from 1928 to 1930, as an exchange lecturer in Paris. While there, he met and became lifelong friends with writer James Joyce. He acted as one of Joyce's assistants while the author was working on *Finnegans Wake* and, at the same time, began his own career as a writer. He published his first poem, "Whoroscope," which concerns time and the ideas of the philosopher René Descartes, in 1930. That same year, he returned to lecture at Trinity College and began to work on a series of stories about the life of a Dublin intellectual that later formed the collection *More Pricks Than Kicks* (1934). After only four terms at Trinity, Beckett left to pursue a career as a freelance writer, traveling throughout Europe and finally settling in Paris, which was to be his primary home for the rest of his life. He also began work on his first novel, *Dream of Fair to Middling Women* (1932), which was highly autobiographical.

Beckett was seriously injured one night when, as he was walking home, he was stabbed. It was during his hospitalization and recuperation that he cemented his friendship with Joyce, who became his caretaker. He also began a long-term association with Suzanne Deschevaux-Dusmesnil, whom he married in 1961. In 1941, when Paris was invaded, Deschevaux-Dusmesnil joined the Resistance with Beckett and they narrowly escaped the arrival of the Gestapo at their apartment. Fleeing to a small town in the south of France, Beckett worked on a farm in exchange for living quarters and continued his writing. After the defeat of the Germans in 1945, he returned to Paris and, at this point, made the decision to write all of his works in French.

Critical Analysis

Taken as a whole, Beckett's works attempt to reduce basic existential problems to a minimalist structure where only the most essential elements are considered. His concerns are commonplace in that they reflect the shared worries of society as a whole, but they are never simple. He ponders such large-scale issues as the nature of life itself, the question of time and its relevance, the concept of eternity, and the sense of isolation, alienation, and loneliness of the individual self.

Beckett's early works are composed of a series of internal monologues: *Molloy* (1951; translated 1955), *Malone meurt* (1951; translated as *Malone Dies,* 1956), and *L'innomable* (1953; translated as *The Unnameable,* 1958). These pieces reflect one of the many paradoxes Beckett explores: the dilemma associated with the fact that the self can never truly know itself. The act of self-observation leads to a split in which the self becomes two individual entities: the observer and the observed. The self is only able to perceive itself through narration, a monologue. This same theme is returned to later in his essentially two-character play, *Fin de partie* (*Endgame,* 1958).

Best known as a playwright, Beckett's major dramatic works, all considered pioneering plays in the emerging tradition of the THEATER OF THE ABSURD, are *En attendant Godot* (*Waiting for Godot,* 1952), *Endgame, Krapp's Last Tape* (1959), *Happy Days* (1961), *Play* (1964), *Not I* (1973), *That Time* (1976), and *Footfalls* (1976). Beckett also wrote a series of radio and television dramas, as well as adaptations of his stage works for film.

Beckett is best known for the play *Waiting for Godot,* an absurdist piece that was first performed on January 5, 1953, in Paris. Two derelict-looking characters, Vladimir and Estragon, sit by the side of a road throughout the two acts, waiting for the mysterious Godot, who never appears (is he to be identified with God? Critics do not agree), and aimlessly discuss possible action. Each of the two acts ends with the same words, except that the roles are reversed. This is the end of Act II:

> **VLADIMIR:** Well, shall we go?
> **ESTRAGON:** Yes, let's go.
> *They do not move.*

The play won worldwide acclaim and was followed by a series of critical successes of plays and novels, some of which he had written much earlier in his life.

Beckett's novels and short stories, such as *Murphy* (1938; translated 1957); *Watt* (1953), which was his last novel initially written in English; and *Texts for Nothing* (1955; translated 1967), also examine the self trapped and isolated in its quest for understanding of identity. The situations are often grotesque, and the overall tone is one of anguish and suffering, lightened by gallows humor.

In 1969, Beckett was awarded the Nobel Prize in literature. He continued to write and to be involved in literary and dramatic projects, publishing his last major work *Stirrings Still* in 1986. Emphysema forced his hospitalization, and, bedridden, he wrote his last poem, "What Is the Word." Shortly after, his declining health kept him from writing and forced him into a nursing home, where he remained until his death on December 22, 1989. Death, however, was not the end of Beckett's publishing career. His first play, the previously unpublished *Eleutheria* (1947), which depicts the author's search for freedom through the character of a young man, was rediscovered and published in English translation in 1995, six years after his death. Beckett had not allowed the play to be printed during his lifetime because he considered it to be a failure. Its publication was the result of a long dispute between Beckett's American publisher and close friend, Barney Rosset, and his family and his French publisher. Critically, this work is of great importance because it shows the beginnings of the ideas that would define Beckett's works and predates, as well as predicts, the beginnings of the theater of the absurd movement.

Other Works by Samuel Beckett

Fehsenfeld, Dow, et al., eds. *The Letters of Samuel Beckett: Volume One, 1929–1940.* Cambridge: Cambridge University Press, 2009.

Gontarski, S. E., ed. *The Theatrical Notebooks of Samuel Beckett, Volume 4: The Shorter Plays.* New York: Grove Press, 1999.

Nohow On: Company, Ill Seen Ill Said, Worstward Ho: Three Novels. Introduction by S. E. Gontarski. New York: Grove Press, 1996.

Works about Samuel Beckett

Ackerly, C. J., and S. E. Gontarsky. *The Grove Companion to Samuel Beckett: A Reader's Guide.* New York: Grove Press, 2004.

Atik, Anne. *How It Was: A Memoir of Samuel Beckett.* Berkeley, Calif.: Counterpoint, 2005.

Bair, Dierdre. *Samuel Beckett: A Biography.* New York: Harcourt Brace Jovanovich, 1978.

Cronin, Anthony. *Samuel Beckett: The Last Modernist.* London: HarperCollins, 1996.

Gordon, Lois. *The World of Samuel Beckett.* New Haven: Yale University Press, 1996.

Knowlson, James. *Damned to Fame: The Life of Samuel Beckett.* New York: Simon & Schuster, 1996.

Bécquer, Gustavo Adolfo (Gustavo Adolfo Dominguez Bastida)
(1836–1870) *poet, prose writer*

Gustavo Adolfo Bécquer was born in Seville, Spain. The son of José Dominguez Bécquer, a somewhat successful painter, Bécquer was orphaned at the age of 11. Apprenticed to be a painter, as was his brother, he eventually gave up the art when his uncle informed him that he had no talent and would be better off as a writer. His brother continued to paint and, although Bécquer turned to writing, he remained deeply interested in visual art throughout his life. One of his major literary innovations was the way he used striking visual descriptions.

For most of his adulthood, Bécquer lived hand-to-mouth in Madrid, publishing his poems and short stories in small journals and magazines. Toward the end of his life, he was given a government position as a censor, which helped improve his quality of living. By this time, he had contracted tuberculosis.

Most of Bécquer's work was never published in book form during his life, only in periodicals. After his death, his friends collected his published and unpublished manuscripts and put out a two-volume book simply titled *Works* (1871). It was only then that, for the first time, Bécquer received critical acclaim.

Bécquer's works can be divided into three major components. The poems or *Rimas* (*Rhymes,* 1860–61), the short stories or *Leyendas* (*Legends,* 1864), and a series of autobiographical literary essays, *Cartas desde mi celda* (*Letters from My Cell*), which he wrote while convalescing at the monastery of Veruela in 1864.

Bécquer called his poems *Rhymes* to indicate his break with earlier traditions of Spanish verse and to show his poems' relationship to folk ballads. His simple but very visual language gives the impression that he is expressing true emotions and getting to the essence of things. He has been compared to the German romantic poet HEINE, although the two writers were probably not familiar with each other's work.

His *Legends* are rich with magical imagery and descriptions of nature and the supernatural. Frequently they take the form of fables and have morals at the end. In his *Legends,* Bécquer is exploring a typical romantic tendency to bring folklore and popular stories into the realm of high art.

Finally, *Letters from My Cell* is a collection of essays in which Bécquer explores his moral, artistic, and spiritual beliefs. Written as he was approaching death, they serve as a kind of psychic autobiography.

Bécquer, underappreciated during his life, went on to become one of the most influential Spanish poets of the 19th century. He was the central figure of Spanish ROMANTICISM. The great Latin American poet RUBEN DARIO openly acknowledged Bécquer's powerful effect on him. Bécquer died at age 34 from tuberculosis, never knowing the lasting influence his work would have.

See also COSTUMBRISMO.

Another Work by Gustavo Adolfo Bécquer

Legends and Letters. Translated by Robert M. Fedorchek. Lewisburg, Pa.: Bucknell University Press, 1995.

A Work about Gustavo Adolfo Bécquer

Bynum, Brant B. *The Romantic Imagination in the Works of Gustavo Adolfo Bécquer.* Chapel Hill:

University of North Carolina, Department of Romance Languages, 1993.

Bei Dao (Zhao Zhenkai) (1949–) poet, novelist

Bei Dao was born in Beijing, China, and received a good education until the Cultural Revolution, when the Communist Chinese government sent intellectuals to the countryside to be "re-educated" with revolutionary ideas. Bei Dao was assigned to labor in a construction company outside of Beijing and wrote poetry in his spare time.

He adopted the pen name Bei Dao, which means "north island," and began to write poetry and short stories. In 1979, he published the short novel *Waves,* in China's first underground literary journal, *Today,* which he cofounded in 1978. The novel was characterized as modern because it interweaves five separate narrative voices to create a subjective point of view.

Bei Dao is best known for his political poems, such as "The Answer" and "Declaration," in which he addresses the oppressiveness of the government regime, using thinly veiled, nihilistic language. Bei Dao's poetry was also criticized for its Western roots, impenetrable and sparse language, and confusing metaphors. One critic dubbed it "misty" in the 1980s, when Communist Party leadership and traditional voices in the literary community took modernism to task. *Today* was shut down in 1980; during a 1983 campaign to wipe out literary "pollution" by modernist and avant-garde writers, Bei Dao and the *Today* poets were among the first denounced. Many poets were suspended from their official jobs, and their poetry banned from publication.

The Communist Party just as quickly revised its thinking on modernism, however, and Bei Dao and his colleagues were rerecognized by the party in 1985. Bei Dao even participated in the Beijing Writers Association, and some of his poems were published in state-sponsored magazines that year, including "The Answer."

Bei Dao continued to write against the mainstream, both in a literary and a political sense. When the prodemocracy movement gained momentum in 1989, he was a leader and activist. Quotations from his poems were chanted and posted at Tiananmen Square. Shortly afterward, he went into exile in Sweden.

Bei Dao currently lives in Hong Kong, where he is professor of humanities at the Center for East Asian Studies of the Chinese University of Hong Kong. His works are widely translated, many in English, including *The August Sleepwalker* (1990), *Old Snow* (1991), *Forms of Distance* (1994), and *The Rose of Time: New and Selected Poems* (2010).

A Work about Bei Dao
Gleichmann, Gabi. "An Interview with Bei Dao." Translated and edited by Michelle Yeh. In *Modern Chinese Literature* 9 (1996): 387–393.

Bely, Andrey (Boris Nikolayevich Bugaev) (1880–1934) novelist, poet

The only child of Nikolai Vasilevich Bugaev, a Moscow University mathematician, and Aleksandra Dmitrivna Egorova, a musician, Andrey Bely was born in Moscow, Russia. Bely's parents had different attitudes about the relative importance of natural sciences and the arts, and he was constantly caught in their conflict. Aiming to please his father, Bely successfully pursued a degree in natural sciences at Moscow University and graduated in 1903.

Bely began to write poetry as a university student. The main support for his initial efforts came from Mikhail Solovyov, the Bugaevs' neighbor and a younger brother of the famous Russian philosopher Vladimir Solovyov. Solovyov provided financial support for Bely's first published collection of poems, *Second Symphony,* in 1902 and suggested the pseudonym Andrey Bely. After the death of his father in 1903, Bely decided to abandon science and devote himself to writing.

Between 1903 and 1910, Bely wrote for *Vesy,* a major journal of the symbolist movement. In his articles, Bely desperately attempted to define and synthesize some kind of philosophy of SYMBOLISM. Bely wrote more than 200 articles, reviews, and essays during this period, as well as another two volumes of *Symphonies.*

In 1905, Bely left Russia and traveled to Munich and Paris, where he was befriended by Jean Jaurès, the famous socialist leader. When he returned to Russia, Bely established a relationship with Asya Turgeneva, who was to be his lover for many years, and in 1910, they went abroad together. They were drawn to Rudolf Steiner's mystical philosophy, anthroposophy. From 1914 to 1916, when Bely was recalled by the Russian government for military duty, the couple were with Steiner in Switzerland.

Although Bely firmly established himself as a poet, he is mostly known for his prose. In *Petersburg* (1913), Bely explores the social and political turmoil of the Russian Revolution of 1905. The novel centers on a plot to deliver a bomb to a high government official. It is a commentary on family, the role of the individual, and spiritualism.

In the Joycean autobiographical novel *Kotik Latayev* (1922), Bely incorporates the story of his own childhood, exploring emotional conflicts between parents and the delicate psyche of a child. Bely's intricate prose brilliantly captures intensity of time, translating the sensory experiences into intriguing and powerful works of fiction.

Bely broke with both Steiner and Turgeneva in 1921 and lived in Moscow from 1923 until his death, producing three more novels and three volumes of memoirs.

Most critics today agree on the literary genius and immense impact of Bely's work. VLADIMIR NABOKOV (quoted in Malmstad and Maguire's introduction to their translation of *Petersburg*) ranked *Petersburg* with James Joyce's *Ulysses*, FRANZ KAFKA's *The Castle*, and MARCEL PROUST's *In Search of Lost Time*, as one of the great books of the 20th century.

Other Works by Andrey Bely
Kotik Letayev. Translated by Gerald J. Janacek. Evanston, Ill.: Northwestern University Press, 1999.

Petersburg. Translated by Robert A. Maguire and John E. Malmstad. Bloomington: Indiana University Press, 1978.

Works about Andrey Bely
Janecek, Gerald. *Andrey Bely: A Critical Review.* Lexington: Kentucky University Press, 1978.
Keys, Roger. *The Reluctant Modernist: Andrey Belyi and the Development of Russian Fiction.* Oxford: Clarendon Press, 1996.

Benn, Gottfried (Kurt Wolff) (1886–1956)
poet, novelist, playwright
Gottfried Benn was born in the German village of Mansfield. His father was a Lutheran minister and his mother was a French-speaking native of Switzerland. Benn attended the Gymnasium at Frankfurt an der Oder. He studied theology and philosophy at the University of Marbach and in 1905 was accepted at Kaiser Wilhelm Akademie, a prominent military medical school. He earned his doctorate in 1912 and married actress Edith Brosin two years later.

Benn had a private practice in Berlin specializing in skin diseases and served in the German army's medical corps in both world wars. He performed numerous autopsies in his career and frequently wrote about morgues in his early poetry. Benn's scientific background instilled a skepticism and self-criticism that often appeared in his literary work.

Benn published five books of poetry between 1910 and 1925. He also wrote a series of works called the "Rönne novellas," which earned critical praise for demonstrating the concept of "absolute prose." In this unique style, Benn replaced a descriptive, psychologically oriented narrative with a blend of associative and visionary elements. In the 1930s, Benn briefly embraced the Nazis before becoming disillusioned with their barbarism. His popularity increased after World War II with the publication of *Statische Gedichte* (*Static Poems,* 1948), a volume of apolitical modernist poems. In 1951, Benn received the Georg Büchner Prize, one of Germany's most prestigious literary awards. At the age of 67, he finally earned enough money from his writing career to quit his medical practice.

Benn's influences included FRIEDRICH NIETZSCHE and his friend ELSE LASKER-SCHÜLER, the expressionist poet. Benn's poetry is melancholy and elegiac, conveying cultural despair. His writings were both praised and denounced for challenging established German literary traditions. Critics are also divided on his significance: Edgar Lohner described Benn as "one of the foremost modern European lyric poets," while Michael Hamburger concluded that "Benn was too restricted in tone to be described as a major writer" in *Gottfried Benn: The Unreconstructed Expressionist* by J. M. Ritchie. As an embodiment of the contradictions of literary modernism, Benn will likely remain a debated German literary figure.

Another Work by Gottfried Benn
Prose, Essays, Poems. Edited by Volknar Sander. New York: Continuum, 1987.

A Work about Gottfried Benn
Ritchie, J. M. *Gottfried Benn: The Unreconstructed Expressionist*. London: Oswald Wolff, 1972.

Bennett, Louise (Louise Bennett-Coverley, Miss Lou, Mrs. Eric Coverley)
(1919–2006) *poet, folklorist*

Louise Bennett was born in Kingston, Jamaica, to Augustus Cornelius Bennett, a bakery owner, and Kerene Robinson, a dressmaker. English poetry influenced the writing she did as a schoolgirl; she wrote poems in standard English until she overheard a country woman on a Kingston tramcar and wrote the first of many poems in Jamaican dialect. Bennett published her first collection of poems, *(Jamaica) Dialect Verses* (1942), in her early twenties.

Bennett primarily writes in Jamaican dialect about Jamaican people's "now" experiences. One speaker usually uses literary techniques—such as allusions to Jamaican folk songs, the Bible, and English literature—and oral performance techniques—such as rhetorical lists—to address an audience. In a 1968 interview with Dennis Scott, Bennett said that people thought of her "as a performing artist primarily" but added, "I did start to write before I started to perform," and "I felt I wanted to put on paper some of the wonderful things that people say in dialect." *Jamaica Labrish* (1966), her most substantial collection of poems, shows Bennett as performer, poet, and social commentator.

Bennett's work as a journalist, actress, folk singer, radio- and television-show host, and drama and folklore lecturer helped generate a large audience for her poetry. But her poetry did not start to receive critical acceptance until the late 1960s. Many distinguished awards followed, and in "Proverb as Metaphor in the Poetry of Louise Bennett" (1984), Carolyn Cooper called Bennett "the quintessential Jamaican example of the sensitive and competent Caribbean artist consciously incorporating features of traditional oral art into written literature."

Other Works by Louise Bennett
Anancy and Miss Lou. Kingston: Sangster's Book Stores, 1966.
Collected Poems. Kingston: Sangster's Book Stores, 1982.
Jamaican Humour in Dialect. Kingston: Jamaica Press Association, 1943.
Laugh with Louise. Kingston: City Printery, 1961.
Miss Lula Sez. Kingston: Gleaner, 1949.

Works about Louise Bennett
Cooper, Carolyn. "Noh Lickle Twang: An Introduction to the Poetry of Louise Bennett." In *World Literature Written in English* (April 1978).
———. *Noises in the Blood: Orality, Gender and the "Vulgar" Body of Jamaican Popular Culture*. Durham, N.C.: Duke University Press, 1995.
Erwin, Lee. "Two Jamaican Women Writers and the Uses of Creole." In A. L. McLeod, ed. *Commonwealth and American Women's Discourse: Essays in Criticism*. New Delhi: Sterling, 1996.

Bernhard, Thomas (1931–1989) *play-wright, novelist*

Thomas Bernhard was born in Heerlen, Netherlands, to Hertha Bernhard. He moved with his mother to Austria at age four; Thomas never met his father, an Austrian carpenter. Hertha's father, Johannes Freumbichler, a novelist, was one of Thomas's earliest influences. Bernhard grew up in poverty and did poorly in school, eventually dropping out at age 15. He studied voice at this time and hoped to start a career in music; however, pneumonia and tuberculosis nearly killed him a few years later. His grandfather and mother died while he struggled to recover from his own health problems. These experiences with death and illness created a pessimism that characterized Bernhard's literary work.

Bernhard studied music and drama in Vienna and Salzburg as a young adult. He published three books of poetry in the late 1950s but received little acclaim until he published his first novel, *Frost* (1963). His first drama *Ein Fest für Boris* (*A Party for Boris,* 1968) premiered on stage in 1970. A tasteless farce about demented invalids who abuse each other, the play reflects Bernhard's vision of humanity's wretchedness. In the following two decades, Bernhard solidified his reputation as a novelist with works such as *Korrektur* (*Correction,* 1975), a novel about a man's increasing obsession with the manuscripts written by a brilliant mathematician friend who committed suicide. Bernhard also gained fame as a playwright for dramas such as *Die Macht der Gewohnheit* (*The Force of Habit,* 1976), a commentary about the empty rituals of high culture. He won numerous literary awards, including the Georg Büchner Prize (1970).

Bernhard was obsessed with insanity, death, and the wretchedness of the human condition. He sharply criticized the moral failures of Austria's history. His works stirred controversy in their attack on the complacency of German theater and their criticism of modern life. Despite his dark themes, Bernhard was illuminating in his use of language and, as literary scholar J. J. Long comments, "a writer of considerable diversity, who was profoundly concerned with both the problems and potential of storytelling."

Other Works by Thomas Bernhard

The Force of Habit: A Comedy. Translated by Neville and Stephen Plaice. London: Heinemann, 1976.
Gargoyles. Translated by Richard and Clara Winston. New York: Knopf, 1970.

A Work about Thomas Bernhard

Long, J. J. *The Novels of Thomas Bernhard: Form and Its Function.* Rochester, N.Y.: Camden House, 2001.

Bernstein, Ingrid

See KIRSCH, SARAH.

Bhatt, Sujata (1956–   ) *poet, translator*

Sujata Bhatt was born in Ahmedabad, India, and grew up in Pune in a large household with her extended family. Her paternal grandfather was a poet, and two of her uncles were famous Gujarati poets. Hearing their stories and listening to their poetry as a child, Bhatt was inspired to write. As a child, she was very proud that she could compose poetry in English, which her family could not do. Her father, a virologist, moved to America in 1968 with the family and wanted Bhatt to become a scientist, too. In school, she obediently took classes in science but slowly gained interest in philosophy, creative writing, and English literature.

Though Bhatt left India at an early age, her childhood years in Gujarat are constantly referred to in almost all her poetry. Written in English, her poetry unabashedly translates sounds of Gujarati words in play with English ones, creating a language-based tension and highlighting the contradictions inherent in translating concepts or ideas from one language to another. Works such as *Brunizem* (1988), however, display her agility in synthesizing the East with the West, a tribute to the positive rewards of a multicultural existence.

In an interview with *PN Review,* Bhatt said that she writes poetry to "break [the] historical silence" surrounding female sexuality, but she also brings out the sensual aspects of seemingly ordinary objects. *Stinking Rose* (1995) is a journey through the myth and history of garlic—its medicinal, herbal, and erotic uses in different cultures through the ages. Her studies in the sciences and her interest in visual arts add dimension to her imagery in matters of light, form, and texture. *A Color for Solitude* (2002) is said to be inspired by the self-portraits of the German painter Paula Modersohn-Becker (1876–1907) during her relationship with poets such as RAINER MARIA RILKE.

Bhatt was briefly a professor of writing at the University of British Columbia, Canada, but left when she moved to Germany. She now works as a freelance writer and also translates other Gujarati poetry into English. Her collection *Brunizem* won the Commonwealth Poetry Prize (Asia), and in 1991, she won the Cholmondeley Award for Poetry (U.K.).

Other Works by Sujata Bhatt

Augatora. Manchester, U.K.: Carcanet Press, 2000.
Monkey Shadows. Manchester, U.K.: Carcanet Press, 1988.
Pure Lizard. Manchester, U.K.: Carcanet Press, 2008.

A Work about Sujata Bhatt

Pandey, M. S. "The Trishanku Motif in the Poetry of Sujata Bhatt and Uma Parameswaran." In *The Literature of the Indian Diaspora: Essays in Criticism.* Edited by A. L. McLeod. New Delhi: Sterling, 2000.

Bing Xin (Ping Hsin; Xie Wanying; Hsieh Wan-ying) (1900–1999) *short story writer, poet*

Bing Xin, the daughter of a naval officer, was born on October 5 in Fuzhou, the capital of China's Fujian province. She was raised in Chefoo in Shandong province and moved to Beijing in 1914 where she attended a Congregational missionary school. She then attended Yanjing University in Beijing. In 1919, during the May Fourth Movement against foreign imperialism, Bing Xin changed her major from medicine to literature, believing that writing fiction would have a positive social impact on Chinese society.

In 1923, she published *Superman,* a collection of short stories, and two poetry collections, *The Stars* and *Waters of Spring.* After these works received critical acclaim, Bing Xin traveled to Massachusetts, where she attended Wellesley College and began to write columns for children that were collected in *Letters to My Little Readers* (1926), which was published in China and was immensely popular. She received her master's degree in 1926 and returned to Yanjing to teach literature. In 1929, she married Wu Wenzao, a sociologist, with whom she had three children. The family moved at the onset of the Sino-Japanese War to Kunming in 1937 and then to Chongqing in 1941.

Bing Xin's short stories are widely known for their sentimental depictions of motherly love and family life. Some modernist critics have written that her work is old-fashioned and too traditional. Nonetheless, most of her stories, such as "Loneliness" (1922), are well observed and address the dilemmas of life and love faced by younger Chinese women. In other stories, such as "Our Mistress' Parlor" (1933), a sarcastic indictment of a shallow Shanghaiese woman, Bing Xin depicts different types of women.

In the 1950s and 1960s, Bing Xin focused on writing children's literature and translating the Indian poet RABINDRANATH TAGORE. Like all artists, she was sent to Hubei for manual labor reeducation during the Cultural Revolution but was reinstated to the party in 1980. She continued to write articles and stories and to serve the party in a number of official positions until her death. Although she was often criticized for being overly traditional, her acutely observed stories of young womanhood earned her a reputation as one of China's foremost women writers.

Other Works by Bing Xin

"Autobiographical Notes" and selected poems. In Special Section on Bing Xin, *Renditions* 16, no. 32 (Fall 1989).

Bingxin Shi Quan Pian = Bing Xin's Complete Poems. Hangzhou: Zhejiang Wen Yi Chu Ban She, 1994.

A Work about Bing Xin

Cayley, John. "Birds and Stars: Tagore's Influence on Bing Xin's Early Poetry." *Renditions* 16, no. 32 (Fall 1989).

Bitton, Erez (Erez Biton) (1942–) *poet*

Erez Bitton was born in Algeria. As a child, playing in an abandoned orchard, he discovered an old grenade. The explosion blinded him and cost him partial use of an arm. Ironically, it was this childhood accident that brought him to an institution for the blind where he received an education not previously available to him.

Bitton's poetry often deals with people who are classified as "other" by a dominant culture, as can be seen in the poem "Summary of a Conversation." As a *Mizrahi,* a Jew who emigrated to Israel from other parts of the Middle East, Bitton had firsthand knowledge of what it meant to be "other."

While the critical establishment views his work as an authentic expression of Middle Eastern Jewry, his poetry defies categorization. He is one of the first poets to use Middle Eastern themes that explore the question of what actually constitutes an authentic or genuine expression of Middle Eastern Jewry. Bitton even challenges the very notions of such categorization. In "Summary of a Conversation," Bitton asserts that the resolution to the dilemma faced by those classified as "other" is found within the self.

Bitton lives in Tel Aviv, Israel, where he has edited *Aperion,* a literary journal dedicated to Mediterranean and Middle Eastern culture. He also performs dramatic recitals of his work to musical accompaniment as an expression the condition of the Mizrahi experience. His most recent publication is *Timbisert, a Morrocan Bird* (2009).

A Work about Erez Bitton

Alcalay, Ammiel. *Keys to the Garden, New Israeli Writing.* New York: City Light Books, 1996.

Bjørnson, Bjørnstjerne (1832–1910)
writer, editor

Bjørnstjerne Bjørnson was born in Kvikne, Norway, to Peder Bjørnson, a Lutheran minister, and Elise Nordraak, a daughter of an affluent merchant. Bjørnson was at first educated by his father and at various country schools. In 1849, to prepare for the university entrance exams, he moved to Oslo where he was planning to study religion, following in his father's footsteps. Bjørnson entered the university in 1852 but soon abandoned his study for the bustling cultural life of Oslo.

He began his literary career as a theater and literary critic for several daily newspapers in Oslo. He later became an editor of the daily *Norsk Folkeblad.* In 1857, Bjørnson took over the management of the Norske Theater in Bergen from HENRIK IBSEN. He returned to Oslo in 1859 and continued to work for newspapers. Bjørnson's liberal editorials, however, finally led to his resignation. In collaboration with Henrik Ibsen, Bjørnson organized the Norwegian Society for Theater, Music, and Language to promote more liberal notions about drama and theater in general.

Bjørnson began writing fiction in the late 1850s, and published several short stories. His short stories were often set in an idyllic, rural environment and idealized the lives of simple peasants. The conflict in the stories is often created when something new or unexpected disrupts the existing order. In "The Railway and the Churchyard" (1858), Knut Aakre, a chairman of the parish and a member of an old and influential family, protects the interests of the village. His neighbor, Lars Hogstad, decides to build a savings bank, which initially brings prosperity to the village. Lars soon realizes that a railroad is necessary to preserve the savings bank. This railroad must go through the old churchyard, and Knut firmly opposes the idea. When the railroad is finally built, a disaster happens: Lars's house is set on fire by sparks from the train. Knut is the first one to help his neighbor. The opposition between the old and the new is the source of tension in the story, but the reader finally sees the synthesis of the two opposing points.

Bjørnson also created a number of historical dramas that were quite popular; however, the political and social issues introduced in these works, along with his staunch atheism, produced charges of high treason. Bjørnson then went abroad, spending several years in Italy, the United States, and Finland. He also completed several novels that centered on social themes such as education, inheritance, dogmatism, and the state of peasantry in Norway. Bjørnson also opposed industrialization and joined ÉMILE ZOLA in protest against the bigotry involved in the Dreyfus affair in France.

Despite declining health which left him paralyzed on one side, Bjørnstjerne Bjørnson continued working until his death in Paris in 1910. His work contributed to the formation of modern drama in Norway; his social and political articles eventually prompted change and caused an upheaval in artistic circles; his short stories and novels promoted understanding of the traditional Norwegian culture. Bjørnson's stories and novels are still popular in Norway and are considered to be among the classics of Scandinavian literature.

Other Works by Bjørnstjerne Bjørnson

The Bridal March, and Other Stories. Translated by Rasmus B. Anderson. North Stratford, N.H.: Ayer Co. Publishing, 1969.
Captain Mansana, and Other Stories. Translated by Rasmus B. Anderson. North Stratford, N.H.: Ayer Co. Publishing, 1980.
Heigen, Einar, ed. *Land of the Free: Bjørnstjerne Bjørnson's America Letters, 1880–1881.* Translated by Eva Lund Haugen. Northfield, Minn.: Norwegian American Historical Association, 2001.
Three Plays. New York: Howard Fertig, 1989.

A Work about Bjørnstjerne Bjørnson

Cohen, Georg. *Henrik Ibsen: A Critical Study. With a 42-Page Essay on Bjørnstjerne Bjørnson.* New York: Classic Books, 1964.

Blasco Ibáñez, Vicente (1867–1928)
novelist

Born in Valencia, Spain, Blasco Ibáñez first began writing about life in that Mediterranean seaport. His is the "regional" novel, and his works depict life in his "patria chica," or place of birth. Blasco Ibáñez writes in the naturalist style: He believes that human behavior is controlled by instinct, emotion, and environment and that we have no free will. His best novel, *La barraca* (1898), takes place in the lovely farmlike regions of Valencia. It presents the animosity held by the half-Moorish peasants toward a stranger in their land.

Around 1902, after writing several novels situated in Valencia, Blasco Ibáñez attempted to describe other areas of Spain, but these works lack the power of his earlier works. His writing became more propaganda than literary expression as he attacked the church, the government, and the military. He carries the reader across Spain, visiting the religious capital, Toledo; Bilbao, an industrial city, and Andalusia in southern Spain, where he describes the hardships suffered by the peasants. His novel, *Sangre y arena* (*Blood and Sand*, 1906) has been called the most complete portrayal of bullfighting ever presented in fiction. Far from an idealistic account, it is a description of all the blood and gore of the fight and depicts the spectators as monsters.

In 1910, in trouble for his unpopular political opinions and his radical journal, *El Pueblo*, Blasco Ibáñez went to South America, where he hoped to devote a novel to each country. After he wrote *Los argonautas* (1914) about Argentina, the outbreak of World War I caused him to return to Europe. He fought for the Allies, earning the French Légion d'Honneur. His later novels deal with the war, for example, *Los cuatro jinetes del Apocalipsis* (*The Four Horsemen of the Apocalypse,* 1916).

Some critics say Blasco Ibáñez has received more recognition than he deserves. His popularity is partly due to his forceful style. His novels are not delicate. It is the powerful descriptions of his hometown, Valencia, in his earlier novels that most attract his readers.

A Work about Blasco Ibáñez

Day, A. Grove, and Edgar C. Knowlton, Jr. *Vicente Blasco Ibáñez*. Boston: Twayne, 1972.

Blixen, Baroness Karen Christence

see DINESEN, ISAK.

Bolaño, Roberto (1953–2003) *novelist, poet*

Born in Santiago, Chile, into a working class family, Roberto Bolaño spent his childhood on the shores of Chile's southern region. His family moved to Mexico City when he was 15, shortly after which he dropped out of high school to work as a journalist. Over the next five years, Bolaño was drawn to left-wing causes, and his newfound ideology brought him back to Chile to support the socialist government of Salvador Allende. Soon after his arrival, however, Bolaño was arrested during the military coup that brought Augusto Pinochet to power. He was imprisoned for eight days, only to be released by two police officers who happened to be childhood friends. For the next four years, Bolaño took to the road as a literary vagabond, living in Mexico, El Salvador, and France before finally settling in Spain, where he married and had two children.

Throughout the 1970s and 1980s, Bolaño wrote poetry while working at day jobs. After realizing he could not properly support his family with the unpredictable nature of his work, he turned to writing novels. Through the 1990s, he produced several critically acclaimed works in short succession, including *Nazi Literature in the Americas* (1996) and *The Savage Detectives* (1998), one of his most celebrated works. Described as "a novel all about poetry and poets," *The Savage Detectives* fo-

cuses on 17-year-old Juan García Madero, who has been asked to join a gang of "literary guerrillas" named the "visceral realists." "He places us there," one critic writes, "in Mexico City, and reminds us of the excitement and boredom, the literary pretentiousness and ignorance, the erotic ambition and anxiety of being a young writer or reader in the company of like-minded friends." The first section of *The Savage Detectives* is Madero's diary, in which he recounts the trials and tribulations of the movement, which is led by two young poets, Arturo Belano and Ulises Lima. The longer second section focuses on first-person interviews with friends, lovers, acquaintances, and enemies of Lima and Belano—people whose lives briefly intersected with the two poets from 1976 to 1996.

In *2666*, published posthumously in 2004, Bolaño is concerned with numerous unsolved serial murders of young women, crimes that have taken place in the city of Ciudad Juárez in Mexico (renamed Santa Teresa in the novel) since 2000. The novel is structured in five parts and revolves around multiple narrators—a journalist, an "unstable" philosophy professor, a group of literary critics, and a host of police officers—who become obsessed or involved with the investigation in various ways, directly and indirectly. There is something secret, horrible, and cosmic afoot" writes a critic, "centered around Santa Teresa and possibly culminating in the mystical year of the book's title. . . . We can at most glimpse it, in those uncanny moments when the world seems wrong."

Suffering from disease for an extended period of time, Bolaño died of chronic liver failure in 2003 at the age of 50, shortly after submitting the first draft of *2666* to his editor. "Bolaño joked about the 'posthumous,'" wrote one critic, "saying the word 'sounds like the name of a Roman gladiator, one who is undefeated.'"

In 2007, two of Bolaño's stories (*The Insufferable Gaucho* and *Clara*) appeared for the first time in English in the *New Yorker*, prompting one critic to add to the author's ironic take on the word *posthumous*, writing: ". . . he would no doubt be amused to see how his stock has risen now that he is dead." Both stories will appear in a new collection. In addition, *Antwerp*, a prose-poem novel written in 1980 when Bolaño was 27, was recently published in English. Called "the big bang of Roberto Bolaño's fictional universe," the novel is divided into 54 sections in which we hear "voices from a dream, from a nightmare, from passersby, from an omniscient narrator" and which "moves in multiple directions and cuts to the bone." Bolaño was awarded the National Book Critics Circle Award in 2008 for *2666*, which was praised by the critics as the first literary masterpiece of the 21st century.

Other Works by Roberto Bolaño

Amulet. Translated by Chris Andrews. New York: New Directions, 2008.

By Night in Chile. Translated by Chris Andrews. New York: New Directions, 2003.

The Skating Rink. Translated by Chris Andrews. New York: New Directions, 2009.

Böll, Heinrich (1917–1985) *novelist, short story writer*

Heinrich Theodor Böll was born in Cologne to Victor and Marie Hermanns Böll. His father was a carpenter, and his mother was from a farming and brewing family. Böll attended a Catholic elementary school and later graduated from the Kaiser-Wilhelm-Gymnasium in Cologne. He studied German and philology for a semester at the University of Cologne before the German army drafted him in 1939. Böll was wounded four times, fighting in World War II. He married Annemarie Cech in 1942.

 The postwar years were lean for Böll and his family. He worked in a carpentry shop and as a temporary employee for the city of Cologne. It was not long, however, before he published several short stories. One of these works received the prize from the German authors' association GRUPPE 47. The success of Böll's novel on generational reckoning, *Billard um halb zehn* (*Billiards at Half-Past Nine*,

1959), helped Gruppe 47 become a stronger voice in German literature. His novel criticizing the government and the church, *Ansichten eines Clowns* (*The Clown*, 1965), marked the start of a new German literary phase in which blunt political reasoning took precedence over formal artistic expression.

Böll's writing career lasted four decades and produced a host of popular and critically acclaimed novels. In a poll taken in the 1970s, West Germans selected him as the fourth-most-influential person in their country. He received the Nobel Prize in literature in 1972, in part for his novel *Gruppenbild mit Dame* (*Group Portrait with Lady*, 1971), about an "author" researching the war experiences of a woman whom he gradually comes to love.

Several themes emerge from Böll's writings. He portrays war as senseless and absurd, refuting the notion of heroism. Böll's opposition of postwar materialism is another common theme. He often challenged authority and criticized the abuses of the Catholic Church. Böll strongly promoted human rights and was considered by many to be the conscience of West Germany. In the words of literary scholar Heinrich Vormweg, "Heinrich Böll created a literary oeuvre which reflects the true history of the Federal Republic as no other has done."

Critical Analysis

Böll's work has always resonated from the effects of the Nazi takeover of Cologne, as well as from the Allied bombing of that city during World War II. His work also deals with the psychological trauma those incidents caused not only in Böll but also in the German psyche itself. His writing has been labelled Trümmerliteratur (literally, rubble literature), writing that deals with the literal rubble that the German people faced as they returned to their homes after the war, as well as the figurative rubble of their ideals and culture. Böll consistently portrays war as senseless and absurd and criticizes the notion of heroism during wartime. In his early work, from what he called the worm's-eye view of World War II, Böll deals with the despair of soldiers' lives and the oppressive cruelties he witnessed in his youth and in military service.

In his 1949 novel *Der Zug war pünktlich* (*The Train Was on Time*), a German soldier takes a train from Paris to Poland when traveling to the front. On his way he meets two other Germans and enters into a dialogue in which they relate their shared horror of war and the effects war has on people, in particular the sense of loss and guilt experienced by the German people following World War II. Böll's literary style is connected to a form of literature called Kahlschlagliteratur (clear-cutting literature), which employed "simple, direct language" that "described but did not evaluate the destroyed world." Böll was also a fierce critic of postwar materialism, capitalism, and the Catholic Church and was considered by many to be the conscience of West Germany.

In his 1974 novel *Die verlorene Ehre der Katharina Blum oder: Wie Gewalt entstehen und wohin sie führen kann* (*The Lost Honor of Katharina Blum, Or: how violence develops and where it can lead*), Böll takes on tabloid publishing and the climate of panic it can create. In the novel, Katharina Blum is employed as a housemaid in Munich. After meeting and sleeping with a man named Ludwig Götten, her life is turned upside down when he is arrested as a thief and a deserter from the military, after Blum had concealed him from the police. The subsequent treatment of Blum by police and by a tabloid newspaper that characterizes her as a "whore" and "heartless bitch," makes her the target of public outrage. Hounded mercilessly by the press, Katharina arranges an interview with the reporter who defamed her and kills him. She subsequently gives herself up to the police.

The Lost Honor of Katharina Blum demonstrates how women are victimized at the hands of institutions controlled by men. Police inspectors are portrayed as representatives of the capitalist state and upholders of male power. Their actions and words exemplify the brutal relations that exist between people in such a society. This brutality subsequently extends into society as a whole, which judges and torments Blum for her alleged behavior, sexual and otherwise. In this novel, Böll explores the theme of an innocent person who is accidentally caught up in the net of the state.

Another Work by Heinrich Böll
Adam, Where Art Thou? Translated by Mervyn Savill. New York: Criterion Books, 1955.

Works about Heinrich Böll
Heinrich Böll, on His Death: Selected Obituaries and the Last Interview. Bonn: Inter Nationes, 1985.
Schwarz, Wilhelm. *Heinrich Böll: Teller of Tales.* New York: Ungar, 1968.

Bonnefoy, Yves (1923–) *poet, critic*
Yves Bonnefoy was born in Tours, France, to a working-class family. His father was a railroad worker, and his mother was a teacher. He received his degree in mathematics and philosophy from the University of Descartes in Tours and then studied mathematics, history, and philosophy at both the University of Poitiers and the Sorbonne.

In 1953, Bonnefoy published his first collection, *Of the Movement and the Immobility of Douve* (1953; translated 1968). These poems were chiefly concerned with human beings' struggle to establish a firm connection among themselves and with the world. Six other collections of poetry followed, including *Ce qui fut sans lumière* (*What Was without Light*, 1987); *Début et fin de la neige* (*Beginning and End of Snow*, 1991); and *La vie errante* (*The Wandering Life*, 1993) about Helen of Troy, the image of beauty threatened by violence.

In addition to poetry, Bonnefoy has written numerous historical and critical texts, such as *The Art and the Place of Poetry* (1989), and is concerned with the connection between poetry and the visual arts.

Bonnefoy has taught at several universities, both in France and abroad, and has been involved in the translation from English to French of 10 Shakespearean plays as well as an edition of the poetry of Yeats. He is also the editor of *Mythologies* (1991), a two-volume scholarly work: One volume explores and reproduces African, American, and Ancient European myths and the histories of religious traditions; the second volume explores the same themes from Greek and Egyptian traditions, as written by French authors. Bonnefoy has received several awards for his poetry, including the Montaigne prize in 1978 and Grand National Prize for Poetry in 1993. He was also awarded the Franz Kafka Prize in 2007.

Other Works by Yves Bonnefoy

In the Shadow's Light. Translated by John Naughton. Chicago: University of Chicago Press, 1991.

Naughton, John, and Anthony Rudolf, eds. *New and Selected Poems.* Chicago: University of Chicago Press, 1995.

Yesterday's Wilderness Kingdom. Translated by Anthony Rudolf. London: MPT Books, 2000.

A Work about Yves Bonnefoy

Naughton, John. *The Poetics of Yves Bonnefoy.* Chicago: University of Chicago Press, 1984.

Borges, Jorge Luis (1899–1986) *poet, short story writer, essayist*

Born in Buenos Aires, Argentina, Borges was the son of Jorge Guillermo Borges and Leonor Acevedo de Borges. The Borgeses were a prominent Argentinean family descended from Juan de Garay, the founder of Buenos Aires.

Borges's father, a lawyer and professor of psychology, had Borges tutored at home until the age of 10 by a British governess. The family also had a large library with many works in English, and Borges read, at a very early age, authors such as Stevenson, Wells, Kipling, and Poe. These writers influenced him dramatically, tempering his bookishness with a love of adventure stories and fantasy. His first publication was a translation into Spanish of Oscar Wilde's fairy tale *The Happy Prince,* which Borges completed when he was nine.

At the beginning of World War I, Borges's family moved to Switzerland, where he attended high school and became fluent in French, German, and Latin in addition to English and his native Spanish. After graduating from high school, Borges

traveled to Spain where he thrust himself into the avant-garde literary discussions in the cafés and befriended a Spanish poet, Cansinos-Assens, a minor but extremely learned poet. Borges's experience during these years sparked his interest in literary experimentation and solidified his desire to become a writer.

Borges returned to Argentina in his mid-20s, and during the next 20 years, he steadily published volumes of poetry, essays, and short stories. His "fictions," as he called them, exhibit his extraordinary literary originality. At their best, his stories are a kind of philosophic science fiction. They have a broad popular appeal and have also received the highest literary respect. Borges was one of the first authors in the 20th century to take popular genres, like the science-fiction tale or the hardboiled detective story, and use them to investigate metaphysical ideas that were traditionally explored only in poetry, philosophy, and "serious" prose fiction. This can be seen in the story from *Fictions* (1962), "The Garden of Forking Paths"—a detective story that is also an intricate exploration of the limits of language.

Many of Borges's stories have little or no plot. They explore instead the different possibilities of an idea. For example, in "The Library of Babel," also from *Fictions,* the narrator explains to the reader how the Library in which he lives works. The Library is infinite and there is no way out. On the shelves are books filled with random letters. Most of the books are filled with nonsense. However, because there is an infinite number of books, sometimes by chance the letters form words or even whole books that make sense. In fact, simply by the laws of mathematics, every possible book in the world must exist in the Library. The trouble is trying to find the important books among the millions of meaningless ones. Borges, who himself spent many years working as a librarian, thus presents his audience with a symbolic tale about the human condition, his message being that if we had enough time, it would be possible to know everything about the world and ourselves, but time is exactly what is limited.

Death and the Compass, another tale from *Fictions,* is the best example of the "other kind" of Borges short story. It is, in essence, a mystery with an intricate and perfectly constructed plot. However, the hero, Lonnrot, is a kind of anti–Sherlock Holmes, a master of logical deduction. In Borges's world, Lonnrot uses this very quality, as he is led to his doom, to solve his own murder. The story can be read as a parable concerning the dangers to the human soul in our highly rational and scientific culture.

In his later life, Borges received many honorary degrees from such universities as Oxford and Harvard, where he also taught. He was the first Latin-American prose writer to become an internationally recognized literary figure. He has had a strong influence on many of the greatest Latin American authors of the 20th century, for example Gabriel García Márquez, Carlos Fuentes, and Julio Cortazar, who follow Borges in the art of irony and prose filled with verbal invention and intellectual game playing, rather than the psychological and social drama of realism.

Critical Analysis

Borges's stories are famous for grappling in brief narratives with huge philosophical issues, for calling the reader's attention to their fictionality, and for conflating dreams and reality. All these qualities are beautifully realized in "The Other Death" (1944). Like many of Borges's narrators, the teller of this story is an intellectual with wide-ranging interests, a writer, and a bit of a detective—at least in metaphysical realms. The narrator's use of historical facts and references to real people past and present gives the story the feel of nonfiction, a characteristic the narrator undermines by his confession at the end that "I am not sure of having always written the truth."

The tale takes place in 1946. Patricio Gannon, a friend of the narrator's, writes to him regarding his plan to translate a poem by Emerson into English. He adds that an acquaintance, Pedro Damián, has died. The narrator notes that he met Damián only once four years earlier and recalls that the old man had fought in the battle of Masoller in 1904.

The narrator decides to write a "tale of fantasy based on the defeat at Masoller." He meets Colonel Tabares, who fought in the battle, and asks the old man to share his memories of the event. The colonel tells the narrator that Damián was a coward who ran away from the battle. This news startles the narrator: "I would have preferred things to have happened differently. Without being aware of it, I had made a kind of idol out of old Damián . . . Tabares's story destroyed everything."

Later, the narrator visits the colonel again to double-check some details for his story. Also visiting the colonel is Dr. Juan Francisco Amaro, who remembers Damián as a hero of the battle. At this point, the colonel says although he was at the battle he does not remember Damián at all.

Strange events continue. The narrator runs into his friend Patricio Gannon in a bookstore. When the narrator reminds him of his promise to translate Emerson's "The Past," Gannon denies that he ever intended to translate the poem (which is about the impossibility of altering the past) and has no memory of Damián. "With rising terror," the narrator says, "I noticed that he was listening to me very strangely." Soon after, the narrator gets a letter from Colonel Tabares, who now remembers Damián's heroism. He visits Damián's cabin to find it is no longer there and that none of the neighbors remember him at all.

The rest of the story involves the narrator's philosophical speculation about what was happening. He finally concludes that Damián passionately wanted to relive the battle and erase his cowardice. God hears his prayer but even God cannot change the past. Therefore, he changes others' *memories* of Damián.

The story ends with the narrator's claim that while others have lost their memories of Damián, "I do not think I am running a similar risk." Then he contradicts himself: "A few years from now, I shall believe I made up a fantastic tale and I will actually have recorded an event that was real." Layer upon layer, "The Other Death" is a dizzying spiral of conundrum and contradiction, a typical Borgesian metaphysical mystery.

Other Works by Jorge Luis Borges

Coleman, Alexander, ed. *Selected Poems.* New York: Penguin, 2000.

Collected Fictions. Translated by Andrew Hurley. New York: Penguin, 1999.

Dreamtigers. Translated by Mildred Boyer and Harold Moreland. Austin: University of Texas Press, 1985.

Irby, James, and Donald Yeats, eds. *Labyrinths: Selected Stories and Other Writings.* New York: Norton, 1988.

Works about Jorge Luis Borges

Barnstone, Willis, ed. *Borges at Eighty: Conversations.* Bloomington: Indiana University Press, 1982.

Bell-Villada, Gene H. *Borges and His Fiction.* Austin: University of Texas Press, 1999.

Brasch, Charles (1909–1973) *poet, critic, translator*

Charles Brasch was born in Otago, New Zealand, the only son of Jewish parents. His father was an established businessman, but from an early age Brasch, to his father's disappointment, aspired to be a poet and writer. Unlike some of his peers, Brasch had little confidence in his innate lyrical gift, and he spent most of his life learning and perfecting the technical aspects of writing poetry. He studied history at Oxford University and worked in the Foreign Office in London before returning to New Zealand permanently in 1945.

In 1947 the journal *Landfall* began publication, with Brasch as its founding editor. For 20 years, Brasch nurtured the talent of young New Zealand writers through his intense editorial scrutiny as well as through contributions from his personal wealth. In addition, each issue of the journal contained an editorial essay by Brasch. *Landfall* is still an important part of New Zealand literary life.

The poems in his first published collection, *The Land and the People, and Other Poems* (1939), betray his preference for accuracy of sense over rhythm; metrically they are a little awkward. Brasch's later poetry finally achieves an impeccable balance between expression in terms of words and cadence. This, however, is the result of a lifetime of hard work.

Brasch's poems deal prominently with his life and travels. Nature and its interaction with human beings constitute an important theme in Brasch's poetry. In the title sequence "The Land and the People," Brasch recounts the past through the reenactment in four poems of the first arrival of people on the islands of New Zealand. The initial arrival is compared to the "original sin," a destruction of nature's paradise. In another poem, "Letter from Thurlby Domain," Brasch sees the ruins of a house as a payment of a debt by human beings to the natural environment they had tried to alter.

Four more collections appeared during his lifetime, including *The Estate and Other Poems* (1957), whose lengthy title poem was written in memory of a friend who died in an accident, and *Ambulando* (1964), in which he began to focus more on his own experience rather than on philosophical subjects and the issue of national identity. As he states in "Cry Mercy":

> Getting older, I grow more personal,
> Like more, dislike more
> And more intensely than ever . . .

His final collection, *Home Ground* (1974) was published after his death, as was an unfinished autobiography, *Indirections: A Memoir* (1980). Brasch's extensive and valuable collection of books and paintings was bequeathed to the Hocken Library in Dunedin, New Zealand.

Other Works by Charles Brasch

Roddick, Alan, ed. *Collected Poems: Charles Brasch.* New York: Oxford University Press, 1991.

Watson, J. L., ed. *The Universal Dance: A Selection from the Critical Prose Writings of Charles Brasch.* Otago, New Zealand: University of Otago Press, 1991.

Works about Charles Brasch

Bertram, James. *Charles Brasch.* New York: Oxford University Press, 1976.

Daalder, Joost. "'Disputed Ground' in the Poetry of Charles Brasch." *Landfall* 26 (September 1972).

De Beer, Mary, et al. "Charles Brasch 1909–73: Tributes and Memories from his Friends." *Islands* 2 (Spring 1973).

Braschi, Giannina (1953–   ) *poet, novelist, professor*

Giannina Braschi was born in San Juan, Puerto Rico, and lived in Madrid, Rome, Paris, and London before settling in New York in the late 1970s. Braschi earned a Ph.D. from the State University of New York. In 1994, her selected works in Spanish were published in English as *Empire of Dreams,* a collection that explores gender and linguistic boundaries. *Yo-Yo Boing!* (1998), a work written in Spanish and English, juxtaposes themes of identity, ethnicity, and globalization with artistic innovations. A *Publishers Weekly* reviewer wrote, "Braschi's melange of prose and poetry, English and Spanish, is admirable for its energy, its experimental format." *Yo-Yo Boing!* was nominated for the Pulitzer Prize and the American Library Association's Notable Book Award.

Another Work by Giannina Braschi

"Three Prose Poems." Translated by Tess O'Dwyer. *The Literary Review: An International Journal of Contemporary Writing* 36, no. 2 (Winter 1993): 147–49.

Works about Giannina Braschi

"Giannina Braschi." *The Literary Review* 36, no. 2 (Winter 1993): 14.

"Yo-Yo Boing!." *Publishers Weekly* 245, no. 35 (August 1998): 49.

Brathwaite, Edward Kamau (Lawson Edward Brathwaite) (1930–   ) *poet, critic, short story writer, teacher, historian*

Born in Bridgetown, Barbados, Brathwaite was educated at Harrison College in Barbados. He won a Barbados scholarship in 1949 to Pembroke College, Cambridge, where he read history. After graduating in 1953, Brathwaite stayed on one more year to earn a Certificate in Education.

In 1955, Brathwaite left England for Ghana and worked as an education officer for seven years. There he founded a children's theater and wrote plays, later published as *Four Plays for Primary Schools* (1964) and *Odale's Choice* (1967). He also published multiple poems in Cambridge University journals and West Indies periodicals, such as *Bim* and *Kyk-Over-Al.* In "Timehri" (1970), Brathwaite remarked on his Ghanaian experiences: "Slowly, ever so slowly, I came to a sense of identification of myself with these people, my living diviners. I came to connect my history with theirs, the bridge of my mind was linking Atlantic and ancestor, homeland and heartland." The historical and geographical themes expressed in these statements reappear in many of Brathwaite's works.

Returning to the Caribbean in 1962, Brathwaite worked as a tutor for the University of the West Indies in St. Lucia. One year later he became a lecturer in history at Mona, Jamaica. He completed his first book of poetry, *Rights of Passage,* during his first year there, and it was published in 1967 as the first volume of a trilogy. The *Rights of Passage,* Brathwaite states, is "based on my own experience of that old triple journey: in my case, from the Caribbean to Europe, to West Africa and back home again. . . . It is a rite and the possession of the Negro peoples of the New World." *Masks* (1968) and *Islands* (1969) soon followed. In the deluge of reviews and commentaries generated by the publication of *Islands,* the trilogy was named one of the most ambitious aesthetic and ethical poetic projects from the Antilles. A *Sunday Times* review of *Islands* positioned Brathwaite as "one of the finest living poets of the Western Hemisphere."

Published as *The Arrivants: A New World Trilogy* in 1973, all three volumes examine African roots to recover West Indian identity. The trilogy explores many themes examined in later works—community, tribal concerns, spiritual growth, and history. Later works, many in dialect, incorporated musical elements of popular culture, such as folk music, jazz, and religious hymns, as well as speech rhythms. Some claimed Brathwaite inadequately recorded intended rhythms in his verse but admit he reads his verse brilliantly.

In subsequent years, Brathwaite successfully published scholarly as well as creative writing. Interested in the relationship of jazz to Caribbean writing, he published *Jazz and the West Indian Novel* in *Bim* in 1967. Other notable scholarly works include *The Folk Culture of Jamaican Slaves* (1969) and *The Development of Creole Society in Jamaica 1770–1820* (1971). Brathwaite's work positioned him as one of the Antilles' most consistent and important English-speaking critics.

Multiple collections of poetry followed, but they received less critical attention than *The Arrivants*. Dissatisfied, some critics said *Other Exiles* (1975) merely collected poems not included in *The Arrivants*. Brathwaite's use of violent demonic imagery to explore Rastafarian subculture and urban slum experiences in *Black and Blues* (1976) earned him a prize at the Cuban Casa de las Américas poetry competition. Critics also quickly recognized Brathwaite's poetic talent in *Mother Poem* (1977). As Brathwaite writes in the preface, "This poem is about porous limestone, my mother, Barbados." Like *Mother Poem, Sun Poem* (1982) is autobiographical: Brathwaite universalizes his cyclical masculine experiences. One year after publishing *Sun Poem*, Brathwaite was appointed professor of social and cultural history at the University of the West Indies. Lecturing and reading his poetry allowed him to travel widely in Europe, Africa, North America, and the Far East.

More recent works, including *The Zea Mexican Diary* (1993), *Trench Town Rock* (1994), and *Dream-Stories* (1994), employ what Brathwaite calls the Sycorax writing style. They alter font, type size, and margins, "allowing [Brathwaite] to write in light and to make sounds visible as if [he is] in video," as stated in an interview with Kwame Dawes in *Talk Yuh Talk: Interviews with Anglo-*

phone Caribbean Poets (2001). Although Brathwaite's poetry has been translated into Spanish, French, German, and the Sranantongo language of Suriname, he recently admitted, "My big regret is that Caribbean criticism has almost totally disregarded my work since *The Arrivants* as long ago now as 1973."

A comparative literature professor at New York University, Brathwaite divides his time between New York and Barbados. To quote editor and interviewer Kwame Dawes, Brathwaite's "critical work is virtually foundational to an examination of a Caribbean aesthetic; his experimentation with music, popular culture, and various forms of poetic expression has proved influential for a significant number of writers. Brathwaite's work is challenging because its meaning resides as much in the sounds of his words as in their semantic construction."

Other Works by Edward Kamau Brathwaite

Ancestors: A Reinvention of Mother Poem, Sun Poem, and X/Self. New York: New Directions, 2001.
Born to Slow Horses. Middletown, Conn.: Wesleyan University Press, 2005.
Third World Poems. London: Longman, 1983.
Words Need Love Too. Philipsburg, St. Martin: House of Nehesi, 2000.

Works about Edward Kamau Brathwaite

Brown, Stewart, ed. *The Art of Kamau Brathwaite.* Bridgend, Mid Glamorgan, Wales: Seren, 1995.
Reiss, Timothy J. *For the Geography of a Soul: Emerging Perspectives on Kamau Brathwaite.* Trenton, N.J.: Africa World Press, 2001.
Savory, Elaine. "The Word Becomes Nam: Self and Community in the Poetry of Kamau Brathwaite, and its Relation to Caribbean Culture and Postmodern Theory." In *Writing the Nation: Self and Country in the Postcolonial Imagination.* Edited by John C. Hawley. Amsterdam: Rodopi, 1996: 23–43.

Brathwaite, Lawson Edward

See BRATHWAITE, EDWARD KAMAU.

Braun, Volker (1939–) *poet, playwright*

Volker Braun was born in Dresden, Germany, less than four months before the start of World War II. His father, a soldier in the German army, was killed in the last year of the war. After completing his schooling, Braun worked as a printer's assistant, a machine engineer, and a construction worker. In 1960, he joined the Communist Party in East Germany and enrolled at the University of Leipzig, where he studied philosophy for four years. After college, Braun worked as a writer and producer for the Berlin Ensemble, the City Theater of Leipzig, and the Deutsches Theater in Berlin.

Braun wrote several works of poetry and prose but achieved his greatest fame as a playwright. His influences include BERTOLT BRECHT and FRIEDRICH SCHILLER. Braun frequently portrayed the individual's struggle for identity in the face of contrary societal expectations. As an idealist, Braun sought to promote a greater acceptance of socialism with his early plays. He opposed reunification in 1989, hoping for the continuance of an East Germany committed to social justice and the environment. Braun's awards include the Heinrich Heine Prize, the Heinrich Mann Prize, and Germany's National Prize. In 2008, he received the 2007 ver.di-Literature Prize for his story, "Das Mittagsmahl" (The Midday Meal).

Another Work by Volker Braun

Das Wirklichgewallte. Frankfurt am Main: Suhrkamp, 2000.

A Work about Volker Braun

Bothe Kathrin. *Die Imaginierte Natur des Sozialismus: eine Biographie des Schreibens und der Texte Volker Brauns (1959–1974).* Würzburg: Konigshausen & Neumann, 1997.

Brecht, Bertolt (1898–1956) *dramatist, playwright*

Bertold Brecht was born in Augsburg, Germany. His father was an administrator of a paper company. Brecht began writing while he was very young and published a few poems at the age of 16. In school, he developed a reputation as a hooligan and a troublemaker. Despite the constant disciplinary problems, he graduated from school and entered the University of Munich in 1917 to study medicine. His studies were interrupted by the outbreak of World War I, and Brecht enlisted in the German army as a medical orderly. After the war, Brecht briefly resumed his studies but eventually abandoned them to pursue a writing career.

In 1919, Brecht joined the Independent Social Democratic Party and began his lifelong association with communism. Starting in 1920, he began to work as a dramatist and playwright at various theaters throughout Germany. Although his early plays were not directly engaged with politics, Brecht often mocked the conventions of bourgeois sensibility and lifestyle. His political engagement, his indictment of capitalism, and his epic style established Brecht as one of the most radical playwrights in Germany.

After Brecht officially joined the Communist Party of Germany in 1929, his works assumed an even more radical stance and directly addressed important political issues. Brecht's affiliation with the Communist Party made him an unpopular figure with government censors and other officials. Many of Brecht's works were banned in Germany even in the years before Hitler came to power.

The political atmosphere in Germany became dangerous for Brecht during the 1930s because of the rise of the Nazis, who were opposed to communism. His works were banned throughout the country, and he was forced into exile. Brecht lived in Denmark, Finland, Russia, and finally the United States. While living in the United States, Brecht tried to write screenplays for the movies, but he had difficulty getting his work accepted. He also found the atmosphere in Hollywood intellectually stifling. In 1947, Brecht was investigated by the anti-Communist congressional Committee on Un-American Activities. Although the committee did not establish any definitive charges against Brecht, his reputation was damaged and he could no longer produce any work in the United States.

In 1948, Brecht returned to Germany, settling in Communist East Germany. Brecht founded his own Marxist theater in East Berlin, where many of his plays were produced. Brecht also experimented with many theatrical conventions, such as lighting, sound, and set. Brecht's reputation spread beyond the borders of Germany, and he became an internationally renowned dramatist. In 1955, he was awarded the Stalin Peace Prize, the highest recognition in the Soviet Union, for his contribution to drama.

Critical Analysis

Brecht's drama reflects his view that theater should provide a forum for social and political change, rather than serve a purely aesthetic function geared toward entertainment. Brecht formulated a new style of acting based on the "alienation effect." He wanted his audience to become objective spectators by disassociating themselves from the characters of the play. Moreover, Brecht argued that actors should disassociate themselves from the characters they portray. Instead of creating an illusion of reality, Brecht wanted his audience to understand that the play is not a reality but a forum for social debate. Brecht believed his style of production would make the political lesson more apparent to the masses.

Mother Courage and Her Children (1941), one of Brecht's most famous historical plays, set during the Thirty Years' War, presents a series of conflicts that occurred between Catholics and Protestants in central Europe between 1618 and 1648. Mother Courage is a woman who depends on the continuation of the war for her economic survival. She is nicknamed Mother Courage for courageously protecting her merchandise under enemy fire. She has three children who die in the war, one by one. Yet, she continues her career as a war profiteer. Staged in East Berlin, the play attracted instant critical attention for its controversial portrayal of war and its dehumanizing effects on people.

The Caucasian Chalk Circle (1948), an adaptation of a medieval Chinese play based on the parable of the chalk circle, centers on a land dispute in a small commune in the Soviet Union after World War II. The main action revolves around the conflict of two women over a child. It is similar to the biblical tale of King Solomon who must resolve a dispute between two women, both of whom claim to be the mother of a child. The play was warmly greeted by audiences and received international recognition.

Among Brecht's most famous plays was *The Threepenny Opera* (1928). This adaptation of John Gay's *Beggar's Opera* presents a universe of beggars, thieves, and prostitutes, a world bereft of honor or trust. Kurt Weill's inventive score adds to the experience of this brittle world, an allegory of Germany's Weimar Republic, the period before Hitler took power. The popular song "Mack the Knife" is from this play.

The Good Woman of Setzuan (1940) tells the tale of three gods who are in search of a truly good person. Their choice is Shen Te, a prostitute. They give her money to start a new life, but she finds that a truly good person cannot survive, so she creates a nasty alter ego, her "cousin" Shu Tai.

Galileo (1939) deals with the historical figure of the famous astronomer, Galileo, who discovers that Earth is not the center of the universe. He holds his findings for eight years but finally reveals them to the pope. The pope subjects Galileo to the Inquisition, and Galileo recants his theory. The play dealt with many political and social issues. The freedom of the individual is juxtaposed against oppressive society, which is dominated by the religious leaders who are not interested in scientific truth because it threatens to overturn their supremacy.

Brecht is also among the finest poets of the 20th century, a talent overshadowed somewhat by his success as a playwright. Brecht published more than 1,500 poems that span more than 30 years, including both world wars. Brecht's poetry combines lyricism with an epic and Marxist view of society and history. In the poem "1940," for example the speaker says that his young son asks him why he should learn mathematics, French, or history, and the speaker wonders why indeed when "two pieces of bread are more than one's about all you'll end up with" and language is unnecessary to convey hunger—a groan will do—and history does not teach us how to survive. Still he tells his son, with false optimism, to study.

Bertolt Brecht is considered to be among the most influential writers of the 20th century. His theoretical works changed the face of the modern theater, and his emphasis on social responsibility of the individual inspired many playwrights to write works of social significance.

Other Works by Bertolt Brecht

Baal. Translated by Peter Tagel. New York: Arcade, 1998.

Brecht on Theater: The Development of an Aesthetic. Translated by John Willett. New York: Hill and Wang, 1994.

Drums in the Night. New York: Methuen Drama, 1988.

Works about Bertolt Brecht

Esslin, Martin. *Brecht, a Choice of Evils: A Critical Study of the Man, His Works, and His Opinions.* New York: Methuen Drama, 1984.

Munsterer, Hans. *The Young Brecht.* New York: Paul and Co., 1992.

Brentano, Catarina Elisabetha Ludovica Magdalena

See ARNIM, BETTINA VON.

Breton, André (1896–1966) *poet, novelist, essayist*

André Breton was born in Tichenbray, France. He studied medicine in Paris and was assigned to a military hospital, where he worked primarily in the psychiatric wards during World War I.

Breton studied the works of SIGMUND FREUD, and Freud's notion of free association greatly influenced Breton's experiments with automatic writing. Aided by French poet Philippe Soupault, he began to work with this concept. He was searching for a higher form of reality that, he assumed, was present at the point where dreams and reality converged. Together, he and Soupault founded the journal *Littérature,* in which they published the works of such writers as LOUIS ARAGON. Breton also used the journal as a vehicle to express his own views, which he went on to publish in a series of three surrealist manifestos in 1924, 1930, and 1942.

The first of Breton's surrealist manifestos is considered to be the founding text of the surrealist movement. Breton assumed a position of leadership within the movement as a result of this text, and he was joined by numerous talented poets and visual artists, all of whom shared the beliefs he had set forth in his text, causing the movement to gain momentum and eventually to spread beyond Europe.

Critical Analysis

In the middle of this creative tempest, Breton published what is considered critically to be his finest work, *Nadja* (1928), which is based, in part, on firsthand experiences. Breton met and spent time with an unknown girl who was living her life in the same manner that Breton had advocated: She made no distinction between factual reality and fictional reality. Her behavior, however, was not socially acceptable, and she was ultimately placed in an asylum.

Surrealism as a movement was eclipsed after World War II by EXISTENTIALISM and was vehemently attacked by such new voices as SARTRE and CAMUS. Breton was subjected to political derision for having denounced the 1936 Moscow trials, thus making himself an enemy of the Communist Party as well as forcing him into conflict with several of his former friends and colleagues, such as Aragon and PAUL ÉLUARD, who rejected surrealism and fervently promoted communism.

Breton continued to proclaim his theme of the need for artists to focus on individual freedom, to develop an anarchist regime in the arts that functions as the exact antithesis of Stalinism and SOCIALIST REALISM and their attempts to harness creativity under totalitarian rule. In particular, he viewed socialist realism, as enforced by Stalin, to be the negation of freedom and was angered and disheartened to see that it could be supported by someone he had respected as much as Aragon. He denounced the idea of artists falling victim to a blind allegiance to repressive ideology. His essay "The Tower of Light" (1952) is solid evidence of Breton's continuing detachment from materialism and his increasing move toward utopian philosophy. He expresses the idea that revolution, to effect change on society, must first promote change in the mind of the individual.

Breton believed that very little had actually been learned as a result of World War I. In a 1942 address to French students at Yale University, Breton expressed these concerns. He also expressed his hope that the outcome of World War II would be different. This vision was shattered, however, by the emergence of the cold war and the added potential of nuclear weaponry to annihilate the human race. In response, Breton's essay "The Lamp in the Clock" (1948) called for a radical reconsideration of exactly what was at stake: the continued survival of humanity.

Breton also expressed his views through poetry. These works, collected as *Selected Poems* (1948; translated 1969), reflect the influence of other poets such as PAUL VALÉRY and ARTHUR RIMBAUD. Breton continued, throughout his life, to focus on the importance of revelation and the links that can be made through the arts between that which is concrete reality and that which exists solely in the realm of the imagination.

Other Works by André Breton

Break of Day. Translated by Mark Polizzotti and Mary Ann Caws. Lincoln: University of Nebraska Press, 1999.

Poems of André Breton: A Bilingual Anthology. Translated by Jean-Pierre Cauvin and Mary Ann Caws. Austin: University of Texas Press, 1982.

Works about André Breton

Caws, Mary Ann. *André Breton.* Boston: Twayne, 1996.

Polizzotti, Mark. *Revolution of the Mind: The Life of André Breton.* New York: Farrar, Straus & Giroux, 1995.

Breytenbach, Breyten (1939–) *poet, novelist, short story writer, essayist*

One of the most controversial figures in South African literary history, Breytenbach was born to an affluent Afrikaner family in the Cape Province. His ancestors settled in South Africa in the early 1700s.

Breytenbach has written wistfully about the poignant beauty of Cape Province. In several of his works, he has written about childhood memories and about the ancestral memory of his people. For example, his great-grandmother, his father, and his mother figure prominently in the retrospective novel *Dog Heart: A Travel Memoir* (1998). His eventual rejection of the Afrikaner tradition echoes all the more loudly because of the depth of his family's connections to the Dutch-settler heritage Afrikaners treasure.

He was seen, even at a young age, to possess great literary and immense talents. His early writings, all written in Afrikaans, such as those in his collection *Catastrophes* (1964), explore his sense of himself as distant from his own people and their traditions. While he was in college in Cape Town in the early 1960s, he was troubled by the encroaching control of the many apartheid laws and chose to go to Europe, where he met and married an Asian woman named Yolande Lien, who figures prominently in his poetry. Breytenbach was trying to return to South Africa in 1965 to accept a literary award when he was told that his marriage was a serious breach of South Africa's law against interracial marriage. His general distaste for apartheid had become personal, and Breytenbach became a founder and organizer of a group called *Okhela,* meaning to "set fire to." The goal of this group was to persuade white South Africans that the apartheid regime could only be brought down from within.

Issues of personal identity, especially regarding the relationship between art and life intrigued Breytenbach even before the frankly autobiographical writings that would develop from his experiences in the 1970s and 1980s. In poetry written during the 1960s, Breytenbach used only lowercase letters, referred to himself in his own poems, and used profanity. All of his writings stress the fictional nature of "real" life.

Since 1961, he has made his home primarily in Paris. Breytenbach entered South Africa illegally in 1975, using the name Christian Jean-Marc Galaska, and was arrested as a terrorist. His trial was an international event, although most of the proceedings occurred within the limitations and secrecy imposed by the Nationalist government. He was sentenced to nine years in prison, and he served seven. His imprisonment became the subject of some of his major works: a loosely structured collection of fragmentary narratives entitled *Mouroir: Mirror Notes to a Novel* (1984) and the autobiographical novel *The True Confessions of an Albino Terrorist* (1984). Another novel, *A Season in Paradise* (1980), and several collections of poetry, notably *Judas Eye* (1988), also investigate Breytenbach's time in South African prisons, although they are not all specifically concerned only with his prison experiences. Pressure from the international community, especially by the then-president of France, François Mitterrand, led to Breytenbach's early release from prison, with the provision that he leave South Africa.

Breytenbach has returned to South Africa since the institution of democratic elections, and he has championed the cause of the Afrikaner in South Africa as a political minority. In this way, one can see a consistency in Breytenbach's political ideology: The oppression of dissident groups, whether that of a minority holding a minority in check or that of a willful majority, should not be allowed to pass unremarked.

Critical Analysis

Breytenbach occupies a unique position in the African literary tradition. Like ANDRÉ BRINK and NADINE GORDIMER he has often written of political oppression and his distaste for the apartheid regime in South Africa. Breytenbach and Brink are also the most well-known writers who publish in Afrikaans, the language of the Dutch settlers, and those most often, and sometimes unfairly, vilified for all of apartheid's wrongs. Like another countryman, J. M. COETZEE, Breytenbach often plays with language at multiple levels. Their willingness to experiment with language, reveling in the multiplicity of possibilities for confusion and misunderstanding, is referred to as "postmodernism": a celebration of fragmentary, rather than unified, meaning, the purpose of which is meant to make readers think about not only what they read but also what they believe. This "playfulness" has often been criticized and stands as one end of the spectrum of opinion on Breytenbach. Ultimately, Breytenbach stands alone, like so many of the protagonists of his novels. Isolation, introspection, scathing self-analysis, and a refusal to use fictions as a crutch for existence mark both his poetry and his prose. For example, in *Dog Heart: A Memoir* (1999), he writes that he needs to see the child he once was to determine how he has become the man he is: "Why, after all these years, do I feel the urge to go and look for the other one, the child I must have been?"

J. M. Coetzee has commented on *Dog Heart* in his collection, *Stranger Shores: Literary Essays 1986–1999* (2001). He sees Breytenbach's text as typical of those narratives which mine his, and South Africa's, past: "Like Breytenbach's other memoirs, *Dog Heart* is loose, almost miscellaneous, in its structure. Part journal, part essay on autobiography, part book of the dead, part what one might call speculative history, it also contains searching meditations on the elusiveness of memory and passages of virtuoso writing . . . breathtaking in the immediacy of their evocation of Africa."

Even in what are recognizably novels, Breytenbach melds the real with the fantastic. For example, *Memory of Snow and Dust* (1989) concerns itself with fables of identity and the uncertainty that lies underneath our solid sense of who we are. The plot involves an Ethiopian journalist who meets and impregnates a mixed-race South African woman while they are in Switzerland for an arts festival, a "neutral" cultural and political space carved out by both custom and art. The journalist agrees to act as a spy for an antiapartheid group and goes to South Africa under an assumed name. But the identity under which he is traveling is accused of murder, and the would-be spy and absentee father cannot clear himself without revealing his own identity and betraying his political comrades. Fictions such as *Memory of Snow and Dust* call into question the seemingly simple injunction that the lives and works of artists are cleanly and clearly separate.

Breytenbach's contributions and importance to world literature are linked to the combination in his works of the personal, political, and cultural in ways that force readers to acknowledge the naturalness of the connections.

Other Works by Breyten Breytenbach

All One Horse. New York: Archipelago Books, 2008.
In Africa Even the Flies are Happy: Selected Poems, 1964–1977. London: Calder, 1978.
Intimate Stranger. New York: Archipelago Books, 2009.
Notes from the Middle World: Essays. Chicago: Haymarket Books, 2009.
Return to Paradise: An African Journal. New York: Harcourt Brace, 1993.
A Veil of Footsteps: Memoir of a Nomadic Fictional Character. Cape Town, South Africa: Human and Rousseau, 2008.
Voice Over: A Nomadic Conversation with Mahmoud Darwish. New York: Archipelago Books, 2009.

A Work about Breyten Breytenbach

Jolly, Rosemary. *Colonization, Violence, and Narration in White South African Writing: André Brink, Breyten Breytenbach, and J. M. Coetzee.* Athens: Ohio University Press, 1996.

Brink, André (1935–) *novelist, essayist, playwright*

André Brink, a white South African, writes in Afrikaans, a national South African language derived from Dutch. His first two novels, *A Dry White Season* (1969) and *Looking on Darkness* (1973), were banned because of their political implications, which prompted Brink to write in English as well.

Brink is part of the Sestiger group (also known as the Sixtyers), a loose network of Afrikaans writers who began their careers in the 1960s and whose works combine Afrikaans literature with European literary trends and an antiapartheid political consciousness. The Sestigers depicted sexual and moral matters and examined the political system in a way that rapidly antagonized the traditional Afrikaner reader. The group opposed the rising authoritarianism of South Africa and provided a voice against racism in the language of the dominant National Party. Brink's works are the most politically committed of the group's collective writings, which led to many of his works being banned until the end of apartheid in the early 1990s.

Much of Brink's work deals with the structures that informed apartheid, such as slavery, interracial relationships, and abuse of police power. In *Cape of Storms* (1992), he uses allegory and myth, which he calls "African magical realism," to depict a historical relationship and the social transition of South Africa. Some critics saw this book as a confused search for identity. His later book, *On the Contrary* (1993), seemed to have an easier time finding its voice within history, perhaps because of Brink's narrative technique, which is based in the oral tradition of African culture. The narrator, Estienne Barbier, speaks to an imaginary woman—an escaped slave whose name might be Rosette and who might or might not exist. The doubt and lack of permanence inherent in the narrator's tale determines the reader's perception of Barbier's life. Her stories, as Brink tells them, seem to determine the content and style of human lives.

Another of Brink's texts, *The Rights of Desire* (2001), deals with racial conflicts. The protagonist, Ruben Olivier, a 65-year-old librarian, is cared for by his black housekeeper, Magrieta, and Antje of Bengal, the ghost of a 17th-century slave who was executed for murdering her master and his wife. Olivier's children force him to take in a lodger, who appears to bring Olivier out of the books and into life. Olivier, thus, represents an Africa that needs to be brought out of the past and into the present.

Brink is emeritus professor of literature at the University of Cape Town. In April of 2000, he received two literary awards: the Hertzog Prize for Afrikaans Literature and the National Book Journalist of the Year award. Brink had previously won the Hertzog Prize in 1994, but turned it down because, he said, "at the time the Akademie appeared to be wholly 'untransformed' and unrepentant about it [apartheid]. To accept the prize seemed like allowing myself to be co-opted into an establishment (the cultural wing of the apartheid regime) with which I could not accept to be identified" (*Monday Paper*). He has now accepted the award because the academy can no longer represent the "old Africaner establishment because that establishment no longer exists" (*Monday Paper*).

Other Works by André Brink

The Blue Door. London: Harvill Secker, 2007.
A Chain of Voices. New York: Morrow. 1982.
A Dry White Season. New York: Morrow. 1980.
A Fork in the Road. London: Harvill Secker, 2009.
Other Lives. Napierville, Ill.: Sourcebooks Landmark, 2008.
Praying Mantis. London: Harvill Secker, 2005.
Rumors of Rain. Napierville, Ill.: Sourcebooks Landmark, 2008.
Writing in a State of Siege. New York: Summit Books. 1983.

Works about André Brink

"André Brink Wins Literary Double." *Monday Paper* (University of Cape Town) 19:12, May 8–15, 2000.
Jolly, Rosemary Jane. *Colonization, Violence, and Narration in White South African Writing: André Brink, Breyten Breytenbach, and J. M. Coetzee.* Athens: Ohio University Press, 1996.

Brinkmann, Rolf Dieter (1940–1975) *poet, short story writer*

Rolf Dieter Brinkmann was born in Vechta, Germany. After completing high school, he worked in a variety of temporary jobs. He began writing at a young age and published his first collection of poems in 1962. He studied at the Teachers' College in Cologne for two years before dropping out. In the late 1960s, Brinkmann edited and translated three anthologies of American post–beat-generation poets. He studied at the Villa Massimo in Rome from 1972 to 1973 with a scholarship from the German government and in 1974 was a visiting lecturer at the University of Texas. The following year, he was killed in London by a hit-and-run driver.

American beat and underground poetry were Brinkmann's heaviest literary influences. The leading German-language pop poet of his day, he helped introduce American pop culture to his country. Brinkmann hoped to free German society from inhibitions and constraints. His poems exhibit a thematic and stylistic break from German tradition. Brinkmann used everyday speech geared to the senses to describe the transitory occurrences of daily life. Scholar Peter Demetz explains that Brinkmann "wanted to quicken the demise of old forms and metaphysical attitudes by a new kind of imagism 'catching momentary impressions' in 'snapshots,' precise, firm, and 'translucent'; he advocated 'no more big emotions,' but 'small momentary excitations.'"

Largely ignored in his lifetime, Brinkmann attained fame after his death. His last collection of poems *Westwärts 1 & 2* (*Westward 1 & 2*, 1975), published posthumously, won the Petrarca Lyric Prize and became a best seller. In the 1980s, critics recognized Brinkmann as a precursor of postmodernism and an articulator of his generation's consciousness.

Another Work by Rolf Dieter Brinkmann

Keiner weiß mehr. Berlin: Kiepeheuer & Witsch, 1968.

A Work about Rolf Dieter Brinkmann

Schafer, Jorgen. *Pop-literatur: Rolf Dieter Brinkmann und das Verhaltnis zur Popularkultur in der Literatur der Sechziger Jahre.* Stuttgart: M & D Verlag fur Wissenschaft und Forschung, 1998.

Broch, Hermann (1886–1951) *novelist, dramatist*

Herman Broch was born to Jewish parents in Vienna, Austria. His father Josef Broch, a flannel merchant, and his mother Johanna Schnabel were both wealthy. In 1904, Broch graduated from the kaiserlich-königlich Staats-Realschule (Imperial and Royal State Secondary School). Acceding to his father's wishes, Broch studied to be a textile engineer at the Spinning and Weaving School in Alsace. He also studied philosophy and mathematics for a semester at the University of Vienna. In 1909, he converted to Catholicism to marry Franziska von Rothermann, a sugar heiress. He became director of his father's Teesdorf textile factory that same year.

As part of the Vienna intellectual scene, Broch became concerned with the disintegration of values. Influenced by FRIEDRICH NIETZSCHE and IMMANUEL KANT, Broch published his first articles on philosophy in 1913. In 1925, he resumed his study of mathematics and philosophy at Vienna University. Three years later, he left the Teesdorf factory to write full time. His first major work was the trilogy *Die Schlafwandler* (*The Sleepwalkers,* 1930–32). He wrote several novels, dramas, and essays in the 1930s, but his works did not fare well financially, due to opposition from the anti-Semitic government. Broch was arrested by Nazis in 1938, but influential friends arranged for his emigration to the United States. In America, Broch wrote his best-known novel, *Der Tod des Vergil* (*The Death of Virgil,* 1945), a lyrical prose recounting of the last hours of the famous poet's life.

Broch's powerful works address the issues of mass psychology, moral decay, ethics, and death. Although an industrialist, he had socialist tendencies and worked to help laborers, needy children, and refugees. He wrote didactic fiction, hoping to improve the condition of humanity and society. In the words of German literary scholar Theodore Ziolkowski, Broch "was conscious of a mission in life, to which he devoted himself with absolute consistency and an almost messianic zeal" (*Herman Broch,* 1964).

Other Works by Herman Broch

The Guiltless. Translated by Charles Wharton Stark. New Haven, Conn.: Yale University Press, 1974.
The Unknown Quantity. Translated by Willa and Edwin Muir. Marlboro, Vt.: Marlboro Press, 1988.

Works about Herman Broch

Lützeler, Paul Michael. *Hermann Broch: A Biography.* Translated by Janice Fureness. London: Quarter, 1987.
Ziolkowski, Theodore. *Herman Broch.* New York: Columbia University Press, 1964.

Bruman, Simone

See SCHWARZ-BART, SIMONE.

Bryusov, Valery (1873–1924) *poet, novelist, critic*

Valery Yakovlevich Bryusov was born in Moscow, Russia, to an affluent middle-class family. He was educated at Moscow University and could speak and write fluently in several European language, including French, English, and German. He was a fundamental figure in the establishment of the Russian symbolist movement (*see* SYMBOLISM), outlining the movement's aesthetic goals in his book *The Russian Symbolists* (1894). Despite being a prolific poet and novelist, Bryusov today is mostly remembered for his role as the editor of the symbolist publication *Vesy* between 1904 and 1909.

Bryusov's verse has often been described as sophisticated and graceful, yet marked by frequent use of cryptic language that praises sensuous delights and bodily pleasures. *Stephanos* (1906) is perhaps the best known of his poetry collections. In addition to composing his own poetry, Bryusov produced a number of magnificent translations of American, French, and Armenian poets into Russian.

Bryusov wrote two novels, *The Fiery Angel* (1908), a mystical novel that depicts a cult of practitioners of black magic in 16th-century Germany, and *Altar of Victory* (1911–12), an obscure postsymbolist novel.

In 1908, after a bitter disagreement with other symbolist writers, Bryusov disassociated himself from the movement. He devoted himself to teaching and to writing a number of respected scholarly works. After the communist revolution, Bryusov indirectly joined the Bolshevik cause and worked for the Soviet literary establishment as a director of several artistic and educational institutions, mainly as a bureaucratic administrator.

Today, Valery Bryusov is mostly remembered for his initial guidance of the symbolist movement and as a literary scholar. His own works are mainly forgotten and only studied in the context of the symbolist movement. His corpus of literary criticism and translations is still respected and used in Russian academic institutions.

Other Works by Valery Bryusov

Diary of Valery Bryusov, 1893–1905. Translated by Joan Delaney Grossman. Berkeley: University of California Press, 1980.

The Republic of the Southern Cross and Other Stories. Translated by Stephen Graham. New York: Hyperion Press, 1977.

A Work about Valery Bryusov

Grossman, Joan Delaney. *Valery Bryusov and the Riddle of Russian Decadence.* Berkeley: University of California Press, 1985.

Büchner, Georg (1813–1837) *dramatist*

Georg Büchner was born in the Hessian village of Goddelau. At the age of three, he moved to Darmstadt with his father, Ernst Karl Büchner, a physician, and his mother, Caroline Louis Reuß Büchner. In 1831, Büchner graduated from the Darmstädter Großherzogliches Gymnasium, one of the finest schools in Hesse, and then studied medicine and natural sciences at the University of Strasbourg. In 1833, he continued his studies at the University of Gießen. Sympathetic with the social misery of the peasant class, he founded a student group committed to radical democratic reform. Büchner anonymously published a pamphlet, *Der Hessische Landbote* (*The Hessian Courier,* 1834), which called for a peasant revolt to end the oppressive rule of the elite class. To avoid arrest, Büchner had to flee to Darmstadt in 1834 and to Strasbourg in 1835.

While at Darmstadt, Büchner wrote the complex historical drama, *Dantons Tod* (*Danton's Death,* 1835). Considered a masterpiece of German literature, this work displays many levels of meaning in its study of the French Revolution and the purpose of history. He later translated two of VICTOR HUGO's works. Büchner's last work, *Woyzeck* (1877), is a drama about an army barber who murders his unfaithful lover. Noted for its originality, the play was a precursor to both expressionism and naturalism in German theater. In 1836, Büchner took a position as a lecturer in comparative anatomy at the University of Zurich. He soon became ill and died in February 1837 from typhoid.

Aside from *Dantons Tod,* all of Büchner's works were published posthumously. His melancholy writing addressed the conflict between the ideals of human freedom and the circumstances of history. Büchner captured the contradictions of his age and in the 20th century became an important influence in the development of German modernism. In his book *Georg Büchner: The Shattered Whole,* scholar John Reddick explains that Büchner's genius stems in part from "the sheer subtlety and complexity of his poetic vision" and "his compulsion to explore questions rather than present answers." The Georg Büchner Prize for literature created by the city of Darmstadt in 1923 is one of the most coveted German literary awards.

Another Work by Georg Büchner

Leonce and Lena. Translated by Hedwig Rappolt. New York: Time and Space Limited, 1983.

A Work about Georg Büchner

Reddick, John, *Georg Büchner: The Shattered Whole.* Oxford: Clarendon Press, 1994.

Bulgakov, Mikhail (1891–1940) *novelist, short story writer, dramatist*

Mikhail Afanasievich Bulgakov was born in Kiev, Ukraine, to Afanasy Bulgakov, a professor of history of religion and a censor, and Varvara Pokrovskaya, a teacher. He was the youngest of six children. When Bulgakov was 16 years old, his father died unexpectedly. Bulgakov studied medicine at the Imperial University of St. Vladimir in Kiev, married Tatiana Lappa in 1913, and received his degree in 1916.

Russia was in the middle of World War I when he volunteered to work as a doctor at the front line for the Russian Red Cross. Along with his wife, a trained nurse, Bulgakov worked in the army for several months. Between 1916 and 1919, he intermittently worked as a doctor in villages and towns throughout Russia. After the Bolshevik revolution in 1917, Russia was engulfed by civil war. Bulgakov served as an army doctor in the forces opposing the revolutionary regime and witnessed firsthand the horrors of war. Discharged in 1919, he settled in the city of Vladikavkaz.

Between 1919 and 1920, Bulgakov gave up his medical career to work as a journalist and dramatist. He wrote feuilletons (short literary articles or sketches that appear in the entertainment section of a newspaper), gave lectures on literature, and produced his first plays. Despite these efforts, Bulgakov and his wife lived in poverty. They survived by cutting and selling Bulgakov's golden chain, given to him by his father, piece by piece. During the summer of 1921, Bulgakov attempted to emigrate from Russia, now controlled by the Communist regime, but health and money problems prevented him from leaving the country. He moved to Moscow, where he lived for the rest of his life.

In 1924, Bulgakov published the first part of *White Guard,* a novel largely based on the experiences during his service in the army at the time of the Russian civil war. Set in Kiev, the novel describes the war's effect on a middle-class family. *White Guard* was not published in its entirety in the Soviet Union until the 1960s, but the complete text, edited by Bulgakov, was published in Paris in 1929. He also published his first collection of short stories, *Diaboliad,* during the same period. Between 1925 and 1927, Bulgakov also published individual short stories based on his experiences as a doctor before and during the war. These stories were later compiled as *Notes of a Young Doctor.*

In 1925, Bulgakov published a novella, *Heart of a Dog.* Bulgakov tells a tale of a stray dog that gains human intelligence when a Moscow professor transplants human glands into the animal's body. The work's elements of surrealism were offensive to Communist orthodoxy of the time and brought Bulgakov under close government scrutiny.

From 1927 until his death in 1940, Bulgakov was in constant conflict with government censors. According to the official Big Soviet Encyclopedia, Bulgakov was considered as a "slanderer of Soviet reality" because of his satirical treatment of the Soviet regime and government officials. Bulgakov continued to work in various theaters in spite of the censorship, but by 1929 his plays *Days of the Turbins, Zoya's Apartment,* and *The Crimson Island* were officially banned. In despair, Bulgakov burned all of his manuscripts. Ill and poverty stricken, he wrote a letter to Joseph Stalin, the leader of the Soviet Union, requesting permission to leave the country, stating, "there is no hope for any of my works" in Russia. His petition was denied; instead, he was granted a minor position in a Moscow theater.

Between 1928 and 1940, Mikhail Bulgakov wrote his most famous and complex novel *The Master and Margarita*. Now considered a major masterpiece of Russian literature, the novel remained unpublished until 1966, more than 25 years after its completion.

After an extended illness that resulted in kidney failure, Bulgakov died in 1940 at the age of 49. Shortly before his death, Bulgakov suffered a nervous breakdown. He eventually lost his sight and his ability to speak and communicated with his wife through gestures. Bulgakov completed *The Master and Margarita* on his deathbed. He did not achieve his current reputation as one of the most influential Russian writers until after his death.

Critical Analysis

As Bulgakov admitted in his diaries, *The Master and Margarita* was mostly influenced by NIKOLAI GOGOL, an earlier master of Russian mysticism. Besides being a devastating political satire, the novel is an allegory of good and evil. The work's main character, Satan, appears in the guise of a foreigner and self-proclaimed black magician named Woland. Along with a talking black cat and a "translator" wearing a jockey's cap and cracked pince-nez, Woland wreaks havoc throughout literary Moscow. The parallel narrative in the work centers on Master, a writer driven to insanity by criticism and political persecution, and his unpublished book about Pontius Pilate. Irreducible to a single theme, *Master and Margarita* comments on authorship, religion, spirituality, politics, and the role of an individual in a socially repressive society.

During the early 1950s, the monument of Nikolai Gogol's grave was renovated by the government. Bulgakov's widow purchased the original headstone and placed it on the grave of her husband. Bulgakov had referred to Gogol as a teacher, writing in one of his letters, "Teacher, cover me with your heavy mantle." The request came true after Bulgakov's death.

Other Works by Mikhail Bulgakov

Black Snow. Translated by Michael Glenny. New York: Harvill Press, 1999.

The White Guard. Translated by Michael Glenny. Chicago: Academy Chicago Publishers, 1995.

Works about Mikhail Bulgakov

Curtis, J. A. E. *Mikhail Bulgakov: A Life in Letters and Diaries.* New York: Overlook Press, 1992.

Proffer, Ellendea. *A Pictorial Biography of Mikhail Bulgakov.* Ann Arbor, Mich.: Ardis, 1984.

Bunin, Ivan (1870–1953) *poet, novelist, short story writer, translator*

Ivan Alexeyevich Bunin was born in Voronezh, Russia, to poor provincial aristocrats Alexei and Ludmila Bunin. The family situation of the Bunins was in constant jeopardy because of the father's heavy drinking and gambling. In 1881, Bunin was accepted into a small grammar school where he received a classical education suitable for entry into the civil service. Bunin's brother, Julian, joined the socialist cause, for which he was sent into exile by government authorities. Bunin briefly joined his brother's revolutionary clique, but he was ultimately disenchanted with politics and left revolutionary circles to concentrate on his writing.

Bunin first published his poems in 1887 and released his first volume of poetry in 1891. To earn money, Bunin worked as a translator. In 1899, he completed translations of the English poet George Gordon, Lord Byron and the American poet Henry Wadsworth Longfellow that were so successful that Bunin was awarded prestigious Pushkin Prize in 1903. Inspired by his friendships with ANTON CHEKHOV and MAXIM GORKY, Bunin turned to prose. Bunin's fiction, influenced by IVAN TURGENEV and LEO TOLSTOY, often addresses the dynamics of family and the social position of an individual in rapidly changing Russia. The revolution of 1905 had a dramatic effect on Bunin: He saw the growing power of the Bolsheviks as a threat to Russian social and cultural traditions.

Despite Bunin's aversion to radical reform, his prose often exposes social injustices. In the internationally acclaimed novel *The Village* (1910), Bunin reveals the horrors of peasant life in Russia. In *Dry Valley* (1911), Bunin analyzes the degeneration of family order and economic stability among the aristocratic gentry in provincial Russia. Bunin's themes, however, are not limited to a social agenda. In his collection of short stories, *The Gentleman from San Francisco* (1915), Bunin's thematic focus explores moral decay, death, and pride. Bunin's fiction is marked by a delicate understanding of human nature, as well as by a keen awareness of the social environment.

As a result of the Bolshevik revolution, Bunin left Russia for France in 1919. In France, he continued his prolific output of prose. *The Well Days* (1930), Bunin's autobiographical novel, was hailed as a masterpiece by a number of critics. In 1933, Bunin was awarded the Nobel Prize in literature.

Bunin lived the rest of his life in Paris, where he died in 1953. His contribution to Russian literature is immeasurable. His elegant prose, combined with lively poetic diction, is remarkable for its literary value, as well as for its social commentary and insight.

Other Works by Ivan Bunin

Edited and translated by Thomas Gaiton Marullo. *Cursed Days: A Diary of Revolution*. Chicago: Ivan R. Dee, 1998.
The Life of Arseniev: Youth. Translated by Gleb Struv and Hamish Miles. Evanston, Ill.: Northwestern University Press, 1994.
Sunstroke: Selected Stories of Ivan Bunin. Translated by Graham Hettlinger. Chicago: Ivan R. Dee, 2002.

Works about Ivan Bunin

Marullo, Thomas Gaiton. *If You See the Buddha: Studies in the Fiction of Ivan Bunin*. Evanston, Ill.: Northwestern University Press, 1998.
Woodward, James B. *Ivan Bunin: A Study of His Fiction*. Chapel Hill: University of North Carolina Press, 1980.

Burkart, Erika (Erika Halter)
(1922–2010) *poet, novelist*

Erika Burkart was born in Aarau, Switzerland. Her father was a writer, hunter, and adventurer. Burkart became a schoolteacher and taught at a primary school from 1942 to 1952. At age 30, however, she gave up teaching to write full time and lived in isolation to better connect with nature—the inspiration for her writing.

Burkart's early volumes of poetry include *Der dunkel Vogel* (*The Dark Bird*, 1953) and *Die gerettete Erde* (*The Saved Earth*, 1960). These collections convey her belief in the divinity of nature and her empathy with the natural world. Burkart's reputation increased after she won the Annette von Droste-Hülshoff Prize in 1957. Her poems in the 1960s express her anxiety about the threats to nature. Her first novel *Moräne* (1970) vividly describes the Swiss countryside and, with its attention to the beauties of nature, reflects the influence of the French writer MARCEL PROUST. Burkart's later works show her continued affinity and concern for the landscape. She was widely admired for her commitment to ecology and her efforts to heal the rift between humanity and nature.

Another Work by Erika Burkart
Der Weg zu den Schaffen. Zurich: Artemis, 1979.

A Work about Erika Burkart
Rudin-Lange, Doris. *Erika Burkart, Leben und Werk*. Zurich: Juris Druck and Verlag, 1979.

Busia, Abena (1953–   ) *poet, essayist, scholar*

Abena Busia was born in Ghana, daughter to the former prime minister. As a youth her family was forced into exile following a coup d'état. Her personal history is marked by the experience of exile, as she traveled the world encountering other people of African descent in the Americas and Europe. Her focus became the points of cultural connection within the African Diaspora (the scattering of African peoples throughout the world through slavery). She received her Ph.D. from Oxford, writing her dissertation on images of Africa in the colonial imagination.

Her collection of poems, *Testimonies of Exile* (1990), speaks to multiple experiences of exile. Her poetry expresses the complexity of her cultural experience: She dresses in traditional Ghanaian attire and speaks with a British accent that reveals the history of colonization yet never betrays the pulsating rhythms and culture of her native Africa.

As a professor she has taught at Yale, UCLA, and University of Ghana and is currently an associate professor at Rutgers University. Much of her recent work focuses on black feminism, exploring the issues of identity, race, and politics. She is currently the codirector of *Women Writing Africa*, a Ford Foundation literary project of the Feminist Press that publishes African women's written and oral narratives.

Another Work by Abena Busia

"What Is Your Nation? Reconnecting Africa and Her Diaspora through Paule Marshall's *Praisesong for the Widow*." In Cheryl Wall, ed., *Changing Our Own Words: Essays on Criticism, Theory, and Writing by Black Women*. London: Rutgers University Press, 1989.

Cabrera Infante, Guillermo (G. Cain)

(1929–2005) *novelist, essayist*

Cabrera Infante was born in Gibara, Cuba. His father was a journalist and typographer. Both of his parents were leaders in the then-underground Cuban Communist Party. When Cabrera Infante was 14 years old, his parents were arrested for holding secret political meetings in their home and spent three months in jail. This infringement on their freedom gave Cabrera Infante a strong dislike for authority. Even after the Cuban revolution, when he was given a number of prestigious literary appointments, he was still unable to abide government censorship and control.

Because his father had lost his job, after Cabrera Infante's parents were released from jail, the family was forced to move to Havana. The urban culture and nightlife of Havana affected Cabrera Infante enormously, and the city at night became the setting for his most famous novel, *Three Trapped Tigers* (1967).

When he was 18, he read *El señor presidente* by Guatemalan novelist Miguel Angel Asturias (1899–1974). Cabrera Infante decided that if Asturias was considered a writer, he could be one too, and he began to write short stories and sketches. During the next few years, he published his writing in and founded several small magazines. At age 23, he was jailed for what the government called "publishing profanities in English." When he was forbidden to publish anything using his name, he assumed the pseudonym G. Cain and continued to write and publish until the Cuban revolution.

It was not until Cabrera Infante was sent to Brussels as a cultural attaché at the Cuban embassy that he completed and published *Three Trapped Tigers,* which gained him international attention. In this book, Cabrera Infante uses humor and wordplay to challenge every type of authority, even the authority of language itself. The book is written using a great deal of Cuban slang, undermining the authority of standard literary Spanish. Cabrera Infante's idiomatic language captures the flavor of nightlife in prerevolutionary Havana one evening in 1958. On first reading, the book appears to be a series of unrelated episodes that are unified only by their setting. However, on careful examination, it becomes obvious that the book is carefully structured so that each episode corresponds to a biblical story, beginning with a creation story and moving on to stories that correspond to the fall from the Garden of Eden, the events related to the Tower of Babel, and the apocalypse. This structuring is both profound, giving depth to the frivolous scenes of nightlife, and irreverent, proposing a highly unorthodox commentary on the Bible and society.

Infante's Inferno (1984), his second novel, centers on a single character. The book follows a young boy growing up in Havana and is semiautobiographical. It focuses on the loves and erotic adventures of the narrator, who claims to be a modern-day Don Juan. The book begins when the boy is 12 years old and follows him, as he matures, through a series of frivolous relationships. Finally, as an adult, he finds an exalted and ideal form of love. Like Cabrera Infante's other works, this book is filled with game playing, literary allusion, and humor. However, it also established him as one of the great erotic writers of Latin America.

Cabrera Infante was a major proponent of interpreting books based on the text alone, without relying on historical context. He believed that once a fact is placed into a work of fiction, it is no longer connected to the reality that may have inspired its author to create it. This idea, combined with his playful literary style, made him one of the major proponents of "art for art's sake" in 20th-century Latin American literature.

Other Works by Guillermo Cabrera Infante

Guilty of Dancing the Chachacha. Translated by the author. New York: Welcome Rain Publishers, 2001.
Holy Smoke. New York: Harper & Row, 1985.
View of Dawn in the Tropics. Translated by Suzanne Jill Levine. New York: Harper & Row, 1978.

Works about Guillermo Cabrera Infante

Hall, Kenneth E. "Cabrera Infante as Biographer." In *Biography* 19:4 (Fall 1996): 394–403. Hawaii: University of Hawaii Press, 1996.
Souza, Raymond D. *Guillermo Cabrera Infante: Two Islands, Many Worlds.* Austin: University of Texas Press, 1996.

Caeiro, Alberto
See PESSOA, FERNANDO.

Cain, G.
See CABRERA INFANTE, GUILLERMO.

Calvino, Italo (1923–1985) *novelist, short story writer, journalist*

Born in Santiago de las Vegas, Cuba, Italo Calvino is the son of Mario Calvino and Eva (Mameli) Calvino, both tropical agronomists. Calvino grew up on the family farm in San Remo, Italy, where his father grew tropical fruit for experimentation and acted as a curator for a botanical garden. Early on, Calvino was enchanted by Rudyard Kipling's stories. He enrolled in the University of Turin with plans to study agronomy, but his plans changed in the early 1940s when he joined the Italian resistance in World War II to fight against the Nazis and fascists.

After the war, Calvino resumed studies at the University of Turin in 1945, this time focusing his attention on literature. He wrote his thesis on novelist Joseph Conrad. In 1945, Calvino combined writing with his wartime efforts by contributing to leftist newspapers such as *Il Politecnico*. He produced his first novel, *The Path to the Nest of Spiders* (1947), two years later. The book, which won him the Premio Riccione award, is based on his time as a partisan fighter, yet it retains an innocence that is part of much of his early narratives. "The problems of our time appear in any story I write," Calvino told the *New York Times Book Review* in 1983.

The Path to the Nest of Spiders lacks the grimness of much of Italian neorealism, both in fiction and in films, partly because of an exuberant, picaresque flavor for which Calvino is indebted to his boyhood reading of Robert Louis Stevenson's *Kidnapped* and *Treasure Island*.

Other notable works followed, including the collection, *Short Stories* (1958) and a three-volume edition of *Italian Folktales* (1956). In his introduction to the latter, Calvino states, "Folktales are real. These folk stories are the catalog of the potential destinies of men and women, especially for that stage in life when destiny is formed, i.e., youth." Calvino's stories and novels use elements of fantasy and fable, displaying the influence of Italian folktales and other traditional narratives. In one of his best-known novels, *Invisible Cities* (1972), for example, an imaginary Marco Polo describes the cities of his empire to Kublai Khan.

One of his most popular novels with readers in the United States was *If on a Winter's Night a Traveler* (1979). In this work, the protagonist is the reader. Calvino's characters are highly self-conscious, and his novels are self-referential. Irish author Silas Flannery, one of the characters in *If On a Winter's Night a Traveler,* states, "I have had the idea of writing a novel composed only of beginnings of novels. The protagonist could be the reader who is continually interrupted."

At his death in 1985, Italo Calvino was the best-known and most-translated contemporary Italian writer. He has accumulated numerous honors and accolades through the span of his career, earning the Italian equivalent of the Pulitzer Prize in literature in 1972.

Critical Analysis

Calvino's greatest works are acts of pure imagination, spinning folktales and ancient fables into modern, sometimes postmodern, fantasies and allegories that touch on both the crisis of identity and art in the contemporary world. After a series of poorly received realist novels written during the 1940s, Calvino wrote, "I began doing what came most naturally to me—that is, following the memory of the things I had loved best since boyhood. Instead of making myself write the book I *ought* to write, the novel that was expected of me, I conjured up the book I myself would have liked to read, the sort by an unknown writer, from another age and another country, discovered in an attic."

The result of this epiphany was *Il visconte dimezzato* (*The Cloven Viscount,* 1952). In it, Calvino focuses on the Viscount Medardo who, on his way to the Turkish wars, is split in half with a cannonball at a battle in Bohemia. One half of Medardo is a savage tyrant who returns to his people in order to split everyone in half, to cut flowers in half, and to cut animals in half. He hates the world and everything in it that is not "halved." The other half of Medardo is a pious and saintly beggar who takes his halfness as a signal to respect everyone else who lacks another half; however, he is so saintly that he only succeeds in irritating people and his preaching bores them. Calvino follows the two halves through the novel; they seek the same girl, with whom they both fall in love, and they inhabit the same semi-feudal parcel of land. They do so until a dénouement that reflects the real nature of Medardo and closes the circle of the story.

Calvino is also interested in the nature of reading itself. *In Se una notte d'inverno unviaggiatore* (*If on a Winter's Night a Traveller*), he alternates the opening chapters of 10 different stories, all written in radically different styles. He opens with a man's discovering that the copy of the novel he has recently purchased is defective, a Polish novel having been included between its pages. When the man returns to the bookshop, he meets a young woman, and they find out that their texts are 10 excerpts that parody the popular genres of contemporary fiction. Of the novel, one critic writes, "Calvino attempts to shift the focus of the reader from the words in his novel and other novels that speak about life to the life that those words show; he tries to alert the reader to the dangers of unrestrained academic analysis while also exposing the reader to this threatened form of entertainment in order to save the pleasure of reading from being destroyed." Calvino sees writing and reading as "pure" acts of equal imagination which are in danger of losing their power in the contemporary world.

Other Works by Italo Calvino

Mr. Palomar. Translated by William Weaver. San Diego: Harcourt Brace Jovanovich, 1985.

Under the Jaguar Sun. Translated by William Weaver. Harvest Books, 1990.

Works about Italo Calvino

Gracia, Jorge. *Literary Philosophers: Borges, Calvino, Eco.* London: Routledge, 2002.

McLaughlin, Martin. *Italo Calvino.* Edinburgh: Edinburgh University Press, 1998.

Weiss, Beno. *Understanding Italo Calvino.* Columbia: University of South Carolina Press, 1995.

Campos, Alvaro de
See PESSOA, FERNANDO.

Camus, Albert (1913–1960) novelist, essayist, playwright

Albert Camus was born in Mondovi, Algeria, on November 7, 1913. Perhaps because he was born to a poverty-stricken family, his education was taken seriously. He attended the university in Algiers, where he became interested in both sports and the theater. He was forced to end his education early, however, by an acute bout with tuberculosis, a disease that continued to plague him throughout his life. The experience of poverty and the fear of death take on major significance in Camus's series of Algerian essays, collected in L'envers et l'endroit (The Wrong Side and the Right Side, 1937), Noces (Nuptials, 1938), and Été (Summer, 1954).

Recovered from his illness, Camus went to work in the early 1950s as a journalist for the anticolonialist newspaper Alger-Républicain, for which he wrote daily articles on the impoverished lives of Arabs in the Kabyles region. He later collected these works in Actuelles III (1958). His journalistic background proved invaluable when he went to France during World War II. While working for the combat resistance network, he began to edit a clandestine journal. The subject of his editorials showed a strong desire to integrate political activism with strict morality.

During the war years, Camus also began to explore what came to be known as his doctrine of the absurd. It was his view that all things in life become meaningless as a result of the fact that the human mind has no rational capacity to understand the experience of death. His novel L'étranger (1942; translated as The Stranger, 1946), for example, explores the concept of alienation. The Myth of Sisyphus (1942; translated 1955) and two plays published in 1944, Cross Purpose (1944; translated 1948) and Caligula (1941; translated 1948), all explore the idea of nihilism.

Although considered an absurdist, Camus had difficulty with the idea that the absurd entailed a lack of morality. His own life and his experiences in occupied France during the war would not allow him to abandon all concepts of moral responsibility. This idea became the focus of Letters to a German Friend (1945). Camus began to rebel against the absurd, seeking ways to create a greater strength of humanity guided by morality. His novel The Plague (1947; translated 1948), for example, details the struggle of those who fight against the bubonic plague, an allegory for the struggle against the evils of war. Instead of focusing on whether or not the battle against evil can be successful, he chooses instead to glorify dignity, as exemplary of humanity's strength in the face of devastation.

Camus also became embroiled in a bitter controversy with fellow philosopher JEAN-PAUL SARTRE as a result of the publication of his controversial essay L'homme révolté (1951; translated as The Rebel, 1954). In this essay, Camus criticized the absolutism of the Christian belief in eternal life in heaven and of the Marxist belief in political utopia. He argued instead that the more moral concept was that of Mediterranean humanism, a doctrine that placed value on nature and temperance in behavior over blind belief and the descent into violence as an acceptable solution to problems. Camus further explores the concept of modern amorality in his novel La chute (The Fall, 1956).

As a playwright, Camus published two political dramas, State of Siege (1948; translated 1958) and The Just Assassins (1950; translated 1958), as well as adaptations of Faulkner's Requiem for a Nun (1956) and DOSTOYEVSKY's The Possessed (1959).

In 1957, Camus was awarded the Nobel Prize for literature. He had become the leading voice for morality and for writing as a means to achieve social change in his generation. He was at the height of his popularity when he died in an automobile accident near Sens, France, on January 4.

Critical Analysis
Camus's The Plague follows the progress of a pestilence that attacks the town of Oran in northern

Africa. The story is told by a narrator who remains nameless throughout most of the novel and whose interest is primarily in the reaction of the townspeople. *The Plague* is an allegorical, philosophical novel that has a good deal more depth and humanity than is usually associated with such works, perhaps because of the humanity inherent in Camus's philosophy. Many critics viewed the novel's title as an allegory for the occupation of France by the Nazis during World War II. Others see the plague as a metaphor for the human condition, stripped of all the trappings that humans impose on reality so as not to have to face it directly. While Camus often bristled at being called an existentialist, his characterization of human existence in this novel certainly deserves the name. Existence, as it is portrayed in *The Plague*, is absurd in the deepest sense of that word. There is no meaning to life beyond what one makes of it; there is no fate or deity to lend relevance to life; the past and the future are mental constructs that people use to avoid facing the naked present and leading what existentialists call an "authentic" existence. Although other writers, such as SAMUEL BECKETT or Jean-Paul Sartre, portray similarly absurd universes, none has Camus's sense of the dignity and courage of humanity in the face of such emptiness.

The plague that besets Oran in the novel whittles life down to its barest essence. The only possible sane response, says the narrator's friend Tarrou, "is to struggle with all our might against death" despite the fact that such a struggle can only result in "a never ending defeat." In ordinary life, without the threat of a plague, people often lose themselves in nostalgia or hope. The past and the future become more real than the present, and people find a multitude of ways—religion, sex, politics, drugs—to ignore the truth that we live for a while, then die. The plague brings the present to the fore, and people see that the only truth and the only reality is humanity, our common struggle against death. Such a struggle is not heroic; it is merely and rightly human. As the narrator says, in the face of the plague the townspeople were "certain that a fight must be put up, in this way or

that, and there must be no bowing down. . . . There was nothing admirable about this attitude; it was merely logical." Along with courage, there is also love. As the plague retreats, the townspeople learn that "if there is one thing one can always yearn for and sometimes attain, it is human love." The narrator says that if in the end some people got what they wanted, it was because "they had asked for the one thing that depended on them solely . . . [humanity's] humble yet formidable love."

Other Works by Albert Camus

Between Hell and Reason: Essays from the Resistance Newspaper "Combat," 1944–47. Translated by Alexandre de Gramont. Middletown, Conn.: Wesleyan University Press, 1991.
The First Man. Translated by David Hapgood. New York: Knopf, 1995.

Works about Albert Camus

Bronner, Stephen Eric. *Camus: Portrait of a Moralist.* Minneapolis: University of Minnesota Press, 1999.
Camber, Richard. *On Camus.* Belmont, Calif.: Wadsworth/Thomson Learning, 2002.
Hawes, Elizabeth. *Camus: A Romance.* New York: Grove Press, 2009.

Canetti, Elias (1905–1994) *novelist, essayist, playwright*

Elias Canetti was born in Ruse, Bulgaria, to a wealthy Jewish merchant family. After the sudden death of his father, he moved with his mother to Vienna, where he learned German, the language he would ultimately choose for his writing.

Canetti produced his first play *Junius Brutus* while studying in Zurich between 1916 and 1921. However, it was during a visit to Berlin in 1928 when, influenced by the ideas of BERTOLD BRECHT, George Grosz, and ISAAC BABEL, Canetti developed the idea for a series of works that would explore human madness. This later became the basis of his novel *Die Blendung* (1935; *The Tower of Babel*, translated 1947 and 1964). The tale of a madman who only feels at home with his books and shuns human contact in any form, the novel was banned by the Nazis as subversive but was well received internationally after World War II.

In 1927, another event influenced Canetti's writing: A crowd of angry protestors burned down the Palace of Justice in Vienna, and Canetti was caught up in the mob. Later, he turned this incident into the basis for his best-known book, *Crowds and Power* (1960), a fictional study of death, disordered society, and mass movements. Drawing not only on his own experience but also on history, folklore, and mythology, this work received critical acclaim that culminated in Canetti's receipt of the Nobel Prize in literature in 1981.

In his later years, Canetti returned to his focus on death. He wrote three largely autobiographical works, including *Die gerettete Zunge* (1978; *The Rescued Tongue,* translated 1980) about his father's death. He lived modestly in Hampstead, England, avoiding critical attention as much as possible to the point of writing his own diary in a code so that intrusive readers would not be able to understand it after his death.

Other Works by Elias Canetti
Crowds and Power. Translated by Carol Stewart. New York: Continuum Pub Group, 1982.
The Play of the Eyes. Translated by Ralph Manheim. New York: Farrar, Straus & Giroux, 1986.
The Wedding. Translated by Gitta Honegger. New York: PAJ Publications, 1986.

A Work about Elias Canetti
Falk, Thomas H. *Elias Canetti.* Boston: Twayne, 1993.

Capécia, Mayotte (1928–1953) *novelist*
Mayotte Capécia was born in Carbet, Martinique, but spent most of her adult years in France. Barely able to read when she arrived in Paris in 1946, Capécia published her first novelette, *Je suis Martiniquaise (I Am a Martinican Woman)* in 1948. According to *Mayotte Capécia, ou l'alienation selon*

Fanon (1999), Capécia drew on a lover's manuscript and used several ghostwriters and editors to construct her novelettes.

Je suis martiniquaise and *La Négresse blanche* (*The White Negress,* 1950), her second novelette, explore themes of miscegenation, racial identity, and exile. They also examine people in Martinique and Guadeloupe during the German occupation of France in World War II. FRANTZ FANON criticized both works for exemplifying the hatred of blacks and used them as examples of Caribbean alienation. Others have also criticized the novels for positioning whites as superior.

Counterattacks in defense of Capécia's work have since surfaced, acclaiming their exploration of race relations in the West Indies. In a 1998 review in *World Literature Today,* Robert P. Smith Jr., asserts, "in spite of their date, Capécia's novelettes remain contemporary in today's complex world of illusion and reality."

Another Work by Mayotte Capécia
I Am a Martinican Woman & The White Negress. Translated by Beatrice Stith Clark. Pueblo, Colo.: Passeggiata Press, 1997.

Works about Mayotte Capécia
Hurley, E. Anthony. "Intersections of Female Identity or Writing the Woman in Two Novels by Mayotte Capécia and Marie-Magdeleine Carbet." *French Review* 70, no. 4 (1997): 575–586.
Sparrow, Jennifer. "Capécia, Conde and the Antillean Woman's Identity Quest." *Journal of the Association of Caribbean Women Writers and Scholars* 1 (1998): 179–187.
Stith Clark, Beatrice. "Who was Mayotte Capécia? An Update." *CLA Journal* 39, no. 4 (1996): 454–457.

Carey, Peter (1943–) *novelist*
Peter Carey was born in Bacchus Marsh, Victoria, Australia. He studied chemistry at Monash University but failed his first-year examinations and dropped out of college. Carey then found work as an apprentice writer in an advertising agency in

Melbourne, and this became the turning point in his life. At the agency, Carey met writers and playwrights, especially Barry Oakley, who would forever influence him. Oakley introduced Carey to the works of writers such as James Joyce, William Faulkner, and SAMUEL BECKETT, which had a powerful influence on Carey's writings. Carey next worked in advertising agencies in London and Sydney before settling down in New York in the late 1980s.

Carey's novels are often described as a mix of seriousness and surrealism. His preference for the macabre and the unusual is exemplified by the assortment of strange and tormented characters in his stories, such as the minister in the grip of a gambling compulsion in *Oscar and Lucinda* (1988). The absurdity of the characters' internal world is complicated by their actual situations in the external world in which they live. Through the clever twisting of his tales, Carey is able to communicate the phantasmagoric but realistic situations of ordinary human experiences. His stories are sardonic commentaries on the bittersweet and inextricably welded relationship between the individual and the society. The often seedy and shadowy nature of Carey's actors makes it hard for some readers to empathize with their tragic and unfortunate experiences. This controversial nature of Carey's novels makes them compelling and thought-provoking to read.

Carey sees himself as an Australian writer, and his works are predominantly set in Australia, either in the countryside or on the streets of big cities. His characters, however, have a variety of backgrounds and origins. They range from the average man on the street to infamous outlaws. Though most of Carey's characters are fictional figures, he has also used historical materials to reconstruct the life and exploits of certain historical figures, such as Ned Kelly in *The True History of the Kelly Gang* (2000). Ned Kelly was a celebrated outlaw who eluded the police for many years before he was captured and hanged in 1880. An unlikely hero, Kelly is a powerful legendary figure who is admired and respected for his filial piety and loyalty. Many of Carey's protagonists share a similar characteristic—they are

social failures and misfits. By narrating their stories, Carey attempts to show that these characters, through their unconventional behavior and personality, challenge a society that does not endorse difference; it is society's inflexible institutions that make the characters victims within their own societies.

In recent years, Carey has continued to write provocative novels. *My Life as a Fake* (2003) is based on a historical event, an Australian literary hoax of the 1940s. *Theft: A Love Story* (2006) has a great deal in common with JOYCE CARY's *The Horse's Mouth*. The protagonist and principal narrator, a painter named Michael Boone, is a self-described "hateful loathsome beast" driven by his desire to restore his sagging reputation. Most recently, *Parrot and Olivier in America* (2010) focuses on the relationship of a French aristocrat and the poor son of an English printer as they come together in the raucous democracy of the New World.

Critical Analysis

Carey is an accessible writer whose works appeal to a mass audience. Carey wrote several short stories before the publication of his first novel (*Bliss*, 1981). These stories won Carey a large following of fans in Australia, especially among the younger generation. One of these stories is "Crabs," a powerful depiction of the sense of alienation. "Crabs" tells the tale of a young man who transforms himself into a tow truck after he realizes that he and his girlfriend are marooned at the drive-in theater. The young man finally realizes in the end that although he has successfully escaped, he is all alone in the world as is everyone else who is still at the drive-in theater.

Carey's later short stories also examine the theme of estrangement. In "The Fat Man in History," for instance, a fat man finds himself caught in a world that favors slim and muscular bodies. In a postrevolutionary era, where humanity is reduced to forms and shapes of its bodies, the protagonist declares obesity to be subversive and challenges the status quo. Through his misfit central characters, Carey is able to poke fun at the mindless fashion trends of contemporary society where men and women are reduced to mere objects. "The Fat Man in History" was published in a collection of short stories of the same title in 1980.

Bliss, which won the Miles Franklin Award in 1982, is a nightmarish and surrealistic tale of a man who dies three times but is resurrected each time to face new challenges. This novel combines light comedy with cynical jabs at the contemporary situation. The story has a political message, as it laments the role of American companies and popular culture in influencing and changing Australia.

Carey's second novel, *Illywhacker* (1985), which is set in Australia's bushwhacking country, conveys a bleak view of Australian society. The narrator, the 139-year-old Herbert Badgery, represents the first generation of Australia's inhabitants whose desire to make good and succeed in society is not fulfilled. Badgery's failure to market the plow he has invented is an allegory of Australia's own failure to extract itself from its economic crisis. The poignancy of Badgery's experiences is worsened by his observation that, two generations later, his descendants, now pet-shop owners, find themselves imprisoned within metaphorical cage similar to those in which the pets are kept constrained.

The most influential of all Carey's books are those that examine the history of Australia's social outcasts, such as the convicts, the poor, and the gang members. *Jack Maggs* (1997), which won the 1998 Commonwealth Writers Prize, is the tale of a young man who inherits money from a convict. It critiques the oppressive influence of English literary writing on Australian literature and represents an attempt to break free of the English conventions of writing.

Carey gains more recognition with every publication. *The True History of the Kelly Gang* won the 2001 Commonwealth Writers' Prize and 2001 Booker Prize and was shortlisted for the Miles Franklin Award. Anthony J. Hassall, after describing a harrowing death by drowning in the final scene of *Oscar and Lucinda,* remarks, "All of Carey's stories offer such fierce and dangerous

pleasures, and despite the terrors they also enact and arouse, they create a wild, apocalyptic beauty." He sums up Carey as "a tribal teller of tales, whose stories strive to articulate an indigenous Australian mythology needed to replace the cultural narratives of successive colonial masters."

Other Works by Peter Carey

The Big Bazoohley. Illustrated by Abira Ali. New York: Henry Holt, 1995.
Collected Stories. St. Lucia: University of Queensland Press, 1994.
His Illegal Self. New York: Vintage, 2009.
Parrot and Olivier in America. New York: Knopf, 2010.
The Tax Inspector. New York: Vintage, 1993.
Theft. New York: Vintage, 2007.
30 Days in Sydney: A Wildly Distorted Account. London: Bloomsbury USA, 2001.
The Unusual Life of Tristan Smith: A Novel. New York: Vintage, 1996.

Works about Peter Carey

Hassall, Anthony J. *Dancing on Hot MacAdam: Peter Carey's Fiction.* St. Lucia: University of Queensland Press, 1998.
Huggan, Graham. *Peter Carey.* New York: Oxford University Press, 1997.
Snodgrass, Mary Ellen. *Peter Carey: A Literary Companion.* Jefferson, N.C.: McFarland: 2010.
Woodcock, Bruce. *Peter Carey.* In *Contemporary World Writers,* 2nd edition. Manchester, U.K.: Manchester U.P., 2004.

Carpentier, Alejo (1904–1980) *novelist*

Alejo Carpentier was born in Havana to European parents. His father, a French architect, and his Russian mother, a medical student, had been living in Cuba for only two years when Carpentier was born. Carpentier's first language was French, and the family returned to Paris while he was still young, so he received both his elementary and secondary education in French schools. Nevertheless, Carpentier felt very strongly attached to his Cuban roots. All of his literature was inspired by what he felt to be the inner spirit of the indigenous Cuban culture.

Carpentier was obsessed with music and was particularly influenced and inspired by the experimental techniques of Igor Stravinsky. Stravinsky's ballet *The Rite of Spring,* which employs tribal rhythms, awakened Carpentier to the creative resources that Afro-Cuban music and culture offered for use as raw material by avant-garde literature. Carpentier went on to become a distinguished musicologist, and his interest in music guided his literary development throughout his career.

When he returned to Cuba in his early 20s, he did not have much time to write fiction because of his political activities. He joined the resistance against Cuban dictator Machado and, in 1927, was arrested. He spent seven months in jail, which ironically gave him time to begin his first novel, *Ecue-Yamba-O!* (1933), which means "God be praised" in the language of the native Cuban religion of Lucumi. This realistic historical novel depicts the struggles of Africans in the new world; however, the book also includes many scenes of mythic and religious rituals that prefigure MAGIC REALISM, one of Carpentier's key contributions to world literature.

Carpentier was released from jail but was not allowed to leave Cuba. Using forged papers, he escaped and returned to France, where he became involved in surrealism and contributed frequently to ANDRÉ BRETON's journal *Révolution surréaliste.* However, he later rejected the shocking absurdity of surrealism for a literary style that was closer to myth.

Carpentier's historical novel, *The Kingdom of This World* (1949), takes place in early 19th-century Haiti under the rule of the Emperor Henri Christophe, a Haitian man who became ruler of the island after the French were overthrown. It is based on research that Carpentier did when he visited Haiti in 1943. While *The Kingdom of This World* still follows many of the conventions of traditional historical novels, in this book Carpentier first displays his particular style of magic realism, using historical facts as a backdrop for a narrative filled with myth and magic.

In his collection of short stories *War of Time* (1958), Carpentier used the same musical and mythological style to tell four vaguely autobiographical tales in which he explores the theme of how individuals interact with the larger forces of history around them. These stories examine how everyday reality can take on mythic force. For example, in "The Pursuit," which takes place in a Havana concert hall during a Beethoven symphony, a young man listens to the music and waits to be assassinated for betraying the Cuban Communist Party to Machado's forces. The story, which has the plot of an espionage tale, is told in a kind of symbolic montage that is itself a sort of symphony.

After the Cuban revolution, Carpentier became an active member of Castro's government and continued to write lyrical novels that, most important, saw individuals as capable of determining their own fate through acts of everyday magic.

Other Works by Alejo Carpentier
Explosion in a Cathedral. Translated by John Sturrock; introduction by Timothy Brennan. Minneapolis: University of Minnesota Press, 2001.
The Lost Steps. Translated by Harriet de Onis; introduction by Timothy Brennan. Minneapolis: University of Minnesota Press, 2001.

A Work about Alejo Carpentier
Gonzalez Echevarria, Roberto. *Alejo Carpentier: The Pilgrim at Home.* Ithaca, N.Y.: Cornell University Press, 1977.

Castellanos, Rosario (1925–1974)
diplomat, novelist, poet, short story writer, playwright, critic
Born in Mexico City, Rosario Castellanos grew up in the town of Comitán, Chiapas, Mexico, close to the Guatemalan border. She was educated at the University of Mexico, where she eventually taught literature, although her work as a novelist and poet was the major source of her income. Her familiarity with the lives of the Indians of Chiapas and

Guatemala caused her to focus on their plight in many of her works.

Castellanos began her writing career as a poet, publishing her first book of poems, *Trajectory of Dust,* in 1948. She continued to write many volumes of poetry, including *Poetry Is Not You* (1972), which focused on human frailty, the limitations of love, and the problems generated by social injustice. Her first novel, *The Nine Guardians,* first appeared in 1958 and was translated into English in 1970. The story tells of a seven-year-old girl who fights the prevailing exploitation of the indigenous (native) people, as well as social and gender prejudice prevalent in the 1930s in Chiapas. *The Nine Guardians* won the 1958 Chiapas Prize.

Castellanos's involvement in the arts and her efforts on behalf of the Mexican feminist movement and indigenous Mexican women led her to be a cultural promoter at the Institute of Science and Arts in Tuxtla Gutiérrez, Chiapas. Her play, *The Eternal Feminine,* published posthumously in 1975, was first performed in Mexico in 1976 and is considered among the most original and important feminist works of literature in Latin America today.

Castellanos's 1960 collection of short stories, *City of Kings,* which focuses on the deceitful treatment of the Chiapa people by white landowners, won the Xavier Vaillaurrutia prize, and her novel, *Labors of Darkness* (1962), earned the 1962 Sor Juana Inés de la Cruz prize, the 1967 Carlos Trouyet Prize in Letters, and the 1972 Elías Sourasky Prize in Letters. When she accidentally died of electrocution while serving as Mexico's ambassador to Israel, Rosario Castellanos was regarded as Mexico's major 20th-century female novelist, a title she continues to hold.

Another Work by Rosario Castellanos

A Rosario Castellanos Reader. Translated by Maureen Ahern et al. Austin: University of Texas Press, 1988.

A Work about Rosario Castellanos

Bonifaz Caballero, Oscar. *Remembering Rosario: A Personal Glimpse into the Life and Works of Rosario Castellanos.* Translated by Myralyn F. Allgood. Potomac, Md.: Scripta Humanistica, 1990.

Castro, Rosalía de (1837–1885) *poet, novelist*

Rosalía de Castro was born in Santiago de Compostela, a region in the northwest of Spain where Galician, similar to Portuguese, was the dominant dialect. She was illegitimate, the child of Teresa de Castro y Abadía, a Galician from a well-off family, and José Martínez Viojo, a seminarian who eventually rose to become the chaplain of Iria. Castro was raised in the countryside with a peasant family and then "reclaimed" by her mother when she was 13. Thus, her early years gave her the opportunity to learn the folklore and songs of Galicia, while her adolescence introduced her to a more traditional education typical for women of her time: learning how to play music, draw, and speak a foreign language.

At the age of 21, Castro married another Galician, Manuel Murguía, a dwarf who had favorably reviewed her first book of poems, *The Flower* (1857). After returning with her husband to her native Santiago in 1859, she bore six children and lived to bury three of them. Her life was difficult, characterized by illness, poverty, and the frustrations associated with being a woman writer in a male-dominated society.

Although her early work is written in the more widely read Castilian, the Spanish language, Castro later chose to write in her beloved Galician, the musical language in which Spanish medieval poetry was written. However, by the 19th century, Galicia was a poor region that provided many of the servants employed by wealthy Castilians, so her work was not appreciated or read by the majority of people. Critics now believe that writing in Galician most likely limited Castro's audience and postponed her current recognition as one of Spain's major 19th-century poets.

Rosalía de Castro was the author of four novels. The first, *Daughter of the Sea,* was published in 1859, and the last, *The First Madman,* was published in 1881, both touching on the pain experienced by children. During this period she published two volumes of poetry written in Galician, *Galician Songs* (1863) and *New Leaves* (1880), with themes of nature, solitude, and the plight of women and the poor. Her final volume of poems, *On the Shores of the Saar* (1884), expressing the disillusionment of adulthood, was written in Spanish and appeared shortly before she died of cancer.

Although Castro's novels contributed to her fame, her poetry established her talent and success. As noted by Salvador de Madariaga, quoted in *The Defiant Muse: Hispanic Feminist Poets from the Middle Ages to the Present,* Castro's poetry can be considered "the best written in Spain in the nineteenth century."

Another Work by Rosalía de Castro

Poems. Translated by Anna-Marie Aldaz and Barbara N. Gantt. Albany: State University of New York Press, 1991.

Works about Rosalía de Castro

Dever, Aileen. *Radical Insufficiency of Human Life: The Poetry of R. de Castro and J. A. Silva.* Jefferson, N.C.: McFarland & Company, 2000.

Stevens, Shelley. *Rosalía de Castro and the Galician Revival.* London: Tamesis Books Ltd., 1986.

Cattopadhyay, Bankim-Chandra
(Bankim Chandra Chatterji) (1838–1894)
novelist

Bankim-Chandra Cattopadhyay was born in Kantalpara, West Bengal, India. His father worked as a tax collector for the government. Cattopadhyay was the first Indian to graduate from Calcutta University (in 1858) at a time when only British people were enrolled. He worked for the government for 30 years while also writing literature. He founded the literary magazine *Bangadarsan* (Mirror of Bengal) in 1872 and was always very involved in supporting Bengali journalism.

Cattopadhyay started to write poetry but soon turned to the novel. His first attempt at the novel was written in Bengali and submitted for a writing contest; it did not win and has never been published. Cattopadhyay's first published novel, *Rajmohan's Wife* (1864), was written in English and is considered to be a reworking of his earlier unpublished novelette. He published numerous romance novels, which display his ability to rewrite historical moments within romantic and melodramatic contexts. His development of the novel in India had an immense impact, as he rejected the conventional Sanskritized literary movement, which supplanted Perso-Arabic words with Sanskrit ones and developed a more Westernized approach to Indian themes. Western ideas, such as romance and sensibility, were seen to be more important than the Indian sense of duty. This shift comes out most strongly in his depiction of women who are often compelled to transgress convention in the pursuit of love. Their love is tragic, however, because it can never be fully realized. In *Durgesnandini* (1865), for instance, the volatile politics between Pathans and Mughals in 16th-century Bengal is offset by a Pathan princess's refusal to accept racial boundaries in her love. Famous for such historical novels, Cattopadhyay is today viewed as the "father of the Indian novel."

Cattopadhyay is also seen as a national poet. The patriotic poem "Vande Materam" ("I Worship Mother") from his novel *Ānandamāth* (*The Abbey of Bliss,* 1882) was adopted throughout India as its unofficial national anthem in the early decades of the 20th century. It was adopted into a song by another famous Bengali poet RABINDRANATH TAGORE. The novel is a powerful story based on the 1773 resistance against Muslim and British conquerors of India by a group of Hindu hermits.

Cattopadhyay's work has been translated into every major Indian language. In 1884, his novel *Bishabriksa,* was translated into English for publication outside India. In 1892, the British government awarded Cattopadhyay the title of *Ray Bahadur* (Brave leader) in honor of his worldwide literary achievements.

Another Work by Bankim C. Cattopadhyay

Krishnakanta's Will. Norfolk, Conn.: New Directions, 1962.

Cavafy, Constantine P. (1863–1933) *poet*

Constantine P. Cavafy was born in Alexandria, Egypt, on April 29, 1863. He died in Alexandria on the same date in 1933. The son of a wealthy English businessman, he moved with his mother to England after his father's death in 1870. He stayed there for seven years, until the family business folded, causing Cavafy and his family to return to Alexandria in poverty. During his time in England, Cavafy became fluent in English and developed a love of English literature that would ultimately influence his decision to become a poet.

Cavafy's first job in 1885 was as a journalist. During this time, he began to publish a few poems on conventional romantic themes. Eventually, he gained steady employment and continued to write poetry. Between 1891 and 1904, he distributed his poetry exclusively to friends. His collected works did not emerge until two years after his death and did not become well known among English audiences until 1952.

After his death, Cavafy's reputation grew, and his poetry, often referred to as disturbing yet beautiful, began to influence other Greek poets. His poetry is known primarily for its themes of love and longing, as well as for its open expression of homosexuality. Often filled with a sense of nostalgia and regret at the decay of culture and the failure of human aspirations, his works are unsentimental.

Cavafy spent most of his life alone. He developed two short-lived relationships, both with men, which shaped the sense of longing in his poems. He also had a long-term acquaintance with the English novelist E. M. Forster. Cavafy died of cancer in Alexandria. It was reported that his final action was to draw a circle on a sheet of paper and enclose within it a period.

Another Work by Constantine P. Cavafy

Before Time Could Change Them: The Complete Poems of Constantine P. Cavafy. Translated by Theoharis Constantine Theoharis. New York: Harcourt Brace, 2001.

A Work about Constantine P. Cavafy

Keeley, Edmund. *Cavafy's Alexandria.* Princeton, N.J.: Princeton University Press, 1995.

Cela, Camilo José (1916–2002) *novelist, short story writer, essayist*

Camilo José Cela was born in Iria Flavia, Spain, the eldest of seven children in a conservative upper-middle-class home. When he was 20, the Spanish civil war erupted, and he was caught in the siege of Madrid. The horrors he saw at that time became the source for much of the imagery he uses in his later novels. He joined Franco's army and, after the fascists' victory, was given a number of important literary and political positions. His work, however, can be seen as an ironic subversion of some of the regime's principles.

Cela's first novel, *The Family of Pascual Duarte* (1942), has been compared to ALBERT CAMUS's novel *The Stranger. The Family of Pascual Duarte* tells the story of a peasant, Pascual Duarte, who is waiting in jail to be executed. Pascual relates, in a distant and emotionally flat tone, a series of horrible acts that he has committed. Cela uses this contrast to explore existential feelings of disconnection. The novel shows the influence of Pío BAROJA Y NESSI in its terse style and complicated structure, and it has inspired many imitators in modern Spanish prose. It is also one of the precursors of OBJECTIVISMO.

Cela went on to write a number of innovative novels that experimented with structure. *San Camilo 1936* (1969), written entirely in the second person, is a long monologue that depicts life in Madrid just before the outbreak of war.

In 1989, Cela won the Nobel Prize in literature. His novels and essays walk a fine line between representing traditional literary and political modes and ironically undermining them. His address to the Nobel Committee expresses his respect both for tradition and for the need to push against its limits: "Let us never forget that confusing procedure with the rule of Law, just as observing the letter rather than the spirit of the Law, always leads to injustice which is both the source and consequence of disorder."

Another Work by Camilo José Cela
The Hive. Translated by J. M. Cohen in consultation with Arturo Barea. New York: Noonday Press, 1990.

A Work about Camilo José Cela
Kirsner, Robert. *The Novels and Travels of Camilo José Cela.* Chapel Hill: University of North Carolina Press, 1964.

Celan, Paul (Paul Antschel) (1920–1970)
poet, essayist, translator

Paul Celan was born Paul Antschel, the only child of German-speaking Jewish parents, in Cernauti, Romania. Young Celan attended German-speaking school and Hebrew school in his childhood. He shared a passion for German poetry with his mother, Fritzi Antschel, especially the ROMANTICISM of Novalis. Celan went to Paris in 1938 to study medicine and then to the University of Czernowitz to learn romance philology. He was particularly attracted by the poetry of GEORG TRAKL and RAINER MARIA RILKE. During World War II, Celan's parents were killed by the Nazis in a concentration camp. Celan was able to survive by working in a forced labor camp until it was liberated by Russian troops in 1943.

In 1944, Celan moved to Bucharest, Romania, where he worked as a translator and editor for a publishing company. In 1947, he emigrated to Vienna, and the following year, he permanently settled in Paris, where he taught German language and literature at the École Normale Superieure. Celan began writing poetry in the late 1940s to relate his experiences of the Holocaust. He was published in several magazines and newspapers throughout West Germany.

Celan gained critical recognition and acclaim in 1952 with the publication of *Poppy and Memories,* a collection that thematically focused on the Holocaust and the Jewish experience under the Nazi regime. The imagery in the collection is nightmarish and surreal, marked by the underlying violence of the place and time, as can be seen in "Death Fugue," the most famous poem in the collection: "Black milk of morning we drink at you at dusktime . . ./We scoop out a grave in the sky where it is roomy to lie."

During the 1960s, Celan extensively translated French poetry into German. In 1960, he was awarded the prestigious Georg Büchner Prize for his poetry. Celan's mental health deteriorated rapidly during these years; apparently, he could not reconcile his Jewish origins and the Holocaust experience with his love for the German language. Although he visited Israel and frequently introduced Jewish themes in his work, the memory of his suffering and the medium of his poetic expression (German) proved to be utterly irreconcilable. He entered a psychiatric hospital in 1965. After being accused of plagiarism, seemingly without grounds, Celan suffered a complete nervous breakdown. He killed himself by drowning in the Seine at the age of 49.

Paul Celan made a tremendous contribution to the German language and the expression of the Jewish experience during and after the Holocaust. The fragmented syntax and minimalism often found in his verse represents the violence and the shattered world of the Holocaust survivor. He is widely read and studied throughout the world.

Other Works by Paul Celan
Glottal Stop: 101 Poems. Translated by Nikolai Popov. Boston: University of New England Press, 2000.
Selected Poems and Prose of Paul Celan. Translated by John Felsteiner. New York: Norton, 2000.

A Work about Paul Celan

Felsteiner, John. *Paul Celan: Poet, Survivor, Jew.* New Haven, Conn.: Yale University Press, 2001.

Céline, Louis-Ferdinand
(1894–1961) *novelist*

Louis-Ferdinand Céline was born Louis Ferdinand Destouches on May 27, 1894, in Courbevoie to a working-class family. He grew up in Paris, where his mother ran a lace shop. In 1912, he enlisted in the army and served in World War I, where he was severely wounded and left with permanent disabilities. He returned to France to study medicine, going on to become a doctor.

Céline became famous as a writer with the publication of his first novel, *Journey to the End of the Night* (1932; translated 1943). Praised by right-wing extremists, the work was largely based on Céline's own adventures: in the trenches during World War I, running a trading post in Africa, working in a factory in the United States, and returning to Paris to practice medicine. His second novel, *Death on the Installment Plan* (1936; translated 1938), which continues the protagonist's story from *Journey to the End of the Night,* was also a critical success. Céline's popularity stemmed largely from the contemporary nature of his writing and its relevance to the understanding of current events and world situations.

In the late 1930s, Céline traveled to the Soviet Union, where he wrote the first of several notorious anti-Semitic, pacifist pamphlets, declaring his disenchantment with war. He began to focus his writing in an attempt to prevent his country from entering World War II. After the war, Céline was accused of having Nazi sympathies. He fled to Germany, where he remained in exile until 1951.

In all of Céline's works, his characters' lives are filled with failure, anxiety, and nihilism. He had difficulty communicating during his life and sank progressively into depression, madness, and rage. His novels display this through their depictions of giants, paraplegics, and gnomes, as well as graphic visions of dismemberment and murder.

Céline died on July 1, 1961, of a ruptured aneurysm. Though his works remain controversial, his attacks against war have influenced such writers as Henry Miller and Kurt Vonnegut, Jr. His influence on world literature stems largely from his willingness to write about controversial subjects and his innovative style (his use of first-person narrative and slang).

Another Work by Louis-Ferdinand Céline

Ballets Without Music, Without Dancers, Without Anything. Translated by Thomas and Carol Christensen. Los Angeles: Green Integer, 1999.

A Work about Louis-Ferdinand Céline

Hewitt, Nicholas. *The Life of Céline: A Critical Biography.* Malden, Mass.: Blackwell, 1999.

Césaire, Aimé (1913–2008) *poet, teacher, playwright, politician*

Aimé Césaire was born into a family of seven children in Basse-Pointe, Martinique. Césaire's father worked as an accountant for the colonial internal-revenue service, and his mother was a seamstress. After earning a scholarship in 1924, Césaire left his local elementary school to attend the Lycée Schoelcher in Fort-de-France, the capital of Martinique. There Césaire met classmate Léon Damas, who later contributed to NÉGRITUDE, and instructor Octave Manoni, whose theories of colonization Césaire later critiqued.

The top student at Lycée Schoelcher in 1931, Césaire earned a scholarship to Paris's prestigious Lycée Louis-le-Grand. There Césaire read widely, including the works of Marx, FREUD, and the precursors of surrealism, LAUTREAMONT and RIMBAUD. With LÉOPOLD SÉDAR SENGHOR, head of the African students, and Damas, Césaire published *L'Étudiant Noir* (*The Black Student*) in 1934 "for all black students, regardless of origin." Now considered the cofounder of négritude with Senghor, Damas claimed that Césaire first used the word *négritude* in a *L'Étudiant Noir* editorial. The small student newspaper appeared five or six times during the next two years until funding difficulties and French authorities stopped publication.

After taking and passing entrance exams to L'École Normale Supérieure in 1935, Césaire went to Yugoslavia with classmate Peter Guberina. A visit to Martinska, or St. Martin's Island, contributed to notes which became *Cahier d'un retour au pays natal* (*Return to My Native Land*), published in 1939, near the time Césaire became a teacher of classical and modern literature at the Lycée Schoelcher. Themes of black West Indian identity run through this and subsequent works, including *Tropiques*, a quarterly journal founded in 1941 with his wife Suzanne and other Martinican intellectuals. Reading *Cahier d'un retour au pays natal* prompted ANDRÉ BRETON to publish "Un grand poète noir" in a 1943 New York–based French-English review. This essay served as the preface to subsequent editions of the original text.

Césaire lived in Haiti and lectured on French poetry after the Provisional French government, which took over in 1943, sent him there as a cultural ambassador. Working in Haiti gave Césaire enough material to write a celebratory historical study on Haiti and his first play written for the stage, *La tragédie du roi Christophe* (*The Tragedy of King Christophe*, 1963). The play draws on the life of Henri Christophe, one of Haiti's earliest leaders, and employs Shakespearean style and tone.

In 1945 Césaire became Mayor of Fort-de-France on a Communist ticket and the following year was the deputy for Martinique in the French National Assembly. In response to criticism of his critiques of French government, Césaire published *Discours sur le colonialisme* (*Discourse on Colonialism*, 1950). The pamphlet critiques racist tendencies in French government and "universal" values based on white civilization, and it calls for political change.

Césaire continued combining literary endeavors with political activism. The surrealistic style of his poetry prompted praise from JEAN-PAUL SARTRE and criticism from Communist Party members, who called it "decadent." Frustrated with attitudes and actions of the French Communist Party, which Césaire accused of "empire building" in the Third World in a *Lettre à Maurice Thorez* (*Letter to Maurice Thorez*), Césaire founded the Martinican Progressive Party in 1958.

Plays published during the 1960s caused some to consider Césaire one of the leading black dramatists of French expression. *Une saison au Congo* (*A Season in the Congo*, 1966) focuses on the demise of Congolese premier Patrice Lumumba and was not as well received by critics or audiences as Césaire's first play, *La tragédie du roi Christophe*. Césaire's radical adaptation of Shakespeare's *The Tempest* as *Une tempête* (*A Tempest*, 1969) focuses on the relationship between the colonizer and the colonized and uses modern language and three acts instead of five. *Une tempête* initially generated much negative commentary by Western critics but was well received by international audiences when performed.

The younger generation of Martinican writers, including Bernabé, CHAMOISEAU, and Confiant, disagree with Césaire's allegiance to writing black literature in French. As Ernest Moutoussamy remarks in *Aimé Césaire, Député à l'Assemblée Nationale, 1945–1993* (1993), "His poetic discourse is that of a prophet, his political discourse is that of a realist and as such makes room for compromise." Césaire died in April 2008 and was granted a state funeral in Fort-de-France, Martinique. France's president, Nicolas Sarkozy, was in attendance.

Other Works by Aimé Césaire

Aimé Césaire: The Collected Poetry. Translated by Clayton Eshleman and Annette Smith. Berkeley: University of California Press, 1983.

Lyric and Dramatic Poetry, 1946–82. Translated by Clayton Eshleman and Annette Smith. Charlottesville: University Press of Virginia, 1990.

Works about Aimé Césaire

Davis, Gregson. *Aimé Césaire.* Cambridge: Cambridge University Press, 1997.

Hale, Thomas, ed. *Critical Perspectives on Aimé Césaire.* Washington, D.C.: Three Continents Press, 1992.

San Juan, E. *Aimé Césaire: Surrealism and Revolution.* Bowling Green, Ohio: Bowling Green State University Press, 2000.

Chamoiseau, Patrick (1953–   ) *nonfiction and fiction writer*

Patrick Chamoiseau was born in Fort-de-France, Martinique. Educated as a lawyer in Martinique and France, Chamoiseau worked as a full-time probation officer for 15 years. In an interview with James Ferguson, Chamoiseau said, "It sounds terrible, but understanding these people's experiences has helped me hugely as a writer, as it has allowed me to look into aspects of life that you wouldn't normally encounter." By writing evenings, weekends, and holidays, Chamoiseau managed to publish prolifically—novels, memoirs, literary criticism, and a collection of short stories.

Chamoiseau sees himself as a "word scratcher" —novelist or writer—who communicates traditions of créolité. To Chamoiseau, "Créolité tries to restore to the modern-day writer that status of storyteller by breaking down the barrier between the written and spoken French and Creole. If a writer can use Creole, then he's much more in touch with the thoughts and expressions of ordinary people."

Chamoiseau's own multivocal novels explore sociolinguistic realities by juxtaposing French and Creole, producing what Pierre Pinalie calls "Fréole," a nonspoken, partially invented, and playful language. In his first published novel, *Chronique des sept misères* (*Chronicle of the Seven Sorrows,* 1986), he examines the lives and stories of Martinican workers. His second novel, *Solibo magnifique* (*Solibo Magnificent,* 1988), a murder suspense story, allegorizes the Creole oral culture. Themes of slavery, class, and colonialism run through Chamoiseau's fictional works.

Inspired by Edouard Glissant's *Discours antillais,* Chamoiseau collaborated with Raphaël Confiant and Jean Bernabé on "Éloge de la créolité." Published in 1989, the first sentence reads, "Neither Europeans, nor Africans, nor Asians, we proclaim ourselves Creoles." The literary manifesto sparked the French-Antillean Créolité movement by challenging many ideas proposed by another Martinican writer, AIMÉ CÉSAIRE, including the NÉGRITUDE literary movement.

"Éloge de la Créolité" generated much controversy, but it was the novel *Texaco,* published in French in 1992, that more staunchly positioned Chamoiseau as an exceptionally talented, internationally significant writer. In *Texaco,* the character Marie-Sophie Laborieux tells the history of the village of Texaco to save it from an urban planner's intended alterations. *Texaco* won France's prestigious Prix Goncourt the year it was published, prompting the translation of a number of Chamoiseau's works into multiple languages.

Apart from novels, Chamoiseau has published two autobiographical narratives on his childhood in Fort-de-France: *Antan d'enfance* (*Childhood,* 1993) and *Chemin-d'école* (*School Days,* 1994). *Antan d'enfance* explores Chamoiseau's magical experience of childhood and foregrounds his mother, who raised five children amidst poverty. The sequel *Chemin-d'école* introduces readers to Chamoiseau's Francophile and Africanist teachers, as well as the imaginative Big Bellybutton, who tells fantastical stories. Like Chamoiseau's other works, *Chemin-d'école* received accolades: "Imaginative and moving," said the *Washington Post.*

In the 1999 afterword to the English translation of the *Chronicle of the Seven Sorrows,* Linda Coverdale asserted, "Chamoiseau is a free-range writer who tries to keep his language 'open' so that readers will feel its humble, questing flexibility, a kind of remarkable mongrelism that proves perfect for the task at hand: presenting a deftly self-conscious form of Creoleness in this chronicle of 'mouth-memory' telling stories to a word scratcher." His most recent work is the autobiographical trilogy *Une Enfance Créole* (2005–09).

Other Works by Patrick Chamoiseau

Creole Folktales. New York: New Press, 1994.
Seven Dreams of Elmira: A Tale of Martinique. Nashville, Tenn.: St. Albans, 2001.
Strange Words. London: Granta Books, 1998.

Works about Patrick Chamoiseau

McCusker, Maeve. *Patrick Chamoiseau: Recovering Memory.* Liverpool: Liverpool University Press, 2007.

Milne, Lorna. "From Creolite to Diversalite: The Postcolonial Subject in Patrick Chamoiseau's *Texaco.*" In Paul Gifford and Johnnie Gratton, eds., *Subject Matters: Subject and Self in French Literature from Descartes to the Present.* Amsterdam, Netherlands: Rodopi, 2000.

———. "Sex, Gender and the Right to Write: Patrick Chamoiseau and the Erotics of Colonialism." *Paragraph: The Journal of the Modern Critical Theory Group* 24, no. 3 (2001): 59–75.

Shelly, Sharon L. "Addressing Linguistic and Cultural Diversity with Patrick Chamoiseau's *Chemin-d'école.*" *French Review: Journal of the American Association of Teachers of French* 75, no. 1 (October 2001): 112–126.

Char, René (1907–1988) poet

One of the early surrealists, René Char was born in Provence and educated at the University in Aix. A controversial figure, he had a great many admirers and an equal number of detractors. As a writer, Char was a key figure in the surrealist movement, from which he later branched off to pursue his own unique direction. His poetry was marked by its extreme economy of language. As a political figure, he was very active in the French Resistance movement.

Char was most deeply affected and inspired by his experience as the leader of a resistance group in Provence during World War II. He understood the tragic nature of war and the difficult attempts of humanity to achieve freedom. These themes are reflected in his works, such as the poems in his collection *Hypnos Waking* (1956). Unlike the majority of his contemporaries, however, Char does not focus on the disillusionment and despair inherent in war. Instead, he is more concerned with humanity's capacity to hope and to love. What bothered him most was immobility, the lack of change that allowed for the acceptance of the status quo.

Char's major contribution to world literature stems from his use of the written word as a means of bringing about positive solutions to social change. In his introduction to *Hypnos Waking*, Jackson Matthews say that Char "has faced the difficult conditions of human freedom, and understood the role of the imagination in the life of man."

Other Works by René Char

Leaves of Hypnos. Translated by Cid Corman. New York: Grossman, 1973.

Poems of René Char. Translated and annotated by Mary Ann Caws and Jonathan Griffin. Princeton, N.J.: Princeton University Press, 1976.

Works about René Char

Caws, Mary Ann. *René Char.* Boston: Twayne, 1977.

Matthews, Jackson. Introduction to René Char, *Hypnos Waking: Poems and Prose.* New York: Random House, 1956.

Piore, Nancy Kline. *Lightning: The Poetry of René Char.* Boston: Northeastern University Press, 1981.

Chateaubriand, François-René, vicomte de (1768–1848) novelist, nonfiction writer

François-René de Chateaubriand and Jean-Anthelme Brillat-Savarin once met at a restaurant to celebrate the publication of Chateaubriand's *The Genius of Christianity.* The chef surprised the diners by already having prepared a new recipe and named it in honor of the author, thus giving birth to the famous Chateaubriand steak.

Chateaubriand was born to nobility, and he grew up in the castle of Combourg, his family's isolated estate in Brittany. His world was devastated by the French Revolution, which forced him into exile. An avid adventurer with a great interest in American Indians, Chateaubriand visited the United States in 1791 to do research for a book on the massacre of the Natchez and to search for the Northwest Passage. However, his journey took him only as far as Niagara Falls, at which point he returned briefly to France before becoming an émigré and living in England until 1800. While there, Chateaubriand decided to pursue a career as a writer and published his first book, *Essai historique, politique, et moral sur les révolutions anciennes et modernes* (*Historical, Political, and Moral Essays on the Ancient and Modern Revolutions,* 1797). The publication of his book *The Genius of Christianity* (1802; translated 1856), with its frank and honest treatment of its subject matter, brought Chateaubriand's name to the forefront of French literature. In spite of his upper-class background, Chateaubriand worked diligently during the French Revolution to eradicate religious barriers, which he viewed as directly responsible for the severe restrictions levied against the poor and the uneducated. *The Genius of Christianity* was his attempt to restore a lost religion to his people. His *The Martyrs* (1809; translated 1812) celebrates Christianity's triumph over paganism.

In addition, two tragic love stories, the unfinished *Atala* (1801) and *René* (1802), stand as prime examples of the ways in which Chateaubriand utilized the melancholy and exotic descriptions of nature and the language of nostalgia that came to characterize the ROMANTIC movement in French literature. Other works that fall under this style of writing include *Les aventures du dernier des Abencérages* (*The Adventures of the Last of the Abencérages,* 1826), a romance novel set in Spain.

As well as his writing career, Chateaubriand was also politically active. He was appointed by Napoléon in 1803 as secretary of the legation to Rome and promoted, in 1804, as minister to Valaise. However, on hearing of the execution of the duc d'Enghien, he became outraged and resigned from his position. He channeled his anger into becoming a bitter anti-Bonapartist, going on to support the Bourbons. He served as ambassador to London in 1822 and as the minister of foreign affairs from 1823 to 1824.

Chateaubriand abandoned political activity in 1830 to devote the final years of his life to composing his own personal history, which he collected as *Memoirs from Beyond the Tomb* (1849).

Although he was often accused of plagiarism and exaggeration by scholars, particularly in his purportedly factual travel narratives, his richly detailed and evocative language greatly enhanced and influenced the romantic movement. In response to this criticism, Chateaubriand once said, "The original writer is not he who refrains from imitating others, but he who can be imitated by none."

Another Work by François-René vicomte de Chateaubriand

Travels in America. Translated by Richard Switzer, Lexington: University of Kentucky Press, 1969.

Works about François-René vicomte de Chateaubriand

Painter, George Duncan. *Chateaubriand: A Biography.* New York: Knopf, 1978.

Smethurst, Colin. *Chateaubriand, Atala and René.* London: Grant and Cutler, 1995.

Chatterjee, Upamanyu (1959–)
novelist

Upamanyu Chatterjee was born in India. He comes from a family of civil servants, and after completing a degree in English Literature, he joined the Indian Administrative Services (IAS) in 1983. This professional move, however, signifies not only the beginning of Chatterjee's career in writing but also the source behind much of the content of his novels.

While in high school, Chatterjee wrote a play adopted from a Hitchcock story called *Dilemma.* It was never published but won the school drama competition despite its open caricaturing of school rules and regulations. Since then, he has written three novels, all of which have received similar critical and political approval in spite of a style that parodies the state legal systems, in which he also holds a job, and its effect on human behavior.

The novel *English, August: An Indian Story* (1988) and its sequel *The Mammaries of the*

Welfare State (2000) are based on a civil servant's experiences working in small-town politics. The adventures of the protagonist, Augustya, take him from a position of naïveté to cynicism after initiation into the politics of the real world. The sequel continues with the life of Augustya, further exposing the parasitic nature of civil servants and the political system of which they are a part. In addition, *mammaries* is a common "Hinglish" (Hindi-English) mispronunciation of the word *memories*. Thus, Chatterjee begins with a joke by teasing the reader from the moment one encounters the title of his book. The third volume in this trilogy, *Way to Go* (2010), tells in outrageous comic style the story of two dysfunctional brothers, Jamun and Burfi, and their father, Shyamanand.

Chatterjee's novels are told in a relentlessly satirical style that is intended to broaden the concept of comedy. He wishes to go beyond satire, parody, and burlesque. His intent is to provide comic relief from the hypocrisies that are inherent in society by revealing the idiosyncrasies produced when idealism meets with reality.

Other Works by Upamanyu Chatterjee

The Last Burden. New York: Penguin, 1997.
Weight Loss. NewYork: Penguin, 2007.

Chatterji, Bankim Chandra
See CATTOPADHYAY, B(ANKIM)-C(HANDRA).

Chatterji, Sarat Chandra (Sarat Chandra Chattopadhyay)
(1876–1938) *novelist*

Sarat Chandra Chatterji was born in Bengal, India. He was born into a very poor family and did not have the opportunity to pursue a higher education. As a young adult, he spent a number of years wandering all over India dressed as a beggar. Despite these trying early years, Chatterji did eventually reclaim his family responsibilities and started to work as a clerk. During his posting in Burma, he

began writing and was eventually able to achieve enough financial stability to return to India.

Chatterji's writing was influenced by Bengali renaissance literature by BANKIM-CHANDRA CATTOPADHYAY and RABINDRANATH TAGORE. Their focus on the beauty of human life and nature can be found in Chatterji's works. In addition, he was an early proponent of women's rights, and many of his works offer unflinching criticism of the gender inequalities of his time. His novel *Palli Samaj* (Village Society, 1915–16) caused a sensation because of its open acknowledgment of a woman's desire for a man after the death of her husband. His "feminist" novels, however, eventually conformed to social norms despite the revolutionary thoughts expressed in his prose work. Chatterji continued his criticism, however, in such essays as "Narir Mulya" (1922–23) that denounce society's maltreatment of women, especially in middle-class Bengal.

Chatterji also wrote numerous political novels. He wrote *Pather Dabi* (*The Right Way,* 1926) while he was president of the Congress Committee of Howrah District in West Bengal, India. Based on the rebel forces in Burma and Singapore, this novel prescribed violence as the only path for a free India and upheld anti-British sentiments. Much controversy surrounded this work, especially because Chatterji then held a post in the Congress Party, which was then still subject to British authority.

Chatterji's romance novels were a sensational success all over India. Much of his national popularity had to do with the fact that his stories were so often adapted for commercial Hindi (not just Bengali) movies. His first novel *Devadas* (1917) introduces a new type of character in Chandramukhi, a "noble" prostitute. This is a story about the suppression of love and desire by those whom society rejects. Her story also reveals social patriarchy's hypocritical views on female chastity. In *Srikanta* (1917–33), Chatterji's most famous work, the union of a singer-dancer and her lover serves to criticize the institution of marriage by examining its social and ethical definition. *Srikanta* is a partly autobiographical collection of episodes in four volumes.

Even today, Chatterji's Bengali novels are the most often translated works into almost all mainstream Indian languages.

Another Work by Sarat Chandra Chatterji

Devdas and Other Stories. Translated by V. S. Naravane. Ottawa: Laurier Press Ltd., 2000.

A Work about Sarat Chandra Chatterji

Naravane, Vishwanath S. *Sarat Chandra Chatterji: An Introduction to His Life and Work.* New Delhi: Macmillan Company of India, 1976.

Chattopadhay, Sarat Chandra

See CHATTERJI, SARAT CHANDRA.

Chekhov, Anton (1860–1904) *short story writer, dramatist*

Anton Pavlovich Chekhov was born in Taganrok, a small provincial town in Russia. His father, Pavel Yegorovich, owned a small grocery where Anton worked after school. Taganrok was on an important commercial route, and Chekhov had an opportunity to meet a variety of people from all walks of life—an invaluable experience for a developing writer. In school, Chekhov particularly excelled in German and scripture. When Chekhov was 16, his father, facing bankruptcy and imprisonment, escaped to Moscow. Eventually, his wife and the younger children joined him, leaving Chekhov behind in Taganrok, where he worked as a tutor and sent most of his money to help his family.

In 1879, Chekhov rejoined his family in Moscow. In that same year, he entered Moscow University to study medicine. While there, Chekhov began to write to help support the family. His first story appeared in 1880 in a comic magazine called *Fragments.* While working for *Fragments,* Chekhov developed a keen ability to capture the speech patterns of characters from all levels of society. Chekhov's characters ranged from thieves to wealthy landowners and every type in between. Chekhov also honed his narrative

technique during the five years he worked for *Fragments.* In the typical Chekhov story, the narrative begins in the present, and the characters' motives are seldom explicitly explained. Everyday life is not simply background in Chekhov's fiction; it forms the dynamic center of the narrative.

Chekhov graduated in 1884 and began to practice medicine. He also continued to write. In 1886, *New Time,* one of the most prestigious and popular newspapers in Russia, began to publish his work. Chekhov developed a warm relationship with the editor of *New Time,* Alexey Suvorin, who encouraged Chekhov and often helped him financially.

In 1887, Chekhov received the prestigious Pushkin Prize for *At Dusk,* a collection of short stories, and completed his first play, *Ivanov,* the story of a young man, very like Chekhov himself, who commits suicide. Chekhov's second play, *The Wood Demon,* was a failure and caused him to stop writing for a period. His first great success in the theater came with *The Seagull* (1896), a tragic tale of love gone awry.

The popularity of his works was such that Chekhov finally achieved financial independence and was able to buy a country estate in Melikhovo and spend money on philanthropic pursuits, such as a free medical clinic he ran between 1892 and 1893 during a devastating outbreak of cholera. Instead of fully concentrating on his writing career, Chekhov extended his medical practice and treated as many as 1,500 patients a year.

In 1897, Chekhov was diagnosed with tuberculosis, and his health deteriorated rapidly. On doctor's orders, Chekhov moved to the small tourist town of Yalta on the Black Sea where the salt air was supposed to help his lungs recover. He found Yalta to be dull and depressing; however, it was there that he created some of his most famous works, including the *The Cherry Orchard.* In Yalta, Chekhov was often visited by his famous friends, such as the writer MAXIM GORKY, the poet IVAN BUNIN, and the composer Sergei Rachmaninoff, which helped alleviate his loneliness and sense of isolation. Despite his doctors' warnings, Chekhov continued to work throughout his long illness. He died on July 14, 1904, at a German health resort.

Critical Analysis

In most of Chekhov's work, one notices a complete absence of an authorial view. A contemporary critic, Aleksandar Chudakov said that other "Critics called into question his narrative patterns in the short stories, the absence of extended introductions, of definite conclusions, of the elaborately detailed prehistories for his characters, or clear-cut motives for their actions." Chekhov's short-story technique was thus innovative not only in terms of subject matter but also style. Eventually, most critics came to recognize the genius of Chekhov's prose, although belatedly, and he was ranked among the giants of Russian literature during his lifetime.

Chekhov's ground-breaking dramatic techniques were not very well received in 1896, and *The Seagull,* one of his most famous plays, was essentially a failure the first time it was performed. When it was later performed by the Moscow Art Theater, however, the play was a critical and popular success because this troupe used realistic acting techniques and an ensemble cast, which were perfectly suited to Chekhov's drama. The Moscow Art Theater eventually staged all of Chekhov's plays. Unlike his fiction, Chekhov's major dramatic work focused on the politics and psychology of bourgeois life. One often finds the same feeling of hopelessness and claustrophobia in the conflicts of the middle-class families in Chekhov's plays as one does in the works of French naturalist writer ÉMILE ZOLA.

The Seagull focuses on such diverse themes as family life, suicide, love, and the mother–son relationship in the context of middle-class dynamics. The action of the play revolves around Arkadina, a famous actress with an established household in the country, whose son, Konstantin, kills a seagull one day. The plot is complicated by the presence of Trigorin, a novelist who is writing a story about Arkadina's household.

Chekhov's last play, *The Cherry Orchard,* was a tremendous success when it was first staged in 1904. The play delineates the tragic downfall of the Ranevskaya family. Madame Ranevskaya, driven by financial despair, reluctantly decides to cut down the cherry orchard on her family estate. In *Cherry Orchard,* Chekhov explores the results of social change on the Russian aristocracy and on the freed serfs. A major theme of the play is independence and the meaning of freedom as it applies to each of the characters.

Chekhov's legacy as a writer and dramatist extended beyond the borders of Russia. His innovative narrative techniques, which contributed to the development of MODERNISM, influenced later generations of writers. His plays, still widely popular today, are produced all over the world. Chekhov taught future generations of writers to present life without authorial commentary—in all its complexity, and in all of its absurdity—and to avoid omniscient explanations and pat answers to life's dilemmas.

Other Works by Anton Chekhov

Five Plays: Ivanov, The Seagull, Uncle Vanya, Three Sisters, and Cherry Orchard. Oxford: Oxford University Press, 1998.

Forty Stories. New York: Vintage Press, 1991.

Works about Anton Chekhov

Gottlieb, Vera, and Paul Allain, eds. *The Cambridge Companion to Chekhov.* Cambridge: Cambridge University Press, 2000.

Malcolm, Janet. *Reading Chekhov: A Critical Journey.* New York: Random House, 2002.

Rayfield, Donal. *Anton Chekhov: A Life.* Chicago: Northwestern University Press, 2000.

Chen Yuan-tsung (1932–   ) *novelist*

Chen Yuan-tsung was born in Shanghai, China, was raised in a wealthy household, and received a Western-style education at a missionary school. During the Sino-Japanese War, she lived in Chongqing but returned to Shanghai, where she lived in 1949, the year of the Communist takeover. Chen stayed in China because of her idealistic belief in the revolutionary cause.

In 1950, at age 18, she acquired her first job at the Film Bureau of Beijing, but this did not last long. The Communist Party leadership began to "send down" young people from cities to the countryside to participate in the so-called agrarian revolution. In 1951, Chen left Beijing for Gansu province in northwestern China to join this revolution and manually work the land. She became a young revolutionary, known as a cadre. She worked at land reform and endured extreme hardships, such as starvation, during Mao Zedong's failed industrial and agrarian initiative known as the Great Leap Forward. She wrote and read as much as possible during this time but suffered during the Cultural Revolution when the oppressive regime persecuted writers, artists, and intellectuals as counter-revolutionaries.

Chen immigrated to the United States in 1972 with her husband, Jack Chen, an artist and writer, and their son and later taught at Cornell. She determined to publish her story from writings she had hidden during her cadre years, which was the tale of millions of young people who came of age in Communist China. She fictionalized her life in the 1980 novel, *The Dragon's Village*. The novel follows Guan Ling-ling, a young woman from a wealthy family who becomes swept up in the revolutionary fervor of pre-Communist China and joins the Red Guards. She encounters both corrupt officials and cadres, but she finds kindness among comrades and endures the same hardships that Chen herself did. Chen lives with her husband in El Cerrito, California. *Return to the Middle Kingdom: One Family, Three Revolutionaries, and the Birth of Modern China* (2008) traces the story of Chen's husband's family through 150 years of Chinese history.

Works about Chen Yuan-tsung

Grunfeld, A. Tom. "The Dragon's Village: An Autobiographical Novel of Revolutionary China." In *Focus* (Spring 1993).

Stone, Judy. "A Talk with the Author/An Author's Ordeal." *New York Times Book Review,* May 4, 1980.

Chernyshevsky, Nikolay (1828–1889)
essayist, fiction writer

Nikolay Gavrilovich Chernyshevsky was born in Saratov, Russia. At first educated by his father, a priest of the Russian Orthodox Church, Chernyshevsky was admitted into a seminary, an institution that prepared students for careers in the clergy. While in the seminary, he demonstrated great ability as a scholar, and his parents decided to send him to a university in St. Petersburg, where he enrolled in the department of philology.

Socially awkward and financially destitute, Chernyshevsky isolated himself from his fellow students. He was an avid reader and dreamed of becoming a great social reformer and philosopher. Between 1855 and 1862, Chernyshevsky worked for a political publication, *The Contemporary,* where he published translations, criticism, and political articles. He was greatly influenced by European socialist thinkers, such as Hegel. Chernyshevsky advocated agrarian reform, emancipation of the serfs, and establishment of communal agrarian communities, which he viewed as a transition to socialism. His politically radical thinking and attacks on government policies, particularly on the institution of serfdom, resulted in almost 20 years of exile to Siberia, where he was sent in 1864. He continued to attack government policies relentlessly and became a member of several underground radical organizations that wanted to reform Russia by any means necessary, including violence against representatives of the government.

Although Chernyshevsky is remembered as a forerunner of the Russian revolutionary movement, he is also noted for his novel, *What Is To Be Done?* (1863). This polemical novel explores the social inequalities of Russian society. The plot concerns a group of young, idealized intellectuals who go to the countryside to ease the lives of peasants through scientific means. The novel condemns moderates for their seeming inability to engage in social transformation and calls for a swift, radical movement. The novel was generally praised by the radical reformers but was condemned by government officials.

Chernyshevsky left a radical legacy for Russian socialism. His works influenced a number of historical figures, including Vladimir Lenin, who participated in the Russian Revolution. Chernyshevsky is considered to be one of the greatest social philosophers of Russia.

Other Works by Nikolay Chernyshevsky

Prologue: A Novel for the 1860's. Translated by Michael J. Katz. Evanston, Ill.: Northwestern University Press, 1995.

Selected Philosophical Essays. Moscow: Foreign Languages Publishing House, 1953; reissued 2002.

A Work about Nikolay Chernyshevsky

Paperno, Irina. *Chernyshevsky and the Age of Realism.* Stanford: Stanford University Press, 1988.

Chughtai, Ismat (1915–1991) *poet, dramatist, novelist, short story writer, scriptwriter*

Ismat Chughtai was born in Aligarh, India. Though she was one of 10 children, Chughtai spent most of her time alone, climbing trees, running after chickens in her backyard and watching the world go by. From an early age, Chughtai collected mental pictures of everyday life whose simplicity underlies the complex emotional portraits of her characters.

Her father worked at court and played a seminal role in allowing Chughtai to pursue a freedom in thought and deed that was denied to most women of her time. In her autobiographical essay, "My Autobiography," she calls herself "Ismat the rebel," perhaps the best description of both her personality and her work. Her unflinching, interrogative look at social rules helped to pave the way for much of the Indian fiction that was written by women in the second half of the 20th century.

Chughtai constantly used the freedoms allowed to her brothers as the model for her own rights. When her parents decided that she would get married when she turned 13, she threatened to renounce Islam. Her father sent her to school, which she entered in fourth grade and received a double promotion immediately. She then left her home to continue her education in Lucknow and finally gained financial independence by becoming a headmistress of a school for girls.

All of Chughtai's work is written in Urdu. The quality and success of her poems changed the previously held conception that only men could write good Urdu poetry. After MUNSHI PREMCHAND, who is considered the father of the Urdu short story ("Afsara"), Chughtai is one of the most popular and prodigious writers of Urdu fiction. She wrote about the lives of the middle class, national politics, and gender at a time when such topics were not explored in popular fiction, especially by women writers. Her works confuse the private realm of a person's mind with the moral codes of the social world. The story *The Quilt* (1942) uses the context of a loveless marriage to question assumptions surrounding female sexuality. The quilt becomes a metaphor for all that is hidden behind the words society uses to construct meaning.

Chughtai's legacy is not limited to the book world. Her husband, a film producer, took her stories to directors and producers who adapted her work for cinema. Chughtai won several National Awards for her Hindi films. She wrote for 11 films and is one of the few female scriptwriters ever to have written for Hindi cinema.

Another Work by Ismat Chughtai

The Quilt and Other Stories. Translated by Tahira Naqvi. New York: Sheep Meadow Press, 1994.

Cixous, Hélène (1937–) *poet, nonfiction writer*

A feminist and theorist, Hélène Cixous was born in the French colony of Oran, Algeria, and grew up in a German-Jewish household. She received a degree in English from the Lycée Bugeaud in Algiers in 1959 and a doctorate in 1968. After graduation, Cixous held teaching posts at several French universities, including the University of Bordeaux, the Sorbonne, and Nanterre, before finally establishing herself at the University of Paris VIII–Vincennes. At the Sorbonne, Cixous participated in the 1968 student uprisings. Later, at Vincennes, she instituted several courses in experimental literature, particularly the significance to women of the relationship between psychoanalysis and language. She also established a center for women's studies at the University at Vincennes and cofounded the structuralist journal *Poétique*.

Cixous was greatly influenced by the progressive ideologies of such intellectuals as Heinrich von Kleist, Franz Kafka, Arthur Rimbaud, Clarice Lispector, Jacques Derrida, Jacques Lacan, Sigmund Freud, and Martin Heidegger. In the 1970s, Cixous, along with other theorists, such as Kristeva, Barthes, and Derrida, began to explore the complex relationships that exist between sexuality and writing. From this study, she produced several influential feminist texts, including "Sortie" (1975) and "The Laugh of the Medusa" (1975).

In 2006, Cixous retired from the University of Paris VII-Vincennes. In 2008, she was appointed A. D. White Professor-at-Large at Cornell University, a post she will hold until 2014. Cixous also was awarded an honorary doctorate in 2009 by University College London and in 2010 by University College Dublin.

Critical Analysis

The essay "Sortie" is of particular importance in that she uses it to establish a basic understanding of the hierarchy of opposites, such as in culture/nature; head/heart; colonizer/colonized; and speaking/writing. She then proceeds to link these opposites to the differences that exist between the male and the female genders in a discussion that calls for the abolition of such dichotomies as a means of empowering women.

"The Laugh of the Medusa" discusses feminine repression as a direct result of male-dominated cultural discourse. Cixous depicts this repression through the image of a dark, unexplored room that stands, metaphorically, for the largely unexplored area of female language and sexuality. It is Cixous's belief that women do not explore these areas of the self out of a deep-rooted fear that has been placed in them by a language deeply rooted in male dominance. She goes on to theorize that women can shed light on this darkened existence simply by questioning their fears. Through this questioning, they will come to find that there is nothing about which to be frightened and that all of their preconceived fears were created by male images and standards that must be viewed as obstacles that can and must be overcome. Cixous also insists that the only way in which women can overcome the obstacles placed before them is to learn to speak with their bodies, using the body as a medium from which they can regain their inner voice. In the absence of a true feminine discourse, as language itself is historically the realm of the masculine, the language of the body takes on significance in its power to change and to reclaim.

In both "The Laugh of the Medusa" and "Coming to Writing" (1977), Cixous tackles many difficult ideas. She explains the idea of feminine discourse, a concept that eludes definition, by arguing convincingly that any attempt to define the term using the language of masculinity would destroy its inherent beauty; therefore, it must be left undefined. She relies heavily on Freudian concepts mingled with certain feminist ideas, such as a rereading of the Medusa myth as an analogy for female empowerment, rediscovered from Greek mythology. She also fervently expresses the idea that the only escape from masculine discourse is to understand and use the link between language and sexuality. Freedom of language results directly from freedom of sexuality. This freedom leads to what Cixous refers to as *jouissance,* a term that relates to a fulfillment of desire that fuses the erotic, the mystical, and the political in a way that goes beyond mere physical satisfaction. It is through this fulfillment, which can be found specifically in writing, that feminine discourse is discovered.

Since her emergence as a strong voice on the literary scene in the 1970s, Cixous has developed even greater complexity in her style and has become somewhat more mysterious in her thinking; however, her radical feminist ideology has softened somewhat as she seeks to explore the idea of collective identities. Her major contribution to world literature lies in her advancement of feminist ideas.

Other Works by Hélène Cixous

Cixous and Jacques Derrida. *Veils.* Translated by Geoffrey Bennington with drawings by Ernest Pignon-Ernest. Stanford: Stanford University Press, 2001.
Hyperdream. Boston: Polity, 2009.
So Close. Boston: Polity, 2010.
Stigmata: Escaping Texts. New York: Routledge, 2005.
The Third Body. Translated by Keith Cohen. Evanston, Ill.: Hydra Books/Northwestern University Press, 1999.

A Work about Hélène Cixous

Penrod, Lynn. *Hélène Cixous.* Boston: Twayne, 1996.

classicism

Classicism as a term is generally accepted as indicative of clarity in style, adhering to principles of elegance and symmetry, and created by attention and adherence to traditional forms. It has often been used synonymously with generic terms such as excellence or artistic quality. The term has its basis in the study, reverence for, and imitation of Greek and Roman literature, art, and architecture. Because the principles of classicism are deeply rooted in the history, rites, rituals, and practices of specific ancient cultures, the term also came to apply to specific cultural, literary, artistic, and academic canons.

The first full-scale revival of classicism occurred during the Renaissance when intensified interest in Greek and Roman culture, especially the literary works of Plato and Cicero, influenced a renewal of classical standards in literature. In the 18th and 19th centuries, following the archaeological discovery of the remains of Pompeii and Herculaneum, there was again a revival of interest first in the culture of Rome and later in the ideas of ancient Greece. This period, generally referred to as neoclassicism, was actually the start of the larger romantic movement (*see* ROMANTICISM). The revival was closely linked to the American and French Revolutions and draws parallels between ancient and modern forms of government.

In Central Europe, during the early part of the 20th century, there was again a spirit of revolution that coincided with a revival of interest in Greek literature. The classical models were somewhat reinvented. This was particularly apparent in the renewed interest in Greek literature and in a tendency among many Greek writers to look to the past—to history, myth, and folklore—as a means of understanding the present situation.

The Greek poet and Nobel laureate GEORGE SEFERIS was particularly interested in awareness of the past and the ways in which history can be used to understand the present. His collection of poems, *Mythistorema* (1935; translated 1960) applied the Odyssean myths to modern situations and circumstances. Homer's *Odyssey* became the symbolic basis for many of his works.

Other poets and novelists, such as TUDOR ARGHEZI and NIKOS KAZANTSAKIS, based elements of their works on principles of classicism and turned their attention to myth as an allegory for modern times. Although his writing was modern in its sense of restlessness and was bold and innovative in its use of often crude, forceful language, Arghezi leaned toward the traditional elements of classicism in his tendency to rely on folklore and mythology. Kazantsakis's epic poem *Odyssey: A Modern Sequel* (1938) picks up Ulysses' tale where Homer leaves off and brings it to a more solid conclusion.

Although classicism cannot be said to have ever been abandoned completely during any period of literary history, its resurgence is cyclical and responsive to historical circumstances. As a result of the early 20th-century interest in revolution and change, similar to the spirit of Greek and Roman times as well as that of the Renaissance, classicism experienced a literary resurgence throughout 20th-century Central Europe.

Works about Classicism

Buxton, John. *The Grecian Taste: Literature in the Age of Neo-Classicism 1740–1820.* New York: Barnes & Noble, 1978.

Knox, Bernard. *Backing into the Future: The Classical Tradition and Its Renewal.* New York: Norton, 1994.

Claudel, Paul (1868–1955) *poet, playwright, essayist*

A prominent figure in the early 20th-century French Catholic renaissance, Paul Claudel was born in Villeneuve-sur-Fère-en-Tardenois, in Aisne, France. He came from a family of farmers, Catholic priests, and landed gentry. A profound religious experience at the age of 18 changed not only his view of the world but also affected his future as a writer. On Christmas day, during services at Notre Dame cathedral, he heard a distinct voice above him proclaim, "There is a God." He became a fervent Catholic and turned to the Bible as his source of inspiration.

As a poet, Claudel's most influential work is his *Five Great Odes* (1910). Claudel uses this poem in five parts to relate poetic inspiration as a gift from God, describing the mystery and wonder of the universe.

As a journalist and literary critic, Claudel also based his beliefs and impressions in his strong religious faith. He regularly attacked musician Richard Wagner, stating that, while he admired Wagner's music, he disliked what it expressed in Wagner's *Der Ring des Nibelungen.* He also wrote on the subject of French literature, particularly admiring BAUDELAIRE and RIMBAUD.

Claudel debuted as a playwright with *Tête d'or* (1889), a drama largely influenced by his own religious experiences. This work was followed by the trilogy of plays, *L'otage* (*The Hostage,* 1911), *Le pain dur* (*Crusts,* 1918), and *Le père humilié* (*The Humiliation of the Father,* 1920), which trace the

degeneration of the nobility. Another dramatic work, *Break at Noon* (1906), dealt with the theme of adultery and was based on an experience in Claudel's own life in which, for a four-year period in the early 1900s, he had engaged in a passionate affair with a married Polish woman. This episode caused him to contemplate the complexities inherent in the theme of forbidden love. One of Claudel's best-known dramas is *The Satin Slipper* (1924), about the epic adventures of Rodrique and the woman he loves.

On May 1, 1950, as a result of his contributions to literature in the form of religion, Claudel was honored by the pope. He died five years later in Paris on February 23.

Another Work by Paul Claudel

Claudel on the Theatre. Translated by Christine Trollope. Coral Gables, Fla.: University of Miami Press, 1972.

Works about Paul Claudel

Caranfa, Angelo. *Claudel: Beauty and Grace.* Lewisburg, Pa.: Bucknell University Press, 1989.

Knapp, Bettina L. *Paul Claudel.* New York: Ungar, 1982.

Cliff, Michelle (1946–) *novelist, poet, short story writer, teacher, critic, editor*

Michelle Cliff was born in Kingston, Jamaica. As a young child, she moved to New York City with her family. After attending public schools and graduating from Wagner College in 1969 with a B.A. in European history, she worked for the New York publisher W. W. Norton from 1970 to 1971. Then she studied at the Warburg Institute in London, earning a master of philosophy degree in 1974. She returned to W. W. Norton as a copy editor and then as a manuscript and production editor. She resigned in 1979 to focus on writing, and in 1980 she published her first book, the prose poem *Claiming an Identity They Taught Me to Despise.*

Themes of race, gender, and power run through Cliff's internationally known poetry, novels, essays, articles, lectures, and workshops. In "Clare Savage as a Crossroads Character" (1990), Cliff acknowledges the autobiographical strands present in her prose poem and earliest novels, *Abeng* (1984) and *No Telephone to Heaven* (1987). *Abeng,* the African word for "conch shell," alludes to Caribbean, United States, and world history. The novel narrates how two runaway slaves, Nanny and Cuffee, lead raids to liberate other slaves. Both *Abeng* and its sequel, *No Telephone to Heaven,* were critically acclaimed for their dexterous linguistic shifts from Jamaican creole to standard English.

Critics name *Free Enterprise* (1993) her strongest novel. In it, female protagonists Annie Christmas and Ellen Pleasant work with freedom fighters to liberate slaves. To quote *Booklist,* "In tall tales and legends, cherished memories, and regrettable misunderstandings, *Free Enterprise* explores the multiple meanings of freedom and enterprise and of a society that enshrines selected meanings of both."

In *Writing in Limbo* Simon Gikandi claims, "The uniqueness of Cliff's aesthetics lies in her realization that the fragmentation, silence and repression that mark the life of the Caribbean subject under colonialism must be confronted not only as a problem to be overcome but also as a condition of possibility—as a license to dissimulate and to affirm difference—in which an identity is created out of the chaotic colonial and postcolonial history."

Other Works by Michelle Cliff

Bodies of Water. New York: Dutton, 1990.
Everything Is Now: New and Collected Stories. Minneapolis: University of Minnesota Press, 2009.
If I Could Write This in Fire. Minneapolis: University of Minnesota Press, 2008.
Into the Interior. Minneapolis: University of Minnesota Press, 2010.
The Land of Look Behind: Prose and Poetry. Ithaca, N.Y.: Firebrand Books, 1985.

The Store of a Million Items: Stories. Boston: Houghton Mifflin, 1998.

Works about Michelle Cliff

Berrian, Brenda F. "Claiming an Identity: Caribbean Women Writers in English." *Journal of Black Studies* 25 (December 1994): 200–216.
Edmonson, Belinda. "Race, Privilege, and the Politics of (Re)Writing History: An Analysis of the Novels of Michelle Cliff." *Callaloo* 16, no. 1 (1993): 180–191.
Gikandi, Simon. *Writing in Limbo: Modernism and Caribbean Literature.* Ithaca, N.Y.: Cornell University Press, 1992.
Schwartz, Meryl F. "An Interview with Michelle Cliff." *Contemporary Literature* 34, no. 4 (Winter 1993): 595–619.

Cocteau, Jean (1889–1963) *poet, novelist, dramatist*

Jean Cocteau was born in Maisons-Lafitte, France. His father, a lawyer and amateur painter, committed suicide when Cocteau was nine. This experience left him with an intense awareness of human frailty and an almost uncanny ability to identify with the world of the dead, as is seen in his early poetry such as *L'ange heurtebise* (1925).

A mediocre student who failed several attempts to pass the secondary-school graduation examination, poetry was Cocteau's first artistic outlet. He published his first volume of poems, *Aladdin's Lamp,* at the age of 19. Influenced by surrealism, psychoanalysis, cubism, and Catholicism, coupled with a frequent use of opium, Cocteau promoted the avant-garde in his works. He counted among his closest friends prominent artists such as Pablo Picasso, composer Erik Satie, and Russian stage director Sergey Diaghilev.

Cocteau met Pablo Picasso and Sergey Diaghilev in 1915. They challenged Cocteau to write a ballet, which is the collaborative work *Parade* (1917), produced by Diaghilev, with scenic design by Picasso and music by Erik Satie. Cocteau went on to firmly establish himself as a writer with the prose fantasy *Le potomak* (1919) about a creature trapped in an aquarium.

Another close and influential friend was the poet and novelist Raymond Radiguet, whose death from typhoid fever caused Cocteau to experiment with opium. Under influence of the drug, he began to write psychological novels such as *Thomas the Impostor* (1923) and his masterpiece, *Les enfants terribles* (*The Incorrigible Children,* 1929) about a group of children trapped in their own scary world.

In 1929, Cocteau was hospitalized for opium addiction, the experience of which he recounts in *Opium* (1930). On his release, he began to work on a series of films that often depicted mirrors as doors to alternate realities. He also befriended the young actor Jean Marais in 1937 and thereafter designed and wrote roles especially for him, producing such works as *Orphée* (*Orpheus,* 1950), a one-act tragedy about death's connection to inspiration, and *Le testament d'Orphée* (*The Testament of Orpheus,* 1961), whose theme was death.

Branded a decadent during World War II, Cocteau continued to lead an active literary life. Always seeking to shock, he had a facelift and began to wear leather trousers and matadors' capes in his declining years. He died on October 11, 1963.

Critical Analysis

Cocteau is perhaps best known for his modern rendering of Sophocles's *Oedipus Rex, The Infernal Machine* (1934). By placing the ancient tale within a contemporary framework, Cocteau manages to draw the modern audience into the tragedy and into an exploration of free will and determinism.

The play opens with a "voice" who retells the tale of Oedipus, the mythological king of Thebes. He ends his introduction with this chilling description:

Watch now, spectator. Before you is a fully wound machine. Slowly its spring will unwind the entire span of a human life. It is one of the most perfect machines devised by the infernal gods for the mathematical annihilation of a mortal.

Despite its sometimes humorous evocation, the workings of fate, that infernal machine, are an ominous presence in the play. In the first act, for example, as Jocasta and Tiresias climb the stairs of the city walls, Tiresias treads on her red scarf, which she wears throughout the play. Jocasta says, "It's the scarf. This scarf is against me. It's always trying to strangle me. One moment, it catches in branches, another moment in the moving wheel of a carriage; then you step on it. I'm afraid of it but I can't part with it. In the end, it will kill me." In the end, of course, Jocasta hangs herself with the scarf.

Cocteau's determinism has the added dimension of Freudian psychology. Oedipus and Jocasta are portrayed as being trapped by their pasts in addition to their fates. Jocasta, grieving over the sacrifice of her infant son, is drawn to strong young men who are the age her son would have been had he lived. Before Oedipus arrives in Thebes, Jocasta wants to feel the muscles of a 19-year-old guard. Oedipus, missing real maternal love, is drawn to older women. He tells Jocasta, "To me the face of a young girl is as empty as a blank page. It doesn't compare with the magnificent, sacred beauty of your face—matured and mellowed by fate."

In addition to overlaying Freudian ideas on the ancient Greek story, Cocteau also incorporates echoes of *Hamlet.* The opening scene on the parapets above the city, when two soldiers are visited by the ghost of their dead king, is very close to the opening scene of the Shakespearean play. Many modern critics, of course, have diagnosed Hamlet with an Oedipus complex.

In the words of the *New York Times* critic Stephen Holden, the play, while less deep and compelling than the Greek original, "finds a lot of mordant humor in the story of mortals who are self-deluded enough to think they have outwitted fate and found lasting happiness."

Another Work by Jean Cocteau

Tempest of Stars: Selected Poems. Translated by Jeremy Reed. Chester Springs, Pa.: Dufour Editions, 1992.

Works about Jean Cocteau

Knapp, Bettina L. *Jean Cocteau.* Boston: Twayne, 1989.

Saul, Julie, ed. *Jean Cocteau: The Mirror and the Mask: A Photo-Biography.* Introduction by Francis Steegmuller. Boston: David Godine, 1992.

Coetzee, J(ohn) M. (1940–   ) *novelist and essayist*

John M. Coetzee was born to a middle-class family in South Africa. His parents were of African and German heritage, but he writes only in English. Like the narrator of his 1997 memoir, *Boyhood,* he spoke both Afrikaans and English fluently as a boy but was an outsider in both communities.

J. M. Coetzee studied undergraduate English in Cape Town but found old, canonized British literature dull. He turned to mathematics for comfort and worked for IBM as a computer systems designer in England in the early 1960s. He returned to literature, however, and came to the United States to study at the University of Texas at Austin, where he received his doctorate in literature in 1969. Coetzee's graduating thesis studied the work of Irish playwright SAMUEL BECKETT, a major influence on his own writing. Also while at the university, he started historical research into the life of explorer and ancestor Jacobus Coetzee, the results of which became his first novel, *Dusklands* (1974).

Critical Analysis

Dusklands simultaneously tells the stories of two main characters, an American bureaucrat in 1970s war-torn Vietnam and an Afrikaner explorer moving into 18th-century South Africa. The book compares America's involvement in Vietnam with the Dutch colonization of South Africa. Coetzee, in essence, explores the imperialist mentality of believing one's own culture superior to others.

In his next novel, *In the Heart of the Country* (1976), Coetzee uses a woman's point of view to tell the story of Magda, who cannot recover from the tragedy of her father's death and her own rape.

The book ends with Magda in a state of hysterical loneliness. In his 1980 book, *Waiting for the Barbarians,* Coetzee turns the colonial experience into allegory, telling the story of an imaginary country being overrun by barbarians.

Coetzee received worldwide recognition with *The Life and Times of Michael K.,* which won England's Booker Prize in 1983. The story introduces another important subject matter of Coetzee's works: the relationship between parents and their children. The narrator, Michael K., escapes from the civil strife and violence of apartheid Cape Town to his mother's farm. He is a simple-minded gardener who lives with his dying mother until their farm is destroyed in the ongoing civil war. Michael and his mother are innocent victims of their political surroundings, but Michael has a simple attitude: He says, "one can live."

Coetzee wrote three more works of fiction in the late 1980s and early 1990s before taking home the Booker Prize again for his 1999 *Disgrace*. In two of these, *Foe* (1986) and *The Master of Petersburg* (1994), he responds to and rewrites great works of European literature. *Foe* is the story of an unnamed woman who tells the story of *Robinson Crusoe* to author Daniel Defoe. This woman, like the colonized people of South Africa, loses her voice in the great machine of colonial history and is unrecognized and forgotten.

Russian author FYODOR DOSTOYEVSKY is the hero of *The Master of Petersburg,* a fictional account of Dostoyevsky tracing the steps of his recently dead stepson, Pavel, around the city of St. Petersburg. The novel is Coetzee's most postmodern work in that it explores the act of writing and the power of language. The character of Dostoyevsky does not use writing's power to help the Russian revolutionaries, however, but to understand and come closer to his dead stepson.

Coetzee's novel *Disgrace* is similar to *The Life and Times of Michael K,* in that its main character, David Lurie, like Michael K., suffers greatly to achieve a small amount of clarity and redemption. David Lurie loses his job as a professor, becomes a caretaker for dying animals, is refused by prostitutes, and considers castrating himself.

Disgrace is Coetzee's first book to deal with postapartheid South Africa directly. Political change does little to improve the lives of the individuals in the novel. Andrew O'Hehir writes in Salon that in Coetzee's novels "political and historical forces blow through the lives of individuals like nasty weather systems." Again and again, Coetzee presents characters who are tossed about violently but who, in every novel, pick up and move on.

The major influences on his work are FRANZ KAFKA and Samuel Beckett. Like Kafka and Beckett's characters, the people in Coetzee's books have a troubled existence in which suffering seems to be the defining characteristic of life.

Among Coetzee's most recent works are *Elizabeth Costello* (2003), a tale about literary celebrity and the irksomeness of fame; *Slow Man* (2005), about a photographer who loses a leg in an automobile accident and must learn to adapt; and *Summertime* (2009), a fictionalized memoir of Coetzee's life.

Coetzee's books have been translated into more than 20 languages. Coetzee has held visiting professorships across the United States, including Harvard, the University of Chicago, and Johns Hopkins University. Besides fiction, he has written many books of essays, including *White Writing: On the Culture of Letters in South Africa* (1988) and *The Lives of Animals* (1999).

J. M. Coetzee's work eloquently deals with South Africa's political history; the nature of writing, language, and power; and how human relationships are divided by the gap between the powered and the powerless. Coetzee won the Nobel Prize in 2003.

Other Works by J. M. Coetzee

Diary of a Bad Year. London: Harvill Secker, 2007.
Giving Offence: Essays on Censorship. Chicago: University of Chicago Press, 1996.
A Land Apart: A Contemporary South African Reader. New York: Viking, 1987.

Works about J. M. Coetzee

Atwell, David. *J. M. Coetzee: South Africa and the Politics of Writing.* Berkeley: University of California Press, 1993.
O'Hehir, Andrew. "'Disgrace' by J. M. Coetzee." *Salon Books* 5 (November 1999). Available online. URL: www.salon.com/books/review/1999/11/05/coetzee. Accessed October 11, 2010.
Viola, Andre. "An Interview with J. M. Coetzee." *Commonwealth Essays and Studies* 14, no. 2 (Spring 1992): 6–7.

Colette (Sidonie-Gabrielle Colette)
(1873–1954) *novelist*

Considered one of the leading French novelists of the 20th century, Colette was born in the village of Saint-Sauveur-en-Puisaye, Burgundy. She was the daughter of a retired army captain, Jules-Joseph Colette, who had lost a leg in the Italian campaign, and the highly unconventional Adèle Eugénie Sidonie Landoy, known as "Sidonie" or "Sido." Her mother's down-to-earth personality, devotion to animals, reading, and gardening greatly influenced Colette.

Colette's career as a novelist began when she was in her early 20s and continued into her mid-70s, during which time she wrote more than 50 books, numerous short stories, and articles for major newspapers and magazines. Always in some way autobiographical in nature, her works blur the boundaries between reality and fiction in an attempt to explore love and female sexuality in a masculine world.

Colette was first encouraged to write by her first husband, writer and music critic Henri Gauthier-Villars. According to some sources, he locked her in her room and would not let her leave until she had completed a requisite number of pages. Regardless of how she started, however, Colette published four of what came to be known as her *Claudine* novels in rapid succession between 1900 and 1903, using her husband's pen name Willy. The novels, all recounting the often prurient adventures of a teenage girl, became so successful that they inspired other products, including a musical adaptation, costumes, soap, cigars, and perfume.

Becoming disillusioned by her husband's repeated adultery, Colette separated from him in 1905 and was divorced in 1906. She went to work as a music-hall performer, doing such memorable things as baring her breasts and simulating sex on stage, an act that resulted in a riot at the Moulin Rouge.

During this period, Colette found a protector, a woman known as "Missy," the niece of Napoléon III, and who was instrumental in establishing Colette's image as a writer, an actress, and a lesbian. "Missy" committed suicide in 1944. Colette was later known, at various points in her life, to have become friends and, most likely, lovers with noted American lesbian Natalie Clifford Barney and Italian author GABRIELE D' ANNUNZIO. Such an independent and gregarious lifestyle eventually filtered into Colette's writing. She remained devoted to her independence, however, and published *La Vagabonde* (1910), a story about an actress who decides to reject the man she loves to protect her ability to live her life as she pleases.

In 1912, Colette married newspaper editor Henri de Jouvenel des Ursins. She wrote theater articles and short stories for his paper and bore him one child, Colette de Jouvenel. Colette had not wanted children and, consequently, neglected her daughter. She also began a questionable relationship with her stepson, Bertrand de Jouvenel, which resulted in much gossip. She depicts this affair in her novel *Chéri* (1920), as told from the point of view of a sexually naive young man.

Critical Analysis

Colette's works are generally divided into four phases. Her early works are the Claudine novels, followed by a time when she wrote predominantly about life in the theater, followed by works about the politics of love, and ultimately followed by her more mature works depicting reminiscences of youth and family. Her fame began to expand in the 1920s, and by 1927 she was often referred to as France's leading female writer. Her mature works,

written during this time, depict a peaceful world and the delicate nature of the mother–daughter bond. *La maison de Claudine* (*My Mother's House*, 1922), *La naissance du jour* (*A Lesson in Love*, 1928) and *Sido* (1929) all celebrate her carefree rural childhood and her mother's strength and vitality. This period marks a distinction from the darker world depicted in her earlier works. Her use of the character/narrator "Colette" in works such as *L'étoile vesper* (1946) and *Le fanal bleu* (1949) further blurred her distinctions between fiction and reality.

Colette received many awards throughout her lifetime. She was the first woman to be granted admission to the prestigious Académie Goncourt, and in 1953 she was elected a grand officer of the Légion d'honneur. A crippling form of arthritis haunted the last 20 years of her life; however, she still managed to publish *Gigi* (1945) at the age of 72. The novel was later made into a film in 1948 and into a musical in 1958, directed by Vincente Minnelli.

Colette died on August 3, 1954, in Paris. Because of her popularity, she was granted a state funeral that was attended by thousands of her admirers but was denied Catholic rites because she had been divorced.

Another Work by Colette
Break of Day. New York: Ballantine Books, 1983.

A Work about Colette
Thurman, Judith. *Secrets of the Flesh: A Life of Colette.* New York: Knopf, 1999.

Collymore, Frank (Colly) (1893–1980)
poet, short story writer, teacher, lexicographer, editor

Frank Collymore was born in St. Michael, Barbados, to Joseph Appleton Collymore, a government customs officer, and Rebecca Wilhelmina, née Clark. Collymore attended Combermere School, a grammar school for boys, from 1903 to 1910 and taught at the same school from 1910 until 1963.

GEORGE LAMMING, the West Indian novelist, poet, and critic, was one of his many students.

Collymore did not publish his first book of poetry, *Thirty Poems,* until 1944. Poems in this and other collections both humorously and seriously examine a variety of topics—landscape, love, war, conformity, and history. After the productive poetry years of the 1940s when he published three books containing 103 poems, Collymore shifted his attention to writing short stories. Eighteen of his short stories appeared in *Bim,* a magazine started by the Young Men's Progressive Club of Barbados. Many of these stories have a dark, even morbid edge, and the mind appears as a recurring theme. In his story *Shadows,* published in *Bim* in December 1942, for example, the narrator asks:

"The mind. What do you and I know of the mind, and of the vast forces which lie around us, in us and yet not wholly of us, secret, prowling, mysterious, fraught with such power as is beyond our knowledge, watching and waiting to encompass us, to overthrow what we call the seat of the reason—the mind whose powers and weaknesses we can never hope to comprehend?"

Working with the editing and publishing of *Bim* from 1942 to 1975 enabled Collymore to influence the production and consumption of West Indian literature significantly, as explained by Lamming in a special introduction to the June 1955 issue:

"There are not many West Indian writers today who did not use *Bim* as a kind of platform, the surest, if not the only avenue, by which they might reach a literate and sensitive reading public, and almost all of the West Indians who are now writers in a more professional sense and whose work has compelled the attention of readers and writers in other countries, were introduced, so to speak, by *Bim.*"

Collymore also used other avenues to introduce readers to West Indian writers; he introduced a

19-year-old DEREK WALCOTT as a true poet in *Savacou* (1949). In a 1986 essay in *Fifty Caribbean Writers,* Edward Baugh asserts, "Collymore earned his reputation as a doyen and godfather of West Indian Literature." In a 1971 essay in *West Indian Poetry 1900–1970,* Baugh goes on to say that Collymore's poetry marked "something of an advance in West Indian poetry," his influences having been "more twentieth-century than those of his coevals [contemporaries]."

Other Works by Frank Collymore

The Man Who Loved Attending Funerals and Other Stories. Edited by Harold Barratt and Reinhard Sander. Portsmouth, N.H.: Heinemann, 1993.
Rhymed Ruminations of the Fauna of Barbados. Bridgetown, Barbados: Advocate, 1968.
Selected Poems. Bridgetown, Barbados: Coles Printery, 1971.

Works about Frank Collymore

Baugh, Edward. "Frank Collymore: A Biographical Portrait." *Savacou: A Journal of the Caribbean Artists Movement* 7–8 (1973): 139–148.
Sander, Reinhard W., Esmond D. Ramesar, and Edward Baugh. *An Index to Bim 1942–1972.* St. Augustine, Trinidad: University of West Indies Extra-Mural Studies Unit, 1973.

Condé, Maryse (1934–   ) *novelist, playwright, essayist, critic, professor*

Maryse Condé was born in Pointe-à-Pitre, Guadeloupe. A bright student with a penchant for reading, Condé attended school in Guadeloupe before continuing her education in France. Studying black stereotypes in Caribbean literature, she earned a doctorate in comparative literature in 1975 from the Université de Paris III (Sorbonne Nouvelle).

Condé taught French in multiple countries, including Guinea, Accra, and Sénégal, from 1960 to 1968. After working as a program producer for the French Services of the BBC from 1968 to 1970, she became an editor at the Paris publishing house

Présence Africaine and, in 1973, began to teach Francophone literature at Paris VII (Jussieu), X (Nanterre), and III (Sorbonne Nouvelle).

While teaching, Condé also wrote. She published numerous novels after the release of her first, *Héremakhonon* (*Welcome Home*) in 1976. In *Héremakhonon*, Veronica, a young Guadeloupian woman who was educated in Paris, goes to West Africa to examine her history. Although multiple similarities exist between Veronica's and Condé's life experiences, Condé denies that Veronica is an autobiographical character. Like the first novel, *Une saison à rihata* (*A Season in Rihata*, 1981) follows a Guadeloupian female protagonist to a fictional West African country repressed by postcolonial regimes. Both novels use multiple points of view to reconstruct history.

Ségou (*Segu*, 1984, 1985), Condé's third novel, written in two volumes, positioned her as a premier contemporary Caribbean writer. Set in the African kingdom of Segu between 1797 and 1860, the novel follows four sons of a royal family to Brazil and the Caribbean while addressing religion, slavery, corruption, incest, and rape. Some criticized the novel as soap-operaesque, but in the *New York Times Book Review*, May 31, 1987, Charles Larson called *Ségou* "the most significant historical novel about black Africa published in many a year." It weaves relatively unknown fragments of African history with compelling personal narratives.

Between *Héremakhonon* and *Ségou*, Condé published numerous theoretical essays on Antillean culture and literature, but afterward she focused on creative writing. The focus of her fiction also shifted from Africa to the African diaspora after *Ségou*. *Moi, Tituba, sorcière noire de Salem* (*I, Tituba, Black Witch of Salem*, 1986) uses first-person narrative to tell the story of an obscure historical figure, Tituba—a black slave from Barbados arrested for witchcraft in the United States during the 17th century. Subsequent works, such as *La vie scélérate* (*The Tree of Life*, 1987) and *Les derniers rois mages* (*The Last Magi*, 1992) continue to explore themes of exile, psychological dislocation, race, class, gender, and history. Condé's most recent work, *Victoire: My Mother's Mother* (2010), is an imaginative retelling of her grandmother's life. An indication of Condé's widespread acclaim, her novels have been translated into English, German, Dutch, Italian, Spanish, Portuguese, and Japanese.

In 1990, Condé took a position at the University of California, Berkeley. Since then, she has worked at the University of Virginia, the University of Maryland, and Harvard. Condé chaired the Center for French and Francophone Studies at Columbia University from 1995 to 2004. Her multifaceted writing techniques and narrative strategies, as well as her work's political and cultural themes, make her one of the most important Caribbean francophone writers.

Other Works by Maryse Condé

Crossing the Mangrove. Translated by Richard Philcox. New York: Anchor Books, 1995.
Land of Many Colors & Nanna-ya. Translated by Nicole Ball. Lincoln: University of Nebraska Press, 1999.
The Story of the Cannibal Woman: A Novel. New York: Washington Square Press, 2008.
Tales from the Heart: True Stories from My Childhood. Translated by Richard Philcox. New York: Soho, 2001.
Who Slashed Celanire's Throat?: A Fantastical Tale. New York: Washington Square Press, 2005.

Works about Maryse Condé

Apter, Emily S. "Crossover Texts/Creole Tongues: A Conversation with Maryse Condé." *Public Culture* 13, no. 1 (Winter 2001): 89–96.
Arowolo, Bukoye. "The Black Caribbean Woman's Search for Identity in Maryse Condé's Novels." In *Feminism and Black Women's Creative Writing: Theory, Practice, and Criticism*. Edited by Aduke Adebayo. Ibadan, Nigeria: AMD, 1996.
Suk, Jeannie. *Postcolonial Paradoxes in French Caribbean Writing: Césaire, Glissant, Condé*. Oxford: Clarendon, 2001.

Constant de Rebecque, Benjamin

(1767–1830) *nonfiction writer, novelist*

Henri-Benjamin Constant de Rebecque was born on October 25, 1767, in Lausanne, Switzerland. His mother died from complications of childbirth one week after he was born. Tutored as a young child, he read daily for eight to 10 hours. He was sent at a young age to the University of Erlangen in Bavaria, where he learned German, one of three languages in which he was proficient by the time he was 18. He later transferred to the University of Edinburgh where he studied under distinguished proponents of freedom, including Adam Smith, Adam Ferguson, and Dugald Stewart. He subsequently moved to Paris to study with the intellectual Jean-Baptiste-Antoine Suard. While there, he became close friends with the great Lafayette, among other influential thinkers.

In 1794, he met GERMAINE DE STAËL, whose influence piqued his interest in politics. He began to publish political pamphlets and was appointed a member of the Tribunal under Napoleon. But Constant was critical of Napoleon's policies, especially his project to make himself consul for life (and later emperor), and when in 1802 Napoleon banished de Staël, Constant accompanied her in her exile from France.

Constant's works of political theory include *De l'esprit de conquête et de l'usurpation* (*On the Spirit of Conquest and Usurpation,* 1814) and *Principes de politique* (*Political Principles,* 1816). One of his principles was the importance of protecting individual liberty against both government and the encroachments of the majority. He also wrote a five-volume treatise, *De la religion* (*On Religion,* 1824–31). Unlike many French thinkers of his time, he believed that religion was a positive force in society and a necessary balance to the power of government.

In 1816, a short novel Constant had written 10 years previously, *Adolphe,* was published. With great economy of style, the work tells the story of a young man's involvement with an older woman and his painful efforts to disentangle himself from the affair. It is presumed that the story has autobiographical elements, though whether the unfortunate Elleanore is based on Madame de Staël or on one of the other women in Constant's life has not been established. Ironically, Constant is better remembered for *Adolphe,* a work to which he attached no great value but which is seen as an important forerunner of the psychological novel, than for his immense work on religion, which occupied decades of his life.

Constant produced dozens of works that defied laws limiting freedom of speech and freedom of the press. He campaigned against the African slave trade and fought for civil liberties alongside Lafayette. Constant's health began to decline rapidly in 1830, and he died on December 8. At his funeral service, people lined the streets to wave the tricolor flags of the Liberal Party in his honor.

Other Works by Benjamin Constant

Adolphe. Translated by Margaret Mauldon. New York: Oxford University Press, 2001.

Political Writings. Translated by Biancamaria Fontana. New York: Cambridge University Press, 1988.

Works about Benjamin Constant

Holmes, Stephen. *Benjamin Constant and the Making of Modern Liberalism.* New Haven, Conn.: Yale University Press, 1984.

Todorov, Tszvetan. *A Passion for Democracy: Benjamin Constant.* New York: Algora, 1998.

Wood, Dennis. *Benjamin Constant: A Biography.* New York: Routledge, 1993.

Cortázar, Julio (1914–1984) *novelist, short story writer, translator*

Julio Cortázar was born in Brussels, Belgium, to Argentinean parents. He moved to Argentina with his family after World War I when he was four years old, having learned by then to speak French as well as Spanish. Not long after returning to Argentina, his father abandoned his family, leaving Cortázar to be raised by his mother. As a student, Cortázar was interested in literature, attending the

Teacher's College in Buenos Aires from which he received a degree in literature in 1935. His earliest jobs were as a secondary school teacher in various towns in Argentina.

In 1945, Cortázar left teaching to become a translator of both English and French writers for various publishing houses in Argentina, but by 1951 he was so much against the Perón regime in Argentina that he turned down the opportunity to have a chair at the University of Buenos Aires and instead went to live in France, where he remained until his death. While in France, he also worked as a translator for UNESCO, dividing each year so that he would translate for six months and write fiction and play jazz trumpet the remaining six months. He lived part of the time in Paris and the rest at his home in the Provençal village of Saignon in the south of France. Cortázar was committed to the revolutionary political movements in Latin America, as witnessed by his visit to Cuba in 1961, his support of the United Chilean Front, and his visit to Nicaragua in 1983.

By his own admission, Cortázar was influenced by SYMBOLIST and surrealist writers such as COMTE DE LAUTREAMONT, ARTHUR RIMBAUD, STÉPHANE MALLARMÉ, ALFRED JARRY, JEAN COCTEAU, and JORGE LUIS BORGES. He was also influenced by Edgar Allen Poe, John Keats, and Virginia Woolf. Both his fiction and interviews with him reveal his belief that reality is actually a collage of the rational and the irrational, the linear and the nonlinear, fantasy and what we generally tend to consider "real," all existing on different planes at the same time. In his humorous and satirical book *Cronopios and Famas* (1962), for example, Cortázar divides the world between *cronopios,* imaginary creatures who represent the magical in life, and *famas,* those who represent conventional reality. In addition, his novel *The Winners* (1960) is composed of various disparate characters who, after winning a lottery, find themselves together on a holiday cruise, their prize. This external voyage becomes a metaphor for the internal, metaphysical confrontation that each character has with himself or herself.

Of all that Cortázar has written, however, he is best known for being the author of the short story "Las babas deldiablo," or "The Devil's Drool," which inspired *Blowup,* Michelangelo Antonioni's 1966 film that won the Grand Prix at Cannes, and the novel *Hopscotch,* which first appeared in 1963. A novel that works on a number of levels, *Hopscotch* consists of a series of numbered chapters that can be read "in normal fashion" or in an entirely different sequence, which Cortázar provides, informing the reader, "In its own way, this book consists of many books, but two books above all." Like a labyrinth or the actual game of hopscotch, the reader who follows the nonlinear "sequence" jumps around while trying to keep his or her balance as the characters search for heaven or hell or the center of the labyrinth. Considered to be one of the major novels written by a Latin American in the 20th-century, *Hopscotch* has been called an "antinovel" in its methods of breaking with traditional form and content while maintaining a comical sense of the absurd.

Julio Cortázar is now considered one of the most important 20th-century Latin American writers, known for his experimentalism and MAGIC REALISM. His short stories and novels, written with wit and a startling sense of fantasy, portray complex characters faced with metaphysical anguish.

Other Works by Julio Cortázar

Blow Up and Other Stories. Translated by Paul Blackburn. New York: Pantheon, 1985.
Final Exam. Translated by Alfred J. MacAdam. New York: New Directions, 2000.
62: A Model Kit. Translated by Gregory Rabassa. New York: New Directions, 2000.

Works about Julio Cortázar

Moran, Dominic. *Questions of the Liminal in the Fiction of Julio Cortázar.* Oxford: European Humanities Research Centre, 2001.
Standish, Peter. *Understanding Julio Cortázar.* Columbia, S.C.: University of South Carolina Press, 2001.

Stavans, Ilan. *Julio Cortázar: A Study of the Short Fiction.* New York: Twayne, 1996.

costumbrismo

Costumbrismo was a main feature of Spanish romanticism. It was, in the most general of terms, the practice of creating literary sketches that captured realistic details about local life and customs. The word *costumbrismo* comes from the Spanish *costumbres,* which means "customs."

Although this practice was a feature in all of Europe's romantic traditions, it was so pronounced and so central to the Spanish romantics that it deserves notice.

Romanticism in Spain in the late 18th and early 19th centuries was a reaction to the previous century's domination by the aesthetic ideas of the Enlightenment. The Enlightenment proposed that there were universal standards for beauty and harmony and that the arts should always follow neoclassical models. Spanish costumbrismo is a reaction against this sort of subtle cultural imperialism. By concentrating on the aesthetic value of the extremely local and idiosyncratic elements of Spanish culture, the writers of the Spanish romantic movement, for example GUSTAVO ALFONSO BÉCQUER, were rebelling against the tyranny of the ideal in favor of their own experiences.

Other romantic writers used costumbrismo for other purposes. For example, the author Mariano José de Larra (1809–37) used costumbrismo as a mode to satirize peculiar Spanish customs and point out the absurdity and barbarity of his contemporaries.

Costumbrismo used slang and local dialects to such a degree that a literary portrait written in Seville was unlikely to be understood by a citizen of Barcelona.

In Enlightenment thought, the individual is always subservient to a norm that may be discovered empirically. The consequence of this line of thinking is that the individual artist is discouraged from expressing idiosyncratic points of view in favor of attempting to express values and ideas that are universally applicable to all humanity. Costumbrismo challenges these ideas by focusing on art's relationship to the specific and immediate environment in which it is made. As a result, many works of costumbrismo are not portable to other times and are not easily translated or understood. On the other hand, costumbrismo has a nuance and a level of vivid, sensuous detail that is often lacking in the didactic works of Enlightenment literature, which are mostly philosophical treatises.

Costumbrismo reintroduced the more personal dramas of everyday life into Spanish literature. In addition, the roots of the 19th-century novel and even of MODERNISM may be seen in costumbrismo.

A Work about Costumbrismo

Tully, Carol Lisa. *Creating a National Identity: A Comparative Study of German and Spanish Romanticism.* Stuttgart, Germany: H. D. Heinz, 1997.

Coverley, Mrs. Eric

See BENNETT, LOUISE.

Crayencour, Marguerite de

See YOURCENAR, MARGUERITE.

Cronin, Jeremy (1949–   ) *poet and essayist*

Jeremy Cronin was born in Durban, South Africa, and studied at the University of Cape Town and the Sorbonne. He was arrested under the 1976 Terrorism Act for participating in underground work for the banned African National Congress in 1976 and spent seven years in a maximum-security prison, three of those years among inmates on death row. While he served his sentence, his wife unexpectedly died. He was released in 1983, the same year that his first collection of poems, *Inside,* was released.

Inside was translated into many languages and won the 1984 Ingrid Jonker Prize. The collection chronicles the relationship between the public life of political struggle and the private life and feelings that accompany this struggle.

Cronin spent three years in exile from South Africa, returning in 1990. His poetry has appeared in many magazines and anthologies, and his collection *Even The Dead* received much critical acclaim after its publication in 1997. The collection is a marked departure from his earlier work and attempts to defy the "amnesia" that prevents people from remembering South Africa's past. Cronin says of his eponymous poem, "Even the Dead," "I am not sure what poetry is. I am not sure what the aesthetic is. Perhaps the aesthetic should be defined in opposition to the anesthetic. . . . Art is the struggle to stay awake." Cronin's pieces determinedly fight the urge to forget the past—he uses the past to forge the trail to the future. His book *Inside and Out* (1999) is a compilation of poems from his previously published volumes, which revisits these themes. Cronin's most recent work is *More Than a Casual Contact* (2006).

Cronin has served as deputy general secretary of the South African Communist Party and lives in Johannesburg. His reinvention of poetic form and style shows the changing landscape of South Africa both physically and politically.

Works Edited by Jeremy Cronin

The Ideologies of Politics. With Anthony de Crespigny. New York: Oxford University Press, 1975.
Thirty Years of the Freedom Charter. With Raymond Suttner. Athens: Ohio University Press, 1987.

Works about Jeremy Cronin

De Kock, Leon. "A Different Cronin." *Electronic Mail and Guardian Review of Books.* August 1997.
Gardner, Susan. *Four South African Poets: Robert Berold, Jeremy Cronin, Douglas Reid Skinner, and Stephen Watson—Interviews.* Grahamstown, South Africa: National English Literary Museum, 1986.

Curnow, Allen (1911–2001) *poet, dramatist, editor*

Allen Curnow was born in Timaru, New Zealand. Although his mother was born in England, on his father's side he was a fifth-generation New Zealander. After studying at Christchurch BHS and the universities of Canterbury and Auckland, Curnow made the decision not to be ordained as an Anglican clergyman, as his father was. Instead, he began his career as a journalist and, between 1951 and 1976, taught English at Auckland University. Curnow edited the first collections of New Zealand poetry, *A Book of New Zealand Verse: 1923–45* (1945, 1951) and *The Penguin Book of New Zealand Verse* (1960).

A MODERNIST poet, Curnow was a friend of the British-American poet W. H. Auden, for whom he named his son Wystan (Auden's first name). For a short period of time, while overseas in 1949, he stayed with the Welsh poet Dylan Thomas with whom he became friends. Curnow's early poetry focuses on social and physical aspects of New Zealand, its landscape, and its place in the larger world, but by the time World War II broke out, Curnow was more concerned with personal as well as universal themes, as reflected in *At Dead Low Water and Sonnets* (1949).

Throughout the 1950s and 1960s, Curnow was considered one of New Zealand's most important poets. His reputation only increased with the 1972 publication of *Trees, Effigies, Moving Objects,* a highly acclaimed sequence of 18 poems. The style of his writing was becoming more open and contemporary as he began to focus on the wild landscape of Lone Kauri Road and Karekare Beach on Auckland's west coast, where he had been spending vacations.

During his long career, Curnow was awarded the New Zealand Book Award for Poetry six times, the Commonwealth Poetry Prize (1988), the Queen's Gold Medal for Poetry (1989), a Cholmondeley Award (1992), the A. W. Reed Lifetime Achievement Award of the Montana

New Zealand Books Awards (2000), and the 2001 Montana New Zealand Award for his last book of poems, *The Bells of Saint Babel's*.

Works about Allen Curnow

Stead, C. K. *Kin of Place: Essays on New Zealand Writers.* Auckland: Auckland University Press, 2002.

Wieland, James. *Ensphering Mind: A Comparative Study of Derek Walcott, Christopher Okigbo, A. D. Hope, Allen Curnow, A. M. Klein and Nissim Ezekiel.* Pueblo, Colo.: Passeggiata Press, 1988.

Czaczkes, Shmuel Yosef

See AGNON, SAMUEL JOSEF.

dada (1916–1920)

Dada, or dadaism, taken from the French word for hobbyhorse, was a nihilistic movement in the arts that spread primarily throughout France, Switzerland, Germany, and the United States between 1916 and 1920. It was founded on principles of anarchy, intentional irrationality, cynicism, and the rejection of social organization.

The origin of the name, like the movement itself, lacks any formal logic. The most widely accepted theory is that, at a meeting in 1916 at the Café Voltaire in Zurich, a group of young artists and war resisters inserted a letter opener into a French–German dictionary. The letter opener pointed to the word *dada.*

The basis of the movement was more substantive than the origin of its name. It was founded as a protest against bourgeois values and as a direct result of mounting sentiments of despair about World War I. One of the chief ambitions of the movement was to discover authentic reality by abolishing traditional culture and values. Comprised of painters, writers, dancers, and musicians, the dadaists were often involved in several art forms simultaneously and sought to break down the boundaries that kept individual art forms distinct. The dadaists did not only want to create art; they wanted to promote revolutionary changes.

They were not interested in public admiration but sought to provoke the public into action. To the dadaists, a violently negative reaction was better than a passive acceptance.

Although as a movement dadaism concerned all forms of the arts, including visual and performance modes, in France it was predominately literary in emphasis, taking the lead from one of its founders, the poet Tristan Tzara. The most noted French publication was the journal *Littérature,* which was published from 1919 to 1924 and contained works by André Breton, Louis Aragon, Philippe Soupault (1897–1990), and Paul Éluard.

The dada movement began to decline in 1922 as many of its proponents began to develop an interest in surrealism.

Works about Dada

Erickson, John D. *Dada: Performance, Poetry and Art.* Boston: Twayne, 1984.

Matthews, J. H. *Theatre in Dada and Surrealism.* Syracuse, N.Y.: Syracuse University Press, 1974.

Dağlarca, Fazil Hüsnü (1914–2008) *poet*

Fazil Hüsnü Dağlarca was born in Istanbul, Turkey, shortly after the start of World War I. He was the fifth child of an army officer, completed his higher education at a military college, and received his own commission as second lieutenant in 1935.

Although Dağlarca received a military education and was an army officer from 1935 to 1950, he showed an aptitude for writing at an early age, publishing his first poems while he was still in middle school. His first complete book of poetry was published in 1935, but he had been publishing poetry in various literary magazines since 1933. He first gained public attention in 1933 for his poem *Slowing Life,* but it was his book *Child of God* (1940) that actually provided the basis of the questions about the universe and God that the bulk of his poetry would attempt to answer. The book's major theme is humanity's amazement at the universe, expressed through the psychological viewpoint of a child who constantly asks questions and searches for answers, while at the same time both admiring and fearing the world itself. God and the nature of God are recurring themes in much of Dağlarca's work.

Dağlarca's military career also provided useful ideas on which he would ultimately focus his poetry. Toward the end of his time as an officer, Dağlarca began to use his writing in an attempt to answer diverse questions on the relationship of humanity to nature in poems such as *The Stone Age* (1945) and *Mother Earth.* Other areas of interest included humanity's relationship to one's own history (in *The War of Independence* [1951], *The Conquest of Istanbul* [1953], and *The Epic of Gallipoli* [1963]) and people's struggles with other people (in *The Agony of the West* [1951], *Song of Algeria* [1961] and *Our Vietnam War* [1966]). Dağlarca's poetry is highly patriotic and firmly entrenched in the ideals of Turkish nationalism.

Dağlarca is one of the Turkey's most prolific and most frequently translated poets. Throughout his career, Dağlarca successfully has tried virtually every form of poetry, including lyric, epic, and inspirational verse; he has also written satire and social criticism. His early poems, in particular, were focused on inspiration and are exemplified by visions of a soul at peace, ready to embrace God. Because Dağlarca watched and lived during a time of conflict, love of God and of the universe were ultimately replaced in his works by a deeper concern for the tragedy of humanity as a whole and a love for all of mankind. His epic poems fall under this category, celebrating the heroic spirit of his nation. Dağlarca's *Epic of the Three Martyrs* (1949) exemplifies and glorifies the Turkish people's struggles.

Dağlarca's style, particularly in his inspirational works, is influenced by a form of Turkish folk poetry known as divan, which has its basis in mysticism and elements of both Islam and Sufism. Folk poets concentrated primarily on native forms and vernacular in much the same manner as the oral literary tradition of the early minstrels. In conjunction with this, early in the 20th century, a nationalist movement sought to create a "Turkish" literature free of borrowed words. This combination of military precision, nationalist sentiment, and mystical allusion is a driving force behind Dağlarca's popularity.

After resigning from the military in 1950, Dağlarca began to concentrate solely on literature and its impact on Turkish culture. Particularly since the Turkish Revolution of 1960, he became increasingly disillusioned by humankind and the failure of intellectuals to contribute adequately to social change. Starting with the publication of *Mother Earth* (1950), his works focus on civic responsibility. Along with a friend, he opened a bookstore in Istanbul that he managed until 1970. On the storefront window glass, he displayed a variety of poems dedicated to current events and social change. Printed in large letters, these poems attracted much attention. When one of his poems of social protest, *Horoz* (1965), prompted legal action against him, Dağlarca responded to his persecutors in yet another poem, *Savci'ya* (1965), which is translated as *To the Public Prosecutor,* thus proving that the literary form can be as viable a weapon as military force.

Another Work by Fazil Hüsnü Dağlarca

Seçme Siirler. Selected Poems. Translated by Talât Sait Halman. Pittsburgh, Pa.: University of Pittsburgh Press, 1969.

Dalit literature

The term *Dalit* literally means "oppressed" and is used to refer to the "untouchable," casteless sects of India. Dalit literature, therefore, is not only about but also written by the educated of this social group. Unlike literature that is defined by its affiliation to a particular style or structure, such as MODERNISM or DADA, Dalit fiction and its literary movement is based on the common ground of social oppression. This movement puts all importance on the lived experience of the writer. Only those who have undergone the trials of being socially ostracized can be said to write Dalit literature of any political or moral relevance. Predictably, such a framework allowed newfound opportunities among women to voice their rebellion against gender oppression.

Dalit writers belong to a historical, social, and political background that spreads throughout India from Gujarat, Tamil Nadu, Maharashtra, and Andhra Pradesh to Punjab. It could be said that Dalit literature achieved a firm foundation in the mid-20th century, but its framework was established in the early 19th century. Today, Dalit writers have their own literary foundations and publish numerous journals. They also have a number of political organizations. The most prominent of these is the Dalit Panthers (begun in the 1970s), which has borrowed much of its ideology from America's Black Panthers.

The form or style of Dalit literature covers a wide range of literary genres. In content, however, there are similarities between authors and their works. The overall message is about community not individuality, revolt not passivity, progress not backwardness. The shared political position of these authors is against the hegemony of upper- and middle-class Hindu beliefs and for the power of the human being against oppressive social rules.

Because of this, cultural concepts such as religion and identity are called into question. The language of these texts is very faithful to local, spoken dialects, and high-flown language is not seen to have adequate political power.

Many national leaders have based their reform on the social cause of the lower castes. For the Dalits, the most famous of these leaders was Dr. Bhimrao Ramji Ambedkar (1891–1956). The emancipation of the Dalits was due in large part to Ambedkar's foundation of educational institutions in the 1960s. These schools were havens where Dalit professors and educated, middle-class Dalit students could come together intellectually. Some famous Dalit writers are MULK RAJ ANAND and NAMDEO DHASAL.

Dalit literature has, since its inception, been translated into several Indian and European languages without compromising on the quality of rebellion that first characterized it. Such literature defies the idea that practice and theory remain separate. The strength of the term *Dalit,* originally used to ostracize a section of Indian society, enabled a successful literary movement that has overthrown social prejudice and won worldwide acclaim.

Works about Dalit Literature

Anand, Mulk Raj. *Anthology of Dalit Literature.* Columbia, Mo.: South Asia Books, 1992.
Moon, Vasant. *Growing up Untouchable in India: A Dalit Autobiography.* Translated by Gail Omvedt. New Delhi: Vistaar, 2002.

D'Annunzio, Gabriele (1863–1938) *poet, novelist, dramatist*

Renowned as a writer and a military hero who strongly supported fascism, Gabriele D'Annunzio was born in Pescara, a town in central Italy. The son of a wealthy landowner, he received his education in Prato at Liceo Cicognini, one of the best schools in Italy during that period.

D'Annunzio published his first collection of poems while he was still in his teens. *Primo vere (First Spring,* 1879) was inspired by the works of the aristocratic, elitist, classical scholar Giosue Carducci, who sought a humanistic approach to literary studies.

In 1881, D'Annunzio enrolled at the University of Rome. Life in the capital city exposed him to a variety of cultural, artistic, and literary stimulation. He contributed articles to several newspapers and became a member of several literary groups. He also married Maria Hardouin di Galese. The daughter of a duke, she expected a specific standard of living, and D'Annunzio produced large quantities of hack writing to maintain her. The works he produced during this time, however, also included some notable pieces strongly influenced by GUY DE MAUPASSANT and the French DECADENCE movement. In particular, the short stories *Canto novo* (1882), *Terra vergine* (1882), and *L'Intermezzo di rime* (1883) express a sensual awareness of life.

D'Annunzio's first novel, *The Child of Pleasure* (1889), was a parody of decadence. He followed this highly successful work with *The Victim* (1891), a novel about sexual depravity. The same year as this work came out, his marriage ended. He moved to Naples and began a series of affairs, the most influential of which was his long-term liaison with the actress Eleonora Duse. He was so deeply inspired by her that he began to produce dramatic works specifically for her, including *La Gioconda* (1899) and *Francesca da Rimini* (1901).

Beginning in 1897, D'Annunzio served a three-year term in parliament, but he was not reelected at the end of his term. Having just purchased an expensive villa in anticipation of maintaining his position, he was able to live off of his savings for only a short period before being forced to flee to France to avoid his debts. He returned to writing during this period, staying away from his native Italy until the start of World War I.

Ever the nationalist, D'Annunzio was prompted by the war to return to Italy. He also began his military career. He wrote powerful speeches and articles, urging his fellow countrymen to support the Allied cause. He began a series of correspondences with Mussolini that provided the leader with much insight into potential military tactics. At one point, however, during 1919, D'Annunzio began to lose faith in Italy and its lack of determination. He took his troops and occupied the town of Fiume, ruling as its dictator for 18 months and professing a desire to declare war against Italy. Ultimately, however, he was forced to retreat.

After losing one eye in a flying accident, D'Annunzio retired to once again work on his writing. He was given the title of Prince of Monte Nevoso in 1924 and was elected president of the Italian Royal Academy in 1937. On March 1, 1938, he suffered a stroke and died the same day. Mussolini, in honor of his contributions to the cause, ordered that he be given a state funeral.

A Work about Gabriele D'Annunzio

Woodhouse, John. *Gabriele D'Annunzio, Defiant Archangel.* New York: Oxford University Press, 2001.

Darío, Rubén (Félix Rubén García Sarmiento) (1867–1916) *poet, short story writer*

Rubén Darío was born in Metapa, Nicaragua (now called Ciudad Darío). While still an infant, his parents divorced, and he was adopted by his godfather, Colonel Félix Ramírez. Though he showed writing talent and ability as a teenager, he was denied a scholarship to study in Europe because his youthful writing was too liberal in its religious views. Instead, after he finished school, he traveled to El Salvador, where he met the poet Francisco Gavidia.

Gavidia introduced Darío to French literature. Darío was particularly interested in VICTOR HUGO and briefly imitated his style. Unable to go to France, he absorbed French culture through its novels and poems. This immersion, first in Hugo and then in the writers of the French symbolist movement (*see* SYMBOLISM), particularly the poet VERLAINE, was a key factor in Darío's development and led to his founding of the movement of Latin American MODERNISM.

Before Darío, Latin American literature was completely dominated by antiquated modes of writing inherited from Europe. In addition, the subject matter was almost exclusively limited to descriptions of local life and scenery. By introducing modernist ideas such as making art for art's sake and developing a unique poetic voice, Darío succeeded in creating a literature of international scope.

In 1888, while living in Chile, Darío published *Blue,* a book of short stories and poems that investigate again and again the role of an artist in an industrial society where all value is based on monetary worth. In the poem "Queen Mab's Veil," Darío uses strong metaphors and symbolic imagery to depict how the artist's inner life can be filled with beauty, even when his or her outer reality is cold and unfeeling. The title of the poem alludes to a speech from Shakespeare's play *Romeo and Juliet* in which Mercutio speaks about the magical quality of dreams.

In *Songs of Life and Hope* (1905), a book of poems, Darío reached another stage in his poetic development. While his earlier books freely use nostalgic images that traditionally represented beauty in poetry, for example, the nightingale, *Songs of Life and Hope* reshapes those images and questions what they mean in a Latin American social and political context. His long poem *To Roosevelt,* written to United States president Theodore Roosevelt, is a meditation on the United States. In it Darío both admires the United States as a model of modern democracy and worries about the possible threat of U.S. imperialism.

In the final years of his life, the poet would write increasingly about politics, his fear of death, and the uncertainty of the fate of humanity. These are the themes that occupy his haunting and beautiful poem "Fatalities," the final poem in *Songs of Life and Hope.*

Darío was the central figure in Latin American modernism and was a forerunner of the cosmopolitan tendencies of such later Latin American authors as JORGE LUIS BORGES, JULIO CORTÁZAR, and OCTAVIO PAZ. He introduced idiomatic language, original metaphors, and formal innovations to the Latin American literary scene. Finally, his body of work stands as a testament to a highly learned and expressive mind, struggling with the great themes of history, spirituality, and art.

Another Work by Rubén Darío
Selected Poems. Translated by Lysander Kemp. Austin: University of Texas Press, 1965.

A Work about Rubén Darío
Ellis, Keith. *Critical Approaches to Rubén Darío.* Toronto: University of Toronto Press, 1974.

Darwish, Mahmud (Mahmoud)
(1942–2008) *poet*
Foremost Palestinian poet Darwish emerged as one of the "Resistance Poets," Palestinians who, in the aftermath of the 1967 Israeli occupation, wrote poetry of struggle. The poem "Identity Card" (1964), an impassioned cry from an Arab quarryman who is determined to keep his dignity despite Israeli occupation, typifies Darwish's early voice. In the 1970s, Darwish's poetry became the definitive expression of the pain of Palestinian exile. He evolved beyond being keeper of Palestine's spiritual flame, and editor Munir Akash called him the "poet of human grief." Darwish's broad vision embraces the literary heritage not only of Arabs but also of Jews and the many other peoples who inhabit the land of his birth. His creative scope encompassed ancient Near Eastern, Native American, and European mythology. A giant in his significance for modern Arabic literature, Darwish was such a literary icon for Palestinians that when he wrote personal poetry, such as the volume of

love poems, *Bed of a Stranger* (1999), some Arab critics responded as if he were turning his back on the plight of his people.

Darwish was born in Barweh, a Palestinian town that was attacked by Israel in its 1948 campaign. Darwish grew up, in Salma K. Jayyusi's words, "as a refugee in his own country." He became active in the Israeli Communist Party and, in 1964, published his first book of poetry, *Leaves of Olive*. In 1971, he resettled in Beirut, where he lived until 1982, when Palestinians were driven out of Lebanon. His memoir, *Memory for Forgetfulness,* is about being trapped in the 1982 Israeli siege of Beirut. In 1996, Darwish was allowed to return to the land of his birth.

Darwish's awards include the Lenin Prize (1983) and France's Knighthood of Arts and Belles Lettres (1997). He served on the Palestinian National Council, founded the prestigious literary magazine *al-Karmel,* has written 30 books, and is translated into 35 languages. In 1999, Israeli authorities finally permitted five Darwish poems to be included in schoolbooks.

Darwish died on August 9, 2008, after undergoing heart surgery in the United States. His body was buried in Ramallah in the West Bank on a hill overlooking Jerusalem.

Other Works by Mahmud Darwish

Adam of Two Edens. Edited by Munir Akash and Daniel Moore. Syracuse, N.Y.: Syracuse University Press, 2000.

Psalms. Translated by Ben Bennani. Boulder, Colo.: Passeggiata Press, 1995.

Victims of a Map: A Bilingual Anthology of Arabic Poetry by Samih al-Qasim, Adonis, and Mahmud Darwish. Translated by Abdullah al-Udhari. London: Al-Saqi Books, 1984.

Davies, Robertson (1913–1995) *novelist, playwright, essayist*

Robertson William Davies was born in Thamesville, Ontario, Canada, to a newspaper owner. He attended Oxford, receiving a degree in literature in 1938. From a young age, he was drawn to the the-

ater, playing small roles outside London; in 1940, he acted at the Old Vic Repertory Company in London and married Brenda Matthews, who was the stage manager for the company. He returned to Canada with his wife soon after to work as a journalist. He was the editor of the *Peterborough Examiner* for 15 years and its publisher from 1955 to 1965.

Davies's love of theater was evident from the many plays he wrote, and he said that he considered his plays comedies rather than tragedies that criticized Canada's provincial attitudes. He won the 1948 Dominion Drama Festival Award for best Canadian play for *Eros at Breakfast,* which made use of allegory (using symbols rather than direct representation) and was more theatrical than realistic. In a similar style, *King Phoenix* is a fantasy based on the mythical King Cole, while *General Confession* is a historical comedy of ideas with the main characters serving as Jungian (derived from Carl Jung) archetypes of self, persona, shadow, and anima. These three plays, with their elaborate costumes and settings and magic transformations, reveal Davies's inclination for spectacle and extravagance.

Although Davies wrote plays, essays, and criticism, it is for his many novels that he is best known and admired. His first trilogy, the Salterton Trilogy—*Tempest-Tost* (1951), *Leaven of Malice* (1954), and *A Mixture of Frailties* (1958)—is an ongoing social comedy set in a small Ontario university town. The novel that begins the Deptford Trilogy, *Fifth Business* (1970), is considered by most critics to be his finest work with its blend of myths, magic, freaks, evil, and theatrical elements. A snowball with a stone concealed in it opens the novel, which then proceeds through the life of a magician whose life is linked through that stone to that of the protagonist, Boy Staunton. The other Deptford novels are *The Manticore* (1972) and *World of Wonders* (1975).

Davies's work often plays with traditional themes and tropes from the Western literary canon. He often works with classical themes set in a modern context, making frequent allusions to works like Milton's *Paradise Lost*. The influence of Shakespeare and Milton is immediately evident. (In fact, Davies's B.Lit. thesis at Oxford was on Shakespearean Theatre.) Davies's work also reflects his interest in Freudian and subsequently Jungian psychology, especially *The Manticore*.

During the course of his career, Davies won a number of major awards for his work, including the Lorne Pierce Medal, the Stephen Leacock Medal for Humour, and the Governor General's Award for *The Manticore*. Davies was the first Canadian to become an Honorary Member of the American Academy and Institute of Arts and Letters. He was a Companion of the Order of Canada.

Reviewer S. A. Rowland writes in *Contemporary Novelists* that Davies "delights in paradox and is himself an example: Among the most innovative of contemporary novelists, he stresses our deep roots in old cultures and 'magical' beliefs."

Other Works by Robertson Davies
The Cunning Man: A Novel. New York: Viking, 1995.
The Lyre of Orpheus. New York: Viking Penguin, 1988.
The Mirror of Nature. Toronto: University of Toronto Press, 1983.
The Rebel Angels. New York: Viking Press, 1982.
The Well-tempered Critic: One Man's View of Theatre and Letters in Canada. Toronto: McClelland and Stewart, 1981.

Works about Robertson Davies
Grant, Judith Skelton. *Robertson Davies: Man of Myth.* New York: Viking, 1994.
Peterman, Michael. *Robertson Davies.* Boston: Twayne, 1986.

decadence
Decadence is a literary and artistic movement that began in Europe during the final decades of the 19th century. Although France produced the most notable of all decadent authors, JORIS-KARL HUYSMANS, whose *À Rebours* (*Against Nature,* 1884) epitomizes the movement, decadence was not confined to France. It spread to Belgium with writers such as Rodenbach, to Germany, with the early works of THOMAS MANN and the writings of STEFAN GEORGE, and Austria, with HUGO VON HOFMANNSTHAL. It was also evidenced in Britain and Ireland in the works of Oscar Wilde, particularly his novel *The Picture of Dorian Gray* (1890). Huysmans's influence on Wilde seems apparent in that Wilde refers to *A Rebours,* calling it the *The Yellow Book* that corrupts Dorian Gray. Other notable members of the French decadent movement include CHARLES BAUDELAIRE and STÉPHANE MALLARMÉ and ARTHUR RIMBAUD.

Characteristic of the decadence movement as a whole, and symptomatic of the obsessions of FIN-DE-SIÈCLE Europe, elements such as decapitation, vampirism, and images of women as evil predators and temptresses were common throughout decadence texts. The themes in these writings are, therefore, inherently diverse and include tales of the supernatural and occult, science fiction, romance, and "faits divers" or "slice of life" sensational crimes.

Seeking to speak out against scientific progress and democracy, decadent authors created their own paradise, often drug induced, and reveled in the poetics of necrophilia. Self-centered and egomaniacal almost to the point of self-annihilation, they tended to be members of the aristocracy who were antidemocratic in politics, misanthropic, and misogynistic (hating or fearful of women). They were often devotees of the occult, and their lifestyles tended to be as flamboyant as their writings were insolent. Many members of the decadent movement ultimately died from their excesses.

A Work about Decadence
McGuinness, Patrick, ed. *Symbolism, Decadence and the Fin de Siècle: French and European Perspectives.* Exeter: University of Exeter Press, 2000.

De Kok, Ingrid (1951–) *poet*
Ingrid De Kok was raised in South Africa, whose geography influenced her later work. She says,

"Growing up in a hard, flat, dry place, a demanding physical environment has probably influenced the way I see a great number of things as well as the way I respond to landscape. I'm interested in geography and space insofar as it relates to the notion of home." This image of home appears in much of her poetry. Her work has appeared in many anthologies and numerous journals in South Africa, England, the United States, and Canada.

De Kok's poetry blends the languages of Afrikaans and English to create images of the South African landscape. In a move that she calls unconscious, she weaves into her poetry the political subjects of loss and apartheid alongside the very personal lives of the people; for example, in her poem, "Mending," from her collection *Familiar Ground* (1988), the narrator says, "The woman plies her ancient art, / Her needle sutures as it darts, / scoring, scripting, scarring, stitching, / the invisible mending of the heart." By blending the traditional sewing metaphor with images of scarring and scoring, De Kok shows not only a garment or body being mended but also a nation.

Her notion of the community in her poetry is influenced by authors such as SEAMUS HEANEY and JEREMY CRONIN, while her interest in form is more influenced by traditional English and American writers such as Emily Dickinson, John Donne, and Robert Frost. De Kok's work has been described as having "fearlessness, guts to transgress, an unfailing ear for the alternation of consonants on the tongue, a turn of thinking and the ability to capture in the most delicate and individual terms a devastating phenomenon."

Other Works by Ingrid De Kok

Seasonal Fires: Selected and New Poems. New York: Seven Stories Press, 2006.
Terrestrial Things. Cape Town, South Africa: Kwela/Snailpress, 2002.

A Work about Ingrid De Kok

Krog, Antjie. "Defenceless in the Face of De Kok's Poetry." *Electronic Mail and Guardian.* Johannesburg, South Africa. January 19, 1998.

Dépestre, René (1926–) *poet, novelist, essayist, journalist, professor, editor*

René Dépestre was born and educated in Jacmel, Haiti, before attending the Lycée Pétion in Port-au-Prince. There he worked with the revolutionary magazine *La Ruche*. At 19, Dépestre published his first revolutionary volume of verse, *Étincelles.*He became a leading voice for young Haitian radicals by, for example, criticizing the Haitian government's exploitative acts in *La Ruche*. After a Haitian student revolution sparked by *La Ruche*'s prohibition in 1946, Dépestre was exiled to France. He published *Traduit du grand large* (*Translated from the High Sea*, 1952), a volume of poetry, before returning to Haiti in 1958. Dissatisfied with Haitian dictator François Duvalier, Dépestre moved to Cuba in 1959 and worked as an editor and professor. After Cuba expelled him in 1978, Dépestre returned to France. He worked for UNESCO during the 1980s and became a French citizen in 1991.

Although Dépestre has lived much of his adult life outside Haiti, he is one of Haiti's most celebrated contemporary poets. His poetry voices Haitian and Caribbean values and explores the relationships between and among identity and ethnicity, slavery, and exploitation. His articles and essays grapple with similar issues, as seen in *Bonjour et adieu à la négritude* (*Hello and Goodbye to Negritude*, 1980), a collection of essays that marks Dépestre's ideological shift from embracing authentic identity to embracing more-open concepts of cultural and personal identities.

Alléluia pour une femme-jardin (*Hallelujah for a Garden-Woman*, 1973) marks an erotic shift in Dépestre's writing. There, for example, Dépestre employs erotic and allegorical representations of women. In *Éros dans un train chinois* (*Eros in a Chinese Train*, 1993), Dépestre develops a new, imaginative, erotic aesthetic called erotic-magical realism that would ideally recreate Haiti. Dépestre's work not only focuses on revolution, but his innovative aesthetics also redefine how to write about revolution.

Other Works by René Dépestre

The Festival of the Greasy Pole. Translated by Carrol F. Coates. Charlottesville: University Press of Virginia, 1990.
A Rainbow for the Christian West. Translated by Jack Hirschman. Fairfax, Calif.: Red Hill Press, 1972.
Vegetations of Splendor. Translated by Jack Hirschman. Chicago: Vanguard, 1981.

Works about René Dépestre

Dayan, Joan. "France Reads Haiti: An Interview with René Dépestre." *Yale French Studies* 83 (1994): 136–53.
Ferdinand, Joseph. "The New Political Statement in Haitian Fiction." In *Voices from Under: Black Narrative in Latin American and the Caribbean.* Edited by William Luis. Westport, Conn.: Greenwood Press, 1984.

Desai, Anita (Mazumdar, Anita)

(1937–) *novelist*

Anita Desai was born in Mussoorie, a tiny hill station on the outskirts of Delhi, India, to a German mother and an Indian father. Though her novels are in English, Desai is fluent in several languages. It has been noted that she spoke German at home, Hindi with friends, and English at school. Desai has taught at Mount Holyoke College, Baruch College, Smith College, and the Massachusetts Institute of Technology. She is a fellow of the Royal Society of Literature in London and a member of the American Academy of Arts and Letters.

Desai's novels are preoccupied with the theme of alienation. Her novel *In Custody* (1985) is set during the fraught political tensions between India and Pakistan during the Partition War and traces the daily lives of middle-class women at home. What unfolds is a female narrative of political struggle that occurs outside of and simultaneous to the one fought in the public space dominated by men. One of the main characters, Nur, is a budding poet whose talent is silenced and hidden by her husband. Her story is one example of the novel's concern with the effects historical events have on family relations and how women are denied public recognition.

Although Desai's earlier novels are based on the question of women's roles in Indian and Pakistani societies, Desai's later novel, *Baumgartner's Bombay* (1988), goes beyond the problem of gender. It is the story of a businessman's search across continents to escape Western anti-Semitism, only to discover traces of it even in India. This novel is more global in perspective in its exploration of the aftereffects of World War II in an Indian context. Her most recent novel, *The Zigzag Way* (2004), focuses on a young American adrift in Mexico. He decides to learn what he can about his grandfather, who once mined in the Sierra Madre.

Desai has also written numerous children's books, of which *The Village by the Sea* (1982) won the Guardian Prize for Children's Fiction in 1983. Her first novel, *Fire on the Mountain,* (1977) won the Indian National Academy of Letters Award. In 1988, she was awarded the Padma Shri by the president of India for her outstanding contribution to Indian literature.

Other Works by Anita Desai

Clear Light of Day. New York: Houghton Mifflin, 2000.
Journey to Ithaca. New York: Knopf, 1995.

Works about Anita Desai

Bande, Usha. *The Novels of Anita Desai.* Prestigé Books, 1992.
Buruma, Ian, ed. *India: A Mosaic.* New York: New York Review of Books, 2000.

Desbordes-Valmore, Marceline

(1786–1859) *poet*

Marceline Desbordes-Valmore was born in Douai, France, to a lower-middle-class family whose lives had been ruined by the French Revolution. She left with her mother for the Antilles in 1801 only to find the conditions there horrible. Faced with riots and an epidemic of yellow fever, her mother died only a few days after their arrival. Desbordes-Valmore returned to Douai in 1802 to embark on a career as a professional singer and actress.

Desbordes-Valmore's life was fraught with tragedy. In 1809, she fell in love with a writer who left her shortly after she gave birth to their child. The child lived only five years. In 1817, she married the actor Prosper Valmore, with whom she had three children, Hippolyte, Ondine, and Inês. The family lived a precarious existence, fleeing the dangers of revolution throughout Europe. Her daughter Inês died in 1846; Ondine's daughter died in 1852, followed by Ondine herself in 1853; and in 1858 Desbordes-Valmore lost her best friend, the musician Pauline Duchambge.

Desbordes-Valmore's poetry was the one reliable source of satisfaction in her life. In it, her griefs found memorable expression and perhaps catharsis. In "Les séparés ("Apart"), for example, the poet addresses an absent lover with a constant refrain: "Do not write!":

> Do not write. Let us learn to die, as best
>   we may.
> Did I love you? Ask God. Ask yourself. Do
>   you know?
> To hear that you love me, when you are far
>   away,
> Is like hearing from heaven and never to go.
>   Do not write!

Between 1819 and 1843, she published several collections of poetry and received recognition from critics such as Charles Augustin Sainte-Beuve (1804–69) and VICTOR HUGO as one of the leading poets of her time. She also wrote a number of works for children. Her poetry is characterized by sincerity, spontaneity, grace, and melancholy.

Another Work by Marceline Desbordes-Valmore

Simpson, Louis, ed. and trans. Selections in *Modern Poets of France: A Bilingual Anthology*. Ashland, Ore.: Story Line Press, 1997.

Works about Marceline Desbordes-Valmore

Boutine, Aimee. *Maternal Echoes: the Poetry of Marceline Desbordes-Valmore and Alphonse de Lamartine*. Newark: University of Delaware Press, 2001.

Johnson, Barbara. *The Feminist Difference: Literature, Psychoanalysis, Race, and Gender*. Cambridge, Mass.: Harvard University Press, 2000.

Sainte-Beuve, Charles Augustin. *Memoirs of Madame Desbordes-Valmore, with a selection from her poems*. Translated by Harriet W. Preston. New York: AMS Press, 1980.

Devi, Mahasweta (1926–) *novelist, short story writer, dramatist, journalist*

Mahasweta Devi was born into a literary family in Dacca, Bangladesh (previously known as East Bengal). As a young child, she migrated to West Bengal (India) with her parents. The local politics of West Bengal and the Bengali language are to this day the source and inspiration for Devi's literature. Her early involvement with the local political theater group "Ganantaya" formed her ambition to spread social and political awareness through her writing. Since then, she has used her prodigious talent to champion the cause of suppressed Indian tribal societies. Most of her work is written in Bengali and has been translated into several Indian languages and into English. In a 1998 interview, she said that her goal is to "fight for the tribals, downtrodden, underprivileged, and write creatively if and when I find the time."

Devi's feminist tone comments on the traditional view of women in Indian society. Female characters in her works are borrowed from an older literary tradition but are transformed to reveal a profound political self-awareness. In the short story "Dopadi," Devi evokes the central female character from the classical epic *Mahabharata*, Draupadi, to tell a story of a fugitive tribal woman, also of the same name, who outwits the local police. Another short story, "Breast-Giver" (1993), is a symbolic comparison between a woman's physical illness and the social illnesses extant in postindependent India.

Mahasweta Devi gave up her position as a professor in English literature at a Calcutta university in 1984. This decision allowed her to begin a new life devoted to social work and writing. In 1997, she was a recipient of the Magsaysay Award (Asia's equivalent to the Nobel Prize) for a lifetime spent in creating literature that extends beyond the literary and intellectual to the social. In 2006, Devi was awarded the Padma Vibhushan, the second highest civilian award from the government of India.

Other Works by Mahasweta Devi

Bait: Four Stories. Kolkata, India: Seagull Books, 2010.

Imaginary Maps: Three Stories by Mahasweta Devi. Translated by Gayatri Spivak. New York: Routledge, 1994.

Works about Mahasweta Devi

"Mahasweta Devi." Available online. URL: http://www.emory.edu/ENGLISH/Bahri/Devi.html. Accessed October 11, 2010.

Spivak, Gayatri. *In Other Worlds: Essays in Cultural Politics.* New York: Routledge, 1987.

Dhammachoti, Ussiri (Atsiri Thammachoat) (1947–) *novelist*

Ussiri Dhammachoti was born in the Hua Hin district, Prachuap Khiri Khan, Thailand. His father was a fisherman who owned several fishing trawlers. Dhammachoti received his primary and secondary education at Sathukan School. When he failed to pass the entrance exams for Chulalongkorn University, he applied to work for the National Statistical Office and was assigned to draw maps for the national population census. In 1970, he reapplied and was admitted to Chulalongkorn University. He graduated with a bachelor's degree in communications arts in 1974 and started a

magazine, which lasted less than a year. He worked for various newspapers, including the *Siam Rath,* for many years before finally quitting his post as publisher in 1998. He is now a freelance writer and writes only in Thai.

Dhammachoti's writings are deeply influenced by his life experiences. His mother's death greatly affected Dhammachoti, whose initial interest in literature was motivated by his mother's love for old Thai literature and poetry. His travels to the northern provinces of Thailand during the years he worked for the National Statistical Office opened the opportunity for him to collect ideas that formed the basis of his works. Dhammachoti's works deal with a variety of themes, such as the impact of the modern world on traditional societies located in the hilly outskirts of Thailand. These themes are often represented in his TV plays, such as *Khun Det* and *Mae Nak Phra Khanong.* His fascination with the local folklore and cultural and religious practices can be observed in his short stories. Dhammachoti also possesses a nostalgic empathy for the people who live in the remote regions of the country. His goal to better their lives is intermixed with his desire to preserve some aspects of their way of life. He sees richness in the traditional history of many of the tribes, like the Miao and Hmong, that should be preserved.

Dhammachoti's stories, such as "Samnuk Khong Pho Thao" ("The Old Man's Conscience," 1972), reflect his compassion for and understanding of not only the poor and downtrodden in Thai society but also the various ethnic groups that live at the borders of the Thai nation. His characters consist of a variety of personality types, ranging from the elite group to the marginalized peoples who lived in the northern region of Thailand. Their differences in background, philosophy, and status, however, do not hinder their attempts to gain a mutual understanding of each other's cultures and tradition.

When Dhammachoti was still an undergraduate, he won the Phlubphla Mali Literary Award from the Literary Circle of Chulalongkorn

University for his short story "Samnuk Khong Pho Thao" in 1972. His collection of short stories *Kuntong . . . Chao Cha Khlab Ma Mua Fa Sang (Kuntong . . . You Will Return at Dawn)* was published in 1978 and won the Southeast Asian Writer Award in 1981. On November 3, 2000, Dhammachoti was awarded the honor of National Artist in Literature.

Another Work by Ussiri Dhammachoti

Of Time and Tide: A Thai Novel. Bangkok: Thai Modern Classic Series, 1985.

Dhasal, Namdeo (Namdev) (1947–   )
poet, novelist

Namdeo Dhasal was born in a small village outside Pune, India. He is a DALIT, which means "casteless" or "untouchable," and grew up very poor. Dhasal had almost no formal education but educated himself on the literature of other Dalit writers who also wrote about the conditions of the oppressed. Because of this focus, at no time can the voice of the poet be distinguished from that of the political rebel. Dhasal's poetry directly addresses the sources of human unhappiness such as poverty, prostitution, and underworld politics of Bombay. His famed knowledge of the city caught the attention of Trinidadian author V. S. NAIPAUL, who used Dhasal as his guide to Bombay and made him an important figure in his book *India: A Million Mutinies Now* (1990).

The city of Bombay is the subject of Dhasal's first collection of poems called *Golpitha* (1973). When the famous Indian playwright Vinay Tendulkar offered to write the introduction to Dhasal's collection, Dhasal insisted that he first come on a walking tour of Golpitha, a red-light district, before writing anything. Dhasal's portraits of the inhabitants in Golpitha vividly capture "life gone wrong" in a world of poverty, filth, and violence. Paradox, however, is a defining feature of Dhasal's style and the harsh realism of his poetry is coupled with images that are both alluring and hopeful. In an untitled poem from *Khel* (*Play,* 1983), for example, "Butterflies of hibiscus" dance under the sun that throws love over a "wounded dog" turning in circles.

Since *Golpitha*, Dhasal has written novels and several collections of poetry. Dhasal writes in Marathi and a hybrid of Hindi and Urdu. His work, written in the language of the streets, has been called a translator's nightmare. In spite of this, Dhasal's poetry has been translated into numerous European languages, and he has traveled widely to read his poetry.

Dhasal was one of the founders of the Dalit Panthers in 1972. In 1990, he joined mainstream politics and became a member of the Indian Republican Party. He received the Padma Shri from the president of India for his outstanding contribution to Indian literature and was chosen to represent India at the first International Literary Festival in Berlin in 2001. In 2004, Dhasal received Sahitya Akademi's Golden Life Time Achievement Award.

Another Work by Namdeo Dhasal

"The Poems of Namdeo Dhasal." In *An Anthology of Dalit Literature.* Edited by Mulk Raj Anand and Eleanor Zelliot. Columbia, Mo.: South Asia Books, 1992.

Dinesen, Isak (Karen Christence Dinesen, Baroness Karen Blixen, Osceola, Pierre Andrézel) (1885–1962)
short story writer, novelist

Isak Dinesen was born in Rungsted, Denmark, to wealth and privilege. Her father, Wilhelm Dinesen, was an army officer and a writer. Her mother, Ingeborg Westenholz Dinesen, was from a prominent business family. Dinesen studied painting at the Royal Academy of Fine Arts in Copenhagen from 1903 to 1906. In 1907, she published several short stories in a Danish monthly, but these works attracted little attention. In 1914, Dinesen married Swedish nobleman Baron Bror Blixen-Finecke and settled on a coffee plantation in Kenya. They later divorced, and Dinesen moved back to Denmark after the plantation went bankrupt in 1931.

Dinesen's writing career thrived after she returned to Rungsted. Critics in Great Britain and the United States praised her first major work, *Seven Gothic Tales* (1934), for its sophistication and imaginative use of fantasy. Dinesen's description of her experiences in Africa, *Den africanske farm* (*Out of Africa*, 1937), was later made into a movie. During World War II, she wrote *Sorg-Acre* (*Sorrow Acre,* 1942), a story set in a rural Denmark that many consider to be her masterpiece.

Dinesen's influences included her father, the Bible, Danish romantic writers, the *Arabian Nights,* and the Icelandic sagas. Many of her works, including *Sorrow Acre,* reflect Dinesen's belief that an individual's fate is in the hands of God. She wrote about the topics of love and dreams in her many imaginative tales of fantasy. However, irony destroys romanticism in many of Dinesen's stories, which critic Curtis Cate describes as "sophisticated," "psychologically subtle," and "philosophically speculative."

Critical Analysis

"Babette's Feast" from Dinesen's short story collection *Anecdotes of Destiny* (1958) is a tale about the power of art. While the story seems firmly grounded in history, the narrator's language suggests the world of a fairy tale or a medieval miracle play.

"Babette's Feast" is set in a small town in Norway in the latter half of the 19th century. The title character is a servant in the home of two elderly women, Martine and Phillipa, the daughters of the founder of a strict Protestant religious sect. Babette, a refugee from the French civil war of 1871, a worker's uprising that led to the execution of more than 20,000 rebels, arrived ragged and exhausted on the sisters' doorstep and begged them to take her in as a cook. The sisters assented, but suspicious of Babette's culinary talents ("In France, they knew, people ate frogs.") showed her how to prepare their simple, spartan fare of "cod and ale-and-bread soup." They told her that "luxurious fare was sinful. Their own food must be as plain as possible; it was the soup-pails and baskets for their poor that signified." Babette becomes invaluable to the sisters and to the town, Christ-like in multiplying the loaves and fishes that fed the poor. "From the day when Babette took over the housekeeping its cost was miraculously reduced, and the soup-pails and baskets acquired a new, mysterious power to stimulate and strengthen their poor and sick."

After 12 years of serving Martine and Phillipa, Babette wins 10,000 francs in a lottery. The sisters are certain that she will leave them and return to France. As they are worrying about how they will manage, Babette asks for a favor. She wants, she says, to cook for them "a French dinner, a real French dinner" for the celebration of the 100th anniversary of their father's birth. The sisters have always deprived themselves of sensual pleasures, dressing and living plainly, and both had rejected suitors years before in order to remain focused on their religious duties. They grant Babette her favor but feel compelled to warn the dinner guests that they are to be subjected to French food. The entire group vows, for Babette's sake, to eat, but they intend to do so without enjoyment.

Babette's feast is, of course, a miracle. The 12 guests, like Christ's disciples, sit down to a meal that changes everything. Only one member of the group, Martine's former suitor, General Loewenhielm, recognizes that the food is exquisitely prepared, the work of a culinary genius. However, the guests notice that the rooms were "filled with a heavenly light, as if a number of small halos had blended into one glorious radiance. Taciturn old people received the gift of tongues; ears that for years had been almost deaf were opened to it. Time itself had merged into eternity." Love blossoms, grudges disappear, and faith is strengthened.

After the dinner, the sisters find that Babette has spent her entire winnings on the dinner. Martine says, "So you will be poor now all your life, Babette?" and Babette answers, "No I shall never be poor. . . . I am a great artist. A great artist, Mesdames, is never poor. We have something, Mesdames, of which other people know nothing."

"Babette's Feast" is like Babette's feast—good for the stomach and the soul. The story was adapted for a major motion picture in 1987.

Another Work by Isak Dinesen

Last Tales. New York: Vintage Books, 1991.

Works about Isak Dinesen

Cate, Curtis. "Isaac Dinesen: The Scheherazade of Our Times." In Olga A. Pelensky, ed., *Isak Dinesen: Critical Views*. Athens: Ohio University Press, 1993.

Thurman, Judith. *Isak Dinesen: The Life of a Storyteller*. New York: St. Martin's Press, 1982.

Ding Ling (Jiang Bingzhi) (1904–1986)
novelist, short story and nonfiction writer

Jiang Bingzhi was born on October 12, 1904, in Hunan Province's Linli County in China. After her father's death, she lived with her uncle in Changde. She was introduced to ideas of revolution and democracy at a young age because Changde was a focal point for the 1911 republican revolution to overthrow the Qing dynasty. At 17, she attended a Communist school in Shanghai and later Shanghai University. In 1923, she left for Beijing, where China's "new culture" was developing. She could not afford to attend lectures at Beijing University, so she read Western and Eastern writers. She also learned to paint, and in 1925, she married Hu Yepin, a revolutionary writer.

In 1927, Ding Ling published to great acclaim her first short story, "Meng Ke," based on her own experience at an unsuccessful film audition. Its publication was quickly followed by "Miss Sophie's Diary," a story about a girl with tuberculosis and her fruitless desire to find love. The next year, she published her first short-story collection, *In the Dark*.

In 1930, Ding Ling and her husband joined the proletarian literary movement in Shanghai, where they joined the newly formed League of Left-wing Writers headed by LU Xun. Hu Yepin was executed by the Nationalists for his involvement in the Chinese Communist Party (CCP) underground, an event that plunged Ding Ling into the revolution. Ding Ling herself was later kidnapped by the Guomingdang (GMD) Nationalist Party.

Amidst her political activity, Ding Ling was also busy writing. She edited *The Dipper*, the league's literary magazine, and published *Flood*, a major revolutionary work of social realist (*see* SOCIALIST REALISM) fiction about peasants exploited by local despots during a disaster. In 1933, she also published the first part of the novel *Mother*, about a spirited heroine during the 1911 revolution, a character based loosely on her own mother.

After her release from Nationalist prison in 1936, Mao Zedong welcomed her with two poems he wrote in her honor at the Yan'an Communist base. She began to work on the *Liberation Daily's* literary supplement. When the Sino-Japanese War broke out in 1937, Ding Ling performed field and propaganda work and wrote stories from the front. An outspoken woman yet a loyal servant of both literature and communism, she voiced opinions on inequities within the supposedly egalitarian party, especially in regard to women, at the Yan'an Forum on Literature and Art in 1942.

During the next decade, Ding Ling continued her literary endeavors, writing, among other pieces, a novel about land reform, *The Sun Shines over the Sanggan River* (1949), which won the Stalin Prize for literature. She also traveled extensively abroad, lecturing on literature and producing essays, literary criticism, and speeches. She frequently wrote about women, both in her stories and in essays, advocating feminist thought, women's sexual freedom, and the rights to seek divorce and not to marry. Her writing was frequently considered scandalous, but it also explored the new dimensions of Chinese womanhood under China's rapidly changing sociopolitical landscape.

In 1955, Ding Ling came under fire from the party leadership. She was accused of heading an antiparty clique and was criticized for the sexual content of her stories. During the brief open period of the Hundred Flowers Campaign in 1956, her plea to make literature independent earned her the label of rightist, as well as party expulsion in 1957. She was "sent down" to do physical labor in a reclamation area in the Great Northern Wilderness in Heilongjiang Province.

When the Cultural Revolution began in 1966, Ding Ling did not escape persecution. She was imprisoned from 1970 to 1975 in Beijing and then removed to a commune in Shanxi. After the revolution, she was officially restored in a 1979 verdict and again became a respected member of the establishment.

As part of the "scar" literature by writers who survived the Cultural Revolution, Ding Ling published essays and stories about her experiences and those of her friends. In 1981, she and her second husband, Chen Ming, moved to a convalescent home in Fukien. Although she was in poor health, she started the literary magazine *China* in 1985. She died on March 4, 1986.

Another Work by Ding Ling
I Myself Am a Woman: Selected Writings of Ding Ling. Barlow, Tani E., and Gary J. Bjorge, eds. Boston: Beacon Press, 1990.

A Work about Ding Ling
Feuerwerker, Yi-tsi Mei. *Ding Ling's Fiction: Ideology and Narrative in Modern Chinese Literature.* Cambridge, Mass.: Harvard University Press, 1982.

Diop, Birago (1906–1989) *poet, folklorist*
Birago Diop was born into an influential family in Dakar, Senegal. His father died prematurely leaving him to be raised by his mother's family. He attended high school before going to France to earn his degree as a veterinarian at the University of Toulouse. In Paris, Diop met many of the founders of NÉGRITUDE, an intellectual and artistic movement that was begun in Paris by black students from the French colonies. The movement celebrated a global African identity, while taking a political stance against colonialism and assimilation. Diop met his compatriot LÉOPOLD SÉDAR SENGHOR, a founder of négritude, who influenced him to write about African cultural values. Diop used his own cultural background as a resource, recounting the stories he was told as a child. In addition, his experience as a veterinarian allowed him to travel throughout remote areas of French West Africa, giving him access to the rural life and values of traditional Africa.

He is most famous for his work *Tales of Amadou Koumba* (1966), an award-winning collection of folk tales that he translated from Wolof, the most prevalent indigenous language in Senegal. He is noted for maintaining its rhythm, imagery, and subtleties in his transcription of these stories and for giving the French world access to these ethnic treasures.

In his poetry, Diop concentrated on the mystical elements in African culture. He released a poetry anthology called *Lures and Glimmers* (1960) that captures the spiritual belief system of many African religions. In 1960, Senghor, the president of Senegal at the time, appointed Diop ambassador to Tunisia. Today, Birago Diop is considered a central contributor of traditional ethnic resources to the négritude movement.

Works about Birago Diop
Gibbs, James. "The Animal Trickster as Political Satirist and Social Dissident." In Edris Makward et al. *The Growth of African Literature.* Trenton, N.J.: Africa World Press, 1998.
Tollerson, Marie. *Mythology and Cosmology in the Narratives of Bernard Dadie and Birago Diop.* Washington, D.C.: Three Continents Press, 1984.

Diop, David (1927–1960) *poet*
David Diop was born in Bordeaux, France, to a Senegalese father on tour of duty and a Cameroonian mother. In his teens, he was deeply impressed by the poetry of AIMÉ CÉSAIRE, the cofounder of NÉGRITUDE, an intellectual movement started

by black students in Paris. These students were writers from the French colonies who celebrated the essence of being African while also criticizing colonialism and assimilation.

As a youth, Diop battled tuberculosis, spending months in hospitals. These solitary moments gave rise to many of his most tender poems. While attending high school, he met Léopold Senghor, another founder of the négritude movement, who later published some of Diop's poems. Diop traveled between Africa and Europe, and many of his poems express a longing for a return to his ancestral land of Africa. In "Africa," for example, he creates nostalgic images of Africa before colonialism, but this was an Africa with which he was not familiar. His only memories were of the aftermath of slavery and assimilation. When Senegal was close to gaining its independence in the late 1950s, Diop moved back to take part in the rebuilding of the country. His revolutionary poems and teachings were his tools of change. Ellen Kennedy, a Négritude historian, quotes Diop as writing that his poems were meant "to burst the eardrums of those who do not wish to hear."

Unfortunately, Diop's life came to a tragic end in a plane crash that also destroyed much of his last, unpublished work. Only 22 of his poems still exist; yet these clearly established him as a powerful contributor to the négritude movement and to world literature.

Another Work by David Diop

Hammer Blows and Other Writings. Translated and edited by Simon Mpondo and Frank Jones. Bloomington: Indiana University Press, 1973.

Djebar, Assia (Fatima Zohra Imalayen) (1936–) *novelist, playwright, filmmaker, short story writer*

An Algerian writing in French, Djebar has produced compelling novels that express Arab women's voices in the postcolonial world. She launched her writing career with the acclaimed novel, *La*

soif (1957; published in English as *The Mischief,* 1958). She and her ex-husband, Walid Garn, wrote a play, *Rouge l'aube* (1969) (*Red Dawn*), about the Algerian war of independence. During the 1960s, Djebar taught history at the University of Algiers. In the 1970s, she embarked on a filmmaking career, in part to reach Algerian women who could not read her work in French, but she returned to fiction writing in the 1980s.

Her intense, lyrical, often sensual prose articulates the voices of Arab women, as individuals and as members of a community with a specific political history. In *Far from Medina* (trans. 1994; originally published as *Loin de Médine: filles d'Ismael,* 1991), she tells of the participation of Muslim women in the first days of Islam. Her rich, intricate historical novel, *L'amour, la fantasia* (1985; *Fantasia: An Algerian Cavalcade,* 1993), tells the history of Algeria from the French colonial onslaught in 1830 to the war of independence, ending in 1961. In this book, Djebar alternates between formal French accounts and oral histories that are based on her field interviews in Arabic with Algerian women who participated in the independence struggle but whose voices are not included in any official history. Djebar conceived the story as part of a quartet that includes its prequel novel, *Ombre Sultane* (1987; *A Sister to Scheherazade,* 1993). "If Algerian Woman in all her complexity and historical reality is the protagonist of Assia Djebar's most ambitious and original work of fiction," writes her translator Dorothy S. Blair in the introduction to *Fantasia,* "this is also an attempt to wrest her own identity as an Algerian woman from the warring strands of her Arabo-Berber origins and her Franco-European education."

Djebar won the Venice Biennale Critics Prize for her film *La Nouba des femmes du Mont-Chenoua* (1979), Prix Maurice Maeterlinck (1995), Neustadt Prize for Contributions to World Literature (1996), and the Yourcenar Prize (1997). In 2005, Djebar was accepted into the Académie française. She is currently a professor of francophone literature at New York University.

Other Works by Assia Djebar

Algerian White. Translated by Marjolijin De Jager and David Kelley. New York: Seven Stories Press, 2001.

So Vast the Prison. Translated by Betsy Wing. New York: Seven Stories Press, 1999.

Women of Algiers in Their Apartment. Translated by Marjolijin De Jager. Charlottesville, Va.: University Press of Virginia, 1992.

Works about Assia Djebar

Merini, Rafika. *Two Major Francophone Women Writers: Assia Djébar and Leila Sebbar: A Thematic Study of Their Works.* New York: Peter Lang, 1999.

Mortimer, Mildred P. *Journeys Through the French African Novel.* Westport, Conn.: Heinemann, 1990.

———., ed. *Maghrebian Mosaic: A Literature in Transition.* Boulder, Colo.: Lynne Rienner Publishers, 2001.

Döblin, Alfred (Linke Poot, Hans Fiedeler)
(1878–1957) short story writer, novelist, playwright

Alfred Döblin was born in Stettin, Germany. His father, a tailor, left the family when Alfred was 10, and his mother was from a lower-middle-class Jewish family. Döblin had difficulty in school and did not pass the Arbitur (school-leaving exam) until age 22. Döblin studied medicine from 1900 to 1905 in Berlin and Freiburg and, in 1911, opened a practice as a family doctor and neurologist. In 1912, he married Erna Reiss and served as an army medical officer during World War I.

Döblin began to write in 1900 and by the early 1910s earned critical acclaim for his expressionist (*see* EXPRESSIONISM) short stories that appeared in the journal *Der Stürm.* His first novel *Die drei Sprünge des Wang-lun* (*The Three Leaps of Wang-lun,* 1915) describes a tragic rebellion in China. Following the war, Döblin wrote theater reviews and plays in addition to his novels. Döblin's novel, *Berlin Alexanderplatz* (1929), was a popular and critical success, inspiring a radio play and a film. The story uses an anonymous omniscient narrative voice, montage, and parody—techniques inspired by James Joyce (1882–1941)—to describe the exploits of an ex-convict in the Berlin underworld.

In 1928, Döblin was elected to the Prussian Academy of the Arts. He and his friend BERTOLT BRECHT were members of a leftist discussion group called Group 1925. After the Nazis gained power in 1933, Döblin lived in France and the United States. In 1941, he converted to the Roman Catholic faith, and in 1945, he returned to West Germany. Although Döblin achieved some critical acclaim for his substantive explorations of human relationships and relationships with God, most of his works were not popular. His novels were complicated, unconventional, and, according to the scholar David Dollenmayer, reflective of Döblin's "deep sense of unease about himself and his place in society, and about modern man and society in general."

Other Works by Alfred Döblin

Destiny's Journey. Translated by Edna McCown. New York: Paragon House, 1992.

Tales of a Long Night: A Novel. Translated by Robert and Rita Kimber. New York: Fromm International Publishing Corporation, 1984.

A Work about Alfred Döblin

Dollenmayer, David. *The Berlin Novels of Alfred Döblin.* Berkeley: University of California Press, 1988.

Donoso, José (1924–1997) novelist, short story writer, poet

José Donoso was born to Dr. José Donoso and Alicia Yáñez in a suburb of Santiago, Chile. Educated by private teachers as a young child, he later attended the prestigious Grange School. Donoso was inspired to write at an early age by uncles who were authors, as well as by the novels of such writers as JULES VERNE and ALEXANDRE DUMAS. After dropping out of school and working for some time on a sheep farm, he completed his education at Princeton University, where he published his first short stories, in English.

When Donoso's first novel, *Coronation,* was released in 1957, his work began to receive serious critical attention. The least experimental of his novels, it relates the transformation of the conservative, middle-class Andrés, as he is drawn out of his orderly, sterile existence and into the realm of obsession and desire. In *Coronation,* the most important themes of Donoso's later fiction are already present: insanity, the complex nature of identity, and the conflict between the demands of instincts and the expectations of society. These same themes are central to *The Obscene Bird of Night* (1970), which represents Donoso's best-known and perhaps most mature work. This book tells the story of the decline of an aristocratic family, as seen through the eyes of Humberto Peñaloza, the private teacher of the family's last offspring. The plot is not presented in any kind of logical sequence, as the disorder of Peñaloza's narrative is intended to reflect the narrator's psychic instability and to question traditional notions of time, space, and reality.

Donoso is a difficult writer to categorize in Latin American and Chilean literature. Although the unorthodox structure of his novels connect them to the phenomenon known as the Boom (a movement in Latin-American fiction involving such authors as GABRIEL GARCÍA MÁRQUEZ and CARLOS FUENTES, who employed experimental narrative techniques in their novels and stories), the domestic settings of his works tie them to the realist tradition.

Donoso has received such recognition for his fiction as the Chilean National Prize for Literature and the William Faulkner Foundation Prize. His stories and novels have been translated into many languages and adapted for film and theater. His work has exercised a critical influence on Spanish-language fiction and represents one of the most varied and compelling attempts to come to terms with the complex history and sociology of Latin America.

Another Work by José Donoso

A House in the Country. Translated by David Pritchard. New York: Knopf, 1984.

A Work about José Donoso

Magnarelli, Sharon. *Understanding José Donoso.* Columbia: University of South Carolina Press, 1993.

Dostoyevsky, Fyodor Mikhaylovich

(1821–1881) *novelist, short story writer*

Fyodor Mikhaylovich Dostoyevsky was born in Moscow, Russia, to Mikhay Dostoyevsky, an army surgeon, and Maria Nechaeva, a daughter of a prominent Moscow merchant. Dostoyevsky had a traumatic childhood. His father was an alcoholic who constantly terrorized the family. When Dostoyevsky was only nine years old, his best friend was raped and murdered, a tragic incident he remembered throughout his life. In 1834 Dostoyevsky entered a prestigious private school in Moscow, where he concentrated on literary studies. He made very few friends and spent most of his time reading. He particularly admired the works of ALEKSANDR PUSHKIN and NIKOLAI KARAMZIN.

At the insistence of his father, Dostoyevsky enrolled in a school for military engineers in St. Petersburg in 1837. That same year, Dostoyevsky's studies were briefly interrupted by the death of his mother. In 1839, his father died; it was rumored that he had been murdered by his own serfs. Both events had a deep impact on Dostoyevsky and later reemerged in his novels.

On completion of his studies in 1845, Dostoyevsky briefly entered the civil service as an engineer but resigned after only a few months to pursue writing. The publication of *Poor Folk* in 1846 immediately gained critical attention, launching his literary career.

Fascinated with French social philosophy, Dostoyevsky began to attend meetings of a radical, utopian group. This group included several prominent figures, mostly artists and intellectuals who were interested in the reformation of Russian society. In 1849, 39 members, including Dostoyevsky, were arrested by the police. After months of interrogation and torture (three members of the group were confined to an insane asylum after their release), Dostoyevsky and other members of the group were sentenced to death. Minutes before the execution, however, Dostoyevsky was pardoned and his sentence reduced to five years of hard labor in Siberia.

The period of exile was perhaps the most crucial experience in Dostoyevsky's life. Spiritually and mentally distraught, Dostoyevsky passionately embraced the doctrines of the Russian Orthodox Church. Deeply affected by his experience as a prisoner, Dostoyevsky became politically reactionary and a staunch supporter of the czar.

As a result, Dostoyevsky was allowed to return to St. Petersburg in 1857, but his exile had taken its toll. He developed epilepsy, and his physical health was very fragile. Along with his brother Mikhail, Dostoyevsky began to edit *Times,* a literary journal that serialized a number of Dostoyevsky's early novels. Among works published during the early 1860s was *The House of the Dead* (1862), a fictional account of prison life based on Dostoyevsky's experiences in Siberia, and *The Insulted and Injured* (1861), a novel that analyzes the shortcomings of naïve utopianism.

Dostoyevsky married Maria Isaev in 1857, but she died in the early 1860s, as did his brother. In 1862, Dostoyevsky left Russia to tour Europe, where he was introduced to gambling, especially roulette, which became an irresistible passion. Gambling compounded his financial troubles, and he returned to Russia in 1864 virtually penniless. Dostoyevsky examined the psychological implications of gambling in his fascinating novel *The Gambler* (1866).

In 1866, Dostoyevsky began working on *Crime and Punishment,* which—harried by debt and desperately in need of money—he completed in a month with the help of a stenographer, Anna Snitkina. Dostoyevsky and Snitkina were married in 1867. With his epilepsy and obsessions,

Dostoyevsky was not the easiest of companions, but the intimacy and love between Dostoyevsky and his wife sustained them for the rest of their lives. The couple traveled extensively throughout Europe but once again had to return to Russia in 1871 because of financial troubles caused by Dostoyevsky's gambling.

Critical Analysis

Dostoyevsky's fiction is notable for its deep and intense understanding of human psychology. In *Notes from the Underground* (1864), Dostoyevsky began his literary experiments with the human psyche through a detailed account of neurotic dementia. In the novel, a minor government official describes his hatred of the society he sees from his "underground" viewpoint. The novel also explores the spiritual conflict between the individual and society. It is also a reaction against the optimistic rationalism of CHERNYSHEVSKY's *What Is to Be Done?.*

In *Crime and Punishment,* Dostoyevsky portrays the spiritual and philosophical struggle of Raskolnikov, a young student who murders a pawnbroker. The novel explores the themes of spiritual suffering, psychosis, and redemption, set against the dark background of the slums of St. Petersburg. Dostoyevsky examines the terms of formation of philosophical concepts and their subsequent effect on the individual. Many critics consider *Crime and Punishment* to be the seminal psychological drama in literary history.

The Idiot (1868) is an indictment of the materialism of the governing classes of Russia. In this striking, realistic portrayal of 19th-century Russian society, Dostoyevsky juxtaposes the ethical idealism of a young man against the crass materialism of the drawing rooms of the middle class. The novel amplifies the growing spiritual unrest of Russian society that attempts to emulate the material values of Western Europe. Dostoyevsky denounces the society in which moral idealism is labeled as mental incompetence. *The Idiot* marks the growing philosophical crises of the realist literature of 19th-century Russia. Yet, though he saw so clearly the flaws in the society that surrounded him, Dostoyevsky denounced political violence and extremism as a way to reform society.

In *The Possessed* (1871), Dostoyevsky comments upon the responsibility of an individual in social matters. The story is about Stavrogin, a charismatic intellectual and atheist, who attracts a group of fanatics who wreak havoc on a small provincial town. It was based on the life of a revolutionary named Sergey Nechayev but may have reminded readers of several radical movements that were current at the time. *The Possessed* was ambivalently received in Russia: With its unflattering picture of political activism, it was hailed as a masterpiece by conservatives, while revolutionary circles denounced it as reactionary.

The Brothers Karamazov (1880) was Dostoyevsky's last and arguably finest novel. As a pioneering work in psychological realism, the novel engages a number of powerful themes: love, hate, patricide, and the search for God, to name a few. *The Brothers Karamzov* follows the destiny of Fyodor Karamazov and his three sons. The most famous chapter of the novel, "The Legend of the Grand Inquisitor," dramatizes the inner struggle between heart and mind in the context of religion. The profound psychological and social implications of the plot assured the everlasting significance of the novel, which was hailed as a great masterpiece virtually from its first publication.

Fyodor Dostoyevsky received unprecedented critical acclaim during the last years of his life. He finally achieved financial solvency and turned his attention to family life. After his death, his widow and children were given a government pension by the czar. Dostoyevsky's funeral was attended by thousands of people. He was hailed as a literary genius, the father of Russian REALISM, and a master of psychological realism. The contribution of Fyodor Dostoyevsky to world literature is almost immeasurable, as his works transformed entire generations of writers and created new dimensions in the world of fiction.

Other Works by Fyodor Dostoyevsky

The Best Short Stories of Dostoyevsky. Translated by David Magarshack. New York: Modern Library, 1992.

Winter Notes on Summer Impressions. Translated by Kyril Fitzlyon. London: Quartet Books, 1986.

Works about Fyodor Dostoyevsky

Amoia, Alba della Fazia. *Feodor Dostoevsky.* New York: Continuum Press, 1993.

Frank, Joseph. *Dostoevsky: The Seeds of Revolt, 1821–1849.* Princeton, N.J.: Princeton University Press, 1976.

———. *Dostoevsky: The Years of Ordeal, 1850–1859.* Princeton, N.J.: Princeton University Press, 1984.

———. *Dostoevsky: The Years of Liberation, 1860–1865.* Princeton, N.J.: Princeton University Press, 1986.

———. *Dostoevsky: The Miraculous Years, 1865–1871.* Princeton, N.J.: Princeton University Press, 1996.

———. *Dostoevsky: The Mantle of the Prophet, 1871–1881.* Princeton, N.J.: Princeton University Press, 2002.

Leatherborrow, William J. *Feodor Dostoevsky: A Reference Guide.* Boston: G. K. Hall, 1990.

Du, Nguyen
See NGUYEN DU.

Ducasse, Isadore-Lucien
See LAUTRÉAMONT, COMTE DE.

Dudintsev, Vladimir Dmitrievich
(1918–1998) *novelist*

Vladimir Dudintsev was born in Kupyansk, Ukraine. After his graduation from the Moscow Law Institute, Dudintsev briefly served in the Soviet army at the outbreak of World War II. Although he wrote a number of short works during the Stalinist era, most of them, as Dudintsev later admitted, were lackluster and mediocre. His real publishing debut came in 1956 with the publication of the novel *Not by Bread Alone*.

Not by Bread Alone tells the story of Lopatkin, a brilliant inventor who was hindered by government red tape. In the West, the novel was hailed for its candid portrayal of negative aspects of the Soviet Union. The work was harshly criticized at a notorious 1957 meeting of the Soviet Writers' Union. (That meeting became the topic of a poem by YEVGENY YEVTUSHENKO, "Again a Meeting": "Again a meeting, noisy, dying / half colloquium / half co-lying . . ." For a long period of time, he was shunned by most of the "official" Soviet writers. Dudintsev found ready support for his work among the political dissidents, but he encountered enormous difficulties publishing in the Soviet Union. His second work, *A New Year's Fairy Tale* (1957), was a science fiction novel set in a Soviet Union of the future.

Dudintsev published his final novel, *White Clothes,* in 1987 at the height of the perestroika movement. *White Clothes* once again criticized government corruption and endless circles of bureaucracy. He also blamed a number of careless, greedy government officials for the environmental disasters in Russia. The novel was widely read and hailed as a work of great social significance.

When Dudintsev died in 1998, he was considered one of the best writers of the Soviet era. He often took great personal risks to expose the social problems of the Soviet Union, and his well-crafted prose is much admired.

Another Work by Vladimir Dudintsev

A New Year's Fairy Tale. In Robert Magidoff, ed., *Russian Science Fiction: An Anthology.* Translated by Doris Johnson. New York: New York University Press, 1964.

Dupin, Amandine-Aurore-Lucile

See SAND, GEORGE.

Duras, Claire de (ca. 1777–1828) *novelist*

Claire de Duras was born to a French noble family. Her father, a count, was a member of the liberal French aristocracy. A supporter of radical ideas, he was executed for failing to support the execution of Louis XVI. After her father's death, de Duras fled with her mother to the United States where they spent some time in Philadelphia, Pennsylvania, with family. She also took a journey to Martinique to receive an inheritance. In both America and Martinique, she saw the realities of slavery. They then traveled to Switzerland and to London, where de Duras met her future husband, Amédée-Bretagne-Malo de Durfort, the duke of Durfort and the future duke of Duras. They were married in 1797.

In 1808, de Duras moved to France with her husband where, as a result of changes brought about by the Restoration, he became an active member of the court in 1814. While her husband was busy with his duties, de Duras held gatherings of thinkers, poets, and intellectuals who discussed their thoughts and ideas about the unjustness of life. It was during these meetings that de Duras began to relate the story of a Senegalese girl, rescued from slavery by a French aristocratic family, whose life of privilege does not protect her from the alienation of racism. The story became popular in the group, and de Duras was encouraged to write it down. This became her first novel, *Ourika* (1823).

Initially published anonymously, *Ourika* grew to become a national obsession. The work opposed the prevailing attitude that slavery was a natural thing and denounced it as an evil institution. The work was also unique in that the narrator was a black woman, which was almost unheard of in French literature at this time. As John Fowles says in the introduction to his translation, it is "the first serious attempt by a white novelist to enter a black mind."

In 1822, de Duras became sick and depressed. She withdrew to her country house, where she wrote two more novels on the subjects of sex and class: *Olivier* (1822) and the epistolary novel

Edouard (1825), both of which feature gentle heroes with feminine characteristics. She was never interested in writing for money or fame; instead, she hoped that her works would promote change. Only after her death did her works and their frank depiction of social concerns begin to gain recognition.

Another Work by Claire de Duras

Ourika: An English Translation. Translated by John Fowles. New York: Modern Language Association of America, 1995.

Works about Claire de Duras

Crichfield, Grant. *Three Novels of Madame de Duras.* The Hague: Mouton, 1975.

Kadish, Doris Y., and Françoise Massardier-Kenney, eds. *Translating Slavery: Gender and Race in French Women's Writing, 1783–1823.* Kent, Ohio: Kent State University Press, 1994.

Duras, Marguerite (1914–1996) *novelist, playwright, screenwriter*

Marguerite Donnadieu was born in Gia Dinh, Indochina, the area that is now Vietnam. She took her pseudonym, Duras, from the name of a French village near where her father had once owned land. Her father died when Duras was only four years old, and her mother, a teacher, struggled to support her three children on her own. Duras spent most of her childhood in Indochina and, when she was still a teenager, had an affair with a wealthy Chinese man. She returns to this period of life repeatedly in her novels.

When Duras was 17, she moved to France to study law and political science at the Sorbonne. After graduating in 1935, she went to work as a secretary at the Ministry of Colonies. In 1939, she married Robert Antelme. With the arrival of World War II, she became a member of the French Resistance. Antelme became a Resistance leader and was captured and imprisoned. He survived Buchenwald, Gandersheim, and Dachau. After his release, Duras, who had been planning to leave

him before his capture, nursed him back to health, living with him in a ménage à trois with Dionys Mascolo. She joined the Communist Party in that period but in 1950, after the Prague Uprising, was expelled for revisionism.

Duras published her first novel, *Les impudents* (1942), in a style greatly influenced by American author Ernest Hemingway. She gained the most recognition, however, during the 1950s with her novels *Un barrage contre le Pacifique* (*The Sea Wall,* 1950) about an impoverished family living in Indochina, and the psychological romance novel *Le marin de Gibralter* (*The Sailor from Gibraltar,* 1952). Her novel *Le square* (1955) earned her both respect as an author and association with what was known as the NEW NOVEL group. However, in her next novel, *Moderato cantabile* (1958), Duras shifted her writing style from traditional topics and themes to what would become her prevailing themes of death, memory, sexual desire, and love.

Toward the end of the 1950s, Duras turned her attention to writing screenplays. The film for which she is best known internationally is *Hiroshima, mon amour* (1959). Directed by Alain Resnais, the film focuses on the theme of complications arising from the love between two people who have experienced the trauma of war. It tells of the brief love affair between Emmanuelle Riva, a married French actress, and Eija Okada, a Japanese architect, during which Riva tells Okada of her forbidden love affair with a German soldier and her subsequent mental breakdown. Innovative in its use of flashbacks and montages, the film received mixed reviews. It earned an Academy Award nomination for best screenplay but failed miserably in the box offices in Japan.

Duras's work became increasingly experimental in the 1960s, especially after the 1968 student revolts. She became interested in the power of language, memories, and alienation. Feminist critics tie her shift in style directly to the concept of feminine writing with its increasing sparseness and suggestiveness. Love, for Duras's characters, becomes an escape that is often linked with alcohol and madness.

In the 1970s, Duras continued to focus on writing screenplays, including the film *Camion* (1982) with French actor Gérard Depardieu. She returned to the novel format in the 1980s with the semiautobiographical *The Lover* (1984), for which she won France's most cherished literary honor, the Prix Goncourt. The novel, made into a film by the same name in 1992, focuses on the sexual initiation of a young girl in Indochina. Duras's works were often associated with events in her life. Her collection of short stories *La douleur* (1985) was based on her relationship with Antelme and Mascolo.

In 1980, Duras met Yann Andréa Steiner. The two lived together until Duras's death. Duras's creativity during this period was often shadowed by her increasing abuse of alcohol. In *Practicalities* (1987), she wrote about her relationship with Steiner, her alcoholism, and her 15-year addiction to aspirin. Steiner finally encouraged her to enter a hospital for treatment in 1982, but when Duras returned home, she began to suffer from hallucinations and a fear that her house had been invaded by strangers. Steiner stayed with her until her death.

Other Works by Marguerite Duras

No More. Translated by Richard Howard. New York: Seven Stories Press, 1998.

The North China Lover. Translated by Leigh Hafrey. New York: The New Press, 1992.

The Ravishing of Lol Stein. Translated by Richard Seaver. New York: Pantheon Books, 1986.

Writing. Translated by Mark Polizzotti. Cambridge, Mass.: Brookline Books, 1998.

Works about Marguerite Duras

Adler, Laure. *Marguerite Duras: A Life*. Translated by Anne-Marie Glasheen. Chicago: University of Chicago Press, 2000.

Schuster, Marilyn R. *Marguerite Duras Revisited*. Boston: Twayne, 1993.

Dürrenmatt, Friedrich (1921–1990)
dramatist, novelist

Friedrich Dürrenmatt was born in Konolfingen, Switzerland, to Reinhold and Hulda Zimmermann Dürrenmatt. His father was the pastor of the Konolfingen church. Dürrenmatt attended secondary school in Großhochstetten and spent his spare time painting, a lifelong interest. After his family moved to Bern in 1935, he attended Freies Gymnasium, a Christian secondary school, and then Humboldtianum, a private school. After graduating in 1941, he studied philosophy, literature, and natural sciences at the University of Zurich and the University of Bern. He served for a year in the Swiss military during World War II and married actress Lotti Geißler in 1946.

Dürrenmatt's first drama, *Es steht geschrieben* (*It Is Written,* 1947) succeeded with critics but not audiences. He attracted more popular success with his play *Romulus der Große* (*Romulus the Great,* 1949). Dürrenmatt wrote three detective novels and his first work of essays, *Theaterprobleme* (1955), in the 1950s. His most popular plays, *Der Besuch der alten Dame* (*The Visit,* 1956, translated 1958) and *Die Physiker* (*The Physicists,* 1962), examine the themes of power, responsibility, and guilt. Dürrenmatt later served on the board of directors of the Zurich Schauspielhaus and continued writing plays until 1988.

Dürrenmatt adapted the satire of Jonathan Swift (1667–1745) and the dramatic technique of BERTOLT BRECHT to his works. He is best known for comic-grotesque satires that explore religious and philosophical issues. He was a pessimist who, according to biographer Roger Crockett, "did not believe that humanity had a promising future on this planet, and he created scenario after scenario to demonstrate this conclusion." Dürrenmatt's numerous awards include the Georg Büchner Prize and the New York Theater Critics' Prize. Even after his death in 1990, *The Visit* and the *The Physicists* were among the most performed plays in Germany.

Other Works by Friedrich Dürrenmatt

The Assignment. Translated by Joel Agee. New York: Random House, 1988.

The Execution of Justice. Translated by John E. Woods. New York: Random House, 1989.

A Work about Friedrich Dürrenmatt

Crockett, Roger A. *Understanding Friedrich Dürrenmatt.* Columbia, S.C.: University of South Carolina Press, 1998.

Eco, Umberto (1932–) *novelist, literary critic*

Born in Alessandria, Italy, Umberto Eco is the son of Giralio Eco, an office worker for a bathtub manufacturer, and Giovanna (Bisio) Eco. He grew up amid World War II, dodging bombs in the countryside as a young teen but also embracing American literature and popular music.

Eco received a doctorate of philosophy from the University of Turin in 1954 at age 22. His thesis on St. Thomas Aquinas and his later work, *The Development of Medieval Aesthetics* (1959), helped stir his passion for the medieval world. His research was invaluable when he wrote his signature work, the novel *The Name of the Rose* (1980).

After his 1954 graduation, Eco worked in Milan preparing cultural programs for RAI, a new state television network. This exposure to television gave him insights into the world of mass media, a subject about which he wrote extensively later in his career. From 1956 to 1964, Eco held a lecturing post at the University of Turin and from 1964 to 1965 at the University of Milan.

In the late 1950s, Eco began to contribute to such Italian daily newspapers and magazines as *L'Espresso,* but it was the publication of his first novel, *The Name of the Rose,* that won Eco worldwide critical acclaim. The novel uses semiotics (the study of signs, codes, and clues) to tell the story of a murder mystery set in a medieval monastery. Eco founded a journal on semiotics in 1971 and has written several books on the subject. In *The Name of the Rose,* he employs semiotic techniques such as using the 10-part Sefirot or Cabbalic system as an underlying structure. The novel became popular with a cross-section of readers from lovers of best sellers to scholars and set records for world sales of an Italian book. In 1986, the novel was made into a major motion picture starring Sean Connery and also received the Strega and Viareggio Prizes, as well as the Medici Prize in France. Eco told *Contemporary Authors* in 1979, "I think that the duty of a scholar is not only to do scientific research but also to communicate with people through various media about most important issues of social life from the point of view of his own discipline."

Eco is also well known for *Foucault's Pendulum* (1988), a novel set in Milan, Paris, and Brazil. It tells the story of a search for a plan of the universe that involves the medieval religious order the Knights Templar and their plans for world domination. The story comes to this conclusion: "There is no map. There is no plan: the secret, he has come to see, is that there is no secret; the answer is that there is no answer."

Baudolino (2000) is the tale of a knight who saves the life of historian Niketas Chroniates and then tells him the unbelievable story of his own life. The protagonist of *The Mysterious Flame of Queen Loana* (2004) is Giambattista Bodoni, an old bookseller who has lost his memory because of a stroke and must reconstruct his past.

Umberto Eco is a significant Italian literary figure. Much more than a best-selling novelist, Eco has made his name, say scholars Norma Bouchard and Veronica Pravadelli, as "a theorist of avant-gardist aesthetics, a scholar of popular culture, a leading semiotician and philosopher of language, [and] a highly respected journalist."

Other Works by Umberto Eco

The Island of the Day Before. Translated by William Weaver. New York: Harcourt Brace Jovanovich, 1995.
The Mysterious Flame of Queen Loana. Translated by Geoffrey Brock. New York: Harvest Books, 2006.

Works about Umberto Eco

Bondanella, Peter. *Umberto Eco and the Open Text: Semiotics, Fiction, Popular Culture.* New York: Cambridge University Press, 1997.
Bouchard, Norma, and Veronica Pravadelli, eds. *Umberto Eco's Alternative.* New York: Peter Lang, 1998.

Ehrenburg, Ilya Grigoryevich
(1891–1967) *novelist, short story writer, poet, travel writer, essayist*

Ilya Grigoryevich Ehrenburg was born in Kiev, Ukraine, into the family of a middle-class Jewish brewer. Facing rapidly growing anti-Semitism in Ukraine, the Ehrenburgs moved to Moscow, Russia, in 1896. Ehrenburg briefly attending the First Moscow gymnasium (high school) but was expelled for participating in revolutionary activities. In 1908, Ehrenburg decided to leave Russia to avoid a trial for his political activities that could, despite his youth, have resulted in a lengthy prison term. Living in Paris, Ehrenburg

participated in the artistic circles of French society.

Ehrenburg started his prolific career with a publication of a poetry collection in 1910. During World War I, he briefly served as a war correspondent. Between 1921 and 1924, he lived in Germany and Belgium. His first novel, *The Extraordinary Adventures of Julio Jurenito and His Disciples* (1921) was a political satire that ridiculed both the capitalist and Communist political systems. In 1928, Ehrenburg published *The Stormy Life of Lazar Roitschwantz*, a novel that depicts wanderings through Europe of a Jewish tailor who barely escapes the anti-Semitism of Russia. Both novels combined sensitivity for the nuances of the plot with biting social commentary.

From 1925 to 1945, Ehrenburg lived in Paris, working for Soviet newspapers and returning to Russia on occasion. In the 1930s, his writings became markedly less radical as he accepted the official doctrines of the Communist Party. In *Out of Chaos* (1934), for instance, he ardently defends the aesthetic goals of SOCIALIST REALISM. In his novel *The Fall of Paris* (1941), he criticizes the capitalist system of France and delineates the social degeneration of French society.

Ehrenburg was honored on several occasions in the Soviet Union. In 1942 and 1948, he was awarded the Stalin Prize and, in 1952, the International Lenin Peace Prize. He also served as a deputy of the Supreme Soviet of the USSR from 1950 and as a vice president of the World Peace Council until his death in 1967. Ehrenburg spent his last days campaigning to publish the works of writers who were suppressed under Stalin's regime. Ehrenburg's fiction, although deeply politicized, reveals a high level of narrative control and a deep understanding of human nature. Despite his positions in the Soviet regime, Ehrenburg was highly respected by Western intellectuals and artists.

A Work about Ilya Ehrenburg
Goldberg, Anatol. *Ilya Ehrenburg, Revolutionary, Novelist, Poet, War Correspondent, Propagandist:*

The Extraordinary Epic of a Russian Survivor. New York: Viking Press, 1984.

Eich, Günter (Erich Günter) (1907–1972)
dramatist, poet

Günter Eich was born in Lebus an der Oder to Otto and Helen Heine Eich. Otto, an accountant, moved the family to Berlin in 1918. Eich finished his secondary education in Leipzig in 1925. He studied Chinese, law, and economics at universities in Leipzig, Berlin, and Paris. Eich published his first poems in an anthology in 1927 and his first volume of poems in 1930. In the 1930s, he worked as a freelance writer and was a pioneer in the writing of German radio plays. In 1940, he married Else Anna Burk, a singer who died a few years later. Eich served in the German air force during World War II. The Americans captured him in 1945 and released him the following year. Starting in 1947, Eich regularly attended the annual meetings of the German literary association, GRUPPE 47. He married the poet ILSE AICHINGER in 1953.

While in a POW camp, Eich wrote "Inventur," a poem that is considered the epitome of the *Kahlschlag* (Clean Sweep) movement. Popular in the 1950s, *Kahlschlag* symbolized the break with past ideologies. German writers embracing this movement sought to address material facts, such as hunger and disease, while cutting corrupt ideals, ideas, and language out of their writing.

Eich's lyric poetry was inspired by Chinese poets such as Li Bai. Favoring the audible over the visual, he attained his greatest notoriety for his radio plays. Eich's best-known play is *Träume* (*Dreams,* 1953). It contains some of his best poetry and addresses his favorite themes: dreams, death, and the divide between reality and unreality. According to the literary scholar Egbert Krispyn, Eich displayed an "uncompromising creative honesty" in his work, which won several awards, including the Munich Grant Prize for Literature and the Friedrich Schiller Memorial Prize of Mannheim.

Another Work by Günter Eich
Pigeons and Moles: Selected Writings of Günter Eich. Translated by Michael Hamburger. Columbia, S.C.: Camden House, 1990.

Works about Günter Eich
Cuomo, Glenn R. *Career at the Cost of Compromise: Günter Eich's Life and Work in the Years 1933–1945.* Atlanta: Rodopi, 1989.

Krispyn, Egbert. *Günter Eich.* Boston: Twayne, 1971.

El Saadawi, Nawal
See SAADAWI, NAWAL.

Éluard, Paul (Eugène-Emile-Paul Grindel) (1895–1952) *poet*

Paul Éluard was born Paul Grindel in Saint-Denis on the outskirts of Paris. When he was 18, he was confined to a sanatorium in Switzerland to recover from a bout of tuberculosis. During this time, he discovered his love for poetry and published his first collection of poems.

Éluard was deeply affected by the tragedy of World War I. He became a pacifist militant and wrote *Poèmes pour la paix* (1918), which details both the need for conflict and the desire to temper it with peace. He also met TRISTAN TZARA, ANDRÉ BRETON, and LOUIS ARAGON, who encouraged him in 1920 to become an active participant in the DADA movement. He later joined the surrealists, becoming one of its major influences. But, simultaneously, he remained true to his own visions of literary integrity, questioning the validity of certain ideas such as automatic writing, a belief that the spiritual realm could convey itself through the writing implement, without the judgment of the writer.

Alongside his opposition to violence and war, Éluard's personal life, in particular his marriage to Maria Benz, became one of the focal points of his writing. She was the inspiration for the passionate celebration of love in his collections *Capitale de la douleur* (1926), *L'amour, la poésie* (1929), and *La*

Vérité immédiate (1932). These works are notable in that they mark a departure from his focus on passive militarism.

Éluard was barred from the Communist Party as a result of a conflict with Aragon. He joined the Resistance, continuing his creative work with collections such as *La victoire de Guernica* (1938) and *Poésie et vérité* (1942). The latter collection contains his most often studied poem "Liberté." Shortly after the liberation and the traumatic death of his wife in 1946, Éluard began to focus his writing on the hope that one day humanity would leave behind its murderous tendencies. He became an impassioned humanist, as evidenced in his works. He died in Charenton-le-Pont.

Other Works by Paul Éluard

Last Love Poems of Paul Éluard. Translated by Marilyn Kallet. Baton Rouge: Louisiana State University Press, 1980.
Selected Poems. Translated by Gilbert Bowen. New York: River Run Press, 1987.

A Work about Paul Éluard

Nugent, Robert. *Paul Éluard.* Boston: Twayne Publishers, 1974.

Elytis, Odysseus (Odysseus Alepoudelis) (1911–1996) *poet*

Odysseus Elytis was born in Iraklion on the island of Crete. The son of a wealthy manufacturer, he shunned the privileged life and devoted himself entirely to seeking truth in his works.

Elytis's first poetry dates back to 1929 and celebrates his childhood visits to the Aegean Sea. He established his reputation as a poet in the 1930s, a decade haunted by the threat of war, by focusing on the intrinsic beauty of humanity and nature. In *Orientations* (1940), Elytis's first and largest collection, he combines elements of the surrealist movement with free association and pagan nature worship. During World War II, Elytis served on the front lines in Albania, fighting against Italian and German forces. This struggle particularly affected him, as did the subsequent horrors of the Nazi occupation of Greece. It was the barbaric nature of war that led him to continue writing poetry that glorified the beauty of his homeland and sought to maintain its integrity against the threat of human destruction. His long poem *Heroic and Elegiac Song of the Lost Second Lieutenant of Albania* (1945) gave voice to Elytis's experiences and feelings. The novel celebrates life and the invisible forces that bind humankind to the natural world while, simultaneously, confronting the very basic conflict of good versus evil.

Elytis is most remembered, however, for *Axion Esti* (1959), a three-part celebration of Greek folklore and history. Translated as *Worth It Be,* this epic poem draws on elements of the Byzantine mass in conjunction with the history of Greece and the biblical creation story. It was later set to music by Theodorakis, who also composed the film score for *Zorba the Greek.* Theodorakis described the poem as a "Bible for the Greek people," which, in a sense, it was, as it later became an anthem for Greek youth.

Elytis spent much of his life in seclusion, focusing only on his poetry. He considered himself to be neither a patriotic poet nor a nature poet. He felt that his duty as a poet was to transform the images offered him by nature to a level where they could exist as reminders to all humanity of the possibility of perfection and beauty in this world. In 1979, he was awarded the Nobel Prize in literature and became a cultural ambassador for the Greek people. He began to travel to give lectures; however, three years later, he confessed to being so busy traveling that he had no time to write. Returning to semiseclusion, he resumed writing, publishing his final collection *West of Sorrow* (1995).

Elytis was so important to the Greek people that radio and television programs were interrupted to announce his death in 1996. Elytis's own definition of death perhaps explains his significance as a writer: "Death is where words no longer have the power to generate, right from the start, the things that they name." For Elytis, poetry was not simply an art; it was also a social responsibility.

Other Works by Odysseus Elytis

The Collected Poems of Odysseus Elytis. Translated by Jeffrey Carson and Nikos Sarris. Baltimore: Johns Hopkins University Press, 1997.

Odysseus Elytis: Analogies of Light. Edited by Ivar Ivask. Norman: University of Oklahoma Press, 1981.

What I Love: Selected Poems of Odysseas Elytis. Translated by Olga Broumas. Port Townsend, Wash.: Copper Canyon Press, 1986.

Emecheta, Buchi (1944–) *novelist*

Buchi Emecheta was born of Ibuza parents in Nigeria. Orphaned at an early age, she spent her childhood in a missionary school. In 1960, at age 16, she married Sylvester Onwordi, to whom she had been engaged since she was 11. In 1962, the couple moved to London; the marriage lasted six years and produced five children.

Many of Emecheta's earliest novels draw on her experiences in Africa and England. Emecheta's early writing style is based on oral tradition. She speaks from her own experiences and vividly describes the people and places encountered by her characters on their journey to self-awareness. Her first novel, *In the Ditch* (1972), tells the story of her life as a struggling immigrant and single mother in London through the character of Adah, a young woman who leaves her husband to find out who she is. In a strange land, she is seen as an outsider. With children in tow, Adah negotiates the welfare system, the job market, and what it means to be deemed a social "problem."

In Emecheta's second novel, *Second Class Citizen* (1974), she continues to chronicle Adah's life, but this time she steps back to see how she arrived in "the ditch." This story concentrates on the inequalities within her culture that manifest themselves as discrimination against women. Adah encounters strict tribal customs that deny education to women. As she bends under the workload of supporting her family and caring for her children, she witnesses the privileges of her student husband. "Second Class Citizen" reveals how gender roles are maintained through culture.

Emecheta's autobiography, *Head Above Water* (1986), tells of her struggle to confront the poor social conditions of blacks in London while simultaneously emerging as a writer.

Emecheta has come under fire from some critics for her refusal to support the pastoral ideas of Africa and Europe. Her raw views often expose the dark side of tribal relations, colonialism, and male/female relations.

She was raised at a time in Nigeria when traditional structures were being challenged by a society that was shifting from rural to urban living. It was also a time when immigration to colonial centers, such as London, presented another test of maintaining or adapting one's identity. Emecheta's novels reflect both the chaos and the opportunities of this unrest and uprooting. Emecheta does not write about an idyllic Africa of the past but instead about contemporary Africa with painstaking accuracy.

She centers the majority of her stories on gender relations and the conflicts between modernity and tradition. These topics often serve as metaphors for the relationship between Africa and the Diaspora (the scattering of people of African descent through slavery) and for the relationship between colonizer and the colonized; for example, in *The Family* (1989), she chronicles the life of an impoverished Jamaican girl who negotiates familial abuse, which is one of slavery's legacies. Emecheta's brave approach to writing about the unspoken has set her apart from other African writers. She has won several literary prizes including her selection in 1983 as one of the Best Young British Writers Award. Emecheta is a strong postcolonial writer who witnesses with a feminist lens; as a result, she has diversified traditional Western feminism by adding a voice that speaks to the specific issues of women from developing countries. She received an honorary Order of the British Empire in 2005.

Other Works by Buchi Emecheta
The Bride Price. New York: George Braziller, 1980.
In the Ditch. Westport, Conn.: Heinemann, 1994.
The Joys of Motherhood. New York: George Braziller, 1980.
Kehinde. Long Grove, Ill.: Waveland Press, 2005.
The New Tribe. Westport, Conn.: Heinemann, 2001.
Second Class Citizen. New York: George Braziller, 1983.
The Slave Girl. New York: George Braziller, 1980.

Works about Buchi Emecheta
Fishburn, Katherine. *Reading Buchi Emecheta: Cross-Cultural Conversations.* Westport, Conn.: Greenwood Publishing Group, 1995.
Uraizee, Joya F. *This Is No Place for a Woman: Nadine Gordimer, Nayantara Sahgal, Buchi Emecheta, and the Politics of Gender.* Lawrenceville, N.J.: Africa World Press, 2000.

Enchi Fumiko (Fumi Ueda) (1905–1986)
playwright, novelist

Enchi Fumiko was born in Tokyo to Ueda Kazutoshi and Tsuruko. Kazutoshi was a well-known linguistics professor who helped put together a major Japanese-language dictionary in 1902. As a young child, Enchi was reclusive and sickly, spending more time in her father's extensive library than at play with other children. Enchi attended Japan Women's University but did not earn a degree. In 1930, she married the journalist Enchi Yoshimatsu and had a child, Motoko, two years later. In 1935, she joined a group of novelists known as Nichireki to learn more about writing. In the 1930s and 1940s, she suffered from breast cancer, uterine cancer, and tuberculosis. At the end of World War II, Enchi's home in Tokyo was destroyed during an air raid.

When Enchi was at university, she developed plays for a Tokyo theater founded by a leader in the modern drama-theater (*shingeki*) movement, Kaoru Osanai (1881–1928). However, by the mid-1930s, she could not find publishers for her plays, so she switched to writing novels. At first, the literary world was receptive to her work; however, for most of the 1940s, she had difficulty finding publishers. Her first major success was *The Starving Years* (1953), about a woman trapped in marriage to a womanizing, chauvinistic man. The novel, however, that won her international acclaim was *Masks* (1958), based on the story of Lady Rokujō from *The Tale of Genji.*

Enchi is known for combining elements from classical Japanese works from the Heian (794–1185) and Edo (1600–1867) periods into modern settings. Many of her stories center on women navigating patriarchal Japan. She has won numerous literary awards, including the Tanizaki Prize in 1969, the Japanese Literature Grand Prize in 1972, and the Order of Culture in 1985.

Other Works by Enchi Fumiko
A Tale of False Fortunes. Translated by Roger K. Thomas. Honolulu: University of Hawaii Press, 2000.
The Waiting Years. Translated by John Bester. Tokyo: Kodansha International, 1971.

A Work about Enchi Fumiko
Vernon, Victoria V. *Daughters of the Moon: Wish, Will and Social Constraint in Fiction by Modern Japanese Women.* Berkeley: Institute of East Asian Studies, University of California Press, 1988.

Enzensberger, Hans Magnus (1929–)
poet, novelist, essayist

Hans Magnus Enzensberger was born in Kaufbeuren, Germany, to middle-class parents and grew up in Nuremberg. As a teenager during World War II, Enzensberger served in the *Volkssturm* (Home Guard). After the war, he worked as an interpreter for the occupying British and American armies, tended bar, and traded on the black market. Enzensberger studied philosophy, literature, and languages at several universities, including the Sorbonne in Paris. After completing his dissertation, he spent two years in radio work and traveled extensively.

Enzensberger's first book of poetry, *Verteidigung der Wölfe* (*Defense of the Wolves*, 1957), sharply criticized West Germany's government and culture, establishing his reputation as one of Germany's most controversial poets. His important influences include BERTOLT BRECHT. He was a member of the literary association GRUPPE 47 and won the Georg Büchner Prize in 1963. In 1965, Enzensberger founded *Kursbuch* (*Coursebook*), a progressive magazine that provided a forum for political and literary debates. He used his essays, poems, and novels to voice his social criticisms and to call for revolutionary change. Literary scholar Peter Demetz describes Enzensberger, in *Postwar German Literature* (1970), as "a highly gifted intellectual" who "wants his reader to think." In 2002, Enzensberger won the Prince of Asturias Award for Communications and Humanities; in 2009 he won the Griffin Poetry Prize Lifetime Recognition Award; and in 2010 he won the Sonningprisen, Denmark's prestigious award, whose organizers described Enzensberger as "one of German literature's most acclaimed contempory writers and analysts."

Other Works by Hans Magnus Enzensberger

Politics and Crime. New York: Seabury Press, 1974.
The Sinking of the Titanic: A Poem. Translated by the author. Boston: Houghton Mifflin, 1980.

A Work about Hans Magnus Enzensberger

Fischer, Gerhard, ed. *Debating Enzensberger: Great Migration and Civil War.* Tübingen, Germany: Stauffenburg, 1996.

Esenin, Sergey

See YESENIN, SERGEY.

Espinet, Ramabai (1948–) *poet, researcher, professor, activist, social commentator*

Born in Trinidad, Ramabai Espinet grew up in a largely creolized, Christian-Indian community in San Fernando. She started reading the works of the English romantics, along with those of Alfred, Lord Tennyson and Henry Wadsworth Longfellow, at an early age. By her late teens, when she moved to Toronto, Espinet had read most of William Butler Yeats's and DEREK WALCOTT's works. These poets, as well as the calypso music from her childhood, have significantly influenced her writing.

Poets Barbara Jones and GABRIELA MISTRAL, who both wrote about women's issues, shaped Espinet's perception of women's poetics, and Espinet subsequently became active in the women's movement in the Caribbean and Canada. In 1990, she published *Creation Fire,* a Caribbean poetry anthology containing a wide range of female Caribbean poets' works in English, French, Dutch, and Spanish.

Themes of identity, gender, and spirituality run through Espinet's own imagistic poetry, which has been published in *CAFRA News, Trinidad and Tobago Review, Woman Speak, Fireweed,* and *Toronto South Asian Review. Nuclear Seasons,* published in 1991, contains her collected poems. In an interview with Kwame Dawes in *Talk Yuh Talk: Interviews with Anglophone Caribbean Poets,* (2001) Espinet said, "In *Nuclear Seasons* the narrative line, for the most part, comes second to the metaphor. But I find myself writing a series of poems more directly now."

Apart from poetry, Espinet has published children's fiction: *The Princess of Spadina: a Tale of Toronto* (1992) and *Ninja's Carnival* (1993). Her essays and short fiction have appeared in journals and anthologies. *The Swinging Bridge* (2003), Espinet's first novel, examines an Indo-Caribbean woman's experiences in Trinidad and Canada.

After dividing her time between Canada and the Caribbean since the 1970s, Espinet now lives in Toronto, where she teaches English and Caribbean studies. She weaves one of her unique projects, "the invention or the renewal of lost myths, especially Caribbean feminist myth," through her varied but connected academic, literary, and activist pursuits. In 2003, Espinet published her first novel, *The Swinging Bridge,* a work that follows several generations of an Indian family from Trinidad.

Other Works by Ramabai Espinet
"Indian Cuisine." *The Massachusetts Review* 35, no. 3–4 (Fall 1994): 563.
"The Invisible Woman in West Indian Fiction." *World Literature Written in English* 29, no. 2 (Autumn 1989): 116–126.

Works about Ramabai Espinet
Birbalsingh, Frank. *Indo-Caribbean Resistance.* Toronto: TSAR, 1993.
Mehta, Brinda J. "Indo-Trinidadian Fiction: Female Identity and Creative Cooking." *Alif: A Journal of Comparative Poetics* 19 (1999): 151–184.
Puri, Shalini. "Race, Rape, and Representation: Indo-Caribbean Women and Cultural Nationalism." *Cultural Critique* (Spring 1997): 119–163.

Espronceda y Delgado, José de (José Ignacio Javier Oriol Encarnación de Espronceda) (1808–1842) *poet*
Born in western Spain, Espronceda was the son of a soldier. He had three brothers, all of whom died shortly after birth. During the first several years of his life, Espronceda and his family were constantly on the move due to the Napoleonic Wars. Espronceda witnessed many of the atrocities of war; his poems are moving, painful, bitter, and tender, reflecting his life experience.

At age 15, Espronceda formed and became president of *Los Numantinos,* a secret patriotic organization. Shortly thereafter, he was arrested and sentenced to prison. The intervention of his father, then a colonel, resulted in his release just weeks later.

In 1826, he traveled to the Portuguese capital of Lisbon, then a center for Spanish liberals. Espronceda tried to enlist in the National Guard but was exiled instead because one of his published poems proved to be too liberal. During this exile, he wrote his only novel, *Sancho Saldaña o el castellano de Cuéllar* (*Sancho Saldaña or the Spaniard of Cuéllar,* 1834). He returned to Madrid, where he founded several liberal/democratic newspapers and wrote one of the most popular Spanish poems of all time, "The Pirate's Song" (1835), which celebrates its antisocial narrator's love of liberty. Other poems of the 1930s that raise questions of social justice include "Under Sentence of Death," "The Executioner," and "The Beggar." In 1840, he published "To Jarifa in an Orgy," a sympathetic address to a prostitute by a disillusioned idealist. After traveling as a delegate to the Spanish embassy, Espronceda took ill and died at age 34.

His two major works were written in his last two years. *The Student from Salamanca* is a narrative poem about a Don Juan-like character. *The Godforsaken World,* which includes the celebrated "Canto a Teresa," addressed to Teresa Mancha, Espronceda's mistress of 10 years, remained unfinished at his death. José de Espronceda's poetry is the epitome of Spanish ROMANTICISM. It is lyrical, patriotic, and youthful. It portrays doubt, sorrow, pleasure, death, pessimism, and disillusion.

Another Work by José de Espronceda y Delgado
The Student of Salamanca/El estudiante de Salamanca. Translated by C. K. Davies, with introduction and notes by Richard A. Cardwell. Warminster, U.K.: Aris & Phillips, 1998.

Works about José de Espronceda y Delgado
Ilie, Paul. "Espronceda and the Romantic Grotesque." *Studies in Romanticism II* (1972): 94–112.
Landeira, Ricardo. *José de Espronceda.* Boulder: University of Colorado, 1984.
Pallady, Stephen. *Irony in the Poetry of José de Espronceda.* Lewiston, N.Y.: Edwin Mellen Press, 1991.

Esterházy, Péter (1950–) *novelist*
A leading contemporary Hungarian author who has changed the face of Hungarian literature, Péter

Esterházy was born in Budapest in 1950, a descendant of a distinguished and aristocratic family that could trace its lineage to the 12th century. As a youth, Esterházy studied mathematics and from 1974 to 1978 worked as a mathematician for the Informatics Institute of the Ministry of Furnaces and Heavy Machinery. Starting in 1974, his prose writings were published in literary journals, and, by 1978, already possessed of a significant reputation as a writer, he began writing full time. Esterházy maintains an unchallenged position as Hungary's most illustrious author and has frequently been mentioned as a candidate for a Nobel Prize.

Esterházy's writings have been translated into more than 20 languages, and he has been awarded more than 32 literary prizes, including the Kossuth Prize, Hungary's most prestigious literary award, in 1996. He is the leading representative of writers born between the end of World War II and the Hungarian Revolution of 1956, known for works that deal with the bitterness and hardships of everyday life under a communist regime. He has made a major impact on the direction of Hungarian fiction by refusing to abide by traditional conventions of narrative prose. Instead, he has adopted the language and style of the world of postmodernism. His writing is brilliantly erudite, humorous, and sophisticated. A cogent commentary on his postmodern style is perhaps best expressed by Ruth Pavey, in her review of *Celestial Harmonies* in the British newspaper *The Independent,* on April 20, 2004. "Book One is subtitled 'Numbered Sentences from the Lives of the Esterházy Family.' The first 'sentence' contains one sentence. The final (371st) 'sentence' contains four sentences. In between, 'sentences' may run to a few pages, but there is no settling down to one subject or span of time. We skip about among the past 10 centuries and among dozens of fathers, all claimed as 'my father' by the narrator."

The following novels, among the many that Esterházy has written, have been translated into English: *Helping Verbs of the Heart* (1985), *The Transporters* (1983), *The Book of Hrabal* (1990), *The Glance of Countess Hahn-Hahn (Down the Danube)* (1991), *She Loves Me* (1993), *A Little Hungarian Pornography* (1984), and *Celestial Harmonies: A Novel* (2004).

Esterházy is best known for *Celestial Harmonies,* an intricate family history that simultaneously mirrors the history of Hungary even as it chronicles the saga of seven centuries of the Esterházy family's significant role in the rise and fall of the Austro-Hungarian Empire. Esterházy writes about his father and the fathers of previous generations of Esterházys—princes, counts, commanders, diplomats, bishops, and patrons of the arts—some of whom were honored and respected, some of whom were justly feared by their contemporaries. In the process of describing his ancestors, Esterházy's postmodernistic style of writing can sometimes confuse the reader, as he characterizes his father as being his father and yet, simultaneously, each of his other ancestors as well. Always mindful of his rich and varied heritage, Esterházy unfolds for the reader the history of his family, its successes and failures, its weaknesses and strengths, and its descent from glory to poverty under the communists. In book 2 of *Celestial Harmonies,* Esterházy describes in detail the life of his father, a man who was born into a life of privilege in 1919 but who ended his days in poverty and debasement under communist rule.

Only a week or two after he had completed *Celestial Harmonies,* Esterházy discovered, to his chagrin and initial disbelief, that from 1957 to 1980, his father had been an informer for the Hungarian secret police. As a result of this discovery, Esterházy immediately set about writing an appendix to *Celestial Harmonies.* The new book was titled *Revised Edition* and was Esterházy's effort to come to terms with the shock provided by the new information. As a result of Esterházy's disclosure of his father's actions, there was much public discussion of the conditions and circumstances that caused those actions, as well as a great deal of anger and pain as people began to realize the extent to which the communist regime had affected their private lives.

While *Celestial Harmonies* and *Revised Edition* focused on Esterházy's father's life, his book *Not Art: A Novel* details his relationship with his mother and their mutual enjoyment of soccer. It was written when his mother was in her 90s, and it celebrates her love of life and how, during her younger years, she had used the thrill and diversion provided by soccer to cope with the vicious attacks that the family endured under communist rule. This book seems to be a postscript to another book, *Helping Verbs of the Heart,* which had been written 20 years earlier. The final sentence in *Helping Verbs* reads: "I will write about all that in more detail later." This is exactly what Esterházy does 20 years later, in 12 short biographical vignettes.

Péter Esterházy has revolutionized Hungarian literature. His complex, postmodernistic writing style is sometimes difficult to comprehend, and he couches many of his messages about life in terms of football—taken from the varying perspectives of a young man and, later on, from the viewpoint of someone who has reached middle age and who can no longer be the energetic player he once was. Much of his writing is characterized by this imagery, and he uses it to great effect to highlight his views on life and society, reflecting an emotional ambivalence between his family's illustrious past and present political realities.

existentialism

Existentialism is a philosophical, artistic, and literary movement that emphasizes individual existence and freedom of choice. Although difficult to define precisely because it encompassed a wide array of diverse elements, certain themes are consistent in works by writers associated with the movement, most particularly the theme of individual existence. Although existentialism is linked explicitly to the 19th and 20th centuries, elements of existentialism can also be found in Socrates' works and in the Bible.

The literary form of the novel became one of the most prominent modes of expression for the movement in the 19th century. Russian novelist Fyodor Dostoyevsky was considered the most prominent existentialist literary figure as exemplified in his novel, *Notes from the Underground* (1864), which focuses on the alienated antihero who must fight against the optimism inherent in rationalist humanism. Logic is eventually shown to be self-destructive. Only Christian love, which cannot be understood through reason and logic, can save humanity. This and other existentialist works found a base in strong Christian theology, as can be seen in the works of German Protestant theologians Paul Tillich and Rudolf Karl Bultmann, French Roman Catholic theologian Gabriel Marcel, the Russian Orthodox philosopher Nikolay Aleksandrovich Berdyayev, and the German Jewish philosopher Martin Buber (existential theists). However, the movement itself encompassed equally strong proponents of atheism, agnosticism, and paganism (existential atheists), all sharing the common theme of individual choice.

Examined historically, existentialism was first anticipated by the 17th-century French philosopher Blaise Pascal, who rejected the rigorous rationalism of his contemporary René Descartes. Pascal contends, in his *Pensées* (1670), that any attempt to explain systematically and rationally concepts as broad as God and humanity must be rooted in arrogance. Like the existentialists, he viewed human existence as a series of paradoxes, the ultimate of which was the human self, a combination of mind and body that inherently contradicts itself.

The 19th-century Danish philosopher, Søren Kierkegaard, was the first writer to refer to himself actually as an existentialist. Regarded as the founder of modern existentialism, he insisted in his works that the highest good for the individual is to find his or her own true path in life. Writing in response to and in negation of G. W. F. Hegel, who claimed to have discovered a way to understand and explain humanity and history rationally and absolutely, Kierkegaard focused on the ambiguity and absurdity of life. He also stressed the importance of committing completely to the choices that are made, often forsaking established societal norms, in the ultimate quest for personal validity. He advocated faith and the Christian way of life as the only means of avoiding despair. Kierkegaard also examined the concept of fear or dread as crucial to greater understanding.

Other existentialist writers and artists went on to echo Kierkegaard's ideas, focusing on the belief that the individual must be allowed to pursue his or her own path, free from the constraints of imposed moral standards. Existentialists argue that there is no objective or rational basis for moral decisions. The German existential philosopher FRIEDRICH NIETZSCHE, for example, theorized that individual choice has a basis in subjectivity and that it is the individual's responsibility to choose the actions that constitute a moral decision. Nietzsche criticized traditional moral assumptions, citing free will as existing in direct opposition to moral conformity. Unlike Kierkegaard, whose ideas led to radically individualistic Christianity, Nietzsche rejected Judeo-Christian ideals, proclaiming the "death of God" and espousing the pagan ideal.

French existentialism grew and flourished independently from German existentialism. Jean Wahl (1888–1974) is considered to be the founder of the French existentialist movement, which was later expanded and brought to greater attention under JEAN-PAUL SARTRE. Sartre adopted the term *existentialism* for his own philosophy and became the leader of the movement in France. It was through his works that, after World War II, existentialism began to gain recognition and followers on an international scale. Sartre's philosophy is atheistic and decidedly pessimistic. He asserts that, although human beings desire a rational basis for their existence, no such foundation exists. Therefore, human life seems contingent and futile. His negativity notwithstanding, he also insisted that existentialism is tied directly to humanism with its emphasis on freedom, choice, and responsibility. Other French writers were profoundly influenced by Sartre and Nietzsche. The works of ANDRÉ MALRAUX and ALBERT CAMUS are generally associated with existentialist ideas because of their focus on the absurdity of life and the apparent indifference of the universe to human suffering. The French THEATER OF THE ABSURD also reflects existentialist ideals, as seen in the plays of SAMUEL BECKETT and EUGÈNE IONESCO.

Works about Existentialism

Giles, James, ed. *French Existentialism: Consciousness, Ethics and Relations with Others.* Atlanta, Ga.: Rodopi, 1999.

Gordon, Haim, ed. *The Dictionary of Existentialism.* Westport, Conn.: Greenwood Press, 1999.

Guignon, Charles, and Derk Pereboom, eds. *Existentialism: Basic Writings.* Indianapolis, Ind.: Hackett Publishing Company, 2001.

MacDonald, Paul S., ed. *The Existentialist Reader: An Anthology of Key Texts.* New York: Routledge, 2001.

expressionism

Expressionism refers to a literary and artistic movement that emerged in Germany in the late 19th century and reached its pinnacle in the late 1920s. Expressionists generally believed that an individual's thoughts and experiences cannot be rendered in objective terms because such representation would distort and sterilize subjective, emotional experience. Under this premise, expressionists rejected REALISM and aimed to depict the world artistically through personal vision. To achieve this, expressionists portray their subjects as experience or emotion rather than through realistic detail. In general, expressionists tended either to simplify or to distort their subjects to expose extreme and fragmented states of human consciousness. Expressionist works are often set in a nightmarish atmosphere to emphasize the dramatic gap between subjective and objective reality.

Expressionism has a more precise meaning in art criticism than it does in literary criticism. In art, the term refers to a school of German and Scandinavian painters of the early 20th century who claimed that human condition cannot be mimetically represented through exact depiction of reality. In the visual arts, one of the most famous examples of a work that depicts expressionistic ideals is Edvard Munch's painting *The Cry* (1893).

Expressionism also found a fertile ground in film: Fritz Lang's expressionist film *Metropolis* (1927), for example, presents a dystopian vision of the future in which the workers are oppressed and held under control by the machines and the elite that controls the machines. *Metropolis* established itself as the foundational classic of world cinema.

In literature, expressionism also originated in Germany. Most literary scholars identify the emergence of expressionism with the works of dramatists Frank Nedekind, Carl Stranheim, and AUGUST STRINDBERG. Expressionism also took root in the poetry of Franz Werfel and the fiction of FRANZ KAFKA. Eventually, literary critics began to refer to every work of literature of the period in which reality is purposefully distorted as expressionist. Consequently, it has become difficult to demarcate the literary expressionists precisely. Although some critics limit the use of the term to the German literary movement of the 20th century, some critics apply the term more liberally to any work that manifests expressionist characteristics.

The German expressionist movement had an intriguing influence on psychology as well, particularly in the works of the Austrian psychoanalytic theorist SIGMUND FREUD. Expressionism tended to explore the dark corners of the human mind, often illuminating anxieties, fears, and secret fantasies. Many critics have attributed this interest to the historical conditions following World War I and the subsequent disillusionment with humanity. Expressionism, thus, also artistically revealed the repressed fears and anxieties of the human psyche.

The expressionist movement was brutally suppressed by the Nazi government. The Nazis viewed the expressionists as a degenerate and subversive group and organized an exhibition of confiscated works of expressionists to demonstrate their "decadence" and "absurdity"; ironically, the exhibition backfired, and thousands of people flooded in to appreciate the works of the famous expressionist artists.

German expressionism influenced a number of writers and artists around the world, including James Joyce and T. S. Eliot. Many modern and POSTMODERN writers, including Tennessee Williams, the Beat writers, and Joseph Heller, were all influenced by the expressionism, which questioned accepted ideas about "objective" reality and brought to literature and art a new psychological dimension—one that is often dark, disturbing, and thought-provoking.

Works about Expressionism

Barron, Stephanie, and Wolf-Dieter Dube, ed. *German Expressionism: Art and Society.* New York: Rizzoli, 1997.

Polcari, Stephen. *Abstract Expressionism and the Modern Experience.* New York: Cambridge University Press, 1993.

F

Fabian
See LAGERKVIST, PÄR.

Fadeyev, Aleksandr Aleksandrovich
(1901–1956) *novelist, short story writer*
Aleksandr Aleksandrovich Fadeyev was born in Krimy, Russia. His father was a village teacher, and his mother a nurse. Fadeyev's family moved to Sarovka, in the far eastern region of Russia, in 1908. Fadeyev attended a small village school where he learned the basic skills, and went on to the Commercial Academy of Vladivostok. After becoming involved in the communist cause in 1918, he left school without graduating. He joined the partisans to defend the Vladivostok region against invading Japanese forces and eventually joined the Red Army, where he was quickly promoted. Fadeyev started his writing career as a journalist for *Soviet South,* a small newspaper in the Russian city of Rostov. He also established a literary journal called *Lava.*

The communist regime assigned Fadeyev as the representative of the Writers' Association. In this capacity, Fadeyev traveled throughout Europe, including Spain during its civil war. When World War II broke out, he worked as a frontline reporter for the two major newspapers in Russia, *Pravda* and *Izvestya.* After the war, he served as the general secretary of the Union of Soviet Writers from 1946 to 1954, editor of several literary journals, and member of the party's Central Committee. He was awarded two Orders of Lenin for his work with the Communist Party.

Fadeyev's fiction often glorifies the struggle of the Soviet Union, specifically of its workers and soldiers, during the Russian civil war and World War II. *The Birth of the Amgunsky Regiment* (1934) describes the war efforts of communist partisans in Far East during the early 1920s. His most seminal work was *The Young Guard* (1945), which deals with the resistance efforts of the young communist workers of Krasnodon during the Nazi occupation.

During the last years of his life, Fadeyev suffered from a number of physical and psychological disorders that were a result of alcoholism. He committed suicide in 1956, leaving a note that revealed his disillusionment with the party and with Stalin. Fadeyev's vivid description of the war experience contributed to the discourse of the Soviet national identity. The heroes of his novels, although highly politicized, display heroism and patriotism in their commitment to defend their homeland.

Another Work by Aleksandr Fadeyev
The Nineteen. New York: Hyperion Press, 1973.

Faiz, Faiz Ahmed (1912–1984) *poet*

Faiz Ahmed Faiz was born in Sialkot, modern Pakistan. His father was a successful lawyer. Faiz studied extensively in the humanities and earned his master's degrees in English and Arabic literatures from Punjab University. Next to MUHAMMAD IQBĀL, he is perhaps Pakistan's best-known poet. He is regarded as the cofounder of the progressive movement in Urdu literature and wrote exclusively in Urdu, a language similar to Arabic.

Faiz was editor of *The Pakistan Times,* a leftist English daily, and of *Imraz,* an Urdu daily. In the 1930s, he was introduced to marxism and became increasingly involved in politics. Through the course of his life, Faiz spent several terms in jail for alleged sabotage against the government. His poetry, however, is a unique intermingling of romantic, sublime, and political themes. He uses traditional images of Urdu love poetry in *ghazal* form, a conventional prose form of the Mughal courts, to address contemporary politics. The customary representation of the *bulbul* (nightingale), the *gul* (rose), and the *baghban* (gardener) in Faiz's *ghazals* were reconfigured to represent the poet, the poet's ideals, and the political system, respectively. At a time when the tensions between Hindus and Muslims in India were rising, Faiz was able to address the state of Muslims in India in this manner.

Faiz's politically motivated works, such as *Zindan Namah* (Prison narrative, 1956) and *Naqshe Faryadi* (Image of complaint, 1941), are written in protest against the government, but Faiz never excludes the power of human love in these verses. This can also be seen in the collection of poems, *Zindan Naman,* which Faiz wrote while in prison. It contains a poem called "Come, Africa" that unites the beating of the heart of the poet with Africa's, evoking a life force that will free the poet and his nation from political and religious intolerance.

Despite being viewed as a militant and subversive by the government of Pakistan, Faiz won the Soviet Lenin Peace Prize in 1962 for his commitment to people's struggles through his poetry.

Other Work by Faiz Ahmed Faiz

The True Subject: Selected Poems of Faiz Ahmed Faiz. Translated by Naomi Lazard. Princeton, N.J.: Princeton University Press, 1988.

Zakir, Mohammed, and Menai, M. N., trans. *Poems of Faiz Ahmad Faiz: A Poet of the Third World.* South Asia. Print House, 1998.

Falkner, Gerhard (1951–) *poet, dramatist, essayist*

Gerhard Falkner was born in Schwabuch, Germany. He prepared for a career as a book dealer before moving to London and the United States. Falkner published his first volume of poetry, *so beginnen am körper die tage* (so begin the days along your body), at the age of 30. After publishing two more poetry collections and a work of prose in the 1980s, he expanded his focus in the following decade to include works for the stage. Falkner wrote the libretto for the opera, *A Lady Dies* (2000), which is based on the death of Princess Diana.

Falkner's influences include critic T. W. Adorno, poet Oskar Pastior, and the DADA movement. Falkner takes a critical view of society in his poems, which reflect a synthesis of several postwar trends in German poetry. His verse is sensual, intellectually full, and written with a disorienting dissection of syntax. In his review of *Voice and Void* by Neil H. Donohue, critic Jerry Glenn describes Falkner as "one of the most talented and explosive poetic voices to have emerged from Germany in recent decades." Although not widely recognized by scholars and critics, Falkner's influence is already evident in the work of younger German poets such as DURS GRÜNBEIN.

Another Work by Gerhard Falkner

Seventeen Selected Poems. Translated by Mark Anderson. Berlin: Qwert, 1994.

A Work about Gerhard Falkner

Donahue, Neil. *Voice and Void: The Poetry of Gerhard Falkner.* Heidelberg, Germany: Universitätsverlag G. Winter, 1998.

Fallaci, Oriana (1930–2006) *novelist, journalist*

An accomplished journalist who had the opportunity to interview some of the most remarkable political figures of the 20th century, Oriana Fallaci was born in Florence, Italy, on June 29, 1930. The daughter of a cabinetmaker and liberal political activist, her childhood coincided with Mussolini's rise to power. Growing up under a fascist regime, she became interested in power and the ways in which it can be both used and abused.

By the time Fallaci was 10 years old, Italy was deeply involved in World War II. One of her greatest influences throughout her life came from this period and the political views of her very liberal father, who opposed Mussolini. Fallaci joined her father as a member of the underground resistance movements that were dedicated to fighting the Nazis, who were allied with Italy. During this period, her father was captured, sent to jail, and tortured. Fallaci continued to fight in his absence, receiving, at age 14, an honorable discharge from the Italian army. The war ended when she was 15, but the effects of having been so directly involved with the struggle remained ingrained in her mind and formed the background for her future work as an author and journalist.

Fallaci began writing at age 16. She received a degree from the University of Florence and went on to become an award-winning writer for several newspapers. Her first journalistic assignment was to a crime column at a daily paper, but she rapidly progressed and soon was interviewing such political figures as U.S. Secretary of State Henry Kissinger, CIA director William Colby, and Iranian leader Ayatollah Khomeini. She also interviewed actors and scientists and conducted intensive research on the U.S. space program.

Aside from her accomplishments as a journalist, Fallaci was also an accomplished novelist. Her works of fiction address the subject of power, particularly in terms of resistance. *Letter to a Child Never Born* (1976), for example, tackles the subject of an unwed pregnant woman who is faced with the difficult choice between having an illegal abortion or keeping the child and facing the social stigma. In this case, the power struggle comes in the form of cultural perceptions and the control they exert on the individual's decision-making processes.

Fallaci maintained a long-term relationship with political activist and Greek resistance leader Alexandros Panagoulis. His death in 1976 prompted her novel *A Man* (1980). Although fictional, this work expresses the challenges of confrontation and resistance to political power structures. Similarly, her novel *Inshallah* (1992) tackles these themes by restructuring the setting to illuminate the same challenges with regard to the civil war in Lebanon. After September 11, 2001, Fallaci wrote two books critical of Islam and Islamic extremists, *The Rage and the Pride* (2001) and *The Force of Reason* (2004). Her harsh critique of Islam created a worldwide controversy, with many Muslims accusing her of racism.

Fallaci's works are important for their contemporary social and political implications and the glimpse they provide of social conditions.

Other Works by Oriana Fallaci
The Egoists: Sixteen Surprising Interviews. Chicago: Henry Regnery Company, 1963.
Interview with History. New York: Liveright, 1976.

Works about Oriana Fallaci
Arico, Santo L. *Oriana Fallaci: The Woman and the Myth.* Carbondale: Southern Illinois University Press, 1998.
Gatt-Rutter, John. *Oriana Fallaci: The Rhetoric of Freedom.* Washington, D.C.: Berg, 1996.

Farah, Nuruddin (1945–) *novelist, playwright, essayist*

When Nuruddin Farah was born, his section of what is now called Somalia, located on the eastern coast of Africa, was a colony of Italy. In 1960, the nation of Somalia was formed by the merger of this Italian colony with what had been known as British Somaliland. He is descended from nomadic peoples who wandered far to feed their herds. His father was a merchant, and his mother was a poet who spoke several languages. Today, Farah has married an exile's nomadic life to a narrative style that wanders far from any conception of "traditional" REALISM. His travels throughout the world mirror his experiments in language use: His novels tend to use fantastic, improbable elements, what some critics refer to as MAGIC REALISM.

Young Farah grew up speaking Somali, Arabic, and Amharic. English is his fourth language. From his mother, he gained a love of the sounds of words, of the power of language, and of the need to use the tapestry of cultures that language represents as a political tool. In many countries like Somalia that have a history of colonialism, the language one uses has political implications. Because English (and Italian and French) are reminders of a time when racism and oppression were the order of the day in such countries, many writers have chosen to avoid what they saw as the "language of the conqueror." Unlike the Kenyan writer, NGŨGĨ WA THIONG'O, however, Farah chooses to write in English for pragmatic reasons. As Charles Larson has observed in *The Ordeal of the African Writer* (2001), relatively few Africans in any country are able to read literary works in any language. Farah is not, however, unaware of the political implications of this choice. His novels often deal with political themes, including language usage.

For example, Farah's third novel, *A Naked Needle* (1976), so infuriated Somali dictator Mohamed Siyad Barre that Farah has lived in exile for more than 20 years. Among other issues, *A Naked Needle* deals with the corruption of those who have ruled the country since independence.

Farah has continued to speak for his country and his people, most notably in his trilogy, *Sweet and Sour Milk* (1979), *Sardines* (1981), and *Close Sesame* (1983), known collectively as *Variations on the Theme of an African Dictatorship*. This trilogy is the fullest and most complex treatment that Farah has yet attempted on his most important theme: the oppression of Somalia's various groups by a succession of despots. Recently, Farah published two books in what will become a trilogy: *Links* (2004), about a Somalian man who lives in America but decides to return to his native land after 20 years of absence to visit his mother's grave, and *Knots* (2007), about a woman who returns to Somalia after the death of her son in America. Both novels deal with the wrenching conditions in this war-torn and impoverished land.

Farah is Somalia's first novelist and its most renowned international literary figure. In addition to his focus on racial inequality and the problems of POSTCOLONIALISM, he has also focused extensively on gender inequities and the problems women face in the Third World. In 1998, he received the Neustadt Prize for Literature, one of the most prestigious literary awards in the world. It carries a $50,000 award and is often seen as a precursor for consideration for the Nobel Prize.

Other Works by Nuruddin Farah

From a Crooked Rib. London: Heinemann, 1976.
Maps. New York: Pantheon, 1986.

A Work about Nuruddin Farah

Alden, Patricio, and Louis Tremaine. *Nuruddin Farah.* New York: Twayne, 1999.

feminism

The term *feminism,* with regard to literature, has a number of distinct associations. Largely grouped under the interdisciplinary field of gender studies, and arising out of increasing understanding of women's issues, different branches of the discipline focus on divergent ideas. The oldest identifiable form of literary feminism grew out of 18th-century liberal philosophy such as that found in Mary Wollstonecraft's *A Vindication of the Rights of Women* (1792), which emphasized female autonomy and self-fulfillment. In the 20th century, liberal feminism worked to achieve economic and social equality for women. More a revisionist than a revolutionary movement, feminism's literary aim was to reform existing structures by getting people to learn and read about women's issues, not to break down those structures to create new ones.

The movement eventually broadened to encompass radical feminism, which accused liberal feminism of not having high enough goals. Arising out of the Civil Rights movement and the surge of Leftist activism in the late 1960s, radical feminism's goal of addressing the women's oppression was revolutionary. As the 1970s progressed, the movement gained a more cultural perspective, the one most widely adopted by feminist writers.

Cultural feminism celebrates women's culture and community. Its goal is to seek out those qualities that are traditionally associated with women, such as compassion, subjectivity, intuition, and closeness to nature, and to claim them as desirable, positive, and even superior traits. Proponents of cultural feminism, including the writers Elizabeth Gould Davis and Ashley Montagu, also believe that these qualities are not innate but are learned.

In France, the feminist social movement began in April 1944 when French women obtained the right to vote. It was advanced greatly by the 1949 publication of SIMONE DE BEAUVOIR's *The Second Sex,* in which she states "One is not born, but rather becomes, a woman. No biological, psychological or economic fate determines the figure that the human female presents in society; it is civilization as a whole that determines this creature."

Simone de Beauvoir was not alone in her support of the emerging feminist trend in France. Other writers soon began to follow her example. HÉLÈNE CIXOUS and her "écriture feminine," developed in her essay "The Laugh of the Medusa" (1975), established a new form of women's writing whereby women could learn to "write from the body" to break free of the bonds of male-dominated rhetoric. Theories of the body became particularly important for feminist thinkers, as a woman's body was traditionally the source of such male-defined constructs as physical weakness, immorality, and unseemliness. One of the main goals of feminism as a literary movement was to redefine the body and society's view of it.

In reference to the concept of the body, many feminist critics turn to the work of writer Julia Kristeva. Although she does not consider herself a feminist writer, her theories linking the mind to the body and linking biology to representation have been pivotal to the movement. Kristeva emphasizes the maternal function of a woman's body and its significance to the development of language and culture. As a result of this function, Kristeva purports, ideals of feminism as espoused by de Beauvoir should be rejected because they negate the importance of motherhood. She also insists that early feminism, which sought total equality, is remiss in its attempts to ignore the inherent differences between genders. She further argues that a unique feminine language, as proposed by Cixous, is impossible. However, in rejecting existing feminisms, Kristeva paves the way for another form of feminism, one grounded in the exploration of multiple identities, arguing that there are as many sexualities as there are individuals.

In the 1990s, the trend toward gender studies, encompassing not only feminism but also lesbian criticism and queer theory, shifted the focus once again to a more inclusive philosophy.

In 1992, a young, bisexual African-American woman Rebecca Walker (daughter of Alice Walker) popularized the term third-wave feminism. (The first wave began in the late 18th century; the second wave began after World War II and continued into the mid-1990s.) Walker's major complaint, and that of other third-wave feminists, was that mainstream feminism did not deal adequately with women like Walker herself—women of color who were young and not heterosexual. In addition, many young feminists of the third wave feel that earlier feminists did not represent the needs of low-income women and tended to focus almost exclusively on the middle class. Third-wave feminists, unlike their second-wave counterparts, take a global perspective and are concerned with empowering women as agents of change in developing countries.

Some Works by Feminist Writers

Gilbert, Sandra M., and Susan Gubar. *The Madwoman in the Attic: The Woman Writer and the Nineteenth-Century Literary Imagination.* New Haven, Conn.: Yale University Press, 2000.

Hirshman, Linda R. *Get to Work: A Manifesto for Women of the World.* New York: Viking Adult, 2006.

Kristeva, Julia. *The Kristeva Reader.* Edited by Tori Moi. New York: Columbia University Press, 1986.

Millet, Kate. *Sexual Politics.* Champaign: University of Illinois Press, 2000.

Moers, Ellen. *Literary Women.* Indianapolis, Ind.: Doubleday, 1976.

Moi, Tori. *Sexual/Textual Politics: Feminist Literary Theory.* New York: Routledge, 2002.

Siegel, Deborah. *Sisterhood Interrupted.* New York: Palgrave Macmillan, 2007.

Woolf, Virginia. *A Room of One's Own.* Fort Washington, Pa.: Harvest Books, 1990.

Works about Feminism

Mohanty, Chandra Talpade. *Feminism without Borders: Decolonizing Theory, Practicing Solidarity.* Durham, N. C.: Duke University Press, 2006.

Richardson, Angelique, and Chris Willis, eds. *The New Woman in Fiction and in Fact: Fin de Siècle Feminisms.* New York: Palgrave, 2001.

Warhol, Robyn R., and Diane Price, eds. *Feminisms: An Anthology of Literary Theory and Criticism.* Piscataway, N.J.: Rutgers University Press, 1977.

Feng Zhi (Feng Chih; Feng Chengzhi)
(1905–1993) *poet*

Feng Zhi was born in China's Hebei Province on September 17. At age 12, he was sent to Beijing to study. He entered Beijing University in 1921 and produced a high volume of poems. In 1924, his first work appeared in *Hidden Grass,* a journal he published with friends in Shanghai. From 1925 to 1932, he edited another journal, *The Sunken Bell.* He graduated from Beijing University two years later and published his first collection, *Songs of Yesterday.* He then moved to Harbin to teach secondary school but returned to Beijing a year later to rejoin the literary community.

Feng Zhi's second collection, *The Northern Journey and Other Poems* (1929), is one of the most famous examples of modern Chinese lyric poetry. Written in melodic, romantic vernacular, it is a lengthy narrative poem about Feng Zhi's social education and his encounters with decadent and morally destitute warlords, prostitutes, and foreign invaders.

The next year, Feng Zhi traveled to Germany to study philosophy and literature in Heidelberg and Berlin. He earned a Ph.D. and translated German poets such as RAINER MARIA RILKE. When he returned to China in 1936, he taught at Tongji University until 1939, when he joined the faculty at South-West United University in Kunming.

In 1941, Feng Zhi published *Sonnets* (1942), a collection of 27 sonnets that earned him fame as the Chinese practitioner of the poetic form. The sonnets are mostly contemplative reflections on life and nature, and because of their tone and internal direction, Feng Zhi is sometimes referred to as a metaphysical poet.

After the 1949 communist revolution, Feng Zhi wrote mostly patriotic poems (in *Collected Poems,* 1955) and focused on scholarship. He joined the Communist Party in 1956 and became director of the Foreign Literature Institute at the Academy of Social Sciences, where he continued his translations and studies of German literature.

Feng Zhi was considered one of modern China's great poets and also was honored with several German literary prizes, such as the Medal of Brothers Green from the German Democratic Republic and the Prize for the Arts by the Center for International Exchanges. He died on February 22, 1993.

A Work about Feng Zhi

Cheung, Dominic. *Feng Chih.* Boston: Twayne, 1979.

Ferré, Rosario (1942–   ) *novelist, short story writer, poet, critic*

Rosario Ferré was born in Ponce, Puerto Rico, to Luis Ferré, politician and eventual governor of the island, and Lorenza Ramírez Ferré. Although Ferré received a conventional, aristocratic education, her childhood nanny, a vivid storyteller, introduced her early on to the worlds of fantasy, legend, and myth. Later in life, she studied under the Peruvian novelist MARIO VARGAS LLOSA and the Uruguayan critic ÁNGEL RAMA, both of whom encouraged her to write.

Ferré's early work, including *The Youngest Doll* (1976), a series of short stories set in Puerto Rico, established her as one of the first Puerto Rican feminist writers. In it, one finds the criticism of feminine stereotypes and an implicit call for the end of the repression of women, both of which themes have come to characterize much of her work. Her writing also deals with the cultural and historical heritage of Puerto Rico. To explore such themes, she incorporates elements of local myth and legend as well as realistic depictions of characters and settings. The title story of one of her best-known books, *Sweet Diamond Dust* (1986), relates the rise and fall of the aristocratic De la Valle family. The alternation of colloquial and formal language and the incorporation of different narrative perspectives in this work are typical of her fiction.

For Ferré writing has been and continues to be a manner of breaking through the societal constraints placed on her as a woman and as an individual. In this sense, she has followed in the tradition of such feminist writers as SIMONE DE BEAUVOIR and VIRGINIA WOOLF. Her questioning of restrictive gender and class divisions in Puerto Rico and the West in general, as well as her sensitive and profound character portrayals, have made her an important figure in contemporary Hispanic and world literature. Ferré won a Guggenheim fellowship in 2004.

Other Works by Rosario Ferré

Flight of the Swan. New York: Farrar, Straus and Giroux, 2002.

The House on the Lagoon. New York: Plume, 1996.

A Work about Rosario Ferré

Hintz, Suzanne S. *Rosario Ferré, A Search for Identity.* New York: Peter Lang, 1995.

Fiedeler, Hans

See DÖBLIN, ALFRED.

fin de siècle

French for "end of the century," fin de siècle first came about as a literary movement in 1871 when German troops withdrew from Paris after the Franco-Prussian War. French anarchists were able to establish the Commune of Paris, which, although it did not last for long, was instrumental in creating an atmosphere in which radical ideas in literature, theater, and the visual arts began to thrive. Paris, at this time, became one of the centers of avant-garde culture. DECADENCE, drug abuse, degradation, and surrealism are commonly associated with the era, as were the fascination with prostitution by male writers, the development of lesbianism as an artistic trend, and an increased focus on sexuality, both heterosexual and homosexual.

Among the most influential writers of this period was VICTOR HUGO, whose works, including *Les Misérables* (1862), were published in the middle of the century and greatly influenced the next generation of artists. In particular, his portrayal of bo-hemians and student revolutionaries was consistent with fin de siècle dark idealism. Other writers, such as GUY DE MAUPASSANT (whose works dealt chiefly with the Franco-Prussian war and fashionable life in Paris) and the prominent SYMBOLIST poets STÉPHANE MALLARMÉ and CHARLES BAUDELAIRE and their often dark and unconventional ideas flourished at the turn of the century as well.

The tone of the fin de siècle movement was dark without the expected, accompanying melancholy. It was a time of political scandal, the most notable of which was the Dreyfus affair in which Captain Alfred Dreyfus was falsely accused and convicted of spying for the Germans during the war. He was sentenced to serve time on Devil's Island, French Guiana. Angered by this, and feeling that the charges were largely a result of anti-Semitism, the writer ÉMILE ZOLA wrote a letter that openly criticized Dreyfus's conviction and subsequent imprisonment. Titled *J'accuse* (January 13, 1898), Zola's letter passionately defended Dreyfus. As a result, the case was reopened and the conviction ultimately overturned. The situation, however, was typical of the prevailing mood of the time, and art was used to effect for social change and rebellion.

Another fin de siècle scandal involved the poet ARTHUR RIMBAUD. He had already caused quite an artistic commotion with his dark, introspective *A Season in Hell* (1873; translated 1932), in which he described his own intense and often tortured existence. He had further scandalized Parisian society when he left his wife for a man, poet PAUL VERLAINE. This affair was an integral part of *A Season in Hell* and also typical of the tumultuousness of the age.

The social, literary, and artistic changes that were occurring at this time affected the theater as well. Actresses began to interpret the works of writers such as COLETTE, whose simulated sexual performance on stage caused a riot at the Moulin Rouge. Women, in particular, began to display their sensuality openly. Bored aristocrats, such as lovers Natalie Barney and poet René Vivien, often gave private yet elaborate shows in their own homes. The concept of *lesbian chic* emerged and flourished in these venues.

As a movement, the fin de siècle officially came to an end in 1905. It had achieved such momentum that it ultimately reached a breaking point; however, many of the influences that came out of the movement and other avant-garde and experimental art forms continued into the next century, shaping future trends in literature, culture, and the arts, not just in France but also internationally.

Works about the Fin de Siècle
Chadwick, Kay, and Timothy Unwin, eds. *New Perspectives on the Fin-de-Siècle in Nineteenth- and Twentieth-Century France.* Lewiston, N.Y.: E. Mellen Press, 2000.
McGuinness, Patrick, ed. *Symbolism, Decadence and the Fin de Siècle: French and European Perspectives.* Exeter, England: University of Exeter Press, 2000.

Fischer, Caroline Auguste (Karoline Auguste Fernandine Fischer)
(1764–1842) *novelist, short story writer*

Little is known about Caroline Auguste Fischer's childhood and youth. Her father, Karl Heinrich Ernst Venturini, was a court violinist at the Duchy of Brunswick. Her mother, Charlotte Juliane Wilhelmine Köchy Venturini, was the daughter of a local tailor. Fischer married Christoph Johann Rudolph Christiani in the early 1790s and moved to Copenhagen. The couple separated in 1798, and Fischer moved back to Germany the following year. In 1803, she had a child with the writer Christian August Fischer (1771–1829). The couple married in 1808 but separated after only seven months.

Fischer used Christian's literary contacts to publish her first novel, *Gustavs Verirrungen* (*Gustav's Aberrations,* 1801). She quickly followed up with two more novels, *Vierzehn Tage in Paris* (*A Fortnight in Paris,* 1801) and *Die Honigmonathe* (*The Honeymoons,* 1802). These works sold well and made her a popular author. After Fischer's second marriage ended, she tried to support herself by running a girls' school in Heidelberg and a library in Würzburg, but these ventures failed. Fischer had only limited success with her later novels and short stories before she quit writing in 1820. She spent her last years in and out of mental institutions and died penniless in 1842.

Fischer often wrote about the incompatibility between pursuing happiness and pursuing virtue. Her stories often portray women forced to choose between creativity and a stifling home life. Fischer's powerful works expose the destructiveness that stereotypes and gender roles had on women in the 1800s. Largely forgotten until the late 20th century, Fischer is now viewed as a significant precursor to modern women's literature in Germany.

Works about Caroline Auguste Fischer
Purver, Judith. "Passion, Possession, Patriarchy: Images of Men in the Novels and Short Stories of Caroline Auguste Fischer." *Neophilologus* 79 (1995).
———."Caroline Auguste Fischer: An Introduction." In Margaret C. Ives, ed., *Women Writers of the Age of Goethe* IV. Lancaster, U.K.: Lancaster University Press, 1991.

Flanagan, Richard (1961–) *novelist, filmmaker*

Richard Flanagan was born in Australia to an Irish Catholic family. He grew up in a mining town on the west coast in the state of Tasmania and left school at 16 to be a bush laborer. In his life since that time, he has been a construction worker at a hydroelectric plant, a Rhodes scholar, and a river guide. He began his writing career by concentrating on history, but his ambition from an early age was to be a fiction writer.

Flanagan considers his major literary influences to be Henry Lawson, Camus, Dostoyevsky, Kafka, Faulkner, South American novelists, and, most recently, Toni Morrison. Supported by a grant from Ars Tasmania, he wrote his first novel, *Death of a River Guide* (1994); it was an unexpected success. As Flanagan states in an interview with Giles Hugo, he is interested in writing about Tasmania not as a nostalgic regional novelist but to find new forms for the richness and complexities of Tasmania's past and present. He draws on oral traditions from his own Irish culture, Aboriginal myths, the landscape, and migrant experience, particularly since World War II. Married to a Slovenian, he is particularly interested in how immigrants from Central Europe have redefined themselves, through many trials, as Tasmanians.

Flanagan's first film, "Sound of One Hand Clapping," is situated in a community of mostly Central European migrant workers. He uses music as an integral role in the film, not as background but as a component of character and action. "Sound of One Hand Clapping" was shown at both the Berlin and Cannes film festivals.

Flanagan's *Gould's Book of Fish* (2002), supported by a grant from the Australia Council, was a best seller and a critical success in Australia and internationally. It won the Commonwealth Writers' Prize for 2002, establishing Flanagan as one of the most imaginative and innovative of contemporary novelists. Flanagan's most recent books are *The Unknown Terrorist* (2006) and *Wanting* (2009). *The Unknown Terrorist* is a thriller, set in Sydney, Australia, featuring a lap dancer and a stranger who may be an al-Qaeda operative. *Wanting*, a historical novel, has been called "a literary-historical game of six degrees of separation" revolving around the life and times of Charles Dickens.

Flaubert, Gustave (1821–1880) *novelist*

Gustave Flaubert was born in Rouen, France. His father was the chief of surgery at the hospital in Rouen, and his mother, who went on to become the most important and influential person in his life, was the daughter of a physician. Flaubert was never satisfied with his bourgeois background and often rebelled against it; these rebellions ultimately led to his expulsion from school and to his finishing his education privately in Paris.

Flaubert's school years, aside from aiding in the development of his rebellious personality, also introduced him to his love of writing. As a teenager, he fell in love with a married woman, Elisa Schlésinger. The relationship was destined to end in disappointment, but his idealized love for Elisa provided the inspiration and subject matter for much of his writing.

While studying law in Paris in the early 1840s, Flaubert suffered from what was diagnosed at the time as a nervous attack, probably a form of epilepsy. He subsequently failed his law exams and decided to devote himself full time to writing.

In 1846, he was introduced to another writer, Louise Colet. This was the start of a relationship that lasted many years. Although they spent very little time together, they corresponded regularly, and she became his mistress. He broke off the relationship in 1855 when she attempted to visit him at his country retreat. Her novel, *Lui* (1859), gives a vengeful account of their relationship.

Although he was living outside of Paris at the time, Flaubert maintained close contact with family and friends in the city and was a witness to the Revolution of 1848. Afterward, he took up an acquaintance with the writer Maxime du Camp. Together, the pair traveled for three years, visiting North Africa, Greece, Syria, Turkey, Egypt, and Italy. On his return to France, Flaubert began work on what would become his greatest achievement, *Madame Bovary,* a novel that took five years to complete.

Critical Analysis

Madame Bovary is a shocking tale of adultery, based on the unhappy affair of the title character, Emma Bovary. The novel was first published in the *Revue de Paris* in 1856 and appeared as a two-volume book in 1857. Like many of his contemporaries' works, Flaubert's novel was attacked for its vivid depiction of what was considered morally offensive behavior. Flaubert was prosecuted for the work on charges of immorality and on the grounds that it was offensive to religion. He came before the same judge who later found CHARLES BAUDELAIRE guilty on a similar charge. Flaubert, however, was not convicted.

Madame Bovary is more than a simple tale of adultery. The protagonist, Emma Bovary, is a dreamer who, as a child, read the works of Sir Walter Scott and the romantics and, as an adult, longs for a life of romance and adventure. She is stuck, instead, in an unhappy marriage to Charles Bovary, a physician, who fails to recognize how miserable his wife is. Seeking escape from her boredom, she turns to extramarital affairs as a source of happiness and adventure. Her pursuit of another life ultimately causes her to fall deeply into debt and leads to her decision to commit suicide. The character was important to Flaubert, who felt her choices exemplified the problem of women who lived in a society trapped in materialism.

As a result of his success with *Madame Bovary,* Flaubert enjoyed much fame as a writer during the 1860s in the court of Napoleon III. He counted among his close friends ÉMILE ZOLA, GEORGE SAND, Hippolyte Taine, and IVAN TURGENEV. All of these writers shared with him similar aesthetic ideals and a dedication to the realistic and nonjudgmental representation of life through literature.

His later works included *Salammbô* (1862), about the siege of Carthage, and *L'éducation sentimentale* (1869), a novel of forbidden romance between a young man and an older married woman set against the backdrop of the 1848 revolution. With his concern for precise form and for detailed observation of human nature, Flaubert began to be associated with a new school of naturalistic writers. He took the approach that it was the goal of the novelist to remain neutral, explaining and teaching but never judging. Many younger writers, such as GUY DE MAUPASSANT and ANTON CHEKOV adopted this outlook.

Although Flaubert was highly respected as a writer, his personal life was shadowed by financial difficulties. After the death of his father, he took up residence with his mother and young niece, who was forced to declare bankruptcy. Flaubert spent much of his fortune assisting her and her family. During his final years, Flaubert lived as a virtual hermit, working on a collection of three stories, *Trois contes,* and on the long novel *Bouvard et Pécuchet.* Before completing the novel, he died from a cerebral hemorrhage.

Other Works by Gustave Flaubert

Early Writings. Translated by Robert Griffin. Lincoln: University of Nebraska Press, 1991.

The First Sentimental Education. Translated by Douglas Garman. Berkeley: University of California Press, 1972.

Flaubert–Sand: The Correspondance. Translated by Francis Steegmuller and Barbara Bray. New York: Knopf, 1993.

The Temptation of St. Anthony. Garden City, N.Y.: Haleyon House, 1950.

Works about Gustave Flaubert

Berg, William J., and Laurey K. Martin. *Gustave Flaubert.* Boston: Twayne, 1997.

Sartre, Jean-Paul. *The Family Idiot: Gustave Flaubert, 1821–1857.* Chicago: University of Chicago Press, 1991.

Wall, Geoffrey. *Gustave Flaubert: A Life.* London: Faber and Faber, 2001.

Fo, Dario (1926–) *playwright*

Dario Fo was born in San Giano, Italy, to Pina (Rota) Fo, an author, and Felice Fo, who divided his time between acting in an amateur theater company and work as a railway station master. As a child, Fo spent vacations with his grandparents on a farm and traveled around the countryside with his grandfather, selling produce from a wagon. His grandfather told imaginative stories infused with local news to attract customers. This was Fo's introduction to the narrative tradition. In his youth, he sat for hours in taverns, listening to glassblowers and fishermen spin tall tales filled with political satire, planting the seeds of his own satirical work.

Fo moved to Milan in 1940 to study art at the Brera Art Academy. During this time, he began to write stories and sketches that were influenced by traveling storytellers. "Nothing gets down as deeply into the mind and intelligence as satire," Fo said in a statement cited by James Fisher. "The end of satire is the first alarm bell signaling the end of real democracy."

Much of Fo's satire focuses on political-religious issues. His one-man show *Comical Mystery* (1969), for example, was a mockery of Catholic hierarchy. The play, considered a cornerstone of his collective work, is his own version of the Gospels with commentary on church corruption.

Sketches in his play include one about a man without legs who shuns a healing from Christ and another depicting a wedding feast at Cana told from the perspective of a drunkard. The show was presented on television in 1977. According to Tony Mitchell in *Dario Fo: People's Court Jester,* the Vatican described the program as the "most blasphemous show in the history of television."

In 1970, Fo performed *I'd Die Tonight If I Didn't Think It Had Been Worth It* (1970), a play comparing Palestinian freedom fighters and Italian partisans. He followed this the same year with *Accidental Death of an Anarchist* (1970), a play about an anarchist who dies while in police custody. The play closed at the Cinema Rossini when police pressured the theater owners.

More than 40 of Fo's plays have been translated into dozens of languages. Fo himself has also performed on radio and film and once hosted a controversial Italian television program in 1962. In 1997, he won the Nobel Prize in literature for his theatrical contributions, which emphasized international topics ranging from AIDS to the Israeli-Palestinian conflict.

In 2006, Fo ran for mayor of Milan but lost in the primary election. He ran as a representative of the Communist Refoundation Party to which both he and his wife belong.

Another Work by Dario Fo

We Won't Pay! We Won't Pay! and Other Plays. Translated by Ron Jenkins. New York: Theatre Communications Group, 2001.

Works about Dario Fo

Fisher, James. "Images of the Fool in Italian Theatre from Pirandello to Fo." Available online. URL: http://persweb.wabash.edu/facstaff/fisherj/new/ItalianTheatre.html. Accessed October 12, 2010.

Mitchell, Tony. *Dario Fo: People's Court Jester.* London: Methuen, 1999.

Fontane, Theodor (Henri Théodor Fontane) (1819–1898) novelist, balladeer

Theodor Fontane was born in Neurippen, Prussia. His parents, Louis Henri and Emilie Labry Fontane, descended from French Huguenots who moved to Prussia in the 1600s. Fontane's education consisted of private tutors and public schools in Swinemünde and Neurippen. As a youth, he joined literary clubs and wrote poems and historical tales. Pursuing the profession of his father, Fontane served as an apprentice to an apothecary from 1836 to 1844. After serving in the Prussian military, Fontane operated his own pharmacy in Berlin until 1849. In 1850, he married Emilie Rouanet-Kummer.

During his lifetime, Fontane achieved his greatest recognition as a balladeer. He published his first two books of ballads in 1850. In 1852, he started to work as a newspaper correspondent. He traveled extensively in the 1860s and 1870s and wrote five travel books based on his experiences; he also wrote theater reviews and briefly served as secretary of the Berlin Academy of Arts in 1876 before he started to write novels. His first novel *Vor dem Sturm: Roman aus dem Winter 1812 auf 1813* (*Before the Storm: A Novel of the Winter of 1812–1813*, 1878) is considered one of the finest historical novels in German literature for its artistic portrayal of the Prussian aristocracy, bourgeoisie, and peasantry during the Napoleonic Wars. He wrote three more historical novels before turning his attention to Berlin society.

Fontane's greatest literary influence was Scottish writer Sir Walter Scott. An accomplished writer of dialogue, Fontane helped pioneer the modernist trend of emphasizing conversation rather than plot. His ironic observations are critical of the prejudices and conventions of society, but his works still exhibit spontaneity, charm, and wit. His novels engage the themes of money, morality, guilt, retribution, and class hierarchy. His biographer Helen Chambers concludes that Fontane made a "unique and refined contribution to world fiction."

Other Works by Theodor Fontane

Effi Briest. Translated by Hugh Rorrison and Helen Chambers. London: Penguin, 2000.

Journeys to England in Victoria's Early Days. Translated by Dorothy Harrison. London: Massie, 1939.

A Work about Theodor Fontane

Chambers, Helen. *The Changing Image of Theodor Fontane.* Columbia, S.C.: Camden House Inc., 1997.

Foscolo, Ugo (Niccolò Foscolo) (1778–1827) playwright, novelist, poet, essayist

Ugo Foscolo was born on the island of Zante in Greece to Andrea Foscolo, a ship's physician, and Diamanatina Spathis. He was brought up speaking both Italian and Greek. Young Ugo changed residences at least twice when his father was named a ship's physician in the Levant and then again when he was made hospital director in Spalato.

Stability was not a big part of Foscolo's life. When his father died in 1788, Foscolo was forced to live with relatives in Zante. When his family was reunited in 1792 in Venice, Foscolo was enrolled in the San Capriano school in Murano, where he mastered Greek and Latin.

In about 1794, Foscolo began to experiment with poetry and to visit Venetian literary salons. Isabella Teotochi, also Greek, ran a salon that attracted great intellectuals. Teotochi eventually became Foscolo's lover, benefactor, and muse. Her decision to annul her marriage and secretly wed another seemed to be the catalyst for Foscolo's 1802 novel *Last Letters of Jacopo Ortis,* a novel in letters modeled after the works of Samuel Richardson and Jean-Jacques Rousseau that depicts the doomed love of Ortis for Teresa.

One of Foscolo's most famous collections of poems is *On Sepulchres* (1807), which speaks about the struggle of civilization and displays the ROMANTIC fascination with ruins: "Even the last ruins, the Pierian sisters gladden / The desert wastes with their singing, and harmony."

Foscolo was one of the major voices of his generation. From his precocious youth to the end of his life, he held tight to romantic ideals.

A Work about Ugo Foscolo

Radcliff-Umstead, Douglas. *Ugo Foscolo*. Boston: Twayne, 1970.

Fraire, Isabel (1934–   ) *poet, translator*

Isabel Fraire was born in Mexico City and raised in New York. A student of philosophy at the Autonomous National University of Mexico, by the early 1960s, she was writing poetry, literary criticism, reviews, and translations, and she became a member of the editorial council of the prestigious review, *Revista Mexicana de Literatura* (Mexican Review of Literature). Although her earliest poems appeared in 1959 in *15 Poems of Isabel Fraire,* her first published book of poems is generally considered to be *Only This Light,* which appeared in 1969.

Fraire's translations from English to Spanish of such American poets as Ezra Pound, T. S. Eliot, Wallace Stevens, E. E. Cummings, William Carlos Williams, and W. S. Auden have been collected in *Seis poetas de lengua inglesa* (Six Poets Writing in English, 1976) and have appeared in many Latin American journals and anthologies. In 1978, she was awarded the Xavier Villaurrutia Prize for her third collection of poetry, *Poems in the Lap of Death* (1977). Of her work, Mexican poet and critic OCTAVIO PAZ has said, "Her poetry is a continual flight of images that disappear, reappear, and return to disappear."

Other Works by Isabel Fraire

Isabel Fraire: Poems. Translated by Thomas Hoeksema. Athens, Ohio: Mundus Artium Press, 1975.
Poems in the Lap of Death. Translated by Thomas Hoeksema. Pittsburgh, Pa.: Latin American Literary Review Press, 1981.

Frame, Janet (1924–2004) *novelist*

Janet Frame was born in Dunedin, South Island, New Zealand, and grew up in Oamuru, South Island. The daughter of a railway-worker father and an encouraging mother who wrote poetry and fiction, she studied to be a teacher at Dunedin Teachers' College and the University of Otago. Her early life was a happy one, despite poverty, her brother's epilepsy, and the drowning of two of her sisters. Before she was able to work as a teacher, however, she was incorrectly diagnosed as being schizophrenic and hospitalized in mental wards for almost 10 years. During this time, she wrote her first collection of short stories, *The Lagoon* (1951), which saved her from being lobotomized when the book won a literary award shortly before the surgery was scheduled. Finally able to leave the hospital, Frame then lived in a friend's garden shed, where she completed her first novel, *Owls Do Cry* (1957), which established her as an important novelist. As Prudence Hockley notes in her review in *500 Great Books by Women* (1994), "The special quality of this novel lies in its poetic, hallucinatory, perceptive voice, imbued with the surreal vision of childhood and madness."

Afraid that she might be forced back to a mental hospital, Frame then left New Zealand in 1956, living in England and Spain until she finally returned to New Zealand in 1963. She is the author of numerous novels, including *Faces in the Water* (1982), a first-person narrative told in the voice of Estina, a woman incarcerated in a mental institution, and a three-volume autobiography, *To the Island* (1982), *An Angel at My Table* (1984), and *The Envoy from Mirror City* (1985). Her style of writing is considered unique, moving between realism and a more nonlinear exploration of the nature of reality. Although her earlier novels focus on the inner world of children, outcasts, and the insane, her later novels are considered poetic and POSTMODERN, with a freshness of language and voice that make them unique. She was awarded every major New Zealand literary prize and considered New Zealand's best-known contemporary novelist.

Janet Frame died from leukemia in 2004 at the age of 79. In that same year, she was given New Zealand's Icon award. Several of Frame's works have been published posthumously, including a volume of poetry, *The Goose Bath* (2006), and a novella, *Towards Another Summer* (2007). In 2008 and 2010, previously unpublished short stories appeared in the *New Yorker*.

Other Works by Janet Frame

The Adaptable Man: A Novel. New York: George Braziller, 1965, 2000.

The Edge of the Alphabet. New York: George Braziller, 1992.

Works about Janet Frame

King, Michael. *Wrestling with the Angel: A Life of Janet Frame.* Washington, D.C.: Counterpoint Press, 2000.

Panny, Judith Dell. *I Have What I Gave: The Fiction of Janet Frame.* New York: George Braziller, 1993.

Freud, Sigmund (1856–1939) *philosopher, psychologist*

Sigmund Freud was born in Freiberg, today in the Czech Republic, to Jewish parents, Jacob Freud, a small-time textile merchant, and Amalia Freud. Although the family was Jewish, Jacob Freud was not at all religious, and Sigmund Freud grew up an avowed atheist. When he was four years old, the family moved to Vienna, Austria, where Freud lived for most of his life. He was a brilliant student, always at the head of his class; however, the options for Jewish boys in Austria were limited by the government to medicine and law. As Freud was interested in science, he entered the University of Vienna medical school in 1873. After three years, he became deeply involved in research, which delayed his M.D. until 1881. Independent research was not financially feasible, however, so Freud established a private medical practice, specializing in neurology. He became interested in the use of hypnosis to treat hysteria and other mental illnesses, and with the help of a grant, he went to France in 1885 to study under Jean-Martin Charcot, a famous neurologist, known all over Europe for his studies of hysteria and various uses of hypnosis. On his return to Vienna in 1886, Freud married and opened a practice specializing in disorders of the nervous system and the brain. He tried to use hypnosis to treat his patients but quickly abandoned it, finding that he could produce better results by placing patients in a relaxing environment and allowing them to speak freely. He then analyzed whatever they said to identify the traumatic effects in the past that caused their current suffering. The way his own self-analysis contributed to the growth of his ideas during this period may be seen in letters and drafts of papers sent to a colleague, Wilhelm Fliess.

After several years of practice, Freud published *The Interpretation of Dreams* (1900), the first major statement of his theories, in which he introduced the public to the notion of the unconscious mind. He explains in the book that dreams, as products of the unconscious mind, can reveal past psychological traumas that, repressed from conscious awareness, underlie certain kinds of neurotic disorders. In addition, he attempts to establish a provisional matrix for interpreting and analyzing dreams in terms of their psychological significance.

In his second book, *The Psychopathology of Everyday Life* (1901), Freud expands the idea of the unconscious mind by introducing the concept of the *dynamic unconscious*. In this work, Freud theorizes that everyday forgetfulness and accidental slips of the tongue (today commonly called Freudian slips) reveal many meaningful things about the person's unconscious psychological state. The ideas outlined in these two works were not taken seriously by most readers, which is not a surprise considering that, at the time, most psychological disorders were treated as physical illnesses, if treated at all.

Freud's major clinical discoveries, including his five major case histories, were published in *Three Essays on the Theory of Sexuality* (1905). In this work, he elaborates his theories about infantile sexuality, the meanings of the id, the ego, and the superego, and the Oedipus complex (the inevitable but tabooed incestuous attraction in families, and the associated fear of castration and intrafamilial jealousy).

In 1902, Freud was appointed full professor at the University of Vienna and developed a large following. In 1906, he formed the Vienna Psychoanalytic Society, but some political infighting resulted in division among members of the group (Carl Jung, for instance, split from the group with bitter feelings). Freud continued to work on his theories and, in 1909, presented them internationally at a conference at Clark University in Massachusetts. Freud's name became a household word after the conference. In his later period, in *Beyond the Pleasure Principle* (1920) and *The Ego and the Id* (1923), he modified his structural model of the psychic apparatus. In *Inhibitions, Symptoms and Anxiety* (1926), he applied psychoanalysis to larger social problems.

In 1923, Freud was diagnosed with cancer of the jaw as a result of years of cigar smoking. In 1938, the Nazi party burned Freud's books. They also confiscated his passport, but the leading intellectuals around the world voiced their protest, and he was allowed to leave Austria. Freud died in England in 1939.

Freud made an enormous contribution to the field of psychology: He established our basic ideas about sexuality and the unconscious and also influenced, to some extent, the way we read literary works by establishing premises for psychoanalytic criticism. His own case studies are often interpreted for their literary merit.

Other Works by Sigmund Freud
Civilization and Its Discontents. Translated by Peter Gay. New York: W. W. Norton, 1989.
The Future of an Illusion. Translated by Peter Gay. New York: W. W. Norton, 1989.

Works about Sigmund Freud
Bernheimer, Charles, and Claire Kahane, eds. *In Dora's Case: Freud-Hysteria—Feminism.* New York: Columbia University Press, 1985.
Erwin, Edward. *The Freud Encyclopedia: Theory, Therapy, and Culture.* New York: Garland Press, 2002.
Mitchell, Stephen. *Freud and Beyond: A History of Modern Psychoanalytical Thought.* New York: Basic Books, 1996.

Freyre, Gilberto de Mello   (1900–1987)
nonfiction writer, sociologist
Born on March 15, 1900, in the city of Recife in the state of Pernambuco in the northeast of Brazil, Gilberto de Mello Freyre is one of the country's leading intellectual figures. After completing his B.A. in Brazil, he continued his studies in the United States where he earned an M.A. at Columbia, studying under anthropologist Franz Boas. After further studies in Portugal, he returned to Brazil and immersed himself in life in his region of origin, becoming good friends with other northeastern writers such as José Lins do Rego.

Freyre is known for his sociological and anthropological texts about Brazilian life. His argument that the specific nature of Portuguese colonization led to a mixed-race society in its colonies is where the concept of Brazil's status as a racial democracy originates. Freyre's most important texts are *The Mansions and the Shanties: The Making of Modern Brazil* (1936) and *The Masters and the Slaves: A Study in the Development of Brazilian Civilization* (1933). His works have left an indelible mark on Brazilian intellectual and popular history.

Another Work by Gilberto Freyre
The Gilberto Freyre Reader. Translated by Barbara Shelby. New York: Knopf, 1974.

Fried, Erich   (1921–1988) *poet, short story writer*
Erich Fried was born in Vienna, Austria, to Hugo and Nellie Stein Fried. In the mid-1920s, his father's shipping company went bankrupt, and the family survived on the money his mother earned selling porcelain figures. After the Nazis sent his father to a concentration camp in 1938, Fried fled to London where he settled permanently. During World War II, he helped his mother and other Jews escape from Nazi-controlled Europe. Fried held many jobs after the war, including dairy chemist, librarian, and worker in a glass factory. He was a commentator for the British Broadcasting System from 1952 to 1968.

Fried published his first collection of poems in 1944. From the 1950s through the 1980s, he published more than 25 volumes of verse and established his reputation as a lyric poet. Fried also translated the works of Dylan Thomas (1914–53), T. S. Eliot (1888–1965), and William Shakespeare (1564–1616) into German. He published the novel *Ein Soldat und ein Mädchen* (*A Soldier and a Girl,* 1960) and wrote Kafkaesque short stories (*see* FRANZ KAFKA). His awards include the Schiller Prize (1965) and the Bremen Literature Prize (1983).

Fried used terse language laced with aphorisms and epigrams to address contemporary issues and events, such as the Vietnam War. National background had little influence on his opinions. Stuart Hood, who translated many of his works into English, stated in an interview, "Fried did not have a problem with nationality. He did not want to be British, German, or Jewish." Fried's positions were thus often paradoxical: He was a German language writer who criticized the policies of West Germany, a Jew who opposed Israel's fight against the Palestinians, and a leftist who was critical of Marxist practice.

Another Work by Erich Fried

Children and Fools. Translated by Martin Chalmers. London: Serpent's Tail, 1992.

A Work about Erich Fried

Lawie, Steven W. *Erich Fried: A Writer Without a Country.* New York: Peter Lang, 1996.

Frisch, Max (1911–1991) *playwright, novelist*

Max Frisch was born in Zurich, Switzerland, to Franz and Lina Wildermuth Frisch. He wrote several unpublished plays as a teenager and studied German literature at the University of Zurich from 1930 to 1933. He then supported himself as a freelance journalist and wrote his first novel, *Jürg Reinhart* (1934). In 1936, Frisch decided to pursue his father's profession and enrolled in the Eidgenössische Technische Hochschule in Zur-

ich to study architecture. He received his degree and opened an architectural firm in 1941. Frisch served intermittently in the Swiss army during World War II and married Gertrud Anna Constance in 1942.

Frisch established his reputation as a dramatist soon after the war with a series of plays that captured the mood of the time. Staying neutral during the cold war, Frisch remained in contact with the literary worlds on both sides of the iron curtain. East German writer BERTOLT BRECHT became one of his most important influences. Frisch traveled extensively throughout his life and gained a reputation as a notable diarist. His novels and plays made him one of the most respected German language writers. The novel *I'm Not Stiller* (1954) deals with the issue of individual freedom and displays the experimental narrative prose that made him famous. His novel *Homo Faber* (1957) is a commentary on the uncontrollable nature of technology. Frisch's later works, such as *Montauk* (1975), reflect a concern with aging and death. He won numerous American, Swiss, and German literary awards, including the Georg Büchner Prize.

Frisch was an original writer with integrity and a concern for truth and relevance. He continually used new contexts to address his common themes: male-female relationships, reality and imagination, social responsibility, and the quest for self-fulfillment. Frisch also had a piercing insight into contemporary life. German literary scholar Wulf Koepke wrote that Frisch's works "exemplify the struggle for survival of the human individual in the face of a society blindly intent on its own extinction."

Another Work by Max Frisch

Sketchbook 1946–1949. Translated by Geoffrey Skelton. New York: Harcourt Brace Jovanovich, 1977.

A Work about Max Frisch

Koepke, Wulf. *Understanding Max Frisch.* Columbia: University of South Carolina Press, 1991.

Fuentes, Carlos (1928–) *novelist, short story writer, dramatist, essayist*

Carlos Fuentes was born in Panama City, Panama, where his father, Rafael Fuentes Boettiger, was the Mexican ambassador. Being the son of a career diplomat, Fuentes spent his childhood moving from city to city, following his father's assignments. He lived in Washington, D.C., where he became acutely aware of his Mexican nationality, in part because of being ostracized and harassed by his schoolmates.

Fuentes received an excellent and international education and is fluent in Spanish, English, and French. At first, it seemed that he would follow his father into the world of diplomacy. He returned to Mexico City to attend law school, but after graduating, he began to dedicate more and more of his time to literary pursuits. His early exposure to the inner workings of the Mexican government and his studies of economics and law gave his later literature a keen political sense and an ability to depict and criticize aspects of the Mexican upper classes.

Though Fuentes began to write as early as the 1940s, it was not until the late 1950s that he became well known. His second novel, *The Death of Artemio Cruz* (1962), received a shocked and confused reaction from its first critics, followed by an almost immediate wave of praise for its groundbreaking style and depth. The book's stream-of-consciousness style evokes the last thoughts of a powerful capitalist, Artemio Cruz, on his deathbed. The book is written in first-person, second-person, and third-person sections that represent the different points of view that Cruz has on his own life.

The use of the fragmented and musical language associated with stream-of-consciousness writing as well as the use of multiple points of view indicate a clear influence by JAMES JOYCE, VIRGINIA WOOLF, and particularly William Faulkner. The book also is clearly structured on Orson Welles's film *Citizen Kane*, which Fuentes saw in New York at an early age.

Another of Fuentes's novels, *Terra nostra* (1975), pushes the envelope of a novel's experimental possibilities even further. It is, essentially, a meditation on Spanish and Latin-American history that uses fiction as its medium. It has no cohesive plot of which to speak and ranges from ancient Rome to the imagined end of the world. The main characters are barely human; they are, in fact, allegorical representations of the primal forces that drive human history.

Fuentes has also written a large number of essays. *La nueva novela hispanoamericana* (*The New Hispanic-American Novel,* 1969), a study of the "new" Latin American novel of the 1960s, is a profound account of what distinguishes the novels of the cultural boom that occurred in Latin America at that time. It delves into the significance of the new style of MAGIC REALISM and thoughtfully examines the strengths and tendencies of what was, at the time, a newly emerging force in world literature.

Along with OCTAVIO PAZ, Fuentes stands as one of the foremost Mexican authors of the 20th century. His erudition and refined intelligence, combined with the gifts of an epic storyteller, earned him in 1987 the Cervantes Prize, the most prestigious award given to a Spanish language author. In 2002, Fuentes published *This I Believe: An A to Z of a Life,* a collection of essays summarizing the author's beliefs. Other recent publications include the political novel *The Eagle's Throne* (2003) and the story collection *Happy Families* (2006).

Critical Analysis

"I learned to imagine Mexico before I ever knew Mexico," Carlos Fuentes once wrote. His "imagined" Mexico has been as influential on Mexicans and on the world as the country itself. In Fuentes's work, the power and politics of Latin America are treated realistically but are merged with mythology and culture, all forming a broad social critique of his subject matter. In *The Death of Artemio Cruz,* for example, the protagonist begins life as a poor worker and a supporter of revolutionary ideals. He gains wealth and becomes a corrupt, ruthless business tycoon, a symbol of international capitalist greed. As he lies on his deathbed, Fuentes follows Cruz's fragmented thoughts and images, which waver between past and present as his family pushes him to reveal the location of his will. As one critic notes, "A dominating theme in [Fuentes's] work is the search for Mexican national identity," and adds, "Of his eleven novels, it is in *The Death of Artemio Cruz* that this mind-set is expressed most strongly." Cruz personifies the image of the successful revolutionary who exploits the ideals of the revolution for economic gain and personal power. This is the image Fuentes seeks to critique, in order to force his readers to consider the nature of power in the face of the struggle for greater equity for all people.

Terra nostra is Fuentes's major novel on Spanish and Latin American history. It moves freely in time from ancient Rome to the apocalyptic end of the 20th century. "Time is the subject matter of all my fiction," Fuentes has said, and *Terra nostra* is an example of this statement. The action of the novel is complex, regarding history as cyclical, not linear, and its primary theme is the problem of absolute authority. Fuentes makes history into "a series of mirrors reflecting forward and back in time and space." Indeed, the mirror is the central image of *Terra nostra*, reflecting not only the idea of "history as mirror" but also the "constant examination of the self in Hispanic culture," the same kind of examination Fuentes carries out in the novel.

In *Terra nostra*, the political and cultural concern is with the shift in power from the old world to the new, from Spain to Spanish America—and to Mexico in particular. Through a focus on a central character who is a composite of all Spanish monarchs, Fuentes explores the origins and structures of power in the Hispanic world as a whole. "With *Terra nostra*," writes critic Raymond Williams, "Fuentes discovered both his tradition and his identity as a Mexican and as a man of the Americas." The novel, however, in its use of second-person narrative, turns the mirror on the reader as well: "I shall create an open book where the reader will know he is read and the author will know he is written."

Other Works by Carlos Fuentes

The Crystal Frontier: A Novel in Nine Stories. Translated by Alfred MacAdam. New York: Farrar, Straus & Giroux, 1997.

The Hydra Head. Translated by Margaret Sayers Peden. New York: Farrar, Straus & Giroux, 1978.

A Work about Carlos Fuentes

Williams, Raymond Leslie. *The Writings of Carlos Fuentes.* Austin: University of Texas Press, 1996.

futurism

Having its origins in literature and poetry, the futurist movement began in Europe on February 20, 1909, when the front page of the French newspaper *Le Figaro* published the *Founding and Manifesto of Futurism* by artist and lawyer Emilio Filippo Tommaso Marinetti. Marinetti's manifesto glorified technology, particularly the speed and power of the newly developed automobile, while at the same time promoting violence and aggression and calling for the destruction of traditional culture. This wide-scale obliteration of the past, according to Marinetti, was to also include the physical demolition of cultural institutions that were linked to traditional society, such as museums and libraries. Marinetti referred to these institutions as "those cemeteries of wasted efforts, those calvaries of crucified dreams, those catalogues of broken impulses!" He also encouraged his followers to "Let the good incendiaries come with their carbonized fingers! . . . Here they are! Here they are! . . . Set the library stacks on fire! Turn the canals in their course to flood the museum vaults!" (*The Futurist Cookbook*) At the time of the publication, Marinetti was the only member of the movement, but he soon gained a large literary and artistic following.

The name *futurism* was coined by Marinetti as a celebration of the change and growth of the future. Futurism stood in contrast to the sentimentality inherent in ROMANTICISM. Futurists openly and intentionally defied tradition and constantly questioned the accepted concepts of art and even the standard definitions of what constitutes art. They embraced technology, particularly anything relating to speed or power, and glorified the energy and violent nature of 20th-century urban life. The power of machinery and a fascination with speed were focal points of the movement, as was the renunciation of the "static" art of previous generations. Futurist literary theory, for example, focused on the ability of language to express. A futurist poet, for example, might frame words so that they would project from the page like gunfire.

Although it began as an Italian movement, futurism quickly spread throughout the world during the early part of the 20th century to places such as Hungary, Poland, the Ukraine, Holland, Portugal, and America. In Poland, Czechoslovakia, and other Eastern bloc countries, futurism was adopted quickly as a movement of protest against established cultural values and political hierarchy.

Futurism not only promoted destruction of cultural institutions; it also glorified war. It favored fascism and aimed to destroy artistic tradition. The motivation behind futurism was largely political. Marinetti and many other futurists were heavily involved in demonstrations urging Italy to enter World War I.

Futurism was also characterized by the numerous manifestos written and published simply for the purpose of explaining the movement itself. These documents took the form of pamphlets and illustrated books of poetry. The rules of futurism as it applied to the arts were defined in these manifestos long before they were actually seen in the arts themselves. The tone of Marinetti's initial manifesto and many others that followed was intentionally inflammatory and, like the movement itself, designed to inspire anger, arouse controversy, and attract attention.

One of the reasons that Italian futurism is not better known today is its relationship to fascism. After World War II, futurism was viewed in a negative light because of this association; however, although Marinetti was a friend of the young fascist Benito Mussolini and both were ardent supporters of fascism, futurism was never, as it has sometimes been claimed, "the official art of fascism." Mussolini was politically active in promoting the futurists, especially during the years 1918 to 1920. He ultimately turned against them, using his political clout to silence them. Many futurists then became disillusioned by the political situation and drifted away from political activism.

Futurism officially ended in 1944 with the fall of Italy and Marinetti's death; however, the legacy of futurism to modern art, including literature, is enormous. Futurism was the first attempt to focus art on technology and machines. Remnants of futurism can be found throughout 20th-century avant-garde art, particularly with regard to many aspects of modern science fiction.

Works about Futurism

Marinetti, F. T. *The Futurist Cookbook.* Translated by Suzanne Brill, edited and with an introduction by Lesley Chamberlain. San Francisco: Bedford Arts, 1989.

Tisdall, Caroline, and Angela Bozolla. *Futurism.* Oxford: Oxford University Press, 1978.

Gabo

See GARCÍA MÁRQUEZ, GABRIEL.

Gandhi, Mohandas K(aramchand)

(1869–1948) *writer, political leader*

Mohandas Karamchand Gandhi was born in Kathiawar, Gujarat, India. He was the youngest son of Karamchand Gandhi, a politician, and Putlibai Gandhi. His mother was an extremely devout Hindu, and Gandhi often said his own beliefs on pacifism were based on his mother's religious teachings. In 1883, at age 13, Gandhi was wedded to Kasturba. Five years later, he was sent to England to study law and, in 1891, was called to the bar but decided to return to India.

After a brief period at work as a lawyer for the Bombay High Court in 1893, Gandhi went to South Africa to work for a Muslim law firm and spent the next 20 years fighting against the maltreatment of South African Indians, a fight that led to the formation in 1894 of the Natal Indian Congress. He later wrote about his experiences in South Africa in *Satyagraha in South Africa* (1924). In this work, Gandhi describes the idea behind *Satyagraha* (Truth Force), which later became the *Satyagraha* movement. This movement was a form of "peaceful resistance" against British colonial rule

and was the most powerful political tool in India's struggle for independence.

By the time he was 45, Gandhi had become an international figure. His wide-ranging influence and prodigious social work gave him the title of "Bapu" (Father) in India and "Mahatma" (Great Soul) all over the world. His teachings on the importance of combining spiritual healing with political struggle have been adopted by international leaders such as America's Martin Luther King and Malcolm X. These ideas are passionately and candidly expressed in his autobiography, *An Autobiography or The Story of My Experiments with Truth* (1929). His experiments with truth, he explains, are a lifelong commitment to achieve purity in mind and action. For Gandhi, however, purity also had political power. His political career was dedicated to encouraging Indians to be nonviolent in their struggle against the violent and oppressive power of the British.

Gandhi's most important contribution to Indian history was his leadership in helping India and Pakistan gain independence from British colonial rule in 1947. His political legacy often overshadows his literary talent, but he wrote prodigiously in both English and Gujarati (his mother tongue). Gandhi wrote numerous essays on topics ranging from vegetarianism to anticasteism to passive disobedience to spiritual healing to religious tolerance. His most important work, *Hind Swaraj* or *Indian Home Rule* (1909), is a compilation of essays on his philosophies and political goals. He was also an editor and contributor to several journals, including an English weekly called *Young India* and a Gujarati monthly called *Navajivan* (*New Life*).

Gandhi spent his later years in and out of prison. In 1948, on his way to evening prayers, he was assassinated by a Hindu fanatic. This event seems, even today, an ironic and tragic end to a life spent spreading the cause for peace and nonviolence.

Other Works by Mohandas K. Gandhi

All Men Are Brothers. New York: Columbia University Press, 1969.

Mahatma Gandhi: Selected Political Writing. Edited by Dennis Dalton. Indianapolis: Hackett Pub. Co., 1996.

A Work about Mohandas K. Gandhi

Wolpert, Stanley. *Gandhi's Passion: The Life and Legacy of Mahatma Gandhi.* New York: Oxford University Press, 2001.

Gao Xingjian (Kao Tsing–jen) (1940–)
novelist, playwright

Gao Xingjian was born on January 4 in Ganzhou in China's Jiangxi Province. Although he was not formally educated, both his parents were interested and educated in the arts, and his mother taught him to read and write. When he entered Nanjing High School in 1951, he wrote prolifically. He graduated with a degree in French from Beijing Foreign Studies University in 1962 and took a job translating books.

Like most Chinese youth of the period, Gao Xingjian became a Red Guard under Mao Zedong's Communist rule and entered cadre schools in Henan and Anhui in 1969. Although China was in the middle of Mao's Cultural Revolution, Gao Xingjian continued to write, largely for psychological relief from the politically oppressive environment, although he later burned all his work from that period.

After the Cultural Revolution, Gao Xingjian was able to publish essays and short stories. In 1975, he was asked to head the French section for the magazine *China Reconstructs,* which helped him build important contacts in the French and Western literary worlds. He made further connections while handling external liaison affairs for the Chinese Writers Association in 1977.

During this time, Gao Xingjian also focused on his own literary endeavors, becoming a playwright for the Beijing People's Art Theater. *Absolute Signal,* his first play, about a thief and his girlfriend, takes place in a train car. It was performed in 1982 and combined traditional dramatic methods with methods used by modern Western playwrights. His 1983 absurdist play *Bus Stop* is based on SAMUEL BECKETT's *Waiting for Godot* and is about a bus that never comes and the hapless passengers who eventually wait years for it. Also interpreted as a critique of the Communist leadership, the play placed Gao Xingjian squarely in the middle of China's debate over MODERNISM. He also authored a piece of critical theory, "A Rough Study of Techniques in Modern Fiction Writing," (1981) which further raised controversy about his sympathy with modern and Western influences. In 1986, Gao Xingjian's plays were banned by the Chinese government from being performed after uproar over the staging of his avant-garde play, *The Other Shore,* essentially a conversation among actors struggling to use a rope to cross from one side of water to another. The dialogue is vague and fluid, a characteristic critics found pointless and subversive.

The next year, Gao Xingjian was diagnosed with terminal lung cancer. The diagnosis turned out to be incorrect, but the brush with mortality and his fear of further persecution by the government drove him to seek spiritual renewal by journeying into the wild, mountainous forests of Sichuan Province. After his wilderness travels, he journeyed to Europe on the invitation of a German organization and became an exile. He moved to France, where he is now a citizen. He has been the recipient of France's prestigious Chevalier d'Ordre des Arts et des Lettres award and has frequently worked on government commissions. He recorded his Sichuan experiences in his novel, *Soul Mountain* (1990), which fictionalizes his journey through the wilderness and his quest for truth and spiritual rebirth. The novel is also known for its innovative voice: The narrator's voice alternately assumes the use of different pronouns—*I, you, he,* and *she*—to create multiple perspectives.

Gao Xingjian is also an accomplished painter. While he has been the recipient of much critical attention and acclaim in the West for his literary work, he has earned his living with his misty and evocative brush paintings that often grace the covers of his volumes.

In 2001, Gao Xingjian became the first Chinese writer to win the Nobel Prize in literature. He accepted the prize as a Chinese writer in exile, and the Chinese government denounced the Swedish Academy for its choice of a writer unknown in China. In awarding the prize, the academy praised Gao Xingjian's "oeuvre of universal validity, bitter insights, and linguistic ingenuity." In 2004, Gao Xingjian's play *Snow in August* was published in English. The play is based on the life of a Buddhist patriarch, Huineng (A.D. 633–713). His recent publications in English include *Buying a Fishing Rod for My Grandfather: Stories* (2007), translated by Mabel Lee.

Another Work by Gao Xingjian
The Other Shore: Plays by Gao Xingjian. Translated by Gilbert Fong. Hong Kong: Chinese University Press, 1999.

A Work about Gao Xingjian
Tam, Kwok-kan. *Soul of Chaos: Critical Perspectives on Gao Xingjian.* Hong Kong: Chinese University Press, 2001.

García Lorca, Federico (1898–1936) *poet, playwright*
Federico García Lorca was born in Fuente Vaqueros, Spain, to a well-to-do family. He was given an excellent education and the opportunity to pursue his artistic interests, which included painting, music, and, most of all, poetry. He spent his childhood in the Andalusian city of Granada, which instilled in him a love of that region's folk traditions. This folk influence would later be seen in his plays and poetry and a series of folk songs he collected and anthologized.

In 1919, he moved to Madrid and, within a short time, earned a reputation as one of the most talented young poets in Spain. His reputation spread throughout the Spanish-speaking world, and such Latin American poets as PABLO NERUDA were inspired and influenced by him.

García Lorca's international reputation had been established, and his career was progressing in Spain. However, personal conflicts and politics within the Spanish literary world caused him to travel to the United States for a year, where he attended Columbia University.

He found New York to be a nightmare, if an exciting one, and he wrote the surrealistic and expressionistic work *Poet in New York* (1940), which was not published until after his death. A castigation of the inhumanity of the modern world, *Poet in New York* remains one of García Lorca's most popular poems in the English-speaking world. It uses surrealist techniques, but unlike the French surrealism of ANDRÉ BRETON, it is filled with emotion and passion.

When García Lorca returned to Spain, he became increasingly involved in theater and wrote a series of plays that reveal the folkloric influences of his youth, creating a theater of strong emotions and symbolism. He also directed a traveling theater company called *La Barraca,* which performed Spanish theater classics in rural areas that had little exposure to culture. This project was one of many liberal political activities in which García Lorca was engaged during the period of the Spanish republic and before the Spanish civil war.

It was also at this time that García Lorca became particularly interested in the emerging women's rights movement. His reputation and fame grew exponentially during this period.

In 1936, while on a trip to Granada to visit his family, García Lorca was trapped by the outbreak of the Spanish civil war and went into hiding. He was captured within a few weeks and executed without trial. The presumed reason was his homosexuality, a crime at the time. However, his liberal agenda was undoubtedly a strong factor as well.

Critical Analysis

García Lorca was obsessed with expressing the intense, vital energy of life, which he did by using subconscious images and strong musical language. In his works, he constantly examined the struggle of opposing forces and the power of dialectical opposites such as good and evil or freedom and repression. These themes interact with his politics to create three major trends in his work: examinations of individuals oppressed by the need to conform to social norms, minorities oppressed by uncaring majorities, and life oppressed by death itself.

In the play *The House of Bernarda Alba* (1936), García Lorca recounts the power relationship between a controlling mother, Bernarda Alba, and her daughter Adela. Bernarda Alba's attempts to separate Adela from her lover end tragically, as do all García Lorca's plays, with her daughter's suicide. Bernarda Alba is a larger-than-life figure who ends up destroying everything she seeks to preserve. The play has distinctive feminist overtones and, along with IBSEN's *Hedda Gabler,* is one of the great early works of feminist literature.

Blood Wedding (1933) recounts the struggle between Leonardo and the citizens of the village in which he lives who react to his nonconformity with murderous rage. The villagers are not given proper names but called only Mother, Father, and so on, indicating that they are not real people but symbols of the rigid conventions of an unjust social morality. Like *The House of Bernarda Alba, Blood Wedding* ends with the tragic death of its most noble character.

In García Lorca's collection of poems *Gypsy Ballads* (1928), he explores the problematic cultural identity of the gypsies in Spain. These poems critique Spanish society for its unfair marginalization of the gypsies. *Gypsy Ballads* also celebrates the beauty and poetry of gypsy culture, pointing out that many things that are quintessentially Spanish, in fact, originated with the gypsies.

Dirge for Ignacio Sánchez Mejías (1937) brings García Lorca's celebration of the power of life into a confrontation with its opposite, the power of death. Ignacio Sánchez Mejías was a friend of García Lorca's who was tragically killed in a bullfight. In the dirge, García Lorca celebrates the matador's vitality and emphasizes the beauty of living on the tightrope between life and death.

García Lorca is one of the most influential poets of the 20th century. NERUDA, PAZ, and many other 20th-century Spanish-speaking poets owe García Lorca a tremendous debt as the central figure of a type of surrealism that is uniquely expressive of emotions. His tragic death at the hands of fascists also stands as an important historical symbol for the need for freedom of expression. He may be seen as a forerunner of the civil rights and women's movements of the latter 20th century, but more important, he was a writer of exquisite poems and plays that truly reveal the preciousness of human life on the edge of death.

Other Works by García Lorca
Four Major Plays. Translated by John Edmunds; introduction by Nicholas Round; notes by Ann MacLaren. New York: Oxford University Press, 1997.
A Season in Granada: Uncollected Poems & Prose. Edited and translated by Christopher Maurer. London: Anvil Press Poetry, 1998.

A Work about García Lorca
Wellington, Beth. *Reflections on Lorca's Private Mythology: Once Five Years Pass and the Rural Plays.* New York: Peter Lang, 1993.

García Márquez, Gabriel (Gabo)
(1928–   ) *novelist, short story writer, screenplay writer, journalist*

Gabriel García Márquez was born in Aracataca, Colombia, a small town near a banana plantation called Macondo. His father, Gabriel Eligio García, was a telegraph operator who had courted his mother in secret by telegraph when she would write home from school. García Márquez lived in Aracataca until the age of eight. During that time, his closest connections were to his maternal grandparents, who had initially tried to prevent their daughter from marrying Gabriel Eligio García because of his conservative political affiliations.

García Márquez's grandmother was a highly superstitious woman and also a brilliant storyteller. She would tell García Márquez the most incredible, exaggerated, and impossible things with the deadpan manner of someone explaining that Earth has a north and a south pole. As a child, García Márquez believed everything she told him and, on some level, never stopped believing. This early experience of blending the real with the fantastic later led García Márquez to develop his unique style of MAGIC REALISM.

His grandfather, who had been a colonel in the Colombian civil war, was a local official. He would spend a great deal of time with his young grandson and often took him to the circus. García Márquez has stated that his grandfather was the most important person in his life and his best friend. The colonel died when García Márquez was eight years old, but García Márquez drew more inspiration for his books from these eight years than from any other period of his life.

García Márquez was sent to boarding school and won a scholarship to go to college in Bogotá, the capital of Colombia. After studying law, he worked as a journalist, traveling throughout South America, Europe, and the United States, eventually settling in Mexico City in 1961.

In Mexico City, he wrote film scripts, including a Western in collaboration with CARLOS FUENTES titled *Tiempo de morir* (*A Time to Die*), to support himself and his wife Mercedes, whom he had married in 1958.

García Márquez had written an unsuccessful first novel called *Leaf Storm* (1955) about life in Macondo, a fictionalized version of García Márquez's birthplace. The novel spans the period from the turn of the century to the 1930s. Though it contains many of the themes in García Márquez's later works, the novel is poorly structured and remains flat.

No One Writes to the Colonel (1961), however, is in many ways García Márquez's first masterpiece. It is a novella that depicts an elderly colonel who waits for a government pension that never arrives. The colonel, lovingly based on García Márquez's grandfather, is a magnificent literary character filled with humor and vitality. It is in this work that García Márquez's control of language and his stylistic innovations caught up with his psychological perception. The combination created a new sort of literature, which was fantastic in its details and yet deeply true in its emotions.

In 2003, an English translation of the first volume of García Márquez's memoir *Living to Tell the Tale* was published. In 2005, the English translation of *Memoria de mis putas tristes, Memoirs of My Melancholy Whores,* was released. According to the publisher, this tale of a 90-year-old man who decides to celebrate his birthday with an adolescent virgin "contemplates the misfortunes of old age and celebrates the joys of being in love."

Critical Analysis

The imaginary town of Macondo is the setting of most of García Márquez's novels and stories. In this way, Macondo is a literary device like the Yoknapatawpha County of William Faulkner. Both places are imaginary worlds, closely based on the setting of the author's childhood, that by being written about repeatedly become literary microcosms, self-contained realities. García Márquez has often spoken of his sense of kinship with Faulkner. He has even said that Faulkner, who grew up in Mississippi near the Gulf of Mexico, is a fellow Caribbean writer.

It was in 1965 that García Márquez began to write his single greatest work *One Hundred Years of Solitude* (1967). He was driving to the beach with his family when suddenly all of the themes that he had been developing since he was a boy solidified into a clear structure. He returned home immediately and began to write.

One Hundred Years of Solitude revisits all of the themes of García Márquez's earlier work as episodes within the epic story of six generations of the Buendia family, the founding family of the town of Macondo.

The book is subtly structured in four sections of five unnumbered chapters each. Each section corresponds to an abstract historical category. The first section explores the mythic and utopian pre-history of the town. Mythical narratives from both the biblical and classical traditions are woven with local superstitions and García Márquez's own inventions. Macondo, though it is a place that seems full of promise, has been founded by José Arcadio Buendia because of a murder he has committed and is trying to forget. This evokes the story of Cain and Abel and shows that Macondo is a place created by an act of transgression.

The second section of the book moves into what could be called historical time. The events in this section closely parallel the history of the actual Columbian civil war in which García Márquez's grandfather fought. However, García Márquez continues to write in his magical style. This combination of historical fact and fantasy has an extraordinarily dramatic effect and is, above all, what makes *One Hundred Years of Solitude* the quintessential example of magic realism.

The third section is an account of how, after the Columbian civil war, a U.S. company comes to Macondo to exploit its banana industry. Though this section can also be said to take place in historical, as opposed to mythic, time, it is different from the previous section. History in the third section has been corrupted by language, particularly the propaganda and media manipulation the banana company uses to exploit the citizens of Macondo. By the time the company is finished, Macondo has been reduced to a wasteland, barely holding on to what is left of its previous vitality.

In the fourth section, the book returns to mythic time, not the utopian time of the beginning but the apocalyptic time of the true end of the world. The final Buendia, the great-great-grandson of the first José Arcadio, lives in Macondo disconnected from history. He does not even know his origins or that he is a Buendia by blood. He spends his time trying to decipher a magical manuscript that holds the secret of his origins and his fate.

García Márquez went on to write multiple novels of the highest literary merit, including *Love in the Time of Cholera* (1988) and *Chronicle of a Death Foretold* (1981). In 1982, he was awarded the world's highest literary award, the Nobel Prize. In his acceptance speech, he spoke of his hopes for a positive political future for Latin America. He emphasized that magic realism is merely an accurate depiction of the miraculous occurrences that take place in Latin American life, occurrences of superhuman wonder and terror.

Other Works by Gabriel García Márquez

Collected Novellas. Translated from the Spanish by Gregory Rabassa and J. S. Bernstein. New York: HarperPerennial, 1991.

The General in His Labyrinth. Translated from the Spanish by Edith Grossman. New York: Knopf, 1990.

Works about Gabriel García Márquez

Martin, Gerald. *Gabriel García Márquez: A Life.* New York: Knopf, 2009.

Miller, Yvette E., and Charles Rossman. *Gabriel García Márquez.* Pittsburgh, Pa.: Department of Hispanic Languages and Literatures, University of Pittsburgh, 1985.

Gary, Romain (1914–1980) *novelist, director, screenwriter, and diplomat*

War hero, novelist, diplomat, husband of a troubled American film star, Romain Gary is one of

France's great literary chameleons, inventing and reinventing himself throughout his career. A vivid and frequently inventive memoirist, the facts of Gary's early life have been subject to some uncertainty. Born Roman (soon altered to Romain) Kacew of Jewish ancestry in Moscow (or possibly Vilnius, Lithuania) on May 8, 1914, the child of actors, Gary grew up in Vilnius and in Warsaw, Poland. He did not know his father and was raised by his mother with whom he was intensely close and who instilled in him an unwavering belief that he would be celebrated. At 14, he emigrated to Nice, France, where he received his baccalaureate. Upon graduation he studied law in Paris and published his first two short stories.

In 1938, he enlisted in the French air force but was the only member of his officer's training class not to receive promotion (perhaps because he had only recently become a citizen but possibly due to anti-Semitism). When France was invaded and defeated by Nazi German forces in 1940, he escaped from France, flying to North Africa where he joined the Lorraine, a bomber squadron in the Free French forces. He served in North Africa for two years until he was relocated to England. At this point, Kacew adopted the pen name "Gari" (Russian for "Burn!"), which he anglicized to "Gary." He flew many hazardous missions in Europe and the Middle East, surviving crashes, wounds, and typhoid. After the liberation of France in 1944, Gary returned to Paris and was decorated with high honors. He received the Croix de guerre, the Légion d'honneur, and was named by Charles de Gaulle as one of the surviving Companions of the Liberation.

During his service, beginning perhaps as early as 1942, the year his mother died, Gary began work on his first novel, the ironically titled *Education européenne* (1944, English title *Forest of Anger*). The novel was written in both French and English and many of the themes that would preoccupy Gary's works are present here. *Education européenne* narrates the struggle of the Polish Resistance fighters against the occupying German forces in the winter of 1942–43. "A sort

of anti-bildungsroman," in the words of one critic, "in the course of which Janek, the fourteen-year-old main character, reluctantly learns to kill." The novel takes an ironic stance toward heroism, expressing a powerful skepticism and disillusionment about the motives for human conflict and struggle. As one of the Resistance fighters remarks, "Men make up pretty stories and then go off and die for them."

Gary married English author Lesley Blanch, and in late 1945 his novel received the prestigious Prix des Critiques and became a best seller. He entered the diplomatic corps and was assigned a post at the French embassy in Sofia, Bulgaria, the first of many. He would be stationed between 1946 and 1961 in Berne, New York (at the United Nations), La Paz, and Los Angeles. His diplomatic career placed him at odds with the French intelligentsia on the Left and forced him to publicly defend French colonial policies with which he privately disagreed.

Despite his diplomatic responsibilities, he continued to produce a steady output of fiction. *Les couleurs du jour* (1952, *The Colors of the Day*) met with good success, and *Les racines du ciel* (1956, *The Roots of Heaven*) won the Prix Goncourt for that year. This was the first of Gary's fictions to be made into a motion picture in 1958, directed by John Huston, starring Trevor Howard, Juliette Greco, and Errol Flynn. *Roots of Heaven* deals with a defiant prisoner being held in solitary confinement in a German prisoner-of-war camp, where he has a vision of elephants as symbols of freedom. After the war, he travels to Africa in search of elephants, only to find them being persecuted, hunted nearly to extinction. In sympathy, he becomes their champion and defender. As Huston observed, "His efforts take on a symbolic significance, and great scientists, artists and politicians from all over the world come to join him. *The Roots of Heaven* was a prophetic book, anticipating the concerns of today's environmentalists."

The advent of the 1960s marked a new phase in Gary's life and career. He wrote his powerful, if frequently self-mythologizing, memoir, *Promesse de l'aube* (1960, *Promise at Dawn*), in which he describes the powerful, frequently painful relationship with his mother, as she imparts to her son an overweening ambition. Critics have described it as a consolidation of Gary's first public identity and as a book that liberated him to reinvent his literary persona.

In the early 1960s, Gary divorced Branch and became involved with (and eventually married) the American actress and darling of French New Wave cinema, Jean Seberg. Raised in Iowa, Seberg was discovered by Otto Preminger in a widely publicized talent search in the late 1950s and became an international star in Jean-Luc Godard's *Breathless* (1960). The skeptical disillusionment that Gary had directed toward war found a new target as he turned his eye on Hollywood (he was posted to the French consulate in Los Angeles at this time) and the liberal politics of Seberg and her circles. In Gary's *The Talent Scout* (1961), the bad social conscience of the young Iowan heroine leads her to become the mistress of a grotesque and terrifying Latin American dictator.

By the end of the 1960s, Seberg, her marriage to Gary faltering, became involved with the Black Panther Party. Seberg's involvement in the black power movement and their presence in the French consulate in Los Angeles would serve as a backdrop for Gary's novel on the subject of racial turmoil in America: *White Dog* (1971). After Seberg's suicide in 1979, it would emerge that a contributing factor had been the FBI's spreading of false rumors about the paternity of Seberg's child, claiming that the child had been fathered by a member of the Black Panther Party. The baby died shortly after birth.

In these years, Gary also began to explore directly questions of Jewish identity. *La danse de Gengis Cohn* (1966, *The Dance of Genghis Cohn*) relates the story of the title character, a Jewish comedian in Berlin who dies in Auschwitz only to haunt as a dybbuk, or ghost, the mind of his German murderer (now a police commissioner) by the name of Schatz. Cohn torments Schatz by speaking through his mouth or materializing suddenly in front of him at the most inappropriate moments. Gradually, however, identities begin to shift and merge, the protagonists apparently switch roles, and at times it seems as if the Nazi were haunting the Jew, as if Schatz had brazenly taken up lodgings in poor Cohn's head. The allegory takes on an added dimension when Gary introduces an explicitly metafictional context. "There's a guy out there," one character relates to the other, "who's trying to get rid of us." "What guy? Where? We can't see him. We're inside" In this way, Gary introduces the author as eradicator, expressing an increasing sense of alienation from his own themes and from his imagination.

Although it would not be discovered until after his death, Gary's use of pseudonymous identity—which had been there from the outset of his career—would become an increasing preoccupation in the 1970s. Not only did he create a new pseudonym for himself, Émile Ajar, but he also kept it from the public and went so far as to engage a distant relation to pose as this mysterious author. He published several popular and critical successes under this name, including *Gros câlin* (1974), *La vie devant soi* (1975), and *Pseudo* (1976). *La vie devant soi* won the Prix Goncourt in 1975, making Gary the only person to have ever won two. He also would publish novels under the pseudonyms of Fosco Sinibaldi and Shatan Bogat. As one critic has observed, "The staging of Ajar and the creation of works in his image are the logical culmination of a career-long investigation into the formation of public images and the dynamics of authorial identity." Or, as Ajar writes in *Pseudo*, "I have problems with my skin because it isn't mine . . . I want to become planetary." Romain Gary died in December 1980 of a self-inflicted gunshot wound.

Other Works by Romain Gary

The Company of Men. New York: Simon and Schuster, 1950.
Lady L. New York: Simon and Schuster, 1958.
The Ski Bum. New York: Harper & Row, 1965.
Tulipe. Paris: Gallimand, 1999.

Gautier, Théophile (1811-1872) *poet, novelist*

Théophile Gautier was born in Tarbes on August 31, 1811. He moved as a young child to Paris with his family, where he studied to become a painter. In June 1829, however, Gautier met with the great novelist VICTOR HUGO, which prompted him to change his aspirations and become a writer. Five months later, his first collection, *Poetries* (1836), was published on the same day that the barricades were erected in Paris.

For financial reasons, Gautier took a position as a journalist in 1836, working as an art critic while continuing to write fiction. His novel *Mademoiselle de Maupin* (1835) caused quite a scandal when it first appeared on account of its description of sexual ambiguity. It is also credited for founding the concept of *art for art's sake,* a phrase Gautier uses in his prologue to the book. The next year, he wrote *La mort amoureuse* (translated into English as *Clarimonde*), about a priest who becomes obsessed with a beautiful vampiress. Gautier also continued to write poetry, publishing the collection *The Comedy of Death* (1838), which shows influences of Shakespeare, GOETHE, and Dante.

In 1839, Gautier decided to try to write for the theater. He created numerous tales of fantasy, but the one for which he is most remembered is his libretto for the ballet *Giselle,* which opened in Paris on June 28, 1841, to overwhelming popular and critical acclaim. *Giselle* continues to be performed frequently in the 21st century.

Gautier was a proponent of the idea of art for art's sake, which is evident in the fact that he originally wanted to be a painter. His love of the visual has transferred to his written works as well.

Others Works by Théophile Gautier

Gautier on Dance. Translated by Ivor Guest. London: Dance, 1986.
Gentle Enchanter: Thirty-Four Poems. Translated by Brian Hill. London: R. Hart Davis, 1960.

A Work about Théophile Gautier

Tennant, Philip E. *Théophile Gautier.* London: Athlone Press, 1975.

Generation of 1898

A group of writers who shared a common concern for Spain's national identity and who worked to revitalize the social, political, and aesthetic structures of their country. The Spanish-American War of 1898 brought an end to the period of Spanish imperialism in the New World. Spain, which had been a world power for hundreds of years, had to face the new reality of being a small provincial nation. The Generation of 1898 urged their fellow compatriots to turn away from the trappings of empire and to search for the "true" Spain of their medieval and Arabic heritage.

ORTEGA Y GASSET, the Spanish philosopher and critic, attributes a span of 15 years to the generation as a movement and further divides it into two groups. The first group includes the forerunners MIGUEL DE UNAMUNO and Ángel Ganivet y García (1865-98); the second group includes the secondary members of the movement such as PÍO BAROJA.

Perhaps the difficulty of conclusively saying who is and is not a member of this movement comes from the fact that one of the main characteristics that members of the Generation of 1898 shared is a strong sense of individuality and nonconformism. The central figures, however, would unquestionably include Baroja, Unamuno, Ganivet, ANTONIO MACHADO, and the Latin American poet RUBÉN DARÍO, who spent a great deal of time traveling in Europe. Other members include Azorín (José Martínez Ruiz, 1873-1967), who was the first to identify the Generation of '98 as a group; Ramón Maria del Valle-Inclán (1866-1936); Juan Ramón Jiménez (1881-1958), who won the Nobel Prize in literature in 1956; and Ramón Pérez de Ayala (1880-1962).

These authors, in addition to individualism, shared strong national feelings mixed with literary and formal experimentation. Out of their rejection of the decedent features of Spanish culture, they embraced MODERNISM in hope that it would cleanse the dead tissue from Spanish art. In politics, they shared a sense of apathy and a mistrust of government control over the individual. In society, they rejected refined manners and taboos. They called for bringing Spanish culture down to earth and embracing Arab and flamenco influences. They wanted a return to the culture of the people rather than the aristocrats. Finally, in art, they introduced new structures and difficult but vital modes of expression.

The writers of the Generation of 1898 opened up the structures of literature and showed the exciting possibilities of experimentation. They influenced 20th-century authors as diverse as GARCÍA LORCA and Ernest Hemingway.

A Work about the Generation of 1898

Shaw, Donald Leslie. *The Generation of 1898 in Spain.* New York: Barnes & Noble, 1975.

Genet, Jean (1910–1986) *novelist, playwright*

A convicted felon who went on to become one of the leaders in the avant-garde theater movement, Jean Genet was born in Paris as the illegitimate son of a woman who abandoned him shortly after birth. Raised in state institutions, he embarked on a life of crime, turning to theft at age 10. He spent time at the Mettray Reformatory, escaping from there at age 19 to join the foreign legion, a position he soon abandoned. From there, Genet wandered throughout Europe spending time in several prisons on charges of vagrancy, theft, homosexuality, and smuggling.

In 1939, Genet began to write about his experiences. His subsequent novels detailed and glorified the underworld, homosexuality, male prostitutes, convicts, and other social outcasts. He wrote his first novel, *Our Lady of the Flowers* (1943; translated 1963), a fictional creation based on the events in his life while he was in prison.

In 1948, Genet was once again convicted of burglary. This, his 10th offense, resulted in an automatic sentence of life imprisonment. By this time, however, his works had gained the attention of fellow writers JEAN-PAUL SARTRE, ANDRÉ GIDE, and JEAN COCTEAU. On hearing of Genet's sentence, they petitioned the president of the republic for Genet's release. His parole was granted, after which his life changed dramatically.

Encouraged by the show of support from such prominent writers, Genet determined to dedicate his life to writing and to abandon crime permanently. He continued to glorify the underworld in which he had lived in his works, but he also began to focus on the beauty and sadness of homosexual love.

In the 1940s, Genet turned his attention to the theater, writing several plays that, at the time, were considered too controversial to be performed in France. His first play, *The Maids* (1947; translated 1954), made a significant impact on the rising trend toward the THEATER OF THE ABSURD. It was based on a true story of two sisters, both maids for the same woman, who murder their mistress. This play was followed by *Deathwatch* (1949; translated 1954), which takes the prison setting so commonly seen in his novels and uses it as a backdrop from which to explore despair and loneliness.

Genet began to abandon traditional ideas of what should constitute acceptable character, plot, and motivation within a theatrical piece. He began to focus on conflicts within society—between illusion and reality, good and evil, and other cultural oppositions—with a fervor that can almost be described as religious. His plays are ritualistic in structure, aimed at arousing the audience's innermost feelings and then offering them the opportunity to undergo a transformation or to reach a catharsis alongside the characters on the stage. Filled with an energy largely created by violence and cruelty, his plays, while shocking, were never vulgar and were diverse in both setting and subject. *The Balcony* (1956; translated 1957), for instance, was set in a brothel; *The Blacks* (1959) in a fantastical court; and *The Screens* (1961; translated 1962) in the middle of the French–Algerian war. All three works, however, focused on the inherent paradoxes of an imperfect life.

Genet's autobiography, *The Thief's Journal* (1949; translated 1964), is a record of his remarkable life and the misery and degradation he suffered at the hands of a bourgeois society. He gave up writing in the 1960s to devote himself to lecturing and supporting the emerging radical activist fervor of the decade. He continued to support radical causes until his death on April 15, 1986.

Other Works by Jean Genet

Funeral Rites. Translated by Bernard Frechtman. New York: Grove Press, 1969.

Prisoner of Love. Translated by Barbara Bray. Hanover. Mass.: University Press of New England, 1992.

Rembrant. Translated by Randolph Hough. New York: Hanuman Books, 1988.

Works about Jean Genet

Knapp, Bettina. *Jean Genet.* Boston: Twayne, 1968.

Sartre, Jean-Paul. *Saint Genet: Actor and Martyr.* New York: Pantheon Books, 1983.

White, Edmund. *Genet: A Biography.* New York: Knopf, 1993.

George, Stefan (1868–1933) *poet*

Stefan George was born in the German village of Rüdesheim to Stephan and Eva George. His father was a prosperous wine merchant. George attended secondary school in Darmstadt and graduated in 1888. He studied modern languages at the University of Berlin for three semesters. Deciding early in life to be a poet, George never engaged in another profession or trade. He rarely remained in one place, frequently traveling to the countries of central and western Europe. While in Paris, he found formative influences in STÉPHANE MALLARMÉ and other French symbolist poets.

George published his first volume of poetry in 1890. In 1892, he founded the journal *Blätter für die Kunst (Journal of the Arts).* George formed many close friendships among the literati, including the Austrian writer HUGO VON HOFMANNS-THAL. He soon attracted a group of disciples known as the George Circle. After the turn of the

century, George increasingly saw himself as an educator to lead the reform of a decadent culture. A brief friendship with a 15-year-old boy, Maximin, further focused George's attention on the beauty and the renewing potential of an elite group of youth. By the 1910s, George's poetry had moved into a prophetic phase. His volume *Das neue Reich (The New Empire)* (1928) revealed his vision for a new Germany. The Nazis sought to use George as a symbol of their state, but he refused their honors and awards. He moved to Switzerland, where he died in December 1933.

George became famous for writing beautiful lyrical poems on such themes as landscape, friendship, and art. He sometimes used terse and forceful language but still produced balladesque works. Early in his career, George wrote of the artist's isolation from nature, but he later sought to teach that man was divine and capable of perfection. He left a lasting influence on German lyrical poetry and expressionist writers. His biographers, Michael and Erika Metzger, explain that George's works "bear witness to the unremitting striving of a man of unique poetic and intellectual powers to find a higher meaning in his existence and ours."

Another Work by Stefan George

The Works of Stefan George. Translated by Olga Marx and Ernst Morwitz. Chapel Hill: University of North Carolina Press, 1974.

A Work about Stefan George

Metzger, Michael M., and Erika A Metzger. *Stefan George.* Boston: Twayne, 1972.

Ghālib, Mirzā (1797–1869) *poet*

Mirzā Asadullāh Khān Ghālib was born in Agra, India. His grandfather immigrated to India from Asia Minor and belonged to a long line of soldiers. Ghālib's father was also a soldier and was killed in battle when Ghālib was five years old. After his father's death, he grew up with his mother's family, who were wealthy landowners. Ghālib was given a private education in languages and sciences and, at age 13, was married and moved to Delhi, where he spent the rest of his life.

Much of Ghālib's finest poetry is in Persian, though he also wrote in Urdu. Ghālib started writing poetry at a very young age and was already moving among literary circles by the time of his marriage. When he was young, he used the name *Asad* and later adopted the name *Ghālib*. He was always hesitant about his choice to become a poet, and he was the first male in his family who did not want to be a soldier. In one of his letters, he describes this decision by comparing his poetic words with the weapons of war. He states that his poetry will be "his ship upon the illusory sea of verse . . . and the broken arrows of my ancestors become my pens." Characteristically witty, Ghālib's allusions are often obscured by the strict rhyme and rhythm constraints of the *ghazal*. (A *ghazal* is defined as a short poem consisting of up to a dozen couplets in the same meter, with a specific rhyme scheme.) Often, however, this necessity only further liberated Ghālib's deliberate play with words and sounds.

Ghālib was never rich, but in middle age, he was invited to join the court of Bahādur Shāh Zafar, the last of the Moghul emperors. Under Bahādur Shāh Zafar's patronage, he began to make a comfortable living from his poetry. The British takeover of India from the Moghuls after the Sepoy Mutiny in 1857 (also known as the First War of Indian Independence) had a tremendous impact on Ghālib's life and work: He lost his position as court poet and instead began writing copious letters to his friends, who were now spread across the subcontinent. Although they were written for private reading, they were collected and published, the first volume of them in the year before he died. Written in Urdu in a colloquial style, these letters are his subjective responses to current events and allow modern readers a glimpse into his time, while taking Urdu literature into a new direction by showing that profound literature could exist outside of the formal *ghazal* and its emphasis on idealism, romance, and universalism.

Another Work by Mirzā Ghālib

Ghazals of Ghālib. Translated by Aijaz Ahmad. New York: Columbia University Press, 1971.

A Work about Mirzā Ghālib

Russell, Ralph. *Ghālib.* Cambridge, Mass.: Harvard University Press, 1969.

Ghosh, Amitav (1956–) *novelist*

Amitav Ghosh was born in Calcutta, India, but grew up in Bangladesh (formerly East Pakistan). As a child, and while on fieldwork research, Ghosh lived in many countries, including Sri Lanka, Iran, England, Egypt, and the United States. Despite his diverse interests (he has studied and taught philosophy, literature, and social anthropology), Ghosh has said that his creative work best captures his ideas. As a child, during summer holidays in Calcutta, Ghosh would spend hours reading books from his uncle's library in his grandfather's house. Because of this initiation into reading and literature, he has acknowledged the lasting influence of RABINDRANATH TAGORE and the Bengali literary tradition in his own writing. Ghosh is a writer, a journalist, and has been a visiting professor at Harvard University since 2005. Ghosh has indicated that he plans to return to India.

After graduation in India, Ghosh went to Oxford University to study social anthropology, where he received a masters, and a doctorate in philosophy in 1982. On his return to India, he began to work for the *Indian Express* newspaper in New Delhi while working on his first novel, *The Circle of Reason* (1986). This and his next novel, *Shadow Lines* (1988), are about the seamlessness of geographical boundaries, and much of the plot of *Shadow Lines* hinges on the question of national identity. The main character suffers from a sudden identity crisis after he is thrown into a situation where he must decide which country (India or Bangladesh) is his, which culture defines him, and which place he can ultimately call his own. This novel won Ghosh India's prestigious Sahitya Akademi Award in 1990.

Many of Ghosh's novels have been the result of years spent in different countries while conducting field research for his college degrees. *In an Antique Land* (1993), for instance, comes out of his research in 1980 while living in a small village in Egypt. *The Glass Palace* (2000), tells the story of an orphaned Indian boy, developed alongside the story of the royal family's exile in India after the British invasion of the kingdom of Mandalay (Burma) in 1885.

Ghosh refused the Commonwealth Writers' Prize for this novel in 2001 in protest against being classified as a "commonwealth" writer. Accepting the award, he said in his letter to the Commonwealth Foundation, would have placed "contemporary writing not within the realities of the present day . . . but rather within a disputed aspect of the past." His works reflect the elements of universal humanity. The cross-cultural references he makes to different nations and cultures render insignificant physical or political boundaries.

Ghosh's 2008 novel, *A Sea of Poppies*, was short-listed for the Booker Prize. Set in India in 1838, this novel follows the fates of the passengers on the *Isis*, a ship out of Calcutta sailing the Bay of Bengal. Aboard ship, characters from a number of different levels of society are united through their time together and their connections to the Asian opium and slave trades.

Another Work by Amitav Ghosh

The Calcutta Chromosome: A Novel of Fevers, Delirium, and Discovery. New York: HarperCollins, 1998.

Works about Amitav Ghosh

Bhatt, Indira, and Indira Nityanandan, eds. *The Fiction of Amitav Ghosh.* New Delhi: Creative Books, 2001.

Dhawan, R. K. *The Novels of Amitav Ghosh.* New York: Prestige Books, 1999.

Gide, André (1869–1951) *novelist*

André Gide was born in Paris on November 22. His father, a law professor at the University of Paris, died when André was 11. Gide was subsequently raised by his wealthy mother on her family's estate near Rouen. Overly protective of her son and concerned over what she believed to be his delicate health, she withdrew him from school and hired private tutors. He was brought up in a strict Protestant tradition, memorizing passages from the Bible at an early age, and undergoing periods of religious fervor. He also developed an abiding affection for his cousin, Madeleine Rondeux, whom he married in 1895. The two stayed married 42 years in what is, according to some accounts, the longest unconsummated marriage in recorded history.

In 1889, after completing his studies and passing his required exams, Gide, never needing to worry about supporting himself financially, decided to devote his life to writing and traveling. He published his first work, *The Notebooks of André Walter* (1891), in the style that was to become his signature: the intimate confessional. He also began to attend gatherings of intellectuals at the Paris apartment of symbolist poet STÉPHANE MALLARMÉ. This was followed by a trip to North Africa in 1893 with a young painter, Paul Albert Laurens. The effect of this journey proved critical to both Gide's life and his works.

Liberated from the confinement of the society in which he was born and raised, he began to examine certain truths about himself, including his homosexuality. When he returned to Paris, however, he quickly began to deny many of these revelations. He took a second trip to North Africa, during which he met Oscar Wilde, an intellectual experience that would forever shape his life and his work. The result of these sexual and intellectual awakenings was the novel *The Fruits of the Earth* (1897).

Although Gide had begun to make discoveries about himself, he was unable to reconcile the reality of his life with his strict moral religious upbringing. On returning to Paris once again, he married his cousin Madeleine Rondeux. The marriage was largely a pretense and fraught with difficulties, as is revealed in his novels *The Immoralist* (1902) and *Strait Is the Gate* (1909). Both works examine the tension between social responsibility and the desire to remain true to the self.

During World War I, Gide worked with the Red Cross in Paris, where he met and fell in love with Marc Allegret. When Madeleine learned of this, she destroyed all the letters Gide had ever sent to her, an act that greatly hurt Gide. In response, he published *Corydon* (1924), a defense of homosexuality, and *If I Die* (1924), his autobiography. These two works shocked and scandalized his closest friends and resulted in Gide's alienation from his previously close social groups. Gide, however, felt personally vindicated by his decision to admit openly his homosexuality and sold his estates to move with Allegret to French Equatorial Africa.

In the 1930s, Gide began to look favorably on principles of marxism and by 1932 had embraced communism largely because of Lenin's decriminalization of homosexuality. However, a visit to the Soviet Union in 1934 left him disillusioned.

A firm antifascist, he spent most of World War II living in North Africa. He was awarded the Nobel Prize in literature in 1947 and, at the time of his death in 1951, he was one of only two authors whose entire collection of works appeared on the Index Liborum Prohibitorum, a listing of books forbidden to be read by Roman Catholics.

André Gide's life was complicated by many facets, and his writing, which reflects the circumstances of his life, is based on an intense scrutiny of himself and the world around him.

Critical Analysis

André Gide's work simultaneously conceals and reveals aspects of the author's life; his novels lay bare the contradictory nature of his upbringing and its effect, as well as his moments of insight, which at times he acknowledged or denied. All of these elements are, according to many critics, structured in the style of an "intimate confessional."

This style is clearly seen in his novel *The Fruits of the Earth*. Described by one critic as a "highly artificial and mock-naïve text," the narrator chronicles his travels to Italy and North Africa in 1893 and 1894 to his "understudy"—that is, his lover Nathaniel. During his travels, Gide formed a friendship with Oscar Wilde (called "Menalcas" in the novel), whom he met in Algiers. He also encountered social and sexual conventions that challenged those with which he was raised. These experiences led Gide to accept his homosexuality, an important theme in the novel. *The Fruits of the Earth* is a celebration of the senses, of self-indulgence in beauty. Like Wilde, Gide saw beauty as an end in itself; nothing else was required. Written while Gide was suffering from tuberculosis, he declared that "today's Utopia" should be "tomorrow's reality."

Gide's inclination toward postmodern techniques of self-referentiality, which reached its height in *The Counterfeiters*, also can be seen as a technique to reveal and conceal elements of his self, as a way to engage in "spiritual self-scrutiny" without committing to the reality of that activity. Revolving around a web of relationships that unfolds throughout the novel, *The Counterfeiters* focuses primarily on schoolmates Bernard, Olivier, and Edouard, who explore their individual sexuality with one another while resisting the temptations of the conventional world. The title of the novel ostensibly comes from Olivier's younger brother Georges, who becomes involved with a ring of counterfeiters; however, the broader thematic application of the term applies to the social network of the novel as a whole, as characters explore their lives in an effort to avoid counterfeit lives and to live authentically, for themselves. This effort is focused primarily on sexuality and in particular on the three schoolmates who struggle with their homosexuality.

Another Work by André Gide

Amyntas. Translated by Richard Howard. New York: Ecco Press, 1988.

Works about André Gide

Fryer, Jonathan. *André and Oscar: Gide, Wilde and the Gay Art of Living*. London: Constable, 1997.

Sheridan, Alan. *André Gide: A Life in the Present*. London: Hamish Hamilton, 1998.

Ginzburg, Natalia (Alessandra Tornimparti) (1916–1991) *novelist, essayist, nonfiction writer*

Natalia Ginzburg, well known for her autobiographical novels detailing her unconventional family and its fight against fascism, was born Natalia Levi in Palermo to a middle-class family. Her religious background was mixed, being Jewish on her father's side and Catholic on her mother's side, and she was raised as an atheist. Because of this, she spent her childhood removed from other children, isolated for her differences. In 1919, she moved to Turin, where her father had accepted a position as a professor at the University of Turin. There, she was immersed in the culture of the time, particularly the activities centered around antifascism. Intellectuals, all opponents of Benito Mussolini, would gather regularly at her family's home to discuss opposition.

Ginzburg graduated from the University of Turin in 1935. Three years later, she married editor and political activist Leone Ginzburg. The couple had two children and lived in seclusion in the region of Abruzzi, where they were involved in numerous antifascist activities. Eventually, they were forced into hiding, alternately in Rome and in Florence, until Leone Ginzburg was arrested in 1944. Imprisoned at the Regina Coeli prison, he died after being subjected to extreme torture.

Ginzburg had begun her career as a writer of short stories. Many of these were published in the Florentine magazine *Solaria*. Her first major work to appear in the magazine was "Un'assenza" (1933), a tale about an unhappy marriage. It was printed when she was only 17 years old. Her first short novel, however, was not written until almost a decade later. She published *The Road to the City* (1942) under the pseudonym of Alessandra Tornimparti while she and her husband were still in hiding.

In 1944, after the death of her husband and the Allied liberation, Ginzburg returned to Rome where she gained employment with the publishing house of Guilio Einaudi. While working as an editorial consultant, she continued to produce novels of her own, including *The Dry Heart* (1947), another tale of unhappy marriage, and *A Light for Fools* (1952), the story of a family's struggles to survive in an era of fascism.

Ginzburg remarried in 1950, this time to Gabriele Baldini, an English literature professor from the University of Rome. While married to him, she produced her humorous and well-known autobiographical work, *Family Sayings* (1963). After his death in 1969, she continued to write, producing essays, biographies, and translations, as well as fiction. She was elected to the Italian Parliament in 1983 and later published more works including *The City and the House* (1984) and *True Justice* (1990). Ginzburg died of cancer on October 7, 1991, leaving behind works that show in vivid detail the social implications of fascism and the history and culture of her world.

A Work about Natalia Ginzburg

Jeannet, Angela M., and Giuliana Sanguinetti Katz, eds. *Natalia Ginzburg: A Voice of the Twentieth Century*. Toronto: University of Toronto Press, 2000.

Giraudoux, Jean (1882–1944) *playwright*

Hippolyte-Jean Giraudoux was born in France in the village of Bellac. He was educated at the École Normale Supérieure. As a child and young man, he traveled extensively to Germany, Italy, the Balkans, Canada, and finally to the United States, where he spent a year as an instructor at Harvard. He returned to France to serve in World War I; he was wounded twice and became the first writer to be awarded the Légion d'honneur.

Giraudoux began his literary career as a novelist, with *Suzanne et le Pacifique* (1921), and he wrote several other works of fiction. He also wrote literary studies such as *Racine* (1930) and political works, including *Full Powers* (1939). But he gained recognition for his stage plays, 15 in all, most of which were initially staged in France by actor-director Louis Jouvet.

Like the great 17th-century French dramatist Racine, whom he deeply admired, Giraudoux often chose classical themes. He titled one of his plays *Amphitryon 38* (1929; translated 1938) in acknowledgement of the 37 versions of the story (about a man whose wife gives birth to twins, of whom one has been fathered not by Amphitryon but by the sky god Zeus) that preceded his own. *Judith* (1931) revisits the biblical story of Judith's outwitting of Holofernes. But unlike Racine, who grandly presents his characters as consumed by fatal passions, Giraudoux treats his characters informally and ironically. He believed that he was living in an age when grandness could not be appreciated, and he adjusted his art accordingly.

Giraudoux's last play, *The Madwoman of Chaillot* (1946; translated 1949), was completed in 1943 but produced and published posthumously. Written during the German occupation of France, it tells an inspirational story of a group of greedy prospectors whose search for oil threatens to destroy a small town and of the "madwoman" who thwarts their plans.

Giraudoux's work is rich in allegory and fantasy and has strong political and psychological undertones. His playful anachronisms and his wit helped release the inhibitions that REALISM had placed on French theater.

Other Works by Jean Giraudoux

Choice of the Elect. Translated by Henry Bosworth Russell. Evanston, Ill.: Northwestern University Press, 2002.

The Five Temptations of La Fontaine. Translated by Richard Howard. New York: Turtle Point Press, 2002.

Lying Woman: A Novel. Translated by Richard Howard. New York: Winter House, 1972.

Plays. Translated by Roger Gellert. London: Methuen, 1967.

Three Plays. Translated by Phyllis La Farge with Peter H. Judd. New York: Hill and Wang, 1964.

Tiger at the Gates [La Guerre de Troie n'aura pas lieu]. Translated by Christopher Fry. London: Methuen, 1983.

Works about Jean Giraudoux

Body, Jacques. *Jean Giraudoux: The Legend and the Secret.* Translated by James Norwood. Madison, N.J.: Fairleigh Dickinson University Press, 1991.

Korzeniowska, Victoria B. *The Heroine as Social Redeemer in the Plays of Jean Giraudoux.* New York: Peter Long, 1991.

Nagel, Susan. *The Influence of the Novels of Jean Giraudoux on the Hispanic Vanguard Novels of the 1920s–1930s.* Lewisburg, Pa.: Bucknell University Press, 1991.

Goethe, Johann Wolfgang von

(1749–1842) *poet, novelist, playwright, essayist*

Johann Wolfgang von Goethe was born in Frankfurt, Germany, to Johann Caspar Goethe, an attorney, and Katherine Elizabeth Goethe, a daughter of Frankfurt's mayor. Goethe's early interest in literature was wholeheartedly encouraged by his mother, an extremely well-educated woman. His childhood was marked by academic brilliance, as well as constant conflict with authority figures in school. Emotionally, Goethe's adolescence was shaped by several unsuccessful love affairs, which greatly contributed to his development as a writer.

At age 16, Goethe enrolled in Leipzig University to study law. During an interruption of his education due to illness, he studied drawing. He transferred to the University of Strasbourg where, in 1771, he obtained a degree in law. Between 1771 and 1774, he practiced law in Frankfurt and Wetzlar, until he was hired by Duke Karl August of Weimar. During his career as an administrator at the Weimar court, Goethe acted as the duke's councilman, a member of the war commission, and director of roads and services, and he directed the financial affairs of the court. A true member of the Enlightenment—the 18th-century movement of confidence in the capacities of human reason—Goethe dedicated his spare time to scientific research, mostly in anatomy. Between 1791 and 1817, Goethe acted as the director of court theaters. He also became an expert on mining, and under his influence and directorship, Jena University enjoyed the status as one of the most prominent and prestigious academic institutions in Europe, particularly in history and philosophy.

Critical Analysis

Goethe's first major work, *The Sorrows of Young Werther,* appeared in 1774. The novel delineates Werther's hopeless love for Lotte Buff, the wife of his close friend. Driven to self-alienation and psychological breakdown, no longer able to live without his beloved, Werther commits suicide. Werther expresses his misery in terms that resonated widely, especially with young readers: "My creative powers have been reduced to a senseless indolence. I cannot be idle, yet I cannot seem to do anything either. When we are robbed of ourselves, we are robbed of everything." Goethe explained his motivation for writing the novel in terms of his heightened spiritual and emotional awareness: "I tried to release myself from all alien emotions, to look kindly upon what was going on around me and let all living things, beginning with man himself, affect me as deeply as possible, each in its own way." The emotions and local color are placed in the foreground of his work. *The Sorrows of Young Werther* is considered to among the most influential texts of German ROMANTICISM.

In Goethe's second major novel, *Wilhelm Meister's Apprenticeship* (1795–96), Goethe continues to explore themes of love and alienation. However, the novel presents a more optimistic outlook on life. Like Werther, Wilhelm suffers a tragic blow after an unsuccessful courtship. Unlike Werther, however, Wilhelm begins to seek out actively other values

in life. He dedicates himself to work and becomes a playwright and an actor. In the end, Wilhelm is spiritually satisfied with his newfound outlet for passion. The novel remains thematically consistent with the romantic school; however, critics have noted the emergence of the conservative side of Goethe's thinking. Unlike many of his contemporaries, Goethe was not impressed by the uprising and violence of the French Revolution. He supported liberty and progress but also maintained that the aristocracy had an important role in society. Many younger readers began to criticize Goethe for what they saw as subservience to the upper classes.

The first part of Goethe's dramatic masterpiece, *Faust,* appeared in 1808. This drama became his passion and he worked on it for more than 30 years. Based on the play by the English Renaissance dramatist Christopher Marlowe, it tells a chilling story of a man who sells his soul for knowledge. Faust makes a contract with Mephistopheles to die as soon as his thirst for knowledge is satisfied. Faust is driven to despair when Margaret, an innocent woman, is condemned to death for giving birth to Faust's illegitimate child. He finally realizes that his lust for knowledge has led to tragic mistakes.

The second part of *Faust* appeared in 1838. Faust marries the beautiful Helen of Troy and creates a happy community of scholars. The bliss of his good deeds brings satisfaction in old age, and Mephistopheles is about to demand satisfaction. But Faust's changed attitudes and good heart are rewarded, as angels descend from the sky in the final scene of the play and take Faust to heaven. The play brought Goethe international success and had a profound influence on modern drama.

During his illustrious career, Goethe produced, in addition, a number of important poetical works. He also provided literary guidance to his close friend FRIEDRICH SCHILLER and produced several of his plays. After his death, he was buried next to Schiller in Weimar.

Although it is difficult to measure the influence of Johann Wolfgang von Goethe, he is certainly among the giants of world literature. His novels, poems, and plays are still widely read and studied. He is a dominant figure of German Romanticism.

Other Works by Johann Wolfgang von Goethe

Italian Journey. Translated by Elizabeth Mayer. New York: Penguin, 1992.

The Sorrows of Young Werther and Selected Writings. Translated by Catherine Hutter. New York: New American Library, 1987.

Theory of Colors. Cambridge, Mass.: MIT Press, 1970.

Vaget, Hans R., ed. *Erotic Poems.* Translated by David Luke. New York: Oxford University Press, 1999.

Works about Johann Wolfgang von Goethe

Eckermann, Johann. *Conversations of Goethe.* Translated by John Oxenford. New York: Da Capo Press, 1998.

Wagner, Irmgard. *Goethe.* Boston: Twayne, 1999.

Williams, John. *The Life of Goethe: A Critical Biography.* Malden, Mass.: Blackwell Publishers, 2001.

Gogol, Nikolay (1808–1852) *novelist, short story writer, dramatist*

Nikolay Vasilyevich Gogol was born in Sorochinez, Ukraine, into a family of minor aristocrats. He was a mediocre student in school and avoided other people. After graduation, he moved to St. Petersburg in search of a position in the civil service. More interested in writing than in a government career, Gogol worked as a minor official for only a brief period of time, quitting his job for a higher-paying position as a history professor at the St. Petersburg University.

In 1831, Gogol published his first collection of short stories, *Evenings on a Farm Near Dikanka.* Based on Ukrainian folk tales, the stories combine elements of the supernatural, humor, and romance. Gogol's first collection was greeted with acclaim from both critics and readers. Fired from his university position for incompetence, Gogol continued his literary work. In *Mirgorod* (1835), he produced more short stories that were based on Ukrainian folklore and history. It was with this

collection that Gogol established himself as the father of Russian REALISM. In his famous story "The Overcoat," he explores the psychology of a clerk who must make enormous sacrifices to buy a new overcoat. It was the first work of Russian literature to bring sympathetic attention to the plight of a social misfit, who would previously have been seen only as a comic character.

In 1836, Gogol presented his first comic play, *The Inspector General,* to an enormous audience that included the czar of Russia. In the play, the officials of a small town expect an important visit from a governor. They mistake Hlestakov, a petty government official en route to his father's estate, for the inspector general. The play, with its hilarious satire on provincial officials, was a huge success in St. Petersburg, but certain censors in the government viewed it as politically dangerous. Afraid of losing his freedom, Gogol left Russia for Europe to continue his work away from government oversight.

Gogol traveled throughout Europe, staying for extended periods in Germany, Switzerland, France, and Italy. While in Paris, he lost one of his closest friends to a cholera epidemic. This tragic event prompted Gogol's return to Russia in 1839. Contrary to his expectations, Russia celebrated his return, and a version of *The Inspector General* was produced in Moscow to mark the occasion. Facing serious health problems, Gogol returned to Europe, became a complete recluse, and turned to studying the sacred texts of the Russian Orthodox Church. His newly found religious sentiments, which some contemporaries described as zeal, eventually surfaced in his work.

Critical Analysis

In 1842, Gogol published the first volume of his masterpiece, *Dead Souls.* Even before publication, it attracted negative attention from the censors, and it came into print only after the personal intervention of the czar. The novel centers on a small-time provincial bureaucrat named Chichikov and satirizes both middle-class greed and the institution of serfdom in Russia. Gogol's critique of serfdom, which essentially consigned peasants to a form of slavery, skillfully portrays the moral decay of Russian society. In hope of advancing his social position and his opportunities for a profitable marriage, Chichikov falsifies his economic status by purchasing "dead souls"—the names of dead serfs. In the second volume, Gogol apparently attempted to incorporate strong elements of spirituality and religion; however, spiritually and psychologically troubled, he destroyed the manuscript. In 1848, he departed on a pilgrimage to Jerusalem, but the journey proved quite unsuccessful in terms of providing the religious consolation Gogol was seeking.

In many respects, Gogol's life translated into his works of fiction. Characters are often mentally distraught, almost to the point of grotesquerie, centering their lives on seemingly insignificant, worldly goals. By the same token, Gogol's critique of Russian society extends far beyond social issues and often illuminates the individual's struggle for spiritual fulfillment.

The last years of Gogol's life were marked by deep physical and psychological suffering. As many experts concur today, Gogol suffered from acute forms of depression and anxiety. Gogol spent the last three days of his life praying. He died in 1852, reportedly from a stroke.

In Russia, Gogol is viewed as one of the major figures of the literary canon. His prose shows a deep understanding and sensitivity, not only to the social order but also to individual psychological dimensions.

Other Works by Nikolay Gogol

Arabesques. Translated by Alexander Tulloch. Ann Arbor, Mich.: Ardis, 1982.
The Collected Tales of Nikolai Gogol. Translated by Richard Pevear and Larissa Volokhonsky. New York: Pantheon, 1998.
Gogol: Three Plays. Translated by Stephen Mulrine. London: Methuen, 2000.

Works about Nikolay Gogol

Fanger, Donald. *Creation of Nikolai Gogol.* Cambridge, Mass.: Harvard University Press, 1982.

Nabokov, Vladimir. *Nikolai Gogol.* New York: W. W. Norton, 1961.
Stilman, Leon. *Gogol.* New York: Columbia University Press, 1990.

Gombrowicz, Witold (1904–1969)
novelist, playwright

Witold Gombrowicz was born on his family's estate in Maolsczyce and then moved to Warsaw, Poland. As a boy, he was introverted and sickly. He felt alienated by the nationalist sentiment of the time and ultimately rejected orthodox culture in favor of the company of peasants, such as maids and stablehands.

Attempting to follow a career that would be accepted by his family, Gombrowicz studied law at the University of Warsaw but began, in secret, to write short stories, which were later published in the collection *Memoirs of a Time of Immaturity* (1933). Although his writing was attacked by critics for its rejection of contemporary viewpoints, it was moderately successful with readers who shared his discontent. Gombrowicz eventually gave up law and began writing full time. In 1938, he published his first play, *Yvonne, the Princess of Burgundy,* and followed it with his first novel, *Ferdydurke* (1938), which is a satirical comment on the absurdities of Polish society in the 1930s with elements of mystery and eroticism.

Gombrowicz was commissioned in 1939 to write a series of articles about Argentina. Two days after he arrived in Buenos Aires, World War II began and Poland was invaded. He stayed in Buenos Aires, working for several small newspapers. There, he published his second play *The Marriage* (1947) and the novel *Trans-Atlantic* (1953).

During a brief respite from censorship in 1956, several of his works were reprinted in Poland, but Gombrowicz did not return to his homeland. His third novel, *Pornografia* (1960), an account of a relationship between two teenagers in rural Poland as viewed by fascinated old men, was followed in 1963 by his receipt of a Ford Foundation Fellowship, which allowed him to leave Argentina. He settled in Berlin, where he wrote his fourth novel, *Cosmos* (1964), an absurdist mystery that has been compared to FRANZ KAFKA's *The Castle,* as well as his final play, *Operetta* (1966), before dying of heart failure in Vence, France.

Gombrowicz's popularity was largely posthumous. His books had been banned, once again, in Poland in the 1960s. After his death, the ban was partially lifted, but Gombrowicz specified in his will that his works were not to be published in Poland unless they were reprinted in their entirety. 1As a result, an underground movement was formed to smuggle foreign editions of his work into Poland. His plays were performed in Polish theaters, but their texts could not be bought in official stores. This contributed to a rise in Gombrowicz's popularity. It was not until 1988, after the collapse of Communist Party rule, that the first full edition of his books was published in Poland.

Other Works by Witold Gombrowicz
Cosmos and Pornografia: Two Novels. Translated by Eric Mosbacher and Alastair Hamilton. New York: Grove Press, 1994.
Diary. Translated by Lillian Vallee. Evanston, Ill.: Northwestern University Press, 1988.
Ferdydurke. Translated by Danuta Borchardt, with a foreword by Susan Sontag. New Haven, Conn.: Yale University Press, 2000.

Works about Witold Gombrowicz
Milosz, Czeslaw. *Who Is Gombrowicz?* New York: Penguin, 1986.
Thompson, Ewa M. *Witold Gombrowicz.* Boston: Twayne, 1979.

Gomringer, Eugen (1925–) *poet*
Born in Cachuela Esperanza, Bolivia, Eugen Gomringer was raised in Switzerland by his grandparents. He studied art history and economics at colleges in Bern and Rome and later worked as a graphic designer. In 1952, Gomringer cofounded the magazine *Spirale.* From 1954 to 1958, he worked as a secretary for Max Bill, the director of the Academy of Art in Ulm, Germany. Since the 1960s, Gomringer has worked as a business manager for the Schweizer Werkbund in Zurich, an artistic adviser for the Rosenthal concern, and as a professor of aesthetic theory at the Art Academy in Düsseldorf.

Gomringer published his first poems in *Spirale* in 1953. His verse helped initiate the concrete movement in poetry. These poems create a concrete reality by using words as building blocks to form three-dimensional semantic, phonetic, and visual explorations. Conventional syntax, description, and metaphor are ignored. The poet Jerome Rothenberg explained that concrete poetry is "a question of making the words cohere in a given space, the poem's force or strength related to the weight & value of the words within it, the way they pull & act on each other." Gomringer's "schweigen" ("Silence") is his most famous concrete poem. The word *schweigen* is printed 14 times to form a rectangle, with the empty space in the middle representing silence.

In addition to poetry collections, Gomringer wrote theoretical tracts explaining his style and calling for a simple, universal language devoid of irrationality. His influence was strong in the 1950s and 1960s, inspiring a range of linguistic experiments. The concrete poetry movement waned in 1972, however, as critics found it too simplistic. Gomringer then gave up poetry to write about art and artists.

Other Works by Eugen Gomringer
The Book of Hours and Constellations. Translated by Jerome Rothenberg. New York: Something Else Press, 1968.
Vera Röhm, with Stephen Bann. London: Reaktion Books, 2006.

Gonçalves Dias, Antônio (1823–1864)
poet, dramatist
Born in 1823, Antônio Gonçalves Dias was the most important romantic poet to write in the Brazilian

literary tradition. He was educated in Portugal at the University of Coimbra but felt strong ties to Brazil. He celebrates Brazil in his poetry collections, such as *Primeiros cantos* (1846) and *Ultimos cantos* (1851), focusing on themes of nature. Specifically, Dias wrote extensively about nativist issues. His glorification of indigenous peoples places him among the many writers of the Indianist movement (*see* INDI-ANISM) of the 19th century in Brazil, along with the novelist JOSÉ DE ALENCAR. Gonçalves Dias's work *Song of Exile* (1843), with its nostalgic first line, "My land has palm trees, where the nightingale sings," is Brazil's best known poem. He is often thought of as Brazil's national poet, although he published only three collections of poetry. He was killed in a shipwreck while returning to Brazil from Portugal.

Works about Antônio Gonçalves Dias

Haberly, David. *Three Sad Races: Racial Identity and National Consciousness in Brazilian Literature.* New York: Cambridge University Press, 1983.

Treece, David. *Exiles, Allies and Rebels: Brazil's Indianist Movement, Indigenist Politics, and the Imperial Nation-State.* Westport, Conn.: Greenwood Press, 2000.

Goncharov, Ivan (1812–1891) *novelist*

Ivan Aleksandrovich Goncharov was born in Simbirsk, Russia. His father, a wealthy grain merchant, died when Goncharov was only seven. Young Ivan was raised by his godfather, Nikolay Tregubov. An average student, Goncharov studied business at the University of Moscow. After he graduated in 1834, he worked in the civil service for nearly 30 years.

In 1847, Goncharov published his first novel, *An Ordinary Story,* which focuses on the conflict between Russian nobility and the newly emergent merchant class. The novel examines the moral implications of income and how it affected social position of the two classes.

Between 1852 and 1855, Goncharov traveled around the world as a personal secretary for Admiral Putyatin. He published his account of the journey as *Frigate Pallada* (1858). His observations about the nations he visited, which included England, parts of Africa, and Japan, are often unflattering, and he expresses his sense of Russian superiority and his distrust of social reform.

In 1859 Goncharov published his most famous novel, *Oblomov,* a masterpiece of Russian REALISM. In the novel, Goncharov satirizes the character of Oblomov, a young aristocrat who is indecisive and apathetic. Goncharov presents the aristocracy as an obsolete class that no longer contributes to the welfare of the state. The novel was so successful that it introduced a new word into the Russian language: *oblomovshina,* meaning "indecision and inertia."

Goncharov's talent was readily acknowledged in Russia by such personages as FYODOR DOSTOYEVSKY. Goncharov, however, was a quarrelsome figure. He accused IVAN TURGENEV and GUSTAVE FLAUBERT of plagiarizing his ideas for their own novels. Goncharov never married. He published his last novel, *The Precipice,* in 1869. The work tells of a sentimental love affair between three men and a mysterious woman. Critical response to the novel was devastating, and Goncharov never published another. He spent the rest of his life virtually alone, writing short stories and essays.

Goncharov died in St. Petersburg in 1891. Through his works, Goncharov depicted the emergent class conflict between aristocracy and the rising middle class. He is mostly remembered for his contribution to realism and his mastery of social satire.

Another Work by Ivan Goncharov

An Ordinary Story: Including the Stage Adaptation of the Novel. Translated by Marjorie L. Hoover. New York: Ardis Publishers, 1994.

Works about Ivan Goncharov

Diment, Galya. *The Autobiographical Novel of Co-Consciousness: Goncharov, Woolf, and Joyce.* Gainesville: University of Florida Press, 1994.

Diment, Galya, ed. *Goncharov's Oblomov: A Critical Companion.* Evanston, Ill.: Northwestern University Press, 1998.

Ehre, Milton. *Oblomov and His Creator: The Life and Art of Ivan Goncharov*. Princeton, N.J.: Princeton University Press, 1974.

Goncourt, Edmond (1822–1896) and Jules (1830–1870) *novelists*

The Goncourt brothers, Edmond and Jules, are most notable for their long history of collaboration as a team of novelists writing in the tradition of naturalism. Edmond was born in Nancy, France, and Jules in Paris eight years later. Close as children, they retained their special bond throughout their lives.

In 1849, "les deux Goncourts," as they would come to be known, began to travel throughout France as artists, painting watercolor sketches and ultimately keeping detailed notes of their travels in a journal. This journal, published as *Journal des Goncourts* (nine volumes, 1887–96; translation of selections by Lewis Galantière, 1937), which they began together in 1851, contains 40 years of detailed accounts of French social and literary life.

The brothers also became successful as art critics and art historians. After a failed attempt at writing for the theater, they began to collaborate on a series of novels, including *Sœur Philomène* (1861), *Renée Mauperin* (1864; translated 1887), *Germinie Lacerteux* (1864), and *Mme. Gervaisais* (1869), all of which became well known as representations of the naturalist school. Their elaborate and often convoluted style as well as their selection of subjects based on their sensational value anticipated naturalist ideas.

After Jules died, Edmond continued to write, publishing three more novels, among them *La fille Élisa* (1877; translated 1959), a tragic story of a girl who becomes a prostitute. As a condition of his will, Edmond provided funding for the establishment of the Académie Goncourt to award and encourage excellence in fiction. The Prix Goncourt for literature is awarded annually to an outstanding author writing in French.

Other Works by Edmond and Jules Goncourt
Pages from the Goncourt Journal. Translated by Robert Baldick. New York: Penguin USA, 1984.
Paris and the Arts, 1851–1896; from the Goncourt Journal. Translated by George J. Becker and Edith Philips. Ithaca, N.Y.: Cornell University Press, 1971.
Paris Under Siege, 1870–1871; from the Goncourt Journal. Translated by George J. Becker. Ithaca, N.Y.: Cornell University Press, 1969.

Works about Edmond and Jules Goncourt
Brookner, Anita. *The Genius of the Future: Diderot, Stendhal, Baudelaire, Zola, the Brothers Goncourt, Huysmans: Essays in French Art Criticism*. Ithaca, N.Y.: Cornell University Press, 1988.
Heil, Elissa. *The Conflicting Discourses of the Drawing-Room: Anthony Trollope and Edmond and Jules de Goncourt*. New York: Peter Lang, 1997.

Goodison, Lorna (1947–) *poet, short story writer, professor, painter, illustrator*

Lorna Goodison was born in Kingston, Jamaica, to Vivian Goodison, a Jamaica Telephone Company technician, and Dorice Goodison, a dressmaker. She was educated at St. Hugh's High School for girls and read the major English writers at an early age. V. S. NAIPAUL's *Miguel Street,* which she read as a teenager, sparked Goodison's appetite for Caribbean literature. In an interview with Kwame Dawes, Goodison said she started writing to read her own writing because so many of the characters she had been reading about differed from those of her experiences.

Goodison wrote while attending the Jamaica School of Art and the Art Students League of New York during her early 20s, but she did not begin to write seriously until the 1970s. Many of her poems juxtapose standard English and Jamaican dialect, and a variety of musical traditions, including rhythm and blues and reggae, influence her writing style. "For Don Drummond," a notable poem in Goodison's first collection, *Tamarind Season: Poems* (1980), reproduces the sound of

Drummond's voice and trombone to mourn the influential Jamaican musician's death.

The poetry collections *I Am Becoming My Mother* (1986) and *Heartease* (1988) explore women's experiences, and *To Us, All Flowers Are Roses: Poems* (1995) focuses on common Jamaican experiences. Goodison's newest collections of poetry include *Guinea Woman* (2000), *Travelling Mercies* (2001), *Controlling the Silver* (2005), and *Goldengrove* (2006). In 2005, Goodison published a collection of short stories, *Fool-Fool Rose Is Leaving Labour-in-Vain Savannah.* The poet Andrew Salkey commented in the journal *World Literature Today,* "The evocative power of Lorna Goodison's poetry derives its urgency and appeal from the heart-and-mind concerns she has for language, history, racial identity, and gender."

Works about Lorna Goodison

Dawes, Kwame, ed. *Talk Yuh Talk: Interviews with Anglophone Caribbean Poets.* Charlottesville: University Press of Virginia, 2001.
Kuwabong, D. "The Mother as Archetype of Self: A Poetics of Matrilineage in the Poetry of Claire Harris and Lorna Goodison." *Ariel* 30, no. 1 (1999): 105–129.

Gordimer, Nadine (1923–   ) *novelist, short story writer, essayist*

Nadine Gordimer published her first short story when she was 13. Since that first publication in 1937, she has published eight collections of short stories and more than a dozen novels. She has also written extensively on political, literary, and cultural issues. She is one of Africa's, and the world's, premier literary talents.

Gordimer was born in a small mining town in South Africa outside of Johannesburg. Her father, Isidore, a Jew, was a jeweler from Lithuania, and her mother, Nan Myers, helped him to become a shopkeeper in the conservative suburban town where Nadine was raised. Her first novel, *The Lying Days* (1953), evaluates the growth and development of a young woman as she confronts the conformity of a comfortable, middle-class existence.

While still a young girl, Gordimer had an experience that was to forever change her life. As she related the incident to Bill Moyers in a 1992 videotaped interview entitled "On Being a Liberal White South African," Gordimer's mother had removed the 11-year-old Gordimer from school "on the pretext of a heart ailment." She was to have little contact with other children until she was 16. Her enforced isolation led to a life filled with reading, writing, and observing. One of the novels she read during this period was Upton Sinclair's *The Jungle,* which recounts the horrible living conditions of workers in Chicago's meat-packing plants in the early 20th century. In the Bill Moyers interview, Gordimer said that reading this book changed her life because she saw, clearly, that literature could change the world, that it could open people's eyes to inequity and foster change.

Critical Analysis

Many of Gordimer's stories and novels examine the status and responsibilities of white, liberal intellectuals in both South Africa and abroad. Novels such as *The Late Bourgeois World* (1966), *A Guest of Honor* (1970), and *Burger's Daughter* (1979) examine the difference between engaging with the world and withdrawing from it. For example, the plot of *Burger's Daughter* concerns the reflections of a young woman whose father had led a life of active political resistance to the inequities of South African culture. His daughter struggles with his legacy and her own wavering commitment to confrontation. The novel raises an issue that is very important in Gordimer's work: Can white South Africans be a part of the world that will come when majority rule becomes a reality? Will "liberalism" alone create a space for whites in the new South Africa? Rosa Burger, the daughter of the title, seems to find her only real fulfillment outside of South Africa and outside of politics. The story that unfolds on her return to South Africa, however, shows that an embrace of the political is necessary, even if the end result is tragic.

Gordimer has been quoted by critic Stephen Clingman, in *The Novels of Nadine Gordimer* (1986), as saying, "If you want to read the facts of the retreat from Moscow in 1812, you may read a history book; if you want to know what war is like and how people of a certain time and background dealt with it as their personal situation, you must read *War and Peace.*" In this and other statements, Gordimer has insisted that the novelist's job is to convey human truth as regards historical events. As Clingman explains, she makes a case for the value of literature in a world of facts and incidents: "This . . . is the primary material that a novel offers: not so much an historical world, but a certain *consciousness* of that world." Gordimer's novels attempt to present complete worlds in which characters are faced with conflicts of class, race, and gender, all of which exist within the dynamics of personal relationships. In other words, she presents the consciousness of a culture by dealing with both the larger political and "smaller" interpersonal relationships that make up her characters' lives. She has, throughout her career, incorporated the historical reality of the South African situation into her work. She has also written many essays that examine the relationship between writers and their worlds, such as those collected in *The Essential Gesture: Writing, Politics, and Places* (1988). Her essays examine many of the ideological implications of what it means to be a writer living in a politically charged environment.

Her first published novel, *The Lying Days* (1953), focuses on the small Jewish world of the Aaron family and its relationship to the various Afrikaners around it. The young woman at the center of the tale, Helen Shaw, views the different cultures (Afrikaner, or Dutch settler, Jewish, and others) with which she interacts as exotic and distinct. The story of this early work also deals with those Jews who sold goods to the black mineworkers in the area outside of Johannesburg.

Her next novel, *A World of Strangers* (1958), was more pointedly political. It deals with the developing anti-apartheid forces of the African National Congress (ANC) in their resistance to the apartheid policies of the increasingly severe Nationalist government. Johannesburg in the mid-1950s was a hotbed of political activity, and writers, such as LEWIS NKOSI and others, were agitating in magazines, such as *Drum,* about active resistance to apartheid. Gordimer's novel details the connection between writing and political engagement, and this early work's insistence on that connection— between the personal and the political—is at the heart of most of her work.

But Gordimer's works are not only political treatises. Her writing is lyrical, and she uses detail to great effect. For example, in *A Sport of Nature* (1987), which tells the story of a white woman who becomes completely immersed in black revolutionary politics, she describes a woman walking through an embassy: "through ceremonial purplish corridors she walked, past buried bars outlined like burning eyelids with neon, reception rooms named for African political heroes holding a silent assembly of stacked gilt chairs. . . ." The images this description evoke are of a "silent," or ineffective, government built on the foundations of "gilt," or pomp.

Her ability to combine rich description, sharply observed dialogue, knowledge of human nature, and political situations has made Gordimer one of the most respected novelists in the English-speaking world. In her own country, she has been consistently controversial in her ongoing literary analysis of the failure of the politics of liberalism, as South Africa has attempted to deal with its multiracial reality. Her international reputation has led to many awards, including Britain's prestigious Booker Prize (for her novel *The Conservationist*) in 1974 and the Nobel Prize in 1991.

Other Works by Nadine Gordimer

Get a Life. New York: Penguin, 2006.
July's People. New York: Viking, 1981.
Jump and Other Stories. New York: Penguin USA, 1992.
Living in Hope and History: Notes from Our Century. New York: Farrar, Straus & Giroux, 2000.

My Son's Story. New York: Farrar, Straus & Giroux, 1990.

The Pick Up. New York: Penguin, 2002.

Writing and Being. Cambridge, Mass.: Harvard University Press, 1995.

Works about Nadine Gordimer

Clingman, Stephen. *The Novels of Nadine Gordimer: History from the Inside.* Amherst: University of Massachusetts Press, 1992 (1986).

Cooke, John. *The Novels of Nadine Gordimer: Private Lives/Public Landscapes.* Baton Rouge: Louisiana State University Press, 1985.

Kamanga, Brighton J. Uledi. *Nadine Gordimer's Fiction and the Irony of Apartheid.* Lawrenceville, N.J.: Africa World Press, 2002.

Newman, Judie, ed. *Nadine Gordimer's Berger's Daughter: A Casebook (Casebooks in Criticism).* New York: Oxford University Press, 2003.

Roberts, Ronald Suresh. *No Cold Kitchen: A Biography of Nadine Gordimer.* Johannesburg, South Africa: STE Publishers, 2005.

Smith, Rowland, ed. *Critical Essays on Nadine Gordimer.* Boston: G. K. Hall, 1990.

Gorenko, Anna Andreyevna

See AKHMATOVA, ANNA.

Gorky, Maxim (Aleksei Maksimovich Peshkov) (1868–1936) *novelist, playwright, short story writer*

Maxim Gorky was born in Nizhnii Novgorod, Russia, to an extremely poor family. His father, a boatyard carpenter, died of cholera when Gorky was only three years old. Gorky's mother died of tuberculosis in 1879. At eight, Gorky began a series of menial jobs in terrible conditions, working as an icon painter, a baker, a watchman, a clerk, and a cabin boy on a Volga steamer—where luckily a kind cook taught him to read. Reading soon took up all his spare time. The pseudonym *Gorky* (Russian for "bitter"), with which he signed his first published short story, "Makar Chudra," in 1892, seems to reflect the pain of his childhood.

The death of his grandmother had a devastating effect on Gorky, and at 21, he attempted suicide. When he recovered from the gunshot wound, he took up wandering, in a period of two years walking all the way to the southern Caucasus and back again to his native city, associating with tramps, prostitutes, and thieves, who became the subjects of his fiction.

At 24, Gorky settled into a job as a reporter for a provincial newspaper and began to publish his stories, which became extremely popular. He was arrested a number of times in this period for his involvement in radical politics. His politics surface in his work as SOCIALIST REALISM.

Gorky admired and was influenced by LEO TOLSTOY and ANTON CHEKHOV. Although Tolstoy and Chekhov focused their works on the upper and middle classes, Gorky concentrated almost exclusively on depicting the social injustices faced by the millions of Russia's workers and peasants. Chekhov also admired Gorky and introduced him to colleagues at the Moscow Art Theater, who persuaded Gorky to write a play for them. Two plays, *The Smug Citizen* and *The Lower Depths,* were produced by the Moscow Art Theater in 1902. Both were very successful with the public, and both brought Gorky negative attention from the czarist authorities. An outcry against inhumanity, *The Lower Depths* is based on outcasts Gorky had met on his travels.

In 1905, Gorky was imprisoned for his involvement in the events of Bloody Sunday (a peaceful demonstration of workers asking the czar for democratic reforms, which ended with dozens dead from gunfire from government troops). He wrote one of his most famous plays, *Children of the Sun*—a satirical look at the ineffective middle classes—while imprisoned. After his release, Gorky traveled to the United States and tried to raise support for the Marxist cause. He lived in exile in Italy until 1913, when he was granted an amnesty by the government. While in Italy, Gorky was visited by Lenin and other radical revolutionaries.

Gorky's *My Childhood* (1913–14) is considered one of the best autobiographical works of Russian literature. In it, Gorky juxtaposes his grandfather's brutality against his grandmother's tender love, skillfully creating individual portraits and demonstrating his great descriptive power. *My Childhood* was followed by two other autobiographical volumes, *In the World* (1915–16) and *My Universities* (1923).

After the Russian Revolution, Gorky often found himself as odds with the hard-line Bolsheviks. Gorky maintained an oscillating position on the Bolshevik policy: He was a spokesman for the Soviet view of art and literature and also worked to preserve Russia's cultural heritage. In 1922, he went back to Italy to live for several years but returned to Russia in 1928 in response to the appeals of his public. There is a question as to whether his death eight years later was from the tuberculosis that had plagued him since his youth or whether Stalin may have been behind it. His funeral in Red Square was a state event.

Gorky achieved tremendous respect and recognition during his lifetime. He not only described social injustice but also acted against it. He did not simply contribute to socialist realism but also left a literary legacy to support it.

Other Works by Maxim Gorky

The Lower Depths and Other Plays. Translated by Alexander Bakshy. New Haven, Conn.: Yale University Press, 1973.

Untimely Thoughts: Essays on Revolution, Culture and the Bolsheviks, 1917–1918. New Haven, Conn.: Yale University Press, 1995.

Yarmolinsky, Avram, and Baroness Moura Budberg, eds. *The Collected Short Stories of Maxim Gorky.* Secaucus, N.J.: Citadel Press, 1988.

Works about Maxim Gorky

Levin, Dan. *Stormy Petrel: The Life and Work of Maxim Gorky.* New York: Schocken Books, 1986.

Yedlin, Tova. *Maxim Gorky: A Political Biography.* New York: Praeger, 1999.

Graham, Peter

See ABRAHAMS, PETER HENRY.

Grass, Günter (1927–) *novelist, poet, playwright*

Günter Grass was born in Danzig, Germany (now Gdansk, Poland). His father, a descendant of German Protestants, owned a grocery store, and his mother was of Slavic origin. Grass entered Conradinum High School in 1937 but was never able to finish his education because of the outbreak of World War II. When the Nazis came to power, Grass joined the Hitler Youth Movement. At 16, he was drafted into the German military. After being wounded, he was interned by the U.S. forces stationed in Bavaria. The reeducation program provided by the U.S. Army had a profound influence on Grass: He was taken on a tour of a Nazi concentration camp at Dachau, near Munich, where he witnessed the horrors of the Holocaust that had been inflicted by the Nazi regime. This experience would be reflected later in Grass's fiction.

After his release, Grass worked as a stonemason, a farmworker, and a potash miner. In 1948, he enrolled in the Düsseldorf Academy of the Arts to study sculpture. He worked as a sculptor for several years, but his interests shifted, and he began to write poetry. In 1955, he officially entered the literary world by winning the third prize in poetry competition sponsored by a German radio station. The prize included the right to attend the meetings of GRUPPE 47, Germany's most important literary circle at the time. Grass then lived in Spain and Paris, where he developed a friendship with PAUL CELAN. He published a volume of poems in 1956, followed by several plays and another book of verse, and he had an exhibition of his art works. His work was well known to a small group of connoisseurs.

With *Die Blechtrommel* (*The Tin Drum*, 1959), the first book of what has came to be known as the Danzig trilogy, Grass was suddenly famous. The novel instantly made Grass into one of the most prominent figures of the German and international literary scenes. The second book of the trilogy, *Katz und Maus* (*Cat and Mouse*), appeared in 1961, and the third, *Hundejahre* (*Dog Years*), in 1963. All the novels in the trilogy achieved critical and popular success. Between 1960 and 1965, Grass received the prestigious Berlin Critics' Prize and the Georg Büchner Prize and was elected into the German Academy of the Arts. In the 10 years following its publication, *The Tin Drum* was translated into more than 15 languages. The book caused offense too: It was publicly burned in Düsseldorf by an organization of religious youth. Grass faced more than 40 civil lawsuits—all eventually unsuccessful—against the Danzig trilogy. The charges ranged from blasphemy to obscenity. The books, however, remained major best-sellers in Germany and around the world.

In the mid-1960s, Grass spent less time writing as he used his acclaim and recognition to campaign for the Social Democratic Party of Germany. The party supported moderate reform, normalization of relations with East Germany, and easing of tensions with the Communist states. *Ortlich Betaubt* (*Local Anesthetic*) was published in 1969, but Grass did not produce another major novel until 1977, when *Das Butt* (*The Flounder*) appeared. It aroused more excitement than any of Grass's works since *The Tin Drum*. Grass's international fame was increased by the appearance of Volker Schlöndorff's film of *The Tin Drum*, which won the Academy Award for Best Foreign Picture in 1979, but, like the novel, it offended some people: The film was banned in Oklahoma, in a decision that was subsequently overturned by a higher court.

Die Rättin (*The Rat*, 1986) is perhaps even more ambitious than *The Flounder*, but Grass continues to be politically involved. In the late 1980s, he was among the few Germans in the political sphere to oppose the reunification of East and West Germany, claiming irreconcilable political, social, and economic differences. Grass also loudly campaigned against the neo-Nazi groups in Germany and actively supported the defense of SALMAN RUSHDIE when Rushdie's book *The Satanic Verses* made him the subject of a death threat.

In 2006, just before the release of his new autobiography, *Peeling the Onion*, Grass stunned the world with his admission that he had been a member of Germany's Nazi Waffen SS during World War II. As Nathan Thornburg of *Time* magazine notes, this was an extraordinary confession for Grass, given his lifelong obsession with the war: "[I]magine making that confession after a lifetime of establishing yourself as Germany's most ardent advocate of full disclosure and penance. There you are, having been jabbing a finger in the German body politic's chest for 60 years, accusing them of failing to own up to their collective responsibility for the war."

Critical Analysis

The Tin Drum presents an irreverent and colorful account of 20th-century German history through the eyes of a mental patient, Oskar Matzerath. A midget, Oskar refuses to grow as a protest against the cruelties of German people, and he communicates with other characters through his drum.

Cat and Mouse, a much shorter work, relates the story of Joachim Mahlke through the voice of Pilenz, a 32-year-old social worker. The story takes place between 1939 and 1944 and essentially recounts the relationship between the life of a self-conscious teenager (the mouse of the title is Mahlke's enormous Adam's apple) and the fearful historical events unfolding around him. Guilt, with its attendant psychological implications, is the predominant theme running throughout the novel.

Dog Years, a novel with similar thematic concerns, examines the crimes of the Nazis and their acceptance by the German society after World War II. The story is presented in terms of an ambiguous friendship between Amsel, a son of prosperous Jewish merchant who becomes a Protestant to escape persecution, and Walter Matern, the son of a Catholic miller. In the trilogy, Grass forced his readers to confront the truth about the Nazi past. By using blasphemous Christian imagery, grotesque sexuality, and ribald scatological humor, he made it impossible to subsume the unspeakable in a featureless tragic view.

Die Plebejer Proben den Aufstand (*The Plebeians Rehearse the Uprising*, 1966) is Grass's fifth play. It is set in Berlin in 1953 in BERTOLT BRECHT's theater. Brecht is directing a rehearsal of his adaptation of Shakespeare's *Coriolanus;* outside, workers are protesting unfair government labor practices. When the workers appeal to Brecht to help their cause, he lets them down by failing to respond: He chooses to perfect the artistic representation of revolution rather than involve himself in real life. The play is both an homage to and a critique of the artist Grass acknowledges as his master.

The Flounder is written on an epic scale, encompassing 4,000 years of European history, with an elaborate narrative technique that has room for poems, recipes, historical documents, autobiographical accounts of Grass's political campaigns and a version of the GRIMM brothers' "Tale of the Fisherman and His Wife."

The Rat is another massive work, this time looking toward the future, examining what hope there is for a world threatened by nuclear disaster and ecological devastation. There are two narrators: a rat who has already witnessed and survived, with her family, the nuclear winter that has obliterated humanity; and a human "I" who still hopes, against the evidence, that people can escape the final catastrophe. The characters, of whom there are many, include some familiar to Grass's readers, among them Oskar Matzerath, 30 years older, and the talking flounder of *The Flounder.*

Günter Grass has received innumerable awards for his contribution to world literature from governments and organizations in Germany, the United States, the United Kingdom, Italy, France, and Russia, including the Nobel Prize in literature in 1999. He is recognized today as perhaps the most important German writer of the second half of the 20th century. His works have been translated into more than 20 languages and still enjoy international status as best sellers. Grass continues his productive career as a writer and a public figure. As the American novelist John Irving said in a 1982 review of *Headbirths, or the Germans Are Dying Out,* "You can't be called well-read today if

you haven't read him. Günter Grass is simply the most original and versatile writer alive."

Other Works by Günter Grass

The Call of the Toad. Translated by Ralph Manheim. New York: Harvest Books, 1993.

Crabwalk. Translated by Krishna Winston. New York: Mariner Books, 2004.

The Flounder. Translated by Ralph Manheim. New York: Harcourt Brace, 1989.

Four Plays. Translated by Ralph Manheim and A. Leslie Wilson. New York: Harvest Books, 1968.

My Century. Translated by Michael Henry Heim. New York: Harvest Books, 2000.

Novemberland: Selected Poems 1956–1993. Translated by Michael Hamburger. New York: Harvest Books, 1996.

On Writing and Politics 1967–1983. Translated by Ralph Manheim. New York: Harcourt Brace, 1985.

Too Far Afield. Translated by Krishna Winston. New York: Harcourt Brace, 2000.

Works about Günter Grass

Irving, John. "Günter Grass: King of the Toy Merchants." In Patrick O'Neill, ed. *Critical Essays on Günter Grass.* Boston: G. K. Hall, 1987.

O'Neill, Patrick. *Günter Grass Revisited.* Boston: Twayne, 1999.

Preece, Julian. *The Life and Work of Günter Grass: Literature, History, Politics.* New York: St. Martin's Press, 2001.

Grimm, Jacob (1785–1863) and Wilhelm (1786–1859) *collectors of folklore and writers of folktales*

Jacob and Wilhelm Grimm were born in Hanau, Germany, to Philipp Wilhelm Grimm, an administrative court official and lawyer, and Dorothea Grimm. After the untimely death of their father in 1796, the Grimm brothers lived with their aunt in Kassel, their mother's hometown, and entered secondary school. Jacob and Wilhelm shared many interests, including reading and listening to German folktales. They entered the University of Marburg within a year of each other to study law. There, the Grimm brothers became interested in folklore, linguistics, and the history of medieval Germany.

Influenced by the sweeping force of German ROMANTICISM, the Grimm brothers began to compile a collection of folktales, many of which existed only as oral accounts passed from generation to generation. They listened carefully to the stories and transcribed them in their journals. They sometimes altered the plots and changed the language of the tales, transforming them into cautionary tales for a new bourgeois readership. In 1812, the Grimm brothers published their first collection of stories, known simply as *Children's and Household Tales*. This collection of 86 stories and went virtually unnoticed by the critics. The second volume, published in 1814, added 70 stories to the original 86 and was far more successful. This two-volume work went through several editions during the Grimms' lifetime. The final version of the work contained more than 200 stories and became one of the best-known works in German and world literature. Unfortunately, writing did not provide a steady income for the brothers, so both worked as librarians in Kassel until 1830.

Today, the brothers Grimm are primarily remembered for their versions of classic fairy tales, such as "Cinderella," the story of a downtrodden young girl who marries a prince; "The Frog Prince," the story of a girl whose kiss turns a frog into a prince; "Snow White," the tale of a girl who eats a poisoned apple and is saved by a prince; and "Rapunzel," the tale of a girl who is rescued from a tower by a prince. Their tales not only capture the innocent magic of folklore, but they also reflect the realistic political and social concerns of German society in the period in which the brothers were writing. In fact, their tales were actually intended for adults. The brothers were in favor of a unified, democratically ruled Germany and were on the side of the emerging middle class against oppressive princes who ruled a loosely knit confederation of states. By capturing the folklore of the German people, the brothers hoped to create a sense of a common past and pride in a German

heritage. As they began to realize that many of their readers were children, they changed some of the stories to emphasize many of the domestic values of the emerging middle class; for example, the Grimms changed the original version of "Rapunzel" to eliminate any suggestion of premarital sex.

In 1819, the Grimm brothers were awarded honorary doctorates from the University of Marburg for their influential work in German folklore. In 1830, they resigned from the library and accepted positions as professors at the University of Göttingen. They lost their positions in 1841, however, when they joined a protest against King Ernst August II, who had revoked the constitution and dissolved parliament on his ascension to the throne of Hannover. Fortunately, their scholarly reputations were such that they immediately received offers from other universities in Germany. The two brothers finally settled at the University of Berlin, where they worked as professors and librarians.

The works of Wilhelm and Jacob Grimm are still widely read today by children and adults alike. Their contribution to German literature as writers and scholars is simply immeasurable; not only did they collect folklore that might otherwise have been lost, but they also made lasting contributions to studies of the German language and linguistics in general. Even more impressive, however, is the successful collaborative effort that existed for three decades. Their tales are known all over the world and have been translated into more than 20 languages. The Grimm brothers influenced entire generations of writers as well as modern poetry in Germany, England, France, and Russia.

Another Work by Wilhelm and Jacob Grimm
The Complete Fairy Tales of the Brothers Grimm. Translated by Jack Zipes. New York: Bantam, 1992.

Works about Wilhelm and Jacob Grimm
Hettinga, Donald. *The Brothers Grimm: Two Lives, One Legacy*. London: Clarion Books, 2001.

Zipes, Jack. *The Brothers Grimm: From Enchanted Forests to the Modern World.* New York: Routledge, 1988.

Grossman, David (1954–   ) *novelist, journalist, essayist, children's story writer*

David Grossman was born in Jerusalem in 1954 to Yitzchak and Michaela Grossman. His father had immigrated to Palestine from the city of Lemberg in Galicia in 1936, and his mother was born in Jerusalem. Grossman studied philosophy and theater at the Hebrew University in Jerusalem. He worked as a reporter and actor for Kol Yisrael, the Israeli Broadcasting Service, but resigned in 1988 to protest restrictions on his journalistic work, particularly as it related to his contact with the Palestinians. Since that time and for the last 20 years, Grossman has not hesitated to openly define and discuss his belief in peace activism.

In 2006, during the war in Lebanon between Israel and Hezbollah, Grossman joined fellow writers A. B. Yehoshua and AMOS OZ in a plea to the Israeli prime minister to reach a cease-fire agreement. Tragically, just a few days later, his son Uri was killed when his tank was hit by a Hezbollah missile. Grossman continues to write and has not diminished his efforts to convince the Israeli government to make some changes to its policies. His wife, Michal, is a well-known psychologist and together with their children they live in Mevasseret Zion, a suburb of Jerusalem.

At the age of eight, Grossman's father introduced him to the Yiddish writer SHALOM ALEICHEM, who brought the daily struggles of the Jews in the European shtetl to life. The young Grossman read voraciously and developed a a consuming attachment to the characters in these colorful descriptions of a bygone era. About life in the shtetl, Grossman writes in his essay "Books That Have Read Me" that his father said to him, "Do you like it? Read, read, it's just how things were with us." So intrigued was the young boy by this literary experience that by the time he was nine years old he had already become a youth reporter.

Grossman says that when, as a youth, he finally realized that the shtetl was also a victim of the Holocaust, that all the descendants of those who had peopled the villages in Shalom Aleichem's stories had been burned to death in the crematoria of the Nazi concentration camps, he came face-to-face with the concept of death for the first time.

David Grossman is one of Israel's best-known authors. He has published seven novels, a play, a number of short stories and novellas, and several books for children and young adults. Grossman uses modernistic narrative techniques such as stream of consciousness and employs fantasy extensively, especially in his children's books. In 2007, according to the Institute for the Translation of Hebrew Literature, Grossman's novels, *The Book of Internal Grammar* and *See Under: Love*, were named among the 10 most important books published since the creation of the state of Israel in 1948. His works have been translated into 25 languages, and he has received several prestigious literary and journalistic awards both in Israel and abroad, among them the Prime Minister's Prize for Creative Work (1984), the Nelly Sachs Prize (1991), the Sapir Prize for Literature for *Someone to Run With* (2001), the Koret International Jewish Book Award for *Her Body Knows: Two Novellas* (2006) and the Emet Prize (2007).

Grossman is an unabashed activist for peace. He is widely recognized for his efforts to bridge the gap between Arabs and Jews, and he dreams of the day when each side will understand the other. His controversial political beliefs are rejected in many circles, and he is known for his outspoken criticism of Israeli policies. He says of himself that he is a man who does not join the choir and that he will never hesitate to take a stand against society if need be.

Grossman has authored many novels and works of nonfiction. His first novel, *Smile of the Lamb* (1983), deals with what life is like for the Palestinians in the West Bank and was made into a film in 1985. *Yellow Wind*, published in 1987, presents a series of interviews with Palestinians in Gaza and the West Bank. His novel *The Book of Intimate*

Grammar (1991) traces three years in the life of Aron Kleinman, an 11-year-old Jerusalem boy, as he observes the changes in his friends wrought by puberty. *Be My Knife* (1998) is a novel in which the two main characters reveal themselves fully to each other through a series of letters as they seek to break the bonds of loneliness. *Someone to Run With* (2000) is a critically successful novel about two teenagers whose adventures reach a climax as they join together to escape from the worlds of drugs, crime, and terrorism. In *Death as a Way of Life: Israel Ten Years After Oslo* (2003), a collection of essays originally published over a 10-year period in *al-Ayyam, Guardian, Newsweek,* and other publications, Grossman expresses his initial joy when the Oslo Accords were signed, only to have it followed by dark disillusionment as his dreams for a lasting peace evaporate.

Critical Analysis

In the powerful and deeply moving novel, *See Under: Love,* Grossman introduces the reader to several unusual characters, including Momik Neuman, a precocious child whose parents were Holocaust survivors who try desperately to scratch out a living in Israel after their recent arrival there. In a determined effort, Momik, puzzled by the silence of his parents on the topic of the Holocaust, resorts to devising a fantasy world to exorcise the Nazi "beast" that haunts them all. Confused by the secrecy surrounding the Holocaust (none of those who had survived it could bring themselves to speak of it), he constructs a complex world of "over there," a world of which his parents speak in whispers, hoping he will not hear. Sadly, however, although Momik wishes to free his parents of the specter of the "beast," his private retreat into the world of horror results in his feeling isolated and becoming detached from real life.

As Momik matures, his tortured mind finds release in writing about the famous Polish author, BRUNO SCHULZ, who was murdered in 1942 in a horrifying revenge scenario. Schulz was killed by a Nazi officer in a fit of vindictiveness because the latter had lost a card game to another Nazi officer who happened to have been Schulz's protector. Momik also recorded the stories told him as a child by his great-uncle Anshel Wasserman. Like Scheherazade, the desperate storyteller of *One Thousand and One Nights,* Uncle Anshel, a famous writer of children's stories, now senile, remained alive in the Nazi concentration camp by spinning fanciful but very meaningful tales for the camp commandant night after night about the good deeds of a band of children. He hoped that these stories about innocent children would ignite a spark of humanity in the heart of the commandant. By means of his uncle's stories, Momik is able to rekindle his own relationship with the world and connect to kindness and decency once again. Grossman ends the book with a moving prayer that is a clear statement of his own personal credo: "We asked so little: for a man to live in this world from birth to death and know nothing of war."

Other Works by David Grossman

Duel. London: Bloomsbury, 2004.
Her Body Knows. New York: Picador, 2006.
Lion's Honey. Edinburgh: Canongate, 2006.
Sleeping on a Wire: Conversations with Palestinians in Israel. New York: Farrar, Straus & Giroux, 1993.
Writing in the Dark. New York: Farrar, Straus & Giroux, 2008.
The Zigzag Kid. New York: Farrar, Straus & Giroux, 1997.

Grünbein, Durs (1962–) *poet, essayist*

Durs Grünbein was born in Dresden and lived in East Germany prior to reunification. In the 1990s, he became a professional poet and traveled throughout the world. He also worked as an essayist and translator. Grünbein is considered one of the most innovative and intellectual of contemporary German poets. The collection of poems *Schädelbasislektion: Gedichte* (*Basal Skull Lesson: Poems,* 1991) is one of his best-known works. *Ashes for Breakfast: Selected Poems* appeared in English in 2005. He has received many literary awards, including the Marburger Literature Prize (1992) and the prestigious Georg Büchner prize (1995). Grünbein's verse reveals an influence from the German poets GOTTFRIED BENN and GERHARD FALKNER.

Science is the prevailing theme in Grünbein's poems and essays. His specific topics include human biology, laboratories, formaldehyde, X-rays, and radioactive decay. Many of his poems portray the exposure of human organs through sonar imaging or autopsies. Although Grünbein views modern science as the dominant power of the present era, he presents it as a threat that diminishes the worth of human beings and reveals the meaninglessness of life. German literary scholar Ruth J. Owen observed that Grünbein portrays the poet as a scientist and successfully challenges "the assumption that science could be an area of human knowledge cordoned off from the poem."

Other Works by Durs Grünbein

Descartes' Devil: Three Meditations. New York: Upper West Side Philosophers, 2010.

Falten und Fallen: Gedichte. Frankfurt am Main: Suhrkamp Verlag, 1994.

A Work about Durs Grünbein

Winkler, Ron. *Dichtung Zwischen Grossstadt und Grosshirm: Annaherungen an das lyrische werk Durs Grünbeins.* Hamburg: Kovac, 2000.

Grünzweig, Dorothea (1952–) *poet*

Dorothea Grünzweig was born in Stuttgart, Germany. She attended colleges in Tübingen, Germany, and Bangor, Wales, where she majored in German studies and English studies. After a research stay at Oxford, she was a lecturer for the University of Dundee in Scotland. Grünzweig later taught at a German boarding school and a German school in Helsinki, Finland. She also wrote reviews and translated Finnish and English literature.

Grünzweig's first collection of poetry, *Mittsommerschnitt* (*Midsummer Cut*, 1997), won the poetry prize of the Neidersachsen/Wolfenbüttel foundation. The next year she contributed poems to *Das verlorene Alphabet* (*The Lost Alphabet*, 1998) anthology. In 2000, Grünzweig gained international exposure after her poems appeared in the English language journals the *Massachusetts Review* and *Arc*. Her other honors include Finland's P.E.N. Club prize (1999) and the Heinrich Heine stipend (2000).

Grünzweig, who divides her time between Germany and Finland, frequently writes poems that have a geographical frame of reference. Inspired by her own experience, she often covers the concepts of original homeland and adopted country. The poems "Spell," "Beginning," and "Insel Seili" ("The Island of Seili") address her other recurring themes of language and speechlessness, and the freezing cold. Her poetry is syntactically complex but creates clear pictures to help illuminate the meaning of her words.

Other Works by Dorothea Grünzweig

Glass Voices lasinaanet. Translated by Derk Wynand. Ottawa: BuschekBooks, 2008.

Vom Eisgebreit: Gedichte. Göttingen: Wallstein, 2000.

Gruppe 47 (Group 47) (1947–1967)

Following World War II the German writers Hans Werner Richter (1908–93) and Alfred Andersch (1914–80) edited a left-wing journal *Der Ruf* (*The Call*). In 1947, the American military government banned the magazine and upset many German literati. In September, these writers joined Richter and Anderson at Bannwaldsee, Bavaria, to discuss plans for another journal. This became the first meeting of Gruppe 47, a loose association of authors whose regular attendees came to include Wolfgang Weyrauch (1904–80), ILSE AICHINGER, HEINRICH BÖLL, GÜNTER EICH, and GÜNTER GRASS. Gruppe 47 met in the autumn of each year through 1967 to discuss and read new literary works. Its only official function was to award the Gruppe 47 Prize, one of Germany's most coveted literary awards at the time.

The German literary scholar Siegfried Mandel described Gruppe 47 as a paradox: "It is one man, Hans Werner Richter, and at the same time an expanding and contracting constellation identifiable by several constant stars." The group avoided an inflexible ideology. Although right-wing writers did not join the group, it had no official social or political program and usually did not initiate new trends. Gruppe 47 was instead more like a barometer of changing literary tastes and social conditions. In general, its members were critical of the values of the West German "economic miracle" and of East German socialism. The 1968 meeting scheduled for Prague was cancelled after Soviet troops invaded Czechoslovakia. Although Richter hosted an informal meeting in 1972, Gruppe 47 never again held a full conference after 1967.

A Work about Gruppe 47

Mandel, Siegfried. *Group 47: The Reflected Intellect.* Edwardsville: Southern Illinois University Press, 1973.

Guan Moye
See MO YAN.

Guillén, Jorge (1893–1984) *poet*

Jorge Guillén was born in Valladolid in the Spanish province of Castile. His poetry reflects the austerity of the region, known for its harsh winters and gray landscape. He was a teacher of Spanish his entire life, on the faculty of such institutions as the Sorbonne, Oxford University, Wellesley College, and Harvard University.

Guillén is generally considered the most intellectual and classic of modern Spanish poets. His poems are terse and lyrical; his work is sober, and he employs more nouns than adjectives. He has been compared to the French poet PAUL VALÉRY, whose works he translated. Guillén tries to describe objects through their "poetic presence" rather than through metaphor, making his work difficult for many to comprehend.

In 1976, the Spanish government honored Guillén with the Cervantes Prize, the highest literary honor of the Spanish-speaking world.

Other Works by Jorge Guillén

Affirmation: A Bilingual Anthology 1919–1966. Translated by Julian Palley. Norman: University of Oklahoma Press, 1971.

Guillén on Guillén: The Poetry and the Poet. Translated by Reginald Gibbons. Princeton, N.J.: Princeton University Press, 1979.

Horses in the Air and Other Poems. Translated by Cola Franzen. San Francisco, Calif.: City Lights Books, 1999.

Our Air/Nuestro Aire: Canticle/Cántico. Translated by Carl W. Cobb. Lewiston, N.Y.: Edwin Mellen Press, 1997.

Guillén, Nicolás (1902–1989) *poet, novelist, editor*

Nicolás Guillén was born and educated in Camagüey, Cuba, and later studied law at the University of Havana. In 1919, the magazine *Camagüey Gráfico* published Guillén's first poems. After meeting the American writer Langston Hughes (1902–67) in January 1930, Guillén published "en negro de verdad" (in an authentic African voice) for the first time when his eight *Motivos de son* (Sound motifs) poems appeared in the *Diario de la Marina* newspaper in April. Later, Guillén dedicated his powerful poem "Sabás" to Hughes.

The publication of *Sóngoro cosongo* (1931) marks what Amilcar Cabral calls the Revitalization Phase. In the prologue, Guillén names his "born again" poetry "versos mulatos," filled with "*color cubano.*" *West Indies, Ltd.* (1934) marks Guillén's shift into the "Radicalization Phase," or fighting phase, during which he wrote *Cantos para soldados y sones para turistas* (Songs for soldiers and sounds for tourists, 1937). In 1938,

Guillén joined the National Committee of the Cuban Communist Party and worked on its journal, *Hoy,* until authorities closed it in 1950. He received the International Lenin Peace Prize in 1954 and the Cuban National Prize for Literature in 1983.

Although Guillén used literature for political ends, he argued that writers should also make "art" when striving to express revolutionary ideas. In *Un poeta en la historia* (n.d.), Alfred Melon, a Universidad de Sorbonne–Nouvelle literature professor, describes Guillén as "one of the major contemporary poets of the world." His work has been translated into more than 30 languages, and it couples experimental aesthetics, such as a conversational tone and free verse, with distinctively Afro-Caribbean experiences.

Other Works by Nicolás Guillén

The Daily Daily. Translated by Vera M. Kutzinski. Berkeley: University of California Press, 1989.

The Great Zoo and Other Poems. Translated by Robert Marquez. New York: Monthly Review Press, 1981.

New Love Poetry: In Some Springtime Place: Elegy. Edited and translated by Keith Ellis. Toronto: University of Toronto Press, 1994.

Works about Nicolás Guillén

Smart, Ian Isadore. *Nicolás Guillén, Popular Poet of the Caribbean.* Columbia: University of Missouri Press, 1990.

White, Clement A. *Decoding the Word: Nicolás Guillén as Maker and Debunker of Myth.* Miami, Fla.: Ediciones Universal, 1993.

Gumilev, Nikolay (1886–1921) *poet*

Nikolay Stepanovich Gumilev was born in Ekaterinburg, Russia, to Stephan Gumilev, a navy doctor, and Anna Lvova, a sister of a navy admiral. The family soon moved to Tsarskoe Selo, where Gumilev would later meet his future wife, ANNA AKHMATOVA. Gumilev grew up playing with his brothers in the countryside. He was sent away to a boarding school in 1900: Academically, he performed very poorly—instead of studying, Gumilev avidly read adventure stories and books about travels to exotic lands. In 1902, Gumilev published his first poem in a small provincial newspaper. He felt triumphant, despite the fact that the publication misspelled his name. After Gumilev graduated, he traveled to Paris where he met several symbolist poets, and where he also published *Romantic Poems,* his first collection of lyric poetry.

In 1909, Gumilev founded a literary journal, *Apollon,* which eventually published some of the best poetry of the period and was the main organ of the ACMEIST movement. In 1910, he and Anna Akhmatova were married. The marriage was stormy from the start; soon afterward, Gumilev left for an extended journey to Africa. By the time he returned, Akhmatova had published many of the poems that went into her first collection, and her fame had begun to exceed her husband's.

Gumilev resumed his position as one of the leaders of the acmeists. Gumilev supported and wrote lyrical poetry that relied on concrete images and opposed the mysticism of SYMBOLISM. In many ways, acmeist poetry, including Gumilev's, was conservative because it relied on rhyme, meter, and traditional poetic devices. Gumilev strove to uphold and advance the literary tradition of Russia, rather than replace it.

In 1913, Gumilev returned to Africa. He explored exotic places, visited local mystics and healers, and was even attacked by a crocodile. The trip to Africa provided Gumilev with vivid images and exotic metaphors that appear throughout his poetry. At the outbreak of World War I, Gumilev returned to Russia and joined the army; he was decorated twice for bravery in combat. After the war, Gumilev returned to St. Petersburg and divorced Akhmatova in 1918. The association of the acmeists was dissolved. Akhmatova's and Gumilev's son, Lev Gumilev, was raised mainly by Gumilev's mother.

Gumilev was recruited by MAXIM GORKY to help with a project in world literature, working with an editor to select important works from other literatures, to write introductory essays for them, and to translate them for publication in Russian. But he was in trouble politically: After the Russian Revolution of 1917, Gumilev had supported the provisional government against the Bolsheviks. When in 1921 the sailors at the Kronstadt naval base, who had helped sweep the Bolsheviks to power, protested against the loss of political freedoms under the Bolshevik government, Gumilev supported their uprising, which was brutally put down. A short time afterward, he was arrested and executed, despite Lenin's intervention. His grave was never found.

Although Gumilev produced a number of notable collections throughout his career, his last work, *The Pillar of Fire* (1921), is considered by most to be his best. *The Pillar of Fire* is marked by exotic and foreign elements. The poems in the collection are explorations of personal experiences of the poet during his travels, as well as the emotional dramas of his personal life. "The Streetcar Gone Astray" imagines a derailed streetcar careering past the landmarks of Russian history and Gumilev's life. This is an example of its imagery (in Carl Proffer's translation):

> *A sign . . . letters poured from blood*
> *Announce—"Vegetables." I know this is*
> * where,*
> *Instead of cabbages, instead of rutabagas,*
> *Corpses' heads are being sold.*

Gumilev left a profound and long-lasting influence on Russian poetry. His images were as unique as they were strange and refreshing. Gumilev's personal life, filled with tragedy, despair, and, at the same time, love and adventure, in many ways reflected the passion of his verse.

Other Works by Nikolay Gumilev

Lapeza, David, ed. *Nikolai Gumilev on Russian Poetry.* Ann Arbor, Mich.: Ardis, 1977.

The Pillar of Fire: And Selected Poems. Translated by Richard McKane. Chester, Pa.: Dufour Editions, 1999.
Selected Works of Nikolai Gumilev. Translated by Burton Raffel and Alla Burago. Albany: State University of New York Press, 1972.
Selections in Proffer, Carl R., and Elledea Proffer, eds. *The Silver Age of Russian Culture* (anthology). Ann Arbor, Mich.: Ardis, 1975.

Works about Nikolay Gumilev

Eshelman, Ralph. *Nikolaj Gumilev and Neoclassical Modernism: The Metaphysics of Style.* New York: Peter Lang, 1993.
Sampson, Earl. *Nikolai Gumilev.* Boston: Twayne, 1979.

Gunesekera, Romesh (1954–) *poet, novelist, short story writer*

Romesh Gunesekera was born in Sri Lanka and moved to the Philippines with his family in the 1960s. When he was 17, he went to England, which became his adopted home, but the spirit of travel has not left him, and he continues to visit both Asia and Europe as a writer-in-residence. Gunesekera's poetry is especially popular in Europe, where it has been translated into almost every major European language. His poems are widely anthologized and are a recurring favorite on BBC radio.

Constantly traveling from a young age, Gunesekera's fiction privileges the role of exile. During his years in the Philippines, for example, he was exposed to writers of the Beat Generation, such as Jack Kerouac and Allen Ginsberg, whom he would not have read otherwise.

Gunesekera started writing when he was 14, beginning with short stories and poetry. Poetry, in fact, is a medium he continues to write in and explore, even when he is working on a novel. His first novel *Reef* (1994), set in the Sri Lanka of the 1950s and 1960s, is an exploration into the memories of the protagonist who leaves Sri Lanka for England to stay with his master, a marine biologist. Their story of relationships, cooking, and domesticity is set against the rise of rebel terrorism between the Sinhalese and the Tamils in Sri Lanka during this time. The other essential character is the reef itself: Its precarious existence serves as a metaphor for the fragile political condition of the nation.

In addition to his novels, a collection of short fiction, and poetry, Gunesekera also writes children's poems. His novel *Sandglass* (1998) won the BBC Asia Award for Achievement in Writing and Literature, and in 1997 he won the Premio Mondello Five Continents Award, Italy's highest literary prize. His most recent novels are *Heaven's Edge* (2002) and *The Match* (2006).

Another Work by Romesh Gunesekera
Monkfish Moon. New York: New Press, 1992.

Gunnarsson, Gunnar (1889–1975)
novelist, dramatist, poet, playwright

A son of a farmer, Gunnar Gunnarsson was born in Fljotsdalur, Iceland. The death of his mother when he was nine years old was a deeply traumatic experience that he remembered for the rest of his life. Gunnarsson grew up in Vopnafjorour, where his family moved while he was still a boy. Until the age of 18, he was educated at various country schools. In 1907, he moved to Denmark, where he studied at Askov Folk High School for two years.

Gunnarsson started his career as a writer at the age of 17, and by 1910 he was devoting all his time to writing. Many of Gunnarsson's early works were written in Danish because Denmark provided a wider audience for his poetry and fiction; however, his works were always set in his native Iceland. During his career as a writer, Gunnarsson published more than 40 novels, as well as short stories, articles, and translations. Although he is very well known in the Scandinavian countries, only a few of his works were ever translated into English. Unfortunately, currently no work of Gunnar Gunnarsson is in print in the United States.

Gunnar Gunnarsson's works depict the courage of the common people of Iceland. His first important work, *Guest the One-Eyed,* a four-volume family saga about three generations of an Icelandic family, was published in 1912 and instantly became a best seller throughout Scandinavia. Recalling the biblical Cain and Abel story, the work describes the parallel lives of a virtuous son, torn between his art and familial obligations to the farm, and an evil son. The work received critical praise in virtually every publication that reviewed it.

World War I deeply affected Gunnarsson's sensibility, and for many years after the war, his fiction reflected a deep, oppositional tension. *Seven Days Darkness* (1920), for example, is about war and the conflicts that it creates within a person, particularly the conflict between national identity and the self.

Between 1920 and 1940, Gunnarsson dedicated his writing to history and culture of the Nordic countries. He gave lectures throughout Scandinavia and Germany and wrote numerous articles on social and cultural problems of unification of the Nordic countries. In many respects, Gunnarsson recognized certain common cultural attributes throughout Scandinavia, but he also insisted on the singularity of particular regions. In 1939, he returned to Iceland, and from then on he only wrote in Icelandic.

Many critics consider *Church on the Mountain* (1923–1928), a five-volume semiautobiographical novel, to be Gunnarsson's masterpiece. The work describes the various twists in the life of an Icelandic farming family. It truly demonstrates Gunnarsson's skill as a storyteller, as well as his rich use of poetic language to portray everyday life. The work has only been partially translated into English, appearing in 1938 as two volumes, *Ships in the Sky* and *The Night and the Dream.*

Gunnar Gunnarsson remains one of the most popular and respected writers not only in Iceland but throughout Europe. He was given honorary degrees by the University of Iceland and the University of Heidelberg. Gunnarsson was instrumental in the formation of Icelandic national identity and was a giant cultural figure in his beloved country.

Other Works by Gunnar Gunnarsson

The Black Cliffs. Madison: University of Wisconsin Press, 1967.

The Good Shepherd. New York: Bobbs-Merrill Company, 1940.

"A Legend." In Sven Hakon Rossel et al., eds., *Christmas in Scandinavia.* Translated by David W. Colbert. Lincoln: University of Nebraska Press, 1996.

Günter, Erich

See EICH, GÜNTER.

Haasse, Hella S. (1918–) *novelist, playwright, essayist*

Hella Haasse is one of the Netherlands most celebrated authors, who has only relatively recently begun to be widely translated and read in English. Haasse was born on February 2, 1918, in Batavia (Jakarta) on the island of Java in what is now Indonesia. She is the daughter of a pianist, Katherina Diehm-Winzenhöhler, and Willem Hendrik Haasse, a financial official for the Dutch East Indies colonial government. Hella Haasse spent most of her childhood in the Dutch East Indies, attending elementary and high school there, although between 1924 and 1928, she and her brother lived with their grandparents in the Netherlands while her mother was treated for tuberculosis in Switzerland.

As a teenager, Haasse developed passions for reading and acting. She wrote plays, read avidly in her father's library, especially the historical fiction of VICTOR HUGO, Walter Scott, and the Dutch novelist Jacob van Lennep. In 1938, Haasse returned to the Netherlands to study Scandinavian languages and literature, but, with World War II looming, she broke off her academic studies and turned to editorial work and theater. In 1939, while serving as an editor of the satirical Amsterdam weekly, *Propria Cures* (Latin for "Mind your

own business"), she met Jan van Lelyveld, and they married in 1944.

Haasse first came to literary prominence in 1948 with the publication of her novel *Oeroeg* (*Forever a Stranger*), a coming-of-age story set in the Dutch East Indies that captured the sense of confusion and uncertainty that many Dutch felt in the face of the Javanese insurgency, the end of Dutch colonial rule, and the establishment of the independent nation of Indonesia. *Oeroeg* was selected as the winner out of 19 entries as part of a contest held by the Amsterdam Association for the Promotion of the Book Trade's Interests. Haasse submitted her manuscript under the Malay pseudonym of "Soeka toelis" (Like to write), but it soon came to light that she was the author. Since *Oeroeg*'s publication, it has become an educational favorite, virtually required reading for generations of college-bound Dutch students. A film adaptation appeared in 1993.

Haasse followed the success of *Oeroeg* with the first of many historical novels, *Het woud der verwachting* (1949, *In a Dark Wood, Wandering*, 1989). Set in 15th-century France during the Hundred Years' War, *In a Dark Wood, Wandering* explores the life of the poet Charles d'Orleans, nephew of King Charles VI, caught first amid the feuding aristocracy of the French court and then a prisoner of war held by the English. The novel blends extensive historical research with a subtle psychological sensibility attuned to the ways in which individuals are shaped by political and filial conflict. Through Haasse's compelling, detailed perspective, d'Orleans, under the pressure of imprisonment and exile, produces his famous poetry of love, loss, and longing.

In 1950, Haasse published *De verborgen bron* (*The Hidden Source*), a short novel, which, like *Oeroeg*, deals with intimate secrets revealed through the protagonist, Jurgen, during a visit to his childhood home. Jurgen concludes, much like the nameless narrator of Haasse's first work, that he really knows nothing about his wife. In 1952, Haasse produced her second sprawling historical novel, *De scharlaken stad* (*The Scarlet City: A Novel of 16th-Century Italy*, 1990), combining the approaches and themes of her previous work. Narrated polyvocally—that is, in 21 chapters, each dedicated to the separate voice of a different historical figure—*The Scarlet City* interweaves the Renaissance world of art and politics, court life and war, and Roman and Vatican intrigue with the central character Giovanni Borgia's search for the actual identity of his father. Michelangelo, Machiavelli, Vittoria Colonna, Pietro Aretino, and Francesco Guicciardini all appear with a kind of fresh intimacy, giving the novel a seamless texture in which historical forces and preoccupations with the uncertainties of identity come together.

A steady output of novels followed and growing interest in Haasse's work was evident in other European countries. In 1958, Haasse received the national Atlantic prize for *De ingewijden* (*The Uninitiated*), the first of many awards. In 1977, she won the Littéraire Witte Prize for *Een gevaarlijke verhouding of Daal-en-Bergse brieven* (*A Dangerous Relationship or Letters from Daal-en-Bergse*, 1976). In 1981, she received the Constantijn Huygens Prize; in 1984, the P.C. Hooft Prize. *Herren van de thee* (*The Tea Lords*, 1992) was nominated for the 1993 AKO Literature and the Arts Council prize for European Literature, and she received the Audience Award for the same

novel. In 2004, Haasse was awarded the Prijs der Nederlandse Letteren for her overall contribution to Dutch literature.

In 1981, Haasse moved with her husband to France. They settled in St. Witz, a town north of Paris, where she remained for nearly 10 years. In 1987, she was made an honorary member of the Belgian Royal Academy of Dutch Language and Literature in Ghent. In 1992, she received the Medal of Honour of Queen Beatrix in Gold for Art and Science in the Family Order of Orange. In 2000, Haasse was made an officer of the Légion d'honneur. In 1990, Haasse and her husband returned to Amsterdam. To mark her 75th anniversary as an author, the Literary Museum in The Hague held a major exhibition dedicated to her life and work.

Critical Analysis

Oeroeg is a bildungsroman set during the 1920s and '30s. Told retrospectively, its nameless narrator charts the course of his life as he grows up on a plantation in Java under the loose supervision of preoccupied and distant parents, a bland official and his nervous spouse. He cultivates a close friendship with the son of one of his father's servants, Oeroeg, who is the same age as he. The narrator and Oeroeg establish a regular friendship until they are sent to different schools, both paid for by the narrator's father, who simultaneously fears that his son is emulating the natives too closely and feels he owes Oeroeg's family a moral debt, as Oeroeg's father died rescuing his master's son. In time, the narrator goes to the Netherlands to further his studies, while Oeroeg joins the anticolonial insurgency. The narrator returns after World War II, now a soldier in the Dutch Indies army, and has a final, utterly disillusioning encounter as Oeroeg tells the narrator that Java is not his home and he should leave.

In *Oeroeg*, Haasse's central theme of the ways in which history (in this case, colonial history) shape and obscure human identity is clearly articulated in a taut narrative form. As the literary critic Hank M. J. Maier has explained, "One can read *Oeroeg* in terms of an allegory of the colonial situation, of the relationship between the rulers and the ruled in the Indies: the protagonist, the Dutch narrator of the tale, grows up as a representative of the ruling class with all the privileges that come with that position, be it largely unknowingly so." Haasse herself explained that she discovered only much later that *oeroeg* is a Sundanese word, meaning "landslide." "I discovered that only in1992 . . . What took place in the second part of the 1940s was of course a fundamental change in the existing relations. For everyone: Indonesians, Indo-Europeans, Dutch—directly involved or not with the decolonization. And it was an oeroeg for me personally." This tracing of how historical forces work through the lives of the European, on both conscious and subconscious levels, has been Haasse's ongoing literary project.

Another Work by Hella S. Haasse

Forever a Stranger and Other Stories. Translated by Margaret M. Alibasah. New York: Oxford University Press, 1996.

A Work about Hella S. Haasse

Schouten, Diny, et al. *Exploring the World of Women.* Amsterdam : Foundation for the Promotion of the Translation of Dutch Literary Works, 1979.

Habibi, Emile (Imil Habibi) (1921–1996)
novelist, short-story writer, political essayist

Acclaimed experimental novelist Habibi writes about Palestinians who, like him, live within Israel after its 1948 statehood and are marginalized and displaced in the land of their birth. *The Secret Life of Sa'eed, the Ill-Fated Pessoptimist* (1974; translated by Salma K. Jayyusi and Trevor LeGassick, 1982), about a Palestinian who becomes an overzealous informant for the Israeli government, is considered his greatest novel, engaging Habibi's typical black humor and cynical wit. The novel's hapless antihero, Sa'eed, faces bewildering choices between Zionist exploitation and Arab stupidities in an Arabic text studded with puns and witty

wordplay. The protagonist's name means "happy"; of course, he is profoundly not happy. Among Habibi's novels are *Sudasiyat al-ayyam al-sitta* (*Sextet on the Six Days,* 1968), about the 1967 Six Day War; *Luka' ibn Luka'* (1980; the title is a nonsensical name combined with its patronymic, which is difficult to translate); and *Ikhtayyi* (*Such a Pity,* 1986), which remembers Palestinian community life before it came into conflict with Israel in 1948.

Habibi helped found the Israeli Communist Party and was elected to three Knesset terms on its platform. His decision to accept the 1992 Israeli Prize for Literature from the Israeli prime minister surprised some among both Arabs and Israeli Jews because his principled opposition to Israel's policies seemed to preclude his acceptance of such an award. A humanist with a broad vision that transcended the sad specifics of his condition as a Palestinian living in Israel, Habibi donated the award money to a Palestinian clinic.

Another Work by Emile Habibi

The Secret Life of Sa'eed, the Ill-Fated Pessoptimist, a Palestinian Who Became a Citizen of Israel. Translated by Salma K. Jayyusi and Trevor LeGassick. Brooklyn N.Y.: Interlink Publishing Group, 1982.

A Work about Emile Habibi

Boullata, Issa J., and Roger Allen. *The Arabic Novel Since 1950: Critical Essays, Interviews, and Bibliography.* Cambridge, Mass.: Dar Mahjar Publications, 1992.

Hagiwara Sakutarō (1886–1942) *poet*

Hagiwara Sakutarō was born in Maebashi, Gumma Prefecture, in Japan. While a student at Maebashi Middle School, he began to show interest in poetry and in 1908 entered the German literature course at the Sixth High School; however, due to illness, he withdrew. In addition to academics, Hagiwara studied the mandolin and guitar, hoping at one time that he might become a professional musician.

Hagiwara's literary career did not take root until 1913, when he published in the magazine *Zamboa*. He experimented with colloquial language, onomatopoeia, and free verse and, in 1917, published his first collection, *Howling at the Moon*, which is regarded as the model for modern lyric poetry. In 1922, he published *The Blue Cat*, a collection of poems that was more reflective and less imagistic than *Howling*. His last collection, *The Iceland* (1934), received mixed reviews. In writing the *Iceland* poems, Hagiwara abandoned the modern, colloquial style of his earlier collections and wrote in classical Japanese. After *The Iceland*, he retired from writing poetry, turning to poetic criticism and studies on Japanese culture.

Hagiwara is known as the father of modern Japanese poetry. He established a new style of poetry that incorporated free verse, colloquial language, and onomatopoeia. His poems are often dark, containing elements of morbid fantasy and FIN-DE-SIÈCLE decadence. He is often contrasted to poet TAKAMURA KOTARŌ.

Other Works by Hagiwara Sakutarō

Face at the Bottom of the World and Other Poems. Translated by Graeme Wilson. Paintings by York Wilson. Rutland, Vt.: C. E. Tuttle Co., 1969.

Principles of Poetry. Translated by Chester C.I. Wang and Isamu P. Fukuchi. Ithaca, N.Y.: East Asia Program, Cornell University, 1998.

Rats' Nests: The Poetry of Hagiwara Sakutarō. Stanwood, Wash.: UNESCO Publishing, 1999.

Ten Japanese Poets. Translated by Hiroaki Sato. Hanover, N.H.: Granite Publications, 1973.

Works about Hagiwara Sakutarō

Gaffke, Carol. *Poetry Criticism: Vol. 18.* Detroit: Gale Research, 1997.

Keene, Donald. *Dawn to the West: Japanese Literature of the Modern Era: Poetry, Drama, Criticism.* New York: Columbia University Press, 1999.

Halter, Erika

See BURKART, ERIKA.

Hamsun, Knut (pseudonym of Knut Pederson) (1859–1952) *novelist, poet, playwright*

Knut Hamsun was born in Lom, Norway, to Peder Petersen, a tailor, and Tora Petersen. The family moved to Hamaroy, a small town 100 miles north of the Arctic Circle, where they took charge of the farm of Hans Olsen, Peder's brother-in-law, who was afflicted with a paralytic illness. Olsen accused the Petersens of owing him money, and as a child, Hamsun was forced to work for his uncle, keeping accounts in the post office, chopping wood, and running the small library in the village. Hamsun read the few books available at the library but had no formal schooling. His father taught him to read and write, and Hamsun occasionally attended a traveling school for a few weeks a year. Hamsun ran away to Lom in 1873 but returned the following year, working small jobs around the village. Hamsun's works reflect the bitterness and hardships of his childhood.

Somehow, Hamsun managed to produce his first novel and have it published in 1877 when he was 18. The same year, Hamsun was hired as a schoolteacher in the small town of Vesteralen. The following year, he published his second novel to no great acclaim. Driven by literary aspirations, he moved to Oslo, where he lived in poverty and worked as a highway construction worker. Destitution forced Hamsun to move to the United States, where he resided between 1882 and 1888, working as a farmhand in North Dakota and as a streetcar attendant in Chicago. These experiences greatly contributed to the formation of Hamsun's literary style.

Hamsun's experiences in the United States inspired him to compose a satirical piece, *Fra det Moderne Amerikas Aandsliv* (*Cultural Life in Modern America*, 1889), which described numerous religions and religious outlooks that Hamsun discovered during his stay. His first breakthrough work, however, appeared in 1890: *Sult* (*Hunger*), which depicts the life of a starving writer in Oslo, became a literary sensation. This sudden success resulted in Hamsun giving a series of lectures in which he criticized such literary figures as HENRIK IBSEN and LEO TOLSTOY for their sentimentality. His next novel, *Mysterier* (*Mysteries*) followed in 1892. *Pan* (1894) was written in Paris, where Hamsun lived from 1893 to 1895.

In 1911, Hamsun relocated to a small farm in Norway. For much of the rest of his life, he divided his time between writing and farming and virtually isolated himself from the outside world. *Markens Grøde* (*The Growth of the Soil,* 1917) tells a story of Isak, a simple man who commits his life to the natural rhythms of rural life and combines the mythological and historical aspects of the Norwegian culture. The novel was well received, not only in Norway but also in Germany, where Hamsun's work developed a huge following. In 1920, Hamsun was awarded the Nobel Prize in literature.

During World War I, Hamsun, unlike most Norwegians, supported the German cause, and before and during World War II he was a vocal supporter of the Nazi Party. During the Nazi occupation of Norway, Hamsun wrote a series of pro-Nazi articles and met with Adolf Hitler and Joseph Goebbels, the Nazi propaganda minister, on whom Hamsun bestowed his Nobel Prize medal as a sign of admiration.

After World War II, Hamsun was arrested by the Norwegian government for his collaboration with the Nazi regime. After spending some time in a psychiatric hospital, he was placed on trial in 1947. He did not rescind his opinions and showed support for Hitler's military policies throughout the trial. Hamsun was heavily fined by the court and censured by the public; sales of his work fell after the trial. Yet, when Hamsun attempted to explain his political views in *På Gjengrodde Stier* (*On Overgrown Paths,* 1949), the work sold out in Norway almost instantly.

Critical Analysis

Despite the controversy about Knut Hamsun's political affiliations, his work has been rediscovered in recent years. Most critics concur that his best work was written before the turn of the century, though *The Growth of the Soil* has its advocates. *Hunger* retains its capacity to shock with its intense depiction of the psychological degeneration of the young writer, whose thoughts become more and more incomprehensible as time passes. This passage is an example of Hamsun's close focus:

> If one only had something to eat, just a little, on such a clear day! The mood of the gay morning overwhelmed me, I became unusually serene, and started to hum for pure joy and for no particular reason. In front of a butcher's shop there was a woman with a basket on her arm, debating about some sausage for dinner; as I went past, she looked up at me. She had only a single tooth in the lower jaw. In the nervous and excitable state I was on, her face made an instant and revolting impression on me—the long yellow tooth looked like a finger sticking out of her jaw, and as she turned toward me, her eyes were full of sausage. I lost my appetite instantly, and felt nauseated.

Hamsun's narrative innovations in this novel, such as the way he shifts between first and third person, have been much imitated, and his anxious, alienated artist prefigures many 20th-century literary heroes.

By the time he wrote *Pan* (1894), Hamsun had become an admirer of FRIEDRICH NIETZSCHE's work, especially Nietzsche's notions about the superman. Written in the form of a hunter's diary, it tells the story of Lieutenant Thomas Glahn's doomed obsession with a mysterious woman. Its stress on the need to escape from urban civilization into the wilderness of nature strongly demonstrates the influence of Nietzsche in its emphasis on the individual.

Undeniably, Hamsun served an important role in presenting the Norwegian culture and struggles to the world in his writings. The focus of Hamsun's work always rested on the relationship between individuals and their respective environments. In terms of style, Hamsun's work was simply exceptional and groundbreaking in its irreverence for the established epistemology of the novel, for the all too readily accepted conventions of fiction. ISAAC BASHEVIS SINGER has observed that Hamsun "is the father of the modern school of literature in his every aspect—his subjectiveness, his fragmentariness, his use of flashbacks, his lyricism. The whole modern school of fiction in the twentieth century stems from Hamsun."

Other Works by Knut Hamsun

Dreamers. Translated by Tom Geddes. New York: New Directions, 1996.
Mysteries. Translated by Sverre Lyngstadt. New York: Penguin, 2001.
Victoria. Translated by Oliver Stallybrass. New York: Green Integer, 2001.

Works about Knut Hamsun

Ferguson, Robert. *Enigma: The Life of Knut Hamsun.* New York: Noonday Press, 1988.
Naess, Harold. *Knut Hamsun.* Boston: Twayne, 1984.
Singer, Isaac Bashevis. Introduction to Knut Hamsun, *Hunger.* New York: Farrar, Straus, 1967.

Han Yongun (Han Yu-chon; Manhae)
(1879–1944) *poet*

Han Yongun was born in Hongsong, Chungchong province, Korea, on August 29. A voracious reader, he taught himself the Chinese classics as a youth. Like many young people of the period, he entered into an arranged marriage at age 13. Later, he entered Komajawa College, where he studied Buddhist philosophy.

In 1904, he became a monk at Paektamsa temple. He hoped to rebuild Buddhism radically in Korea with modern reforms such as a choice for celibacy, establishing a solid economic base, and taking Buddhism to the masses. As president of the Buddhist Studies Association in 1913 and in 1918, he established the Buddhist monthly, *Mind.*

His poem of the same name is considered by some to be the first modern poem, written in free verse, and highly metaphysical.

Han Yongun was an active leader of the 1919 Korean Independence Movement, which culminated in a demonstration against Japanese colonial rule on March 1, 1919. His works were frequently patriotic, invoking Buddhist themes to reiterate Korean culture and to inspire resistance against Japanese rule. Examples of such poems are "Submission" and the title poem from his most famous work, a collection of 88 poems titled *The Silence of Love* (1926). In these free-verse Buddhist poems addressing a *nim,* or love, the object of love is ambiguous. Critics believe that the *nim* is alternately a woman ("And You"), the Korean people ("To My Readers"), or a Buddhist object of nature ("Preface"). Although the *nim* itself may remain nameless, themes of patriotism, devotion, and a pantheistic love are evident. One of the most famous poems from the collection, "Ferryboat and Traveler," examines the relationship between joining and parting in love.

Han Yongun wrote in the Chinese style, in *sijo,* or the traditional Korean verse, and in free verse. The poems from *The Silence of Love* are known for their innovative free verse. Another literary innovation was using poetry as a vehicle for social and political change, a marked departure from the lyrical and apolitical Korean literary tradition.

Han Yongun died of neuralgia on June 29 at age 65, just one year before Korea gained liberation from Japanese rule.

Another Work by Han Yongun

Love's Silence and Other Poems. New York: Ronsdale Press, 1999.

A Work about Han Yongun

Yu, Beongcheon. *Han Yong-un and Yi Kwang-su: Two Pioneers of Modern Korean Literature.* Detroit: Wayne State University Press, 1992.

Handke, Peter (1942–) *playwright, novelist, critic*

Peter Handke was born in Altenmarkt, Austria, to Maria Handke, an impoverished farmer, and was raised by his stepfather, Bruno Handke, a soldier in the German army and later a carpenter. Handke attended a standard Austrian elementary school. Between 1954 and 1959, he lived and studied at a Roman Catholic seminary, intending to become a priest. The admission to the seminary of a poor country boy, gained through a rigid examination, was a source of pride for Handke and his parents. Handke, however, was extremely unhappy at the seminary and later expounded on the state-sponsored lies taught by the priests.

Between 1961 and 1965, Handke studied law at the Karl-Franzens University in Graz. When Handke's first novel was accepted for publication by a prestigious publishing company, he immediately quit the law, leaving the school before the final exam. Handke began his writing career as a literary critic and writer for the Austrian radio. In 1966, shortly after the publication of his first major work, *Die Hornissen* (*The Hornets*), the 23-year-old Handke publicly criticized contemporary German literature and GRUPPE 47, the group of leading German writers, at a literary seminar held at Princeton University. He claimed that Group 47 established a codified set of aesthetics that rigidly defined what literature should be. Handke has remained a controversial figure in literature for much of his career. In 1969, he started Verlag der Autoren, a publishing house that supported radical writers and filmmakers.

Critical Analysis

Handke established himself as a renovator of the German theater with the production of *Publikumsbeschimpfung* (1966; translated as *Offending the Audience*, 1971). The play completely departs from traditional theatrical conventions, such as plot, theme, and character. The four actors literally set about offending the audience by lecturing the spectators about their expectations, naïveté, and conventional role. The play caused a sensation, but many critics saw Handke's gesture as pretentious and concluded that his drama would never gain a wide appeal in Germany.

The Hornets has not been translated into English. Instead of using the traditional units of demarcations, the novel is structured into 67 free-standing, episodic parts that seemingly have no connection, narrative or otherwise, among them. At the center of the convoluted narrative is the blind narrator, Gregor Benedikt, who attempts to reconstruct the events leading to his blindness. Instead of using visual images, Handke relies on imitation of words and sounds to recreate Gregor's environment. While deconstructing the traditional conventions of the novel, *The Hornets* comments on the structure of the traditional novel. Although the novel brought critical recognition to Handke, it baffled and surprised most of its readers.

Der Hausierer (*The Peddler,* 1967) further challenges the traditional methodology of the novel. The novel is divided into chapters, which are further subdivided into theoretical and narrative sections. The theoretical sections present the theory behind the detective novel. The narrative parts elusively delineate a fragmented murder mystery but do not present a motivation for the murder, nor is the crime solved in the end. Indeed, the only clues to reading the narrative are provided in the theoretical parts of the work. *The Peddler* was called unreadable by many critics and never achieved wide success with the general reading public.

A prolific writer, Peter Handke has produced more than 20 plays, several screenplays, and several works of fiction. He has also directed and acted in films. He has received numerous prizes for his writing, including the Corinthian Culture Prize in 1983, the Franz Kafka Prize in 1979, and the Great Austrian State Prize in 1988.

By the 1980s, Handke had achieved recognition as a leading contemporary author in Austria. Many of his plays were translated into French and English. In the mid-1990s, however, his name once again became controversial when he wrote a series of articles supporting Serbia in the Balkan Wars and condemning the NATO bombings.

Later, at the funeral of Slobodan Milošević (the former president of Serbia who was accused of war crimes) in 2006, Handke gave a speech that caused great controversy throughout the world. Handke is reported to have said he was happy "at being close to Milošević who defended his people," but he denies that those were his words. In a letter to a French newspaper, he translated his words from the Serbian. His version of the remarks follows: "The world, the so-called world, knows everything about Yugoslavia, Serbia. The world, the so-called world, knows everything about Slobodan Milošević. The so-called world knows the truth. This is why the so-called world is absent today, and not only today, and not only here. I don't know the truth. But I look. I listen. I feel. I remember. This is why I am here today, close to Yugoslavia, close to Serbia, close to Slobodan Milošević." Despite his controversial political stance, Handke's work is still praised and read throughout the world. Peter Handke has established himself as one of the leading figures of POSTMODERNISM.

Other Works by Peter Handke

Crossing the Sierra de Gredos: A Novel. Chicago: Northwestern University Press, 2009.
Don Juan: His Own Version. New York: Farrar, Straus and Giroux, 2010.
The Goalie's Anxiety at the Penalty Kick. New York: Farrar, Straus and Giroux, 2007.
On a Dark Night I Left My Silent House. Translated by Krishna Winston. New York: Farrar, Straus & Giroux, 2000.
Once Again for Thucydides. Translated by Tess Lewis. New York: New Directions, 1998.
A Sorrow Beyond Dreams: A Life Story. Translated by Ralph Manheim. New York: Farrar, Straus & Giroux, 1975.

Works about Peter Handke

Demeritt, Linda C. *New Subjectivity and Prose Forms of Alienation: Peter Handke and Botho Strauss.* New York: Peter Lang, 1987.
Firda, Richard. *Peter Handke.* Boston: Twayne, 1993.

Konzett, Matthias. *The Rhetoric of National Dissent: In Thomas Bernhard, Peter Handke, and Elfriede Jelinek.* Rochester, N.Y.: Camden House, 2000.

Harris, Wilson (Kona Woruk) (1921–)
novelist, critic, poet

Wilson Theodore Harris was born to a middle-class family in New Amsterdam, a colony of British Guiana that is now the independent country of Guyana. He studied English literary classics and classical literature while attending Queen's College in Georgetown, the capital of Guyana, from 1934 to 1939. Harris also studied and practiced land surveying, which informed his fiction; the surveyor is one of Harris's recurring fictional characters. He also uses the land as an innovative fictional tool.

While working as a land surveyor, Harris began to publish poems, stories, critical essays, and reviews in the literary journal *Kyk-over-al*. He published two small books of poems, *Fetish* (1951) and *Eternity to Season* (1954), before leaving Guyana for Britain in 1959 to become a full-time writer. His first novel, *Palace of the Peacock* (1969), one of his best known, is an exploration of intercultural and interracial relationships, as well as of history and mythology in Guyana.

Harris continues to explore these intercultural, interracial, and transhistorical themes in Guyana in subsequent novels: *The Far Journey of Oudin* (1961), *The Whole Armour* (1962), *The Secret Ladder* (1963), and *Heartland* (1964). Commenting on Harris's poetry and novels in *New World Guyana Independence Issue*, Louis James asserts, "For Harris, time and space are exploded, and as in atomic physics, matter is transformed into energy and vice versa, a person may turn into a place, a place into an aspiration."

Harris's own comments in *Explorations* (1981), a collection of critical writings, explain what motivates the symbols, mythological allusions, nonlinearity, imagistic juxtaposition, and multiple speakers that reappear in his novels. He states that, "Within the art of fiction we are attempting to explore . . . it is a 'vacancy' in nature within which agents appear who are translated one by the other and who . . . reappear through each other, inhabit each other, reflect a burden of necessity, push each other to plunge into the unknown, into the translatable, transmutable legacies of history." In other words, Harris's literary devices require the reader to participate actively with him in exploring culture and history.

In his next novels, Harris focuses on memory and the mind, still using the setting of Guyana, and explores the land's symbolic potential. Some of these novels include *The Eye of the Scarecrow* (1965) and *The Waiting Room* (1967), both of which were written in the form of a diary or journal. *Tumatumari* (1968) and *Ascent to Omai* (1970) explore the female and male consciousness, respectively.

In Harris's later novels, he begins to use different settings, such as London, Mexico, Edinburgh, and India. Themes of resurrection, metaphors of painting, and characters reoccur in these novels: *Companions of the Day and Night* (1975), *Da Silva da Silva's Cultivated Wilderness* (1977), *Genesis of the Clowns* (1977), *The Tree of the Sun* (1978), and *The Angel at the Gate* (1982). *Da Silva da Silva's Cultivated Wilderness* exemplifies the autobiographical traces found in his other works, such as the *Genesis of Clowns;* like Harris, Da Silva is a South American artist of mixed racial background who lives in London.

While writing, Harris worked as a lecturer and writer-in-residence at different universities, including the University of the West Indies, the University of Texas at Austin and Yale University in the United States, and New Castle University in Australia. His critical works include *Fossil and Psyche* (1974), *The Womb of Space: The Cross-Cultural Imagination* (1983), and *The Radical Imagination* (1992). In *Wilson Harris and the Caribbean Novel* (1975), Michael Gilkes asserts, "The work of Wilson Harris deserves serious attention for this reason above all: it suggests the possibility of a response to the West Indian cultural and historical reality which is neither a revolt against, nor

a passive acceptance of, a divisive situation." Harris was knighted in 2010.

Other Works by Wilson Harris

Bundy, A. J. M., ed. *Selected Essays of Wilson Harris: The Unfinished Genesis of the Imagination.* New York: Routledge, 1999.
The Four Banks of the River of Space. Boston: Faber, 1990.
The Ghost of Memory. London: Faber & Faber, 2006.
Mask of the Beggar. London: Faber & Faber, 2003.
Resurrection at Sorrow Hill. London: Faber & Faber, 1993.

Works about Wilson Harris

Cribb, Timothy J. "Toward the Reading of Wilson Harris." *Review of Contemporary Fiction* 17, no. 2 (Summer 1997): 59–62.
Johnson, Kerry L. "Translations of Gender, Pain, and Space: Wilson Harris's *The Carnival Trilogy, Meddelanden fran Strindbergssallskapet*" 44, no. 1 (Spring 1998): 123–143.
Kutzinski, Vera M. "New Personalities: Race, Sexuality, and Gender in Wilson Harris's Recent Fiction." *Review of Contemporary Fiction* 17, no. 2 (Summer 1997): 72–76.

Hašek, Jaroslav (1883–1923) *novelist*

Jaroslav Hašek was born in Prague in 1883 to a middle-class family. His childhood was uneventful, but his later years were fraught with alcoholism and mental instability. He is best known for his satiric masterpiece *The Good Soldier Schweik* (1921). He also created the Party of Peaceful Progress Within the Limits of Law, a political party, the financial proceeds from which he spent at the local pub.

At the start of his literary career, Hašek was widely published in political journals. In 1907, he became the editor of *Komuna,* a noted anarchist magazine. He married, but his wife later left him when he became involved in stealing dogs and forging pedigrees. After attempting suicide, Hašek spent a brief period in a mental institution. In

1915, he began to work as a cabaret performer but was called to serve in the Austrian army during World War I. All of these experiences were used to create the character of Schweik, a drunkard and a liar who ultimately outwits the army. Other exploits from Hašek's own life that found their place in his work include his imprisonment in camps in Ukraine and the Urals during the war, his work as a propagandist with the Czech Legion, and his ultimate return to Prague and nationalist politics.

Critically acclaimed as one of the world's greatest satires, *The Good Soldier Schweik* was first rejected by the literary establishment because the character of Schweik was considered too low class. An incompetent soldier, Schweik is arrested for making snide remarks about the assassination of Archduke Ferdinand and, in another escapade, is thrown out of an insane asylum when the doctors suspect him of merely feigning madness. The general public, however, responded favorably to his antics. Four volumes of Schweik's adventures were completed, the last published posthumously and finished by Hašek's friend Karel Vanek.

Another Work by Jaroslav Hašek

The Bachura Scandal and Other Stories and Sketches. Translated by Alan Menhennet. Chester Springs, Pa.: Dufour Editions, 1992.

Works about Jaroslav Hašek

Parrott, Cecil. *The Bad Bohemian: The Life of Jaroslav Hašek, Creator of The Good Soldier Svejk.* London: Bodley Head, 1978.

———. *Jaroslav Hašek: A Study of Svejk and the Short Stories.* Cambridge: Cambridge University Press, 1982.

Hasluck, Nicholas (1942–) *novelist, poet*

Nicholas Hasluck, born in Canberra, Australia, was the son of Sir Paul and Dame Alexandra Hasluck, both established writers. His father served on numerous missions to the United Nations and was governor-general of Australia between 1969 and 1974. His parents' achievements in writing and their involvement in public life have influenced Hasluck's own writing career. After studying law at the universities of Western Australia and Oxford in 1963 and 1966, respectively, Hasluck worked briefly as an editorial assistant in London before returning to Australia in 1967 to become a barrister.

Hasluck's literary works reflect his concerns with political and social issues within Australian society. In his 1982 novel, *The Hand That Feeds You,* a cynical commentary on contemporary Australian society, Hasluck observes that the push for development and progress meets reluctance because people prefer easy options, such as reliance on the welfare system. His literature presents a world of espionage and subversion. The characters of his novels, such as Dyson Garrick, are compelling figures whose goals are usually hampered by external factors that lead them to choose between their dreams and their lives. His poetry, however, is diffuse and slightly satirical. In the poem "Anchor" (1976), the "anchor" refers to turning points or moments suspended in time at which a person's life arrives and departs from a new juncture, departing from the old path. This poem illuminates Hasluck's awareness of the transient nature of life and the importance of events in determining changes in one's life.

The newspaper *The West Australian* refers to Hasluck as "A writer who obviously thinks the truth and the relationship between art and life are important matters . . . one of those rare writers who can meditate on these issues and at the same time write highly entertaining stories." Hasluck's novel *Our Man K* (1999) shows most aptly his desire to achieve a balance between reality and fiction. Drawing on historical materials, Hasluck recreates Egon Kisch (1855–1948), a Czech reporter who went to Australia in the 1930s to address an antiwar congress, as his central character. Kisch was a key figure during the war years, and his controversial character and his satirical writings form the basis for Hasluck's fiction. Hasluck's *The Bellarmine Jug,* a detective thriller set in Holland, won the

Age Book of the Year Award in 1984. *The Country Without Music,* a fiction that examines the earlier history of Australia when it was still a penal colony, was the joint winner of the 1990 Western Australia Premier's Award for Fiction. In 2000, Hasluck was appointed as a judge on the supreme court of Western Australia.

Other Works by Nicholas Hasluck
Anchor and Other Poems. Fremantle, Australia: Fremantle Arts Center Press, 1976.
The Blue Guitar. New York: Holt, Rinehart and Winston, 1980.
A Grain of Truth. Melbourne, Australia: Penguin, 1987.
The Hat on the Letter O. (Revised Edition) Fremantle, Australia: Fremantle Arts Center Press, 1990.
Quarantine. Melbourne and Sydney: Macmillan Press, 1978.
Truant State. Victoria: Penguin, 1987.

Hauptmann, Gerhart (1862–1946)
playwright, novelist
Gerhart Hauptmann was born in Obersalzbrunn, Germany, a fashionable resort town, to Robert and Marie Hauptmann, owners of a small hotel. Hauptmann entered a gymnasium in Breslau but had to leave because of conduct problems and poor academic performance. Hauptmann was artistically inclined from an early age and initially rejected formal education. Disturbed by the attitudes of young Hauptmann, his family sent him to live with his uncle, a pious estate owner. Hauptmann spent several years living and working alongside the peasants on his uncle's estate, learning their simple way of life and their deep religious devotion. Hauptmann eventually changed his attitude toward formal education but remained adamant in his goal of becoming an artist. He attended an art academy in Breslau, initially intending to become a sculptor. Hauptmann's artistic goals changed, however, and he briefly studied history at the University of Jena between 1882 and 1883.

Hauptmann studied art in Rome but was forced to return to Germany because of ill health in 1884. While in Rome, Hauptmann decided to become a writer. In 1885, Hauptmann married Marie Thienemann, an attractive heiress. Thienemann's wealth provided the financial support for Hauptmann's artistic goals. After settling in Berlin, Hauptmann immersed himself in the literary and intellectual currents of the day.

Gerhardt Hauptmann's early influences were derived from the works of German ROMANTICISM. In Berlin, however, Hauptmann came into a contact with progressive intellectuals who rejected romanticism and fervently advocated REALISM. Indeed, Hauptmann's early plays reflect the profound influence of HENRIK IBSEN, the master of dramatic realism. Consequently, Hauptmann's themes are often related to the social and political conditions of German society.

Critical Analysis
In 1889, Hauptmann's debut play, *Vor Sonnenaufgang (Before Dawn)* attracted attention from many and shocked its audiences with its candid realism. The play depicts the relationship between Alfred Loth, a young socialist who studies the working conditions in the Silesian coal mines, and Helene Kraus, a sister-in-law of his former college comrade who takes control of the mines. Helene's family is corrupted by the power and money that the coal mines bring. Alfred Loth leaves Helene after an intense emotional struggle that results in her suicide. Hauptmann highlights the intense opposition and conflict created by corruption and exploitation of workers.

Die Weber (The Weavers, 1892) dramatizes a revolt of the Silesian weavers that occurred in 1844. The audience was amazed to find no leading hero in the cast of more than 70 characters. Hauptmann wrote the play without a leading character to dramatize the struggle of ordinary people. Viewed as politically dangerous, *The Weavers* was at first banned by the authorities. When the play was finally performed, it established Hauptmann's reputation as one of the world's leading dramatists.

Another play, *The Beaver Coat* (1893), is a broad comedy in Berlin dialect about a woman who cleverly tricks pompous bureaucrats; it was a great hit with the public. But Hauptmann began to withdraw from realism and to focus on the destiny of individual characters rather than tackling social problems with *Hanneles Himmelfahrt* (*The Assumption of Hannele*, 1894), about a peasant girl's visionary dream life, and *Die versunkene Glocke* (*The Sunken Bell*, 1897), a mystical verse drama. In many respects, this shift is associated with turmoil in Hauptmann's personal life. He developed a romantic relationship with a 14-year-old girl, Margaret Marschalk. In 1904, Hauptmann divorced his wife and married Marschalk after she became pregnant. The deep spiritual and psychological conflict of this relationship is reflected in such tragedies as *Fuhrman Henschell* (*Drayman Henschell*, 1898), which shows the psychological deterioration brought about in its central hero by domestic conflict.

Although mainly remembered as a dramatist, Hauptmann was also a prolific novelist. *Der Narr in Christo, Emanuel Quint* (*The Fool in Christ, Emmanuel Quint*, 1910), Hauptmann's most famous novel, reflects in the story of a Silesian carpenter Hauptmann's fascination with the figure of Christ. Indescribable in terms of a single thematic focus, the novel combines elements of mysticism, fantasy, symbolism, and folklore to create a complex world of religious and spiritual ambiguity.

Gerhardt Hauptmann was recognized for his contributions to world literature when he was awarded the Nobel Prize in 1912. He remained in Germany throughout the Nazi period, his adherence to the principles of social justice and socialism remaining strong in the face of the Nazi harassment and threats. Despite constant recommendations by Hauptmann's peers, the Nazi regime adamantly denied him the Schiller Prize, the most prestigious prize for literature in Germany. By the time he died, his Silesian homeland had been annexed by the Russian army.

Other Works by Gerhart Hauptmann

Lineman Thiel and Other Tales. Translated by Stanley Radcliffe. Chester Springs, Pa.: Dufour Editions, 1989.

Plays: Before Daybreak, The Weavers, The Beaver Coat. Edited by Reinhold Grimm and Caroline Molina y Vedia. New York: Continuum, 1994.

Three Plays: The Weavers, Hannele, The Beaver Coat. Translated by Horst Frenz and Miles Waggoner. New York: Ungar, 1977.

Works about Gerhart Hauptmann

Maurer, Warren G. *Understanding Gerhart Hauptmann.* Columbia: University of South Carolina Press, 1992.

Osborne, John. *Gerhart Hauptmann and the Naturalist Drama.* London: Routledge, 1998.

Havel, Václav (1936–) *nonfiction, playwright*

Best known internationally as the former president of the Czech Republic, Václav Havel was born in Prague. The son of intellectuals who were closely tied to political uprisings, Havel was prohibited by the Communist government from finishing school after his compulsory education. Havel, therefore, apprenticed as a lab technician and continued taking night classes.

After serving two years in the military, Havel took a job as a stagehand at the ABC Theater and later at The Balustrade, where he became resident playwright and where his first plays, including his well-known *The Garden Party* (1963) were produced. *The Garden Party* was a satire of modern bureaucratic routines.

Havel enrolled at the Academy of Dramatic Arts and graduated in 1967. He also joined the editorial board of *Tvárin*, a literary magazine that conflicted with the conservative Writers' Association. The magazine disappeared in 1969, the same year Havel's passport was confiscated because of his supposed subversive writings.

In many of his plays, Havel used satire to comment on social and political issues. In *The Memorandum* (1965), for example, the creation of an improved language results in a breakdown of human relationships. *The Increased Difficulty of Concentration* (1968), moreover, attacks sociological terminology. After the Soviet invasion in 1968, Havel wrote a series of one-act plays, *Audience* (1978), *Private View* (1978), and *Protest* (1978), in which the main character is a playwright in trouble with the authorities.

Throughout the 1970s, a period of political unrest, Havel helped start the human-rights organization Charter 77 and the Committee for the Defense of the Unjustly Prosecuted. His plays were banned, but the manuscripts circulated privately and were printed in Western Europe, bringing attention to the Czechoslovakian struggle. As a result, Havel was subjected to police harassment and numerous arrests.

After the fall of communism, Havel was president of Czechoslovakia from 1989 to 2003. His contribution to politics grew directly from his active participation in politically motivated literature. His lifelong dedication to human rights and democratic reforms are reflected in his plays, which serve as inspiration to others that the power of one person can change history.

In 2007, Havel published a political memoir, *To the Castle and Back,* in the form of what he called "a special kind of collage." The book deals primarily with his 14 years at Prague Castle, where the presidents of Czechoslovakia have their offices. Paul Berman, writing for the *New York Times Book Review,* described the book as "an artful, sly and touching self-portrait, cleverly and neurotically disguised as an artless heap of dry scribbled notes and wastebasket throwaways."

Another Work by Václav Havel

The Garden Party and Other Plays. New York: Grove Press, 1993.

Works about Václav Havel

Kriseova, Eda. *Vacláv Havel: The Authorized Biography.* New York: St. Martin's Press, 1993.
McRae, Robert. *Resistance and Revolution.* Ottawa: Carleton University Press, 1997.

Hayashi Fumiko (Miyata Fumiko)
(1903–1951) *novelist, poet, children's story writer, reporter*

Hayashi Fumiko was born to Hayashi Assatarō Miyata and Kiku in Shimonoseki, Yamaguchi Prefecture, in Japan. Her schooling was sporadic until she entered Onomichi Girls High School in Hiroshima Prefecture. However, because her family could not pay her school fees, Hayashi worked nights at a canvas-sail factory to pay for her own education. After graduating, Hayashi had a number of unsuccessful relationships with men until she settled down with Rokutoshi Tezuka in 1926. She was obsessive about her writing, often sacrificing her health for her work. She died of a heart attack.

While Hayashi was attending high school, she contributed poems to local newspapers. Her aspirations to become a professional writer took her to Tokyo, Japan's literary center, in 1924, and she began to publish children's stories. However, she achieved greater success as a poet, producing her first collection, *I Saw a Blue Horse,* in 1929. A year later, she published one of her best received works, the fictional diary *Vagabond's Song,* which was based on her early life. During the war, Hayashi became a war correspondent and witnessed the fall of Nanking. The war became a source of inspiration, and afterward she entered her most productive period, writing numerous short stories, essays, and novels about people struggling against the adversity of war. Her final novel, *Drifting Clouds* (1951), follows in this vein, portraying a young woman trying to navigate the changing social structure of postwar Japan.

Hayashi gained special fame for the quantity of literature she produced and for her ability to capture subtle emotions in her writing. Her stories typically portray the lives of the underdogs struggling in prewar and postwar Japan.

Other Works by Hayashi Fumiko

"Narcissus." Translated by Kyoko Selden. In Noriko Lippit and Kyoko Selden, eds., *Stories by*

Contemporary Japanese Women Writers. Ardsley, N.Y.: M. E. Sharpe, 1982.

"Tokyo." Translated by Ivan Morris. In Donald Keene, ed., *Modern Japanese Literature.* New York: Grove Press, 1956.

Works about Hayashi Fumiko

Ericson, Joan E. *Be a Woman: Hayashi Fumiko and Modern Japanese Women's Literature.* Honolulu: University of Hawaii Press, 1997.

Tanaka, Yukiko, ed. *To Love and to Write: Selections by Japanese Women Writers 1913–1938.* Seattle: Seal Press, 1987.

Hayashi Kyōko (Miyazaki Kyōko)
(1930–   ) *novelist, essayist*

Hayashi Kyōko was born in Nagasaki but spent her first 14 years in Japanese-occupied Shanghai. In 1945, a few months before Japan's defeat, Hayashi moved to Nagasaki, where she attended high school and worked in a munitions factory. When the atomic bomb was dropped on Nagasaki, Hayashi fell victim to severe radiation sickness. After several months, she had recovered enough to re-enter high school, graduating in 1947. She then studied nursing but shortly abandoned it and moved to Tokyo. There, she met and married a journalist in 1951 and gave birth to a son.

Hayashi began her writing career in 1962 when she was hired by the magazine *Bungei Shuto (Literary Capital).* Her first story, "Ritual of Death," based on her experiences on August 9, 1945, appeared in the magazine in 1975. Three years later, she published a short-story collection, *Cut Glass and Blown Glass,* which depicts atomic bomb experiences. In her next collection, *Michelle's Lipstick* (1980), the stories are narrated by a girl in Shanghai. Developing her concerns about the long-term effects of war, Hayashi published her third collection, *Home in Three Worlds,* in 1984.

As a *hibakusha* (a survivor of the atomic bombing), Hayashi lives with fears about the effect of radiation on her son, her health, and the human race. Her writing usually focuses on the atomic bombing and her experiences in Shanghai and reflects a personal belief that the past exists in the present. She has won the Gunzō New Writer's Prize, the Akutagawa Award, the Kawabata Yasunari Literary Award, and the Woman Writer's Award.

Other Works by Hayashi Kyōko

"The Empty Can." Translated by Margaret Mitsutani. In *The Crazy Iris and Other Stories of the Atomic Aftermath.* Edited by Kenzaburō Ōe. New York: Grove Press, 1985.

"Yellow Sand." Translated by Kyoko Iriye Selden. In *Stories by Contemporary Japanese Women Writers.* Edited by Noriko Mizuta Lippit and Kyoko Selden. New York: M. E. Sharpe, 1982.

Works about Hayashi Kyōko

Bhowmik, Davinder L. "Temporal Discontinuity in the Atomic Bomb Fiction of Hayashi Kyōko." In *Ōe and Beyond: Fiction in Contemporary Japan.* Edited by Stephen Snyder and Philip Gabriel. Honolulu: University of Hawaii Press, 1999.

Treat, John Whittier. "Hayashi Kyōko and the Gender of Ground Zero." In *The Woman's Hand: Gender and Theory in Japanese Women's Writing.* Edited by Paul Schalow and Janet Walker. Stanford, Calif.: Stanford University Press, 1996.

Hayslip, Le Ly (1949–   ) *novelist*

Le Ly Hayslip was born in Ky La, a village near Da Nang, Vietnam. She was the seventh child in a peasant farm family, grew up during the Vietnam War, and received only a third-grade education. When she turned 14, she was accused of sympathizing with the revolutionaries by the South Vietnamese government and of being a government spy by the Vietcong. Originally sentenced to death by the Vietcong revolutionaries, her life was spared and Hayslip fled to Saigon, where she met her first husband, Ed Munro, an American civilian working in Vietnam. They married when she turned 21 and escaped to the United States in 1970.

Hayslip's first memoir, *When Heaven and Earth Changed Places,* is a heartrending account of her life beginning with her turbulent childhood and ending with her return to Vietnam after an absence of 16 years. The book, published in 1989 and well received, explores the ironic balance between the bittersweet anguish of Hayslip's past and her renewed hope and forgiveness for her homeland. Hayslip published her second memoir, *Child of War, Woman of Peace,* in 1993. Her eldest son, James, was her coauthor. The memoir relates the author's life after she moved to the United States.

Hayslip's literary success lies in her ability to blend both Eastern and Western values. Her poignant story became the setting for the award-winning film *Heaven and Earth* (1993), directed by Oliver Stone. Stone was so moved by Hayslip's account that he funded the building of a clinic in Hayslip's home village in Da Nang.

Hayslip, who now lives in California, continues to encourage both Vietnamese and Americans to overcome the stigma of the Vietnam War by engaging in projects to build schools and medical facilities in impoverished parts of Vietnam. Her East Meets West Foundation, formed in 1988, continues to give humanitarian relief to individuals and groups to help them rebuild their lives.

Head, Bessie (1937–1986) *novelist*

Bessie Head was born in Pietermaritzburg, South Africa. She was the illegitimate daughter of a wealthy white Scottish woman and a South African stablehand. Head was born in the mental institution where her mother died. She was taken from her mother at birth and raised in a foster home in the colored community of Cape Province. When she turned 13, she began six years of study at St. Monica's Home, an Anglican missionary school for colored girls.

Head received a teaching certificate in 1955 and taught in an elementary school for two years. She then worked for a succession of newspapers in Cape Town, Johannesburg, and Port Elizabeth. Though married in 1960, she soon divorced in 1964. Her involvement in the Pan Africanist Congress, a political party that emerged around the same time as the African National Congress, led to her brief arrest and constant surveillance by the government. She left South Africa for Botswana in 1964 and remained in exile until her death. Although Head always felt a sense of nostalgia for South Africa, she never wanted to return to her homeland, dreading the prospect of fighting apartheid.

Head's writings are epitomized by tumultuous emotions, unsettling trauma, and hope, as seen through the optimism and resilience of her characters. Her works deal with issues of alienation, racial discrimination, poverty and interpersonal relationships. Her ability to convey a variety of perspectives through her characters is a testimony to her creativity and talent. Head's most renowned novel is *Question of Power,* published in 1973. The story revolves around an expatriate named Elizabeth who lives in Botswana. Elizabeth's various imagined encounters with a lover land her in a mental hospital, and her hellish experiences are metaphorical allegories of racism and gender discrimination. Bessie Head's greatest contribution to world literature lies in her ability not only to examine the problems related to the issue of gender discrimination in South Africa but also to offer solutions to the problems.

Other Works by Bessie Head

The Collectors of Treasures. London: Heinemann, 1992.

Daymond, M. J., ed. *The Cardinals: With Meditations and Short Stories.* London: Heinemann, 1996.

Maru. London: Heinemann, 1996.

Tales of Tenderness and Power. London: Heinemann, 1989.

When Rain Clouds Gather. London: Heinemann, 1996.

A Woman Alone: Autobiographical Writings. London: Heinemann, 1991.

Works about Bessie Head

Abrahams, C., ed. *The Tragic Life: Bessie Head and Literature in Southern Africa.* Trenton, N.J.: Africa World Press, 1990.

Eilersen, Gillian. *Bessie Head: Thunder Behind Her Ears: Her Life and Writing.* Cape Town: David Philip, 1995.

Garrett, James. "Writing Community: Bessie Head and the Politics of Narrative." *Research in African Literature* 30:2 (Summer 1999).

Hébert, Anne (1916–2000) *poet, novelist*

Anne Hébert was born in Quebec. Her earliest influences include her father, a civil servant, and her cousin, the poet Hector de Saint-Denys Garneau. Though Hébert moved to Paris in the 1950s, she made several trips back to Canada. She died of cancer in the city of Montreal.

Hébert's work began to receive critical attention in the 1940s and 1950s with the publication of her first book of poetry in 1942, *Les songes en equilibre;* her next book of poems appeared in 1953, titled *Le tombeau des rois.* Her first novel, *Kamouraska,* about a 19th-century murder, appeared in 1970 and was translated into English in 1974. Another of Hébert's novels, *Héloïse* (1980), concerns a vampire in Paris. *Les fous de bassan* (1982, translated as *In the Shadow of the Wind*) tells the story of a double rape and murder from multiple points of view. Hébert won the Governor General's Literary Award twice, for *Poèmes* in 1960 and for the novel *Les enfants du Sabbat* (*The Children of the Sabbath*) in 1975, and received many other awards. She is one of the best-known and most translated Québecois writers.

Another Work by Anne Hébert

Anne Hébert: Selected Poems. Translated by A. Poulin, Jr. Brockport, N.Y.: BOA Editions, 1987.

A Work about Anne Hébert

Knight, Kelton, W. *Anne Hébert: In Search of the First Garden.* New York: Peter Lang, 1998.

Heine, Heinrich (1797–1856) *poet*

Heinrich Heine was born in Düsseldorf, Germany, to a Jewish family. After the failure of his father's business, Heine went to live with his uncle Solomon in Hamburg to train for a career in commerce. Heine disliked commerce and decided to study law, which he did at the universities of Bonn, Berlin, and Göttingen, finally taking a degree in 1825. To enter civil service, which was closed to Jews at that time in Germany, Heine converted to Protestantism; however, he never practiced law or held a government post of any sort.

Heine's own writing was deeply influenced by the philosophy of G. W. F. Hegel, who was a professor at the University of Berlin. Heine was fascinated with the early ideas of socialism and with the improvement of workers' conditions and frequently corresponded with Friedrich Engels and Karl Marx, both admirers of Heine's work. In 1831, he embarked for Paris as a journalist.

Heine found the bustling, artistic world of Paris a startling contrast to the repressive atmosphere in Germany. In Paris, Heine reported on French cultural life, wrote travel books, and reviewed German works on politics and philosophy. His affinity for socialism and vocal criticism of German politics quickly brought him to the attention of censors. In 1835, the federal German Diet attempted to enforce strictly a ban on all of his works throughout Germany. Heine was surrounded by government spies, and his stay in Paris eventually became a permanent exile.

Heine's poems range from bitter political satires to love lyrics. *The Book of Songs* (1827), one of the early lyrical collections, established Heine's success in Germany. The collection reveals a heavy influence of traditional folk poetry but also a stylistic shift from the lyrical traditions of the romantic movement to a dimension of social criticism. *Germany: A Winter's Tale* (1844) presents a satire in verse that attacks reactionary aspects of German society. At the end of the long narrative poem, the Goddess of Hamburg reveals a gloomy vision of Germany's future to the narrator, who is half submerged in a chamber pot.

The death of Heine's uncle in 1844 left him with a small pension; the French government also subsidized him. The same year, Heine was overcome by a terrible disease that left him paralyzed and partially blind. Heine continued to work and, in 1851, produced one of his finest collections of verses, *Romanzero.* The collection was different from anything he had done before. In *Romanzero,* Heine attempted to reconcile and combine the elements of Christianity and paganism. Thematically, Heine attempted to avoid the political controversy that his previous collections caused in Germany.

Heinrich Heine remained a controversial figure long after his death. A proposal to erect a statue commemorating his works caused riots in Germany. The works have been closely identified with German national identity, and he had an enormous influence on later poets, such as RAINER MARIA RILKE. The Nazis allowed publication of Heine's works; they did not reveal the identity of the author, however, because of his Jewish background. Although Heine contributed to German romanticism, his later works clearly show a deviation from the traditional themes and motifs of this movement. Today, Heinrich Heine is included in the canon of German literature as an influential poet crucial to the development of national literature, as well as an important social thinker.

Other Works by Heinrich Heine

The Harz Journey. Translated by Charles Leland. New York: Marsilio Publishers, 1995.
The Romantic School and Other Essays. New York: Continuum, 1985.
Songs of Love and Grief. Translated by Arndt Walter. Chicago: Northwestern University Press, 1995.

Works about Heinrich Heine

Hermand, Joest. *Heinrich Heine's Contested Identities: Politics, Religion, and Nationalism in Nineteenth Century Germany.* New York: Peter Lang, 1999.
Kossoff, Philip. *Valiant Heart: A Biography of Heinrich Heine.* London: Cornwall Books, 1983.

Herzen, Aleksandr Ivanovich (1812–1870) *philosopher, essayist*

Aleksandr Herzen was born in Moscow, Russia, as an illegitimate child of Luisa Gaag, a German immigrant, and Ivan Yakovlev, a retired army officer and minor aristocrat. His father paid for Herzen to receive an excellent education from private tutors, and Herzen became fluent in several European languages. He was particularly interested in the history of the French Revolution and the poetry of ALEKSANDR PUSHKIN. In 1829, he began to attend the Moscow University in preparation for a job in civil service.

In 1834, Herzen was implicated in an antigovernment conspiracy. Placed under arrest and, after months of interrogations, exiled to Perm, Herzen did not return to Moscow until 1840. During his years in exile, Herzen began his prolific career as a writer, but most of the works written during this period could not be published in Russia because of their politically incendiary, liberal content. Influenced by the French socialist philosophers, particularly Claude Saint-Simon (1760–1825), Herzen often criticized the institution of serfdom and dominant autocracy in Russian government. Unable to continue his work in Russia, Herzen moved to Paris in 1847, never to return.

That year, Herzen published a novel, *Who Is to Blame?* (1847), about a young liberal who becomes disillusioned with Russia and its political institutions. After his relocation abroad, Herzen abandoned fiction writing in favor of social and political works. During his brief stay in France, Herzen supported the French revolution of 1848. After the failure of the revolution, Herzen wrote *From the Other Shore* (1850), an analysis and critique of the European revolutionary movements of the time.

In 1852 Herzen moved to London, where he founded the Free Russian Press, which published a series of journals. Herzen was finally able to express freely his political opinions. Between 1857 and 1862, Herzen published a liberal journal, *Kolokol* (*The Bell*), which was banned in Russia but smuggled in. For a time, the journal acquired tremendous popularity and wide readership in Russia. It may have been influential in Czar Aleksandr II's 1860 liberation of the serfs. Herzen supported the traditional, communal institutions of Russia, which he considered as precursor for a free, socialist society—contrary to the government's agenda. However, by the 1860s, Herzen's views seemed conservative to many Russian political factions, and *The Bell*'s influence waned. Herzen turned to writing his autobiography, *My Past and Thoughts* (1852–55), in which he included an account of Russia under serfdom and the attendant social-resistance movements of the period.

British playwright Tom Stoppard has made Herzen the subject of a trilogy, *The Coast of Utopia*. In a 2002 article in the *Observer*, Stoppard says:

> Herzen had no time for the kind of mono-theory that bound history, progress and individual autonomy to some overarching abstraction like Marx's material dialecticism. What he did have time for . . . was the individual over the collective, the actual over the theoretical. What he detested above all was the conceit that future bliss justified present sacrifice and bloodshed.

Works by Aleksandr Herzen

From the Other Shore. Translated by Moura Budberg. New York: Oxford University Press, 1989.

My Past and Thoughts: The Memoirs of Alexander Herzen. Translated by Constance Garnett. Berkeley: University of California Press, 1999.

Who Is to Blame? A Novel in Two Parts. Translated by Michael R. Katz. Ithaca, N.Y.: Cornell University Press, 1984.

Works about Aleksandr Herzen

Acton, Edward. *Alexander Herzen and the Role of the Intellectual Revolutionary.* New York: Cambridge University Press, 1979.

Partridge, Monica. *Alexander Herzen.* Paris: Unesco, 1984.

Hesse, Hermann (1877–1962) *novelist, poet*

Hermann Hesse was born in Calw, Germany, to Johannes and Marie Hesse, Pietist missionaries and religious publishers. Hesse's parents traveled to India on several occasions to conduct missionary work. The travels to India provided a profound formative experience for young Hesse, one that deeply influenced his writings. At first, Hesse was educated by his parents and was expected to follow their path. In 1891, he entered a Protestant seminary at Maulbronn to prepare for life as a missionary and preacher. Hesse, however, found himself spiritually and psychologically unfit for a religious career, and he left the seminary without taking a degree.

Hesse became a professional writer in 1904 when he published *Peter Camenzind,* a novel about a man who—like Saint Francis of Assisi—leaves a big city to devote his life to meditation. The novel was a great success, and Hesse was subsequently able to dedicate his time to writing. After a visit to India in 1911, Hesse began to study Eastern religions. *Siddhartha* (1922), a novel about young Guatama Buddha who rebels against the repressive traditions of his Brahmin father and ultimately finds enlightenment, reflects Hesse's interests in Eastern philosophy. *Siddhartha* remains the most widely read work of Herman Hesse.

In 1912, Hesse moved to Switzerland, where he remained throughout World War I. He openly attacked the attitudes of militarism and nationalism that beleaguered Europe and promoted the rights of prisoners of war. Because of Hesse's antiwar attitudes, he was regarded as a traitor by many in Germany. *Demian* (1919), a novel published by Hesse under the pseudonym of Emil Sinclair, reflected Hesse's personal crises during the years of World War I. In the novel, Demian, a young man, is torn between the world of sensuality and pleasures and the orderly, restrained world of middle-class existence. The novel also revealed Hesse's interest in psychoanalysis and the works of Carl Jung, a pupil of SIGMUND FREUD. The work was well received, particularly by veterans of World War I.

Der Steppenwolf (1927) tells a story of Harry Haller, a man undergoing a midlife crisis, who recognizes another personality within himself called Hermine. Hermine introduces Haller to a sensuous life of drinking, sex, and drugs. The novel's psychological complexity and the problematic treatment of spiritual persona appealed to many readers. *Der Steppenwolf* became a seminal text for the American Beat poets, and the American rock band Steppenwolf is named after the novel.

During the Nazi regime, Hesse's works were still published in Germany and were privately defended by Joseph Goebbels, the Nazi propaganda minister; however, after Hesse refused to remove the brutal scenes of anti-Semitism and violence against the Jews from the reprint of *Narcissus and Goldmund* (1930) in 1941, he was blacklisted by the Nazis. Hesse also assisted political refugees during World War II. He wrote *The Glass Bead Game* (1943), a novel about a futuristic, imaginary community in which wisdom is communicated through a series of complex games, in response to the Nazi regime in Germany.

Hermann Hesse was awarded the Nobel Prize in literature in 1946. He wrote more than 50 poems and essays between 1945 and 1962 for several Swiss newspapers. His works remain popular throughout the world. During the 1970s, Hesse was a cult figure for many young readers because of his focus on Eastern religions and his criticism of middle-class attitudes and values. He influenced many contemporary writers. He is one of the most popular writers of the German-speaking world.

Critical Analysis

Herman Hesse's masterpiece *Steppenwolf* reflected the particular circumstances of his life at the time of its writing. His opposition to the rise of National Socialism, a failed marriage, his search for self, his deteriorating social life, and a strong influence of Jungian thought contributed to the development of the novel.

In *Steppenwolf*, the central character, Harry Haller, divorced and suicidal, encounters a stranger with an advertisement for a "magic theatre"; the stranger offers him a pamphlet entitled *Treatise on the Steppenwolf*. The pamphlet gives an explanation of the indefinable nature of every person's soul, which Harry is either unable or unwilling to recognize. It also discusses the "suicides," people who, deep down, knew they would take their own life one day. On the other hand, the pamphlet also hails their potential to be great, to be one of the "Immortals." After a second encounter, this time with a woman named Hermine, who introduces Haller to Pablo, he is brought to Pablo's "magic theatre"; in the theater he learns that "the thousands of possible Harrys in the mirror are the diverse dimensions of himself." In the last scene, Harry meets Mozart, who teaches him to accept the world as it is and to learn to laugh at the "distortions," represented by Mozart's playing his music on a gramophone.

The major themes in the novel are the "multilayered soul of human nature," and the possibility of transcendence and healing through suffering—a theme that reveals the influence of Buddhism on Hesse's work. This theme is also found in Pablo's instruction to Haller to abandon his personality in order to enter the magic theater. To do this, Haller learns to laugh at his personality "until it shatters into so many small pieces." In addition, transcendence in the novel is connected to group cohesion; Haller attempts to separate himself from culture, believing he is better than others. The novel appears to suggest that in order to rise above a culture, a person must first become one with that culture. Hesse's *Steppenwolf* is a novel that blurs the lines between reality and fantasy and offers transcendence over eternal suffering.

Other Works by Hermann Hesse

Gertrude. Translated by Hilda Rosner. New York: Noonday, 1998.
Poems. Translated by James Wright. New York: Farrar, Straus & Giroux, 1970.
Soul of the Age, Selected Letters of Hermann Hesse. New York: Noonday, 1992.

A Work about Hermann Hesse

Mileck, Joseph. *Hermann Hesse: Life and Art*. Riverside: University of California Press, 1981.

Higuchi Ichiyō (Higuchi Natsuko)
(1872–1896) *short story writer*

Higuchi Ichiyō was born in Tokyo to Higuchi Noriyoshi and Taki. When Higuchi was very young, she was sent to private school, where she learned the Chinese classics and developed her writing skills; in addition, her father taught her Japanese classical poetry at home. When her father died, however, the family fell on hard times. They moved to the Yoshiwara pleasure district and opened a shop that eventually failed. Higuchi died of tuberculosis at age 24.

During her time in school, Higuchi developed a passion for writing. In 1892, the novelist and magazine publisher Tōsui Nakarai launched Higuchi's career by helping her publish articles in well-regarded literary magazines. She quickly earned the esteem of established writers and critics. Higuchi began to publish short stories in a variety of literary journals; however, she produced her greatest writing after she had moved her family to the Yoshiwara district in 1893. Her most enduring works—"Child's Play," "Troubled Waters," and "Separate Ways" (1895)—bring to life the characters and lifestyles of the district in the late 19th century.

Higuchi is the only woman whose works have been consistently included among the great works of the Meiji period (1868–1912). She is particularly known for her short stories that depict life in the Yoshiwara district and for her revival of the written style of Ihara Saikaku (1642–1693).

Other Works by Higuchi Ichiyō

"Muddy Bay." Translated by Hisako Tanaka. *Monumenta Nipponica* 14 (1958): 173–204.

"The Thirteenth Night" and "Child's Play." In *In the Shade of Spring Leaves: The Life and Writings of Higuchi Ichiyō, a Woman of Letters in Meiji Japan*. Translated by Robert Lyons Danly. New Haven, Conn.: Yale University Press, 1981.

Works about Higuchi Ichiyō

Copeland, Rebecca L. *Lost Leaves: Women Writers of Meiji Japan*. Honolulu: University of Hawaii Press, 2000.

Danly, Robert Lyons. *In the Shade of Spring Leaves: The Life and Writings of Higuchi Ichiyō, a Woman of Letters in Meiji Japan*. New Haven, Conn.: Yale University Press, 1981.

Hikmet, Nazim (1902–1963) *poet, playwright, novelist, memoirist*

Nazim Hikmet was born in Salonica, Greece, where his father was serving in the foreign service. His mother was an artist, his grandfather a poet. Introduced to poetry at an early age, Hikmet published his first poems at age 17. In 1922, attracted to the ideas of social justice promised by the Russian Revolution, he went to Moscow. There he met VLADIMIR MAYAKOVSKY, the FUTURIST poet who became one of his greatest influences.

Hikmet's life from this point on was fraught with political conflict as a result of the leftist political views that were contained in his writings. In 1924, after the Turkish War of Independence, he returned to Istanbul but was soon arrested and sentenced to 15 years of hard labor for working with a "leftist" magazine. He managed to escape in 1926 by fleeing, once again, to Russia. He continued to write in exile and attempted to return home in 1928, hoping for political amnesty. Instead, he was immediately arrested and sentenced to six years in prison; in 1933, he was released. During this period, Hikmet established himself as a major poet and playwright, publishing, among other works, *The Epic of Sheik Bedrettin* (1936). It was this poem, based on a rebellion by Turkish peasants against the Ottoman Empire in the 15th century, that led to another arrest; this time Hikmet was sentenced to 61 years in prison.

Hikmet continued to write in prison, sending out manuscripts secretly in letters to family and friends. Most of his poetry was inspired by universal humanism, compassion, and a love for the country that had exiled him. Among these works was his epic masterpiece, *Human Landscapes* (1941–45). In 1950, he was awarded the World Peace Prize and granted his freedom. This freedom was illusory, however: Two attempts were made on his life as he tried to flee the country. He escaped to Russia aboard a Romanian freighter and remained as a political refugee until his death from a heart attack in 1963.

Other Works by Nazim Hikmet

The Epic of Sheik Bedreddin and Other Poems. Translated by Randy Blasing and Mutlu Konuk. New York: Persea Books, 1977.

Poems of Nazim Hikmet. Translated by Randy Blasing and Mutlu Konuk. New York: Persea, 1994.

A Work about Nazim Hikmet

Goksu, Saime, and Edward Timms. *Romantic Communist.* New York: St. Martin's Press, 1999.

Hiraoka Kimitake

See MISHIMA YUKIO.

Ho Xuan Huong (1776–1820) poet

Ho Xuan Huong was born in Quynh Doi village, Nghe An province, Vietnam. Her father, Ho Phi Dien, was a member of the Hanoi scholar–gentry class. Her first husband was the prefect of the Vin Tuong district and encouraged her to write poetry. Ho had a good understanding of Chinese and Vietnamese writing that allowed her to write well in both classical Chinese and popular *nom* genres. Scholars of Vietnamese literature believed that Ho was a woman ahead of her time. With verve, Ho attacked the hypocrisy of Confucian Vietnamese society by showing her contempt for social conventions. She was seen not only as a feminist but also as a courageous defender of women's rights in early conservative Vietnam. Her simple yet forceful language appealed to a wide audience.

Sexuality is a dominant theme in Ho's poems. Her casual and playful exploration of sensual pleasures attracted and infuriated the conservative members of Vietnamese society. Ho was simultaneously seen as a wanton female and a heroine who stood steadfast to her own beliefs and values. Her poem "Jackfruit" is a compelling tale about the panic of an unmarried girl who discovers she is pregnant. In "Sharing a Husband," Ho describes the suffering of girls who are resigned to a subsidiary status in their husbands' homes. Ho's subversive attacks on the social hierarchy ironically won her the respect of those in power. She was respected for her fearlessness in criticizing the injustice of Vietnamese society, an action that few men, even those in power, would dare to undertake. Ho triumphed as a heroic female poet in a society that was overwhelmingly dominated by men.

Other Works by Ho Xuan Huong

"The Man-and-Woman Mountain." In Jacquelyn Chagnon and Don Luce, eds., *Quiet Courage: Poems from Viet Nam.* Washington, D.C.: Indochina Mobile Education Project, 1974.

"On Being a Concubine." In Jacquelyn Chagnon and Don Luce, eds., *Quiet Courage: Poems from Viet Nam.* Washington, D.C.: Indochina Mobile Education Project, 1974.

"Poking Fun at a Bronze." In Jacquelyn Chagnon and Don Luce, eds., *Quiet Courage: Poems from Viet Nam.* Washington, D.C.: Indochina Mobile Education Project, 1974.

Hoffmann, E. T. A. (pen name of Ernst Theodor Hoffmann) (1776–1822) novelist, fairy-tale writer

Ernst Theodor Amadeus Hoffmann was born in Köningsberg, Prussia (today Kaliningrad, Russia), to Christoph Ludwig and Lovisa Hoffmann. Ludwig left Lovisa while Ernst was still an infant. Responsibility for raising young Hoffmann fell on the shoulders of his maternal uncle, Otto Wilhelm Doerffer, a jurist. Young Hoffmann shared two passions: music and literature. Hoffmann was particularly influenced by the novels of JOHANN WOLFGANG VON GOETHE and the plays of

FRIEDRICH SCHILLER and William Shakespeare. In music, Hoffmann adored the operas of Wolfgang Amadeus Mozart (Hoffmann added the letter *A* to his first name in honor of Mozart).

Hoffmann studied law at Köningsberg's university but seemingly without inspiration. On graduation, Hoffmann moved to Glogów in Silesia to study law under the guidance of his uncle Johann Ludwig Doerffer, an established provincial judiciary. Between 1798 and 1800, Hoffmann served as an intern in the high court of Berlin. Hoffmann was quite successful in his law career, and he was promoted to supervise the jurisdiction of Posen in South Prussia. In 1816, Hoffmann attained a high position in the Supreme Court at Berlin.

Hoffmann began his artistic career as a composer rather than as a writer. He worked as a musical director, composer, and theatrical critic until 1814 when he finally recognized that he would never be a great composer. Many of Hoffmann's stories, however, reflect his passion for music. In "Don Juan" (1813), for instance, a hotel guest undergoes a supernatural transformation while watching a performance of Mozart's opera *Don Giovanni*. In "Councilor Krespel" (1816), a young girl dies when she is forced to produce the perfect voice.

Hoffmann's themes often deal with the magical, grotesque, or supernatural experience. His fiction is considered to be among early works of horror and fantasy. Furthermore, it was difficult for Hoffmann to reconcile his two seemingly conflicting roles as bureaucrat and artist, and this internal conflict is often reflected in his works. "The Golden Pot" (1816) presents the conflict between the world of the artist and the mundane, spiritually destructive world of the bourgeoisie. In another tale, "Das Fräulein von Scuderi" (1819), Hoffmann depicts a respectable goldsmith who becomes a heartless criminal at night.

In time, Hoffmann was seen as the heart of late German ROMANTICISM. Quite ironically, many of Hoffmann's literary masterpieces were transformed into musical masterpieces. The best known of these is the "Nutcracker and the Mouse King" (1816). The famous German composer Offenbach composed an opera based on the life and tales of Hoffmann, *The Tales of Hoffmann*, which is still widely popular.

Of his longer works, *The Devil's Elixir* (1816), the most popular, depicts the travels and adventures of an 18th-century Capuchin monk, Brother Medardus. This strange tale combines Gothic and grotesque elements and portrays several shocking situations, such as rape and scandalous murder–intrigues of the pope's court. The work was praised for its intricate plot and psychological complexity.

E. T. A. Hoffmann was perhaps one of the most influential writers in the world. Many of the psychological theories of Carl Jung and SIGMUND FREUD are based on Hoffmann's work, specifically Freud's theory of the uncanny. Furthermore, Hoffmann was one of the most influential figures for Russian romanticism, inspiring numerous writers and composers to the present day. In the United States, Hoffmann became the main inspiration for the dark, nightmarish fiction of Edgar Allan Poe. Despite his failure as a composer, Hoffmann's work as a writer inspired some of the world's greatest and most remembered musical masterpieces. His work has been translated into more than 20 languages.

Other Works by E. T. A. Hoffmann

The Life and Opinions of the Tomcat Murr. Translated by Anthea Bell. New York: Penguin, 1999.
The Tales of Hoffmann. Translated by R. J. Hollingdale. New York: Penguin, 1990.

A Work about E. T. A. Hoffmann

McGlathery, James. *E. T. A. Hoffmann*. Boston: Twayne, 1997.

Hofmannsthal, Hugo von (Loris, Loris Melikow, Theophil Morren)
(1874–1929) *poet, dramatist, essayist*

Hugo von Hofmannsthal was born in Vienna, Austria, to Hugo August Peter Hofmann, the director of a large investment bank, and Anna Maria Josefa Fohleutner, a brewing heiress. Hofmannsthal studied with private tutors and attended the Akademisches Gymnasium, one of Vienna's most prominent schools. There, he published poetry and wrote his first play at age 16. Hofmannsthal studied law and French at Vienna University and earned a doctorate in romance literature in 1899. Two years later, he married Gerty Schlesinger, the daughter of the general secretary of the Anglo-Austrian Bank.

Hofmannsthal's early poems and essays made him a literary sensation in Vienna. In the early 1890s, Hofmannsthal became part of a prominent circle of young writers known as Young Vienna. For a short time, he had close ties with the poet STEFAN GEORGE. Hofmannsthal wrote his best poems in the mid-1890s. His early works, such as *Der Tor und der Tod* (*Death and the Fool*, 1893), were characterized by Viennese aestheticism and FIN-DE-SIÈCLE melancholy.

After the turn of the century, Hofmannsthal abandoned aestheticism and turned from poetry to plays and essays. The composer Richard Strauss (1864–1949) used Hofmannsthal's play *Elektra* (1904) for the libretto, or text, of an opera. Hofmannsthal later wrote five more librettos for Strauss. After World War I, Hofmannsthal's increasing anxiety over the decline of Western civilization can be seen in his play *Der Turm* (*The Tower*, 1925), in which Hofmannsthal addresses the question of whether a decaying society can be renewed through revolutionary violence.

Although Hofmannsthal's later critics saw him as an elitist defender of outdated conservative values, his works still command popular and critical attention. German literary scholar Claude Hall described Hofmannsthal as "a great theatrical showman who aimed at reproducing the macrocosm of the world and his dreams in the microcosm of the stage."

Other Works by Hugo von Hofmannsthal

The Lyrical Poems of Hugo von Hofmannsthal. Translated by Charles Wharton Stark. New Haven, Conn.: Yale University Press, 1918.

Selected Plays and Libretti. Michael Hamburger, ed. New York: Pantheon Books, 1963.

Works about Hugo von Hofmannsthal

Coghlan, Brian. *Hofmannsthal's Festival Dramas.* Cambridge: Cambridge University Press, 1964.
Vilain, Robert. *The Poetry of Hugo von Hofmannsthal and French Symbolism.* New York: Oxford University Press, 2000.

Hölderlin, Friedrich (1770–1843) *poet, novelist*

Friedrich Hölderlin was born in Lauffen am Neckar, Germany. His father, an administrator at a local monastery, died when Hölderlin was two years old. His mother, Johanna Christina Hölderlin, married the mayor of Nürtingen, Johann Christoph Gok, a few years later. In childhood, Hölderlin read intensely, including the classics and was fluent in Greek and Latin by the age of 12. At 14, he began to write poems. In 1788, under the guidance of his stepfather, Hölderlin entered the University of Tübingen to pursue studies in theology. He graduated with a master's degree.

During Hölderlin's studies at the university, his interests in theology began to fade. He became a close friend of Friedrich Wilhelm Hegel (1770–1831), an important philosopher whose theories became the foundation for revolutionary thinking. Hölderlin also became involved in liberalism and passionately admired the ideals of the French Revolution. In 1793, Hölderlin met FRIEDRICH VON SCHILLER, one of the most important literary figures of German ROMANTICISM, who agreed to publish several of Hölderlin's poems.

In 1793, Hölderlin began work as a private tutor. Employed by Jacob Gontard, a wealthy Frankfurt banker, he fell in love with Gontard's wife, Susette. Although the love affair was platonic, it had a deep impact on the psyche of the young poet. In many of his famous poems, Susette appears as the mysterious "Diotima." Hölderlin eventually left Frankfurt in 1798, but the two continued to meet secretly and to corresponded frequently with each other.

Hölderlin briefly worked in France as a private tutor. During this period, his mental health was becoming unstable. In 1802, Hölderlin returned to Germany in the advanced stages of schizophrenia. After learning about Susette's death in 1805, Hölderlin suffered a complete psychological breakdown and spent the last 36 years of his life in an unstable state of mind. He died in poverty and virtual obscurity.

Critical Analysis

Combining the elements of classicism and romanticism, Hölderlin did not exclusively belong to either of the two dominant literary movements of his day. He tended to use classical verse form and syntax in his poetry, following the teachings of Friedrich Klopstock (1724–1803), who attempted to perfect the German language by modeling it to a classical form. From the romantics, Hölderlin borrowed a rich but convoluted tradition of mystical nature, pantheism, and Christianity. He referred to notions of the cosmos and history to assign some poetic meaning to a world that was collapsing before his eyes. By following and enriching the German philosophical tradition, he greatly contributed to the formation of German idealism, a term usually used to define liberal, philosophical trends during and after the French Revolution.

Hölderlin's most famous novel, *Hyperion* (1797–99), focuses on the young Greek of ancient mythology who takes up arms to fight the Turkish oppression in his homeland. The novel virtually has no plot; *Hyperion*'s beauty rises from its lyrical, dithyrambic (highly emotional) language combined with a deep knowledge of Greek antiquity. The romance of the novel is developed in the form of letters between Hyperion and his beloved. *Hyperion* has often been celebrated as a masterpiece of German literature. It certainly impressed Friedrich Schiller when the young Hölderlin presented the manuscript of the novel to the famous poet, who encouraged Hölderlin to continue his work.

The vast majority of Hölderlin's work deals with heroic themes or subjects. In his poetry, he preferred to maintain classical verse measures. He dedicated an ode to French emperor Napoleon Bonaparte (titled "Bonaparte" (1798), in which he compares Bonaparte to a poet:

> *Poets are holy vessels*
> *In which the wine of life,*
> *The spirit of heroes is preserved.*
> *But this young man's spirit,*
> *The quick—would it not burst,*
> *Any vessel that tried to contain it?*

Hölderlin's verse, especially in its attention to the preservation of classical Greek measures, seems, at the same time, both heroic and rugged. The lyricism is achieved through carefully selected images and irregular lines. Hölderlin's verse became popular, especially among students of philosophy for its liberal inclinations and romantic celebration of life.

In a series of poems to his beloved Diotima, Hölderlin reveals a delicate control of the classical image. In "Diotima" (1797), Hölderlin reveals the full potential of his poetic mind: "Beautiful thing, you live as do delicate blossoms in winter/ In a world that's grown old hidden your blossom, alone." The Diotima poems are considered among the greatest lyrical poems in the German language. Hölderlin dedicated the last years of his life to translating Sophocles' works into German. His translations are still considered superb.

Friedrich Hölderlin did not achieve the recognition that his works enjoy today until the early part of the 20th century. Hölderlin was the favorite poet of FRIEDRICH NIETZSCHE, and Martin Heidegger referred to Hölderlin as "a poet's poet." Today, Hölderlin is considered second only to GOETHE. In many respects, Hölderlin is still being rediscovered for the beauty of his poetic form and the magnificent control of his poetic lines.

Other Works by Friedrich Hölderlin

Hymns and Fragments. Princeton, N.J.: Princeton University Press, 1984.

Selected Poems and Fragments. New York: Penguin, 1998.

Works about Friedrich Hölderlin

Fioretos, Aris. *The Solid Letter: Readings of Friedrich Hölderlin.* Stanford, Calif.: Stanford University Press, 2000.
Unger, Richard. *Friedrich Hölderlin.* Boston: Twayne, 1984.

Höllerer, Walter (1922–2003) *poet, critic*

Walter Höllerer was born in the Bavarian town of Sulzbach-Rosenberg. During World War II, he served in the German military on the Mediterranean front. After the war, he studied at universities in Erlangen, Göttingen, and Heidelberg, earning a doctorate in 1949 in comparative literature. Höllerer then began a long career as a professor of German and comparative literature at Frankfurt University, the Technical University of Berlin, and the University of Illinois. He cofounded and edited the journals *Akzente* (*Accents*) and *Sprache im technischen Zeitalter* (*Language in the Technological Age*). In 1977 he founded the Archives for Contemporary German Literature in Sulzbach-Rosenberg.

Höllerer's first collection *Der andere Gast* (*The Other Guest,* 1952) contains many poems written in classical meters. Four years later, he edited *Transit* (1956), a significant anthology of German poetry. Höllerer published three more volumes of verse in the 1960s. During the following decade, he wrote the novel *Die Elephantenuhr* (*The Elephant Clock,* 1973), a complicated work that reflects his perception of chaos in the contemporary world. His comedy *Alle Vögel alle* (*All the Birds,* 1978) is a composition that was influenced by his conception of semiology.

In addition to his writing and editing, Höllerer attained recognition in his versatile career as a scholar, critic, and literary theorist. He was also a prominent member of the German writers' association GRUPPE 47. Although his early poetry contained traditional forms, Höllerer later became more progressive, writing experimental lyrical poems. His view of literature emphasized its role in communicating art, science, and everyday life. Because he spent much time and energy promoting the careers of young authors, Höllerer's influence in German literature will likely remain strong well into the 21st century.

Another Work by Walter Höllerer

Gedichte 1942–1982. Frankfurt am Main: Suhrkamp, 1982.

A Work about Walter Höllerer

Frisch, Max. *Dramaturgisches: ein Briefwechsel mit Walter Höollerer.* Berlin: Literarisches Colloquium, 1976.

Hosseini, Khaled (1965–) *novelist*

Khaled Hosseini was born in Kabul, Afghanistan, on March 4, 1965. His father was a diplomat working in the Afghan Foreign Ministry. His mother taught Persian literature and worked as a school vice principal. They lived in the Wazir Akbar Khan district of Kabul, an affluent and cosmopolitan area. At the time, Afghanistan was a peaceful country, not yet invaded by the Soviet Union nor taken over by the Taliban. Hosseini attended the Esteqlal and Malalaï Lycées, which are supported by the French government and teach the official French school curriculum.

Briefly, the Hosseinis lived in Tehran, Iran, where Khaled was exposed to Persian culture and poetry. Even though he was quite young when they lived in Iran, Khaled befriended the family cook and taught him to read and write. The man was a member of the Hazara ethnic group, an oppressed minority in Afghanistan, and their friendship opened Khaled's eyes to the concept of social injustice, which eventually became a major theme in his writing.

In 1976, Hosseini's father was transferred to the Afghan embassy in Paris. Two years after their move, communists overthrew the government of Afghanistan. Political turmoil followed, and in December 1979 the Soviet Union entered Afghanistan in an attempt to restore their communist allies to power. They were met with armed resistance, some of which was supported by the United States. The Soviets labored for 10 years in Afghanistan, and nearly 5 million Afghanis fled the regime. The Hosseinis, including Khaled and his four siblings, an aunt, and a grandmother, applied for political asylum in the United States and moved to San Jose, California, in 1980.

When he arrived in California, Hosseini spoke no English. Nevertheless, he was enrolled in Independence High School and graduated in 1984. He graduated from Santa Clara University with a degree in biology in 1988 and then earned a medical degree in 1993 from the University of California, San Diego. In 1996, Hosseini completed his residency at Cedars-Sinai Hospital in Los Angeles.

Following his marriage to Roya, also an Afghan immigrant, Hosseini moved back to San Jose to practice medicine. He continued to practice medicine until a year and a half after the publication of his first book, *The Kite Runner* (2003).

The Kite Runner began as a short story. Encouraged by his father-in-law to develop further the story of two boys from different social classes, Hosseini reworked the story as a novel. *The Kite Runner* is set before the Soviet invasion. Given all the chaos and bloodshed of the war with the Soviets and the repression and brutality of the theocratic society established by the Taliban, Hosseini felt that the country he had known as a child had been forgotten by the world.

The book tells the story of Amir, the son of a rug exporter, and his friend Hassan as they live through the fall of Afghanistan's monarchy, the invasion by the Soviets, and the establishment of the Taliban regime. The story concludes after the American invasion of Afghanistan in response to the September 11, 2001, terrorist attacks. The characters are intimately drawn, and readers often report recognizing aspects of themselves in Hosseini's work. The universality of the story set in such an unfamiliar place and time makes it both deeply resonant and curiously exotic.

Although *The Kite Runner* was published to generally good reviews, sales at first were slow. With no initial endorsements from influential sources, advertising was mainly by word of mouth. Eventually, the American Booksellers Association's Book Sense, listed *The Kite Runner* as a new and noteworthy book, and in February 2003 Borders gave it their Original Voices Award and placed the book prominently in stores. With the publication of the paperback edition in May 2003, sales rose sharply, and the book became a *New York Times* best seller. In 2007, the novel was released as a major motion picture.

Also in 2007, Hosseini published his second novel, *A Thousand Splendid Suns*, which follows the experiences of two women during the same period of Soviet and Taliban occupation in Afghanistan. Khaled Hosseini has retired from his medical practice and now lives in Northern California with his wife and two children, where he continues to write.

A Work about Khaled Hosseini

Stuhr, Rebecca. *Reading Khaled Hosseini*. Santa Barbara, Calif.: Greenwood Publishing Group, 2009.

Houellebecq, Michel (1958–) *novelist, poet, filmmaker*

Houellebecq has been a polarizing figure in contemporary French literature. Born on France's Réunion Island in February 1958, Michel Houellebecq is a practiced controversialist who has been described as a shock novelist, postmodern reactionary, neo-romantic, and a nihilist. He has been decried as a misogynist, awarded a number of major literary prizes, and is the subject of a French literary journal, *Houelle*, which is dedicated to his life and work.

Houellebecq came to national and international prominence in 1998 with the publication of *Les particules élémentaires* (*The Elementary Particles; Atomised* in the U.K.), a deliberately insolent best-selling novel (a wry, disaffected, pornographic portrait or allegory of French culture since the late 1960s and a treatise on cloning) that has inspired venomous criticism and equally strident defense, both in France and abroad. The controversy has been fueled by the author's frequent and frequently provocative interviews. As Julian Barnes has reported on Houellenbecq's impact, "He is *mediatique* (mediagenic) by being *anti-mediatique*." That is to say, he thrives on media attention by not caring how the media covers him.

One difficulty with any account of the life of Michel Houellebecq stems from the way he has readily deployed elements of his autobiography in his fiction and the way the elements of his biography have been routinely presented as part of his nihilistic, or cynical, personality. He was evidently alienated from his parents at an early age. As he has described them, his father was a mountain guide and his mother was an anesthesiologist; they divorced within a few years of his birth. According to his Web site, they "soon lost all interest in his existence." He has described them as "hippies." From 1964 onward, he was raised outside of Paris by his paternal grandmother. By his own account, he was lonely, depressed, and repulsed by the social and academic world around him. He has stated that he was rejected for military service due to morphine addiction, yet he graduated from college receiving a degree in agronomy in 1980 and soon after married the sister of a classmate. Prolonged unemployment, divorce, and alcohol and drug abuse led to repeated hospitalizations for clinical depression.

Beginning in the late 1970s, Houellebecq began to show literary ambitions. In 1985, he published his first poems in *Nouvelle Revue de Paris* under the editorship of the poet/musician/filmmaker Michel Bulteau. This led to the publication of a study of the American author H. P. Lovecraft, known for his weird fictional amalgams of horror, fantasy, and science fiction. In *H. P. Lovecraft, contre le monde, contre la vie* (*H.P. Lovecraft,*

Against the World, Against Life, 1991, 2005), Houellebecq described a kindred spirit, someone sickened by and alienated from the world, profoundly skeptical of human progress, and he expressed an interpretation of Lovecraft's worldview that neatly coincided with his own. A collection of poems, *La poursuite du bonheur* (*The Pursuit of Happiness,* 1992) followed, winning the Prix Tristan Tzara, an international poetry award.

In addition to his poetic pursuits, Houellebecq was employed by the French National Assembly repairing computers and debugging software. In 1994, his first novel *Extension du domaine de la lutte* (*Whatever*) appeared and garnered a solid following and the 1995 Prix Flore for best first novel. Frankly reminiscent of Albert Camus's *The Stranger,* the novel is narrated by an anonymous, 30-year-old, depressive sex-obsessed computer engineer with an especially repellent appearance who makes unsolicited advances toward every woman he meets. The intellectual core of the novel expresses one of Houellebecq's abiding themes, that the sexual revolution and liberal capitalism are linked in modern life, analogous to one another. "In a totally liberal economic system certain people accumulate considerable fortunes," he writes, [while] "others stagnate in unemployment and misery. In a totally liberal sexual system certain people have a varied and exciting erotic life; others are reduced to masturbation and solitude." Bored and incapable of experiencing pleasure even as he obsesses about its pursuit, the narrator expresses a generational disaffection with deadpan sarcasm and mordant wit that resonated with French readers as no author had since Camus.

A second collection of poetry, *Le sens du combat* (*The Meaning of the Fight,* 1995), won a second Prix Flore in 1996. Houellebecq also worked as a music critic for a French rock music magazine, *Les Inrockuptibles.* In 1998, the year that *Les particules élémentaires* appeared, he received the Grand Prix National des Lettres Jeunes Talents on the basis of his work up to that time, and later that year, amid the celebrity and controversy of his second novel, he won the Prix Novembre. Also in 1998, he married Marie-Pierre Gauthier and moved to Ireland.

His follow-up novel, *Plateforme* (*Platform*, 2001), sold more than 400,000 copies in its first few months, dominating the French literary marketplace and creating even more controversy than his previous work. In *Plateforme*, the provocation came in the first instance not from the sexual content itself but from the first-person narrator's (whose name is Michel) defense of exotic eroticism and sex tourism. The novel describes with graphic gusto the hedonistic pleasures of Thai prostitution and sex-and-sunshine travel packages that cater to Western males. While there is no shortage of targets that come in for Michel's contempt (the publisher of a popular series of French travel guides, Guide du Routard, was one of the first to condemn the book for its sneering), there is also a good deal of anti-Muslim spleen vented by various characters in the novel, which ends with a resort being blown up by Islamic fundamentalists. This aspect of the book triggered an international incident when Houellebecq gave an interview with the literary monthly *Lire* in which he echoed the sentiments of his characters saying, "The most stupid religion is Islam." In the months following the September 11, 2001, attacks on the World Trade Center and the Pentagon, Houellebecq was placed on trial for "inciting racial hatred," and while he was acquitted, the incident reinforced his image as a provocateur of the politically incorrect.

Since *Plateforme*, the American publisher McSweeney's has reissued the Lovecraft study. Also, a novel, *La possibilité d'une île* (*The Possibility of an Island*, 2006), has appeared.

Critical Analysis

The Elementary Particles, the book that gained Houellebecq international renown, expresses the central tenet of his literary vision—the theme that connects him to Camus and Beckett—an existential disaffection based on a sense of fundamental hopelessness with respect to humanity. It is essentially a tale of two half-brothers, Bruno and Michel, abandoned by their hedonistic mother and parceled out to different grandmothers. Abused as a boy, Bruno grows into "a frustrated satyr," as one critic described him, his life one interminable round of sexual obsession. Michel has no interest at all in the social, reclusively pursing high-level research into cloning. As Bruno's life spins out of control, Michel's carries on with an icy, orderly regularity. As critic Nancy Hutson has observed, "Like all of Houellebecq's novels, *Elementary Particles* explores the eternal themes of nihilism: sexual miseries and misfortunes, the absence of love, the wish for death, horror at mortality and the passage of time." As one character states, "In the end, there is nothing but solitude, cold and silence. In the end, there is nothing but death."

This perspective is precisely what Houellebecq found so compelling about H. P. Lovecraft, of whom he wrote, "Few beings have ever been so impregnated, pierced to the core, by the conviction of the absolute futility of human aspiration. The universe is nothing but a furtive arrangement of elementary particles. A figure in transition toward chaos. That is what will finally prevail." In his interpretation of Lovecraft, Houellebecq expresses the central metaphor of his novel and his work, the essential atomism of the universe, and the futile and pointless chaos of desire.

Other Works by Michel Houellebecq

Lanzarote. Translated by Frank Wynne. London: William Heinemann, 2003.

Rester vivant, méthode (*To Stay Alive: A Method*). Translated by Richard Davis. Paris: La Différence, 1991.

A Work about Michel Houellebecq

Cruickshank, Ruth. *Fin de millénaire French Fiction: The Aesthetics of Crisis*. Oxford: Oxford University Press, 2009.

Hsieh Wan-ying

See BING XIN.

Hu Shih (Hu Hongxin) (1891–1962) *poet, scholar, critic*

Born on December 17 in Shanghai, Hu Shih was educated first by private tutors and then in Shanghai schools. He entered China College in 1906, where he published essays and poems in a school paper, *Emulation,* which he later edited. Hu Shih traveled to the United States to study agriculture at Cornell University in 1910 but soon switched to literature and philosophy. He completed his Ph.D. in philosophy at Columbia University under the department head, John Dewey.

Greatly influenced by his studies of imagist poetry, American literature, and his experiences in the United States, Hu Shih wrote an article considered by many to have brought about the era of modern Chinese literature. "Suggestions for a Reform of Literature" was published in 1919 in the popular journal *New Youth* and made him one of the leading intellectuals of the anti-imperialist May Fourth Movement. In his article, Hu Shih encouraged writing that addressed substantive and timely issues and that was innovative and fresh and used accessible language, particularly *baihua,* the Chinese vernacular.

Hu Shih himself was one of the first to attempt *baihua* poetry in a 1920 volume titled *Experiments.* Although the literary quality of the poems is considered only fair, the style was, nonetheless, a pioneering work in modern poetry. Hu Shih incorporated innovations such as writing without traditional meters, transcribing Western names into verse, and writing in a pragmatic and impersonal style.

As one of the leading literary intellectuals in the 1920s and 1930s, Hu Shih criticized official corruption and vice in the ranks of leadership. He also expressed grave concern over the condition of workers, especially the particularly disadvantaged—women, rural poor, and factory laborers. He was known as a radical for being a Confucian realist who combined classical Confucian and Daoist thought with modern pragmatism, individualism, and secular humanism. He also supported opening China to Western ideas and influence while maintaining China's classical traditions and thought.

At the time, Hu Shih was considered China's foremost man of letters, as well as a cultural icon. As a result, he enjoyed prestige and acclaim. After serving as ambassador to the United States from 1938 until 1942, he presided over the prestigious Beijing University from 1946 until 1949 when he moved to the United States to direct the Gest Oriental Library at Princeton.

Hu Shih continued his focus on scholarship, studying the 18th-century Chinese classic by Cao Xueqin, *Dream of the Red Chamber,* praising its autobiographical angle. His studies prompted the onset of his own persecution in China because officials felt that his scholarship that addressed the novel's literary form undermined its political importance as an exposé of feudal society and the traditional family system. Party conservatives also viewed him as overly Westernized. As he was politically moderate, Hu Shih was also reviled for his increasing distance from revolutionary thought.

Hu Shih, however, remained undeterred. Throughout his career, he produced reference and scholarly works, including *An Outline of the History of Chinese Philosophy* in 1919. He also translated a wide selection of writers from the Americans Bret Harte and John Dewey to the French writer Alphonse Daudet. Hu Shih moved to Taiwan in 1958 to serve as the president of the country's highest cultural institution, the Academia Sinica. He remained in Taiwan until his death.

Another Work by Hu Shih

A Hu Shi Reader. New Haven, Conn.: Yale Far Eastern Publications, 1991.

Works about Hu Shih

Goldman, Merle. *Modern Chinese Literature in the May Fourth Era.* Cambridge, Mass.: Harvard University Press, 1977.

Grieder, Jerome B. *Hu Shih and the Chinese Renaissance: Liberalism in the Chinese Revolution, 1917–1937.* Cambridge, Mass.: Harvard University Press, 1970.

Huang Chunming (Huang Ch'un-ming)
(1939–) *short story writer, satirist*

Huang Chunming was born in Yilan, a small coastal town in Taiwan on February 13. He ran away from home after his mother's death and wandered from place to place, performing odd jobs. This pattern continued with his schooling as he drifted from college to college until he graduated from Pingtung Normal College and as he worked at various jobs, as schoolteacher, freelance musicologist, radio program editor, television producer, and documentary filmmaker. As a writer, he has created a small but distinctive body of work that is known for its national and popular appeal.

In the late 1960s, Huang Chunming's main theme was the agrarian fight against the disintegrating effects of modernization on their communities. Because he traveled frequently through the countryside, he was in tune with the particular trials of agrarian workers. Although concerned with the fate of individuals who were faced with a rapidly changing and increasingly modern society, he was not a traditionalist; he simply objected to the often dehumanizing aspects of progress. One of his most famous stories, "His Son's Big Doll" (1968), illustrates how commercialization undermines individual dignity—a father accepts a job as a walking costumed advertisement and dreads being discovered by his young son. Other stories, such as "The Drowning of an Old Cat" (1967), directly address official corruption.

Huang Chunming's literary style is simple, similar to folk writing, and although it largely portrays realistic images of rural life, it is modern. His views—universal and anti-imperialistic—and his progressive politics render him a modern teller of folk stories.

A self-described vagabond and free spirit, Huang Chunming presently spends most of his time as a scholar and practitioner of folk culture. He researches and compiles Taiwanese folk songs and documents Taiwanese festivals on film, in addition to writing stories that celebrate the common people and folk life.

Other Works by Huang Chunming

The Drowning of an Old Cat and Other Stories. Translated by Howard Goldblatt. Bloomington: Indiana University Press, 1980.
The Taste of Apples. Translated by Howard Goldblatt. New York: Columbia University Press, 2001.

Works about Huang Chunming

"Father's Writings Have Been Republished: Or, The Sexuality of Women Students in a Taibei Bookstore." In Helmut Martin and Jeffrey Kinkley, eds., *Modern Chinese Writers: Self-Portrayals.* Armonk, N.Y.: M.E. Sharpe, 1992.
Goldblatt, Howard. "The Rural Stories of Huang Chunming." In Jeannette L. Faurot, ed., *Chinese Fiction from Taiwan: Critical Perspectives.* Bloomington: Indiana University Press, 1980.

Huchel, Peter (1903–1981) *poet*

Peter Huchel was born in Berlin to Friedrich Huchel, a civil servant, and Marie (Zimmermann) Huchel. He grew up in Mark Brandenburg and studied literature at Humboldt University, the University of Freiburg, and the University of Vienna. Huchel supported himself as a writer and translator before serving in the German army during World War II. From 1945 to 1948, he edited, produced, and directed for East German radio and in 1948 edited *Sinn und Form* (*Meaning and Form*), making it one of the most respected liberal European literary journals. He was fired in 1962, however, for not following the government's SOCIALIST-REALISM principles in his editorial policy. Huchel later moved to West Germany and married Nora Rosenthal in 1953.

Huchel published his early poems in journals in the 1920s. In 1932, he won the literary prize of the leftist journal *Die Kolonne* (*The Column*). After World War II, he published many of his early poems in *Gedichte* (*Poems*, 1948). His later collections included *Chausseen Chausseen*

(*Highways Highways,* 1963) and *Die neunte Stunde* (*The Ninth Hour,* 1979). Huchel won numerous literary awards, including the National Prize in 1951.

His influences included the poets Oskar Loerke and Wilhelm Lehmann. Many of his poems about nature describe the magic and mystery of the landscape near his hometown of Mark Brandenburg, and critics have praised the effective use of rhyme, meter, assonance, and alliteration in his early verse. After falling out of favor with the East German government, Huchel became withdrawn and isolated. His later writing used less rhyme and meter, and his poems were elegiac, melancholy, and pessimistic. Despite the opposition he faced, Huchel retained his principles and integrity. Literary scholar Ian Hilton wrote that "Huchel swam against the tide to remain stubbornly independent—and survived, albeit with difficulty."

Another Work by Peter Huchel

Selected Poems. Translated by Michael Hamburger. Manchester, U.K.: Carcanet Press, 1974.

A Work about Peter Huchel

Hilton, Ian. *Peter Huchel: Plough a Lonely Furrow.* Dundee, Scotland: Lochee Publications, 1986.

Hugo, Victor (1802–1885) *novelist, poet, dramatist*

Now best known internationally for his novels on which the acclaimed Broadway musicals *Les Misérables* and *Notre Dame de Paris* were based, Victor Hugo was born in Besançon on February 22. His father, an army general, taught him a great admiration of Napoleon, as a young child; however, as a result of his parent's separation, he moved to Paris to live with his mother and her lover, Hugo's father's former commanding officer. The lover was executed in 1812 for plotting against Napoleon, an event that set up a conflicting ideology within the impressionable young Hugo.

As a youth, Hugo's views tended toward the conservative, but he grew to become deeply involved in republican politics, the essence of which

provided the theme for many of his works. From 1815 to 1818, while attending the lycée Louis-le-Grand in Paris, he began to write poems and tragic verses. He also translated the works of Virgil and, in 1819, with the help of his brothers, founded the literary review *Conservateur Littéraire.* Inspired by FRANÇOIS RENÉ DE CHATEAUBRIAND, Hugo began to publish poetry, gaining both recognition and a pension from Louis XVIII. His debut novel *Han d'Islande* (1823) appeared shortly thereafter.

Hugo married Adèle Foucher in 1822. Their wedding was eventful because Hugo's brother, distraught over losing a longtime rivalry for her affections, went insane on the day of the ceremony and spent the remainder of his life institutionalized. This event had a profound effect on the psychological motivations for several of Hugo's characters.

Critical Analysis

Hugo came into contact with a number of liberal writers in the 1820s, and his own political views began to shift from criticizing Napoleon to glorifying him. He also became involved in the literary debate between French CLASSICISM and ROMANTICISM. Although he was not directly involved in political movements at this time, Hugo nevertheless expressed his admiration for romanticism and its values in his works. The preface to his drama, *Cromwell* (1827), placed him at the forefront of the romanticists. His play *Hernani* (1830), about two lovers who poison each other, caused a riot between classicists and romanticists.

Hugo gained lasting fame with *Notre-Dame de Paris* (1831; translated 1833), the story, set in 15th-century Paris, of a deformed and hunchbacked bell-ringer, Quasimodo, who falls deeply in love with a beautiful gypsy girl, Esmeralda. His love, however, is a tragic one: Esmeralda is in love with another man, Captain Phoebus, and an evil priest, Claude Frollo, is in love with her. When Frollo discovers that Esmerelda loves Phoebus, he murders his rival, and Esmeralda is accused of the crime. Quasimodo provides sanctuary for his distraught love in the cathedral, but Frollo finds her. When she rejects him, he leaves her to be executed. Grief-stricken, Quasimodo throws the priest from the cathedral tower and vanishes. Later, it is discovered that there are not one but two skeletons in Esmeralda's tomb, locked in an eternal embrace, a beautiful gypsy and the hunchback who loved her. The story was well received and has since become a prominent cultural myth.

Following the success of *Notre-Dame de Paris,* Hugo published several volumes of lyric poetry, all of which were also successful. He was considered by many to be the greatest poet of the day. These poems were inspired by an actress, Juliette Drouet, with whom Hugo had an affair that lasted until her death in 1882. His principal poetic works include *Les orientales* (1829), *Feuilles d'automme* (*Autumn's Leaves,* 1831), *Chants du crépuscule* (*Twilight Songs,* 1835), and *Voix intérieures* (*Inner Voices,* 1837). The poems in these collections are rich in language and intensely sexual, but they also carry a trace of Hugo's growing bitterness toward life.

Becoming disillusioned with the political and cultural values of France, Hugo finally took a stand and became involved in republican politics. In 1841 he was elected to the prestigious Académie Française, an achievement largely overshadowed a few short years later by the death of his beloved daughter Léopoldine. So distraught was Hugo over her loss that it was a full decade before he began to publish again. Instead, he devoted his time and energy to politics and the promotion of social justice.

In 1851, Napoleon III claimed complete power in France. Fearing for his life as a result of his openly republican beliefs, Hugo fled with Juliette Drouet first to Brussels and then to the Channel Islands. This exile, which was to last 20 years, provided him with the opportunity to produce some of his best-known works including, most notably, *Les misérables* (1862; translated 1862). An epic tale of social injustice told from the perspective of Jean Valjean, imprisoned and labeled a criminal for life because he stole a loaf of bread, the novel spectacularly depicts the conditions of post-Napoleonic France.

The political upheaval in France after Napoleon III fell from power and the proclamation of the Third Republic allowed Hugo to return to France in 1870. Labeled a national hero, he was elected as member of the National Assembly and then as a senator of the Third Republic. The last two decades of Hugo's life, however, were marked by tragedy that included the deaths of his sons, his wife, and his mistress. He continued to write poetry and remained active in politics until his health began to fail. Hugo died in Paris on May 22, 1885. His funeral was a national event attended by 2 million people. Hugo is buried in the Panthéon.

Other Works by Victor Hugo

The Distance, The Shadows: Selected Poems. Translated by Harry Guest. London: Anvil Press Poetry in association with Wildwood House, 1981.

History of a Crime. Translated by Huntington Smith. New York: T. Y. Crowell and Co., 1888.

The Last Day of a Condemned Man. Translated by Geoff Woollen. London: Hesperus Press, 2003.

La Légende des Siécles. Mamaroneck, N.Y.: Gerard Hamon, 1965.

Oeuvres Poetiques, Vol. 2 Avec: Les Châtiments et Les Contemplations. New York: French and European Publications, 1987.

Things Seen. Translated by David Kimber. London: Oxford University Press, 1964.

Works about Victor Hugo

Frey, John Andrew. *A Victor Hugo Encyclopedia.* Westport, Conn.: Greenwood Press, 1999.

Porter, Laurence M. *Victor Hugo.* Boston: Twayne, 1999.

Huysmans, Joris-Karl (Charles-Marie-Georges Huysmans) (1848–1907) *poet, novelist, essayist*

Joris-Karl Huysmans, a writer and art critic first associated with the NATURALIST movement who became prominent in the French decadent movement (see DECADENCE), was born in Paris on

February 5. His father died when Huysmans was eight years old, a traumatic experience that would influence his later works, many of which, such as *À rebours* (*Against Nature*, 1884), *Là-bas* (*Down There*, 1891), and *La cathédrale* (*The Cathedral*, 1898), trace the author's conversion to Catholicism through satanism.

Huysmans's first work, *Le drageoir aux épices* (*A Dish of Spices*, 1874), was comprised of a series of prose poems that were stylistically similar to those of CHARLES BAUDELAIRE. He published it at his own expense, taking on the pseudonym of Joris-Karl Huysmans. The work captured the attention of writer ÉMILE ZOLA and was followed by Huysmans's publication of several naturalistic novels, including *Marthe, histoire d'une fille* (Martha, the story of a girl, 1876), *Les soeurs Vatard* (*The Vatard Sisters*, 1879), and *En ménage* (1881). He also served in the Franco-Prussian War and wrote *Sac au dos* (1880) about his experiences.

In 1877, Huysmans began to turn away from naturalism. *À rebours* explores decadence. This misogynistic work, while important in its own right, was also influential in the decadent movement. Oscar Wilde refers to it as the "poisonous yellow book" that causes the downfall of his famous protagonist Dorian Gray. The dark comedy tells of a wealthy aristocrat, Des Esseinres, who experiments with exotic, often erotic, pleasures to the point at which he cannot face the real world for fear that it will be mediocre in comparison. He attempts to overcome nature by turning it into an object of art.

Huysmans's later novels, including *Là-bas,* are highly autobiographical and trace the spiritual search of a man named Durtal, who experiments with satanism and attends a Black Mass. The work went on to become prominent for its depiction of satanic rites and for its mention of several well-known occultists of the FIN DE SIÈCLE in Paris.

In the early 1890s, Huysmans experienced a crisis of faith and returned to the Catholic Church. His novels *En route* (1895) and *La cathédrale* trace his spiritual journey. Taken as a whole, his works are both erotic and spiritual in nature and rich and intoxicating in language. Huysmans remained a staunch Roman Catholic until his death from cancer on May 12.

Another Work by Joris-Karl Huysmans

The Road from Decadence: From Brothel to Cloister: Selected Letters of J. K. Huysmans. Translated by Barbara Beaumont. Columbus: Ohio State University Press, 1989.

A Work about Joris-Karl Huysmans

Ridge, George Ross. *Joris-Karl Huysmans.* Boston: Twayne, 1968.

Hwang Sun-won (1915–2001) *poet, fiction writer*

Hwang Sun-won was born on March 26 in Taedong, a county in modern-day North Korea. He published his first poem in 1931 while he was still in high school; by the end of the 1930s, he was regularly publishing poems and short stories. Graduating from Waseda University in Japan with a B.A. in English in 1939, he published his first short-story collection, *The Swamp*, in 1940. The volume is largely comprised of nostalgic stories of country folk that focus on childhood or the loss of innocence. Hwang Sun-won wrote in the dialect of his home province of Pyongannam and in a sparse and minimalist style that would become his trademark.

Hwang Sun-won is known for his reverence for life and humanity and for maintenance of an optimistic outlook even when writing critically. Although he began his career with the sentimental stories of rural Korea, the content of his work changed as Korea moved through history. In 1945, Korea was liberated from Japanese colonial rule and the postliberation period provided the backdrop for his first novel, *Living with the Stars* (1945). The next year, Hwang Sun-won and his family moved to Seoul, where he taught high school.

Affected by the outbreak of civil war in 1950, Hwang Sun-won wrote pieces, such as the novel *Trees on a Cliff* (1960), that reflect upon the tragic consequences of war for humanity. After the war divided Korea into north and south, he wrote *The Descendants of Cain* (1959), a novel featuring characters on a farm and highlighting the class disparity between landowners and tenant farmers. Although a traditional love story, it primarily criticizes the Communist North Korean regime's land-reform policies. Eventually, Hwang Sun-won turned his attention to the dehumanizing urban areas, where an increasing number of Koreans had settled.

Hwang Sun-won taught at Kyung Hee University from 1955 to 1993. He received many prizes and awards for his work, including the Freedom Literary Award in 1955 and the Republic of Korea Literary Award in 1983. His son, HWANG TONG-GYU, carries on his literary legacy as a respected poet.

Other Works by Hwang Sun-won

The Book of Masks. Translated by Martin Holman. London: Readers International, 1976.

The Stars. Translated by Edward W. Poitras. Singapore City: Heinemann Asia, 1980.

A Work about Hwang Sun-won

Epstein, Stephen J. "Elusive Narrators in Hwang Sun-won." In *Korean Studies,* 19 (1995).

Hwang Tonggyu (Hwang Tong-gyu)
(1938–   ) *poet*

Hwang Tonggyu was born on April 9 in Seoul to one of Korea's most famous writers, HWANG SUN-WON. He studied English literature at Seoul National University, graduating in 1961, and continued his graduate studies at Dongguk University. He completed further scholarship abroad, first at Scotland's Edinburgh University (1966–67) and then at the University of Iowa (1970–71).

Hwang Tonggyu's extensive training abroad affected his writing style. He blends the lyricism of traditional Korean poetry with Western modernism. As a result, his works are both contemplative and critical. He published his first volume of poems, *One Fine Day,* in 1961, followed by *Sad Songs* in 1965, moving from the abstract to concrete examinations of daily life. By the time he released *Snow That Falls on the Three Southern Provinces* in 1975, he had shifted from writing about daily life to Korea's social and political climate in quiet protest poems, such as "Song Under Martial Law." This shift evolved into a growing search for self that often manifested itself in dark and harrowing verse, such as "Lips." These poems in turn, evolved into a deep examination of metaphysics and death ("Flight").

Hwang Tonggyu continues to write, and his works are widely translated into many languages, especially English, German, and French. As a specialist in English-language poetry, he also translates Western works such as Robert Lowell and T. S. Eliot. He currently teaches English and American poetry at Seoul National University. In 1987, he served as an exchange professor at New York University. He lives in Seoul with his wife and two children.

Other Works by Hwang Tonggyu

Strong Winds at Mishi Pass. Groveport, Ohio: White Pines Press, 2001.

Wind Burial: Selected Poems of Hwang Tonggyu. Laurenberg, N.C.: St. Andrew's Press, 1990.

Hyder, Qurratulain (Qurrat-ul-Ain Haider) (1926–2007) *novelist, journalist*

Born in 1927 in India, in Uttar Pradesh, Qurratulain Hyder, known as Ainee Apa to her friends, came from a family of authors. Her father, Sajjad Haidar Yaldram, and her mother, Nazr Zahra (later Nazr Sajjad Haider), were both distinguished authors. Hyder began writing at the age of 11, and by 1948, at the age of 21, she had published her first novel, *Meray Bhi Sanam Khanay (My Temples, Too).* Hyder graduated from the Lucknow University in 1947 and lived in Pakistan and England before her permanent return to India in 1960. During her years away from India, she held brief positions as a guest lecturer at the universities of California, Chicago, Wisconsin, and Arizona. Hyder was part of the editorial staff at the newspaper *Illustrated Weekly of India*, as well as the managing editor of *Imprint* magazine in Bombay.

Hyder's creative voice was immediately heralded as an expression of stylistic modernity (she was best known for her use of stream-of-consciousness narrative), yet one also rooted in the traditions of the Indo-Muslim experience in content, giving voice to the nation's struggle to narrate the tale of its postwar rebirth, which followed India's independence from British rule and the partition of India and Pakistan. These were mandated by the Indian Independence act of 1947. Her work, written in the Urdu language, was also hailed as a continuation of and an innovative contribution to Urdu's long literary tradition, which began in the 14th century. Writing in her native language was risky at the time, because Urdu literature was long dominated by poetry, not prose. By the time she began writing, Urdu was a language in decline in India, mainly spoken and read in Pakistan. Hyder was a prolific writer; her body of work includes 12 novels and novellas and four collections of short stories. She was also a renowned translator of foreign classics, as well as of her own works into English, which she undertook because she did not trust her work in the hands of others. Hyder is also credited with discovering and translating an 18th-century Indo-Muslim novel by Hasan Shah entitled *Nashtar*, which she retitled *The Nautch Girl*. Shah's novel is now considered a seminal work in Indo-Muslim literature. For Hyder, language represented not only a people but its history as well. These are both important elements in her notion of a "composite culture," comprising the close relationship between India and Pakistan, a relationship she struggled to nurture, despite the many political and cultural divisions between these countries.

Ultimately, Hyder's international reputation rests on her 1960 novel *Aag Ka Duriya (River of Fire)*. In it, the history of the Indo-Pakistani culture is told, beginning in the fourth century C.E. and concluding 2,500 years later in 1956, during the post-independence partition era of India and Pakistan. The history is told through the lives of ordinary people who appear in different ages under different names, experiencing the major events of each era. Hyder was not only praised for her use of language but also for her depiction of people of high and low social status: maharajahs, folk singers of Bengal, fakirs, the phaeton pullers, and boatmen. Upon Hyder's death, critic Aamer Hussein declared that *River of Fire* is to Urdu fiction what GARCÍA MÁRQUEZ's *One Hundred Years of Solitude* is to Hispanic literature, particularly its creation of what is considered an authentic and empowering narrative of Urdu culture and history which for many Urdu people articulated the "truth" of their experience.

Many of the novels and short stories that followed explored similar historical and cultural terrain; for example, *Aakhir-e-Shab ke Hamsafar (Travellers unto the Night)*, first published in 1989, is set in Bengal, India. Its narrative follows important historic moments and periods of the region, including the rise in nationalistic feelings, the growth of revolutionary movements, independence, and ultimately the creation of the People's Republic of Bangladesh, formed after the war of independence in 1971. Hyder won the Jnanpith Award, the highest literary award given in India, for the novel. In 2005, she was conferred the Padma Bhushan, the third highest civilian honor awarded by the government of India, for her contribution to Urdu literature and education. She died in India in 2007 following a long battle with chronic lung disease. Hyder's epitaph reads: "(I) have returned everything to you, I have not taken anything (away with me) upon departure. Now do not accuse me O People, Look at me (examine me) I have departed empty-handed!"

Other Works by Qurratulain Hyder

Fireflies in the Mist. New York: New Directions, 2010.
The Sound of Falling Leaves. New Delhi: Sahitya
　　Academy, 1994.

A Work about Qurratulain Hyder

Hasan, Mushirul, and Asmin Roy. *Living Together
　　Separately: Cultural India in History and Politics*.
　　New Delhi: Oxford University Press, 2005.

Ibsen, Henrik (1828–1906) *dramatist, playwright, poet*

Henrik Ibsen was born in Skien, Norway, into a wealthy merchant family. While Ibsen was very young, his father suffered financial losses, and the family verged on poverty, no longer able to afford Ibsen's education. Young Ibsen developed a deep distrust for society and engaged in drunkenness and gambling. He also fathered an illegitimate child at the age of 18. To evade the social repercussions of his relationship with a servant girl, he was forced to support the child financially.

In 1850, Ibsen moved to Oslo to prepare for entrance into the university, but he failed to pass the entrance examinations. Becoming involved in radical politics, he joined a revolutionary group, but after the group was broken up by the government, Ibsen disengaged himself from politics for the rest of his life. During these years in Oslo, Ibsen began to write articles for various journals. He also wrote poetry and a play, neither of which was successful.

In 1851, Ibsen was appointed "stage poet" for a small provincial theater in Bergen. Ibsen wrote several early plays based on the history and folklore of Norway. Although these works were by no means Ibsen's greatest efforts, the theater management soon recognized Ibsen's talent as a playwright. In 1852, the theater sent Ibsen on a study tour to Denmark and Germany.

Returning to Norway in 1857, Ibsen was appointed director of the newly formed Norwegian Theater in Oslo. After several unsuccessful productions, the theater went bankrupt. Ibsen was reappointed to the Oslo Theater, where he attempted to establish his reputation as a playwright with a series of historical dramas. They were poorly received, and Ibsen was often publicly humiliated by their criticism.

The Norwegian government provided Ibsen with a grant to study in Italy and Germany. He left in 1863 and lived abroad until 1891. Ibsen's reputation as a playwright was established in the late 1860s with production of several successful pieces, including *Brand* (1866), in which a minister takes his calling too seriously, and *Peer Gynt* (1867), in which a man lacking in character finds redemption in the love of a woman. In 1866, Ibsen was granted an annual pension from the Norwegian government. When Ibsen returned to Norway in 1891, he was known as one of the world's greatest dramatists.

Critical Analysis

Henrik Ibsen's drama often focused on the realistic psychological complexities of the individual, and his work was much more focused on character than on plot. One of the central conflicts in Ibsen's drama is between characters who seek to realize themselves emotionally and spiritually and the barriers that have been created by outdated conventions of bourgeois society. Ibsen was often seen as a progressive, liberal thinker by younger generations outside Norway; in Norway, however, Ibsen was generally viewed as a conservative playwright, writing against the tide of increasing pressures of modern times. The themes of Ibsen's work are still debated by contemporary audiences and scholars.

Peer Gynt (1867) tells the story of a young man raised on the traditional fairy tales of Norway. Peer leads an irresponsible life, drinking, lying, and ruining young women's reputations. The epic play describes Peer's fantastical journey through the world. Peer becomes a slave dealer and a prophet and finally finds himself alone, wandering through the desert. When Peer returns home, he finds himself spiritually ruined because of the immoral life that he led in the past. In the end, Peer is saved by the love of Salvig, one of the women he abandoned. The play is a combination of psychological realism and folklore. This popular play was set to music by the famous Norwegian composer Edvard Grieg (1843–1907).

Ibsen's most famous work of realism, *A Doll's House* (1879), presents a tragic conflict in a middle-class family. Nora, the mother of three children, is treated like a doll by her husband. Faced with a familial conflict, Nora suddenly matures, realizing that she needs to leave her family to fulfill herself spiritually. The play created much controversy throughout Europe: Ibsen's representation of a woman who leaves her family in pursuit of spiritual fulfillment was seen as disturbing and unconventional. The realistic portrayal of the middle-class household also hurt bourgeois sentimentality. Despite the criticism, the play caused quite a sensation, and it toured Europe and America. The play remains Ibsen's most widely read and produced work.

Hedda Gabler (1890), the story of a woman who cannot resolve a conflict between her inner self and what society demands of her, was roundly condemned by many when it was first produced. A contemporary critic, Hjalmer Boyeson, called her "a complete perversion of womanhood." But Hedda is a character of tremendous complexity who continues to intrigue audiences.

Ibsen's most controversial play, however, was *Ghosts* (1881), which tells the story of the wife of a terrible drunk who sacrifices herself to the undesirable marriage because of social conventions. Their son is unknowingly engaged in a love affair with his half-sister, an illegitimate child of the father and a servant woman. The mother sends her son away, hoping that he will change. The son returns years later, the very picture of his father. He begins to suffer from syphilis, which he inherited from his father. The mother is faced with the difficult choice of administering poison to her son at his request or watching him go through complete psychological and physical degeneration. The subject of venereal disease was not seen as appropriate for theater. The play was bitterly criticized by the conservative segments of the public. *Ghosts* attacks the accepted social conventions of marriage and presents them as destructive to individual happiness.

Although Henrik Ibsen's talent was recognized during his lifetime, today his works enjoy the unanimous acclaim of the critics. Some of Ibsen's topics are still seen as controversial by many audiences. Ibsen is probably among the most influential playwrights in the development of modern drama. He anticipates the modern themes of alienation and the smothering pressure to conform that society exerts on individuals.

Other Works by Henrik Ibsen

Brand. Translated by Robert David McDonald. New York: Theater Communications Group, 1997.

Four Great Plays: Ghosts, An Enemy of the People, The Wild Duck, A Doll's House. Translated by R. Sharp. New York: Bantam, 1981.

Hedda Gabler and Other Plays. Translated by Una Ellis-Fermor. New York: Penguin, 1988.

Works about Henrik Ibsen

Clurman, Harold. *Ibsen.* New York: Da Capo Press, 1989.

Rose, Henry. *Henrik Ibsen: Poet, Mystic, and Moralist.* New York: Haskell, 1972.

Idris, Yūsuf (1927–1991) novelist

Yūsuf Idris was born in a small Egyptian village in the district of Sharqiyyah. His father was a middle-class farmer, and Idris's family moved frequently in the 1930s. He was brought up in his grandmother's house, where he was the only child in the household. When Idris was five years old, he attended primary school in a nearby village. He was the youngest student in the school, and his inability to relate to the other students or to his grandmother led Idris to seek consolation in reading folktales and popular stories. His interest in storytelling increased when he was sent to live with his elderly uncle, who had a rich supply of stories.

The outbreak of World War II forced Idris to move to different schools to avoid the violence. When the war ended, he studied medicine at Cairo University, becoming increasingly involved in the students' nationalist movement, which had its center in the department of medicine. Idris's political activities led to his arrest and exposed him to the political turmoil following the war.

In the 1940s, he became friends with the Chekhovian writer Muhammad Yusri Ahmad, who recognized and encouraged Idris's gift for storytelling. In 1950, Idris published his first short story. During the next 10 years, he wrote prolifically. In his first collection of short stories, *Arkhas layali* (*The Cheapest Nights,* 1954), Idris focuses mainly on people from impoverished and oppressed backgrounds, and he examines different character types from various occupations, social classes, and age groups. Idris did not write with the intention to shock readers with the oppressive circumstances of his characters' existence but rather to illuminate the subtle optimism and endurance that his characters possessed. For example, in "The Cheapest Nights," the title story of his collection, the main protagonist, besieged with increasing problems that exacerbate his poverty, eventually discovers that his only means of finding salvation is to try and create peace from his situation.

Idris's works resonate with vivid depictions, bold ideas, and intelligible presentation. His creative imagination, which he developed as a child, is artistically mixed with his sharp observation and understanding of the human situation. Idris's writings are celebrated because he presents familiar characters and situations from new perspectives. His writing style is powerful and provocative, and his novels and short stories explode with energy. Idris's political views and his determination to revolt against injustice remained strong, and his views often found expression in the stories he wrote.

Other Works by Yūsuf Idris

In the Eye of the Beholder: Tales of Egyptian Life. Edited by Roger Allen. Minneapolis: Bibliotheca Islamica, 1978.

The Piper Dies and Other Stories. Translated by Dalya Cohen-Mor. Potomac, Md.: Sheba Press, 1992.

Rings of Burnished Brass. Translated by Catherine Cobham. Cairo: American University in Cairo Press, 1992.

Three Egyptian Short Stories. Translated by Saad al-Gabalawy. Timonium, Md.: York Press, 1991.

Works about Yūsuf Idris

Allen, Roger M. A., ed. *Critical Perspectives on Yūsuf Idris.* Boulder, Colo.: Lynne Rienner, 1994.

Cobham, Catherine. "Sex and Society in Yūsuf Idris: 'Qa al-Madina'." *Journal of Arabic Literature* 6 (1975).

Cohen-Mor, Dalya. *Yūsuf Idris: Changing Visions.* Potomac, Md.: Sheba Press, 1992.

Kurpershoek, P. M. *The Short Stories of Yūsuf Idris: A Modern Egyptian Author.* Leiden, Netherlands: E. J. Brill, 1981.

Ihenfeld, Christa
See WOLF, CHRISTA.

Imalayen, Fatima Zohra
See DJEBAR, ASSIA.

Indianism

Indianism, or the valorization of the native peoples of the Americas, was a popular sentiment in Latin American literature. Although Indianism can be seen as far back as the 17th century in the poetry of Diogo Garção Tinoco of Brazil and even earlier in the writings of Bartolomé de Las Casas, a defender of the Indians in the Americas who wrote extensively during the early 1500s, the movement reached its height in the 19th century. One reason for this may be that the newly independent countries of Latin America were searching for a way to distinguish their literary history from that of Europe. In doing so, many authors looked to the continent's indigenous past as a source. In Brazil, ANTÔNIO GONÇALVES DIAS (1823–64) was the first great Indianist writer of this period. He wrote romantic literature often with Indianist themes, such as his first major work, *First Cantos,* and his later novel *Memories of Agapito Goiaba.* He also wrote a dictionary of the Tupi language, that of the native people of Brazil. Additionally, another major Brazilian author of the period, novelist JOSÉ MARTINIANO DE ALENCAR wrote historical novels with Indian main characters that celebrated the native peoples as the defining origin of the Brazilian nation. Alencar's three major Indianist novels are *The Guarani Warrior* 1857), *Iracema* (1865), and *The Ubirajara. Iracema* is the only work available in English; and it is a love story of an Indian princess and a Portuguese officer. Dominican author Manuel de Jesús Galván (1834–1910) also used the historical novel as a vehicle for Indianist writing. His novel, *Enriquillo,* written between 1879 and 1882, is a fine example of this genre.

Works about Indianism

Haberly, David. *Three Sad Races: Racial Identity and National Consciousness in Brazilian Literature.* New York: Cambridge University Press, 1986.

Tapia, John Reyna. *The Indian in the Spanish-American Novel.* Durango, Colo.: University Press of America, 1981.

Treece, David. *Exiles, Allies, Rebels: Brazil's Indianist Movement, Indigenist Politics, and the Imperial Nation-State.* Westport, Conn.: Greenwood Press, 2000.

Ionesco, Eugène (1912–1994) *playwright*

Considered by critics as the founding father of the French THEATER OF THE ABSURD, Eugène Ionesco was born in Slatina, Romania, on November 26. His beginnings as a writer came when he received a grant to study in Paris, where he wrote his thesis on "Sin and Death in French Poetry since Baudelaire" in 1938. He remained in France, where he began to concentrate on writing for the theater.

Ionesco was a staunch anti-Communist and a fervent believer in human rights. His plays dramatize the theme of the individual's struggle against conformity. Although more openly humorous and less despairing, his works are often compared to those of SAMUEL BECKETT. His best-known and often-produced play, *La cantatrice chauve* (1949; *The Bald Soprano,* 1965), takes its initiative from the empty clichés that Ionesco found while trying to learn English from a language textbook. He used the nonsensical sentences to illustrate the emptiness of a life that is stifled by the formalities of language and custom.

Ionesco referred to his works as "antiplays" that fuse tragedy and comedy. *The Lesson* (1951; translated 1958) tells of a teacher who dominates and ultimately kills his student through his oppressive mastery of language. *The Chairs* (1952; translated 1958) relates the tale of an old couple who attempt to pass on their life experience to a gathering of invited guests. With the exception of a deaf mute, the guests never arrive. The couple, however, believing that the audience is assembled, say their piece and then kill themselves, reflecting the lack of attention given to the playwright's message by a nonthinking audience.

Ionesco's breakthrough work in the English-speaking theater was *Rhinoceros* (1959; translated 1960), a play that depicts totalitarianism as a disease that ultimately turns human beings into savage rhinoceroses. Ionesco's protagonist, Bérenger, an ordinary man who holds onto his humanity, reappears in several of Ionesco's other works.

Aside from writing plays, Ionesco also wrote about the theater in his *Notes and Counternotes* (1962; translated 1964). He published his memoirs in *Present Past, Past Present* (1968; translated 1971), and wrote one novel, *The Hermit* (1973). He was elected to the prestigious Academie française in 1970 and died at the age of 84.

Critical Analysis

The Rhinoceros is often interpreted as an allegory about the rise of fascism. During the course of the play, nearly all residents of a town are transformed into great, ugly, violent beasts, just as ordinary Germans were transformed into monsters as they embraced the Nazi Party line before and during World War II. Clearly, however, *The Rhinoceros* can be read much more broadly, as an allegory for the general failure of humans to live authentic lives in an absurd universe. Like many other existentialist writers, Ionesco sees the cosmos as meaningless, without purpose or reason. In such a universe literally anything can happen. Therefore, the question becomes, "On what basis do human beings make moral choices under such circumstances?"

In *The Rhinoceros*, we witness characters transform into beasts out of the fear of being alone, out of the lust for power, out of the need to conform, out of weakness. We also witness the transformation of the rhinos themselves from ugly, ungainly beasts to creatures of great beauty, a change that mirrors the progressive inability of the townspeople to see the true nature of what they have become. Only the play's unlikely protagonist,

Bérenger, resists the lure of conformity, of going along with the crowd. Although he is originally portrayed as a weak-willed alcoholic, it becomes clear that Bérenger may be the only character who sees life for what it really is. If he escapes into drink, the others escape into something far more dangerous.

Like CAMUS in *The Plague*, Ionesco sees love as the only basis for moral choice in an absurd universe. It is his love of humanity that allows Bérenger to resist becoming a rhinoceros. He comes to understand that only by leading a committed life, a life in service of humanity, can one survive as fully human in an absurd universe. The play ends on Bérenger's line, "I'm not capitulating."

Another Work by Eugène Ionesco

A Hell of a Mess. Translated by Helen Gary Bishop. New York: Grove, 1975.

A Work about Eugène Ionesco

Hayman, Ronald. *Eugène Ionesco.* New York: Ungar, 1976.

Ipellie, Alootook (1951–2007) *poet*

Born in Nunavit in northern Canada, Alootook Ipellie was one of the foremost Inuit writers and artists. He began his career as an announcer for CBC radio, moving to Ottawa, Ontario, in 1973. Since that time, he wrote poetry and essays, contributed to Inuit newspapers and magazines such as *Nunavut* and *Nunatsiaq News,* and edited the *Inuktitut,* a quarterly magazine published by the Inuit Tapirisat of Canada that features articles on traditional ways of life and current issues of interest to Inuit readers and is published in English and Inuktitut.

Published in 1993, Ipellie's major work, *Arctic Dreams and Nightmares,* is a collection of 20 short stories that celebrate the Inuit way of life. The book also includes Ipellie's drawings—he was a celebrated artist and illustrator as well as a writer—and an introductory essay.

A Work by Alootook Ipellie

"The Igloos Are Calm in the Camp." *Canadian Literature* Issue 167 (Winter 2000), 43.

Works about Alootook Ipellie

Kennedy, Michael P. J. "Alootook Ipellie: The Voice of an Inuk Artist." *Studies in Canadian Literature* 21, no. 2 (1996): 155–64.

———. "Review of Arctic Dreams and Nightmares by Alootook Ipellie." *Canadian Journal of Native Studies* 14, no. 1 (1994): 181–83.

Iqbāl, Muhammad (1877–1938) *poet, essayist*

Muhammad Iqbāl was born in Sialkot, India (now modern Pakistan), into a middle-class orthodox Muslim family. Iqbāl was an exceptional student and won numerous scholarships that allowed him to complete his advanced education in England and Germany. In 1905, Iqbāl left for England, intending to become a lawyer. He quit his position as a lecturer at Government College, Lahore, and after three years obtained a master's degree in philosophy from Cambridge University and a doctoral degree from the University of Munich. He returned to India in 1908 and started to teach philosophy again but quit after only two years, saying that the government did not allow enough freedom of expression to Muslims.

Iqbāl began writing poetry for personal satisfaction. His peers saw his talent and convinced him to submit his poems to a journal for young writers called *Makhzan,* which was published by a close friend of his. The admiration of the older poets for his poetry encouraged Iqbāl to contribute to every single issue.

Critical Analysis

Though never actively involved in political events, Iqbāl's works are a testimony to his deep concern for Muslims around the world. Troubled by the mounting tension between Indian Muslims and Hindus in prepartition India, much of his poetry was written based on his own desire to find a solution to end India's religious conflicts. He often attended large political gatherings in Lahore, where people united with the common goal of leading India to freedom from British colonial rule. Later, prior to his death, Iqbāl's poetry played a pivotal role in the years leading to Pakistan's freedom from Britain and India.

The influence of religion at home and his studies in Persian mysticism and philosophy, however, are as important as religious politics in the formation of Iqbāl's unique poetic voice, which is at once extremely mystical, bombastic, and patriotic. It gracefully navigates between religious zealousness and the sublime in nature and humanity. In Iqbāl's poetry, the idea of love, or *Ishq* in Urdu, is deeply connected to the principles of *self* and *personality.* These concepts illustrate Iqbāl's views on the close relationship between poetry and pan-Islamism.

Iqbāl believed that the affirmation of an individual's intellect, desires, and ambitions would lead directly to the progress of the international Islamic community. In his opinion, the slower progress of the East, compared to Western civilization, resulted from blindly believing in systems of thought that had refused to recognize the power of the self in the individual. To remedy this, Iqbāl's poetry sought to teach that the act of loving the self would give birth to individual personality. An individual, therefore, is not a passive follower of fate or faith but the chief protagonist in his or her own life.

As with all his poetry, however, the theme of unity is essential. This reflects Iqbāl's involvement with the modernist school of Islam, which sought to create a bridge between the older traditions of Islam and the new one being shaped under current cultural influences. In *Rumuz-i-Bekhudi* (*Mysteries of Selflessness,* 1914–18), the poet calls life a "wave of consciousness," which can "thread between the past and now, / And the far future." For Iqbāl this thread is always the message of God as prescribed in the Qur'an.

Iqbāl's vision of Islam was multifaceted in that he sought to bring science, philosophy, psychology, and politics under one rubric. His poems embody many different Western and non-Western philosophical, political, and religious concepts. The central point, however, is the need to believe in personal action and its role in aiding the betterment and progress of the world's Muslim community. Although Iqbāl's use of the concept of freedom evokes the Renaissance belief in a universal humanity, he wrote primarily for a Muslim audience.

The connection of the terms *progress* and the *individual* can be traced to Iqbāl's admiration of Western philosophies where the emphasis is on the self, its role in the freedom of expression, and its potential as a source of power against oppression. In one of his Urdu poems from *Bang-i-Dira* (*The Sound of the Caravan Bell,* 1925) he highlights the importance of capitalizing on the gift of human intellect. Only nature is passive and that is only because it does not have intellect. In this collection, the bell serves to symbolically awaken readers to the accomplishments of Islam. Islam, therefore, is projected as the timeless answer to personal freedom and religious salvation.

The element of revival was already begun in Iqbāl's first prose work *Asrar-i-Khudi* (*Secrets of the Self,* 1911–12). This Persian masterpiece was unlike anything Iqbāl had written before because of its profound psychological and philosophical message. In this work, Iqbāl proposes that the awakening of the soul and the self must happen before Islam itself can undergo any changes. Its publication bewildered his contemporaries because it was radically different from his earlier, nationalist poetry.

Though less political in its approach, *Asrar-i-Khudi* does not detract from Iqbāl's prescription that change and advancement will bring harmony to the world. This theme is continued in a later work, *Rumuz-i-Bekhudi*, where individual selflessness is shown to be an expression of one's social duty. This idea is best captured in the lines "A common aim shared by the multitude / Is unity which, when it is mature, / Forms the Community; the many live / Only by virtue of the single bond."

During Iqbāl's adulthood, Muslims were facing religious crises across the globe. The precarious, double-edged positioning of Muslims in India reinforced Iqbāl's collaboration with the international Muslim Nationalism Movement, which worked under the slogan: "Freedom and Unity, Pan-Arabism and Pan-Islamism." Many critics, in fact, have claimed that Iqbāl's decision (in the 1910s) to write almost exclusively in Persian was a gesture to join with the wider Islamic community for whom Persian was the true language of Islam.

Stylistically, GHĀLIB and Iqbāl have a lot in common and are regarded as Urdu literature's greatest poets. Both wrote *ghazals,* which are metrical poems similar to the Western sonnet. While Ghālib's *ghazals* are extremely metaphysical and obscure in tone, Iqbāl writes almost like an orator. When he started writing in Urdu again in 1935, Iqbāl began to address the cause of Indian Muslims with new vigor. Even the element of lyricism is absent in his poems, and his tone more didactic than ever before.

The fiery spirit behind his later work marked the final stage in Iqbāl's contribution to bridging the gap between the Middle Ages and the modern in Urdu poetry. The new emphasis given to freedom, personal achievement, individual action, and self-development transformed the traditional Islamic belief in the negation of earthly life. Iqbāl, however, was not a reactionary and did not completely eschew previous Islamic ideas or the poetic conventions of older Urdu poetry: He highlighted existent ones and was able to show that the future for the Islamic world could be changed because the past supported it. As Muhammad Sadiq points, "Iqbāl gave [Islamic Internationalism] a new edge. . . . He does not think ahead of his day, therefore, he thinks in terms of it . . . to meet the challenge of the present." Iqbāl's value as a poet, therefore, lies in his ability to use his heritage to help his contemporary world envision its future.

In 1922, despite his open criticism of British rule, Iqbāl accepted the offer of knighthood by the queen of England. The highly mystical and philosophical undertones in his poetry explain why a poet who favors one religion and expounds one political path is still read by people of all religions and all political beliefs. In 1930, Iqbāl became president of the Muslim league. He was one of the first Muslim leaders to propose the possibility of an independent Muslim country called Pakistan. This idea was Iqbāl's solution for ending religious dissent in India, and it became a reality in 1947, after his death.

Other Works by Muhammad Iqbāl

Complaint and Answer: Iqbāl's Dialogue with Allah. Translated by Khuswant Singh. Delhi: Oxford University Press, 1981.

Dreams in a Time of War: A Childhood Memoir. New York: Pantheon, 2010.

Something Torn and New: An African Renaissance. Jackson, Tenn.: Basic Civitas Books, 2009.

Tulip in the Desert: A Selection of the Poetry of Mohammad Iqbāl. Translated by Mustansir Mir. London: Hurst & Co., 2000.

Wizard of the Crow. New York: Anchor, 2007.

A Work about Muhammad Iqbāl

Malik, Hafeez, ed. *Iqbāl, Poet-Philosopher of Pakistan.* New York: Columbia University Press, 1971.

Ishigaki Rin (1920–2004) *poet, short story writer*

Ishigaki Rin was born in Tokyo. When she was four, her mother died, which led to an unstable home life. During this early period, she contributed poems to girls' magazines. After graduation from Akasaka Higher Elementary School, she began to work at Nihon Kyōgyo Bank in 1934, where she remained until 1975.

While working at the bank, Ishigaki began to publish poems in union periodicals. In 1944, together with a number of other women writers, she launched the poetry magazine *Dansō,* under the guidance of poet Fukuda Masao. During this period, she also tried her hand at short-story writing. In the postwar period, she composed poetry in the style of REALISM, leading to her first poetry collection *Watashi no Mae ni Aru Nabe to Okama to Moeru Hi to* (The pots, pans and burning fire before me) (1959). In a poem of the same name, she wrote about cooking as an expression of love for the people around her. Her second poetry collection, *Hyōsatsu nado* (Nameplates, etc.)(1968), focused on the pain of life as one of its themes; for example, in the poem "Cliff," she wrote about the women who committed suicide in Saipan at the end of World War II by leaping from a cliff into the sea. The collection won the H-shi Award, named after modern poet Hirazawa Teijirō. She has also won the Toshiko Tamura Prize for a general collection, *Ishigaki Rin Shishū* (Ishigaki Rin's poetry anthology) (1971), and the Globe Award for the poetry collection *Ryakureki* (An abbreviated history) (1979). Other publications include *Yūmoa no Sakoku* (The national isolation of humor) (1973), a collection of essays and early short stories, and the poetry collection *Yasashii Kotoba* (Sweet words) (1984).

Ishigaki's poetry is renowned for its frankness and sympathy for humankind while exercising humorous social criticism. She is also unique in her frank portrayal of Japan's defeat in World War II.

Another Work by Ishigaki Rin

Anthology of Modern Japanese Poets. Edited and translated by Alexander Besher, Hiroaki Sato, and Yoichi Midorikawa. Chicago: University of Chicago Press.

J

Jaccottet, Philippe (1925–) *poet, novelist*
Philippe Jaccottet was born in Moudon, Switzerland,was educated in Lausanne, and developed an early enthusiasm for poetry, beginning his career by publishing French translations of Homer, Góngora, HÖLDERLIN, LEOPARDI, and UNGARETTI.

Jaccottet met his literary mentor, Gustave Round, in 1941 and, after a trip to Italy where he met Ungaretti, settled in Paris. He made friendships in the literary community with such writers as FRANCIS PONGE, YVES BONNEFOY, André du Bouchet (1924–) and Jacques Dupin (1927–). Their influence caused him to be wary of EXISTENTIALISM and surrealism, and he took refuge in his own works in the more coherent and traditional style of CLASSICISM.

Jaccottet's first published poetry collection was *Requiem* (1947), but his first significant collection was *Frightens and Other Poetries* (1953), whose poems deal with the passage of time, the anguish of death, and the loss of love. His first prose work, *A Walk Under the Trees* (1957), established his fascination with landscapes.

Several other prose works followed these early successes. *The Ignoramus* (1958) and *Elements of a Dream* (1961) explore the tenuous nature of human existence. With *Airs* (1967), he returned to poetry, focusing on lighter themes. A passage from his *Cahier de verdure* (*Notebook of Green,* 1990) gives a sense of the intensity with which he endows encounters with the natural world:

> This time it was a cherry tree. Not a cherry tree in full bloom, referring to some kind of clear approach, but a cherry tree loaded with fruits, caught sight of one evening in June, on the other side of a huge cornfield. It was once more as if someone had appeared there and were talking to you without really talking to you, without even pointing at you: someone or, rather, somebody, and a "beautiful thing" indeed . . .

Jaccottet has also written several works of criticism, as well as poetry and prose dealing with significant events in his life. He continues to write and work as a translator.

Other Works by Philippe Jaccottet
Selected Poems. Translated by Derek Mahon. Winston-Salem, N.C.: Wake Forest University Press, 1988.

Under Clouded Skies; and, Beauregard. Translated by David Constantine and Mark Treharne. Newcastle upon Tyne: Bloodaxe Books, 1994.

A Work about Philippe Jaccottet

Cady, Andrea. *Measuring the Visible: The Verse and Prose of Philippe Jaccottet.* Atlanta, Ga.: Rodopi, 1992.

James, C. L. R. (1901–1989) *historian, novelist, playwright, journalist*

One of the leading 20th-century literary and political voices of the Caribbean, Cyril Lionel Robert James was born in Trinidad in 1901. In his early years, he demonstrated a passion for classic English literature and cricket. In 1910, he received a national scholarship to Queen's Royal College, a secondary boy's school, from which he graduated in 1918. During the 1920s, James worked as a schoolmaster, cricket reporter, and writer of fiction. One of his students was Eric Williams, later Trinidad and Tobago's first prime minister. He began publishing stories and essays in two journals, *The Beacon* and *Trinidad*. His literary breakthrough came with the publication of one of his first short stories, "La Divina Pastora" (1927), in the *Saturday Evening Review*.

In 1932, James moved to Great Britain with the manuscript of a novel, *Minty Alley* (1936), and settled first in Leicester and then in London, where he covered cricket for the Manchester *Guardian*. Acknowledged as one of the first novels of the West Indies written by an indigenous person of African descent, *Minty Alley* portrays the local residents in one of Trinidad's barrack-yards, exploring class division, urban violence, and sexual mores, themes that have become commonplace in modern Caribbean literature.

It was also during these years that James's marxist political interests began to take more definite shape. James became a leading voice in the Trotskyist movement; he was active in the Independent Labor Party; and he began to connect his thinking about labor to the Pan-Africanist

movement, opposing colonialism through the popular mobilization of African and Caribbean masses. Applying marxist revolutionary thought to the problems of the colonies took center stage in James's mind as he wrote *World Revolution (1937)*, a critique of Soviet communism, and his landmark study of Toussaint Louverture and the Haitian Revolution, *The Black Jacobins: Toussaint L'Ouverture and the San Domingo Revolution* (1938). The book demonstrated that Louverture's overthrow of slavery in Haiti in the 18th century came about through the mass mobilization of slaves. The threat of similar revolts in other colonies compelled the European political establishment to outlaw slavery. As James would later claim, *The Black Jacobins* was written to show "how the African Revolution would develop." He was also interested in the revolutionary potential of theater, producing in 1938 a dramatic version of the life of Louverture starring the African-American actor Paul Robeson.

In 1938, James moved to the United States, lecturing on the looming war in Europe and what was then termed the Negro Question. He concluded his tour in Mexico, meeting with the exiled Russian revolutionary Trotsky and formulating a position on the roles that people of African descent should play in revolutionary struggles. James spent much of the 1940s involved in Socialist Party politics. He wrote a string of theoretical position papers: "Dialectical Materialism and the Fate of Humanity" (1947); *The Revolutionary Answer to the Negro Problem in the USA* (1948); and *The Class Struggle* (1950). Within a marxist context, James and his coauthors expressed a deepening sense of the autonomous significance of racial matters. In *The Revolutionary Answer to the Negro Problem in the USA*, they wrote, "We say, number one, that the Negro struggle, the independent Negro struggle, has a vitality and a validity of its own; that it has deep historic roots in the past of America and in present struggles." In this period, he married Constance Webb, the second of his three wives, and traveled in New York literary circles, becoming close to writers such as

Richard Wright, Ralph Ellison, St. Claire Drake, James T. Farrell, and Carl Van Vechten. James also immersed himself in a study of American history and literature.

In the early 1950s, during the anticommunist hysteria of the McCarthy era in the United States, James, whose visa status had long been in question, was interned on Ellis Island and eventually deported. During his internment, he wrote *Mariners, Renegades and Castaways: The Story of Herman Melville and the World We Live In* (1953), a remarkable study in which James portrays the classic 19th-century American author as, in the words of one critic, "a masterful interpreter of America's transition to capitalist modernity." At the end of this study, James appended an essay protesting his internment, in which he wrote, "I publish the protest with the book on Melville because as I have shown, the book as written is a part of my experience. It is also a claim before the American people, the best claim I can put forward, that my desire to be a citizen is not a frivolous one."

After his deportation, James returned to England, then to the Caribbean in time to see many former colonies gain independence. He published a remarkable book, *Beyond a Boundary* (1963), on sport, culture, and politics that dealt with one of the abiding passions of his life: cricket. Part memoir, part analysis of how the game of cricket has shaped West Indian identity, *Beyond a Boundary* linked James's boyhood experiences on the cricket pitch to his cricket journalism for the Manchester *Guardian* and to his sense of the game's revolutionary potentials.

He was allowed to return to the United States in the late 1960s. At that time, he taught in Washington, D.C., at Federal City College and involved himself in the nascent black studies movement that grew out of the Civil Rights and Black Power movements. Always productive, James continued to write He spent his last years in London, where he died in 1989.

Other Works by C. L. R. James

A History of Negro Revolt. New York: Haskell House Publishers, 1977.

At the Rendezvous of Victory. Westport, Conn.: Lawrence Hill & Co., 1980.

Notes on Dialectics. Westport, Conn.: Lawrence Hill & Co., 1980.

Spheres of Existence. Westport, Conn.: Lawrence Hill & Co., 1980.

Jarry, Alfred (1873–1907) *playwright, poet, novelist*

Best known for his play *Ubu roi* (*King Ubu*, 1896), Alfred Jarry was an eccentric whose fantastic works are considered to be forerunners of the THEATER OF THE ABSURD. Born in Lavalle, Mayenne, he inherited much of his eccentricity and a trace of insanity from his mother. By age 15, he had already collaborated with several classmates to write *Ubu roi* as a means of ridiculing a disliked mathematics professor. Originally performed with marionettes, the play was later produced in Paris where its anarchist themes and coarse language incited a riot.

Jarry created his own absurdist logic, which he called Pataphysics, a science governing the laws of exceptions and reaching beyond metaphysics to encompass that which cannot be defined. He attributed his logic to a science-fiction type character known as Dr. Faustoll. He even invented a Pataphysical calendar, which begins on September 8, 1873, Jarry's birthdate.

Inspired by H. G. Wells's novel *The Time Machine*, Jarry turned to science fiction and wrote the essay "How to Build a Time Machine" (1900). His final novel, *Le surmâle* (*The Supermale*, 1902), was a comic fantasy of a superman who ate superfood and performed feats of erotic endurance before dying in the embrace of a machine.

Jarry's life eventually began to mirror his art. From Père Ubu, his protagonist in *Ubu roi*, he picked up eccentric and destructive habits. Referring to himself frequently in the third person, he drank excessively, hallucinated frequently, and shouted orders and obscenities at friends and acquaintances.

By the time Jarry was 34, he had become a familiar figure in Paris, where he walked the streets and carried a green umbrella, a symbol of middle-class power in *Ubu roi.* He also wore cycling clothes and brandished two pistols, which he often used to threaten fellow pedestrians.

Jarry's way of life ultimately took its toll. He died on All Saint's Day, 1907, from alcoholism and tuberculosis, leaving behind a legacy to modern science fiction, as well as two sequels to *Ubu roi,* one of which, *Ubu echaîné* (*Ubu Bound,* 1900) was not performed until 1937. *Ubu cocu* (*Ubu Cuckolded,* 1944) was published posthumously.

Another Work by Alfred Jarry

Adventures in 'Pataphysics. Translated by Paul Edwards. London: Atlas, 2001.

A Work about Alfred Jarry

Lennon, Nigey. *Alfred Jarry: The Man with the Axe.* Los Angeles: Panjandrum Books, 1984.

al-Jayyusi, Salma al-Khadra (1946–   )
anthologist, literary critic, poet

Salma al-Khadra al-Jayyusi was born in East Jordan to a Palestinian father and a Lebanese mother. She spent most of her childhood in Acre and Jerusalem. After graduating from the American University of Beirut with a B.A. in Arabic and English literature, she went to London for her Ph.D. Jayyusi has traveled widely and lived in many places around the globe. She has taught at various universities in the Middle East and the United States and founded the Project of Translation from Arabic Literature in 1980. This project stemmed from al-Jayyusi's discovery that Arabic literature was not widely known around the world, and in cases where translations could be found, they were poorly done.

She is best known for her literary critique of Arabic literature and poetry. Having traveled widely during her life, she is able to interpolate in her poems the richness of her experiences within other cultures. Despite her ability to immerse herself in other traditions, Al-Jayyusi is committed to presenting the essence of Arabic literary tradition

to the literary world. Her first collection of poems, *Return from the Dreamy Fountain,* was first published in 1960. Even though it was well received by readers, Al-Jayyusi decided to focus her next efforts on collecting rarely known Arabic works and bringing them to the attention of the world. In 1977, she published a two-volume critical literary history of Arabic poetry, *Trends and Movements in Modern Arabic Poetry.* She hopes that by continuing to introduce books such as the above to the world, she can grant readers a better understanding of the richness of Arabic literature.

Other Works Edited by Salma al-Khadra al-Jayyusi

Anthology of Modern Palestinian Literature. New York: Columbia University Press, 1992.
The Legacy of Muslim Spain. Leiden; New York: E. J. Brill, 1992.

Jelinek, Elfriede (1946–   ) *novelist, poet, playwright, musician*

The Austrian author Elfriede Jelinek was not widely known beyond German-speaking audiences until 2004 when she was awarded the Nobel Prize in literature. As one American reviewer explained, the response to her selection was one of cautious support with a mixture of puzzlement, outrage, and enthusiasm. Though some of her work had been translated into English, and her 1983 novel *Die Klavierspielerin: Roman* (*The Piano Teacher*) was adapted into a highly regarded French-language film *La Pianiste* (2001), by Austrian director Michael Haneke, most English-speaking audiences were unfamiliar with her writing.

In Austria, Jelinek is known as a marxist/feminist critic of her own country for its Nazi past and its culture, which she has described as "rather authoritarian Catholic." Jelinek feels that because Austria has a dearth of political thinkers, the role of "social admonisher" has fallen to artists. Her work also has an explicit, sadomasochistic aspect derived from her sexual politics, expressed in such novels as *Die Liebhaberinnen* (*Women as Lovers,*

1975) and *Lust* (1989), politics that have caused controversy. "I describe the relationship between man and woman as a Hegelian relationship between master and slave," Jelinek has stated in an interview. "As long as men are able to increase their sexual value through work, fame or wealth, while women are only powerful through their body, beauty and youth, nothing will change."

Jelinek was born in Mürzzuschlag in the Austrian province of Styria on October 20, 1946. Her father, a Czech of Jewish descent, was a chemist who avoided Nazi persecution because he worked in a strategically vital industry. Her mother was Roman Catholic from an affluent Viennese family, and Jelinek was raised in Vienna, studying music: organ, piano, recorder, and composition. In the 1960s, she enrolled at the Vienna Conservatory but suffered a nervous breakdown before completing her exams; the conservatory eventually certified her as an organist in 1971. During this same period, Jelinek also took classes in drama and art history at the University of Vienna and began to write poetry.

Her first book, *Lisas Schatten* (*Lisa's Shadow*, 1967), was a collection of poems. Her first novel, *Wir sind Lockvögel, Baby!* (*We're Decoys, Baby!*), appeared in 1970. It has been described by Tobe Levin as the "first full-length pop novel in the German language," and its tone and approach constitute a scathing critique of modern media and pop culture. The German literary critic Reinhard Urbach observed that *We're Decoys, Baby!* "is a collage of clichés from pulp fiction, soap opera and comics, but the content illustrates the flip side of innocence. Where one expects romance, rape occurs. And cynicism takes the place of pathos. The form is in constant conflict with the content." This would become a trademark of Jelinek's work, the exposure of the ways that modern culture masks violence as romance. Jelinek's fiction continually exposes the hidden violence of popular culture to Austria's Nazi past, the way that postwar Austrian society glossed over its violent past.

Jelinek's next novel, *Michael. Ein Jugendbuch für de Infantilgesellschaft* (*Michael: A Young Person's Guide to Infantile Society*, 1972), maintains the caustic sarcasm of her first novel but uses a more conventional format (each chapter is like an episode from a sitcom) to expose the mechanisms through which mainstream media manipulate and shape public consciousness and individual desire.

In the early 1970s, Jelinek spent time traveling and lived in Berlin and Rome. She married Gottfried Hüngsberg, a data systems engineer, and began dividing her time between Vienna, where she lived with her mother until her death in 2000, and Munich, where her husband lives and works. Her next three novels, *Die Liebhaberinnen* (1975; *Women as Lovers*, 1994); *Die Ausgesperrten* (1980; *Wonderful, Wonderful Times*, 1990); and *The Piano Teacher* firmly established her reputation and garnered for Jelinek a wider audience and critical reputation in Germany.

Jelinek also ventured into drama during this period. Her radio play *Wenn die Sonne sinkt ist für manche schon Büroschluss* (*When the Sun Sinks It's Time to Close Shop*) was very favorably received in 1974. In the 1980s, Jelinek wrote a number of plays that were performed in Austria, Germany, and Switzerland but which also drew critical ire for their attacks on Austrian society, including, *Burgtheater: Posse mit Gesang* (*Burgtheater: Satiric Comedy with Music*, 1985) and *Krankheit oder moderne Frauen* (*Sickness or Modern Women*), written in 1984 and first produced in Bonn in 1987.

Jelinek's subsequent work continued to demonstrate how mass media and entertainment shape the basic ways in which people perceive the world and create a populace that is complacent and indifferent to political and social injustice. In *Lust* (1989) and in *Gier: Ein Unterhaltungsroman* (*Greed: A Light Entertainment*, 2000), male power and violence against women are squarely targeted.

Despite the controversy her work has aroused, Jelinek has been the recipient of a number of literary awards. Most notably she has received the Heinrich Böll Prize (1986); Peter Weiss Prize (1994); Bremen Literature Prize (1995); Georg Büchner Preis (1998); Berlin Theatre Prize (2002); Heinrich Heine Prize (2002); Lessing Prize for

Criticism (2004); Mülheim Dramatists Prize (2002, 2004, and 2009); and the Nobel Prize in literature in 2004. Jelinek also has proved herself an able translator of works into German; some of the authors she has translated include Thomas Pynchon, Georges Feydeau, Eugène Labiche, and Christopher Marlowe.

In awarding Jelinek the Nobel Prize, the committee cited the way she "deliberately opens her work to the clichés that flood the news media, advertising and popular culture—the collective subconscious of our time. She manipulates the codes of pulp literature, comics, soap operas, pornography and folkloristic novels . . . so that the inherent madness in these ostensibly harmless consumer phenomena shines through." In her Nobel lecture, "Sidelined," Jelinek turned that critical eye on herself and her own use of language and observed its double-edged nature. Likening language to a dog, she explained: "[T]his dog, language, which is supposed to protect me, that's why I have him, after all, is now snapping at my heels. My protector wants to bite me. My only protector against being described, language, which, conversely, exists to describe something else, that I am not—that is why I cover so much paper—my only protector is turning against me."

Critical Analysis

Elfriede Jelinek's work typically presents difficulties for readers because it is fundamentally provocative in a deliberate effort to promote social change. Its frank examination of sexual and political themes, presented in violent or sadomasochistic ways, has frequently antagonized and shocked Jelinek's audience. Because much of her criticism of media has to do with the way popular culture masks violence and subjection under the guise of "entertainment" and "pleasure," Jelinek's own writing is always suspicious of pleasure and aggressively challenges the reader, calling pleasure—even reading pleasure—into question. In *Greed: A Light Entertainment*, for example, the title deliberately misleads the reader, as a form of false advertising. The novel is neither light nor entertaining. Indeed,

the narrator frequently addresses the reader directly, antagonistically: "You can complain all you like about boredom while you're reading this," she writes, "but please not to me."

Similarly, *Lust* created controversy because it was marketed as "female pornography." However, readers soon became aware that its sexual acts did not titillate but were rather presented in a dry, mechanical way so as to strip them of, as one critic has noted, "any titillating aura." The sexual in Jelinek is strategically redirected toward pain, mutilation, and self-cancellation as part of her effort to criticize a male-dominated culture. In *The Piano Teacher*, we are presented with the psychopathology of Erika, a failed artist who mutilates herself.

> When SHE's home alone, she cuts herself, slicing off her nose to spite other people's faces. She always waits and waits for the moment when she can cut herself unobserved. No sooner does the sound of the closing door die down than she takes out her little talisman, the paternal all-purpose razor. . . . She is very skilled in the use of blades; after all, she has to shave her father, shave that soft paternal cheek under the completely empty paternal brow, which is now undimmed by any thought, unwrinkled by any will. This blade is destined for HER flesh.

In this example, Jelinek explores her character's psychology. The reader is made to perceive how the personal, individual pathology is applied to society at large, transformed into a cultural complaint and critique. For Jelinek, ideology is visited upon the body as violence, and her characters, novels, and plays express this central insight in many ways.

Another Work by Elfriede Jelinek
Einar. Translated by P. J. Blumenthal. Sausalito, Calif.: Post-Apollo Press, 2006.

Works about Elfriede Jelinek
Fiddler, Allyson. *Rewriting Reality: An Introduction to Elfriede Jelinek*. Oxford: Berg, 1994.

Johns, Jorun B., and Katherin Arens, eds. *Elfriede Jelinek: Framed by Language.* Riverside, Calif.: Ariadne Press, 1994.

Jhabvala, Ruth Prawer (1927–   )
novelist, short story writer, scriptwriter

Born in Cologne to Polish parents, Ruth Prawer Jhabvala possesses a triple or quadruple heritage—European (Jewish), British, Indian, and now American; she has made her home on three continents and absorbed several cultures. She was educated in England at Hendon County School and at the University of London's Queen Mary College, where she obtained an M.A. In 1951, she married Cyrus Jhabvala, a Parsi architect, and she lived with him in New Delhi from 1951 to 1975. (The Jhabvalas have three daughters.) In 1975 she emigrated to the United States, but she visits England frequently and spends winters in India.

In addition to a dozen novels and a half-dozen volumes of short stories, Ruth Prawer Jhabvala has written many film scripts. In 1962, she met Ismail Merchant and James Ivory; theirs has proved a long-lasting team, responsible for such films as *Shakespeare Wallah* (1965), *A Room with a View* (1986), *Howard's End* (1992), and *The Remains of the Day* (1993). For *A Room with a View,* Jhabvala won an Academy Award. Two of her own novels, *The Householder* and *Heat and Dust,* have also been filmed.

Critical Analysis

Jhabvala's literary career spans 45 years and exhibits several phases. Often compared with Jane Austen and E. M. Forster because she writes comedies of manners, her influences include Charles Dickens, George Eliot, Thomas Hardy, Tolstoy, Turgenev, and Proust. Her early novels are more narrowly focused than her later ones and often center on joint or extended Indian families and their problems. East/West conflict is another major theme and the chief reason for comparing her with Forster.

Esmond in India (1957) tells of a philandering British civil servant who has an Indian wife and a British mistress, befriends a number of middle-class Indian women, and exhibits a love/hate relationship with the subcontinent. *The Householder* (1960) focuses on the marriage of Prem and Indu; Prem discovers he must defeat his mother-in-law and rise above himself to fulfill his marriage. *Heat and Dust* (1975), which won the Booker Prize, is one of this author's most complex, sophisticated works, interweaving two love stories 50 years apart—that of Olivia, who runs off with an Indian prince, and that of her granddaughter. The novel raises the question "What is identity?" and probes the relations between history and reality, history and fiction, and fiction and reality. *A New Dominion* (1971) is experimental, employing omniscient narration (like Jhabvala's earlier fiction) but supplementing this by shifting from one character's viewpoint to another's. This novel and *Heat and Dust* are both reminiscent of Forster's *A Passage to India.*

Later novels are more complex in narration, more detached, and darker in mood. They exhibit film techniques learned from scriptwriting. The first Jhabvala novel to be written in the United States, *In Search of Love and Beauty* (1983), is a quest novel exploring all three of its author's heritages—German, British, and Indian—against an American background. The later novels also handle another favorite Jhabvala theme: the fraudulent guru or swami who cheats his devotees. In *Three Continents,* American female twins turn over their lives and fortunes to sham gurus with disastrous results.

Jhabvala's fiction has received mixed reviews. A craftswoman whose every word counts, she is prized as such in the Western world; Indians, however, are often nettled by her outsider's "inside" view of them and the subcontinent, and they chafe at her detachment—which is really self-defense, as she makes clear in the introduction to *Out of India.* She admits that, while immersed in India, she was never of it. After reviewing differing evaluations of Jhabvala, Ralph Crane observes simply, "She is a writer whose work will stand the test of time."

In 2005, Jhabvala published *My Nine Lives: Chapters of a Possible Past,* which she calls a work of "autobiographical fiction." In this book, Jhabvala imagines alternative paths that her life might have taken.

Another Work by Ruth Prawer Jhabvala

East into Upper East: Plain Tales from New York and New Delhi. Washington, D.C.: Counterpoint Press, 2000.

Works about Ruth Prawer Jhabvala

Crane, Ralph J. *Ruth Prawer Jhabvala.* New York: Twayne, 1992.

Sucher, Laurie. *The Fiction of Ruth Prawer Jhabvala: The Politics of Passion.* New York: St. Martin's Press, 1989.

Jiang Bingzhi

See DING LING.

Jiménez, Juan Ramón (1881–1958) *poet*

Juan Ramón Jiménez was born in southern Spain but spent most of his life in Madrid. He devoted his life to poetry, publishing his first volume at age 20. In about 1916, when he fell in love and married, he stopped writing in fixed meters and switched to free verse. He wanted to remove everything but the pure poetic essence from his verse. His constant inspiration came from his wife.

Jiménez was a member of the GENERATION OF 1898, a literary and cultural movement in the first two decades of the 20th century. Each author of the movement had his own idea of how to write "well," but all agreed that the improvisation, pomp, and regionalism of earlier Spanish literature must be replaced by a more modern, simpler literature that seeks its inspiration abroad. Jiménez's poetry is an example of the move toward this simplicity. Much of his work, such as *Arias tristes* (*Sad Arias,* 1903) and *Melancolía* (*Melancholy,* 1912), is very sad.

Although known for his voluminous output of poetry, Jiménez is also the author of the beautiful story of a little donkey called *Platero y yo.* It was first published in 1917 and has been translated into English. Jiménez was awarded the Nobel Prize in literature in 1956.

Other Works by Juan Ramón Jiménez

The Complete Perfectionist. Translated by Christopher Maurer. New York: Doubleday, 1997.

Florit, Eugenio, ed. *Selected Writings of Juan Ramón Jiménez.* Translated by H. R. Hays. New York: Farrar, Straus & Giroux, 1999.

Light and Shadows: Selected Poems and Prose. Translated by James Wright and Robert Bly. Buffalo, N.Y.: White Pine Press, 1987.

Works about Juan Ramón Jiménez

Kluback, William. *Encounters with Juan Ramón Jiménez.* New York: Peter Lang, 1995.

Wilcox, John. *Self and Image in Juan Ramón Jiménez.* Champaign: University of Illinois Press, 1987.

Johnson, Pauline (Tekahionwake) (1861–1913) *poet*

Pauline Johnson was born on the Six Nations Reserve near Brantford, Ontario, Canada. Her mother was a nonnative who came to Canada from Ohio, and her Mohawk father was a chief of the Six Nations Reserve. Johnson had two older brothers and a sister. She was influenced at early age by such canonical writers as John Milton (1608–74) and Sir Walter Scott (1771–1832) but was also exposed to native stories by her father and grandfather. This combination of influences had a great impact on her development as a writer.

When Johnson's father died, the family moved to Brantford, Ontario, where Johnson began to write poems and short stories. She published these stories in local newspapers to make money. In addition, Johnson became famous for her poetry recitals, her gift for performing poetry, a legacy of the storytelling she learned from her father and grandfather. She toured Canada and the United States and also traveled abroad, performing her work and often sharing the bill with famous musicians or comedians.

Johnson's popular books of poetry include *The White Wampum* (1895), *Canadian Born* (1903), and *Flint and Feather* (1912). In all her work, Johnson celebrates her native heritage: "My aim, my joy, my pride is to sing the glories of my own people." In 1911, Johnson published *Legends of Vancouver*, a collection of stories and legends of the Squamish people as told to her by her friend Squamish chief Joe Capilano. Johnson died at the age of 52 of breast cancer. The monument to her grave can be found in Vancouver's Stanley Park.

Another Work by Pauline Johnson
Ruoff, LaVonne Brown, ed. *The Moccasin Maker*. Norman: University of Oklahoma Press, 1998.

A Work about Pauline Johnson
Strong-Boag, Veronica Jane, and Carole Gerson. *Paddling Her Own Canoe: The Times and Texts of E. Pauline Johnson (Tekahionwake)*. Toronto: University of Toronto Press, 2000.

Johnson, Uwe (1934–1984) *novelist, critic*
Uwe Johnson was born in Cammin, Poland, to Erich Johnson, an administrative official of the Nazi Party, and Erna Johnson. Johnson attended an elite elementary school that provided intensive training in the Nazi ideology for its students. After the end of World War II, the Johnsons moved to Rechnitz, Germany, to avoid the advancing Soviet army. Johnson's father was arrested in 1946 by Soviet officials for participation in the Nazi regime. The family never saw him again.

Between 1952 and 1954, Johnson studied German language and literature at University of Rostock, East Germany. Johnson joined the junior ranks of the Free German Youth, an East German Communist organization for high school and college students. Johnson was expelled from the university when he refused, despite strong pressure from the Communist officials, to make false claims during a public speech at a Free German Youth meeting about the Young Congregation, a movement of Christian youth. Later, Johnson was allowed to continue his studies at Karl Marx University of Leipzig, where he finished his bachelor's degree in 1956. He was not allowed to pursue doctoral studies.

Johnson began his literary career translating English works into German. He also worked for various publishing houses in East Germany, appraising the merit of proposed projects. Johnson constantly struggled to find employment and had several altercations with the Communist regime of East Germany, which prevented any possibility of a teaching career. Completely disenchanted, Johnson moved to West Berlin in 1959.

Uwe Johnson's work definitely has political dimensions; however, it is not easy to assess what these exactly are. His work has been criticized by the government and some writers of West Germany as procommunist and has been similarly derogated in East Germany as anticommunist: It seems that Johnson opposed the regimes of both countries. He saw the government of East Germany as socially oppressive, dictatorial, and dominated by Stalinism. At the same time, Johnson was disgusted with the government of West Germany, which he frequently characterized as fascist. Indeed, the national government of West Germany was dominated by ex-Nazis and was in many ways as repressive as the government of East Germany. Johnson lived in West Berlin because it was not under the direct jurisdiction of the national government in Germany.

Critical Analysis
Johnson's first novel, *Mutmassungen über Jakob* (*Speculations about Jacob*, 1959), was an instant success when it appeared in West Germany. The plot of the novel centers on Rohlfs, a member of the East German Security Force, who enters the life of the Cresspahl family. Heinrich Cresspahl's daughter, Gesine, left for West Germany and works for NATO. Throughout the novel, Rohlfs attempts to influence the family to recruit Gesine as a spy for East Germany. By no means a one-sided

perspective, the novel discusses the personal and political challenges brought about by the division of Germany. The novel also gained popularity in East Germany and was not censored by government officials.

Das dritte Buch über Achim (The Third Book about Achim, 1961) tells the story of Karsch, a West German journalist who travels to East Germany to visit his ex-lover Karin, a successful actress. While in East Germany, Karsch meets Achim, Karin's boyfriend, a professional biker and a star in East Germany. Karsch faces a difficult decision when a publishing company approaches him to write Achim's life story in a way that would glorify socialist life in East Germany. Once again, the book does not provide a clear political message and seems to present an objective reflection of a divided Germany. The work was hailed as an achievement in contemporary German literature and especially was praised by GÜNTER GRASS, another controversial and famous German writer.

Uwe Johnson lived for a time in the United States and finally settled in the United Kingdom. He found the environments of both Germanys stifling and not conducive to his work. He continued to write novels and received numerous awards, including the Fontane Prize in 1960, the Wilhelm Raabe Prize in 1975, the Georg Büchner Prize in 1971, and the Thomas Mann Prize in 1978. Johnson was a member of the Academy of Arts in West Berlin and of the German Academy for Language and Literature. After the reunification of Germany in 1990, interest in Johnson's work dramatically increased. Gary Baker remarks,

> Uwe Johnson is significant not only for his unique literary style and linguistic creativity but also for the thematic issues addressed in his works. He was the first German author to treat, in fiction, the division of Germany after the war. He explored its psychological, political, and cultural manifestations in a network of characters and places unmatched in complexity and authenticity.

Other Works by Uwe Johnson

Anniversaries: From the Life of Gesine Cresspahl. Translated by Leila Vennewitz and Walter Arndt. New York: Harcourt Brace, 2000.
A Trip to Klagenfurt: In the Footsteps of Ingeborg Bachmann. Translated by Damion Searls. New York: Hydra Books, 2002.

A Work about Uwe Johnson

Baker, Gary. *Understanding Uwe Johnson.* Columbia: University of South Carolina Press, 1999.

Jünger, Ernst (1895–1998) *novelist, essayist*

Ernst Jünger was born in Heidelberg, Germany, and grew up in Hannover. The son of a pharmacist, he ran away from home in 1913 to look for more exciting possibilities in life. After joining the French Foreign Legion and serving in North Africa, he joined the German army at the outbreak of World War I and served as an officer on the Western front. Between 1919 and 1923, Jünger continued his military career and served as an officer in the Weimar Republic army. After retirement, he studied entomology at Leipzig, Germany, and Naples, Italy. He eventually became a famous entomologist (several insects were named after him).

During the 1920s, Jünger joined the pro-Nazi movement and contributed to several right-wing publications. His first book, *The Storm of Steel* (1920), argued that Germany's suffering during World War I was a prelude to a rebirth of a powerful nation and great victory ahead. In *Adventurous Heart* (1929) and *The Workers* (1933), Jünger examined the social and emotional structure of the worker. In these works, Jünger rejects humanism and claims that struggle for power among world nations is imminent. Although Jünger supported the right-wing movement, he rejected offers of friendship from Adolf Hitler during the 1920s, refused to serve as the head of the Nazi Writers' Union in 1933, and vocally opposed anti-Semitism. For these reasons, the Nazi government prohibited further publication of his work in 1938.

During World War II, Jünger served as a captain in the German army. Stationed in Paris, he associated with several artists, including the famous painter Pablo Picasso. After the death of his son at the Italian front, he became completely disenchanted with war.

After the war, Jünger published a number of works in which he supported European unity and promoted the rights of the individual. In *The Glass Bees* (1957), for example, he paints a world in which machines threaten the rights of individuals. In his books, Jünger often dispassionately painted historical and social developments that resulted in violation of human rights; hence, he was sometimes accused of indifference and elitism. Despite criticism, he achieved a reputation as a great German writer.

He was awarded numerous prizes, including the Great Order of Merit (1959), the Immermann Prize (1964), and the Goethe Prize (1982), as well as an honorary degree from the University of Bilbao, among others. By the time of his death at the age of 103, Jünger had published more than 20 books. His works have been translated into more than a dozen languages.

Other Works by Ernst Jünger

Aladdin's Problem. Translated by Joachim Neugroschel. New York: Marsilio, 1992.

A Dangerous Encounter. Translated by Hilary Barr. New York: Marsilio, 1993.

A Work about Ernst Jünger

Nevin, Thomas. *Ernst Jünger and Germany: Into the Abyss, 1914–1945*. Durham, N.C.: Duke University Press, 1997.

K

Kabbani, Nizar (Qabbani) (1923–1998)
poet, essayist

Born in Damascus, Syria, to a respected middle-class Muslim family, Kabbani published his first volume of poetry in 1944. He immediately gained fame for his bad-boy erotic daring and his "hip" language that expressed Arabic youth culture. Kabbani's poetry often incites rebellion against what he saw as repressive political and social mores. In 1954, the Syrian parliament considered demoting him from his diplomatic post for the disrespect to religion some found in his poem, "Bread, Hashish, and the Moon," but the motion failed.

At the height of his literary career, from the 1950s to the 1970s, Kabbani, often writing in a female voice, expressed the joys of love and eros for a generation of men and especially women. He saw himself as a champion of women's liberation and sexual freedom.

In the 1980s, Kabbani wrote three volumes of poetry, titled "Trilogy of the Children of the Rocks" (1988), celebrating the teenage rebels of the Palestinian *intifadah.* His poetry conveys deep Arab pride as well as sharp criticism of many aspects of Arab life and culture, such as the sexual double standard for men and women. His most scathing poetic attacks, such as "Scribblings in the Margins of the Notebook of Defeat," are aimed at repressive Arab governments that curtail the human rights of the Arab peoples. He also wrote strident poems against Israeli and American policies toward Arabs, such as the poem "I Am a Terrorist" in which he says that Arab men are labeled terrorists by the Western media for defending their homes and their people's dignity.

Kabbani graduated from the University of Damascus with a law degree in 1945 and joined Syria's diplomatic corps. He was posted in Egypt, Turkey, Britain, Lebanon, Spain, and China before he resigned in 1966 and moved to Beirut, where he established his own publishing company.

From a brief early marriage in Syria, he had two children, one of whom died in a car accident as a young man; Kabbani eulogized him in poetry. Kabbani married again, this time to an Iraqi schoolteacher, Balqis al-Rawi. His poem, "Choose," was widely considered by the Arabic reading public to be Kabbani's marriage proposal to Balqis. The handsome poet—he was nicknamed "the blond rebel"—and the beautiful woman who was his muse captivated public attention. They had two children. Kabbani wrote some of his finest poetry of love and sensuality in the 1970s. The poem "I Bear Witness That There Is No Woman But You," for example, provocatively turns the Muslim testimony of faith in one God into a testimony of a man's love for one woman. When Balqis was killed at her office in a Beirut bombing in 1981, he publicly mourned her in several anguished poems.

After her death, Kabbani left the Arab world for Europe, living in Geneva, Paris, and London, where he settled down to a life of exile. In 1997, a street was named after him in his old neighborhood in Damascus. When he died, his body was flown back to Damascus for burial, as he had requested in his will.

Kabbani wrote more than 50 books of poetry as well as several volumes of essays and one drama, a political satire. During his lifetime, his readings drew crowds in the tens of thousands. Many Kabbani poems were adopted as song lyrics by some of the most popular figures in Arabic music so that his words continue to be heard through song. In today's pop music scene, Iraqi icon Kazem al-Saher has acquired rights to sing many of Kabbani's poems. Kabbani's work has been translated into Spanish, French, Italian, Persian, and English. In 1994, he was awarded the Oweiss Prize for Cultural Productivity in the United Arab Emirates.

Other Works by Nizar Kabbani

Arabian Love Poems: Full Arabic and English Texts. Translated by Bassam K. Frangieh and Clementina Brown. Boulder, Colo.: Lynn Rienner, 1999.

On Entering the Sea: The Erotic and Other Poetry of Nizar Qubbani. Translated by Lena Jayyusi et al. New York: Interlink, 1996.

Kafka, Franz (1883–1924) *novelist, short story writer*

Franz Kafka was born in Prague, Czech Republic, to Hermann Kafka, a dry-goods merchant, and Julie Kafka. Kafka's family spoke German and belonged to a small but old community of German-speaking Jews in Prague. Hermann Kafka was a domineering, almost tyrannical figure in the Kafka household. He took out his anger and

frustration on young Franz, who recalled the terrifying experiences later in his life. Indeed, many biographers and critics of Kafka note that Kafka's work often deals with a conflict between father and son or with people pleading innocence in front of authority figures. Kafka's childhood was marked by the constant domestic conflicts and by the social atmosphere of Prague that branded Jews as second-class citizens and outcasts. Kafka's attitude toward his Jewish heritage was ambiguous and is an obliquely expressed conflict in his works.

Kafka was educated in German elementary schools. In 1901, he enrolled in Ferdinand-Karls University to study law, graduating with a doctorate in 1906. Kafka's career as a writer began about 1904 when he was working as a legal clerk. At work, Kafka composed mundane reports on industrial health hazards and the legal implications of industrial injuries; at night, however, Kafka composed elaborate, sometimes fantastic tales. Between 1907 and 1923, Kafka worked in the insurance business and achieved remarkable success; indeed, he was so valued by his employers that they arranged a deferment from the draft during World War I.

In 1917 Kafka was diagnosed with tuberculosis. He continued to work but suffered a serious setback when he contracted influenza in 1919. Kafka also met constant disappointment from publishers who rejected his work. After several turbulent but unsuccessful relationships with women, in 1922 Kafka finally married Dora Diamant, a young woman from a respected Orthodox Jewish family in Prague. The couple moved to Berlin, where Kafka, by then confined to bed, worked on his journals and wrote numerous letters to his friends and family. By 1924, Kafka was moved to a sanatorium just outside of Vienna. He died of tuberculosis in obscurity and poverty.

Kafka asked his friend and fellow writer Max Brod to destroy all manuscripts after his death. Fortunately, Brod disobeyed the last wish of his friend. Thus, with the exception of few short stories, most of Kafka's major work was published posthumously.

Critical Analysis

"The Metamorphosis" (1915) is probably Kafka's best-known and most critically acclaimed short story. In the story, Gregor Samsa, a traveling salesman, awakes one day to discover himself transformed into a giant grotesque insect. No longer able to communicate with his parents or the outside world, Gregor physically degenerates day by day; mentally, however, he does not seem to change. Gregor is finally killed by his father. "The Metamorphosis" presents a range of themes found in the works of MODERNISM, such as alienation of the individual, failure of communication, and attachment to a landscape that has grown ungovernably hostile. At the time of its publication, however, most readers did not know how to interpret the strange allegorical plot of the story. Today, the story is often cited as central to the modernist movement, and it reflects the ideas that the movement embodied.

Kafka's novel *The Trial* (1925) depicts the suffering and psychological torment of Josef K., who is arrested one morning without reason. Throughout his "trial," Josef never discovers the crime of which he is accused. He is dragged through a seemingly endless investigation in a court system that reveals nothing. Josef does not confront an identifiable authority figure, but he is constantly burdened by laws he cannot comprehend. At the end of the novel, Josef becomes a martyr to the law when he is stabbed to death. Truth is no longer relevant in the faceless system of law that delivers arbitrary judgment and punishment. Kafka addressed a similar theme in the short story "The Penal Colony" (1919); here, truth becomes an instrument of punishment, as the victims of truth are killed by a machine that inscribes the nature of their crimes on their bodies.

The protagonist of Kafka's novel, *The Castle* (1926), is simply identified as K. K arrives in a small village, claiming to be a land surveyor and bears the official authority of the government. K seeks to meet Klamm, the ruler of the mysterious castle that supposedly has sovereignty over the village. K develops a strange relationship with Arthur and Jeremiah, Klamm's assistants, who refuse to arrange a meeting with their supervisor. K finally befriends and uses Frieda, a former mistress of the castle, who leaves K after discovering his true intents. *The Castle* focuses on several important themes, including bureaucracy, love, guilt, and law. All these themes are strangely interconnected in the landscape where the individual is incapable of retaining a stable identity. Although Kafka never finished *The Castle*, it remains as one of his most important works.

Franz Kafka received no recognition for his incredible talent during his lifetime. Today, however, Kafka is considered one of the leading figures of modernism and of world literature in general. He left a body of works of great complexity and literary genius, and one that continues to enrich readers and critics today. Kafka was rediscovered in the 1950s and is among the most admired of modern writers. Perhaps more than any other writer, Kafka captures the nightmare reality and absurdity of modern existence and the strange, alienated feel of a world without reason.

Other Works by Franz Kafka

Amerika. Translated by Willia Muir. New York: Schocken Books, 1996.
The Complete Stories. New York: Schocken Books, 1995.
Franz Kafka: The Diaries, 1921–1923. New York: Schocken Books, 1989.

Works about Franz Kafka

Adler, Jeremy. *Franz Kafka.* New York: Overlook Press, 2002.
Brod, Max. *Franz Kafka: A Biography.* New York: Da Capo Press, 1995.

Kanik, Orhan Veli (1914–1950) *poet*

Orhan Veli Kanik was born in Istanbul, Turkey. The son of a conductor for the Presidential Symphony Orchestra, he received a diverse and liberal education but withdrew from the University of Istanbul before completing his degree. His talent as a writer was nurtured at a young age, and he was fortunate to have among his mentors the leading poet, literary critic, and historian Ahmet Hamdi Tapinar. Tapinar encouraged Kanik to write, leading him to publish his poetry in the school paper *Sesimiz* (Our voice) while Kanik was in his early teens. Kanik served with the armed forces during World War II and obtained a job as a translator after the war, but he left this position to lead a bohemian life, more in tune with his poetry and his philosophy.

Kanik was born into a family of writers and artists. His younger brother, Adnan, was also a writer until he was sent to prison in 1949 for a political offense. Orhan, however, was able to avoid conflicts with the authorities and to publish *Leaf,* a literary journal. The journal ran for 28 issues and ceased publication with a special memorial edition on Kanik's death.

Kanik was never a prolific writer, but he had a great influence on the development of Turkish poetry. His own work was more influenced by Japanese haiku than by traditional Turkish or Western forms. Kanik believed that a strict adherence to traditional forms had made much of Turkish poetry sterile. He sought to reinvent tradition with a sense of vibrancy that would resonate with the needs of common humanity. He broke free of conventional modes, discarding rhyme and meter, and focused instead on an almost nihilistic viewpoint that, simultaneously, managed to incorporate a reaffirmation of the joy of life. He wrote entirely in free verse, tackling the issues relevant to everyday life in plain language that was devoid of metaphors and clichés.

Although NAZIM HIKMET had earlier brought the use of free verse to Turkish poetry, it was Kanik who established its relevance by introducing ideas of the French modernist movement to his poetry. Alongside fellow poets Oktay Rifat and Melih Cevdet Anday, he started the artistic movement POETIC REALISM, which focuses on the emergence of the common man as hero. By stripping away the traditional adornments of poetry, the poet is free to use everyday life as subject matter.

Kanik died from a cerebral hemorrhage after collapsing in Istanbul on November 14, 1950. Many believed that his death was a result of his love of alcohol, citing a famous line from one of his poems, "I wish I were a fish in a bottle of booze." Kanik's death came as a shock to the people of Turkey. After a well-attended funeral ceremony, he was buried on a hill where he could rest forever, "Listening to Istanbul."

Another Work by Orhan Veli Kanik

I, Orhan Veli: Poems by Orhan Veli. Translated by Murat Nemet-Nejat. Brooklyn, N.Y.: Hanging Loose Press, 1989.

Kao Tsing-jen
See GAO XINGJIAN.

Karamzin, Nikolai Mikhailovich
(1766–1826) *historian, short story writer, novelist*

The birthplace of Nikolai Karamzin is uncertain, but most research suggests a small village along the Volga River in Russia. Karamzin's mother died when he was very young, and he was raised by his father, Mikhail Karamzin, a retired army captain and minor aristocrat. A village priest taught him to read and write. When Karamzin was 13, his father sent him to study in Moscow. He was a brilliant student, and attended university lectures when he was just 16. Although he was eager to study at the university, Karamzin's father insisted that he pursue an army career. Karamzin enlisted as an officer in the Preobrozhentsky regiment in St. Petersburg in 1783.

In St. Petersburg, Karamzin spent his time in literary circles and eventually became a translator. He published his first translation at the age of 17 and was paid with two volumes of the English novelist Henry Fielding's works. He left the army in 1784 after the death of his father. In 1789, he left Russia and traveled across Europe, visiting Germany, Switzerland, France, and England.

On his return to Russia in 1790, Karamzin established a literary journal, *Moscow Journal,* in which he published his *Letters of the Russian Traveler* (1792), a collection that was based on his travels in Europe, and "Poor Liza" (1792), a short novel about a peasant girl. Several other stories that Karamzin wrote at this time brought French sentimentalism to Russia and were widely imitated.

Karamzin was not particularly interested in politics, but when he established a new journal in 1801, *Vestnik Evropy* (*The Messenger of Europe*), it became the leading political journal in Russia. It was the most widely read publication in Russia during the early 1800s. The journal's popularity brought financial success, which freed Karamzin to begin his enormous historiographic work, *History of the Russian State* (1819–29). This 12-volume work, which covered Russian history up to 1613, was the most complete history of Russia of the time. The Russian emperor, Aleksandr I, appointed Karamzin official historiographer in 1803 with a pension of 2,000 rubles a year, a considerable sum.

Between 1810 and 1811, Karamzin worked on *Memoir on Ancient and Modern Russia* (1811). In this work, Karamzin related his political beliefs, as well as his personal conversations with Aleksandr I. He believed that autocracy was the appropriate form of government for Russia, making a careful distinction between autocracy and despotism, based on the importance of the law.

Karamzin left a long-lasting legacy when he died in 1826. He had become one of the closest friends of the emperor and remained a defender of the monarchy. More important, Karamzin's work influenced such important writers as ALEKSANDR PUSHKIN and MIKHAIL LERMONTOV. He also established a historiographic tradition that did not previously exist in Russia, and his account of Russian history was an important part of the Russian self-image into the 20th century.

Works about Nikolai Karamzin

Black, Joseph Lawrence. *Nicholas Karamzin and Russian Society in the Nineteenth Century: A Study in Russian Political and Historical Thought.* Toronto: University of Toronto Press, 1976.

Hammarberg, Gitta. *From the Idyll to the Novel: Karamzin's Sentimentalist Prose.* New York: Cambridge University Press, 1991.

Lewis, S. Mark. *Modes of Historical Discourse in J. G. Herder and N. M. Karamzin.* New York: Peter Lange, 1995.

Karnad, Girish (1938–) *playwright*

Girish Ranghunath Karnad was born in Maharashtra, India, but has lived most of his life in the southern state of Karnataka. Most of Karnad's work is written in Kannada, the language spoken in Karnataka, but he has translated all his major plays into English. He is a playwright, story writer, poet, and director of films.

After completing his college studies in math and statistics in 1958 at Karnataka University, Karnad went to Oxford University to earn a master's degree in philosophy, politics, and economics. It is here that Karnad first started to explore his artistic talents and began writing poetry.

When Karnad returned to India, he started to work at Oxford University Press in 1963. After the success of his second play *Tughlaq* (1964), he decided to quit the press and has since devoted his life to writing drama. At one point (1974–75), he was the director of the Film Institute of Pune, India.

Karnad has written 10 plays, all of which are extremely politically driven but read like folktales. His very first play *Yayati* (1961), written while studying at Oxford, is taken from a story in the great Hindu epic *The Mahabharata*. It recounts the events that follow a son's attempt to rescue his father from a curse, thus throwing the entire family into a moral dilemma. There is a strong sense of the past in Karnad's work, and he borrows extensively from Indian mythology and history. His play *Tughlaq,* for instance, shows the transformation of the old Mughal emperor (Mohammad bin Tughlaq) from a sensitive ruler into an unjust oppressor. His folktale *Cheluvi* (1992), which was also made into a movie, is about a girl who turns into a tree, thus becoming a symbolic vehicle of nature's outcry against humanity's inconsiderate actions.

Karnad's plays have always carried social messages. At a time when most of his peers were switching to the more-lucrative film industry, Karnad steadfastly stuck to writing about social reform for the theater. In 1994, he won the Sahitya Akademi Award for his social drama, *Taledanda* (1990), and the Jnanpith Award in 1999 for his contribution to modern Indian drama.

Other Works by Girish Karnad

The Dreams of Tipu Sultan and Bali: The Sacrifice—Two Plays by Girish Karnad. New Delhi: Oxford University Press India, 2004.

Three Plays: Naga-Mandala; Hayavadana; Tughlaq. New York: Oxford University Press, 1996.

A Work about Girish Karnad

Dodiya, Jaydipsinh. *The Plays of Girish Karnad: Critical Perspectives.* New Delhi: Prestige Books, 1999.

Kaschnitz, Marie Luise (pseudonym of Freifrau Marie Luise von Kaschnitz-Weinberg) (1901–1974) *poet, short story writer*

Marie Luise Kaschnitz was born in Karlsruhe, Germany. Her parents were Max Freiherr von Holzing-Berstett, a general and nobleman, and Elsa von Seldenek. Kaschnitz grew up in Berlin and Potsdam. She trained to be a book dealer and later worked at a publishing house in Munich. In 1925, she married Guido von Kaschnitz-Weinberg, an archaeology professor. They traveled extensively and lived for several years in Rome.

Although best known as a poet, Kaschnitz's first work was a novel, *Liebe beginnt* (*Love Begins*, 1933). After World War II, she emerged as a lyric poet with her first collection *Gedichte* (*Poems*, 1947). Starting in the 1950s, she also published short-story collections and radio plays based on biblical legends. After Kaschnitz's husband died, she wrote

Wohin denn ich (*Where Do I Go Now?* 1963), a moving collection of poems inspired by her loss.

A central theme in Kaschnitz's writings is the search for self. She often describes the plight of the individual in an impersonal, alien world. Influenced by her Christian faith and World War II, she frequently dealt with the issues of guilt and death. She used traditional forms but also experimented, developing her own unique style. Kaschnitz received the guest chair for poetry at the University of Frankfurt and won numerous awards, including the prestigious Georg Büchner Prize.

Other Works by Marie Luise Kaschnitz

Circe's Mountain: Stories by Marie Luise Kaschnitz. Translated by Lisel Mueller. Minneapolis: Milkweed Editions, 1990.

Selected Later Poems of Marie Luise Kaschnitz. Translated by Lisel Mueller. Princeton, N.J.: Princeton University Press, 1980.

A Work about Marie Luise Kaschnitz

Pulver, Elsbeth. *Marie Luise Kaschnitz.* Munich: C. H. Beck, 1984.

Kauraka Kauraka (1951–1997) *poet*

Kauraka Kauraka was born in the village of Avatiu, Rarotonga, the Cook Islands. Kauraka's poetry reflects the interesting cultural roots of his heritage. His mother was a descendant of the Manihiki, and his father was part Manihiki, Mangaian, and Chinese. Kauraka went to New Zealand for his high school and college education and later went to Japan as a professional singer and musician for the Betela Dance Troupe. Kauraka graduated from the University of the South Pacific in Fiji in 1980 and became the language curriculum adviser to the Education Department in Rarotonga. He received his M.A. degree from the Anthropology Department in the University of Hawaii at Manoa in 1987. He became a full-time writer retelling, translating, and writing stories of the Pacific Islands. Kauraka founded Sunblossom Press in the Cook Islands and devoted his life to writing about the richness of Polynesian cultural tradition.

Kauraka's poetry reflects the ancient beliefs and traditions of his rich heritage. The images and metaphors in his poems are essentially Polynesian in nature. His talent for music shows distinctly in his poetry, which has a sing-song quality. Nature imagery (such as gardenias and coconut trees) and animal symbols (such as snakes, dolphins, and birds) constitute important elements of his poems. In "Return to Havaiki" (1985), Kauraka uses the images of the *ngoio* (black noddy tern) and "great sky mushrooms" to reflect the natural richness of his Polynesian home, Manihiki.

Kauraka's experiences while traveling also give his poetry a unique blend of cross-cultural elements that reveal his desire to share cultural complexities, especially those of Polynesia. He often questions the abandoning of traditional culture to embrace unquestionably the cultural practices of modern Western society. In "Darkness within the Light" (1985), Kauraka beseeches the New Zealander of indigenous descent not to forsake his traditional roots. In another poem, "Children of Manuhiki, Arise" (1985), he laments the powerful influence of modernity on the younger generation of Polynesians who no longer heeds the oral traditions of their ancestors.

Kauraka's poems also bespeak the need to use the past to understand the future. All of these characteristics can be seen in the poems in Kauraka's collection, *Dreams of a Rainbow* (1987), which he wrote when he was still a graduate student in Hawaii. His respect for the traditional past was most aptly described in "Po, The Great" and "Three Warriors." In "Po, The Great," he celebrates the power of Po, the parent of all mythical gods of the Pacific Islands; in "Three Warriors," he personifies the three virtues of Polynesian heroes.

Kauraka's most important contribution lies in his ability to create a dialogue between different groups of people. Through poetry, he establishes a platform on which the older and more traditional generation interacts with the younger, modern one. His poetry leads to a better understanding of world culture and interaction between not only two different cultures but also two generations within a culture.

Other Works by Kauraka Kauraka

Manakonako = reflections. Auckland: Mana Publications, 1991.
Manihikian traditional narratives = Na fakahiti o Manihikian. New Zealand: Te Ropu Kahurangi, 1988.
Taku Akatauira = My dawning star: poems. Suva, Fiji: Mana Publications, 1999.

A Work about Kauraka Kauraka

Simpson, Michael, and John Untfrecker. *Dreams of the Rainbow: Poems by Kauraka Kauraka.* Honolulu: University of Hawaii at Manoa, East–West Center, 1986.

Kawabata Yasunari (1899–1972) *novelist and short story writer*

Kawabata Yasunari was born to Kawabata Eikichi and Gen in Osaka. When he was young, his father, mother, grandmother, and sister died, leaving him in the care of his nearly blind and terminally ill grandfather. In 1915, having also lost his grandfather, Kawabata moved to a middle-school dormitory, and then, having determined to become a writer, he studied Japanese literature at Tokyo Imperial University. In the 1930s, Kawabata became actively involved in the literary community, supporting young writers, working for magazines, and becoming a member of the censorious Literary Discussion Group, organized by the government as Japan entered World War II. Kawabata went into semiretirement in the late 1960s. In 1972, he was found dead, an apparent suicide, in his seaside apartment.

In 1921, Kawabata published his first story, "A View of the Yasukuni Festival," which garnered the attention of influential writer Kan Kikuchi (1888–1948). Even with his support, however, Kawabata's early stories were largely unsuccessful, perhaps due to their experimental style. In 1926, however, he published a novella written with more traditional literary idioms. The success of *The Izu Dancer,* about a walking tour of the Izu Peninsula near Tokyo, established Kawabata as a writer. A distinctive feature of his novels is the theme of unrequited longing. In *Snow Country* (1947), the protagonist Shimamura engages in an unfulfilling love affair with a geisha while secretly longing for a woman involved with another man. In 1950, Kawabata published one of his best works, *Sound of the Mountain* (1950), which won the literary prize of the Japanese Academy. The story, which catalogs the rambling thoughts of an aging patriarch, is distinctive for its stream-of-consciousness narrative.

Kawabata was a member of the literary movement called Shinkankakuha (Neo-Perceptionists). The movement attempted to find methods of bringing individual senses to life, chiefly through stream-of-consciousness narrative. Typically, his stories lack a traditional plot structure but excel in lyrical quality. His unique narrative style garnered attention internationally, and in 1968 Kawabata was the first Japanese writer to receive a Nobel Prize in literature.

Other Works by Kawabata Yasunari
Beauty and Sadness. Translated by Howard Hibbett. New York: Knopf, 1975.
The House of the Sleeping Beauties and Other Stories. Translated by Edward Seidensticker. Tokyo: Kodansha International, 1969.

A Work about Kawabata Yasunari
Gessel, Van C. *Three Modern Novelists: Sōseki, Tanizaki, Kawabata.* Tokyo: Kodansha International, 1993.

Kazantzakis, Nikos (1883–1957) *poet, philosopher, novelist*
Nikos Kazantzakis was born in Iráklion, Crete, and is considered one of the most important 20th-century Greek philosophers. He graduated from Athens Law School in 1906 and fought as a volunteer for the Greek army during the Balkan wars.

After the wars ended, he traveled to Spain, Egypt, China, Japan, and Russia, publishing travelogues of his journeys.

Kazantzakis is much better known as a philosopher than as a writer. His work was influenced by the writings of NIETZSCHE, elements of marxism, and the basic philosophical beliefs of Christianity and Buddhism. He attempted to combine and harmonize these different ideas in his book *Askitiki* (1927), which is considered the basis of his own philosophy. His epic poem *Odyssey: A Modern Sequel* (1938) is also among his well-known earlier works. It picks up Ulysses's tale where Homer left off and brings it to a more solid conclusion.

It was in the later years of his life, however, that Kazantzakis became famous for his novels, including *Zorba the Greek* (1946) and *The Last Temptation of Christ* (1955). Both of these works have since been made into films. The controversial nature of *The Last Temptation of Christ,* in which Jesus must face the greatest temptation of all, led to the Roman Catholic Church's banning of the book and to Kazantzakis's excommunication from the Greek Orthodox Church in 1955. The film version, produced in 1988, also caused much protest from conservative Christian organizations.

In 1956, Kazantzakis was awarded the International Peace Award. He died one year later in Germany, the same year that the first of his novels to be made into a film, *He Who Must Die* (1957) was presented at the Cannes Film Festival.

Critical Analysis
The Last Temptation of Christ possibly holds the distinction of being the book most hated by people who have not read it. At the time of Kazantzakis's excommunication from the Greek Orthodox Church for having written the novel, the Orthodox Church of America condemned the work, admitting that they had based their decision on magazine articles, not on the work itself. The 1988 film by Martin Scorsese suffered the same fate: Thousands who had not seen the film condemned it out of hand, infuriated by Kazantzakis's central idea—that Christ was not a plaster

saint but a human being beset with all the frailties, hopes, passions, and doubts all people share.

Kazantzakis's perspective is that Christ's death on the cross is such a magnificent sacrifice *because* of his humanity, *because* he was tempted to be an ordinary man and live an ordinary life. The author holds that the idea that a deity would rather be human elevates humanity and highlights the heroism and beauty of human life. Thus, for Kazantazakis, Christ is the existential hero who chooses his fate, not the "son of God" who must follow his father's wishes but the "son of man" who is free to refuse but does not.

As infuriating to the novel's detractors, perhaps, is Kazantzakis's other "heretical" idea: that Judas was Christ's friend who betrays him out of love. When Christ tells Judas what he must do, Judas replies, "I've asked you before, Rabbi—is there no other way?" Jesus says, "No, Judas, my brother. I too should have liked one; I too hoped and waited for one until now—but in vain. No, there is no other way. The end of the world is here. This world, this kingdom of the Devil, will be destroyed and the kingdom of heaven will come. I shall bring it. How? By dying. There is no other way." Although Judas fears he will not be able to do his duty, Jesus tells him, "You will, Judas, my brother. God will give you the strength, as much as you lack, because it is necessary—it is necessary for me to be killed and for you to betray me. We two must save the world. Help me." Judas too is free to choose, and he too chooses heroically. Like Zorba the Greek, a man who loves life and lives with zest and joy, Kazantzakis's Christ is a richly human figure.

Other Works by Nikos Kazantzakis

At the Palaces of Knossos: A Novel. Translated by Themi and Theodora Vasils. Athens: Ohio University Press, 1988.
Buddha. Translated By Kimon Friar and Athena Dallis-Damis. San Diego, Calif.: Avant Books, 1983.

Works about Nikos Kazantzakis

Bien, Peter. *Nikos Kazantzakis, Novelist.* Bristol: Bristol Classical Press, 1989.

Dombrowski, Daniel. *Kazantzakis and God.* Albany: State University of New York Press, 1997.

Kemal, Yaşar (1923–) *novelist, poet*

Yaşar Kemal was born in Hemite, a hamlet in the province of Adana in southern Turkey. When Kemal was five, his father was murdered while praying in the mosque. Kemal found solace in his love of music and poetry. When he turned nine, he attended a school in the neighboring village. He completed his primary education in Kadirli where his family resettled, becoming the first villager from Hemite to complete his primary education.

Kemal wrote his first story in 1947 and worked as a public letter writer for the next three years. In 1950, he moved to Istanbul, where he found a job as a reporter for the daily newspaper *Cumhuriyet (Republic)*. Kemal's unique style of writing won him not only national but also international recognition. He was a fervent activist for human rights in Turkey, and his works and activities enhanced his fame as a spellbinding storyteller.

Kemal's enchantment with the Anatolian tradition of folk minstrels features prominently in his writings such as *Salman the Solitary* (translated 1998), in which the traveling bard assumes the narrator's role. Kemal's love of music and creativity allow him to enhance his talent as an animated and powerful storyteller. He writes with energy and devotion, drawing on the rich tradition of his Turkish heritage and the literary tradition of Anatolia. His works, though heavily imbued by his strong leftist political views, still preserve a certain idyllic quality, which bespeaks of optimism and romanticism.

In an interesting way, Kemal represents the romantic bard of the Anatolian past who writes and sings of social injustice. He has found balance between his appropriation of the genre of traditional literature and his concern with modern issues. His best-known novel is the epic *Memed, My Hawk* (1955), which won the Varlik Prize 1956 for Best Novel. Kemal has been short-listed for the Nobel

Prize in literature many times, and his collection of articles won the annual Journalists' Association Prize. In recent years, Kemal has been awarded numerous literary prizes including the Z. Homer Poetry Award (2003), the Savanos Prize (Thessalonika-Greece) (2003), the Turkish Publishers Association Lifetime Achievement Award (2003), and the Presidential Cultural and Artistic Grand Prize (2008).

Other Works by Yaşar Kemal

Anatolian Tales. Translated from the Turkish by Thilda Kemal. New York: Mead, 1969.

Iron Earth, Copper Sky. Translated from the Turkish by Thilda Kemal. London: Collins and Harvill Press, 1974.

Seagull. Translated from the Turkish by Thilda Kemal. New York: Pantheon Books, 1981.

A Work about Yaşar Kemal

Bosquet, Alain. *Yaşar Kemal on His Life and Art: Yaşar Kemal with Alain Bosquet.* Translated from the French by Eugene Hibert and Barry Tharaud. Albany, N.Y.: Syracuse University Press, 1990.

Keneally, Thomas (1935–) *novelist, playwright*

Thomas Keneally was born at Kempsey on the north coast of New South Wales, Australia. His father was a postman. He attended a Christian Brothers' school for his primary and high school education, and, at 17, he began to study for the Catholic priesthood. He abandoned this vocation in 1960 before his official ordination. Keneally taught for four years at the University of New England at Armidale before becoming a full-time writer. He was one of the few Australians who could rely on his writing to support himself and his family. Keneally has received three Commonwealth Literary Fund Awards, and his books have won four Miles Franklin Awards. He was awarded the Order of Australia in 1983 for his contributions to Australian literature, and the Prime Minister's Literary Award for *The Widow and Her*

Hero (2008). Keneally now lives in New York and Sydney.

Keneally's writing appeals to both Australian and international audiences because it deals with human issues that transcend all geographical and social boundaries. Using a mixture of humor and tragic irony, Keneally is able to capture the constant struggle of society to come to terms with its actions, its relationships with others, and its uncertainty. Keneally's past clearly influences his works. His first novel, *The Place at Whitton* (1964), is a mystery tale set in a Catholic seminary, while *Blood Red, Sister Rose* (1974) involves a heroine who resembles Joan of Arc. These two novels highlight the importance influence of the Catholic vocation as a phase in his past.

One of the major subjects represented in Keneally's works is his concern with history and its lessons. Using historical materials, he is able to examine historical events and their impact through the perspectives of his central characters in novels such as *Schindler's Ark* (1982) and *Bring Larks and Heroes* (1967). *Schindler's Ark* tells the true story of Oskar Schindler, a German industrialist who saved thousands of Jews from death during the Holocaust. This book was adapted and made into a movie, *Schindler's List,* in 1993. In *Searching for Schindler: A Memoir* (2007), Keneally describes how he wrote the novel and how its success affected him. *Bring Larks and Heroes* narrates the story of Australians who fought in Vietnam during World War II.

Keneally's earlier novels tend to have a predominantly Australian setting. Books such as *The Fear* (1965) and *The Chant of Jimmie Blacksmith* (1972) are set in Australia. In *The Fear,* Keneally examines the experiences of a young boy growing up during World War II. The fears of war reaching Australian shores loom heavy in the imaginative mind of the boy as he begins to conjure imaginary visions of war atrocities and prisoner-of-war camps. *The Chant of Jimmie Blacksmith,* however, is a study of a history of interracial relations between the Aborigines and the Europeans. His later novels, beginning with *Blood Red, Sister Rose,* are set in locations including France, England, Yugoslavia, and the United States.

Keneally's novels cover a wide range of genres from fables to macabre murders and mysteries. His versatility can be observed in his writings from concise and didactic parables to ornately elaborate narratives. In all Keneally's novels, he is concerned with the connection between the past and the present. His motivation to write stems from his curiosity regarding the irony that human beings often find themselves in conflict with the conventions and values of the systems of authority that they help create. For instance, Schindler in *Schindler's Ark* tries to do the humane thing by assisting many Jews to escape even though the fear of being discovered by the fanatical Nazi government hovers constantly over his head.

Keneally's heroes and heroines act with integrity and honor despite their individual flaws. They are tragic figures trapped between the demands of unsympathetic institutions of authority and their own personal desires. In their attempts to do the right thing, they often flounder either in the seas of their guilt or under the destructive claws of the authority. Examples of these can be found in two of Keneally's characters, Ramsey and Maitland. Ramsey, in *The Survivor* (1969), finds himself caught in a vicious abyss of guilt and remorse for 40 years after he deserted his close friend and companion during an Antarctic expedition. Maitland, a priest–teacher in *Three Cheers for the Paraclete* (1968), finds himself the subject of a series of religious hymns poking fun at the absurdity of religious rules. The tragic nature of the characters' experiences is partially alleviated by Keneally's injections of humor into the harsh reality of their experiences. The message that Keneally clearly sends to his readers is the recognition that in spite of their poignant experiences, these heroic characters are active shapers of their own worlds. This is perhaps a main reason that Keneally's novels are so appealing to readers all over the world: Readers are able to empathize with Keneally's protagonists. The human condition is a complex web,

and people are victims as well as active participants in their destinies.

Keneally also writes in other genres such as drama, children's stories, nonfiction, and film scripts. His plays include *Halloran's Little Boat* (1968), which is an adaptation of his book *Bring Larks and Heroes,* and *Bullie's House* (1981), which examines early interactions between Australian Aborigines and the European settlers. In *Bullie's House,* the Aborigines show the white settlers their precious totems hoping that the latter would in return share their knowledge and technology, which the whites never quite do on equal terms. Keneally's greatest contribution lies in his ability to capture in essence and intensity the dramatic clash of two cultures, which constitutes an important theme in world literature.

Other Works by Thomas Keneally
A Commonwealth of Thieves. New York: Anchor, 2007.

The Great Shame: and the Triumph of the Irish in the English-speaking World. New York: Nan A. Talese, 1999.

The Playmaker. London: Sceptre, 1988.

A Season in Purgatory. New York: Harcourt Brace Jovanovich, 1977.

Three Cheers for the Paraclete. New York: Viking, 1969.

Towards Asmara. London: Hodder and Staughton, 1989.

Victim of the Aurora. New York: Harcourt Brace Jovanovich, 1978.

Works about Thomas Keneally
Beston, John. "Novelist's Vital Professionalism," *Hemisphere* 17, no. 10 (1973): 23–26.

Breitinger, Eckhard. "Thomas Keneally's Historical Novels," *Commonwealth News (Aarhus)* 10 (1976): 16–20.

Kertész, Imre (1929–) *novelist, translator*

The 2002 Nobel laureate in literature and a Holocaust survivor, Imre Kertész was born to

Jewish parents in Budapest, Hungary, in November 1929. At age 14, in 1944, he was taken with other Hungarian Jews to the Nazi concentration camp at Auschwitz in Nazi-occupied Poland and then later to the camp at Buchenwald in Germany. When the Allies liberated the camps in 1945, Kertész returned to Hungary and found work as a journalist for a Budapest newspaper *Világosság*. He was dismissed in 1951 when the newspaper became an official organ of the Communist Party and Kertész refused to comply with the new policies. After fulfilling his military service, Kertész supported himself as a writer and Hungarian translator of German-language authors, such as FRIEDRICH NIETZSCHE, SIGMUND FREUD, and Ludwig Wittgenstein.

Written in the 1960s, Kertész's first novel, *Sorstalanság* (*Fateless*), was published in 1975 and largely ignored until it was translated into German in 1990 (the English translation appeared in 1992). Loosely derived from Kertész's time in the death camps, *Sorstalanság* features a 15-year-old narrator, György Köves, who is arrested and deported to a Nazi concentration camp, where he relates his experiences of suffering and atrocity with a striking degree of emotional detachment that achieves a kind of poignancy. "I will continue to live my unlivable life," Köves observes. "[T]here is no absurdity that one cannot live quite naturally."

In subsequent novels, Kertész returns to Köves's story, having him age accordingly, as he continues to try to make sense of his wartime experience. In *A kudarc* (*Fiasco* 1988), with wry self-referentiality, Kertész tells the story of a writer whose first novel (entitled "Fatelessness") has been roundly rejected and who relieves himself of his story by attributing it to the hero of a Kafkaesque novel within the novel. In *Kaddis a meg nem született gyermekért* (1990, *Kaddish for a Child Not Born*), Köves returns, now middle-aged, speaking of and to the child he never had. Using the motif of the Kaddish, the Jewish prayer for the dead, to memorialize the never-to-be-born, Kertész explains with implacable logic why he will be the end of

his line. "What happened to me, my childhood," he explains, "must never happen to another child." "Not since Kafka or Beckett," one reviewer noted, "has a writer packed so much metaphysics into so tight a space."

In 1991, Kertész published a collection of short prose, *Az angol lobogó*, followed by *Gályanapló* (1992, *Galley Diary*), a fictional diary of the years from 1961 to 1991. A second installment of the diary covering 1991–95 appeared in 1997, *Valaki más: a változás krónikája* (*I—Another: Chronicle of a Metamorphosis*). *A holocaust mint kultúra* (1993, *The Holocaust as Culture*), the first of three collections of essays and lectures, also appeared.

In its Nobel citation, the Swedish Academy praised Kertész's resistance to social and political conformity: "For him Auschwitz is not an exceptional occurrence that like an alien body subsists outside the normal history of Western Europe," the Academy noted. "It is the ultimate truth about human degradation in modern existence." While always careful to remind readers and critics of the essentially fictional character of his work, Kertész has expressed the imaginative and thematic centrality of his wartime experience. In *Galley Diary*, he writes,

> If I think about a novel, I again think about Auschwitz. Whatever I think about, I always think about Auschwitz. Even if I am seemingly speaking about something completely different, I am speaking about Auschwitz. I am a medium for the spirit of Auschwitz. Auschwitz speaks through me. Everything else seems stupid to me, compared to that.

Since winning the Nobel Prize, Kertész has continued to explore the terrain of his own life and its complex intermingling with fictional modes. In *Felszámolás* (2003, *Liquidation*), a quasi-detective story in which an editor searches for a lost literary masterpiece, he describes a Budapest New Year's Eve party at which the partygoers play a game of lager poker. The "players sit around the table and each person says where they have been. Only the place name, nothing else. That was the basis for determining the value of the chips." B., the central character and the author of a play also called "Liquidation," folds. He doesn't want to cheat. Auschwitz, he knows, is "untrumpable."

In 2008, *Detektívtörténet* (*Detective Story*) appeared, and it represents a departure from Kertész's previous work. It is the first-person account of Antonio Rojas Martens, a low-ranking member of the secret police in a nameless South American dictatorship. Although the setting is new, this novel is thematically similar to his prior works. Martens is on death row, awaiting his execution for murder, attempting to come to terms with his fate.

In his Nobel acceptance speech, Kertész expressed his abiding interest in the Holocaust:

> In short, I died once, so I could live. Perhaps that is my real story. If it is, I dedicate this work, born of a child's death, to the millions who died and to those who still remember them. But, since we are talking about literature, after all, the kind of literature that, in the view of your Academy, is also a testimony, my work may yet serve a useful purpose in the future, and—this is my heart's desire—may even speak to the future. Whenever I think of the traumatic impact of Auschwitz, I end up dwelling on the vitality and creativity of those living today. Thus, in thinking about Auschwitz, I reflect, paradoxically, not on the past but the future.

This thematic orientation remains constant whether Kertész's fiction adheres closely to the facts of his experience or departs from them.

Other Works by Imre Kertész

A nyomkereső (*The Pathfinder*). Translated by Tim Wilkinson. Hoboken, N.J.: Melville House Publishing, 2008.
The Union Jack. Translated by Tim Wilkinson. Hoboken, N.J.: Melville House Publishing, 2010.

Kincaid, Jamaica (Elaine Potter Richardson) (1949–   ) *novelist, short story writer*

Jamaica Kincaid was born in St. John's, Antigua, and named Elaine Potter Richardson by her mother, Annie Richardson. Shortly after Kincaid's birth, Annie married David Drew, a carpenter and cabinetmaker, after whom Kincaid models her fictional fathers, not her biological father, Roderick Potter. Annie Richardson taught her daughter how to read and sent her to the Moravian school. Shortly after her 17th birthday, Kincaid traveled to the United States to work and study.

Elaine Potter Richardson officially changed her name to Jamaica Kincaid in 1973, partially to heighten her anonymity as a writer. In 1976, she started to work as a staff writer for the *New Yorker*, after George W. Trow, the *New Yorker*'s "Talk of the Town" editor, introduced Kincaid to the magazine's editor, William Shawn. Before long, Kincaid began to write the "Talk of the Town" column and by 1992 was using the metaphor of gardening to write about the effects of colonialism.

Critics have praised Kincaid's lyrical originality, her characterization, and the modernist narrative techniques in her depiction of Caribbean life, including colonialism, separation, and mother-child relationships. Kincaid voiced a lack of interest in First World approval, assuming a self-exiled literary position (in a 1990 interview with Donna Perry). Ironically enough, critical attention and acclaim from First World critics—especially for her short story collection, *At the Bottom of the River* (1983), and her novels, *Annie John* (1985) and *Lucy* (1990)—steadily increased. To quote R. B. Hughes in *Empire and Domestic Space in the Fiction of Jamaica Kincaid*, "Kincaid's novels illustrate alternative, conceptual, emancipatory spaces within idealised colonial territory. Her doing so depends upon her '. . . displacing the discursive structures of the (colonial) master subject,' and depends too '. . . on a sense of possibilities and self-representation beyond the territory defined by the dominant [culture].'"

Kincaid's more recent publications include *Mr. Potter* (2002), a novel about a poor chauffeur on Antigua who fathers many children, and the travel book *Among Flowers: A Walk in the Himalaya* (2005), about Kincaid's trip to Nepal with a group of botanists to gather the seeds of flowering plants.

Other Works by Jamaica Kincaid

Annie, Gwen, Lilly, Pam and Tulip. New York: Whitney Museum of Modern Art, 1986.
Autobiography of My Mother. New York: Farrar, Straus & Giroux, 1995.
A Small Place. New York: Farrar, Straus & Giroux, 1988.

Works about Jamaica Kincaid

Covi, Giovanna. *Jamaica Kincaid and the Resistance to Canons.* In Carole Boyce Davies and Elaine Savory Fido, eds., *Out of the Kumbla: Caribbean Women and Literature.* Trenton, N.J.: Africa World Press, 1990: 345–354.
Edwards, Justin D. *Understanding Jamaica Kincaid.* Columbia: University of South Carolina Press, 2007.
Paravisini-Gebert, Lizabeth. *Jamaica Kincaid: A Critical Companion.* Westport, Conn.: Greenwood, Press, 1999.

Kirsch, Sarah (Ingrid Bernstein)
(1935–) *poet, short story writer*

Sarah Kirsch was born in Limlingerode, a village in the Harz Mountains. Her father worked in telecommunications for the East German government. Kirsch became a socialist at a young age. She earned a diploma in biology from the University of Halle and attended the Johannes R. Becher Institute for Literature in Leipzig from 1963 to 1965. Participating in the East German effort to build solidarity between workers and writers, Kirsch worked in factories and collective farms during the 1960s. She married the writer Rainer Kirsch in 1958.

Kirsch's first publication was a radio play for children that she cowrote with her husband in 1963. They also collaborated on her first poetry collection, *Gesprach mit dem Saurier* (*Conversation with a Dinosaur*, 1965), a volume of children's poems with a political edge. Her poems in *Landaufenthalt* (*A Stay in the Country*, 1967) combine descriptions of nature with political commentary. In the late 1960s, Kirsch defended the value of lyric poetry in the socialist state. Although her stand drew government criticism, the debate started a "lyric boom" among poets. In 1976, she protested when East Germany revoked the citizenship of the singer Wolf Biermann. As a result, she lost her membership in the Communist Party and moved to West Berlin.

Kirsch is known for her unique style that combines musicality and facility of language. She used intense nature images to describe human experiences and to bridge the gap between love poetry and the poetry of social production. She was especially concerned about the role of women in modern society in both private and public realms. Kirsch's influences include BETTINA VON ARNIM and the Russian poet ANNA AKHMATOVA. Despite her political difficulties, Kirsch won numerous awards for her poetry and short-story collections in the 1970s and 1980s, including the Friedrich Hölderlin Prize. Her latest collection, *Krähengeschwätz* (*Crows' Chattering*), was published in 2010.

Another Work by Sarah Kirsch

The Panther Woman: Five Tales from the Cassette Recorder. Translated by Marion Faber. Lincoln: University of Nebraska Press, 1989.

A Work about Sarah Kirsch

Hopwood, Mererid, and David Basker, eds. *Sarah Kirsch.* Cardiff: University of Wales Press, 1997.

Kiš, Danilo (1935–1989) *novelist, poet*

Danilo Kiš was born in Subotica, on the border of Yugoslavia and Hungary. His father, a Hungarian Jew, died in Auschwitz. Most of his family was killed during World War II except his mother, a Christian from Montenegro. Raised in Hungary and Montenegro, Kiš studied literature at the

University of Belgrade and eventually worked as a teacher in France.

Kiš's work was greatly influenced by the loss of his family. His novels *Garden, Ashes* (1965) and *Hourglass* (1972) are monuments to his father's life and death. *A Tomb for Boris Davidovic* (1976) is a collection of stories about victims of Communist terror set in a politically oppressed Eastern Europe. In the title story of this collection, Boris repeatedly flees from prison and changes his name, only to be recaptured. The frequency of this pattern is both comic and tragic. This and the rest of the stories in the volume are short biographical sketches of a victim as hero, fighting against history and a pervasive sense of doom. The characters range from idealistic to opportunistic, from sadistic to compassionate, and the stories themselves from the absurd to the horrific.

Another of Kiš's works, based largely on personal narrative, is *Early Sorrows* (1969), a collection of stories about the often tragic childhood experiences of a Jewish boy in a small Serbian town near the Hungarian border during World War II. Kiš illustrates the dramatic change in the boy's life from peaceful serenity to horror and brutality after soldiers enter his village.

Kiš's work gained large international audiences primarily because noted writer Susan Sontag introduced Kiš to English-speaking readers. He has also been compared with Jorge Luis BORGES, to whom he explicitly admitted a debt, once indicating that the history of the short story can be divided into two distinct eras: before Borges and after Borges.

Other Works by Danilo Kiš

The Encyclopedia of the Dead. Translated by Michael Henry Heim. New York: Farrar, Straus & Giroux, 1989.
Hourglass. Translated by Ralph Manheim. Evanston, Ill.: Northwestern University Press, 1997.

A Work about Danilo Kiš

Birnbaum, M. D., and R. Trager-Verchovsky, eds. *History, Another Text.* Ann Arbor: University of Michigan Press, 1988.

Klausner, Amos
See Oz, Amos.

Kogawa, Joy (1935–) *poet, novelist*
Joy Kogawa was born in Vancouver. As a second-generation Japanese-Canadian, or *nisei,* her work, including poetry, fiction, children's literature, and nonfiction, often reflects the perspectives of Japanese-Canadians. Kogawa and her family were evacuated to Slocan, British Columbia, and later to Coaldale, Alberta, during World War II. Kogawa received her education at the University of Alberta and taught elementary school in Coaldale. She also studied at the University of Toronto and at both the Anglican Women's Training College and the University of Saskatchewan. She married in 1957, had two children, and divorced in 1968.

Joy Kogawa has published several collections of poetry, essays, children's literature, and novels. Among her more notable works are the novels *Obasan* (1981), which focuses on the lives of Japanese-Canadians during World War II, and *The Rain Ascends* (1995), about a Protestant clergyman who abuses children. Kogawa has been active in lobbying the Canadian federal government to acknowledge and redress its decision to intern 20,000 Japanese Canadians during World War II.

Another Work by Joy Kogawa
Itsuka. Toronto: Viking, 1992.

A Work about Joy Kogawa
Davidson, Arnold E. *Writing against the Silence: Joy Kogawa's* Obasan. Toronto: ECW Press, 1993.

Köhler, Barbara (1959–) *poet, essayist*
Barbara Köhler was born in Burgstädt, Germany. After passing the Arbitur (school-leaving exam), she studied literature at the Johannes R. Becher Institute in Leipzig. Her first collection of verse, *Deutsches Roulette* (*German Roulette,* 1991), established her as one of Germany's most innovative young poets. She followed up with a second

collection, *Blue Box* (1995), and published internationally in journals such as *Poetry* magazine. She has also written for several newspapers. Köhler's several literary awards include the Leonce and Lena Prize (1991), the Else Lasker-Schuler Prize (1994), and the Clemens–Brentano Prize (1996).

Köhler's verse displays a restless yet precise passion, as seen in the poem "Self-portrait" (1991), and also combines traditional and contemporary forms. Her poems "Gedicht" ("Poem," 1991), "Ingeborg Bachmann Stirbt in Rom" ("Ingeborg Bachmann Dies in Rome," 1991), and "IV" (1991) reveal Köhler's common themes of yearning, mourning, and the memories of unhappy women, respectively. Köhler's writing shows an understanding of poetry's potential in bringing out the richness and fullness of language.

A Work about Barbara Köhler

Paul, Georgina, and Helmut Schmitz, eds. *Entgegenkommen: Dialogues with Barbara Köhler*. Atlanta: Rodopi, 2000.

Kokoschka, Oskar (1886–1980) *painter, poet, playwright*

Oskar Kokoschka was born in Pochlarn, Austria, to Gustav Kokoschka, a goldsmith, and Romana Loidl, a great storyteller who inspired his love for nature. Kokoschka graduated from state school, but he dreamed of becoming an artist and entered the Vienna School of Arts and Crafts, where he studied from 1905 to 1909. The revolutionary nature of his art was deemed scandalous by some instructors and administrators, and he was expelled after painting a particularly controversial painting.

Kokoschka's work often openly expressed sexual themes and other controversial motifs; indeed, the imagery in Kokoschka's poetry often resembled the strange and unusual images found in his graphic works. In 1908, Kokoschka published his first book of poetry, *The Dreaming Youth*. Along with the poems, the book contained reproductions of paintings that he specifically completed for the book. Kokoschka's early work was heavily influenced by SYMBOLISM; however, he is often credited with the foundation of EXPRESSIONISM.

The aim of the movement was to represent the subjective psychological experience through literature and other forms of art. *Murder, the Women's Hope* (1916), a short play completed by Kokoschka in 1907, became the basis for expressionist drama. In the play, first performed in 1909, the nameless Man confronts his impulsive sexual drives and attempts to free himself from the physical dependence associated with bodily functions. In a kind of crude sexual fantasy, the Man strangles the nameless Woman and then slaughters her female companions. The clearly demarcated antagonism between the male and female, violence, and sexual submission were persistent themes of Kokoschka's work. *Orpheus and Eurydice* (1923) pursues similar themes and comments on the turbulent relationship between Kokoschka and Alma Mahler, the widow of the famous composer Gustav Mahler (1860–1911). In many instances, however, his work was simply too overwhelming for the sensibility of the general public, and it never gained a wide appeal.

Kokoschka's painting became renowned for its surreal, dreamlike images, and it gained some popularity. He held an appointment as an art instructor between 1911 and the outbreak of World War I in Vienna and Berlin. Kokoschka served in the cavalry of the Austrian army during World War I and was wounded several times. After retiring from the army, Kokoschka continued working extensively on his paintings.

During the 1930s, Kokoschka's works were openly attacked by pro-Nazi newspapers in Austria and Germany. Kokoschka left Austria for Czechoslovakia in 1931 and then emigrated to England after the fall of Czechoslovakia to the Nazis. In Nazi Germany, Kokoschka's work was banned and was ridiculed by the authorities as an example of "degenerate art." During this time of turmoil, Kokoschka mostly wrote essays on art and expressionist aesthetics.

After the end of World War II, Kokoschka returned to Austria and worked as an art instructor and theater designer. His gained international popularity by the 1950s, and his works were exhibited throughout the world. In 1971, Kokoschka published *My Life,* an autobiography in which he also presents his views on art and culture and provides engaging accounts of his personal relationships with famous artists of the expressionist movement.

Oskar Kokoschka is mainly remembered today for his paintings; however, his work in literature laid the ground for the seminal expressionist movement. His striking, often disturbing works challenge our epistemological notions about art and aesthetics. Today, Kokoschka's visual art and literary works are considered to be among the masterpieces of the 20th century.

Other Works by Oskar Kokoschka

Oscar Kokoschka Drawings, 1906–1965. Miami: University of Miami Press, 1970.
Plays and Poems. Translated by Michael Mitchell. New York: Ariadne Press, 2001.

Works about Oskar Kokoschka

Calvocaressi, Richard, and Katharina Schultz. *Oskar Kokoschka, 1886–1980.* New York: Solomon R. Guggenheim Foundation, 1986.
Whitford, Frank. *Oskar Kokoschka: A Life.* New York: Atheneum, 1986.

Kostrowitsky, Wilhelm Apollinaris de
See APOLLINAIRE, GUILLAUME.

Kumagai Yumiko
See KURAHASHI YUMIKO.

Kundera, Milan (1929–) *novelist*
Milan Kundera was born on April 1 in Brno, Moravia. The son of a concert pianist and musicologist, Kundera studied music and was a jazz musician in his youth. He soon turned to writing, publishing his first volume of poetry, *Clovek Zahrada Sirá (Man: A Broad Garden)* in 1953. This work, as well as two later poetry collections—*Poslední Máj (The Last May,* 1955) and *Monology (Monologues,* 1957)—were condemned by Czechoslovakian officials because of their ironic tone and erotic imagery. Kundera has repeatedly denied any political motivation behind his works.

Kundera was a Communist Party member twice, from 1948 to 1950 and from 1956 to 1968. Both times, he was expelled from the party for his supposedly unorthodox or anticommunist opinions. During this time, he also studied and taught in the Film Faculty of Prague's Academy of Music and Dramatic Arts. His political entanglements and disagreements with the Communist Party, however, ultimately led to the threat of a loss of his employment. Kundera was involved in the liberalization of Czechoslovakia in 1967 to 1968. After the Soviet occupation, he was attacked by the authorities for his liberal beliefs and ousted once again. In 1969, he was fired from his job, and his works were banned from legal publication in Czechoslovakia.

Kundera is best known internationally for his novel *The Unbearable Lightness of Being* (1984), which was made into a film of the same name in 1988 by American film director Philip Kauffman.

Kundera is a prolific writer. In his early career, several volumes of short stories, as well as a successful one-act play, *The Owners of the Keys* (1962), were followed by the publication of his first novel, *The Joke* (1967; translated 1982). This comedic work takes an ironic look at the private lives of various people in Czechoslovakia during the years of Stalinism. It has been translated into numerous languages and has achieved international acclaim. This was followed by a second novel, *Life Is Elsewhere* (1969; translated 1974), about a hopeless romantic who embraces the 1948 Communist takeover. This novel was banned immediately from Czech publication. Kundera's subsequent novels, including *The Farewell Party* (1976), *The Book of Laughter and Forgetting* (1979; translated 1980), and *The Unbearable Lightness of Being* were banned in Czechoslovakia but were published in France and other countries. *The Book of Laughter and Forgetting* was among his most successful novels, perhaps because it pointed to one of the harsher truths of Kundera's homeland: humankind's propensity to deny or erase historical truths.

In a collection of essays titled *The Art of the Novel* (1988), Kundera writes that a novel must be "autonomous," that it should be created independently of any political belief system. In 1975, in response to the suppression of his work, Kundera was allowed to emigrate to France. He took a teaching post at the University of Rennes, where he remained on the faculty until 1978. In 1979, the Czech government revoked his citizenship. Kundera continues to write works that are humorous yet skeptical and pessimistic in their depictions of humanity, whether under Communist rule or elsewhere.

Beginning in 2008, Kundera became embroiled in a controversy. Evidence was found that seemed to suggest he had denounced a young Czech pilot and spy for the West to the Czech police. Kundera has denied this accusation, and 11 well-known writers came to Kundera's defense. They included SALMAN RUSHDIE, FERNANDO ARRABAL, Philip Roth, CARLOS FUENTES, GABRIEL GARCÍA MÁRQUEZ, J. M. COETZEE, ORHAN PAMUK, Jorge Semprún, and NADINE GORDIMER. Kundera's most recent book, *The Curtain: An Essay in Seven Parts* (2005), is a series of essays on the novel and great novelists.

Critical Analysis

Kundera's best received work to date is the philosophical novel *The Unbearable Lightness of Being*. Set during and after what is known as the Prague Spring (a period of relative democratization in Soviet Czechoslovakia in 1968 that ended in a military crackdown by the Soviet army), the novel focuses on four main characters—Tomas, Tereza, Sabina, and Franz. The novel is postmodern in many respects. For example, the narrator repeatedly calls attention to the fictionality of his work: "It would be senseless for the author to try to con-vince the reader that his characters once actually lived. They were not born of a mother's womb; they were born of a stimulating phrase or two or from a basic situation." The novel moves back and forth in time and visits the same situation more than once from the perspective of different characters. The story is held together more by metaphor than by plot or character, the central metaphor being the title itself. The characters are lightly drawn; we come to know them deeply but narrowly, and they do not feel "real" in the same way characters do in more traditional realistic fiction.

Kundera begins the novel with a philosophical discussion of the concept of the eternal return as put forth by the German philosopher NIETZSCHE. The idea is that "everything recurs as we once experienced it, and that the recurrence itself recurs ad infinitim." However, what interests Kundera is the opposite concept, especially as it pertains to human existence. A human life does not recur and is thus "like a shadow, without weight, dead in advance, and whether it was horrible, beautiful, or sublime, its horror, sublimity, and beauty mean nothing." Then Kundera asks the question, posed again and again in the novel: is lightness, weightlessness, good or bad, positive or negative? As Tomas reflects on his choices, the narrator tells us:

> We can never know what to want, because, living only one life, we can neither compare it with our previous lives nor perfect it in our lives to come.

Yet, Kundera implies, would it be any better if we could do it all again? Would our choices be different? Improve?

In the novel, this motif or metaphor of lightness and its opposite concept of burdensomeness or weight are played out in the lives and choices of the central characters and especially in their love lives. Kundera presents the characters first from the outside, in terms of their behaviors, then from within, placing their behavior in the context of past events, often incidents from childhood. He is particularly interested in the sad and funny failures of communication. In a chapter entitled "Words Misunderstood," he traces Sabina and Franz's utterly different understandings of the same events and actions.

The Unbearable Lightness of Being is a tour de force. Beautifully written, it asks in very simple terms the most difficult philosophical questions and explores the questions in richly drawn situations; it is at once funny and sad, deeply erotic, political, and metaphysical.

Other Works by Milan Kundera

Encounter. New York: Harper, 2010.
Identity. Translated by Linda Asher. New York: Harper Flamingo, 1998.
Ignorance: A Novel. New York: Harper, 2003.
Slowness. Translated by Linda Asher. Boston: Faber and Faber, 1996.
Testaments Betrayed. Translated by Linda Asher. Boston: Faber and Faber, 1996.

Works about Milan Kundera

Misurella, Fred. *Understanding Milan Kundera: Public Events, Private Affairs.* Columbia: University of South Carolina Press, 1993.
Petro, Peter, ed. *Critical Essays on Milan Kundera.* New York: G. K. Hall, 1999.

Kunene, Mazisi (1930–2006) *poet*

Mazisi Kunene was born in Durban, South Africa. He began writing poetry as a boy and by the age of 10 was already submitting poems to local newspapers and magazines. Kunene taught for four years in Natal, where he obtained his master's degree. In 1959, he went to London to further his studies in the School of Oriental and African Studies at the University of London. In London, he founded the Anti-Apartheid Movement and became the director of education for the South African United Front. Kunene spent 34 years in exile in England and the United States for his leadership in the antiapartheid movement. He finally returned to South Africa in 1993 and became a professor in the department of Zulu Language and Literature in the University of Natal. In the same year, he was appointed Africa's poet laureate in the United Nation's Education, Science and Cultural Organization.

Kunene's poetry shows how the concerns and themes of his Zulu heritage can be used to enhance an understanding of South African history and society. His poems, such as "Encounter with the Ancestors" (1982), draw on the rich images and symbols of Zulu myths. They reveal ideas such as the virtues and wisdom of ancestors, which have been transmitted from generation to generation in Zulu oral tradition. His poetry expresses the relevance of these motifs in South African society today.

Kunene's intimate involvement in the political movement against apartheid is also an essential element of his works, which, perhaps, explains why his first volume of poems, *Zulu Poems* (1970), was banned for many years in South Africa. One of his two epic poems, *Emperor Shaka the Great*, celebrates the heroism and strength of Shaka Zulu, the founder of the Zulu nation. Kunene's favorable depiction of Shaka as a hero challenges the Eurocentric portrayal of the man as a tyrannical despot. His other epic poem *Anthem of the Decades* was published in 1981. Both poems were first published in the Zulu language and later translated into English.

In recognition of Kunene's contributions to African literature, the Mazisi Kunene Library was jointly established by Create Africa South and the Kunene family. Its aims are to fund study in the Zulu language, to publish and distribute Kunene and other writers' works in the Zulu language, and to provide research facilities for scholars interested in South African history and society. Kunene's writing stands apart from other African voices that speak of alienation and anger. His works, especially the two epic poems, showcase the glory and richness of the African traditions and challenge Western readers to accept and appreciate the importance of African cultures. His use of Zulu language and style also provides a medium through which African cultural symbols and thought are effectively transmitted without appropriating

English or other European diction. Kunene's final volume of poetry, published in 2007, is *Echoes from the Mountain: New and Selected Poems.*

Another Work by Mazisi Kunene
The Ancestors and the Sacred Mountain. London: Heinemann, 1982.

Works about Mazisi Kunene
Barnett, Ursula. *A Vision of Order: A Study of Black South African Literature in English (1914–1980).* Amherst: University of Massachusetts Press/London: Sinclair Browne, 1983.
Goodwin, K. L. *Understanding Poetry: A Study of Ten Poets.* London: Heinemann, 1982.
Haynes, John. "Kunene's Shaka and the Idea of a Poet as Teacher." *Ariel* 18, no. 1 (1987): 39–50.
Maduka, Chidi. "Poetry, Humanism and Apartheid: A Study of Mazisi Kunene's *Zulu Poems,*" *Griot* 4, nos. 1–2 (1985): 57–72.

Kunert, Günter (1929–) *poet, short story writer*
Günter Kunert was born in Berlin four years before the Nazi rise to power. Because his mother was Jewish, he faced discrimination and was prevented from completing grammar school. After the war, he attended Berlin Kunsthochschule, an art institute. While a teenager, he switched his focus from art to literature and published his first poems and prose in the *Ulenspiegel* (*Joker*) magazine. An idealistic socialist at an early age, Kunert joined the Socialist Unity Party in East Germany in 1949. Three years later, he married Marianne Todten, whose critical assistance greatly benefited his writing career.

Kunert's first collection of poetry, *Wegschilder und Mauerinschriften* (*Road Signs and Wall Writings,* 1950), made a significant literary impact. In 1952, the German poet BERTOLT BRECHT, one of Kunert's influences, praised him as a gifted young poet. During the following three decades, Kunert published more than 20 works of poetry, prose, and essays as well as one novel. In the mid-1960s, he became critical of East Germany's socialist

government. In the 1970s, he joined SARAH KIRSCH and CHRISTA WOLF in protesting the revoking of the singer Wolf Biermann's citizenship. Kunert was then harassed and lost his party membership. He moved to West Germany in 1979.

Kunert is considered a master of the epigram, the parable, the satire, and the use of aphoristic form to express a principle in a short work. His writing is serious, ironic, and grotesque. He takes a firm stand against misuse of the language. Kunert frequently dealt with contemporary concerns—such as greed, poverty, and injustice—and is committed to remembering the victims of past persecutions. Although his writing becomes increasingly pessimistic after the mid-1960s, Kunert is known for the integrity of his work. His many awards include the Johannes R. Becher Prize.

Another Work by Günter Kunert
Windy Times: Poems and Prose. Translated by Agnes Stein. New York: Red Dust, 1983.

Kurahashi Yumiko (Kumagai Yumiko) (1935–) *novelist, short story writer*
Kurahashi Yumiko was born in Kōchi, Shikuoka Prefecture, to dentist Kurahashi Toshirō and his wife, Misae. Kurahashi entered Kyoto Women's College in 1953 and, in 1955, enrolled in Japanese Women's Junior College of Hygiene in Tokyo to become a dental hygienist at her father's practice. However, she surprised her family when, upon graduation, she enrolled as an undergraduate in the French Department of Meiji University. Upon completing the program, she started graduate school but returned home when her father died in 1962. Two years later, she married photographer Kumagai Tomihiro and later attended the University of Iowa's creative writing program under a Fulbright Fellowship in 1966.

Kurahashi's writing garnered notice while she was still an undergraduate. Her short story "Party" (1960) won both the Meiji University Chancellor's Award in 1960 and the Women's Literary Award in 1961. She quickly followed with her first novel,

Blue Journey (1961), a story about a woman's search for the man to whom she is engaged. In 1969, Kurahashi published *The Adventures of Sumiyakist Q*, which portrays the attempts of a man to convert people secretly to an imaginary ideology called Sumiyakism. Shortly after her return from studying in the United States, Kurahashi initiated a series of novels centered on the life of a woman named Keiko with the publication of *A Floating Bridge of Dreams* (1969). In this ongoing series, Kurahashi creates a parallel fictional world that continues through several generations of Keiko's family.

Kurahashi is known both for writing complex stories that are presented with striking clarity and for her inclusion of controversial subjects, such as incest and partner swapping, in her stories. In addition to her prizes for "Party," she won the Tamura Toshiko Award in 1963 and the Izumi Kyōka Memorial Prize in 1987.

Other Works by Kurahashi Yumiko

"The Monastery." Translated by Carolyn Haynes. In Van C. Gessel and Tomone Matsumoto, eds., *The Shōwa Anthology: Modern Japanese Short Stories.* Tokyo: Kodansha International, 1985.

The Woman with the Flying Head and Other Stories of Kurahashi Yumiko. Translated by Atsuko Sakaki. Armonk, N.Y.: M. E. Sharpe, 1998.

A Work about Kurahashi Yumiko

Sakaki, Atsuko. "(Re)canonizing Kurahashi Yumiko: Toward Alternative Perspectives for 'Modern' 'Japanese' 'Literature.'" In Stephen Snyder and Philip Gabriel, eds., *Ōe and Beyond: Fiction in Contemporary Japan*. Honolulu: University of Hawaii Press, 1999.

Labrunie, Gerard

See NERVAL, GERARD DE.

Lagerkvist, Pär (Fabian) (1891–1974)
poet, playwright, novelist, short story writer

Pär Lagerkvist was born in Växjö, Sweden, to Anders Johan, a railway linesman, and Johanna (Blad) Lagerquist. Although he embraced Darwinism and political radicalism at a young age, Lagerkvist was influenced throughout his life by his parents' pietistic Christian faith. He attended the University of Uppsala in 1911 and 1912. In addition to writing, he briefly worked as a theater critic for a Stockholm newspaper in the late 1910s. He married Karen Dagmar Johanne Soerensen in 1918 and, after they divorced, married Elaine Luella Hallberg in 1925.

Lagerkvist first emerged on the literary scene as a poet. The second of his nine collections, *Ångest* (*Anguish*, 1916), described the despair and pain of World War I. The volume challenged the Swedish romantic tradition in verse and is considered the beginning of poetic modernism. Lagerkvist continued his search for aesthetic revolt and renewal in his dramas. He wrote 13 plays, including *Himlens Hemlighet* (*The Secret of Heaven*, 1919), which addressed the search for meaning in life. In the 1930s, Lagerkvist's dramas, plays, and short stories dealt with the issues of evil and fascism. After 1940, he focused on writing novels. *Dvärgen* (*The Dwarf*, 1944), considered by many to be his best work, explores the evil and creativity of humans.

Lagerkvist wrote more than 40 major works and has been translated into 34 languages. He was elected to the Swedish Academy of Literature in 1940 and won the Nobel Prize in literature in 1951. His influences include the dramatist AUGUST STRINDBERG, and naivism, cubism, and fauvism in French painting. His literary career lasted a half-century and encompassed all major genres but still displayed a remarkable internal consistency. Lagerkvist wrote about faith, skepticism, death, and evil, and explored the mysteries of existence. The scholar Robert Donald Spector observed that in Lagerkvist's works "his major theme is a quest for a god who will replace the deity of his youth."

Critical Analysis

As a poet, Lagerkvist first gained attention for his second collection, *Anguish*. The primary source of his personal anguish originated from the despair and death caused by World War I and the questions he believed the war raised about the fundamental nature of humanity. In the collection,

Lagerkvist explores the search for meaning in a world devastated by war. "Anguish, anguish is my heritage," he writes, "the wound of my throat / the cry of my heart in the world." Here Lagerkvist is extending his personal anguish into the world, regarding all of humanity as sharing anguish as they experience the horror of war. In these poems, Lagerkvist also explores the themes that would become central to his life and work: the question of good and evil from the perspective of Christian theology and the search for a meaningful life in a world in which the machine of war killed millions. *Anguish* is considered to be one of the first examples of EXPRESSIONISM in Sweden, as well as of MODERNISM, as it gave vent to Lagerkvist's inner thoughts with no particular application of accepted poetic structure and questioned the certainty of religious thought and its assumed "universality." Although the poems reject the status quo, they leave nothing to replace it but a void framed by a singular question: Why?

As a novelist, Lagerkvist's most renowned and most personal work was *Barabbas* (1950). The novel relates the fictional life of the title character who, according to the Bible, was released instead of Jesus at the crucifixion. The name of the character translates to the "Son of Man," making Lagerkvist's intentions very clear: readers are meant to identify with the struggle of Barabbas, to question their own beliefs and conduct a search for meaning as he does. In the beginning, Barabbas does not respect Jesus or his sacrifice, which he regards as meaningless. After his release, he struggles with the Christian faith, trying to understand, and finally comes to reject it as too idealistic. He claims he "wants to believe" but cannot bring himself to make the leap of faith. After a long physical and spiritual journey, Barabbas is arrested and eventually crucified, along with a group of Christians, and is considered by those who survive as a martyr for the faith. The inherent absurdity of this outcome highlights Lagerkvist's struggle with Christianity and the question of good and evil: A man who rejects faith can nevertheless be recognized and praised for the ultimate act of faith.

Another Work by Pär Lagerkvist

Guest of Reality. Translated by Robin Fulton. New York: Quartet, 1989.

A Work about Pär Lagerkvist

Spector, Robert Donald. *Pär Lagerkvist.* Boston: Twayne, 1973.

Lagerlöf, Selma (1858–1940) *novelist*

Selma Lagerlöf was born in Marbacka, Sweden. She was educated at home by her father, a retired army officer, and her grandmother. Lagerlöf's grandmother told her traditional tales of Sweden, which played an important role in the formation of her artistic imagination. In 1882, Lagerlöf went to the Royal Women's Superior Training Academy in Stockholm to prepare for a career as a teacher. After graduation, she taught in a school for girls for 10 years.

While teaching, Lagerlöf began writing her first novel. She sent early chapters to a literary contest in a local magazine and was awarded a publishing contract for the entire novel. Financially supported by her lifelong friend, the Baroness Sophie Aldesparre, Lagerlöf completed her first novel, *The Story of Gösta Berling* (1891). Gösta, a young adventurous hero, suffers a series of ordeals before he marries the dashing heroine, Countess Elizabeth, and finds peace in his life. The story was significant in the Swedish romantic revival of the late 1890s.

Lagerlöf's work appealed to people of all ranks. Her work was founded on the rich traditions and deep cultural history of the Swedish people. With financial assistance from the Swedish Academy and a pension from Sweden's King Oscar, Lagerlöf resigned from teaching to concentrated on her writing. A journey to Egypt and Palestine between 1899 and 1900 inspired the publication of her first major and critically acclaimed work, *Jerusalem*. The collection of stories describes the destructive effects of a conservative, religious revival on a small Swedish community. The Ingmar family takes a journey to Jerusalem, and one of the family members is sold into slavery by another. Still another Ingmar renounces his engagement to the love of his life so he can marry a rich woman. The collection placed Lagerlöf on a prominent level in the literary world of Sweden.

In 1906, Lagerlöf published her best-known work, *The Wonderful Adventures of Nils*. The work was commissioned by the Swedish board of education to teach geography in the primary school. It tells the story of a naughty but courageous young boy, Nils, who is magically reduced to the size of a gnome. He travels throughout Sweden on the back of a gander who escapes the farm to join the flock of wild geese. From them, Nils learns courage, companionship, and commitment. Although this story is a fairy tale, it also provides, as it was meant to do, useful information about Swedish geography and life in Sweden. The story is loved and admired throughout the world.

In 1909, Selma Lagerlöf became the first female writer to win the Nobel Prize for literature. When the Soviets invaded Finland in 1939, Lagerlöf donated the Nobel medal to raise money for the Finnish army. A truly amazing and courageous person, she helped a great number of German writers and artists to escape Nazi persecution by arranging to smuggle them into Sweden. This remarkable woman is not only a national writer of Sweden but also its national hero. She used her artistic talent to depict the cultural history and customs of her country. Selma Lagerlöf's work is still widely read throughout the world today, with the sad exception of the United States.

Other Works by Selma Lagerlöf

Girl from the Marsh Croft, and Other Stories. Translated by Greta Andersen. Iowa City: Penfield Press, 1996.
Invisible Links. Translated by Greta Andersen. Iowa City: Penfield Press, 1995.
Memories of Marbacka. Translated by Greta Andersen. Iowa City: Penfield Press, 1996.

A Work about Selma Lagerlöf

Edstrom, Vivi Bloom. *Selma Lagerlöf.* Boston: Twayne, 1982.

La Guma, Alex (1925–1985) *novelist, short story writer*

One of South Africa's premier chroniclers of life under apartheid in South Africa, Justin Alexander La Guma was born into a trade unionist household. This early involvement with socialist politics combined with his status as a Cape Town "coloured" (a person of mixed race ancestry according to apartheid laws established in 1948) conspired to make of La Guma a writer concerned with issues of class and race in all his writings.

His parents made him aware of his mixed-race heritage by stressing the various cultures that were his heritage. His maternal grandmother had come to South Africa from Indonesia; his maternal grandfather came from Scotland. His father was originally from what is now known as the Malagasy Republic. When La Guma was only 13 years old, he tried to get to Spain to fight against the fascists in the Spanish civil war, but he was turned down. Two years later, in 1940, he tried to enlist as a soldier to fight against Nazi Germany, but he was refused because of his slight build and unhealthy appearance. At 17, he went to work doing manual labor in a box factory where he developed a lifelong awareness of the real concerns of working people.

In 1955, La Guma worked for a left-wing newspaper in Cape Town as a journalist until the apartheid government banned his work; he wrote political columns, reported on the absurdities of apartheid laws, and even penned a regular political cartoon. After the murders of unarmed blacks in 1960 by white policemen, an event since referred to as the Sharpeville Massacre, all antigovernment groups were banned, and La Guma himself was jailed for more than six months. He was later sentenced, in 1962, to five years under house arrest. The punishment meant that he could not leave his home, meet with any of his friends, or in any way communicate with those whose ideology he shared. In his novel, *The Stone Country* (1967), La Guma fictionalizes this experience, and several stays in prison in 1960 and 1961 when South Africa was under a state of emergency and many people were detained without being formally charged.

La Guma was banned from employment as a journalist during the early 1960s, and he turned to writing fiction as a result. The publication, in 1962, of a collection of short stories entitled *A Walk in the Night and Other Stories* marked the advent of something truly different in the South African literary tradition. In the lead story in the collection, the novella from which the collection takes its name, La Guma allows his characters to speak in a sanitized version of the Cape Town dialect that the real underclass spoke. Another story in the collection, "Tattoo Marks and Nails," focuses on a prison cell and is a precursor to *The Stone Country*. Although he was not the first South African writer to focus on working people and their problems, La Guma's concentration on the realistic representation of the poorest and most vulnerable of his culture's people marked him as a uniquely South African voice. For example, although PETER ABRAHAMS can very easily be seen as a literary pioneer for his focus on the poorest of South Africa's noncitizens in *Mine Boy* (1946) and other texts, La Guma allows the streets to speak for themselves. In many ways, he signals a resistance to the forms of the European literary tradition that had, to that date, influenced the vast majority of South African works written in English.

La Guma is an important figure in the literary tradition of South Africa because he points up something about the way people in the United States understand places like South Africa. Important critics such as LEWIS NKOSI and J. M. COETZEE observed long ago that those of us who read about foreign cultures often view foreign texts as "sociological" documents; for example, a 1974 essay by Coetzee examines the reduction of the literary text to an example of an exotic culture. These astute critics also have observed that—worse—"weak" literature all too often is celebrated because its politics are right. But La Guma's works have both a deceptive, realist style and true literary merit. He is rightly read as much

for the quality of his writing as for his content. As Cecil Abrahams states "He [La Guma] sees his task as similar to that of the African story-teller, namely that of recording events as told to him and fashioning the tale in such a manner that there is both a moral and an entertaining purpose involved."

Other Works by Alex La Guma

In the Fog of the Season's End. London: Heinemann, 1972.
Time of the Butcherbird. London: Heinemann, 1979.

Works about Alex La Guma

Abrahams, Cecil. *Alex La Guma*. Boston: Twayne, 1985.
Coetzee, J. M. "Man's Fate in the Novels of Alex La Guma." *Studies in Black Literature* 5.1 (Spring 1974).

Laing, B. Kojo (1946–) *novelist, poet*

B. Kojo Laing was born in Kumasi in the Ashanti region of Ghana. He was the eldest son of six children and was baptized Bernard Ebenezer, but he later dropped his Christian name in favor of his African identity. Laing's father was the first African rector of the Anglican Theological College in Kumasi. Although Laing's family belonged to the educated middle class, they were by no means rich. Laing had to sell snacks on the street in Accra when he was a child. His disgust with this experience influenced his perception of the city and is distinctly expressed in his writings. Laing spent the first five years of his early education in Accra and was later sent to Scotland in 1957, where he had both his primary and secondary education. In 1968, he graduated from Glasgow University with a master's degree, then returned to Ghana to join the civil service. Laing left the service in 1979 to work as an administrative secretary of the Institute of African Studies for five years and then headed Saint Anthony's School in Accra in 1985, where he still works today.

Laing emerged as an important poet in the 1970s but did not become very widely known until 1986 when he published his first novel, *Search Sweet Country* (1975). His search for spiritual meaning is most intensely expressed in this novel, which is an analogy of his own experience as a civil servant in the Ashanti region. In the novel, Laing explores the complexities of human relationships and the different responses of people from different backgrounds to the reign of a corrupt military government. The bittersweet flavor of Laing's writing reveals his continuous attempt, through language, to bridge the differences between physical reality and spiritual ideals.

Laing's love of nature is also clearly reflected in his writing. One of his favorite pastimes is hunting, which provides him with a source of imagery. In *Woman of the Aeroplanes* (1988), for example, Laing uses images that symbolize the natural, surreal, and human worlds. An example of Laing's use of nature imagery in the novel is his humorous personification of the lake, which becomes extremely jealous of the ducks that swim in its waters and refuses to ripple.

Laing was also deeply influenced by his life experiences, such as his father's religious devotion and early death and his own journeys and failed relationships. His poem "Funeral in Accra" commemorated his father's death and marked his rite of passage from youth to adulthood. This poem was published in 1968 together with two other poems, "African Storm" and "Jaw." These poems contain the metaphors of his psychological struggle between alienation and dislocation.

Laing's main contribution to world literature is his ability to create a hybrid of languages and images from both the traditional African and modern Western worlds. His works, such as *Godhorse* (1989), appropriate the common symbol of technology, such as the car, and by simplifying its locomotive movements, compare it with daily human actions, such as walking or transplanting crops in the fields. By carefully and cleverly blending mixed symbols and language, Laing reveals the complexity of interdependent relationships within society.

Another Work by B. Kojo Laing

Major Gentl and the Achimota Wars. London: Heinemann, 1992.

A Work about B. Kojo Laing

Ngaboh-Smart, Francis. *Beyond Empire and Nation: Postnational Arguments in the Fiction of Nuruddin Farah and B. Kojo Laing.* New York: Rodopi, 2004.

Laird, Christopher (1945–   ) *poet, writer, editor, producer, director*

Born in Trinidad, Christopher Laird is the author of poetry that has appeared in *The New Voices,* the *Caribbean Writer,* and *Kairi.* As editor of *Kairi,* he has striven to increase the visibility of writers from and about Trinidad and Tobago. Laird has also done a number of extensive interviews with cultural personalities, including novelist George LAMMING, carnival artist Peter Minshall, and actor and dramatist Slade Hopkinson.

Laird's poetry has been anthologized in *Voiceprint: An Anthology of Oral and Related Poetry from the Caribbean* (1989). In "Hosay," a seven-part poem published in *Voiceprint,* the speaker draws attention to himself with speech and musical rhythms, but then concludes the poem saying,

> *I am silent now.*
> *I done talk.*
> *Until a mounting fire*
> *stretches me taut*
> *to move the air again.*

As video producer, director, writer, and editor, Laird examines Caribbean culture. One of Laird's projects, *Caribbean Eye* videos, explores regional Caribbean philosophies, celebrations, and styles of music and drama. *Caribbean Carnivals* (1991), *Dramatic Actions* (1991), and *Women in Action* (1991) are three of the 13 half-hour, made-for-television *Caribbean Eye* videos from Trinidad's Banyan Studios.

In 1992, Laird codirected *And the Dish Ran Away with the Spoon* with Tony Hall. Produced as part of the BBC/TVE Developing World Series, the video uses poetry, interviews, music, and clips from television shows to highlight effects of American television broadcasts on local Caribbean cultures. It won best documentary and best video at Images Caraïbes, the Caribbean Film & Video festival, and also best documentary at the Prized Pieces competition of the National Black Programmers Consortium of the United States. Laird's varied projects significantly facilitate the exploration and appreciation of Caribbean culture.

Other Works by Christopher Laird

Brown, Stewart, Mervyn Morris, and Gordon Rohlehr, eds. Selections in *Voiceprint: An Anthology of Oral and Related Poetry from the Caribbean*. Harlow, U.K.: Longman, 1989.
"Faith, Beauty and Blood." *Caribbean Writer* 5 (1991): 49–50.
"Jamestown Beach, Accra." *Caribbean Writer* 3 (1989): 44–45.

Lamartine, Alphonse de (1790–1869)
poet, novelist

Alphonse Marie Louis de Lamartine was born to a family of minor nobility in Mâcon on October 10, 1790. He received a traditional education and, after spending a brief period of time in the army, traveled to Italy where he discovered much of the aesthetics of love and nature that would prevail in his works and that tie him closely to French ROMANTICISM.

His first published work, *Méditations poétiques* (1820), met with immediate success. In the 24 poems that compose this collection, Lamartine expressed his feelings about religion, love, and nature. Subsequent works, such as *Harmonies* (1830), developed his theme of lyricism and his musical tones. He also expressed his religious views in such works as *Jocelyn* (1836), a novel in verse, and

La chute d'un ange (*An Angel's Fall,* 1838), an epic poem that describes an evil tyranny.

Politically, Lamartine tried to remain distant from party conflicts; however, his idealist philosophy tended toward democracy and the campaign for social justice. His *Histoire des Girondins* (*History of the Girondists,* 1847), a work that promoted and glorified the aims of a political group of moderate Republicans known as the Girondists during the French Revolution met with immense popular success. After competing unsuccessfully against Napoleon III for the presidency, Lamartine left politics to devote his life to writing.

Another Work by Alphonse de Lamartine

Poetical Meditations/Méditations Poétiques. Translated by Gervase Hittle. Lewiston, N.Y.: Edwin Mellen Press, 1993.

Works about Alphonse de Lamartine

Boutin, Aimee. *Maternal Echoes: The Poetry of Marceline Desbordes-Valmore and Alphonse de Lamartine*. Nework: University of Delaware Press, 2001.
Fortescue, William. *Alphonse de Lamartine: A Political Biography*. New York: St. Martin's Press, 1983.
Lombard, Charles M. *Lamartine*. Boston: Twayne, 1973.

Lamming, George (William) (1927–)
novelist, poet, critic, teacher, lecturer, broadcaster, trade union activist

George Lamming was born and raised in Carrington's Village, a former sugar estate on the outskirts of Barbados's capital, Bridgetown. Although Lamming's mother married after his birth, Lamming said, "it was my mother who fathered me." Lamming attended Combermere High School on a scholarship. There, teacher and writer FRANK COLLYMORE encouraged his writing. When Lamming's courses ended in 1946, Collymore helped Lamming obtain a teaching position at El Colegio de Venezuala, a boarding school for boys of South American origin, in Port of Spain, Trinidad. That year Lamming also started publishing poetry in *Bim,* a literary magazine edited by Collymore. From 1947, the BBC's "Caribbean Voices" series broadcast Lamming's poems and occasional short prose pieces. Themes Lamming explored during this period—frustration with West Indian cultural life and artists' preference for imported culture—reappear in later works as well.

In 1950, Lamming sailed to England with other West Indian immigrants, including the novelist Samuel Selvon, and briefly worked in a factory and hosted a book program for the BBC West Indian Service while writing. Lamming dedicated his first novel, *In the Castle of My Skin* (1953), to his mother and Frank Collymore. This fictional account of the West Indian experience quickly garnered critical acclaim in the United States and England. In the preface, U.S. novelist Richard Wright describes Lamming's prose as "quietly melodious," and in an essay entitled "George Lamming's *In the Castle of My Skin*" (1954), the novelist Ngũgĩ wa Thiong'o calls the work "one of the great political novels in modern 'colonial' literature."

Lamming's subsequent works explore West Indian history, culture, and politics. After completing *The Emigrants* (1954), a novel that follows a group of young men of Lamming's generation from the West Indies to London, Lamming returned to the Caribbean to gather material for his third novel, *Of Age and Innocence* (1958), set on the fictitious island of San Cristobal. This novel examines relationships formed during colonial history, as does Lamming's fourth novel, *Season of Adventure* (1960). In a 1989 interview archived online by *Banyan Limited,* Lamming said that *Season of Adventure* was "probably the first" and "only" novel "which is in a sense devoted to the elevation of the steelband not only as a moment of great culture and triumph, but also showing the way in which cultural activity can be so decisive in political life." Published the same year as *Season of Adventure, The Pleasures of Exile* (1960), a collection of essays, examines West Indian colonialism.

Two more novels published in the early 1970s, *Water with Berries* (1971) and *Natives of My Person* (1972), use allegory to examine guilt produced by colonialism and carried by English and Caribbean characters. Some critics consider the latter work as Lamming's major work, while others criticize its ideological representation of characters. In 1974, Lamming edited *Cannon Shot and Glass Beads: Modern Black Writing,* an anthology examining black responses to white racism.

In later years, Lamming devoted his attention to lecturing and essays, regularly contributing to the journal *Casa de las Américas,* published in Havana. Since entering academia as a writer-in-residence and lecturer at the University of the West Indies in 1967, Lamming has been a visiting professor at the University of Texas at Austin and the University of Pennsylvania, a teacher at the University of Miami's summer Institute for Caribbean Creative Writing, and a lecturer in Denmark, Tanzania, Kenya, and Australia. Regarded as one of the most perceptive commentators on the West Indies, Lamming is also considered one of the most important Caribbean West Indian novelists.

Other Works by George Lamming

Coming, Coming Home: Conversations II: Monographs. Philipsburg, St. Martin: House of Nehesi, 2000.

"Concepts of the Caribbean." In Frank Birbalsingh, ed., *Frontiers of Caribbean Literatures in English.* New York: St. Martin's Press, 1996.

Drayton, Richard, and Andaiye, eds. *Conversations: George Lamming Essays, Addresses and Interviews, 1956–1990.* London: Karia Press, 1992.

Sovereignty of the Imagination—Conversations III. Philipsburg, St. Martin: House of Nehesi Publishers, 2009.

Works about George Lamming

Hulme, Peter. "Reading from Elsewhere: George Lamming and the Paradox of Exile." In Peter Hulme and William H. Sherman, eds., *The Tempest and Its Travels.* Philadelphia, Pa.: University of Pennsylvania Press, 2000.

Phillips, Caryl. "George Lamming." *Wasafiri: Journal of Caribbean, African, Asian and Associated Literatures and Film* 26 (Autumn 1997).

Silva, A. J. Simoes da. *The Luxury of Nationalist Despair: George Lamming's Fiction as Decolonizing Project.* Atlanta, Ga.: Rodopi, 2000.

Lampedusa, Giuseppe Tomasi di
(1896–1957) *novelist*

Giuseppe Tomasi di Lampedusa was born in Palermo, Italy, to Prince Guilio di Lampedusa and his wife, Beatrice. He grew up in a palace and had a great fondness for his upbringing, which he was able to capture in his writing. He had an extremely close, nearly suffocating relationship with his mother through much of his life. From age 16 to 18, he attended the Liceo-Ginnasio Garibaldi school, where he proved to be an excellent scholar in philosophy, history, and Italian. He went on to study law at the University of Rome.

From 1916 to 1918, Lampedusa fought in the Italian Alps in World War I and was wounded and captured. After the war, he traveled extensively in Italy as well as to London, Paris, and other European cities. In the 1920s, he immersed himself in a self-directed course of study in European history and literature. His favorite writers included William Shakespeare, John Keats, and CHARLES BAUDELAIRE.

In 1954, Lampedusa began a course of lectures on literature, one of which was published as the book, *Lessons on Stendahl* (1977). He then turned to novel writing and began *The Leopard,* a book about the Italian aristocracy, which was published posthumously in 1958. As a diversion from this book, Lampedusa began his autobiography. It was a chance to write about his beloved family palace, which had nearly been destroyed in an air attack during World War II.

Lampedusa had an active and varied life that contributed to the richness of his work. He left his mark in the worlds of education, literature, and history. David Gilmour, his biographer, writes, "his work will survive because he wrote about the central problems of the human experience."

A Work about Giuseppe Tomasi di Lampedusa
Gilmour, David. *The Last Leopard: A Life of Giuseppe di Lampedusa.* New York: Pantheon, 1988.

Langgässer, Elisabeth (1899–1950) *poet, novelist, short story writer*

Elisabeth Langgässer was born in Alzey, Germany, to Eduard and Eugenie Dienst Langgässer. Her father, an architect, was a Jew, but she was raised as a Catholic. After Eduard's death in 1909, the family moved to Darmstadt, where Langgässer attended the Viktoria-Schule. After passing the school-leaving exam in 1918, she taught at a primary school in Grieshein. In 1935, she married the theologian Wilhelm Hoffmann.

Langgässer wrote book and theater reviews before publishing her first poetry collection, *Der Wendekreis des Lammes* (*The Tropic of the Lamb,* 1924). Her first novel, *Proserpina* (1933), won the Literary Prize of the Association of Women's Citizens. In 1936, the Nazis forbade her from further publication because she was of Jewish descent; she defied the ban with a short-story collection in 1938. After World War II, she gained wider popularity and critical acceptance. Her novel *Das Unauslöschliche Siegel* (*The Indelible Seal,* 1946) earned praise from writers THOMAS MANN and HERMANN BROCH.

The influence of FRANZ KAFKA and James Joyce is evident in Langgässer's works. Many considered her a religious writer, but she often included nonreligious aspects such as war and economic hardship in her writing. Langgässer's poems explore the conceptions of *soul* and *psyche* and investigate the evil side of human nature. Not afraid of paradoxes, she also dealt with the irrationality, beauty, and brutality of human passions. The literary scholar Hermann Boeschenstein writes that Langgässer "is able to do what has often been termed the prerequisite to the revitalization of modern religious literature; she repeats the old truths in an exciting new way."

Another Work by Elisabeth Langgässer
The Quest. New York: Knopf, 1953.

A Work about Elisabeth Langgässer

Gelbin, Cathy S. *An Indelible Seal: Race, Hybridity and Identity in Elisabeth Langgässer's Writings.* Essen: Die Blaue Eule, 2001.

Lao She (Shu Qingchun) (1899–1966)
novelist

Shu Qingchun was born Shu She-yü on February 3 in Beijing. When foreign allied forces attacked Beijing in the 1900 Boxer Rebellion, his father was killed. His mother did laundry so that Shu Qingchun could be privately tutored. He graduated from Beijing Normal in 1918 and became headmaster of a primary school, managing it so efficiently that he was appointed a government post in 1920. He returned to teaching and did social work with various Beijing organizations while studying English at Yenching University. In 1924, he taught Chinese at the Oriental School of London University and assisted in translating a 16th-century Chinese novel.

Inspired by the writing of Charles Dickens, Shu began to write (under the pseudonym Lao She), completing his first novel, *The Philosophy of Lao Zhang* (1926), while in London. The book was published as a serial in Shanghai to critical and popular acclaim because of its patriotism and realistic portrayal of a civil servant, two students, and a contemptible schoolmaster.

In 1930, Lao She returned to China and taught Chinese at Qilu and Shandong Universities, where he continued to write prolifically. His most popular work was the social critique *Lo-t'o Hsiang-tzu* (*Rickshaw Boy,* 1936), a novel about making a living in Beijing. In 1940, he completed the trilogy about Japanese-occupied Beijing, *Four Generations Under One Roof.*

As one of the country's foremost patriotic writers, Lao She was active in the anti-Japanese movement during the Sino-Japanese War. He was elected director of general affairs of the All-China Resist-the-Enemy Federation of Writers and Artists. In 1946, he traveled to the United States as a visiting lecturer and wrote his last novel, *The Drum Singers,* published in the United States in 1952. He returned to celebrate China's new Communist regime in 1949 and wrote plays, all of which became classics of socialist literature, including *Dragon Beard Ditch* (1950), *Teahouse* (1956), *All the Family Are Blessed* (1959), and *Beneath the Red Banner* (1964).

Although he served high posts in the Chinese Writers Association, Lao She was no exception to the suppression of writers during the Cultural Revolution. Unable to contend with the disgrace of public denunciations and criticisms, he committed suicide on August 24, 1966. He was posthumously "rehabilitated" by the Communist Party in 1979, and his complete works were published.

Other Works by Lao She

Blades of Grass: The Stories of Lao She. Honolulu: University of Hawaii Press, 1999.

Cat Country: A Satirical Novel of China in the 1930s. Translated by William A. Lyell. Columbus: Ohio State University Press, 1970.

Heavensent. Translated by Xiong Deni. San Francisco: China Books and Periodicals, 1986.

Teahouse: A Play in Three Acts. Translated by John Howard-Gibbon. Beijing: Foreign Languages Press, 1980.

Works about Lao She

Vohra, Ranbir. *Lao She and the Chinese Revolution.* Cambridge, Mass.: East Asian Research Center, Harvard University, 1974.

Wang, David Der-Wei. *Fictional Realism in Twentieth-Century China: Mao Dun, Lao She, Shen Congwen.* New York: Columbia University Press, 1992.

Larsson, Karl Stig-Erland (Stieg)
(1954–2004) *novelist, journalist*

Before his death from a heart attack at age 50, Stieg Larsson was known mainly as an investigative journalist in his native Sweden. In his spare time, he managed to complete the three novels of the Millennium Trilogy, which was signed by a Swedish publisher not long before his death. The first novel, *The Girl with the Dragon Tattoo*

(2005), quickly became an international publishing sensation; the following two—*The Girl Who Played with Fire* and *The Girl Who Kicked the Hornet's Nest*—have sold similarly well. The heroine of the series, Lisbeth Salander, is a young woman of the counterculture who has survived a horrific childhood to become a brilliant, brave, and often cold-blooded investigator. The critic Marilyn Stasio wrote, "Salander surely stands for the female life force, the enraged and implacable avenger of victims." The hero, Mikael Blomkvist, is a good-hearted crusading journalist, similar in some respects to Larsson himself.

As a journalist, Stieg Larsson was known for exposing Sweden's right-wing extremist groups. He helped found the Swedish antifascist organization, Expo Foundation, and was editor in chief of its magazine, *Expo*, until his death. The Millennium Trilogy is a fictional examination not only of the fascism and extremism hidden in Swedish society but also of violence against women. Reviewing *The Girl with the Dragon Tattoo* in the *New York Times Book Review*, Alex Berenson wrote, "The novel offers a thoroughly ugly view of human nature, especially when it comes to the way Swedish men treat Swedish women." Some critics have called the trilogy heavy-handed and confusing, but most have maintained that Larsson wrote a superior brand of political crime fiction. David Kamp, in a review of the series as a whole, described Larsson as a "cerebral, high-minded activist and self-proclaimed feminist who happened to have a God-given gift for pulse-racing narrative."

A Work about Stieg Larsson

Forshaw, Barry. *The Man Who Left Too Soon: The Biography of Stieg Larsson*. London: John Blake, 2010.

Lasker-Schüler, Else (1869–1945) *poet, novelist*

Else Lasker-Schüler was born in Elberfeld, Germany, to Aron Schüler, a banker, and Jeanette Schüler. The youngest of six children, Else was deeply devoted to her mother, who encouraged Else's early interest in poetry. Paul, Lasker-Schüler's older brother, also helped develop her strong passion for poetry. As a Jewish family, the Schülers had difficulty in the social environment of Germany. Because of constant teasing by the Catholic and Lutheran children, Else had to quit elementary school and was tutored at home by her parents.

In 1890, Lasker-Schüler suffered the painful loss of her mother. Four years later, she married Jonathan Lasker. Lasker-Schüler separated from her husband in 1899 after refusing to acknowledge him as the father of their son Paul. Along with her son, she moved to Berlin in 1899 where she immediately became immersed in the artistic and cultural life of the city. Lasker-Schüler frequented various literary cafés throughout Berlin where she composed poetry, made sketches, and conversed with other artists. For the next 10 years, although she associated with various literary groups, such as the expressionists (*see* EXPRESSIONISM), her work does not appear to have been influenced by them.

In 1913, Lasker-Schüler traveled to Russia with the goal of securing the release of her longtime friend Johannes Holzmann, who had been arrested for revolutionary activities and leadership in anarchist circles. Her mission was unsuccessful, but it provided plenty of material for her writings. During World War I, Lasker-Schüler lost many friends, such as the Austrian poet GEORG TRAKL. As a result of these experiences, she became deeply committed to pacifism.

In 1932 Lasker-Schüler received the Kleist prize, one of the highest literary honors in Germany. The atmosphere in German society, however, was becoming dangerous for her with the rise of the National Socialists (Nazi) Party. One of the newspapers controlled by the Nazis commented on Lasker-Schüler's award: "The pure Hebrew poetry of Else Lasker-Schüler has nothing to do with us Germans." Fearing for her life, Lasker-Schüler promptly left Germany for Switzerland. Arriving without luggage, she spent six nights sleeping on a bench in a Zurich park but survived by giving poetry readings and selling her drawings and sketches, as well as on generous gifts from her friends and readers. She spent several years living in Switzerland and Jerusalem, where she died in 1945.

Lasker-Schüler's early poetry was first published about 1899. Through the years, her poetry became more and more complex, often treating concrete ideas with abstract images. Her first collection of poetry, *Styx* (1902), reveals some qualities of the Expressionist school that are characterized by decorative and emotional imagery, as seen in "Coolness" (1902): "In the white blaze / Of bright roses / I want to bleed to death." As Ruth Schwertfeger notes, "Preoccupation with spiritual reality dominates Lasker-Schüler's thinking."

Lasker-Schüler clearly considered herself a Jewish poet: In the poem "My People," published in *The Seventh Day* (1905), she openly identifies herself with the Jewish people: "I have traveled the diaspora / From my blood's fermentation / Constantly over in me again." Lasker-Schüler's fascination with her Jewish roots also led to her constant longing for Jerusalem, which she visited five times during her life.

Lasker-Schüler's banishment from Germany was a painful experience and one to which she returns over and over in her poetry. In "Banished" (1934) she longs for Germany, which she always considered her homeland: "Where is the breath my life exhaled? / Exiled dreamer I glide between pale hours / Companion to wild game. I used to love you." Lasker-Schüler considered herself a German to the end of her life.

Else Lasker-Schüler's poetry did not become widely popular until the end of the World War II. Today, she is considered to be among the best poets of Germany. In 1953, at a poetry reading dedicated to the memory of Else Lasker-Schüler, the poet Gottfried Benn referred to her as "the greatest lyric poet Germany ever had." Lasker-Schüler's work is not well known outside of German-speaking countries because, as many critics and scholars claim, the complexity of her verse renders it virtually untranslatable. Recent translations, however, have been more successful, and her works are now available in more than 12 languages.

Other Works by Else Lasker-Schüler

Selected Poems. Translated by Jeanette Demeestere-Litman. New York: Green Integer, 2000.
Star in my Forehead. Translated by Janine Canan. New York: Consortium, 1999.

A Work about Else Lasker-Schüler

Yudkin, Leon I. *Else Lasker-Schueler: A Study in German Jewish Literature.* Washington, D.C.: B'nai B'rith Book Service, 1991.

Laurence, Margaret (Jean Margaret Laurence) (1926–1987) *novelist, short story writer*

The Canadian novelist Margaret Laurence was born Jean Margaret Wemyss on July 18, 1926, in Neepawa, Manitoba, Canada. Her mother, Verna Jean Simpson, died when Margaret was four. Her father, Robert Harrison Wemyss, died when she was nine, after which she was raised by her maternal grandparents.

Laurence's childhood was difficult. She hated her maternal grandfather, who was a cold, formidable man. To escape the oppressive atmosphere in which she lived, Laurence read and wrote avidly from a young age. Having already selected writing as her career, she got a job at her local paper when she was 17. Three years later, she went to Winnipeg United College, now the University of Winnipeg, to study English.

After graduating in 1947, Laurence returned to journalism, becoming a reporter for the *Winnipeg Citizen*. That same year, she married John Laurence, an engineer. In 1949, the Laurences moved to England, and a year after that to Somalia, then the British Protectorate of Somalia. In 1952, they moved again to the Gold Coast, now known as Ghana. While living abroad in Africa, Laurence had two children, Jocelyn (born in 1952) and David (1955).

It was during this time in Africa that Laurence began to write in earnest, and her primary topic was her experience as a white minority in Africa. Her stories were heavy with Christian symbolism and dealt with the ethics of colonialism.

Laurence's first novel, *This Side Jordan* (1960), which took its title from the Book of Joshua and the imagery of crossing over into the Promised Land, focuses on how British imperialism affected Africans in the postcolonial era. The Gold Coast was attempting to gain its freedom from the United Kingdom, and such transitions, Laurence felt, were neither easy nor quickly accomplished. In the story, Nathaniel, a young African schoolteacher, works in a very poor secondary school because he does not have the training to get a job in a better school. His family constantly tries to pull him back into the old tribal ways, while he attempts to pull himself forward into the new Africa. The novel allows a degree of uncertainty as to whether Nathaniel completes his journey or is overcome by the obstacles in his way.

In 1957, just before the Gold Coast gained its independence, the Laurence family moved to Vancouver, British Columbia. Here, although Laurence continued to write about Africa for a time, she felt that she had done all she could with the subject. She then turned her focus on "her own people," the Scottish Presbyterians of Manitoba. Laurence was concerned with internal freedom, a person's ability to deal with and move beyond his or her compulsive actions and live a fuller life.

Laurence separated from her husband in 1962 and moved to England, first to London and then to Elm Cottage in Penn, Buckinghamshire. Her second and best-known novel, *The Stone Angel*, was written during this time and published in 1964. *The Stone Angel* became the first in a series of novels set in the fictional Manitoba town of Manawaka, which also includes *A Jest of God* (1966); *The Fire-Dwellers* (1969); *A Bird in the House* (1970); and *The Diviners* (1974), Laurence's final and most complex novel. Highly regarded, it is the story of Hagar, a 91-year-old woman who is looking back over her life, a life devoid of joy, kindness, or love. Hagar prized conviction over all else, and the choice seems empty. *The Stone Angel* is often assigned to Canadian high school students as required reading.

Acknowledged as one of Canada's most widely read novelists, Margaret Laurence gained her popularity primarily from her powerful ability to create memorable characters. The critic David Stouck has written that "Margaret Laurence's fictions stand out for their unforgettable portraits of women wrestling with their personal demons, striving through self-examination to find meaningful patterns to their lives."

Laurence and her husband did not officially divorce until 1969, the same year Margaret was granted the position of writer-in-residence at the University of Toronto. In 1971, she was named a Companion of the Order of Canada. Eventually, she returned to Canada, buying homes in both Lakefield and Peterborough, Ontario. From 1981 until 1983, Laurence was chancellor of Trent University in Peterborough.

In 1986, Laurence was diagnosed with late-stage lung cancer. Because the cancer had spread, there was no hope for a cure. In order to spare everyone needless suffering, Laurence committed suicide in her Lakefield home on January 5, 1987.

Other Works by Margaret Laurence

The Christmas Birthday Story. Toronto: Knopf Books for Young Readers, 1980.

Dance on the Earth: A Memoir. Toronto: McClelland & Stewart, 1989.

Heart of a Stranger. Toronto: McClelland & Stewart, 1980.

Jason's Quest. Toronto: McClelland & Stewart, 1970.

Long Drums and Cannons: Nigerian Dramatists and Novelists, 1952–1966. Alberta: University of Alberta Press, 2001.

The Olden Days Coat. Toronto: Tundra Books, 2004.

The Prophet's Camel Bell. Toronto: McClelland & Stewart, 1967.

Six Darn Cows. Toronto: Lorimer, 1979.

The Tomorrow-Tamer: Short Stories. Toronto: New Canadian Library, 1970.

Works about Margaret Laurence

King, James. *The Life of Margaret Laurence.* Toronto: Vintage Canada, 1998.

Powers, Lyall. *Alien Heart: The Life and Work of Margaret Laurence.* East Lansing: Michigan State University Press, 2004.

Lautréamont, comte de (Isadore-Lucien Ducasse) (1846–1870) *poet*

Isadore Ducasse, who adopted the pen name and title of comte de Lautréamont, was born in Uruguay on April 4, 1846, to French parents. His father was a consular officer; his mother died when he was 18 months old. When he was 10 years old, his father left him with relatives in France, where he attended school and earned a reputation as a sullen, introverted student who disliked math and Latin. Lautréamont, however, became interested in literature and, as an independent thinker, developed ideas and attitudes that would eventually earn him a permanent place in French literary history.

After leaving school at age 19, Lautréamont traveled abroad, made some literary contacts, and then returned to Paris to begin his first major work, *Les chants de Maldoror* (1869). The title of this work has been subject to various interpretations, ranging from "dawn of evil" to "evil from the beginning." It is a macabre prose poem in which the main character celebrates evil with religious fervor. Themes within the work include rebellion against God, the image of Christ as a rapist, and a bitter protagonist whose decomposing and disfigured body is a haven for animals who have taken up residence in it while he still lives.

For the publication of *Maldoror,* he assumed the pseudonym Lautréamont, a name that is taken perhaps from Eugène Sue's novel *Lautréamont,* whose protagonist is similar in attitude to the main character in *Maldoror.* Part of the work was first printed privately in 1868, most likely with financial assistance from Lautréamont's father. The entire work was printed in 1869, but the publishers, fearing prosecution because of the blasphemous nature of the piece, opted not to make the text available for purchase.

Lautréamont tried in vain to convince the publishers to make his work available. He also began

another collection, this time celebrating hope and faith, but he died before completing it.

Nine years after his death, Lautréamont's works were finally published. They met with little notice, however, until members of the surrealist movement in the 1920s began to focus on Lautréamont as a thematic forerunner of their own ideals.

Another Work by comte de Lautréamont

Maldoror; and Poems. Translated by Paul Knight. Hardmonsworth, U.K.: Penguin, 1978.

A Work about comte de Lautréamont

Bachelard, Gaston. *Lautréamont.* Translated by Robert S. Dupree. Dallas, Tex.: Dallas Institute of Humanities and Culture, 1986.

Lawson, Henry (Larsen, Henry Hertzberg; Henry Archibald) (1867–1922) *short story writer, poet*

Henry Lawson was born on the goldfields of Grenfell, New South Wales, Australia. He was the eldest son of a Norwegian sailor, Peter Lawson, and his wife, Louisa. His mother was actively involved in publishing and was a famous leader of the women's rights movement in Australia. Lawson's early life was difficult: His family was poor, and an ear infection caused him to lose his hearing by the time he turned 14. His parents eventually separated, and his mother moved to Sydney. Lawson later moved to Sydney as well and became deeply influenced by his mother's radical friends.

Lawson's writings reflect his bitter life experiences. His inability to communicate because of the deafness led him to develop a keen habit of observing people. Lawson's works are about watching people and observing their actions. He used his powers of observation and his past experiences to enhance his writing. The major themes of Lawson's poems revolve around the Australian bush. Growing up in the bushland, Lawson knew the hardships of bush life and drew inspiration from the lessons learned coping and living with nature and the land, as can be seen in most of his short stories, including "The Drover's Wife," published in his collection *While the Billy Boils* (1896). Lawson found an affinity with the bush that he could not feel from human company. The celebratory tone of such poems as "The Roaring Days" (1889) and "Andy's Gone with Cattle" (1888) contrasts with the estrangement that the poet clearly felt in observing people.

Lawson's writings also reflect his deep concern for political and social issues. Some of his major poems of political and social protest include "The Watch on the Kerb" (1888) and "The Men Who Made Australia" (1901), which highlight the alienation and despair that are shared among most of Australia's struggling population. These same themes can be seen in his short stories "In the Storm That Is to Come" (1904) and "The Union Buries Its Dead" (1896).

Lawson's isolation increased as he failed to find happiness in marriage. He resorted to heavy drinking and spent most of his later life in a state of delirium and mental instability. His writing declined as his health collapsed. He began to write autobiographical works as he sought to hang on to his sanity. At his death, he was the first Australian writer to be granted a state funeral. Lawson's contribution to Australian and world literature lies in his accurate but starkly depressing portrayal of the difficult lives of the Australian lower classes, especially the much neglected regions of the Australian countryside and bush areas.

Other Works by Henry Lawson

The Bush Undertaker and Other Stories. Sydney: Angus and Robertson, 1994.
Henry Lawson: Short Stories. Edited by John Barnes. New York: Penguin, 1986.

Works about Henry Lawson

Philips, A. A. *Henry Lawson.* Boston: Twayne, 1970.
Wright, Judith. *Henry Lawson.* Melbourne, Australia: Oxford University Press, 1967.

Le Clézio, Jean-Marie Gustave

(1940–) *novelist, short story writer, essayist*

Jean-Marie Gustave Le Clézio was born on April 13, 1940, in Nice. His father is ethnically French, born on Mauritius, the island off the east coast of Africa that was Dutch, French and, then English and that gained its independence in 1968. The author regards himself as both French and Mauritian and has dual citizenship. He calls Mauritius his "little fatherland." For a couple of years, Le Clézio's family lived in Nigeria where his father worked as a doctor during World War II; they returned to France in 1950.

Le Clézio grew up speaking French and English. He studied in Bristol and Nice, earning his master's degree in English at the University of Provence Aix-Marseille I in 1964. His doctoral thesis on Mexico's early history was completed at the University of Perpignan in 1983. Le Clézio has lectured at many universities, including those in Bangkok, Mexico City, Boston, and Albuquerque.

Le Clézio's first novel, *The Interrogation* (1964), received much attention, mostly because he tried, in the aftermath of the French nouveau roman, to lift words above impoverished everyday speech and renew their power to invoke the essence of life. The book tells the story of Adam, a hermit who drags himself about a French beachside town trying to establish whether he has just left the army or whether he has been discharged from a mental hospital. Adam is just the first of many of Le Clézio's protagonists tormented by a vision of the world that becomes progressively more horrifying. *Fever*, a collection of short stories, continues the theme. "Life is full of madnesses," states Le Clézio in the introduction. "They're only little everyday madnesses, but they're terrible if you look at them closely."

From the very beginning of his literary career, Le Clézio stood out as an ecologically engaged author, as can be seen in *Terra amata* (1967), *The Book of Flights* (1971), and *The Giants* (1975). Literary fame came with *Désert* (1980), which won the Académie française's Grand Prix Paul Morand. Announcing a drastic change in his style, this book contrasts glimpses of a lost culture in the North African desert with unwanted immigrants' views of Europe. Long stays in Mexico and Central America (1970–74) were significant for Le Clézio's work, as he left the big cities in search of a new spiritual reality in contact with native populations. Le Clézio's effort to translate the major works of the Mayan tradition testifies to his fascination with Mexico's magnificent past. Later, the author's attraction to the dream of earthly paradise becomes apparent. *The Prospector* (1993) uses the islands of the Indian Ocean as the setting for an adventure story, whereas the novel *Raga* (2006) takes up the issue of how globalization erases the traditional ways of life on the islands of the Indian Ocean.

Le Clézio then shifted the focus of his fiction to his own family history. *Onitsha* (1991) reconstructs his early childhood, telling the story of his family's reunion after the war years, whereas *Revolutions* (2003) melds the themes of memory, exile, and growing up amid culture clashes. Le Clézio juxtaposes various times and distant places related to his own family history: His main character spends his student years in Nice, London, and Mexico, and his life is contrasted with the experiences of an ancestor from Brittany who emigrated to Mauritius in the 1790s and the story of a female slave from the beginning of the 19th century. There is also an interpolated narrative about childhood memories of an older relative, which are passed on to the author's fictional self.

Le Clézio received many literary prizes: Prix Théophraste Renaudot (1963), Prix Larbaud (1972), Grand Prix Jean Giono (1997), Prix Prince de Monaco (1998), and Stig Dagermanpriset (2008). Le Clézio won the Nobel Prize in literature in 2008. The Swedish Academy called him the "author of new departures, poetic adventure and sensual ecstasy, explorer of a humanity beyond and below the reigning civilization."

Since the 1990s, Le Clézio and his wife have divided their time among Albuquerque in New Mexico, the island of Mauritius, and Nice.

Other Works by Jean-Marie Gustave Le Clézio

The Mexican Dream, or, the Interrupted Thought of Amerindian Civilizations. Translated by Teresa Lavender Fagan. Chicago: University of Chicago Press, 1993.

The Round & Other Cold Hard Facts. Translated by C. Dickson. Lincoln: University of Nebraska Press, 2002.

Léger, Alexis Saint-Léger
See PERSE, SAINT-JOHN.

Leiris, Michel (1901–1990) *novelist, nonfiction writer*

Noted for his work as anthropologist and writer, Michel Leiris was born in Paris to an upper-class family. He became a serious student of chemistry but was soon drawn to the Bohemian world of Parisian cafés and cabarets where he first encountered and then became enamored with the growing surrealist, and DADA movements.

Leiris was first introduced to surrealism by his close friend André Masson. He focused for a time on writing poetry in the surrealist fashion but by the 1920s abandoned the movement. With GEORGES BATAILLE and others, Leiris formed the Collège de Sociologie. Leiris had an abiding interest in the cultures of Central America, Africa, and the Caribbean, and the college formed a launching point for his extensive fieldwork in Ethiopia and the Sudan. Many of his writings come from his experiences there, including *L'Afrique fantôme* (1933), a travel account of his voyages.

Leiris's other writings include a four-volume autobiography, *La règle du jeu,* the first volume of which was originally published in English as *Manhood.* The entire work was eventually translated and titled *Rules of the Game.* He also wrote a detailed biography of Francis Bacon and conducted several anthropological studies.

Leiris lived out his life in Paris with his wife, the owner of Galerie Louise Leiris, a prominent art institution of the postwar era. It is because of her interest in the arts that Leiris also wrote extensively on the modern artists of the period, such as Miró, Giacometti, Bacon, Lam, and Duchamp.

Other Works by Michel Leiris

Aurora: A Novel. Translated by Anna Warby. London: Atlas, 1990.

Broken Branches. Translated by Lydia Davis. San Francisco: North Point Press, 1989.

Nights as Day, Days as Night. Translated by Richard Sieburth. New York: Rizzoli, 1988.

Rules of the Game. Translated by Lydia Davis. Baltimore: Johns Hopkins University Press, 1997.

A Work about Michel Leiris

Hand, Sean. *Michel Leiris: Writing the Self.* New York: Cambridge University Press, 2002.

Leopardi, Giacomo (1798–1837) *poet, essayist, philosopher*

Giacomo Leopardi was born in Recanti, now Marche, Italy, to Count Monaldo Leopardi and Marchesa Adelaide Antici. His upbringing was so sequestered that he was 20 years old before he left his home unaccompanied. Leopardi was a precocious youth and at 12 had surpassed the educational level of his tutors. He was a bibliophile and a polyglot who learned seven languages, including, Greek, Latin, and German. As a young man, he made translations and wrote commentary on the classics and at age 15 produced his first book, *History of Astronomy.* Although he grappled with blindness and a hunchback, his passion for writing saw him through his maladies.

Leopardi's crowning masterpiece was the book of poetry *I canti* (1831). His poems were very personal statements of his life, loves, and loneliness. In his poem "To Italy," he states, "If but the gods be willing / Endure as long as your renown endures." In his poem "The Solitary Life," he strikes a more despairing note: "On earth, unhappy people find no friend / Or refuge left for them except cold steel."

Giacomo Leopardi is considered the greatest literary figure of 19th-century Italy for his poetry, essays, and translations. According to Leopardi's biographer J. H. Whitfield, no Italian poet aside from Dante has attracted such a circle of devoted admirers as Leopardi. Whitfield summarizes Leopardi's contribution to Italian literature: "[he] sees the poet as potentially a philosopher, and the philosopher as potentially a poet; and though it has been fashionable, especially in Italian criticism, to set the two as opposites, the marriage of the terms is most nearly achieved in the case of Leopardi."

Other Works by Giacomo Leopardi

The Canti: With a Selection of His Prose. Manchester, U.K.: Carcanet, 1998.

Leopardi: Selected Poems. Translated by Eamon Grennan. Princeton, N.J.: Princeton University Press, 1997.

Works about Giacomo Leopardi

Nisbet, Delia Fabbroni-Gianotti. *Heinrich Heine and Giacomo Leopardi: The Rhetoric of Midrash.* New York: Peter Lang, 2000.

Press, Lynne, and Pamela Williams. *Women and Feminine Images in Giacomo Leopardi.* Lewiston, N.Y.: Edwin Mellen Press, 1999.

Whitfield, J. H. *Giacomo Leopardi.* Oxford: Blackwell, 1954.

Lermontov, Mikhail (1814–1841) *poet, novelist*

Mikhail Yuryevich Lermontov was born in Moscow, Russia, to Yuri Lermontov, a retired army captain, and Maria Lermontov, a descendent of an aristocratic family. After the death of his mother in 1817, Lermontov was sent to his affluent grandmother, Elizabetha Stolypin. He received an excellent education from private tutors, and in 1827, he enrolled in a prestigious academy in Moscow that was sponsored by the royal family. Young Lermontov, surrounded by the most prominent intellectuals and writers in Russia, began to compose poetry in 1828. In 1830, he traveled with his grandmother to the family estate outside Moscow, where, in idyllic surroundings, he read intensively and wrote poetry.

Lermontov was heavily influenced by ROMAN-TICISM. George Gordon, Lord Byron (1788–1824) and ALEKSANDR PUSHKIN were his favorite poets. After a few unsuccessful years at the Moscow University, Lermontov joined the army as a junior officer in 1832. After the death of Aleksandr Pushkin in a duel in 1835, Lermontov wrote a commemorative poem, "On the Death of the Poet," in which he suggested that the government had been involved in the scandal that led to the duel and may even have paid Pushkin's opponent. The poem was widely popular but was considered incendiary by the authorities. Lermontov was demoted and exiled to the Caucasus, an isolated, mountainous region of Russia. The material for most of Lermontov's prose came from his experiences in the Caucasus. Lermontov composed a heroic poem, "The Song of the Merchant Kalashnikov" (1837), about a man whose heroism consists in following his inner principles rather than the pressures of society. Lermontov returned to St. Petersburg in 1838, after his grandmother made numerous petitions on his behalf. In 1840, Lermontov was sent back to the Caucasus, as a punishment for dueling.

Lermontov enlisted in a regiment that was responsible for putting down a violent rebellion by Chechen forces. After receiving an award for bravery in combat, he was allowed to return to St. Petersburg in 1841. While in St. Petersburg, he published a collection of poems and completed *Demon* (1828–41), a long narrative poem about a love affair between a fallen angel and a mortal. The poem reveals Lermontov's aversion to religion and his love for rugged, primitive landscape.

Shortly before his death, Lermontov completed one of the greatest novels in Russian literature, *A Hero of Our Time* (1840). Based on Lermontov's experiences in the Caucasus, this classic work of psychological realism examines the psyche and emotions of the disenchanted aristocrat Pichorin.

Nearly all of Lermontov's works were critically acclaimed and widely popular during his lifetime, but his personal relationships were often turbulent and dramatic. He made many enemies during his short life, largely because of his cynical and, at times, cruel disposition. Like his hero Aleksandr Pushkin, Lermontov was shot and killed in a duel.

Lermontov's reputation as a poet is only second to Pushkin's in Russia. His stirring poetry is remarkable for its lyricism and for its skillful and ingenious use of metaphor. Lermontov made a dramatic contribution to the poetic tradition of Russia, revealing new ways in which the Russian language could be extended, molded, and shaped into a dramatic lyrical form. He is not very well known outside Russia because his poetry is extremely difficult to translate; today, however, he is recognized as one of the most influential and seminal figures of the Russian literary landscape.

Other Works by Mikhail Lermontov

A Hero of Our Time. Translated by Vladimir Nabokov. New York: Knopf, 1992.

Major Poetical Works. Translated by Anatoly Liberman. Minneapolis: University of Minnesota Press, 1984.

Works about Mikhail Lermontov

Garrard, John. *Mikhail Lermontov.* Boston: Twayne, 1982.

Golstein, Vladimir B. *Heroes of Their Times: Lermontov's Representation of the Heroic Self.* New Haven, Conn.: Yale University Press, 1992.

Levi, Carlo (1902–1975) *journalist, novelist, painter, sculptor*

A multitalented man best known for his antifascist memoir, *Christo si è fermato a Eboli* (*Christ Stopped at Eboli,* 1945), Carlo Levi was born in Turin, Italy, on November 29, 1902. His parents were assimilated, affluent Italian Jews, Ercole Levi and Annetta Treves; the father a prominent physician and the mother the sister of Claudio Treves, a leader of the Italian Socialist Party.

In 1917, Levi graduated from Liceo Alfieri, a prestigious preparatory school, and began his studies at the University of Turin, where he received a medical degree in 1924. Although trained as a doctor, he never formally practiced medicine (although his memoirs record his treatment of various patients in France and in southern Italy), because he pursued other interests, chiefly painting and politics. He exhibited his art first in 1923 in the expressionist exhibition "Six Painters of Turin."

Levi's college years were dominated by the rise to power of the fascist dictator Benito Mussolini. Levi's Jewish background and family's involvement in Socialist Party politics (his uncle was one of Mussolini's rivals) led him toward antifascism, opposing the anti-Semitism, fear, and intimidation carried out by Mussolini and his squads of armed henchmen known as Blackshirts. Traveling in artistic, intellectual, and political circles that opposed the rising tide of Italian fascism, Levi began to cultivate connections between his aesthetics and his politics. Indeed, as Stanislao G. Pugliese has noted, Levi connected painting and antifascism in his belief that new art forms must be developed in order to counter the Italian culture that had produced and promoted fascism.

In 1924, Levi went to Paris, ostensibly to conduct postgraduate medical research, but soon circulating in Parisian artistic circles. There he was exposed to the work of the Fauvists, an early avant-garde movement characterized by the use of vivid, nonnaturalistic color and form, and Postimpressionist painters such as Amedeo Modigliani and Giorgio de Chirico. Soon Levi began regularly exhibiting his paintings at the Venice Biennale (a room was designated exclusively for his work in 1954). In Paris Levi forged friendships with Russian composers Igor Stravinsky and Sergei Prokofiev and a large circle of European intellectuals, all the while continuing to develop his intellectual and artistic resistance to fascism. He lived in Paris from 1924–28 and again from 1932–34.

During the early 1930s, Levi was active in political opposition and journalism, contributing to Giustizia e Libertà (Justice and Liberty), an antifascist movement that he founded with the Rosselli brothers. He served as coeditor of an underground publication, Lotta politica (Political struggle). In April 1935, Levi was arrested by the Italian state for his antifascist activities and his opposition to the mobilization of Italian troops in the prelude to the Italo-Abyssinian War (1935–36) and sentenced to "internal exile." He was placed under surveillance in the small town of Aliano in Lucania, a remote, impoverished area of southern Italy. The two-year experience further radicalized Levi and brought him into contact with a rural peasantry and way of life wholly alien to the sophisticated urban world of Turin and Paris. The record of this experience would become Christ Stopped at Eboli, the work that in the years after World War II would catapult Levi to international renown, a fame he would not duplicate with any of his many, varied subsequent works.

In 1937, Levi returned to Turin and learned of the assassination in France of the Rosselli brothers and in response painted the "Autoritratto con la camicia insanguinata" ("Self-portrait with a Bloody Shirt"). He worked as a set designer and art director on Aldo Vergano's film, Pietro Micca. After his release from exile, Levi again moved to France. While living there he wrote the essay "Paura della libertà" ("Fear of Freedom," 1946), in which he saw the sources of the looming global conflict evolve out of fear and in a turning away from moral and spiritual autonomy. He returned to Italy in 1941, establishing himself in Florence, only to be arrested again on political charges in 1943. He was incarcerated at Le Murate prison until Mussolini was deposed in the summer of that same year. During these years, he worked as coeditor of La Nazione del Popolo, the publication of the Tuscan Committee of National Liberation (CTLN), a wing of the Italian resistance to German occupation, and as editor of the Action Party's L'Italia Libera.

The appearance of Christ Stopped at Eboli, Levi's memoir about his banishment to Lucania, a barren region just north of the arch of the Italian boot, transformed his life and made him famous. The title derives from a local saying meant to express the idea that Lucania was pagan and bereft of culture and that Christianity and humanism in general never reached Lucania but stopped nearer to civilization in the town of Eboli.

With fame, other works followed. His essays written during the war were collected in *Of Fear and Freedom* (1946) and in *L'orologio* (*The Watch*, 1950), a quasi-fictional account set in Rome in 1946 at a political moment between the fall of the Mussolini and the fall of Ferruccio Parri, when the last cabinet of "men of the Resistance" yielded power to the first Alcide De Gasperi government. As a leftist, Levi viewed the De Gasperi administration, which was a coalition government led by the centrist Christian Democratic Party, as a wrongheaded compromise of the ideals of the antifascist resistance movement. This was a moment in which the novelist's voice—a voice that more or less coincides with the political views of Levi himself—lamented at how the potential for radical reform was exchanged for politics as usual. *The Watch* has been called a novel, but as all of Levi's writing is formally unstable it is more accurately, as one reviewer observed, "a narrative mural." Like Levi, the protagonist of *The Watch* is employed by a Roman newspaper, and this affords the novelist an opportunity to present a panoramic tableau of high and low in postwar Italy, populated with political idealists, blackmarketers, beggars, and literati.

Levi led an active political life as well, serving in the Italian senate from 1963 to 1972 as an independent parliamentary deputy on the Communist Party list. He died at age 72 in early January 1975.

Critical Analysis

In *Christ Stopped at Eboli,* Levi vividly depicted the desolate clay wasteland village of Gagliano (his fictional name for Aliano), with its malaria-ridden, one-room huts in which humans and farm animals shared living quarters. He discovered a largely pagan society, preoccupied with goat-devils and werewolves, structured to keep its inhabitants debt-ridden and trapped in grinding poverty. Levi's northern Italian sensibilities were shocked by what he saw, and he concluded that Italy consisted of two civilizations: one peasant and essentially pre-Christian, the other post-Christian and essentially statist (corrupted by statism, the practice or doctrine of giving a centralized government control over economic planning and policy). The publication of this work brought before the Italian public the economic, medical, and social impoverishment of the people of Lucania as no one had before and propelled Levi to national and then international prominence as a spokesperson for the commitment to modernize the lives and communities of southern Italy by providing them the autonomy to take control of their lives.

Christ Stopped at Eboli resonated throughout Europe and especially in the United States where Depression-era documentaries and documentary-style fiction about the dust bowl and Southern sharecropping (such as John Steinbeck's *The Grapes of Wrath*) had already gained social and literary currency. Like neorealist cinema exemplified by Roberto Rossellini's *Rome, Open City* (1945), the lightly fictionalized *Christ Stopped at Eboli* (while not as violent) offered an unsentimental but lyrical and compassionate portrait of ordinary people struggling to scratch out a living against overwhelming odds. For many Americans in the late 1940s, Levi—not really much of a novelist—came to represent the voice of contemporary Italian literature, so much so that one 1949 review of modern Italian novelists began, "Despite the current American impression, contemporary Italian literature does not begin with Carlo Levi."

Other Works by Carlo Levi

The Linden Trees: A Narrative of Travel in Germany. Translated by Joseph M. Bernstein. New York: Alfred A. Knopf, 1962.

Words Are Stones: Impressions of Sicily. Translated by Angus Davidson. New York: Farrar, Straus & Cudahy, 1958.

Works about Carlo Levi

Baldassaro, Lawrence. *Carlo Levi* (*New Directions in European Writing*). Oxford: Berg Publishers, 1997.

Ward, David. *Antifascisms: Cultural Politics in Italy, 1943–46: Benedetto Croce and the Liberals, Carlo*

Levi and the "Actionists." Cranbury, N.J.: Associated University Presses, 1996.

Levi, Primo (1919–1987) *novelist, nonfiction writer*

Best known for his autobiographical *If This Is a Man* (1947), an account of survival in a Nazi concentration camp, Primo Levi was born in 1919 to a middle-class Jewish family in Turin. Growing up under Benito Mussolini and his fascist, anti-Semitic regime, Levi learned little about his heritage. He was able to enter the University of Turin to study chemistry just before laws were enacted in 1938 to prohibit Jews from academic study. He graduated in 1941 at the top of his class, one year after Italy allied with Germany during World War II.

During the war, Levi began to write articles for *Giustizia e Liberata,* a resistance magazine. He was captured in December 1943 while attempting to make contact with a partisan group in northern Italy. He was first interred at a transitional camp in Fossoli but was soon deported to the major concentration camp at Auschwitz. Traveling to the camp in a convoy of 650 prisoners, he was one of only 24 survivors. Forced to work in one of the laboratories, he was spared the gas chambers but not the memory of those around him who did not survive.

After the camp was liberated by the Soviets in 1945, Levi returned to Turin where he secured work as a chemist. He returned to his family's old manor home and began to write. *If This Is a Man* was written in the form of a memoir documenting his internment at Auschwitz. Although the subject matter was gruesome and intense, part of Levi's appeal was his ability to abstract himself from his surroundings and take on the role of an objective, scientific observer. The work was not without compassion, but neither did it seek to capitalize on the tragedy of life in a concentration camp. The book was an instant success, selling more than a half-million copies in Italy before being translated into eight languages as well as being adapted for radio broadcast and theatrical production.

A sequel to the book, *The Truce* (1963), detailed Levi's eight months spent wandering the remains of a war-torn Europe immediately after his liberation. The focus of the work is the difficulty a survivor faces when he or she is allowed to return, after great trauma, to a normal life.

By 1961, Levi had become the general manager of a paint factory, which enabled him to save enough money to retire in 1977 and devote himself full time to his writing. All of his works are in some way autobiographical. *The Periodic Table* (1975) uses the elements as a background; each element represents an event that is then recorded in memoir form as a meditation on the past. In all, the work is comprised of 21 separate entries, ranging from his encounter with an official from Auschwitz to a homage to his Jewish heritage. *If Not Now, When* (1989) focuses on the emerging sense of Jewish pride, coupled with an historical account of Russian action against the Nazis.

Levi's final work, *The Drowned and the Saved* (1986), is a collection of essays relating the ever-present memory of the Holocaust to the fact that anti-Semitism still exists even though the war is over. It was published one year prior to Levi's death, an apparent suicide. He struggled for much of the last 40 years of his life to reconcile the fact that he had survived life in a concentration camp.

Levi's greatest contribution to world literature is the legacy he left behind. His works give great insight into the life of a Jew and a survivor.

Another Work by Primo Levi

The Voice of Memory: Interviews, 1961–1987. Translated by Robert Gordon. New York: New Press, 2001.

A Work about Primo Levi

Kremer, Roberta S., ed. *Memory and Mastery: Primo Levi as Writer and Witness.* Albany: State University of New York Press, 2001.

Li Feigan

See BA JIN.

Lim, Shirley Geok-Lin (1944–   ) *novelist, poet*

Shirley Geok-Lin Lim was born in historic Malacca, a small town on the west coast of Malaysia. Lim's childhood was marked by feelings of abandonment, deprivation, and suffering, caused by her mother's abandoning her and her five brothers when they were still young. As the only girl in the family, Lim often felt neglected and marginalized; she nevertheless completed her high school education in a Catholic convent and went on to the University of Malaya. She taught for two years before going to the United States to obtain graduate degrees at Brandeis University in Massachusetts. Lim taught briefly at Westchester College before moving to Santa Barbara in 1990. She is currently professor of English and Women's Studies at the University of California and was professor of English and head of the English Department at the University of Hong Kong.

Lim is an animated writer who is able to draw on her rich cultural origins and experience to elevate her poetry and prose. Her writings bespeak the emotional longing she holds for her homeland, even as they dramatize her grappling with issues of ethnicity, gender, and identity as an Asian American living in the United States. In her poem, "Bukit China" (Malay name for "Chinese Hill") (1994), for example, Lim examines the theme of displacement and loss as experienced by her Chinese forefathers who crossed the South China Sea in the distant past to seek fortune in the reputedly rich "Southern Ocean" in Southeast Asia. Issues of ethnicity and identity are most poignantly expressed in her collection *Life's Mysteries: The Best of Shirley Lim* (1995). In one poem in the collection, "A Pot of Rice," Su Yu reaffirms her own identity as she cooks a pot of rice in her New York apartment to offer to her dead father. In another poem, "Transportation in Westchester," the subject of interracial relationships takes on a new shape when the Asian-American protagonist realizes her own prejudice through her interactions with African Americans.

Lim has received many awards, honors, and prizes for her critical and literary contributions. Her first book, *Crossing the Peninsula and Other Poems* (1980), won the Commonwealth Poetry Prize in 1980; a work she edited, *The Forbidden Stitch: An Asian-American Women's Anthology* (1989), was the recipient of the 1990 American Book Award.

Other Works by Shirley Geok-Lin Lim

Among the White Moon Faces: An Asian-American Memoir of Homelands. New York: The Feminist Press, 1996.

Another Country and Other Stories. Singapore: Times Books International, 1982.

Joss and Gold. New York: The Feminist Press, 2001.

Sister Swing. Tarrytown, N.Y.: Marshall Cavendish, 2006.

What the Fortune-Teller Didn't Say. Albuquerque, N. Mex.: West End Press, 1998.

Writing Southeast Asia in English: Against the Grain, Focus on Asian English Language Literature. London: Skoob Books Publications, 1994.

Lispector, Clarice (1920–1977) *novelist*

Clarice Lispector was born in Ukraine on December 10 but moved to Recife, Brazil, when she was only two months old and remained there for the rest of her life. Although it is likely that her parents, Ukrainian Jews, spoke Yiddish at home, she often denied it because she so strongly identified herself as Brazilian. The family later moved to Rio de Janeiro where she eventually completed her college studies. At the age of 23, she married her former classmate, Maury Gurgel Valente, who had become a diplomat. As a result of his career, they traveled widely, allowing her the opportunity for many new experiences, which certainly contributed to her career as a writer.

One year after her marriage, Lispector published her first novel, *Near to the Wild Heart.* The book was very well received, and she wrote several novels throughout her lifetime, including among the best-known, *Family Ties* and *The*

Passion of G.H. In addition she wrote short stories. Her final book, a short novel, *The Hour of the Star,* recounts the life story of a poor Brazilian girl and considers the issues of otherness and understanding.

Lispector's work has been more popularized outside of Brazil than that of many other female Brazilian authors who remain mostly unknown in the United States. This is largely because of HÉLÈNE CIXOUS, a French writer who is currently a university professor in the United States. She has written several books of criticism and even a novel inspired by Clarice Lispector's work. Lispector's novels tend to concern family relationships, moral uncertainty, and social isolation that so many 20th-century novelists have focused on. Lispector died in Rio de Janeiro, Brazil, on December 9, 1977, one day short of her 57th birthday, having made extraordinary contributions to Brazilian literature.

Another Work by Clarice Lispector
Family Ties. Arlington: The University of Texas Press, 1972.

Works about Clarice Lispector
Cixous, Hélène. *Reading with Clarice Lispector.* Minneapolis: University of Minnesota Press, 1990.

Moser, Benjamin. *Why This World: A Biography of Clarice Lispector.* New York: Oxford, 2009.

Peixoto, Marta. *Passionate Fictions: Gender, Narrative, and Violence in Clarice Lispector.* Minneapolis: University of Minnesota Press, 1994.

Liu E (Liu Tieh Yun) (1857–1909) *poet, novelist*
Liu E was born the son of a scholar official in Liuhe in the Jiangsu Province. He was a good student with diverse interests and was very open to new ideas. He worked variously as a doctor, a merchant, and a government administrator, in addition to writing. He had friends in high places but was also adaptive to Western influ-

ences during the late Qing (Ch'ing) dynasty when China was especially guarded against them. This would ultimately damage his career and reputation.

Liu E wrote and published poetry and fiction throughout his life but is known primarily for writing one of the first Chinese novels in a vernacular language, *The Travels of Lao Can (Ts'an).* As a serial that began publication in 1903, and as a complete book in 1907, it is considered to be one of the first modern novels because of its accessible vernacular language and its satiric and pointed critique of official corruption. The novel opens with the title character Lao Can's allegorical dream that equates China with a leaking, sinking ship. Lao Can offers potential solutions in his dream, including the use of new technical instruments and other Western innovations. After the dream ends, the novel then follows Lao Can, an itinerant and eccentric doctor, on his travels through the country. Inspired by his dream to effect change, Lao Can encounters cruel officials who are insensible to the plight of the Chinese people and closed to the possibility of improvements.

Liu E suffered at the hands of official corruption himself, and the parallels to Lao Can are many; in fact, many of the officials in the novel bear names very similar to Liu E's own colleagues. When Liu E suggested building a railway in the city of Zhili, he was attacked by conservative officials. Eventually, in 1908, he was banished to Xinjiang, China's western barren lands, for associating with foreign merchants during the Boxer Rebellion. He died in exile.

A Work about Liu E
Holoch, Donald. "The Travels of Laocan: Allegorical Narrative." In M. Dolezelova-Velingerova, ed., *The Chinese Novel at the Turn of the Century.* Toronto: University of Toronto Press, 1980.

Lorca, Federico García
See GARCÍA LORCA, FEDERICO.

Lu Xun (Lu Hsün; Zhou Shuren) (1881–1936) *short story writer, essayist*

Zhou Shuren, who adopted the pen name Lu Xun, was born September 25 into a family of declining social status in Shaoxing, Zhejiang Province. His grandfather directed his schooling, which was less rigid than a traditional education. By age 11, he was an avid reader of popular literature and nonfiction but lacked interest in classical Confucian texts.

In 1893, when Zhou Shuren's grandfather was charged for taking bribes in the examination system and imprisoned, he went to live with his mother's family. He was deeply affected by the shift from a wealthy lifestyle to a poor one, later writing that it illuminated his understanding of the world.

In 1902, Zhou Shuren moved to Japan. Eager to better the conditions of China's people, he studied medicine at Sendai Medical College but maintained interests in literature and philosophy and read Western publications. He was especially influenced by Russian writers such as GOGOL and CHEKHOV. However, when he watched a newsreel from the Russo-Japanese War of 1904–05 of a captured Chinese spy being tortured, he changed his course of study; the inhumanity in the footage affected Lu Xun deeply. Subsequently, he participated in democratic and nationalistic activities and focused on writing as a means to effect social change, believing that literature would uplift the collective Chinese "spirit."

While still in Tokyo, Lu Xun edited the journal *New Life* and published essays in the Communist journal *Henan* on Western philosophy, sometimes collaborating with his brother, the writer Zhou Zuoren. In 1909, he returned to China and taught middle-school biology in Hangzhou and Shaoxing. After the Nationalist Revolution in 1911, Lu Xun accepted a position with the education ministry, where he studied and compiled Buddhist sutras. He began to publish poems and fiction in the popular journal *New Youth* in 1918, including "The Diary of a Madman," a short story about a man who suffers from paranoid delusions of the widespread practice of cannibalism. It is considered the first Chinese modernist short story because of its subjective,

first-person narrative. He also submitted "random essays" and "random thoughts," which were published as such in the magazine. He accepted a lectureship at National Beijing University in Chinese literature in 1919 but soon returned home to take care of personal matters. There, he was moved to write stories about the debilitating effects of the old Chinese way of life on conditions in his hometown.

By 1921, back in Beijing and teaching at Beijing Normal University, he became established as a fiction writer and one of the leading writers of the May Fourth Movement, with more than 50 stories published in *New Youth*. He also wrote his first collections of stories, *The Outcry* (1923) and *Hesitation* (1926). The stories in these collections were inspired by the folk tales and myths of Lu Xun's childhood, but they were often dark and brooding. Perhaps his most famous work is the novella *The True Story of Ah Q* (1922), about a lonely laborer from a poor village. Despite failing at all his endeavors, Ah Q blindly interprets each failure as a victory and is eventually unfairly executed because of his foolishness. The story demonstrates Lu Xun's contempt for the similar myopia of Chinese society toward its sociopolitical and economic plight.

Lu Xun left Beijing in 1926 for Guangdong and Macau and often engaged in debates with the new breed of communist writers who advocated SOCIALIST-REALISM in literature. He grew disillusioned with the Nationalist Party and became a Communist in 1929. He was active as a founder of the League of Left-Wing Writers in 1930 but never joined the Communist Party itself. He turned to translating Soviet theory and attacking Nationalists, antileftists, and Western writers. He became one of the leading socialist intellectuals, teaching at various universities, including Xiamen and Zhongsan, and editing numerous journals, including *Wilderness, Tattler,* and *Torrent.* Even when he contracted pulmonary tuberculosis in 1933, he continued to contribute articles on a near-daily basis to the newspaper *Shen Pao.* He died on October 19, 1936, in Shanghai. At his funeral, he was eulogized as the "national soul," and the Communist

Party canonized him posthumously. Today, he is revered as one of China's greatest writers whose contributions to modernism and communist literature are held up as the highest literary ideals.

Other Works by Lu Xun

Call to Arms (Chinese/English Edition). Beijing: Foreign Language Press, 2000.

Diary of a Madman and Other Stories. Translated by William Lyell. Honolulu: University of Hawaii Press, 1990.

Lu Xun: Selected Poems. Translated by W. J. F. Jenner. Beijing: Foreign Languages Press, 1982.

Selected Stories of Lu Xun (Chinese/English Edition). Beijing: Foreign Language Press, 2000.

Works about Lu Xun

Lee, Leo Ou-fan. *Voices from the Iron House: A Study of Lu Xun.* Bloomington: Indiana University Press, 1987.

Lyell, William A. *Lu Hsun's Vision of Reality.* Berkeley: University of California Press, 1976.

Machado de Assis, Joaquim Maria
(1839–1908) *short story writer*

Machado de Assis was born in Rio de Janeiro, Brazil, on June 21. The son of a mulatto father and a white mother, Machado de Assis's racial background has often been remarked upon. He lost his mother when he was very young and became extremely attached to his stepmother, who encouraged his education and put him through public school. After his father died in 1851, she accepted a job in a local college, and Machado de Assis was forced to leave school and work, but it is likely that he continued attending some classes intermittently at her place of employment. Machado de Assis published his first poem, "Ela," in a journal at age 16, thus beginning a long and prolific literary career. He became one of the most important Brazilian literary figure of the second half of the 19th century.

Machado de Assis published 200 short stories in newspapers and magazines and chose 68 to be published in anthologies. Many critics consider him to be the master of the Brazilian short story, and his influence on other writers has been widespread. In his short stories, he takes up many themes from Brazilian life and also addresses various areas of the human psyche; for example, in "The Fortune-teller," published in a collection titled *Various Stories,* from 1897, he writes about the question of destiny. The story tells about three friends: a couple and their single male friend. The wife and the male friend are having an affair, and they are afraid the husband may have found out. Each goes separately to see a fortune-teller about their destiny, with surprising results. In an earlier story, "The Mirror," from an 1882 collection, he writes about the interior and exterior life of one man. The story is told in the first person; the main character recounts the process of his realization that all humans are actually two people. The person we are inside is not the person we dress in the mirror. His narrative is psychologically compelling, again with a startling finish. Although Machado de Assis rarely touches on the issue of race in his stories (something for which GILBERTO FREYRE criticized him, stating that his style was too Europeanized), he does treat the question of slavery in some of his short stories. Brazil was the last country in the Northern Hemisphere to abolish slavery in 1888, so this was a public question that marked the author's lifetime. In an 1899 collection of short stories, Machado de Assis published the story "Father against Mother" that examines the struggle between a poor man and a mulatto slave woman. He and his wife will be forced to give up their baby because of lack of finances if he cannot raise money. He is a slave catcher by profession. At the last moment, he sees a mulatto slave woman whose reward price is very high. However, she is pregnant and begs him not to take her back. In the conclusion, he is forced to make a difficult choice in this ethical dilemma.

Machado de Assis was friendly with many great literary figures of his day. He enjoyed meeting with these friends and discussing intellectual issues. From this, came the idea of founding the Brazilian Academy of Letters. He and his circle of peers founded the academy in 1897. At the initial meeting, they elected him as the academy's first president, a position he held until his death. Because of his great importance to Brazilian literature, the Brazilian Academy of Letters is also called the House of Machado de Assis.

Other Works by Joaquin Maria Machado de Assis

The Devil's Church and Other Stories. Arlington: University of Texas Press, 1977.
The Posthumous Memoirs of Brás Cubas. New York: Oxford University Press, 1997.

A Work about Joaquin Maria Machado de Assis

Schwarz, Roberto. *Misplaced Ideas: Essays on Brazilian Culture.* New York: Verso, 1992.

Machado y Ruiz, Antonio (1875–1939)
poet

Born in Seville, Spain, the son of liberal intellectuals, Antonio Machado y Ruiz became a French teacher and lived in the province of Castile, where he found the somewhat stark landscape more in keeping with his seriousness than that of Andalusia, the more verdant province of his birth. His poems portray the sober, dramatic Castilian landscape, and it is its nature that guides him. Machado, like JUAN RAMÓN JIMÉNEZ, was a member of the GENERATION OF 1898, a group of writers who sought a moral and cultural rebirth for Spain. They analyzed the problems of the

social framework of Spain and prescribed cures. A fondness for simplicity and landscape characterizes Machado's work. With his brother, the poet Manuel Machado (1874–1947), he also wrote plays.

Machado attended the Institución Libre de Enseñanza, considered the best learning institution of its kind in Spain at that time. The education he received there had a profound influence on his work. There, he developed his love of nature and adopted tolerance, respect, patriotism, and austerity as his way of life.

In 1888, he and his brother began to attend theater, befriending actors and even doing a little acting. In 1893 his father died. The subsequent death of his grandfather left the family in a precarious financial situation and interrupted Machado's education. He then tried unsuccessfully to work in a bank and, in 1898, moved with his brother to Seville, where he began to write poetry.

The principal influences on his poetry were Juan Ramón Jiménez, GUSTAVO ADOLFO BÉCQUER, and ROSALÍA DE CASTRO. In his first book of poems, *Soledades* (1903), the poet searches for himself in time, in love, and in death. An important theme in all his work is time, something that he perceives as alive and personal. He often searches for love and lost youth.

Machado was forced to leave Spain in 1936 because of his political beliefs. He crossed the Pyrenees on foot and died a month later in France.

Other Works by Antonio Machado y Ruiz

Barnstone, Willis S., ed. and trans. *Six Masters of the Spanish Sonnet: Francisco de Quevedo, Sor Juana Inés de la Cruz, Antonio Machado, Federico García Lorca, Jorge Luis Borges, and Miguel Hernández.* Carbondale: Southern Illinois University Press, 1993.
The Landscape of Soria. Translated by Dennis Maloney. Fredonia, N.Y.: White Pine Press, 1985.
Trueblood, Alan S., ed. *Antonio Machado: Selected Poems.* Cambridge, Mass.: Harvard University Press, 1988.

Works about Antonio Machado y Ruiz

Cobb, Carl. *Antonio Machado.* Boston: Twayne, 1971.

Johnston, Philip G. *The Power of Paradox in the Work of Spanish Poet Antonio Machado.* Lewiston, N.Y.: Edwin Mellen Press, 2002.

Machado y Ruiz, Manuel (1874–1947)
poet, playwright, critic

Manuel Machado y Ruiz was born in Seville, Spain. His family were prominent and wealthy members of the city's middle class. His grandfather was a university professor and an expert in Spanish music and folklore. The Arabic inflections of Seville and his grandfather's studies of folk traditions led Machado y Ruiz to emphasize Arab imagery in his poetry.

Though he published few poems, he was one of the central figures of Spanish MODERNISM. His poetry resembles the work of RUBÉN DARÍO, the key figure of Latin American Modernism, but with more emphasis on the cultivation of aesthetic pleasure and less on inner anguish.

Machado y Ruiz was a member of the GENERATION OF 1898 and, like other members of that movement, he was concerned with revitalizing Spain's national identity. He believed this would be achieved by celebrating Spain's inner Arab spirit, which had been repressed by hundreds of years of Catholic rule.

His use of symbolism shows a clear influence of the poet VERLAINE, whose works he read when he was a young man studying in Paris. By combining modern trends from Europe and Spanish folk traditions, Machado y Ruiz was a forerunner to the poet GARCÍA LORCA.

Machado y Ruiz also modernized a number of plays by the Spanish dramatist Lope de Vega in collaboration with his brother ANTONIO MACHADO Y RUIZ. Machado y Ruiz had a sophisticated literary sensibility, and his literary style influenced lyric poetry in Spain and the world into the 20th century.

A Work about Manuel Machado y Ruiz

Brotherston, Gordon. *Manuel Machado: A Revaluation.* Cambridge: Cambridge University Press, 1968.

Madariaga, Salvador de (1886–1978)
historian, essayist

Born in La Coruña, Spain, to a Spanish colonel, Madariaga held many jobs during his lifetime. He studied engineering in Paris and returned to his homeland to work for the Spanish railways. Then he went to London, was an editor for the *Times,* and wrote articles about World War I that were later published as *La guerra desde Londres* (*The War from London,* 1917).

In 1922, he was named head of the disarmament section of the League of Nations. He taught at Oxford (1928–31) and then was Spanish ambassador to the United States and France. He resigned in 1936 but did not participate in the Spanish civil war (1936–39). In disagreement with the Spanish dictator, Generalísimo Francisco Franco, he never returned to Spain while Franco was in power. During World War II, he worked for the BBC, broadcasting in Spanish, French, and German to Europe. He visited Spain in 1976 and was received into the Academia Española 40 years after his election into it, the ceremony having been postponed until after Franco's death.

Madariaga wrote in Spanish, French, and English. His works include historical works (biographies of Hernán Cortés, Columbus, and Simón Bolívar) and literary criticism (*Guía del lector del Quijote,* 1926). In *Englishmen, Frenchmen, Spaniards* (1928), he comments on national characteristics. His book *España* (1930) is an important historical interpretation of Spain and exemplifies Madariaga's ambition to familiarize the rest of the world with Spain.

Other Works by Salvador de Madariaga

Anarchy or Hierarchy. New York: Macmillan, 1978.

Don Quixote: An Introductory Essay in Psychology. Westport, Conn.: Greenwood, 1980.

Latin America between the Eagle and the Bear. Westport, Conn.: Greenwood, 1976.

A Work about Salvador de Madariaga

Preston, Paul. *Salvador de Madariaga and the Quest for Liberty in Spain.* Oxford: Clarendon Press, 1987.

Maeterlinck, Maurice (1862–1949) *poet, playwright, novelist, essayist*

Count Maurice-Polydore-Marie-Bernard Maeterlinck was born in Ghent, Belgium, to an affluent family. Educated at a Jesuit college, he originally studied to be a lawyer but practiced law only for a brief time before turning his interests and talents to writing.

During a trip to Paris, Maeterlinck came in contact with several members of the literary community, such as Villiers de l'Isle Adam, who became one of Maeterlinck's greatest literary influences. Maeterlinck eventually moved to Paris to pursue his writing career.

Although his later works were mostly dramatic in nature, his earliest published efforts were poetic, his first published work being the collection of poems *Ardent talons* (1889). He published his first play, *La princesse Maleine,* in 1899, and it was well received, particularly by Octave Mirbeau, the literary critic of *Le Figaro,* whose praise of the work transformed Maeterlinck into an almost overnight success.

Maeterlinck's works are characterized by symbolist (*see* SYMBOLISM) themes, including a concern with the metaphysical, mysticism, and an awareness of death. This is particularly evident in *The Intruder* (1890) and *The Blind* (1890). Even his ostensibly love-themed works such as *Pelléas et Mélisande* (1892), *Alladine et Palomides* (1894), and *Aglavaine et Sélysette* (1896) share this same bleak undertone, as do the works in which he developed his mystical ideas: *The Treasure of the Humble* (1896), *Wisdom and Destiny* (1898), and *The Buried Temple* (1902). Even some of Maeterlinck's later works, such as *Joyzelle* (1903) and *Marie Magdeleine* (1909), focus prevalently on death, but by World War I, he began to dwell on an almost fantasylike optimism. This optimism can be found in his play *The Burgomaster of Stilemonde* (1918). His *Oiseau bleu* (*The Blue Bird,* 1908), intended for children, also struck a positive note. His best-known play, however, is *Monna Vanna* (1902), set in an exotic 15th-century Pisa, which deals with a moral dilemma of a beautiful wife.

In 1911, Maeterlinck was awarded the Nobel Prize in literature. In his later years, he turned his attention to writing philosophical essays and, in 1932, was awarded the title of count in Belgium.

Another Work by Maurice Maeterlinck

The Life of the Bee. Translated by Alfred Sutro. New York: Dodd, Mead, 1970.

A Work about Maurice Maeterlinck

Knapp, Bettina. *Maurice Maeterlinck.* Boston: Twayne, 1975.

magic realism

Magic realism is a style of fiction writing that combines elements of fantasy and reality without any clear delineation between the two. Though elements of fantasy in literature can be found throughout history, it is the particular relationship between the fantastic and the real that characterizes magic realism's unique flavor. Though it had some precedent in European literature, particularly in the work of FRANZ KAFKA, magic realism was primarily developed in post–World War II Latin America.

The Latin-American literary ancestor of magic realism was JORGE LUIS BORGES, who used fantasy in his short stories as a means of exploring philosophical mysteries. In the 1960s, the generation after Borges—GABRIEL GARCÍA MÁRQUEZ, CARLOS FUENTES, MARIO VARGAS LLOSA, and ALEJO CARPENTIER, all important contributors to the development of the magical-realist style—came to the world's attention. It was clear there was a

Latin-American renaissance in progress and that magic realism would make an important contribution to world literature.

Critical Analysis

Magic realism demonstrates the presence of a hidden layer of reality behind the appearance of the natural world and human society. This effect is achieved both by presenting the incredible in a straightforward manner and by describing the commonplace as mysterious. Both Gabriel García Márquez and Alejo Carpentier have said that magic realism is an effect that is based not in fantasy but in Latin-American reality.

A humorous example of this can be found in García Márquez's novel *One Hundred Years of Solitude* (1967), in which a child is born with the tail of a pig. García Márquez chose this particular "stigma" specifically because of its unreality. The episode reinforces the carefully balanced themes of what is real versus the absurd and fantastic. After the book was published, people from all over Latin America came forward, admitting to having been born with a pig's tail. Having read *One Hundred Years of Solitude,* they realized that it was only natural and that they were no longer embarrassed to admit it. The outrageousness of the incident and the readers' reactions to it force readers to consider the absurdity in everyday life and society.

Many of the Latin-American magic-realist writers spent time in Europe, particularly France, and were exposed to surrealism and its use of the absurd. Though the influence of surrealism on magic realism is unquestionable, it is magic realism's relationship to truth that sets it apart. The surrealists used fantasy and absurdity to attack conventional ideas of reality; the magic realists created substitute ideas of reality in hope of coming closer to psychological and metaphysical truths.

In this way, the fantastic elements of magic realism take on the stature of myths. Myths, although not able to be proved by science or history, have a kind of accuracy about the nature and needs of humanity and the world. Because of their connection to some inner aspect of human consciousness, myths have a power beyond that of mere fantasy. Magic realism attempts to use this mythic force.

Another distinguishing feature of magic-realist novels is their relationship to history. Carlos Fuentes and Mario Vargas Llosa, as well as García Márquez and Carpentier, combine specific details of Latin-American history with fantastical elements in their works.

In *Terra nostra* (1975), Fuentes uses magic realism as a means to recount and analyze the history of Spain and Latin America. The book is unquestionably about the history of the Hispanic world, but the use of the fantastic allows Fuentes to give the events a sense of universality.

Vargas Llosa, however, embellishes history with fantasy for the purpose of making an ideological critique in a dramatic and nondidactic way. To a lesser degree, this is also García Márquez's strategy in *One Hundred Years of Solitude,* in which he combines the actual events of Columbian history with a mythical story of the imaginary town Macondo to critique Latin-American politics and U.S. imperialism. Perhaps it is this perfect synthesis of the two powers of magic realism that makes *One Hundred Years of Solitude* the generally acknowledged masterpiece of the genre.

Isabel Allende, though not one of the inventors of magic realism, adopted a style similar to García Márquez's. In her novel *The House of the Spirits* (1982), Allende uses magic realism to convey a feminist perspective on Latin-American history and culture. Some readers have even seen in Allende's novels a feminist critique of magic realism itself.

American writer Toni Morrison has also been called a magic realist. Her work, particularly her novel *Beloved* (1987), employs the characteristic use of the fantastic to reveal metaphysical truth and confront the historical injustice of slavery.

Magic realism, when it is most successful, goes beyond itself to penetrate into unrecognized truths. It engages history in a way that REALISM cannot. Realism, our sense of what is subjective and what is objective in reality, is, in a certain sense, determined by history. The extraordinary success of magic realism demonstrated, both in Latin America and throughout the world, that traditional realism, dominant into the 20th century, is no longer necessarily the best mode for expressing the drama of contemporary life.

Works about Magic Realism

Angulo, María-Elena. *Magic Realism: Social Context and Discourse.* New York: Garland, 1995.

Mellen, Joan. *Magic Realism.* Detroit: Gale Group, 2000.

Mahfouz, Naguib (1911–2006) *novelist*

Naguib Mahfouz was born in the al-Jamaliyyah district of Cairo, Egypt, the youngest child of a civil servant. When Mahfouz was six years old, his father moved the family to a more prosperous suburb. Mahfouz read extensively as a child. His father's wealth allowed him to acquire many translated books that were not part of his school curriculum. When the 1919 revolution in Egypt took place, Mahfouz was only eight years old. The revolution had broken out because the British colonial government prevented an Egyptian nationalist from traveling to the Versailles Conference to demand Egypt's independence. Despite Mahfouz's young age, he was greatly affected by the event, and he idolized the heroes of the revolution for their bravery and courage.

After completing his secondary education, Mahfouz studied philosophy at the University of Cairo. He was invited after his graduation to continue his studies in the master's program. By the 1930s, Mahfouz was writing articles about the intellectual ideas and issues of the time, such as the pursuit of science in conjunction with socialist ideology to foster a better future for Egypt and the replacement of the absolutist monarchic government with a social-democratic one. He eventually turned away from his university career and entered the civil service, where he remained until his retirement in 1971. His work gave him time to pursue his writing, which was his first love.

Throughout his writing career, Mahfouz continued to read avidly the works of many European and Russian writers such as ALBERT CAMUS, FYODOR DOSTOYEVSKY, LEO TOLSTOY, and MARCEL PROUST.

Mahfouz's writings were clearly affected by the turmoil caused by the political changes in Egypt. A supporter of the political revolution of the 1960s, Mahfouz found many kindred spirits in revolutionary movement of this time but was deeply disturbed by the methods activists employed to achieve their goals. He attempted to represent the spirit of the revolution and its ideals through his works. His stories bespeak the uncertainty of the 1960s, which peaked with the outbreak of the war between Egypt and Israel in 1967. The war signaled the final failure of the ideas and structures of the Egyptian government and also prompted many writers, including Mahfouz, to engage in more reflective writings.

In 1988, Mahfouz became the first Arab author to win the Nobel Prize in literature. The award recognized Mahfouz's contribution to developing the novel in the Arab literary world, but it also put Mahfouz and his family under intense scrutiny by the news media. His worsening health led him to seek medical care in London, and when he returned, he narrowly escaped an attempt on his life by a group of Islamic fundamentalists in 1994. Although he suffered a stab wound in the attack, he remained a faithful advocate of free expression. Mahfouz sustained a head injury in July 2006 and died in August of that year. On August 31, the Egyptian government granted him a full state funeral.

Critical Analysis

The early stage of Mahfouz's writing was marked by his deep concern with philosophical issues such as class struggle, identity, poverty, and colonial oppression. These themes are represented in his works of the 1940s and 1950s, such as *Kifah Tiba* (*Struggle at Thebes,* 1944), *Al-Qahirah al-jadidah* (*Modern Cairo,* 1946), and the Cairo Trilogy, *Al-Thulathiyya: Bayn al-Qasrayn* (*Palace Walk,* 1956), *Qasr al-Shawq* (*Palace of Desire,* 1957), and *Al-Sukkari-yya* (*Sugar Street,* 1957). In *Kifah Tiba,* he examines the significance of the country's early history during the time of its struggle for independence. By reflecting on the character and rash actions of the youthful pharaoh, Mahfouz was able to compare his pharaoh protagonist with the young King Farouk of Egypt. In *Al-Qahirah al-jadidah,* on the other hand, Mahfouz analyzes the lives of various characters whose continuous quest for better lives brings them into conflict with the dominant British colonial class. Themes such as the exploitation of the lower classes by the colonial rulers are further elaborated and portrayed in another of Mahfouz's novels, *Zuqaq al-Midaqq* (*Midaq Alley,* 1947).

In his early work, Mahfouz masterfully portrays the varied view of many different characters. In the Cairo Trilogy, a monumental work of 1,500 pages, he traces the major events of Egyptian history through his narrative about the 'Abd al-Jawwad family. He explicates a complex web of relationships set against the background of Egypt's bitter struggle against British colonialism. The novel examines complicated and fragile human relationships against the backdrop of major political events such as the political revolution of 1919. It also explores important themes, such as generational differences, tradition versus modernity, and sexual equality. Mahfouz's protagonists continued to find their own identities as they faced and reacted to the changes of the times. In a certain way, Mahfouz's life was a reflection of this haplessness of humanity to change.

In the second phase of Mahfouz's literary career, he became more outspoken, especially when expressing his political views. This stage was clearly influenced by his reaction to the political events from the 1960s to the 1980s. Between 1961 and 1967, he published six novels, in which he began to enhance his narration to convey the complexities and urgency of colonial oppression and the disillusionment that accompanied this period of chaos and disorder. He also began to write from the point of view of the protagonists of his stories. In tersely realistic style, he expressed his characters' emotional estrangement from their peers and their community. As a result, his explicitness brought a new dimension to Mahfouz's stories. He was able to showcase his talent in creating a variety of human characters with varied and complex personalities and points of view. In *Miramar* (1967), for example, Mahfouz conjures a setting in which characters from different occupational backgrounds and age groups come together. The story focuses on the character of Zahra, a lovely peasant girl who exudes innocence, simplicity, and optimism. Zahra personifies the optimism of Egypt in the postwar period, which is marred by the harsh reality of corruption and vice that leads to the suicide of one main character and the continuous impoverishment of the others.

Mahfouz's works reflect his personality and his experiences in Egypt where he spent most of his life. His concern with the human condition and other philosophical issues clearly influenced his writings. The major themes in his works include the constant human need for acceptance and solace, the vicious cycle of social oppression from which the poor could never escape, and the irreconcilable differences between the ideologies of the upper and lower classes. Even though Mahfouz wrote of the struggle and suffering of the poor, his stories are mostly narratives of the urban middle class, especially the lives and problems of intellectuals. In addition, Mahfouz's middle-class background and his long-term residence in cities gave him the experience and knowledge with which to create familiar settings.

Other Works by Naguib Mahfouz

Akenaten. New York: Anchor, 2000.
Arabian Nights and Days. Translated by Denys Johnson-Davies. New York: Doubleday, 1995.
The Beggar. Translated by Kristin Walker Henry and Nariman Khales Naili al Warrah. Cairo: American University in Cairo Press, 1986.
Children of the Alley. Translated by Peter Theroux. New York: Doubleday, 1996.

The Thief and the Dogs. Translated by Trevor Le Gassick and Mustafa Badawi. Cairo: American University in Cairo Press, 1984.

The Time and the Place. Translated by Denys Johnson-Davies. New York: Doubleday, 1991.

Works about Naguib Mahfouz

Gordon, Haim. *Naguib Mahfouz's Egypt: Existential Themes in his Writings.* Westport, Conn.: Greenwood Press, 1990.

Le Gassick, Trevor, ed. *Critical Perspectives on Naguib Mahfouz.* Washington, D.C.: Three Continents Press, 1991.

Peled, Mattityahu. *Religion My Own: The Literary Works of Naguib Mahfouz.* New Brunswick, N.J.: Transaction Books, 1983.

Somekh, Sasson. *The Changing Rhythm: A Study of Naguib Mahfouz's Novels.* Leiden, The Netherlands: Brill, 1973.

Maillet, Antonine (1929–) *poet, playwright, novelist*

Antonine Maillet was born in the Acadian community of Bouctouche, New Brunswick. Her work often draws on her Acadian upbringing and employs a particular Acadian dialect. In 1950, she received a B.A. from the University of Moncton and, nine years later, completed an M.A. She continued her studies at Laval, earning a Ph.D. in literature in 1970. She taught literature and folklore, first at Laval and then at Montreal. She also worked for Radio-Canada in Moncton as a scriptwriter and host. She is currently a chancellor of the University of Moncton.

While in school, Maillet worked on her writing, producing her first play, *Poire-acre,* in 1958. That same year, her first novel, *Pointe-aux-Coques* was published. Since that time, she has published close to 50 novels, plays, and poems and has become one of the most important living French-Canadian writers. Her novel *The Tale of Don L'Original* (1972) won the Governor General's Award for Fiction. In 1979, Maillet became the only Canadian author to win France's most prestigious literary award, the Prix Goncourt, for her novel *Pélagie-la-Charette* (1979), a historical novel about the British army's destruction of Acadian settlements in 1755.

Other Works by Antonine Maillet

The Devil Is Loose! New York: Walker & Co., 1987.

La Sagouine. Translated by Wayne Grady. Fredericton, New Brunswick, Canada: Goose Lane Editions, 2007.

Works about Antonine Maillet

Aresu, Bernard. "Pélagie la Charrette and Antonine Maillet's Epic Voices." In Makoto Ueda, ed., *Explorations: Essays in Comparative Literature.* Lanham, Md.: University Press of America, 1986.

Briere, Eloise A. "Antonine Maillet and the Construction of Acadian Identity." *Postcolonial Subjects: Francophone Women Writers.* Edited by Mary Jean Green et al. Minneapolis: University of Minnesota Press, 1996, 3–21.

Maláika, Nazik al- (1923–2007) *poet, critic*

Al-Mala'ika was born in Baghdad to a literary family; her mother was a nationalist poet in the independence movement against British rule. She earned a B.A. in Arabic at the Teacher's Training College, Baghdad (1944), and an M.A. in comparative literature from the University of Wisconsin (1956). With her husband, she helped found the University of Basra in Iraq. Al-Mala'ika taught at the University of Kuwait from 1970 to 1982 and thereafter lived in Iraq until living conditions, affected by the Gulf War (1991), deteriorated so much that she could not maintain her health, so she moved to Cairo.

Al-Mala'ika's literary criticism and poetry helped to break the hold of traditional forms on modern Arabic poetry. Her first collection, *Ashiqat al-lail* ("Lover of night," 1947) offered poetry of highly sensitive emotion, idealism, despair, and disillusion, themes typically associated with Arabic literary romanticism of the 1930s and 1940s. In the introduction to her second collection,

Shazaya wa ramad ("Shards and ashes," 1949) she suggests a break with the centuries-old rhyme patterns of Arabic poetry and proposes that the "poetic foot" be cut loose from the two-hemistitch verse form that has anchored Arabic poetry since its beginnings. Her belief is that this form and the poetic conventions associated with it have come to inhibit rather than spur creativity. *Shazaya wa ramad* and subsequent poetry collections depart from traditional forms. "Cholera" was her first poem to demonstrate what is considered, in Arabic literature, to be "free verse." Her 1962 book of literary criticism *Qadaya al-shi'r al-mu'asir,* (the title means "Issues in Contemporary Arabic Poetry"), in which she refines and elaborates the proposal for modern verse begun in the introduction to *Shazaya wa ramad,* is a milestone text and is hotly debated. Al-Mala'ika continued to write poetry into the 1970s, departing from the dark, romantic tendencies of her early work to a more philosophical stance. Religious and spiritual themes enter her later poetry, which is often marginalized, as very few modern Arab poets and critics take religious inspiration seriously.

Only a small amount of her work is available in English, in anthologies such as Kamal Boullata's *Women of the Fertile Crescent* (1981).

Another Work by Nazik al-Mala'ika

Jayyusi, Salma, ed. Selections in *Modern Arabic Poetry.* New York: Columbia University Press, 1987.

A Work about Nazik al-Mala'ika

Jayyusi, Salma. *Trends and Movements in Modern Arabic Poetry.* Boston: Brill, 1977.

Malange, Nise (1960–) *poet, screenwriter*

Nise Malange was born in Cape Town, South Africa. She went to the United States, where she obtained a degree from the University of Iowa. Malange specialized in scriptwriting and film and video production while she was in Zimbabwe. She is currently the director of the Culture and Working Life Project at the University of Natal in Durban. She is also the national vice president of the Congress of South African Writers. In addition, Malange works as a consultant within the labor movement and writes to forward the cause of women's rights in South Africa. Malange writes poetry and plays and has presented papers on African arts and cultures at international conferences. She won the prestigious Norwegian Award for Poetry in 1987.

Malange's poems are inspired by her personal experiences as a disenfranchised black woman in South Africa. Her turbulent youth, spent during the years of apartheid, has had a distinct impact on her writing. Issues such as domestic violence, disenfranchisement, and education for girls are common themes in her works. Her play *Pondo Women Cleaners* (1987) addresses the pain and suffering of a marginal group of disenfranchised women. Malange believes that literature can be used for the mobilization of the masses, and her poetry examines the oppression and struggle of women in a male-dominated society. Through her poetry, Malange also reaches out to her readers, imploring them to derive strength from their common experiences. She believes that literature has the power to influence and help them to improve their lives.

Malange represents one of the prominent members of a new generation of African poets known as the "oral poets." Her desire to inspire ordinary people to voice their opinions against social evils such as oppression and class differences is most effectively carried out in her active participation in community work and workshops that she helps organize.

Other Works by Nise Malange

"Ditsela! Ditsela," *Pathways* 1 (May 1997).
"Nightshift Cleaner, Nightshift Mother," *Illuminations: An International Magazine of Contemporary Writing* 8 (Summer 1989).

Mallarmé, Stéphane (1842–1898) *poet*

A symbolist (*see* SYMBOLISM) poet whose works are often considered by critics to be the best example of "pure poetry," Stéphane Mallarmé was born in Paris into a family of French civil servants. As a student, he distinguished himself in the study of languages. After graduation, he visited England, was married in London, and then returned to France, where he accepted the first in a series of teaching posts. He taught English in several provincial schools in Tournon, Besançon, Avignon, and Paris until his retirement in 1893.

Mallarmé made many close contacts within the artistic community. Chief among these was his sustained friendship with Manet, which began in 1873 and continued until the artist's death in 1883. He wrote two articles on Manet, which are considered to be incisive symbolist analyses of impressionism.

In the 1880s, Mallarmé became the center of a group of French writers who lived and worked in Paris. This group, which included ANDRÉ GIDE and PAUL VALÉRY, met to share ideas on poetry and art. Mallarmé's ideas often contradicted each other. According to Mallarmé, nothing lies beyond reality; however, within this state of nothingness, there exists that which is the essence of perfection. This takes the shape of what he refers to as the "perfect form." He believed it was the poet's task to find these essences within the void of nothingness and to clarify them with the language of poetry.

Mallarmé's ideas were not always well received. Readers and critics alike found him to be unnecessarily complicated and often obtuse. He would challenge his readers to use their minds when they read his works by, among other things, looking up common words in the dictionary to find archaic meanings for them. He would then employ these words in their long-lost form within his poems.

Critical Analysis

Mallarmé began to write poetry in his early teens. His first poems were published in magazines in the 1860s, and his first important poem, "L'Azur," was published when he was only 24. He was profoundly influenced by the works of CHARLES BAUDELAIRE, particularly by Baudelaire's advocacy of the obscure and his emphasis on the element of mystery within a poetic work. Mallarmé, however, went beyond this concept, stressing the inherent magical quality and the sacredness of poetry. He spent long periods of time obsessing over the minute details of each of his poems, reveling in the importance of even the smallest and seemingly most insignificant details of language and imagery. His poetry was allusive and often hard for readers to grasp. His language was compressed in such a way that a finished poem often seemed more an interpretation than a poem that could be easily defined, which demanded an awareness of the process of poetic creation.

Language and art held a close association in many of Mallarmé's works. His association with the visual arts is readily evident in his poetry collection, *The Afternoon of a Faun* (1876), his best-known work. It was illustrated by Manet and inspired both Debussy's 1894 musical composition of the same name and the subsequent ballet by Nijinsky. The poems in the collection were written while Mallarmé was working at Tournon, a town he found both ugly and unpleasant. In contrast to the author's own surroundings, the poem presents the rambling erotic thoughts of a faun as it whiles away the hours of a drowsy summer afternoon in a place of great beauty.

Perhaps Mallarmé's greatest achievement came in his contribution to those writers who came after him. This influence was not restricted to French poetry but spread internationally among a diverse group of writers. Wallace Stevens credits Mallarmé as a source of great inspiration, as does T. S. Eliot. His influence is readily apparent in James Joyce's *Finnegans Wake*.

The condensed figures and unorthodox syntax of Mallarmé's poetry set it apart from much of the rest of the works of his time. He framed each of his poems around one central symbol, idea, or metaphor. All of the additional imagery simply served to help illustrate and develop the main idea. His use of free verse was influential on the FIN DE SIÈCLE movement in France, the 1890s decadent movement, and 20th-century MODERNIST poetry.

Mallarmé's other works include *Hérodiade* (1896) and *A Funeral Toast,* the latter of which was written as a memoriam to the French author THÉOPHILE GAUTIER, whose works Mallarmé greatly admired. He also wrote an experimental poem *Un coup de dés jamais n'abolira le hasard* (1897), which was published posthumously. In his later years, he became close friends with Whistler and devoted himself to creating what he referred to as his "grand oeuvre" or "great work." Unfortunately, Mallarmé died in Paris on September 9, 1898, before he could complete this impossible masterpiece.

Other Works by Stéphane Mallarmé

Collected Poems. Translated by Henry Weinfield. Berkeley: University of California Press, 1994.
Mallarmé in Prose. Translated by Jill Anderson. New York: New Directions, 2001.

Works about Stéphane Mallarmé

Lloyd, Rosemary. *Mallarmé: The Poet and His Circle.* Ithaca, N.Y.: Cornell University Press, 1999.
Stafford, Hélène. *Mallarmé and the Poetics of Everyday Life: A Study of the Concept of the Ordinary in His Verse and Prose.* Atlanta, Ga.: Rodopi, 2000.

Malouf, David (1934–   ) *poet, novelist, playwright*

David Malouf was born in Brisbane, Australia, to a Lebanese father and an English mother. He attended the Brisbane Grammar school and later received an honors degree in language and literature at the University of Queensland, where he taught English until 1962. His expertise and skill in the use of the English language inspired him to write poems. He published his first poem, "Interiors," in *Four Poets* in 1962.

Malouf is considered both a primitive and a romantic for his uses of nature. His themes include nature, the use of language as a transforming device across cultures, identity, isolation, unity, and belonging. He uses imagery, metaphor, symbolism, and analogy to express these themes.

In "Twelve Night Pieces" from *Poems 1975–76* (1976), he writes, "From wetness of earth and earth rot morning / Glory climbs to the sun . . ." to reveal the morning glory as a symbol of human connection with nature. In "The Bicycle" from *The Bicycle and Other Poems* (1970), he uses the analogy of the mechanical bicycle and the natural human experience of traveling through life: "Now time yawns and its messengers appear/ like huge stick insects, wingless, spoked with stars. . . ."

Malouf's novels carry the theme of identity for which the hero longs through union with another. In Malouf's first novel, *Johnno* (1975), Johnno and Dante long for their fathers' love. In *Conversations at Curlow Creek* (1996), Michael Adair wants to be united with his brother and his love, Virgilia. *An Imaginary Life* (1978), *Remembering Babylon* (1993), *Child's Play* (1982), and *Flyaway Peter* (1982), the novels for which Malouf won the Australian Literature Society's Gold medal, all talk about the predicament of isolation.

Malouf is celebrated as a poet, essayist, novelist, and playwright. He won the Australian Literature Society gold medal for the verse collection *Neighbours in a Thicket* (1974). He also won the Townsville Foundation for Australian Literary Studies Award and the Grace Leven Poetry Prize. The novel *Remembering Babylon* was nominated for the 1993 Booker Prize. Malouf speaks about his passion for writing in his autobiography, *12, Edmonstone Street* (1985). In 2009, Malouf's novel *Ransom* was published. It tells the story of the *Iliad* from the death of Patroclus to the burial of Hector.

Other Works by David Malouf

Dream Stuff: Stories. New York: Pantheon, 2000.
Selected Poems, 1959–1989. London: Chatto and Windus, 1994.

A Work about David Malouf

Indyk, Ivor. *David Malouf.* New York: Oxford University Press, 1993.

Malraux, André (1901–1976) *novelist, nonfiction writer*

André Georges Malraux was born in Paris, France, on November 3, into a wealthy family. His parents separated when he was a child and he was brought up by his mother. His father was a stockbroker who committed suicide in 1930. As a youth, Malraux studied a wide variety of subjects, such as archaeology, art history, and anthropology. However, what interested him the most was oriental languages, histories, and cultures, which he studied at the École des Langues Orientales.

At the age of 21, Malraux married Clara Goldschmidt, also a writer, and together they traveled to Cambodia and spent time in Indochina, attempting to rediscover the Khmer statuary. He was arrested, however, for taking bas-reliefs from a temple. His three-year sentence was rescinded, and he returned briefly to France. It was during this period that he became highly critical of French colonial authorities governing Indochina. As a result, Malraux began the first of many political endeavors that, alongside and often directly linked to his literary achievements, eventually distinguished his remarkable life. He helped to first organize the Young Annam League, an anticolonial organization in Saigon in 1925. He also founded and edited the politically active and outspoken anticolonial Saigon newspaper *Indochina in Chains*.

On returning to France, Malraux published his first novel, *The Temptation of the West* (1926). The work, set in the early stages of the Chinese revolution and revolving around letters exchanged between a young European and an Asian intellectual, focuses on the parallels between Eastern and Western culture. He followed this work with two novels, *The Conquerors* (1928), which dealt with a revolutionary strike in Canton, and *The Royal Way* (1930), a successful adventure story set in the jungles of Indochina.

Malraux supported himself by working as an art editor in Paris for Gallimard Publishers. He was able to take several archaeological expeditions to Afghanistan and Iran, which led to his discovery of the lost city that may have been home to the Queen of Sheba. He continued to write, with death and revolution two of his major themes. *Man's Fate* (1933), one of his best-known novels, won the Prix Goncourt. The novel depicts a communist uprising in Shanghai and focuses on the dignity of human solidarity in both life and death.

In the 1930s, Malraux became known politically for his support of antifascist and leftist organizations. He fought for the Republicans during the Spanish civil war and wrote about these experiences in his novel *L'espoir* (*Days of Hope*, 1937). The book, published prior to the end of the war, stops with the March 1937 battle at Guadalajara. In 1938, *L'espoir* was revised as a screenplay under the title *Sierrade teruel;* however, the film was not released in France until after the conclusion of World War II.

The 1940s marked a shift in Malraux's life. He divorced his wife and broke away from communism, as he did not agree with the Nazi–Soviet pact. He began to concentrate on writing nonfiction and was openly opposed to Stalin's ideas. He served with a French tank unit during World War II and, though twice captured by the Gestapo, managed to escape both times.

After the war, Malraux became a vocal supporter of Charles de Gaulle. He wrote a number of books on art and aesthetics and married a concert pianist. When De Gaulle came into power, Malraux was appointed minister of cultural affairs, and his first act in office was to order the cleaning of the Louvre. This act was highly controversial in that many people saw it not as an improvement but as an act of vandalism. Malraux eventually retired from the forefront of politics to write his memoirs, including the autobiographical *The Fallen Oaks* (1971). He wrote regularly until his death on November 23, 1976.

Another Work by André Malraux

The Walnut Trees of Altenburg. Translated by A. W. Fielding. Chicago: University of Chicago Press, 1992.

A Work about André Malraux

Cate, Curtis. *André Malraux: A Biography.* New York: Fromm International, 1998.

Mandelstam, Osip Yemilyevich
(1891–1938) *poet*

Osip Mandelstam was born in Warsaw, Poland, but grew up in St. Petersburg, Russia. His father was a successful leather merchant, and his mother a piano teacher. Although the Mandelstams were Jewish, the family was not very religious. Mandelstam received an excellent education at home from various tutors and later from the Tenishev Academy. He traveled extensively throughout Europe between 1907 and 1910 and studied French literature at the University of Heidelberg. Between 1911 and 1917, Mandelstam studied philosophy at the University of St. Petersburg. He published his first poem in 1910 in the journal *Apollon.* With the advent of revolution, Mandelstam abandoned his studies to concentrate on poetry.

Influenced by his close relationship with ANNA AKHMATOVA and NIKOLAY GUMILEV, Mandelstam readily joined the acmeists (*see* ACMEISM) and established his reputation as a poet with his collection *Kamen* (*Stone,* 1913). Like Akhmatova, Mandelstam often mixed classical images with those of contemporary Russian culture. Mandelstam's poetry also exalted the architectural and literary achievements of classical Greece and Rome. In his next two collections, *Tristiya* (1922) and *Poems 1921–25* (1928), he reaffirmed his position as one of the best poets in Russia. Although both collections contained images and themes previously found in *Stones,* Mandelstam, influenced by political upheaval in Russia, expanded his poetic perspective to more universal themes of life, death, and exile.

In 1918, Mandelstam began to work for the education ministry of the new communist regime, but his support for the regime soured and stopped completely after the 1921 execution of his friend Gumilev. In the 1920s, he supported himself by writing children's books and translating works by English and French writers. He married Nadezhda Kazin in 1922 and in 1928 published three books: a poetry collection, entitled simply *Poems,* and two collections of critical essays. After a trip to Armenia in 1930, Mandelstam published his last major collection of poetry, *Journey to Armenia,* in 1933. An epigram about Stalin he wrote in 1934—"And every killing is a treat / For the broad-chested Ossete"—resulted in Mandelstam's being arrested and exiled to Voronezh. Nadezhda accompanied him and helped transcribe the agonized poems he composed there. In 1938, he was arrested again for "counterrevolutionary" activities. This time he was sentenced to five years of hard labor. Mandelstam died that year in the Gulag and was buried in a common grave.

International acclaim for Mandelstam's work did not come until the 1970s, when his works were published in Russia and the West. Mandelstam's poems of exile were not published until 1990 in *The Voronezh Notebooks.* Their lyrical approach to almost unimaginable pain is astonishing, as in the poem "Black Candle" (1934):

> *It is your fate, for your narrow shoulders to*
> *   turn red*
> *under the lashes,*
> *red under the lashes, to burn in the frost . . .*
> *And as for me, I burn after you like a black*
> *   candle,*
> *burn like a black candle and dare not pray.*

The magnificence of Mandelstam's verse is still being rediscovered today. He is now considered to be one of the best Russian poets of the 20th century. The critic Simon Karlinsky, for example, remarked in a review of Bruce McClelland's translation of *Tristiya* in the *New York Times Book Review:* "In Mandelstam, Russian poetry at last has a poet of stature comparable to Pushkin's—a claim that even the most fanatical admirers of Blok, Mayakovsky or Pasternak would not dream of making."

Other Works by Osip Mandelstam

50 Poems/Osip Mandelstam. Translated by Bernard Meares, with an introduction by Joseph Brodsky. New York: Persea Books, 2000.

The Noise of Time: The Prose of Osip Mandelstam. Translated by Clarence Brown. San Francisco: North Point Press, 1986.

Osip Mandelstam's Stone. Translated and introduced by Robert Tracy. Princeton, N.J.: Princeton University Press, 1981.

Tristia. Translated by Bruce McClelland. Barrytown, N.Y.: Station Hill Press, 1987.

The Voronezh Notebooks: Poems 1935–1937. Translated by Richard McKane and Elizabeth Mc-Kane. Chester Springs, Pa.: Dufour Editions, 1998.

Works about Osip Mandelstam

Cavanagh, Clare. *Osip Mandelstam and the Modernist Creation of Tradition.* Princeton, N.J.: Princeton University Press, 1995.

Harris, Jane Garry. *Osip Mandelstam.* Boston: Twayne, 1988.

Mandelstam, Nadezhda. *Hope Against Hope.* Translated by Max Hayward. New York: Modern Library, 1999.

———. *Mozart and Salieri: An Essay on Osip Mandelstam and the Poetic Process.* New York: Vintage, 1994.

Manhae

See HAN YONGUN.

Mann, Heinrich (1871–1950) *novelist, playwright, essayist*

Luiz Heinrich Mann was born in Lübeck, Germany. His father, Thomas Johann Heinrich Mann, was a successful grain merchant. His mother, Julia da Silva-Bruhns Mann, was of Brazilian descent. As a teenager, Mann became an apprentice to a bookseller and worked for a publishing house. After an inheritance made him financially independent, he started his literary career in 1891. He lived in Italy, Germany, and France before moving to the United States in 1940 to escape the Nazis. He married the actress Maria Kanová in 1914 and, after their divorce, married Nelly Kroeger in 1939.

Mann, a prolific essayist, was one of the few German writers to oppose his country's participation in World War I. He attained literary fame with his novel *Der Untertan* (*The Patrioteer,* 1918), a satirical critique of Germany under Kaiser Wilhelm. His novel *Professor Unrat* (1905) was translated as *The Blue Angel* and made into a popular movie in 1928. In the 1930s, Mann wrote two successful historical novels on King Henry of Navarre. In 1949, he won the National Prize of East Germany and died a year later after accepting the presidency of that country's Academy of Arts.

Mann's influences included FRIEDRICH NIETZSCHE and 19th-century French writers such as GUSTAVE FLAUBERT. He and his brother THOMAS MANN criticized, supported, and influenced each other's writing careers. Mann employed caricature and sarcasm in his works to convey his social and political criticisms. A socialist, he used his novels and plays to oppose authoritarianism, militarism, and fascism. Less successful than his brother, Mann was sometimes an uneven and impatient writer who lacked precision and polish. Nonetheless, as the scholar Rolf Linn points out, Mann's work represents "an almost complete intellectual and political history of Germany in the first half of the twentieth century" and "through it the best thought of nineteenth century France entered German thinking."

Another Work by Heinrich Mann

Henry, King of France. Translated by Eric Sutton. New York: Knopf, 1939.

A Work about Heinrich Mann

Linn, Rolf N. *Heinrich Mann.* Boston: Twayne, 1967.

Mann, Thomas (1875–1955) *novelist, critic, essayist*

Thomas Mann was born in Lübeck, Germany. His father was a wealthy, prominent citizen who was twice elected as mayor of Lübeck. His mother, Julia da Silva-Bruhns, was born in Brazil of mixed German and Portuguese ancestry. After the death of Mann's father in 1891, his family relocated to Munich. Mann was an avid reader during childhood and particularly admired realistic literature. Mann attended the University of Munich; on graduation, he worked for the German Fire Insurance Company.

While at university, Mann immersed himself in the writings of ARTHUR SCHOPENHAUER and FRIEDRICH NIETZSCHE, two very influential German philosophers and cultural critics. Mann also became obsessed with the musical works of Richard Wagner, a composer whose operas and orchestral works were inspired by German myth and legend. Mann's early literary influences, were LEO TOLSTOY and FYODOR DOSTOYEVSKY, whose psychological realism Mann particularly admired.

In 1929, Mann won the Nobel Prize in literature. When Adolf Hitler came to power in Germany, Mann, along with his family, moved to Switzerland, where Mann worked as an editor for various literary journals. In 1938, Mann moved to the United States, working as a visiting professor at Princeton University. While at Princeton, Mann completed several critical works, including a study of Dostoevsky. Mann eventually moved to California but left the United States in 1952, bitterly disappointed by the persecution of communists and communist sympathizers by the U.S. government.

Critical Analysis

Mann's first major work, *Buddenbrooks* (1900), shows the influence of Richard Wagner in its use of leitmotif, using a word or an image over and over again in the work as a thematically unifying element. The novel follows several generations of the Buddenbrook family, a wealthy and powerful German family that disintegrates and degenerates with each successive generation. The novel especially focuses on the last Buddenbrook, the decadent artist Hanno. The work demonstrates Mann's affinity for the epic quality of the novel, which he inherited from early Tolstoy works. *Buddenbrooks*

was well received throughout Germany and established Mann as a prominent writer.

In 1912, Mann completed a much shorter but also less conventional work, *Death in Venice*. The story recounts a strange relationship between Tadzio, a 14-year-old boy, and Gustav von Aschenbach, a mature German writer. Aschenbach becomes obsessed with the boy, who falls ill during an epidemic. Aschenbach decides to brave the epidemic and nurse the boy but contracts the disease himself and dies. Throughout the story the narrator asks this question:

[D]o you believe, my dear boy, that the man whose path to the spiritual passes through the senses can ever achieve wisdom and true manly dignity?

Aschenbach, who has never before allowed himself to experience passion, literally dies for it and of it. The ambiguities in the relationship between Aschenbach and the boy, as well as the story's multilayered symbolism, have made *Death in Venice* a frequent subject of debate among scholars and critics.

During World War I, Mann adamantly supported the policies of the kaiser, the leader of Germany, and vehemently attacked liberalism. After the end of World War I, however, Mann's political opinions changed, and he vocally supported parliamentary democracy and the newly formed Weimar Republic.

The Magic Mountain (1924), Mann's second great work, reflects the political conflict found in the writer's contemporary world. In the novel, Hans Castorp visits his cousin at a fashionable tuberculosis sanatorium and decides to stay there even though he is not ill. The stay spans more than seven years, during which time Castorp talks with the other patients in the sanatorium and learns valuable lessons about the meaning of life and death. Castorp is caught in a conflict between two opposing political forces represented by two characters: a young Italian liberal humanist, Settembrini, and Naptha, a radical reactionary figure who supports faith beyond reason. The differences between the two men culminate in a duel: Settembrini fires into the air, and Naptha, overwhelmed by rage, kills himself. The duel between the two opposing forces symbolically reflects the conflict in Mann's own society. The work also reflects Mann's concern about fascism and the growing popularity of the Nazis in his native Germany. The novel received tremendous critical acclaim and became a best-seller in Germany.

Joseph and His Brothers appeared as a trilogy written between 1933 and 1943. Set in the biblical world, the story emerges as a religious and political allegory of conflict between individual liberty and political oppression. The story describes the progress of Joseph who matures into a wise political leader ready to lead his people to freedom. The novel was written during the height of the Nazi regime and reflects Mann's personal hatred for fascism and oppression.

Mann's last great novel, *Doctor Faustus* (1947), delineates the life of a famous composer, Adrian Lewerkuhn. The work is set against the grim background of crumbling German culture and society between the First and the Second World Wars. Mann's exploration of the roots of fascism in Germany was well received around the world but was resented by some in Germany itself.

When Thomas Mann returned to Europe in 1953, he refused to live in Germany—the government of which had deprived him of his citizenship in 1936—and settled in Switzerland. In 1949, Mann was awarded the Goethe Prize, the highest literary honor in Germany. Mann's exploration of the relationship of the extraordinary person to the society has never been surpassed.

Other Works by Thomas Mann

Confessions of Felix Krull: The Confidence Man. New York: Vintage Press, 1992.
Death in Venice and Other Stories. Translated by David Luke. New York: Bantam Books, 1988.

Works about Thomas Mann

Heilbut, Anthony. *Thomas Mann: Eros and Literature.* Riverside: University of California Press, 1997.

Robertson, Ritchie. *The Cambridge Companion to Thomas Mann.* Cambridge: Cambridge University Press, 2002.

Mansfield, Katherine (Kathleen Mansfield Beauchamp) (1888–1923)
short story writer, poet

Katherine Mansfield was born Kathleen Mansfield Beauchamp in Wellington, New Zealand, to an affluent, middle-class family, but in 1909 she left for London to pursue a career as a writer. There, she met and married George Bowdon, a music teacher, but left him a few days after the wedding. Her first complete volume of short stories was published in 1911, under the title *In a German Pension.* These stories were based on Mansfield's stay at a Bavarian health resort, where she lived for a time after she left her husband and where she suffered a miscarriage.

Shortly after her return to London, she met John Middleton Murry, a critic, poet, and editor, whom she married in 1918. In that same year, she was diagnosed with tuberculosis. In London, she met a number of artists and writers, including D. H. Lawrence, who modeled one of his characters in his novel *Women in Love* after Mansfield, and Virginia Woolf. The painter Dorothy Brett described Mansfield as having "a sort of ironic ruthlessness toward the small minds and less agile brains. . . . Katherine had a tongue like a knife, she could cut the very heart of one with it." (She was much more subtle and ambiguous in her writing.) In fiction writing, Virginia Woolf treated Mansfield as such a serious rival that, after her death, Woolf said there was "no point in writing. Katherine won't read it."

When her brother Leslie was killed during World War I, Mansfield began to write stories about her family and growing up. Some of her best stories, such as "The Garden Party," are set in New Zealand at the turn of the century.

"The Garden Party," published in 1922, deals with social class, death, and the artist's sensibility. The Sheridan family is hosting an elaborate garden party when a delivery man brings the news that a worker who lived in one of the little cottages near the Sheridan house has been killed in an accident. Mrs. Sheridan, once assured that the man did not actually die in her garden, insists that the party go on, telling her daughter, Laura, "People like that don't expect sacrifices from us." Later, Mrs. Sheridan sends Laura to the Scott house with the leftovers from the party, and at the "pokey little hole . . ." she accidentally enters the room where the body is laid out. Gazing at the dead man, she thinks, "He was given up to his dream. What did garden parties . . . matter to him?" The story exemplifies Mansfield's delicate, poetic style, her tendency to focus on a life-changing moment, and her habit of ending on a note of ambiguity.

In "The Fly" (1923), a businessman is reminded by a visitor of the death of his son six years earlier in World War I. Unable to summon up the grief he wants to feel, he picks up a photograph of his son. At this moment, he notices a fly that has fallen into the inkpot. He rescues the fly and watches as it begins the tedious process of cleaning itself off. Just as it is "ready for life again," the man drops more ink on it. He repeats the process, amazed at the fly's courage and resilience, until the final blot of ink kills the fly, at which point the man is seized by "a grinding feeling of wretchedness." He calls for fresh blotting paper but cannot remember what he had been thinking about before he began to torment the fly. Although the man cannot remember, the reader knows that the fly stands for all those who are helpless victims of a cruel fate.

Although *Poems* (1923) and *The Letters of Katherine Mansfield* (1928) were published posthumously, Mansfield is primarily remembered for her seven books of short stories, and she has exerted a lasting influence on modern short-story writers. She crafted her stories very carefully, writing and rewriting. Her writing is always subtle and often ironic and witty. As she defied conventions in her life, so her stories question conventional ideas about social class, family life, and marriage.

Katherine Mansfield died of tuberculosis in 1923 near Fontainebleau, France. The first significant writer to emerge from New Zealand, she is claimed by nationalist critics in both New Zealand and Britain but is best thought of as a product of colonialism. Her biographer Antony Alpers says of her New Zealand stories:

> They were really insights into the social isolation that used to be common in New Zealand . . . and they were written in a cultural isolation that was total for their author: no one who read them in London could have known what they in fact achieved. . . . The stories were something that only a New Zealander could have written at that time. They succeeded in relating character to environment in a land of "no tradition."

Critical Analysis

Mansfield's delicate, indirect style is beautifully exemplified in "Miss Brill," published in 1922 in the collection *The Garden Party*. The story is told in a stream-of-consciousness narration, allowing the reader to follow the thoughts of the story's protagonist, Miss Brill, a lonely spinster living in genteel poverty in Paris. Other characters are revealed only through what they say and do in Miss Brill's presence. As is the case with many of Mansfield's stories, Miss Brill experiences an epiphany, a moment that changes everything forever.

As Miss Brill dresses for her Sunday walk in the park, she decides to add a touch of elegance to her outfit by wearing her fur. Her fur, which she addresses almost as if it were a dear little pet, is a fox fur collar. These collars, once popular, were fashioned so that the fox's body circles the woman's neck, his teeth grasping the end of the tail. Suitably decked out, Miss Brill walks to her "'special' seat in the park." Her greatest enjoyment is listening in on others' conversations, "listening as though she didn't listen" and "sitting in other people's lives just for a minute." One incident in particular reveals much about Miss Brill. An elderly couple stands near her, a woman in an ermine toque (hat) and a gentleman in gray. Miss Brill thinks that the hat no longer suits the old woman, who had "bought [it] when her hair was still yellow. Now everything, her hair, her face, even her eyes, was the same colour as the shabby ermine. And her hand . . . was a tiny yellowish paw." As the woman greets the man in gray, he blows smoke from his cigarette in her face and walks away. Although the woman continues to smile, Miss Brill imagines her thinking, "The Brute! The Brute!" attributing a history to the couple, a romance, perhaps, an abandonment. It is at this moment that Miss Brill experiences her greatest moment of joy. She realizes that, "It was like a play. . . . They were all on stage. They weren't only the audience, not only looking on; they were acting. Even she had a part." This insight gives Miss Brill a new sense of purpose, of importance, as she imagines telling the people in her straitened everyday existence that she is an "actress." "Yes, I have been an actress for a long time." However, as she is watching a charming young couple, Miss Brill overhears the young man call her "a silly old thing" and the girl say her fur "looks like a fried whiting [fish]."

Mansfield subtly evokes Miss Brill's devastation. As she returns to her home, she sees it anew. It is now a "dark little room . . . like a cupboard." As she tosses the fur into its box, she imagines she can hear it crying. Thus, the old fox fur becomes a symbol of Miss Brill herself, outdated, worn, dispensable. All her joy is gone, and now she sees herself in the old, faintly ridiculous people she has watched with a touch of superiority in the park. Mansfield leaves the reader to judge the depth of Miss Brill's self-deception.

Other Works by Katherine Mansfield

Bliss and Other Stories. London: Wordsworth, 1996.
Something Childish. North Pomfret, Vt.: Trafalgar Square, 2000.

Works about Katherine Mansfield

Alpers, Antony. *The Life of Katherine Mansfield.* New York: Viking Press, 1980.
Kobler, J. F. *Katherine Mansfield: A Study of the Short Fiction.* Boston: Twayne, 1990.
Tomalin, Claire. *Katherine Mansfield: A Secret Life.* New York: Knopf, 1988.

Manzoni, Alessandro (1785–1873) *poet, novelist*

Italian patriot Alessandro Manzoni, best known for his fiercely nationalistic novel *The Betrothed* (1827) was born on March 7 in Milan. His father was a wealthy landowner, and his mother was the daughter of Cesare Beccaria, a well-known jurist and author of an influential treatise on crime and punishment. His parents separated in 1792, and, as a child, he moved with his mother to Paris where he received his education at several Catholic schools. His earliest works are characterized by a deeply anticlerical sentiment, as well as by strong support for Jacobean and democratic ideologies. He later rejected deism for an equally fervent devotion to Roman Catholicism. Manzoni returned to Italy in 1810, where he met and married Enrichetta Blondel.

Although he published several early works, Manzoni's most prolific period as a writer came between the years of 1812 and 1815. During this time, he began the poetry collection *Inni sacri,* which he concluded 10 years later with the final piece, *La Pentacoste* (1822). His poetry is noted for its warmth of religious feeling. He also wrote two tragic dramas, *Il conte di Carmagnola* (1820) and *Adelchi* (1822), as well as an ode to Napoleon upon his death, "Il Cinque Maggio" (1822).

Manzoni's best-known work, *I prommessi sposi* (1827; translated *The Betrothed* 1951), was written between 1821 and 1827, during which the author was influenced by Sir Walter Scott. Developed from a series of theoretical writings, the historical novel is set in 17th-century Milan and provides a lavishly detailed and fiercely patriotic look at life in Italy. In Lombardy, a local tyrant thwarts the love between two peasants. After initial publication of the work, Manzoni continued to make revisions to create a stylistically superior version of the text, publishing the final revised edition in 1840. It now stands as a prime example of modern Italian prose. In revising, Manzoni sought to remove all traces of non-Tuscan idiom. This act revived the age-long conflict as to which dialect should be the standard for Italian prose, an issue in which Manzoni was interested. Manzoni was convinced that Tuscan should be the standard, national Italian literary language.

Beginning in 1842, Manzoni turned away from writing fiction and concentrated on theoretical works and as well as his involvement in politics. In 1860, he was elected senator of the new Italian kingdom. He was also assigned as president for the commission for the unification of the Italian language. For his work in this capacity, he was granted Roman citizenship.

Manzoni died on May 22, 1873, in Milan. He is best remembered for his constant contribution to improving the Italian prose style, as well as for his patriotic ideology and religious fervor. His legacy is such that, on the first anniversary of his death, the composer Verdi wrote his *Requiem* in honor of Manzoni.

A Work about Alessandro Manzoni

Barricelli, Gian Piero. *Alessandro Manzoni*. Boston: Twayne, 1976.

Marinetti, Filippo Tommaso
(1876–1944) *nonfiction writer*

Emilio Filippo Tommaso Marinetti, one of the founders and a leading proponent of the Italian FUTURIST movement, was born in Alexandria, Egypt. The son of a wealthy lawyer, he was educated in a strict French Jesuit school in Alexandria. He completed his studies in Paris and then studied law at Pavia and Genoa universities. His devotion to literature soon overshadowed his plan for a career as a lawyer.

At 16, while still at the Jesuit College, Marinetti began to develop his skills as a writer, publishing a literary magazine from 1892 to 1894.

He experimented with the emerging poetic form of free verse, publishing his first poems in that style in 1898. By 1900, he had abandoned all pretense of aspiring to the legal profession and devoted himself full time to the study of French and Italian poetry and literature. In 1905, he founded another literary magazine, *Poesia,* which was published in Milan until 1909. Through this journal, he embarked on a crusade to liberate poetry from the traditional constraints of language, form, and meter by providing an outlet for emerging nontraditional writers. Still a virtual unknown, Marinetti gained instant recognition with a single publication in *Le Figaro* on February 20, 1909. His essay *Foundation and Manifesto of Futurism* initiated a controversial shift in the nature of literature. In the work, he glorified the rapid pace of the future—machines, danger, speed, violence, and war. Other artists, unaware that Marinetti was not only the movement's leading theorist but also its sole member, soon joined the trend so that by 1910, a small but vocal group of artists, writers, and musicians were known as the first wave of futurists.

A brilliant publicist, Marinetti spurred the growth of the movement by inundating the public with a series of manifestos, each one progressively more vehement and filled with promises of the future. His earliest manifestos were published in *Poesia,* but subsequent works were printed in his new journal *Lacerba* after its inception in 1913.

Alongside his manifestos, Marinetti was also hard at work as a novelist. His works, which followed the tenets set forth by his own concept of futurism, most particularly the denigration of women, often caused controversy. The publication of his experimental novel, *Marfarka the Futurist* (1910), resulted in his arrest and imprisonment on charges of pornography.

Marinetti continued to work to expand the goals of futurism to encompass all areas of the arts, including literature, music, painting, architecture, costume design, and photography. Two years after meeting his future wife, Benedetta Cappa, he published another manifesto, *Against Marriage* (1919);

however, he broke from his own reasoning and the two were finally wed in 1923.

The end of futurism and the end of Marinetti's life coincide. Italy's defeat in the war changed the popular opinion of violence and conflict, and, with the loss of Marinetti in 1944, the movement was unable to sustain its brief but explosive momentum.

A Work about Filippo Tommaso Marinetti

Blum, Cinzia Sartini. *The Other Modernism: F. T. Martinetti's Futurist Fiction of Power.* Berkeley: University of California Press, 1944.

Maron, Monika (1941–) *novelist, short story writer*

Monika Maron was born in Berlin during World War II. Her father was a communist who served as East Germany's minister of the interior. Her mother was a Pole of Jewish descent. After Maron completed grammar school, she studied drama and art history. She worked at a factory and for East Berlin television before spending six years as a journalist for *Für Dich* and *Wochenpost*. She became a full-time writer in 1976.

Maron's first novel, *Flugasche (Flying Ash,* 1981), was banned in East Germany for its critical portrayal of conditions there; it was, however, successful in the West. The novel describes the efforts of a journalist to shut down a power plant that is poisoning residents of an industrial city. *Flugasche* is the first book to address the problems of pollution in East Germany. Maron's second novel *Die Überläuferin (The Turncoat,* 1986) continues her theme of criticizing the East German state. In this work, she describes a woman's psychological collapse while living in dehumanizing conditions. Maron wrote a third novel in 1991 to form a trilogy about East Berlin. Part of a rebellious and critical generation of German writers, her criticism of East Germany also appears in her short stories and essays. In 1992, Maron won the coveted Kleist Prize.

Other Works by Monika Maron

Animal Triste (European Women Writers). Lincoln: University of Nebraska Press, 2000.
Pavel's Letters. London: Random House, 2003.
Silent Close No. 6. Translated by David Newton Marinelli. Columbia, La.: Reader's International, 1993.

Masaoka Shiki (Masaoka Tsunenori) (1867–1902) *poet, diarist, critic*

Masaoka Shiki was born in Matsuyama in present-day Ehime Prefecture to Masaoka Hayata and Yae. He began to write prose and poetry while still in grade school there. He left Matsuyama in 1883 to attend University Preparatory College in Tokyo. In 1890, he entered the Literature Department of Tokyo Imperial University but left in 1893 to devote himself to literature. During his university period, he traveled around Japan, and in 1895, he volunteered to become a war correspondent in China during the Sino–Japanese War (1894–95). In the last years of his life, tuberculosis virtually confined Masaoka to a sickbed. He succumbed to this illness in 1902.

While still at university, Masaoka published three analytical books that were highly critical of modern haiku poetry, in particular attacking the stature of widely acclaimed haiku master Bashō Matsuo (1644–94). By 1896, he had softened his perspective and published *Buson the Haiku Poet,* which praised the style of Buson Yosa (1716–83). In 1897, he started the magazine *Hototogisu* to provide an outlet for modern haiku. He then wrote a critique of tanka poetry called *Letters to the Tanka Poets,* published in 1898. His most highly regarded poetry was written from his sickbed toward the end of his life and published posthumously in a volume called *Poems from the Bamboo Village* (1904).

Masaoka is known more for revitalizing the haiku and tanka forms of poetry than for writing poetry. He espoused a new style of poetry based on *shasei* (copying life). He claimed the traditional poetic conventions that restricted haiku and tanka were killing them as art forms.

Other Works by Masaoka Shiki

Masaoka Shiki: Selected Poems. Translated by Burton Watson. New York: Columbia University Press, 1997.
Peonies Kana. Translated by Harold J. Isaacson. New York: Theatre Arts, 1972.

A Work about Masaoka Shiki

Beichman, Janine. *Masaoka Shiki.* New York: Kodansha International, 1986.

Maupassant, Guy de (1850–1893)
novelist

Although some accounts vary, Henri-René-Albert-Guy de Maupassant was most likely born at the Château de Miromesniel in Dieppe, France, to a noble family. He spent his childhood in Normandy, where, graced with an almost photographic memory, he began to gather the rich and vivid details that he would later use in his stories about the Norman people.

In 1869, Maupassant went to Paris, where he began to study law, but he left school at age 20 to serve in the Franco–Prussian War. When he returned to Paris, he became obsessed with the idea of becoming a writer and sought out the company of other writers including GUSTAVE FLAUBERT, from whom he learned much about the writer's craft. He also began to search his memories for ideas of his own and soon published the short story "La main ecorchée" (1875), in which he richly details the haunting image of a mummified hand. The story was based on an experience Maupassant had as a teenager when he actually saw a mummified hand up close. The details of his description reveal not only the vividness of Maupassant's memories but also his adherence to accuracy.

Aligning himself with the naturalist school (see *naturalism*), Maupassant published collections of poetry, the first of which was *Des verse* (1880). It was his short stories, however, that gained critical and popular acclaim. In a journal edited by ÉMILE ZOLA, Maupassant published what has come to be regarded as one of his greatest works, "Boule de suif" ("Ball of Fat," 1880). Set during the Franco-Prussian War, it is the sad tale of a prostitute and her inhumane treatment by the bourgeois passengers with whom she must travel on a coach. She is forced to spend the night with a Prussian officer so that he will allow the coach to proceed. The next day, she is scorned by her fellow travelers, even though it is her action that allows them to complete their journey.

Throughout the 1880s, Maupassant wrote more than 300 short stories, six novels, and three travel books. All of his works are marked by his attention to detail, objectivity, and a remarkable sense of comedic timing. Most often, they focus on everyday events in the lives of common people, while revealing the hidden sides of human nature. Two of his best-known works include *A Woman's Life* (1883), which details the frustrating and unhappy existence of a Norman wife, and *Pierre et Jean* (1888), a psychological tale of two brothers. The latter inspired debate about its morality, as the hero of the tale is successful only because he commits acts that are morally questionable.

Another of Maupassant's works, *Le horla* (*The Hallucination,* 1887), established him as a master of the horror tale. The main character, probably suffering from syphilis, believes he has summoned the Horlas, invisible cousins to vampires, and, in an attempt to get rid of them, burns down his house, killing his servants. When this does not work, he commits suicide. Maupassant himself suffered from syphilis, contracted at age 20, and the increasing madness brought on by the disease is readily apparent in his later works. One-tenth of his total literary output is in the form of horror stories and, of these, the main recurring theme is madness.

Maupassant attempted to end his own life on January 2, 1892. The attempt was unsuccessful but did lead to his admission to a private asylum, where he died one year later.

Critical Analysis

One of the best-loved and most frequently anthologized of de Maupassant's short stories is "The Necklace," published in 1884. The story is typical of de Maupassant in its realism and psychologically astute depiction of character. In a few deft strokes de Maupassant is able to evoke a fully rounded character. In "The Necklace," the protagonist, Mathilde Loisel, "was one of those pretty and charming girls born, as though fate had blundered over her, into a family of artisans." She marries a man she considers beneath her and begins a life of considerable unhappiness because she cannot afford the kind of luxury she believes she should have. To add to her woes, she has an old school friend, Madame Forestier, who is wealthy and Mathilde can no longer visit her because she cannot bear the contrast in their lives and surroundings.

Her husband, "a little clerk in the Ministry of Education" who is infuriatingly delighted with their modest lives, hopes to please her by securing an invitation to the home of the Minister of Education. Mathilde, however, scorns the invitation, because she does not have a suitable dress for the occasion. Her husband sacrifices money he had been saving for a gun to allow her to buy a dress, but to his intense disappointment she still refuses to attend the gathering because she has no jewelry to wear. Eventually, Mathilde decides to borrow a necklace from Madame Forestier, who graciously lends her "a superb diamond necklace." Mathilde wears the necklace to the party and is a huge success. "She was the prettiest woman present, elegant, graceful, smiling, and quite above herself with happiness."

The story has an aura of doom, so that the reader is not surprised when disaster strikes: Mathilde loses the necklace on the way home from the party. She and her husband borrow 40,000 francs, replace the necklace without ever telling Madame Forestier about the loss, and then work for 10 years to pay off their debts. While Mathilde and her husband were once merely genteelly poor, they now experience grinding poverty, depicted by de Maupassant with the unblinking accuracy characteristic of Émile Zola. Mathilde "came to know the heavy work of the house, the hateful duties of the kitchen. She washed the plates, wearing out her pink nails on the coarse pottery and the bottoms of pans. She washed the dirty linen, the shirts and dish-cloths, and hung them out to dry on a string; every morning she took the dustbin down into the street and carried up the water, stopping on each landing to get her breath. And, clad like a poor woman, she went to the fruiterer, to the grocer, to the butcher, a basket on her arm, haggling, insulted, fighting for every wretched halfpenny of her money."

The story ends with a twist typical of de Maupassant. When the debt is finally paid, Mathilde encounters Madam Forestier, who does not recognize her former friend, so changed is she by poverty. When Mathilde confesses the loss of the necklace, her friend replies, "Oh, my poor Mathilde! But mine was imitation. It was worth at the very most five hundred francs! . . . " The reader is left to contemplate the justice or lack thereof in Mathilde's terrible punishment for a moment of vanity and an evening of joy.

Other Works by Guy de Maupassant

A Life: The Humble Truth. Translated by Roger Pearson. New York: Oxford University Press, 1999.
The Necklace. Translated by Jonathan Sturges. London: Pushkin, 1999.

A Work about Guy de Maupassant

Lerner, Michael G. *Maupassant.* New York: George Braziller, 1975.

Mayakovsky, Vladimir (1893–1930) *poet*

Vladimir Vladimirovich Mayakovsky was born in Bagdadi, Georgia. Vladimir Konstantinovich, Mayakovsky's father, was employed as a forest ranger. Mayakovsky started school in 1902 but was not very interested in his studies. His older sister Ludmila, a student in Moscow, brought home political pamphlets, which Mayakovsky read avidly. When Mayakovsky's father died in 1906, his mother, Alexandra Alexeevna, moved her family to Moscow. Mayakovsky was instantly absorbed by the political situation of Moscow: At age 14, he was a full member of the Moscow Bolshevik Party.

Expelled from school in 1908 for nonpayment of tuition, Mayakovsky served as a messenger and lookout for the Bolsheviks. He was arrested for his activities but soon was released on probation. A year later, he was again placed in jail for his association with the revolutionaries. He wrote his first poem in solitary confinement. In 1911, he decided to study art and was admitted to the Moscow Institute for the Study of Painting, Sculpture, and Architecture. Painter David Burliuk introduced Mayakovsky to modern painting and poetry and was the first person to read Mayakovsky's poetry.

Mayakovsky joined the futurist movement, denouncing the rich literary tradition of Russia. He labeled ALEKSANDR PUSHKIN and MAXIM GORKY, for instance, "insignificant." He did not rebel against only the literary canon but also against the conventional use of language. Many of Mayakovsky's poems contains words that do not actually exist in the Russian language. Mayakovsky published his first two poems, "Night" and "Morning," in 1912; they were published the same year in a collection with other poems and some prose pieces entitled A Slap in the Face of Public Taste.

In 1913, Mayakovsky produced his first play, Vladimir Mayakovsky: A Tragedy. The play consists of a number of poetic monologues that explore the self-perception of the poet, and the leading part was played by Mayakovsky himself. It was not a big success with the public. Mayakovsky's first major poem, "A Cloud in Trousers," appeared in 1915. The poem is a tale of love and uses unusual images to denounce the traditional romantic representation of the poet in such lines as: "I am spit of the filthy night on a palm of a beggar."

Between 1915 and 1918, Mayakovsky produced a number of poetic works that dealt mostly with political ideology and were clearly propaganda for the Communist Party, which took control of the country in October 1917. He was an enthusiastic supporter of the Bolshevik regime and wrote in 1924 a poem in praise of Lenin.

In 1925, Mayakovsky visited the United States, attending meetings of labor unions, giving lectures about workers' rights, and sometimes joining the picketers during a strike. Mayakovsky described these experiences in two collections of poems, Poems of America and My Discovery of America (1926). In 1927, Mayakovsky established a literary journal, Novy Lef, in which he attacked Maxim Gorky. The short-lived journal published purely political poems that criticized capitalism, the West, and the "vices of the bourgeoisie." After a trip to Europe in 1929, Mayakovsky produced Poems About a Soviet Passport, a collection that recounted the reactions produced by his passport as he traveled across Europe. During 1928 and 1929, he also produced a number of propaganda pieces that dealt with various mundane issues of the proletariat, such as the joys of electricity, the advantages of running hot water, and the necessity of five-year plans. But his political verse alternated through the 1920s with much more personal love poems.

Mayakovsky received numerous awards from the Soviet government. Yet, he wrote two plays, The Bedbug (1928) and The Bathhouse (1930), that satirized Soviet bureaucracy and were suppressed by the authorities. His most successful play, Moscow on Fire (1930), appeared just a few days after his death, and recounted the events of the revolution of 1905.

In 1930, Mayakovsky shot and killed himself in his Moscow apartment. He seems to have been motivated by disappointment in love as well as by anxiety about the reception of his work. After his death, his body was placed on display for three days, and more than 150,000 mourners came to say their farewells. Stalin eulogized him, and generations of Soviet students memorized his poems. Today, critical opinion of his works remains mixed, as it was during his lifetime. Mayakovsky completely broke away from literary tradition, establishing his own unique style for poetry and drama; at the same time, he attacked and denounced a number of writers and poets who did not adhere to the principles of SOCIALIST REALISM.

Other Works by Vladimir Mayakovsky

The Bedbug and Selected Poetry. Translated by Max
   Hayward. Bloomington: Indiana University Press,
   1975.
For the Voice. Cambridge, Mass.: MIT Press, 2000.
Listen! Early Poems. Translated by Maria Enzberger.
   San Francisco: City Lights Books, 1991.
Mayakovsky: Plays. Translated by Guy Daniels. Evan-
   ston, Ill.: Northwestern University Press, 1995.

Works about Vladimir Mayakovsky

Bowra, C. M. "The Futurism of Vladimir Mayakovsky." In *The Creative Experiment.* New York:
   Grove Press, 1958.
Terras, Victor. *Vladimir Mayakovsky.* Boston: Twayne,
   1983.

Mazumdar, Anita

See DESAI, ANITA.

Meeks, Brian (1953–) *nonfiction writer, poet, fiction writer*

Born in Montreal, Canada, to a Trinidadian
mother and Jamaican father, Meeks grew up in Jamaica. There he attended Jamaica College before
doing undergraduate work at the University of the
West Indies, St. Augustine, Trinidad, during the
politically turbulent early 1970s. After earning a
doctorate from the University of the West Indies
at Mona, Meeks acted as a media and political
education consultant for the People's Revolutionary Government of Grenada. He also edited *The
Free West Indian* during the early 1980s. Musicians
Bob Marley, John Coltrane, and Miles Davis
significantly influenced Meeks's work. In the ac-
knowledgments to *Radical Caribbean: From Black
Power to Abu Bakr* (1996), Meeks thanked Gordon
Rohlehr and KAMAU BRATHWAITE for teaching
him "the importance of rigorous study and appreciation of popular culture as both central cause
and effect of the political process."

Themes of human agency, revolution, and radical
Caribbean activism reappear in Meeks's intellectual

works. *Caribbean Revolutions and Revolutionary
Theory: An Assessment of Cuba, Nicaragua and Grenada* (1993) traces revolutionary concepts from
the French Revolution to reconsider revolutionary
meaning. In *Radical Caribbean: From Black Power to
Abu Bakr,* Meeks maps two decades of radical movements in the Caribbean to examine why revolutions
occur. An *International Affairs* reviewer wrote, "In
the case of Grenada [Meeks's] account of the tragic
fall of the revolution goes beyond anything which
has been written before." Meeks's 2003 novel, *Paint
the Town Red,* is set in Jamaica in the 1970s.

Before returning to the University of the West
Indies at Mona, where he is currently a senior lecturer in comparative politics and political theory
and head of the Department of Government,
Meeks taught at James Madison College, Michigan
State University. In addition, Meeks has written
poetry, which has been published in many anthologies. His consistent intellectual contributions
make him one of the most influential contemporary Caribbean political theorists.

Other Works by Brian Meeks

*Narratives of Resistance: Jamaica, Trinidad, the Carib-
   bean.* Kingston, Jamaica: University of West Indies
   Press, 2000.
"NUFF at the Cusp of an Idea: Grassroots Guerrillas
   and the Politics of the 1970s in Trinidad and Tobago." *Social Identities* 5, no. 4 (1999).
"The Political Moment in Jamaica: The Dimensions
   of Hegemonic Dissolution." In Manning Marable,
   ed., *Dispatches from the Ebony Tower.* New York:
   Columbia University Press, 2000.

A Work about Brian Meeks

Allahar, Anton, ed. *Caribbean Charisma: Reflections
   on Leadership, Legitimacy, and Populist Politics.*
   Boulder, Colo.: L. Rienner Publishers, 2001.

Mehta, Gita (1943–) *novelist*

Gita Mehta was born in Delhi, India. Her parents
were deeply involved in India's political struggle

for independence against the British. Her father, Biju Patnaik, is one of India's most famous freedom fighters who went on to become the political leader of the state of Orissa, India. Mehta was sent to boarding school at an early age, as both her parents were constantly in and out of jail due to their political activities.

Mehta was educated in India and England, and her novels reflect her preoccupation with the ongoing relationship between Western and Eastern cultures. She explores this theme in her nonfiction book *Karma Cola: Marketing the Mystic East* (1979) in which she looks into the fascination that Eastern cultures hold for "hippies" from the West. As the title suggests, the novel is based on the global economy and explores the commodification of one culture by another.

Her first fictional work, *Raj: A Novel* (1989), is a historical novel about a young girl from a noble family who comes of age during the British Raj. Through her experiences, it becomes obvious that the roots of British and Indian culture cannot be easily untangled in colonial India, especially among the privileged classes who have benefited from British education. What develops alongside the maturity of the heroine is India's own birthing process into independence from the British. Mehta's *Snakes and Ladders: Glimpses of Modern India* (1997) further explores aspects of India's change after its independence. *Eternal Ganesha,* a nonfiction work published in 2006, explores the significance and mythology of the Hindu deity Ganesh.

In addition to writing novels, Mehta is a journalist and documentary filmmaker. She has directed four films on the Bangladesh war and one on the Indo–Pakistan war for the BBC and NBC.

Another Work by Gita Mehta

A River Sutra. New York: Vintage Books, 1994.

A Work about Gita Mehta

Byer, Kathleen Collins. "The Lama and the Vanaprasthi: Rudyard Kipling's *Kim* and Gita Mehta's *A River Sutra*." In A. L. McLeod, ed., *The Literature of the Indian Diaspora: Essays in Criticism.* New Delhi: Sterling, 2000.

Memmi, Albert (1920–) *novelist*

Albert Memmi was born in the Jewish quarter of Tunis, Tunisia. His father was a Jewish-Italian saddler, and his mother was a Berber (a member of the non-Arab minority of North Africa). When Memmi was four years old, he went to rabbinical school and studied there for three years. In 1927, he attended the school of the Alliance Israélite Universelle in the rue Malta Srira in Tunis. Memmi would often help his father in his workshop where he listened to stories told by an old family friend. While attending school, Memmi was actively involved with local Jewish youth groups; this strongly influenced his perceptions, which would later surface in his writings, especially those relating to colonial issues. Memmi graduated from the Lycée Carnot in 1939 and was awarded the honor prize in philosophy. From 1941 to 1942, he studied philosophy at the University of Algiers. After the invasion of France by Nazi Germany when anti-Semitic laws were implemented by the collaborationist Vichy government of France, Memmi was expelled from the university and sent to a forced labor camp until 1945. After World War II, he moved to Paris and continued his studies at the Sorbonne. After Tunisia gained full independence, Memmi settled in Paris, where he took on various professorial positions. He retired from teaching in 1987.

Memmi's works were heavily influenced by the political and social situations that shaped his life, and his dual position as a member of the French educated elite and an impoverished and marginalized Jew also influenced his writings. In his first novel, *La statue de sel* (*The Pillar of Salt,* 1953), Memmi's main protagonist, Mordecai, pours out his despair and sorrow. He is plagued by poverty and solitude, living as an estranged "outsider" who tries to make sense of his existence in a foreign land. Memmi's political views, his sociological training, and his own experiences, especially during World War II, allow him to discuss and explore the complexity of colonialism, particularly in his 1957 work, *The Colonizer and the Colonized,* in which he examines the social and psychological foundations of the views held by the colonizer and the colonized. To Memmi, the two groups constitute a framework in which neither group can exist without the other: The colonizer and the colonized are interdependent, but each group is a complex organization.

Memmi's works clearly show his genius as one of the leading intellectuals in postcolonial theory and thinking. He wrote all of his works in French, but many have been translated and published in English.

Other Works by Albert Memmi

Dependence: A Sketch for a Portrait of the Dependent. Translated by Philip A. Facey. Boston: Beacon, 1984.

Desert. Pueblo, Colo.: Passeggiata Press, 1992.

Jews and Arabs. Translated by Eleanor Levieux. Chicago: J. P. O'Hara, 1975.

The Liberation of the Jew. Translated by Judy Hyun. New York: Viking Press, 1966.

Racism. Translated by Kwame Anthony Appiah. Minneapolis: University of Minnesota Press, 1999.

The Scorpion. Translated by Eleanor Levieux. New York: Orion, 1971.

A Work about Albert Memmi

Roumani, Judith. *Albert Memmi.* Philadelphia: Temple University Press, 1987.

Menchú, Rigoberta (1959–) *memoirist*

Rigoberta Menchú was born in the village of Uspanadan in the western highlands of Guatemala to Vicente Menchú, a Quiche Maya Indian and an organizer of the Committee of Peasant Unity, and Juana Menchú Tum, also a Quiche Indian. She began to work at age five to help her mother pick coffee beans. At age nine, she was helping her father hoe and plant maize, and at 12, she joined in the communal work of her people by participating in the harvesting of maize. By then, her eldest and youngest brothers had died, the former from having breathed in the fumes of pesticide that had been sprayed at the farm where he worked, and the latter from malnutrition.

At age 13, Menchú, who was eager to learn to read and speak Spanish, the language of her oppressors, decided to accept a position as a maid in the distant capital. The exploitation she experienced as a maid, as well as her father's imprisonment at this time for his efforts at organizing against the landowners who were intent on depriving the Quiche Indians of their land, contributed to her later transformation into a leader of her people. Menchú's political activism began when she was still a teenager, involving herself in social reform through the Catholic church, the women's rights movement, and a local guerrilla organization. In 1979, she joined the Committee of Peasant Unity (CUC), as her father had recently done. Yet, it was not until the Guatemalan army brutally killed her father, her brother, and her mother in separate incidents in 1980 and 1981 that she became prominent in the CUC. Aware of the horrendous torture each of her family members received before being burned to death, Menchú was forced to go into hiding in 1981, first in Guatemala then in Mexico.

Since then, Menchú has dedicated her life to resisting oppression in Guatemala and fighting for the rights of all its Indian peasant groups. She was one of the founders of the United Representation of the Guatemalan Opposition (RUOG) in 1982, and the following year, she recounted the story of her life and the ways of her people to the anthropologist, Elisabeth Burgos-Debray, who proceeded to transcribe the tapes and edit them into the internationally known book, *I, Rigoberta Menchú* (1983), which was translated into English by Ann Wright and published in 1984. However, an unexpected controversy erupted in 1999 after anthropologist David Stoll raised questions concerning the authenticity of Menchú's autobiography in *Rigoberta Menchú and the Story of All Poor Guatemalans.* In response to Stoll's book, Arturo Arias edited *The Rigoberta Menchú Controversy* (2001), a compilation of the various newspaper reports, articles, and letters—including one by Stoll—written in response to this ongoing controversy.

After the publication of her autobiography, Menchú continued her activism, becoming a member of the National Committee of the CUC in 1986 and, in 1987, participating as the narrator of *When the Mountains Tremble,* a film protesting the suffering of the Maya people. Menchú was awarded the Nobel Peace Prize in 1992 and, in 1996, became a Goodwill Ambassador for UNESCO.

In 2006, Menchú, along with six other Nobel Peace Prize winners—Jody Williams, Shirin Ebadi, Wangari Maathai, Betty Williams, and Mairead Corrigan Maguire—founded the Nobel Women's Initiative to support the rights of women around the world.

Another Work by Rigoberta Menchú

Crossing Borders. Translated by Ann Wright. New York: Verso, 1998.

A Work about Rigoberta Menchú

Schulze, Julie. *Rigoberta Menchú Tum: Champion of Human Rights.* New York: John Gordon Burke, 1997.

Michaux, Henri (1899–1984) *poet*

An accomplished painter and poet, Henri Michaux was born on May 24 to a bourgeois family in Namur, Belgium. As a student, he was indifferent at best and held himself apart from his peers. He found comfort in art, languages, and literature, all of which helped him through World War II and the German occupation of Belgium.

Although Michaux attempted to write poetry while he was still in school, he concentrated mostly on reading everything from the works of the saints to avant-garde poetry. He considered entering the priesthood but instead followed the advice of his father and embarked on the study of medicine. Dissatisfied, he left to work as a sailor on a merchant vessel, disembarking only two days before the ship capsized. He returned to Belgium where, after a series of miserable jobs, he discovered the works of the COMTE DE LAUTREAMONT.

Inspired, Michaux moved to Paris, where he began to paint and secured a job in a publishing house while developing himself as a writer. After the death of his parents in 1929, he traveled extensively and became fascinated by Eastern religion. His writing career was firmly established due to favorable criticism from ANDRÉ GIDE. Among his best-known collections are *My Properties* (1929), a work that explores the imagination and consciousness, and *Plume* (1930), a comic exploration of self-identity.

Michaux married during World War II but lost his wife in a house fire. After this, he began to experiment with drugs. He became a French citizen in 1955, abandoned drugs, and began to focus his writing on the themes of drug addiction, human anguish, and despair; in *Miserable Miracle* (1956), for example, he details the journeys of the imagination as it searches for self-knowledge while under the influence of mescaline.

Michaux was admired by both the surrealists and the U.S. beat poets. Toward the end of his life, he turned more and more to Eastern meditation as he focused on the study of the human spirit. Michaux died on October 18, having contributed greatly to both the origins of the surrealist movement and U.S. beat literature.

Another Work by Henri Michaux

Tent Posts. Translated by Lynn Hoggard. Los Angeles: Sun and Moon Press, 1997.

A Work about Henri Michaux

Broome, Peter. *Henri Michaux.* London: Athlone Press, 1977.

Mickiewicz, Adam (1798–1855) *poet, playwright*

Adam Bernard Mickiewicz was born in Nowogródek, Poland. Regarded as one of the greatest Polish poets and activists for Polish independence, much of his past remains a mystery, including the possibility that he might have been of Jewish descent on his mother's side. Biographical data, particularly regarding his relationships with women and his interest in mysticism, were kept quiet during the years of Communist rule in Poland. Spirituality of any kind was looked on unfavorably, and much of Mickiewicz's history was deliberately hidden to maintain his flawless public image. After his death, Mickiewicz's son, Władysław, destroyed documents that might have negatively affected his father's public image. Mickiewicz's actions and writings, however, reveal not only a romantic poet and great artist but also a political activist. Mickiewicz's major poetic and dramatic works were written during a three-year period before his attention shifted to political writing.

Mickiewicz received a government-sponsored education in Polish literature and history. He made friends with many fellow students who were members of secret youth organizations. On graduating, he took a high-school teaching position in Kovno to repay his government scholarship, but when authorities discovered secret student organizations at the school, an investigation resulted in a six-month prison term and a five-year exile in Russia.

Mickiewicz's banishment had a positive influence on his career as a writer and activist. He befriended Russian poet ALEKSANDR PUSHKIN and traveled to Germany where he attended Hegel's lectures and met GOETHE. Hearing news of the November uprising in 1830, he attempted unsuccessfully to return to Poland. When the uprising failed, Mickiewicz, along with many other Polish artists, moved to France.

In Paris, he began to focus on political journalism, appealing to Polish emigrants to unite in the common cause. In 1839, he took a position as lecturer on Roman literature at the University of Lausanne and, in 1840, on Slavonic literatures at the Collège de France. He was suspended from his post in 1844 for his antichurch attitude and mystic or supernaturally oriented ideas.

Mickiewicz's poetry was first collected in two volumes called *Vilna* (1822–23) and reflected his love of Polish folklore and tradition, particularly folk songs and legends. This love is evident in his plays *The Forefathers Eve* (1823) and *Grazyna* (1825). Mickiewicz's poetic novel *Konrad Wallenrod* (1828) is based on the history of the Teutonic knights. His work always contains a sense of patriotism and a desire for Poland to one day regain its independence.

Mickiewicz was also a poet of prophecy, a trend held in high regard in Poland throughout the 18th and 19th centuries. He linked his patriotism and nationalism to mysticism and spirituality. Influenced by Andrzej Towianski, a known mystic, Mickiewicz came to believe that Israel was a fellow sufferer of Poland and that Poland was the "Christ" of all nations. He believed that the kingdom of God would prevail in the middle of the 19th century and that the chosen nations would be the Poles, French, and Jews. This commitment to Judaism is often linked to his mother's ancestry and is evident as well in his positive representation of Jewish characters such as Jankiel, the patriotic Jew in *Pan Tadeusz* (1834). Written while he was in exile, this epic poem, his last strictly poetic work, attempts to recapture the Poland of his childhood as an idealized place and time. After the publication of this work, Mickiewicz made what he referred to as a "moral decision" to commit himself to prophecy and political activism, viewing the writing of poetry as trivial in light of Poland's tragic political situation.

More than just a poet and playwright, Mickiewicz was a spiritual leader to the Polish nation. His writings provided hope to not only the people of his native Poland as they struggled under Russian, Prussian, and Austrian rule but also to his many fellow exiles in the emigré circles in Paris.

Other Works by Adam Mickiewicz

Forefathers. Translated by Count Potoki of Montalk. London: Polish Cultural Foundation, 1968.

The Great Improvisation. Translated by Louise Varèse. New York: Voyages, 1956.

Olzer, Krystyna, ed. *Treasury of Love Poems by Adam Mickiewicz.* New York: Hipprocrene Books, 1998.

Works about Adam Mickiewicz

Gardner, Maria. *Adam Mickiewicz, the National Poet of Poland.* New York: Arno Press, 1971.

Welsh, David J. *Adam Mickiewicz.* Boston: Twayne, 1970.

Midang

See SO CHONG-JU.

Milosz, Czeslaw (1911–2004) *poet, novelist*

Czeslaw Milosz was born on June 30 in Seteksniai, Lithuania. Recipient of the Nobel Prize in literature in 1980, he is considered one of Poland's greatest modern poets, though his works, like many of his contemporaries', were once banned in his native land.

Milosz received his early education in Roman Catholic schools. In 1917, at the start of the October Revolution, he left war-torn Russia to live with his grandparents in Szetejnie. He earned a law degree from King Stefan Batory University, where he became politically active, cofounding a leftist literary group called Zagary. On graduation, he began working for a Polish radio station but was ultimately fired from his position for associating with Jews.

Milosz's greatest early influence was his uncle, Oscar Milosz, a noted French-Lithuanian metaphysical poet. He published his first collection of poetry, *Poemat O Czasie (Poem in Frozen Time,* 1933) at age 22. A second volume followed shortly thereafter, and in 1934 he received an award from the Union of Polish Writers for his poetry. World War II intervened and Milosz served as a radio operator. He returned home only to be captured in the Russian occupation of his city. He managed to escape to Poland where he joined the resistance in Warsaw.

Although he was ultimately exiled from Poland, Milosz became well known as a poet in literary circles but suffering greatly, however, from government censorship. He assembled an anthology of English and American poetry that he was not allowed to publish; in addition, so many changes were made to a screenplay he cowrote that he re-fused to allow his name to appear in the credits. In 1945, he joined the Polish diplomatic service, serving in New York and Washington. A year later, his works were banned in Poland, and the government withheld his passport in 1950 as a result of his leftist views and his critical stance against the Communist regime in Poland.

Milosz was allowed to leave Poland in 1951 to seek political asylum in Paris. He obtained refuge at "Kultura," a haven for exiled political writers and artists, with other influential Polish émigrés. Alone and financially destitute, he wrote *The Captive Mind* (1953), in which he harshly criticized Stalinism and "The vulnerability of the twentieth century mind . . . and its readiness to accept totalitarian terror for the sake of a hypothetical future" (Milosz). Although officially banned in Poland and viewed with much negativity by French left-wing intellectuals, the book was astoundingly successful. It was printed by Kultura's underground publishing house, and copies were shipped secretly to Poland.

For five years after the publication of *The Captive Mind,* Milosz did not produce any works. His exile left him feeling alone. He wrote his second novel *Issa Valley* (1955), which tells of childhood in Lithuania, as a means of reconnecting to his past. He was finally able to reunite with his family and, in 1960, moved once again, this time to the United States, where he took a post in Slavic languages and literature at the University of California at Berkeley.

In 1981, Milosz returned home for the first time since 1951. Martial law was declared, however, in December of that same year, and his works were once again banned in Poland. After winning the Nobel Prize, his recognition grew to the point that his poem *You Who Wronged a Simple Man* was used on Solidarity flyers and also inscribed on a monument to Gdansk shipyard workers who had been killed during the 1970 protests. Milosz died at home in Krakow in 2004, age 93.

Other Works by Czeslaw Milosz

The History of Polish Literature. Berkeley: University of California Press, 1983.

Milosz's ABCs. Translated by Madeline G. Levine. New York: Farrar, Straus & Giroux, 2001.

Road-side Dog. Translated by Czeslaw Milosz and Robert Haas. New York: Farrar, Straus & Giroux, 1998.

A Work about Czeslaw Milosz

Nathan, Leonard, and Arthur Quinn. *The Poet's Work: An Introduction to Czeslaw Milosz.* Cambridge, Mass.: Harvard University Press, 1991.

Miron, Gaston (1928–1996) *poet*

Gaston Miron was born in Sainte-Agathe-des-Monts, Québec. He is one of most famous contemporary Québecois poets and has played a significant role in fostering Québecois writing. He cofounded *Hexagon,* which he directed from 1953 to 1983, and he has lectured on Québecois writing and has read his work throughout Europe and North America.

Miron's poems are rich in rhythms, melodies, and evocative words; yet at the same time, they convey an impassioned militant independence. In 1954, he began his major poetic cycle with "Agonique Life," "Walk with Love," and "Bateche." Fragments of these works were eventually published in the early 1960s, and in the 1970s, university presses continued to publish collections of the cycle. Miron's work is today regularly reprinted, translated, and anthologized, reaching a wide and diverse audience. For his work as an editor and essayist, in addition to his work as a poet, he received numerous awards, including the Academy of Letters of Quebec Medal (which recognized Miron's role in celebrating Québecois culture). In 1995, he received an honorary doctorate from the University of Montreal. Miron is considered one of the most significant poets of Quebec.

Another Work by Gaston Miron

The March to Love: Selected Poems, Gaston Miron. Edited and translated by Douglas J. Jones. Pittsburgh, Pa.: International Poetry Forum, 1986.

Mishima Yukio (Hiraoka Kimitake) (1925–1970) *novelist, short story writer, playwright*

Mishima Yukio was born in Tokyo to Hiraoka Azusa and Shizue Hashi. Shortly after his birth, Mishima's paternal grandmother, Natsuko, took him to raise. In accordance with his grandmother's wishes, he attended the elitist Gakushūin, a school founded to educate the imperial family. Mishima was a good student and displayed a talent for writing even while he was young.

While still at Gakushūin, he published his first prose work, *A Forest in Full Bloom* (1941), a historical novel. Mishima disclaimed this story as imitative of Austrian poet Rainer Maria RILKE, but critics received it favorably. Having made a literary entrance, Mishima widened his literary circles, becoming associated with the Japanese romantics.

As World War II raged, Mishima prepared himself to go to war. However, when he went for his final physical, he was misdiagnosed with tuberculosis. As a result, he sat out the war, working in a navy library, and was accepted to Tokyo Imperial University in 1944.

After World War II, the romantics were out of favor in a world dominated by the struggle to recover from the war. Mishima's work was regarded as too introspective, so he had difficulty publishing his stories. However, in 1946 he met KAWABATA YASUNARI, who helped him publish two stories. The first of these— "The Middle Ages" (1946)—was a portrayal of the grief the historical figure Ashikaga Yoshimasa felt over the death of his son, Shogun Ashikaga Yoshihisa. The second story—"Cigarettes" (1946)—was based on Mishima's experiences at Gakushūin. The protagonist becomes a target of members of a rugby club when he reveals that he has joined the literary club. Shortly thereafter, Mishima received his degree from Tokyo Imperial University and went to work for the finance ministry. After less than a year, he left the ministry and joined a group of leftist writers, who helped him once again to publish his work.

In 1948, he published his first novel, *Thieves,* a story of love among a group of upper-class youth. The novel was not well received but demonstrated the development of a romantic style that reached its fulfillment in Mishima's next novel.

Confessions of a Mask (1949) established Mishima as a writer of merit. The story is about a man who struggles with a growing awareness of his homosexuality and attempts to throw off the mask of heterosexuality. In this novel, Mishima tackles for the first time the issue of false appearances, a theme that recurs in his later works.

Although *Confessions of a Mask* launched Mishima's career, the stories that followed were not of the same caliber. Two years passed before he published his next major work, *Forbidden Colors,* a novel that describes the homosexual subculture of Tokyo in the immediate postwar period.

In 1956, Mishima published his best-received work, *The Temple of the Golden Pavilion.* The story centers on a temple acolyte who is handicapped by a stutter. Frustrated by the inaccessibility of beauty, he decides to destroy the temple, a symbol of beauty, and burns it to the ground. This novel won Mishima the Yomiuri Prize for literature.

Mishima married Yōko Sugiyama, the daughter of a well-known painter, in 1958 and settled into a comfortable life. During this period his nationalistic beliefs began to resurface, and he wrote "Patriotism" (1956), a short story based on an attempted coup d'état by imperial army officers in 1936. "Patriotism" was the first in a series of stories that deal with characters who either betray or uphold ideals.

These nationalistic stories helped build to the climax of Mishima's life—his ritualistic suicide within the compound of Japan's Self-Defense Forces in Tokyo in protest of the demilitarization of Japan. On November 25, 1970, Mishima and three members of the militaristic group he organized, the Shield Society, took Gen. Kanetoshi Mashita hostage. After a speech from a rooftop in which Mishima called for a return of the emperor to power, he retired into the building and committed *seppuku* (a ritualistic suicide using a sword).

Critical Analysis

Yukio Mishima's short story "Patriotism" is a disturbing and compelling experience for most readers. The story begins with a paragraph that reads as if it had been taken from an obituary:

> On the twenty-eighth of February 1936 . . . Lieutenant Shinji Takayama . . . took his officer's sword and ceremonially disemboweled himself in the eight-mat room of his private residence in the sixth block of Aoba-Chō, in Yotsuya Ward. His wife Reiko followed him, stabbing herself to death. The lieutenant's farewell note consisted of one sentence: Long live the Imperial forces. His wife, after apologies for her unfilial conduct in thus preceding her parents to the grave, concluded, "The day which, for a soldier's wife, had to come, has come. . . . " The last moments of this heroic and dedicated couple were such as to make the gods themselves weep. The lieutenant's age, it should be noted, was thirty-three, his wife's twenty-three; and it was not half a year since the celebration of their marriage.

This paragraph is intended to shock the reader. One's first reaction is, "What a tragedy, especially for the poor wife who was forced to join her husband." However, that reaction is challenged by the description of the couple as "heroic and dedicated." It is this clash of viewpoints—the western horror of suicide and Mishima's admiration for the ancient Japanese warrior code of the samurai—that makes "Patriotism" such a thought-provoking story.

After the first paragraph, the entire story is a flashback to the political events that led to Shinji's decision to commit seppuku and to the act itself. The story is told with surprising lyricism, and the two protagonists go to their deaths peacefully and joyfully and with all due ceremony, careful not to break the code. The couple make passionate love, knowing that they are about to die, and the love-making is all the more intense because they know it will be their last time. Also surprising is the willingness with which Reiko joins her husband in death. When he announces that he will "cut his stomach," she replies, "I am ready . . . I ask permission to accompany you." She has known this

moment may come and she is completely prepared. She is not portrayed as a victim, either of
her husband's pride or of a culture that demands
such loyalty from wives, but as an active participant in the ceremony, following her husband's
lead with a gentle joy and profound sense of duty.
When Shinji agrees that Reiko will join him, "a
sudden release of abundant happiness welled up in
both their hearts. Reiko was deeply affected by the
greatness of her husband's trust in her."

Mishima's description of the act of suicide itself
is both graphic and loving, brutal and beautiful. If,
as Hippocrates said, art is long while life is short,
then Mishima's characters turn death itself into art,
reinforced, of course, in 1970, by Mishima himself
committing seppuku.

Other Works by Yukio Mishima

After the Banquet. Translated by Donald Keene.
   New York: Knopf, 1963.
Madame de Sade. Translated by Donald Keene.
   New York: Grove Press, 1967.
The Sailor Who Fell from Grace with the Sea. Trans-
   lated by John Nathan. New York: Knopf, 1965.

Works about Yukio Mishima

Nathan, John. *Mishima: A Biography.* Cambridge,
   Mass.: Da Capo Press, 2000.
Scott-Stokes, Henry. *The Life and Death of Yukio
   Mishima.* New York: Farrar, Straus & Giroux, 1974.
Yourcenar, Marguerite. *Mishima: A Vision of the
   Void.* Translated by Alberto Manguel. New York:
   Farrar, Straus & Giroux, 1986.

Miss Lou
See BENNETT, LOUISE.

Mistral, Gabriela (Lucila Godoy Alcayaga) (1889–1957) *poet, essayist*

Gabriela Mistral was born in a rural community
in northern Chile to Jerónimo Godoy Villanueva
(former schoolteacher, guitar player, and song-
writer) and Petronila Alcayaga Rojas. As a child

Mistral was falsely accused by her schoolmaster,
also her godmother, of stealing paper from a supply cabinet. After the incident, she never returned
to the local school and received most of her early
education from her mother and an older sister. By
age 15, she had completed her teacher training and
had begun to teach reading and writing to Indian
children and adults in remote villages.

In 1914, Mistral began to publish poems in various journals in Chile and overseas. It was at this
time that she adopted her pseudonym as a tribute
to two writers she admired: the Italian GABRIELE
D'ANNUNZIO and the Frenchman Frédéric Mistral.
As she devoted much of her energies to her career
as a school administrator, which she considered her
real vocation, it was not until 1922 that she published a larger selection of her poems under the
title *Desolation.* Her first book drew immediate
praise from critics, other writers, and audiences.
In it, the poet addressed many of the themes that
would preoccupy her throughout her life: maternal
affection, the joys and trials of love, the suffering
of the poor. Her second book, *Tenderness* (1925),
includes much of the children's verse that originally
appeared in *Desolation* and that Mistral strove to
develop as a genre in its own right. *Felling* (1938)
represented a break from the style of her earlier
works: While the poetry remains essentially simple,
the stanzaic structure of poems in this and the last
book Mistral published, *Wine Press* (1954), tends
to be more variable and complex. It is the simplicity, emotive force, and subtle profundity of Mistral's
poetry that make it so moving and unique. The
poem "Mourning" from *Wine Press* begins, "In one
single night there burst from my breast / the tree of
mourning; it heightened and grew."

Later in life Mistral received international recognition as a poet, an educator, and an ambassador, and in 1945 she was awarded the Nobel Prize
in literature. She is considered one of the most
important figures in early 20th-century Chilean
and Latin American poetry, and her influence has
proven extensive. Both as an educator and as a
poet, she made poetry accessible to all classes of
society and, in this way, has contributed directly

and indirectly to much of the great poetry that has appeared in Chile and other Hispanic countries in the last several decades.

Other Works by Gabriela Mistral

Agosin, Marjorie, ed. *A Gabriela Mistral Reader.* Translated by Maria Jacketti. Fredonia, N.Y.: White Pine Press, 1992.

Selected Poems. Translated and edited by Doris Dana. Baltimore: Johns Hopkins University Press, 1971.

Works about Gabriela Mistral

Arce de Vázquez, Margot. *Gabriela Mistral: The Poet and Her Work.* Translated by Helene Masslo Anderson. New York: New York University Press, 1964.

Fiol-Matta, Licia. *A Queer Mother for the Nation: The State and Gabriela Mistral.* Minneapolis: University of Minnesota Press, 2002.

Mistry, Rohinton (1952–) *novelist*

Rohinton Mistry was born in Bombay, India, and is of Parsi descent (a community exiled after the Islamic conquest of Iran and one of the smallest existing ethnic minorities in India). After his studies in mathematics and economics at Bombay University, Mistry left India and immigrated to Canada in 1975. He entered the University of Toronto, where he graduated with a bachelor's degree in English and philosophy. This blend of interests may explain the recurring commentary on class status that is an important theme in his works, which are strongly expressive of his upbringing in Bombay and Zoroastrian beliefs.

Mistry's future with writing was sealed after he won first prize in a writing, contest held at the University of Toronto. Following this success, Mistry wrote two collections of short stories, later compiled together in *Swimming Lessons and Other Stories from Feroz Shah Baag* (1987). These works portray both the problems and tribulations of being a Bombay Parsi. Most of the characters are Bombay Parsis who are under pressure to find a balance between their split identities as Zoroastrian Parsis and Indian Parsis.

Mistry's first novel, *Such a Long Journey* (1991), is a continuation of these issues, and it won the Commonwealth Writers' Prize. His novels are written in English but are saturated with a multilingual (English–Hindi–Parsi) colloquialism that is peculiar to Bombay city-talk. Mistry's characters are harmonious hybrids out of the clash between histories and communities. His second novel, *A Fine Balance* (1995), for example, traces the lives of four characters of different castes and religions who must defy social, even individual, prejudices to help each other survive the 1947 partition of India and Pakistan.

Unlike other Indian authors living abroad who, because of distance or exile from India, write about problems surrounding migration or postcolonial subjectivity (*see* POSTCOLONIALISM), Mistry's works are remarkably free of these perspectives. The India of his books is equally recognizable to Indian readers for its authenticity as it is rewarding to an international audience that has little opportunity to read Parsi authors in English.

Critical Analysis

Mistry's work has often been called "Indo-Nostalgic"; that is, for many critics his writing carries a strong undercurrent of longing for the Indian subcontinent, a love for its geography, culture, and an appreciation for its history. While this may be true, there is also an evident appreciation for Western culture and history. In addition, "Indo-Nostalgic" writing does not often engage in the exploration of cultural identity or multiculturalism; instead, it often reveals "palpably deep (and perhaps somewhat romanticized) feelings for their childhoods in the subcontinent," exploring the themes of "rediscovery" or "reconnection" within the context of the West. This approach is characteristic of Mistry's writing, as it tends to explore India's past in a manner that is critical, but also decidedly wistful.

Mistry's breakthrough novel, *Such a Long Journey,* is set in Bombay (now Mumbai), India. Through the experiences of the novel's protagonist, Gustad Noble, we are introduced to everyday life in Bombay in the early 1970s as Noble interacts with his family, dealing in particular with his children's many tribulations, as well as a host of eccentric neighbors and his close friend and coworker, Dinshawji. The narrative takes place within the larger context of India's political turmoil under the leadership of then Prime Minister Indira Gandhi, of whom Mistry has been notably critical. Noble's own "long journey" begins when he unwittingly becomes involved in the politics surrounding the Bangladesh separatist movement in India and Pakistan.

Mistry's second novel, *A Fine Balance*, set from 1947–77, follows its four characters against the frenzied backdrop of post-independence India, always with an eye for those most affected by the turmoil. In *A Fine Balance*, one critic writes, "One can read the sentence: 'the lives of the poor are rich with symbols.' One might just as well say: the book of the poor, not forgetting the fact that the book is indeed about the poor, who remain poor throughout, even if their lives [are] made richer by symbols." Although Mistry's nostalgia is heartfelt, his aim always is to speak about difficult truths.

Other Works by Rohinton Mistry

Family Matters. New York: Vintage, 2003.
The Scream. Toronto, Ontario: McClelland & Stewart, 2008.
The Tales of Ferozsha Baag. London: Faber, 1992.

Works about Rohinton Mistry

Bahrucha, Nilufer E. *Rohinton Mistry.* Jaipur, India: Rawat Publications, 2003.
Batra, Jagdish. *Rohinton Mistry: Identity, Values, and Other Sociological Concerns.* New Delhi: Prestige, 2008.
Bhautoo-Dewnarain, Nandini. *Contemporary Indian Writers in English: Rohinton Mistry.* Cambridge: Cambridge University Press, 2006.
Dodiya, Jaydipsing, ed. *The Fiction of Rohinton Mistry: Critical Studies.* London: Sangam, 1998.

Mo Yan (Guan Moye) (1956–) *short story writer, novelist*

Mo Yan was born on February 17 in Gaomi township in China's Shandong Province, a poor rural community. He often went without food and clothing in the harsh northern climate. Like most young people of his generation, he joined the People's Liberation Army (PLA) in 1976, at age 20, serving as a police commissar and a propaganda officer. He also began writing, publishing his first story, "Rain Falling Thick and Fast in the Spring Night," in 1981.

Mo Yan often describes his writing as an outgrowth of the extreme poverty and isolation of his childhood, as well as of his family's strong oral tradition. He chose an ironic pen name that belied his desire to express himself (*Mo Yan* means, "don't speak"). In 1986, he graduated from the PLA's Armed Forces Cultural Academy's literature department and joined the Chinese Writers Association. By then, he had completed his first book of stories, *The Crystal Carrot* (1986). He also finished *Red Sorghum* (1987), his best-known work, which addresses the plight of China's rural poor while describing an unusual love story set among the sorghum fields of his hometown. Taking place during the Japanese occupation of China, *Red Sorghum* contains patriotic themes. Zhang Yimou's film version won the top prize at the Berlin Film Festival in 1987.

Mo Yan's second novel, *The Garlic Ballads* (1987), addresses corrupt practices by Chinese officials. He writes in *World Literature Today* that it is "a book about hunger, and it is a book about rage." His third novel, *The Republic of Wine*, is both an examination of greed and a reflection upon Mo Yan's own struggles with alcoholism.

Mo Yan's writings are vividly rendered and are often exceedingly graphic in their portrayal of human excess, desire, decadence, and waste. However, his compassion for the Chinese peasant is always present. Most criticisms of Mo Yan's works are aimed at the continuation of patriarchal themes in his work.

Mo Yan remained an employee of the PLA until 1997 when he joined the editorial staff of the *Beijing Procuratorial Daily.* His book of short stories, *Shifu, You'll Do Anything for a Laugh,* was published in English in 2001; the English translation of his novel *Big Breasts and Wide Hips* (2003) was published in 2004. He lives in Beijing.

Other Works by Mo Yan

Life and Death Are Wearing Me Out: A Novel. New York: Arcade Publishing, 2008.
"My American Books." In *World Literature Today* 74:3 (Summer 2000).

Works about Mo Yan

Goldblatt, Howard. "'The Saturnicon': Forbidden Food of Mo Yan." In *World Literature Today* 74:3 (Summer 2000).
Inge, M. Thomas. "Mo Yan through Western Eyes." In *World Literature Today* 74:3 (Summer 2000).
Wang, David Der-Wei. "The Literary World of Mo Yan." In *World Literature Today* 74:3 (Summer 2000).

modernism

The term *modernism* generally refers to the literary and cultural movements associated with the early part of the 20th century from the start of World War I in 1914 to the start of World War II, though there are claims that it began in the middle of the 19th century with the publication of Baudelaire's *Les fleurs du mal* and Flaubert's *Madame Bovary* in 1857, as a response to urbanization, the increasing commodification of life, and the devaluation of art. The modernist movement in literature was created by a change in the way writers looked at the world around them. Influenced by the horrors of World War I and the rise in societal materialism, as well as socioeconomic and religious suppression, these writers' perceptions, not only of the world as a whole but also of humanity's place in that world shifted radically. They needed new ways to express their shifting perceptions.

Modernist writers experimented, often radically, with form. In poetry, formalized rhymes and meters became free verse. Novelists began to write more loosely, for example, forsaking a logical sequence of thoughts for a stream-of-consciousness style. In particular, the conventions of REALISM were discarded in favor of distorted time sequences and collages of imagery. These new forms and styles were often complex and posed a challenge to readers, who then had to struggle to find their own positions relative to the fragmented nature of the works. This creation of a feeling of isolation and dislocation in the reader was one of the main ideas behind modernism.

Modernist writers wanted their readers to think differently about the cultural and political changes occurring throughout Europe and America at the start of the 20th century. The horrors of World War I as well as the discovery of hidden forces motivating and governing human behavior (made by thinkers such as Karl Marx, SIGMUND FREUD, and FRIEDRICH NIETZSCHE) led to a search for hidden meanings elsewhere in society. There was also a shift towards mysticism as an alternative to traditional ideology.

A widespread loss of confidence in the concept of identity was also foremost among the philosophical questions that plagued modernist writers. Long-standing scientific beliefs about the origin of humanity were challenged. The industrialization and mechanization of society was rapidly displacing people from their jobs. Christianity was becoming widely associated with capitalism and with an oppressive, often hypocritical, view of morality. At the same time, the critical study of biblical texts and the rising popularity of Darwin's theory of evolution gave rise to further religious challenge. Finally, a growing awareness of other cultures also influenced modernist concepts and world views, leading to changes in the perception of reality, which began to seem like an external concept rather than an innate one.

Like many other eras of social and political upheaval, the early 20th century found its expression through the arts, with modernism at the heart of that ideology. World War II brought a new period of social change, thus marking the end of this particular movement and paving the way for other trends.

Latin-American Modernism

Modernismo, or Latin-American modernism, was a mostly poetic literary movement, distinct from European and American modernism, that began at the end of the 19th century and lasted until the end of World War I. It resembles French SYMBOLISM and borrowed extensively from the ideas of Charles Baudelaire, especially those concerning art for art's sake.

Modernism rose in a cultural framework defined by a disillusionment with ROMANTICISM and a desire for a renewal of spiritual ideals. Its central figure is poet RUBÉN DARÍO, who, in the 1880s, revitalized Latin-American poetry through his unique diction and his upholding of artistic beauty as life's ultimate ideal.

The modernist poem valued sensations over ideas. This was a revolutionary position in Latin America where, up until that time, most poetry had been either didactic or sentimental. Modernist writers also employed a collection of symbols, borrowed from the French and from antiquity, to represent their ideas in a more visceral fashion. The swan was the most prominent of these symbols. White and graceful, it was a symbol of ideal beauty; at the same time, its neck—hooked in the form of a question mark—represented the doubts of modern humanity.

The erotic, which earlier Latin-American writers had avoided, was embraced by modernists. The sensual aspects of love were celebrated, and erotic passion was equated with the artist's desire to create.

The modernists proposed that artists were in contact with a higher being and were able to unlock life's mysteries by the powers of art. To this end, they concentrated a great deal of effort on developing formal virtuosity and inventing new kinds of versification.

The high modernism of Darío and his followers, with its French influences, was a highly aestheticized movement, cosmopolitan, and not tied to national or patriotic issues. Modernism took a different turn in Brazil, where writers such as Mario de Andrade (1893–1945) and Oswald de Andrade (1890–1954) sought to create a new nation by assimilating the eclectic influences of its history, including indigenous and African cultures, in a new tapestry of national identity. Avant-garde movements in Nicaragua, Mexico, and Cuba also incorporated indigenous and African-based popular cultures.

The modernist movement, and Darío in particular, prepared the way for such poets as PABLO NERUDA and OCTAVIO PAZ. It is important to note, however, that modernists had not yet completely accepted the idea of a world without absolute values and meanings as their 20th-century descendents would. Their poetry was rigorously structured in imitation of their conception of reality. It remained logical and was essentially neoclassical in its ambitions. Unlike their descendents, modernists reacted to the uncertainty of the world by trying to create an art form that reassured them that a moral order could exist. As the 20th century progressed this idea became more and more untenable.

Chinese Modernism

Modernism in China had a more progressive meaning than in Europe and Latin America. Its beginnings can be dated to 1899, when Liang Qichao (Liang Ch'i-ch'ao) (1873–1929), a leading intellectual, called for a "revolution in poetry" and the overthrow of traditional literature, which was written in a formal literary language. He advocated the use of both old and new vernacular mixed with literary Chinese. Other writers, such as Huang Zunxian (Huang Tsun-hsien) (1848–1905), advocated further reforms, such as the addition of colloquial vocabulary and references to modern life in poetry. These reforms were augmented by an increased number of translations of foreign works that had a modernity all their own.

By 1916, despite China's political chaos, writers found unprecedented freedom to experiment and modernize. The decade saw the birth of many literary journals. One of the most influential was Chen Duxiu's *New Youth,* which he founded in 1915 and which served as a focal point in the modernist movement. Chen Duxiu blamed the Confucian classics, which formed the foundation of Chinese literary tradition, for China's inability to modernize.

1917 marks a milestone in the development of China's literary modernism: In January, Chen Duxiu published HU SHIH's "Some Tentative Suggestions for the Reform of Chinese Literature." Its suggestions were indeed modest, but the article was held up as a modernist manifesto. Hu Shihs advised against the use of clichés and advocated timeliness in topics, but the most important innovation he urged was to write in the Chinese vernacular language, known as *baihua,* that is, to use the national language to create a national literature. Hu Shih insisted that the use of a "dead" language produced a "dead" literature.

Hu Shih's article took the literary world by storm. By the time that the second beginning of modernism rolled around on May 4, 1919, experiments in *baihua* literature were already underway. Hu Shih published several *baihua* poems in January 1918, and in May, LU XUN published what is regarded as the first Chinese modernist short story, "Diary of a Madman." A vicious satire that attacks the old Chinese morality, the story is about a paranoid man who suspects all of conspiring to kill and eat him.

The political climate in China urged further change in its literature. After World War I, the 1919 Treaty of Versailles awarded parts of China in concession to Japan. This outraged the Chinese people, and many began to turn their attention to China's weaknesses in the new world and to mobilize in protest. A demonstration on May 4, 1919, drew thousands, including many students and scholars. The task of rectifying China's humiliation instilled literary modernism with a sense of political urgency; writers committed to writing with a cause—that of national pride.

Some of the main themes of modernism were to write in an accessible and truthful language (*baihua*), to think and write critically as a means for change in society and government, to celebrate individualism, and to experiment with new forms.

The short story rose to prominence as a vehicle for modernism. The May Fourth era had begun, and it was a time of great productivity, openness to foreign literature and ideas, and a deep commitment to social change. Writers such as DING LING used modernism to explore modern ideas, such as feminist independence.

Eventually, the May Fourth era gave way to the ascendancy of SOCIALIST REALISM under the Communist regime. Modernism experienced a revival after the easing of restrictions in the 1970s and 1980s, and it is still currently as much the subject of examination and debate in China as is POSTMODERNISM, as Chinese writers reexamine history through literary innovation. Since the Cultural Revolution, modernism has focused on form, such as SYMBOLISM in poetry (as in the writing of BEI DAO) and the avant-garde in theater (as in the plays of Nobel laureate GAO XINGJIAN). Also, a number of writers have turned to explorations of MAGIC REALISM, satire, and stream-of-consciousness writing. Much of the writing that is done in China and in exile by Chinese writers continues the modernist experiment.

Works about Modernism

Ellison, David Richard. *Ethics and Aesthetics in Modernist Literature: From the Sublime to the Uncanny.* New York: Cambridge University Press, 2001.

Fekkema, Douwe, and Elrud Ibsch. *Modernist Conjectures: A Mainstream in European Literature, 1910–1940.* New York: St. Martin's Press, 1988.

Goldman, Merle, ed. *Modern Chinese Literature in the May Fourth Era.* Cambridge, Mass.: Harvard University Press, 1985.

Gross, John, ed. *The Modern Movement: A TLS Companion.* Chicago: University of Chicago Press, 1993.

Larson, Wendy, and Anne Wedell-Wedellsborg. *Inside Out: Modernism and Post-Modernism in Chinese Literary Culture.* Aarhus, Denmark: Aarhus University Press, 1993.

Lee, Leo Ou-fan. "Beyond Realism: Thoughts on Modernist Experiments in Contemporary

Chinese Writing." In Howard Goldblatt, ed., *Worlds Apart: Recent Chinese Writing and its Audiences.* Armonk, N.Y.: M. E. Sharpe, 1990.

Login Jrade, Cathy. *Rubén Darío and the Romantic Search for Unity: The Modernist Recourse to Esoteric Tradition.* Austin: University of Texas Press, 1983.

Montale, Eugenio (1896–1981) *poet*

Winner of the 1975 Nobel Prize in literature, Eugenio Montale was born in Genoa, Italy. The youngest of five children born to Domenico Montale, an import businessman, Montale's formal education was cut short by poor health, but summers spent observing the harsh landscape surrounding his family's villa on the Ligurian riviera soon affected the tone and vision of his poetry. He had originally aspired to a career as an opera singer, but a brief tour as an infantry officer during World War I caused him to set his plans aside.

Montale continued to read fervently, devouring the works of philosophers such as Benedetto Croce and Henri Bergson but also delighting in the classics of both Italian and French fiction. Returning from the war, he again began to sing, but the death of his voice teacher in 1923 caused him to abandon his desire to pursue an operatic career and to look instead toward a literary career.

In 1927, Montale moved to Florence where he secured employment with a publishing house before moving on, in 1928, to accept the position as director of the Gabinetto Viesseux research library. He worked primarily as a critic and is best known in this field for assisting James Joyce in promoting ITALO SVEVO as an emerging Italian voice. At the same time, Montale also began to establish his own literary voice as a poet; he published his first collection of poems, *Bones of the Cuttlefish* (1925), in which he focused on the scenery of his childhood summers in Liguria. Subsequent collections, such as *The Occasions* (1939), became increasingly introspective and focused on personal emotions set against a background of current events.

In 1938, Montale, who had always vocally opposed fascism, was dismissed from his cultural position because of his refusal to join the Fascist Party. He withdrew from public circles and ceased to write, working instead on translations of other writers. In particular, he became very much affected by T. S. ELIOT's poem *The Waste Land.* Montale believed that this work expressed succinctly the confusion and pessimism felt by people living in the time between World War I and World War II. Eliot, in turn, knew of Montale's works and translated his poem *Arsenio* into English at the same time that Montale was working on Eliot's piece. The two writers, separated by vast cultural and geographic distances, seemed to share a similar view of the world. Much of Montale's poetry, like Eliot's, focuses on the dilemma of everyday life and explores modern history, philosophy, and the nature and effect of love on the human condition.

Montale's third collection, *The Storm and Other Poems* (1956), engaged similar themes. His fourth collection, however, took on a slightly more autobiographical tone, containing elements drawn directly from the author's life. This work, *Satura* (1962; translated 1971), also experimented with dialogue and nontraditional form. Some of the poems are satirical in nature, particularly in their look at the empty promises made by certain proponents of ideologies.

In 1967, Montale was made a member for life in the Italian Senate. Shortly thereafter, in 1975, he was awarded the Nobel Prize. His two final works were both diaries written in verse. *Diaro del '71 e del '72* (1973) and *Diaro di quattro annini* (1977) both express aspects of Montale's own life as an artist and as a human being. He died in Milan on September 12, four years after his final publication.

Another Work by Eugenio Montale

Collected Poems: 1920–1954. Translated by Jonathan Galassi. New York: Farrar, Straus & Giroux, 1998.

A Work about Eugenio Montale

Ó Ceallacháin, Éanna. *Eugenio Montale: The Poetry of Later Years.* Oxford: Legenda, 2001.

Mootoo, Shani (1958–   ) *writer, painter, video artist*

A Trinidadian writer and artist of ethnic Indian origin who makes her home in Canada, Shani Mootoo was born in Dublin, Ireland, in 1958. At the time, her father, D. R. K. Mootoo, was studying medicine at the Royal College of Surgeons. Although the new parents stayed in Dublin, the infant of three months was sent to Trinidad to live with her paternal grandparents. Mootoo's grandmother, Basdevi, was third-generation Indo-Trinidadian; they lived in San Fernando on the southwestern coast of the island. At the age of five, Mootoo was reunited with her parents, her father having received his medical degree in 1961.

Mootoo has claimed that she was sexually abused by an uncle as a child—an abuse that her parents and grandparents refused to acknowledge. This became a great source of pain and family tension. Rebellious and more interested in the African aspects of Trinidadian culture, Mootoo has said that she began writing at the age of 10 but received little encouragement from her parents. "When I was ten I wrote what I considered to be a novel," she recalls. "At the time I thought my father was the most powerful man in the world. So I asked him to publish it." These efforts met with disapproval, and Mootoo turned to painting and other visual media.

Mootoo received a degree in fine arts from the University of Western Ontario in 1980. She intended to pursue an advanced degree but, as she said in an interview, "My parents wouldn't let me go. My brother had to get his medical degree and that was more costly." Mootoo returned briefly to Trinidad to teach at Naparima Girl's High as a literature, art, and drama teacher in 1981 but shortly thereafter returned to Canada more or less permanently, settling in Vancouver. One reason Mootoo moved to Vancouver was because of the restrictive, conventional aspects of Trinidadian society and her family life. In Vancouver, she could live openly as a lesbian: "I'm not very good at hiding," she said.

In Vancouver she immersed herself in the arts scene, producing paintings and multimedia video works for museum installations and screenings. A number of these works have been shown at the Venice Biennale and the Museum of Modern Art in New York City as well as museums around Canada. Some of these titles are: *English Lesson* (1991); *Lest I Burn* (1991); *A Paddle and a Compass* (1992); *The Wild Women in the Woods* (1993); *Her Sweetness Lingers* (1994); *Guerita and Prietita* (1995); and *a.m.* (1996). They range from three to 30 minutes in length and were made by Mootoo or in collaboration with other artists.

As with all her work, Mootoo's painting is deeply personal and wrestles directly with the trauma of her childhood in Trinidad. In the early 1980s, she approached Jack Shadbolt, an important Canadian painter and one of the central figures in the Vancouver art world and the Vancouver School of Art, and asked him for feedback on her work. In an interview, Mootoo said that Shadbolt observed the corrosive anger in her work. Mootoo said that he told her, "'If you don't look at what's inside of you right now eating you up like that you won't paint it for very long.' And I knew what he was talking about. He was talking about a lot of the sadness and the deep, deep distress from the sexual abuse as a child."

In this same period, during the mid-1980s and early 1990s, Mootoo kept a diary connected to her past, and she would occasionally show entries to Persimmon Blackbridge, a fellow artist and mentor who also wrote fiction, and who, unbeknownst to Mootoo, passed them on to Press Gang Press, a small Vancouver publisher. Mootoo was hesitant, given the private nature of her materials, but the publishers persisted, and the result was a collection of short stories *Out on Main Street* (1992). In this collection, Mootoo announced one of her central themes: to expose how traditional gender roles are rigidly regulated and policed in Trinidadian society and how transgressions of these norms (for example, lesbianism) result in generational conflict and sometimes brutality and violence. Canada, in these stories, becomes a place of refuge and tolerance.

Out on Main Street was critically well received, and with this encouragement Mootoo produced her first novel, *Cereus Blooms at Night* (1996), for which she received international acclaim and a wide expansion of her audience. *Cereus Blooms at Night* is a powerful story, which some reviewers have likened to American novelist Toni Morrison's *Beloved*, with its themes of female suffering and retribution. With increased visibility, Mootoo became a contributing editor for the national broadcast of the CBC (Canadian Broadcasting Company) program "This Morning." Several works have followed: *The Predicament of Or* (2001), a book of poems, and the novels *He Drown She in the Sea: A Novel* (2005) and *Valmiki's Daughter* (2008). *Valmiki's Daughter* returns to familiar terrain for Mootoo. It relates the story of a well-off Trinidadian family—in particular, a doctor, Valmiki, and his daughter, Viveka—both of whom are concealing their true sexual identities. As a writer and an artist, Mootoo continues to mine her Caribbean experience for her fictional themes.

Critical Analysis

As the critic Evelyn O'Callaghan has observed, Shani Mootoo's work shares affinities with other Trinidadian and Carribean writers, such as V. S. NAIPAUL, though she does this from a much more strongly female and feminist point of view. Virtually all of her books "deal with those who feel themselves to be outsiders at home and who come to see the migrant condition as the only viable alternative." Canada becomes the space where Mootoo can find the creative and social distance to critique the society that has set her into motion. Mootoo connects the ways in which questions of gender and sexual orientation are typically silenced in West Indian culture, creating the social conditions in which individuals marked by these differences are made to suffer or to seek open expression of their identity through migration.

Set on the lush island of Lantanacamara (a fictionalized Trinidad), *Cereus Blooms at Night* tells the story of Mala Ramchandin, who has been sexually abused by her father and has an affinity with snails: "For Mala, snails and the natural world she connects with are far more benevolent than

the sort of danger she encounters from human beings. Nature is never hateful, but human beings are." The violence that Mala witnesses visited upon snails soon is visited upon her, and she is forced to conceal her pain. The title of the novel refers to a beautiful flower that blossoms only once a year, at night. As the symbolism of the title suggests, survival in the teeth of abuse, abandonment, and madness is the theme of the novel. "I'm a survivor of incest," Mootoo has remarked, "and I'm a lesbian, so I know how easy it is—too easy—to remain in the place of the victim."

The novel explores the nature of colonialism through a meddlesome missionary couple, the Thoroughlys, who arrive from Great Britain and raise a young boy away from his family in order to bring him up as a "proper Christian gentleman." Mootoo shows how this process makes the boy ashamed of his own background, frequently in intimate, bodily terms. "His mother, smelling of coals and charred eggplant and a sweat that embarrassed him with its pungency of heated mustard seed, had left the clay oven at the back their quarters. She quickly pulled her orhanie [head covering formerly worn by East Indian women] over her head and nose and mouth." In scenes such as this, Mootoo depicts the evolution of colonial mentality through the cultivation of a sensibility that rejects the native and indigenous. Mootoo then narrates the ways in which her central characters attempt to liberate themselves from the effects of colonialism. The novel found a responsive audience. It was nominated for a number of prestigious literary prizes, including the Ethel Wilson Fiction Prize in 1997, the Chapters/Books in Canada First Novel Award, the Giller Prize, and the Booker Prize.

Other Works by Shani Mootoo

"Hybridity and Other Poems." In *Performing Hybridity*. Minneapolis: University of Minnesota Press, 1999.

Works about Shani Mootoo

Brüning, Angela. "The Corporeal and the Sensual in Two Novels by Shani Mootoo and Julia Alvarez."

In *Beyond the Blood, the Beach & the Banana: New Perspectives in Caribbean Studies.* Edited by Sandra Courtman. Kingston, Jamaica: Ian Randle: 2004.

Gagnon, Monika Kin. "Out in the Garden: Shani Mootoo's Xerox Works." In *Other Conundrums: Race, Culture and Canadian Art.* Vancouver: Arsenal Pulp Press, 2000.

Morante, Elsa (1918–1985) *novelist*

Elsa Morante, best known for her critically acclaimed novel *La storia* (1974), was born in Rome. She left home at the age of 18 to live with an older man, her education incomplete. A year later, however, she met the writer ALBERTO MORAVIA, whom she married after a brief affair with a younger man. Moravia recognized Morante's natural gift as a writer and introduced her to many of the leading Italian writers and intellectuals of the time.

Morante's first published work, *Il gioco segreto* (1941), was a collection of short stories, several of which she had already published in magazines and journals. She followed this with a children's book, *Le bellissime avventure di Cateri dalla trecciolina* (1942). Although both works were well received, they received little critical attention. She spent the latter half of World War II hiding from fascist authorities in the countryside. This rural environment later played a great role in her fiction.

Late in the 1940s, William Weaver, an American translator, befriended both Morante and Moravia and introduced their works to an American audience. Simultaneously, Morante began to translate the works of writer Katherine Mansfield. Influenced by Mansfield's style, Morante wrote *Menzogna e sortilegio* (1948; translated 1951) which, with the help of Weaver, was translated into English as *House of Liars.* The work presented what would come to be Morante's common themes of memory, dreams, and obsessions, and the novel gained immediate critical success.

Morante was never a prolific writer and was critical of her own work, much of which she destroyed. Her major work, *La storia* (1974),

translated into English as *History*, was set in Rome during and after World War II and dealt with the impact of historical events on the individual human beings who lived them. Each of the work's eight sections begins with an omniscient narrator who relates the events of the war as they are happening and then describes how these events affect the lives of individuals, both physically and psychologically. The novel was awarded the Viareggio Prize and was adapted to film in 1985.

Morante's final novel, *Aracoeli* (1982), a sensitive treatment of homosexuality, was also highly acclaimed. She continued to write, publishing essays and short stories, until her death in Rome.

Another Work by Elsa Morante

Arturo's Island: A Novel. Translated by Isabel Quigley. South Royalton, Vt.: Steerforth Press, 2002.

Moravia, Alberto (Alberto Pincherle) (1907–1990) *novelist, short story writer, essayist, playwright*

Alberto Moravia was born in Rome to Carlo Pincherle Moravia, an architect and painter, and Teresa DeMarsanich, a countess. At age 9, Moravia's health deteriorated when he became ill with coxitis, tuberculosis of the bone. After several months in bed, he recovered somewhat and was taken to Viareggio on vacation. In *Life of Moravia* (1990), a book he wrote with Alain Elkann, Moravia said, "In Viareggio, many things happened: I found out what sex was. More or less the basic experience I narrated in *Agostino*, though the situations and characters there are the fruit of invention."

Moravia published his first novel, *The Time of Indifference*, in 1929, which gained him recognition. This EXISTENTIALIST novel is the story of siblings who explore the themes of alienation and a society that they perceive as shallow and false. Moravia won more praise for his two novels *Agostino* (1944) and *Luca* (1948). He fused the two works and published them in English under the title *Two Adolescents*. The story of Agostino, depicting themes of a teen's sexual exploration, loss of innocence, and disillusionment with the world, melds into the story of Luca, a 15-year-old boy, chronicling the angst and rebellion of the teen. It follows him through his sexual initiation, a grave illness, and ultimate redemption.

Another important theme in Moravia's novels is the condemnation of society's values. His works, such as *The Wheel of Fortune* (1935) and *Two Women* (1958), were censored and ultimately banned by the fascist government for their allegorical representation of capitalism and fascism as destroyers of innocence.

Moravia told an interviewer for *The Guardian,* "A writer has few themes if he is faithful to himself. He should not have much to say, but what he has to say he should give depth to and say in different ways." One recurring theme in Moravia's novels is the relationship between perception and reality, between one's internal thoughts and the outside world. Of his own reality, in terms of his writing, Moravia says, in *Life of Moravia,* "My books never satisfy me completely. I've always had the impression I could improve them, make them better."

Although Moravia may not have been satisfied with his writing, his list of prestigious honors confirms his talent. *Agostino* was awarded the Corriere Lombardo Prize in 1945. In 1952, he won the Chevalier de la Légion d'Honneur and the Strega Prize.

Another Work by Alberto Moravia

The Voyeur: A Novel. Translated by Tim Parks. New York: Farrar, Straus & Giroux, 1987.

A Work about Alberto Moravia

Peterson, Thomas E. *Alberto Moravia.* Boston: Twayne, 1996.

Mori Ōgai (Rintarō Mori) (1862–1922)
novelist, short story writer, poet, essayist

Mori Ōgai was born in the remote town of Tsuwano to a physician during the last years of Japan's feudal system. A gifted student, he was studying the Chinese classics by the age of five, and at 19, he graduated from Tokyo Imperial University with a medical degree and joined the army. The government sent Mori in 1884 to study medical hygiene at German universities. While there, he also read widely in Western literature. Shortly after his return, he served as a medical officer during the Sino-Japanese War (1894–95) and the Russo-Japanese War (1904–05). In 1907, he became surgeon-general. Mori retired from the army in 1916 to become director of the Imperial Household Museum and head of the Imperial Art Academy.

On his return from Germany, Mori wrote several novellas, including *The Dancing Girl* (1890), a story about an affair between a Japanese student and a German woman in Berlin. Although his early stories were romantic, Mori became increasingly interested in history as a medium for storytelling. *The Wild Geese* (1911–13), a romantic story of unrequited love, is relayed as an "old tale." Then, four days after the ritualistic suicide of Gen. Maresuke Nogi, who loyally followed Emperor Meiji into death in 1912, Mori wrote "The Last Testament of Okitsu Yagoemon," which examines the Confucian ideal of blind loyalty to one's master. This short story created a new Japanese literary genre called *rekishi shōsetsu* (historical fiction), which Mori used to explore ideals and character in the rapidly changing society of early 20th-century Japan.

Mori's renown stems from his medical accomplishments, complex prose style, and creation of a new genre, adopted by such writers as AKUTAGAWA RYŪNOSUKE and Yasushi Inoue. Mori also contributed to the modernization of Japanese theater by translating more than 50 European plays. For these accomplishments, he is regarded, along with NATSUME SŌSEKI, as one of the greatest influences on modern Japanese literature.

Other Works by Mori Ōgai

Dilworth, David, and J. Thomas Rimer, eds. *Saiki Kōi and Other Stories.* Honolulu: University of Hawaii Press, 1977.
Rimer, J. Thomas. *Youth and Other Stories.* Honolulu: University of Hawaii Press, 1994.

Works about Mori Ōgai

Marcus, Marvin. *Paragons of the Ordinary: The Biographical Literature of Mori Ōgai.* Honolulu: University of Hawaii Press, 1993.
Rimer, John Thomas. *Mori Ōgai.* Boston: Twayne, 1975.

Mrożek, Slawomir (1930–) *playwright, short story writer*

Slawomir Mrożek was born in Borzecin, near Kraków, Poland. The son of a postal carrier, Mrożek first began his career as a journalist and cartoonist, writing satirical short articles that used wordplay and grotesque situations as a backdrop for their humor.

While writing for a Kraków newspaper, Mrożek began to write satirical short stories. The first collection of his works, *Slon* (1957; translated *The Elephant,* 1967) satirized various aspects of Polish communism in the 1960s. It was immediately successful both critically and publicly. The title story pokes fun at a small-town zoo which, when it is allocated government money to acquire an elephant, decides to save the government the money by inflating a large elephant-shaped balloon. They tell visitors that the elephant is very sluggish and that is why it hardly ever moves. Their scheme works until a gust of wind blows the elephant away. Other stories in the collection include a tale in which a lion refuses to take part in the eating of Christians because it knows that one day the Christians will rise to power and remember its actions. Another story focuses on an uncle who cannot tell his nephew what a giraffe looks like because he only reads books on marxism. When he looks through all of his Marxist books, he discovers they say nothing about giraffes, and the nephew, therefore, concludes that giraffes do not exist.

In the late 1950s, Mrożek left journalism to write plays. His first drama was *The Police* (1958). As a playwright, he is most noted for his subtle parody and his use of stylized language. His dramas present simple situations and human behaviors that are taken to the absurd. Mrożek's works

belong to the style of theater known as the THEATER OF THE ABSURD, which creates dramatic effect through distortion and parody.

In 1963, Mrożek emigrated to France and then to Mexico. His first full-length drama, *Tango* (1964; translated 1968), was first staged in 1964 and was eventually performed throughout Europe. The play presents a satirical psychological observation of totalitarianism.

In the 1990s, Mrożek focused his attention on war, the disintegration of morality, and a political system based on genocide. *Love in Crimea* (1994) focuses on the fall of the Russian empire; *The Beautiful Sight* examines the Balkan War from the point of view of two European tourists vacationing at the seaside in the former Yugoslavia who become annoyed by the interruption of the war; and *The Reverends* looks at religious hypocrisy.

After the 1990s, Mrożek continued to write and express his views about the tragedy still facing much of Eastern Europe in the 21st century. His works are influential both from their political standpoint and in their accurate representation of history in the making.

Other Works by Slawomir Mrożek

The Mrożek Reader. Edited by Daniel Gerould. New York: Grove Press, 2004.
Striptease; Tango; Vatzlav: Three Plays by Slawomir Mrożek. New York: Grove, 1981.

A Work about Slawomir Mrożek

Stephan, Halina. *Translating the Absurd: Drama and Prose of Slawomir Mrożek.* Amsterdam: Rodopi, 1997.

Müller, Heiner (1929–1995) *dramatist*

Heiner Müller was born in Eppendorf, Saxony, into a working-class family. His father, a socialist, was beaten, arrested, and lost his job during the Nazi regime. Müller too became a socialist and was a civil servant in East Germany and later worked as a journalist and technical writer for the East German Writers' Union. He honed his skills as a dramatist working at the Maxim Gorki Theater in East Berlin in the late 1950s.

Müller wrote three plays with his wife, Inge Müller. The pair won the Heinrich Mann Prize in 1959. Their collaborative work *Der Lohndrücker* (*The Wage Shark*, 1957) was a critique of working conditions in East Germany. Because the Müllers refused to whitewash negative aspects of the socialist state, their own government disapproved of their plays, but their works were more successful in the West. After the government forced Müller to abandon contemporary subjects, he began to write adaptations of classical works in the 1960s; however, he added his own interpretations to the plays of Sophocles, Shakespeare, and the Soviet dramatist MIKHAIL SHOLOKHOV. These adaptations finally brought Müller fame in East Germany: He won the prestigious Büchner Prize in 1985.

Müller's writing reflects a strong influence from BERTOLT BRECHT. Although his dialectical dramas elicited official disapproval in East Germany, Müller's work with classic dramas earned him widespread acclaim. His biographer Jonathon Kalb notes in *The Theater of Heiner Müller* (1984) that Müller saw "that overvaluation of originality, the bourgeois-era cult of the absolutely new, was a factor in the devaluation of history (in the West and East), and responded with a string of texts that refused to treat originality with proper capitalistic seriousness." He is also known for combining lyrical prose with poetry to create language in his plays. Müller frequently depicted the individual's struggle with society, and his works address the causes of late 20th-century German angst.

Another Work by Heiner Müller

A Heiner Müller Reader: Plays, Poetry, Prose. Edited and translated by Carl Weber. Baltimore: Johns Hopkins University Press, 2001.

A Work about Heiner Müller

Kalb, Jonathon. *The Theater of Heiner Müller.* Munich: C. H. Beck, 1984.

Müller, Herta (1953–) *novelist, poet, essayist*

Herta Müller, the Romanian-born German novelist who won the Nobel Prize in literature in 2009, is best known for her powerful literary rendition of cruelty and horror in communist Romania during the repressive Nicolae Ceauşescu regime. She was born on August 17, 1953, in the Banat district in western Romania, into a family of Romania's German minority. Her grandfather had been a wealthy farmer whose property was confiscated by the communist regime, forcing his son to work as a truck driver to support his family. Müller's mother spent five years (1945–50) in a forced labor camp in the Soviet Union. The novel *Everything I Possess I Carry with Me* (2009) was partly inspired by what happened to Müller's mother after the deportation to the camp in present-day Ukraine.

Müller left her village of Nitzkydorf to study German and Romanian literature at the University of Timişoara, where she joined the Aktionsgruppe Banat, an organization of Romanian-German writers who sought freedom of expression under the Ceauşescu dictatorship. After graduating, Herta got a job as a translator in an engineering factory. She worked there for two years, until she was fired in 1979 for refusing to cooperate with the infamous Securitate—the Romanian secret police. After refusing to be an informant, she was exposed to various forms of harassment, facing interrogations and persecution. During those hard times, Müller wrote the short stories that would comprise her first book. The book, *Nadirs* (1982), was released in a state-censored version that had been radically modified. Müller was trying to make ends meet by teaching and giving private German lessons when an uncensored manuscript of *Nadirs* was smuggled to the West and published to instant critical acclaim. Fearing the secret police, Müller had to meet her German proofreader in the forest so that no one could overhear their discussions. After a trip to the Frankfurt Book Fair where she spoke out publicly against the Romanian dictatorship, she was forbidden to publish in Romania. In *Nadirs*, as well as in the *Oppressive Tango* (1984),

Müller depicted the hypocrisy of village life and its ruthless oppression of nonconformists. Her focus on the intolerance and corruption of the German minority in Romania earned her harsh criticism and accusations of destroying the idyllic image of German rural life in Romania.

After being refused permission to immigrate to West Germany in 1985, Müller managed to leave two years later. Her husband, novelist and essayist Richard Wagner, joined her, and they settled in Berlin. In the following years, Müller started lecturing at universities in Germany and abroad. She received many honorary positions and was elected to membership in the German Academy for Writing and Poetry in 1995.

Many of Müller's works reflect aspects of her own history, as well as her family and friends' personal experiences and intimate recollections. Her 1996 novel, *The Land of Green Plums,* was written after the deaths of two friends who were killed, Müller suspected, by the secret police. Also, one of its characters was based on a close friend from Aktionsgruppe Banat. This novel contains her richest portrayal to date of life under the Romanian dictatorship, and she links the repressive childhood of her narrator with the brutal oppression of the state. The novel *Passport* (1986), which was written while Müller was waiting for permission to immigrate to Germany, chronicles the efforts of a Romanian-German peasant family to get passports to leave the country. Like her earlier works, this tale exposes the brutal corruption of the village by showing how its officials, from postmaster to priest, demanded material goods and sexual favors from those petitioning to leave the country. *Traveling on One Leg* (1989) portrays the problems of resettlement in the West and the feelings of alienation that plague the political exile. Many of the essays in *A Warm Potato Is a Warm Bed* (1992) are reflections on political events and complicated issues of homeland. Another volume of essays, *The Devil Is Sitting in the Mirror* (1991), includes a series of lectures that Müller gave at the University of Paderborn in 1989–90 and discusses the tensions and conflicts that give rise to the poetic imagery in her work. The volume includes a number of collages combining image and text.

The novel *Even Back Then, the Fox Was the Hunter* (1992) tells the story of a teacher harassed by the Romanian secret police and explores the disintegration of identity in a nation governed by fear. Müller's most recent collection of essays, *Hunger and Silk* (1995), mainly deals with her earlier life as a nonconformist and dissident. Müller has been an outspoken critic of those East German writers who collaborated with the secret police, and she even withdrew from the World Association of Writers, PEN, in 1997, as a protest against the decision of its German section to merge with its former DDR branch.

Müller's works are characterized by pure poetic language and metaphors that recur and evolve throughout her tales. The oppressiveness of bleak themes is alleviated by the beauty of her prose and the flashes of humor behind some of her imagery. She has won a dozen literary prizes, including the Marieluise-Fleißer Prize (1990), the Kranichsteiner Literary Prize (1991), the Kleist Prize (1994), and the European Literary Prize "Aristeion" (1995). Müller has given guest lectures at universities, colleges, and other venues in Paderborn, Warwick, Hamburg, Swansea, Gainesville (Florida), Kassel, Göttingen, Tübingen, and Zürich, among other places. She lives in Berlin.

The Nobel Prize to Herta Müller coincided with the 20th anniversary of the fall of communism. The spokesman of the Swedish Academy compared Müller's use of German as a minority language with another famous German-speaking author, FRANZ KAFKA. Michael Krüger, head of Müller's publishing house, stated: "By giving the award to Herta Müller, who grew up in a German-speaking minority in Romania, the committee has recognized an author who refuses to let the inhumane side of life under communism be forgotten."

Another Work by Herta Müller
The Appointment. Translated by Michael Hulse and Philip Boehm. New York: Metropolitan Books, 2001.

A Work about Herta Müller

Haines, Brigid, ed. *Herta Müller*. Cardiff: University of Wales, 1998.

Munonye, John (1929–1999) *novelist*

John Munonye was born in Akokwa, Imo State, Nigeria. He was the fourth of seven children. Munonye's father, a farmer, worked hard to send him to Christian schools. He first completed his undergraduate education at the University of Ibadan before leaving for London to obtain his masters in education at the University of London's Institute of Education. Munonye returned to Nigeria in 1954 and worked as a teacher for three years. He was promoted to the positions of administrator and school inspector in 1958, and he became principal of the Advanced Teachers College in 1970.

Munonye's writings reflect the cultural and psychological conflict he experienced balancing traditional Igbo values and Western ideology. His themes consist of the predicament of the common person's struggle in a rapidly modernizing world, colonial experience, cultural conflict, family friction, and love. In *The Oil Man of Obange* (1971), for example, Munonye tells the tragic tale of a palm-oil seller's sacrifice for his children in colonial Nigeria. Jeri, the main protagonist, literally works himself to death to give his children a Western education. In *The Only Son* (1966), Munonye began a trilogy that examines issues of religious differences and the generation gap between old and young people in Nigerian society.

Munonye's literary achievements tend to be overshadowed by the popularity of fellow Nigerian CHINUA ACHEBE, whom he used as a model for his writings. Unlike Achebe, however, Munonye incorporated humor into his reflections of the somber realities of life in colonial Nigeria. Munonye was a member of the first generation of Nigerian writers to write about their pasts in the initial stages of Nigeria's independence. His writing represents a voice among many, which bespeaks a clear optimism tainted by apprehension.

Works about John Munonye

Lindfors, Bernth. *Dem-Say: Interviews with Eight Nigerian Authors*. Austin, Tex: African and Afro-American Studies and Research Center, 1974.

Nnolim, Charles E. "Structure and Theme in Munonye's *The Oil Man of Obange*." *African Literature Today* 12 (1982): 163–173.

Munro, Alice (1931–) *novelist, short story writer*

Alice Munro was born Alice Laidlaw in Wingham, Ontario, to Robert Laidlaw and Ann Chamney. During the depression, her father bred silver foxes. Munro began college at the University of Western Ontario but left in 1951 to marry James Munro. During the 1950s and 1960s, she privately wrote short stories. Her first collection, *Dance of the Happy Shades,* was published in 1968 and drew on her own experiences; for example, the story "Boys and Girls" begins, "My father was a fox farmer. That is, he raised silver foxes, in pens; and in the fall and early winter. . . ."

After the success of her first work, Munro continued publishing stories and novels. She writes "regional" fiction, realistic, domestic stories about ordinary people grounded in a particular region, Western Ontario; she was inspired by southern U.S. writers such as Eudora Welty. Her second work, *Lives of Girls and Women* (1971), is an episodic novel set in Jubilee, Ontario, and explores the emotional and imaginative development of the protagonist Del Jordan. Geoffrey Wolff of *Time* magazine noted the homespun realism of the work: "The book is a fiction for people who like to read brittle, yellow clips from newspapers published in towns where they never lived, who like to look through the snapshot albums of imperfect strangers."

Who Do You Think You Are? (1978), considered Munro's best work, is a collection of interrelated stories that follow the life of a character named Rose through childhood, college, marriage, and back to her childhood home. It explores the dark secrets underneath the surface of small-town life, such as incest and abuse: "He shakes her and hits her against the wall, he kicks her legs. She is incoherent, insane, shrieking. *Forgive me! Oh please, forgive me!*" One of Munro's hallmarks is the coherence of her short story collections, as critic Ildiko de Papp Carrington notes: "Although eight of the ten stories in *Who Do You Think You Are?* were originally published separately, the collection constitutes an organic whole." The collection was short-listed for the Booker Prize. Munro's 2002 collection of short stories, *Hateship, Friendship, Courtship, Loveship, Marriage,* continues her exploration of life in rural Ontario. Critic Beverly Rasporich contends that "the fictional world that Munro creates is an expanding, visionary location but at the same time always recognizably hers." In 2009, Munro was awarded the Man Booker International Prize for her entire body of work.

Critical Analysis

A story that is clearly semiautobiographical, Munro's 1968 tale "Boys and Girls" is also a richly ambiguous adolescent initiation story. Just as Munro's father once raised foxes, so does the narrator's father in this story and the narrator is at pains to point out that she is no city child, unused to life and death on the farm. She and her brother, in fact, like to watch their father skin the foxes.

When the narrator goes to bed at night in the attic room she shares with her younger brother, she lies awake inventing stories about herself as she grows older. In most of the stories, she is a swashbuckling hero, rescuing people from all sorts of dangers. During the day, she says, she much prefers her father's "world" to that of her mother and enjoys working outdoors with him. "Work done out of doors, and in my father's service, was ritualistically important." She hates helping her mother in her "hot dark kitchen."

One evening the narrator hears her mother complaining to her father about how little help she gets from her daughter. "It's not like I had a girl in the family at all." Later the narrator says she began to hear more on the theme of being a girl: "I

no longer felt safe . . . The word girl had formerly seemed to me innocent and unburdened like the word child; now it appeared that it was no such thing. A girl was not, as I had supposed, simply what I was; it was what I had to become. It was a definition, always touched with emphasis, with reproach and disappointment." The narrator fights against this new definition but finds ineluctably that her nighttime fantasies begin to change. Now she is the one who is rescued.

At the end of the story, the narrator, in a desperate and foolish act, allows the escape of a horse that was about to be slaughtered in order to provide meat for the foxes. Although she has already told the reader that she knows and accepts the fate of farm animals, she does not say why she is impelled to try to save the horse. However, it is clear that hers is a symbolic gesture. She wants the horse to escape her fate just as she wishes to escape being a girl.

She does not succeed. That evening, after her father and brother have captured and killed the horse, her brother reveals that the narrator deliberately let the horse go. Her father asks her why she would do such a thing. She does not reply. "'Never mind,' my father said. He spoke with resignation, even good humor the words which absolved and dismissed me for good. 'She's only a girl,' he said." The narrator continues, "I didn't protest that, even in my heart. Maybe it was true."

In this story, Munro does a brilliant job of tracing the social creation of a gendered identity. The narrator, like most prepubescent girls, is androgynous. She thinks of herself as a person and wants for herself the free and active life that her father has. She sees no reasons she should not grow up to be a person with the freedom to choose what she likes to do. Yet the social pressure to be a "girl" is so strong that it even invades her dreams. Her final gesture is fruitless.

Other Works by Alice Munro

Runaway. New York: Vintage, 2005.
Selected Stories. New York: Knopf, 1996.
Too Much Happiness. New York: Knopf, 2009.
The View from Cable Rock. New York: Vintage, 2008.

A Work about Alice Munro

Howells, Coral Ann. *Alice Munro*. New York: St. Martin's Press, 1998.

Murakami Haruki (1949–   ) *novelist, short story writer*

Murakami Haruki was born in Kyoto, Japan, to Murakami Chiaki and Miyuki, both teachers, who often discussed classical poetry and medieval war tales at home. Thus instilled with a love of literature, Murakami entered the drama program at Waseda University with the intention of becoming a scriptwriter. After graduating, Murakami, with his wife, Yōko, opened a prosperous jazz club called Peter Cat in Tokyo. Then in 1986, Murakami moved to Europe, where he lived for most of a decade.

Reputedly inspired by a baseball game he attended in 1978, Murakami began to write novels, publishing his first a year later. *Hear the Wind Sing* (1979) is a retrospective story based on bar conversations between the unnamed protagonist, *boku* (I), and his friend "the Rat." The book won *Gunzō* magazine's New Novelist Prize.

His next novels further developed the character of *boku,* an everyman who represents the inner workings of the mind. In 1985, *Hard-Boiled Wonderland and the End of the World* split the world of *boku* in two: the real and the fantastic. Murakami then spent two years at Princeton University where he researched his next two books, *South of the Border, West of the Sun* (1998) and *The Wind-up Bird Chronicle* (1997). Since the 1995 sarin gas attack on a Tokyo subway, Murakami has published two volumes of interviews with both the victims and the members of the religious sect that took responsibility for the attack.

In 2002, *Kafka on the Shore* was first published in English. The novel alternates chapters, telling two different but interrelated stories, one about the 15-year-old writer FRANZ KAFKA. In 2004, *After Dark* was published in English. This novel focuses on a single night in metropolitan Tokyo. His nonfictional *What I Talk about When I Talk about Running* was published in 2008.

Murakami is regarded as one of the first Japanese authors at ease with the Westernization of Japan, largely due to his incorporation of foreign words into his prose and his open portrayal of postwar Japan. He has won the Tanizaki Jun'ichirō Prize and the Yomiuri Literary Award.

Other Works by Murakami Haruki

The Elephant Vanishes. Translated by Alfred Birnbaum and Jay Rubin. New York: Vintage International, 1993.
Norwegian Wood. Translated by Jay Ruben. London: Harvill Press, 2000.
A Wild Sheep Chase. Translated by Alfred Birnbaum. Tokyo: Kodansha International, 1989.

Works about Murakami Haruki

Aoki Tamotsu. "Murakami Haruki and Contemporary Japan." Translated by Matthew Strecher. In John W. Treat, ed., *Contemporary Japan and Popular Culture*. Honolulu: University of Hawaii Press, 1996.
Rubin, Jay. "Murakami Haruki's Two Poor Aunts Tell Everything They Know About Sheep, Wells, Unicorns, Proust, and Elephants." In Stephen Snyder and Philip Gabriel, eds., *Ōe and Beyond: Fiction in Contemporary Japan*. Honolulu: University of Hawaii Press, 1999.

Musil, Robert von Edler (1880–1942) *novelist, playwright*

Robert Musil was born in Klagenfurt, Austria, to Alfred Musil, a professor of engineering at the Technical University of Brunn and an arms manufacturer, and Hermine Musil. Robert Musil's childhood was difficult: His father was devoted to his career, and his mother was involved in an affair with Robert Musil's private tutor for many years. In elementary school, Musil had a nervous breakdown as a result of frequent family dramas at home. At the age of 12, he was sent away to a military academy by his father and, between 1898 and 1901, attended the Technical University of Brunn. Forced to study engineering by his domineering father, Musil finally revolted, left for Germany, and decided to study philosophy instead. In 1908, he received a doctorate in philosophy from the University of Berlin.

Musil began his writing career as a student at the University of Berlin. In 1906, he published his first novel, *Young Torless,* which was based on his experiences in the military academy. Although Musil's work was somewhat popular, he could not support himself by writing; from 1911 to 1914, he worked as a librarian in Vienna. He served in the Austrian army during World War I and, after being wounded, edited the army newspaper. After the war, Musil worked in various administrative capacities for the ministry of defense, but he lost his position and became a full-time writer and journalist in the 1920s.

After producing a number of short plays and satires, Musil concentrated on writing his major work, *The Man Without Qualities* (1930–43). This monumental novel describes the social, cultural, and political life during the last days of the Habsburg empire. In a style often compared to MARCEL PROUST'S, Musil focused on the emotional and intellectual development of the individual and concentrated on such themes as sexuality and survival. Ulrich, the protagonist of the novel, a highly educated but psychologically immature man, desires to find his place in modern life. He undergoes a deep emotional transformation, marked by an almost psychologically incestuous relationship with his sister Agathe.

Married to a Jewish woman, Musil feared persecution by the Nazis and fled Austria for Switzerland in 1938. In Switzerland, he published a number of short essays; however, he remained an obscure writer. Robert Musil died in poverty and without due recognition. Most of his works have been rediscovered and published since his death. Today, Musil is considered one of the great writers of Austria. His works have been translated into more than 20 different languages.

Other Works by Robert Musil

Diaries, 1899–1941. Translated by Philip Payne. New York: Basic Books, 2000.

Five Women. Translated by Eithne Wilkins. New York: David R. Gordon, 1999.
Precision and Soul: Essays and Addresses. Chicago: University of Chicago Press, 1995.

A Work about Robert Musil

Jonsson, Stephen. *Subject Without a Nation: Robert Musil and the History of Modern Identity.* Durham, N.C.: Duke University Press, 2001.

Musset, Alfred de (1810–1857) *poet, playwright*

Best known for his poetry, Alfred de Musset was inspired by Shakespeare and a love affair with GEORGE SAND. He can also be credited as having written the first modern French dramas. Born in Paris to a distinguished family, Musset graduated with honors from Collège Henri IV and briefly pursued a career in medicine before a dislike of blood prompted him to first try painting and then, ultimately, writing.

He published his first work, the ballad *A Dream,* in 1828, which was followed a year later with his first collection of poetry, *Contes d'Espagne et d'Italie* (1830). The collection gained him the favor of VICTOR HUGO and earned his acceptance into the circle of ROMANTIC poets. In 1830, Musset was asked to write for the stage, but his first play, *La nuit vénitienne* (*A Venetian Night,* 1830), was not successful.

In 1833, Musset met and began a passionate affair with poet George Sand. His autobiographical piece, *La confession d'un enfant du siècle* (*Confession of a Child of the Century,* 1835), details their relationship. She abandoned him, however, after falling in love with another man during a trip to Venice. Returning to France alone and in despair, Musset used his feelings to produce some of his greatest theatrical works, including *Lorenzaccio* (1834) and *No Trifling With Love* (1834). He has been praised for his multidimensional female characters and his in-depth understanding of love. His works are commonly compared, in terms of popularity in France, to those of Racine and Molière.

Poor health began to haunt Musset in the 1840s in the form of a heart ailment that came to be referred to by scientists as Musset's symptom. Aggravated by excessive drinking and the depression caused by several failed affairs, his health caused a decline in his literary output. He spent the last two years of his life confined to his apartment and died on May 2, 1857.

Another Work by Alfred de Musset

Fantasio and Other Plays. Translated by Michael Feingold. New York: Theatre Communications Group, 1993.

A Work about Alfred de Musset

Bishop, Lloyd. *The Poetry of Alfred Musset: Styles and Genres.* New York: Lang, 1997.

Nabokov, Vladimir (1899–1977) *novelist, dramatist, literary critic, translator, poet*

Vladimir Vladimirovich Nabokov was born in St. Petersburg, Russia, into a wealthy, aristocratic family. His father, Vladimir Dmitrievich Nabokov, was a prominent liberal politician; his mother, Elena Ivanovna Nabokova, was a descendant of a wealthy, noble family. Nabokov learned French and English from various tutors and learned to read and write English before his native Russian. He described himself as "a perfectly normal trilingual child in a family with a large library." Nabokov's father served in the first Duma (the parliamentary body of Russia) and later held a post in the Provisional Government. After the Communists took control of the government, Nabokov's family left Russia in 1919 and temporarily settled in England. Nabokov's mother sold her jewels to finance his education at Trinity College, Cambridge, which he attended from 1919 to 1922. Nabokov graduated with honors from Cambridge, receiving a degree in Russian and French. The Nabokov family then moved to Berlin, Germany, when Nabokov's father accepted a position as the editor of the Russian newspaper. Nabokov's father was assassinated by right-wing monarchists in 1922.

Between 1922 and 1923, Nabokov published two collections of poetry and, in 1924, produced his first play, *The Tragedy of Mr. Morn.* In 1925, he married Vera Slonim. Although he worked in several genres of literature, Nabokov particularly excelled in fiction. In 1926, *Mary,* his first novel, was published in Berlin; two years later, he published his second novel *King, Queen, Knave.* Between 1929 and 1938, Nabokov published four novels and a collection of short stories.

The year 1938 was crucial for Nabokov's literary career. After moving to France, Nabokov decided he would try to write a novel in English; his first such work was *The Real Life of Sebastian Knight* (1914), a "biography" of a fictional writer, narrated by his brother.

In 1940, Nabokov emigrated to the United States, narrowly escaping the advancing Nazi troops. Between 1941 and 1959, Nabokov taught creative writing, literature, and Russian at Wellesley College, Stanford, Harvard, and Cornell. During the 1940s, he published short stories in *The New Yorker* and a scholarly work on NIKOLAI GOGOL. During these years, Nabokov's output of fiction was relatively small, partly because he was still adjusting to writing in English. In 1951, he published a memoir, *Conclusive Evidence.*

Nabokov's most famous novel, *Lolita,* was written during the early 1950s and published in France in 1955. The novel explores the psychological ramifications of a man's love affair with his 12-year-old stepdaughter. Although a number of critics immediately recognized the artistic virtues of the novel, it was banned in France in 1956 for its subject matter. When *Lolita* was finally published in the United States, it remained on *The New York Times* best-seller list for six months. The novel was adapted into a film by Stanley Kubrick in 1962 and again by Adrian Lyne in 1997. *Lolita* remains one of the most powerful novels of 20th-century American literature. As critic Charles Rolo said in the *Atlantic Monthly* in 1958, *Lolita* is "an assertion of the power of the comic spirit to wrest delight and truth from the most outlandish materials."

In 1961, Nabokov moved to Montreux, Switzerland, where he remained until his death in 1977. During the 1960s and 1970s, he continued to write novels and translated his earlier works from Russian to English. One of the main criticisms of his work was its seeming lack of concern for social issues. Nabokov did not refute such criticism: "I have never been interested in what is called the literature of social comment." Indeed, his work comments on the experience of the individual, often exploring the character's psychological dimensions. "The true conflict is not between the characters in the novel, but between author and reader," he maintained. By the time of his death, Nabokov had established a worldwide reputation as a great writer and scholar.

Critical Analysis

It is nothing short of a wonder that Nabokov's *Lolita* has been translated into film not once but twice. Both films visualize the perverted attraction of Humbert Humbert toward a 12-year-old "nymphet" (Nabokov's coinage) Lolita. However, there is almost nothing visual about the novel. It is compelling in its words, words, words—multisyllabic, polylinguistic, puns, plays, allusions, a rich mixture of language in all its forms and potentialities. All this—and *this* is what the novel is really about—is lost in a film.

What makes the novel so infinitely readable is its narrator. Humbert is a slippery character who changes from moment to moment. Is he a despicable cad who seduces a child? Is he a sophisticated and educated European with exquisite taste? Is he a bumbling old man making a fool of himself over a youthful but not at all innocent vixen? Is he writing pornography? Autobiography? Apologia? Did any of this really happen? (Well of course not; this is a novel. Still, are readers meant to believe this seduction really happened or is Nabokov, as Humbert, toying with us, drawing us into a farce—or a tour de force?)

Critics often have tried to say once and for all what *Lolita* is really about. The Canadian author Robertson Davies claims that the theme of *Lolita* is "not the corruption of an innocent child by a cunning adult, but the exploitation of a weak adult by a corrupt child." Martin Amis has called *Lolita* a story of tyranny told through the eyes of a tyrant and sees the novel as Nabokov's view of Stalinism. The critic Lionel Trilling warned that the narrator's voice is seductive and dangerous: "We find ourselves the more shocked when we realize that, in the course of reading the novel, we have come virtually to condone the violation it presents."

Lolita is all this and more. It is a work about the power of fiction to draw in the reader, to repel and compel us. It is both a serious work of art and an elaborate joke. Nabokov has said, "I would say that of all my books *Lolita* has left me with the most pleasurable afterglow—perhaps because it is the purest of all, the most abstract and carefully contrived." His choice of words is telling. The story of a pederast is "the purest of all," the vivid tale of humiliation and perversion is "abstract," the apparently jumbled memoir "contrived." Then, with typical wit and not a little pride, Nabokov quips, "I am probably responsible for the odd fact that people don't seem to name their daughters Lolita any more. I have heard of young female poodles being given that name since 1956, but of no human beings."

Other Works by Vladimir Nabokov

Ada. New York: Vintage Press, 1990.
Despair. New York: Vintage Press, 1989.
Pale Fire. New York: Vintage Press, 1989.
Speak, Memory: An Autobiography Revisited. New York: Vintage Press, 1989.

Works about Vladimir Nabokov

Cornwell, Neil. *Vladimir Nabokov.* Plymouth, U.K.: Northcote House Publishers, 1999.
Grayson, Jane, et al., eds. *Nabokov's World* (2 vols). London: Palgrave MacMillan, 2002.
Shapiro, Gavriel. *Nabokov at Cornell.* Ithaca N.Y.: Cornell University Press, 2003.

Naidu, Sarojini (1879–1949) *poet*

Sarojini Naidu was born in Hyderabad, India, into an extremely Westernized family, which gave her the opportunity to pursue a lifestyle and education uncommon to most women of her time. Naidu wrote only in English and started writing poetry as a young girl. She went to England in 1895 to study at King's College, London, and returned to India in 1898.

Naidu's poetry was originally very well received in England because it portrayed an India with which Victorian England was familiar. Her poems were romantic portrayals of an aesthetically appealing, nonpolitical India that was friendly to its colonizers, the British, especially when Britain's rule was threatened.

As Naidu developed as a poet and became more involved in the political activities of the Indian National Congress Party, her poetry also changed. *The Golden Threshold* (1905), for example, presents a collage of poems about Indian life as seen through the native eye. The poems focus strongly on the social conditions of the nation under colonial rule. Because these poems were such a departure from Naidu's earlier works, which showed the influence of great Western poets such as Wordsworth and Keats, Naidu was called "the nightingale of India," an epithet given her by MOHANDAS GANDHI.

By her third and final collection of lyric verse, Naidu was already beginning to spend less time writing poetry and more time being actively involved in politics. She was a close friend of Gandhi and was often the only woman who would accompany him on his many political marches and rallies. Such involvement on her part also made her a powerful figure for women's causes. One of her contributions was working to abolish *purdah,* a social rule that forced women to seclude themselves inside homes and wear clothing that completely covered their bodies.

Naidu dedicated her last volume, *The Broken Wing* (1915–16), to India's patriotic freedom fighters. This work completed her transformation from a poetess of remarkable Western education and romantic sensitivity to one whose only concern was to encourage the patriotic zealousness of her time. She was the first Indian woman to become the president of the Indian National Congress in 1925, and in 1947, she was made governor of the state of Uttar Pradesh.

Other Works by Sarojini Naidu

The Bird of Time; Songs of Life, Death and the Spring. New York: J. Lane Company, 1916.
The Sceptred Flute: Songs of India. New York: Dodd, Mead & Co., 1923.

A Work about Sarojini Naidu

Naravane, Vishwanath S. *Sarojini Naidu: An Introduction to Her Life, Work, and Poetry.* New Delhi: Orient Longman Ltd., 1996.

Naipaul, V(idiadhar) S(urajprasad)

(1932–) *novelist, travel writer, essayist*
Born in Chaguanas, Trinidad, V. S. Naipaul is descended from Hindu Indians. His grandfather worked in a sugarcane plantation, and his father, Seepersad, was a journalist and short story writer. As a child, Naipaul spent most of his time in the matriarchal Tiwari clan house in Chaguanas or in the streets of Port of Spain. He attended Queen's

Royal College, Trinidad, and University College, Oxford, where he studied English literature.

After graduation, Naipaul stayed in England and worked for the BBC and the *New Statesman,* a literary journal. Inspired by his father, Naipaul began to write about his childhood experiences. Multiple publications followed, and selections of his published reviews and articles appear in *The Overcrowded Barracoon* (1972) and *The Return of Eva Perón with The Killings in Trinidad* (1980).

Western critics positively reviewed Naipaul's first novels, but others, especially those from the Caribbean and developing countries, vehemently criticized the treatment of colonial people in his writings. His first three novels—*The Mystic Masseur* (1957), *The Suffrage of Elvira* (1958), and *Miguel Street* (1957) which Naipaul wrote first but published last—ironically and satirically portray the absurdities of Trinidadian life while exploring the lives of East Indian community members.

Critical Analysis

A House for Mr. Biswas (1961), Naipaul's fourth work, earned substantially more recognition than his earlier novels. It focuses on Biswas, a sensitive man who is loosely modeled after Naipaul's father, who struggles with displacement, disorder, and alienation to establish his own identity. The hierarchical relations in Biswas's house symbolize and comment on colonial relationships. Many of Naipaul's subsequent novels also explore themes of alienation as his characters strive to integrate cultural tensions, especially those between native and Western-colonial traditions and influences.

The same year Naipaul published *A House for Mr. Biswas,* he received a grant from the Trinidad government to travel in the Caribbean. Extensive travel followed in the 1960s and early 1970s. His excursions to countries including Uganda, Argentina, Iran, Pakistan, Malaysia, and the United States informed his writing. *Mr. Stone and the Knight's Companion* (1963), which takes place in England, was Naipaul's first novel set outside the West Indian context.

More serious place-specific cultural studies replaced the more comedic aspects of Naipaul's earlier novels. The three short stories in *In a Free State* (1971), which won the Booker Prize in 1971, take place in different countries. Naipaul uses a novella as well as travel-diary excerpts in these three stories to explore individual and universal freedom. The novel *Guerrillas* (1975) follows an uprising in the Caribbean, and *A Bend in the River* (1979), which has been compared to Joseph Conrad's *Heart of Darkness,* examines the future of a newly independent state in Central Africa. The introspective *The Enigma of Arrival* (1979) juxtaposes autobiography and fiction to construct an almost anthropological exploration of the life of a writer of Caribbean origin living in rural England.

Although some praised Naipaul's complex and sometimes scathing cultural analyses of his journeys as honest and visionary, others criticized them as pessimistic portrayals of the developing world, as seen in two of his travel books on India: *An Area of Darkness* (1964) and *India: A Wounded Civilisation* (1977). Other nonfiction works include the more widely accepted *India: A Million Mutinies Now* (1990), *The Middle Passage: Impressions of Five Societies—British, French, and Dutch —in the West Indies* (1963), and *Among the Believers: An Islamic Journey* (1989), which critically assesses Muslim fundamentalists in non-Arab countries.

The Mimic Men, published in 1967, is considered by critics to be Naipaul's best novel. It traces the life of Ralph Singh, a politician in early retirement who explains his own position: "The career of the colonial politician is short and ends brutally. We lack order. Above all, we lack power, and we do not understand that we lack power." Set in the Caribbean island of Isabella and in England, the novel has generated many questions concerning authenticity, politics, and psychology.

After the publication of *The Loss of El Dorado* (1970), which describes Trinidad's colonial history, Naipaul returned to Trinidad. Still dissatisfied, the writer returned to England. There he began to feel that the boundary between fiction and reality was no longer as clear as it once had been. As he wrote, "Fiction, which had once liberated me and enlightened me, now seemed to be pushing me toward being simpler than I really was." He explained this concept further in *Reading and Writing: a Personal Account* (2000): "So, as my world widened, beyond the immediate personal circumstances that bred fiction, and as my comprehension widened, the literary forms I practiced flowed together and supported one another; and I couldn't say that one form was higher than another." *A Way in the World* (1994), for instance, which contains nine thematically linked but segmented narratives, draws on the genres of fiction, history and memoirs, and documentary to address personal and sociopolitical issues. Naipaul's more recent nonfiction works include *A Writer's People: Ways of Looking and Feeling* (2007), an appreciation of various writers important to him, such as GUSTAVE FLAUBERT, Virgil, and DEREK WALCOTT, and *The Masque of Africa: Glimpses of African Belief* (2010), which he describes as a travel book.

In 2001, Naipaul published the novel *Half a Life* (2001), which follows the first 40 years in the life of Willie Chandran, a Hindu who leaves India to be educated in England and eventually settles in Africa. In the sequel, *Magic Seeds* (2004), Chandran returns to India to join a revolutionary group.

Naipaul's distinctive incorporation of multiple genres in literary works has earned him the reputation of formal innovator. Themes of alienation, mistrust, and self-deception run through many of his works, but his latter works tend to embrace more than criticize.

In 1990, Naipaul, who has British citizenship, was knighted by Queen Elizabeth. After being a perennial nominee for the Nobel Prize in literature, Naipaul received the award in 2001. To quote Timothy F. Weiss, Naipaul,

through an autobiographical art, has tapped experiences that have come to define aspects of people's lives in the colonial and postcolonial word. Spanning several decades, his works are about more than the problems of the developing world that are a deep concern running through every book; they are about a rapidly changing world order and a changing definition of home and belonging in that new order.

Other Works by V. S. Naipaul
Between Father and Son: Family Letters. New York: Vintage Books, 2001.
Half a Life. New York: Knopf, 2001.
"To a Young Writer." *New Yorker* (June 26–July 3 1995).

Works about V. S. Naipaul
French, Patrick. *The World Is What It Is: The Authorized Biography of V. S. Naipaul.* New York: Vintage, 2009.
Gupta, Suman. *V. S. Naipaul.* Plymouth, U.K.: Northcote House in Association with the British Council, 1999.
Khan, Md. Akhtar Jamal. *V. S. Naipaul: a Critical Study.* New Delhi: Creative Books, 1998.
King, Bruce. *V. S. Naipaul.* London: MacMillan, 1993.
Weiss, Timothy S. *On the Margins: the Art of Exile in V. S. Naipaul.* Amherst: University of Massachusetts Press, 1992.

Narayan, R(asipuram) K(rishnaswamy)
(1906–2001) *novelist, short story writer*
R. K. Narayan was born in Madras, India. His father was a teacher who was repositioned in various South Indian states, which meant that Narayan frequently changed schools. Though he was not a model student, education was an important part of growing up in the Narayan household. Narayan was the third of eight children; to relieve some of the burden of bringing up so many children, his father sent Narayan to live with his maternal grandmother in Madras.

Narayan has often claimed that listening to his grandmother's stories inspired his own love for storytelling. Because writing was not considered a worthwhile profession at the time, his family received his decision to become a writer with shock and dismay. The creative spirit is not exclusive to R. K. Narayan in his family: His brother, R. K. Laxman, is one of India's most famous and highly published cartoonists and has illustrated several of Narayan's books. Like Laxman, Narayan depicts India through the eyes of a character from an "older" world, one that is detached from the modern world and is constantly bewildered by its machinations.

Narayan proved to be resourceful through his writing from the very beginning. While working on his first book *Swami and Friends* (1935), he was able to support himself by contributing short stories to magazines. This book first introduces Narayan's Malgudi village and its inhabitants. This fictional world appears to be completely estranged from the outside world, and its isolation clearly brings out more clearly the emotional ties that keep this village community together.

When Narayan began to write, he was one of numerous writers who created a turning point in Indian literature. For the first time, Indian writers were writing only in English, and many of them were writing for a national and international audience. At a time when writing in English was considered politically incorrect and when Indian politics were the most appropriate theme, Narayan placed himself outside of these constraints. He chose to use both English (the only language in which he wrote) and India's rural settings to create a version of an Indian life that was relatively free from colonial politics. One of his most popular works, *Malgudi Days* (1942), for instance, borrows the Malgudi of *Swami and Friends* to explore the effects of Western influence through human relationships. Later, a television series was based on these stories. The mythical village of Malgudi is set at the crossroads of an old India meeting a new one. These stories capture the image of the ordinary person amid simple surroundings to suggest an organic shift from a colonial India to an independent one. The central characters in *The English Teacher* (1945) and his story "Mithaiwalla" ("The Vendor of Sweets," 1967) are heroes set in this same transition.

The story "Mithaiwalla" focuses on the conflict that arises between a father and his son as they must learn how to understand their changing relationship without letting their differences create an emotional rift. In *The English Teacher*, a teacher's moral struggle against a decadent form of education is made more complicated by his growing responsibilities as a father. Also set in a small town, this novel explores the links between personal and social relationships. Being a good teacher, the protagonist learns, is contingent upon his maturity as a father and husband. The darker sides to Narayan's fiction are, however, always clothed in a humor that strives for frankness and compassion rather than judgment.

Narayan's novel *The Guide* (1958) won the Sahitya Akademi Award (India's highest literary award) and was made into a Hindi movie of the same name that has now become an Indian classic. It was the first Indian–English work to receive the award. In addition to writing fiction, Narayan interpreted and translated into English many of India's classic epics. His versions of *The Mahabharata* (1978) and *The Ramayana* (1972) made these texts available to new readers both in and outside India.

Narayan won the Padma Bhushan (given in recognition of contributions to the nation) in 1964. In 1980, he was awarded the A. C. Benson Medal by the Royal Society of Literature and made an Honorary Member of the American Academy Institute of Arts and Letters. In 1986, he joined Indian politics and became a member of Parliament; he was awarded this post for his contribution as outstanding litterateur and held the position for six years.

Other Works by R. K. Narayan

The Financial Expert. Chicago: University of Chicago Press, 1995.
My Days: A Memoir. New York: HarperCollins, 1999.

A Work about R. K. Narayan

Kain, Geoffrey R., ed. *R. K. Narayan: Contemporary Critical Perspectives.* East Lansing: Michigan State University Press, 1993.

Natsume Kinosuke

See NATSUME SŌSEKI.

Natsume Sōseki (Natsume Kinosuke)
(1867–1916) *novelist, short story writer, essayist*

Natsume Sōseki was born Natsume Kinosuke in Tokyo, Japan. He was adopted shortly after his birth but was returned to his family home at age nine. While still very young, he studied Chinese literature and haiku, venturing into English literature at Tokyo Imperial University. After graduation, he began to teach in public schools. A turning point came in 1900 when the government sent him to England to continue his study of English literature. When he returned, he became a lecturer at Tokyo Imperial University. However, he soon resigned his teaching position to take up writing full time for the *Asahi Shimbun Newspaper* in 1907. He died nine years later from a stomach ulcer.

Shortly after returning from England, Natsume began his career with the comic novel *I Am a Cat* (1905). The story portrays the antics of a cat that lives with a teacher, indirectly revealing the relationship of the teacher and his wife. Within the next two years, he produced a number of short stories and novels, including a perennial favorite of Japanese students called *Botchan* (1906). In this novel, Natsume created a lovably bumbling protagonist who faces a series of awkward situations. Toward the end of his life, Natsume wrote what has become one of the most CELEBRATED novels of Japanese literature, *Kokoro* (1914). This psychological novel took up the issue of individualism in a country in the throes of modernization.

Natsume is considered, along with Ogai MORI, to be the father of MODERNISM in Japanese literature, largely because of his effective portrayal of intellectuals at the turn of the century. Natsume's early writing was by and large satirical, but as he began to address issues such as alienation and morality, he adopted a more serious and often pessimistic tone.

Other Works by Natsume Sōseki

Botchan. Translated by Alan Turney. Tokyo: Kodansha International, 1992.

Grass on the Wayside. Translated by Edwin McClellan. Chicago: The University of Chicago Press, 1969.

The Miner. Translated by Jay Rubin. Stanford, Calif.: Stanford University Press, 1988.

The Wayfarer. Translated by Beongcheon Yu. Detroit: Wayne State University Press, 1967.

Works about Natsume Sōseki

Doi, Takeo. *The Psychological World of Natsume Sōseki.* Translated by William Jefferson Tyler. Cambridge, Mass.: Harvard University Press, 1976.

Iijima, Takehisa, and James M. Vardaman Jr., eds. *The World of Natsume Sōseki.* Tokyo: Kinseido Ltd., 1987.

naturalism (1860–1900)

Naturalism is perhaps best described as a literary movement in which writers attempted to be true to reality, accurate in their representation of life, and methodical and nonjudgmental in their observations of the various phenomena of life. The French writer ÉMILE ZOLA first used the term *naturalism* to explain the application of elements of the scientific method to the examination of all aspects of life. In his essay *Le Roman expérimental* (1880), Zola wrote that the novelist should approach the craft of writing in the same manner as the scientist approaches the study of nature.

Proponents of naturalism believe that both hereditary and environmental influences combine to determine human behavior. For a writer to depict life as it really is, the ultimate goal of naturalist literature, he or she must present characters whose motivations can be clearly understood based on the surrounding causes. In other words, Zola and those who followed him replaced the classical idea of fate as the major factor behind human circumstances with the more scientific concept of determinism in which human beings are responsible for their own actions. Thus, some, if not all, human values can be seen to proceed in direct relationship to situational needs such as food, water, and shelter, placed in combination with environmental, sociological and psychological factors. The literature of the naturalist school, therefore, dealt more commonly with the observation of reality as it actually presents itself than with the construction of elaborate fantasies.

Naturalism in literature developed as a direct response to ROMANTICISM. Dissatisfaction with the representations of social conditions in literature led to a desire on the part of certain writers to create a body of work that stood in more direct correlation to actual life. Romanticism focused on high lyricism and was concerned with the beauty of language and self-expression, human emotions and personal values. Naturalism, on the other hand, was more concerned with cause-and-effect relationships and logical outcomes to given circumstances. This trend was not entirely new; Realism had anticipated some of these concerns. However, naturalism was also a reaction to REALISM. The naturalists believed that realist literature, while it sought to portray life accurately, was not a true representation of the harsh realities faced by the lower social classes. Whereas the realists displayed a tendency within their work to aestheticize societal problems, making them more palatable to the bourgeois readership, naturalists developed more accurate portrayals of reality, making no attempt to pass judgment or to suggest a solution. They abandoned religion and philosophy, believing neither discipline capable of effecting change on society. Instead, they believed that literature had the power to create change simply by making the reader aware of the extent of the problem.

Common, therefore, among naturalist works is the emphasis on characters who are poor, undereducated, and trapped in lives filled with filth and corruption. These are the people whose lives are most controlled by social and cultural influences and whose decisions are most affected by the fulfillment of basic needs. As a result, much naturalist literature is a dreary representation of the harsh realities of life. Although similar to realism in many ways, naturalism goes beyond realism in its belief that social and biological factors take the place of free will entirely, as can be witnessed in the trappings of lower-class existence.

In addition to Zola, other noted French naturalists include the GONCOURT brothers, J. K. HUYSMANS, and GUY DE MAUPASSANT. The Goncourts' works, such as *Soeur Philomène* (1861) and *Renée Mauperin* (1864; translated 1887) were based largely on notes from their travels and presented an accurate vision of life as they observed it. Prior to his absorption in DECADENCE, Huysmans's early works, such as *Marthe* (1876), can also be classified as naturalist pieces.

In the theater, the naturalist movement is most closely associated with the Théâtre Libre movement of the late 19th century. Again, the goal of drama, like that of literature, became the desire to represent life as accurately as possible. By placing a greater degree of emphasis on scenic design, which was realistically detailed, and costume design, which reflected the style and quality of the characters, as well as the development and encouragement of more natural acting methods, the movement was an attempt to break free from the conventions of artificial theatricality prevalent in the past.

The naturalist movement in France did not confine itself to one art form but existed in theatrical performances and the visual arts as well. Neither was the movement restricted to France. Similar movements occurred in the latter part of the 19th century throughout Europe and in America.

Works about Naturalism

Baguley, David. *Naturalist Fiction: The Entropic Vision.* New York: Cambridge University Press, 1990.

Bronson, Catharine Savage, ed. *Nineteenth Century French Fiction Writers: Naturalism and Beyond, 1860–1900.* Detroit: Bruccoli Clark Layman, 1992.

Nelson, Brian, ed. *Naturalism in the European Novel: New Critical Perspectives.* New York: St. Martin's Press, 1992.

Pagano, Tullio. *Experimental Fictions: From Émile Zola's Naturalism to Giovanni Verga's Verism.* Madison, Wisc.: Fairleigh Dickinson University Press, 1999.

Naubert, Benedikte (1756–1819) *novelist, writer of fairy tales*

Born into an academic family in Leipzig, Germany, Benedikte Naubert received an education unusual for a woman of her time. She was one of the most prolific and widely read authors of her age: Her publications—family novels, historical novels, and fairy tales—extend to 80 titles. Because of prejudice against women writers, she chose to publish anonymously. She influenced the historical novels of Sir Walter Scott and was appreciated by the romantics. The stories in Naubert's *Neue Volksmarchen der Deutschen* (1789–92), based on folktales, were original in combining the fantastic with the everyday and giving a voice to female narrators and protagonists. The brothers GRIMM were indebted to her, but their tales told a very different story about the ideal rise of women in the emerging bourgeois family. A few of her novels were translated into English during her lifetime, and one of her most interesting stories, *Der kurze Mantel,* has more recently been translated as "The Cloak" in *Bitter Healing: German Women Writers: 1700–1830* (Blackwell and Zantop, eds., 1990).

Ndebele, Njabulo (1948–) *novelist*

Njabulo Ndebele was born in Western Native Township near Johannesburg, South Africa. His father, a Zulu, was a schoolteacher who later became an inspector of schools, and his mother, a Swazi, was a nurse. Ndebele's mixed parentage has an important influence on his perception of what it means to be African, which is revealed in his works. Ndebele moved with his family to a small mining town in Charterston Location in 1954 where he completed his primary-school education. Because Ndebele's parents did not think the apartheid South African government would allow Ndebele to exploit his intellect, they sent him to

black-ruled Swaziland to attend high school. He went to Cambridge University for two years for his master's degree and taught briefly at the University of Lesotho before going on to the University of Denver for his Ph.D. In 1983, Ndebele returned to Africa where he filled several administrative and teaching positions before finally becoming vice chancellor of the University of Cape Town in September 2000, a position he held until 2008.

Ndebele's most significant contribution to world literature is his desire to bring African literature out of its protest mood. In a series of articles, he questioned the conventional African approach to writing, which challenged white colonials' domination by appealing to their guilt. The most influential of these articles was "New South-African Literature or the Rediscovery of the Ordinary," published in *South African Literature and Culture: Rediscovery of the Ordinary* (1991). Ndebele believes that African writers should write for their fellow African readers, appealing to an African collective consciousness and heritage. African literature should not merely attack apartheid or oppression but should find a common ground where all Africans can express their values.

Ndebele's stories depict his various attempts to search for African values and to promote them as the essence of African identity that transcends all differences. In the short story, "Uncle" (1983), for example, the character Lovington teaches his nephew to recognize a new "map" of South Africa, drawn using traditional South African values, not colonial European laws. Within this framework, Ndebele also celebrates Africa's past by remembering heroic figures, such as King Moshoeshoe. In another short story, "The Music of the Violin" (1983), Ndebele presents music as a mock battleground where the indiscriminate adoption of Western culture is criticized by a child who sees the contradiction more clearly than his anglophile parents.

Ndebele's attempts to address the multidimensional aspects of colonialism on South Africa represent a refreshing approach to the different facets of colonialism that have been presented by past African writers as one dimensional. Perhaps the most remarkable contribution Ndebele makes to the literary world is his poignant and vivid description of the daily lives of ordinary Africans. By concentrating on daily struggles of ordinary people for survival rather than the sensational power struggles developing at the higher levels, Ndebele is able to show that little defeats and victories take place in spite of the larger nationalistic struggle. The true hero in Ndebele's mind is the ordinary person who, through diligence and resourcefulness, continues to survive.

Ndebele has won various writing awards including the Noma Award for Publishing in Africa, the SANLAM First Prize for outstanding fiction, and the Pringle and Mofolo–Plomer Awards. He published a novel, *The Cry of Winnie Mandela,* in 2003, and another essay collection, *Fine Lines from the Box: Further Thoughts on Our Country,* in 2007.

Other Works by Njabulo Ndebele

Bonolo and the Peach Tree. New York: Manchester University Press, 1992.

Death of a Son. Johannesburg: Viva, 1996.

Fools and Other Stories. London: Reader's International, 1986.

Rediscovery of the Ordinary: Essays on South African Literature and Culture. Johannesburg: Congress of South African Writers, 1991.

Sarah, Rings and I. Johannesburg: Viva, 1993.

Works about Njabulo Ndebele

Shava, Piniel. *A People's Voice: Black South African Writing in the Twentieth Century.* London: Zed Books, 1989.

Trump, Martin. *Rendering Things Visible: Essays on South African Literary Culture.* Athens: Ohio University Press, 1990.

Necker, Anna Louise Germaine

See STAËL, GERMAINE DE.

negritude

In the early 1930s, French-speaking African and Caribbean writers living in Paris started the literary and ideological negritude movement with the leadership of poet AIMÉ CÉSAIRE from Martinique, poet Léon-Gontran Damas from French Guiana, and poet and later president of Senegal (1960–80) LÉOPOLD SÉDAR SENGHOR. Inspired by Harlem Renaissance writers in the United States, such as W. E. B. DuBois and Langston Hughes, and West Indian thinkers and poets, such as Jacques Roumain, René Maran, and Jean Price-Mars, black intellectuals began to examine critically Western values to reassess black cultural value and identity.

The publication of *Légitime Défense* (*Legitimate Defense*) in the early 1930s, a journal with a strong Marxist and anticolonial bent, prompted Senghor, Damas, and Césaire to print *L'Étudiant noir* (The black student) in 1934 "for all black students, regardless of origin, African, Antillean or American." According to Damas, the word *négritude* first appeared in an editorial by Césaire in *L'Étudiant noir.* For Césaire in his long poem, *Cahier d'un retour au pays natal* (*Return to My Native Land,* 1939), negritude originated in "Haiti, where Negritude first stood up and swore by its humanity." The term gained popularity after appearing in Césaire's poem, but some say the spirit of negritude was first expressed poetically by Damas in *Pigments* (1937).

After World War II, the group founded *Présence Africaine,* a publishing house and journal edited by Alioue Diop. One year later, Senghor's *Anthologie de la nouvelle poésie nègre et malgache de langue française* (Anthology of new Negro and Malagasy poetry in French, 1948) appeared. It included existentialist philospher JEAN-PAUL SARTRE's well-known essay, "Orphée noir" ("Black Orpheus"), which describes negritude from a Marxist perspective.

Initially, the negritude movement primarily influenced French-speaking colonial writers, but it gradually became more global. The core group expanded to include a number of African and West Indian poets, including Jacques Rabémananjara, a poet and playwright from Madagascar who met

Senghor and Césaire in Paris in the 1950s, and Guy Tirolien, a West Indian poet who met Senghor in a German prison camp during the war. Many involved in the negritude movement critically examined assimilation, world wars, and the suffering of black people in their writing. They also promoted political and intellectual freedom, as well as the value of African life and traditions.

Senghor published his systematic statements on négritude in *Liberté I: Négritude et Humanisme* (1964), a collection of essays. On negritude, Senghor wrote, "To establish an effective revolution, *our* own revolution, we first had to cast off our borrowed clothes—the clothes of assimilation—and to assert our *négritude*." Césaire took an even more revolutionary interpretation of negritude than Senghor, as can be seen in his *Discours sur le colonialisme* (*Discourse on Colonialism*), (1950) which displays his Marxist allegiances.

The spread of the negritude movement to black student writers in France, Africa, and the Caribbean during the 1930s, 1940s, and 1950s receded in the 1960s when fewer and fewer negritude themes appeared in writers' works. More recently, however, such writers as Abiole Irele, Biodun Jeyifu, and Omafume Onoge have been returning to the literary and ideological issues of negritude. Some have criticized the movement's reliance on NATIVISM and ahistoricism, as well as its representation of women and its failure to achieve revolutionary change. Many, however, still recognize negritude's significance as an empowering, historically grounded, and pertinent literary movement.

Works about Negritude

Ahluwalia, Pal. "'Negritude and Nativism': In Search of Identity." *Africa Quarterly* 39, no. 2 (1999).

Arnold, James A. "Négritude Then and Now." In James A. Arnold, ed., *A History of Literature in the Caribbean: Vol. I, Hispanic and Francophone Regions.* Philadelphia: Benjamins, 1994.

Asante-Darko, Kwaku. "The Co-Centrality of Racial Conciliation in Negritude Literature." *Research in African Literatures* 31, no. 2 (2000).

Claxton, Hadiya. "Colonialism, Negritude, and Experiences of Suffering." *JAISA: The Journal of the Association for the Interdisciplinary Study of the Arts* 5, no. 1 (Fall 1999).

Jack, Belinda E., and Sada Niang. "Literature and the Arts—Negritude and Literary Criticism: The History and Theory of 'Negro-African' Literature in French." *African Studies Review* 41, no. 2 (1998).

Jeyifo, Biodun. "Greatness and Cruelty: 'Wonders of the African World' and the Reconfiguration of Senghorian Negritude." *The Black Scholar* 30, no. 1 (Spring 2000).

Neruda, Pablo (Neftali Ricardo Reyes Basoalto) (1904–1973) *poet*

Pablo Neruda was born in Parral, Chile. His father, Jose del Carmen Reyes, was a railroad engineer. His mother, Rosa Basoalto, died of tuberculosis a few days after Neruda was born. In 1920, at age 16, Neruda moved to Santiago to study French literature at the Instituto Pedagogico; however, after three years of study he left school without graduating. It was at this time that Neruda adopted his pseudonym, taking the last name of Czech short-story writer Jan Neruda (1834–91).

In 1924, Neruda published *Twenty Love Poems and a Song of Despair,* which remains one of the most popular poetry collections in the Spanish-speaking world. Neruda's approach to love poetry is visceral and original; his emotions are vibrant and his sorrows poignant but without the least sentimentality. *Twenty Love Poems and A Song of Despair* combines rich and musical diction, striking images and a strong sense of connection with the natural in human love.

As Neruda's literary reputation grew, he also began a political career. He was appointed as the Chilean consul in Rangoon, the capital of Burma, in 1927. He pursued his political career quite seriously throughout his life, serving as a senator and even running for president of Chile. He was a communist and worked to forward his ideals through both government service and poetry.

The collection *Residence on Earth* (1931, 1935, 1947) marked a significant change in style from his earlier books. It is written in the style for which Neruda is best known and that, during his life, was called Nerudaism—it is filled with irrational leaps of thought, eccentric uses of language, and powerful images presented without explanation. However, unlike the absurdist poetry of such French Surrealists as ANDRÉ BRETON, *Residence on Earth* is extremely emotional and expressive. Neruda's style of surrealism is not intended to shock or to make his reader laugh; rather, he uses the absurd to represent the complexity of the human mind and modern life.

Canto General (1950) represented another radical change in Neruda's poetry. Abandoning the obscurity of his earlier work, he attempted to create an epic poem about the grandeur of South America. *Canto General* is a free-verse poem written in a biblical cadence. It is a poetic catalogue of both the human and natural aspects of South American reality. In the poem, Neruda was trying to do for the Latin-American world what Walt Whitman had done for the United States in *Leaves of Grass:* to create an epic of democracy, not centered on a single elite hero but celebrating the majesty of every citizen.

In 1971, Neruda won the Nobel Prize in literature. Along with JORGE LUIS BORGES, Neruda was one of the first Latin-American writers to become a major presence in international literary circles. Radically transforming his literary style again and again throughout his life, and working tirelessly for his political beliefs, his achievement is truly astounding. Neruda, who fought against oppression his entire life, died in Santiago in 1973, 12 days after a coup d'état deposed the liberal government of President Allende and brought fascism to Chile.

Other Works by Pablo Neruda
Elementary Odes of Pablo Neruda. Translated by Carlos Lozano. New York: G. Massa, 1961.
Late and Posthumous Poems, 1968–1974. Edited and translated by Ben Belitt. New York: Grove Press, 1988.

Memoirs. Translated from the Spanish by Hardie St. Martin. New York: Farrar, Straus & Giroux, 1977.

Works about Pablo Neruda
De Costa, Rene. *The Poetry of Pablo Neruda.* Cambridge: Harvard University Press, 1982.
Nolan, James. *Poet-Chief: The Native American Poetics of Walt Whitman and Pablo Neruda.* Albuquerque: University of New Mexico Press, 1994.

Nerval, Gérard de (Gérard Labrunie) (1808–1855) *poet*
Considered to be among the early French romantic poets, as well as an early Bohemian, Gérard de Nerval was born in Paris. The death of his mother when he was only two years old greatly affected the tone of his works, which are characterized by a fascination with dreams, visions, and fantasies, particularly those related to death, as well as the madness that these can produce. Throughout his life, he suffered from manic depression and an artistic vision that was destined to destroy him.

Nerval was greatly influenced by the German romantic poets. He translated the works of GOETHE and also was interested in the occult and the poetry of the French Renaissance. The mystic world fascinated him, particularly esoteric, gnostic, and oriental philosophy.

Living in a heightened state of reverie, he began to suffer periods of madness. After an extreme manic episode in 1841, Nerval was hospitalized. During this time, he wrote *Christ on the Mount of Olives* (1841), which forms part of his final collection, and assumed the name *Nerval,* taken from an imaginary genealogy that he had created to replace his own family history. He fantasized that he was descended from Nerva, a Roman emperor, by way of Napoleon. It is this voice, a collected wisdom of the ages, through which he speaks in his poems.

His final poetic work, a collection of sonnets called, collectively, *The Chimeras* (1854), emphasizes themes of death and despair. The work is comprised of three parts. In the first section, six poems deal with the concept of a lost love who appears as bride, priestess, sorceress, queen, muse, and ultimately death. This latter vision ties directly to the death of Nerval's mother. The second section, "Christ on the Mount of Olives," details Christ's betrayal by both humankind and God. The final part, "The Golden Verses," reaffirms life after a deep depression.

Written while Nerval was undergoing a period of deep depression, *The Chimeras* was published only one year before the poet committed suicide.

His last great work, the short story collection *Les filles du feu* (*The Daughters of Fire*, 1854), celebrates lost love and mythical aspects of women. The manuscript of *Aurélia,* an autobiographical and almost surrealistic story of breakdown and vision, was found in his pocket when he hanged himself at dawn on January 26, 1855.

Another Work by Gérard de Nerval

Selected Writings. Translated by Richard Sieburth. Hardmondsworth, U.K.: Penguin Books, 1999.

A Work about Gérard de Nerval

Lokke, Kari. *Gérard de Nerval: The Poet as Social Visionary.* Lexington: French Forum, 1987.

Neto, António Agostinho (1922–1979)
poet

António Agostinho Neto was born in Kaxikane, a Kimbundu village in the Icolo e Bengo region of Angola. His political awareness began at an early age: He became involved in cultural and political activities following his high-school graduation in 1944 when he was working in the Health Service in Luanda. In Lisbon, where Neto was attending university, he became very involved in the independence political activities of the overseas African students. He was arrested and imprisoned twice, in 1951 and 1955. By the time of his second imprisonment, he had become such a well-known figure that French intellectuals such as JEAN-PAUL SARTRE and SIMONE DE BEAUVOIR pressured the Portuguese government to release

him. After his release, Neto returned to Angola in 1959 and became the leader of the Popular Movement for the Liberation of Angola (MPLA). He spent most of his political career in and out of exile and prison until November 1975, when he declared Angola's independence. He was sworn in as Angola's first president, a position that he held until his death.

Neto's poetry clearly resonates with themes that most concern him, such as the nationalist struggle, his African roots, and assimilation. His writings also reveal his attempt to reconcile ideas of individual freedom and colonial domination. In "Nausea" (1974), for example, he examines the anguish of the colonized character João, whose anger intermixed with helplessness results in a physical state of unease. Neto's rejection of assimilation is best expressed in his poems "Marketwoman" (1974) and "Friend Mussunda" (1974), in which the characters, common people, celebrate the collective idea of "Africanness" and renounce colonial attempts to assimilate them.

Neto remains one of the most influential, founding poets of Angolan literature, and his poetry bespeaks the common African themes inherent in the relationship between the colonized and the colonizer.

Other Works by António Agostinho Neto

Ainda o Meu Sonho. Luanda: Uniao dos Escritores Angolanos, 1980.
Cikectabea de Poemas. Lisbon: Casa dos Estudantes do Imperio, 1961.
Sacred Hope. Dar es Salamm: Tanzania Publishing House, 1974.

Works about António Agostinho Neto

Burness, Donald. *Fire: Six Writers from Angola, Mozambique and Cape Verde.* Washington, D.C.: Three Continents, 1977.
Enekwe, Ossie O. "The Legacy of António Agostinho Neto." *Okike,* 18 (June 1981).
Martinho, Fernando. "The Poetry of Agostinho Neto." *World Literature Today,* 53 (Winter 1979).

new novel

The new novel, or nouveau roman, emerged in France in the 1950s. Representative authors include CLAUDE SIMON, NATHALIE SARRAUTE, ALAIN ROBBE-GRILLET, MARGUERITE DURAS, and Michel Butor. The term was introduced by critic Roland Barthes and theorized by Robbe-Grillet in his *For a New Novel* (1963). The main concept of the movement was to create fiction that opposed the constraints of conventional fiction and broke the rules that defined what a novel was.

To break realistic molds of storytelling, the new novelists abandoned the idea of continuity and standard chronological order, such as in Sarraute's 1951 work *Portrait of a Man Unknown*. They borrowed freely from poetry and the visual arts to produce works that were linguistic collages, as in Simon's *The Wind* (1959). The importance of memory and free association of ideas were often stressed as well.

The new novelists represented a vast and divergent array of stylistic and ideological perspectives. They had different aims and goals with regard to their works and, for the most part, were often opposed to being grouped together even in theoretical terms. The movement, in essence, suggested a move away from tradition and realized an attempt to experiment with new literary forms.

See also OBJECTIVISMO.

A Work about the New Novel

Babcock, Arthur E. *The New Novel in France: Theory and Practice of the Nouveau Roman.* Boston: Twayne, 1997.

Ngũgĩ wa Thiong'o (James Ngugi)

(1938–) *novelist, essayist, playwright*

Ngũgĩ wa Thiong'o was born in Kamiriithu in the Kiambu district of central Kenya, a district in which a large number of white people lived. Living where the two worlds of the black African and the white Christian met clearly had its impact on Ngũgĩ's works. Although his parents were Gikuyu, the largest ethnic group in Kenya, they did not practice traditional religion, nor were they Christians. In 1948, Ngũgĩ was exposed to the Gikuyu religion and values when he began school, which taught him about European subjects, traditional Gikuyu values, and Gikuyu history. Ngũgĩ became especially interested in Gikuyu traditions after undergoing the Gikuyu rite of passage ceremony. He also developed a strong interest in reading European classics, especially adventure stories.

Ngũgĩ's eloquent prose resonates with the emotions and conflicts of his personal life and the life of his country. It is not surprising, therefore, that his themes include alienation, love, loss, and struggle. His first novel, *Weep Not, Child* (1964), was the first English language novel to be published by an East African. The main protagonist, Njoroge, lost his opportunity to further his studies after having to face the dilemma of choosing between his idealistic dreams and opposing the harsh reality of colonial domination.

The colonial government's mission to destroy the independent guerrilla army of the Mau Mau peasant rebellions in the 1950s greatly affected Ngũgĩ and his family. Ngũgĩ's brother joined the Mau Mau, his stepbrother was shot, and his mother was arrested, interrogated, and tortured. Ngũgĩ faced the dilemma of advancing his education (something very few black Africans had accomplished and which the colonial government made possible) and dealing with the government's persecution of his family. He depicts this conflict within himself and his community in, and uses the rebellions as a backdrop for, his novel *The River Between* (1965), which is about an unhappy love affair in a rural community whose Christian converts and non-Christian natives are at odds.

In 1977, Ngũgĩ's active involvement in his village's communal theater led to his arrest and imprisonment. He was accused of promoting his strong political views via his play *I Will Marry When I Want* (1977). In addition, his novel *Petals of Blood* (1978), strongly depicts the exploitation and corruption of the colonial government in Kenya at that time. Ngũgĩ was released from prison a few years later, and though he was a devout Christian, he rejected Christianity and changed his name to wa Thiong'o in honor of his Gikuyu heritage. He also began to write his novels in Gikuyu, publishing the first modern novel written in that language, *Devil on the Cross* (1980). Ngũgĩ argued that African literature written in a colonial language was not African literature.

Ngũgĩ left Kenya in 1982. He continues to write about Gikuyu culture. In his later and strongly influential work, *Matigari* (1987), for example, Ngũgĩ narrates a satirical tale of a guerrilla fighter who seeks to find true liberation through the use of arms. The story is based on a famous Gikuyu folktale. Ngũgĩ also encourages fellow African writers to continue to write in their native languages. He now teaches at the University of California, Irvine, where he has taught since 2002.

In early August 2004, Ngũgĩ began a month-long tour of East Africa. Three days after his arrival, robbers entered his apartment, stole money and a computer, beat Ngũgĩ, and raped his wife. In 2006, *Wizard of the Crow*, Ngũgĩ's first novel in 20 years, was published in English. The *Washington* Post called this sprawling novel "an epic African political satire." In 2010, he published *Dreams in a Time of War: A Childhood Memoir. Publishers Weekly* called it "no ordinary coming-of-age tale."

Other Works by Ngũgĩ wa Thiong'o

Decolonizing the Mind: The Politics of Language in African Literature. Westport, Conn.: Heinemann, 1986.

Something Torn and New: An African Renaissance. New York: Basic Civitas Books, 2009.

Works about Ngũgĩ wa Thiong'o

Cantalupo, Charles, ed. *Ngũgĩ wa Thiong'o: Texts and Contexts.* Lawrence, N.J.: Africa World Press, 1995.

Gikandi, Simon. *Ngũgĩ wa Thiong'o.* (Cambridge Studies in African and Caribbean Literature). Cambridge: Cambridge University Press, 2009.

Nicholls, Brendon. *Ngũgĩ wa Thiong'o, Gender, and the Ethics of Postcolonial Reading.* Surrey, U.K.: Ashgate, 2010.

Nguyen Du (1765–1820) poet

Nguyen Du was born in Thing Long, Ha Tinh Province, central Vietnam. The first 35 years of Nguyen Du's life were spent trying to survive the chaos of the Tay Son rebellion that began in 1771. Nguyen Du, a member of the northern scholar classes, was a loyal supporter of the then defunct Le dynasty and was extremely critical of the Tay Son rebellion, denouncing the rampant corruption and immoral behavior of the Tay Sons in his poetry. The Tay Son rebellion ended in 1802 with the ascension of the Nguyen emperor, Gia Long, to the Vietnamese throne in Hue. This southern-based dynasty (Ly), however, did not win Nguyen Du's support, despite his serving the dynasty for 20 years. Nguyen Du saw the Ly dynasty as an illegitimate successor to the Le dynasty, and his unwillingness to serve can be observed in his writings. He uses metaphors such as the bitterness of remarrying to illustrate his reluctance to serve a new master while he still felt loyal to the old. Nguyen Du served as an envoy in the 1813 mission to China, and he was to depart on another mission to China in 1820 when he died unexpectedly.

Nguyen Du's poetry deals with timeless issues that characterized Confucian Vietnamese society, such as personal morality and political obligations. His poems, such as the epic *Truyen Kieu* (*The Tale of Kieu*) bespeak his constant concern with morality and his respect for individual fortitude. The publication date of the poem is unknown. The poem relates the life of Kieu, whose determination in the face of misfortune and suffering earn her happiness in the end. Nguyen Du's poetry celebrates the high ideal of morality above love and selfish desire. Poems such as *The Tale of Kieu* and *The Guitar Player of Long Thanh* reflect his Buddhist ideology that places sacrifice, sorrow, and suffering as necessary obstacles to overcome before happiness can be obtained. Nguyen Du's poetry remains today a valuable repository of information and insight into late 18th- and early 19th-century perceptions of morality.

Other Works by Nguyen Du

"Calling the Wandering Souls." In Jacqui Chagnon and Don Luce, eds., *Quiet Courage: Poems from Viet Nam.* Washington, D.C.: Indochina Mobil Education Project, 1974.

The Tale of Kieu: A Bilingual Edition. Translated by Huynh Sanh Thong. New Haven, Conn.: Yale University Press, 1987.

A Work about Nguyen Du

Woodside, Alexander. Introduction to *The Tale of Kieu: A Bilingual Edition.* Translated by Huynh Sanh Thong. New Haven, Conn.: Yale University Press, 1987.

Nichol, b[arrie] p[hilip] (1944–1988) *poet*

bpNichol, as he styles his name, was born in Vancouver, British Columbia, and grew up in three locations—Vancouver, British Columbia; Winnipeg, Manitoba; and Port Arthur, Ontario. While working toward a certificate from the University of British Columbia in elementary education (which he received in 1963), Nichol audited creative-writing courses. After teaching elementary school in British Columbia, he moved to Toronto in 1967.

Nichol's first published poem, "Translating Apollinaire," appeared in 1964. He soon gained notoriety for his concrete poetry. (Concrete poetry is written so that the words form a definite shape. George Herbert's "Easter Wings," in which the lines of poetry are arranged to form angel's wings, is a famous example. Another predecessor is GUILLAUME APOLLINAIRE with his *Calligrammes*). One of Nichol's concrete poems is "Blues," in which the word *love* is set six times, vertically, horizontally, and backwards, with a diagonal row of *e*'s across the center suggesting a cry of pain or perhaps astonishment. (The poem may be seen online at http://www.thing.net/~grist/l&d/bpnichol/ky-ebp01.htm.)

Nichol did not gain wide recognition, however, until the publication of *The Martyrology* (1972), a long narrative poem in five volumes that abandoned the concrete form of Nichol's previous work. (Subsequent books of *The Martyrology* were published in 1976, 1982, 1987, and 1992.) Nichol also published prose works, visual books, and miscellanies, usually through small presses. He liked to revisit themes and to work in series, as he did in the three volumes, *Love: A Book of Remembrances* (1972), *Zygal: A Book of Mysteries and Translations* (1985), and *Truth: A Book of Fictions* (1990). *Truth,* like the last volume of *The Martyrology,* was published posthumously; Nichol had just finished assembling the manuscript when he died.

In all of his work, Nichol explores the possibilities for meaning to be created by the structural and textual characteristics of words on the page—that is, their formal arrangement and layout. Concrete poetry marks an extreme form of this possibility, as can be seen in Nichol's poems.

In 1970, Nichol won the Governor General's Award for poetry. In addition to his many volumes of poetry, he also wrote 10 episodes of the children's program *Fraggle Rock*. His concrete poetry is the subject of a 1969 documentary film by MICHAEL ONDAATJE, *Sons of Captain Poetry*.

Other Works by bpNichol

An H in the Heart: A Reader. Edited by George Bowering and Michael Ondaatje. Toronto: McClelland & Stewart, 1994.

bpnicholcomics. Vancouver: Talonbooks, 2002.

A Work about bpNichol

Barbour, Douglas. *b.p. Nichol and His Work.* Toronto: ECW Press, 1992.

Nietzsche, Friedrich (1844–1900)
philosopher

Friedrich Nietzsche was born in Rocken, Germany, to Karl Ludwig Nietzsche, a Protestant pastor, and Franziska Nietzsche. Karl Ludwig died when his son was only five. The family moved to Naumburg, where Nietzsche attended *Domgymnasium,* a private preparatory school connected with a cathedral. At *Domgymnasium,* Nietzsche demonstrated great potential as a scholar and was consequently offered a scholarship to Schulpforta, the most famous high school in all of Germany. Nietzsche attended Schulpforta for six years; he was considered to be one of the best students in his class. Although he apparently failed a mathematics class in his final year of studies and jeopardized his graduation, in Robert Holub's 1995 biography, a teacher is quoted in defense of Nietzsche: "Do you wish perhaps that we allow the most gifted student that the school had since I have been here to fail?"

After graduating from Schulpforta in 1864, Nietzsche studied classical philology at the University of Bonn and the University of Leipzig. While studying at both universities, Nietzsche was influenced by the German philosopher Arthur Scho-penhauer. The philosophical works that Nietzsche wrote later in his life were in many ways a response to Schopenhauer's philosophical ideas. In 1867, Nietzsche interrupted his studies for compulsory military service, but was declared unfit for duty in 1868 after falling off a horse. While recovering from the injury, he was befriended by the famous composer Richard Wagner and his wife, who became his mentors.

In 1869, at age 24, Nietzsche was appointed as a professor of classical philology at the University of Basel, Switzerland, where he remained for the next 10 years. The appointment was quite unusual because he never completed his dissertation. To accept this position, he had to renounce his Prussian citizenship and, because he never became a citizen of Switzerland, he remained a person without a country for the rest of his life. In 1870, at the outbreak of the Franco-Prussian War, he enlisted in the Germany army as a medical orderly, but he contracted diphtheria and had to resign the post.

Critical Analysis

During the 1870s, Nietzsche became progressively dissatisfied with his work as a philologist.

Although he remained at the University of Basel until 1879, he contributed very little to classical philology. In 1872, he published *A Birth of Tragedy,* which Robert Holub calls "an odd mixture of classical philology, half-baked enthusiasm for Schopenhauer, and Wagner veneration." Using little philological evidence, Nietzsche attempted to connect the rise of tragedy with a coupling of Dionysian and Apollonian principles, to hinge the downfall of tragedy to rational thinking, and to present Richard Wagner as the renovator of German tragic art. His colleagues greeted *The Birth of Tragedy* with disparagement and perplexity, finding little relevance to philology in the work.

Nietzsche, suffering from numerous health problems and, utterly disappointed with his career as a philologist, retired from the university in 1879. With much more success, he turned his energy to cultural criticism, particularly focusing on the role of Christianity in the formation of Western ideas about psychology and social behavior. *Human, All Too Human* (1878–80) is the first published work in which he defends his famed perspectivism, the view that truths and all interpretations are formulated from particular perspectives. He claimed that, contrary to the claims of moralist theory, morality is not inherent in or determined by reality; it is, in fact, the invention of human beings. Moreover, Nietzsche sets morality against historical background, describing how the view of morality changed over time. The work explicitly contrasts Christian and Greek moral thought, typically claiming that Greek thought had been vastly superior.

Nietzsche further elaborates his critique of Christian morality in *Daybreak* (1881). In this work, he claims that Christianity somehow reshapes our notion of morality by implicating psychological guilt and constantly seeking spiritual reassurances—both acts that are destructive to the psychological and social health of society. In his famous work *The Gay Science* (1882), Nietzsche makes his perhaps most famous statement, proclaiming the death of God. Nietzsche once again renounces the Christian doctrine of afterlife and proposes an alternative system in which an individual should appreciate this life in its aesthetic terms. He suggests that ideal is the full experience of one's life, with all the turns of fate and flaws. Furthermore, he proposes the doctrine of eternal recurrence in this work: a concept that describes time as circular rather than linear, in which cyclical events recur over and over again.

Needless to say, Nietzsche's profound atheism was viewed as disturbing by his contemporaries. Yet, Nietzsche secured a small following, especially among the young members of the intelligentsia, with the publication of his major work *Thus Spake Zarathustra* (1883–94). The work, a combination of poetry, prose, and epigrams, describes the journey of Zarathustra who comes down from a mountain after years of meditation to offer his thoughts to the world. The work, structured as a parody of the Bible, praises all things denounced by Christian teachings, such as vanity, war, cruelty, and pure aestheticism. The work, often described as a culmination of Nietzsche's philosophical career but which breaks with conventional philosophical discourse, is his most widely read and appreciated work. Although *Thus Spake Zarathustra* was not widely appreciated during Nietzsche's lifetime, it influenced generations of philosophers and artists after his death.

Throughout his life, Nietzsche remained a prolific writer. He lived in seclusion in Italy and Switzerland, maintaining very few contacts. In 1889, he suffered a complete nervous breakdown after witnessing a brutal beating of a horse on a street in Turin. He was transferred from clinic to clinic for the next 10 years, but, unable to work or recover his health, he finally died just as his popularity began to spread all over the world.

Today, Nietzsche is remembered as one of the most influential philosophers and writers of the 19th century. His works have been translated into virtually every major language around the world. Nietzsche questioned the accepted notions of morality and values in the context of Christianity to emphasize the importance of the material, aesthetic world. It is not surprising that many artists found his message attractive and powerful. Many of his works are still read, discussed, and debated in universities all over the world.

Other Works by Friedrich Nietzsche

The Anti-Christ. Translated by H. L. Mencken. London: Sharp Press, 1999.
Twilight of the Idols or How to Philosophize with a Hammer. Translated by Duncan Large. Oxford: Oxford University Press, 1998.
The Will to Power. Translated by Walter Kaufmann. New York: Random House, 1987.

Works about Friedrich Nietzsche

Holub, Robert. *Friedrich Nietzsche*. Boston: Twayne, 1995.
Kauffman, Walter. *Basic Writings of Nietzsche*. New York: Random House, 1968.
Safransky, Rudiger. *Nietzsche: A Philosophical Biography*. New York: Norton, 2001.

Nkosi, Lewis (1936–2010) *novelist, literary critic*

Lewis Nkosi was born in Durban, South Africa. Before he turned eight, his parents died. He lived with his maternal grandmother, who worked as a washerwoman to support Nkosi's early education. During this time, Nkosi developed a love for literature, especially the works of 19th-century French novelists. Between 1952 and 1954, he was enrolled in a boarding school run by missionaries, and his Zulu language teacher gave him a thorough background in Zulu culture and history. After graduating, he worked briefly at a Zulu newspaper before being invited, in 1956, to join *The Drum*, an influential newspaper actively involved in the antiapartheid movement. Nkosi's acceptance of a Nieman Fellowship at Harvard University led to his exile from his homeland in 1961.

At Harvard, Nkosi wrote a play, *The Rhythm of Violence* (1964), as an entry for a drama competition. The play relates the violence and racism surrounding and following the first bombing in

Johannesburg by African National Congress and Pan-Africanist Congress members. After Harvard, Nkosi worked as a literary editor of *The New African* in London from 1965 to 1968. Between 1970 and 1974, he took a four-year course in English literature at the University of London, spent several years in Europe and accepted a professorship in English at the University of Wyoming.

White supremacy and racial tension are recurring themes in Nkosi's writings. In his most acclaimed work, *Mating Birds* (1986), he satirizes the hypocrisy of the white court that condemned Sibiya, the main protagonist, to death mainly because he was black. In the novel, Sibiya narrates the series of events leading to his conviction of the rape of a white woman and his impending execution. By appropriating the plight of Sibiya, Nkosi contests the legitimacy of white justice and values in South Africa, which he portrays as being driven by self-interest. Another novel, *The Underground People,* about the personal and the political in the lives of antiapartheid activists, followed in 1993.

In 1965, Nkosi published a collection of essays, *Home and Exile,* which won a prize at the Dakar World Festival of Negro Arts in 1966. The essays in this collection deal with a variety of issues and themes, ranging from Nkosi's experience in exile to his views on African theater, black American poetry, and other African writers' works.

Nkosi's main contributions lay in his ability to communicate the complexity and subtle aspects of racial politics and relationships in South Africa to a general reading public.

Other Works by Lewis Nkosi

The Black Psychiatrist. Lusaka: Lusaka Theatre Playhouse, 1983. Available online at http://weber studies.weber.edu/archive/Vol.%2011.2/ 11.2Nkoski.htm.
Malcolm. London: ICA and Bush Theatres, 1972.
Mandela's Ego. Cape Town, South Africa: Struik Publishers, 2009.

Tasks and Masks: Themes and Styles of African Literature. Harlow, U.K.: Longman, 1981.
The Transplanted Heart: Essays on South Africa. Benin City, Nigeria: Ethiope Publishing, 1975.

Works about Lewis Nkosi

Jacobs, Johan. "Lewis Nkosi: *Mating Birds.*" *Critical Arts,* 5:2 (1990).
Masuwa, Kristina Rungano. "South African Writing: Lewis Nkosi." *Wasafiri,* 19 (1994).
Watts, Jane. *Black Writers from South Africa: Towards a Discourse of Liberation.* New York: St. Martin's Press, 1989.

Nobre, António (1867–1900) *poet*

Born in Oporto, Portugal, to middle-class parents, Nobre suffered from ill health and died of tuberculosis at an early age. His illness changed his life and poetry. As a youngster, he spent many summers in northern Portugal. In 1898, he studied law in Coimbra, Portugal, but failed his courses and went on to Paris to attend the Sorbonne, where he received his degree in political science in 1895. Nobre traveled widely, always seeking better health. His finest poems were written while he was living in Paris's Latin Quarter.

Only one volume of poetry was published during Nobre's lifetime: *Só* (1892). It consists mainly of verse written in Portugal and Paris between 1884 and 1892. These poems express the loneliness and poverty the poet experiences on the death of his father. Two more volumes, containing a mixture of narcissism, folklore, realism, whimsy, and pessimism, appeared after the poet's death.

Another Work by António Nobre

Primeiros Versos e Cartas Inéditas. Lisboa: Editorial Notícias, 1983.

Noonuccal, Oodgeroo (Kath Walker)
(1920–1993) *poet, writer, political activist*
Oodgeroo Noonuccal was born in the land of Minjerribah on the coast of Brisbane, in Australia,

to the Aboriginal couple Edward and Lucy Ruska. Kath Walker was her English name, but she returned later in her life to her traditional name Oodgeroo Noonuccal to identify with the Aboriginal people of Noonuccal, with whom she grew up. (Oodgeroo is the Aboriginal name for the paperbark tree.) Noonuccal attended the Dunwich State School on North Stradbroke Island. Her formal education ended when she turned 13, and she became a domestic servant, as did most Aboriginal girls. In 1939, Noonuccal joined the Australian Women's Army Service (AWAS) and advanced to the rank of corporal.

The struggles of the Aboriginal people inspired Noonuccal to write when she was very young. JUDITH WRIGHT, an Australian poet, read Noonuccal's poems and introduced her to the Jacaranda Press in Brisbane. Noonuccal's first volume of poems, *We Are Going* (1964), was the first published work by an Aborigine. She writes of the oppression of the Aboriginal people and their sense of pride, using a free-verse style identified as "protest verse." In the poem "We Are Going," for example, the members of an Aboriginal tribe are given voice: "We are as strangers here now, We belong here." Noonuccal's second book, *The Dawn Is at Hand* (1966), is filled with rich imagery describing the tortures of the Aboriginal people.

Noonuccal's themes include the wrongs committed against the Aborigines, world peace, and a new life for her people. Noonuccal was one of Australia's best-known poets and was also known internationally as a political activist. She was a member of the realist writers' group (*see* REALISM) and wrote against social injustice. Noonuccal also wrote folk tales for children on the life and beliefs of the Aboriginal people. *Father Sky and Mother Earth* (1981) describes the bond of the Aboriginal people with nature. Fellow Australian poet Judith Wright wrote of Noonuccal's poems, "They were memorable, they were memorized and they will be remembered" (1994).

A Work about Oodgeroo Noonuccal

Collins, John, ed. *Noonuccal and Her People: Perspectives on Her Life's Work.* St. Lucia: University of Queensland Press, 1996.

Nooteboom, Cees (Cornelis Johannes Jacobus Maria Nooteboom) (1933–)
novelist, poet, short story writer, travel writer

Cees Nooteboom was born on July 31, 1933, in The Hague, the Netherlands, to Hubertus Nooteboom and Johanna Pessers. He has an older sister, Hanneke (1932), and a younger brother, Huub (1940). Not much is known about Nooteboom's early life. "Other people can trot out their entire childhood, complete with dates, schools and events, as though they were their own computer, I can't do that. Sometimes I wonder whether I was ever really there," he has said.

His father left during World War II and remarried. Nooteboom's half-brother, Hugo, was born that same year. In 1945, Hubertus Nooteboom died from injuries suffered when The Hague was bombed by the British Royal Air Force.

Following the war, Nooteboom's mother married a Roman Catholic and moved the family to Tilburg, where Nooteboom attended Sint Odulphus Lyceum, then the Gymnasium Immaculatae Conceptionis in Venray. After two years in the Catholic school in Vernay, the family moved to Hilversum, and Nooteboom attended the Roman Catholic Lyceum voor het Gooi and then the Augustinianum in Eindhoven. Nooteboom was an adept student with a love of learning. His was a classical education that included learning Greek and Latin.

Nooteboom graduated in his early 20s and was struck with wanderlust. "One fine day, and I know how romantic and old-fashioned that sounds, but it is what happened, I packed a rucksack, took leave of my mother and caught the train to Breda. An hour later—you know how small the Netherlands is—I was standing at the side of the road on the Belgian border sticking my thumb in the air, and I have never really stopped since," he said. His first major trip took him through Scandinavia to Provence, France, and he used those experiences to write his debut novel *Philip en de anderen* (Philip and the Others), published in 1955, now considered a classic of Dutch literature.

In 1954 Nooteboom moved to Amsterdam, and in 1956 he wrote his first significant newspaper article. In 1957 he married Fanny Lichtveld, but their marriage was annulled seven years later. Throughout the 1960s, Nooteboom had a regular column in *de Volkskrant*, a national daily Dutch morning paper.

Nooteboom's second novel, *De ridder is gestorven* (The Knight Has Died), was published in 1963. The novel is about a Dutch novelist who kills himself and leaves a manuscript unfinished, with a request that another writer finish it. The unfinished manuscript, it turns out, is also about a Dutch novelist who commits suicide and leaves an unfinished manuscript for someone else, creating a story that is like Russian nesting dolls, with a large doll that opens to reveal a smaller one, which also opens. Nooteboom's novels are often typically postmodern, in that they explore writing and literature as their major subjects.

After *The Knight Has Died,* Nooteboom did not write another novel for 17 years. Instead, he traveled the world. This served him well, as he became the travel editor for *Avenue,* a Dutch literary magazine, which enabled him to publish both his poetry and travel writings. His work in journalism also combined with his travel experiences to give Nooteboom the perspective and depth of knowledge to become a political commentator and strong advocate for the European Union.

In 1980, Nooteboom published *Rituals*, his first novel to be translated into English. The book follows three men in Amsterdam attempting to create meaning in a world empty of religion and God by adopting ritualistic rules for their lives. The novel marked the beginning of a very prolific time in Nooteboom's life. He wrote poems, novels, and novellas, including *Een lied van schijn en wezen* (*A Song of Truth and Semblance*, 1981), *Mokusei* (1982), *In Nederland* (*In the Dutch Mountains,* 1984), and *De zucht naar het Westen* (1985).

Nooteboom's popularity rose sharply after the publication of *Het volgende verhaal* (*The Following Story*) in 1991. The book received acclaim on German television and quickly went on to become a best seller. Nooteboom's previous work was suddenly in demand in translation. In 1993, Nooteboom received the European Aristeion prize for *The Following Story.*

His most recent novel *Lost Paradise: A Novel* (2007) takes its inspiration from John Milton's *Paradise Lost.* It follows two unrelated travelers, one on a plane to Berlin and one on a train in Holland, whose paths intersect. The story touches on the ways in which the divine illuminates people's lives and weaves a tale of longing, regret, and the basic human impulse to reject the inescapable.

In 2009, Nooteboom was honored with the Prijs der Nederlandse Letteren, the most prestigious literary award in the Netherlands.

Other Works by Cees Nooteboom

All Souls Day. New York: Harcourt, 2001.

The Captain of the Butterflies. Los Angeles: Sun & Moon Press, 1997.

Nomad's Hotel: Travels in Time and Space. New York: Mariner Books, 2009.

Roads to Santiago. New York: Harvest Books, 2000.

Nortje, Arthur (1942–1970) *poet*

Arthur Nortje was born in the town of Oudtshoorn, Cape Province, South Africa. His mother was unmarried, and Nortje never knew who his father was. He attended school on scholarship and showed an early interest and propensity for writing poetry. In 1961, he moved to Cape Town, where he attended the University College of the Western Cape. The sharp class and racial distinctions that existed in the university led Nortje to resent the arbitrary nature of social segregation. He belonged to the "colored" group, the offspring of parents with mixed racial backgrounds, and his distaste for the opulent upper class is clear in his poetry, such as in "Thumbing a Lift" (1962), which won a Mbari Poetry Prize from Ibadan University.

Nortje briefly taught high school in Port Elizabeth before going to Oxford University in 1965, again on scholarship, one sponsored by the politically radical National Union of South African Students. After earning his B.A., he moved to British Columbia in Canada in 1967 to teach and then returned to London in 1970 to embark on his postgraduate study. He died on December 8.

Loneliness is perhaps the most acute emotion that surfaces in all Nortje's poems, which also speak of desolation and loss. His sense of estrangement from his homeland, following his self-imposed exile from South Africa, and his unfortunate encounter with love resonate through his characters and their experiences. Nortje's unfulfilled love for a young woman who separated from him to migrate to Canada, left him in despair. Discrimination intensified his anguish, loneliness, and alienation, which he depicts in political poems that condemn apartheid and its inherent hypocrisy. For example, in *Dead Roots* (1973), Nortje's first collection, a number of poems, such as "Continuation," relate his deterioration into depression and his dependency on drugs. In another poem, "The Long Silence," Nortje poignantly contrasts the forlorn resignation of the oppressed Africans with the "success" of the apartheid government. Though Nortje's literary career was brief, he successfully brought to the world a voice and a vision that, while pained and pessimistic, were very realistic.

Other Works by Arthur Nortje

The Collected Poems of Arthur Nortje. Edited by Dirk Klopper. Pretoria: University of South Africa Press, 2000.
Deep Roots. London: Heinemann, 1973.

Works about Arthur Nortje

Berthoud, Jacques. "Poetry and Exile: The Case of Arthur Nortje." *English in Africa* 11, no. 1 (1984).
Bunn, David. "'Some Alien Native Land': Arthur Nortje, Literary History, and the Body in Exile." *World Literature Today* 70 (Winter 1996).

Dameron, Charles. "Arthur Nortje, Craftsman for his Muse." In Christopher Heywood, ed., *Aspects of South African Literature.* London: Heinemann, 1976.
Leitch, Raymond. "Nortje: Poet At Work." *African Literature Today* 10 (1979).

Nwapa, Flora (1931–1993) *novelist*

Flora Nwapa was born in Oguta, East Central State, Nigeria. Her parents were both teachers, and Nwapa grew up in a popular and wealthy family. She graduated from the University of Ibadan in 1957 and received her postgraduate diploma in education from the University of Edinburgh the following year. Nwapa returned to Nigeria and worked as an education officer in Calabar for a short time before assuming the position of geography and English teacher at Queen's School in Enugu from 1959 to 1962. She remained in Lagos until the Nigerian civil war—the attempt by the Igbo people of Nigeria's eastern area to establish a separate country called Biafra—broke out in 1967. Like many members of the Igbo elite, Nwapa and her family were forced to return to the eastern region. Three years after the war ended, she became the minister of Health and Social Welfare of the east central state from 1970 to 1971 and then the minister of Lands, Survey and Urban Development from 1971 to 1974.

Nwapa was the first African woman writer to publish her works in English. She is also the first African woman to use the Igbo as the basis of her stories. She established Tana Press in 1976, which became the first indigenous publishing house to be owned by a black African woman in West Africa. The company published mainly adult fiction, but Nwapa soon set up another publishing house, Flora Nwapa and Co., that specialized in children's fiction. Nwapa took her role as an educator seriously: She continued to teach at colleges and universities throughout her life and published works dealing with moral and ethical issues. She taught at various institutions in the United States, including New York University, Trinity College, and University of Michigan. Nwapa died at age 62 in Enugu, Nigeria. At the time of her death, she had just completed her final manuscript of *The Lake Goddess* (1995) about the goddess Mammy Water, who was a source of inspiration for Nwapa's fiction.

Nwapa is best known for her recreation of Igbo life and traditions from a woman's point of view. In many ways, she could be considered one of Nigeria's and Africa's first feminist writers. She conveyed the positive optimism of her female protagonists and their strength and freedom to choose their own paths. For instance, in *Idu* (1970), Idu's quest for personal fulfillment leads her to take her own life in defiance of her community's belief that motherhood is the sole purpose of a woman's existence. Idu, however, prizes her life with her husband above all else, including her child's welfare. Her suicide is a commentary on a woman's love.

Critical Analysis

Nwapa's debut novel, *Efuru* (1960), retells an Ibo folktale about Efuru, a woman whose life mirrors that of the lake goddess she worships. Efuru has beauty and wealth but few children like the goddess. Efuru, however, has to struggle to find her place in the society in which she lives. The novel is indicative of Nwapa's portrayal of strong female characters who are adventurous, independent, materially comfortable, and also have the freedom to make their own decisions. These portrayals of women in Ibo society, however, go against conventional views as presented in traditional Ibo texts, which tend to show Ibo women as weak, promiscuous, and fickle minded. Nwapa challenged these traditional views and set the foundation for later women writers to challenge and question the depiction of Ibo women in literature.

Nwapa also wrote short stories, poetry, and children's books. Her stories were not restricted to themes that dealt only with women's rights or a woman's place in society; she also drew on experiences from the Nigerian civil war, folktales, and other political conflicts that occurred during her lifetime. In *Never Again* (1975), which is set in the Nigerian civil war, her main character starts off as a fervent supporter of the Biafran cause but ends up trying to piece her life together and questioning her actions. In her children's stories, Nwapa drew on her rich reservoir of legends and folktales to emphasize the morals of the stories. Her major contribution to world literature rests in her characterization of the heroine as independent and strong and in her descriptions of the continual subjugation of women in Africa.

Other Works by Flora Nwapa

Efuru. London: Heinemann, 1966.
Never Again. Trenton, N.J.: Africa World Press, 1992.
One Is Enough. Trenton, N.J.: Africa World Press, 1992.
This Is Lagos and Other Stories. Trenton, N.J.: Africa World Press, 1992.
Wives at War and Other Stories. Trenton, N.J.: Africa World Press, 1992.
Women Are Different. Trenton, N.J.: Africa World Press, 1992.

Works about Flora Nwapa

Brown, Lloyd W. *Women Writers in Black Africa.* Westport, Conn.: Greenwood Press, 1981.
Emenyonu, Ernest. "Portrait of Flora Nwapa as a Dramatist." In Marie Umeh, ed., *Emerging Perspectives on Flora Nwapa.* Trenton, N.J.: Africa World Press, 1998.

Ōba Minako (Shiina Minako)
(1930–2007) novelist, short story writer, essayist, poet, playwright

Ōba Minako was born in Tokyo to Shiina Saburō and Mutsuko. From a very young age, Ōba nurtured an interest in reading. Her love of books was so intense that, even as she fled World War II air raids, she always grabbed a book to pass the time. Ōba witnessed the mushroom cloud of the atomic bomb dropped on Hiroshima and tended radiation sickness victims as they escaped the city. After the war, she studied American literature at Tsuda Women's College, where she met Ōba Toshio, whom she later married. The turning point in Ōba's life came when her husband was stationed in Alaska for 11 years. Removed from the restrictions placed on women in Japan, Ōba had the freedom to travel and to pursue a graduate-level education, although she never earned a degree.

Ōba completed her first short story, "A Picture with No Composition," in 1963 while she was attending a graduate art program at the University of Wisconsin. Four years later, she wrote "The Rainbow and the Floating Bridge" while attending a graduate art program at the University of Washington in Seattle and then "The Three Crabs" once she returned home to Alaska. In 1969, Ōba wrote "Fireweed," notable for its Alaskan setting and her depiction of an untraditionally ferocious nature. Her major works include *The Junk Museum* (1975), *Urashima Grass* (1977), *Without a Shape* (1982), and *Birds Singing* (1985), none of which have yet been translated into English.

Like the novelists ŌE KENZABURŌ and GABRIEL GARCÍA MÁRQUEZ, Ōba is noted for reusing characters and events from earlier stories. She frequently portrays strong female protagonists who challenge social mores, particularly with regard to women's roles. She has won numerous awards for her fiction, including the Gunzō New Writer's Prize, the Akutagawa Prize, and the Tanizaki Jun'ichirō Prize.

Other Works by Ōba Minako

"The Pale Fox." In *Worlds of Fiction*. Edited by Roberta Rubinstein and Charles R. Larson. New York: Macmillan, 1993.

"The Smile of a Mountain Witch." In *Stories by Contemporary Japanese Women Writers*. Translated by Noriko Mizuta Lippit and Kyoko Irye Selden. Armonk, N.Y.: M. E. Sharpe, 1982.

A Work about Ōba Minako

Wilson, Michiko Niikuni. *Gender Is Fair Game: (Re)Thinking The (Fe)Male in the Works of Ōba Minako*. Armonk, N.Y.: M. E. Sharpe, 1999.

objectivismo

In the later half of the 20th century, *objectivismo* was a movement in Spain that was closely related to the French NEW NOVEL and particularly to the writings of ALAIN ROBBE-GRILLET and JOSÉ CAMILO CELA. *Objectivismo,* or objectivism, refers to the attempt to write novels that were completely free of subjective material and, therefore, closer to material reality. This involved the rejection of all conventional modes of narrative literature such as plot, chronological progression, and metaphorical description. The novels of *objectivismo* would, for example, feature extravagant, long descriptions of a piece of furniture or a geographic location and then repeat the same descriptions periodically throughout the book. Cela's *La colmena* (*The Hive,* 1951) is a prime example.

Strongly influenced by existential philosophy of Heidegger, the main point of *objectivismo* is that reality, before human interpretation, is just there. Before any of the narrative meaning that human beings give to it, the most important feature of reality is its simple presence.

By refusing to concentrate on action or meaning, *objectivismo* texts have a sort of physical presence, in the philosophical sense of the word *physical.* More important, the texts imply that the author and human personality are essentially illusions. By an aesthetic act of will, the author may overcome these illusions and present a text free of his presence. The novels of Rafael Sánchez Ferlosio (1924–   ), such as *El Jarama* (1956; translated as *The One Day of the Week,* 1962), and the early work of Juan Marsé, are examples.

Literary critic Roland Barthes was a major influence on both the New Novel and *objectivismo.* He believed that too much importance had been given to the author's intentions in interpreting literature. He argued that, in fact, meaning, specifically the intentional meaning of the author, was an impermanent and changing thing based more on cultural context than anything else. *Objectivismo* is a literary style that supports and is supported by this idea.

The novels of *objectivismo* are texts that push the reader to supply interpretations. They are presented with compressed and repetitive events that are explained only in glimmers so that any meaning the reader gleans will not be definitive.

A Work about *Objectivismo*

Robbe-Grillet, Alain. *For a New Novel: Essays on Fiction.* Translated by Richard Howard. New York: Grove Press, 1966.

Ōe Kenzaburō (1935–   ) *novelist*

Ōe Kenzaburō was born in a small village in Ehime Prefecture on the island of Shikoku. By the time he entered school, Japan was at war, so he underwent strict moral training intended to instill unquestioning loyalty to the emperor. Before the end of the war, his father died, leaving him in the care of his mother. Under her guidance, Ōe developed an interest in literature, including Western novels. In 1954, he formalized that interest, entering the French literature department of Tokyo University.

While at Tokyo University, Ōe began to write plays for a student drama group. In 1957, he converted one of his plays into a short story, "A Peculiar Occupation," about a student who takes on a part-time job of exterminating dogs used for experiments. That story brought him to the attention of established writers, and he quickly found acceptance in the literary world. During the next two years, he published a number of stories, including *Nip the Buds, Shoot the Kids,* about a group of abandoned boys, which won the Akutagawa Prize, ensuring Ōe's place among the literati.

Ōe increasingly became politically active, notably opposing nuclear proliferation and the Japan–United States Mutual Security Treaty. His political concerns carried over into his writing and, in 1961, parodying a 17-year-old extremist who had assassinated a leader of a Socialist faction, he wrote the short story "Seventeen."

Ōe's literary career took a radical turn in 1963. Three years after his marriage to Itami Yukari, the sister of renowned film director Itami Jūzō, his son Hikari was born with a birth defect that damaged his brain. From this point, Ōe turned to more personal reflection in his writing.

Critical Analysis

In 1964, Ōe published one story and one novel that dealt specifically with the birth of his son. "Agwhee the Sky Monster" is the short story of a composer wrestling with a decision he made to let his son, diagnosed with a potentially fatal birth defect, die. The story is told from the perspective of a young college student who has been hired to watch over the composer. Ōe's novel *A Personal Matter* is widely regarded as his greatest work. In this novel, rather than killing the child, the protagonist, Bird, decides to save his son's life. The story trails the twists and turns of Bird's dilemma until he finally makes the decision to keep his child.

In his next major novel, *The Silent Cry* (1967), Ōe explores simultaneous story lines. The first involves a sibling rivalry in which one brother attempts to destroy a powerful supermarket chain and sleeps with both his brother's wife and his younger sister. The second story is set 100 years earlier. In it, their great-grandfather's younger brother foments an uprising against feudal authorities and has an affair with his brother's wife.

Although *The Silent Cry* received attention for its originality, critics regard his 1979 *A Game of Contemporaneity* as the pinnacle of this style of juxtaposing timeframes. The story is told in a series of letters from the narrator, Tsuyuki, to his sister, Tsuyumi. Tsuyuki is to develop a record of the history and myths of their village and, in doing so, relays a number of stories in fragmented form to his sister.

A Game of Contemporaneity also represented another significant development in Ōe's writing—myth making. Most of his later works reflect this style, particularly *The Burning Green Tree* (1993–95), a trilogy that focuses on the story of a man named Gii. Having lived abroad in his youth, Gii moves to a village in Shikoku. Soon thereafter, a local medicine woman dies, and the villagers believe that Gii has inherited her healing powers.

In 1994, Ōe received the Nobel Prize in literature. During his Nobel speech, he called himself the last of the postwar writers—those who had witnessed the hardship of war but still retained hope for the future. He concluded his lecture, "As one with a peripheral, marginal and off-center existence in the world I would like to seek how—with what I hope is a modest, decent and humanist contribution—I can be of some use in a cure and reconciliation of mankind."

Other Works by Ōe Kenzaburō

The Catch and Other War Stories. Selected by Shoichi Saeki. New York: Kodansha International, 1981.
The Changeling. New York: Grove Press, 2010.
Somersault. New York: Grove Press, 2003.
Teach Us to Outgrow Our Madness: Four Short Novels. Translated by John Nathan. New York: Grove Press, 1977.

Works about Ōe Kenzaburō

Napier, Susan. *Escape from the Wasteland: Romanticism and Realism in the Fiction of Mishima Yukio and Ōe Kenzaburō.* Cambridge, Mass.: Harvard University Press, 1991.
Wilson, Machiko N. *The Marginal World of Ōe Kenzaburō: A Study in Themes and Techniques.* Armonk, N.Y.: M. E. Sharpe, 1986.

Ogot, Grace (1930–) *novelist*

Grace Ogot was born in Butere near Kisumu, district Central Nyanza, Kenya. She attended several girls' schools before training at the Nursing Training Hospital at Mengo, Uganda, from 1949 to 1953. From 1958 to 1959, she was a midwifery tutor and nursing sister at Makerere Hospital. She married Bethwell Ogot, history lecturer at Makerere University, in 1959. Two years later, Ogot became the principal of the Women's Training Center in Kisumu. In 1963, she returned to Makerere Hospital as nursing officer. She was also actively involved in activities that supported the women's movement. She was a member of the Maendeleo ya Wanawake Organization of Women and the Executive Committee of the Kenya Council of Women.

Ogot's writings reflect not only her feminist leanings but also her belief in the importance of perpetuating tradition and history in the face of technological progress and modernization. Her novel *The Promised Land* (1959) describes the Luo (an ethnic group in Kenya) migration from Uganda to the eastern shore of Lake Victoria during the colonial period. Migration, which is a dominant motif in this novel, highlights the sense of alienation and displacement experienced similarly by those who are victims of colonial exploitation and male domination. Ogot uses strong female characters, such as Nyapol, to comment on the hypocrisy of male domination by discrediting the male personalities in her novels and short stories. Nyapol's husband Ochola's mental deterioration in the new settlement is contrasted with Nyapol's strength and perseverance, and this challenges the misrepresentation of African females as meek and passive.

Ogot's volume of short stories, *Land Without Thunder* (1968), which was more successful and popular than *The Promised Land,* reinforces her attempts to undermine patriarchal authority by challenging ideas of male dominance. By developing the reversal of roles in her fiction, Ogot creates a platform for the female voice and discloses the male biases inherent in traditional African literature. In "The Old White Witch," for example, the white matron's shock at discovering that her female charges are more defiant and vociferous in their resistance to her domination than the men challenges the stereotypical view that men form the foundation of the African resistance movement.

Ogot's greatest contribution to African and world literature lies in her criticism of a male-dominated Africa and in her accurate and insightful depiction of many marginalized indigenous groups, such as the Luo, in Kenya.

Other Works by Grace Ogot

The Graduate. Nairobi: Uzima Press, 1980.
The Island of Tears. Nairobi: Uzima Press, 1980.
Miaha. Nairobi: Heinemann, 1983.
The Other Woman: Selected Short Stories. Nairobi: Transafrica Publishers, 1976.
The Strange Bride. Translated by Okoth Okombo. Nairobi: Heinemann, 1989.

Works about Grace Ogot

Conde, Maryse. "Three Female Writers in Modern Africa: Flora Nwapa, Ama Ata Aidoo and Grace Ogot." *Présence Africaine* 82 (1972).
Lindfors, Bernth. "Interview with Grace Ogot." *World Literature Written in English* 18, no. 1 (1979).

Okara, Gabriel (1921–) *novelist, poet*

Gabriel Okara was born at Bumoundi in the Ijo country of the Niger Delta in Nigeria. His parents were both members of the Ekpetinma clan. Okara received his early education at St. Peter's and Proctor's Memorial School and later attended the Government College of Umuahia. His education was temporarily interrupted by the outbreak of World War II, but he resumed his studies during the war at Yaba Higher College. Under the guidance of renowned sculptor Ben Enwonwu, Okara became a painter; then later he turned to bookbinding, journalism, and creative writing. His first poems were published in the Ibadan-based journal *Black Orpheus* in the 1950s. He has been a part-time lecturer at the University of Nigeria, a government official, general manager of the Rivers State Broadcasting Corporation, and a founding member of the Association of Nigerian Authors.

Though Okara had no formal training in writing, his works effectively blend intense expression with masterful diction. Okara has written only one novel, *The Voice* (1964), which was critically acclaimed for its experimental and unorthodox style. This satire contains a strange narrative of events detailing a romantic hero's search for righteousness in a corrupted world. An eccentric writer, Okara amuses and inspires through his creative rendering of themes—colonialism, racism, and the fear of losing one's heritage—that consume most African writers of his time. He has also written two children's books: *Juju Island* and *Little Snake and Little Frog* (both 1982).

Folktales and myths are a strong source for Okara's poems, which attempt to revitalize the enchantment of Nigerian folklore through their representation of primordial acts of bravery and wisdom. Okara uses an unusual blend of ambiguous symbols and powerful imagery to relate these acts. The poem "You Laughed and Laughed and Laughed," for example (anthologized in Biddle), juxtaposes the cold laughter of the civilized world against the ancestral strength of Africa:

> Then I danced my magic dance
>   to the rhythm of talking drums
>   pleading, but you shut your
>   eyes and laughed and laughed and
>   laughed . . .

The poem relates how that cold laughter is ultimately thawed ("Now it is my turn to laugh"):

> . . . you whispered;
>   'Why so?'
>   And I answered:
>   'Because my fathers and I
>   are owned by the living
>   warmth of the earth
>   through our naked feet.'

His poems, which are written in a simple lyrical form, are also characterized by energy and vibrancy paralleled by a constant underlying protest against social injustice. "The Fisherman's Invocation," for instance, highlights Okara's concerns with the tribulations of nation building during the Nigerian civil war.

Okara received first prize in the British Council's 1952 short story competition for his piece, "Iconoclast." In 1953, his poem, "The Call of the River Nun," won the best entry prize at the Nigerian Festival of Arts, and he won the Commonwealth Poetry Prize for "The Fisherman's Invocation" in 1979. Okara was also awarded an honorary doctorate by the University of Port

Harcourt in Rivers State in 1982 in recognition for his efforts to involve Nigerians in their cultural and literary heritage.

Other Works by Gabriel Okara

Biddle, Arthur, ed. *Global Voices: Contemporary Literature from the Non-Western World.* Englewood Cliffs, N.J.: Prentice-Hall, 1995.
The Fisherman's Invocation. London: Heinemann Educational Books, 1978.
The Voice. New York: Holmes and Meier, 1987.

Works about Gabriel Okara

Anozie, S. O. "The Theme of Alienation and Commitment in Okara's *The Voice.*" *Bulletin of the Association for African Literature in English* 3 (1965).
Egudu, R. N. "A Study of Five of Gabriel Okara's Poems." *Okike* 13 (1979).
Shiarella, J. "Gabriel Okara's *The Voice*: A Study in the Poetic Novel." *Black Orpheus* 2:5–6 (1970).

Ondaatje, Michael (1943–) *poet, novelist*

Born in Colombo, Ceylon (now Sri Lanka), of Dutch, English, Sinhalese, and Tamil descent, Philip Michael Ondaatje is the youngest child of Mervyn Ondaatje, a tea-and-rubber-plantation superintendent, and Enid Doris, who ran a dance and theater school. In 1962, Ondaatje emigrated to Canada, where he studied English and history at Bishop's University in Quebec; he has baccalaureate and master's degrees.

Ondaatje is one of a few Canadian writers who also is published in the United States and Britain and is known internationally. His early poems appeared in *New Wave Canada: The New Explosion in Canadian Poetry* (1967). His poetry collection *Secular Love* (1984) explores the pain of the failure of his first marriage and celebrates his second.

In his first foray into fiction, *The Collected Works of Billy the Kid* (1970), Ondaatje retells the story of the outlaw William H. Bonney through a mixture of poetry, prose, photographs, and other illustrations. In *Coming through Slaughter* (1976), too, he interweaves biography, history, and fiction to relate the story of jazz cornetist Buddy Bolden, who went insane. *In the Skin of the Lion* retells the story of the building of Toronto's Prince Edward Viaduct. In 1978, after a 24-year absence, Ondaatje returned to his homeland, now Sri Lanka. In journals, he recorded family anecdotes and stories that developed into his "fictional memoir" *Running in the Family* (1982), which is composed of vivid, rhapsodic reminiscences.

In many of his novels, Ondaatje uses his central characters to explore a violent reality, mixing the ordinary and the fantastic to create a surreal montage, as can be seen in *The English Patient* (1993). Here a quartet of characters—Hana Lewis, a Canadian nurse; the "English patient," burned beyond recognition, who is in fact a Hungarian count; thief and double agent David Caravaggio; and sapper Kip Singh, who has been sent to clear the area of enemy mines—shelter in a dilapidated Italian villa during the last days of World War II. Douglas Barbour remarks, "As the complexly ordered fragments of the novel accumulate, their pasts, their presents, and their possible futures intertwine in an intricate collage," creating in the process, as Lorna Sage observes, "an improbable civilization of their own, a zone of fragile intimacy and understanding. . . ."

Fascinated by history, documentation, and biography, Ondaatje reinvents history through imagination. The dominant features of his style are a dynamic beauty and a scarcely contained violence. He has won many awards, including the Governor General's Award three times, the Booker Prize, and the Toronto Book Award. In 2007, Ondaatje published *Divisadero*, a novel about a family living on a farm in Northern California and how a traumatic event affects the rest of their lives.

Another Work by Michael Ondaatje
Anil's Ghost: A Novel. New York: Vintage, 2004.

A Work about Michael Ondaatje
Barbour, Douglas. *Michael Ondaatje*. Boston: Twayne, 1993.

Onetti, Juan Carlos (1909–1994) *novelist, short story writer*

Juan Carlos Onetti, the son of Carlos Onetti and Honoria Borges, was born in Montevideo, Uruguay. Considering that he would go on to become a major novelist, the most remarkable thing about Onetti's childhood was that he never finished high school. He dropped out in his early teens and spent the next 20 years working at odd jobs and living the life of a bohemian. However, he continued to read constantly and educated himself in modern politics and literature.

Onetti was particularly fond of the novels of the Norwegian writer KNUT HAMSUN. His first novel, *El pozo* (*The Pit,* 1939), resembles Hamsun's novel *Hunger* (1890). Both works follow an alienated protagonist (similar to protagonists found in works by JEAN-PAUL SARTRE and ALBERT CAMUS) through an unfriendly city, concentrating on the main character's thoughts and his disconnection from everyone around him. Present in *Hunger* but far more pronounced in *El pozo* is the introduction of elements of fantasy in what is mainly a realistic narrative. *El pozo* was completely unsuccessful when it was first published; now, it is recognized as a precursor to the MAGIC REALISM movement and as perhaps the first truly modern Latin-American novel.

In *La vida breve* (*A Brief Life,* 1950), Onetti again focuses on a main character, Juan María Brausen, who is alienated from society and completely absorbed by his own thoughts. Brausen is himself a writer, and the reader watches him create narratives within the narrative. The novel takes place in the fictitious town of Santa Maria and combines REALISM with philosophical asides and elements of fantasy. Onetti would go on to write about Santa Maria again and again in his fiction. In this way, he resembles and is a precursor to GARCÍA MÁRQUEZ. Both authors worked at not only telling distinct stories but also creating an imaginary world. Unlike the mythic grandeur of García Márquez's Macondo, Onetti's imaginary world is restrained, tinged with the melancholy of philosophical dilemmas.

In 1974, Onetti was imprisoned by the Uruguayan government for selecting a controversial short story as the winner in a contest sponsored by the magazine *Marcha*. He was held for three months and finally released due to the outrage of the international community. He moved to Spain the next year and became a Spanish citizen.

Late in his life Onetti's pessimism increased. In *Dejemos hablar al viento* (*Let The Wind Speak*, 1979), he once again revisited Santa Maria, this time narrating its destruction by fire and a cleansing wind. This act of symbolically uncreating the imaginary world he had been building all his life resonates with both sorrow and purification. It is a final abandonment of nostalgia and a preparation for death.

In 1980, Onetti was awarded the Miguel de Cervantes Prize, the most prestigious award given in the Spanish-speaking world. He was the first Latin-American novelist to hit on the particular mixture of fantasy, reality, and formal experimentation, which such writers as CARLOS FUENTES, García Márquez, and VARGAS LLOSA later developed into their own styles of magic realism. He is a writer of subtle humor and great philosophical insight.

Other Works by Juan Carlos Onetti

Goodbye and Stories. Translated by Daniel Balderston. Austin: University of Texas Press, 1990.
Past Caring? Translated by Peter Bush. London: Quartet Books, 1995.
The Shipyard. Translated by Nick Caistor. London: Serpent's Tail, 1992.

Works about Juan Carlos Onetti

Adams, Ian M. *Three Authors of Alienation: Bombal, Onetti, Carpentier.* Austin: University of Texas Press, 1975.
San Roman, Gustavo. *Onetti and Others: Comparative Essays on a Major Figure in Latin American Literature.* Albany: State University of New York Press, 1999.

Ortega y Gasset, José (1883–1955)
philosopher

José Ortega y Gasset was born in Madrid, Spain. Both his mother and father's families were powerful and successful publishers. Ortega y Gasset was trained to be a journalist, as well as to take over his family's publishing empire. However, when he graduated from the University of Madrid, despite an innate talent, he found the prospect of a career in journalism unsatisfying. Instead, he chose to study philosophy in Germany.

In 1914, at the outbreak of World War I, he published his first book *Meditations on Quixote*. The book is a collection of essays on topics ranging from the purely literary to features of life in modern-day Europe. All of the essays mix cultural commentary with the philosophical underpinnings that Ortega y Gasset had absorbed through his study of German philosophy, particularly that of Kant.

During the next 40 years, until his death, Ortega y Gasset was extremely prolific. His complete works, published in 1983, are 12 volumes of more than 500 pages each. He was also an important political figure in Spain, working tirelessly for moderate liberal reform until his impatience with extremism led him to retire in 1933.

Two of Ortega y Gasset's works stand out from the rest as having had a very large influence on later 20th-century thought. The first of these is *The Dehumanization of Art* (1925), in which he examines a unique modern phenomenon, the unheard-of unpopularity of modern art, and its rejection by the masses. Why, he asks, does the art that is generally acknowledged by critics and intellectuals as deserving of aesthetic merit receive such a negative reaction from common society? He finds that, unlike the highest forms of visual art from the past, modern art emphasizes the fictional aspect of the art medium and deemphasizes the "human concerns" of art's subject matter. Although this brings increased pleasure to knowing viewers who are educated to appreciate "pure" aesthetics, it alienates the uneducated viewers who want to find in art something to relate to their own lives.

In *The Revolt of The Masses* (1929), Ortega y Gasset examines another 20th-century phenomenon, the modern practice of sightseeing. Why, he asks, do countless people wish to go to sights, such as palaces or the Vatican, that formerly were accessible only to the privileged few? In former times, these places were used for specific functions. However, the masses go not to use the places as they were intended but simply to assert their own presence. Though somewhat elitist by today's standards, *The Revolt of The Masses* can be best understood as an indictment of the fascist tendencies of many European countries, including Spain, between the world wars. Ortega y Gasset feared, often correctly, that unfettered rule by the populace would end in brutality and fascism.

Ortega y Gasset is one of the most important Spanish philosophers of the 20th century. His efforts brought modern philosophical thought into Spanish culture. His influence has been worldwide, and his thought has influenced literature, philosophy, and art history.

Other Works by José Ortega y Gasset

History as a System, and Other Essays Toward a Philosophy of History. With an afterward by John William Miller. New York: Norton, 1961.

Man and Crisis. Translated by Mildred Adams. New York: Norton, 1962.

Meditations on Hunting. Translated by H. B. Westcott. New York: Scribner, 1986.

The Mission of the University. Translated by Howard Lee Nostrand. Piscataway, N.J.: Transaction Publishers, 2001.

The Origin of Philosophy. Translated by Toby Talbot. Champaign: University of Illinois Press, 2000.

Velasquez, Goya, and the Dehumanization of Art. New York: Norton, 1972.

A Work about José Ortega y Gasset

Díaz, Janet Winecoff. *The Major Themes of Existentialism in the Work of José Ortega y Gasset.* Chapel Hill: University of North Carolina Press, 1970.

Osceola

See DINESEN, ISAK.

Ostrovsky, Nikolai (1904–1936) *novelist*

Nikolai Alexeevich Ostrovsky was born in the small village of Viliya, Russia. His father worked as a seasonal laborer, and the family was very poor. In 1914, his family resettled in the town of Sheptovka, where Ostrovsky briefly attended elementary school. As a young teenager, he worked at various jobs and ran errands for the Bolshevik underground. He joined the Red Army in 1918 and fought for the Bolshevik cause. In 1920, he was seriously wounded in battle and subsequently contracted typhus.

Ostrovsky was officially declared an invalid in 1922. Bedridden by his physical breakdown, he dedicated his time to completing a correspondence course with Sverdlov University in Moscow, but a month after completing his course, he lost his vision and became partially paralyzed. He then began to write articles for newspapers and journals, to speak on the radio, and to begin his only full-length novel.

Ostrovsky completed *How the Steel was Tempered* in 1930. The novel, published in 1934, is firmly grounded in SOCIALIST REALISM and depicts the struggles of workers and soldiers in forging the Soviet Union, and its artistic aim of the novel is reflected in the simple, utilitarian language of the writer. Immediately hailed as a masterpiece of socialist art, the novel garnered him the Order of Lenin in 1935. His second novel *Born of the Storm,* about the civil war in the Ukraine, was incomplete when he died at the age of 32.

Ostrovsky achieved immense literary success with only one published novel. Although he was not prolific in his contribution to Russian literature, he did influence a new generation of fiction writers who attempted to glorify the building of a communist state.

Oz, Amos (Amos Klausner) (1939–)
novelist, short story writer, essayist

Amos Oz was born in a poor neighborhood of Jerusalem to conservative Zionist parents who both emigrated from Europe and met in Jerusalem.

A sabra, or native Israeli, Oz grew up speaking and writing modern Hebrew. Oz's mother died when he was a teenager, and he left home at the age of 15 to join Kibbutz Hulda, one of Israel's oldest communes. There, striking out on his own, he changed his name from Klausner to Oz, a Hebrew word meaning "courage" or "strength."

At the commune, Oz was allowed to write just one day a week. Later, as his success grew, he was allowed to increase his writing time. He described life on a kibbutz in his first novel, *Elsewhere, Perhaps* (1973), and in *A Perfect Peace* (1982), set in a kibbutz in the 1960s. These and other of Oz's works explore the conflicts and tensions in modern Israeli society, examining human nature, its frailty, and its variety. Many of his stories take place either on a kibbutz or in Jerusalem, where he creates microcosms of Israeli society.

Oz is a full Professor at Ben-Gurion University of the Negev and was awarded the prestigious Israel Prize for Literature in 1998, the 50th anniversary year of Israel's independence.

Critical Analysis

Oz's breakthrough novel, *My Michael*, is representative of his dual interest as a writer: first in the trials and tribulations of those who live in Jerusalem, and second in the ancient politics of the land that is holy for three major religions and continues to fuel current debates and conflicts.

The novel focuses on Hannah and Michael, who married soon after Israel gained its independence in 1949 and find themselves unhappy 10 years later with married life. Hannah seeks adventure, recalling events from her childhood, while Michael, a geologist, remains earthbound and pragmatic, losing himself in his work. Oz uses the basic conflict in the marriage, in particular Hannah's struggle for independence, as a direct analogy for the newly formed state of Israel, struggling to define and defend itself from its enemies. Bedridden after the birth of their son, Hannah realizes that her condition offers a chance for a kind of freedom. In her bed she imagines herself as another person, Yvonne Azulai, who lives a life she can only dream of. Oz details the tribulations of this couple in concise sentences that demonstrate a preference for realistic depictions of particular details that illuminate only the essence of the conflict.

In *Panther in the Basement* (1995), Oz focuses on Proffi, a 12-year-old Israeli boy who becomes swept up in the events taking place in 1948, the final year of the British occupation of Palestine and the birth of the Promised Land. In the fervor surrounding the politics of the transition, Proffi and his friends form a secret organization called F.O.D., Freedom or Death. In the midst of planning to blow up 10 Downing Street in London—the home of the British prime minister—Proffi strikes up an unexpected friendship with a British soldier, Sergeant Dunlop. When the relationship is discovered, his friends brand him a traitor. "Instead of a panther in the basement," Proffi writes, "they saw me as a knife in the back." The tensions and aspirations underlying the formation of Israel are played out in the dreams and conflicts of the members of F.O.D.

Other Works by Amos Oz

Fima. Translated by Nicholas de Lang. New York: Harvest Books, 1994.

Rhyming Life and Death. New York: Houghton Mifflin, 2009.

Suddenly in the Depth of the Forest (A Fable for All Ages). London: Chatto and Windus, 2005.

To Know a Woman. Translated by Nicholas de Lang. California: Harcourt Brace, 1992.

A Work about Amos Oz

Cohen, Joseph. *Voices of Israel: Essays on and Interviews With Yehuda Amichai, A. B. Yehoshua, T. Carmi, Aharon Applefeld, and Amos Oz*. Albany: State University of New York Press, 1990.

Pa Chin
See BA JIN.

Pagis, Dan (1930–1986) *poet*
Dan Pagis was born in Bukovina, once a part of Austria, Romania, and the Soviet Union. Today, Bukovina is part of Ukraine and Romania. Pagis spent his early years in the home of his grandparents. He had few friends but was a very enthusiastic reader from the age of six, spending much of his time in his grandparents' apartment library. At the age of 11, Pagis was deported to a Nazi camp, where he spent three years. He emigrated to Palestine in 1946 and, after only four years in Israel, began to write in his new language of Hebrew.

Said to be one of the most vibrant voices in modern Israeli poetry, Pagis is also internationally recognized as a major poet of his generation. He has been called a poet of the unspeakable because many of his poems are infused with the horror of the Holocaust. Much of Pagis's subject matter is grim, containing images of genocide, but Pagis also explores other horizons, evoking biblical texts, centuries-old mysticism, and the medieval Iberian peninsula. Writers of his generation were known as the emigré writers, consisting of those born in the Diaspora (Jewish communities outside Palestine).

Along with other Israeli writers of his generation, Pagis helped to bring a more natural colloquial style to Hebrew poetry. His many volumes of poetry have been described as "a poetry of allusion" in which he uses irony and plays on words to mask sorrow. Yet, his poems also celebrate the human spirit and contain compassion for his persecutors. His work remains popular and is celebrated not only in his home in Israel but also around the world.

Other Works by Dan Pagis
Points of Departure. Translated by Stephen Mitchell. Philadelphia: Jewish Publication Society, 1981.

The Selected Poetry of Dan Pagis. Translated by Stephen Mitchell. Berkeley: University of California Press, 1996.

Variable Directions: Selected Poetry. Translated by Stephen Mitchell. San Francisco: North Point Press, 1989.

Works about Dan Pagis
Alter, Robert. "Dan Pagis and the Poetry of Displacement." In *Judaism: A Quarterly Journal of Jewish Life and Thought* 180, 45:4 (Fall 1996).

Jacobson, David C. "The Holocaust Survivor in Israeli Poetry: Dan Pagis." Paper delivered at academic conference: Symposium on Trends in Contemporary Israeli Literature, University of Michigan, Ann Arbor, Michigan, 1977.

Marcel Pagnol (1895–1974) *playwright, filmmaker, novelist*

Pagnol was born in 1895 in Aubagne, France. His father, Joseph, was an English teacher, and his mother, Augustine Lansot, a seamstress. The Pagnol family were proud of their descent from Spanish swordsmiths who fled from Toledo, Spain, during the 15th-century religious persecutions known as the Inquisition. The life and work of the author and filmmaker would later reflect the progressive thinking of his ancestors.

In 1900 his father was hired at l'école des Chartreux, in Marseille. To his parents' amazement, Pagnol learned to read at an early age, but he was not allowed to open a book until the age of six, on orders from his mother "for fear of cerebral explosion." In 1904, his family rented a house in the village of La Treille called the Bastide Neuve. The village and the surrounding area would become a creative hub for Pagnol throughout his life and would eventually serve as his final resting place.

Pagnol's creative life began early, writing his first play for a local theater group at the age of 15. In 1913, at the age of 18, he began his studies in literature at the University of Provence Aix-Marseille I. At the start of the World War I, Pagnol was called up into the infantry, but he was soon discharged due to a poor constitution. While at university, he cofounded *Fortunio* magazine in 1913. Renamed *Cahiers du Sud* (Journal of the South) in 1925, it became one of the foremost literary reviews in the world. In 1916, Pagnol graduated with a degree in English and married Simonne Colin. For the next six years, he worked as an English teacher at Pamiers, Aix-en-Provence, and Marseille. In 1922, he moved with Colin to Paris, where he continued teaching but devoted his free time to playwriting. In collaboration with playwright and screenwriter Paul Nivoix, his childhood friend who introduced the provincial Pagnol to the cultural life of Paris, Pagnol wrote the five-act satire *Les Marchands de gloire* (*The Merchants of Glory*) in 1925.

First performed at the Théâtre de la Madeleine in April 1925, *The Merchants of Glory* focuses on the character of Edouard Bachele, a provincial civil servant who uses the emotional capital of the alleged "heroic" death of his son on the French battlefield in World War I to gain fame and authority. Elected as a member of parliament, his power and ambition grow until the sudden appearance of his son. After recovering from amnesia in a German hospital, Bachele's son reveals that his actions were not as heroic as once believed, placing in jeopardy his father's campaign for a position as minister. A controversial play that takes to task civilian profiteers who exploit the heroism of soldiers, *The Merchants of Glory* threw Pagnol into the spotlight of the Paris stage. This success was followed by the plays *Jazz* (1926) and *Topaze*, the latter of which established his international reputation and caused him to turn his attention to film.

An exploration of ambition focusing on a naïve schoolteacher who is dominated by desire for money, *Topaze* opened in October 1928 at the Théâtre des Variétés and ran for two years. In the play, Mr. Topaze loses his teaching position when he refuses to raise the grades of one of his students, a child of a wealthy family. He finds work as a tutor in the home of Suzy Courtois, the mistress of a dishonest local politician named Régis Castel-Bénac. Mr. Topaze is deceived into signing onto one of Régis's deals but is told to remain silent. Because the business is legally in Topaze's name, however, he decides to run it for his own profit. Pagnol concludes in the play that cynicism is the only realistic attitude in a world ruled by profit. *Topaze* was adapted for film five times: a Hollywood and French adaptation were released simultaneously in 1933; two French-language versions directed by Pagnol himself appeared in 1936 and 1951; and *Mr. Topaze* (aka *I Like Money*), a British adaptation directed by and starring Peter Sellers, was released in 1961.

While *Topaze* began its run at the Théâtre des Variétés, Pagnol completed *Marius*, a play focusing on the provincial characters he recalled from his childhood in Marseille. Pagnol admitted to feeling "exiled in Paris" during this time, and despite the warnings of friends and critics who believed the accents and culture of Marseille would not translate well in Paris, *Marius* opened in March 1929, playing to sold-out audiences for 800 performances. The play would subsequently be adapted for a feature film, which was released in 1931. Marius forms the first part of the "Fanny" or "Marseille" trilogy of plays (and later films), which include *Fanny* (1931) and *César* (1935), which had the distinction of beginning its life as a film and then in 1946 was adapted for the stage. This trilogy of stage and film productions highlights one of Pagnol's central themes: to depict a poetic interpretation of reality that "makes strange" ordinary life, allowing the viewer to see it from another perspective. He wrote affectionately about the people of Provence and their dreams and fears. He used the settings of the city, the harbor, and the countryside as a background, and he focused particular attention on the village of La Treille, where he spent many summers as a child. This trilogy represented the typical characteristics of the south of France: the old "dreamer," the homebound wife, and the young rebel. The story is set against the colorful background of the Vieux Port of Marseille. In the first play, the central character Marius dreams of "far islands beneath the wind" and leaves Fanny to go to sea. When he returns, Fanny has married the elderly and kindly Panisse, for the sake of her and Marius's, child, César. Twenty years later, after the death of Panisse, Marius and Fanny are reunited by their son. Pagnol's stories and characters continue to resonate with French audiences, inspiring new, popular adaptations of his work.

In 1926, Pagnol separated from Simonne Colin, though they would not officially divorce until 1941. He married Jacqueline Bouvier in 1945, who had two children. When his daughter, Estelle, died at the age of two, Pagnol slipped into a long depression. After the failure of his next play, he turned to writing a series of autobiographical novels collectively called *Souvenirs d'enfance* (*Childhood Memories*). The four volumes explore Pagnol's life from birth to approximately 1910, focusing on his experiences in Marseille and La Treille. *La gloire de mon père* (*My Father's Glory*) and *Le château de ma mère* (*My Mother's Castle*) were both published in 1957, followed by *Le temps de secrets* (*The Time of Secrets*) in 1959 and *Le temps d'amour* (*The Time of Love*), published posthumously in 1979. The success of *Childhood Memories* encouraged Pagnol to continue writing, completing a second series that focused on the realities of Provençal peasant life at the turn of the 20th century. The most popular of this series, *Jean de Florette* (1963) was adapted for film in 1986, part of the heritage cinema movement of that decade that celebrated the history, culture, and geography of France.

Pagnol died in Paris on April 18, 1974. He is buried in the municipal cemetery at La Treille, along with his mother, father, brothers, and wife Jacqueline Bouvier.

Critical Analysis

Pagnol's work in theater, film, and literature share in common his abiding love for the French provinces and the lure of a romanticized rural life they present, as well as his distaste for the rough politics of urban (that is, mainly Parisian) life. His play *The Merchants of Glory* is a prime example of Pagnol's scathingly critical assessment of the mind of the city dweller whose self-interested ambitions override his natural morality to the extent that he is willing to use the alleged death of his son to further his career. This is further exemplified in *Topaze*, in which an otherwise provincial character is gradually corrupted by the greed and power of his lover and her father and comes to believe that all behavior is justified in the name of economic profit.

The idealized memories of his childhood in French villages color Pagnol's characters and the narratives of all his stories. In his series *Childhood Memories*, we are presented with a vision of France that for Pagnol has sadly passed on: a 19th century vision that cherishes honor and hard labor as principal virtues. However, it would be problematic to suggest that Pagnol's love for the provinces is as straightforward as it appears. In his *Marseille* trilogy the character of Marius stands in as a rural avatar of Pagnol. This is a man who, while mainly happy with his lot in a sleepy harbor town, looks out at the sea and thinks, "Whenever I go to the dock and look at the horizon, I am on the other side. If I see a boat on the ocean, it pulls me like a cord . . . like a belt pulling my sides, and I don't know where I am, I cannot think of anything else. . . ." Like Marius, Pagnol's desire to travel, to have new experiences, led him to Paris and to theatre, film, and finally novels.

Pagnol's provincial narratives also acknowledge that the values of villagers can be as suspect as those of their city neighbors. The novels *Jean de Florette* and *Manon des Sources* focus on the machinations of a group of villagers concerning a plot of land with a crucial water source. For Pagnol, it is the natural world that governs the actions of people who, when removed from the influences of the city, ultimately return to the values underlying a closer relationship with nature by way of rural life. For French culture, Pagnol's work will always represent a depiction of a heritage that imagines a country in which the values of its ancestors will always prevail.

Other Works by Marcel Pagnol

Jean de Florette and Manon of the Springs. New York: Farrar, Straus & Giroux, 1988.

Works about Marcel Pagnol

Marcel Pagnol Web Site. Available online. URL: http://www.marcel-pagnol.com.

Pak Mogwol (Park Yong-jong)
(1916–1978) *poet, essayist, translator*
Park Yong-jong was born in Kyongju in Korea's Kyongsangnam province on January 6, 1916, and was educated through middle school. He is best known for his lyrical and nostalgic poems, which were popular with the Korean masses. His early pastoral poems of rural beauty, such as "Green Deer" and "The Mountain Peach Blossoms," were sentimental and evocative of his own childhood. Many were homages to his hometown and were infused with patriotic sentiments. He derived his rhythms from folk life and was deeply interested in folk culture.

Pak Mogwol moved from the countryside to the bustling metropolis of Seoul after Korea's liberation from Japanese colonialism in 1945. With his move, he made a similar shift in his poetry by moving toward REALISM, depicting city life, and pitting ordinary human beings against urban desolation. In "Sketch," for example, he tenderly describes a cast of haggard urban dwellers. In later years, Pak Mogwol's style and focus shifted once more—this time toward spiritualism and an acceptance of death—in poems such as "An Ordinary Day," in which the narrator marks his own grave.

In 1962, Pak Mogwol accepted a position teaching Korean literature at Hanyang University. He continued to write, producing essays, poems for children, translations, and the lyrical Korean poetry of which he is considered by many to be the modern master. He also edited the monthly journal, *The Image.* Pak Mogwol was honored with many awards, including the Free Literature Prize in 1955 and the Republic of Korea Literary Arts Prize in 1968. He died on March 24, 1978.

Another Work by Pak Mogwol

Selected Poems of Pak Mogwol. Translated by Kim Uchang. Fremont, Calif.: Asian Humanities Press, 1990.

Pamuk, Orhan (1952–) *novelist*
Orhan Pamuk was born in Istanbul, Turkey, and except for three years in New York, he spent his entire life there. Pamuk studied architecture at the Istanbul Technical University for three years but ultimately finished formal studies at the Institute of Journalism at Istanbul University. He began writing regularly in 1974 and published *Cevdet Bey*

and His Sons in 1982, marking the beginning of his career. The novel was a family saga written in the REALIST style.

Pamuk's novels are very popular and at the same time highly controversial. His novel *Kara Kitap* (*The Black Book,* 1995), about a week in the life of the lawyer Galip whose wife Ruya has left him, became both a best seller and an object of condemnation. Its postmodern style and ambiguous politics angered leftists and fundamentalists alike.

Snow, published in English in 2004, is a dense, discursive novel about Ka, a Westernized poet who returns to his native Turkey after many years of absence. The novel focuses on the conflict between secular and religious factions in the eastern town of Kars, where Ka has gone both to reunite with a lost love who is recently divorced and to investigate a serious of suicides among girls forbidden to wear head scarves while studying at the university.

Pamuk's works have been translated into more than 20 languages. He is the recipient of major Turkish and international literary awards, including the 1984 Madarali Novel Prize for his second novel, *Sessiz Ev* (*The Silent House,* 1983); here, Pamuk shifted from the realist style of his first novel to a more in-depth psychosociological style. Pamuk won the 1991 Prix de la Découverte Européenne for the French translation of *Sessiz Ev.* His most notable subjects are Istanbul, Turkey's culture and politics, and human rights, and his novels, when taken as a whole, show a mixture of modern and traditional styles. In "Orhan Pamuk," Andrew Finkel states that "The point [of Pamuk's novels] seems to be that a person does not have to abandon the past in order to be part of the future."

Pamuk has been embroiled in several controversies in recent years. In 2002, a Turkish newspaper accused him of plagiarizing major portions of his novels *My Name Is Red* and *White Castle.* Pamuk will not comment on the accusations.

In 2005, Pamuk commented on the mass killings of Armenians by the Ottoman Empire in the early years of the 20th century. As a result of his comments, Pamuk faced criminal charges and other forms of harassment, including book burnings.

Eventually the charges were dropped, partly because the case raised questions about whether or not Turkey should be allowed to join the European Union. In 2006, Pamuk was awarded the Nobel Prize in literature, the first Turkish citizen to have won the prize.

Other Works by Orhan Pamuk
Istanbul: Memories of a City. Translated by Maureen Freely. New York: Alfred A. Knopf, 2005.
The Museum of Innocence. Translated by Maureen Freely. New York: Alfred A. Knopf, 2009.
Other Colors: Essays and a Story. Translated by Maureen Freely. New York: Alfred A. Knopf, 2007.
The White Castle. Translated by V. Holbrook. New York: George Braziller, 1991.

Pardo Bazán, Emilia de (1851–1921)
short story writer, novelist

Pardo Bazán was born in La Coruña, Galicia. Her parents encouraged her studies, and her father's library supplied her with a great variety of reading material. She was fascinated by books about the French Revolution and loved *Don Quixote,* the Bible, and Homer's *Iliad.* She began to write poetry as a young child. Taught by private tutors, she refused to take music classes or to play the piano, as was traditional for young women; instead, she spent time reading and writing. Married at age 17, she moved to Madrid, where she became part of the social scene. Later, she went to France and traveled through Europe, learning French and German. She was influenced by French literature. In 1876, she gave birth to the first of three children and dedicated her only book of poems to this child. Her first novel, *Pascual López* (1879), was written on the birth of her second child. In 1880, she contracted hepatitis and went to Vichy to recuperate. There, she met the French poet and novelist VICTOR HUGO.

La cuestión palpitante (1883), a collection of articles explaining NATURALISM, (the theory that human behavior is controlled by instinct, emotion, and social and economic determinism), created a scandal, and her husband asked her to stop writing and to retract several statements. Two years later, in 1884, she left him and published *La dama joven* about matrimonial crises. *La Tribuna,* (1882), her third novel, is considered to be her first naturalist work. It is a study of the environment and workers in the cigar factories in La Coruña, similar to works by BENITO PÉREZ GALDÓS (1843–1920). The two authors had a romantic relationship lasting some 20 years.

In 1890, she established the magazine *El nuevo teatro crítico.* At this time, denouncing educational differences between the sexes, she began a lifelong campaign for female emancipation. In 1906, she won a major battle in this area, becoming the first woman to preside over the literary section of the Ateneo of Madrid (a pioneering cultural institution) and the first female professor of literature at the Central University of Madrid.

Pardo Bazán was given the title of *condesa* (countess) for her literary achievements.

Other Works by Emilia Pardo Bazán

The House of Ulloa. Translated by Lucia Graves. New York: Penguin USA, 1991.
Torn Lace and Other Stories. Translated by Maria Cristina Urruela. New York: Modern Language Association of America, 1997.
The Tribune of the People. Translated by Walter Borenstein. Lewisburg, Pa.: Bucknell University Press, 1999.
The White Horse and Other Stories. Translated by Robert M. Fedorchek. Lewisburg, Pa.: Bucknell University Press, 1993.

Works about Emilia Pardo Bazán

Gonzalez-Arias, Francisca. *Portrait of a Woman As Artist: Emilia Pardo Bazán and the Modern Novel in France and Spain.* New York: Garland, 1992.
Hemingway, Maurice. *Emilia Pardo Bazán: The Making of a Novelist.* Cambridge: Cambridge University Press, 1983.
Tolliver, Joyce. *Cigar Smoke and Violet Water: Gendered Discourse in the Stories of Emilia Pardo*

Bazán. Lewisburg, Pa.: Bucknell University Press, 1999.

Park Yong-jong
See PAK MOGWOL.

Pasolini, Pier Paolo (1922–1975) *director, writer, poet, novelist, critic*

Pier Paolo Pasolini was born in Bologna, Italy, to Carlo Alberto Pasolini, an Italian army officer, and Susanna Colussi, a grade-school teacher. He attended the University of Bologna as an art history major before he switched to literature. He wrote his thesis on the poet Giovanni Pascoli. Pasolini was drafted into the Italian army in 1943 in the middle of his studies but served only a week. When his army unit was captured by the Germans, Pasolini escaped into the Italian countryside, after which he began to write poetry. During this time, he discovered he was homosexual.

Pasolini began to write novels in the 1950s. His early novels included *The Ragazzi* (1955), about poor young people in the slums of Rome, and *A Violent Life* (1959), which expresses his radical political beliefs. The former, a portrayal of the underside of Roman life, was considered so graphic and controversial that it led to charges of pornography.

In the 1960s, Pasolini turned to writing for film. He preferred the medium of film to paper, having once said, "Since Chaplin's *Modern Times,* movies have anticipated literature. . . . The movie has much more freedom." One of his key films is *The Gospel According to St. Matthew* (1964), which features his mother in the role of the older Virgin Mary. His final film was *One Hundred and Twenty Days of Sodom* (1975), which uses sex as a metaphor for the class struggle; this film stirred up controversy for its portrayal of Italian hedonistic society.

Pasolini was brutally murdered under ambiguous circumstances. Some believe a teenage prostitute bludgeoned Pasolini to death and then ran over him with Pasolini's car. Others believe he was assassinated, perhaps for his political beliefs. A provocative and controversial artist, writer, and filmmaker, Pasolini gained popularity after his death. Several of his works were released posthumously.

Other Works by Pier Paolo Pasolini

Petrolio. Translated by Ann Goldstein. New York: Pantheon, 1997.

Pier Paolo Pasolini: Poems. Translated by Norman MacAfee. New York: Noonday Press, 1996.

Roman Poems. Translated by Lawrence Ferlinghetti and Francesca Valente. San Francisco: City Lights Books, 1986.

Works about Pier Paolo Pasolini

Friedrich, Pia. *Pier Paolo Pasolini.* Boston: Twayne, 1982.

Rohdie, Sam. *The Passion of Pier Paolo Pasolini.* London: British Film Institute, 1996.

Pasternak, Boris (1890–1960) *novelist, poet, translator, short story writer*

Boris Leonidovich Pasternak was born in Moscow to Leonid Pasternak, a celebrated painter, and Rosa Kaufman, a concert pianist. The family was established in the intellectual and cultural circles of Moscow. Indeed, LEO TOLSTOY was a family friend and played a role in the formation of Pasternak's literary style. An excellent student, Pasternak received the Russian equivalent of valedictorian rank and in 1908 began to study law at Moscow University. While there, he became very interested in philosophy and decided to pursue his studies at the University of Marburg in Germany in 1912.

Pasternak successfully completed his studies and in 1914 published his first volume of poetry, *The Twin in the Clouds.* Two subsequent collections, *Over the Barriers* (1916) and *My Sister, Life* (1917), established his reputation as a major Russian poet. His poetic works combined the elements of SYMBOLISM and FUTURISM, with verse that is lyrical and emotional, and contains some of the most profound images and metaphors found in Russian poetry.

At first, Pasternak supported the Bolshevik revolution, but he soon was disenchanted with the failed promises of the communist regime. During the 1920s, he began his prolific career as a fiction writer. In *The Childhood of Lovers* (1924), Pasternak explores the psychological makeup and emotions of a young girl. He published a short autobiographical work, *Safe Conduct* (1931), and a brilliant collection of poetry, *Second Birth* (1932). Because of his interest in exploring ethical themes and his political disillusionment, he came under repeated attacks from the government during the 1930s and was forbidden to publish. He supported himself by translating English and German poets into Russian. During these years, Pasternak gained the respect of Russian intellectual circles.

Pasternak received the Nobel Prize in literature in 1958 as a result of his most celebrated work, *Doctor Zhivago* (1957). The epic novel recounts the experiences of a young doctor, Yuri Zhivago, during the upheavals of the early 20th century. The novel's insights into the Communist regime quickly brought about government criticism and censure. It was first printed in Italy in 1957, followed by an English translation in 1958 and its publication in 1959 in the United States. Forced by the Soviet government to refuse the Nobel Prize, Pasternak was expelled from the Soviet Writers' Union and exiled to an artists' community outside Moscow. He died virtually abandoned by everyone except close friends. Critical acclaim for his work did not come in Russia until years after his death.

Pasternak is now recognized as one of the greatest writers of the 20th century. He left a legacy of courage and genius that is still admired today. He sacrificed his life for his work, to which his own countrymen were denied access until the 1970s.

Critical Analysis

In Russian, the root word *zhiv* means "life"; Dr. Zhivago—the novel's protagonist—embraces life in epic style, exploring a world of political and personal revolutions. Part autobiography (Zhivago is a poet) and part historical romance, *Dr. Zhivago* is a chronicle of a people and of an age.

The title character, Yuri Zhivago, functions as Pasternak's noble everyman; the events of his life are intimately connected with the tumultuous events affecting Russia, Europe, and the world of the early 20th century. Indeed, the status of his turbulent and ultimately doomed romance with Lara Guishar parallels that of World War I (1914–18), the Russian Revolution (1917), and the Russian Civil War (1917–21). The sheer complexity of the epic narrative, populated by dozens of major and minor characters who step in and out of Zhivago's life, lends the novel an impression of chaos that mirrors the turmoil of a country seemingly always on the brink of revolution. At the end of the novel, Zhivago's fate (death from a weak heart) and his unfulfilled love for Lara (they marry other people, Lara returning only for his funeral) are compared with the fate of Russia in the first half of the century.

The connection, however, is not Pasternak's attempt at propaganda: Zhivago's ideals, founded in his quasi-mystical worldview, run counter to the brutality of these events and the materialism that the philosophies that fuel them expound upon. By the time he completed *Dr. Zhivago*, Pasternak's idealism regarding the promise of the Russian Revolution had soured, especially under the brutal reign of Joesph Stalin, who forced him into exile. The novel, with its criticism of Stalinism, in particular in references to the infamous prison camps, reflects that disillusionment, along with Pasternak's frustration with his own life and work. Despite this, Pasternak loved Russia. "He was prepared to forgive his country all its shortcomings," writes Isaiah Berlin, "all, save the barbarism of Stalin's reign; but even that, in 1945, he regarded as the darkness before the dawn which he was straining his eyes to detect—the hope expressed in the last chapters of *Doctor Zhivago*."

A Work about Boris Pasternak

Barnes, Christopher. *Boris Pasternak: A Literary Biography*. Cambridge: Cambridge University Press, 1998.

Paton, Alan (1903–1988) *poet*

Alan Paton was born in Pietermaritzburg, Natal, South Africa. His father was James Paton, a Scot who had migrated to South Africa in 1895, and his mother was a descendant of English immigrants. His parents were not well educated, but they were staunchly religious, and Paton grew up reading the Bible. His strict father often beat his sons, and the trauma of Paton's childhood deeply affected his views about authority and corporal punishment. His father's influence is not altogether negative, however; he encouraged Paton to love books and nature. Paton was an avid reader of Charles Dickens, Walter Scott, and Rupert Brooke. He attended high school at the Maritzburg College from 1914 to 1918 and completed his college education at Natal University College in 1924. Paton worked as a teacher at the Ixopo High School for White Students, where he met his first wife. In 1935, Paton was appointed principal of the Diepkloof Reformatory for young offenders. This experience formed the basis of his political consciousness. Paton resigned from his job and, in 1953, formed the South African Liberal Party (disbanded in 1968).

Paton's most famous novel is *Cry, the Beloved Country,* which was published in 1948. By the time of Paton's death, the book had sold more than 15 million copies worldwide. It was also adapted into two films. Kumalo's journey in the book reflects Paton's concern with major themes that influenced his life, such as authority, racial discrimination, and religion. Paton's empathetic portrayal of Kumalo, a black Anglican priest, led many white South Africans to criticize his work for being too sentimental. At the peak of apartheid in South Africa, his disdain of racial discrimination and his idealized vision of eventual reconciliation of the two racial groups were deemed too revolutionary. Paton was a sort of liminal figure because he stood on the line that borders the two worlds of white and black South Africans. Most of the white Afrikaners rejected him for his sympathy for the black Africans, and some of the latter viewed his writing with suspicion, evidently shown in the mixed reactions to his portrayal of characters and interracial relationships in *Cry, the Beloved Country.* Paton's next international success, *Too Late the Phalarope* (1953), further explores the themes of racial and political inflexibility.

Paton's work against apartheid won him the annual Freedom Award in 1960. His other works include autobiographies and biographies of famous political figures such as Jan Hofmeyer, the cabinet minister. Paton's main contribution to African literature lies in his balanced perspective and optimism, untainted by the bitterness that often accompanies other African writings.

Other Works by Alan Paton

Journey Continued: An Autobiography. New York: Scribner, 1988.
Save the Beloved Country. New York: Scribner, 1989.
Towards the Mountains. New York: Scribner, 1980.

Works about Alan Paton

Alexander, Peter F. *Alan Paton: A Biography.* Oxford: Oxford University Press, 1994.
Chapman, Michael. *South African Literatures.* London: Longman, 1996.

Pavese, Cesare (1908–1950) *novelist, poet, translator*

Cesare Pavese was born in Santo Stefano Belbo, Italy, to Eugenio Pavese, a clerk at a law court in Turin, and Consolina Mesturini. His rural Italian roots are a big part of his identity, and his poetry and fiction are infused with images connected to his poor beginnings. As a young boy, he spent summers in the country and the rest of the year in Turin. When Pavese was six, however, his father died of a brain tumor. His mother, determined to give him a good education, enrolled him in the Liceo Massimo D'Azeglio school. Augusto Monti, his Italian and Latin teacher there, became an influential mentor in his life. Monti encouraged his bright pupil to read the works of Vittorio Alfieri, an 18th-century Italian dramatist whose works explored themes of political freedom and the dangers of tyranny. Monti introduced Pavese to

politics, specifically the need for civic awareness, and helped instill in him a disdain for totalitarianism. In 1927, Pavese enrolled in the Faculty of Letters at the University of Turin. He wrote his thesis on U.S. poet Walt Whitman and graduated with a degree in literature in 1930. Other writers played a key role in Pavese's career as he translated many works of famous writers, beginning in 1931 with his translation of Sinclair Lewis's *Our Mr. Wrenn.* Other notable translations include Herman Melville's *Moby-Dick* (1932), Daniel Defoe's *Moll Flanders* (1938), and Charles Dickens's *David Copperfield* (1939).

Pavese did not, however, limit himself to translating. *Hard Labor,* his collection of verse, was published in 1936. In her biography *Cesare Pavese,* Aine O'Healy says the collection is "one of Pavese's most challenging and ambitious works, and it contains the nucleus of all the thematic preoccupations of his subsequent writing," such as rural versus urban life, parenthood, and work.

Heavily influenced by Whitman and other poets, Pavese set out to create serious narrative poetry. His poem "South Seas," for example, is a recounting of a walk in the countryside with his cousin; yet, it takes on epic proportions.

Pavese's entry into novel writing took place toward the end of his life. His first novel, *The Beautiful Summer* (written in 1940), is a coming of age story about a working-class girl in Turin. *Among Single Women,* a novel that studied the "false tragic world of the upper class," followed in 1949. Pavese returns to the coming-of-age story in *The Devil in the Hills* (1948), but this time uses three young men as his characters and human freedom and limitation as his themes. These collective works earned Pavese the Strega Prize for fiction in 1950.

Pavese's contributions in the areas of poetry and fiction are noteworthy. His novels, translated into many languages, helped establish Italian neorealism, a movement in art, literature, and film characterized by its preoccupation with everyday, working-class life and leftist politics. In addition, his translations helped American classical literature reach a wider Italian audience. When he committed suicide in 1950, Pavese left this diary entry: "I have done my public share—as much as I could do. I have worked. I have given people poetry. I have shared the sufferings of many."

Another Work by Cesare Pavese
The Selected Works of Cesare Pavese. Translated by R. W. Flint. New York: Farrar, Straus & Giroux, 1968.

A Work about Cesare Pavese
Áine O'Healey. *Cesare Pavese.* Boston: Twayne, 1988.

Pavlova, Karolina Karlovna (1807–1893)
poet, novelist

Karolina Pavlova was born in Yaroslavl, Russia, but spent her childhood and most of her adulthood in Moscow with parents of German origin. Her father, Karl Yanish, was a professor of chemistry and physics, a physician, an amateur astronomer, and a scholar of literature and painting. Pavlova received a marvelous education as a child: She was an avid reader, was fluent in four languages by age 12, and often helped her father collect astronomical data.

Pavlova began her literary career in the late 1820s, translating ALEKSANDR PUSHKIN's poetry into German and French. When she began to compose poetry, she also did so in French and German. Her translations were quite popular in the fashionable salons of Moscow, and Pavlova was inspired to compose poetry in Russian.

In 1836, she married N. F. Pavlov, a mediocre writer who was in constant trouble with authorities because of his political activities. Pavlova's poetry was at its most popular in the 1840s, and in 1848 Pavlova successfully published a novel, *A Double Life.* She soon found herself bankrupt, as her husband gambled away her inheritance. Indignant, Karl Yanish wrote a letter to government officials, describing the antigovernment activities of Nikolay Pavlov, who was subsequently imprisoned and sentenced to exile. Public indignation forced Pavlova to leave Moscow in 1853. She briefly settled in St. Petersburg until she finally left Russia in 1861 and settled in Dresden, Germany.

Her poems were collectively published only once during her lifetime, in 1863, but were overlooked. In 1915, however, VALERY BRYUSOV edited a collection of her poems, and Pavlova's work became popular and appreciated, especially in literary circles. *A Double Life* is the only work of Pavlova's translated into English. In the West, Pavlova's work is not well known, although some scholars have begun to reexamine her poetry, particularly in the context of feminism.

A Work about Karolina Pavlova
Fusso, Susanne, ed. *Essays on Karolina Pavlova.* Chicago: Northwestern University Press, 2001.

Paz, Octavio (1914–1998) *poet, essayist*

Octavio Paz was born in Mexico City, Mexico. His father, Octavio Paz, Sr., a lawyer, diplomat, and journalist, had represented the Mexican revolutionary Emiliano Zapata when he was tried in the United States. His mother, Josefina Lozano, was a first-generation Mexican born to Spanish parents. Paz was educated in his early years in a French school. In addition, his aunt tutored him in French and recommended French books for him to read. As a boy, his favorite authors were VICTOR HUGO and Jean-Jacques Rousseau. This affinity with French culture stayed with Paz throughout his life and influenced both his poetic style and his thought.

In his 20s, Paz's poetry was noticed by PABLO NERUDA, and he was invited to Spain to attend the Second Antifascist Writers Congress. He traveled in Europe and befriended ANDRÉ BRETON, French surrealist writer from whom Paz absorbed the ideas and psychological and philosophical concepts of surrealism. Paz approached these ideas with classical sensibility and measured logic.

In *Labyrinth of Solitude* (1950), a collection of essays, Paz speculates on the sociology of the Mexican national character. He finds that Mexico is a nation yet to arrive at a final national identity. It is a culture fragmented by the conflicts between the old world and the new. Because the culture is fragmented, its citizens are unable to connect with each other, and they find themselves trapped by solitude. Paz proposes a solution, which he takes directly from surrealism: The only way to escape solitude is through romantic love as an act of the imagination. Paz goes on to say that, for escape to be possible, Mexican women must be allowed more freedom to develop their own identities. *Labyrinth of Solitude,* thus, has an international appeal.

Though Paz's essays have come to be appreciated as much as his poems, his first success and literary impact was as a poet. His poem *Sun Stone* (1957) is perhaps the apex of his poetic vision and his powers of formal design. Its structure is cyclical and is metaphorically based on the famous Aztec calendar stone, a cosmological object that represents the Aztecs' religious and physical conception of the universe. It also has a practical purpose in that it can be used to help a person calculate the seasons. Paz, in essence, tried to create a poem that would represent analogously the universe of modern consciousness in all its grandeur and, at the same time, be accessible to an individual on a very personal level.

In both his poetry and his essays, one of Paz's primary concerns is how individuals connect to their society. He applied his formidable critical powers to the art of literature in his collection of essays *The Bow and the Lyre* (1953). His analysis explores poetic language, the role of the writer, and the social importance of literature. The book is filled with learned detail that Paz uses as he strives to synthesize poetry's historical and universal aspects.

In 1990, Octavio Paz won the Nobel Prize in literature. He was considered a mentor to many Mexican authors in the generation that came after him, most importantly to CARLOS FUENTES. The two Mexican authors shared the qualities of a powerful imagination and a deep concern for history.

Another Work by Octavio Paz

A Draft of Shadows, and Other Poems. Edited and translated by Eliot Weinberger, with translations by Elizabeth Bishop and Mark Strand. New York: New Directions, 1979.

Works about Octavio Paz

Grenier, Yvon. *From Art to Politics: The Romantic Liberalism of Octavio Paz.* Lanham, Md.: Rowman & Littlefield, 2001.
Ivask, Ivar. *The Perpetual Present: The Poetry and Prose of Octavio Paz.* Norman: University of Oklahoma Press, 1973.
Quiroga, Jose. *Understanding Octavio Paz.* Columbia: University of South Carolina Press, 1999.

p'Bitek, Okot (1931–1982) *poet*

Okot p'Bitek was born in Gulu, northern Uganda. He attended Gulu High School and King's College in Budo before taking a two-year course at the Government Training College in Mbarara in 1952. He taught English and Religious Knowledge at Sir Samuel Baker's School near Gulu, where he was also the choirmaster. His interest in music began around this period and continued throughout his life. P'Bitek became increasingly interested in his African heritage and tradition. In 1962, he moved to Oxford University to pursue a degree in social anthropology and examine closely the richness of the African tradition. P'Bitek became active in politics, especially during the 1960s when a movement was established to gain independence for Uganda. He returned briefly to Uganda to change the agenda of the Ugandan Cultural Center in Kampala and then moved to Nairobi to teach at the university. He finally returned to Makerere University as a professor of creative writing in 1982 but died tragically five months later.

P'Bitek's poetry shows the rich influence of his interests in traditional African song, music, and oral tradition. He wrote his first poem, "The Lost Spear" (1952) while he was still a student in Mbarara. The poem retells the traditional Lwo folk story regarding the spear, the bead, and the bean.

P'Bitek's writings also express his concern with contemporary political issues and display his resourcefulness in blending these concerns with his musical talent. In *Song of Lawino* (1966), for example, p'Bitek employs strong imagery and lyrical rhythms to denounce Africans, especially politicians, who embrace Western ideology and discard their African heritage.

P'Bitek did not reject technological advancement and progress in Uganda, but he disagreed that these should come at the cost of losing Acoli cultural values. P'Bitek's contribution to world literature lies in his belief and efforts in bringing native language to the forefront of poetry writing in Africa, and his works express his concern that African nations be built on the basis of African beliefs, culture, and values, not on Western ones.

Other Works by Okot p'Bitek

African Religions in Western Scholarship. Kampala: East African Literature Bureau, 1970.
Hare and Hornbill. London: Heinemann, 1978.
The Horn of My Love. London: Heinemann, 1974.

Works about Okot p'Bitek

Heron, G. A. *The Poetry of Okot p'Bitek.* London: Heinemann, 1976.
Ofuani, Ogo. "The Poet as Self-Critic: The Stylistic Repercussions of Textual Revisions in Okot p'Bitek's *Song of Ocol.*" *Research in African Literatures* 25, no. 4 (Winter 1994): 159–75.

Pederson, Knut

See HAMSUN, KNUT.

Perec, Georges (1936–1982) *novelist*

Georges Perec was born on March 7 in Paris, where he lived for most of his life. His father was killed in 1940 in World War II. Perec and other members of his family sought refuge in the country, but his mother disappeared from Paris in 1942, and it was later discovered that she died at Auschwitz. Perec was raised by his aunt and uncle, served in the army, married, and published his first works in magazines.

Perec's first novel, *The Things* (1965), was awarded the Prix Renaudot. He followed this achievement with 20 more books, no two of them having the same pattern. He joined a Paris-based writing group, OULIPO, the Workshop of Potential Literature, whose main goal was to expand literary possibilities by borrowing from the fields of mathematics and logic. Perec became intrigued by the palindrome, a sentence or word that reads the same both forward and backward. Perec wrote one palindrome consisting of more than 5,000 letters.

Perec's literary output includes novels, short stories, and word games. He also composed a 466-word text using *a* as the only vowel. This experiment led to his fascination with the lipogram, a text in which one or more letters may not appear. *La Disparition* (1969) is a novel lipogram in E, meaning that the letter *e* is never used. This made translating difficult, as the literal English title, *The Disappearance*, would contain the forbidden letter. It was translated in 1994 by Gilbert Adair as *A Void.*

Largely secretive with regard to his private life, Perec did publish *W, or The Remembrance of Childhood* (1975), an odd assortment of memoirs interspersed with sections about a dystopian island called W, where life revolves around sports. His masterpiece, however, is *Life, A User's Manual* (1978), which tells stories about the residents of an apartment building. Perec built the work based on a complex system detailing the number and the length of the chapters, as well as the appearance of certain random elements within each of the stories. *Life, A User's Manual* was awarded the Prix Medici.

Another Work by Georges Perec

53 Days. Translated by David Bellos. London: Harvill, 1992.

A Work about Georges Perec

Bellos, David. *Georges Perec: A Life in Words.* London: Harvill, 1993.

Peretz, Isaac Lieb (1852–1915) *poet, novelist, playwright*

Isaac Lieb Peretz was born in Zamosc, Poland. Considered one of the founders of modern Yiddish literature, he was largely self-educated, gaining much of his knowledge through extensive reading. A career as a successful lawyer left little time for Peretz to write until a false accusation forced him to seek new employment. He was hired as a cemetery official for the Jewish cemeteries in Warsaw, Poland.

Peretz's career change left him with ample time to pursue his writing. He published fiction, plays, and poems and inspired younger writers to pursue their goals. He became active in socialist spheres and was often accused of radicalism. Attracting negative attention from the authorities, he was imprisoned once for his socialist activities.

A voice for the Jewish Enlightenment in Poland, a movement that stressed understanding and embracing Jewish heritage and culture, Peretz wrote his early work in Hebrew and his later work in Yiddish. Much of his work makes the point that, although Jews in Poland were materially poor, their lives were spiritually rich. He glorified the worker and showed compassion for the poor. For example, *Stories and Pictures* (1900; translated 1906), considered his finest work, is a series of Hasidic sketches in which Peretz offers a sympathetic look at Jewish life. With a tone that is sometimes loving, sometimes critical, he describes situations common not only to the Polish Jews of his time but also to all of humanity.

Peretz's heroes are the oppressed and the suffering who exemplify virtue, faith, and unselfishness that are often lacking in humanity as a whole. The hero of the short story "Bontsche the Silent" (in *Man's Search for Values* [translated by A. S. Rappoport, 1987]), for instance, is a virtuous man who spends his entire life suffering in silence. He receives his reward in the afterworld, where he is told that he can have whatever he desires; however, all the man can think of requesting is a hot roll and fresh butter for breakfast every morning. In this way, Peretz also exemplifies the simple pleasures of life that are most often taken for granted.

Another Work by Isaac Lieb Peretz

Selected Stories. Translated by Eli Katz. New York: Zhitlowsky Foundation for Jewish Culture, 1991.

A Work about Isaac Lieb Peretz

Wisse, Ruth R. *I. L. Peretz and the Making of Modern Jewish Culture.* Seattle: University of Washington Press, 1991.

Pérez Galdós, Benito (1843–1920) *novelist, playwright, historian*

Benito Pérez Galdós was born on Grand Canary Island. He was the youngest of 10 children, and his mother was determined that he would be a lawyer, thereby bringing middle-class respectability to the family. Though an intelligent child and very talented in both the literary and visual arts, he did not apply himself at school and had no interest in being a lawyer. Nevertheless, when he was 18, his mother sent him to the University of Madrid to study law. Madrid was a true awakening for the young writer. Though Pérez Galdós had spent most of his youth in the Canary Islands, it was Madrid that became the focus of his novels, and he eventually became the quintessential writer of that city in the 19th century.

In 1865, he abandoned law school and became a journalist for the newspaper the *Nation*. His years reporting on the news of Madrid served as a literary apprenticeship in that the skills he acquired later helped him to develop his incredible REALISM. After Madrid, Pérez Galdós spent some time in Paris, where he began his first novel, *The Shadow* (1871), an odd phantasmagoric novel of psychological investigation. Its use of fantasy was uncharacteristic for Pérez Galdós and the realist style he would develop.

In 1873 Pérez Galdós wrote the first of a series of five works entitled *National Episodes,* in which he dramatizes events from 19th-century Spanish history as a way to explore issues of morality. In his concern for the moral character and national identity of Spain, he can be seen as a precursor and influence on the writers of the GENERATION OF 1898.

Pérez Galdós's historical interest became the major direction of his later works. Almost all of this series' 46 novels depict the reality of his time or the recent past while commenting on how the forces of history affect individual lives. *The Disinherited Lady* (1881) is a perfect example. On the surface it is a realistic account of a woman's life in late 19th-century Spain; however, it is also a symbolic meditation on how the Spanish tendencies of self-deception and dreaming have led to certain political tragedies.

Later in his career, such novels as *Compassion* (translated 1962) would turn to examine more closely issues of the spirit and faith. Pérez Galdós continued to write in the realist mode, of which he was an exceptional master, but now, instead of layering his realism with political and historical ideas, his books began to focus on the metaphysical forces behind life.

Pérez Galdós wrote to illuminate the relationships between the individual and the forces of society. Those forces variously took the forms of history or metaphysical questions in his novels; however, they always represented the vast interconnected web of forces that make up reality. He could be compared to the French novelist BALZAC. The two authors were exacting realists who used realism in an attempt to communicate their visionary insights.

Other Works by Benito Pérez Galdós

The Golden Fountain Café. Translated by Walter Rubin. Pittsburgh, Pa.: Latin American Literary Review Press, 1989.

Our Friend Manso. Translated from the Spanish by Robert Russell. New York: Columbia University Press, 1987.

A Work about Benito Pérez Galdós

Ribbans, Geoffrey. *History and Fiction in Galdós's Narratives.* Oxford: Clarendon Press, 1997.

Perse, Saint-John (pseudonym of Marie-René-Auguste-Alexis Saint-Léger) (1887–1975) *poet, diplomat*

Saint-John Perse was born on the island of St. Léger des Feuilles near Point-à-Pitre, Guadeloupe. His father was a lawyer, and his mother's family owned plantations. In 1899, his family moved to France and settled in Pau. While studying law at Bordeaux, Perse befriended PAUL CLAUDEL and other writers. He published his first collection of poems, *Éloges* (1911) shortly after graduating.

Perse wrote his epic poem *Anabase* (*Anabasis*, 1924) while he was working as a diplomat in China from 1916 to 1921. The title refers to the classical Greek writer Xenophon's account of an army's march through the ancient East. American-born English poet T. S. Eliot (1888–1965) thought so highly of this work that he translated it into English and wrote a preface in which he called it "a piece of writing of the same importance as the later work of James Joyce." Perse composed more poems from 1921 to 1932 while he was secretary to French statesman Aristide Briand. In 1940, the Nazi secret police seized and destroyed manuscripts in his Paris apartment, and the collaborationist Vichy regime revoked Perse's citizenship and dismissed him from office.

Perse first fled to England and then settled in the United States, where he worked as a consultant on French poetry at the Library of Congress. He published many works after moving to the United States, including *Exil* (*Exile*, 1942), a collection of four poems. His collection *Amers* (*Seamarks*, 1957) has been called one of the greatest works to emerge from World War II, and its section titled "Etroits sont les vaisseaux" ("Narrow are the vessels") is considered one of the great erotic sequences in French literature.

The New York Times Book Review (July 27, 1958) wrote that "If one reads through all" Perse's poems, "one is immediately aware that each is, as it were, an instrument of one great oeuvre." As B. Lindblad, president of the Royal Academy of Sciences, said before Perse's acceptance speech for the 1960 Nobel Prize in literature, "with sublime intuition" Perse knows "how to describe in brilliant metaphors the reaction of the soul of humanity."

Other Works by Saint-John Perse
Anabasis. Translated and with a preface by T. S. Eliot. Fort Washington, Pa.: Harvest Books, 1970.

Collected Poems. With translations by W. H. Auden et al. Princeton, N.J.: Princeton University Press, 1983.

Exile, and Other Poems. Translated by Dennis Devlin. New York: Pantheon Books, 1953.

Selected Poems. Edited by Mary Ann Caws. New York: New Directions, 1982.

Works about Saint-John Perse
Krause, Joseph. "The Two Axes of Saint-John Perse's Imagery." *Studi Francesi* 36, no. 1 (January–April 1992): 81–95.

Sterling, Richard L. *The Prose Works of Saint-John Perse: Towards an Understanding of His Poetry.* New York: Peter Lang, 1994.

Pessoa, Fernando (Alberto Caeiro, Ricardo Reis, Álvaro de Campos) (1888–1935) *poet*

Born in Lisbon, Portugal, to a cultured family, Pessoa was educated in South Africa and spoke English fluently. At age 15, he composed English sonnets in the style of Shakespeare.

In 1905, he returned to Portugal, attended the University of Lisbon, and became a commercial translator, an occupation that he held his entire life. He was one of the founders of *Orpheu* and *Presença*, two highly influential literary journals. At the time of his death, his work was not known outside of Portugal.

Pessoa began to write poetry in 1912. His poems express a longing for Portugal's glorious past, and they reflect the influence of the classical tradition and French SYMBOLISM. His earlier poems are nostalgic for a mythic past, whereas his later works deal more with consciousness and sensation.

His two main themes are the inherent limitations of one's power to apprehend reality and the elusive nature of personal identity. He invented literary alter egos to explore these themes. Pessoa wrote under 73 different names, and each persona reflects an individual outlook and Pessoa's belief that there is no one integrated personality. It is interesting to note that there is a recurrence of masks in his poems. His family name comes from the Latin *persona,* which refers to the masks worn by actors and, by extension, to the role the actors play. Also interesting is the fact that, in Portuguese, his family name means both "person" and "nobody."

Among his poetry collections are *Sonnets* (1918), *English Poems* (1922), and *Mensagem* (1934).

Another Work by Fernando Pessoa
Fernando Pessoa. Translated by Jonathan Griffin. Oxford: Carcanet, 1971.

A Work about Fernando Pessoa
Montero, George, ed. *The Man Who Never Was.* Providence, R.I.: Gavea Brown, 1982.

Pincherle, Alberto
See MORAVIA, ALBERTO.

Ping Hsin
See BING XIN.

Pirandello, Luigi (1867–1936) *playwright, novelist, short story writer*

Luigi Pirandello was born in Caos, Italy, to Stefano Ricci-Gramitto, a sulfur dealer, and his wife, Caterina. His father expected him to join the family business, but Pirandello pursued academics instead. In 1887, he studied at the University of Palermo, then the University of Rome, before receiving a Ph.D. in Roman philology in 1891 from the University of Bonn in Germany. His dissertation explored the Sicilian dialect of his native region. After his university training, Pirandello returned to Rome and translated Goethe's *Roman Elegies*. He also published his first original work, *Joyful Ill*(1889), a collection of romantic and sentimental poetry.

In 1894, he entered an arranged marriage with Antoinetta Portulano, the daughter of his father's business associate. His wife suffered a severe nervous breakdown and violent outbursts. In 1919, once Pirandello became financially solvent in his work, she was sent to a sanitarium. The turbulent union produced three children and fueled the sense of tragedy and despair found in Pirandello's work.

In 1908, Pirandello became a professor of Italian literature at the Girls' Normal School in Rome. In 1921, he had dual theatrical successes with his plays *Six Characters in Search of an Author* and *Henry IV*. *Six Characters* experiments with theatrical conventions. The story revolves around actors and a director rehearsing Pirandello's own play *The Rules of the Game*. During the rehearsal, a group of six people arrive, looking for someone to dramatize their story. As the tale unfolds, themes of morality, incest, and death intermingle. According to Susan Bassnett-McGuire in her book *Luigi Pirandello*, this work is a "two-fold process [that] takes place first in the author's mind and then on the stage when the actors and director take over."

When the play *Henry IV* (known in the United States as *The Living Mask*) came out, it was considered the Italian *Hamlet*. It is the most frequently performed of all of Pirandello's works in English. It centers on a costume party at which each guest is required to portray a famous historical character. One man chooses to be Henry IV. During the evening, he falls from a horse, hits his head, becomes deluded into believing he is actually the monarch, and is sequestered in a country villa set to resemble a medieval castle. His family, convinced that he is mad, plans to cure him of his insanity, but it is revealed that the man has been merely wearing the mask of insanity for a number of years and enjoying the ruse. In her introduction to *Three Plays*, Felicity Firth summarizes the theme in *Henry IV*:

"[E]ach individual creates for himself a personal vision of the truth in order to make life bearable. . . ."

Luigi Pirandello is one of Italy's most respected playwrights. His ability to capture his own multitiered vision of truth has entertained audiences for many years. While he encountered initial resistance for his self-consciousness and experimentalism, he won the Nobel Prize in literature in 1934 and has become one of the most influential 20th-century dramatists. In 1935, Pirandello wrote of his critics, "The world of international literary criticism has been crowded for a long time with numerous Pirandellos—lame, deformed, all head and no heart, gruff, insane and obscure—in whom, no matter how hard I try, I cannot recognize myself, not even in the slightest degree."

Critical Analysis

Few artists of the 20th century explore their themes as openly and as consistently as Luigi Pirandello. In all of his work, but especially in his plays, he drives home the point that, in the words of Gregory J. Howard, " 'Truth' is elusive, slippery, and more to the point, highly relative."

Pirandello's interest in questions of truth—fueled by events in his personal life—focuses primarily on the issue of "insanity": that is, who defines insanity? What is "sanity"? In his 1918 play, *Right You Are! (If You Think You Are)*, Pirandello explores this issue at a depth that rivals his better-known plays, such as *Six Characters in Search of an Author*. In it, Ponza and his mother-in-law, Signora Frola, battle over what appears to be a nonexistent woman, who is Ponza's wife and Frola's daughter. The community members who witness this conflict (Ponza prohibits Frola from seeing his wife) come to the consensus that either Ponza or Frola is mad.

Laudisi, the protagonist, orchestrates the investigation, challenging the community's belief that the power of sheer empirical observation will ultimately lead them to the "Truth." In one telling moment, Laudisi invites people to touch him, then declares:

Now, you have touched me, have you not? And you see me? And you are absolutely sure about me, are you not? Well now, madam, I beg of you; do not tell your husband, nor my sister, nor my niece, nor Signora Cini here, what you think of me; because, if you do, I would all tell you that you are completely wrong. But, you see, you are really right; because I am really what you take me to be; though, my dear madam, that does not prevent me from also being really what your husband, my sister, my niece, and Signora Cini take me to be—because they also were absolutely right!

In presenting the idea that people "experience" Laudisi differently, *Right You Are! (If You Think You Are)* raises fundamental questions for the audience—namely, the interplay between absolutism and relativism, which Pirandello leaves us to explore and draw our own conclusions.

Other Works by Luigi Pirandello

Firth, Felicity, ed. *Three Plays: "Enrico IV," "Sei Personaggi in Cerca d'Autore," "La Giara."* New York: St. Martin's Press, 1988.

Tales of Madness: A Selection from Luigi Pirandello's Short Stories for a Year. Translated by Giovanni R. Bussino. Brookline Village, Mass.: Dante University of America Press, 1984.

Three Major Plays. Translated by Carl R. Mueller. Hanover, N.H.: Smith & Kraus, 2000.

Works about Luigi Pirandello

Bassanese, Fiora A. *Understanding Luigi Pirandello.* Columbia: University of South Carolina Press, 1997.

DiGaetani, John Louis, ed. *A Companion to Pirandello Studies.* Westport, Conn.: Greenwood, 1991.

poetic realism

Poetic realism began in Germany, Scandinavia, and Central Europe, having its origins in the works of Poul Müller (1794–1838) and developing in the poetry and fiction of Theodor Storm (1817–88) and Theodor Fontane (1819–98), but its influence spread to Eastern European countries and to Russia as well. It developed as a result of dissatisfaction with the constraints and embellishments of ROMANTICISM, and in response to the often bleak social conditions of the late 19th century.

The major difference between poetic realism and other REALISM movements was the tendency for writers who associated with poetic realism to view the harsh realities of the world through a veil of artistic illusion, allowing some elements of the romantic movement to appear in their works. Higher poetic themes—such as love, aesthetics, death—were placed in the context of everyday life. Russian exponents of this principle notably include ALEKSANDR PUSHKIN.

As the age of realism progressed and war became more common among Central and Eastern European countries, as well as in America, poetic realism lost many of its ties to romanticism, moving away from a veil of illusion to a clear view of the human condition.

In the 1890s, poetic realism began to fade into the background and to be replaced throughout much of Central Europe by photographic realism, or NATURALISM. Reality was seen without the veil of illusion, and life was viewed impersonally, with no attempt to gloss over the unpleasant aspects of human existence. This change, however, arrived later in the Balkans and Russia, where poetic realism held sway until the middle of the 20th century. Even after the start of World War II, poetic realism explored the subjects of poverty and suffering and, at the same time, expressed hope within the bleakest of circumstances.

In the Balkans, poetic realism found an even greater expression in the visual arts, as represented by the works of Marko Celebonovic (1902–87), Nedjeljko Gvozdenovic (1902–88), Pedja Milosavljevic (1908–87), and Ivan Tabakovic (1898–1977). The tendency, however, in both the literature and art of this period was for artists to attempt to come to terms with reality, as opposed to escaping it.

Twentieth-century Russian poets who are considered poetic realists include Andrey Voznesensky (1933–   ), YEVGENY YEVTUSHENKO, and Joseph Brodsky (1940–96). In France, as well as in the Balkans, poetic realism continued to filter itself into the emerging field of film.

Works about Poetic Realism

Bernd, Clifford. *Poetic Realism in Scandinavia and Central Europe.* Columbia, S.C.: Camden House, 1995.

Pizer, John David. *Ego-Alter Ego: Double And/ As Other in the Age of German Poetic Realism* Durham: University of North Carolina Press, 1998.

Ponge, Francis (1899–1988) *poet, essayist*

French poet and essayist Francis Ponge was born in Montpellier, France, on March 27. He first studied law in Paris and then literature in Strasbourg. In the years between World War I and World War II, he worked as a journalist and newspaper editor. In 1937, Ponge became a member of the Communist Party. He was actively involved during World War II in the organization of a resistance movement among journalists. He left the party in 1947 and lived for two years in Algeria prior to returning to Paris to teach. He retired in 1965 to give lectures in several countries.

Ponge's poetry first gained attention in the late 1940s when it was praised in an article by JEAN-PAUL SARTRE. Ponge's poems were meticulous observations rather than emotional works. He described his ideas in rational terms that still remained lyrical. His collections include *The Voice of Things* (1942; translated 1972) and *La rage de l'expression* (1952). He often looked at common objects as a means of expressing larger concerns such as in "L'Orange," from his collection *Le parti pris des choses* (1942), in which an ordinary orange becomes a metaphor for ways of dealing with oppression.

Ponge died in Paris on August 6, 1988, leaving behind a legacy to world literature of the deeper understanding of the inherent simplicity of life.

Other Works by Francis Ponge

The Delights of the Door: A Poem. Translated by Robert Bly. New York: Bedouin Press, 1980.

Selected Poems. Translated by C. K. Williams. Winston-Salem, N.C.: Lake Forest University Press, 1994.

A Work about Francis Ponge

Sorrell, Martin. *Francis Ponge.* Boston: Twayne, 1981.

Poot, Linke

See DÖBLIN, ALFRED.

Popa, Vasko (1922–1991) *poet*

Vasko Popa was born in Grebenats, Banat, in Serbia. Although little is written of his life, he is one of the most widely translated modern Serbian poets. His works often describe the tragic experiences of the modern urban man in a time of war, and they express the fears and insecurities of humans trapped in a world that is becoming less and less welcoming.

Popa's poetry is best known for its classical elements as it brings to life the myth of Kosovo as it appeared in the traditional epic songs, by translating them into the language of modern Yugoslav poetry. In *Earth Erect* (translated 1973), for example, Popa describes his country outside of war as "A field like no other / Heaven above it / Heaven below."

Classical images of Serbia's national culture dominate Popa's poetry, thus leading to its success not only in his own country but even more so abroad, where his works have been used as song lyrics for both children's classical folk-song anthologies and contemporary Serbian "rock" music. From surrealist fable to traditional folktale, combining autobiography with myth, Popa's poetry embodies the spirit of a country struggling to maintain its identity.

Other Works by Vasko Popa

Earth Erect. Translated by Anne Pennington. Iowa City: International Writing Program, University of Iowa, 1973.

The Golden Apple: A Round of Stories, Songs, Spells, Proverbs and Riddles. Translated by Andrew Harvey and Anne Pennington. London: Anvil Press Poetry, 1980.

Homage to the Lame Wolf: Selected Poems, 1956–1975. Tranlated with an introduction by Charles Simic. Oberlin, Ohio: Oberlin College, 1979.

Works about Vasko Popa

Alexander, Ronelle. *The Structure of Vasko Popa's Poetry (UCLA Slavic Studies, Vol. 14).* Columbus, Ohio: Slavica Publishers, 1986.

Lekic, Anita. *The Quest for Roots: The Poetry of Vasko Popa (Balkan Studies, Volume 2).* New York: Peter Lang, 1993.

postcolonialism

Postcolonialism is a complex phenomenon that has generated many interpretations. From a historical perspective, it refers to literature and cultures that have redefined themselves following the experience of Western colonization. It most commonly applies to the cultures of South Asia, Africa, and the Caribbean that have gained their independence since the Second World War (1939–45). Postcolonialism in Latin America has a longer history, going back to the 19th century. It also refers to a body of theory written primarily by diasporic academics—from the Caribbean, the Middle East, South Asia, and Africa—who now reside in Europe and the United States. Edward Said's seminal work *Orientalism* (1978) casts a postcolonial eye on the discourse of the "Orient" generated by colonialism. This work has inspired many revisions and reinterpretations of colonial discourse. Similarly groundbreaking are Hohmi Bahba's *Dislocations of Culture* (1994), which looks at the ways in which writers formed under colonialism turn the language of the colonizer into new forms of identity and resistance; and Gayatri Spivak's *In Other Worlds* (1987), which applies postmodern, poststructuralist, and feminist theories to the reading of postcolonial discourse and literature.

Although most colonized countries won their independence during the 20th century, Latin America has a unique postcolonial history. Colonized in the 16th century primarily by Spain and Portugal, it experienced postcolonial movements in the 19th century when many of its countries won their independence and sought to define their cultural specificity. This was achieved by, for example, incorporating elements that had been rejected or marginalized by the colonizers, such as indigenous and African cultures, or else by turning to northern Europe and North America, instead of Spain or Portugal, for cultural models and ideals. However, especially toward the end of the century, Latin America experienced forms of economic and cultural colonization that were imported from Great Britain, France, and the United States that posed new challenges to national definition and visions of independence. During the 20th century, many Latin-American liberation movements and many prominent writers and intellectuals were inspired by Communist responses, especially that of Cuba, to colonialism and its aftermath.

After the Second World War, the European empires that had dominated a large part of the world during the 19th century, exporting their cultures and their literary forms, began their retreat. Independence movements led not only to political and national redefinitions but to creative responses to Western influences and oppression. Since the independence of India in 1947, inspired by the writings of Mohandas K. Gandhi, South Asia has seen an extraordinary renaissance of writers from different religions and regions, exploring South Asian and diasporic identity. Many of these writers are internationally known. V. S. Naipaul, for example, was awarded the Nobel Prize for literature in 2002. Since independence, African literature has also found an international audience and includes Nobel Prize winners such as Nadine Gordimer and Wole Soyinka. Books by writers from many different parts of the world are being published at an ever-increasing speed; many different voices are being heard, including those of women and the politically disenfranchised.

The NEGRITUDE movement in France of the 1940s and 1950s, led by AIMÉ CÉSAIRE and LÉOPOLD SENGHOR, valorized African identity and revitalized African and Caribbean poetry. When he became president of independent Senegal in 1960, Senghor used the concept of *négritude* as part of his political agenda, creating debate and controversy among other African and Caribbean writers about the meaning of being African.

In the 1950s and 1960s, the Civil Rights movement in the United States added impetus to the revival of African culture, long suppressed by slavery and its aftermath, and encouraged or inspired liberation movements throughout the world. In South Africa, often at the cost of imprisonment or death, black and white writers increasingly dared to oppose apartheid. Also, since the 1970s, liberation movements by indigenous peoples in Australasia and Latin American have transformed dying oral cultures, based on myth and ritual, and created new genres, such as the oral testimonial. *I Rigoberta Menchu: An Indian Woman in Guatemala* by RIGOBERTA MENCHÚ is one of many such testimonials that have brought to international attention the plight of indigenous cultures. Similarly, since the 1970s, the outcast Dalits of India have begun to reinvent their own culture and DALIT LITERATURE.

The question of language is crucial to postcolonial writers who were forced to learn the language of the colonizers, most often English, Spanish, or French. (In some cases, there are competing colonial languages, for example French and English in Canada, and Afrikaans and English in South Africa). After independence, for whom were these writers writing and in what language should they write? Some followed the example of the Martinican novelist Raphaël Confiant (1951–   ), who chose to write in his native Creole and then changed to French. For most writers, it was a question of finding a wider audience. CHINUA ACHEBE, considered to be the first African novelist, chose to write in English to reach not only Western readers but also many African readers who speak hundreds of different languages but whose lingua franca is English. Addressing different constituencies, the Kenyan NGŨGĨ WA THIONG'O writes in both English and Kikuyu.

Postcolonial writers have shown to what extent they have been able to use their colonial languages in new and liberating ways. Their styles vary according to their specific cultural and historical circumstances. Drawing on oral and spiritual traditions alien to the modern, secular West, some writers, such as the Colombian GABRIEL GARCÍA MÁRQUEZ and the Indian-born SALMAN RUSHDIE have combined myth and modernity, the sacred and the profane to create what has been called MAGIC REALISM, a popular postcolonial genre. Magic realism acknowledges the overlapping of cultures and the often absurd and ironic juxtapositions of competing beliefs, economic systems, and voices in the fragmented discourse of the postmodern and postcolonial world.

Postcolonialism has produced a strong immigrant and diasporic literature. For economic and political reasons, South Asians, Indonesians, Africans, Turks, and Caribbeans have established themselves in the West and have produced a new definition of what constitutes, for example, English or French or German or Dutch literature. Writers cannot easily be pinned down to a national identity. Dual nationality is common. Salman Rushdie wanders from Bombay to London to New York, always redefining the urban ground beneath his feet through the prism of his changing cultural experiences, including an India long left behind. The Trinidadian-born V. S. Naipaul reimagines the India, Africa, and Caribbean of his parents' diasporic past and chooses to live in England. MICHAEL ONDAATJE moves from Sri Lanka to England to Canada. Other Indian, African, and Caribbean writers situate themselves within a tradition that includes, but is not reduced to, the colonial experience. Some of them emulate ARUNDHATI ROY, a recipient of the Booker Prize, who has resisted the path of literary celebrity in the Indian diaspora and has remained in India, using her influence to support oppressed minorities —including tribal women—in their local cultural and political struggles.

Beginning with the collapse of the Berlin Wall in 1989, the disintegration of the empire of the Soviet Union, established since the Second World War, has produced its own, European form of postcolonial experience and literature. The fall of the Soviet Union has meant the reconfiguration of social and national identities in Eastern and Central Europe. Economic disorder and political unrest, especially due to the war in the former Yugoslavia and neighboring states, have also changed forms of literary expression and have increased the immigration of writers to Western Europe and the United States.

Electronic communications, the expansion of capitalism after the fall of the Soviet Union, and the economic liberalization of China have globalized the economy. For some peoples of the former colonial world, especially those opposed to Western forms of modernization, globalization, often interpreted as Americanization, is perceived as a threat to local cultures, religions, and forms of expression. For others, globalized forms of communication and dissemination of ideas are sources of new kinds of agency and self-determination. Because of their colonial histories, postcolonial writers remain especially alert to the dangers as well as the possibilities of globalization.

Works about Postcolonialism

Appiah, Kwame Anthony. *In My Father's House: Africa in the Philosophy of Culture.* New York: Oxford University Press, 1993.

Ashcroft, Bill, Gareth Williams, and Helen Tiffin. *The Empire Writes Back: Theory and Practice in Postcolonial Literatures.* New York: Routledge, 2002.

Fanon, Frantz. *Black Skin, White Masks.* Translated by Charles Markmann. New York: Grove Press, 1991.

———. *The Wretched of the Earth.* Translated by Constance Farrington. New York: Grove Press, 1996.

Glissant, Edouard. *Caribbean Discourse: Selected Essays.* Translated by J. Michael Dash. Charlottesville, Va.: Caraf Books (University of Virginia Press), 1992.

Gugelberger, Georg M., ed. *The Real Thing: Testimonial Discourse and Latin America.* Durham, N.C.: Duke University Press, 1997.

King, Anthony D., ed. *Culture, Globalization, and the World-System: Contemporary Conditions for the Representation of Identity.* Minneapolis: University of Minnesota Press, 1997.

Lazarus, Neil. *Resistance in Postcolonial African Fiction.* New Haven, Conn.: Yale University Press, 1990.

Ngũgĩ wa Thiong'o. *Decolonising the Mind: The Politics of Language in African Literature.* Portsmouth, N.H.: Heinemann, 1986.

Stratton, John. *Writing Sites: A Genealogy of the Postcolonial World.* Ann Arbor: University of Michigan Press, 1990.

Viswanathan, Gauri. *Masks of Conquest: Literary Study and British Rule in India.* New York: Oxford University Press, 1998.

postmodernism

Postmodernism emerged after World War II as a reaction against MODERNISM, which upheld the potentially restorative and integrating power of literature. Postmodernists do not attempt to correct or remedy the chaos and cacophony of language, but rather they imitate and often celebrate it. Many postmodernists, for example SAMUEL BECKETT and PETER HANDKE, emphasize the alienation of the individual in the modern social environment and seem highly aware of the domineering presence of technology—computers, telephones, faxes, weapons of mass destruction—in daily life. Although the intellectual beginnings of postmodernism are often identified with the French school of structuralist criticism, the aesthetic ideas of postmodern writers and artists can be found in contemporary works around the globe.

Postmodernist works often combine elements of diverse genres, such as television, cartoons, and music, that have a potential appeal to popular culture, and they often challenge the ideological assumptions of contemporary society. Opposing the notions of mimetic representation, postmodernists agree that language has its own singular reality.

The postmodern movement is identified with its own critical theories, namely deconstruction and cultural criticism. Cultural criticism questions the notions of "high" and "low" cultures and tends to treat all works of art, from comic books to statues, as equally legitimate cultural expressions. Deconstruction (often referred to as poststructuralism), the postmodern movement primarily based on the work of French philosopher Jacques Derrida (1930–   ), questions the notion of a single, unified meaning in a literary work. Through an act of close reading, the deconstructionists attempt to show that texts are self-contradictory and lack a single, unified center.

The postmodern movement is by no means limited to the arts. Our notions about the relationship between ideology and power underwent dramatic change based on the work of the French philosopher Michel Foucault (1926–84). Julia Kristeva (1941–   ), a psychoanalytic gender critic, changed our notions of femininity and its relationship to arts. Psychology also experienced dramatic changes, primarily in the field of psychoanalysis. Jacques Lacan (1901–81) refined SIGMUND FREUD's ideas about the relationship of language, gender, and psyche.

In certain ways, postmodern thinkers demonstrate that the line between science and arts is not as self-demarcating as some would like it to be. Many postmodern scientists question the notion of a single, unified reality. The artificial intelligence expert Marvin Minsky (1927–   ) insists that computers can think. Chaos theory, developed by the chemist Ilya Prigogine (1917–   ), disrupts our concept of a unified universe. Currently, many postmodern thinkers are examining the role of computers and hypertext in our understanding of epistemology. These ideas closely relate to our changing understanding about the structure of language and discourse.

Postmodernism has influenced virtually every genre of literature, theater, and film. Even of greater significance, postmodernism has confronted our epistemological conceptions about language, image, and signs.

Works about Postmodernism

Appignanesi, Chris. *Introducing Postmodernism*. New York: Totem Books, 2001.

Docherty, Thomas, ed. *Postmodernism*. New York: Columbia University Press, 2002.

Eagleton, Terry. *The Illusions of Postmodernism*. Oxford: Blackwell, 1996.

Grenz, Stanley. *A Primer on Postmodernism*. Grand Rapids, Mich.: Wm.B. Eerdmans Publishing Co., 1996.

Heartney, Eleanor. *Postmodernism*. New York: Cambridge University Press, 2001.

Premchand, Munshi (Dhanpat Rai Srivastana) (1880–1936) *novelist, short story writer*

Premchand was born outside the city of Benares, India. His family was very poor. The plight of the poor and the downtrodden is one of the prevalent themes in Premchand's work. He is perhaps the most famous Hindi–Urdu novelist of Indian literature and is considered to be the father of the Urdu short story. One of the strongest influences in Premchand's earlier work was Gandhian politics. His later novels are a blend of his own faith in marxism and his growing disillusionment with GANDHI's brand of grassroots activism.

In 1899, Premchand became a schoolteacher and continued this profession for 20 years. Copies of his first collection of short stories *Passion for the Fatherland* (1908), written in his first penname Navab Rai, were burned by British officials because of their strong patriotic (anti-British) message. After this event, he wrote by the pen name, Premchand. In 1915, Premchand stopped writing in Urdu completely and switched to writing in Hindi. This further increased his popularity because the Hindi language is spoken by a larger population in India.

By the time he wrote *Godān* (*Gift of the Cow*, 1936), published the year he died, Premchand had broken from his earlier optimistic portrayals of village life. Instead, he saw more clearly the dismal economic situation of India's rural poor. *Godān* offers a stark look at the lack of social and economic reform in villages, while metropolitan India is busy with modernization. Hori, the main character, and the village setting are realistic portraits that reveal the growing chasm between urban and rural India.

Because Premchand had his own publishing house, he encountered little difficulty in publishing his more controversial works. These works, such as *Nirmala* (1928), address the social and psychological problems imposed on women by society's norms. In particular, Premchand challenges the standard treatment of widows and prostitutes; at the time, widows were forced into financially dependent relationships with their family members because they were not given employment and were not allowed to remarry.

While serving as editor of the literary magazine *Hans* in the 1930s, Premchand used his position to create a mutual ground for literature and progressive politics. In 1936, he briefly served as president of the All India Progressive Writers' Association (AIPWA). This group was one of India's first attempts to form a collective of leftist, socialist writers. Premchand's novels were also an international success. His novel *Godān* has been translated into almost every Western language.

Other Works by Munshi Premchand

Gaban: The Stolen Jewels. Translated by Christopher R. King. Delhi: Oxford University Press, 2000.
Nirmala. Translated by Alok Rai. New York: Oxford University Press, 1999.

A Work about Munshi Premchand

Rai, Amrit. *Premchand: His Life and Times.* New York: Oxford University Press, 2002.

Proust, Marcel (1871–1922) *novelist*

Best known for his stream-of-consciousness autobiographical novel *À la recherche du temps perdu* (*In Search of Lost Time,* 1912; first published in English as *Remembrance of Things Past*), Marcel Proust was born in Auteuil, just outside of Paris, on July 10, 1871. The son of a wealthy doctor and his wife, a Jewish woman from a highly cultured background, Proust received an excellent education at the Lycée Condorcet. In spite of severe asthma, which plagued him throughout his life, he served one year in the military before attending the Sorbonne, where he received a degree in law.

Proust's literary skills became evident while he was still in his early teens. After graduation from the Sorbonne, he began to frequent the aristocratic salons in the wealthy sections of Paris. He also began to write for several of the symbolist (*see* SYMBOLISM) magazines. His first books, *Portraits de peintres* (1896) and *Pleasures and Regrets* (1896), came out in rapid succession and established him as an emerging literary voice.

Between 1895 and 1899, Proust worked steadily on an autobiographical novel, which he never completed and which was never published. He returned to this genre with greater success later in life. Proust supported himself with family money and with money that he earned translating the works of English art critic John Ruskin. He also worked briefly as a lawyer, becoming active with ÉMILE ZOLA in the Dreyfus affair. One of the prime examples of anti-Semitism in late 19th-century France, this case dealt with a false accusation of treason against Jewish army captain Alfred Dreyfus.

Proust's asthma increased in severity as he grew into adulthood, and he often spent large periods of time under the devoted care of his mother, to whom he became almost neurotically attached. The death of his father in 1903, followed by the death of his mother two years later, combined with the loss of his lover caused Proust to withdraw from his high-profile society life almost to the point of his becoming a total recluse. He took up residence in a soundproof flat and, until 1919, lived there, devoting himself entirely to his writing. He rarely left his dwelling except during the summer months, when he would retreat to coastal Cabourg. Financially secure, he was finally able to begin work in earnest on his masterpiece.

Inspired by the autobiographical works of GOETHE and CHATEAUBRIAND, Proust began work on *In Search of Lost Time*. He spent the majority of his time during this period locked in his bedroom writing late into the night and sleeping by day. He produced the first of seven volumes of the work in 1912.

Critical Analysis

In Search of Lost Time has no clearly constructed plot line. It is told entirely in a stream-of-consciousness style by a nameless narrator who, while he is not exactly Proust, resembles the author in many ways. He begins his journey in the novel completely ignorant, only beginning to rediscover his childhood memories after he is given a Madeleine cake soaked in linden tea, similar to those his aunt had given to him when he was a young boy. Memory becomes the central focus of the work, which traces the lives of the narrator's family as well as two other families, one aristocratic, the other Jewish. The smallest details within the work often prove to be the most important, and the characters are richly detailed.

Aside from his novels, Proust is also noted for his elaborate and lengthy letters. Collected volumes of his correspondence reveal his varied interests and his primary belief that a writer must be constantly seeking new information. He is considered by many critics to be one of the leading pioneers of the modern novel, and his influence can be seen in the works of Virginia Wolf, SAMUEL BECKETT, CLAUDE SIMON, and others. His skills as a literary critic remained undiscovered in his lifetime; it was not until the posthumous publication of *Contre Sainte-Beuve* (1954) that his nonfiction works received any serious attention.

The publication of the second volume of Proust's autobiographical masterpiece was delayed due to the start of World War I. It did not become available until 1919. This volume and the ones that followed, however, earned him international acclaim. It is a massive work, totaling more than 3,000 pages. Proust dedicated the final decade of his life to its perfection. On his deathbed,

he was still making corrections, leaving the final volumes without what he considered to be their finishing touches. Proust died in Paris on November 18.

Other Works by Marcel Proust

The Captive. Translated by Charles Kenneth Scott-Moncrieff. New York: A. & C. Boni, 1929.

The Complete Short Stories of Marcel Proust. Translated by Joachim Neugroschel. New York: Cooper Square Press, 2001.

Selected Letters: 1880–1903. Translated by Ralph Manheim. New York: Doubleday, 1983.

Selected Letters Volume 2: 1904–1909. Translated by Philip Kolb. London: Collins, 1989.

Works about Marcel Proust

Carter, William C. *Marcel Proust: A Life.* New Haven, Conn.: Yale University Press, 2000.

Hindus, Milton. *A Reader's Guide to Marcel Proust.* New York: Syracuse University Press, 2001.

Shattuck, Roger. *Proust's Way: A Field Guide to In Search of Lost Time.* New York: W. W. Norton, 2000.

Pushkin, Aleksandr (1799–1837) *poet, novelist, short story writer*

Aleksandr Sergeyevich Pushkin was born in Mihailovskoe, Russia, to aristocratic parents, Sergey Pushkin and Nadezhda Osipovna. On his mother's side, Pushkin descended from an African slave, given to Peter the Great as a state present from the Ottoman Empire. He had close relationships with his grandmother and his nurse, who brought him up on Russian folktales, and with the serfs on his family's estate. He was given a classical education from one of the best schools available in Russia, the Lyceum Tsarskoye Selo. It was there that he began to write poetry. He graduated with honors in 1817.

After graduation, Pushkin began to pursue a life of pleasure, freedom, and revolutionary thought in St. Petersburg. He published poetry that was considered scandalous at the time and brought the attention of the czar. In 1820, he published the long narrative poetic romance *Ruslan and Ludmilla,* which combined the traditional elements of a Russian fairy tale with the exquisite control of poetic language. The poem was immediately recognized as a masterpiece of Russian literature and brought fame to Pushkin.

That same year, Pushkin published *Ode to Liberty,* a poem that satirized famous figures of the czar's court and was viewed as politically and socially radical by the censors. Pushkin was exiled by the czar's police and forced to relocate in Ekaterinoslavl in southern Russia. This banishment provided an opportunity for Pushkin to travel to the exotic Caucasus and Crimea and gave him inspiration for his short stories, "The Prisoner of the Caucasus" (1822) and "The Fountain of Bakhchisarai" (1824). Both stories center on the beautiful and inspiring mountainous landscape, and they reveal a strong influence of the poetry of the notorious Lord Byron. During his exile, Pushkin led a riotous lifestyle, and he was then ordered to return to his family's estate in Mikhailovskoe.

Far away from the court and stimulating society, in the solitude of Mikhailovskoe, Pushkin began to work without distractions. There he conceived his historical epic work, *Boris Godunov* (completed 1825; published 1831). The poem, broad in its scope, presents a tragic story of a downfall of a Russian czar. The poem was popularly received and was transformed into an opera by Modest Mussorgsky. Pushkin gave a public reading of the poem for which the government immediately reprimanded him. After the death of Alexander I in 1825, the new czar, Nicholas I, offered to be the personal censor of Pushkin; all future poems and stories were to be read directly by him before publication. Pushkin found this arrangement restrictive, however, and the czar ordered that he be put under constant government surveillance for the rest of his life.

Critical Analysis

Aleksandr Pushkin is considered the greatest poet of Russia. Often relying on historical foundations, his work established and shaped the country's poetic language. Influenced by the English romantic poets, such as Wordsworth and Lord Byron, however, Pushkin's attitude was ironic in the manner of Voltaire. His work was unprecedented in its scope, in imagery, and in its use of common Russian language.

In the long narrative poems *Poltava* (1829) and *The Bronze Horseman* (1837), Pushkin extols the achievements of Peter the Great. In both poems, the earthly figure of Russia's emperor is transformed through lyricism into a heroic deity who builds the Russian Empire.

Eugene Onegin (1833) is considered to be the definitive masterpiece of Russian literature. A novel in verse, *Eugene Onegin* dramatically describes the ill-fated relationship between lovers. The complex rhyme scheme and unprecedented, delicate treatment of poetic meter still amaze readers of Pushkin. Besides its poetic language, the work also contains a biting commentary on the social order of Russia during the 1820s. Some critics consider *Eugene Onegin* among the greatest works of all literature.

Although Pushkin is primarily known for his verse, his short stories also attained critical recognition. His stories and poems are based not only on historical facts but also on the deep cultural traditions of the Russian people. In "The Golden Cockerel" (1833), he introduces the traditional elements of a fairy tale into his prose, finding inspiration for his work in the bedtime stories that were told to him in childhood. He transformed several of these fairy tales into works of high poetic merit.

The Queen of Spades (1834) reveals deep psychological torments of a gambler who decides to risk his entire fortune in a game of cards. *Eugene Onegin* and *The Queen of Spades* were adapted into operas by Russian composer Tchaikovsky, while "The Golden Cockerel" became the basis for an opera by Rimsky-Korsakov. The adaptability of Pushkin's verse into music demonstrates the lyrical quality of the poet's work.

In 1837, Pushkin was wounded in a duel over an alleged affair between his wife and a young

Frenchman; he died several days later, leaving a legacy for generations of Russian writers and for every major poetic movement. Pushkin clearly showed the poetic capacity of the Russian language, he also memorialized the rich cultural heritage of his motherland. Indeed, Pushkin is now considered to be an incomparable part of Russian language and culture.

A Work about Aleksandr Pushkin

Feinstein, Elaine. *Pushkin*. London: Weidenfield and Nicolson, 1998.

Q

Qabbani

See KABBANI, NIZAR.

Quasimodo, Salvatore (1901–1968) *poet*

Salvatore Quasimodo, recipient of the 1959 Nobel Prize in literature, was born in the small town of Modica, Sicily. The son of a railroad worker, he began to develop a love of writing in his early childhood. His family, however, felt that it would be much more practical for him to pursue an education in a technical field; therefore, he moved to Rome in his late teens to study engineering. Financial difficulties forced him to abandon his education in 1923, but a series of odd jobs eventually led to a secure government position as a civil engineer in 1926. Stable in his employment, Quasimodo was then able to return to his thoughts of becoming a writer. His brother-in-law, the novelist Elio Vitorini, introduced Quasimodo into literary circles where he soon befriended fellow writers EUGENIO MONTALE, and GUISEPPE UNGARETTI.

Quasimodo published his first poetry in magazines. His first volume of collected works, *Water and Land* (1930), contained several poems that had been written when he was as young as 18 as well as numerous, more recent pieces. This collection falls into what has been defined as the early phase of Quasimodo's career. Divided by World War II, his works are distinctly marked as falling into two separate stylistic categories. Before the war, as in this collection, his writing style was complex and tended toward the metaphysical. Most of his poetry during this period was nostalgic, filled with images of Sicily as a backdrop for feelings of loneliness and melancholy. At the same time, he also concerned himself with themes of childhood memory and a love for the beauty and culture of Italy. He connects this culture to influences of various invaders, such as the Greeks and Romans, and the profound and lasting effect they had on his own literary heritage.

As Quasimodo's early poetic style developed, he began to come under the influence of the SYMBOLIST movement. *Sunken Oboe* (1932) and *Scent of Eucalyptus* (1933) both contain poems that exemplify the movement's adherence to suggestive imagery and mysticism. As a result, much of his work during this period is considered difficult to analyze because of the complex and metaphysical nature of his imagery content.

In 1938, becoming more involved in his writing, Quasdimodo left his government post to become an assistant to Cesare Zavattini, a well- known editor of several popular literary periodicals. He continued to work on his own poetry and to publish his works regularly in collections such as *Greek Lyrics* (1940), a compilation of ancient Greek lyrical poetry. In this work, he once again returned to the idea of past influences, making associations between modern style and ancient language. Quasimodo also became enamored of the academic lifestyle at this point. He devoted himself entirely to his writing, expanding his focus to include essays on poetry and other forms of literature as well as translations of classical poetry and drama, including the works of Shakespeare, Homer, Virgil, and Sophocles. In 1941, he gained employment as a professor of Italian literature at the Giuseppe Verdi Conservatory in Milan, allowing him to continue to spread his own poetic ideals to future generations.

The start of World War II marked a shift in Quasimodo's writing. He became a member of an anti-Fascist group and spent a brief period of time in prison. There, he began to develop a more humanistic approach to his work, becoming more concerned with social conditions, contemporary issues, and the atrocities of war and human suffering. His best-known work, *And Suddenly It's Evening* (1942), marks the beginning of this change in style.

Quasimodo briefly joined the Italian Communist Party at the end of the war, but he quickly resigned in protest of the party's insistence that he dedicate his talents to producing political poetry. In response, he published *Day after Day* (1947), a collection of poems in which he focuses on the hardships faced by Italian citizens during World War II and on his own disdain for his country and the role that it played in the war. Vivid in description, this work is often considered one of the strongest volumes of antiwar poetry to come out of any country during this period. It reflects strongly Quasimodo's own concerns for the fate of Italy, as well as his fear that the country will lose its culture and beauty. This falls in direct parallel to his early works and their tendency to exemplify those same values of cultural and natural beauty.

In the later years of his life, Quasimodo continued to focus on issues pertaining to the tragedy of human conditions and social injustices; however, he also began to return to some of his earlier nostalgia, this time not for places but for people whose lives impacted his own. Quasimodo had one child, a daughter Orietta, born in 1935 to Amelia Specialetti, a woman to whom he was never married. His first wife, Bice Donetti, had passed away in 1948. Although he remarried to the dancer Maria Cumani, they permanently separated in 1960, leaving him with three lost loves. His fond but often bittersweet memories of these women, as well as reminiscences over several friends who died before him, form much of the driving force behind his final volume of poetry, *To Give and To Have* (1966).

He continued to be active as a writer and a critic until his death. While in Amalfi where he was judging a poetry competition, Quasimodo suffered a cerebral hemorrhage. He was returned to Naples for treatment, where he died, leaving behind a legacy of poetry best known for its fight against the social injustice and tragedy of war.

Other Works by Salvatore Quasimodo

Complete Poems. Translated by Jack Bevan. New York: Schocken Books, 1984.

The Poet and the Politician, and Other Essays. Translated by Thomas G. Bergin and Sergio Pacifici. Carbondale: Southern Illinois University Press, 1964.

Queirós, José María de (Eça de Queirós) (1845–1900) *novelist*

Born in Portugal, Eça de Queirós was the illegitimate son of a magistrate and was raised by his grandparents. He was sent to boarding school at the age of five. This parental neglect may explain the satirical nature of his works.

After law school, he worked as a journalist and then entered the consular service in 1872. He resided mostly abroad, and his *Letters from En-gland* (1870) provide us some amusing views on life in Victorian England.

Considered Portugal's greatest novelist, he was influenced by ROMANTICISM and NATURALISM.

He uses very expressive, realistic language and is known for his character descriptions. His major novels are critical portrayals of upper-class Portuguese society. In *O crime do padre Amaro* (1876; *The Sin of Father Amaro*) and his masterpiece *Os Maias* (1888), Queiroz depicts the corruption he saw among the clergy and in high society. He is critical of the intellectual elite, which he believes suffers from moral deficiency. His works seem to say that Portugese society could not change unless there was a major catastrophe.

Other Works by José María de Eça de Queirós

The Illustrious House of Ramires. Translated by Anne Stevens. New York: New Directions, 1994.

The Relic. Translated by Margaret Jull Costa. New York: Hippocrene Books, 1995.

A Work about José María de Eça de Queirós

Coleman, Alexander. *Eça de Queirós and the European Realism.* New York: New York University Press, 1980.

Queiróz, Raquel de (1910–2003)
journalist, novelist

Raquel de Queiróz was born November 17 in Fortaleza, a town in the state of Ceará in Brazil. Her great-grandmother was the cousin of another famous Brazilian writer, JOSÉ DE ALENCAR, also from the state of Ceará in northeastern Brazil. At age seven, she moved with her family to Rio de Janeiro, but they returned to Ceará just two years later, and she would remain there until she graduated from college in 1921.

Queiróz began to write early, and she had a long career as a journalist. She also wrote novels, the first of which, *The Fifteen,* was published in 1930. The novel was very well received, and it gave Queiróz a literary name in Brazil. She received the Graça Aranha Foundation prize for the novel in Rio de Janeiro in 1931. Just a few years later, she formed friendships with Graciliano Ramos

and Jorge Lins do Rego, also from the northeast. Through the exceptional writing of Queiróz and others from this region, the northeastern novels of Brazil were born. In the 1930s, Queiróz married literary figure and poet José Auto da Cruz Oliveira. They had a daughter and later separated. She continued to write in various genres throughout her life, including journalistic chronicles, novels, short stories, theater, and even children's literature. One of her best-known novels, *The Three Marias* (1939), is often considered semiautobiographical because it recounts the story of a young woman through her developmental years, from the age of 12 until she turns 20.

Queiróz was also very politically active, and she represented Brazil at the session of the General Assembly of the United Nations in 1966, where she worked especially on the Human Rights Commission. On August 4, 1977, the Brazilian Academy of Letters elected her as its first female member, paving the way for future female authors in Brazil.

Other Works by Raquel de Queiróz

Castro-Klaren, Sara, Sylvia Molloy, and Beatriz Sarlo, eds. Selections in *Women's Writing in Latin America.* Boulder, Colo.: Westview, 1992.

A Work about Raquel de Queiróz

Ellison, Fred P. *Brazil's New Novel: Four Northeastern Masters.* Berkeley: University of California Press, 1954.

Queneau, Raymond (1903–1976) *poet, novelist*

Raymond Queneau was born in Le Havre, France. A man of many diverse intellectual interests, he was a mathematician, scholar, humorist, linguist, and poet. When he was 17, Queneau went to Paris, where he briefly associated with ANDRÉ BRETON's surrealism. He composed the manifesto *Permettez!* (1920) but soon broke with the group to write about the link he saw between surrealism and EXISTENTIALISM.

In his works, Queneau often uses colloquial speech patterns and phonetic spelling of words. Fascinated by languages, he felt that written French needed to free itself from archaic rules and restrictions. His first novel, *Le chiendent* (*The Bark Tree*, 1933), was noted for its use of slang and casual language. Because of this, Queneau's works are difficult to translate, as the language itself is critical to the interpretation.

Queneau is best known internationally for his novel *Zazie dans le métro* (1959), the story of a young girl who comes to visit Paris and stays with her heterosexual uncle, who is employed as a dancer in a gay bar. Her one desire is to ride the metro, which she cannot do because the workers are on strike. Instead, she embarks on a journey toward adulthood. The novel was adapted to film in 1960, gaining both positive and negative critical attention for its bold use of language and its break from cultural norms.

After this first film endeavor, Queneau collaborated on several other occasions with "New Wave" film directors. His work in this genre marks his most notable contribution to world literature. In addition, one of his poems was made popular when it was set to music by Juliette Greco. Queneau was elected to the Goncourt Academy in 1952. He died on October 26, 1976, having left his mark in the destruction of traditional literary norms.

Another Work by Raymond Queneau
Stories and Remarks. Translated by Marc Lowental. Lincoln: University of Nebraska Press, 2000.

A Work about Raymond Queneau
Guicharnaud, Jacques. *Raymond Queneau.* Translated by June Guicharnaud. New York: Columbia University Press, 1965.

Quental, Antero Tarquínio de
(1842–1891) *poet*

Antero Tarquínio de Quental was born in Ponta Delgada, Portugal. He was from an aristocratic family of intellectuals, writers, and religious leaders. Nevertheless, all his life Quental was a rebel and had decidedly liberal leanings.

He was the key figure in the Generation of Coimbra, a group of students at the University of Coimbra who attempted to revitalize postromantic Portuguese literature. The Generation of Coimbra had a great deal in common with Latin-American MODERNISM, and Quental had many affinities with RUBÉN DARÍO, modernism's key figure.

Quental's *Modern Odes* (1865) abandons romantic decadence and returns to a vocabulary of classical images and symbols, presenting a heightened, purified view of reality with a pessimistic tone.

Though not an innovator, Quental was a master of the sonnet. He proved this in his *Complete Sonnets* (1886), a collection of 109 sonnets that serve as a spiritual autobiography.

Quental, though a minor figure, was an important voice of modernism and social reform in 19th-century Portugal.

Rao Srinivasa, Srirangam
See SRI SRI.

Rabéarivelo, Jean-Joseph (1903–1937)
poet

Jean-Joseph Rabéarivelo was born in Tananarive, Madagascar. His mother was a member of an aristocratic Madagascar family that had been impoverished by the French takeover of the island. Rabéarivelo was educated by his uncle in French schools but left school at 13. He worked in various occupations, including as a librarian, which gave him the opportunity to read widely. He began to write poetry, mostly in French but some in his native Malagasy, at first under pseudonyms. He also began to write for journals, and when his article on Madagascar poetry was accepted by the international journal *Anthropos* in 1923, Rabéarivelo decided to become a full-time writer. During the same year, he became a proofreader for a printing press, a job he kept until his death in 1937. He married in 1926 and had five children; his grief over the death of his youngest daughter in 1933, expressed in a short story entitled "Un conte de la nuit," may have contributed to his death. After struggling with addictions, Rabéarivelo committed suicide by poisoning himself.

A sensation of despair and foreboding overhang Rabéarivelo's poetry, which was influenced by the work of CHARLES BAUDELAIRE and the French symbolists (*see* SYMBOLISM) as well as by traditional Malagasy form. His melancholy resonates through his poems, as in "Valiha," which both celebrates and grieves for a transformation of nature into art, when bamboo shoots, rustling in the wind, are turned into a musical instrument, the traditional stringed valiha of Madagascar:

> There they will sound
> until an artist comes
> who will break their godlike youth
> and flay them in his village
> and stretch out their skins
> with shards of calabashes . . .

The isolation and sadness of the speakers of his poems derive from Rabéarivelo's personal life experiences. His sorrow was further accentuated by his perceived failure in life, giving his poems a poignant bitter-sweetness. His despair is tinged with a quiet resilience that was derived from his love of freedom and nature, echoing the chants of Madagascar's highlands. Gerald Moore and Ulli Beier remark, "In his poetry he has destroyed and dismembered reality. And out of the fragments he has built a new mythical world; it is a world of death and frustration, but also transcended by a sad beauty of its own."

Another Work by Jean-Joseph Rabéarivelo

Translations from the Night: Selected Poems of Jean-Joseph Rabéarivelo. Edited by John Reed and Clive Wake. London: Heinemann Educational, 1975.

Works about Jean-Joseph Rabéarivelo

Adejunmobi, Moradewun. *Jean-Joseph Rabéarivelo, Literature, and Lingua Franca in Colonial Madagascar.* New York: Peter Lang, 1996.

Moore, Gerald and Ulli Beier, eds. *Modern Poetry from Africa.* New York: Viking, 1963.

Rabinowitz, Sholem

See ALEICHEM, SHALOM.

Ravikovitch, Dahlia (1936–2005) *poet*

Dahlia Ravikovitch was born in Ramat Gan, a suburb of Tel Aviv (now in Israel), and spent her early years on a kibbutz (a communal farm or settlement in Israel) before attending high school in Haifa. She later studied at the Hebrew University of Jerusalem. Ravikovitch published her first collection of poems, *The Love of an Orange,* in 1959 when she was still in the army. She worked as a journalist, teacher, and television reviewer.

Ravikovitch's early poems are often romantic, evoking distant places, love, and mythological figures. Her later work contains increased satire and sarcasm but still maintains intellectual understanding and sensitivity.

After the Israeli war in Lebanon in 1982, Ravikovitch became active in the Israeli peace movement, and her poetry often tackles the difficult subject of war. She said, "Everyone wants peace but everyone thinks someone else should bring it." Yet, it remains difficult to categorize her work—she takes on womanhood, human rights,

and war, alongside inner life and loneliness as some of her themes.

Ravikovitch was considered one of Israel's best poets. She also wrote some prose and several children's books, translated poetry by William Butler Yeats, Edgar Allan Poe, and T. S. Eliot into Hebrew, and was the recipient of the Shlonsky, Brenner, Ussishkin, and was Bialik Prizes. She committed suicide in Tel Aviv in August 2005.

Other Works by Dahlia Ravikovitch

A Dress of Fire. Translated by Chana Bloch. Camp Hill, Pa.: Horizon House Publishers, 1978.

Hovering at a Low Altitude: The Collected Poetry of Dahlia Ravikovitch. London: Norton, 2009.

The Window: New and Selected Poems. In collaboration with Ariel Bloch. New York: Sheep Meadow Press, 1989.

Works about Dahlia Ravikovitch

Cooperman, Alan. "Making Peace Where Politicians Fear to Tread." *U.S. News and World Report* (June 30, 1997). Available online. URL: http://traubman.igc.org/makepeace.htm.

Lowin, Joseph. "Born to Dream: A Discussion into English of Dahlia Ravikovitch's 'The Reason for Falling.'" From the Literary Corner (17 April 2002) of The National Center for the Hebrew Language. Available online. URL: www.ivrit.org/literary/born_to_dream.htm.

realism

Realism in literature is a worldwide movement that had its most profound effects in fiction and drama in the late 1800s. Born out of the ideas of the ROMANTIC novel but infused with concrete details and accurate descriptions of society, the characters of realist fiction are drawn from the events and contexts of modern life and face everyday obstacles. Realism, as it has spread throughout the world, has mutated into POETIC REALISM, NATURALISM, SOCIALIST REALISM, MAGIC REALISM, and (in Italy) VERISMO. Realism has molded the expectations of readers worldwide,

French Realism

Realism is most commonly traced to the French novelist HONORÉ DE BALZAC and his series of novels and stories which, grouped together, form *The Human Comedy* (1840). Balzac's intention was to portray, as accurately as possible, all aspects of French life and culture, from the lowest prostitute to the highest political leader. His attention to detail in setting and characterization provided the foundations for the movement, although the actual plots of his works, often absurd and almost unbelievable, were far from the goals to which realism ultimately aimed.

In 1857, GUSTAVE FLAUBERT's *Madame Bovary* became the prototype for the realist novel. Like Balzac's work, Flaubert's novel was the result of systematic research; however, instead of fanciful plots, he focused instead on the issue of female adultery and the unhappy married life of a country woman, Emma Bovary. Considered mild according to modern standards, Flaubert's love scenes were so detailed that they resulted in the author facing charges of obscenity. He was called the anatomist of the heart.

Russian Realism

The shift from romantic idealism to realism in Russian literature was primarily initiated by the prose of NIKOLAY GOGOL, which addressed aspects of everyday life of the common people in Russia. In many respects, realism in Russia coincided with the development of a large class of government officials and merchants. The works of realism often depict the lives and conflicts of the Russian middle class and deal with themes such as marriage, money, and class relations. For the realists, literature needed to reflect the problems and issues pertinent to the economic, political, and social life of the nation.

In the 1850s, during the early phase of the realist movement, such writers as ALEKSANDR OSTROVSKY and IVAN GONCHAROV began to shift artistic focus toward the previously neglected merchant class, while poets such as Nikolay Nekrasov (1821–78) created long narrative poems that focused on the social ills suffered by the poor. The early works of realism often also depicted the moral degeneration of the Russian aristocrats.

Most of the realist masterpieces produced in Russia emerged during the movement's late phase, which is sometimes referred to as the golden age of Russian literature. The highly sophisticated prose of IVAN TURGENEV, for instance, focuses on the social dynamics of minor aristocrats and middle-class families. Turgenev also provided an unprecedented level of literary attention to the Russian peasantry. FYODOR DOSTOYEVSKY, however, concentrated on psychological realism. His novels carefully examine the emotional motivations and desires of his characters. Another giant of realism, LEO TOLSTOY, combined astute social commentary with observations about spirituality and religion. Most critics view ANTON CHEKHOV as the last seminal figure of Russian realism. Like many other realists, Chekhov focused on the problems and moral dilemmas faced by middle-class families. Chekhov believed that the middle class was the backbone of Russian society and, therefore, centered his work on it.

Chinese Realism

In China, realism accompanied modernism in literature into the 20th century. In a sense, many modernist writers, such as HU SHIH, were realists in their use of objectivity to reflect the modern "condition."

Several literary groups and organizations formed during the May Fourth era, a period of unprecedented intellectual openness, innovation, and experimentation in China. Among them was a group of scholars who comprised the Literary Association. They also came to be known as the realist school. Mao Dun (1896–1981; also known as Mao Tun) was the leader of this group and its most prominent practitioner. He took over the journal *Short Story Monthly* and converted it to a journal of vernacular literature (*baihua* literature). The use of the vernacular was an important component of realism in that it best captured the language of the Chinese people and contributed to an accurate representation.

Mao Dun and the realist school openly advocated "art for life's sake," which was a continuation of the idea that literature could effect social change. In contrast to the romantic tradition of "art for art's sake," the objective representation of reality had a sociopolitical purpose, and many realist writers had agendas for reform. BA JIN, an ardent anarchist and Communist, for example, was known for his realistic portrayals of Chinese society, as can be seen in *Family* (1931), his chronicle of the falling gentry. Mao Dun's 1933 work, *Midnight,* was another such work: Considered a major political novel of the era, it was noted for its objectivity, optimism for change, and revolutionary appeal.

Realism often manifested itself in short stories and novels about daily life and included criticism of government or society. BING XIN's short stories, such as "Loneliness" (1922), about young women confronting issues in love and life, were extremely popular, and because of her realistic portrayals, they often provided psychological insight readers could relate to.

The poetry school of realism also provided realistic depictions of Chinese life, adding innovative form and language. Realistic poetry focused on the preservation of natural rhythms as found in vernacular speech, as opposed to the poetic and formal diction of formalists or the experimental language of symbolist poetry. Realism's poets included Hu Shih, Li Jinfa (1900–76), and Dai Wangshu (1905–50), whose works were published in the journal *Poetry*.

By the onset of the communist revolution, realism had faded into the more direct objectives of socialist realism. Works took on a distinct socialist tenor, but components of realism, such as the close representation of reality to provide social critique, as well as writing in the vernacular, persisted. These powerful elements of realism render it a continuing popular force in Chinese literature today, although it frequently appears in new, slightly changed forms.

Works about Realism

Anderson, Marston. *Limits of Realism.* Berkeley: University of California Press, 1989.

Fanger, Donald, and Caryl Emerson. *Dostoevsky and Romantic Realism: A Study of Dostoevsky in Relation to Balzac, Dickens, and Gogol.* Evanston, Ill.: Northwestern University Press, 1998.

Lukacs, Georg. *The Theory of the Novel.* Translated by Anna Bostock. Cambridge, Mass.: MIT Press, 1974.

Mortimer, Armine Kotin. *Writing Realism: Representations in French Fiction.* Baltimore, Md.: Johns Hopkins University Press, 2000.

Reid, J. H. *Narration and Description in the French Realist Novel: The Temporality of Lying and Forgetting.* New York: Cambridge University Press, 1993.

Reis, Ricardo

See PESSOA, FERNANDO.

Remarque, Erich Maria (pseudonym of Erich Paul Kramer) (1898–1970) *novelist*

Erich Maria Remarque was born in Osnabruck, Germany, to Anna Marie and Peter Maria Kramer, a bookbinder. Despite the modest income of the family, Remarque was educated in the best private school in town, but his studies at the University of Munster were interrupted by the outbreak of World War I and his subsequent draft into the army at the age of 18. Remarque fought on the Western front and was wounded several times.

After discharge from the military, Remarque completed a pedagogy course offered by the government to veterans and soon began his writing career as a journalist for a sports magazine, *Sportsbild,* and then became its assistant editor.

Remarque's first novel, *All Quiet on the Western Front* (1929), is his most famous work. It realistically depicts the horrors faced by soldiers of both sides during World War I. The novel begins in 1917, after Paul Baumer, the protagonist, loses half of his friends in battle. Encouraged by their teacher to enlist in the German army, Baumer and his classmates find themselves in the trenches under constant attack by French machine guns and poisonous clouds of mustard gas. Baumer's romantic and nationalistic perspective of war, which the reader finds in the beginning of the novel, is replaced by sudden physicality, violence, and, ultimately, a sense of the futility of war. Today, *All Quiet on the Western Front* is considered one of the best depictions of war and a masterpiece of German literature. The work was internationally acclaimed and read worldwide. In Germany, however, the novel was politically controversial: Not only did it enrage members of the rising Nazi party, it was also labeled as defeatist and unpatriotic by many veterans whose sensibilities were injured by the frankness Remarque depicted.

In 1931, Remarque published *The Way Back*. A chilling sequel to *All Quiet on the Western Front*, the novel presents the collapse of the German government and army after the war and the return of the veterans into a world that has been shattered forever. In the 1930s, Remarque's position in Germany became precarious because of the rise of the Nazi regime. *All Quiet on the Western Front* was banned and was among the works that were publicly burned by the Nazis in 1933. The premier of the film adaptation was violently disrupted by Nazi gangs. In 1938, after accusations of pacifism, the Nazi government stripped Remarque of citizenship. Remarque fled to the United States and settled in Switzerland after World War II.

Remarque's later works did not receive the same critical acclaim as *All Quiet on the Western Front* but achieved a wide popularity among readers. He continued to describe a European society plagued by social and political upheavals. Remarque also addressed the oppression of the Nazi rule: *Arch of Triumph* (1946) portrays a German physician who flees from the Nazi rule. Remarque also closely collaborated with filmmakers in the United States, and several of his novels were adopted into screenplays.

Today, Erich Maria Remarque's work continues to remind readers of the horrors of war. His works are widely read and have been translated into more than 20 languages. A remarkable and heroic writer, Remarque was not afraid to express his views, despite the constant threats and harassments by the Nazi regime. Remarque died in Locarno, Switzerland.

Other Works by Erich Maria Remarque
The Black Obelisk. Translated by David Lindley. New York: Fawcett Books, 1998.
Three Comrades. Translated by A. W. Wheen. New York: Fawcett Books, 1998.

A Work about Erich Maria Remarque
Barker, Christine. *Erich Maria Remarque.* New York: Barnes and Noble, 1980.

Reyes, Neftali Ricardo
See NERUDA, PABLO.

Rhys, Jean (Ella Gwendolyn Rees Williams) (1890–1979) *novelist, short story writer*
Jean Rhys was born in Roseau, Dominica, West Indies, to William Rees Williams, a Welsh doctor, and Minna Williams (née Lockhart). She attended a Dominican convent school until immigrating to England at age 16, where she attended Cambridge's Perse School and London's Academy of Dramatic Art before joining a touring theater company. Three-and-a-half black notebooks, filled after a romantic break in 1913, were the basis for the novel *Voyage in the Dark* (1934).

During the 1920s, Rhys was loosely a part of the Left Bank writers, including such writers as James Joyce, Hemingway, and Ford Madox Ford, who represented the artistic and intellectual realm of politics. Ford helped Rhys publish her first work, *The Left Bank and Other Stories* (1927). Four more novels followed in the 1930s. Themes of denial, dissonance, rejection, discrimination, and alienation run through these and others of Rhys's works, which employ a controlled style, literal and figurative imagery, and first- and third-person points of view. Inquiries made by actress Selma Vaz Dias in 1949 to perform a dramatic adaptation of the modernist *Good Morning, Midnight* (1939) and in 1956 to broadcast the same novel as a radio play encouraged Rhys to complete her fifth novel, *Wide Sargasso Sea* (1966), the story of which is derived from Charlotte Brontë's *Jane Eyre* and tells the haunting tale of Rochester's first wife. In *The Letters of Jean Rhys* (1984), Rhys called the novel "a demon of a book" that "never leaves" her; the critics called the book a masterpiece.

During the years, British, American, and Caribbean critics have attempted to position Rhys's works as distinctively British, American, or Caribbean, respectively. In *Fifty Caribbean Writers* (1986), Jean D'Costa summarizes Rhys's importance to world literature when she says that "Rhys's works offer much to the analysts of society, of sexuality, of the psyche, of British imperial history, of Anglo-European letters, and of the Creole societies."

Other Works by Jean Rhys

After Leaving Mr. Mackenzie. New York: Harper & Row, 1982.

The Collected Short Stories. Introduction by Diana Athill. New York: Norton, 1987.

Smile, Please: An Unfinished Autobiography. Berkeley, Calif.: Donald S. Ellis/Creative Arts, 1983.

Works about Jean Rhys

Lykiard, Alexis. *Jean Rhys Revisited.* Exeter and Devon: Stride Publications, 2000.

Mellown, Elgin W. *Jean Rhys: A Descriptive and Annotated Bibliography of Works and Criticism.* New York: Garland Press, 1984.

Savory, Elaine. *Jean Rhys.* New York: Cambridge University Press, 1999.

Richardson, Elaine Potter
See KINCAID, JAMAICA.

Richler, Mordecai (1931–2001) *novelist, short story writer, essayist*

Born in Montreal, Canada, in 1931, Mordecai Richler has written extensively about the Jewish enclave where he was raised, centered on St. Urbain Street in the Mile End area of the city. Many critics have noted that this neighborhood and Montreal in general are less locations than they are characters in Richler's novels, and Richler has said that he feels "forever rooted in Montreal's St. Urbain Street. That was my time, my place, and I have elected myself to get it right." The critic Robert Fulford has compared Richler's Montreal neighborhood to the American novelist William Faulkner's Yoknapatawpha County. Both novelists create whole worlds out of these places, one imaginary, one deeply imagined.

Richler's grandfather was a rabbinical scholar who immigrated to Canada in 1904 from Galacia in the Austro-Hungarian Empire, after having escaped from one of the many pogroms then rampant. He established a scrap metal business that employed several of his 14 children, including Richler's father, Moses. Moses married the former Lily Rosenberg, herself the daughter of a rabbi. The marriage was an unhappy one. Lily felt that she had married beneath her, and in 1943 she had the marriage annulled on the grounds that she was underage and had married without her father's consent. Although Lily was only 17 when she married, the marriage was arranged and thus could not have occurred without her father's consent.

Richler's family, observant Orthodox Jews, had hoped that young Mordecai would study to become a rabbi. He had attended Jewish parochial school, but by the time he had begun high school at Baron Byng (which is portrayed as Fletcher Field High School in several of his novels), Richler had lost his interest in religious studies. According to friends, he was a bit of a prankster in high school, something like his character Duddy Kravitz. As his grades were not good enough to allow him to enter McGill University, he matriculated instead at Sir George Williams College, now Concordia University. Richler did not stay long. He has said that he was afraid that his studies would destroy his creativity.

In 1949, Richler (like many of his characters) traveled in Europe. While there, he published his first short story, "Shades of Darkness (Three Impressions)," and wrote the draft of a novel that he later destroyed. Broke, Richler returned to Montreal in 1951. He worked for the Canadian Broadcasting Corporation (CBC) as a salesman and an editor while he shopped for a publisher of his novel, *The Acrobat*. Finally published in 1954, *The Acrobat* received good reviews but did not sell well.

Richler returned to Europe in 1954 and remained there for the next 20 years. Two novels followed, *The Acrobat: Son of a Smaller Hero* in 1955 and *A Choice of Enemies* in 1957. Then, in 1959, Richler published what has been called his breakthrough work, *The Apprenticeship of Duddy Kravitz*. Kravitz, the novel's antihero, is an ambitious Jewish boy from the St. Urbain area of Montreal, a young man who is determined to own land and escape his impoverished life in the ghetto. The novel is a bawdy and raucous satire of pretension, hypocrisy, and greed, and it sets the tone for much of Richler's later works.

In the 1960s, Richler published two more comic works, *The Incomparable Atuk* (1963) and *Cocksure* (1968). Atuk is an Inuit poet who is lionized by Toronto's liberal, intellectual elite and who dives into the city's greed, corruption, and phoniness with both mukluks. Among the funniest scenes are those in which Atuk's family members, whom he has brought to Toronto and locked in the basement so they can manufacture "authentic" Inuit art, escape and run amok in the big city. In 1968, *Cocksure*, labeled obscene by many, won (along with Richler's essay collection *Hunting Tigers under Glass*) the Governor General's Award. Richler's 1971 novel *St. Urbain's Horseman*—considered by many critics and readers one of his finest works—also won the Governor General's Award in 1972.

Richler returned to Montreal in 1972 and continued to reside there until his death in 2001. Throughout the 1970s, Richler wrote for television and film, earning an Academy Award nomination for his 1975 screenplay for *The Apprenticeship of Duddy Kravitz*. He also wrote an extremely popular children's book, *Jacob Two-Two Meets the Hooded Fang*, which won the first Ruth Schwartz Children's Book Award in 1976. Other Jacob Two-Two books followed. In 1990, Richler published *Solomon Gursky Was Here*, a novel based on the rise of the Bronfman family, distillers of Seagram's whiskey. The *New York Times* critic Francine Prose wrote that in this, his ninth novel, Richler is after "something ambitious and risky, something slightly Dickensian, magical realist: 'Two Hundred Years of Jewish-Canadian Solitude." She adds, "The novel is at once an extended joke about, and a homage to, that amateur historian in every Jewish family who can prove Columbus was Jewish and who knows what Abraham Lincoln and F.D.R. were called before they changed their last names." Richler also made a name for himself as a journalist and social critic. "Acerbic" is the word most frequently used to describe Richler's social criticism; he wrote with particular acidity against Québéquois separatists—those who wished to secede from Canada and become an independent nation. A 1991 article Richler wrote for the *New Yorker* made, according to Brian Fawcett, "an *international* laughingstock of Quebec's language laws." The article was expanded to book length and published in 1992 as *Oh Canada! Oh Quebec!* Richler's final novel, *Barney's Version*, won the prestigious Booker Prize in 1997.

Richler was married twice. His first marriage was brief; his second marriage in 1960, to Florence Wood, lasted until his death. The couple had three sons and two daughters. Four of Richler's children are writers; the fifth is both a cartoonist and a writer. Richler, who died at the age of 70 in 2001, was once asked how he wished to be remembered. He replied, "Yesterday, the world mourned the passing of devastatingly handsome, incomparably talented Mordecai Richler, taken from us in his prime, aged 969."

Critical Analysis

Barney's Version is a tour de force, a work that could only have been written late in life by a writer in his prime and in complete command of his craft. Ostensibly, the novel is a memoir by 67-year-old Barney Panofsky, written in self-defense, to counter the memoir of Terry McIver, Canadian novelist and Barney's great antagonist. Barney has much in common with Richler himself, and his curmudgeonly digressions are among the most entertaining parts of the novel, as he skewers everything from Canadian literary culture to vegetarian restaurants. Barney is wealthy, cynical, and a moral scourge who has not always behaved very well. His version of events becomes even more fascinating when the reader realizes three facts: Barney is a notoriously unreliable person and narrator; he is clearly losing his memory; and he may or may not have murdered his best friend.

The novel is scathing, and little escapes Richler's (or Barney's) poison pen. Open the novel almost anywhere, and the reader can find a passage like this one:

> Yes, carbon paper, if any of you out there are old enough to remember what that was. Why, in those days we not only used carbon paper, but when you phoned somebody you actually got an answer from a human being on the other end, not an answering machine with a ho, ho, ho message. In those olden times you didn't have to be a space scientist to manage the gadget that flicked your TV on and off, that ridiculous thingamabob that now comes with twenty push buttons, God knows what for. Doctors made house calls. Rabbis were guys. Kids were raised by their moms instead of in child-care pens like piglets. Software meant haberdashery. There wasn't a different dentist for gums, molars, fillings, and extractions—one nerd managed the lot. If a waiter spilled hot soup on your date, the manager offered to pay her cleaning bill and sent over drinks, and she didn't sue for a kazillion dollars, claiming "loss of enjoyment of life." If the restaurant was Italian it still served something called spaghetti, often with meatballs. It was not yet pasta with smoked salmon, or linguini in all the colours of the rainbow, or penne topped with a vegetarian steaming pile that looked like dog sick. I'm ranting again. Digressing. Sorry about that.

At the same time that *Barney's Version* is outrageously funny, it is also painful and poignant as Barney comes face to face with not only his failings but also his mortality. When his nemesis McIver dies, Barney says, "I'm of two minds about funerals. At my age, staring down into one of those six-foot-deep pits gives me the chills, but there is some satisfaction to be squeezed out of witnessing the burial of somebody else. . . . But to my astonishment, I wept hot tears at McIver's funeral. We had once been young and footloose together in Paris, roistering provincials, and, looking back, I regret that we never became friends."

According to Abraham Levitan writing for the *Yale Review*:

> Richler's . . . prose rings with so much raw comedy that one barely realizes its deep-seated sadness until the final pages. It is the melancholy of *Barney's Version*, however, that lends the story its majesty, redeeming Richler from the potential saccharine superficiality of such a sprawling subject.

Another Work by Mordecai Richler
Mordecai Richler Was Here: Selected Writings. Cambridge, Mass.: Da Capo Press, 2007.

Works about Mordecai Richler
Kramer, Reinhold. *Mordecai Richler: Leaving St. Urbain.* Montreal: McGill-Queens University Press, 2008.

Posner, Michael. *The Last Honest Man: Mordecai Richler: An Oral Biography.* Toronto: McCelland & Stewart, 2005.

Vassanji, M. G., and John Ralston Saul. *Mordecai Richler (Extraordinary Canadians).* Toronto: Penguin Canada, 2009.

Rifaat, Alifa (1930–1996) *short story writer*

Born in Cairo, Egypt, Rifaat was raised in the traditions and culture of Islam and rarely traveled outside her home country, with the exception of brief visits as an adult to such countries as England, Germany, and Canada. Her largely isolated upbringing, reinforced by her language, as well as the influence of such texts as the Qur'an, the Hadith, and other Arabic texts all served to form her worldview and the major themes evident in her writing.

Despite her commitment to Islam, Rifaat was nevertheless a controversial author in her country throughout her career; this was due in large part to her criticism of Muslim men, who she felt were not properly fulfilling their role within Islamic tradition in terms of the sexual needs of their wives, and her largely negative description of purdah, gender segregation and women's obligation to conceal their bodies, in her stories. Rifaat was praised by Western critics for her passionate depiction of these lives.

Rifaat's experience of Islamic law was direct: Early in her life she expressed a desire to attend college in the pursuit of an education and a career in the arts. Her parents, however, arranged for her to be married, an arrangement to which she finally submitted. Following a brief education at the British Institute in Cairo, Rifaat embarked on a writing career, while also raising three children and tending to her husband. She first published a series of short stories under a pseudonym in 1955 in the magazine *al-Risala*. Her husband's discovery of and vehement opposition to her writing stalled her career for some time. It was not until 1972 that she began publishing again, this time under her own name. Many of the short stories Rifaat wrote during the 1970s and 1980s focus primarily on women's inner thoughts and dreams; she explored the emotional lives of Muslim women and the psychological damage done to them by Muslim men, as well as by an oppressive system of social mores that does not take into account the need for personal, sexual, and emotional fulfillment in women. Rifaat and other female writers who began publishing in the 1960s and 1970s in Arabic were among the first Muslims to express such concerns. Yet, it is also important to note that because of her relative isolation from Western culture and her commitment to Islam, Rifaat did not look to the feminism of the West for a model of how women's lives should change. As a result, she did not question the role of women according to her faith; instead, she depicts the hardships imposed on women because of men's shortcomings within that culture and calls for change.

An author of several short story collections, including *Hawatandbi-Adam (Eve Returns with Adam to Paradise)* (1975) and *Girls of Baurdin* (1995), Rifaat is best known in the Western world for her book *Distant View of a Minaret* (1983), a collection of 15 short stories that explore the everyday life of women in Muslim society in Egypt. Although the stories are not directly connected, in concert they construct a compelling exposé of Rifaat's cultural world. Rifaat's stories are deceptively simple. In the title story, for example, a wife dwells on her husband's unwillingness to satisfy her sexually and the fact that the view from her window, which once gave her an expansive view of all of Cairo, is reduced to a view that is limited to that of a single minaret (tower of a mosque) because of the new buildings that tower over the city. Upon discovering that her husband has had an "attack" (no further description is given) and sensing the "odour of death in the room," she sends her son to bring the doctor. After doing this she returns to "the living room and poured out the coffee for herself. She was surprised how calm she was." The deliberately unassuming style of the language conceals the radical implications of the story in the context of Islamic culture: the culture of the West encroaching on traditional Muslim culture and the implied "death" of traditional concepts of gender roles, leaving women "free." Rifaat died in Egypt in 1996.

Works about Alifa Rifaat

Al-Ali, Nadje Sadig. *Gender Writing/Writing Gender: The Representation of Women in a Selection of Modern Egyptian Literature*. Cairo: American University in Cairo Press, 1994.

Rilke, Rainer Maria (1875–1926) *poet, playwright, translator*

Rainer Maria Rilke was born in Prague, Czechoslovakia, to Josef Rilke, a minor railroad official, and Sophie Entz, a descendant of an aristocratic family. His mother dressed him in girls' clothes and called him Sophie until the age of eight to compensate for the loss of her infant daughter. Sophie Entz was a devout Catholic and often went on pilgrimages to shrines and other holy places; young Rilke accompanied her. This early experience with Catholicism left Rilke with a profound distrust and dislike of Christianity.

Rilke's parents separated when he was nine, and he was sent to a military academy by his father. Because of ill health, Rilke left the academy and traveled to Leinz, Austria, to study business. He was apprenticed to his uncle's law firm as a clerk. Rilke decided against a career in business and attended universities in Prague, Berlin, and Munich, where he studied art history, philosophy, and literature. He developed a talent for languages and became fluent in Russian, French, English, Danish, and Czech. Rilke developed a close relationship with several Russian intellectuals and accompanied them on a trip to Russia in 1899, where he met LEO TOLSTOY and studied Russian spiritual mysticism.

Critical Analysis

Today, Rilke is considered one of the greatest lyrical poets of the German-speaking world. He began his career as a poet in 1894 when he published a small, conventional volume of poems, *Leben und Leiden*. While working as a correspondence secretary for Auguste Rodin in Paris, Rilke composed *The Book of the Hours: The Book of Monastic Life*. Saint Francis of Assisi is a major figure in the work. Rilke transforms this conventional image of Christian humility and piety into a kind of pagan nature spirit who permeates all things. Furthermore, Rilke praises traditional Christian values, such as poverty and spiritual purity, and often presents God as a humble, homeless man: "For blessed are those who never went away / And stood still in the rain without a roof."

Among Rilke's prose works, *The Tale of the Love and Death of Coronet Christoph Rilke* (1906), a long prose poem, became a great popular success. Set during the 1660s, the dynamic prose of the work tells of a young coronet who joins the European forces in their fight against the Ottoman Empire. The young coronet falls in love with a young lady, but he is killed during a sudden attack by the Turks the next day. Rilke, however, does not utterly glorify the military. The poem includes brutal scenes of violence and conveys the monotony of long military marches.

Rilke was a master of several genres. His famous novel *The Notebooks of Malte Laurids Brigge* (1910) takes the form of the diary of a Danish poet who arrives in Paris and describes his reactions to the cultural and intellectual life in the city. The novel uses flashbacks to describe the events of Laurids's childhood and the various European cities that he had visited. Lacking a traditional plot, the novel focuses on episodes in Laurids's life that create confrontation in his development as a writer. Eventually, Malte Laurids realizes that he has to transform himself metaphorically into an open vessel, receiving the outside events without preconceptions, to become a truly great poet.

Rilke's last seminal collections of poetry, *Duino Elegies* and *Sonnets to Orpheus,* were both published in 1923. Both works no longer dealt with ordinary images; instead, they concentrated on the larger themes of life and death, spirituality, philosophy, and materiality. Rilke presented material and spiritual worlds as entities and the individual as an observer entrapped between the both realms, only momentarily able to capture them. The alienated artist, however, can build a bridge between two worlds by creating a material translation of the spiritual realm. Indeed, the theme of alienation is one of the most dominant ones in the collection: "We are not at one / Are not in agreement like birds of passage / Overtaken and delayed, we force ourselves suddenly on the winds / and fall onto an indifferent pond."

Rainer Maria Rilke established himself as one of the most important figures of German literature. Although he is mainly remembered as a poet, he made a tremendous impact in virtually every genre. Rilke's influence on his generation of poets is simply enormous: he composed a significant corpus of poetic works in Russian and French, and he translated innumerable literary works from English, French, Russian, and Danish into German. Today, Rainer Maria Rilke is considered as the most important 20th-century poet of the German-speaking world: "Rilke was a large man, expansive in his concern for the fate of human beings in a difficult world," as Patricia Brodsky notes. Rilke's death was as strange as his life; he died from an infection that was contracted from a prick of a rose's thorn.

Other Works by Rainer Maria Rilke

Ahead of All Parting: Selected Poetry and Prose of Rainer Maria Rilke. Translated by Stephen Mitchell. New York: Modern Library, 1995.
The Book of Images. Translated by Edward Snow. Portland, Oreg.: North Point Press, 1994.
Rilke's Book of Hours: Love Poems to God. Translated by Joanna Macy. New York: Riverhead Books, 1997.

Works about Rainer Maria Rilke

Brodsky, Patricia. *Rainer Maria Rilke.* Boston: Twayne, 1988.
Freedman, Ralph. *Life of a Poet: Rainer Maria Rilke.* Chicago: Northwestern University Press, 1998.

Rimbaud, Arthur (1854–1891) *poet*

Arthur Rimbaud was born on October 20, 1854, in Charleville, a town in provincial France. He was the son of an army captain who deserted his family when Rimbaud was only six years old, forcing the family into poverty. This abandonment became a central theme in Rimbaud's poetry and was represented by the figure of a mythical father who was a man of action and an adventurer. Rimbaud's mother was afraid that her son would become hardened by his experience, especially when he became intrigued by the social conditions in which he was forced to live and began to sneak out to play with his peers. She eventually secured the means to move her family to the best part of town but still forbade Rimbaud to associate with boys his own age. She appears in his works as a controlling and domineering figure.

Deprived of the company of his peers, Rimbaud devoted himself to his studies until July 1870 when, with the outbreak of the Franco-Prussian War and the departure of his favorite teacher who left to serve with the army, he became despondent and fled his home to begin a life of rebellion.

Rimbaud spent a year of his life as a vagabond, denouncing women and the church, living on the streets in the most squalid conditions he could find. He studied the so-called immoral poets, such as BAUDELAIRE, and read everything from philosophy to the occult. He also began writing poetry, some of which he sent to PAUL VERLAINE who, in 1871, invited the aspiring poet to visit him at his home in Paris.

Although the rest of the Parisian literary world rejected him, Rimbaud and Verlaine became lovers. In 1872, Verlaine left his wife and moved with Rimbaud to London. Their relationship was a difficult one, but it continued off and on for more than two years, giving Rimbaud a sense of spiritual and emotional disillusionment. After a drunken argument between the couple in Brussels, Verlaine shot Rimbaud in the wrist. Rimbaud, who had grown tired of the relationship, notified the police. Verlaine spent 18 months in prison. Rimbaud's guilt and disillusionment prompted him to write *A Season in Hell* (1873; translated 1932).

Rimbaud's affair with Verlaine eventually ended, and Rimbaud abandoned writing completely when he was not yet 20 years old. Returning to his earlier rebellious nature, he became a trader and gunrunner in Africa. He died 18 years later, on November 10, in Marseille, France, following the amputation of his right leg.

Rimbaud's literary legacy, however, lives on. He is known as the precocious boy-poet of SYMBOLISM and is credited with being one of the creators of free verse because of the rhythmic experimentation in his poem *Illuminations* (1886; translated 1932). Rimbaud's poetry is remarkable in its subtle suggestiveness. His work draws largely on subconscious sources, delving deeply into the human psyche. He helped to popularize synesthesia, a device commonly employed by symbolist poets in which one sensory experience is described in relation to another. In his "Sonnet of the Vowels" (1871; translated 1966), for example, each vowel is assigned a particular color and other sensory associations.

In addition, Rimbaud's influence can be seen in diverse works of modern literature, particularly that of the Beat poets. He has also been cited as the source of inspiration for modern musicians, such as Bob Dylan, Jim Morrison, and Patti Smith.

Another Work by Arthur Rimbaud
Rimbaud: Complete Works, Selected Letters. Translated by Wallace Fowlie. Chicago: University of Chicago Press, 1987.

Works about Arthur Rimbaud
Cohn, Robert Greer. *The Poetry of Arthur Rimbaud.* Columbia: University of South Carolina Press, 1999.
Robb, Graham. *Arthur Rimbaud.* New York: Norton, 2000.

Rinser, Luise (1911–2002) *novelist, short story writer*

Luise Rinser was born in Pitzling, Bavaria. Her parents Josef and Luise Sailer Rinser were strict Catholics. After she finished grammar school in 1930, Rinser studied psychology and pedagogy at the University of Munich. She earned her teaching diploma in 1934 and spent four years teaching elementary school. After her first husband, conductor Horst-Günther Schnell, died fighting in World War II, Rinser married composer Carl Orff in 1954.

Rinser began to write in the 1930s and published her first story, "Die Lilie" ("The Lily") in 1938. Her first published volume *Die gläsernen Runge* (*Rings of Glass*, 1941) gained popular approval but was banned by the Nazis for promoting values different from those approved by the government. In 1944, Rinser was sent to a concentration camp for opposing the war effort. She described her prison experiences in *Gefängnis- Tagebuch* (*Prison Diary,* 1946). After World War II, Rinser wrote short stories and worked as a literary critic and columnist. Her novel *Mitte des Lebens* (*Nina,* 1956) became a major international success and was translated into 22 languages. In the 1970s and 1980s, she published six diary volumes and a best-selling autobiography. A political activist, she ran for president of West Germany in 1984 as the Green Party candidate.

Rinser's influences include the baroque Catholic tradition, Eastern philosophy, Carl Gustav Jung, and Ernest Hemingway. A major theme in her works is the plight of the disadvantaged and oppressed. Her specific topics include the fight for female equality in a patriarchal society and power politics in the Catholic Church. Critic Albert Scholz writes in "Luise Rinser's Gefängnistagebuch" that Rinser "is strongest and most effective in her positive attitude toward the fundamental questions of the present day, in her striving for truth, and in her portrayal of authentic human beings working and suffering."

Another Work by Luise Rinser

Abelard's Love. Translated by Jean M. Snook. Lincoln: University of Nebraska Press, 1998.

A Work about Luise Rinser

Falkenstein, Henning. *Luise Rinser.* Berlin: Colloquium Verlag, 1988.

Robbe-Grillet, Alain (1922–2008) *novelist*

Alain Robbe-Grillet was born in Brest, France, to a family of scientists and engineers. Before becoming a writer, he worked in a German tank factory during World War II and earned a degree from the National Institute for Agronomy. He worked as an agronomist, supervising several banana plantations in the West Indies, until 1955, when he took a job at Les Editions de Minuit, a well-known publishing house, as a literary consultant.

Robbe-Grillet had actually begun to write much earlier in his life, completing his first novel, *A Regicide,* in 1949, although it was not published until 1978. An illness in 1951 prompted his writing of *The Erasers* (1951), the work that established him as a novelist and gained him recognition and a leading position in the NEW NOVEL group. Robbe-Grillet followed this work with *The Voyeur* (1955) and *In the Labyrinth* (1959).

In response to the growing debate as to what constitutes the new novel, he wrote *For a New Novel* (1963). According to Robbe-Grillet, the perspective of the new novel is highly subjective and expresses the angle of vision of individual characters, not of the novelist or reader. He also condemned the use of metaphors, for which he received much criticism from his contemporaries JEAN-PAUL SARTRE and ALBERT CAMUS who felt that his ideas were out of touch with reality.

Critical Analysis

Robbe-Grillet's works often lack the traditional or conventional elements of literature: a solid dramatic plot, character development, and coherent chronology. Instead, his works are often composed of recurring images and events from daily life.

Although Robbe-Grillet has worked in several literary genres, he is first and foremost a writer of mysteries, albeit nontraditional ones. His novel, *The Erasers,* which earned him the Fénéon Prize in 1954, mixed a traditional mystery story with shifting perspectives and vividly detailed descriptions of common, natural objects, such as a tomato slice. In his most famous work, *Jealousy* (1957), which is considered to exemplify the new novel, the main character spies on his possibly adulterous wife. The plot is secondary, if not nonexistent, and Robbe-Grillet devotes the bulk of the work to studying the importance of the narrator to the creation of the text.

In addition, many of Robbe-Grillet's so-called mysteries, including *The Voyeur,* leave the reader without any concrete resolution. In this case, the novel (which was awarded the Critic's Prize in 1955, in spite of the fact that many members of the jury did not feel the work could be classified as a novel) is about a traveling watch salesman named Mathias who is never explicitly identified as the murderer.

Using the same fractured structure that he employed in his novels, Robbe-Grillet wrote and directed several works for the screen, including *Trans-Europ-Express* (1966), which incorporates ideas from Alfred Hitchcock films and the popular gangster genre, and *Topology of a Phantom City* (1976), which uses freeze-frame cinematography to focus on specific elements. The tale of a police investigation into the murder of a French prostitute, this film is often told from the first person perspective of David, the narrator, who is also the perpetrator of the crime.

Another of Robbe-Grillet's trademark devices was the use of bizarre descriptions of sexual violence. Many of these were based on images taken from the visual arts. *La belle captive* (1975) was inspired by the paintings of René Magritte, for example. In *Snapshots* (1976), he includes a story in honor of a work of painter Gustave Moreau,

"The Secret Room," in which he vividly describes a chained and abused woman.

In his later novels, Robbe-Grillet turned his attention to the spy genre. *Djinn* (1981) recounts the fractured tale of a man who works for an American spy. In the process, he is forced to question his own existence when he is told that he is not real at all but merely the product of a dream.

In 1984, Robbe-Grillet published the first part of an autobiographical trilogy, *Ghosts in the Mirror*. In this work, he acknowledges CLAUDE SIMON's idea that everything is autobiographical to some extent, indicating that much of his work is drawn, at least in part, from elements of his own life and memory. Robbe-Grillet died on February 18, 2008.

Another Work by Alain Robbe-Grillet

Project for a Revolution in New York: A Novel. Translated by Richard Howard. New York: Grove Press, 1972.

A Work about Alain Robbe-Grillet

Smith, Roch C. *Understanding Alain Robbe-Grillet.* Columbia: University of South Carolina Press, 2000.

Roberts, Charles (1860–1943) *poet, short story writer*

Charles G. D. Roberts was born in Douglas, New Brunswick; the eastern Canadian landscape would have a profound impact on his work. He graduated from the University of New Brunswick and published his first book of poetry, *Orion and Other Poems,* in 1880. From 1879 to 1895, Roberts worked as a teacher in New Brunswick, as editor of the literary magazine *The Week,* and as a professor at King's College of Windsor, in Nova Scotia.

Regarded by many as the father of Canadian poetry, although he also wrote prose, Roberts, along with three contemporary writers, styled themselves the "Poets of the Confederation" and strove for a distinctly Canadian voice.

During this period, he wrote one of his most celebrated collections, *In Divers Tones* (1887). Although in this and other works Roberts attempted to establish a Canadian national literature, he was profoundly influenced by British Victorian poets. The title of *In Divers Tones,* for example, is taken from Alfred, Lord Tennyson's long poem *In Memoriam.*

In 1897, Roberts moved to New York. He began, in part for financial reasons, to write prose; in particular, he pioneered the genre of the modern animal story. These stories are collected in the volumes *Earth's Enigmas* (1896) and *Eyes of the Wilderness* (1933). Roberts returned to Canada in 1925, settling in Toronto, and returned to writing poetry as well. Roberts was knighted in 1935.

Another Work by Charles Roberts

Keith, W. J., ed. *Selected Poetry and Critical Prose.* Toronto: University of Toronto Press, 1974.

romanticism

The term *romanticism* is applied to literary, intellectual, and artistic movements of the late 18th to mid-19th centuries that share a number of common characteristics, including strong emotion, imagination, freedom from classical correctness in art forms, and rebellion against social conventions. Many romantics advocated a return to nature and a belief that humanity, specifically the individual, was innately good or worthy, rather than inherently sinful, as the church had held for centuries. Romanticism was also, in part, a revolt against the age of reason and the ideals of rationalism.

Psychologically, romanticism was marked by a focus on emotions over intellect (the sense that the artist is an individual and thus the supreme creator of his or her own work) and on a deep feeling of national pride. Whereas the thinkers and writers of the Enlightenment paid homage to the classical writers by emphasizing reason, logic, order, and restraint, the romantics valued emotional experience. Romantic works emphasize subjective experience, individuality, and imagination. Romantics value emotional experience, individual style, and spontaneity in the individual expression of experience.

Imagination and emotions are linked to nature rather than to reason and logic. The romantics believed that human nature was generally good but was corrupted by society. Considering this philosophical viewpoint, it is not surprising that many romantics depicted and praised various aspects of nature because the natural environment outside the confines of civilization was supposedly a force that encouraged the possibility of authenticity and goodness. Nature, often seen as the antithesis of materialism and the social conflicts produced by civilization, became a prominent theme in the works of romantics. The romantics also revered childhood, which they saw as a natural state before the intervention of the corrupting forces of modern society.

Romantic writers, opposing the established order, also insisted on political and moral changes. Many took inspiration from the French Revolution of 1789, before the horrors of the Reign of Terror. Critics have sometimes attributed the romantic opposition to REALISM to the political affiliations of the movement. Many romantics became politically disenchanted after a series of failed European revolutions of the early 19th century. However, broadly speaking, the term *romanticism* applies to the arts, philosophy, and politics.

Romanticism in Germany

Romanticism originated in Germany and England during the 18th century as an opposition to the Enlightenment and neoclassicism. Eighteenth-century German philosopher FREDRICH VON SCHILLER was the first to apply the term to the literary movement.

In Germany, romanticism played an especially significant role in the development of national literature. JOHANN WOLFGANG VON GOETHE and Friedrich von Schiller are perhaps the most important figures associated with German romanticism. In his poetry and prose, Goethe created powerful emotional scenes often set against the background of wild, untamed nature. Likewise, Schiller created powerful emotional scenes, combining elements of folklore and traditional genres of literature. Many romantics also began to compose works celebrating the vernacular German and German culture. E. T. A. HOFFMANN and the GRIMM brothers wrote fairy tales that not only included fantastic and irrational elements but also celebrated the traditional culture of the German people. The humble heroes of their tales exemplified the courage, morality, and ingenuity of the common people. Achim von Arnim (1781–1831) and Clemens Brentano (1778–1842) collaborated on a collection of German tales that were orally transmitted to them by various common folk throughout Germany. Romanticism began during the process of unification of the German states, and thus greatly contributed to the establishment of a unified German national identity.

In certain ways, romantic literature in Germany was linked with the romantic tradition in music: Wilhelm Müller's (1784–1827) *Die Winterreise* was transformed into a series of musical pieces by Franz Schubert (1797–1828). Ludwig Uhland (1787–1862) wrote lyrical ballads that praised nature and human passions based on the traditional tales of German peasants.

German romanticism was perhaps one of the most influential movements in the history of European literature, affecting innumerable writers in England, France, Russia, and later America. The works of German romantics are still read and appreciated throughout the world. Romantics were visionary in their concern for emotions and psychology and their humanistic emphasis on the individual, particularly the individual who occupies a humble rank on the social ladder.

Romanticism in France

Romanticism arrived later in France than it did in Germany and England. The reasons for this are largely political. During the French Revolution and the Napoleonic Wars, France was too involved in its own internal struggles to be greatly affected by the outside world. In 1815, however, with the restoration of the monarchy, the return of the French nobility from exile brought about significant changes in literature and culture, as well as in politics. Many of those nobles who returned had lived for many years of exile in England. On arriving in France, they brought with them a variety of English cultural traditions, including the poetry of English romantic poet George Gordon, Lord Byron (1788–1824). Up until this point, French literature had for the most part held to the 17th-century literary ideal of neoclassicism. In a time when large-scale sociopolitical changes were occurring with great force, the works of Racine and Corneille and the expression of perfect harmony and clarity that had their roots in the Greek and Roman traditions were soon usurped by the rebellious beauty of romanticism.

Romanticism did not arrive in France without precedents, however. The works of the 18th-century writer Jean-Jacques Rousseau anticipated the trend by focusing on the social aspects of the human condition and questioning whether the concept of the soul could be dealt with rationally. In *Les confessions* (1770), for example, Rousseau's subject, himself, becomes the most important figure in literature, granting the "I" form of identity a sense of supremacy that was lacking in literature to that point.

FRANÇOIS-RENÉ CHATEAUBRIAND expresses the alienation of young aristocrats after the revolution, and with his *René* and *Atala* explores the themes of melancholy and exile. GERMAINE DE STAËL's *De l'Allemagne* introduced German mysticism and romanticism into France and contested universalist ideals in the name of a national literature. In French theater, VICTOR HUGO is credited with having set forth a definition of the movement in the *Préface* to his play *Cromwell* (1827). Hugo championed freedom of speech and freedom of the artist and individuality in all of his works, most notably in the novels *Les misérables* (1862) and *Notre Dame de Paris* (1831).

In general, the romantic shared a few common goals. The focus on political freedom and the exploration of individual psyche, even to the point of the bizarre and the supernatural, became of utmost importance. The peculiar and the macabre were stressed as equally valid aspects of humanity. Gothic literature and the fantastic experienced a rise in popularity in the 1830s. Poetry, in particular, turned to nature as a source of primary inspiration. The romantic poet often felt the need to suffer to understand art as it related to the human condition. Political activism and the push for social change were also important aspects of the movement.

See also COSTUMBRISMO.

Works about Romanticism

Daniels, Barry V. *Revolution in the Theatre: French Romantic Theories of Drama*. Westport, Conn.: Greenwood Press, 1983.

Lacoue-Labarthe, Phillipe, ed. *The Literary Absolute: The Theory of Literature in German Romanticism*. Albany: State University of New York Press, 1988.

Moses, Claire Goldberg. *Feminism, Socialism and French Romanticism*. Bloomington: Indiana University Press, 1993.

Schulte-Sasse, Jochen, ed. *Theory as Practice: An Anthology of Early German Romantic Writings*. Minneapolis: University of Minnesota Press, 1997.

Rosas, Oscar (1864–1925) *poet*

Oscar Rosas was born in Florianópolis, Brazil. He was a minor member of the Brazilian symbolist movement whose leading figure was JOÃO CRUZ E SOUSA. Symbolism in Brazil was a manifestation of Latin American MODERNISM, a larger movement best exemplified by RUBÉN DARÍO.

Later in life, Oscar Rosas became increasingly politically active, eventually serving in the Brazilian house of representatives. In 1925, he was attacked in a fight over politics and eventually died from the wound he sustained.

Rosenstock, Samuel

See TZARA, TRISTAN.

Roy, Arundhati (1961–) *novelist, nonfiction writer*

Arundhati Roy was born in Bengal, India, and grew up in Kerala. In 1986, her mother, Mary Roy, became famous for her court case that demanded equal rights for women in inheritance laws. Mary Roy also ran a liberal school, called Corpus Christi, where Arundhati Roy received her primary education. Born into a religious family, Roy was brought up in a traditional Syrian Christian household. When she was 16 years old, she left home and went to Delhi to study architecture.

Her first novel, *The God of Small Things* (1997), won the 1997 Booker Prize. She is the first nonexpatriate and the first Indian woman to win this award, and she has claimed that it will be the only novel she writes. Her novel, in fact, begins with the quote stating that this story will "be told as though it's the only one." *The God of Small Things* uses MAGIC REALISM to depict Kerala's multireligious communities. Roy's brand of magic realism steers away from mere illusion, however, because of the text's lingering question on social identity. The secret love affair between two main characters highlights the still-existing burden of caste and religious (especially Syrian Christian) divisions in Kerala. Roy poses time and place as protean categories in the narrator's memory as she tries to understand her roots within a family that is separated within itself by outside social forces.

Roy has also written many screenplays, including *In Which Annie Gives It Those Ones* (1988) and *Electric Moon* (1992), for which she became known for her straightforward and highly opinionated style. Since then and after her novel, she has dedicated herself to writing newspaper and journal articles about social issues in India. As a writer, she claims, this is the best form of activism of which she is capable. In 1999, her essay "The Greater Common Good," on the dispossession of tribal peoples during construction of the Narmada Dam, caused global concern. Her journalistic writing has given several underprivileged communities of India access to international media attention and has helped these kinds of social issues gain worldwide support. Roy was awarded the Sydney Peace Prize in May 2004 for her work on various social issues. In 2007, she announced that she was working on a new novel.

Critical Analysis

The God of Small Things tells the story of a Syrian Christian family in Ayemenem, Karala, India. The children, the "two-egg" twins Esta and Rahel, and their mother, Ammu, have returned home after Ammu has doubly disgraced herself first by marrying without her family's permission and then divorcing her husband.

Roy herself has likened the novel to a work of architecture, and, indeed, much of its distinctiveness lies in its structure, which moves backward and forward in time. The central events of the tragic story are the deaths of two characters—Esta and Rahel's half-English cousin Sophie Mol and their beloved friend, the untouchable Velutha. The novel begins with Rahel's returning to her family home in Ayemenem, 23 years after the terrible day in 1969 when the children's lives were shattered. The structure of the novel follows the structure of her remembering, moving between past and present. Although the reader knows from the beginning that Sophie and Velutha die, how and why are revealed only gradually.

Rahel is the narrator, sometimes in the voice of an adult, more often in the voice of a child for whom the world is a magical living entity, a place where huge concrete airport ashtrays shaped like kangaroos come alive and nibble on cashews—and where dead cousins do cartwheels in their coffins. Roy has been praised for the extraordinarily inventive language with which she manages to evoke the world through a child's eyes. Words take on new weight when they are capitalized or separated or run together. Rahel's uncle Chacko sometimes speaks in his "Reading Aloud" voice. Rahel misunderstands her uncle when he uses a legal term in Latin (*locus standi*) and later repeats that her mother had no "Locust Stand I." When a bat lands on Rahel's aunt Baby Kochamma at Sophie's funeral, "The singing stopped for a 'Whaisit?' 'Whathappened' and for a 'Furrywhirring' and a 'Sariflapping.'"

As with many postcolonial Indian authors who write in English, Roy takes great and imaginative freedoms with the language. She repeats phrases and motifs, lending a rhyme and rhythm to her prose that edges into poetry. She embellishes her writing with lavish, odd, yet perfectly apt similes and metaphors. At Sophie's funeral, the "yellow church swelled like a throat with the sound of sad singing." A huge moon is "as big as the belly of a beer-drinking man." Even in the most horrific chapter of the novel, Roy shocks with this description of the police who are descending on Velutha:

> A forked canal. . . . A tree trunk fallen over it. The Touchable Policemen minced across. Twirling polished bamboo batons.
>   Hairy fairies with lethal wands.

The private tragedy of *The God of Small Things* mirrors the tragedy of postcolonial India. Chacko tells the twins that they are all "anglophiles," lovers of things British, who are "trapped outside their own history and unable to retrace their steps because their footsteps had been swept away." Chacko suggests, and the novel confirms, that colonialism has become internalized, that Indians have come to regard themselves—as their conquerors did—as inferior beings. Esta and Rahel cannot help noticing the extent to which their world revolves around Sophie Mol, because she is English. She is a "littleangel" while they are "littledemons."

The God of Small Things is a beautiful work about a series of unimaginable horrors that destroy a family. That contrast, between the lush language and the stark story, results in an unforgettable work of literature.

Other Works by Arundhati Roy

The Algebra of Infinite Justice. London: Flamingo, 2001.

The Cost of Living. London: Flamingo, 1999.

Introduction to 13 December, A Reader: The Strange Case of the Attack on the Indian Parliament. New York: Penguin, 2006.

Listening to Grasshoppers: Field Notes on Democracy. New Delhi: Penguin, 2009.

An Ordinary Person's Guide to Empire. Cambridge, Mass.: South End Press, 2004.

Power Politics. Cambridge, Mass.: South End Press, 2002.

Public Power in the Age of Empire. New York: Seven Stories Press, 2004.

War Talk. Cambridge, Mass.: South End Press, 2003.

Works about Arundhati Roy

Jones, Sonya L. "The Large Things of Arundhati Roy." In *The Literature of the Indian Diaspora: Essays in Criticism.* Edited by A. L. McLeod. New Delhi: Sterling, 2000.

Mullaney, Julie. *Arundhati Roy's* The God of Small Things: *A Reader's Guide.* London: Continuum International, 2002.

Sharma, A. P. *The Mind and Art of Arundhati Roy.* London: Minerva Press, 2003.

Shawan, R. K. *Arundhati Roy: The Novelist Extraordinary.* London: Sangam Books, 1999.

Rushdie, Salman (1947–) *novelist, essayist*

Ahmed Salman Rushdie was born to wealthy, liberal, secularized Muslim parents, Anis Ahmed Rushdie and Negin Rushdie, in Bombay, India, but has lived much of his life in England. He is an agnostic Muslim and feels torn between different cultures. Referring to his short story collection *East, West* (1994), Rushdie told the *Daily Telegraph*, "The most important part of the title is the comma. Because it seems to me that I am that comma."

Rushdie's first three novels, *Grimus* (1975), *Midnight's Children* (1980), and *Shame* (1983), won critical approval. *Midnight's Children* was a multiple award winner: the Booker Prize, an award from the English Speaking Union, the James Tait Black Prize, and a special "Booker of Bookers" award as the best novel in the first 25 years of the Booker Prize.

Rushdie gained international fame even with nonreaders with his novel *The Satanic Verses* (1988), which rewrote the story of the Islamic prophet Muhammad, depicting him as a skeptic and a man driven by sexual desire. The prophet's scribe, "Salman," is initially faithful but says that when faced with religious hypocrisy, "I began to get a bad smell in my nose."

Satanic Verses enraged Islamic fundamentalists, leading Iran's spiritual leader at the time, the Ayatollah Ruhollah Khomeini, to issue a *fatwa*, or religious decree, pronouncing a death sentence against Rushdie for offending God. "Anyone who dies in the cause of ridding the world of Rushdie," said Khomeini, "will be a martyr and will go directly to heaven." After Khomeini's pronouncement, some bookstores that were believed to be carrying Rushdie's book were bombed, and riots occurred in places where he was believed to be staying. One translator of the book was stabbed to death. Many writers vocally announced their support for Rushdie, and politicians around the world condemned the death sentence. Critic Amir Mufti says, "The violence of the novel's reception . . . is an accurate indicator of the anger generated by its insistence on a sweeping rearrangement and rethinking of the terms of Muslim public culture." Pradyumna S. Chauan says, "*The Satanic Verses* was, and still remains, a major contribution to the contemporary novel."

Despite the death threat, which eventually was lifted, Rushdie continued to write. He even made unannounced public appearances, including one onstage during a well-attended, multimedia concert by the rock group U2.

After writing a nonfiction account of travels in Nicaragua, *The Jaguar Smile* (1987), Rushdie took a sympathetic interest in the United States, setting his novel *Fury* (2001) there. It is the story of Malik Solanka, professor and dollmaker, who tries to lose himself in New York City but discovers that one's deeds take on a life of their own as he watches his dolls become extremely popular. Solanka sees parallels between God's strange relationship to the humans he created, who have free will, and his own relationship to his dolls: "Nowadays, they started out as clay figurines. Clay, of which God, who didn't exist, made man, who did."

Solanka also struggles to control his own anger, often amplified by the chaos of the city: "He was never out of earshot of a siren, an alarm, a large vehicle's reverse-gear bleeps, the beat of some unbearable music." Rushdie argued in newspaper editorials in the years prior to *Fury* that America has generated hostility from both left-wing and right-wing groups around the globe precisely because it is an embodiment of freedom and change. In America's ability constantly to reinvent itself, Rushdie sees parallels to the dangerous power of fiction making and to his own status as a cultural nomad, a theme that arises repeatedly in his collection *Imaginary Homelands: Essays and Criticism 1981–1991* (1991).

In 2005, Rushdie published *Shalimar the Clown*, a complex novel that spans continents and generations and explores the roots of terrorism in a post–9/11 world. In 2008, *The Enchantress of Florence* was published. It is, according to Rushdie, his "most researched book," one that took "years and years of study." The novel moves between Renaissancee Florence and Emperor Akbar's court in Sikri at the height of the Mughul empire. The two settings are linked by the story of the magically beautiful hidden princess, Qara Köz.

Critical Analysis
Much of Rushdie's work is classifiable as MAGIC REALISM, combining realistic issues and events with elements of magic or mythology. *Grimus,* for instance, sends its Native American protagonist, Flapping Eagle, in search of his sister and involves him with magicians, intelligent stone frogs, extraterrestrials, and a host of other fantastic devices.

In *Midnight's Children,* political satire mixes with Hindu fantasy and psychic abilities as it is revealed that 1,001 children born at the stroke of midnight on August 15, 1947, the day of Indian independence from Britain, gained such superpowers as telepathy and telekinesis. Two of those children, one wealthy and one poor, are switched at birth, leading to political complications.

The Muslim Indian narrator, Saleem Sinai, says he is "handcuffed to history," the events of his life "indissolubly chained to those of my country." Sinai's psychic powers, says critic Dubravka Juraga, enable him "to empathize with members of all segments of India's complex, multilayered society," from a starving man to a rich man who bullies serfs and even to real-life political figures such as Prime Minister Nehru. Throughout the course of the novel, Saleem struggles to retain his own identity. Scholar Michael Reder remarks, "as Saleem's story demonstrates, individuals can fall victim to a discourse—such as a national myth—in which they themselves are denied a role." Individual identity is constrained by historical circumstances.

Shame, patterned after GABRIEL GARCÍA MÁRQUEZ's *One Hundred Years of Solitude,* combines Pakistani civil war with the fairy–tale-like story of a little girl so wracked by shame that her blushes can set objects on fire. An accusatory narrative voice sometimes interrupts Rushdie's main narration, demanding to know whether Rushdie is close enough to Indian and Pakistani culture to tell this tale: "We know you, with your foreign language wrapped around you like a flag: speaking about us in your forked tongue, what can you tell but lies?" Critic Timothy Brennan calls this "Rushdie's most fully realized and densely crafted novel."

In *Haroun and the Sea of Stories* (1990) Rushdie artfully blends references to *The Thousand and One Nights* with Rushdie's philosophy that reality is open to many interpretations and his love of fiction as a playground of the mind where countless ideas, even heretical ones, can be displayed. It is the story of a boy who hopes to rescue his father by returning to him the gift of storytelling: "And because the stories were held here in liquid form, they retained the ability to change, to become new versions of themselves." Rushdie and his characters savor the ability to rework old tales and old beliefs.

Rushdie's blending of different cultural influences has been a chief interest of his critics, who have seen in him both a testament to the relevance of tradition and folklore and a reminder that the entire idea of nationhood is in some sense a fiction, maintained by common beliefs and touchstone stories. Further, as critic Timothy Brennan observes, by rewriting sacred stories with the imagination and freedom of a fiction writer rather than the ferocity of a heretic or adherent of a rival religion, Rushdie "unravels the religion from within." Scholar M. Keith Booker, in his introduction to a collection of essays on Rushdie, writes that "Rushdie has undoubtedly been one of the most important writers in world literature in the past quarter century . . . [and] a major commentator on Indian and other postcolonial cultures."

Other Works by Salman Rushdie

The Ground Beneath Her Feet. New York: Henry Holt, 1999.

The Moor's Last Sigh. Thorndike, Maine: Chivers Press, 1995.

Works about Salman Rushdie

Booker, M. Keith, ed. *Critical Essays on Salman Rushdie.* New York: G. K. Hall, 1999.

Cundy, Catherine. *Salman Rushdie.* Manchester, U.K.: Manchester University Press, 1996.

Harrison, James. *Salman Rushdie.* New York: Twayne, 1992.

Russian symbolism

See SYMBOLISM.

Saadawi, Nawal El (1931–) *essayist, memoirist, novelist*

Nawal El Saadawi has authored some of Arab feminism's landmark texts. Her indictment of female genital mutilation in *The Hidden Face of Eve* is perhaps the aspect of El Saadawi's work best known in the West; the English translation rearranges the Arabic text to begin with the author's searing memory of her clitorectomy at age six. Well known, too, are her attacks on Islamic fundamentalism and theory of ancient Egypt as originally matriarchal. Less well known in translation, perhaps because it is less palatable to her Western readership, is the fact that El Saadawi denounces the patriarchy of all three Near Eastern religions—Islam, Christianity, and Judaism. Her protest against U.S. and global capitalism's exploitation of women in the developing world is another important theme in her work, which tends to be glossed over in English-language references in favor of emphasis on her critiques of Arab sexual mores. El Saadawi's travelogue, *My Travels Around the World* (1992), which contains powerful condemnation of Western imperialism, is out of print.

In her fiction, El Saadawi's protagonists are victimized women, beaten by overwhelming male domination in a world devoid of female friendship and male allies. In life, El Saadawi earned her M.D. (1955) at Cairo University in a climate made possible by other Egyptian feminist men and women. Her parents, of rural Egypt, supported her career choice. In *Memoirs of a Woman Doctor* (1989) and other works, El Saadawi drew on her clinical experiences for writing about women's sexual oppression. Abortion, honor killings, child molestation—El Saadawi's indictment of patriarchy leaves no taboo unbroken. *Women and Sex* (1971) got her fired as Egypt's director of health education, and Sadat imprisoned her in 1981 for feminist activism, releasing her after international outcry. This is the basis of her *Memoirs from the Women's Prison* (translated by Miriam Cooke, 1986).

El Saadawi's husband Sherif Hetata, translates her novels into English. She has a daughter and a son from two earlier marriages; the family is active in the Arab Women's Solidarity Association, founded by El Saadawi. Currently living in Cairo, she has seen her work translated into a dozen languages. *Woman at Point Zero* (translated by Hetata, 1983) is the most widely read of her novels. Some critics see its story of a friendless, poverty-stricken woman driven to murder by a life in which she has suffered every possible sexual abuse from child molestation to rape and forced prostitution as a stunning portrayal of patriarchy at its worst, while others find its popularity an example of the way in which El Saadawi's complex, highly political feminist analysis is susceptible to being reduced to grist for sensationalist stereotypes of Arab women as sexual victims.

Other Works by Nawal El Saadawi

Daughter of Isis. Translated by Sherif Hetata. London: Zed Books, 1999.

The Nawal El Saadawi Reader: Selected Essays 1970–1996. London: Zed Books, 1997.

Works about Nawal El Saadawi

Malti-Douglas, Fedwa. *Men, Women, and God(s): Nawal El Saadawi and Arab Feminist Poetics.* Berkeley: University of California Press, 1995.

Tarabishi, George. *Woman Against Her Sex: A Critique of Nawal El-Saadawi, with a Reply by Nawal El-Saadawi.* London: Al Saqi Books, 1988.

Sachs, Nelly Leonie (1891–1970) *poet*

Nelly Leonie Sachs was born in Berlin to Jewish parents, William and Margarethe (Karger) Sachs. Her father was a wealthy industrialist and inventor. Sachs attended Hoch Toechterschule but received most of her education privately. She developed an early interest in dancing and literature and began writing poetry and puppet plays as a teenager.

Sachs's first volume of poetry *Legenden und Erzählungen* (*Legend and Tales,* 1921) reflected her interest in the common roots of Judaism and Christianity. She was later influenced by German and Jewish mysticism, including the writings of Jakob Böhmne, and Hasidism. In the 1930s, Sachs published her poetry in newspapers and Jewish journals. With the help of friends, she escaped from Nazi Germany to Sweden in 1940. Sachs wrote her most significant poetry about the horrors of World War II and the Nazi death camps; these poems are included in volumes such as *In den Wohnungen des Todes* (*In the Habitations of Death,* 1946) and *Sternverdunkelung* (*Eclipse of the Stars,* 1949) and earned her worldwide acclaim.

While in Sweden, Sachs also translated the works of several Swedish poets, such as Erik Lindegren and Johannes Edfelt, into German.

The primary theme of Sachs's literary work is the Holocaust. Critics have noted that her poems elevated the Jews' suffering to a cosmic plane. Scholar Elisabeth Strenger writes in her essay "Nelly Sachs and the Dance of Language," that in Sachs's poems, "Jewish mystical voices cry out over the uninitiated language of the German oppressors." Sachs includes deep religious feeling, mourning, and elements of dance in her language. Her work provides an important poetic testimony to the Holocaust. She shared the Nobel Prize in literature in 1966 with SAMUEL JOSEPH AGNON.

Another Work by Nelly Sachs

The Seeker and Other Poems. Translated by Ruth Mead, Matthew Mead, and Michael Hamburger. New York: Farrar, Straus & Giroux, 1970.

A Work about Nelly Sachs

Bahti, Timothy, and Marilyn Sibley Fries. *Jewish Writers, German Literature: The Uneasy Examples of Nelly Sachs and Walter Benjamin.* Ann Arbor: The University of Michigan Press, 1995.

Sa'id, Ali Ahmad

See ADONIS.

Saint-Exupéry, Antoine de

(1900–1944) *novelist, nonfiction writer*

Best known internationally for his children's fantasy *Le petit prince* (1943; translated as *The Little Prince,* 1943), Antoine de Saint-Exupéry was born in Lyons and educated in Switzerland at Jesuit schools. Obsessed with aviation, he joined the French air force in 1921 but left to become a commercial pilot in 1926. His novels and other works express his humanist beliefs regarding fairness and compassion to all humankind, as well as a deep respect for the art of flying.

As a commercial pilot, Saint-Exupéry's job involved flying airmail routes over North Africa, the South Atlantic, and South America. He based his first novel, *Southern Mail* (1929; translated 1933), on these experiences. He married a young widow from Buenos Aires in 1931, publishing his second novel, *Vol de nuit* (*Night Flight,* translated 1932), that same year.

During World War II, Saint-Exupéry returned to the military, joining the French air force once again. However, on June 22, 1940, an armistice was signed between France and Germany, ending the Phoney War. In an enormous victory for Germany, Paris was occupied. Saint-Exupéry went to New York as a voice of the Resistance to try to encourage the United States to enter the war. Wanting action, he rejoined the Free French in 1944. *Flight to Arras* (1942; translated 1942) is an account of his wartime experiences.

Saint-Exupéry was last seen alive when he departed to fly a reconnaissance mission over southern France in 1944. His plane vanished without a trace. After his death, two notebooks that reflect on his life and ideas were published as *Wisdom of the Sands* (1948; translated 1950).

Works about Antoine de Saint-Exupéry

Saint-Exupéry, Consuelo de. *The Tale of the Rose*: *The Passion That Inspired* The Little Prince. New York: Random House, 2001.

Schiff, Stacy. *Saint-Exupéry: A Biography.* New York: Alfred A. Knopf, 1995.

Saint-John Perse

See PERSE, SAINT-JOHN.

Salih, Tayeb (1929–2009) *novelist, short story writer, broadcast journalist*

Salih's name points his readers toward his connection to the Islamic African world. The word *tayeb* in Arabic denotes purity, goodness, and piety. In addition, the prophet Salih is an important prophet in the Qur'an. Salih's contribution to world literature is his ability to fuse Western and Islamic-African realities in interesting and accessible ways.

Salih was born into a farming community in the northern section of Sudan, a country that has had a troubled history of conflict with its larger, wealthier, northern neighbor, Egypt. The Sudan of which he writes is a country divided by racial, national, and religious schisms. The seeds of the geopolitical problems of the region stem from its European colonial heritage but are also tied to issues of religious and cultural differences that national boundaries too rarely reflect.

Salih was raised in a traditional Islamic home, which meant that he studied the Qur'an regularly. He had originally intended to follow his father's lead and pursue a career in agriculture, but his path led him to a career in broadcasting. Notably, Salih led the dramatic production division of BBC's Arabic Service. This experience undoubtedly helped him to put the struggle for "true" Sudanese independence into a larger geopolitical context.

His most well-known work is the novel *Season of Migration to the North,* which was first published in 1969. The novel operates as a sort of "response" to Joseph Conrad's *Heart of Darkness* in that it traces the journey of an Islamic African named Mustafa as he visits the "horror" of London, the heart of the imperial center of the colonial world. The novel also echoes *Othello* and other literary encounters between dominant groups and "marginal" characters, stressing the deep chasms of cultural misunderstanding that appear when one encounters those who are different. As Mustafa puts it in the novel, "May God have mercy on someone who has turned a blind eye to error and has indulged in the outward aspect of things."

Like the Egyptian writer, NAGUIB MAHFOUZ, with whom Salih shares many thematic interests, Salih is not primarily a "protest" writer but one whose narratives speak to the richness of the culture out of which he has sprung and to the need to embrace the whole experience of a people.

Another Work by Tayeb Salih

The Wedding of Zein and Other Stories. Washington, D.C.: Three Continents Press, 1985.

A Work about Tayeb Salih

Boullata, Issa. *Critical Perspectives on Modern Arabic Literature.* Washington, D.C.: Three Continents Press, 1980.

Samman, Ghada (1942–) *novelist, short story writer, essayist, journalist, poet*

Born in Damascus, Syria, Samman has written more than 30 books, including six short story collections. One of these, *The Square Moon* (1994), uses supernatural elements. Her novel *Beirut '75* (1975) was considered prophetic for seeing the tensions under the surface of seemingly prosperous Lebanon; Samman wrote it just before the outbreak of the civil war that would rack the country for 15 years (1975–90). Her 1976 novel, *Beirut Nightmares,* placed her in a group of novelists who stayed in Lebanon during the civil-war years. Composed in more than 200 "nightmares," ranging in length from 10 lines to 10 pages each, *Beirut Nightmares* is a riveting experiment in form, as well as a stunning portrait of civil war from the apartment window of one woman trapped by crossfire. Samman's novel *al-Riwaya al-mustahila* (1997), has not been translated into English. In addition to short stories and novels, she has written poetry, including *Love Across the Jugular Vein* (Arabic) in 1980, which treats love relationships in an ironic, wry tone that is, at the same time, infused with warmth and honesty.

Having lost her mother as a young girl, Samman was raised by her father, a law-school dean. She earned her B.A. in English literature at the University of Damascus and her master's at the American University of Beirut. She studied in London for a time and lived in Europe from 1967 to 1969. Because of problems with Syria's strict regulations on Syrians abroad, Samman was unable to return to Syria. She settled in Lebanon where, in 1977, she established her own publishing company.

Samman cuts a striking figure as one of the best-known feminists of the Arab world. The heroines of her novels tend to be strong women breaking out of traditionally feminine roles. Her writing shows fierce awareness of the economic exploitation of the poor, in addition to an abiding concern with gender. Samman's tone is typically ironical, urbane, witty, and sometimes cynical, conveying profound commitment to social and political issues and attention to the craft of writing. Samman's work is translated into Russian, Romanian, Italian, Persian, German, Spanish, and English.

Other Works by Ghada Samman

Arab Women in Love & War: Fleeting Eternities. Translated by Rim Zahra. Scotts Valley, Calif.: BookSurge Publishing, 2009.

The Night of the First Billion. Translated by Nancy N. Roberts. Syracuse, N.Y.: Syracuse University Press, 2005.

The Square Moon. Translated by Issa J. Boullatta. Fayetteville: University of Arkansas Press, 1998.

Works about Ghada Samman

Cooke, Miriam. *War's Other Voices.* Cambridge: Cambridge University Press, 1988.

Zeidan, Joseph. *Arab Women Novelists.* Albany: State University of New York Press, 1995.

Sand, George (Amandine–Aurore–Lucile Dupin) (1804–1876) *novelist*

Noted for her skill as a writer as well as for her numerous love affairs with prominent men, such as ALFRED DE MUSSET and Frédéric Chopin, French romantic (*see* ROMANTICISM) novelist George Sand was born in Paris and raised and educated at her grandmother's country estate, which Sand inherited in 1821. In 1822, she married Baron Casimir Dudevant. Financially and socially secure, Sand bore two children with Dudevant, but she never found happiness with him nor reconciled her intellectual and artistic goals with those of wife and mother. She left her family in 1831 to return to Paris and embarked on a career as a writer.

Sand wrote and edited for several journals, including the prominent *Le Figaro, Révue de Deux Mondes,* and *La République.* Through her employment, she became acquainted with several well-known poets, artists, and philosophers. Her early works, in particular, show the influence these associations had on her. This was particularly true throughout the 1830s when, in response to rapidly expanding industrialization, Sand and her associates sought, through their works, to cure society of the evils of new technology. She was joined in this cause by Franz Liszt, with whom she became very good friends. Several other prominent figures with whom Sand was involved during this period and whose views distinctly reveal themselves in her writings include the revolutionary Michel de Bourges and Pierre Leroux.

One relationship in particular marked the start of Sand's career as a novelist: Her affair with fellow writer Jules Sandeau led them to coauthor and publish a novel, *Rose et Blanche* (1831), under the pseudonym Jules Sand. She assumed the name *George* for her second novel, *Indiana* (1832), which recounts the tale of a young woman who is both abused by her much older husband and deceived by her treacherous lover. The work was an instant success and was soon followed by the publication of popular novels in the 1830s, such as *Lélia* (1833), which exalted free love over conventional marriage.

In the 1840s, Sand began to break away from the molds provided for her by the men in her life and started to establish her unique writing voice. She became firmly committed to the ideals of socialism and, as a result, her works often provoked controversy. Alongside economic and social themes, Sand often questioned the preconceived notions of gendered identity. Her autobiography, *Histoire de ma vie* (1855), for example, raises questions about gender and sexuality that emerged from her complicated and unconventional life.

Sand's works were extremely popular during her lifetime. She wrote novels, memoirs, essays, short stories, and even children's fairy tales that often carried a deeper, more mature meaning. She died on June 8, having paved the way for female novelists, and left behind a lasting influence on fellow writers Fyodor Dostoyevsky, Gustave Flaubert and Marcel Proust.

Critical Analysis

Sand's *Indiana*, the first work she wrote independently, is, in some measure, a political novel, in that it protests how the Napoleonic Code deals with the rights of married women. The heroine, Indiana Delmare, a woman of Creole descent, has been forced by her brutal father to marry a much older man, Colonel Delmare. She is young, naive, and miserable. When the handsome and charming Raymon de Ramière appears on the scene, Indiana falls madly in love. De Ramière is reminiscent of other rakes in French literature, in that the moment Indiana begins to return his love, he loses interest in her. Not realizing this, Indiana eventually leaves her husband and goes to de Ramière, only to find that he has already married another. She has "risked everything" for him—and he no longer cares at all for her.

Rescued by her cousin Ralph, who has loved her all his life, Indiana returns with him to the island of her birth. Both consumed with despair, Indiana and Ralph make a suicide pact, but on the evening they decide to die, Ralph confesses to Indiana that he has loved her his whole life. She returns his love, saying, "Be my husband in heaven and on earth, and let this kiss pledge me to you for all eternity." The chapter ends with Ralph's carrying Indiana to the place where they proposed to jump into a waterfall. The final chapter of the novel is told by Ralph to a visitor. He says that he lost his way looking for the waterfall, and when dawn came, he and Indiana began a life together, unmarried. They dedicate their lives to freeing slaves on the island.

In an important subplot, Indiana's fate is foreshadowed by her foster sister, Noun, who lives with the Delmares. She is "sparkling with health, lively, brisk, and overflowing with the full-blooded ardour and passion of a Creole." As Indiana is gradually falling in love with de Ramière, she does not realize that he and Noun are already lovers. When he finds Noun is pregnant, he abandons her. She commits suicide, but Ralph and Colonel Delmare conspire to convince Indiana that the death was an accident. Thus, in the structure of the novel, Noun becomes a surrogate for Indiana, and a warning that the young woman fails to comprehend.

Feminists have long argued over whether *Indiana* is a feminist work. If one looks at the character of Indiana herself, it would be hard to conclude that it is. She is neither strong nor independent. Still, the overall impact of the novel is undeniably feminist, and on several occasions Indiana herself rises to the level of a role model, particularly when she tells her husband:

> I know I am the slave and you're the lord. The law of the land has made you my master. You can tie up my body, bind my hands, control my actions. You have the right of the stronger, and society confirms you in it. But over my will, Monsieur, you have no power. God alone can bend and subdue it . . . [and] if you don't control a woman's will, your power over her is a mockery.

Later she tells her husband, "I am prepared to help you and follow you because that is what I intend. You can condemn me but I shall never obey anyone but myself."

Indiana never quite lives up to the independence and boldness she achieves in this scene, but it is impossible not to sympathize with her and to despise the social system that so traps and smothers her. Also, it is easy to imagine that she might have been quite a different person had she been educated to think for herself and accustomed to freedom.

Indiana is also a significant example of a new tradition of 19th-century women novelists. It goes against the grain of the male-authored novels of the time, in which the adulterous wife is always doomed.

Other Works by George Sand

The Castle of Pictures and Other Stories: A Grandmother's Tales. Translated by Holly Erskine Hirko. New York: Feminist Press at the City University of New York, 1994.
Horace. Translated by Zack Rogow. San Francisco: Mercury House, 1995.

Works about George Sand

Jack, Belinda Elizabeth. *George Sand: A Woman's Life Writ Large.* London: Chatto and Windus, 1999.
Massardier-Kenney, Françoise. *Gender in the Fiction of George Sand.* Atlanta, Ga.: Rodopi, 2000.

San Juan, Epifanio (1938–) *poet, novelist*

Epifanio San Juan was born in Manila, Philippines. He received his B.A. degree from the University of the Philippines in 1958, left for the United States in 1960, and received his M.A. and Ph.D. from Harvard University in 1962 and 1965, respectively. He has taught in various universities, and is currently the professor and chair of the Department of Comparative American Cultures at Washington State.

San Juan has written poetry, fiction, and literary criticism, in both Tagalog and English. His works address important issues, such as class conflict and political struggle in Filipino history, which had remained largely uninvestigated. He seeks to define the central role of race and racism in America, using his experience as an Asian intellectual living in the United States. San Juan believes that literature constitutes an important critical tool that should be used to examine and reflect social change.

San Juan has written more than 100 scholarly articles, published in journals in Europe, Japan, the Philippines, and the United States. Although he is an accomplished poet and novelist, he is better known for his work in comparative cultural studies. His 1972 work, *Carlos Buloson and the Imagination of the Class Struggle,* on Carlos Bulosan, a famous Filipino-American writer of the

1940s and 1950s, narrates the biography of a talented Filipino writer who published several important and influential works before his death in 1956. Bulosan did not manage to return to the Philippines or to become a U.S. citizen, but his works are celebrated for their depictions of the Filipino experience.

Another work, *From Exile to Diaspora: Versions of the Filipino Experience in the United States,* (1998) examines the diasporic experience of Filipinos, who constitute one of the major immigrant groups to the United States within the past century. In this work, San Juan argues that even in their overseas location, Filipinos continue to assess and reexamine their colonial past in view of their present. Their zeal for democracy and equality remains as vital to their existence in their new adopted home as in their homeland. This book as well as *The Rise of the Filipino Working Class and Other Essays* (1978), attribute a great degree of agency to the Filipino people.

San Juan was awarded the Fulbright lectureship from 1987 to 1988. His book, *Racial Formations/Critical Transformations* (1992), won both the National Book Award and the Human Rights Award in 1993. He was also the recipient of the 1994 Katherine Newman Award from the Society for the Study of Multi-ethnic Literatures in the United States.

Other Works by Epifanio San Juan

From the Masses, to the Masses: Third World Literature and Revolution. Minneapolis, Minn.: MEP Publications, 1994.

On the Presence of Filipinos in the United States and Other Essays. Salinas, Calif.: SRMNK Publishers, 2007.

Saramago, José (1922–2010) *novelist*

José Saramago was born in Azinhaga, Portugal. His parents, José de Sousa and Maria da Piedade, were landless subsistence farmers. His last name, different from his father's, was written on his birth certificate as a joke by the public official who registered his birth. José de Sousa, the father, was called Saramago as a nickname because Saramago was a kind of wild green that was eaten in Azinhaga by the very poor.

Saramago was extremely close to his grandfather who, though illiterate, was an eloquent storyteller. The two of them, old man and young boy, would go on summer nights to sleep beneath a large fig tree by their house, and the grandfather would tell stories into the night. This formative experience instilled in Saramago a love of narrative and fantasy. Years later, he would begin to write in an attempt to preserve his memories of his grandfather and grandmother and his experiences of hearing stories under the fig tree.

Having moved to Lisbon, where Saramago's father worked as a policeman, Saramago went to elementary school and excelled. However, after a few years, his parents could no longer afford a liberal education for their son. He was sent to a technical school instead, where he trained to be a mechanic. Even at technical school, Saramago sought out the poems and stories contained in the literary anthologies that were used to teach grammar. He spent his evenings in the public library, reading whatever books he came across and practicing his French.

It was at this time that Saramago discovered the work of FERNANDO PESSOA, who was the inspiration for Saramago's novel *The Year of the Death of Ricardo Reis* (1984). Ricardo Reis was one of Pessoa's pseudonyms, and Saramago's novel explores the meaning of Pessoa's work in the face of the fascism that plagued Portugal in the 20th century.

Saramago worked for a few years as a mechanic and then managed to get a job as a civil servant. In 1950, he lost this job because of his affiliation with the Communist Party. He managed to find some work as a journalist and in the publishing industry, but as the political situation became more and more radically conservative, it became impossible for Saramago to find work anywhere. It was this situation that prompted him in 1976 at age 54 to dedicate himself to writing novels full time.

For the next 20 years, Saramago produced a steady stream of exceptional novels that blend allegorical symbolism, politics, and a unique narrative style. Finally, in 1998, Saramago was awarded the Nobel Prize in literature, the first Portuguese citizen to receive that award.

On June 10, 2010, Saramago died at his home in Lanzarote in the Canary Islands. His last published work was *The Notebook* (2010), a year's worth of blog entries. Begun in November 2008, *The Notebook* deals with topics ranging from the American election to the Israeli retaliation bombing of Gaza, from the world financial crisis to conversations with friends.

Critical Analysis

Saramago's novels share certain affinities with the MAGIC REALISM of some novels of Latin America, whose political contexts often center on colonialism. Though Portugal was a colonial power and not a colony, its separation from the rest of Europe, due to the fascist regimes that held power after World War II, created many similarities between Saramago's Portugal and Latin America.

He explores these political themes in his novel *The Stone Raft* (1986), in which the Iberian Peninsula breaks off from Europe and starts to float south on the ocean. *The Stone Raft* is a utopian novel in which the image of Portugal floating toward Africa represents Saramago's political vision of a world in which the oppressors in Europe come together with the oppressed peoples of developing nations.

In 1991, Saramago wrote *The Gospel According to Jesus Christ*. This book presents Christ in a very humanized form, emphasizing his family relationships and his love affair with Mary Magdalene. The novel was written as a critique of the strict Catholicism of Portugal and as an exploration of metaphysical doubt. The Portuguese government reacted strongly against it for its anti-Catholic views and vetoed its presentation for the European Literary Prize. In protest, Saramago moved to the Canary Islands.

In 1995, Saramago wrote *Blindness,* which is probably his most widely read book in the English-speaking world. It recounts an epidemic of a mysterious blindness that strikes people in an unnamed country seemingly at random. In his Nobel lecture, Saramago said of the book,

> Blind. The apprentice thought, "we are blind," and he sat down and wrote *Blindness* to remind those who might read it that we pervert reason when we humiliate life, that human dignity is insulted every day by the powerful of our world, that the universal lie has replaced the plural truths, that man stopped respecting himself when he lost the respect due to his fellow-creatures.

Saramago's recent publications include *Small Memories* (2006), an autobiographical work that looks back at his childhood, and *Death with Interruptions* (2009), which portrays the disruption when Death takes a holiday, then returns with a whole new process of announcing herself. *The Elephant's Journey,* the tale of a trip across Europe during the Reformation, was published posthumously in English in 2010 by Houghton Mifflin Harcourt.

Largely unknown outside of Europe before winning the Nobel Prize, Saramago quickly became the most popular Portuguese writer worldwide. His perceptiveness about human nature coupled with his strong moral and political concerns make his novels compelling. Saramago uses magic realism in a way that revitalizes his readers and stirs them to moral action.

Other Works by José Saramago

All the Names. Translated from the Portuguese by Margaret Jull Costa. New York: Harcourt, 1999.

Baltasar and Blimunda. Translated from the Portuguese by Giovanni Pontiero. San Diego: Harcourt Brace Jovanovich, 1987.

Journey to Portugal. Translated from the Portuguese and with notes by Amanda Hopkinson and Nick Caistor. London: Harvill Press, 2000.

Sargeson, Frank (1903–1982) *novelist*

Frank Sargeson was born to a middle-class family in Hamilton, New Zealand, completed his training as a solicitor in Auckland in 1926, and traveled in Britain and Europe for two years. He returned to New Zealand and took on various odd jobs before settling on his family land near Takapuna, remaining there for the rest of his life and making his living as a full-time writer. Between 1936 and 1954, Sargeson published 40 stories, most of which were completed before 1945. He continued writing in the postwar period, but he was unable to produce many works. Sargeson's writings reveal him as a writer who continued to develop and improve his art as he grew older. In his 60s, he experienced a new zest for writing, which culminated in the publication of his first complete collection of stories, *Collected Stories, 1935–1963* (1964). By the time Sargeson turned 70, he had begun to write a number of autobiographies and memoirs, veering away from the macabre and dark satirical style that characterize his writings of the previous decade. His trilogy of memoirs is, in comparison, anecdotal and lighthearted. These memoirs, which traces Sargeson's life as a writer from 1930 to 1970, are titled *Once Is Enough* (1973), *More Than Enough* (1975), and *Never Enough* (1977).

Sargeson's earlier works are remarkable for their stark depiction of human characters whose limited vision and lack of imagination represent the New Zealand working-class society. His central characters, usually the narrators of the stories, are often undistinguished and ordinary with puritanical upbringing that dictates actions and choices. Readers can appreciate these stories through Sargeson's mastery in conveying the poignant but realistic social circumstances of the working-class majority. In stories such as "The Making of a New Zealander" (1940) and "That Summer" (1946), the main characters are represented by unsettled laborers and unemployed men whose limited visions do not allow them to recognize and challenge the social forces that constitute the causes of their unhappy lives.

In the 1960s, Sargeson began to experiment with a different narrative technique. Using dark humor, he examines a new set of characters now taken from the middle classes whose better social positions ironically do not give them any advantage over the less-educated working classes of Sargeson's earlier short stories and novels. For instance, in the novel *The Hangover* (1967), Sargeson describes the dark world of a young university student caught between his duty to obey his puritanical but demented mother and his desire to indulge in the sensual pleasures of the city. The narratives of Sargeson's stories, unlike his earlier works, are elaborate and verbose.

In the 1970s, Sargeson returned to a form of narrative reminiscent of his earlier writings but dealing with subjects closer to his heart. These were mainly autobiographies and critical writings. He managed to complete two novellas before his death in 1982: *Sunset Village* (1976), a comic crime mystery, and *En Route* (1979), a story relating a journey of self-discovery, which was published together with a novella by Edith Campion, another New Zealand author, in a joint volume entitled *Tandem*. Sargeson's achievements in fiction enable New Zealand writing to be appreciated and recognized all over the world.

Other Works by Frank Sargeson

Conversation in a Train, and Other Critical Writing. New York: Oxford University Press, 1990.
I Saw in My Dream. Auckland, N.Z.: Auckland University Press, 1974.
Joy of the Worm. London: MacGibbon and Kee, 1969.
Man of England Now; With, I for One . . ., And, a Game of Hide and Seek. London: Martin, Brian and O'Keefe, 1972.
Memoirs of a Peon. London: MacGibbon and Kee, 1965; Auckland, N.Z.: Heinemann, 1974.
Never Enough: Places and People Mainly. Wellington, N.Z.: Reed. 1978.
Sunset Village. London: Martin, Brian, and O'Keefe, 1976.

Works about Frank Sargeson

King, Michael. *Frank Sargeson: A Life.* New York: Viking, 1995.

McEldowney, Dennis. *Frank Sargeson in His Time.* Dunedin, New Zealand: McIndoe, 1976.

Sarmiento, Félix Rubén García

See DARÍO, RUBÉN.

Sarraute, Nathalie (1900–1999) *novelist, essayist*

Pioneer and leading theorist of the French *nouveau roman* or NEW NOVEL, Nathalie Sarraute was born in Ivanova, Russia, on July 18 to intellectual parents: Her father worked in the field of sciences, and her mother published novels under the pseudonym of Vichrovski. They divorced, however, when Sarraute was two years old, and she went to live with her mother in Paris where, at a young age, French became her primary language. Her mother eventually remarried and the family returned to Russia when Sarraute was eight years old. She remained in close contact with her father, spending one month each year with him. When he began to encounter difficulties in Russia over his political views, he emigrated to France. Sarraute followed two years later to live with him in Paris and did not return again to her native Russia until 1936.

Sarraute received the bulk of her education at the Sorbonne, where she studied literature and law. In 1921, she spent a year at Oxford, prior to traveling to Berlin, where she continued to study legal science. She married Raymond Sarraute, a fellow law student, in 1925 and became a member of the French bar in 1926. She remained an active member until 1941 when she quit law to pursue a career as a writer.

Sarraute began writing while she was actively practicing law. Her first work, *Tropismes* (1932), was completed in 1932. It contains 24 short sketches based on nameless characters who are trapped by their interdependence on each other. Initially, the work was not well received or understood. It was rereleased in 1957 at the height of the popularity of the new novel style and saw greater success and critical acclaim.

During the 1950s and 1960s, Sarraute, alongside fellow writers such as ALAIN ROBBE-GRILLET, CLAUDE SIMON, MARGUERITE DURAS, and Michel Butor, worked to pioneer the new-novel format. Exemplified by such works as Sarraute's *Portrait d'un homme inconnu* (*Portrait of an Unknown Man,* 1951), which JEAN-PAUL SARTRE dubbed an antinovel, the new novel discarded the conventional ideas of structure. In her works, Sarraute routinely abandoned chronological order and shifted point of view freely to focus instead on the conscious and subconscious minds of her characters.

Central to Sarraute's works is the idea of interpersonal relationships. *Portrait of an Unknown Man* explores a daughter's difficult relationship with her miserly father. *Martereau* (1953) recounts the internal tensions that arise in a family structure that is made up of individuals whose personalities are vastly different. In both of these works, the constantly shifting point of view calls into question the narrator's reliability. In *Le planétarium* (1959), Sarraute does away with the narrator entirely in what is considered to be both an ironic comedy of manners and a parable of the creative process.

In the mid-1950s, Sarraute began to work on critical essays as she continued to write fiction. In *L'ère de soupçon* (*The Age of Suspicion,* 1956), she attempts to analyze her own creative process and the goals she had for her works. In later years, she also devoted time to writing critical analyses on the works of other authors, including PAUL VALÉRY and GUSTAVE FLAUBERT. Sarraute expanded her writing further to include work on a number of radio and stage plays and on her partial autobiography, *Childhood* (1983), which was adapted for the stage. Sarraute died at the end of a lengthy and productive career in Paris on October 19, 1999.

Other Works by Nathalie Sarraute

Collected Plays. Translated by Maria Jolas and Barbara Wright. New York: George Braziller, 1981.

Here: A Novel. Translated by Barbara Wright. New York: George Braziller, 1997.

Works about Nathalie Sarraute

Barbour, Sarah. *Nathalie Sarraute and the Feminist Reader: Identities in Process.* Lewisburg, Pa.: Bucknell University Press, 1993.

Knapp, Bettina. *Nathalie Sarraute.* Atlanta, Ga.: Rodopi, 1994.

Sartre, Jean-Paul (1905–1980) *novelist, playwright, essayist*

Best known for his ties to EXISTENTIALISM, a philosophy that emphasizes the ultimate importance of human freedom, as well as for his long-term relationship with fellow French philosopher and writer SIMONE DE BEAUVOIR, Jean-Paul Sartre was born in Paris on June 21. The son of a naval officer who died when Sartre was very young, he spent his early years living with his mother and his grandfather. After his mother's remarriage in 1917, he moved to La Rochelle, where he attended school. He graduated from the École Normale Supérieure in 1929. He was a student at the time of his first meeting with de Beauvoir, and their relationship, along with Sartre's studies and exposure to other existential philosophers, proved to be important influences on both his life and his works.

After graduation, Sartre secured employment as a teacher. In 1945, he left teaching to devote his time exclusively to writing. He also traveled extensively in Egypt, Greece, Italy, and Berlin, where he studied the works of German philosophers Martin Heidegger and Edmund Husserl. At this time, Heidegger's most important work, *Being and Time* (1927), had been released. Uniting Søren Kierkegaard's and FRIEDRICH NIETZSCHE's views on existentialism with Husserl's concept of phenomenology, Sartre began developing his own existential philosophy. During the late 1930s, Sartre began to gather around him a small group of intellectuals; together, they spent hours at cafés on the Left Bank, discussing philosophy and the importance of freedom.

In 1939, Sartre was drafted to serve in World War II. Less than a year later, he was captured and imprisoned in Germany, where he remained until 1941. Here, Sartre experienced firsthand the ramifications of the loss of what he valued most, his personal freedom. On returning to Paris, he joined the Resistance and put his growing talents as a writer to good use penning articles about the Resistance for magazines such as *Les Lettres Française* and *Combat.*

Sartre was deeply affected by his experience in the war and when it was over, decided to devote himself full-time to writing and political activism. He founded *Le Temps Modernes* (1946–   ), a monthly journal dedicated to literature and politics. Although he never became a member of the Communist Party, he worked closely with communists in hopes of finding a solution to the problems of poverty and the poor social conditions of the working class. In his writing, he spent a great deal of time and effort trying to reconcile existentialism with marxism.

Aside from his work as a writer, Sartre exemplified his own beliefs by speaking out for freedom for oppressed peoples, such as the Hungarians in the mid- to late 1950s and the Czechoslovakians in the late 1960s. He became involved in numerous humanitarian causes and, as a result, twice had bombs set off in his place of residence. In 1967, he served as leader of the war-crimes tribunal, which investigated the actions of U.S. soldiers in Indochina, and, in 1968, he supported the student anti-Vietnam War protestors. He was also arrested in 1970 for selling an underground newspaper publication.

In 1975, Sartre's eyesight began to fail, and his health declined rapidly. No longer able to write, he nevertheless remained vocal and active; toward the end of his life, he was completely blind. He died on

April 15, 1980, in Paris. His legacy remains as one of the strongest and most influential voices of the existentialist movement.

Critical Analysis

Sartre's first novel, *La nausée* (1938), was greatly influenced by Husserl's concept of phenomenology, a movement devoted to describing experiences exactly as they present themselves with no reliance on theories, assumptions or deductions. Transferring this concept to human existence, Sartre's novel explores the idea that life has no essential purpose and that the main character is haunted by feelings of horror and nausea as he attempts to come to terms with the banality of life. During this period, Sartre also published a collection of short stories and a novella, *Le mûr* (1938; published in English as *Intimacy*), which dealt with similar themes of identity and freedom.

Sartre's nonfiction work *L'être et le néant* (*Being and Nothingness*, 1943) begins to formulate the foundation of his own philosophy. He relates the idea of existence to his belief that it is composed of two distinct parts. In the first part are those things that exist simply because they are. They exist "en-soi" or *in* themselves. Human beings, however, belong to the second part, existing "pour-soi" or *for* themselves. According to Sartre, the demarcation between the two parts of existence is based on the fact that humans possess consciousness, in particular an awareness of mortality; thus, human beings exist in a constant state of dread. Sartre's premise, which he examines in later works, was this: To give meaning to those things that exist "en-soi," it is necessary for humans first to detach themselves from those things.

The importance of accepting responsibility for one's own actions is, therefore, also an essential part of Sartre's philosophy. His first dramatic work, *Les mouches* (*The Flies*, 1943), examines this theme against the backdrop of ancient Greece, using the mythological characters of Electra and Orestes. Orestes, choosing to act by killing his murderous mother, rejects the guilt that has paralyzed his city since Agamemnon's death. His second play, *Huis-clos* (*No Exit*, 1944), presents three characters in a room with no way out, learning to face the truth that "Hell is other people."

Sartre also wrote works of literary criticism that explore the responsibility of artists in relation to their art, beginning with *Qu'est-ce la littérature?* (*What Is Literature?*, 1947). He followed this in the same year with a study of Baudelaire, and in 1952 he published a biography of Jean Genet, *Saint-Genet, comédien et martyr* (*Saint Genet, Actor and Martyr*). Sartre admired Genet for being free of the constraints of convention and making his own personal distinctions between right and wrong. Sartre was among a group of writers (including Albert Camus and Jean Cocteau) who in 1948 successfully petitioned for Genet's release from a life sentence for burglary. From 1960 to 1971, he worked on a massive critical biography of Gustave Flaubert, *L'idiot de la famille* (*The Family Idiot*). The work reached five volumes but remained unfinished, as in the last years of his life Sartre's failing eyesight prevented him from writing.

In 1963, Sartre published his memoir of childhood, *Les mots* (*The Words*), in which he explored how language and literacy changed the consciousness of the growing child. In that year, the Nobel committee chose to honor Sartre with the Nobel Prize in literature, but Sartre refused to accept the award, feeling that it represented bourgeois values he rejected. Nonetheless, his reputation continued to grow, and his funeral drew thousands of mourners.

Other Works by Jean-Paul Sartre

Colonialism and Neo-Colonialism. Translated by Steve Brewer, Azzedine Haddour, and Terry McWilliams. London: Routledge, 2001.
Notebook for an Ethics. Translated by Davis Pellauer. Chicago: University of Chicago Press, 1992.
Truth and Existence. Translated by Adrian van den Hoven. Chicago: University of Chicago Press, 1992.

Works about Jean-Paul Sartre

Gordon, Haim. *Sartre's Philosophy and the Challenge of Education.* Lewiston, N.Y.: E. Mellen Press, 2001.

Howells, Christina, ed. *The Cambridge Companion to Sartre.* New York: Cambridge University Press, 1992.

Kamber, Richard. *On Sartre.* Belmont, Calif.: Wadsworth/Thomson Learning, 2000.

McBride, William L., ed. *Sartre's Life, Times and Vision-du-Monde.* New York: Garland Press, 1997.

Satyanarayana, Visvanatha (1895–1976)
poet, novelist, dramatist

Visvanatha Satyanarayana was born in Andhra Pradesh, India. He wrote in Telugu and is the author of more than 100 works. This alone places him among the most important figures in Telugu fiction. He has also rewritten ancient Hindu epics such as the *The Ramayana,* which dates from the fourth century B.C. When his version of the epic, *Ramayana—The Celestial Tree* appeared in 1953, it was seen as controversial because of his transformation of the original, formal Sanskrit into a more conventional style. This translation, however, made it accessible to a wider audience, and in 1971, it won him the Jnanpith Award (India's highest literary award).

Satyanarayana was widely read in European literature. One of his novels, *Veyipadagalu* (*A Thousand Hoods,* 1933–34), was inspired by the novels on industrialization by British writers Thomas Hardy (1840–1928) and D. H. Lawrence (1885–1930). Satyanarayana saw in their work his own belief that great literature is not only about issues but also form. Like them, Satyanarayana believed important themes such as social reform should not overshadow the mechanics of the literary genre and that the social message should not subsume the aesthetic element of the literary work.

Satyanarayana's literary legacy includes poetry, short stories, essays, plays, and novels. In 1970, he was made a Fellow of the Sahitya Akademi, which is reserved for the "immortals of Indian Literature."

A Work about Visvanatha Satyanarayana

S. P. Sen, ed. *History in Modern Indian Literature.* Calcutta, India: Institute of Historical Studies Press, 1975.

scapigliatura

A mid-19th-century Italian bohemian movement in art and literature, often associated with the French DECADENCE movement, *scapigliatura* takes its name from the title of a novel by one of the group's founding members, Cletto Arrighi, *The Scapigliatura and February 6th* (1862). In the book, the term refers to the restlessness and independent spirit of its characters, all ranging in age from 25 to 30 years old. Founded in Milan, the movement was greatly influenced by the works of BAUDELAIRE, and Edgar Allan Poe, as well as those of the French symbolist poets and German romantic writers (*see* SYMBOLISM and ROMANTICISM).

The main characteristics of the movement include an intense aversion to the sentimentalism and conformity of romanticism. In particular, artists of the *scapigliatura* movement held a common conviction that truth was the only valid form of poetry and art; anything less than brutal honesty was seen as substandard and unimportant. The works that came from this school featured bizarre and often pathological elements, as well as direct, realistic narration and vivid, often grotesque description, a theme held in common with French decadent writers. A second aim of *scapigliatura,* similar to many avant-garde and bohemian movements, was the rejection of bourgeois values and of the right to ownership of property.

The group was never large, consisting only of a select few artists, poets, and musicians. Its primary leader was Iginio Ugo Tachetti, who began his education in classical studies and was well acquainted with English literature. After a brief stint in the army, he began writing short stories and spending his free time in Milan, where he met with other members of the group, including the novelists and chief spokespeople for the movement, Giuseppe Rovani and Emilio Praga. Tachetti's works exemplified much of what the group sought to attain. He died young, at age 30, refusing to the end to accept hypocrisy, tradition, or conventions.

In the end, the group's most lasting influence on world literature came in its advancement of the avant-garde. The writers associated with the movement were largely considered isolated avant-garde writers who chose to live their lives and dedicate their art to revolt against middle-class conformity.

A Work about *Scapigliatura*

Del Principe, David. *Rebellion, Death, and Aesthetics in Italy: the Demons of Scapigliatura.* Madison, Wisc.: Fairleigh Dickinson University Press, 1996.

Scherzer, Rosalie

See AUSLANDER, ROSE.

Schiller, Friedrich von (1759–1805) *playwright, essayist, poet*

Friedrich von Schiller was born in Marbach, Württenberg (present-day Germany), to Johannes Kaspar Schiller, an army officer and surgeon, and Elizabeth Schiller. Johannes Schiller was a pious Lutheran and a harsh disciplinarian. He disapproved of his son's interests in literature and theater and many times forbade him to write poetry. At age 14, Schiller entered an academy to study law but subsequently decided to study medicine instead. His medical education was short-lived, however: He was expelled in 1780 for writing a controversial essay, *On Relation Between Man's Animal and Spiritual Nature,* which openly questioned the official theological dogma of the church.

On his return to Marbach, Schiller was forced to join his father's regiment of the army. Despite his father's strong efforts to suppress this "foolish" activity, Schiller continued to write. Schiller did not find the life of the soldier appealing and

consciously avoided his duties as much as possible. Thoroughly resisting his father, Schiller continued to write and was almost arrested for neglecting his military duties.

Schiller's first play, *The Robbers* (1781), depicts a noble outlaw, Karl Moor, who violently and passionately rejects the conservative and reactionary notions of his father in his quest for justice. The play simultaneously reflected Schiller's own conflict with his father and the ideological struggle between the conservative and liberal political forces in Germany. The play was warmly greeted not only in Germany, especially among the university students, but also among the romantic writers in England. The play remains a ground-breaking work in the corpus of German romanticism. The major theme of liberty that appears in *The Robbers* permeates virtually all of Schiller's major works. The play *Don Carlos* (1787) similarly depicts a conflict between a father and son. *Don Carlos* is set during the reign of Philip II of Spain. It portrays the inner struggle of his eldest son, torn between passionate love and the vile political intrigues of his father's ministers in the court.

Between 1783 and 1784, Schiller worked as a playwright and stage manager for the theater in Mannheim. With the assistance of JOHANN WOLFGANG GOETHE, Schiller was appointed professor of history at the University of Jena in 1789. For the next three years, Schiller worked almost exclusively on history, writing an account of the Thirty Years' War. Schiller had to give up the professorship because of declining health. He worked as an assistant to Goethe, then the director of the theater at the Weimar Court.

Schiller also distinguished himself as a poet. "Ode to Joy" (1785), later set to music by Ludwig van Beethoven, is currently the anthem of the European Union. In *Wilhelm Tell* (1804), Schiller describes the close relationship with nature shared by the Swiss hero. The characteristics of Schiller's works—in their attention to nature, human emotions, and the ideals of liberty and political freedom—became the working definition of ROMANTICISM.

Schiller's interest in history resulted in several historical plays. *Mary Stuart* (1800) describes the turbulent relationship between Elizabeth I and Mary Queen of Scots in the final days before Mary's execution. The captive, wild environment of the castle of Fothernghay provides a dark, melancholy background that amplifies Mary as a tragic, romantic figure in the play. The dramatic trilogy *Wallenstein* (1796–1799) depicted Germany during the Thirty Years' War. Schiller captured the deep fragmentation of society along the lines of religion. The German national identity and the idea of nationhood is juxtaposed against the ruinous conflict created by the religious strife and political scheming of the rulers.

Schiller also wrote essays on topics ranging from religion and politics to art and humanity's relationship with nature. Many of Schiller's ideas were influenced by the works of the famous 18th-century German philosopher Immanuel Kant. In *On the Aesthetic Education of Man* (1795) Schiller deals with the bloody aftermath of the French Revolution and how it changed an understanding of notions of freedom. The key to freedom, the essay argues, is the fundamental aesthetic development of the individual and society. According to the essay, the experience of the sublime and the beautiful—two important philosophical categories in the works of Kant—is truly fundamental to one's education. A true sense of freedom and liberty is tightly connected to this experience.

In *On the Naïve and Sentimental in Literature* (1795), Schiller creates a series of dialectical dichotomies, such as feeling and thought, nature and culture, finitude and infinity, and finally sentimental and naïve modes of writing. Although describing himself as a sentimental or "reflective" writer, Schiller paid homage to his close friend Goethe, whom he described as the ultimate archetype of the naïve genius. Here, *naïve* is not used in the conventional sense of the word, but rather as a philosophical term that describes something that is utterly pure and good and closely connected with nature.

Friedrich von Schiller is considered today to be one of the foremost German writers. His drama and poetry are significant contributions to the literature of the romantic movement, although his reputation and legacy is recognized significantly more in Europe than it is in the United States. His magnificent control and elegant use of the German language inspired generations of readers, writers, and poets, and his works have had a long-lasting impact on the formation of the German national literature, as well as the German national identity.

Other Works by Friedrich von Schiller

Essays. New York: Continuum, 1993.
Schiller's Five Plays: The Robbers, Passion and Politics, Don Carlos, Mary Stuart, and Joan of Arc. Translated by Robert McDonald. New York: Consortium Books, 1998.

Works about Friedrich von Schiller

Carlyle, Thomas. *The Life of Friedrich Schiller: Comprehending and Examination of His Works*. Portland, Ore.: University Press of the Pacific, 2001.
Sharpe, Lesley. *Friedrich Schiller: Drama, Thought, and Politics*. Cambridge: Cambridge University Press, 1991.

Schmitz, Ettore
See SVEVO, ITALO.

Schulz, Bruno (1892–1942) *novelist, artist*
Bruno Schulz, who is considered a major 20th-century Polish prose writer, was born in 1892 and shot to death by a Nazi officer in 1942. Born to Jewish parents in the provincial Galician town of Drohobycz, in what was then Poland, Schulz was interested in graphics and studied architecture at Lvov University and in Vienna. From 1924 to 1941, Schulz taught drawing at a Polish high school in his hometown. Although he was unhappy in his profession, he had no other source of income.

Schulz's life was solitary and isolated, peopled through his imagination and the many identities that his religion and cultural connections provided. His first writings were short stories about the people with whom he came into contact in his hometown, and, at first, some of his colleagues discouraged him from continuing to write. However, his work was brought to the attention of the novelist Zofia Nalkowska, who recognized his talent and encouraged him to continue. His first book, a novel-memoir, *The Cinnamon Shops* (1934), is better known in English-speaking countries as *The Street of Crocodiles*. Three years later, *Sanitorium Under the Sign of the Hourglass* (1937) was published. Shulz created his own illustrations for his early works. In 1938, he received the prestigious Golden Laurel award from the Polish Academy of Letters for *The Cinnamon Shops*.

During the early years of World War II, as part of the nonaggression pact agreed upon in 1939 by Russia and Germany, the city of Drohobycz had fallen under the control of Soviet authorities. However, after the breaching of that agreement, the Nazis occupied the city and created a large Jewish ghetto there. Although Schulz was confined to the town ghetto after the German occupation, he was protected by a Nazi officer, Felix Landau, who admired his artistic talents. During the last weeks of his life, Schulz painted a mural in his unique style for Landau's home (later painted over and forgotten). Schulz met a tragic end at the hand of another Nazi officer, Karl Günther, who was Landau's rival.

There are two versions of the incident that led to Schulz's horrible death. In one, Günther lost to Landau at a game of cards and shot Shulz in a fit of angry revenge. Another version suggests that Landau had shot Günther's "favorite Jew," a dentist, and in a fit of revenge Günther killed Landau's "favorite Jew."

The ghetto was liquidated in 1943, and thereafter the city was once again occupied by the Soviets; it remains part of Ukraine today. The existence of the mural—found in 2001 after a long search by Benjamin Geissler, a German documentary filmmaker—led to a major disagreement between Yad Vashem, the Israeli memorial museum to Jews who died in the Holocaust, and Ukrainian authorities.

After the mural was restored, representatives of Yad Vashem purchased segments of the mural and smuggled them out of the country. Yad Vashem contended that it had purchased the segments legally and had a moral right to the fragments because Schulz's death was a result of his Judaism, not his nationality. The Ukrainian government, however, did not accept that contention, and there was a backlash of anger against Yad Vashem on the part of both Poles and Ukrainians, for whom Schulz is a beloved writer. Eventually, a compromise was reached between the two parties: the existing fragments that had remained in the Ukraine are now in the Bruno Schulz Museum in Drohobycz, and the fragments at Yad Vashem have been declared Ukrainian property. However, these are on long-term loan to Yad Vashem, where they can be seen by museum visitors. The fascinating history of the mural has been dramatized in Geissler's film *Finding Pictures*.

It is believed that at the time of his death Schulz was in the middle of writing a novel called *The Messiah*, but the manuscript has never been found. The same fate was shared by some of his short stories, which had been submitted to magazines but were never found. In 1975, a collection of his letters written in Polish was published. His two best-known works, *The Street of Crocodiles (Cinnamon Shops)* and *Sanatorium Under the Sign of the Hourglass*, as well as *The Complete Fiction of Bruno Schulz*, have all been translated into English. *The Street of Crocodiles* is a collection of short stories about Schulz's father and the city of Drohobycz. His father is portrayed as battling the forces of routine conformity in the town in a literary rendition that moves from the real and down to earth to the fantastic and surreal at the author's will. *Sanatorium Under the Sign of the Hourglass* is a collection of short stories in a novel format that, in a dreamlike, poetic fashion, deals with the death of the narrator's father.

Schulz's life and works have intrigued many writers. David Grossman, the Israeli author, wrote about Schulz in his novel *See Under: Love*. In it, Grossman imagines that Schulz did not remain in his hometown to be shot, but instead undertook a bizarre, imaginary sea journey. The American author Cynthia Ozick has written a novel, *The Messiah of Stockholm*, in which the main character believes that he is Schulz's son and can get his hands on his father's unfinished final novel. Amir Gutfreund, an Israeli writer, included two short stories about Schulz in his collection of stories titled *The Shoreline Mansions*, and the Polish writer and critic Jerzy Ficowski researched Schulz's life and work for 60 years before publishing *Regions of the Great Heresy*, a biographical portrait of Schulz's life. Not only does Schulz's life, death, and work intrigue writers, but it also has led to several film and theatrical adaptations of his works.

Neither Schulz's writing nor his art is easily categorized, but they have been characterized as sublime and evocative, highly original, and profound. He maintained an intensely private inner world—essentially a blend of his Eastern European cultural origins combined with his childhood dreams, magic, and erotica. In his writings, Schulz's world is an entity entirely its own, unregulated by the laws of time. In fact, Schulz used time for his own purposes, removing it from the world of reality and treating it as an independent reality with a life of its own. Appreciation for the quality of Schulz's literary skills and his art has increased steadily with time, and in the final decade of the 20th century, his works were highlighted at two major museum exhibitions in Jerusalem and Warsaw.

Another Work by Bruno Schulz

The Complete Fiction of Bruno Schulz. New York: Walker and Company, 1989.

Works about Bruno Shulz

Banks, Brian R. *Muse & Messiah: The Life, Imagination & Legacy of Bruno Schulz*. London: Inkermen Press, 2006.
Ficowski, Jerzy. *Regions of the Great Heresy*. Translated and edited by Theodosia Robertson. New York: W. W. Norton & Company, 2003.
Grossman, David. *See Under: Love*. Translated by Betsy Rosenberg. New York: Washington Square Press, 1989.

Schwarz-Bart, Simone (Simone Bruman) (1938–) *novelist*

Simone Schwarz-Bart was born Simone Bruman in Charente-Maritime, France, to a governess and a military man, according to a 1973 *Elle* interview; however, the novelist has since named the Guadeloupean capital Pointe-à-Pitre as her birthplace. Bruman was educated at Pointe-à-Pitre, Dakar, and Paris, where she met and married her husband, novelist André Schwarz-Bart, in the early 1960s.

Simone and André Schwarz-Bart coauthored *Un plat de porc aux bananes vertes* (*A Dish of Pork with Green Bananas*, 1967), which employs nonlinear narratives, and *La mulâtresse Solitude* (*A Woman Named Solitude*, 1972), a fictional biography of a mulatto female struggling to exist in society. In 1972, Simone Schwarz-Bart also published *Pluie et vent sur Télumée Miracle* (*The Bridge of Beyond*, 1972), in which Télumée, the novel's female heroine, explores and consequently revises the painful history of her people.

One year after her return to Guadeloupe in 1978, Schwarz-Bart published *Ti Jean l'horizon* (*Between Two Worlds*, 1979). In this novel, she uses MAGIC REALISM (elements of dreams, magic, fantasy, or fairy tales) and science fiction to tell the adventures of Ti Jean, a Guadeloupean folk hero, and to deconstruct traditional myths of Antillean identity.

All of Schwarz-Bart's novels have been internationally well received in multiple publications, including *The New York Times Book Review*, *Savacou*, and *Nouvelle Revue Française*. Her fictional retelling of personal Caribbean histories contributes to international contemporary expressions and examinations of the painful repercussions of patriarchal domination and exile.

Other Works by Simone Schwarz-Bart

In Praise of Black Women, Volume 1: Ancient African Queens, with André Schwarz-Bart. Translated by Rose-Myriam Réjouis, Stephanie K. Turner, and Val Vinokurov. Madison: University of Wisconsin Press, 2001.

In Praise of Black Women, Volume 2: Heroines of the Slavery Era, with André Schwarz-Bart. Translated by Rose-Myriam Réjouis, Stephanie K. Turner, and Val Vinokurov. Madison: University of Wisconsin Press, 2002.

In Praise of Black Women, Volume 3: Modern African Women, with André Schwarz-Bart. Translated by Rose-Myriam Réjouis, Stephanie K. Turner, and Val Vinokurov. Madison: University of Wisconsin Press, 2003.

Your Handsome Captain. Translated by Jessica Harris. In *Plays by Women: An International Anthology.* Edited by Francoise Kourilsky and Catherine Temerson. New York: Ubu Repertory Theatre Publications, 1989.

Works about Simone Schwarz-Bart

Karamcheti, Indira. "The Geographics of Marginality: Place and Textuality in Simone Schwarz-Bart and Anita Desai." In *Feminist Explorations of Literary Space.* Edited by Margaret R. Higonnet and Joan Templeton. Amherst: University of Massachusetts Press, 1994, pp. 125–146.

McKinney, Kitzie. "Memory, Voice, and Metaphor in the Works of Simone Schwarz-Bart." In *Postcolonial Subjects: Francophone Women Writers.* Edited by Mary Jean Green et al. Minneapolis: University of Minnesota Press, 1996, pp. 22–41.

Sebald, W. G. (1944–2001)
novelist, educator

W. G. Sebald, the distinctive novelist of memory, the Holocaust, and Germany during World War II, was born Winfried Georg Maximilian Sebald on May 18, 1944, in Wertach im Allgäu, Germany, a village of about 1,000 inhabitants in the Alpine region of Bavaria. One of four children (the only son), Max, as Sebald was known familiarly, was the son of a soldier, Georg, from a glassmaking family, and Rosa, the daughter of a local chief of police. Sebald's father joined the army in 1929, rising to the rank of captain under the Nazi regime. Sebald has said that his father was held as a prisoner of war until 1947 and then lived apart from his family, working in a neighboring town. Consequently, Sebald was raised by his policeman grandfather during his formative years. "My parents came from working-class, small-peasant, farm-laborer backgrounds," Sebald told an interviewer, "and had made the grade during the fascist years; my father came out of the army as a captain. For most of those years, I didn't know what class we belonged to."

Sebald's family continued to prosper as Germany rebounded in the post–World War II era, occupying a "proper" place in lower-middle-class German society. It was this social stratum, as Sebald has described it, that maintained the most steadfast silence about the war and the Nazi atrocities. Sebald attended high school in Obersdorf, and it was there that his class was first shown newsreels of the Allied liberation of Belsen, one of the Nazi concentration, or death, camps. "Until I was 16 or 17," Sebald said, "I had heard practically nothing about the history that preceded 1945. Only when we were 17 were we confronted with a documentary film of the opening of the Belsen camp. There it was, and we somehow had to get our minds around it—which of course we didn't. . . . So it took years to find out what had happened."

Sebald studied German literature at Freiburg University, taking his degree in 1965. The Auschwitz trials took place in Frankfurt while Sebald was at university, and Sebald came to the profoundly unsettling realization that the defendants were very similar to the people with whom he had grown up. The witnesses for the prosecution, Jews who had survived the horrors of Auschwitz, forcefully confirmed for Sebald the reality of the Holocaust, namely the Nazi slaughter of millions of Jews, as never before and impressed upon him the widespread cultural amnesia of postwar Germans.

In 1966, Sebald became an assistant lecturer at the University of Manchester and four years later took a lectureship in German in the school of European studies at the recently founded University of East Anglia. "I scarcely spoke English, and coming from a backwoods, I found it difficult to adapt," he said. "But I stuck it out; I got to like the place." In 1967, he married his wife Ute, and they had a daughter, Anna. Reportedly, his lectures at East Anglia were sardonic and challenging, delivered with a dry, ironical wit. He began paradoxically to feel at home in East Anglia, where he took long rambles and became a connoisseur of the isolation of the area. Having settled in the village of Wymondham, Sebald wrote a series of monographs that garnered for him a formidable reputation as a critic of German-language literature.

In 1987, he was appointed to a chair of European literature at East Anglia and, in 1989, became the founding director of the British Center for Literary Translation. While Sebald moved up in the academic ranks, however, European studies was in decline. The shrinking pool of British students with the interest or the language skills to study German added to Sebald's sense of isolation.

Living in England, however, gave Sebald a new vantage from which to reflect upon Germany, especially the history of political persecution—the incarceration and systematic extermination of whole peoples and groups in society—which his neighbors carefully avoided mentioning after the war. Sebald became even more aware of the difficulties and pitfalls of this subject. When Germans began to address the Nazi past, many did so in, as Sebald has observed, "not always acceptable forms." Therefore, Sebald took it upon himself to address the Holocaust and war years with the utmost subtlety and care. Also, he became all the more interested in the Holocaust as a result of living in England, where he began to encounter real people to whom these nightmarish events actually had happened. One character in Sebald's *The Emigrants* (1993) is based partly on his Manchester landlord, who was a Jewish refugee. "You could grow up in Germany in the postwar years without ever meeting a Jewish person," Sebald has remarked. "There were small communities in Frankfurt or Berlin, but in a provincial town in south Germany, Jewish people didn't exist. The subsequent realization was that they had been in all those places, as doctors, cinema ushers, owners of garages, but they had disappeared—or had been disappeared." Living in England allowed Sebald to go through a process of realization, which in turn allowed him to produce the extraordinary fiction of the 1990s that would bring him literary renown.

In 1988, he published *Nach Der Natur: Ein Elementargedicht*, a prose poem about the destruction of nature, published in English as *After Nature* (2002). It was followed by an elliptical novel *Schwindel Gefuhle* (*Vertigo*, 1990), in which a morose narrator, who is evidently a stand-in for Sebald himself, ambles through European cities (Vienna, Venice, Milan, Verona) trying in vain to connect the past with the present. Eventually, he traverses the Austrian border into Bavaria and into the village of W. One reviewer called it "a quest novel, but in a wary, suspicious mode." *Die Ausgewanderten: Vier Lange Erzahlungen* (*The Emigrants*, 1992) records its narrator's investigations into the mysterious memories of others, four emigrants who move from country to country but carry the history of 20th-century war and atrocity with them. Each of these stories dramatizes in subtle and violent ways, as one reviewer noted, the "treacherous enchantment of memory itself." *Austerlitz* (2001) deals with Jacques Austerlitz, who is brought up by Welsh Calvinist foster parents and in middle age suddenly "recovers" lost memories from his youth during the 1930s. Specifically, Austerlitz recalls having arrived in England and Wales from Prague on the Kindertransport, a refugee network in Britain of some 10,000 unaccompanied Jewish children in 1938–39. Austerlitz's recovery of his long-buried memories becomes an act of historical excavation into a painful episode, one in which survival requires dislocation and the erasure of identity.

Sebald was inspired by watching a BBC documentary on Susi Bechhofer, who in the 1990s, like the fictional Austerlitz, in midlife remembered coming to Wales on the Kindertransport.

By the end of the 1990s, Sebald's work was regularly being translated into English and had garnered a large American audience. He was widely considered a candidate for the Nobel Prize when in December 2001 he was killed at the age of 57 in an automobile accident in Norfolk, England, near his home. The former poet laureate of Great Britain, Andrew Motion has commemorated this loss in a poem entitled, "WG Sebald" in which he addresses his departed friend.

> . . . , I watch you start
> a new journey, . . .
> keeping your attention fixed on every dead
>   thing,
> yourself included, as it accelerates and
>   passes
> ahead of you into the future, . . .

Critical Analysis

Die Ringe des Saturn: Eine Englische Walfahrt (*The Rings of Saturn,*1995) takes up the abiding themes of Sebald's work in the context of an English walking tour. "In August 1992, when the dog days were drawing to an end," he begins, "I set off to walk the county of Suffolk, in the hope of dispelling the emptiness that takes hold of me whenever I have completed a long stint of work. . . . At all events, in retrospect I became preoccupied not only with the unaccustomed sense of freedom but also with the paralysing horror that had come over me at various times when confronted with the traces of destruction, reaching far back into the past, that were evident even in that remote place." Melancholy, depression, paralysis are all symptoms of history and the specter of annihilation and destruction it carries with it. These are the feelings that set Sebald's stories in motion, stories invariably about humans in motion, searching the past to account for the ways in which it haunts the present.

In *The Rings of Saturn*, the narrator observes East Anglia's abandoned fisheries, polluted tides, decayed estates, seeing in them the inevitable course of destruction and erasure beneath the veneer of prosperity. The narrator contemplates "the immense power of emptiness." Whether addressing the vagaries of memory, the legacy of Nazi atrocity, or the inevitable corrosive changes in English land, Sebald finds a powerful and haunting way to articulate this emptiness.

Other Works by W. G. Sebald

Campo Santo. New York: Random House, 2005.
On the Natural History of Destruction. New York: Random House, 2003.

Works about W. G. Sebald

Denham, Scott, and Mark McCulloh, eds. *W. G. Sebald: History, Memory, Trauma (Interdisciplinary German Cultural Studies 1).* Berlin: Walter de Gruyter, 2006.
Long, J. J. *W. G. Sebald: Image, Archive, Modernity.* New York: Columbia University Press, 2008.

Seferiadis, Giorgos
See SEFERIS, GEORGE.

Seferis, George (Giorgos Seferiadis)
(1900–1971) *poet*

George Seferis was born Giorgos Seferiadis in Smyrna, Turkey. As a child, he attended school in Smyrna and at the Gymnasium in Athens and, in 1918, moved with his family to Paris, where he attended the University of Paris to study law and where he also developed an interest in literature.

After graduating, Seferis returned to Athens in 1925. One year later, he was admitted to the Royal Greek Ministry of Foreign Affairs. In addition to his success as a writer, he had a long and successful diplomatic career. His final diplomatic post was as Royal Greek Ambassador to

Great Britain from 1957 to 1962. Throughout his career, Seferis received numerous awards and recognitions. Included among these were honorary doctoral degrees from Cambridge University in 1960, Oxford University in 1964, the University of Salonika in 1964, and Princeton University in 1965.

His background in law and diplomacy, combined with his love of literature, allowed Seferis to make a profound impact on Greek poetry. His travels throughout the world gave him numerous ideas and provided the rich backgrounds for many of his works. What he experienced through war and through political negotiation influenced his decision to write poetry, almost exclusively with the themes of alienation, wandering, and death. Seferis's poetry is often surrealistic and always highly symbolic, sometimes to the point of being cryptic and difficult to interpret. He often invokes classical Greek themes as a means of exploring 20th-century Greek lifestyles and social consciousness.

Seferis's earliest poetry collections exist in two volumes. *Strophe* (*Turning Point*, 1931) consists of rhymed lyrical poems that were strongly influenced by the symbolist movement (*see* SYMBOLISM). His second collection, *E Sterma* (*The Cistern*, 1932), portrays through vivid imagery the idea that humankind must keep its true nature hidden from the everyday world that seeks to alienate and ignore humanity.

In his later poetry, Seferis shifts his focus to include a pervasive sense of awareness of the past, in particular Greek history. This awareness is not merely that of a historian but rather is indicative of the poet's desire to relate past events to those of the present and, ultimately, the future. This theme first becomes apparent in *Mythistorema* (1935; translated 1960), a collection consisting of 24 short poems that, when read as a group, translate the Odyssean myths into modern situations and circumstances. Seferis continued to develop these themes, using Homer's Odyssey as his symbolic basis, in several subsequent collections: *Book of Exercises* (1940), *Logbook I* (1940), *Logbook II*

(1944), *Thrush* (1947), and *Logbook III* (1955). One notable exception to his use of Odysseus as a solitary source, however, occurs in "The King of Asine," one of the poems in *Logbook*. This poem is considered by many critics to be Seferis's greatest achievement because of its historical importance. This historical source consists of a single reference in Homer's *Iliad* to the King of Asine, who remains otherwise an all-but-forgotten character in Greek history.

Seferis did not limit himself to poetry and diplomatic relations, however. In addition to his collected poetic works, he published one book of essays, *Dokimes* (1944; translated *Essays on the Greek Style*, 1962). He also translated several works by T. S. Eliot and produced *Copies* (1965), a collection of translations from American, English, and French poets.

In the later years of his life, Seferis returned to writing in a style similar to that of his early poetry. His final collection of poems, *Three Secret Poems* (1966), contains, much like his first collection *Strophe*, 28 short lyrical poems that are highly surrealistic in nature. In 1963, Seferis was the first Greek writer to win the Nobel Prize in literature "for his eminent lyrical writing, inspired by a deep feeling for the Hellenic world of culture."

Another Work by George Seferis

Keeley, Edmund, ed. *Complete Poems of George Seferis*. Translated by Philip Sherrard. Greenwich, U.K.: Anvil Press Poetry, 1989.

Works about George Seferis

Hadas, Rachel. *Form, Cycle, Infinity: Landscape Imagery in the Poetry of Robert Frost and George Seferis*. Cranbury, N.J.: Bucknell University Press, 1985.

Kelley, Edmund, and Philip Sherrard, eds. *George Seferis*. Princeton, N.J.: Princeton University Press, 1995.

Tsatsos, Ioanna. *My Brother George Seferis*. Translated by Jean Demos. St. Paul, Minn.: North Central Publishing Company, 1982.

Seifert, Jaroslav (1901–1986) *poet*

Jaroslav Seifert was born in Prague, Czechoslovakia. He quit school at a young age to work for the Communist newspaper *Rudé Pravo*, where he acquired an extensive knowledge of Czechoslovakian history and culture, as exemplified in his first volume of poetry, *The City in Tears* (1920). The poems in this collection are characterized by simplicity and sensuality.

Seifert traveled throughout Europe, where he became familiar with literary trends. He initially regarded poetry as a tool for social change, and his early work expressed support for communism. Later, influenced by DADA and FUTURISM, his focus shifted toward poetry that was guided by sensual rather than intellectual motivations.

Because of his refusal to conform to orthodox political beliefs, Seifert's works were often censored by the Czechoslovakian government. He cofounded a society of avant-garde literary figures in Prague and, in 1929, was finally expelled from the Communist Party for refusing to oppose the elected Czechoslovakian government.

Seifert joined the Social Democrats, and his poetry began to change once again. *The Carrier Pigeon* (1929) focused on daily life, rejecting metaphor in favor of REALISM. During World War II, the publication of *Bozena Nemcová's Fan* (1939), with its passionate opposition to the Nazi occupation of Prague, put Seifert back in favor with the Communist Party, but by 1950 he was once again evicted from the party and charged with subjectivism.

Seifert then became a spokesperson for artistic freedom. In the 1970s, he headed the Union of Czech Writers and acted to oppose a ban on foreign publishing. *The Plague Column* (1977), which warned of the dangers of neo-Stalinism, was published in Cologne, West Germany, as a result of Czechoslovakian censorship. His final published work was his memoir, *All the Beauties of the World* (1981).

In 1984, Seifert became the first Czechoslovakian to receive the Nobel Prize in literature. Age and failing health prevented him from traveling to Stockholm to accept his award in person, and the Czechoslovakian government would not grant his son an exit visa to pick up the award for him. He died in Prague two years later.

Other Works by Jaroslav Seifert

Dressed in Light. Translated by Paul Jagasich and Tom O'Grady. New York: Dolphin-Moon Press, 1990.

The Early Poetry of Jaroslav Seifert. Translated by Dana Loewy. Evanston, Ill.: Hydra Books, 1997.

Sembène, Ousmane (1923–2007) *novelist, screenwriter*

Ousmane Sembène was born in Ziguinchor, in the Casamance region of southern Senegal. The son of a fisherman who was too poor to put his son through school, Ousmane left school before finishing to take various odd jobs, including those of bricklayer, fisherman, plumber, and apprentice mechanic. He was drafted into the French colonial army during World War II and served in both Italy and Germany. After the war, he returned to work as a manual laborer, first in Dakar, Senegal, and later in Marseilles, France. While in France, he was strongly influenced by French leftist thought and eventually became a trade-union leader. He joined the French Communist Party and became an active member until 1960 when Senegal gained its independence. After a year of instruction in cinema studies in Moscow, he devoted most of his attention and time to making films.

Sembène first made his mark as a novelist with *Le docker noir* (*The Black Dockworker,* 1956) and moved into the film industry after 1962. In both his novels and his screenplays, he develops the themes of the nationalist struggle against colonialism, corruption, and racial discrimination. These are the issues that plagued most African writers who had firsthand experience of colonialism. What distinguishes Sembène is that he continues to write and explore these themes long after the colonial struggle ended. He completed three novels during the 1950s and 1960s. His most popular and, arguably, best novel is *Les bouts de bois de Dieu* (*God's Bits of Wood,* 1960), a story that vividly depicts the African workers' struggle against colonial oppression and exploitation. The book is set during the 1947 and 1948 Dakar-Niger Railway strike, an event that Sembène witnessed. He develops a sophisticated view of workers' rights and industrial relations, using a Marxist approach in this novel. *Xala* (1973) ironically bespeaks the anguish and disappointment following the postcolonial independence where Africans realized that their new leaders were incapable of making genuine progress or fulfilling promises that they pledged during the struggle.

Sembène's novels and screenplays are informed by his own personal experiences and encounters. He was most effective in depicting the complexities of the colonial and postcolonial struggle of many African nations, which, in many cases, did not end with the gaining of independence. Sembène wrote all his works in French; approximately half have been translated into English.

Other Works by Ousmane Sembène
The Black Docker. London: Heinemann, 1987.
The Money-Order; with White Genesis. London: Heinemann, 1972.
Niiwam and Taww. Oxford: Heinemann, 1992.
Tribal Scars and Other Stories. London: Heinemann, 1974.

Films by Ousmane Sembène
Camp de Thiaroye. 1988. With Thiero Faty Sow.
L'Empire Sonhrai. 1963. In French.
Le Mandat (The Money-Order). 1968. In French and Wolof. English version, 1969.
Xala. 1974. In French and Wolof.

Works about Ousmane Sembène
Conde, Maryse. "Sembène Ousmane-Xala." *African Literature Today* 9 (1978).
Peters, Jonathan. "Sembène Ousmane as Griot: *The Money-Order with White Genesis*." *African Literature Today* 12 (1982).

Pfaff, Françoise. *The Cinema of Ousmane Sembène, A Pioneer of African Film.* Westport, Conn.: Greenwood, 1984.

Senghor, Léopold Sédar
(1906–2001) *poet*
Léopold Sédar Senghor was born in the little coastal town of Joal, Senegal. As a boy, he moved around the circle of Serere farmers and fishermen and listened to the tales they told of precolonial Africa. These stories would greatly influence his poetry. He attended a Roman Catholic mission school in French West Africa when he was young and entered the Collège Libermann in Dakar in 1922 to study for the priesthood. He was, however, found participating in protests against racism and expelled from the school. Senghor finally completed his secondary education in a public school in 1928 and left Senegal after winning a scholarship to study in France.

Senghor studied contemporary French literature at the prestigious École Normale Supérieure in Paris. He was greatly influenced by the vibrant atmosphere of intellectual ferment in 1930s Paris. Black African writers were rediscovering their roots in exile away from their homeland, and this led them to establish the intellectual movement called NEGRITUDE, which encouraged black students, artists, and writers to explore their common cultural roots and tradition. Senghor and his writer-friend AIMÉ CÉSAIRE were the cofounders of négritude and the newspaper, *L'étudiant noir* (The black student).

Senghor established his literary and political career in the aftermath of World War II. In 1946, he and his mentor, Lamine Guèye, were both appointed as representatives of Senegal in the French Constituent Assembly in Paris. Senghor managed to be reelected and served in the assembly until 1958. When Senegal gained its independence in April 1960, Senghor became its first president. His rich cultural background and his keen intellect made him an effective leader, but his success did not last long. The persistence of Senegal's economic crisis and the futility of Senghor's programs led to his forced retirement in 1980. He resettled in Verson, France, where he spent the rest of his life.

Senghor's poems, written in French and translated into many languages, reflect his inner conflict between his Western predisposition and his determination to preserve the wealth of his African heritage. The poems in his first book, *Chants d'ombre* (Songs of shadow, 1945), are extremely effective in their dramatization of his search for identity. In these poems, he manages to extricate himself from the vicious cycle of self-doubt and find balance by retreating to his childhood and the past. This theme of the returning to his origins is best presented in the poem "Que m'accompagnent kôras et balaphong" ("To the Music of koras and balaphon"), which also exhibits Senghor's aptitude for music. He believed that good musical rhythm was essential in poetry and often insisted that his poems should be read to the accompaniment of African music.

Senghor's personal experience as an exile living in France also influenced his writings. His sense of alienation derives from his dilemma as an educated African who felt torn between his black attributes and background and his Western intellectual inclinations. He felt distinctly the need to promote his black identity in the margins of Western society to establish his presence. Senghor's volume *Hosties noires* (Black victims, 1948) contains many poems written in the war years. A common thread runs through these poems: Senghor's growing disappointment and exasperation with losing his European "heritage." Senghor knew he could never be French, but his desire to retain his "Frenchness" was intermixed with a realization that his true roots lay in Africa. Senghor's ingenuity lies in his fluency in French, his extraordinary exploration of the range of human emotions, and his intellectual critique of French colonialism in Africa.

Other Works by Léopold Sédar Senghor

The Collected Poetry. Translated by Melvin Dixon. Charlottesville: University Press of Virginia, 1991.

Irele, F. A., ed. *Selected Poems of Léopold Sédar Senghor.* New York: Cambridge University Press, 1977.

Works about Léopold Sédar Senghor

Kluback, William. *Léopold Sédar Senghor: From Politics to Poetry.* New York: Peter Lang, 1997.
Spleth, Janet. *Léopold Sédar Senghor.* Boston: Twayne, 1985.
Vaillant, Janet G. *Black, French, and African: A Life of Léopold Sédar Senghor.* Cambridge, Mass.: Harvard University Press, 1990.

Sereny, Gitta (1921–) *biographer, journalist*

Gitta Sereny was born in Vienna, Austria, on March 13, 1921, to Hungarian Protestant parents. Her father died when she was just two years old. Sereny's family was well off, and she was educated at a number of different schools, including a boarding school in England. While traveling back to Vienna from her English school, Sereny stopped in Nuremberg and witnessed a Nazi rally, which left her greatly impressed. She later read *Mein Kampf*, Hitler's manifesto, to better understand the rally she had seen.

Hitler's annexation of Austria in 1938 had a great impact on Sereny's life. Her mother, although not Jewish, was involved in the Jewish community and had planned to marry a Jewish economist, Ludwig von Mises. As the Nazi regime took power, Sereny witnessed the oppression of the Jewish people and was sympathetic to their plight, unlike many of her fellow Austrians. She and her mother moved to Switzerland to escape persecution, and at 17 Sereny ran away to Paris.

In Nazi-occupied France, Sereny worked as a nurse and assisted the Resistance in returning British airmen across enemy lines. Sereny got word that she was going to be arrested for helping the Resistance, and before she could be caught she fled to Spain and then sailed for the United States. There, she got work as a child-welfare officer for the United Nations and returned to Europe to search for children whom the Nazis had kidnapped and adopted out to German parents as a way to seed the German population with "approved" Aryan stock. The children sent to live with new families met criteria that the Nazis felt made their genetics valuable. Often, the German parents were the only parents the children had ever known; tragically, returning them to their birth parents was an act of traumatic kidnapping all over again.

Following the end of World War II, Sereny married an American photographer, Don Honeyman, and began work as a journalist and biographer. She focused her work on dealing with the devastating aftermath of Nazi Germany and pursuing an explanation for the human evil to which the Holocaust bears witness. In 1945, Sereny attended the Nuremberg Trials, military tribunals in which Nazi politicians and soldiers were punished for war crimes. It was during these trials that she first saw Albert Speer, the Minister of Armaments and War Production for the Nazis, who later became the subject of her most famous book.

Sereny's first book, *The Case of Mary Bell: A Portrait of a Child Who Murdered*, was published in 1972. Mary Bell was an 11-year-old girl who murdered two young boys. She was kept in a detention center until she was 23. Sereny attempts to uncover why Bell committed these acts, interviewing the girl, her family, and her community extensively in search of a cause for her psychosis.

Sereny's published work on Nazi Germany began with *Into That Darkness: From Mercy Killing to Mass Murder, a Study of Franz Stangl, the Commandant of Treblinka* (1974). She chose Stangl because she felt that of all the Nazis, he was the most likely to have "a semblance of moral awareness," and this self-awareness would shed some light on those who had committed such terrible crimes. She became, in some ways, Stangl's confessor, taking a sympathetic approach to a man she felt was trying to understand the enormity of his guilt.

In 1977, Sereny was involved in the controversy surrounding David Irving, an English historian of dubious merit who wrote the book *Hitler's War*, in which Irving claimed that Hitler was unaware of the Holocaust in which Jews were being slaughtered until October 1943. Sereny denounced him and wrote an exposé in the *Sunday Times*. Following that article, she received a letter from Albert Speer, the man she had seen on trial at Nuremberg, stating that Irving was dangerous. It was clear that Speer wanted to tell Sereny his story.

Sereny befriended Speer, corresponding for a number of years through letters, phone calls, and personal interviews. Speer had originally been an architect and ended up as Germany's Minister of Armaments. Although his impact on the war had been immense, Speer was not part of the planning and execution of the death camps. However, he certainly knew about the plan and did not raise any objections. Sereny's biography of Speer, *Albert Speer: His Battle with Truth* (1995), details his organizational genius; the personal, emotional troubles that brought him into Hitler's close confidence; and the lasting crisis of conscience that made him seek out a journalist to begin with. In 1995, the book received the James Tait Black Memorial Prize.

Gitta Sereny's latest book, *The German Trauma: Experiences and Reflections, 1930–2001* was published in 2002. She was made a Commander of the Order of the British Empire in 2004 for her work in journalism.

Other Works by Gitta Sereny

Cries Unheard: The Story of Mary Bell. New York: Picador, 2000.

The Invisible Children: Child Prostitution in America, West Germany and Great Britain. New York: Alfred A. Knopf, 1983.

Serote, Mongane Wally (1944–) *poet, essayist, novelist*

Mongane Wally Serote was born in Sophiatown, South Africa. He received his early education in Alexandra Township and later attended the

Morris Isaacson High School in Soweto. In 1974, after a succession of different jobs, he left South Africa on a Fulbright scholarship, which enabled him to study for a master's degree in fine arts at Columbia University in New York. Before leaving he had been awarded the Ingrid Jonker Prize for Poetry following the publication of his collection *Yakhal'inkomo* (1972).

Serote's novel *Gods of Our Time* (1999) documents the latter years of the liberation struggle in South Africa and conveys the bewilderment and uncertainty of those involved in the historic events of the time. In his text, Serote mimics the dislocated sensation of living in a time when people often disappeared without a trace by using a multitude of characters who enter the pages in an apparently random manner and then, inexplicably, disappear again. Much of Serote's work chronicles a disconnection with the past and attempts a realignment and reconfiguration with that past. His collection of poetry *The Night Keeps Winking* (1982) was banned in his home country. It contains vivid imagery of the cruelty of life under apartheid, but also lyrical notes:

> If life is so simple
> why can't it be lived
> if it is so brief
> why can't it be lived

After living in exile in Botswana and Britain, he returned to South Africa when the end of apartheid came. In 1991, he received an honorary doctorate from the University of Natal. He won the Noma Award for Publishing in Africa in 1993. Mongane Serote was elected to South Africa's Parliament in 1994 and became the chair of the Arts, Culture, Language, Science and Technology Parliamentary Portfolio committee. Serote continues to chronicle the history of the South African experience. Serote is currently the CEO of the Freedom Park Foundation, a national heritage site in Pretoria, South Africa.

Other Works by Mongane Wally Serote

History Is the Home Address. Cape Town, South Africa: Kwela Books, 2007.
Scatter the Ashes and Go. Johannesburg, South Africa: Ravan, 2002.
To Every Birth Its Blood. Westport, Conn.: Heinemann, 1983.

Works about Mongane Wally Serote

Brown, Duncan. "Interview with Mongane Wally Serote." *Theoria: A Journal of Studies in the Arts, Humanities and Social Sciences* 80 (October 1992): 143–149.
Horn, Peter. "A Volcano in the Night of Oppression: Reflections on the Poetry of Mongane Serote." Available online. URL: http://homepages.compuserve.de/PeterRHorn/volcano.htm.

Seth, Vikram (1952–) *novelist, poet*

Vikram Seth was born in Calcutta, India, but grew up in Delhi. His father, Prem Seth, is an executive in a business company, and his mother, Lalitha Seth, is a judge. After completing his schooling in India, Seth went to England and America for further studies. At Stanford University in 1975, while studying for his doctorate in economics but frustrated by the tediousness of filling in data for a project, Seth decided to take a temporary leave from economics and thought to try writing a novel instead. He went to a bookstore and was so inspired by a PUSHKIN novel that he decided to write one himself.

What began as a break became Seth's lifetime profession—a cross-cultural exploration of the question of identity and human relationships. He has written about North America, Tibet, China, England, and India: In each instance, he does not create, as in the works of SALMAN RUSHDIE, postmodern cultural hybrids through his characters; rather, Seth's works can be said to be deliberately straightforward and direct without undermining the lyricism of his language. He does not complicate human nature but frankly and compassionately tries to communicate it. In *An Equal Music* (1998), which is set in England, the imminent separation of the lovers is an outcome destined by music and is not a result of a larger social or political cause. In this novel, the theme of love is contained within the context of the feelings the couple have for each other. The romantic intimacy between individuals in a drama devoid of politics places this work in a modernist framework.

Seth's difference from contemporary Indian writers of English can be found in a descriptive style that is as uncomplicated in form as it is in content. This, however, does not mean that he has not written on political issues: The poem "A Doctor's Journal Entry for August 6, 1945," from *All You Who Sleep Tonight* (1990), is a vivid exposition of a doctor's reaction to the atomic bomb at the moment of its fall into Hiroshima. Caught between saving himself and needing to do his duty to others as a doctor, the narrator realizes that silence and death are his only options.

Seth's first literary venture was not, as he intended, a novel. *Golden Gate* (1986) is written completely in rhyme and won him the Commonwealth Poetry Prize in 1986. *Golden Gate* follows the formal tradition of older poetry and is a satire of cosmopolitanism in sonnet form. It was inspired by the vibrancy of San Francisco and the lives of the youth who eke out a living there. Seth's second novel, *A Suitable Boy* (1993), is set in postindependent India in the 1950s. While a mother performs an exacting search for a perfect husband for her daughter, ethnic violence between Hindus and Muslims divides a nation. *A Suitable Boy* is the longest novel ever written in English. Because of its length and scope, covering the lives of four extended families, Seth was hailed as a "latter-day Tolstoy" by international critics when it was released.

Seth also studied classical Chinese poetry at Nanjing University (China) and has written about his travels in China and Tibet. Seth's travelogues uncover traces of India, found even in the remotest mountain in Tibet. After his studies in China, Seth published a collection of Chinese poems that he translated into English.

Seth has proven to be a truly versatile writer. Just as uncomplicated in form as he is in content, he has written in almost every literary genre. He has often said that rather than trying to combine different genres at one time, he prefers to pick a different form for a different theme. He has written six books of poetry, three novels, and a libretto, *Arion and the Dolphin* (1999), for an opera by British composer Alec Roth. His attention to form has twice placed him in the *Guinness Book of Records:* for *Golden Gate,* the first novel in English written entirely in sonnet form, and for *A Suitable Boy.*

In 2005, Seth published *Two Lives* (2005), a nonfiction memoir that focuses on the lives of his great-uncle and German-Jewish great aunt. A new novel, *A Suitable Girl*, is scheduled for publication in 2013. Seth has referred to the novel as a "jump sequel," because it is set in the present and does not begin in 1952 where *A Suitable Boy* ends.

Critical Analysis

A Suitable Boy opens with a wedding and the simple edict of a mother to a daughter, "You too will marry a boy I choose." The scene and the words are deceptively straightforward; the daughter, Lata Mehra, and the mother in question, Rupa Mehra, live within the rigid context of Indian culture, with its peculiar web of permissions, prohibitions, and traditions that establishes the complexity of that statement, determining a limited number of outcomes. The simplicity of the conceit also belies the complexity of the novel itself, its foundation being a vigorous REALISM that supports an intricate plot structure.

Lata is bound to submit to her mother's choice, and the plot of the novel is fueled by the puzzle of who Lata will marry and the question of her right to choose her own husband. Issues of the impact and meaning of caste in love and marriage drive Seth's story of four middle- and upper-class families, three of which are related by marriage. Another crucial issue, religion, complicates Lata's fancy for a boy named Kabir—an interest that is soon crushed by Rupa when she discovers that he is Muslim. The stories of these families raise a host of issues in *A Suitable Boy*: "the value of work, the process of change, the injustice of poverty, and the direction taken by the newly independent and democratic India," one that is not the "magical India full or miraculous coincidences . . . but rather a workaday nation of legal systems and industry."

A Suitable Boy is also a comic novel. The tone is lighthearted, and any complications that hint at darkness are resolved by the typical devices of comedy, including flexibility of time and the happy coincidence. The novel ends with what might be regarded as a cliché: a marriage. Indeed, critics point out the conventionality of the narrative weakens its impact. However, it is Seth's genius for synthesis that makes *A Suitable Boy* so effective. "What we have here," writes one critic, "is not simply a love story, nor an epic, nor a realist historical novel," but "an Indian novel in English." Seth's inclusive use of genres and his disdain for experimental techniques have made his novel an international best seller and a powerfully emotional narrative.

Another Work by Vikram Seth

From Heaven Lake. New York: Vintage Books, 1987.

Works about Vikram Seth

Atkins, Angela. *Vikram Seth's "A Suitable Boy": A Reader's Guide*. New York: Continuum International, 2002.

"The Gate and the Banyan: Vikram Seth's Two Identities." In *The Literature of the Indian Diaspora*. Edited by A. K. McLeod. New Delhi: Sterling, 2000.

Pandurang, Mala. *Vikram Seth: Multiple Locations, Multiple Affiliation*. New Delhi: Rawat, 2001.

Shalamov, Varlam (1907–1982)
poet, essayist

The son of a priest, Varlam Tihonovich Shalamov was born in Vologda, Russia. As a young man, Shalamov joined the communist cause and actively participated in the Russian Revolution. Between 1926 and 1929, Shalamov studied law at the Moscow University. In 1929, he was arrested for distribution of the so-called "Lenin's Will," a document that stated that Lenin opposed the appointment of Joseph Stalin to the leadership of the Communist Party and the Soviet Union. Shalamov was released in 1932 but was arrested once again in 1937 at the height of the period of Stalin's political repressions.

Shalamov spend the next 17 years in a labor camp in Kolyma, a remote location in Siberia. After he returned in 1952, he began to publish poems in various journals. In the meantime, he secretly worked on *Kolyma Tales,* which appeared in dissident circles around Moscow in 1966. *Kolyma Tales* describes Shalamov's experiences in Stalin's labor camps. The stories were officially published in London in 1977. After the London publication, the collection caused a scandal for the Soviet government, and Shalamov was forced to renounce his work publicly. He died alone in a nursing home five years before *Kolyma Tales* was officially published in the Soviet Union.

Varlam Shalamov's *Kolyma Tales* is considered by many to be a centerpiece of dissident fiction in Russia. His tales had a direct political impact in the Soviet Union, as they exposed the scandalous treatment of political prisoners in the Soviet Union and the injustices of the Soviet judicial system. Today, Shalamov is admired by many, and his work continues to bear relevance to the treatment of political prisoners by various totalitarian governments around the world.

Another Work by Varlam Shalamov

Graphite. Translated by John Glad. New York: Norton, 1981.

Shields, Carol Ann (1935–2003) *novelist, short story writer*

Carol Ann Shields (née Warner) was born in the United States in 1935. Her university years were divided between academic study in the United States, England, and Canada. She received her master's degree in English literature from the University of Ottawa. In 1957, she married Donald Hughes Shields, a Canadian engineering student and moved to Canada, where she spent the rest of her life. She had four daughters and one son. Her daughter, Anne Giardini, is also a writer. Shields died of breast cancer in 2003.

Shields taught English at several Canadian universities. She was a member of the faculty of the University of Ottawa, the University of British Columbia, and the University of Manitoba in Winnipeg, where she and her husband settled in 1980. It was there that she wrote her major books, and she frequently used Winnipeg as a backdrop for her novels. In 1996, she became the fifth chancellor of the University of Winnipeg. Ms. Shields authored more than 20 works, including plays, poetry, essays, short fiction, novels, a book of criticism on Susanna Moodie, and a biography of Jane Austen. Her works have been translated into 22 languages.

As the mother of five children, Shields believed that motherhood and writing were intertwined. She once said, "I couldn't have been a novelist without being a mother. It gives you a unique witness point of the growth of personality. It was a kind of biological component for me that had to come first. And my children give me this other window on the world."

Carol Shields's best-known novel, *The Stone Diaries* (1993), earned her a Pulitzer Prize for fiction from the United States in 1995 and the Governor General's Award in Canada in 1993. This is the first time anyone has ever won both awards for the same work. *Stone Diaries* was nominated for the U.S. National Book Critics Circle Award and the 1993 Booker Prize and was named one of the best books of the year by *Publishers Weekly*. It also was chosen as a Notable Book by the *New York Times Book Review*. Ms. Shields authored several novels and short story collections, including *Small Ceremonies* (1976), *The Orange Fish* (1989), *Swann* (1987), *Various*

Miracles (1985), *Happenstance* (1980), *The Republic of Love* (1992), *Larry's Party* (1997), and *Unless* (2002). Her novel *Swann* was made into a film in 1996, and *Larry's Party* became a musical stage play.

Shields received many honors and awards. She was the recipient of a Canada Council Major Award and was appointed a fellow of the Royal Society of Canada and a member of the Order of Manitoba. She also received the 1990 Marion Engel Award and the Canadian Author's Award and was appointed an officer of the Order of Canada in 1998. She was elevated to Companion of the Order in 1993. In 1998, she won the Orange Prize for Fiction, given to the best book by a woman writer in the English-speaking world, for her 1997 novel *Larry's Party*. She was nominated for the 2002 Giller Prize, the Governor General's Award, the Booker Prize, and the 2003 Orange Prize for Fiction for her last novel, *Unless*, published in 2002. *Unless* was awarded the Ethel Wilson Fiction Prize. Also, in 2002, her biography of Jane Austen received the prestigious Charles Taylor Prize for literary nonfiction.

Shields is a shrewd observer of everyday life, and friendship and the inner lives of women play a significant role in her writing. Her novels deal with the day-to-day issues that people face and explore universal themes such as loneliness and lost opportunities. At the same time, she is cognizant of the beauty of life and the rewards it offers. In *Dropped Threads* (2001), coauthored with colleague Marjorie Anderson, she encourages women to write about experiences that they have been unable to share with others. In an interview, Shields shared the rationale for the creation of *Dropped Threads*. "Our feeling was that women are so busy protecting themselves and other people that they still feel they have to keep quiet about some subjects." Shields spoke often of redeeming the lives of ordinary people by recording them in her own works. ". . . I think those women's lives were often thought of as worthless because they only kept house and played bridge. But I think they had value."

Shields is known for her dissection of the inner lives of women. Her last novel, *Unless*, was published just a year before her death, when she had been battling cancer for almost five years. This novel, which is semiautobiographical, deals with the ordinary woman and the fact that she vacillates between two worlds—the humdrum daily life of a wife and mother and a vivid intense, internal life. The main character, Reta Winters, is a writer and translator. Reta is troubled by her daughter's decision to become a beggar, living on the street, and wearing a sign with the word "Goodness" written on it. Exploring this strange scenario leads Reta to an expression of her views about literature and language and her belief that women have been underestimated by the literary world. According to Bill Robinson, of the Web site MostlyFiction Book Reviews, *Unless* is ". . . a novel in praise of 'the pleasures of ordinary existence. . . .' where the everyday is a constant source of beauty and enlightenment."

Unless is a novel, according to Tim Adams's tribute to Shields in the *Observer* of Sunday, July 20, 2003, ". . . which almost heroically held fast to the quietly comic details of love and life in the face of the alternatives. The title itself reflected this ever anxious concern. 'Unless,' Shields suggested, is the 'worry word of the English language.' It saves you from your fate: 'Unless you're lucky, unless you're healthy, fertile, unless you're loved and fed, unless you are clear about your sexual direction, unless you are offered what others are offered, you go down in the darkness, down to despair.'"

Adams continues: "Ms. Shields was always a beguiling writer. She'd have you think her concerns were only little affairs of the heart, the minor compromises men and women make with love, the ways in which her characters might find hope and comfort in the domestic and everyday. She was able to invest this detail, however, with such generosity, and with that it amounted to a worldview (not for nothing did she look to Jane Austen as a model)."

Critical Analysis

In *The Stone Diaries*, the protagonist, Daisy Goodwill Flett, considers herself an ordinary woman whose life is similar to that of millions of other women. Daisy, however, is determined to tell her story, in diary form, in an effort to give meaning to her own life. In the telling of her story, Daisy imparts significance to a life that might otherwise not be worthy of notice. As Joan PreFontaine writes in her review on BooksILoved.com, "Why would we want to read about the rest of Daisy's existence, which is, for the most part, conventional and predictable, based on filling others' expectations and fighting despair . . . Shields has a way of addressing her character's inner realities with lyrical affection and quiet irony. Because the story is told from many points of view over time, we are offered a complex, historical understanding of Daisy's life. All this is conveyed in prose that flows smoothly and fluidly and is enchantingly sharp and full of the wit and the keen powers of observation of its author."

The effectiveness of Shields's use of the diary form is heightened by the fact that she is almost able to convince her readers to accept the work as an actual autobiography, rather than a work of fiction. To lend the novel an aura of authenticity as an autobiography, Shields adds photographs (some actually of her own children), a family tree, and a collection of unconventional, often fantastic family anecdotes and experiences. In fact, New York *Newsday* says of the book that it is, "A kind of family album made into a work of art."

Perhaps what makes Daisy different from many women of her generation (she was born in 1905 and died in 1985) is her awareness that something is lacking in her life. She struggles to find purpose in it, even though she does not always know how to achieve it. At one point, she works as a gardening columnist and develops a rich inner life. Ultimately, however, she loses her job to a man and once again finds herself seeking direction. In a sense, Shields's novel is about the predictable and conventional life of a woman during the unsettling mid-decades of last century. She uses the imagery of stone in both Daisy's life and that of her father to bring home the reality of death and the awareness that people cannot always find the fullest expression of reality in their lives. All too often, things are not what they seem. The reader is given a window into Daisy's heart through Ms. Shields's amazing use of language as she proves that even the most mundane life has extraordinary qualities.

Other Works by Carol Ann Shields

Anniversary. Written with Dave Williamson. Winnipeg, Canada: Blizzard Publishing, 1998.

The Box Garden. New York: Penguin, 1996.

A Celibate Season. Written with Blanche Howard. Saint Louis Mo.: San Val, 1999.

Collected Stories. New York: Harper Perennial, 2005.

Coming to Canada. Quebec: Carleton University Press, 1995.

Departures and Arrivals. Winnipeg, Canada: Blizzard Publishing, 1990.

Dressing Up for the Carnival. New York: Penguin, 2000.

A Fairly Conventional Woman. Toronto: Macmillan of Canada, 1982.

Fashion Power Guilt and the Charity of Families. Written with Catherine Shields. Winnipeg, Canada: Bain & Cox, 1995.

Intersect. Ontario: Borealis Press, 1974.

Others. Ontario: Borealis Press, 1972.

Thirteen Hands. Winnipeg, Canada: Blizzard Publishing, 1993.

Shiga Naoya (1883–1971) *novelist, short story writer, essayist*

Shiga Naoya was born in Ishimaki, Miyagi Prefecture, Japan, to Shiga Naoharu and Gin. When he was still very young, his grandparents took him to their residence in Tokyo. A member of an affluent and influential family, Shiga entered the elitist Gakushūin, a school established to educate the imperial family. He became interested in Christianity and joined a Christian study group while in middle school, and in 1906, he entered the English literature department of the Tokyo Imperial University. In 1914, Shiga married Sadako Kadenokōji. His father disapproved of the marriage, and Shiga responded by renouncing his inheritance, thus severing his ties with his family.

Shiga's formal literary career began with his publication of the short story "The Little Girl and the Rapeseed Flower" (1904) while he was still in high school. In 1910, Shiga and a group of friends from Gakushūin started a literary magazine as an outlet for their writing, and Shiga regularly contributed short stories. In 1912, he published *Ōtsu Junkichi,* his first long work. While critics called the novella uneven, its honesty of emotion ranks it among Japan's finest literary works. Five years later, while recovering from having been hit by a train, Shiga wrote his masterpiece "At Kinosaki," a reverie on the deaths of small animals. Shiga excelled in the arena of short stories, but he struggled with novel writing. Despite other attempts, he wrote only one full-length novel—*A Dark Night's Passing*—over a 16-year period, from 1921 to 1937. In the last 20 years of his life, Shiga entered into semiretirement, periodically writing personal essays based on his observations.

Shiga is regarded as the supreme stylist of his day. Using an economy of words, he depicted vivid vignettes based closely on his personal experiences. His literary power stems from his objectivity and honesty in portraying his characters' emotions. In 1949, he received the Order for Cultural Merit.

Other Works by Shiga Naoya

Morning Glories. Translated by Allen Say and David Meltzer. Berkeley, Calif.: Oyez, 1976.

The Paper Door and Other Stories. Translated by Lane Dunlop. San Francisco: North Point Press, 1987.

Works about Shiga Naoya

Mathy, Frances. *Shiga Naoya.* Boston: Twayne, 1974.

Starrs, Roy. *An Artless Art: The Zen Aesthetic of Shiga Naoya.* Richmond, Surrey: Japan Library, 1998.

Shiina Minako

See Ōba Minako.

Sholokhov, Mikhail (1905–1984) *novelist, short story writer*

Mikhail Aleksandrovich Sholokhov was born in a small village of Kruzhlinin, Russia. Sholokhov's father engaged in a number of farm-related trades; his mother was an illiterate Ukrainian peasant who learned to read and write late in her life to correspond with her son. Sholokhov was educated in several schools but left his educational pursuits to join the army in 1918. He fought on the Bolshevik side during the Russian civil war. He took part in the suppression of an anti-Bolshevik rebellion by the Don Cossacks (a semiautonomous group who was granted limited local independence by the czar, often in exchange for services in the military). Indeed, almost all of Sholokhov's prose is based on this experience during the war.

At the end of the war, Sholokhov relocated to Moscow where, between 1922 and 1924, he worked as a stonemason and an accountant. He occasionally participated in writers' seminars and published his first story, *The Birthmark,* in 1924. The same year, he decided to dedicate himself completely to writing; only a year later, he published his first collection of short stories, *Tales of the Don,* which depicted the bitter transformation of village life during the civil war.

Sholokhov's fame as a novelist came with the serialized publication of *And Quiet Flows the Don* (1928–40). Although the novel won the Stalin Prize in 1941, it was initially criticized for its objectivity in depicting the civil war. The work traces the tragic life of Cossack Grigory Melekhov and his ill-fated love. Along with the spiritual destruction of the protagonist, Sholokhov also depicts the downfall of traditional Cossack communities. His other major work, *Virgin Soil Uplifted* (1932–60), describes the agricultural collectivization in the Soviet Union. Although now recognized by many critics as mediocre at best, the novel received the Lenin Prize in 1960.

Sholokhov achieved high rank in the Communist Party. He accompanied the Soviet leader Nikita Khrushchev on a trip to Europe and the United States in 1959, and in 1961, he was elected as a member of the Central Committee. Many writers have criticized Sholokhov's work for its unscrupulousness in following official doctrines; still others questioned the authorship of *Tikhiy Don.* Despite these troubles, Sholokhov was the first officially sanctioned Soviet writer to receive the Nobel Prize in literature in 1965. By Sholokhov's death in 1984, more than 79 million copies of his work were published in 84 languages.

A Work about Mikhail Aleksandrovich Sholokhov

Ermolaev, Herman. *Mikhail Sholokhov and His Art.* Princeton, N.J.: Princeton University Press, 1982.

Shu Qingchun

See LAO SHE.

Shute, Nevil (Nevil Shute Norway) (1899–1960) *novelist*

Between 1924 and 1960, Nevil Shute Norway, who used the pen name Nevil Shute, wrote 24 novels and an autobiography. He was born in Ealing, Middlesex, England, in 1899. His father, Arthur Hamilton Norway, held an important position in the British postal system and eventually became the head of the post office in Dublin, where he was present during the Easter Uprising, a rebellion in 1916 that was aimed at ending British rule in Ireland. Shute served as a volunteer stretcher bearer during the uprising and was commended for his bravery.

The young Norway attended Dragon School, Shrewsbury School, Balliol College, Oxford, and the Royal Military Academy in Woolwich. He applied for membership in the Royal Flying Corps but was rejected because he stammered. However, he did serve as a soldier in the Suffolk Regiment during World War I. An aeronautical engineer and a pilot, Shute worked for major British airplane companies such as de Havilland and Vickers.

Shute worked on developing and building airships—lighter-than-air aircraft—that stay aloft by means of gas pumped into a large balloonlike cavity. He was part of the team working on constructing the R100, a privately funded airship project for Vickers, both as a stress engineer and eventually as deputy chief engineer. Sadly, and much to Shute's chagrin, the R100 was eventually discontinued due to a catastrophic accident that downed the R101, a governmentally funded sister airship, killing 48 people. Shute details these frustrations in his autobiography, *Slide Rule* (1954). Shute was a strong proponent of private enterprise and believed deeply in the importance of self-reliance and individual responsibility. It was, he believed, the lack of these essential qualities in government that may have led to the tragedy that brought about the end of R101 and, indirectly, the end of R100 as well.

In 1931, during the same year that he married Frances Mary Heaton, a doctor, Shute founded Airspeed, Ltd., an aircraft construction company in Portsmouth. He had a difficult time finding the necessary capital to fund his new company, but he eventually succeeded by exercising those qualities of character in which he so firmly believed. His company manufactured the Envoy, an airplane that was selected as King George VI's private plane in 1937, thus becoming part of what was known as the King's Flight.

During World War II, Shute joined the Royal Naval Volunteer Reserve and worked on the development of secret weapons for the Directorate of Miscellaneous Weapons Development. At the same time, because he had already developed a reputation as a budding writer, the Ministry of Information sent him to Normandy to observe the invasion of Europe by the Allied Expeditionary Forces on June 6, 1944. Later, he was sent to Burma to write articles about the war.

After the war, Shute was disturbed by the election of a socialist government in Britain and, in 1950, decided to settle in Australia, in Langwarrin, southeast of Melbourne. He had a short-lived career as a racing driver and wrote about his experiences in *On the Beach* (1957), probably his most famous novel, which deals with the end of life on Earth as a result of the explosion of an atomic bomb.

For the most part, Shute's characters are drawn from the middle class. They are generally university-educated professionals who are representative of life in England during the first half of the 20th century. Shute writes in a highly readable style, with clearly delineated plots, and his books frequently involve aviation. Other themes with which Shute deals in his novels *Lonely Road(1932)*, *The Chequer Board (1947)*, and *Round the Bend* (1951) include the dignity of labor and bridging of barriers in class, race, and religion. *Trustee from the Toolroom* (1960) reflects Shute's appreciation for honesty and integrity in the workplace.

While Shute loved Australia, he had a negative view of the United States and England (especially postwar England under socialist governments), and his books *Beyond the Black Stump* (1956), *The Far Country* (1952), and *In the Wet* (1953) reflect these positions.

Shute's novels can be divided into three periods: those written before World War II, those written during the war, and those written after he emigrated to Australia. His popularity as a writer peaked in the 1950s and the 1960s, and many of his books were made into films. In fact, *On the Beach* was filmed twice, once in 1959 and once in 2000. The first film version starred Gregory Peck and Ava Gardner and deviated from the plot of the novel. Consequently, Shute repudiated the film, which also elicited negative comments from some reviewers for its apparent opposition to any form of nuclear armament—which was not Shute's intention. *Pied Piper* (1942) and *A Town Like Alice* (1950) were also made into very popular films. Shute was a fellow of the Royal Aeronautical Society. He died in Melbourne in 1960.

Critical Analysis

Shute is best known for *On the Beach,* a novel that deals with the fatal and irreversible effects of atomic radiation. Set in Melbourne, Australia, in 1964 (then five years in the future), the plot deals with the people of Australia, all doomed to die from the effects of a radioactive cloud that resulted from nuclear explosions in the Northern

Hemisphere during World War III. While the bombs did not explode in the Southern Hemisphere, the fallout has already killed all life in the Northern Hemisphere, and it is only a matter of time before the radioactive cloud reaches the populated areas of the Southern Hemisphere. Because Melbourne is the southernmost city in Australia, the cloud has not yet arrived, but it is expected within four months.

The novel deals with the reaction of the Australians to their impending deaths. They have all been supplied with suicide pills or injections to avoid the torture of radiation sickness. There is, however, no hope for survival at all, and this is what makes the novel unusual since most of Shute's characters in his other novels are self-sufficient and capable of enduring hardships and challenges and eventually succeeding. The last survivors from the Northern Hemisphere, Captain Dwight Towers and his American nuclear submarine crew, have escaped from the radiation-afflicted Northern Hemisphere. They undertake trips to the north of Australia where they find no signs of life. Ultimately, they travel as far north as Seattle to investigate what seems like a Morse code signal, only to find that the signal is nothing more than a broken window sash hitting a telegraph key.

Although Shute was concerned with the proliferation of atomic weapons and the havoc they could wreak, he was not entirely opposed to nuclear armaments. Rather, he was concerned that small, irresponsible states might set off a nuclear conflagration through the use of such weapons in local conflicts. His daughter, writing about the novel some 40 years after its first publication, believes that this novel had a profound influence on many people and resulted in the founding of the Campaign for Nuclear Disarmament in England and the Peace Movement in the United States.

Shute offers no solution to the problem he presents. There is no miraculous salvation. All the characters in the novel are doomed to die. Most of the novel explores how the various characters will deal with the knowledge of their impending death. Captain Towers plays an important role in helping Moira, a woman who loves him, to adopt more elevated moral principles. Others attempt to go about the business of living as if things will go on normally forever. They plant gardens and continue their daily activities for as long as possible. The power of the novel is expressed in the dignity of the main characters in the face of inevitable death. They do not complain or feel sorry for themselves. They do not attempt to flee farther south but valiantly accept their fate. This approach is typical of Shute's personal strength of character and his belief in the power of the human spirit.

Other Works by Nevil Shute

Landfall: A Channel Story. New York: William Morrow and Company, 1940.

Marazan. New York: Cassell and Company, 1926.

Most Secret. Mattituck, N.Y.: Amereon, 1942.

No Highway. New York: William Morrow and Company, 1948.

An Old Captivity. New York: William Morrow and Company, 1940.

Pastoral. New York: William Morrow and Company, 1944.

The Rainbow and the Rose. New York: Signet, 1958.

Requiem for a Wren. New York: William Morrow and Company, 1955.

Ruined City. London: Heinemann, 1938.

The Seafarers. Kerhonkson, N.Y.: Paper Tiger, 2000.

So Disdained. New York: Ballantine, 1928.

Stephen Morris. Mattituck, N.Y.: Amereon, 2002.

Vinland the Good. Kerhonkson, N.Y.: Paper Tiger, 1946.

What Happened to the Corbetts. Sheridan, Ore.: Heron Books, 1939.

A Work about Nevil Shute

Giffuni, Cathy. *Nevil Shute, a Bibliography.* Adelaide: Auslib Press, 1988.

Sienkiewicz, Henryk (1846–1916) *novelist, short story writer*

Henryk Sienkiewicz was born in Wola Okrzejska, part of the Russian area of Poland. His father's family were revolutionaries who fought for Polish independence, and his mother's family included history scholars.

Sienkiewicz's talent for writing emerged at a young age. His earliest works were satirical sketches on social consciousness. In 1876, he visited America, publishing his travel accounts in Polish newspapers and gaining material for future works.

Returning to Poland, Sienkiewicz turned to historical studies, writing a trilogy about 17th-century Poland, which included *With Fire and Sword* (1884), *The Deluge* (1886), and *Pan Michael* (1888). A prolific writer, he followed these works in rapid succession with novels on a variety of contemporary subjects. *Without Dogma* (1891) was a psychological study of decadence, while *Children of the Soil* (1894) focused on the lives of peasants.

In 1896, Sienkiewicz published *Quo Vadis*. This novel, for which he is most widely recognized internationally, told of the persecution of Christians at the time of Nero. He returned to historical subjects in *Krzyzacy* (1900), recounting the Poles' victory over the Teutonic knights in the Middle Ages, and *On the Field of Glory* (1906), a sequel to his previous trilogy. His final works, *Whirlpools* (1910) and *In Desert and Wilderness* (1912), again deal with contemporary issues.

In 1905, Sienkiewicz was awarded the Nobel Prize in literature for his "outstanding merits as an epic writer." Living in a time of cultural oppression, Sienkiewicz encouraged patriotism through his writing. Evidence of his success can be found in reports of Polish citizens pinning pages of his books to their clothing as a reminder of the fight for freedom. Sienkiewicz also wrote open letters to his people addressing political injustice, and in 1901, he helped to expose the persecution of Polish schoolchildren by the Prussians. He did not live to see the success of all he had fought to attain. He died two years before Poland's boundaries were restored.

Other Works by Henryk Sienkiewicz

Charcoal Sketches and Other Tales. Translated by Adam Zamoyski. Chester Springs, Pa.: Dufour Editions, 1990.

The Little Trilogy. Translated by Miroslaw Lipinski. New York: Hippocrene Books, 1995.

Works about Henryk Sienkiewicz

Giergielewicz, Mieczyslaw. *Henryk Sienkiewicz: A Biography.* New York: Hippocrene Books, 1991.

Kryanowski, Jerzy, ed. *The Trilogy Companion: A Reader's Guide to the Trilogy of Henryk Sienkiewicz.* New York: Hippocrene Books, 1992.

Simenon, Georges (1903–1989) *novelist*

Best known as a skilled writer of highly literate detective fiction, Georges Simenon was born in Liège, Belgium. The son of an accountant, he was forced to quit school because of his father's poor health. His mother died in 1921, and he worked for a time as a baker and a bookseller before launching his writing career with an apprenticeship at a local newspaper, *Gazette de Liège*.

Simenon began publishing when he was only 17 years old. He joined with a group of painters, writers, and artists who called themselves The Cask. This group spent the majority of their time drinking, experimenting with drugs, and having deep philosophical discussions. He recounts his experiences with this group in his novel *Le Pendu de Saint Pholier* (1931).

In 1922, Simenon moved to Paris, where he published numerous short stories and novels under a variety of pen names. Between 1922 and 1939, he produced more than 200 works of pulp fiction. The first work published under his real name was *The Strange Case of Peter Lett* (1931), in which Simenon introduces the character of Inspector Maigret, the Paris police detective about whom he would ultimately pen 84 mysteries, 18 of them written in the early 1930s. Simenon left the character behind for an eight-year hiatus at the start of World War II.

During the German invasion of France, Simenon moved to Fontenay, where he wrote successfully for the film business. After the war, under suspicion of having been a Nazi collaborator, he moved to the United States, where he wrote several mysteries with American settings, including *Belle* (1954) and *The Hitchhiker* (1955).

Simenon returned to Europe to live in Switzerland in 1955. Several of the Maigret novels enjoyed success as films. He announced his retirement in 1973, just after the publication of one last Maigret work, *Maigret et Monsieur Charles* (1972). He continued to write some nonfiction, including *Lettre à ma mère* (1974), which focuses on his relationship with his mother. Simenon died on September 4, 1989, leaving instructions that his body be cremated without ceremony. His legacy to literature lives on in the psychological depth he brought to the genre of detective fiction.

Other Works by Georges Simenon

Maigret Loses His Temper. Translated by Robert Eglesfield. San Diego, Calif.: Harcourt Brace Jovanovich, 1993.

The Rules of the Game. Translated by Howard Curtis. San Diego, Calif.: Harcourt Brace Jovanovich, 1988.

Works about Georges Simenon

Assouline, Pierre. *Simenon: A Biography.* Translated by Jon Rothschild. New York: Knopf, 1997.

Becker, Lucille. *Georges Simenon Revisited.* Boston: Twayne, 1999.

Simon, Claude (1913–2005) *novelist*

Closely associated with the emergence of the nouveau roman in the 1950s, Claude Simon was born in Antananariro in the then French colony of Madagascar. His father was killed during World War I, leaving Simon to be raised by his mother and her family in Perpignan, a French city near the Spanish border.

Simon studied for a career in the navy but was ultimately dismissed and left to study art at both Oxford and Cambridge Universities. In the early 1930s, he visited the Soviet Union. Upon his return, he served with the French army. During World War II, he was captured by the Germans but managed to escape and join the Resistance.

It was not until after the end of World War II that Simon began his career as a writer. His first novel, *Le tricheur* (*The Cheat*, 1945), was followed by the autobiographical novel *La corde raide* (*The Tightrope,* 1947). These two works and Simon's two subsequent novels are traditional in structure, with easily identifiable plots and characters. Simon gained international recognition, however, with his "new novel"–styled *Le vent* (*The Wind,* 1959). Here Simon began to develop a style in which the plot is really just one event viewed from several perspectives.

In *L'herbe* (1958) Simon began to emphasize visual perceptions. Nothing much happens in the novel, even though it is set in France in 1940, the tumultuous year of the German invasion. An old woman, Marie, is dying; her recollections, mainly of houses and gardens, form the substance of the book. A sequel, *La route des Flandres* (1960), is about Marie's nephew Georges, juxtaposing his wartime experiences with his present postwar reality. Much of Simon's work is largely biographical or historical in origin. Stylistically, he grew to favor a stream-of-consciousness style that was often devoid of regular punctuation and used parentheses excessively. For his works and contribution to the field of literature, Simon was awarded the Nobel Prize in literature in 1985.

Other Works by Claude Simon

The Georgics. Translated by Beryl and John Fletcher. New York: Riverrun Press, 1991.

The Invitation. Translated by Jim Cross. Normal, Ill.: Dalkey Archive Press, 1991.

The Jardin des Plantes. Translated by Jordan Stump. Evanston, Ill.: Illinois University Press, 2001.

The Trolley. Translated by Richard Howard. New York: New Press, 2002.

A Work about Claude Simon

Brewer, Maria Minich. *Claude Simon: Narratives Without Narrative.* Lincoln: University of Nebraska Press, 1995.

Singer, Isaac Bashevis (Icek-Hersz Zynger) (1904–1991) *novelist, short story writer*

Isaac Bashevis Singer was born in Radzymin, Poland. Singer's father was a Hasidic rabbi, and his mother came from a family of rabbis. When he was four, he moved with his family to Warsaw where he received a traditionally Jewish education, combining academics with the study of Jewish law in Hebrew and Aramaic texts. An avid reader, he was also influenced by the works of Spinoza, GOGOL, DOSTOYEVSKY, and TOLSTOY. Singer entered the Tachkemoni Rabbinical Seminary in 1920 but ultimately gave up this vocation to become a writer.

He began his writing career as a journalist in Warsaw, where he worked as a proofreader for *Literarische Bleter,* a newspaper edited by his eldest brother Joshua Singer, who was more politically active than his brother and highly disillusioned with the Soviet political system. This disillusionment affected the younger Singer's awareness of the continuous sociopolitical and cultural upheaval in Poland.

Singer's chief subject was Jewish life, history, and tradition, centered primarily on the period before the Holocaust. He examines the importance of the Jewish faith through the lives of his characters.

Singer's earliest fictional works were short stories and novellas. His first novel, *Satan in Goray* (1932), was published in Poland. It addresses the theme of the power of the 17th-century false messiah Shabbatai Zvi. Written in a linguistic style similar to the medieval Yiddish book of chronicles, the novel is set in the 17th century during the time of the Cossaks and is based on the mass murder of Jews, peasants, and artisans. The characters are often at the mercy of circumstance but are also the victims of passion. The story examines the danger of messianic fever, or overzealous prophet-worship. The destructive nature of passion and obsession are common themes in Singer's work.

Fearing Nazi persecution, Singer became a foreign correspondent and emigrated to the United States just after the publication of his first novel. He left behind his first wife, Rachel, and their son,

Israel. Settling in New York, he obtained employment with the Yiddish newspaper *Jewish Daily Forward.* In 1940, he married Alma Haimann, a German émigré, and was granted American citizenship in 1943.

His first collection of stories that was published in English was *Gimpel the Fool* (1957). He also published numerous stories in the *Jewish Daily Forward,* which were later collected in *In My Father's Court* (1966) and *More Stories from My Father's Court* (2000). The latter collection was published posthumously. In these stories, Singer depicts his own childhood in the overpopulated poor Jewish quarters of Warsaw before and during World War I. Singer's father is depicted as a pious man who studies the Talmud with great fervor; his mother is pictured as more practical, focusing on everyday problems.

The Family Moskat (1950) was Singer's first novel to be published in English. It forms the first volume of a trilogy along with *The Manor* (1967) and *The Estate* (1969). These novels describe how families are destroyed by the changing demands of society and a decline in religious faith.

Although Singer wrote all of his works in Yiddish, he collaborated with a number of well-known literary figures in the translation of his work, among them Saul Bellow and, most frequently, Cecil Hemley. He often published fiction under the pen name Isaac Bashevis and journalism under Warshofsky.

In 1978, Singer was awarded the Nobel Prize in literature. In 1984, his short story "Yentil the Yeshiva Boy" was made into the popular film *Yentl.* The 1989 film *Enemies, a Love Story* was also based on one of his novels. Singer died in Surfside, Florida, on July 24, 1991.

Critical Analysis

Singer's beloved short story "Gimpel the Fool" is a parable about perspective. It begins like a typical folktale about a silly fellow, save that it is told in the first person. "I am Gimpel the fool," the narrator tells us. "I don't think myself a fool. On the contrary. But that's what folks call me." As

Gimpel narrates the many ways in which he is duped and led astray by the townspeople, it is hard not to agree with their assessment. At the same time, Gimpel reveals that he is not as stupid as he seems. He says at one point that people become angry if he does not believe them—so he believes them, adding, "I hope at least that did them some good." Another time, he says, "I knew very well that nothing of the sort had happened." But he goes along anyway: "Maybe something had happened. What did I stand to lose by looking?"

As the tale progresses, Gimpel becomes something like the saintly fool, a man whose sheer goodness overcomes his canniness and his own self-interest. He lets himself be fooled but takes the best of what is dished out to him. He even comes to love his unfaithful wife.

Only after his wife dies is Gimpel tempted to do evil. The devil appears and convinces Gimpel, who is a baker, to repay the townspeople for their years of torment by tainting their bread. He bakes the tainted bread, but his wife comes to him in a dream and says, "You fool! Because I was false is everything false too?"

Gimpel throws away the tainted bread, sells all his possessions, and becomes a wanderer and a storyteller, beloved of little children. He also learns that "There are really no lies. Whatever doesn't really happen is dreamed at night. It happens to one if it doesn't happen to another, tomorrow if not today, a century hence, if not next year." Old and white-haired, he concludes that when his time to die comes, he will "go joyfully. Whatever may be there, it will be real, without complication, without ridicule, without deception. God be praised, there even Gimpel cannot be deceived."

Surely, Singer suggests, it is better to expect the best than the worst, to take the good with the evil, to make others happy, to love children whether your own or not, to give gifts, even to the ungrateful. It is all in one's perspective.

Other Works by Isaac Bashevis Singer

The Penitent. New York: Farrar, Straus & Giroux, 1983.
Reaches of Heaven. New York: Faber, 1982.
Scum. Translated by Rosaline Dukalsky Schwartz. New York: Farrar, Straus & Giroux, 1991.
The Slave. Translated by the author and Cecil Hemley. New York: Farrar, Straus & Giroux, 1962.

Works about Isaac Bashevis Singer

Friedman, Lawrence. *Understanding Isaac Bashevis Singer*. Columbia: University of South Carolina Press, 1988.
Hadda, Janet. *Isaac Bashevis Singer: A Life*. New York: Oxford University Press, 1997.

Škvorecký, Josef (1924–) *novelist*

Josef Škvorecký was born in 1924 in Náchod, Bohemia, Czeckoslovakia. He received his Ph.D. from Charles University in Prague. Škvorecký was fired from his job when his first novel, *The Cowards* (1958; translated 1970), was published; the novel was banned in Czechoslovakia soon after its publication for its ironic portrayal of the everyday lives of people living under communist rule. Undaunted, Škvorecký began freelancing, writing novels, film scripts, and nonfiction.

In response to the defeat of the Czech reform movement, Škvorecký left Czechoslovakia to settle in Canada in 1969. With his wife, he founded a Czechoslovakian publishing house in Toronto, where he began to build a solid reputation as a novelist. During a 20-year period, he developed a reputation as one of Canada's finest novelists, receiving the Governor General's Award for Fiction in 1984.

All of Škvorecký's novels have some basis in his experiences in Czechoslovakia and are often semi-autobiographical. Some of his works also focus on the problems of romantic love in a harsh sociopolitical climate. *The Engineer of Human Souls* (1984) is a comic novel that tells the tragic tale of novelist Danny Smiricky, a Czech immigrant living in Canada. *The Bride of Texas* (1995) is a historical novel about Czechoslovakian immigrants during the American Civil War who fought alongside the Union army.

Škvorecký taught at the University of Toronto from 1971 to 1991. Retired from teaching, he continues to write. A recent novel, *Dead Man on Campus* (2000), is an autobiographical novel merged with a murder mystery.

Other Works by Josef Škvorecký

The Bass Saxophone: Two Novellas. New York: Ecco Press, 1994.

Dvořák in Love: Alight-Hearted Dream. New York: Norton, 1988.

Ordinary Lives. Toronto: Key Porter Books, 2009.

When Eve Was Naked: Stories of a Life's Journey. New York: Picador, 2003.

A Work about Josef Škvorecký

Solecki, Sam. *Prague Blues: The Fiction of Josef Škvorecký.* New York: Ecco Press, 1990.

So Chōng-ju (Midang) (1915–2001) *poet*

So Chōng-ju was born in Sonuna village in Korea's North Cholla Province. After receiving a high school education without graduating, he entered the monastery but soon left to pursue a career in writing.

So Chōng-ju, who was influenced by the Western writers FRIEDRICH NIETZSCHE and CHARLES BAUDELAIRE, is considered one of Korea's first modern poets. He made a ripple in the Korean literary community by being the first writer to invoke sexual imagery, as in the poem "The Snake" (1938). Poems such as these marked his early sensual period.

So Chōng-ju also masterfully chronicled ordinary life. In the 1950s and 1960s, he drew on his Buddhist training and entered a Zen stage. Writing under his Buddhist name, Midang, he wrote of epiphany and Zen insight in "Legendary Karma Song" (1960) and "Beside a Chrysanthemum" (1955). He also focused on aesthetics and the natural world, both areas of Buddhist scholarship. Eventually, as So Chōng-ju aged, he returned to more personal poetry, reflecting upon his life and experiences and confronting the specter of his own mortality. "In Looking at Winter Orchids" (1976), for example, the narrator draws a parallel between his own mortality and flowers past bloom.

So Chōng-ju is one of the best-loved poets of modern Korea. He also achieved renown in the international community, which culminated in his nomination for the Nobel Prize in 1994, becoming the first Korean writer to receive this honor. A respected scholar, So Chōng-ju was a professor at Buddhist University and Dongguk University in Seoul. When he died on December 24, at the age of 85, the country mourned his death as a premier man of letters.

Another Work by So Chōng-ju

Poems of a Wanderer: Selected Poems of Midang So Chōng-ju. Translated by Kevin O'Rourke. Dublin: Dedalus Press, 1995.

socialist realism

Socialist realism was first recognized as an emerging literary movement in the Soviet Union in response to a May 1932 article in the *Literary Gazette*. The article stated that, in response to modern times and a general trend toward embracing socialist doctrine, "The masses demand of an artist honesty, truthfulness, and a revolutionary, socialist realism in the representation of the proletarian revolution." This article was followed shortly thereafter by a 1933 article by MAXIM GORKY, "On Socialist Realism," which emphasized the importance of artists taking "a new direction essential to us—socialist realism, which can be created only from the data of socialist experience." However, socialist realism was not officially defined as a literary and political term until 1934 when, at the First All-Union Congress of Soviet writers, it was officially adopted as the accepted standard for art and literature. In a speech at the congress, Gorky called on writers to "make labor the principal hero of our books."

Socialist realism was based on the principle that the arts should serve the purposes of communism and communist ideologies, both by glorifying worker heroes and by educating readers about the benefits of communist life. A first generation of socialist realists, including Maxim Gorky and Andrey Platonov (1899–1951), were not under state control and created works that portrayed the suffering of the poor and oppressed. However, socialist realism under Stalin persecuted writers who did not adhere to the party line. Writers, as well as visual and performing artists, were required to join the state-controlled Union of Soviet Artists and, as a condition of membership, were required to agree to abide by the union's restrictions. The movement began and spread quickly alongside the growth and expansion of communist ideology and government, becoming a dominant form of artistic expression in much of Eastern and Central Europe, but it also included writers from the United States, Latin America, Africa, and Asia.

Many writers and visual artists living under Communist governments found the demands of socialist realism stifling, so they emigrated to other countries. Others, such as the Polish writer SLAWOMIR MROŻEK, without leaving, found ways to keep their creativity alive through the use of indirect satire. The first collection of Mrozek's works, *Slon* (1957; *The Elephant*, 1967), was an anthology of very short stories that satirized various aspects of Polish communism in the 1950s. It was immediately successful with both critics and the general public but was not favored by strict socialists. Stalin's death in 1953 led to some relaxation of government control of the arts, but socialist realism continued as the official accepted literary and artistic practice into the 1980s.

Socialist realism is no longer a major movement, and very few works, if any at all, written today would fall under this category. It seems that socialist realism dissolved well before the collapse of the Soviet Union, and very few works of socialist realism, with the major exception of the first wave, are either read or appreciated today.

Socialist Realism in China

The growth of communism in the 1920s introduced socialist realism to China. A lack of mass awareness was discussed by writers, and quasi-socialist associations, such as the League of Left-Wing Writers (1930), were founded. But socialist realism did not materialize as an explicit literary and political directive in China until 1942, when Mao Zedong's talks at the Yenan Forum on Art and Literature gave the movement its foundation. By circumscribing the role of literature in a socialist society, Mao Zedong shaped communist literature for the remainder of the century. He drew heavily upon Soviet influence, and his primary tenet was the service of literature to revolutionary thought and politics.

Mao Zedong believed writers should not criticize the revolution but should emphasize the positive. Another main point at the Yenan talks was that literature must serve the masses. However, Mao Zedong also indicated that literature should not "lower" itself culturally to simple propaganda but should rise to a new artistic standard that concurrently served the revolutionary cause and urged the study of folk traditions.

Socialist realism was best served by writers indigenous to the movement. However, there were many writers who had been working for years who converted to communism, such as DING LING and BA JIN. Adaptation to the newly stringent requirements of socialist realism was difficult. Some writers, including Ding Ling, Ba Jin, and the unfortunate scapegoat Wang Shiwei, were eventually purged by the party for a lack of mass awareness and other literary "crimes." The new writers were untrained students of revolution, such as Hao Ran, who wrote party-line fiction such as the three-volume novel *Bright Sunny Skies* (1965). Held up as a hallmark of literature for and by the masses, the novel follows three players— a landlord, a party secretary, and a fallen party member—in the difficult task of collectivizing their local economy.

Socialist realist works were to depict the revolutionary journey accurately. However, they also needed to portray revolutionary heroes or heroines, focus on the masses, and glorify the work of the revolution, such as industrialization, the militia of the People's Liberation Army, and agrarian reforms. The novels tended to be long and predictable, with idealistic young heroes, such as Yang Mo's romantic and revolutionary *Song of Youth* (1958). The military was the most popular topic, as in Chin Ching-mai's *The Song of Ou-Yang Hai* (1966), about a real-life People's Liberation Army soldier who acted selflessly. Ts'ao Ming's *The Motive Force* (1949) told the story of the rehabilitation of a destroyed hydroelectric plant and glorified industrial reconstruction in Manchuria.

The Communist Party had to launch periodic campaigns against forces that they deemed threatening to socialist realist literature. Two of the most infamous were the criticisms and purgings of Ding Ling and Hu Feng in 1955. Ding Ling, who was once lauded for her 1949 socialist-realist novel on land reform, *The Sun Shines Over Sanggan River,* was sent to labor reform for explicit and immoral writings and for her urgings for literary openness. Hu Feng was imprisoned for his criticisms of thought reform and the dogmatic views of party leaders regarding literature. Some writers, like Wang Shiwei, were even executed.

A brief respite against such persecution occurred from April 1956 to May 1957 in a period of tentative liberalization called the Hundred Flowers. In *Literature of the Hundred Flowers,* Mao Zedong said, "In the arts, let a hundred flowers bloom and in scholarship, let a hundred schools of thought contend." Here, Ding Ling and other writers who had been working under the demands of socialist realism for nearly a decade took the ills of the movement to task. Among the issues they raised were whether all literature had to be overtly political and whether poetry could be lyrical. The flowering was immediately followed by a purging anti-Rightist campaign.

The Cultural Revolution that began in 1966 and was led by Jiang Qing, Mao Zedong's wife, produced a high volume of works of propaganda that were of dubious artistic quality. Many cultural relics were destroyed; intellectuals, writers, and other artists were sent to labor reform camps; self-criticisms were forced; and mass persecutions were common.

After the Cultural Revolution, socialist realism had some mending to do. The first wave of writings from "rehabilitated" writers, such as Ding Ling and Ba Jin, were known as "scar literature" and revealed the wounds that resulted from the oppressive dictates of Chinese socialist-realist literature. Socialist realism persists in some form today, but with the changing face of Communist China it is hardly recognizable. Writers such as Mo Yan document stories of ordinary life under communism with darkness and humor.

Works about Socialist Realism
Bisztray, George. *Marxist Models of Literary Realism.* New York: Columbia University Press, 1978.
Herdan, Innes. *The Pen and the Sword: Literature and Revolution in Modern China.* London: Zed Books Ltd., 1992.
Kemp-Welch, A. *Stalin and the Literary Intelligentsia, 1928–39.* New York: St. Martin's Press, 1991.
Lahusen, Thomas. *How Life Writes the Book: Real Socialism and Socialist Realism in Stalin's Russia.* New York: Cornell University Press, 1997.
Mao Zedong. *Selected Works of Mao Tse-Tung.* New York: Pergamon Press, 1977.
Robin, Régine. *Socialist Realism: An Impossible Aesthetic.* Translated by Catherine Porter; foreword by Léon Robel. Stanford, Calif.: Stanford University Press, 1991.
Yang Lan. *Chinese Fiction of the Cultural Revolution.* Hong Kong: Hong Kong University Press, 1998.

Södergran, Edith (1892–1923) *poet*

Edith Södergran was born in St. Petersburg, Russia, to Finnish–Swedish parents. Her father, Matts Södergran, was a mechanic and engineer who worked for Alfred Nobel for a time. Her mother, Helena Lovisa, was the daughter of a wealthy Swedish ironmaster. Södergran was educated at a German school in St. Petersburg and spent her summers at Raivola, Russia. As a teenager, she wrote poems in German, Swedish, French, and Russian. Södergran battled tuberculosis throughout her adolescence and spent several years in sanitariums in Switzerland and Finland.

An unhappy love affair with a Russian physician inspired Södergran's first collection of poetry *Dikter* (*Poems*, 1916). Her verse blended numerous influences, including HEINRICH HEINE, ELSE LASKER-SCHÜLER, Walt Whitman, and Russian SYMBOLISM. Södergran's collection *Septemberlyran* (*September Lyric*, 1918), written after her wealth was erased by the Russian Revolution, was partially about the Finnish civil war. Her friendship with critic Hagar Olsson inspired the verse in *Rosenaltaret* (*The Rose Alter*, 1919). After Södergran adopted Rudolf Steiner's anthroposophy doctrines and Christianity, she ceased writing poetry until her final days. She died after long bouts with illness and malnutrition.

Södergran developed a cult following after her death. Young poets made pilgrimages to her Raivola home until it was destroyed in World War II. Södergran's works have been translated into French and German. Her poems combine childlike humor, frankness, and a passion for beauty, and she is credited with liberating Nordic verse from the restrictions of traditional rhyme, rhythm, and imagery. George Schoolfield's biography *Edith Södergran* (1984) contains a quote from Swedish poet Gunnar Ekelöf in a letter to W. H. Auden, describing Södergran as "a very great poet . . . brave and loving as your Emily Brontë."

Another Work by Edith Södergran
Love and Solitude: Selected Poems, 1916–1923. Translated by Stina Katchadourian. Seattle: Fjord Press, 1985.

A Work about Edith Södergran
Schoolfield, George C. *Edith Södergran: Modernist Poet in Finland.* Westport, Conn.: Greenwood Press, 1984.

Solovyov, Vladimir (1853–1900)
philosopher, poet, translator
Vladimir Sergeyevich Solovyov was born in Moscow, Russia. His father, S. M. Solovyov, was a famous

historian. Solovyov received an excellent education while growing up and attended the Moscow University, where he received a doctoral degree in philosophy. Afterward, he became a professor at the Moscow University until 1881, when he was forced to resign after publicly criticizing the death sentence passed on the assassins of Czar Aleksandr II.

Solovyov's poetry was closely connected with his philosophical and scholarly works, for which he is primarily remembered today. Deeply influenced by Plato, he adopted many of the Platonic ideals in the development of his own philosophy in conjunction with the beliefs of the Russian Orthodox Church. Although Solovyov was hardly a liberal in his political beliefs, he supported land reforms and other democratic reforms to ease the suffering of the Russian masses. His views became more and more reactionary as the Russian antigovernmental opposition became more and more violent.

Although initially sympathetic to the democratic cause and socialism, Solovyov's philosophy took a bitter turn toward the end of his life and became firmly grounded in Christian mysticism. He began to write about the end of history and the coming of the Antichrist.

A Work by Vladimir Solovyov
Politics, Law, and Morality: Essays by V. S. Solviev. London: Yale University Press, 2000.

A Work about Vladmir Solovyov
Kostalevsky, Marina. *Dostoevsky and Soloviev: The Art of Integral Vision.* London: Yale University Press, 1997.

Solzhenitsyn, Aleksandr (1918–2008)
novelist, historian
Aleksandr Isayevich Solzhenitsyn was born in Kislovodsk, Russia. His father died in a hunting accident six months before Solzhenitsyn's birth, and his mother supported the family by working as a typist. Solzhenitsyn studied mathematics and physics at the Rostov University,

graduating with honors in 1941. While studying sciences, he also completed correspondence courses in literature at the Moscow State University. During World War II, he served as a captain of the artillery and was decorated for bravery. After writing a letter in which he criticized Stalin, he was sent to the political prison camps, where he remained from 1945 to 1953.

Most of Solzhenitsyn's work deals with his experiences during imprisonment. His first published novel, *One Day in the Life of Ivan Denisovich* (1958), appeared in the leading literary journal of the Soviet Union, *Novy Mir*. The novel dramatically portrays a day in the life of a political prisoner in one of the Stalin's labor camps. After the publication of the novel, Solzhenitsyn attracted negative attention from the government. His second novel, *Cancer Ward* (1968), was initially rejected. The novel describes the lives of patients suffering and dying from cancer as an allegory for Stalinist persecutions; it was viewed as too radical by the authorities. *The First Circle* (1968), set during the late 1940s and the early 1950s, depicts a group of scientists who are forced to work on secret government projects in the labor camps.

By 1966, all of Solzhenitsyn's works were censored. In 1965, the KGB confiscated numerous manuscripts, and when Solzhenitsyn complained to the Soviet Writers' Union, he was expelled. Fortunately, Solzhenitsyn's works were smuggled abroad and were immediately recognized as dramatic testimony to Stalin's purges and persecutions. In Russia, Solzhenitsyn's work was secretly distributed in underground editions. Although he was awarded the Nobel Prize in literature in 1970, Solzhenitsyn was forced by the Soviet government to decline it. After *Gulag Archipelago* was published abroad in 1973, Solzhenitsyn was arrested and charged with treason. *Gulag Archipelago* contains personal testimony, interviews, and memories of the victims of Stalinist oppression. For the first time, the world could read about the unimaginable extent of Stalin's labor camps, where millions of political prisoners slaved for years. Solzhenitsyn was stripped of Soviet citizenship and forcibly deported to Switzerland.

Solzhenitsyn accepted his Nobel Prize in 1974, after his deportation from Russia. In 1990, his citizenship was reinstated, and all charges against him were dropped. He returned to Russia in 1994 and settled near Moscow.

Solzhenitsyn's work is considered groundbreaking, particularly for its fearless exposure of the oppressive nature of the Soviet political system. Solzhenitsyn remains the central figure of dissident literature, as well as one of the best-known Russian writers of the 20th century. His prose is distinct not only for its content but also for its well-developed narrative, highly descriptive diction, and realistic dialogue.

In 2001 and 2002, Solzhenitsyn published *Two Hundred Years Together*, a two-volume history of Russian-Jewish relations. The book sparked controversy, and many historians regard it as not only anti-Semitic but also factually inaccurate. Solzhenitsyn claimed that Jews were overrepresented among the early Bolshevik leaders of Russia. He also accuses Jews of cowardice for failing to serve during World War II. He says, "I had to bury many comrades at the front, but not once did I have to bury a Jew."

In 2007, Russian president Vladimir Putin conferred on Solzhenitsyn the State Prize of the Russian Federation for his humanitarian work. Solzhenitsyn died of heart failure in 2008.

Critical Analysis

Solzhenitsyn's *The Gulag Archipelago* is a nonfictional account of the imprisonment and murder of millions of citizens of the Soviet Union by their own government, primarily during Stalin's rule from 1929 to 1953. Solzhenitsyn's subject is "that amazing country of Gulag which, though scattered in an archipelago geographically, was, in the psychological sense, fused into a continent—an almost invisible, almost imperceptible, country inhabited by the zek people [prisoners]." Written between 1958 and 1968, Solzhenitsyn used his own experiences of a Gulag labor camp from 1945 to 1953 and accounts related to him by 227 other survivors.

"GULag" is an acronym for the Russian *Glavnoye Upravleniye ispravitelno-trudovyh Lagerey*, which literally translates into "Chief Administration of Corrective Labor Camps." At one level, *The Gulag Archipelago* traces the history of the Soviet concentration camp and forced labor system from 1918 to 1956, beginning with its origins in Lenin's initial creation of an economy based partially on a prison-camp system. Solzhenitsyn also follows the typical course of a *zek* through the system, starting with the arrest, "show" trial, internment, and "transport to the 'archipelago'; treatment of prisoners and general living conditions; slave labor gangs and the technical prison camp system; camp rebellions and strikes; the practice of internal exile following completion of the original prison sentence; and ultimate (but not guaranteed) release of the prisoner."

Subtitled "An Experiment in Literary Investigation," *The Gulag Archipelago* almost caused Solzhenitsyn to lose his life. Due to the KGB's surveillance of him, Solzhenitsyn only worked on parts of the manuscript and hid sections of the work throughout Moscow and the surrounding suburbs. Despite the seriousness of its subject and the risk Solzhenitsyn took in writing it, the work is noted for its humor. "Rather than a grim rendering of crimes and atrocities," one critic writes, "*The Gulag Archipelago* often contains sarcastic and ironic gallows humour. Precisely because of this dark humour, the prose often turns human and profoundly moving without ever falling into sentimentality or self-pity."

A Work about Aleksandr Solzhenitsyn

Scammell, Michael. *Solzhenitsyn: A Biography.* New York: Norton, 1984.

Souza, Eunice de (1940–) *poet, novelist, critic*

Eunice de Souza was born in Pune, India. She is of Goan Roman Catholic origin. Her father, an aspiring novelist, filled their house with books and inspired de Souza's love for literature and writing. In addition to writing four collections of poetry, she has put together anthologies of poems by other Indian poets. De Souza also writes folktales for children, is a regular contributor to newspapers and magazines, and is a respected literary critic. She was the head of the English department at St. Xavier's College, Mumbai, where she helped start an annual literary festival called Ithaka.

De Souza's anthology of Indian women poets of the 20th century is called *Nine Indian Women Poets* (1997). One of her inspirations for starting the project was her discovery of an obscure, ancient poem by a female monk. She began the anthology in the hopes that such moments of literary history would never again be neglected. *Nine Indian Women Poets* uncovers the contribution of women poets, such as Kamala Das and SUJATA BHATT, and their role in advancing an old tradition of women writing in India. The anthology also reveals the different ways modern poetry has developed as a mode of expression for women in India.

De Souza's own poetry is in English, combined with a sharp, witty and scathing language from Mumbai's streets, that reflects the author's own personality. Famous for her highly opinionated and critically discerning work, de Souza is often hailed as a feminist. She herself claims that poetry and propaganda do not belong together and that she would have to admit she prefers writing about her pet parrots.

In recent years, de Souza has turned her hand to editing. In 2004, she published, *101 Folktales from India* and *Purdah: An Anthology.* In 2005, she published *Early Indian Poetry in English: An Anthology 1829–1947* and *The Satthianadhan Family Album.*

Other Works by Eunice de Souza

Conversations with Indian Poets. New York: Oxford University Press, 2001.
Dangerlok. New Delhi: Penguin Books, 2001.
Dev & Simran. New York: Penguin Books, 2003.

Soyinka, Wole (Akinwande Oluwole Soyinka) (1934–   ) *playwright, poet novelist, essayist*

Soyinka was born to Samuel Ayodele, a teacher, and Grace Eniola Soyinka, a shopkeeper, in western Nigeria. Both of his parents were Yoruba, a major tribal group in this West African country. He showed immense intellectual ability at an early age and was eventually able to go to England to study at the University of Leeds. Soyinka returned to Nigeria after graduating and worked to develop a Yoruba-based theater. He was influential in training many young people as the head of the Drama School of Ibadan University until he was arrested in 1967. Soyinka worked and wrote for the freedom of Biafra, a section of Nigeria, and his writings led to his imprisonment for almost two years. He details the experience in his text *The Man Died: The Prison Notes of Wole Soyinka* (1972), in the preface, of which, he says, "Books and all forms of writing have always been objects of terror to those who seek to suppress the truth."

Books were smuggled in to him while he was imprisoned. Soyinka read them ceaselessly and then wrote on these and other loose pieces of paper. In a sense, he inscribed his life in between the lines of other texts. Ultimately, the books were smuggled out, and the experience, as well as much poetry, was reconstituted. Some of the poetry can now be read in collections such as *A Shuttle in the Crypt* (1972). Soyinka's act of writing himself into existence within an unforgiving environment, using whatever materials were available, is an apt metaphor for how he has dealt with the legacy of colonialism in Nigeria. Like his countryman CHINUA ACHEBE, Soyinka draws on his cultural inheritance to make sense of the postcolonial world he inhabits.

He has written several autobiographical books that also portray Nigeria from the 1940s to the 1960s. Soyinka depicts his coming of age in *Ake: The Years of Childhood* (1981) and his early adulthood in *Ibadan, The Penkelemes Years, A Memoir: 1946–1965* (1994).

Critical Analysis

In his play, *Death and the King's Horseman* (1975), Soyinka depicts a proud Yoruba leader who must make an impossible choice. His king has died, and he is expected to will himself to death and follow his king. A colonial administrator imprisons the king's "horseman" (a form of commander, and a very revered position), and the Yoruba takes this interference as a sign that his gods do not wish him to die. But the very people who had worshiped him now shun and insult the once-renowned warrior. In the most affecting portion of the play, the protagonist, Olori Elesin, sways and becomes one with the rhythmic pulse of the drums as they beat him on his way to the welcome embrace of eternity. Elesin's death is sad, yet honorable, even magnificent. His gesture is not futile—he does not act out of personal pride or desperation—rather, his embrace of this appropriate end fulfills the proper Yoruba tradition and leaves an honorable legacy.

Soyinka adapted the historical events of a 1946 incident to ground his play, but it is important to note that he refuses the label of a "clash of cultures" for his representations of such events. In much the same way that he inscribed himself into books while in prison, he takes the historical reality of colonialism and "writes" himself and his people into it. In this way, he examines the legacies left to his country while still insisting on the cultural vigor of his own people. Further, this form of writing his people into European versions of history allows Soyinka to avoid merely politicizing in favor of a joyous embrace of the power of theater itself.

Many of his plays deal with political themes. For example, *Madmen and Specialists* (1975) is set during the civil war in Nigeria in the 1960s and depicts the struggle between an interrogator and his prisoner.

Soyinka's poetry also deals with political subjects, but it is also often concerned with everyday Nigerian existence. For example, in the poem "Telephone Conversation," from the collection *Reflections* (1980), the speaker of the poem tries to entice a young woman into a date. The young woman wants to know just how dark, how "black" he is before she will agree. The young man simply wants her to see him for herself.

Soyinka's political thought is best viewed in his collection of essays, *The Open Sore of a Continent* (1996), which examines Nigeria's descent into turmoil in the 1990s. His outspoken criticism of the government led to a death sentence on the now-exiled writer. He published *You Must Set Forth at Dawn: A Memoir* in 2001.

It would be difficult to overstate the importance of Wole Soyinka to world literature. He was the first black African to win the Nobel Prize for literature (1986) and has a dazzling variety of texts that point to his prolific ability and his immense versatility.

Other Works by Wole Soyinka

Climate of Fear. New York: Random House, 2005.
Idanre and Other Poems. New York: Hill and Wang, 1967.
Madmen and Specialists. New York: Hill and Wang, 1971.
Myth, Literature, and the African World. Cambridge, U.K.: Cambridge University Press, 1976.

Works about Wole Soyinka

Katrak, Ketu. Wole Soyinka and Modern Tragedy: A Study of Dramatic Theory and Practice. Westport, Conn.: Greenwood Press, 1986.
Wright, Derek. Wole Soyinka Revisited. Boston: Twayne, 1993.

Sri Sri (Srirangam Rao Srinivasa)
(1910–1983) *poet, novelist*

Sri Sri was born in Vishakapatnam, Andhra Pradesh, India. After finishing his education in Madras, he became a subeditor for a daily newspaper and also worked for All India Radio. He wrote his first poem when he was seven and his first novel when he was nine.

Sri Sri is best noted for his radical attempts to use literature for social critique. His poetry is stylistically uncomplicated and composed of simple vocabulary, a trademark of "progressive poetry," a new school of Telugu poetry that Srinivasa started in the mid–1950s. The new movement attracted young writers because of its aim to change the style, content, and mythical and religious topics of traditional Telugu poetry. These poets were often called the militant young poets of Telugu literature. Their poetry characteristically resisted any romanticization and, instead, was concerned with reform and progress.

Sri Sri wrote creative, journalistic, and critical works that were collected into a six-volume anthology in Telugu titled *Sri Sri Sahityamu* (1972). The difference in genre, however, did not change the thematic kernel of his writing, which is to uncover the reasons for social inequalities. The poem "Hogwash" is a list of questions, posed to an imaginary "Sir." The speaker of the poem refuses to believe that the other man's economic privilege is a product of his own "illusion." Rejecting silence, he asks: the landlord's / Rolls Royce, / an illusion? / the prince's / fat wallet, / an illusion? / Sir / how can it be?

Sri Sri's contribution to Telugu literature was not only his original work. Profoundly influenced by dadaism (see DADA) and surrealism, he translated the works of CHARLES BAUDELAIRE (1821–61), ANDRÉ BRETON (1896–1966), and Salvador Dalí (1904–89) into Telugu. In 1966, Sri Sri was awarded the Lenin Peace Prize for his collection of poems called *Creation by the Sword*. In 1970, he became the first president of the Revolutionary Writers' Association of India.

Another Work by Sri Sri

Mahaprasthanam. Machilipatnam, India: Nalini Kumar Publishing House, 1950.

A Work about Sri Sri

Dharwadker, Vinay, and A. K. Ramanujan, eds. *The Oxford Anthology of Modern Indian Poetry.* London: Oxford University Press, 1994.

Srivastav, Dhanipat Rai
See PREMCHAND, MUNSHI.

Staël, Germaine de (Anna Louise Germaine Necker, Baronne de Staël-Holstein) (1766–1877) *novelist*

Anna Louise Germaine Necker was born in Paris to Swiss parents active in contemporary political and intellectual life. As a young child, she was tutored privately in her home and spent much time attending her mother's celebrated intellectual salon, where she had the opportunity to become acquainted with such leading intellectual figures as Edward Gibbon and Denis Diderot. As finance minister to Louis XVI, her father, Jacques Necker, directly experienced the turmoil of the revolution of 1789. He was a major influence on his daughter.

At age 20, Mademoiselle Necker married a Swedish diplomat, Baron Staël-Holstein. The baron was 17 years older than she and, though a titled nobleman, penniless. She supported the moderates during the revolution, but when her life was threatened, she fled to England and helped others escape the terror. Her major work on the revolution, *Considerations sur la Révolution française* (*Thoughts on the French Revolution*), was not published until after her death. When she returned to Paris, her home became an intellectual and political salon of great power where writers, critics, and other artists gathered together to discuss not only politics and literature but also fashion trends and the development of social manners and customs. Although Staël and her husband separated in 1797, they remained on friendly terms.

Critical Analysis

Staël was a writer from a very young age. Influenced by Jean-Jacques Rousseau, she published the short stories "Mirza" and "Zulma" in 1795. Among the issues raised in these stories are the difficulties of being a writer when women were increasingly confined to a domestic role and the iniquities of the slave trade. In 1796, she published the major treatise *De l'influence des passions* (*On the Influence of the Passions*), following it in 1800 with *De la littérature* (*On Literature*). This work, which relates literature to social and political structures, transformed literary theory and founded comparative studies.

In 1794, Staël became romantically and intellectually involved with BENJAMIN CONSTANT, whose ideas were a great source of inspiration to her. Under his influence, she began to read the works of AUGUST WILHELM SCHLEGEL (1767–1845) and his brother Friedrich (1772–1829) and dared to oppose Napoleon's policies.

Staël's first major novel, *Delphine* (1802), gained her attention both popularly and politically. Following the release of a nonfiction study of the effects of social conditions on literature, the novel is a politically challenging look at the destiny of women in a male-dominated, aristocratic society. Above all, the work questions the accepted norms of society as they pertain to the rights of women as intellectually independent people. Staël denied allegations that her work was intended to provoke a political response, claiming to be more intent on observations of fact than on causing open opposition to the norm. Napoleon, however, considered the work such a threat to the traditions of French society that he exiled Staël in 1803.

Staël retreated to Coppet on Lake Geneva, where she had an estate. There, she surrounded herself with a circle of highly influential and intelligent friends and associates. She traveled as much as possible, and a trip to Italy provided her with the inspiration for her second major novel, *Corinne* (1807). This work strips away all of the trappings of neoclassicism to express itself fully in the style of French ROMANTICISM. It is a tragic love story about an Italian woman, an intellectual, who falls for an English lord. The novel challenges, once again, the accepted norms for women in society—its main character, Corinne, is a celebrated poet, who ultimately loses her lover because he desires a less complex and more domestic partner. Other early feminist themes pervade the text as well, such as the rights of women to chose whom to love and to be intellectuals. These themes are developed alongside descriptions of Italy's artistic and architectural

beauty and of evocations of the ideal of individual freedom not hampered by gender or class.
The novel stands as one of Staël's most influential
works, affecting not only the development of the
French novel but also literary trends in England
and the United States.

Staël's principal theoretical work, *De l'Allemagne* (*On Germany,* 1810) was also the result of
her travels. It again brought her to Napoleon's attention. Although government censors did not see
the book as a threat, Napoleon disliked it because
he resented the comparisons Staël made between
French and German cultures to the detriment of
the French. In 1811, he ordered the destruction of
the entire first edition, stating that it had no business being published in the first place because it
was "un-French." Several copies of the book escaped destruction, however, and made their way
to England, where they were published in a new
edition and were well received. *De l'Allemagne* introduced German Romantic literature and idealist
philosophy into France and was a major influence
on the French Romantic movement.

In 1811, after a series of affairs with influential men, de Staël secretly married a young officer nearly half her age, Jean Rocca. Together they
had one child, a boy, who was born mentally
retarded. By this time, Staël had two other children, a boy fathered by a revolutionary whom
she had helped escape to England in 1793 and
a daughter, most probably fathered by Constant.
Harassed repeatedly by the police, Staël exiled
herself and her family, fleeing to Russia and then
to England.

In 1815, Staël returned to Coppet and republished *De l'Allemagne.* Although her health was
declining rapidly, she enthusiastically participated
in the political life of France and, in spite of her
long-standing history of problems with Napoleon,
warned him of a threat that had been made on his
life.

Staël suffered a stroke on July 14, 1877, and
died in Paris. One of her best-known works, *Ten
Years of Exile* (1821), which was largely autobiographical, was published posthumously.

Another Work by Germaine de Staël

*An Extraordinary Woman: Selected Writings of Ger-
maine de Staël.* Translated by Vivian Folkenflik.
New York: Columbia University Press, 1987.

Works about Germaine de Staël

Besser, Gretchen Rous. *Germaine de Staël Revisited.*
Boston: Twayne, 1994.
Hogsett, Charlotte. *The Literary Existence of
Germaine de Staël.* Carbondale: Southern Illinois
University Press, 1987.

Stead, Christina (1902–1983) *novelist, short story writer*

Christina Stead was the child of English parents who immigrated to Rockdale, New Sydney,
Australia, where she was born. After the death of
her mother, Ellen Butters Stead, when Christina
was two years old, she was raised and influenced
by her father, David George Stead, a naturalist
who worked as an economist for the Australian
fisheries. When her father remarried Ada Gibbons,
Stead was expected to help care for the six children whom their marriage produced. She received
her education in Sydney, graduating from Sydney
University Teacher's College in 1922. After working for a short time at the university as a demon-
strator in experimental psychology and then in
Sydney Schools as a teacher of abnormal children,
Stead became a secretary until she decided to leave
Australia in 1928, working as a clerk first in London
and then in Paris.

During her years in Europe, Stead began writing fiction, producing a collection of rather bizarre short stories, *Salzburg Tales* (1934), and
a novel, *Seven Poor Men of Sydney* (1934). Soon
after this, she met William Blake, an American
financier, writer, economist, and socialist, whom
she eventually married in 1952 and lived with
until his death in 1968. Stead and Blake lived in
Spain until the threat of civil war and then moved
to the United States, living in New York and then
Hollywood, where Stead worked as a screenwriter
for MGM during World War II. They returned to

Europe after the war, living in various countries until Blake's death. Stead finally returned to Australia in 1974, where she lived and wrote until her own death.

Although Christina Stead is the author of numerous novels and several collections of short stories, she is best known for her brilliant portrayal of a dysfunctional family in *The Man Who Loved Children* (1940). Loosely based on the lives and relationships of her father and her stepmother and their children, including herself, the novel depicts Sam and Hetty Pollit, each of whom seems unable to speak in a language that the other understands, so they employ their children as their means of communication, having them convey messages and carry notes back and forth between their parents. Also suffering from economic reversals after the death of Hetty's wealthy father, the family's struggles with angry creditors, Sam's passivity when it comes to fighting to keep his government job, Hetty's unwanted sixth pregnancy, the stepdaughter Louisa's defiance of her father, and an anonymous false accusation Sam receives that the baby is not really his, the family is unable to survive the passionate destructiveness and selfishness of the parents, whose battles become physical and life threatening. Louisa, who longs to save the children from their parents, wants to kill them both but manages to poison only Hetty, who actually realizes what is happening and thus chooses it as well. Sam, however, cannot believe that Louisa is indeed responsible for his wife's death, and Louisa is finally driven to escape from her father to survive. Stead's success in capturing the psychological truths of each character and the vividness with which she conveys their animosity has made *The Man Who Loved Children* a memorable book for which she has received the most acclaim, especially after its reissue in 1965 by an American publisher.

Another Work by Christina Stead

Letty Fox: Her Luck. New York: New York Review of Books, 2001.

Works about Christina Stead

Rowley, Hazel. *Christina Stead: A Biography.* New York: Henry Holt & Company, 1995.

Sheridan, Susan. *Christina Stead.* Bloomington: Indiana University Press, 1988.

Stendhal (Marie-Henri Beyle)
(1783–1842) *novelist, essayist*

Best known for his two masterpieces, *Le rouge et le noir* (*The Red and the Black,* 1830) and *La chartreuse de Parme* (*The Charterhouse of Parma,* 1839), Stendhal was born as Marie-Henri Beyle in Grenoble to a wealthy lawyer. His mother passed away in childbirth when Stendhal was very young. At age 16, he moved to Paris ostensibly to study, but he entered the military before ultimately settling on a career as a writer.

Stendhal enlisted in Napoleon's army in May 1800 and served for 18 months as a lieutenant, fighting in Russia, Germany, and Italy. His dreams, however, were not centered on achieving military accolades; he hoped to become one of the greatest comic poets of all time. When he resigned from active service, he took a post in civil and military administration, which he held until the fall of the French empire in 1814. At that point, he was given a 50 percent pay cut, making his income inadequate to his needs. He searched for other employment for several years but was unable to secure anything in France. Ultimately, he decided to move to Italy, where his first book, a travel piece entitled *Rome, Naples, and Florence in 1817* (1817), was published. This was also the first time he chose to use the pen name of Stendhal.

Stendhal returned to Paris in 1821, taking advantage of his success as a writer and the steadily improving conditions in France. He frequented salons where he could discuss the latest ideas on art, literature, and politics. He continued to do well as a writer, publishing *On Love* (1822) and *Racine and Shakespeare* (1823) in quick succession. *On Love,* a psychology of love, is a collection of thoughts and ideas that show Stendhal as an early sympathizer, particularly with regard to his feelings on women's education. *Racine and Shakespeare* is an important romantic manifesto that insists that literature should reflect its historical moment. These works were well received, but his first novel, *Armance* (1827), a psychological study of impotence, was scorned by the critics.

Critical Analysis

The Red and the Black was a breakthrough for Stendhal. Inspired by a newspaper account of the trial of a young man for attempted murder of a married woman, it advanced the development of the novel in its complex and ironic interweaving of the psychological and the historical. It tells the story of Julien Sorel, a peasant, in the context of the post-Napoleonic period between 1815 and 1830. Sorel uses seduction and hypocrisy to rise in society, but believing that his mistress has betrayed him, he shoots the one woman he ever really loved. Finally, he rejects his lies and masks and, a condemned man, stands before the court to attack social inequality and oppression:

> Gentlemen, I have not the honour to belong to your social class. You see in me a peasant in revolt against the baseness of his fate. . . . I see men who would like in my person to punish and dishearten for ever that class of young people who, born in a lowly and poverty-stricken class, had the chance to educate themselves and the courage to associate with those circles which arrogance of the rich calls society. . . .

After the revolution of 1830 and the rise to power of King Louis-Philippe, Stendhal was appointed French consul in the small Italian port town of Civitavecchia. While there, he wrote *Memoirs of an Egoist,* (published 1892), in which he provides a vivid depiction of life in and among the salons, museums, and theatres of Paris. This work, along with two others, *Lucien Leuwen: The Green Huntsman,* which depicts the corruption under the reign of Louis-Philippe, and the largely autobiographical piece *The Life of Henry Brulard,* which was left unfinished, remained in manuscript at Stendhal's death, but were published in the 1890s.

Stendhal's political views were often motivated by his own success or failure under a prevailing regime. If he was doing poorly, he tended to mock and criticize the ruling body for his lack of success. However, as soon as he began to thrive, his views shifted and he became moderately conservative. He composed his second great work, *The Charterhouse of Parma,* between 1836 and 1839, which is concerned with a search for identity. The protagonist, Fabrizio del Dongo, defines himself in areas as diverse as the battlefield at Waterloo and a Carthusian monastery. He experiences the frustrations of war, politics, love, and the loss of his child. He finally withdraws to the Charterhouse of Parma, where he dies. The work was published to great acclaim, rapidly gaining popularity, and critical success.

The Charterhouse of Parma was destined to be Stendhal's last major accomplishment. In 1841 he suffered a stroke, which forced him to take a leave of absence from his post and return to Paris. Late in the evening of March 22, 1842, Stendhal was taking a walk down a Paris street when he collapsed, unconscious, to the ground. He died a few hours later on March 23.

Another Work by Stendhal

Lamiel, or the Ways of the Heart. Translated by Jacques Le Clercq. New York: H. Fertig, 1978.

Works about Stendhal

Keates, Jonathan. *Stendhal.* London: Sinclair-Stevenson, 1994.
Pearson, Roger. *Stendhal's Violin: A Novelist and His Reader.* New York: Oxford University Press, 1992.
Talbot, Emile J. *Stendhal Revisited.* Boston: Twayne, 1993.

Storni, Alfonsina (Alfonsina Tao-Lao)
(1892–1938) *poet, dramatist, journalist*

Alfonsina Storni was born in Sala Capriasca, Switzerland, and moved with her cultured Italian-Swiss parents to Argentina at the age of four. When her father died in 1900, she was obligated to work in a cap factory, as an actress, and later as a schoolteacher. Her first poems were published in 1910, the year she moved to Buenos Aires. In 1911, she gave birth to an illegitimate child and later worked as a journalist and a teacher to support herself and her son.

Storni's first book of poems, *The Restlessness of the Rose Bush,* appeared in 1916, and her poetry between 1916 and 1921 reflects an intense romantic subjectivity. Her poetry was well received—in 1920, she won First Municipal Poetry Prize and Second National Poetry Prize.

By 1925, Storni's poetry was becoming more objective, as reflected in *Ochre* (1925), which focuses on the sea, and in *World of Seven Wells* (1934). Between 1926 and 1934, many of her plays were performed in theaters in Buenos Aires. During this period, she also authored, under the pseudonym Tao-Lao, various critical articles that appeared in the newspaper *La Nación.*

Her last books of poems, *Magnetized Circles* (1938) and *Mask and Trefoil* (1938), reflect her cynicism, her feminist rebelliousness, and her powerful language. By then, Storni had been dealing with breast cancer for three years, and when the cancer returned in 1938, she chose to commit suicide by filling her pockets with stones and drowning herself in the sea at Mar del Plata. She sent her final poem, "I Want to Sleep," now considered to be a suicide poem, to *La Nación* so that it would be received at the same time she entered the sea.

Another Work by Alfonsina Storni

Selected Poems of Alfonsina Storni. Translated by Mary Crow and Norman Ton. Fredonia, N.Y.: White Pine Press, Inc., 1996.

A Work about Alfonsina Storni

Phillips, Rachel. *Alfonsina Storni: From Poetess to Poet.* United Kingdom: Boydell & Brewer, Inc., 1975.

Strindberg, August (1849–1912)
playwright, short story writer, novelist

August Strindberg was born in Stockholm, Sweden, to Carl Oscar Strindberg, a shipping agent, and Ulrika Eleanora Norling, a woman of working-class origins. Norling had been Carl Oscar's domestic servant but later became his mistress and mother to August. Strindberg's childhood was quite unhappy: He experienced the loss of his mother at age 13, endured poverty and family conflicts, and suffered abuse from his stepmother.

In 1867, Srindberg entered the University of Uppsala but failed to pass a preliminary examination in chemistry and had to leave. He worked at the Royal Dramatic Theater as an assistant manager and then returned to the University of Uppsala, where he finally received his degree in 1872. On graduation, Strindberg worked in Stockholm as a journalist and, from 1864 to 1882, served as an assistant librarian at the Royal Library.

Strindberg was married three times. His first, unsuccessful marriage was to the Baroness Siri von Essen, a member of the Swedish aristocracy in Finland, with whom he had three children. He married a second time in 1893 and a third time in 1901. These unions also ended in divorce, and he lost custody of his children.

Strindberg's first nationally successful novel, *The Red Room* (1879), focuses on the rise of industrialism in Sweden. The protagonist of the novel, Arvid Falk, is an aspiring youth who dreams of becoming a writer. Although he is talented, Falk rejects the uncertainties of a writer's life for a stable middle-class existence. Strindberg suggests that it is almost impossible to devote ones life to aesthetic pursuits in a world controlled by capitalistic values. The novel was popular throughout Sweden and established Strindberg as one of the foremost writers of Scandinavian literature.

During the years between 1883 and 1887, while living in France and Switzerland, Strindberg faced financial troubles and found himself on the verge of a nervous breakdown. This psychological imbalance culminated in clinical paranoia and a dependence on absinthe, a liquor made from wormwood. In 1884, Strindberg published *Getting Married,* a novel based on his experience during marriage. This frank portrayal of the institution of marriage outraged many in Sweden. Strindberg was put on trial charged with blasphemy, but he was eventually acquitted. He developed a deep distrust of women, whom he saw as persecutors, and believed that his wife was behind a plot to have him committed to a mental institution.

Critical Analysis

Strindberg's most famous play, *Miss Julie* (1888), was also one of his most controversial works. Julie, the daughter of a prosperous count, allows Jean, a male servant, to seduce her during a night of festivities. Jean understands that marriage between him and Julie is impossible. Fearing for his position, Jean psychologically corners Julie, and she commits suicide. *Miss Julie* combines the elements of NATURALISM and REALISM that made it a masterpiece. It depicts a Darwinian struggle between the sexes that is further amplified by the respective social roles and positions of the two main characters. Many critics have compared *Miss Julie* to HENRIK IBSEN's *A Doll's House.* Both plays are classified as works of realism, but the representations of femininity found in the two plays are strikingly different. Julie is ultimately dominated by Jean, while Nora, even in defeat, is dominated by no one. Today, *Miss Julie* is Strindberg's most frequently performed play.

Between 1892 and 1897, Strindberg experienced one mental crisis after another. Constantly under attack by critics, and haunted by the guilt of loosing custody of his children, Strindberg was on a verge of a complete collapse. Still, he eventually recovered and entered the most productive period of his career. Between 1898 and 1909, Strindberg wrote 36 plays, most of which deal with life, death, and various aspects of marriage.

In a *A Dream Play* (1901), however, Strindberg breaks with the realism of the previous works. All actions are presented in the form of the thoughts, dreams, and psychological perceptions of Daughter of Indra, a mysterious, luminous figure who seemingly descends from heaven. The play seems to foreshadow the many theories of Austrian psychoanalyst SIGMUND FREUD about the separation of the conscious from the unconscious and the active role of the former in the formation of the individual psyche. Most critics rejected the play as absurd, although some realized the genius of Strindberg's work.

Between 1907 and 1908, Strindberg experimented with various forms of theater. He introduced chamber music as part of his plays, and he exchanged the traditional single protagonist for a small group of equally important characters. These and other innovations had a long-lasting and dramatic influence on traditional conceptions of theater.

During his life, August Strindberg wrote more than 70 plays in addition to numerous novels, short stories, and essays. Today, he is considered to be among the most influential playwrights and theoreticians of the modern period. The controversial subjects of his plays challenged audiences to question what was suitable for theater and how plays should be performed. Strindberg's works have been the single most important source of inspiration for the German EXPRESSIONIST movement and for many contemporary playwrights as well.

Other Works by August Strindberg

Five Plays. Translated by Harry Carlson. Riverside: University of California Press, 1996.
Inferno and from Occult Diary. New York: Penguin, 1988.
Miss Julie and Other Plays. Oxford: Oxford University Press, 1999.

Works about August Strindberg

Lagercrantz, Olaf. *August Strindberg.* New York: Farrar, Straus & Giroux, 1984.
Meyer, Michael. *Strindberg: A Biography.* Oxford: Oxford University Press, 1987.

Suleri, Sara (Sara Suleri Goodyear)
(1953–) *novelist, critic*

Sara Suleri was born in Karachi, Pakistan. Her father, Ziauddin Ahmed, is Pakistani and an active political journalist. Her mother, Mair Jones, is Welsh and a professor of English literature. Suleri completed her master's degree at Punjab University and went on to Indiana University, where she received her doctorate degree in English in 1980. She became a professor at Yale University in 1981 and is the founder and editor of the *Yale Journal of Criticism.*

Her first novel, *Meatless Days* (1989), has several obvious similarities to her own life and is claimed by many critics to be an autobiographical memoir, though the author herself denies it. The narrator of the novel searches for her identity as it changes in time, memory, and space. Moving between Asia and America, the narrator depicts with longing what can be lost in transformations through cultural exchange and remembered relationships. Her search for her own identity, however, underlies the equally important search for Indian and Pakistani female identity in a history that has silenced them. *Meatless Days* is a personalized narrative on the search for women's presence and their voices.

Suleri is also the author of the critically distinguished work *The Rhetoric of English India* (1992). This book looks into the formation of colonial and postcolonial India and Pakistan through the English language by examining the works of authors such as Rudyard Kipling (1865–1936), E. M. Forster (1879–1970), V. S. NAIPAUL, and SALMAN RUSHDIE.

Another Work by Sara Suleri

Boys Will Be Boys: A Daughter's Elegy. Chicago: University of Chicago Press, 2003.

A Work about Sara Suleri

Smith, Sidonie, and Watson, Julia, eds. "Women Skin Deep: Feminism and the Postcolonial Condition." In *Women, Autobiography, Theory: A Reader.* Madison: University of Wisconsin Press, 1998.

Svevo, Italo (Ettore Schmitz) (1861–1928)
novelist, short story writer

Considered one of the pioneers of the Italian psychological novel, Italo Svevo was born Ettore Schmitz in the town of Trieste, then part of the Austrian Empire. The son of a German Jewish glassmaker and his Italian wife, Svevo was sent to Germany at age 12 to attend boarding school. He later returned to Trieste to continue his education, which was abruptly terminated when he was in his late teens as a result of his father's failure in business. Svevo took a position as a clerk but continued to spend much of his free time reading and, ultimately, writing as well.

Svevo published his first novel, *Una vita (A Life,* 1892), when he was 31 years old, using his pseudonym for the first time. The work gained attention immediately for its revolutionary introspective, analytic style. Svevo continued to publish works in this style, which were later classified as psychological novels; at the time, however, the newness of his tone made his works difficult to comprehend, resulting in their being ignored by critics once their curiosity wore off. Svevo's second novel, *As a Man Grows Older* (1898), received a similar lack of attention, at which point he officially gave up writing to pursue a career in his father-in-law's business. (He continued to write short stories throughout this period.)

Svevo's business career required him to travel, and many of his trips were to England. To improve his command of English, he employed as a tutor the young writer James Joyce, who was living in Trieste and teaching at the Berlitz school. In spite of their age difference, they rapidly forged an enduring friendship. Joyce allowed Svevo to read portions of his work in progress, *Dubliners,* and, in his turn, Svevo gave Joyce both of his novels to read. Joyce found the works to be enthralling and encouraged Svevo to resume his writing endeavors. As a result, his best-known work, *La coscienza di Zeno (Confessions of Zeno,* 1923), was published. Written in the first person, it represents an attempt by the narrator to discover through analysis the source of his nicotine addiction. Again, the work was ignored, but two years after publication, Joyce arranged for publication of a French translation. Svevo became famous in France, and his popularity slowly grew in Italy, helped by the support of

EUGENIO MONTALE, as the psychological novel gained acceptance.

Svevo was in the process of working on a sequel to *Zeno* when he was killed in an automobile accident on September 13, 1928. His contribution to Italian literature, however, included a stream-of-consciousness style, which was present in both *Zeno* and several posthumously published short stories, as well as his advancement of the genre of the psychological novel in Italy.

Another Work by Italo Svevo

Emilio's Carnival (Senilità). Translated by Beth Archer Brombert. New Haven, Conn.: Yale University Press, 2001.

Works about Italo Svevo

Gatt-Rutter, John. *Italo Svevo: A Double Life.* Oxford: Clarendon Press, 1988.
Svevo, Livia Veneziani. *Memoir of Italo Svevo.* Translated by Isabel Quigly. London: Libris, 1989.
Weiss, Beno. *Italo Svevo.* Boston: Twayne, 1988.

symbolism

Predominant in France at the end of the 19th century, and evident in Belgium as well, the symbolist movement, strongly influenced by CHARLES BAUDELAIRE's essays on poetry and art, originated with the work of a group of French poets, including PAUL VERLAINE, STÉPHANE MALLARMÉ, and ARTHUR RIMBAUD. It reached its peak around 1890, and the principles on which it was founded continued to influence MODERNIST movements of the early 20th century.

Symbolism began as a reaction against the prevailing literary trends of REALISM and NATURAL-ISM. Because of the tendency of symbolist poets to focus on the artificial and grotesque as opposed to the natural, as well as their common thematic use of ruin and decay, the writers of this movement were also commonly associated with the subsequently emerging DECADENT movement.

Beginning in the 1830s, realism became the dominant form of literary expression in France. It was later followed by the similar but revised naturalist movement. Both schools of thought based their works entirely on factual observations of contemporary society and sought to portray life without glamorization or pretense. Toward the end of the century, particularly in Paris, symbolists began to challenge this style, believing that words and language as they currently existed were superficial. Therefore, they declared that to represent and transform the reality of modern life, the poet must recreate language. Through the use of symbols, poets could create patterns of meanings based on symbolic representation and allusion rather than direct statement. The symbolists affirmed the transcendent possibilities of the imagination.

There are a number of specific themes common to symbolist poetry, but the main focus is on the difficult role of the poet in modern urban life. The symbolist poets shared with the decadents a common FIN DE SIÈCLE sense of brooding melancholy and darkness.

Early symbolists experimented with form, resulting in the development of poetic free verse, poetry that, whether rhymed or unrhymed, disregards conventional rules regarding poetic meter. It often borrows patterns from natural speech in place of the more affected diction common to traditional poetry. This form is still the prevailing standard in modern poetry.

Another technique, which has existed since Homer but was exploited especially by French symbolists, is synesthesia, describing one sensation in terms of another (for example, describing sound with colors). Symbolist poets used synesthesia as a means of uncovering the correspondences between different sensory impressions, as in Baudelaire's famous "Correspondances" from *Les fleurs du mal* (*The Flowers of Evil*, 1857).

While the symbolist movement had its origins in poetry, its influence eventually began to extend to fiction, drama, music, and the visual arts. The prominent members of the school, such as Rimbaud, Verlaine, and Mallarmé, can all trace their influence to the works of Charles Baudelaire, who was influenced by Edgar Allan Poe, as their precursor; in turn, they influenced the writings of Paul Claudel, Paul Valéry, Maurice Maeterlinck, and others. Similar movements arose outside of France, and symbolism's effects reached as far as the United States in the works of writers such as Dylan Thomas and e.e. Cummings.

Russian Symbolism

Symbolism began in Russia a little later than in France and flourished until the Russian Revolution (1917). Deeply rooted themselves in mysticism, the Russian symbolists viewed themselves as a nexus between the Russian people and some higher spiritual realm. Like its French counterpart, Russian symbolism manifested itself in drama, poetry, prose, and graphic art; however, it achieved its full force almost exclusively in poetry. Like their French models, the Russian symbolists experimented with verse forms and especially with free verse.

The symbolists rejected realist notions about the social purposes of art. For the symbolists, the artist was a semidivine figure whose work would guide the Russian people to an ideal future. Symbolists often viewed the imagination as a different level of reality, and they used obscure images and strange metaphors to convey their feelings of detachment from the reality of everyday life.

Aleksandr Blok, Vladimir Solovyov, and Andrey Bely were the leading figures of symbolism in Russia, but it is Solovyov who is considered the most important originator of the movement in Russia. Solovyov created a new form of mysticism based on the worship of the Eternal Feminine, dually identified as nature and as the muse that endowed poets with inspiration. Solovyov's work was the single most important foundation for the Russian symbolist movement.

The symbolist movement served an extremely important function in Russian literary history by bridging the gap between realism and acmeism. Although poets such as Anna Akhmatova later rejected symbolism, the movement was an extremely important early influence on her generation of poets and on later generations as well.

Works about Symbolism

Fowlie, Wallace. *Poem and Symbol: A Brief History of French Symbolism*. University Park: Pennsylvania State University Press, 1990.

Frantisek, Deak. *Symbolist Theater: The Formation of an Avant-garde*. Baltimore: Johns Hopkins University Press, 1993.

McGuinness, Patrick, ed. *Symbolism, Decadence and the Fin de Siècle: French and European Perspectives*. Exeter, U.K.: University of Exeter Press, 2000.

Pyman, Avril. *A History of Russian Symbolism*. New York: Cambridge University Press, 1994.

Szymborska, Wislawa (1923–) *poet*

Wislawa Szymborska was born in Bnin, now a part of Kornik, in western Poland. In 1931, she moved with her family to Krakow where, during the German occupation of Poland in World War II, she attended classes illegally. After the war, she studied Polish literature and sociology at the Jagiellonian University. She worked as a poetry editor and columnist for the Krakow literary magazine *Zycie Literacia* until 1981.

Szymborska's first published poem was "Szukam slowa" ("I Am Looking for a Word," 1945). She finished her first collection of poetry three years later, but the communist Party's strict cultural policy deemed the work to be too complex, and it was not published. As a result, Szymborska concentrated on making her work more political, and her first collection, *Dlagtego Zyjemy,* appeared in 1952.

Szymborska's early works conformed to the style of socialist realism. Later, she became disillusioned with Communism and expressed her pessimism about humanity's future in her poems. Her 1996 poem "Tortures," with the line "Nothing has changed" that opens each stanza, connects the cruelties of the 20th century with the entire human experience over the ages: "Tortures are as they were, it's just the earth that's grown smaller."

In 1996, Szymborska won the Nobel Prize in literature "for poetry that with ironic precision allows the historical and biological context to come to light in fragments of human reality." She is one of the few female poets ever to have received this prize. Szymborska has published 16 collections of poetry. Her poems have been translated into numerous languages and have also been published in multiple anthologies of Polish poetry.

A private person by nature, Szymborska avoided public appearances but served as an inspiration for other female writers. In her acceptance speech for the Nobel Prize, she described her role not only as an artist but as a member of a larger humanity: ". . . inspiration is not the exclusive privilege of poets or artists generally. There is, has been, and will always be a certain group of people whom inspiration visits. It's made up of all those who've consciously chosen their calling and do their job with love and imagination. . . . Whatever inspiration is, it's born from a continuous 'I don't know.'"

Other Works by Wislawa Szymborska

Here. New York: Houghton Mifflin Harcourt, 2010.

Miracle Fair: Selected Poems of Wislawa Szymborska. Translated by Joanna Trzeciak. New York: Norton, 2001.

Monologue of a Dog. New York: Houghton Mifflin Harcourt, 2005.

Poems New and Collected. Translated by Stanislaw Baranczak and Clare Cavanagh. Orlando, Fla.: Harcourt Brace, 1998.

T

Tabucchi, Antonio (1943–) *novelist, short story writer, translator*

A scholar and translator, Antonio Tabucchi is especially known for his work on the Portuguese poet FERNANDO PESSOA. He is a true master of the short story and has often been mentioned as a contender for the Nobel Prize in literature.

Tabucchi was born in Pisa, in the Italian region of Tuscany. He was educated at the University of Pisa and then went to the Scuola Normale Superiore di Pisa. From 1978 to 1987, Tabucchi worked as a lecturer in literature at the University of Genoa. In 1991, he became professor of Portuguese at the University of Siena.

As a novelist, Tabucchi made his debut in 1975 with *Piazza d'Italia*, which, in tragicomic style, sought to trace a short history of Italy's triumphs and tribulations from 1860, when the country was first unified, to the end of the World War II in 1946. Turbulent and eventful, this history is written from the losers' point of view.

During his years at university, Tabucchi traveled widely around Europe on the trail of his favorite authors. On one of his journeys, he found the poem "Tobacco Shop" in Paris, signed by Alvaro de Campos, which was one of the so-called heteronyms (an imaginary character, created by the poet so that he could write in different styles)

of Fernando Pessoa. The Portuguese poet, who was relatively unknown during his lifetime, became Tabucchi's principal interest for at least the next 20 years. Tabucchi edited Pessoa's poems and published critical studies of his work, as well as the novel *The Last Three Days of Fernando Pessoa* (1994). In the collection of short stories, *In Dreams of Dreams*, Tabucchi imagines dreams of famous writers and artists. One of the dreamers is Pessoa, who meets his poetical personality, Alberto Caeiro, in South Africa, on March 7, 1914. The future Portuguese bard begins to write poetry the very next day, in accordance with Caeiro's advice.

The question of identity has been a central theme in Tabucchi's fiction; he thinks that the most notable characteristic of 20th century literature has been the "fracture" between art and life, or reality and illusion, within the modernist antihero who has doubts about his genuine self. In *Indian Nocturne* (1984), the narrator travels to India to search for his friend, Xavier, who turns into the narrator's alter ego and eventually claims the narrative, imposing his voice as the dominant one.

Tabucchi wrote *Requiem: A Hallucination* (1992) as his homage to Lisbon. In *Pereira Declares: A Testimony* (1994), he deals with more serious issues. In Lisbon in 1938, a cultural editor takes a stand against the regime of António Salazar, the

Portuguese dictator. The book became a best seller, and in Italy the figure of the editor Pereira was turned into a symbol of resistance, adopted by the left-wing opposition who opposed the media magnate Silvio Berlusconi and his right-wing coalition in the 1994 parliamentary campaign. Berlusconi was elected Italy's prime minister three times, once in 1994, once in 2001, and again in 2008.

Tabucchi's novels and stories deal with painful episodes of European history, such as the Spanish civil war or fascism. His writing is clear, but much is left unsaid, and the mood is often melancholic and dreamlike.

Tabucchi's awards include the Inedito Prize in 1975, the Pozzale Luigi Russo Prize in 1981, the French Prix Médicis étranger in 1987, the Viareggio and Campiello Prizes in 1994, and the Nossack Prize from the Leibniz Academy in 1999.

Tabucchi's books and essays have been translated into 18 languages. He spends six months of the year in Lisbon with his wife, a native of the city, and their two children and the rest of the year in Siena, Italy, where he teaches Portuguese literature. Tabucchi regularly contributes articles to the cultural pages of the Italian and Spanish newspapers. In the 1990s, he was one of the founders of the International Parliament of Writers, which, among other activities, maintains a network of refuge cities for displaced writers and their families.

Other Works by Antonio Tabucchi

Little Understandings of No Importance. Translated by Francis Frenaye. New York: New Directions Publishing Corporation, 1989.

Vanishing Point (The Woman of Porto Pim and the Flying Creatures of Fra Angelico). Translated by Tim Parks. New York: Vintage, 1993.

Tagore, Rabindranath (Rabindranath Thakur) (1861–1941) *poet, novelist, dramatist, essayist*

Rabindranath Tagore was born in Calcutta, India, into an affluent family that was also very invested in Indian politics. His great-grandfather

Dwar-kanath Tagore was a businessman; Tagore's father, Debendranath Tagore, however, was more involved in religion than in politics and revived an old religious movement called the Brahmo Samaj. Rabindranath Tagore combined his grandfather's visions for the country with his father's religious asceticism, and his works, therefore, represent a unique synthesis of powerful national politics and spiritual poeticism. Tagore is the author and composer of India's national anthem, as well as the lyrical composer of a song by BANKIM CHATTOPADHYAY called "Vande Materam" (Hail Motherland), which was adopted as India's unofficial national anthem during its problems before independence from British rule.

In his memoir *My Reminiscences* (1911), Tagore calls his memory a "picture-chamber . . . a series of pictures [which] correspond, but are not identical." A pioneer in integrating East–West poetic, political, and even scientific structures, Tagore is one of the key figures in the intellectual movement called the Bengal renaissance. The Bengal renaissance consisted of a group of writers who took advantage of colonial education and Western culture while at the same time contributing to Indian literature for an Indian audience.

This attitude reflected Tagore's own belief that education is interdisciplinary, bringing together science with humanism and politics with spirituality, and it was realized in the foundation of Shantiniketan (Abode of Peace), a school on the outskirts of Calcutta. This place, under the guidance of Tagore, who also taught there, grew into a meeting place for national and international scholars of music, painting, singing, and languages. Today, it thrives as one of West Bengal's prominent educational institutions.

In 1921, Tagore also founded Shriniketan (Abode of Plenty), a school that sought to bring Western scientific progress to India. At the same time, the preservation of nature was very important to Tagore, and this was enhanced by the foundation of Shriniketan, whose objective was to bring agricultural progress to the countryside. Tagore's works reflect his deep concern and respect for nature, and the need to bridge the gap between human and natural existence. In one of his letters he says that "I feel . . . I was one with the rest of the earth, that grass grew green upon me, that the autumn sun fell on me and its rays . . . wafted from every pore of my far-flung evergreen body." This is one of the most important themes in his poetry.

Tagore translated many of his own works into English. With the aid of W. B. Yeats and Thomas Sturge Moore, he brought out a translation of his religious and spiritual poetry called *Gitañjalī* (*Offering of Songs*, 1910). They were a huge success, and their publication caught the attention of renowned figures such as Albert Einstein, Ezra Pound, and ANDRÉ GIDE, with whom Tagore kept up regular correspondences. Their admiration of his work secured Tagore's position as an international poet. *Gitañjalī* borrows from India's ancient and traditional religious poetry. Written from a modern perspective, these poems take a new look at the conventional understanding of the relationships between nature, God, and spirituality. In these poems, the search for human spirituality goes beyond traditional religion.

Tagore's most famous novel, *The Home and the World* (1915–16), is about rural politics, though its tone is extremely nonpolitical. As the title suggests, the novel delves into how the domestic and political realms of power overlap. In this story, the woman protagonist defies social norm by coming out of the inner rooms of the house to join the men in their discussion of politics in the living room. She also allows herself to act on the gallant advances made to her by her husband's friend. The change in friendship between the two men is complicated through the female protagonist's fluctuating romantic attachment to both men. As the two male friends become increasingly estranged due to politics, it is the woman of the home who reveals the true meaning of faithfulness, loyalty, and commitment. Her honesty and open curiosity humanize the novel's ruthless description of rural politics, and her story stresses the importance of domestic issues in the political struggles of the outside world.

By the time of his death, Tagore was idolized as one of India's leading political figures, a national poet, a painter, and an educational visionary. He experimented with almost all literary genres and left behind a prodigious assortment of novels, short stories, songs, poetry, plays, essays, as well as correspondence with friends, family, and international contemporaries such as W. B. Yeats and Ezra Pound. In 1913, Tagore was awarded the Nobel Prize for literature for his translation of *Gitañjalī*. In 1919, he refused England's offer of knighthood in protest against human-rights violations under British rule.

Other Works by Rabindranath Tagore
The Broken Nest. Columbia: University of Missouri Press, 1971.
The Hungry Stones and Other Stories. New York: Macmillan, 1916.
Nationalism. London: Macmillan Publishers, 1917.
Selected Poems. Translated by William Radice. London: Penguin, 1985.

A Work about Rabindranath Tagore
Kipalani, Krishan. *Rabindranath Tagore: A Biography.* London: Oxford University Press, 1962.

Takamura Kotarō (1883–1956) *poet*
Takamura Kotarō was born in Tokyo to sculptor Takamura Kōun and his wife, Waka. His father, hoping that his son would follow in his footsteps, sent Takamura to Tokyo Fine Arts School in 1897. Even so, Takamura was already demonstrating an interest in literature and had begun to write and publish haiku and tanka. In 1906, he left to study in the United States, England, and France. When he returned to Japan, he fell in with dissolute artists and writers. In 1914, he married Naganuma Chieko. During the war, he acted as the head of the Japanese Literature Patriotic Association. Takamura took defeat hard and retreated to a country cabin in Iwate Prefecture for seven years, some believe to come to terms with the guilt he expressed over

having encouraged young soldiers to battle and thus their deaths.

Takamura's first poems were written in traditional poetic forms. He began to write free verse, however, when he returned to Japan. His first poem of note, "The Lost Mona Lisa," published in 1911, was about the disappearance of a prostitute. His first collection of poetry, *The Road Ahead*, published in 1914, challenged conceptions of poetry by using subjects and diction that were not traditionally considered appropriate. *Chieko's Sky*, his second collection, was published in 1941 and consisted of love poems to his wife.

Takamura always considered himself first and foremost a sculptor, but he is more highly regarded as a poet who helped redefine the landscape of modern poetry. His most significant poetry is in free verse. In particular, his love poems to his wife garner the greatest praise for their moving emotional content and for their clear expression.

Other Works by Takamura Kotarō

A Brief History of Imbecility: Poetry and Prose of Takamura Kotarō. Translated by Hiroaki Sato. Honolulu: University Press of Hawaii, 1992.

Chieko and Other Poems of Takamura Kotarō. Translated by Hiroaki Sato. Honolulu: University Press of Hawaii, 1980.

Works about Takamura Kotarō

Keene, Donald. *Dawn to the West: Japanese Literature in the Modern Era: Poetry, Drama, Criticism*. New York: Holt, Rinehart and Winston, 1984.

Rabson, Steve. *Righteous Cause or Tragic Folly: Changing Views of War in Modern Japanese Poetry*. Ann Arbor, Mich.: Center for Japanese Studies, University of Michigan, 1998.

Tanikawa Shuntaro (1931–) *poet*

Tanikawa Shuntaro was born in Tokyo, Japan, to Tanikawa Tetsuzo, a philosopher, and Tanikawa Taki (Osada), a pianist. Tanikawa began writing poetry in his teens after a high-school friend asked him to contribute to a poetry magazine. When his father asked him what he intended to do instead of entering college, Tanikawa handed him notebooks that he had filled with poems. Recognizing talent, his father gave the poems to Miyoshi Tatsuji, Japan's leading poet at the time, who helped get them published in the *Bungakkai* (*Literary World*) magazine when Tanikawa was still in his teens. Tanikawa's first book collection, *Twenty Billion Light Years of Loneliness* (1952), was published when he was 21.

Tanikawa says his early work was influenced by volumes of poetry from his father's library, but his work breaks with the major traditions of Japanese verse. He does not write haiku, although his strong, startling imagery is similar to the form's vivid word pictures. In a poem entitled "Colours," he ends with this surprising image: "Despair is a simple colour / Pure white." Many of his poems allude to icons of American popular culture, such as jazz musician Miles Davis and actor James Dean. His central theme is the isolation of the individual who stands alone facing an incomprehensible universe. In "The Isolation of Two Million Light Years," he comments, "The human race, on its little ball, / Sleeps, wakes, and works, / Wishing at times for companionship with Mars."

Tanikawa is Japan's most popular poet. He has published more than 60 volumes of poetry; has written scripts for television and film, children's books, song lyrics, and plays; and has translated Charles Schultz's comic strip "Peanuts" into Japanese. He has won many Japanese literary awards as well as an American Book Award for the English translation of *Floating the River in Melancholy* (1988). According to Geoffrey O'Brien of the *Village Voice*, Tanikawa "receives praise and the kind of lavish editions reserved in America for the long deceased."

Other Works by Tanikawa Shuntaro

Naked (Asian Poetry in Translation). Yokohama, Japan: Saru Press International, 2005.

Shuntaro Tanikawa: Selected Poems. Translated by William I. Elliott and Kazuo Kawamura. New York: Persea Books, 2001.

A Work about Tanikawa Shuntaro

Morton, Leith. "An Interview with Shuntaro Tanikawa," *Southerly* 58, no. 1 (Autumn 1998): 6–31.

Tanizaki Jun'ichirō (1886–1965) *novelist, short story writer, playwright, essayist*

Tanizaki Jun'ichirō was born in Tokyo to Tanizaki Kuragorō and Seki. While he was a boy, his father lost the family fortune, so when Tanizaki, a gifted student, gained entrance to the prestigious Metropolitan Middle School and the First Higher School, his family could not afford tuition. To continue his education, Tanizaki worked as a houseboy for a wealthy family until he had an affair with a maid and was dismissed. In 1908, he entered the Japanese literature department of Tokyo Imperial University but was expelled for failing to pay his fees. In 1915, he married Ishikawa Chiyo, whom he divorced 15 years later. He quickly married reporter Furukawa Tomiko. However, this marriage lasted less than a year because he had begun to court another woman, Nezu Matsuko, whom he eventually married.

While attending university, Tanizaki published his first short story, "The Tatooer" (1910), which won the acclaim of critics. It was not until 1924 that Tanizaki produced his first novel, *Naomi,* which depicts a man who makes an ill-fated attempt to turn his lover into a Western woman. Five years later, Tanizaki's focus shifted to traditional Japan in his novel *Some Prefer Nettles* (1929). In 1933 he crafted a chilling masterpiece, "The Story of Shunkin," a short story about a servant who blinds himself to preserve in his mind the image of his mistress, who has become disfigured in an attack.

During the war years, Tanizaki worked on his most lyrical novel, *The Makioka Sisters* (1948). In the last year of his life, he published *Diary of a Mad Old Man,* the story of a scheming, aging man who suffers a stroke during a liaison with a woman.

Tanizaki insisted that fiction should be artifice. His stories, while reflecting the issues and trends of the time, were entirely created worlds rather than fictionalized accounts of personal experiences or historical events. His stories typically revolve around male protagonists and their relationships with women. In 1949, Tanizaki received the Imperial Order of Culture.

Other Works by Tanizaki Jun'ichirō

The Key. Translated by Howard Hibbett. New York: Knopf, 1961.
Seven Japanese Tales. Translated by Howard G. Hibbett. New York: Knopf, 1963.

Works about Tanizaki Jun'ichirō

Gessel, Van C. *Three Modern Novelists: Sōseki, Tanizaki, Kawabata.* Tokyo: Kodansha International, 1993.
Ito, Ken K. *Vision of Desire: Tanizaki's Fictional Worlds.* Stanford, Calif.: Stanford University Press, 1991.

Tao-Lao, Alfonsina

See STORNI, ALFONSINA.

Thakur, Rabindranath

See TAGORE, RABINDRANATH.

Thammachoat, Atsiri

See DHAMMACHOTI, USSIRI.

theater of the absurd

Taking its name from the idea of the absurd as something not grounded in logic or reason, the theater of the absurd is related to aspects of EXISTENTIALISM. The movement itself actually refers to a style of drama that began in Paris and flourished in the late 1940s and 1950s.

The roots of theater of the absurd can be traced back as far as the morality plays of the Middle Ages, the Spanish religious allegories, the nonsensical writings of Lewis Caroll, and the macabre and grotesque drama of ALFRED JARRY. It was anticipated by DADAISM and the surrealist movement of the 1920s and 1930s and gathers much of its theoretical accountability from ANTONIN ARTAUD's text *The Theatre and its Double* (1938; translated 1958). The term itself comes from the use of the word *absurd* by existentialist philosophers such as ALBERT CAMUS and JEAN-PAUL SARTRE in reference to the lack of a rational explanation for the human condition.

Although Alfred Jarry's *Ubu Roi* (1888) anticipates much of the foundation on which absurdist drama rests, the three playwrights most closely associated with the movement's popularity are JEAN GENET, EUGÈNE IONESCO, and SAMUEL BECKETT. Their works take on a nightmarish quality as they examine contemporary alienation and human anxiety over the absence of social coherence or transcendental meaning. Many playwrights, such as Beckett, wrote in French though it was not their native language, and communicated a sense of linguistic estrangement.

According to some sources, Beckett was the most influential writer of the period. His *Happy Days* expresses humanity's fear of death through the character of a woman who, in the first act, is buried up to her waist in a mound of dirt. By the second act, the mound has grown so that only her head remains visible, a metaphoric vision of the ultimate journey from life to death and burial.

Other playwrights of this school wrote of similar anxieties. Ionesco emphasizes the fear of mediocrity and the inability to communicate in *The Bald Soprano* (1950). Genet's works, on the other hand, fuse illusion with reality in an often violently erotic manner to exemplify the absurd roles that people play in daily existence.

The influence of theater of the absurd, created by a group of international writers living in Paris, extends beyond France to the works of Czechoslovakian playwright VÁCLAV HAVEL, British writers Harold Pinter and Tom Stoppard, and U.S. dramatists Edward Albee and Sam Shepard.

A Work about Theater of the Absurd

Esslin, Matin. *Theatre of the Absurd.* New York: Overlook Press, 1969.

Theodorescu, Ion N.

See ARGHEZI, TUDOR.

Tian Jian (Tien Chien; Tong Tianjian)
(1916–1985) *poet*

Tong Tianjian was born on May 14 in Anhui province's rural Wuwei County, in China. He moved to Shanghai in 1933 and studied foreign languages at Guanghua University, where he edited the journals *New Poetry* and *Literary Mosaic*. He published poems written during his college years in *Before Dawn* in 1935.

Tian Jian's poetry was known as declamatory poetry because of its political nature and revolutionary ideas. Much of his work was influenced by the Japanese occupation of Nanking and the Sino-Japanese War and had a very nationalistic slant.

Before the Sino-Japanese War, Tian Jian focused on the lives of Chinese peasants, for whom he wrote two volumes of poetry, *Pastoral Songs* (1936) and *Stories of the Chinese Countryside* (1936). The latter is a long poem comprised of three parts: "Hunger," "On the Yangtze River," and "Go Ahead." Tian Jian used the river as a metaphor for China and depicted the hardships of peasant life and resistance against the old regime.

In the spring of 1937, Tian Jian traveled to Japan and returned to China after the Sino-Japanese War began later that year. He served as a war correspondent with the Service Corps on the Northwestern Battlefield. He wrote poems influential for their military fervor and rhythms during the war in two volumes, *Odes to Soldiers on Patrol in a Sandstorm* (1938) and *Poems Dedicated to Fighters* (1943).

Tian Jian joined the Chinese Communist Party in 1943. He held high-level information posts and participated in land reform. He also continued his literary pursuits. He began a drive for "street verse," edited a new party literary magazine called *New Masses,* and joined the Chinese Writers Association after its 1949 formation. He then taught at the Central Institute of Literature in Beijing.

During the Korean War, Tian Jian served again as a war correspondent and visited Eastern Europe and Africa in 1954. He produced many volumes of poetry and essays, including *A Hero's Battle Song* (1959), *Travels in Africa* (1964), and *A Sketch on a Trip to Europe* (1956), before the onset of the Cultural Revolution, when he was suppressed.

After the revolution ended, Tian Jian began to write poetry again in 1976. His work celebrated the new life of "liberated" peasants, such as *China in her Prime* (1986). Tian Jian died August 30, 1985, in Beijing.

Toer, Pramoedya Ananta (1925–2006)
novelist

Pramoedya Ananta Toer was born in Blora, a small town on the north coast of Java, Indonesia. His father was a former teacher and an activist of the Blora branch of the PNI (Indonesian National Party). His mother was the daughter of a mosque official and a former student of his father. Toer was the eldest of nine children. He graduated from the Radiovakschool in Surabaya in 1941. To avoid conscription into the Dutch army, Toer fled back to Blora. During the first four months of the Japanese occupation, he looked after his ill mother and his younger siblings. When his mother died, the family moved to Jakarta.

Toer wandered over much of Java after he had been passed over for promotion. He returned to Jakarta after he learned about the declaration of independence by Sukarno, Indonesia's former president, in August. Following the reorganization of the Indonesian army in late 1946, he became the editor of the journal *Sadar,* the Indonesian edition of *The Voice of Free Indonesia.*

Toer was imprisoned for two years for possessing anti-Dutch political documents and was one of the last men to be released in 1949. He was immediately given a position by the government literary bureau, Balai Pustaka, an appointment he temporarily postponed because of his father's death. Between 1950 and 1951, Toer was an editor for the modern-literature department of Balai Pustaka and for the magazines, *Indonesia* and *Kunang-Kunang (Firefly).* He became a member of the Lekra (Institute for People's Culture), an affiliated organization of the Indonesian Communist Party, and lectured in the Res Publica University in Jakarta. He also edited "Lentera," the literary column in the daily paper *Bintang Timur.*

His sympathy for the despised Chinese in Indonesia landed him in trouble with Sukarno's "Guided Democracy" government. He was arrested in 1969 and sent to Buru Island, where he spent 10 years in exile. He was released in 1979 but was placed under house arrest by the new government a few years later. Toer's works had been banned in Indonesia since 1965, but they were extremely popular outside Indonesia, were printed in at least 28 languages, and won him international fame as a defender of truth and human rights. Finally in 1997, with the toppling of the Suharto regime, Toer was released from house arrest, and the ban on his works was lifted. He died in April 2006 at the age of 81.

Critical Analysis

Toer's works are extremely valuable to the study of Indonesian history. In *The Girl from the Coast,* Toer tells the story of his grandmother, derived from his interactions with her, others' perceptions of her, and his own imagination. Interwoven into the tale is a complex exploration of class conflict and gender relations at the village level. As in many of Toer's works, he intersperses his story with references to historical events, such as Kartini's death, enabling the reader to place episodes within a temporal context. Kartini was a princess of the Javanese royal family who was extremely influential in providing education for all. This story, which was first published in Indonesian in 1987, is the first in an untitled semiautobiography. Unfortunately, the second and third parts have been lost.

Toer's voice clearly emerges in his works. He writes with an intensity that emanates emotions ranging from anguish and melancholy to soft compassion and harsh indignation. His writings appeal through their sheer reflection of lived experiences that are both real and sadly universal. Toer is able to draw his readers into his world by enabling them to live vicariously through his own experience and tragedy. In *The Fugitive* (1962), a novel of betrayal and bravery during the Japanese occupation of Indonesia during World War II, the plight of Raden Hardo, the hero of the tale, bears similarity to Toer's own experience during the war. His attachment to Javanese attitudes and cultural beliefs is also revealed. The characters in the story, such as Hardo and Dipo, clearly resemble heroic characters that can be found in the Javanese traditional art form, the *wayang,* a shadow-puppet theatrical medium of performance.

Toer's storytelling skill is best exemplified in his 1999 work, *Tales from Djakarta: Caricatures of Circumstances and Their Human Beings.* In this collection of short essays, he is able to paint with great accuracy and biting wit the scenes of daily life in 1950s Jakarta, the capital of Indonesia. Through his writing, the bustling city with its ironic contrast of the luxurious quarters of the rich and the simmering squatters of the poor comes to life. He narrates with sarcastic wit the plight of the common people, some of whom rise above their station and others who miserably fail. Toer's stories do not always end in tragedy; for instance, in "Maman and His World" (1999), Maman, a poor *kampung* boy is able to build and own his own factory through hard work and perseverance. Maman's kindness and generosity also enable him to enlarge his wealth. Toer's heroes are taken from a variety of backgrounds, but his most poignant ones are those who remain untouched by avarice and other vices.

Toer was first propelled to fame when he completed the novel *Kranji-Bekasi Jatuh* in 1947. During his imprisonment in the Bukit Duri jail from 1948 to 1949, he wrote the short-story collections *Percikan Revolusi* and *Perburuan.* The latter won him first prize from Balai Pustaka. His greatest works are *Bumi Manusia, Anak Semua Bangsa,* and *Jejak Langkah.*

Toer's popularity in the literary world bespeaks his power to write convincingly and realistically about the plight of the common person not only in Indonesia but all over the world. His characters are universal, and his use of historical contexts and periods enables readers to better understand Indonesia's past.

Other Works by Pramoedya Ananta Toer

Child of All Nations (Buru Quartet, Volume 2). Translated by Max Lane. New York: Penguin USA, 1996.

Footsteps (Buru Quartet, Volume 3). Translated by Max Lane. New York: Penguin USA, 1996.

House of Glass (Buru Quartet, Volume 4). Translated by Max Lane. New York: Penguin USA, 1997.

The Mute's Soliloquy: A Memoir. Translated by Willem Samuels. New York: Hyperion, 1999.

This Earth of Mankind (Buru Quartet, Volume 1). Translated by Max Lane. New York: Penguin USA, 1996.

Works about Pramoedya Ananta Toer

Hering, Bob, ed. *Pramoedya Ananta Toer 70 Tahun: Essays to Honour Pramoedya Ananta Toer's 70th Year.* Indonesia: Yayasan Kabar Seberang, 1995.

Koh, Young Hoon. *Pemikiran Pramoedya Ananta Toer dalam Novel-novel Mutakhirnya.* Kuala Lumpur: Dewan Bahasa dan Pustaka, 1996.

Tolstoy, Leo (Count Lev Nikolayevich Tolstoy) (1828–1910) *novelist, short story writer, dramatist*

Leo Tolstoy was born in the town of Yasnaya Polyana, Russia, into a landowning family. His mother, Princess Volkonskaya, died when he was two years old, and his father when he was nine. He and his siblings were raised by relatives and educated by private tutors. At 16, Tolstoy entered the University of Kazan, but after dabbling in oriental languages and law, he returned to the family estate in 1847. A restless and high-spirited youth, he soon tired of the country and spent the next several years in St. Petersburg and Moscow, living a profligate life and keeping a diary in which he recorded even the most outrageous of his adventures. In 1852, seeking adventure, he joined his brother in the army. He was cited for bravery in the defense of Sebastopol. He left the army in 1856 and returned to the family estate with the idea, radical for the time, of educating and emancipating his serfs.

Tolstoy's early education included grounding in several European languages and literatures, and he continued to enlarge this knowledge over the next several years with extensive travels. He read widely and was particularly taken with the ideas of the 18th-century French writer Jean-Jacques Rousseau. He was also well acquainted with the English novelists Laurence Sterne and Charles Dickens, who helped form his approach to the novel, while Rousseau and the New Testament influenced his later religious and philosophical works.

Tolstoy had begun his literary career with the publication, while he was still in the army, of an autobiographical work, *Childhood* (1852), and this was followed by *Boyhood* in 1854 and *Youth* in 1857. Material for these works came from his prodigious memory, substantially abetted by reference to the detailed diary he had begun in 1847. Though the facts of Tolstoy's early life form the basis of these books, their rearrangement and modification show us the budding writer of fiction learning his craft. Other short stories, based on his army experiences, followed in 1855 and 1856. In 1862, Tolstoy married Sofiya Bers, with whom he would have 13 children. His obsessive honesty led him to give her his diaries to read, and the young bride was, at the least, startled. She later got even by giving Tolstoy *her* diary to read. But marriage had

a settling influence, and in the next 15 years following that, Tolstoy produced his greatest works, *War and Peace* (1865–69) and *Anna Karenina* (1875–77).

Tolstoy's approach to his work of this period was to observe carefully even the most minute details of his characters' lives and to record them faithfully, building the story in the same way that real life reveals itself. The great English critic and essayist Matthew Arnold said that if life could write its own story, it would write like Tolstoy. The two novels are not led by preconceived literary ideas of how structure, plot, and narrative are to be delineated; they happen, as life happens.

Critical Analysis

War and Peace is the story of five aristocratic Russian families, their associates, and the effects of Napoleon's wars from 1805 to 1820. The novel also contains essays that reflect Tolstoy's philosophy of history. The central love story involves Natasha Rostova and Pierre Bezukhov. Natasha finds fulfillment in marriage and motherhood, serving as an example of the value of life's simple processes. Meanwhile, Pierre searches for the philosophical system that will explain to him the meaning of life, but he comes, for a while at least, to believe that no such system exists outside of the common routines of existence.

In the essays on history and in the novel's chaotic plots, Tolstoy repudiates the theory that great men make history and that events are shaped by human intention. He views Napoleon and the Russian emperor Aleksandr as pompous men whose bumblings cause great misery. The pretenses of noble society are shown to be hollow as well. The character Prince Andrey Bolkonsky eschews the false values and artificialities of social life, substituting for a while the values of heroism and bravery in battle. He is severely wounded at Austerlitz and, while attempting to recuperate, realizes that these values as well are worthless. Tolstoy's own values are exemplified by the less sophisticated characters. Critics often have noted that Tolstoy describes his characters' thinking and behavior in minute detail, like a painter adding small brushstrokes, until, through sheer accretion, a full portrait appears. As the novel proceeds through its many years, the characters age; Natasha, for instance, grows from a giddy and self-centered girl to a portly and concerned mother.

Anna Karenina, though set in the same aristocratic milieu as *War and Peace,* is not as panoramic in scope. Based on the true story of a young woman's suicide in Tolstoy's province, it tells of the aristocratic Anna, who conducts an adulterous love affair with the dashing army officer Aleksey Vronsky. For him, she leaves both her husband and her beloved little boy. In contrast to her self-defeating romantic attachment is the true love of Kitty and Konstantin Levin. Kitty is the sister of the unhappy Dolly Oblonsky, whose careless husband Stiva has been unfaithful to her.

Anna is Stiva's sister and in some ways is as careless as he; she wants romance and persuades herself that it is owed her. Society does not accept Anna's self-assertion in the face of convention, and she is ostracized. When she comes eventually to see the flaws in her lover, she has lost the love of her good but dull husband and sees no way out of her guilt-ridden life except suicide. Levin and Kitty meanwhile have bonded with a true love that accepts the daily limitations of being human.

Underlying both these works and the great changes that took place in Tolstoy's life soon after the publication of *Anna Karenina* are the philosophical musings of Jean Jacques Rousseau, apostle of what has come to be known as ROMANTICISM. Central to this doctrine is the idea of the *noble savage,* which holds that only those not infected with civilization's postures and deceptions are truly good. Civilization includes high society, secular and sacred institutions, commerce and money, legalisms and rank. Though Tolstoy used his reading of Rousseau to profound effect in his two great novels, when he

tried to put these theories into practice, he ran into serious trouble, both artistic and personal. Among other things he was excommunicated from the Russian Orthodox Church, and he seriously alienated most of his family, particularly his wife, by repudiating the great novels and attempting to give away all his worldly goods. His writing suffered from his preoccupations, although his two later novellas, *The Death of Ivan Ilyich* (1886) and *The Kreutzer Sonata* (1891), are still widely read. A third long novel, *Resurrection,* was published in 1899, and at about this time he wrote a play, *The Living Corpse.*

Tolstoy proceeded into an ascetic and anarchistic old age. Although his philosophical meditations do not have the standing today they once had, his influence was profound, especially on the young MOHANDAS GANDHI: Passive resistance toward evil was a principle advocated by Tolstoy that Gandhi used with great effect to liberate India from foreign rule. Tolstoy's later convictions and behavior so contradicted his earlier ones that he sought literally to run away from them. Hounded by the demons of his own philosophy, he died while attempting to escape media attention in a provincial railroad station.

Works about Leo Tolstoy

Berlin, Isaiah. *The Hedgehog and the Fox: An Essay on Tolstoy's View of History.* New York: Simon & Schuster, 1986.

Bloom, Harold, ed. *Leo Tolstoy: Comprehensive Research and Study Guide.* Broomall, Pa.: Chelsea House, 2001.

Gifford, Henry. *Tolstoy.* New York: Oxford University Press, 1982.

Orwin, Donna Tussing, ed. *The Cambridge Companion to Tolstoy.* New York: Cambridge University Press, 2002.

Shirer, William. *Love and Hatred: The Stormy Marriage of Sonia and Leo Tolstoy.* Upland, Pa.: DIANE Publishing Co., 1994.

Troyat, Henri. *Tolstoy.* Translated by Nancy Amphoux. New York: Grove Press, 2001.

Tong Tianjian
See TIAN JIAN.

Tornimparti, Alessandra
See GINZBURG, NATALIA.

Torres Bodet, Jaime (1902–1974) *novelist, poet*

Jaime Torres Bodet was born in Mexico City. He was the son of Alejandro Torres Girbent, a theatrical producer, and Emilia Bodet. Torres Bodet believed it was important for a writer to work a "regular" job and to be involved in the world. He was an educator and would eventually be appointed minister of education for Mexico.

He and his literary group, the Contemporaneos, were seminal in bringing modern European literature to the attention of Mexican intellectuals in the first half of the 20th century. His novel *Movie Star* (1933) contrasts the world of psychology and imagination with the reality of everyday life in a modern style that brought intellectual vitality to the Mexican novel.

Later in his life, when he was involved in his political career, he dedicated himself almost exclusively to the writing of poetry. In 1965, he published a volume titled *Poems by Jaime Torres Bodet*, which included his own selection of his 50 most important poems. His poetry demonstrates his ideas about the importance of everyday life as a subject for literature. In it, he writes passionately about simple experiences.

Torres Bodet is remembered for his great expressive force in writing. He received the National Literature Award in 1966, and the Mexican government issued a commemorative stamp in his honor in 1975. Torres Bodet's poetry is considered thoughtful, sensitive, and humanistic.

Another Work by Jaime Torres Bodet
Selected Poems. A bilingual edition with translations by Sonja Karsen. Bloomington: Indiana University Press, 1964.

A Work about Jaime Torres Bodet
Karsen, Sonja. *Jaime Torres Bodet: A Poet in a Changing World.* Saratoga Springs, N.Y.: Skidmore College, 1963.

Trakl, Georg (1887–1914) *poet*

Georg Trakl was born in Salzburg, Austria, into a middle-class Protestant family. Although his early childhood was quite happy, Trakl began to show signs of trouble in his adolescence. In his youth, he was close to his sister Grete, so close that many have speculated about an incestuous relationship. In high school, Trakl frequented brothels, drank, and used opium heavily. After failing his courses in high school, he was forced to repeat a year and eventually dropped out.

He apprenticed to a local pharmacist, many believe, to have easier access to drugs. By his early adulthood, he showed clear signs of mental illness and emotional disturbance.

Trakl moved to Austria, where he studied to be a pharmacist. In Vienna, he began to write his first serious poems, publishing them in several literary journals. He also met prominent artists of the expressionist movement (*see* EXPRESSIONISM), including OSKAR KOKOSCHKA. Shortly before completing his degree, Trakl lost all financial support as a result of his father's death.

Trakl published only one collection of poetry during his lifetime, *Poems* (1913). The poems, permeated by dark themes of sorrow and decay, reveal his deep disgust with imperialist society. Two posthumous collections, *The Autumn of the Lonely* (1920) and *Song of the Departed* (1933), reveal similar themes, often distorting reality to amplify the disturbed emotional state of the poet. The bleak verses are pierced by nightmarish images of twilight, death, and somber religious symbolism.

At the outbreak of World War I, Trakl was recruited into the Austrian army in the capacity of a pharmacist. He was hospitalized on several occasions for depression, attempted suicide, and was released seemingly without any improvement.

Three days after having witnessed several locals hanged from a tree by the Austrian army, Trakl intentionally overdosed on cocaine.

Although Trakl was by no means a prolific poet, he left a significant contribution for the expressionist movement. His poetry is widely read and appreciated in Germany, the United States, and Europe as a whole. Trakl's work has been translated into nine languages.

Other Works by Georg Trakl

Autumn Sonata: Selected Poems of Georg Trakl. Translated by Daniel Simko. London: Asphodel Press, 1998.
Poems and Prose. Translated by Alexander Stillmark. New York: Libris, 2001.
A Work about Georg Trakl
Williams, Eric, ed. *The Dark Flutes of Fall: Critical Essays on Georg Trakl.* Rochester, N.Y.: Camden House, 1991.

Tsushima Yūko (Tsushima Satoko)

(1947–) short story writer, novelist
Tsushima Yūko was born in Tokyo to novelist Dazai Osamu and his wife, Michiko. Soon after her birth, her father committed suicide with his lover. Her mother raised her, her older sister, and an older brother, who was mentally handicapped, on her own. When Tsushima was very young, she attended a music school for children. In 1965, she began to study English literature at Shirayuri Women's College in Tokyo, graduated in 1969, and went on for one year of postgraduate study at Meiji University. She married in 1972 but later separated from her husband after having two children.

Tsushima's writing career began while she was still an undergraduate when she won a university prize for her story, "Requiem for a Dog and an Adult" (1969). Her first novel, *The House Where Living Things Are Gathering,* followed in 1973. She continued to write at a rapid rate, producing short story collections that appeared almost annually, including *A Bed of Grass* in 1977. Her second novel, *Child of Fortune* (1978), is about

a 36-year-old music teacher raising a child on her own. The novel *Driven by the Light of Night* (1986), about the efforts of a woman to retain the memories of her dead son, marked a new direction in Tsushima's writing. She picked up the theme of bereavement and memory again in *To the Daylight* (1988).

Tsushima's protagonists are generally single mothers who experience an awakening, and her novels typically explore the internal world of female protagonists. Tsushima herself has claimed that her writing stems from a desire to articulate herself, which was repressed during childhood because of her nonverbal relationship with her handicapped brother. She has won many literary prizes, including the Kawabata Yasunari Prize in 1982 and the Yomiuri Newspaper Prize in 1987.

Other Works by Tsushima Yūko

The Shooting Gallery and Other Stories. Translated by Geraldine Harcourt. New York: Pantheon Books, 1988.
"Water's Edge." In *Reexamination of Modern Subjectivity in Japanese Fiction.* Saitama-ken Sakado-shi, Japan: Center for Inter-cultural Studies and Education, Josai University, 1994.
Woman Running in the Mountains. Translated by Geraldine Harcourt. New York: Pantheon Books, 1991.

Tsvetaeva, Marina (1892–1941) *poet*

Born in Moscow, Marina Ivanovna Tsvetaeva grew up in an affluent family. Her father was an art history professor at the University of Moscow, and her mother a talented pianist. Tsvetaeva's family frequently traveled abroad, and she attended schools in Italy, Switzerland, Germany, and France. In school, Tsvetaeva excelled in literature, history, and languages. She published her first collection of poems, "Evening Album" (1910), at the age of 18. The collection explored the themes of childhood and subsequent transition to adulthood. It was noticed and praised by VALERY BRYUSOV.

In 1912, Tsvetaeva married Sergei Efron; two daughters were born, in 1912 and 1917. Tsvetaeva opposed the Bolshevik revolution of 1917, and Efron volunteered to serve in the oppositional forces of the White Army. Tsvetaeva remained in Moscow, where she suffered from poverty and hunger. Her daughter Irina died of starvation in 1920. In spite of all, Tsvetaeva wrote intensely, producing six verse dramas and several narrative poems including *The Demesne of the Swans,* an epic about the Russian civil war, and many lyrics. Eventually, Tsvetaeva and her family emigrated from Russia, spending time in Berlin and Prague and settling in Paris in 1925, the year her son Gyorgy was born.

During these years Tsvetaeva published five collections of poetry, the last—and the last published in her lifetime—being *After Russia* (1928), a collection that dealt with the themes of national identity and displacement. Tsvetaeva was the only source of income for her family in Paris, and she eventually turned to writing prose because it paid more than poetry. She wrote critical essays, memoirs, and short stories. Tsvetaeva's prose, however, never achieved the level of skill and literary genius found in her verse. Furthermore, Tsvetaeva did not identify herself with the Russian émigré community. After writing a friendly and admiring letter to the Soviet poet MAYAKOVSKY, Tsvetaeva was ostracized from the émigré community and found it virtually impossible to have her work published. Efron had become more sympathetic to the Soviets, as had their daughter Alya, and in 1937 Alya and Efron returned to Russia.

Tsvetaeva was never able spiritually and emotionally to separate from Russia, as her nostalgic and expressive poems "Homesick for Motherland" (1935) and "Motherland" (1936) indicate. Tsvetaeva's last collection of verse, *Poems to the Czechs* (1938–39), explored the anguish of the Nazi occupation of Czechoslovakia. Tsvetaeva returned to Russia in 1939, with Gyorgy, and soon found herself in the same predicament as she had been during the 1920s. Besides the occasional translation work that was provided to Tsvetaeva by BORIS PASTERNAK, she was unable to find employment. Efron and Alya were arrested for espionage during the height of the Stalinist purges. Alone, impoverished, and in deep despair, Tsvetaeva committed suicide in 1941.

Tsvetaeva's use of traditional poetic diction and classical images went against the cultural politics of SOCIALIST REALISM. For Tsvetaeva, poetry was a personal rather than a social experience. Her contribution to Russian literature was not recognized until years after her death. Now, however, she generally ranked with ANNA AKHMATOVA, OSIP MANDELSTAM, and BORIS PASTERNAK as one of the four greatest Russian poets of the 20th century.

Other Works by Marina Tsvetaeva

Earthly Signs. Translated by Jamey Gambrell. New Haven, Conn.: Yale University Press, 2002.

Milestones. Translated by Robin Kemball. Evanston, Ill.: Northwestern University Press, 2002.

Poem of the End: Selected Narrative and Lyrical Poetry, with Facing Russian Text. Translated by Nina Kossman. Ann Arbor, Mich.: Ardis, 2000.

The Ratcatcher: A Lyrical Satire. Translated by Angela Livingstone. Evanston, Ill.: Northwestern University Press, 2000.

Selected Poems. Translated by Elaine Feinstein. New York: Penguin Books, 1994.

Works about Marina Tsvetaeva

Dinega, Alyssa E. *A Russian Psyche: The Poetic Mind of Marina Tsvetaeva.* Madison: University of Wisconsin Press, 2002.

Feiler, Lily B. *Marina Tsvetaeva: The Double Beat of Heaven and Hell.* Durham, N.C.: Duke University Press, 1994.

Schweitzer, Viktoria. *Tsvetaeva.* Translated by Peter Norman. New York: Farrar, Straus & Giroux, 1993.

Turgenev, Ivan Sergeyevich (1818–1883) *novelist, dramatist, short story writer*

Ivan Turgenev was born in Orel, Russia, to Sergey and Varvara Turgenev, rich aristocratic landowners. Turgenev's childhood was defined by the domineering personality of his mother. In 1827, the family relocated to Moscow, and Turgenev, who up to that point had been educated by his mother, was now tutored by prominent intellectuals and writers of the period. A brilliant student, he was admitted to Moscow University at the age of 15. The family moved to St. Petersburg in 1834, where Turgenev continued his studies.

While studying in St. Petersburg, Turgenev met a number of important literary figures, among them ALEKSANDR PUSHKIN and NIKOLAY GOGOL. In 1838, he moved to Berlin to continue his studies of philosophy and literature. While in Germany, Turgenev developed a warm friendship with Mikhail Bakunin, a famous anarchist and social theoretician. Turgenev returned to Russia in 1841 and began work on short stories about the lives of peasants. He published his first story, "Khor and Kalinich," in 1847. Many of these stories, depicting daily lives and suffering of common people, appeared together as *A Hunter's Sketches* in 1852. The collection revealed Turgenev's love of nature as well as his concern for the social conditions of common Russians. In *A Hunter's Sketches,* he criticized the institution of serfdom, in which the social status of peasants was equivalent to that of slaves. It was widely rumored that reading this story was what inspired Aleksandr II to emancipate the serfs.

In 1856, Turgenev traveled extensively throughout Europe. He had a following in French literary circles and developed friendships with such influential writers as FLAUBERT and ZOLA. After a hostile response to his novel *Fathers and Sons* (1862), Turgenev left Russia and settled in Paris. By 1870s, Turgenev was recognized as one of the world's leading writers.

The decade 1850–1860 was the most productive in Turgenev's career as a writer. Turgenev always concentrated on social and political issues in his work, as his novels *Rudin* (1856), *A Nest of Gentlefolk* (1859), and *On the Eve* (1860) readily attest. Turgenev often juxtaposes the daily struggles of the peasants with disruption in the social structure of country aristocrats. The parallel placement of spiritual and physical struggles in the narrative often plays an important role in his work. His most famous novel, *Fathers and Sons,* deals with nihilism and the role of the individual within a family and the social dynamics of the state. The work was widely criticized for its "social irresponsibility" and supposed "misrepresentation" of Russia's youth. Despite this criticism, Turgenev continued to examine social issues in his work. His novels *Smoke* (1867) and *Virgin Soil* (1877) deal with the transformation of Russian society and its subsequent effects on the peasantry and country gentry.

Turgenev also wrote a number of plays. *A Month in the Country* (1855) contained a number of dramatic innovations in style and subject matter. This play became a catalyst for the dramatic works of Anton CHEKHOV. In the comical play *A Provincial Lady* (1851), Turgenev satirically treats the moral and ethical beliefs of country aristocrats. Both plays demonstrate Turgenev's ability to illuminate a social issue without demonizing a certain class or social group. Turgenev's criticism is often intricately interwoven into the fabric of the segment of society represented on stage.

When Turgenev died in 1883, his contribution to world literature was already recognized, and his literary influence extended far beyond the borders of Russia. Henry James, for instance, considered Ivan Turgenev one of the greatest writers of the 19th century. Turgenev's work also inspired social changes in Russia and contributed to the development of liberal political thought.

Critical Analysis

Fathers and Sons is Turgenev's response to the cultural rift he saw between those who demanded more Western influence in Russian culture in the mid-1800s and those who defended traditional Russian culture and the Russian Orthodox Church. The confrontation between the new and the old becomes the novel's central theme, as well as its primary structural device. The thematic hub of the novel is the concept of nihilism, championed by the protagonist Yevgeny Bazarov, a philosophy that claims that life lacks objective meaning, purpose, or intrinsic value. With this theme, Turgenev anticipates many of the cultural movements of the late 19th and early 20th century.

In terms of the novel's organization, critic Avrahm Yarmolinsky writes, "The total effect of *Fathers and Sons* does not measure up to that of individual scenes, so that the whole is less than the sum of its parts"; that is, most critics agree that the power of the novel ultimately resides in its individual scenes, not in the larger structure of the work. *Fathers and Sons* focuses on friends Bazarov and Pavel Kirsanov as they travel and argue about the nature of nihilism and its value to Russia. Their relationship personifies the struggle between the "fathers" (defended by Pavel) and their nihilist "sons." Indeed, the novel is built in the manner of a physical journey in which Turgenev's constructs a dynamic "around the fulcrum of each of the two sons in relationship with his father. Therefore, there is a type of structure that involves Arkady and Bazarov meeting Arkady's father, and then leaving to meet Bazarov's father." In addition, at certain points in the novel, Bazarov and Kirsanov function as each other's son or father. Thus, the theme of the novel transcends biology and ventures into the realm of philosophy and spirituality.

Turgenev demonstrates nihilism's unsustainablity as a philosophy through Bazarov's unrequited love for Anna Odintsova, which challenges his stance on the uselessness of emotion, and through the happiness of Pavel's brother Arkady's marriage to Katya. Bazarov's untimely death from typhus also allows him redemption; through his parent's unconditional love and his friend's grief, his "cosmic despair" is resolved.

Another Work by Ivan Turgenev

Three Novellas About Love. Translated by Tatiana Litvinov. Moscow: Raduga, 1990.

A Work about Ivan Turgenev

Knowles, Anthony Vere. *Ivan Turgenev.* Boston: Twayne Publishers, 1988.

Tuwim, Julian (1894–1953)
poet

Julian Tuwim was born in Lodz, Poland. His father's family was strongly Jewish and included several Zionists. His mother, however, was an assimilationist who insisted that Tuwim be educated in a strictly Polish manner. He never attempted to conceal his Jewish identity and upbringing; as a result, during the years preceding World War II, he was subjected to numerous brutal attacks by extreme Polish nationalists.

Tuwim lived in exile in France, South America, and the United States throughout the Nazi era. He was an active antifascist, and part of one of his poems became the anthem of the Polish resistance movement.

Tuwim was also one of the leaders of the Skamander group, a group of experimental poets. He became a major figure in Polish literature largely as a result of his collection *Slowa we Krwi* (*Words Bathed in Blood*, 1926). The poetry in this volume fervently expresses the sense of emptiness that accompanies the violence of urban life. Although Tuwim clearly sympathized with the poor and underprivileged, he did not become as actively involved in the proletariat revolutionary movement as he had in speaking out against fascism. Instead, his poems voiced the protest of an isolated intellectual. He used his works to illustrate the dangerous effects of capitalism.

In addition to *Slowa we Krwi*, Tuwim also wrote a collection of poems for children called *Locomotive* (1938; translated 1940) and published translations of PUSHKIN, for which he won the Pen Club Award in 1935, and of other Russian poets. Many of Tuwim's poems were also set to music and became extremely popular.

Another Work by Julian Tuwim

The Dancing Socrates, and Other Poems. Translated by Adam Gillon. Boston: Twayne Publishers, 1968.

Tzara, Tristan (Samuel Rosenstock)
(1896–1963) *poet, essayist*

Known primarily as one of the founders of DADA, Tristan Tzara was born in Moinesti, Romania, on April 16. While living in Zurich during World War I, he wrote *La première aventure céleste de Monsieur Antipyrine* (*The First Heavenly Adventure of Mr. Antipyrine,* 1916) and *Twenty-Five Poems* (1918). These two works are commonly considered to be the first dadaist texts. He also wrote the movement's manifesto, *Seven Dada Manifestos* (1924).

Tzara eventually moved to Paris, where he became involved with fellow writers ANDRÉ BRETON, LOUIS ARAGON, and Philippe Soupault. Together this group shocked readers and critics alike with their nihilistic works, which sought to subvert the conventional structures of language and society.

In the early 1930s, Tzara began to tire of nihilism and turned, instead, to the newly emerging surrealism as a more constructive form of artistic expression. In 1936, he joined the Communist Party and became actively involved in seeking ways to integrate surrealism with Marxist doctrine.

During World War II, Tzara joined the French resistance movement. His political activities brought him into close contact with the realities of oppression and made him brutally aware of human suffering. His later works, such as *The Approximate Man* (1931), *Speaking Alone* (1950), and *The Inner Face* (1953), reflect this new understanding of the human condition.

Tzara continued to be active as both a poet and an essayist until his death in Paris on December 24, 1963.

Another Work by Tristan Tzara

Approximate Man and Other Writings. Translated by Mary Ann Caws. Detroit: Wayne State University Press, 1973.

Works about Tristan Tzara

Lindsay, Jack. *Meetings with Poets: Memories of Dylan Thomas, Edith Sitwell, Louis Aragon, Paul Eluard, Tristan Tzara.* New York: Ungar, 1969.

Peterson, Elmer. *Tristan Tzara: Dada and Surrational Theorist.* New Brunswick, N.J.: Rutgers University Press, 1971.

U

Ueda Fumi

See ENCHI FUMIKO.

Unamuno y Jugo, Miguel de

(1864–1936) *novelist, playwright, poet, essayist*

Miguel de Unamuno y Jugo was born in Bilbao, Spain. He grew up and was educated there until he was 16, absorbing the Basque culture and independent spirit of that city. At 16, he went to Madrid to study literature and philosophy at the university.

Unamuno went on to become a professor of Greek and Spanish literature at the University of Salamanca. Because he spoke out publicly against the dictatorship of Primo de Rivera in the 1920s, he was banished and fled to France. He lived just over the Spanish border in the town of Hendaye so that he could continue to express his views against the regime to his fellow Spaniards.

In 1930, he was able to return to Spain. During the Spanish civil war, he sided with Franco, although he eventually spoke out against the dictator. Unamuno was one of the most famous members of the group of Spanish writers known as the GENERATION OF 1898. Like other members of the movement, he sought to present a revital-

ized model of Spanish nationalist identity be expunging certain decadent cultural habits that had infiltrated Spanish culture. To this end, he was against bullfights and the veneration of the Hapsburg and Bourbon royalty that had ruled Spain for the past few centuries. He called for a return to the Spanish traditions of the Middle Ages before the Spanish Inquisition had homogenized Spanish culture.

He was the most versatile of the Generation of 98, writing novels, poetry, and philosophy with equal skill. In line with his political views, Unamuno's most important essays examine Spanish history and the potential roles the Spanish nation might play in the modern world.

His novels and poetry focus more on the plight of the modern individual. In *Mist* (1914), a typical novel and one of his most successful, Unamuno traces the life of Augusto Perez, a man who lacks a strong personality and any self-knowledge. Gradually, Unamuno depicts how Perez arrives at self-knowledge through the pain of unsuccessful romances. The mist of the title becomes a metaphor both for Perez's personality and the forces that obscure it.

Unamuno's most famous poem is "Atheist's Prayer," which portrays the irony of praying to a god whom one cannot truly believe exists. It is representative of Unamuno's typical blend of intensely spiritual feeling and skepticism.

Along with JOSÉ ORTEGA Y GASSET, Unamuno is the member of the Generation of 1898 who has the largest international reputation. He is certainly the most internationally known novelist of his generation. His influence on later Spanish authors who followed his particularly open style of narrative structure and ideas was immense. He demonstrated a mode of philosophical literature that was particularly suited to the themes of existential philosophy and, along with PÍO BAROJA Y NESSI, pioneered the modern Spanish novel.

Other Works by Miguel de Unamuno y Jugo

The Agony of Christianity; and, Essays on Faith. Translated by Anthony Kerrigan. Princeton, N.J.: Princeton University Press, 1974.

Our Lord Don Quixote: The Life of Don Quixote and Sancho, with Related Essays. Translated by Anthony Kerrigan. Princeton, N.J.: Princeton University Press, 1976.

A Work about Miguel de Unamuno y Jugo

Ilie, Paul. *Unamuno; An Existential View of Self and Society.* Madison: University of Wisconsin Press, 1967.

Undset, Sigrid (1882–1949) *novelist, short story writer, essayist*

Born in Kalundborg, Denmark, Sigrid Undset grew up in Christiana (present-day Oslo), Norway. Her father, Ingvald Undset, was an archaeologist and historian who encouraged her interest in history and literature. Her mother, Anne Charlotte, the daughter of a Danish attorney, had to support the family after Ingvald died in 1893. To help her mother, Undset took a job as a secretary at age 16. She cultivated her literary talent during the 10 years she worked in offices. In 1909, she started to write full time.

Undset's first novels and short stories drew from her work experience and portrayed women trying to decide between career and family. In the 1920s, she turned to historical novels and published her masterpiece, the *Kristin Lavransdatter* (1920–22) trilogy. Undset's next set of works on medieval Norwegian history, translated into English as *The Master of Hestviken* (1928–30), earned her the Nobel Prize in literature. In the 1930s, Undset returned to writing about modern concerns and became one of the first Norwegians to oppose fascism. During World War II, she fled to the United States to escape Nazi occupation.

Undset was a keen observer of contemporary events. Her works about women caught between public and private spheres deal with careers, love, marriage, and infidelity. Undset's historical novels display an impressively detailed knowledge of medieval Norway. Her search for ethics and religion led to her conversion to Catholicism in 1925. Although Undset's religious views offended some, her biographer Mitzi Brunsdale pointed out in *Sigrid Undset* (1988) that even Undset's critics praised her sincerity: "She assailed not only Norwegian social conditions but the dangerous materialism and sentimental humanitarianism that she felt threatened all Western civilization."

Another Work by Sigrid Undset

Gunnar's Daughter. Translated by Arthur B. Chater. New York: Penguin USA, 1998.

A Work about Sigrid Undset

Brunsdale, Mitzi. *Sigrid Undset: Chronicler of Norway.* New York: Berg Publishers, Ltd., 1988.

Ungaretti, Giuseppe (1888–1970) *poet*

Giuseppe Ungaretti was born in Alexandria, Egypt. He spent his childhood in North Africa, however, where the nomadic culture influenced many of his future life choices as well as his writing. Educated in Paris, he lived a free-spirited life along with many other members of the emerging literary and artistic avant-garde. Their ideas, particularly those of the French symbolists, would eventually impact the direction of his poetry.

During World War I, Ungaretti served in the Italian infantry. He fought with the 3rd Army on the lower Isanzo front from 1915 to 1918. In the spring of 1918, he was transferred to the Western front where the Italian army fought with much distinction. It was this experience that gave the aspiring poet the background for his mature works, particularly his war poetry, such as *Vigil* (1915) and *Brothers* (1916).

Writing in the style of the symbolists, in which the works are reduced to their simplest and most essential elements, Ungaretti's major themes are love and the precarious and temporary nature of the human existence. This is particularly evident in *I Am a Creature* (1916). He chose each word carefully, stressing the musicality of language and avoiding elaborate structure within his poems. His style was so unique that it prompted an entire poetic movement that became known as hermeticism.

Ungaretti's poetry is collected in English translation in a series titled *The Life of Man* (1969). As well as writing poetry, he also translated the works of Shakespeare and Racine and held teaching posts in Brazil and Rome.

Another Work by Giuseppe Ungaretti

Selected Poems: Bilingual Edition. Translated by Andrew Frisardi. New York: Farrar, Straus & Giroux, 2002.

Valéry, Paul (1871–1945) *poet, essayist*

A writer who devoted his life and work to worshiping what he referred to as the "idol of intellect," Paul Valéry was born in the small Mediterranean seaside town of Sète on October 30. The son of a customs clerk, he spent his childhood by the sea. He grew to be fascinated by the rhythmical quality of waves and the intrinsic natural beauty of water. This early childhood aesthetic delight translated itself into a later interest in both architecture and poetry.

As an adult, Valéry left the seacoast to travel to Paris, where he made the acquaintance of a small group of friends who shared his interests and encouraged his artistic endeavors, among whom was fellow writer ANDRÉ GIDE. The two became lifelong friends and influenced each other greatly. Valéry was also influenced by STÉPHANE MALLARMÉ and the symbolist poets. His earliest works were published in symbolist journals, where they were well received, but Valéry chose initially to place his artistic endeavors secondary to his study of mathematics and the sciences. He did, however, publish a collection of vignettes, such as *Mr. Head* (1895), depicting human intellect as distinct and segregated from the world as a whole. This theme would manifest itself in much of Valéry's later work.

A failed romance prompted Valéry to withdraw completely from the arts, maintaining some of his artistic friendships but taking a job in the civil-service branch of the French war office and focusing solely on scientific pursuits. He wrote no poetry during this period. He wrote only his observations on the scientific aspects of language and consciousness and one substantial work on Leonardo da Vinci. He praised Leonardo as being a perfect example of man because of his ability to remain emotionally detached in his mastery of both science and the arts.

In 1912, 20 years after his retreat from poetry, Valéry was encouraged by André Gide to revise some of his earlier works. Five years later, the poems were collected and published to widespread acclaim. Of particular interest both popularly and critically was the publication of his long poem *The Youngest Fate* (1917). The work details the awakening of human consciousness and intellect symbolically through the youngest fate, which represents the earliest stage of human development. This work solidly emphasizes Valéry's *idol of intellect,* which he eventually defined as a state of pure reason existing separately from the emotional demands of society. He also stressed the conflict between the human desire to think and the human will to act.

The works produced in 1917 gained Valéry widespread fame as a poet. He continued to publish poetry throughout the rest of his life, but the majority of his work remained focused on the sciences, as well as cultural and political concerns. His interest in the sciences brought him into direct contact with many influential thinkers, including Einstein and Faraday. He became a prominent personality in Parisian high society where his wit and intelligence provided much entertainment at otherwise dry social functions. The degree to which he knew and understood politics also made him an extremely popular speaker on current events.

In 1925, Valéry was elected to the Académie Française, and the position of professor of poetry at the Collège de France was created specifically for him. He died soon after the liberation of France at the end of World War II. He was given a state funeral, in keeping with his honored place in French society.

Another Work by Paul Valéry

Sea Shells. Translated by Ralph Manheim. Boston: Beacon Press, 1998.

Works about Paul Valéry

Kluback, William. *Paul Valéry: A Philosopher for Philosophers: The Sage.* New York: Peter Lang, 2000.

Putnam, Walter. *Paul Valéry Revisited.* Boston: Twayne, 1995.

Vallejo, César (1892–1938) *poet, novelist*

César Abraham Vallejo was the youngest of 11 children born to a family in Santiago de Chuco, a small Andean town north of Peru. His parents, Francisco de Paula Vallejo and María de los Santos Mendoza, were both children of Chimu Indian mothers and Spanish Catholic priests. Vallejo's family was very poor, and financial problems haunted the poet throughout his life.

In 1910, he enrolled in the University of Trujillo, but his studies were repeatedly interrupted due to financial hardship. Vallejo took different jobs, such as teaching and a clerical position in a sugar estate's accounting department, to survive. His job at the sugar estate showed him the poverty and poor working conditions of the workers, an experience that helped refine Vallejo's sense of solidarity with and empathy for those who suffer.

It was in Trujillo that Vallejo first came into contact with writers, and there he wrote his first poems, including the draft of his first book of poetry, *The Black Heralds* (1918). The poetry in this collection shows both MODERNIST and ROMANTIC tendencies and was well received. He received his master's degree in 1915 in Spanish literature and, in 1917, moved to Lima, where he became acquainted with many important Peruvian writers and intellectuals of the day, including the anarchist Manual Gonzalez Prada.

After the crushing loss of his mother in 1920, and having lost a teaching position, he returned home to visit. Disturbances broke out while he was there—an official was assassinated and a store was burned down—and he was accused of being an instigator. Even though there was an overwhelming supportive response in the form of letters by important intellectuals and newspaper editors, Vallejo still served 105 days in jail. This experience, as well as the changes occurring in European literature, affected his next collection of poetry, *Trilce* (1922), which marked a fundamental change in Hispanic-American literature. By separating himself from the more traditional models he had followed in the past, and by pursuing unexplored experiences of the human condition, Vallejo helped renovate poetic language and form.

Having lost yet another job and fearing being put back in jail, Vallejo moved to Paris in 1923. Although he met such important vanguard figures as Vicente Huidobro, Juan Gris, Pablo Picasso, JEAN COCTEAU, and ANTONIN ARTAUD, Vallejo eventually abandoned his own experimental writings due to his readings in marxism. By 1927, he was engaged in the communist cause and became an intellectual and political activist. In 1930, he was arrested at a train station for producing communist propaganda and was ordered to leave France.

Vallejo went to Madrid where, in 1931, he joined the Spanish Communist Party and wrote his novel *Tungsten* (1931). He returned to Paris in 1933 via a resident permit that banned him from becoming involved in any type of political activities.

In 1934, he married Georgette Phillipart, with whom he had been living since 1929. In 1936, the fascist uprising in Spain sparked in Vallejo a period of unparalleled creativity. In 1937 he was voted Peruvian representative at the Second International Congress of Writers for the Defense of Culture, which took place in Spain. There he had a chance to see firsthand the horror of the civil war, and out of this experience in the next few months came a tragedy, *La piedra cansada* (The Exhausted Rock), and more than 80 poems, including the 15 poems that form *Spain, Take This Cup from Me*.

In his poem "Black Stone on Top of a White Stone" Vallejo wrote: "I shall die in Paris, in a rainstorm." These words were prophetic. His last words expressed his desire to go to Spain and fight against the fascist forces that were tearing through the country. At the time of his death, much of his work was still unpublished. In 1939, his *Spain, Take This Cup from Me* and *Human Poems* were published posthumously. His poetry is characterized by experimentation with language, which often makes it difficult to read; real historical elements; and intense images of human pain and connection. His poem "To My Brother Miguel In Memoriam," for example, poignantly draws a parallel between the brothers' childhood games of hide-and-seek and Miguel's death: "Miguel, you went into hiding . . . but, instead of chuckling, you were sad." Vallejo is remembered as being Peru's greatest poet, as well as one of the seminal voices of 20th-century Hispanic-American poetry, and one of the most original Spanish voices of all time.

Other Works by César Vallejo

The Black Heralds (Discoveries). Translated by Richard Schaaf and Katherine Ross. Pittsburgh, Pa.: Latin American Literary Review Press, 1990.

Bly, Robert, ed. *Neruda and Vallejo: Selected Poems*. Translated by John Knoepfle and James Wright. Boston: Beacon Press, 1993.

César Vallejo: The Complete Posthumous Poetry. Translated by Clayton Eshleman and Jose Rubin García. Berkeley: University of California Press, 1992.

Trilce. Translated by Rebecca Seiferle. New York: Sheep Meadow Press, 1992.

Tungsten. Translated by Robert Mezey. Syracuse, N.Y.: Syracuse University Press, 1989.

Works about César Vallejo

Niebylski, Dianna C. *The Poem on the Edge of the Word: The Limits of Language and the Uses of Silence in the Poetry of Mallarmé, Rilke and Vallejo*. New York: Peter Lang, 1993.

Sharman, Adam, ed. *The Poetry and Poetics of César Vallejo: The Fourth Angle of the Circle*. Lewiston, N.Y.: Edwin Mellen Press, 1997.

Vargas Llosa, Mario (1936–) *novelist*

Mario Vargas Llosa was born in Arequipa, Peru. Shortly after his birth, his father and mother separated, and his mother took him to live in Bolivia. His grandfather was the Peruvian consul there, and Vargas Llosa spent the next eight years in a privileged and happy atmosphere. He read adventure stories and, because he could not stand it when the books came to an end, he invented additional chapters.

When Vargas Llosa was 10 years old, his parents reconciled, and he returned to Peru. As a teenager, he began to write poems. His father, wishing to discourage his son from being a writer, sent him to the Leoncio Prado Military School. This traumatic experience had the opposite effect on Vargas Llosa: Forced to keep his literary interests secret, he became more committed to his writing and developed a strong need to rebel against conventional society.

When Vargas Llosa's first novel *The Time of the Hero* (1962) was published, it won several literary prizes and was highly praised. It also caused a great controversy at the Leoncio Prado Military School because of his harsh criticism of the military. A thousand copies were burned publicly on orders of the school administration.

The Time of the Hero focuses on sections of society and taboos frequently avoided by Peruvian writers. In the book, Vargas Llosa pays a great deal of attention to his character's fantasies, which become an active part of the plot. One of Vargas Llosa's main interests is how real life and fantasy combine to form a reality which would not exist without both of them.

In 1967 Vargas Llosa met GABRIEL GARCÍA MÁRQUEZ in Caracas. The two men, both central figures in the MAGIC REALISM movement, held a series of public discussions on the art of fiction writing. At this time, Vargas Llosa was arriving at his mature conception of the purpose of the novel in society. He saw the novel as a mode for the writer to struggle with and attempt to change human reality. He viewed the novel both as a means to preserve moments of time from one's personal past and to exorcise personal demons.

Vargas Llosa became increasingly concerned with politics during the 1970s and, in 1981, wrote *The War of the End of the World*, which examines and harshly criticizes the tendency toward political fanaticism so prevalent in Latin-American history. Set in 19th-century Brazil, it blends an actual historical event with fantasy and the psychological exploration of its characters. The overall effect is to make visceral the atrocity of an event that otherwise might have been become a history remembered without emotion. Vargas Llosa's techniques emphasize that history is itself a kind of fiction and our view of it can change the future.

In 1990, Vargas Llosa took his political interests from the world of literary discourse and decided to put them into action. He ran for president of Peru against Alberto Fujimori. Unfortunately, he lost, and Fujimori went on to impose an authoritarian and corrupt government on the people of Peru.

Vargas Llosa continues to write. His novel *The Feast of the Goat* (2002) examines the reign of Dominican dictator Gen. Rafael Trujillo with Vargas

Llosa's characteristic blend of history, fantasy, and political insight. His novel *The Way to Paradise* was published in 2003. *The Way to Paradise,* like *The Feast of the Goat,* is fictionalized biography, this time of an early 19th-century workers' rights activist, Flora Tristan, and her grandson, the painter Paul Gauguin. *The Bad Girl* (2006) is the story of an odd love affair that spans continents and 40 years of history. In 2010, *El sueno del celta* was published. And in October 2010, Vargas Llosa won the Nobel Prize in literature for "his cartography of structures of power and his trenchant images of the individual's resistance, revolt and defeat."

Critical Analysis

The War of the End of the World documents and explores the war of Canudos. It is a novelization of a real conflict in the 19th century between the government of Brazil and a group of 30,000 members of a community who founded Canudos under the messianic leadership of Antônio Vicente Mendes Maciel, or Antônio Conselheiro (Anthony the Counselor).

In the midst of an economic decline following a drought and the end of slavery in northeastern Brazil, the province's poor are attracted by the charisma and fiery religious teachings of the counselor who preaches that the end of the world is coming and that the political chaos that underlies the collapse of the empire of Brazil is the sign. Seizing a hacienda (estate) in Canudos, the area hardest hit by economic decline, the Counselor's followers build a town and defeat several government military missions intended to remove them. As the state's violence against them increases, they also turn increasingly violent, eventually seizing the weapons used against them. In an epic final battle, 3,000 soldiers are sent to destroy Canudos, resulting in a bloody conflict with the poor, while politicians of the old order witness the destruction of their world in the resulting literal and figurative inferno.

Writing about *The War of the End of the World*, Vargas Llosa claims, "[Great novels] hold up a mirror that seems to reflect real life but in fact deforms real life, adds fresh touches, reshapes it." In the novel, he focuses on the residents of Canudos, relegating the Counselor to an increasingly smaller role as the novel progresses. As he disappears from the narrative, his legend and his influence grow to the point that his followers refer to him as "Blessed Jesus the Counselor." Most of the incidents are seen through the eyes of the followers, as Vargas Llosa interweaves a large cast caught up in a complex web of events in such way that he offers the reader a fully realized picture of what it was like to live in those times. The critic Harold Bloom has included *The War of the End of the World* on his list of books comprising what is called the Western canon.

Other Works by Mario Vargas Llosa

Aunt Julia and the Scriptwriter. Translated by Helen R. Lane. New York: Farrar, Straus & Giroux, 1982.

The Bad Girl. New York: Farrar, Straus & Giroux, 2007.

A Fish in the Water: A Memoir. Translated by Helen Lane. New York: Farrar, Straus & Giroux, 1994.

Vassilikos, Vassilis (1934–   ) *novelist, poet, screenwriter, politician, diplomat*

The prolific Greek author of more than 100 books and Greece's former ambassador to UNESCO, Vassilis Vassilikos is largely known beyond the Hellenic world for his astute political novel, *Z* (1966), which is a fictionalized account of the assassination in May 1963 of the Greek politician Gregoris Lambrakis and the government conspiracy surrounding it. Vassilikos was born on November 18, 1934 (some sources say 1933), in the northern Greek seaport of Kavala. During the German occupation of Greece during World War II, he was educated in that city and attended the Valagianni School; he graduated from Anatolia College in Thessaloniki. Vassilikos studied law at Aristotle University of Thessaloniki. He began publishing poetry during this period. In 1959, after receiving his law degree, he left Greece for the United States,

where he studied directing for television at the Yale School of Drama and at the School of Radio and Television in New York. He returned to Greece and began working as a journalist, actor, and director or assistant director for Greek and foreign productions (theater, television, documentary).

The first major work that brought Vassilikos international attention was a trilogy of novellas, *The Plant, the Well, the Angel. The Plant* relates the eerie story of Lazaros, who steals a plant from a mysterious young woman and brings it home to his parents' modern apartment building where it proceeds to flourish until it takes over the entire building, choking off the water supply and elevator. Lazaros eventually goes to seek out the girl from whom he stole the plant only to find that her home has been torn down to make way for a huge construction project. By turns comic and horrifying, this tale and the other novellas fall somewhere between the real and the surreal, the literal and the allegorical; they made a powerful impression on readers in the early 1960s, winning the Group of Twelve Prize. The social criticism would become even more explicit in Vassilikos's next major work, *Z*, which dealt with the political assassination of an opposition leader and government attempts to silence any protest of his death.

Vassilikos spent the years from 1967 to 1974, the period during which the Greek state was ruled by a dictatorial military junta known as the colonel's dictatorship, in self-imposed exile. His leftist views and his novel *Z* made him, like many other leftist writers and intellectuals, an obvious target of the regime. This period also coincided with the peak of Vassilikos's international renown, as the success of the novel was amplified by the even greater acclaim of the graphic and brutal film adaptation made in France in 1969 by fellow Greek exile, Costa-Gavras; the film won the Jury Prize at the Cannes Film Festival and then took the Oscar for Best Foreign Film. Vassilikos has said that he felt that the success of the film contributed to the instability and ultimate downfall of the Greek dictatorship. Because the film presented the active role the dictatorship took in the assassination of politician Gregoris Lambrakis and the government cover-up that followed it, the international credibility of the regime was severely compromised. "In my opinion (and not just my own)," Vassilikos has said, "[the film] was a catalyst in causing trouble for the dictatorship."

In 1973, a translation of Vassilikos's essays from the mid-1960s on his view of Greece from exile appeared. This was entitled *Outside the Walls*, and it included petitions to then–prime minister George Papandreou to release a number of political prisoners on the left. *The Recorder (Interviews, 1970–1971)* transcribes a series of interviews that Vassilikos conducted with Greek immigrants in northern European countries. His experiences of exile also found their way into fictional works such as *Café Emigkrek* (1967), whose title is a portmanteau word combining émigré and Greek, and narrates the conversations of Vassilikos and his colleagues in a Paris café attempting to diffuse the heartache of exile. Similarly, *The Harpoon Gun* (1971) takes up the theme of exile but on a much more ambitious scale. It consists of two novels and 13 stories loosely organized by the common experience of exile. The title story, inspired by a film by Costa-Gavras, *State of Siege*, recounts the kidnapping of an American military attaché by a group of antigovernment Greeks demanding the release of 10 political prisoners. Kidnapping is presented as a form of harpooning. The concluding story, "Self-slaughter," recounts the mysterious death of another Greek political exile in Scandinavia. Through all of these stories, the themes of desperation, self-negation, and alienation express the wages of exile.

After the fall of the dictatorship, Vassilikos returned to Greece and rejoiced in the freedoms the Greek people began once again to enjoy. "No writer is persecuted," he told the *New York Times*. "We are free to write what we like." However, he also observed that the people had turned their attention to matters other than literary expression; that during the dictatorship statements about human freedom took on great resonance and power. "The least nuance about liberty took on larger proportions," he said. "People go back to books when there is no free press." In a sense, the political tensions that made his work so vital in Greece and such an example to the larger world were no longer present.

Vassilikos's first novel after returning to Greece, *The Monarch* (1974), concerns an exiled Middle Eastern king, living in Rome, planning a resistance movement, and the target of an assassination. The story tells of the king's relation with a journalist who is assigned to write the king's biography.

Vassilikos also entered into the political arena, serving from 1981 to 1984 as deputy general manager of ET-1 (Greek national television) and town councilor for the municipality of Athens. From 1996 to 2004, he was the goodwill ambassador of Greece to UNESCO, and from 2001 to 2005 he served as president of the Society of Authors in Greece.

Additionally, Vassilikos's years in exile have led to literary connections with countries in which he has resided. He has translated into Greek the works of French novelist ANDRÉ GIDE and American poet James Merrill. Vassilikos appears in Merrill's poetry and was instrumental in forging the poet's connections to Greece.

Vassilikos has played the role of leading man of Greek letters, receiving numerous honorary degrees and awards. He won the 1970 International Prize Mediterranean. In 1980, for political reasons, he declined a National Short Story Award for "The Last Goodbye"; the story was later made into a successful film. He received an honorary doctorate from the University of Patras, was made a Commander of Arts and Letters by the French Republic (1984), and is a member of the International Parliament of Writers in Strasbourg; he also serves on the Board of the French Writers (Maison des Ecrivains, France, 1990–1993).

Vassilikos is married to the well-known Greek soprano, Vasso Papantoniou. They have one daughter.

Critical Analysis

Vassilis Vassilikos began his career as a journalist and poet, and he frequently combines his journalistic and poetic impulses in his fiction, sometimes aiming for surrealist effects, sometimes for the purposes of political allegory or critique. This was evident in *The Plant, the Well, the Angel* and in *Z*, where the title was defiantly meant to signify the Greek word *zei*, which means "he is alive." In other words, the assassinated political figure, and the opposition movement he represented, is far from dead, despite government suppression. Vassilikos often inserts himself in his fictions and fictionalizes his life, in part to remind his reader that his territory is the fluid borderland between life and literature.

As his life was marked by political exile, his fiction since *Z* has repeatedly returned to this theme. Perhaps this is best exemplified by his ongoing fictional autobiography, *The Few Things I Know About Glafkos Thrassakis* (1975–78, published in four volumes, updated and revised, 1989), which appeared in English in 2002. His English translator, Karen Emmerich, has described this work as a "fictional biography of a nonfictional individual." Vassilikos calls it an "autonovegraphy" or "novistory." Narrated by an anonymous biographer (who reminds the reader how much he looks like his subject), the novel purports to tell the life story of the Greek writer Glafkos Thrassakis, which is in turn the literary pseudonym of Lazarus Lazaridis, who resembles Vassilis Vassilikos himself. As one reviewer observed, "Biographer and subject, subject and author, fiction and fact: masks and doubles proliferate. The result is a deft and witty reflection on writing as well as a moving portrait of the artist as political exile."

Other Works by Vassilis Vassilikos

And Dreams Are Dreams. Translated by Mary Kitroëff. New York: Seven Stories Press, 1996.
The Photographs. Translated by Mike Edwards. New York: Harcourt Brace Jovanovich, 1971.

A Work about Vassilis Vassilikos

Beaton, Roderick. *An Introduction to Modern Greek Literature*. New York: Oxford University Press, 1995.

Verga, Giovanni (1840–1922) *novelist, dramatist*

Giovanni Verga was born in Catania, Sicily. He intended initially to pursue a career in law; he abandoned his studies to concentrate on writing novels. His early works were romantic in tone, but his later and, subsequently, better-received novels beginning with *The Malavogolia Family* (1881) were written in the emerging Italian realist style known as VERISMO.

Modeled after ÉMILE ZOLA's *Rougon-Macquart* series, *The Malavogolia Family* was initially intended to be part of a larger sequence of novels collectively titled *The Vanquished*, dealing with the life of Sicilian fishermen. Although only one other novel was completed in the saga, *Maestro Don Gesualdo* (1884), the works firmly established Verga as a leading writer in the verismo school. His attention to detail in his faithful depictions of late 19th-century life in both Sicily and southern Italy gained him much praise.

Although Verga began his career writing novels, he is best known for his dramatic works. His first play was an adaptation of his short story "Cavalleria rusticana" (1884). A tale of lust, love, and murder, the play, set in his native Sicily, gained popularity when it was further adapted as an opera by the composer Mascagni. *Cavalleria rusticana* continues to be performed throughout the world.

Verga's second dramatic work, *In Porter's Lodge* (1885), again treats the themes of love and violence. This time, he moves the setting to the city of Milan, thus exemplifying the universality of his themes. In fact, the major criticism against Verga's dramas has been that he indulges in the violent nature of reality, focusing on murder, lust, adultery, suicide, and other crimes of passion at the expense of the poetry and humor of Sicily. This is equally true in several of his later plays including *The She-Wolf* (1896) and *The Wolf Hunt* (1902). However, it is his unsentimental depiction of reality that make his plays successful. Verga's one attempt at social drama, *The Fox Hunt* (1902), received little attention critically and was a failure in production.

Verga wrote his last play, an adaptation of his novel *Dal tuo al mio,* in 1905. The remainder of his life, during which many translations of his works were produced internationally, passed quietly. He died in 1922, well remembered for his contributions to Italian realistic literature.

Other Works by Giovanni Verga

Appelbaum, Stanley, ed. *Sicilian Stories/Novelle Siciliane: A Dual-Language Book.* New York: Dover, 2002.

The House by the Medlar Tree. Translated by Raymond Rosenthal. Berkeley: University of California Press, 1984.

Little Novels of Sicily: Stories. Translated by D. H. Lawrence. South Royalton, Vt.: Steerforth Press, 2000.

verismo

Similar in form to other REALIST movements of the late 19th and early 20th centuries, the Italian *verismo* movement developed as a means of objectively presenting life in simple language, with vivid details and natural dialogue. In particular, writers of the movement focused on the social conditions and hardships of the lower classes, bringing to focus much of the tragedy of the dominant human condition.

Two primary novelists of the *verismo* movement were Luigi Capuana (1839–1915) and GIOVANNI VERGA. They were influenced by the French realist movement, especially the writings of HONORÉ DE BALZAC, and, closer to home, the short-lived Milanese Bohemian movement SCAPIGLIATURA. Capuana is actually credited with having begun the movement with his collection of short stories *Studies of Women* (1877), a work which was extremely psychologically motivated as well as objective in its depictions to the point of almost excluding all traces of human emotion. Verga's works, while also objective in nature, tended to be softer than Capuana's, lending a trace of emotional warmth to an otherwise dismal portrait of 19th-century Sicily and its social conditions.

As the movement grew, other writers also began to adopt some of its traits, generally focusing their works on the places they knew the best, such as their hometowns, and the prevailing social conditions faced by the lower-class residents. Minor writers of the movement who are worthy of note included Matilde Serao (1865–1927) and Grazia Deledda (1871–1936), who was awarded the Nobel Prize in literature in 1926.

Verismo also found expression in opera. In the last decade of the 19th century, violence and melodrama found their way to the stage in the form of operatic works taken directly from everyday life. Here, the influence of the movement is felt most strongly. In particular, Puccini's *Tosca* (1900) shows strongly the impact of *verismo*.

A Work about *Verismo*

Sergio, Pacifici, ed. *From Verismo to Experimentalism: Essays on the Modern Italian Novel.* Bloomington: Indiana University Press, 1970.

Verlaine, Paul (1851–1896) *poet*

A leading poet of the French symbolist movement (*see* SYMBOLISM), Paul Verlaine was born in Metz. In 1881, he moved to Paris, where he attended school and read CHARLES BAUDELAIRE's *Flowers of Evil,* which influenced his decision to become a writer.

Verlaine studied law for two years but abandoned his studies to pursue writing. He befriended several young poets with whom he spent long hours in philosophical discussions. Excessive consumption of absinthe, the favored drink among writers and artists, eventually led to the demise of many of his relationships and to his own ultimate hospitalization.

Verlaine's father refused to support his son's bohemian way of life, but Verlaine managed to forge an existence based primarily on drinking and writing. His first published works, *Poèmes saturniens* (1866) and *Fêtes galantes* (1869), echoed the emerging symbolist style.

In 1870, although he had already begun to display homosexual tendencies, Verlaine married Mathilde Maute de Fleurville. For her, he wrote *La Bonne Chanson* (1870), in which he expressed his darkest fears and hopes for happiness. The marriage ended when Verlaine began an affair with the younger French poet ARTHUR RIMBAUD. Verlaine left his wife to return to a bohemian existence with Rimbaud until, after a drunken argument, he shot Rimbaud in the wrist. Verlaine was sentenced to 18 months in prison, during which time he wrote what is arguably his finest collection, *Songs Without Words* (1874).

In 1873, Verlaine converted to Catholicism. He moved to England to teach French and began work on the collection *Wisdom* (1881). These poems reflect his new faith in God. He left his teaching post in 1889 and adopted his favorite student.

In 1883, Verlaine's student died of typhus. His mother's death followed in 1886. Again Verlaine sought refuge in alcohol. He continued to write but spent his royalties on prostitutes and constantly reflected on his loss of Rimbaud, whom he claimed to dream about every night.

Verlaine achieved great fame as a poet and was elected France's Prince of Poets in 1894. His way of life ultimately got the better of him, and he died two years later on January 8, in complete poverty.

Another Work by Paul Verlaine

Women and Men: Erotica. Translated by Philip Shirley. New York: Stonehill, 1980.

A Work about Paul Verlaine

Chadwick, Charles. *Verlaine.* London: Athlone Press, 1973.

Vigny, Alfred de (1797–1863) *playwright, poet, novelist*

Best known for his *Chatterton* (1835), one of the most influential plays of the French romantic period (*see* ROMANTICISM), Alfred de Vigny was born in Loches, Indre-et-Loire, to Leon Pierre de

Vigny, a former officer of the king's army. As a student, he wrote several neoclassical tragedies based on the lives of such figures as Anthony and Cleopatra, but he destroyed these works and, at age 16, followed in his father's footsteps by entering the military. He soon became disillusioned with military life, however, finding it less glamorous than it is portrayed in fiction. He spent most of his time in the barracks reading classical texts and writing poetry.

Vigny met VICTOR HUGO in 1820 and became enamored of the new trend toward romanticism. He published a collection of poetry, *Poèmes antiques et modernes* (1826), and a historical novel, *Cinq-Mars* (1826), inspired by the works of Sir Walter Scott.

In 1827, Vigny resigned from military service and went to Paris to write. He wrote of his disappointment with the military experience in *Servitude et grandeur militaires* (*The Military Necessity,* 1835). In this work, he condemns the savage nature of war but praises the friendships that develop between soldiers.

Vigny planned to marry Delphine Gay who, 20 years later, became the inspiration for many of his poems, but his mother opposed the idea, and he married instead Lydia Bunbury. In 1827, after an English Shakespearean theater group came through France, he became interested in theater, writing adaptations of Shakespeare's plays. He wrote his first original play, *La maréchale d'Ancre* (1831), based on Louis XIII.

His best-known work, *Chatterton* (1835), was written for his mistress, actress Marie Dorval. It describes the death of a young poet who was incapable of surviving in a brutal, materialistic world. Its success gained Vigny recognition as a literary rival to Hugo, with whom his friendship had declined. Although he remained successful in his literary career, the end of his life was difficult. His marriage and his affair both turned sour, and he was rejected by the French Academy five times before being accepted in 1845. He published only a few poems in later years, dying in Paris on September 17, 1863.

Other Works by Alfred de Vigny

Alfred de Vigny's "Chatterton". Translated by Philip A. Fulvi. New York: Griffon House, 1990.

Stello: A Session with Doctor Noir. Translated by Irving Massey. Montreal: McGill University Press, 1963.

Works about Alfred de Vigny

Dolittle, James. *Alfred de Vigny.* Boston: Twayne, 1967.

Shwimer, Elaine K. *The Novels of Alfred de Vigny: A Study of Their Form and Composition.* New York: Garland Press, 1991.

Villiers de L'Isle-Adam, Auguste
(Mathias de Villiers) (1838–1889)
novelist, playwright

A believer in God as well as in the mysteries of the occult, Villiers was a visionary who anticipated SYMBOLISM, promoted idealism, lived his beliefs in spite of the harsh reality of the world around him, and remained proud of his heritage. Born in Brittany on November 28, he came from a family whose ancestors had defended and rebuilt France, fought in the Crusades, and exemplified what Villers believed to be the true ideals of virtue. The temporary nature of physical existence, the importance and reality of the spirit world and its forbidden mysteries, as well as the beauty and nobility of intellect all find their way into his writing.

Villiers's works, influenced by the gothic elements of ROMANTICISM, are also commonly associated with the then-emerging symbolist movement. Although extremely prolific, he is most noted for the play *Axel* (1890), the short-story collection *Sardonic Tales* (1883; translated 1927), and the novel *L'Eve Future* (1886). In these works, Villiers turns to magic and the supernatural in a search for idealism that is lacking in the material world.

Loved and admired by fellow writers PAUL VERLAINE and MAURICE MAETERLINCK, Villiers was unknown to most of the world and scorned by many who did know him and believed him to be a madman. His early works, of which there were many, such as the spiritual romance *Isis* (1862) and the macabre *Claire Lenoir* (1867), went unnoticed by the public and the critics. *L'eve future* (1886), his parody of science and technology, finally gained him some measure of recognition in 1886.

Villiers died on August 19 while working on the final revisions to the posthumously published *Axel.* The recognition that had been denied him in life, as is often true for those individuals whose work is visionary, found him in death, and he paved the way for much of the emerging symbolist work that followed.

A Work about August Villiers de L'Isle-Adam

Conroy, William Thomas. *Villiers de l'Isle-Adam.* Boston: Twayne, 1978.

Voinovich, Vladimir (1932–) *novelist*

Vladimir Vladimirovich Voinovich was born in the city of Dushanbe, the capital of Tajikistan, in the Soviet Union. His father was a journalist, and his mother a mathematics teacher. Although his father wrote poetry and prose, virtually none of it was published. From an early age, Voinovich loved books and he later remarked about his childhood, "Our principal wealth was our books. . . ." Voinovich grew up during World War II and began to work at age 11. As he admits, he had little formal schooling and was principally educated by his father. He worked at various jobs, such as carpenter and metal worker, before starting to write.

Working with various composers, Voinovich began his writing career in 1960 by writing approximately 50 songs; he also wrote poetry and was published nearly at once. In 1961, his first short story, "We Live Here," was published in *Novy Mir,* a prestigious literary journal. Early in his career, the poignant realism of Voinovich's prose alarmed the Soviet government, which resulted in Voinovich being openly badgered in newspapers throughout the country. Voinovich emigrated from Russia in 1980. He was stripped of his Soviet citizenship in 1981 by decree of Leonid Brezhnev, the leader of the Soviet Union.

No longer restricted by censors, Voinovich was prolific and productive while he lived in Germany and the United States. His best-known novel, *The Life and Extraordinary Adventures of Private Ivan Chonkin,* was published in Paris in 1975. Combining political criticism and humor, the novel satirizes the absurdity of the Soviet regime. Voinovich experimented with various genres of fiction, ranging from striking realism to dystopian science-fiction visions of a communist future. *Moscoe 2042* (1986) exaggerated and reflected the reality of the crumbling Soviet regime. In this novel, the narrator time-travels into 21st-century Moscow and discovers a culturally and socially degenerate society that supposedly achieved the theoretical goals of communism.

After the fall of the communist regime, the government returned Russian citizenship to Voinovich. He currently lives in Moscow and in Munich, Germany. Voinovich is a member of the prestigious Bavarian Academy of Arts and the Mark Twain society. His prose has been translated into 10 languages. Voinovich has been awarded the State Prize of the Russian Federation (2000) and the Andrei Sakharov Prize for Writer's Civic Courage (2002).

Another Work by Vladimir Voinovich
Fur Hat. Translated by Susan Brownberger. New York: Harvest Books, 1991.

W

Walcott, Derek (Alton) (1930–) *poet, playwright, producer, teacher, journalist, painter*

Derek Alton Walcott was born in Castries, St. Lucia, an ex-British colony. His grandmothers were slave descendants, and his grandfathers were English and Dutch. Both Walcott's father, Warwick, a Bohemian poet and artist, and his mother, Alix, who ran Castries' Methodist school and recited Shakespeare in the house, influenced the pursuits of Derek and his twin brother, Roderick, who later became a distinguished playwright. Walcott's mentor Harold (Harry) Simmons, a painter, folklorist, and family friend, gave the young man painting and drawing lessons, as well as access to his library of poetry and art books and his collection of classical records. By the age of eight, Walcott decided he wanted to become a poet.

Educated at St. Mary's College, a high school for boys in Castries, Walcott published his first poem at age 14 in *The Voice of St. Lucia*. As an 18 year old, he published his first volume of poetry, *25 Poems* (1948), followed by his long poem *Epitaph for the Young* (1949). *25 Poems* attracted the attention and encouragement of FRANK COLLYMORE. Looking back at his earlier verse writing in "What the Twilight Says," a 1970 autobiographical essay, Walcott wrote that he strove to "legitimately [prolong] the mighty line of Marlowe and Milton."

In 1950, the British awarded Walcott a Colonial Development and Welfare Scholarship to the University College of the West Indies in Jamaica. While there, Walcott published a small collection of poetry, entitled *Poems*. He stayed at the University College of the West Indies to do graduate work in education after earning a B.A. in English, French, and Latin. Before leaving, Walcott designed and directed the student drama society's presentation of *Henri Christophe* (1950), Walcott's first and best-known play, previously produced in 1950 by the St. Lucia Arts Guild, which Walcott founded.

From 1953 to 1957, Walcott worked as a teacher at the Grenada Boys' School, St. Mary's College, and Jamaica College, and in 1956, he started working in journalism as a feature writer for *Public Opinion*, a Jamaican weekly in Kingston. Later, he became a feature writer and drama critic for the Trinidad *Guardian*. Sponsored by a Rockefeller Foundation theater fellowship, he went to New York in 1958 and studied directing and set design. Dissatisfied, he settled in Trinidad one year later. In 1960, he founded the Little Carib Theatre Workshop (which later became the Trinidad Theatre Workshop). There he trained actors and produced a number of his earlier plays, many on the myths and rituals of West Indian folk life.

Walcott's plays examine Caribbean identity and life by employing verse and prose, elements of pantomime, realism, fable, and fantasy. In "What the Twilight Says," Walcott wrote that he wanted to use "a language that went beyond mimicry," "which begins to create an oral culture, of chants, jokes, folk-songs, and fables." Of his many plays, Walcott's *Dream on Monkey Mountain* (1967) is among his most impressive. It won an Obie Award as the best foreign play of 1971 after being staged in New York. Three other plays—*The Last Carnival,* which looks at the recent decades of Trinidad's history; *A Branch of the Blue Nile,* about a conflict in the central character's mind between drama and the church, with characters partly based on the actors Walcott worked with at the Trinidad Theatre Workshop); and *Beef, No Chicken,* a comedy about the absurdities of postcolonial politics in the Caribbean—appear in *Three Plays* (1986).

In addition to playwriting, Walcott has worked with Galt MacDermott, known for the musical *Hair,* and has written musicals: *The Joker of Seville* (first performed in 1974; an adaptation of Tirso de Molina's *El Burlador de Sevilla* from Roy Campbell's English translation); and *O Babylon!* (first performed in 1976; a portrayal of Rastafarians in Jamaica that examines capitalism).

Drawing on various literary and dramatic traditions—classical and contemporary, African, Asiatic, and European—Walcott writes in standard English and West Indian dialect. His work uses imagery and traditional literary techniques to explore themes of exile, injustice, oppression, and identity formation while reconstructing history. *In a Green Night* (1962), his first widely distributed and commercially published volume of poetry, fuses traditional verse with examinations of Caribbean experiences. In a review cited in the Academy of American Poets Poetry Archive, Robert Graves asserted, "Derek Walcott handles English with a closer understanding of its inner magic than most (if not any) of his English-born contemporaries."

Since the 1970s, Walcott has periodically lived and worked in the United States, serving as a visiting lecturer at several universities, including Columbia, Rutgers, Yale, Princeton, Harvard, and Boston University. In 2009, Walcott began a three-year residency at the University of Alberta in Canada.

Meanwhile, Walcott has continued to write prolifically. Between 1970 and 1974, he published essays on literary culture, including "What the Twilight Says: An Overture" (1970), "Meanings" (1970), and "The Muse of History" (1974). His publications consistently garner critical acclaim. They include *Sea Grapes* (1976) and *The Star Apple Kingdom* (1979), collections in which he turned from the lush celebrations of the Caribbean landscape that characterized his earlier poems to examine the cultural tensions of island life, and *Midsummer* (1984), which focuses on the poet's own situation, living in America and isolated from his Caribbean homeland. In his most ambitious work, the epic poem *Omeros* (1990), Walcott uses terza rima, a rhyme scheme of interlocking tercets most famously used by Dante in *The Divine Comedy,* and Creole idioms to retell the Homeric legends in a modern Caribbean setting.

In 1992, two years after *Omeros*'s publication, Walcott received the Nobel Prize in literature. Rex Nettleford, a former classmate of Walcott's at the University of West Indies, vice chancellor of the University of West Indies, and artistic director of Jamaica National Dance Theatre Company, said in 1992, "he's the West Indian writer most deserving of recognition. His work signifies the cultural integrity emerging from tremendous cross-fertilization in Caribbean life and history. It reminds us that we have no common mint of origin, only a common mint of relations." D. S. Izevbaye comments that his "skill in creating new meanings out of old, that is, the creation of a new language based on his commitment to standard English and a mythohistoric interpretation of West Indian identity, is a central part of Walcott's achievement."

Critical Analysis

Another Life is Walcott's first poem of epic dimensions. Although autobiographical elements figure prominently in this text, Walcott did not think of the poem as merely his own life story but as "a biography of a West Indian intelligence." *Another Life* is a fascinating mixture of Walcott's artistic influences and, more broadly, historical and cultural events that have shaped life in the West Indies. Attentive readers will find references to Homeric epics, James Joyce, Ezra Pound, and T. S. Eliot, as well as numerous allusions to major works of visual art. A West Indian intelligence, however, is much more than a constellation of Western writers and painters. The poem's opening lines present an image of the sea as a book in which the poet finds inspiration to write about the West Indian experience:

> Verandahs, where the pages of the sea are a
> book left open by an absent master in the mid-
> dle of another life

For Walcott, a West Indian intelligence is the effect of the clash between the West and the New World. It is created through the experience of slavery and colonization and the memory of African and Native Caribbean ancestors. West Indian landscape—the sea, mountains, villages, and beaches—also shapes this kind of intelligence and, as the beginning of the poem suggests, is the starting point for understanding the complicated history of the region.

Published 16 years later, *Omeros* is Walcott's epic masterpiece. Although this poem incorporates many characters from Homer's *Odyssey*, it is not simply a rewriting of that work. Rather, it is a tribute to the West Indian landscape and a celebration of the Caribbean experience—the people's joy, faith, and hardships. Most of the themes explored in Walcott's earlier work are taken up in *Omeros* with new intensity. For instance, a people's history, a theme characteristic of any epic and a question of continued interest to Walcott, is not merely a background to the narrated events but becomes a protagonist itself. Walcott paints a dense and complex image of history represented as Sunday, a man strolling around a Lisbon harbor. Unexpected things happen when Sunday winds his watch:

> Sunday hears his own footsteps, making
> centuries recede, . . .

A couple of pages later, Walcott compares Caribbean history to "an infinite Sunday" and writes that "for those to whom history is the presence of ruins, there is a green nothing." It is a curious statement that explains the difference between the understanding of history in the Caribbean and in the West. For Walcott, as for other Caribbean writers, history is not a chronological chain of events but rather a loop that makes it impossible to trace events in an orderly fashion. His opaque poetic language helps him communicate this idea of chaotic, reversed history.

Other Works by Derek Walcott

The Bounty. New York: Farrar, Straus, & Giroux, 1997.
Tiepolo's Hound. New York: Farrar, Straus & Giroux, 2000.
What the Twilight Says: Essays. New York: Farrar, Straus, & Giroux, 1999.
White Egrets. New York: Farrar, Straus & Giroux, 2010.

Works about Derek Walcott

Breslin, Paul. *Nobody's Nation: Reading Derek Walcott.* Chicago: University of Chicago Press, 2001.
Burnett, Paula. *Derek Walcott: Politics and Poetics.* Gainesville: University Press of Florida, 2000.
Izevbaye, D. S. "The Exile and The Prodigal: Derek Walcott as West Indian Poet." *Caribbean Quarterly* 26 (March–June 1980).
King, Bruce. *Derek Walcott, a Caribbean Life.* New York: Oxford University Press, 2000.

Walker, Kath

See NOONUCCAL, OODGEROO.

White, Patrick (1912–1990) *poet, novelist*

Patrick Victor Martindale White was born in Knightsbridge, London, to Victor Martindale and Ruth Withycombe. He came to Australia as an infant and grew up in Kings Cross, Sydney. In 1925, he went to England to attend Cheltenham College and returned to Australia in 1929. White's interest in writing came early as a child, and he also wanted to be an actor. His mother encouraged him to write while in primary school, and when he was nine, he was published in the children's page of a newspaper.

White's collection of poems, *The Ploughman* (1935), gained prominence, and other of his poems were published in the *London Mercury*. He rewrote his novel *The Immigrants,* which was published as *Happy Valley* in 1939, for which he won the Australian Literature Society's gold medal. In 1939, he came to the United States and published *The Living and the Dead* (1941).

White's main themes are alienation, the Australian landscape, the cultures of Europe and Australia, and the Aborigines. His central theme is the search for meaning and value in life. He was influenced by the French poet CHARLES BAUDE-LAIRE and came to be known as a symbolist (*see* SYMBOLISM) writer. He uses symbolism to convey a sense of the splendor of Australia, which to many people seemed dull. White's narrative techniques include autobiographical elements, dramatization, symbolism, merging of his self with his characters, and flashbacks. For White, plot was not as important as character development.

White was also known to be a transcendentalist because of his portrayal of an Australia above the ordinary. He wrote the novel *The Tree of Man* (1955) with the goal of finding a secret core or purpose of Australia. In the novel, Stan and Amy long for a new beginning for their country, beyond ordinary politics. In *The Aunt's Story* (1948), White writes about the national homelessness of Theodora, who is placed between the two cultures of Britain and Australia. He also expresses his doubts about Europe because of nuclear armament and the Holocaust. Ellen in *A Fringe of Leaves* (1976)

feels ill at ease in Europe. The Australian landscape is a major presence in this novel. As he writes of his own reaction to Europe in his autobiography, *Flaws in the Glass* (1981), "It was landscape that made me long to return to Australia."

In *Voss* (1957), we see a primitive picture of the Aborigines. Voss, the main character, communicates with the Aborigines in a language of nature, as if they were not human. In *A Fringe of Leaves,* we also read of Eliza Fraser, who is stranded on an island and is living with the Aborigines. She becomes one with them, and her cannibalism is a metaphor for European destruction of Aboriginal culture.

Patrick White won the Nobel Prize in literature in 1973, the only Australian to have this honor. In 1965, he won the Australian Literature Society's gold medal for *Riders in the Chariot* (1961). He received the Australia Day Councils' Australian of the Year Award for 1974. He is considered to be one of the most intellectual, original, and preeminent Australian novelists. White died in Sydney in 1990 after a long illness.

Critical Analysis

In 1973, Patrick White won the Nobel Prize in literature. The Nobel judges cited "an epic and psychological narrative art, which has introduced a new continent into literature." The honor accorded to White was fully justified by his novel *The Eye of the Storm*, released shortly after the prize was awarded.

In the novel, Elizabeth Hunter, an ailing Australian matriarch, blind and invalid, is visited by her two children who moved to Europe. Known as cruel and promiscuous in her past, Hunter continues to reign over her estate. The premise of the work is deceptively simple: Hunter has a "mystical experience" during a summer storm in Sydney that subsequently transforms all her relationships. Her new existence becomes charged with a meaning that reveals itself to those around her, including her three nurses, her housekeeper, her solicitor, and her two adult children. From this slight sketch, White draws out a broad canvas of personalities, all orbiting around the powerful gravitational pull of Hunter. In *The Eye of the Storm,* White is more concerned with difficult relationships within a dysfunctional family than with issues of spiritual transcendence, which had dominated his earlier work.

The central purpose of White's work was to explore the underlying problems of humanity, namely, the impossibility of building a bridge from one life to another and the possibility of an individual's relationship with God. He developed a distinctive style, sometimes with surrealist overtones, to match his powerful and emotional themes. As in the storm scene in *The Eye of the Storm,* White often used religious experience in exploring humanity's relationship with the unknown. This purpose fuels his approach to language, which, according to one critic, "reels out into impressionistic passages and then coils back into precision, like jazz music leaving and returning to the beat, the narration passing from one mind to another but never into omniscience." Ultimately, his work focuses upon ways in which transcendence might be achieved for the individual. White's work was once deemed too spiritual and intellectual for Australian audiences, but it has found renewed interest in the new century.

Other Works by Patrick White

Selected Writings. Edited by Alan Lawson. St. Lucia: University of Queensland Press, 1994.
The Twyborn Affair. New York: Penguin, 1980.

Works about Patrick White

Marr, David. *Patrick White: A Life.* New York: Knopf, 1991.
Wolfe, Peter, ed. *Critical Essays on Patrick White.* Boston: G. K. Hall, 1990.

Wicomb, Zoë (1948–) *short story writer, novelist*

Born near Cape Town, Wicomb was educated at universities in South Africa and in Great Britain. Although everyone in the rural town in which she was raised spoke Afrikaans, the dialect spoken by the Afrikaner descendants of South Africa's Dutch settlers, she taught herself to speak English by "copying the radio." She wanted to be a writer of English stories and, encouraged especially by her father, Robert, she wrote "horrible little poems." The dismantling of apartheid and the first truly free elections in South Africa's history (in 1992) have meant that the country's writers must look beyond apartheid for subjects. Wicomb is one of a wave of "new" South African authors whose work does not revolve around colonialism, in general, or apartheid issues, in particular. She writes feelingly and lyrically about personal identity and the connectedness, or lack of it, between and among people of color.

Wicomb has written two books. The first, *You Can't Get Lost in Cape Town* (1987), is a series of related short stories set in and around the strikingly beautiful Cape Province. The central character of this "novel in parts" is an educated, young, mixed-race ("coloured") woman. In the closing story in the collection, "A Trip to the Gifberg," Wicomb's first-person narrator details the occasionally difficult interaction with her Griqua (tribal African) mother as they journey to a mountain that her mother had always meant to visit. The older woman, uneducated and accustomed only to the old ways, had often looked up at the "unattainable blue of the mountain" from a seat on her porch. The personal relationship, especially when her mother is "genuinely surprised that our wishes do not coincide," speaks to the political and public lack of any real connection between even those whose "color" had previously defined them as a coherent group.

In both this work and in her second novel, *David's Story* (2001), Wicomb explores the various landscapes, physical and emotional, of her characters' existence as neither black nor white in the "new," postapartheid Africa. Like many other writers of contemporary South Africa, the overthrow of the racially based segregation policies of the apartheid-era government has compelled and allowed Wicomb to deal with increasingly difficult issues of personal identity. For example, the protagonist of *David's Story* has to come to grips with his self-identification as a political activist when his opponent, apartheid, has been defeated. David confronts the power of an unpleasant past in a present where all is supposed to be "better."

Wicomb's third novel, *Playing in the Light* (2006), is set in contemporary South Africa and tells the story of a woman who believes herself to be white but finds out that her parents were "coloured" (the South African term for mixed race). Wicomb's recent collection of short stories, *The One That Got Away* (2009), explores a variety of human relationships. The stories are set in both Cape Town and in Glasgow, Scotland, where Wicomb now lives. Wicomb is one of a group of South African writers who speaks to issues beyond the sociological and the political, and her growing status among critics and writers outside of South Africa attests to her power and reach.

Another Work by Zoë Wicomb

"Shame and Identity: The Case of the Coloured in South Africa." In *Writing South Africa: Literature, Apartheid, and Democracy, 1970–1995.* Edited by Derek Attridge and Rosemary Jolly. Cambridge: Cambridge University Press, 1998, pp. 91–107.

Wiesel, Elie (1928–) *novelist, nonfiction writer*

Elie Wiesel was born in Sighet, Transylvania. When he was 15, his family was sent to Auschwitz, a Nazi death camp. His mother and younger sister died there, but his two older sisters survived, and Wiesel and his father were transferred to Buchenwald, where his father perished shortly before the liberation of the camps in 1945.

When World War II was over, Wiesel lived in a French orphanage until 1948 when he began to study journalism at the Sorbonne in Paris. The French writer and Nobel laureate François Mauriac persuaded Wiesel to break his silence and write about his time in the concentration camps. The resulting memoir, *Night* (1958), established Wiesel as a writer. A passage from the book recalls his shattered childhood: "Never shall I forget the little faces of the children, whose bodies I saw turned into wreaths of smoke beneath a silent blue sky. Never shall I forget those flames which consumed my faith forever."

Wiesel has written more than 40 works on the Holocaust and humanity's responsibility to fight racism and genocide. These works include several novels and two additional volumes of memoirs.

Wiesel became an American citizen in 1963 and, in 1978, was appointed chairman of the President's Commission on the Holocaust. He has since founded the U.S. Holocaust Memorial Council, received more than 100 honorary degrees, and defended causes ranging from those of the Soviet Jews to Cambodian refugees, famine and apartheid victims in Africa, and victims of war in Yugoslavia. He has received numerous awards for his literary and human-rights activities, including the Nobel Peace Prize in 1986.

In 2007, Wiesel was attacked while staying in a hotel in San Francisco by a Holocaust denier. Wiesel was not injured, and his attacker was arrested, tried, and ordered to undergo psychiatric treatment. In 2008, the Elie Wiesel Foundation for Humanity revealed that nearly all the foundation's assets were lost through Bernard Madoff's investment firm.

In 2009, Wiesel toured Buchenwald, the German concentration camp where his father was executed by the Nazis. He visited the tragic site in the company of President Barack Obama and German chancellor Angela Merkel.

In 2010, Wiesel stirred up a great deal of controversy as a result of a full-page ad he took out in the *New York Times* expressing his opinion that Jerusalem belongs to Jews and that Muslims have no claim to the city. In part, the ad read, "For me, the Jew that I am, Jerusalem is above politics. It belongs to the Jewish people and is much more than a city, it is what binds one Jew to another in a way that remains hard to explain. When a Jew visits Jerusalem for the first time, it is not the first time; it is a homecoming. The first song I heard was my mother's lullaby about and for Jerusalem. Its sadness and its joy are part of our collective memory."

While Wiesel justifies his opinion by saying that there is no mention of Jerusalem in the Qur'an, Muslim scholars disagree.

Wiesel continues to write. In 2009, he published *A Mad Desire to Dance,* a dense and difficult novel about a 60-year-old Holocaust survivor who tells his story to his psychiatrist. In the same year, Wiesel published *Rashi,* a biography of a French Talmudic scholar. In 2010, *The Sonderberg Case* tells the story of a theater critic who must cover the trial of a German expatriate, Walter Sonderberg, whose plea in the case is, "Guilty . . . and not guilty."

Critical Analysis

Wiesel's trilogy—*Night (1960), Dawn* (1961), and *Day* (1962)—examines his life during the Holocaust. "In *Night,*" he writes, "I wanted to show the end, the finality of the event. Everything came to an end—man, history, literature, religion, God. There was nothing left. And yet we begin again with night."

Night is narrated by Eliezer, a Hungarian Orthodox Jewish teenager who, following the passing of a law stating that Jews who were unable to prove their citizenship would be deported, is imprisoned on a train bound for Poland. He escapes and returns to his village to tell "the story of my own death." His village is subjected to harsher and harsher restrictions until 1944, when Eliezer and his family are transported to the death camp Auschwitz II-Birkenau, where they are separated—women from men—leaving Eliezer with his father. The remainder of *Night* focuses on Eliezer's efforts not to be separated from or lose sight of his father. He narrates his grief and shame as he witnesses his father's slow decline and, finally, his resentment and guilt, because his father's existence threatens his own. The brutal, dehumanizing effect of concentration camps is rendered in vivid intensity in the novel as Eliezer ponders the value of his life over that of his father.

The central themes of *Night* are the death of God, children, innocence, and identity. Ellen Fine argues that "The *défaite du moi,*" the dissolution of the self, is a recurring theme in the novel. In a particularly disturbing scene, all three themes work in concert; in it, a child is hung for unnamed crimes, and the camp is forced to watch the execution. As Eliezer passes the boy, he observes: "Behind me, I heard the same man asking: *Where is God now?* And I heard a voice within me answer him: . . . *Here He is—He is hanging here on this gallows.*" The critic Alfred Kazin describes this crucial moment in the novel as the literal death of God, the sacrifice that appears to accomplish nothing for the remaining prisoner, and the scene that made *Night* famous.

Other Works by Elie Wiesel

And the Sea Is Never Full: Memoirs. Translated by Marion Wiesel. New York: Knopf, 1999.

The Fifth Son. Translated by Marion Wiesel. New York: Schocken Books, 1998.

The Testament. Translated by Marion Wiesel. New York: Schocken Books, 1981.

A Work about Elie Wiesel

Kolbert, Jack. *The Worlds of Elie Wiesel: An Overview of his Career and Major Themes.* Selinsgrove, Pa.: Susquehanna University Press, 2001.

Williams, Ella Gwendolyn Rees

See RHYS, JEAN.

Wittig, Monique (1935–2003) *poet, novelist, essayist*

A prominent name in feminist and lesbian literature, Monique Wittig was born in France. She earned a degree in languages from the University of Paris and published her first novel, *L'opopomax* (1964) shortly thereafter. In the late 1960s, she became increasingly outspoken about women's rights, helping to organize the separatist group Féministes Révolutionaires, for which she became the spokeswoman in 1970. She also took part in numerous organized protests and published a second novel, *Les guérillères* (1970).

In 1973, Wittig became increasingly unable to reconcile her own goals as a writer with the idea of separatism. Although she understood its importance for some women, she also felt that oppression, whether based on gender differences or sexual orientation, exists primarily as a result of the preconceived concept that heterosexuality is inherently at the foundation of society. The way to negate discrimination, therefore, is to negate this belief, an idea that became major theme in Wittig's writing.

In 1976, Wittig moved to the United States and began working on the journal *Questions Féministes* with SIMONE DE BEAUVOIR. She received her Ph.D. in 1986 and took a position on the faculty at the University of Arizona at Tucson in 1990.

Wittig's works, including the well-known pieces *One Is Not a Woman Born* (1981) and *The Lesbian Body* (1973), speak of gender equality and rights for women. She believed in expressing her views in her works as a means of abolishing gender distinctions in society.

Other Works by Monique Wittig

Lesbian People: Material for a Dictionary. New York: Avon Books, 1979.
The Straight Mind and Other Essays. Boston: Beacon Press, 1992.

A Work about Monique Wittig

Gray, Nancy. *Language Unbound: On Experimental Writing by Women.* Urbana: University of Illinois Press, 1992.

Wolf, Christa (Christa Ihenfeld)

(1929–) *novelist, short story writer, essayist*
Christa Wolf was born in Landsberg an der Warthe, Germany (today Gorzów Wielkopolski, Poland). During World War II, her father Otto Ihelenfeld, a salesman, was forced to move the family to Mecklenburg. After completing grammar school in 1949, Wolf studied literature at the Universities of Leipzig and Jena. She joined East Germany's Socialist Unity Party (SED) and worked as a

journal editor and reader for publishing houses. In 1951, she married essayist Gerhard Wolf.

In the 1950s, Wolf began to write essays and coedited two anthologies on East German literature with her husband. Her first major literary success *Der geteilte Himmel* (*The Divided Heaven*, 1963) dealt with the issue of divided Germany and made her the best-known writer in East Germany. Wolf followed the SED's call for writers to work in factories and incorporate working themes into their books. However, she later wrote novels that were critical of East Germany. In 1976, Wolf lost her membership in the East German Writers' Union for protesting the revocation of singer Wolf Biermann's citizenship. Wolf continued writing and, in 1980, won the prestigious Büchner Prize. She frequently addressed political topics in her numerous essays and, in 1989, joined writer VOLKER BRAUN in opposing German reunification.

Wolf's important influences include Anna Seghers and INGEBORG BACHMANN. She writes with frankness and believes that literature should help the reader grow personally. Wolf combines elements of pessimism with resourceful approaches to feminism and individualism. She addresses contemporary concerns but does not allow East Germans to escape dealing with their Nazi past. In 1997, scholar Marit Resch wrote in *Understanding Christa Wolf* (1997) that "one of Wolf's most important messages to all German citizens today is that it is imperative to discuss and honestly examine the totality of GDR [East German] history, not just politically expedient excerpts of it." In 2002, Wolf was awarded the Deutscher Bücherpreis (German Book Prize) for her lifetime achievement.

Other Works by Christa Wolf

Accident: A Day's News. Translated by Heike Schwarzbauer and Rick Takvorian. London: Virago, 1989.
Cassandra: A Novel and Four Essays. Translated by Jan van der Heurck. New York: Farrar, Straus & Giroux, 1984.

A Work about Christa Wolf

Resch, Margit. *Understanding Christa Wolf: Returning Home to a Foreign Land.* Columbia: University of South Carolina Press, 1997.

Wolff, Kurt

See BENN, GOTTFRIED.

Woruk, Kona

See HARRIS, WILSON.

Wright, Judith (1915–2000) *poet*

Judith Wright was born to Philip Arundel Wright and Ethel Wright in Thalgarrah Station in Australia. Wright's mother died in 1927, and a governess educated Wright. From 1929 to 1933, she attended the New England Girls' School in Armidale. She started writing poems when she was very young, and her first poems appeared in 1933. In 1934, she attended the University of Sydney.

Many of Wright's poems appeared in leading journals including the *Sydney Morning Herald, Bulletin,* and *Meanjin Papers.* Significant themes of her poetry include relationships with nature, Australian culture, Aboriginal culture, human rights, and reverence for life. *The Moving Image* (1946), her first collection of poems written during World War II, considers death and evil.

Wright writes in lyric form, as in *Woman to Man* (1949), which compares poetic imagination to the love between a man and woman: "Then all worlds I made in me: / all the world you hear and see." *The Two Fires* contains poems on the threat to humanity by humanity itself by means of nuclear weapons. There is also an emphasis on the exploration of language and the importance of myth. Her poetry is influenced by T. S. Eliot, Wallace Stevens, and W. B. Yeats, as can be seen in the wasteland images and prosaic language of *Phantom Dwelling* (1985).

Wright is renowned as poet, short story writer, environmentalist, and children's writer. *Going-on Talking: Tales of a Great Aunt* (1998), her last book, was for children. She has received several honors: In 1949 she won the Grace Leven Prize for Poetry; she was elected to the Australian Literature Council; she won the Robert Frost Memorial award in 1976; she won the World Prize for Poetry in 1984; and, her greatest honor, she received the Queen's gold medal for poetry. Wright has published more than 56 volumes of poetry and short stories. She is acclaimed as one of Australia's greatest writers.

Another Work by Judith Wright

Collected Poems, 1942–1985. Sydney: Angus & Robertson, 1994.

Works about Judith Wright

Strauss, J. *Judith Wright.* Melbourne: Oxford University Press, 1995.
Walker, S. P. *Flame and Shadow: A Study of Judith Wright's Poetry.* St. Lucia, B.W.I.: University of Queensland Press, 1991.

X-Y

৩৯৪৬৯

Xie Wanying

See BING XIN.

Yacine, Kateb (1929–1989) *novelist, poet, playwright*

Kateb Yacine was born in Condé-Smendou, near Constantine, Algeria. *Kateb* means "writer" in Arabic, which designates Yacine's family as highly literate. Yacine was raised on both tales of Arab achievements and Algerian legends. These childhood memories had an important influence on his writings. Yacine's father sent him to a French high school rather than a Qur'anic school when he was a young boy. In 1945, he participated in a nationalist demonstration in Sétif, which led to his expulsion from the Collège de Sétif. He was sent to prison without trial for a few months. During this time, he discovered his love for poetry and revolution. In 1950, he moved to France after paying several short visits to the country. His involvement in the Algerian revolution forced him to leave France in 1955, shortly after he had been offered a job at a publishing company. Yacine lived in many countries including Germany, the Soviet Union, Tunisia, and Vietnam, before returning finally to Algeria in 1970. He formed a theatrical company after his return and began to write plays. Yacine died in Grenoble, France.

At age 17, Kateb published his first book, *Soliloques* (1946), a collection of poems, and in 1948, he published the long poem "Nedjma ou le poème ou le couteau," in which the character of Nedjma (the name means "star"), a mysterious woman, first appears. Kateb used the figure of Nedjma in many later poems and plays.

Revolution constitutes an important theme in Yacine's works. His visits to different countries greatly enhanced his determination to spearhead the Algerian nationalist struggle for independence. In the love story, *Nedjma* (1956), which recounts a tale of intraclan struggle set against the background of French colonial Algeria, the main protagonist Nedjma is loved by four revolutionaries. Nedjma, the name of the cousin with whom Yacine fell in love, is a mysterious character, obviously influenced by early childhood fantasies that were resurrected from his memories of Algerian legends.

Yacine's writings explore other important themes as well, such as change and the resilience of Algerian traditional values. Yacine's heroes are often Marxist revolutionaries, including historical characters in other cultures and societies, such as Ho Chi Minh and Mao Zedong. Ho Chi Minh is featured in Yacine's play, *L' Homme aux sandales de caoutchouc* (*The Man in the Rubber Sandals*) (1970).

Until his death, Yacine believed it was the responsibility of the writer to educate the public that the constant struggle between the proletariat (the working class) and the bourgeoisie (the upper and middle classes) was unceasing. Yacine wrote all his works in French.

A Work about Kateb Yacine

Salhi, Gamal. *The Politics and Aesthetics of Kateb Yacine: From Francophone Literature to Popular Theatre in Algeria and Outside.* Lewiston, N.Y.: Edwin Mellen Press, 1999.

Yamada Eimi (Yamada Futaba)

(1959–) *novelist, short story writer, cartoonist*

Yamada Eimi was born in Tokyo. As a high school student, she became a devoted reader and chose Japanese literature as her area of study when she attended Meiji University in 1978. However, she never graduated, having already begun writing in her junior year manga for high-school girls. Yamada soon tired of producing manga and decided to take up fiction writing. She adopted a sensational lifestyle as a bar hostess, a nude model, and a "queen" of a sado-masochists' club. She began to write seriously when her relationship soured with an African-American soldier based in Japan.

Her first work, the autobiographical novella *Bedtime Eyes*, published in 1985, was about a relationship between a Japanese woman and an African-American soldier based in Japan. A year later, Yamada produced eight stories, including "Jessie's Spine," about a Japanese woman's difficult relationship with her African-American lover's son. Increasing her rate of production even more, she published another eight short stories and three novels in 1987. One of the novels, *A Foot-bound Butterfly*, is a story about the experiences of a young girl as she navigates adolescent pressures.

Yamada is a prolific writer whose stories revel in the exotic. Her characters are generally young women living on the edge and often involved in relationships with African Americans. She incorporates an unusually large amount of slang English into her stories to evoke vivid imagery. As such, Yamada's stories represent a new voice in Japanese literature. She has won the Bungei Award, and the Tanizaki Prize, one of Japan's most coveted literary awards.

Other Works by Yamada Eimi

"Kneel Down and Lick My Feet." Translated by Terry Gallaher. In Alfred Birnbaum and Elmer Luke, eds., *Monkey Brain Sushi: New Tastes in Japanese Fiction.* New York: Kodansha International, 1993.
Trash. Translated by Sonya L. Johnson. New York: Kodansha International, 1995.

A Work about Yamada Eimi

Cornyetz, Nina. "Power and Gender in the Narratives of Yamada Eimi." In Paul Gordon Schalow and Janet A. Walker, eds., *The Woman's Hand: Gender and Theory in Japanese Women's Writing.* Stanford, Calif.: Stanford University Press, 1996.

Yáñez, Mirta (1947–) *poet, screenwriter, critic*

Mirta Yáñez was born in Havana, Cuba, and attended the University of Havana, where she later taught. Considered to be one of Cuba's best contemporary poets who has written for Cuban film and television, she is also one of Cuba's foremost literary critics and has written extensively about feminism in Cuban literature.

In 1996, she assembled a collection of writing by Cuban women, and in 1998, it was released in the United States with the title *Cubana*. This collection of 16 stories and an introductory essay by Yáñez gives the reader a moving glimpse into the difficult social situation of Cuban woman today.

Yáñez lives in Havana where she writes and lectures. In 2004, she edited a volume of short stories, *Making a Scene: An Anthology of Stories by Cuban Women.*

Yathay Pin (1944–   ) *novelist*

Yathay Pin was born in Oudong, a village about 25 miles north of Phnom Penh, Cambodia. Yathay's father, Chhor, was a small trader, and his family, though not impoverished, was poor. Yathay was the eldest of five children. His father had high expectations of him: Knowing that Yathay was an excellent student, Chhor sent him to a good high school in Phnom Penh. Yathay received a government scholarship after completing high school, and he went to Canada to further his studies. In 1965, Yathay graduated from the Polytechnic Institute in Montreal with a diploma in civil engineering. He went back to Cambodia and joined the Ministry of Public Works. He married his first wife soon after, and they had one son. His first wife and second baby died in childbirth in 1969. Afterward, Yathay married his wife's sister, Any, and they had two sons. In 1975, the Khmer Rouge overthrew the Lon Nol government in Phnom Penh and began a regime of terror. The communist Khmer Rouge persecuted educated professionals and intellectuals and accused them of being bourgeois capitalists. Yathay and his family, consisting of eight members, were sent to work as unpaid agricultural workers in the countryside. By 1977, most of his family members had perished from malnutrition, overwork, or sickness. Yathay, who had managed to disguise his educated background for a few years, was finally betrayed by an acquaintance. Fearing execution, he made a run for freedom by walking over the mountains that separated Cambodia from Thailand. Yathay safely reached Thailand two months later; he had, however, lost his wife in a forest fire. From his Cambodian past, Yathay has one surviving son whom he fears is already dead. Yathay now works as a project engineer in the French Development Agency in Paris. He has also remarried and now has three sons.

Yathay's best and only known work is *Stay Alive, My Son* (1987), which is an acrid account of his hellish experience in Cambodia under the terror of the Khmer Rouge regime. His harrowing tale of anguish and distress is one among many voices that have since emerged from the writings of Cambodian refugees who have lived to tell about the horrors. *Stay Alive, My Son* is a remarkable book not merely because it is a moving tale but also because it is a true story. Only the late Haing Ngor's memoir, *A Cambodian Odyssey* (1987), can rival its poignant reality.

Yesenin, Sergey (Esenin, Sergei) (1895–1925) *poet*

Born in Konstantinovo, Russia, in a peasant family, Sergey Aleksandrovich Yesenin was raised by his maternal grandparents. He vigorously engaged in all the physical activities afforded by the countryside, such as swimming, hunting, and riding horses. He began to compose verse when he was only nine. After finishing grammar school in 1909, he was sent to a seminary to be trained as a teacher. While in seminary, he became serious about writing poetry and, upon the advice of a teacher, left for Moscow to pursue writing as a career.

After an unsuccessful marriage that lasted only a year, Yesenin moved to St. Petersburg in 1914. His first poetry collection, *Radunitsa (Mourning for the Dead)* was published in 1916. The poems were composed in the traditional lyrical style, emphasizing rhyme, meter, and metaphor. Yesenin focused on his personal experience with nature, family relationships, and love. To the disapproval of the exponents of SOCIALIST REALISM, Yesenin's poetry continued to stress image rather than message. His fame spread quickly, and he even read his poetry for the empress and her daughters. Nonetheless, he welcomed the October Revolution of 1917, seeing it as a vindication of the peasant values he celebrated in his collection *Inoyiya (Otherland, 1918).* But before long he was disillusioned with Bolsheviks, criticizing them in poems such as "The Stern October Has Deceived Me."

Yesenin's application to join the Communist Party was rejected in 1919, supposedly due to his lack of political discipline.

In 1922, Yesenin published *Pugachev,* a tragic epic poem about an 18th-century peasant rebellion. The same year, he married American dancer Isadora Duncan, who had opened a ballet school in Moscow. Duncan and Yesenin traveled together in Europe and the United States and had spectacular public quarrels. After their 1923 separation, Yesenin returned to Moscow where he gave poetry recitals in cafes and drank heavily, sober only when he was actually composing verse.

The collections published in 1924 and 1925 demonstrate a major shift in Yesenin's poetry. *Moscow of the Taverns* (1924) and *Soviet Rus* (1925) comment on social and cultural changes in Communist Russia. Although Yesenin's diction remains lyrical and imaginative, he has moved away from the solipsistic study of the individual.

Subdued by alcoholism, Yesenin developed major psychological problems during the last year of his life. His marriage to Sofia Tolstoy, granddaughter of LEO TOLSTOY, was essentially unsuccessful. Yesenin committed suicide by hanging himself. His suicide note was a poem written in his own blood. His works, popular though they were, were banned under Stalin but were republished in Russia in 1966.

Other Works by Sergey Yesenin

The Collected Poems of Yesenin. Translated by Gregory Brengauz. Tallahassee: Floridian Publisher, 2000.
Confessions of a Hooligan: Fifty Poems. Translated by Geoffrey Thurley. Manchester, U.K.: Carcanet Press, 1973.

Works about Sergey Yesenin

McVay, Gordon. *Isadora and Esenin: The Story of Isadora Duncan and Sergei Esenin.* Ann Arbor, Mich.: Ardis, 1978.
Visson, Lynn. *Sergei Esenin, Poet of the Crossroads.* Wurzburg: Jal-Verlag, 1980.

Yevtushenko, Yevgeny (1933–) *poet, dramatist*

Yevgeny Yevtushenko was born in Irkutsk, Russia. When he was 11, his family moved to Moscow. From an early age, he loved literature and decided to pursue a career in a literary field. He studied at the Gorky Institute of Literature from 1951 to 1954. He was closely attached to his father and sometimes accompanied him on geological expeditions. In 1948, they traveled to distant regions of Kazakhstan and Altai. The experiences of this trip appear in Yevtushenko's first published collection of verse, *Zima Junction* (1956).

Yevtushenko became internationally renowned with the publication of *Babi Yar,* a long narrative poem that denounces Nazi anti-Semitism and memorializes victims of the Holocaust. The poem also criticizes actions of the Russian people toward the Jews. For this reason, the poem did not appear in Russia until 1984. Yevtushenko proceeded to publish verse of a more political nature. In *Heirs of Stalin* (1961), he warns readers about the dangers that Stalinism poses even after Stalin's death. In 1963, Yevtushenko published *A Precocious Autobiography* in English. The work was criticized by the government for its open criticism of Soviet policies, and he was not allowed to leave the country for two years.

In 1972, Yevtushenko shifted his artistic interests from poetry and produced a hugely successful play, *Under the Skin of the Statue of Liberty.* Yevtushenko is a prolific artist and expanded his artistic scope to directing, acting, and photography. He also edited poetry for *Ogonek,* a journal that published many previously repressed writers and poets.

Yevgeny Yevtushenko has achieved enormous success during his lifetime. He was appointed as an honorary member of American Academy of Arts and Sciences in 1987. In 1989, he was elected as a member of the Congress of People's Deputies, and he has served as vice president of an organization of Russian writers (PEN). After the collapse of the Soviet Union, Yevtushenko played a central role in the erection near the former KGB headquarters of a monument to the victims of Stalinism.

Yevtushenko now divides his time between Russia and the United States, where he teaches poetry at several U.S. universities. He is also working on a three-volume collection of Russian poetry.

Other Works by Yevgeny Yevtushenko

The Collected Poems, 1952–1990. Translated by James Ragan. New York: Henry Holt, 1991.
Don't Die Before You're Dead. Translated by Antonina W. Bouis. New York: Random House, 1995.
Yevgeny Yevtushenko: Early Poems. Translated by George Reavey. New York: Marion Boyars, 1989.

Yosano Akiko (Shō Hō) (1878–1942) *poet, essayist, critic, children's story writer*

Yosano Akiko was born in the city of Sakai near Osaka, Japan, to a merchant family. When she was young, she helped out with the family business, reading Japanese classical literature from her father's library in her spare time. After she completed a junior-high-school education, she began to write poetry. During this time, she wrote a letter to Tokyo poet Tekkan Yosano (1873–1935) to establish a professional relationship. She later married him. In an effort to further education for women, Yosano helped establish a high school for women in 1921. Seven years later, she started a poetry magazine called *Tōhaku* (Cameria-Camelia). She died of a cerebral hemorrhage in 1942.

Yosano's first poem was published in an anthology of Osaka-area poets in 1896. She continued to work with these local poets until she met Tekkan, who published a literary magazine *Myōjō* (*Morning Star*). In 1901, she left Osaka for Tokyo and began to publish poems, novels, and essays at a rapid rate. During this period, she published her most famous collection of poetry, *Midaregami* (*Tangled Hair*, translated 1987). She also wrote essays on social and political issues, translated *The Tale of Genji* into modern Japanese, and created a collection of children's stories.

Yosano primarily wrote tanka and free verse that expressed honest emotions. To develop honesty in her writing, she based her poems on her personal experiences and feelings, notably her love for Tekkan. Her style challenged traditional poetry themes and methods of expression, thereby establishing her own modern poetic style. By the time of her death, Yosano had written approximately 50,000 tanka.

Other Works by Yosano Akiko

River of Stars: Selected Poems of Yosano Akiko. Translated by Keiko Matsui Gibson. Boston: Shambhala Publications, 1997.
Tangled Hair: Love Poems of Yosano Akiko. Translated by Dennis Maloney. Fredonia, N.Y.: White Pine Press, 1991.
Travels in Mongolia and Manchuria. Translated by Joshua A. Fogel. New York: Columbia University Press, 2001.

Works about Yosano Akiko

Rodd, Lauren Rasplica. "Yosano Akiko and the Taisho Debate over the 'New Woman.'" In *Recreating Japanese Women, 1600–1945.* Edited by Gail Lee Bernstein. Berkeley: University of California Press, 1991.
Ueda, Makoto. *Modern Japanese Poets and the Nature of Literature.* Stanford, Calif.: Stanford University Press, 1983.

Yourcenar, Marguerite (Marguerite de Crayencour) (1903–1987) *novelist, poet, essayist*

Born to an aristocratic family in Brussels, Belgium, Yourcenar spent much of her childhood traveling with her father. After his death, she became independently wealthy and was able to pursue writing, a passion that had begun to manifest itself when she was a teenager. Her historical novels, which deal with modern themes such as the psychological manifestations of homosexuality and deviant behavior, gained her international fame and recognition.

Chinese legend fascinated Yourcenar in her early works, as did the role and life of the artist. In her early short story collection, *Oriental Tales* (1938), she draws from Chinese and Sanskrit legend to write about art and the artist's frustration. In one particular piece, "How Wang-Fo Was Saved," she recounts the tale of an aging painter who is imprisoned by a ruler who fears the power of art.

Memoirs of Hadrian (1951) is among the best known of Yourcenar's works. Detailing the reflections of a dying man and set on the eve of Hadrian's death, the emperor recounts his memories in a letter addressed to the person who will take his place. The novel took 15 years to complete and was published shortly after Yourcenar moved to the United States at the start of World War II.

Yourcenar took a position in New York at Sarah Lawrence College as professor of French literature and began to live with her translator Grace Frick. The two remained partners for the duration of Yourcenar's life. She continued to write, publishing *Le coup de grâce* (1939), the story of a Prussian officer who, because he secretly loves her brother, decides to kill the woman who has fallen in love with him. She also published *The Abyss* (1976), in which she creates a fictional Renaissance man who is essentially a combination of the historical figures Da Vinci, Paracelsus, Copernicus, and Giordano Bruno. Like many of the male characters she presents, he is depicted as a homosexual.

Yourcenar wrote only one work with a contemporary setting. The novel, *Denier du rêve* (*A Coin in Nine Hands*, 1934), revolves around the attempted assassination of Mussolini. The novel is also unique in that it revolves around several female characters and examines the female psyche. The majority of Yourcenar's characters in her works are men who are trapped between the demands of society and the desire for passion.

Yourcenar also wrote two volumes of family memoirs, *Souvenirs pieux* (*Dear Departed*, 1974) and *Archives du Nord* (*Northern Archives*, 1977), as well as a number of essays, poems, and plays. As a translator, she worked to translate English and American novels as well as Negro spirituals into her native French. In 1980, Yourcenar became the first woman ever to be elected to the Académie Française. She died seven years later on December 17 in Maine.

Other Works by Marguerite Yourcenar
Dreams and Destinies. Translated by Donald Flanell Friedman. New York: St. Martin's Press, 1999.
How Many Years. Translated by Maria Louise Ascher. New York: Farrar, Straus & Giroux, 1995.
Mishima: A Vision of the Void. Translated by Alberto Manguel. Chicago: University of Chicago Press, 2001.

Works about Marguerite Yourcenar
Horn, Pierre L. *Marguerite Yourcenar.* Boston: Twayne, 1985.
Saint, Nigel. *Marguerite Yourcenar: Reading the Visual.* Oxford: Legenda, 2000.

Yu Guangzhong (Yü Kwang-chung)
(1928–) *poet, essayist*

Yu Guangzhong was born in Nanjing, China, the capital of Fukien Province. He studied foreign languages at Ginling and Xiamen Universities in China before moving to Hong Kong with his family in 1948.

In 1950, Yu Guangzhong fled to Taiwan as a student refugee. He attended Taiwan's most prestigious institution, the National Taiwan University, where he began to write poetry. He graduated in 1952 and that same year published his first collection of poems, *Blues of a Sailor*. Highly sentimental and nostalgic, it was very popular.

Yu Guangzhong worked as an army interpreter until 1956 when he turned to teaching. Eventually, he decided to pursue a graduate degree in the United States. He earned a Masters of Fine Arts from the University of Iowa in 1959. He returned to Taiwan in 1959 and taught at Taiwan Teachers University and the Political University of Taiwan. Later, he taught at the Chinese University in Hong Kong.

Yu Guangzhong remained committed to literature, however, and formed the Blue Star Poetry Society with a friend, Qin Zihao. In the 1960s, he moved away from the sentimental style of his past writing and studied both traditional Chinese and modern forms of poetry. He published an article, "Good-bye, Mr. Nothingness!" on this subject, advocating change but discouraging the complete Westernization of Chinese literature.

Yu Guangzhong continued to teach English literature at National Taiwan Normal University until 1972 when he became the chair of the Department of Western Languages and Literature at National Chengchi University. Since then, he has lived in the United States twice as a Fulbright scholar and is the author of many volumes of poetry, including *Stalactite* (1960), *Associations of the Lotus* (1964), and *A Bitter Gourd Carved in White Jade* (1974). He is also a prolific translator of poetry and a prominent literary critic and essayist. Today, he is considered one of Taiwan's premier men of letters.

Yun Tongju (Yun Hae-hwan) (1917–1945)
poet

Yun Tongju was born on December 30, 1917, in Myongdong, North Kando province of Korea. He regularly published children's poems while studying literature at Yonhui College and wrote poems for a volume he hoped to publish later. After graduating in 1941, he chose to continue his studies in English literature.

Like many students in Japanese-occupied Korea, Yun Tongju traveled to Japan, first enrolling at Rikkyo University in 1942 and then transferring to Doshisha University in Kyoto. At the time, resistance to Japanese colonial rule was high, and

restrictions on Koreans in Korea and Japan were increasingly stringent. Yun Tongju was forced to take a Japanese name and read, write, and speak in Japanese. He wrote secretly in his native language.

Yun Tongju actively participated in the Korean independence movement. As a result, in July 1943, he was arrested for subversive activity by the Japanese government. It is thought he was mistreated and abused in Japan's Fukuoka prison, where he died under unknown circumstances at the age of 28.

His one volume of poetry, *Sky, Wind, Stars and Poetry,* was published posthumously in 1948. The poems closely reflected Yun Tongju's feelings as a subject of Japanese colonialism. Particularly because he studied in Japan, he had to deal with a marked isolation from his native country and culture. His poems capture his displacement and resentment. "Counting the Stars" is replete with melancholic remembrances of the past, while "Awful Hour" examines the depths of the narrator's sense of alienation, perhaps in a period of intense solitude.

Yun Tongju's writing is the poetry of an exile. He searched for spiritual integrity and a Korean identity under an oppressive foreign regime. As he was battling outward influences of oppression, his inner struggle manifested itself in tortured, anguished, highly personal poems that seem to document both his individual struggle between self-love and self-hate and Korea's national crisis to articulate its independence. Because his writing is a testament to Korea's struggle against colonialism and provides a moving portrait of a young person's inner struggles, they were extremely popular, especially among younger readers.

Yun Tongju did not live to see Korea's liberation in 1945. In 1968, his alma mater, Yonhui College, erected a monument in his honor.

Z

Zagajewski, Adam (A. Z., Antoni Kamiński) (1945–) *poet, essayist, literary critic*

Adam Zagajewski was born in Lvov, then part of Soviet Russia, to Tadeusz Zagajewski and Ludwika Turska. Soon after his birth, the family was repatriated to a small town in Silesia, southern Poland, where Zagajewski spent his teenage years. In 1963, he moved to Cracow to study psychology and philosophy at the Jagiellonian University, graduating with a masters degree in psychology in 1968 and a degree in philosophy two years later. His philosophical sensibility is noticeable in his essays as well as in his poetry as one of the ways of capturing the experience of the world.

Zagajewski's Cracow years (1963–82) mark the first stage of his literary career and his involvement in reactionary student activity. In 1968, Zagajewski founded "Teraz" (Now), a large and important poetic group belonging to the New Wave movement in Poland. In 1972, Teraz published its manifesto *Świat nie przedstawiony* (The unrepresented world). It recognized the complicity of language with Communist propaganda and asked for the renewal of poetic expression. Criticizing the excessive use of metaphor and allusion in favor of a direct, expressive, and forceful language, the New Wave poets wanted to make an intervention into social life and help turn literature toward reality. Zagajewski's first collections of poems *Komunikat* (*Announcement*, 1972) and *Sklepy mięsne* (*Meat Shops*, 1975) take up the problems of life under the Communist regime and contain Zagajewski's most explicit political poems. In December 1975, he signed "The Letter of 59," a protest issued against the government and the planned changes to the country's constitution that violated basic human rights. After a short ban , Zagajewski's poems continued to appear in underground literary magazines (*Znak, Tygodnik Powszechny, Zapis*).

In 1982, after martial law was declared in Poland, Zagajewski immigrated to Paris where he spent the next 20 years. He joined the staff of the literary magazine *Zeszyty Literackie* (Literary review), which published many other émigré authors such as Czesław Miłosz, Zbigniew Herbert, Tomas Venclova, and Iosif Brodsky. In the 1980s, his poetry became more reflective and philosophical, taking up themes of exile and displacement and the condition of contemporary human beings. The title poem from the collection *Jechać do Lwowa* (*To Go to Lvov,* 1985) is marked by the pervasive longing for the place of his birth that Zagajewski only knew through his parents' stories and recollections. In *Two Cities* (1991, 1995), Zagajewski meditates upon the condition of homelessness, evokes memories of his two lost homelands—Lvov and Cracow, and reconstructs his family history interwoven with the political events in Poland. Paris provided Zagajewski with the necessary distance to reevaluate his political engagement in Poland and in the New Wave movement. In the collection *Solidarity, Solitude* (1986, 1990), Zagajewski distances himself from his early stance, arguing that political engagement of poetry is at odds with the autonomy of poetic language.

In 1988, Zagajewski accepted an appointment to the University of Houston where he taught creative writing. Zagajewski and his wife, Maja Wodecka, returned to Poland in 2002 and now live in Cracow. Zagajewski still teaches at the University of Chicago, where he is a member of its Committee on Social Thought.

In the United States, Zagajewski's work was published in such journals as *Chicago Review, Callaloo, New England Review,* and *World Literature Today.* His poem "Try to Praise the Mutilated World" was the only poem selected for the post–9/11 issue of *the New Yorker.* The line "you must praise the mutilated world," which speaks of the necessity to embrace the world broken by wars, communism, and other historical turmoil, resonated with Americans.

Among Zagajewski's many awards are the Kościelski Award (Geneva, 1975); the Kurt Tucholsky Prize (Sweden, 1985); Prix de la Liberté (France, 1987); Guggenheim Fellowship (1992); the Konrad Adenauer Foundation Award (2002); and the Neustadt International Prize for Literature (2004).

Other Works by Adam Zagajewski

Another Beauty. Translated by Clare Cavanagh. New York: Farrar, Straus & Giroux, 2000.
Canvas. Translated by Renata Gorczynski, Benjamin Ivry, and C. K. Williams. New York: Farrar, Straus & Giroux, 1991.
Eternal Enemies. Translated by Clare Cavanagh. New York: Farrar, Straus & Giroux, 2008.
Solidarity, Solitude: Essays. Translated by Lillian Vallee. New York: Ecco Press, 1990.
Tremor: Selected Poems. Translated by Renata Gorczynski. New York: Farrar, Straus & Giroux, 1985.

Two Cities: On Exile, History, and the Imagination. Translated by Lillian Vallee. New York: Farrar, Straus & Giroux, 1995.

Works about Adam Zagajewski

Anders, Jaroslaw. *Between Fire and Sleep: Essays on Modern Polish Poetry and Prose.* New Haven, Conn.: Yale University Press, 2009.
Shallcross, Bożena. *Through the Poet's Eye: The Travels of Zagajewski, Herbert, and Brodsky.* Evanston, Ill.: Northwestern University Press, 2002.

Zamyatin, Yevgeny (1884–1937) *novelist*

Yevgeny Ivanovich Zamyatin was born in the small provincial town of Lebedyan, Russia. His father was a priest, and his mother an extremely well-educated woman who loved music. As a young child, Zamyatin read Dostoevsky and Turgenev. Zamyatin graduated Voronezh Gymnasium in 1902 with the Gold Medal (the highest academic honor in Russia, equivalent to valedictorian), which he pawned for 25 rubles some months later. He moved to St. Petersburg and worked in the shipyards. Zamyatin joined the Bolsheviks, and his political beliefs got him into trouble. He was beaten by the police, placed in solitary confinement for several months, and was finally banished from St. Petersburg by the czar's police force.

Zamyatin's literary debut in 1908 was a subversive short story "Alone," for which he was briefly exiled to Lakhta. In 1914, he was tried for political subversion and expression of antimilitarist sentiments on the basis of his short story "At the End of the World." He was eventually acquitted. In 1917, MAXIM GORKY offered Zamyatin a position with *Vsemirnaya Literatura,* a journal specializing in world literature. Zamyatin was in charge of the English and American sections in the journal. Throughout this period, he continued to publish short stories.

Zamyatin described his literary works as neorealism, a style according to Zamyatin that concentrates on the grotesque and brutal aspects of life. Zamyatin's most famous work, *We* (1924), is one of the earliest dystopian novels. The setting of the novel is a future One State, governed by perfect laws of mathematics. All citizens have numbers instead of names, and their consumption (including sex) is completely regulated by the state. *We* comments on the structure of Soviet society, as well as the role of an individual within this social matrix. After the publication of *We,* Zamyatin could no longer publish his work in the Soviet Union. He moved to Paris in 1931. Zamyatin was readmitted to the Writers' Union but died in 1937 before he could return to Russia.

Zamyatin never received proper recognition for his work during his lifetime. His style had an enormous influence on many writers, including George Orwell and Ursula Le Guin. Zamyatin's work has been translated into more than a dozen languages.

Another Work by Yevgeny Zamyatin
The Dragon: Fifteen Stories. Translated by Mirra Ginsburg. New York: Random House, 1967.

Zhao Zhenkai
See BEI DAO.

Zhou Shuren
See LU XUN.

Zola, Émile (1840–1902) *novelist, essayist*
Noted both as the founder of the naturalist movement (*see* NATURALISM) and for his active participation in the Dreyfus affair, Émile Zola was born in Paris, France. His father died when he was seven years old, leaving the family with severe financial problems. He spent his childhood in the south of France, in Aix-en-Provence, returning with his mother to Paris at age 18. He befriended French painter Paul Cézanne and, influenced by ROMANTICISM, began to write. His mother had great hopes that he would pursue a career in law and ease the family's financial burdens, but he failed his exams. Popular legend holds that there were times in which Zola's family was so poor that he would capture birds on his windowsill to provide meat for the supper table.

Unable to pursue law, Zola secured employment first as a clerk for a shipping firm, then at the Louis-Christophe-François-Hachette publishing house, all the while working toward his goal of becoming a published author. His journalistic writings included art criticism and literary reviews as well as political articles in which he openly expressed his animosity toward Napoleon III.

Zola's earliest published works of fiction include *Contes à Ninon* (*Stories for Ninon,* 1864) as well as several essays, plays and short stories. He attracted little attention for his work until the publication of his scandalous and sordid autobiographical work *La confession de Claude* (*Claude's Confession,* 1865). This attention, however, came not so much from the public as it did from the authorities. As a result, Zola was fired from his job at the publishing firm, but he gained recognition as an emerging author.

Thérèse Raquin (1867), Zola's first novel to be considered a major work, was published two years later and was a moderate success. He followed it immediately with the first of a series of works collectively referred to as the *Rougon-Macquart* cycle (1871–93), which revolves around the life of a family living under Napoleon III and the Second Empire. Zola initially presented this idea to his publisher in 1868. The family is split into two branches: the working-class Rougons, and the Macquarts, who are alcoholics and smugglers. In the course of time, some would rise to the highest levels of society, and others would fall victim to the evils of society and the malformations of their own character. The series reached 20 volumes, each one slightly different in theme but all of them sharing a common element of detailed research. Zola conducted interviews and attempted to experience as much as he could firsthand to understand and present his characters fully. He was particularly interested in the effects of heredity and social determinism. This marked the beginning of the new naturalist period of French literature.

The novel that brought him fame was *L'assommoir* (*The Drunkard,* 1877). After its publication, he bought property and continued to compile detailed notes about all aspects of life. *Germinal* (1885) was written based on notes compiled on labor conditions for coal miners. Having centered his novel on a worker's strike, Zola again attracted the attention of the authorities, who viewed his work as advocating and encouraging revolution.

On January 13, 1898, Zola became even more openly involved in controversy. He published an open letter entitled *J'accuse* in which he defended Albert Dreyfus, a Jewish officer who had been sent to prison for allegedly giving military secrets to Germany. This letter was ultimately instrumental in gaining Dreyfus a new trial and his eventual release, but not until Zola was forced to flee to England to escape imprisonment for writing it. He returned in 1899, after Dreyfus was released.

On September 28, 1902, Zola was found dead in his home of carbon monoxide poisoning. Strong evidence points to the possibility that this was not an accident but a murder, carried out by those who disagreed with his views.

Critical Analysis

"I want to shout out from the housetops that I am not a *chef d'école* [school principal], and that I don't want any disciples," Zola remarked, but with the publication of *The Drunkard*, the seventh book in his 20-volume series *Natural and Social History of a Family During the Second Empire*, his status as a leader in the genre of NATURALISM, whether Zola accepted it or not, was firmly established.

In his preface to the series, Zola wrote:

I wish to explain how a family, a small group of human beings, conducts itself in a given social system after blossoming forth and giving birth to ten or twenty members, who, though they may appear, at the first glance, profoundly dissimilar one from the other, are, as analysis demonstrates, most closely linked together from the point of view of affinity. Heredity, like gravity, has its laws.

The Drunkard focuses on Gervaise Macquart, who, living in Paris, attempts to start up a laundry business and bears a daughter, Nana, only to fall on hard times due to her husband's descent into extreme alcoholism following a debilitating accident. The instability that ensues forces Macquart deeply into debt and causes her to close her laundry. She follows her husband's slide into alcoholism; Nana eventually runs away, leaving Paris, ensuring the continuation of the vicious cycle.

As he usually did, Zola amassed a significant amount of research for this novel, resulting, in the opinion of many critics, in his most realistic novel to date. Zola used the street slang of the time to capture the authenticity of 19th-century working-class Paris. His descriptions of these particular conditions drew widespread praise for their REALISM. Indeed, *The Drunkard* was taken up by temperance workers across the world as a tract against the dangers of alcoholism; Zola himself, however, always insisted there was more to his novel than a critique of alcohol abuse. The novelist also drew criticism from some quarters for the brutal honestly of his work, believing him to be too coarse and vulgar in his portrayal of working-class people. Zola rejected both of these criticisms; his response was simply that he wished to present a true picture of real life.

Other Works by Émile Zola

The Masterpiece. Translated by Thomas Walron. New York: Oxford University Press, 1993.

Pot Luck. Translated by Brian Nelson. New York: Oxford University Press, 1999.

A Work about Émile Zola

Brown, Frederick. *Zola: A Life.* New York: Farrar, Straus & Giroux, 1995.

Zynger, Icek-Hersz

See SINGER, ISAAC BASHEVIS.

SELECTED BIBLIOGRAPHY

Abrahams, Cecil. *Alex La Guma*. Boston: Twayne, 1985.

Abrahams, C., ed. *The Tragic Life: Bessie Head and Literature in Southern Africa*. Lawrenceville, N.J.: Africa World Press, 1990.

Abramson, Glenda. *The Writing of Yehuda Amichai: A Thematic Approach*. Albany: State University of New York Press, 1989.

Ackerly, C. J., and S. E. Gontarsky. *The Grove Companion to Samuel Beckett: A Reader's Guide*. New York: Grove Press, 2004.

Adams, Ian M. *Three Authors of Alienation: Bombal, Onetti, Carpentier*. Austin: University of Texas Press, 1975.

Adereth, Max. *Elsa Triolet and Louis Aragon: An Introduction to Their Interwoven Lives and Works*. Lewiston, N.Y.: Edwin Mellen Press, 1994.

Adler, Jeremy. *Franz Kafka*. New York: Overlook Press, 2002.

Adler, Laure. *Marguerite Duras: A Life*. Translated by Anne-Marie Glasheen. Chicago: University of Chicago Press, 2000.

Aichinger, Isle. *The Bound Man and Other Stories*. Translated by Eric Mosbacher. New York: Noonday Press, 1956.

Akutagawa Ryunosuke. *Tales Grotesque and Curious*. Translated by Glen W. Shaw. Tokyo: Hokuseido, 1948.

Al-Ali, Nadje Sadig. *Gender Writing/Writing Gender: The Representation of Women in a Selection of Modern Egyptian Literature*. Cairo: American University in Cairo Press, 1994.

Alberti, Rafael. *The Owl's Insomnia: Poems Selected and Translated by Mark Strand*. New York: Atheneum, 1973.

Alcalay, Ammiel. *Keys to the Garden, New Israeli Writing*. New York: City Light Books, 1996.

Alexander, Peter F. *Alan Paton: A Biography*. Oxford: Oxford University Press, 1994.

Alldridge, James C. *Ilse Aichinger*. Chester Springs, Pa.: Dufour Editions, 1969.

Alpers, Antony. *The Life of Katherine Mansfield*. New York: Viking Press, 1980.

Amoia, Alba della Fazia. *Feodor Dostoevsky*. New York: Continuum Press, 1993.

Anand, Mulk R. *Anthology of Dalit Literature*. Columbia, Mo.: South Asia Books, 1992.

Anastasia, Olga, ed. *Isak Dinesen: Critical Views*. Athens: Ohio University Press, 1993.

Anders, Jaroslaw. *Between Fire and Sleep: Essays on Modern Polish Poetry and Prose*. New Haven, Conn.: Yale University Press, 2009.

Anderson, Marston. *Limits of Realism*. Berkeley: University of California Press, 1989.

Angulo, Maria-Elena. *Magic Realism: Social Context and Discourse*. New York: Garland, 1995.

Anyidoho, Kofi, Abena Busia, and Anne V. Adams, eds. *Beyond Survival: African Literature and the Search for New Life.* Lawrenceville, N.J.: Africa World Press, 1998.

Arenas, Reinaldo. *The Ill-Fated Peregrinations of Fray Servando.* Translated by Andrew Hurley. New York: Avon, 1987

Arghezi, Tudor. *Poems: Tudor Arghezi.* Translated by Andrei Bantas. Bucharest: Minerva Publishing House, 1983.

———. *Selected Poems of Tudor Arghezi.* Translated by Michael Impey and Brian Swann. Princeton, N.J.: Princeton University Press, 1976.

Arico, Santo L. *Oriana Fallaci: The Woman and the Myth.* Carbondale: Southern Illinois University Press, 1998.

Arnold, James A., ed. *A History of Literature in the Caribbean.* Philadelphia: Benjamins, 1994.

Assouline, Pierre. *Simenon: A Biography.* Translated by Jon Rothschild. New York: Knopf, 1997.

Atik, Anne. *How It Was: A Memoir of Samuel Beckett.* Berkeley, Calif.: Counterpoint, 2005.

Atkins, Angela. *Vikram Seth's "A Suitable Boy": A Reader's Guide.* New York: Continuum International Inc., 2002.

Attridge, Derek, and Rosemary Jolly, eds. *Writing South Africa: Literature, Apartheid, and Democracy, 1970–1995.* Cambridge: Cambridge University Press, 1998.

Atwell, David. *J. M. Coetzee: South Africa and the Politics of Writings.* Berkeley: University of California Press, 1993.

Auslander, Rose. *Selected Poems of Rose Auslander.* Translated by Ewald Osers. London: London Magazine Editors, 1977.

Babcock, Arthur E. *The New Novel in France: Theory and Practice of the Nouveau Roman.* Boston: Twayne, 1997.

Bachelard, Gaston. *Lautreamont.* Translated by Robert S. Dupree. Dallas, Tex.: Dallas Institute of Humanities and Culture, 1986.

Bahti, Timothy, and Marilyn Sibley Fries. *Jewish Writers, German Literature: The Uneasy Examples of Nelly Sachs and Walter Benjamin.* Ann Arbor: The University of Michigan Press, 1995.

Bair, Dierdre. *Samuel Beckett: A Biography.* New York: Harcourt Brace Jovanovich, 1978.

———. *Simone de Beauvoir: A Biography.* New York: Touchstone, 2002.

Baker, Gary. *Understanding Uwe Johnson.* Columbia: University of South Carolina Press, 1999.

Barbour, Douglas. *b. p. Nichol and His Work.* Toronto: ECW Press, 1992.

———. *Michael Ondaatje.* Boston: Twayne, 1993.

Barbour, Sarah. *Nathalie Sarraute and the Feminist Reader: Identities in Process.* Lewisburg, Pa.: Bucknell University Press, 1993.

Barker, Christine. *Erich Maria Remarque.* New York: Barnes and Noble, 1980.

Barlow, Tani E., and Gary J. Bjoge, eds. *I Myself Am a Woman: Selected Writings of Ding Ling.* Boston: Beacon Press, 1990.

Barnes, Christopher. *Boris Pasternak: A Literary Biography.* Cambridge: Cambridge University Press, 1998.

Barnett, Ursula. *A Vision of Order: A Study of Black South African Literature in English (1914–1980).* Amherst: University of Massachusetts Press, 1983.

Barnstone, Aliki, and Willis Barnstone, eds. *A Book of Women Poets from Antiquity to Now.* New York: Schocken Books, 1980.

Barnstone, Willis, ed. *Borges at Eighty: Conversations.* Bloomington: Indiana University Press, 1982.

Barnstone, Willis, and Tony Barnstone, eds. *Literature of Asia, Africa, and Latin America.* Upper Saddle River, N.J.: Prentice Hall, 1999.

Barron, Stephanie, and Wolf-Dieter Dube, eds. *German Expressionism: Art and Society.* New York: Rizzoli, 1997.

Bassanese, Fiora A. *Understanding Luigi Pirandello.* Columbia: University of South Carolina Press, 1997.

Baudelaire, Charles. *Baudelaire: Poems.* Translated by Laurence Lerner. London: J. M. Dent, 1999.

Bauer, Nancy. *Simone de Beauvoir, Philosophy and Feminism.* New York: Columbia University Press, 2001.

Bauermeister, Erica, Jesse Larsen, and Holly Smith, eds. *500 Great Books by Women.* New York: Penguin, 1994.

Beasley, W. G., ed. *Modern Japan: Aspects of History, Literature and Society.* Berkeley: University of California Press, 1975.

Beaton, Roderick. *An Introduction to Modern Greek Literature.* New York: Oxford University Press, 1995.

Beichman, Janine. *Masaoka Shiki.* New York: Kodansha International, 1986.

Beizer, Mikhail, trans. Michael Sherbourne. *The Jews of St. Petersburg. Philadelphia:* Jewish Publication Society, 1989.

Bell-Villada, Gene H. *Borges and His Fiction.* Arlington: University of Texas Press, 1999.

Bellos, David. *Georges Perec: A Life in Words.* London: Harvill, 1993.

Benn, Gottfried. *Prose, Essays, Poems.* New York: Continuum, 1987.

Berlin, Isaiah. *The Hedgehog and the Fox: An Essay on Tolstoy's View of History.* New York: Simon & Schuster, 1986.

Bermel, Albert. *Artaud's Theatre of Cruelty.* New York: Taplinger, 1977.

Bernstein, Gail L., ed. *Recreating Japanese Women, 1600–1945.* Berkeley: University of California Press, 1991.

Bertram, James. *Charles Brasch.* Wellington: Oxford University Press, 1976.

Besser, Gretchen Rous. *Germain de Stael Revisited.* Boston: Twayne, 1994.

Bhagvan, Manu, and Anne Feldhaus. *Speaking Truth to Power: Religion, Caste and the Subaltern Question in India.* New York: Oxford University Press, 2010.

Birbalsingh, Frank, ed. *Frontiers of Caribbean Literatures in English.* New York: St. Martin's Press, 1996.

———. *Indo-Caribbean Resistance.* Toronto: TSAR, 1993.

Birch, Cyril, ed. *Chinese Communist Literature.* New York: Frederick A. Praeger, 1963.

Birnbaum, M. D., and R. Trager-Verchovsky, eds. *History, Another Text.* Ann Arbor: University of Michigan Press, 1988.

Bishop, Lloyd. *The Poetry of Alfred Musset: Styles and Genres.* New York: Peter Lang, 1997.

Bisztray, George. *Marxist Models of Literary Realism.* New York: Columbia University Press, 1978.

Blackwell, Jeannine, and Susanne Zantop, eds. *Bitter Healing: German Women Writers: 1700–1830.* Lincoln: University of Nebraska Press, 1990.

Bloom, Harold, ed. *Isaac Babel: Modern Critical Views.* Broomall, Pa.: Chelsea House, 1987.

Boeschentein, Hermann. *A History of Modern German Literature.* New York: Peter Lang, 1990.

Bohn, William. *Apollinaire and the International Avante-Garde.* Albany: State University of New York Press, 1997.

Bondanella, Peter. *Umberto Eco and the Open Text: Semiotics, Fiction, Popular Culture.* Cambridge: Cambridge University Press, 1997.

Bonifaz, Oscar C. *Remembering Rosario: A Personal Glimpse into the Life and Works of Rosario Castellanos.* Translated by Myralyn F. Allgood. Madrid: Scripta Humanistica, 1990.

Bouchard, Norma, and Veronica Pravadelli, eds. *Umberto Eco's Alternative.* New York: Peter Lang, 1998.

Boullata, Issa. *Critical Perspectives on Modern Arabic Literature.* Washington, D.C.: Three Continents Press, 1980.

Bower, Kathrin M. *Ethics and Rememberance in the Poetry of Nelly Sachs and Rose Auslander.* Rochester, N.Y.: Camden House, 2000.

Brasch, Charles. *Indirections: A Memoir 1909–1947.* Edited by James Bertram. Wellington, N.Z.; New York: Oxford University Press, 1980.

Breslin, Paul. *Nobody's Nation: Reading Derek Walcott.* Chicago: University of Chicago Press, 2001.

Brewer, Maria M. *Claude Simon: Narratives Without Narrative.* Lincoln: University of Nebraska Press, 1995.

Brock, Peggy, ed. *Women, Rites and Sites: Aboriginal Women's Cultural Knowledge.* Boston: Allen and Unwin, 1900.

Brod, Max. *Franz Kafka: A Biography.* New York: Da Capo Press, 1995.

Brodsky, Patricia. *Rainer Maria Rilke.* Boston: Twayne, 1988.

Bronner, Stephen E. *Camus: Portrait of a Moralist.* Minneapolis: University of Minnesota Press, 1999.

Brotherson, Gordon. *Manuel Machado: A Revaluation.* Cambridge: Cambridge University Press, 1968.

Brown, Frederick. *Zola: A Life*. New York: Farrar, Strauss & Giroux, 1995.

Brown, Lloyd W. *Women Writers in Black Africa*. Westport, Conn.: Greenwood Press, 1981.

Brown, Stewart, ed. *The Art of Kamau Brathwaite*. Bridgend, Mid Glamorgan, Wales: Seren, 1995.

Brown, Stewart, et al. *Voiceprint: An Anthology of Oral and Related Poetry from the Caribbean*. Essex, England: Longman Group UK Limited, 1989.

Brunsdale, Mitzi. *Sigrid Undset: Chronicler of Norway*. New York: Berg Publishers, Ltd., 1988.

Burness, Donald. *Fire: Six Writers from Angola, Mozambique and Cape Verde*. Washington, D.C.: Three Continents Press, 1977.

Burnett, Paula. *Derek Walcott: Politics and Poetics*. Gainesville: University Press of Florida, 2000.

Buruma, Ian, ed. *India: A Mosaic*. New York: New York Review of Books, 2000.

Buxton, John. *The Grecian Taste: Literature in the Age of New-Classicism 1740–1820*. New York: Barnes and Noble, 1978.

Bynum, Brant B. *The Romantic Imagination in the Works of Gustavo Adolfo Bécquer*. Chapel Hill: University of North Carolina, Department of Romance Languages, 1993.

Cady, Andrea. *Measuring the Visible: The Verse and Prose of Philippe Jaccottet*. Atlanta, Ga.: Rodopi, 1992.

Calvocaressi, Richard, and Katharina Schultz. *Oskar Kokoschka, 1886–1980*. New York: Solomon R. Guggenheim Foundation, 1986.

Camber, Richard. *On Camus*. Belmont, Calif.: Wadsworth/Thompson Learning, 2002.

Caranfa, Angelo. *Claudel: Beauty and Grace*. Lewisburg, Pa.: Bucknell University Press, 1989.

Carlyle, Thomas. *The Life of Friedrich Schiller: Comprehending and Examination of His Works*. Portland, Oreg.: University Press of the Pacific, 2001.

Cate, Curtis. *André Malraux: A Biography*. London, England: Hutchinson, 1995.

Cavafy, Konstantin. *Before Time Could Change Them: The Complete Poems of Constantine P. Cavafy*. Translated by Theoharis Constantine Theoharis. Orlando, Fla.: Harcourt Brace, 2001.

Caws, Mary Ann. *René Char*. Boston: Twayne, 1977.

Celan, Paul. *Selected Poetry and Prose of Paul Celan*. Translated by John Felstiner. New York: Norton, 2000.

Chadwick, Charles. *Verlaine*. London, England: Athlone Press, 1973.

Chagnon, Jacqui, and Don Luce, eds. *Quiet Courage: Poems from Viet Nam*. Washington, D.C.: Indochina Mobil Education Project, 1974.

Chambers, Helen. *The Changing Image of Theodor Fontane*. Columbia, S.C.: Camden House Inc., 1997.

Champagne, Roland A. *Georges Bataille*. Boston: Twayne, 1998.

Chapman, Michael. *South African Literatures*. London, England: Longman, 1996.

Chartier, Armand B. *Barbey d'Aurevilly*. Boston: Twayne, 1977.

Chen Yuan-tsung. *Return to the Middle Kingdom: One Family, Three Revolutionaries, and the Birth of Modern China*. New York: Sterling Publishing, 2008.

Cheung, Dominic. *Feng Chih*. Boston: Twayne, 1979.

Chevalier, Tracy, ed. *Contemporary World Writers*. Detroit: St. James Press, 1993.

Chung, Chong-wha, ed. *Modern Korean Literature, An Anthology, 1908–1965*. New York: Kegan Paul International, 1995.

Cixous, Helene. *Reading with Clarice Lispector*. Minneapolis: University of Minnesota Press, 1990.

Cliff, Michelle. *The Land of Look Behind: Prose and Poetry*. Ithaca, N.Y.: Firebrand Books, 1985.

Clurman, Harold. *Ibsen*. New York: Da Capo Press, 1989.

Cobb, Carl. *Antonio Machado*. Boston: Twayne, 1971.

Coghlan, Brian. *Hofmannsthal's Festival Dramas*. Cambridge: Cambridge University Press, 1964.

Cohen, Georg. *Henrik Ibsen, A Critical Study. With a 42-Page Essay on Bjørnstjerne Bjørnson*. New York: Classic Books, 1964.

Cohen, Joseph. *Voices of Israel: Essays on and Interview with Yehuda Amichai, A. B. Yehoshua, T. Carmi, Aharon Applefeld, and Amos Oz*. Albany: State University of New York Press, 1990.

Cohn, Robert G. *The Poetry of Arthur Rimbaud.* Columbia: University of South Carolina Press, 1999.

Collins, John, ed. *Noonuccal and Her People: Perspectives on Her Life's Work.* St. Lucia, B.W.I.: University Queensland Press, 1996.

Collymore, Frank. *The Man Who Loved Attending Funerals and Other Stories.* Edited by Harold Barratt and Reinhard Sander. Portsmouth, N.H.: Heinemann, 1993.

Conde, Maryse. *Tales from the Heart: True Stories from My Childhood.* Translated by Richard Philcox. New York: Soho, 2001.

Conroy, William T. *Villiers de L'Isle-Adam.* Boston: Twayne, 1978.

Cooke, Miriam. *War's Other Voices.* Cambridge: Cambridge University Press, 1988.

Cooke, Nathalie. *Margaret Atwood: A Biography.* Toronto: ECW Press, 1998.

Copeland, Rebecca L. *Lost Leaves: Women Writers of Meiji Japan.* Honolulu: University of Hawaii Press, 2000.

Cornwell, Neil. *Vladimir Nabokov.* Plymouth, Mass.: Northcote House Publishers, 1999.

Cook, David, and Michael Okenimkpe. *Ngugi wa Thiong'o: An Exploration of His Writings.* London, England: Heinemann, 1983.

Couste, A. *Julio Cortázar.* South America: Oceano Group, 2002.

Coutinho, Edilberto. *Gilberto Freyre.* Rio de Janeiro, Brazil: Agir, 1994.

Cox, Brian, ed. *African Writers.* New York: Charles Scribner's Sons, 1997.

Crane, Ralph J. *Ruth Prawer Jhabvala.* Boston: Twayne, 1992.

Crichfield, Grant. *Three Novels of Madame de Duras.* The Hague: Mouton, 1975.

Crockett, Roger A. *Understanding Friedrich Dürrenmatt.* Columbia: University of South Carolina Press, 1998.

Cronin, Anthony. *Samuel Beckett: The Last Modernist.* London, England: HarperCollins, 1996.

Cruickshank, Ruth. *Fin de millénaire French Fiction: The Aesthetics of Crisis.* Oxford: Oxford University Press, 2009.

Csaire, Aime. *Lyric and Dramatic Poetry, 1946–82.* Translated by Clayton Eshleman and Annette Smith. Charlottesville: University Press of Virginia, 1990.

———. *Aimé Césaire: The Collected Poetry.* Translated by Clayton Eschleman and Annette Smith. Berkeley: University of California Press, 1983.

Cuomo, Glenn R. *Career at the Cost of Compromise: Gunter Eich's Life and Work in the Years 1933–1945.* Atlanta, Ga.: Rodopi, 1989.

Currie, William. *Metaphors of Alienation: The Fiction of Abe, Beckett and Kafka.* Ann Arbor, Mich.: University Microfilms, 1973.

Curtis, J. A. E. *Mikhail Bulgakov: A Life in Letters and Diaries.* New York: Overlook Press, 1992.

Czeslaw, Milosz. *Who Is Gombrowicz?* New York: Penguin, 1986.

Daglarca, Fazil H. *Secme Siirler. Selected Poems.* Translated by Talat Sait Halman. Pittsburgh: University of Pittsburgh Press, 1969.

Dana, Doris, ed. *Selected Poems of Gabriela Mistral.* Translated by Doris Dana. Baltimore: Johns Hopkins University Press, 1971.

Dance, Daryl C., ed. *Fifty Caribbean Writers: A Bio-Bibliographical Critical Sourcebook.* Westport, Conn.: Greenwood Press, 1986.

Daniels, Barry V. *Revolution in the Theatre: French Romantic Theories of Drama.* Westport, Conn.: Greenwood Press, 1983.

Danly, Robert L. *In the Shade of Spring Leaves: The Life and Writings of Higuchi Ichiyo, a Woman of Letters in Meiji Japan.* New Haven, Conn.: Yale University Press, 1981.

Davies, Carole B., and Anne Adams Graves, eds. *Nagambika: Studies of Women in African Literature.* Lawrenceville, N.J.: Africa World Press, 1986.

Davies, Carole B., and Elaine Savory Fido, eds. *Out of the Kumbla: Caribbean Women and Literature.* Lawrenceville, N.J.: Africa World Press, 1990.

Davis, Gregson. *Aimé Césaire.* Cambridge: Cambridge University Press, 1997.

Dawes, Kwame, ed. *Talk Yuh Talk: Interviews with Anglophone Caribbean Poets.* Charlottesville: University Press of Virginia, 2001.

Day, A. Grove, and Edgar C. Knowlton, Jr. *Vicente Blasco Ibáñez.* Boston: Twayne, 1972.

Del Principe, David. *Rebellion, Death, and Aesthetics in Italy: The Demons of Scapigliatura.* Madison, Wis.: Fairleigh Dickinson University Press, 1996.

Demetz, Peter. *After the Fires: Recent Writing in the Germanies, Austria, and Switzerland.* New York: Harcourt Brace Jovanovich, 1986.

———. *Postwar German Literature: A Critical Introduction.* New York: Pegasus, 1970.

Dever, Aileen. *Radical Insufficiency of Human Life: The Poetry of R. de Castro and J. A. Silva.* Jefferson, N.C.: McFarland, 2000.

Dharwakder, Vinay, and A. K. Ramanujan, eds. *The Oxford Anthology of Modern Indian Poetry.* London, England: Oxford University Press, 1994.

Dhqwan, R. K. *The Novels of Amitav Ghosh.* New York: Prestige Books, 1999.

DiGaetani, John L., ed. *A Companion to Pirandello Studies.* Westport, Conn.: Greenwood Press, 1991.

Dodiya, Jaydipsinh, ed. *The Fiction of Rohinton Mistry: Critical Studies.* London, England: Sangam, 1998.

Dodiya, Jaydipsinh. *The Plays of Girish Karnad: Critical Perspectives.* New Delhi: Prestige Books, 1999.

Doherty, Justin. *The Acmeist Movement in Russian Poetry: Culture and the Word.* Oxford: Oxford University Press, 1995.

Doi, Takeo. *The Psychological World of Natsume Soseki.* Translated by William Jeffeson Tyler. Cambridge: Harvard University Press, 1976.

Dolezelova-Velingerova, M., ed. *The Chinese Novel at the Turn of the Century.* Toronto: University of Toronto Press, 1980.

Dolittle, James. *Alfred de Vigny.* Boston: Twayne, 1967.

Dollenmayer, David. *The Berlin Novels of Alfred Doblin.* Berkeley: University of California Press, 1988.

Donahue, Thomas J. *The Theater of Fernando Arrabal: A Garden of Earthly Delights.* New York: New York University Press, 1980.

Dooling, Amy D., and Kristina M. Torgeson. *Writing Women in Modern China: An Anthology of Women's Literature from the Early Twentieth Century.* New York: Columbia University Press, 1998.

Edstrom, Vivi Bloom. *Selma Legerlof.* Boston: Twayne, 1982.

Edwards, Justin D. *Understanding Jamaica Kincaid.* Columbia: University of South Carolina Press, 2007.

Ehre, Milton. *Isaak Babel.* Boston: Twayne, 1986.

Eich, Gunter. *Pigeons and Moles: Selected Writings of Günter Eich.* Translated by Michael Hamburger. Columbia, S.C.: Camden House, 1990.

Eilersen, Gillian. *Bessie Head: Thunder Behind Her Ears: Her Life and Writing.* Cape Town, Claremont: David Philip, 1995.

El-Enany, Rasheed. *Naguib Mahfouz: The Pursuit of Meaning.* New York: Routledge, 1993.

Ellis, Keith. *Critical Approaches to Rubén Dario.* Toronto: University of Toronto Press, 1974.

Ellison, David R. *Ethics and Aesthetics in Modernist Literature: From the Sublime to the Uncanny.* New York: Cambridge University Press, 2001.

Ellison, Fred P. *Brazil's New Novel: Four Northeastern Masters.* Berkeley: University of California Press, 1954.

Elytis, Odysseus. *The Collected Poems of Odysseus Elytis.* Translated by Jeffrey Carson and Nikos Sarris. Baltimore: Johns Hopkins University Press, 1997.

Erickson, John D. *Dada: Performance, Poetry and Art.* Boston: Twayne, 1984.

Ermolaev, Herman. *Mikhail Sholokhov and His Art.* Princeton, N.J.: Princeton University Press, 1982.

Erwin, Edward. *The Freud Encyclopedia: Theory, Therapy, and Culture.* New York: Garland, 2002.

Espinet, Ramabai, ed. *Creation Fire: A CAFRA Anthology of Caribbean Women's Poetry.* Toronto: Sister Vision, 1990.

Esslin, Martin. *Brecht, a Choice of Evils: A Critical Study of the Man, His Works, and His Opinions.* New York: Methuen Drama, 1984.

———. *Theatre of the Absurd.* New York: Overlook Press, 1969.

Ezenwa-Ohaeto. *Chinua Achebe: A Biography.* Bloomington: Indiana University Press, 1997.

Falb, Lewis W. *Jean Anouilh.* New York: Frederick Unger, 1977.

Falk, Thomas. *Elias Canetti*. Boston: Twayne, 1993.

Faurot, Jeannette L., ed. *Chinese Fiction from Taiwan: Critical Perspectives*. Bloomington: Indiana University Press, 1980.

Fehsenfeld, Dow, et al., eds. *The Letters of Samuel Beckett: Volume One, 1929–1940*. Cambridge: Cambridge University Press, 2009.

Fekkema, Douwe, and Elrud Ibsch. *Modernist Conjectures: A Mainstream in European Literature 1910–1940*. New York: St. Martin's Press, 1988.

Felsteiner, John. *Paul Celan: Poet, Survivor, Jew*. New Haven, Conn.: Yale University Press, 2001.

Ferguson, Robert. *Enigma: The Life of Knut Hamsun*. New York: Noonday Press, 1988.

Ferre, Rosario. *Sweet Diamond Dust and Other Stories*. New York: Plume, 1996.

Feuerwerker, Yi-tsi Mei. *Ding Ling's Fiction: Ideology and Narrative in Modern Chinese Literature*. Cambridge, Mass.: Harvard University Press, 1982.

Fioretos, Aris. *The Solid Letter: Reading of Friedrich Holderlin*. Stanford, Calif.: Stanford University Press, 2000.

Firda, Richard. *Peter Handke*. Boston: Twayne, 1993.

Fishburn, Katherine. *Reading Buchi Emecheta: Cross-Cultural Conversations*. Westport, Conn.: Greenwood Press, 1995.

Flores, Angel. *Spanish American Authors*. New York: H. W. Wilson Company, 1992.

Flores, Angel, and Kate Flores, eds. *The Defiant Muse: Hispanic Feminist Poems from the Middle Ages to the Present*. New York: The Feminist Press, 1986.

Fong, Gilbert C. F. *The Other Shore: Plays by Gao Xingjian*. Hong Kong: The Chinese University Press, 1999.

Fortescue, William. *Alphonse de Lamartine: A Political Biography*. New York: St. Martin's Press, 1983.

Fowlie, Wallace. *Poem and Symbol: A Brief History of French Symbolism*. University Park: Pennsylvania State University Press, 1990.

Franco, Jean. *An Introduction to Spanish-American Literature*. Cambridge: Cambridge University Press, 1994.

Frank, Joseph. *Dostoevsky: The Seeds of Revolt, 1821–1849*. Princeton, N.J.: Princeton University Press, 1976.

———. *Dostoevsky: The Years of Ordeal, 1850–1859*. Princeton, N.J.: Princeton University Press, 1984.

———. *Dostoevsky: The Years of Liberation, 1860–1865*. Princeton, N.J.: Princeton University Press, 1986.

———. *Dostoevsky: The Miraculous Years, 1865–1871*. Princeton, N.J.: Princeton University Press, 1996.

———. *Dostoevsky: The Mantle of the Prophet, 1871–1881*. Princeton, N.J.: Princeton University Press, 2002.

Frantisek, Deak. *Symbolist Theater: The Formation of an Avant-Garde*. Baltimore: Johns Hopkins University Press, 1993.

Freedman, Ralph. *Life of a Poet: Rainer Maria Rilke*. Chicago: Northwestern University Press, 1998.

French, Patrick. *The World Is What It Is: The Authorized Biography of V. S. Naipaul*. New York: Vintage, 2009.

Frey, John A. *A Victor Hugo Encyclopedia*. Westport, Conn.: Greenwood Press, 1999.

Friedman, Lawrence. *Understanding Isaac Bashevis Singer*. Columbia: University of South Carolina Press, 1988.

Friedrich, Pia. *Pier Paolo Pasolini*. Boston: Twayne, 1982.

Fusso, Susanne, ed. *Essays on Karolina Pavlova*. Chicago: Northwestern University Press, 2001.

Garrard, John. *Mikhail Lermontov*. Boston: Twayne, 1982.

Gatt-Rutter, John. *Italo Svevo: A Double Life*. Oxford: Oxford University Press, 1988.

———. *Oriana Fallaci: The Rhetoric of Freedom*. Washington, D.C.: Berg, 1996.

George, Stefan. *The Works of Stefan George*. Translated by Olga Marx and Ernst Morwitz. Chapel Hill: University of North Carolina Press, 1974.

Gessel, Van C., and Tomone Matsumoto, eds. *The Showa Anthology: Modern Japanese Short Stories*. Tokyo: Kodansha International, 1985.

Giergielewicz, Mieczyslaw. *Henryk Sienkiewicz: A Biography*. New York: Hippocrene, 1991.

Gifford, Henry. *Tolstoy*. New York: Oxford University Press, 1982.

Gifford, Paul, and Johnnie Gratton, eds. *Subject Matters: Subject and Self in French Literature from Descartes to the Present*. The Netherlands: Rodopi, 2000.

Gikandi, Simon. *Writing in Limbo: Modernism and Caribbean Literature*. Ithaca, N.Y.: Cornell University Press, 1992.

Giles, James, ed. *French Existentialism: Consciousness, Ethics and Relations with Others*. Atlanta: Rodopi, 1999.

Goldberg, Anatol. *Ilya Ehrenburg, Revolutionary, Novelist, Poet, War Correspondent, Propagandist: The Extraordinary Epic of a Russian Survivor*. New York: Viking Press, 1984.

Goldblatt, Howard, ed. *Worlds Apart: Recent Chinese Writing and Its Audiences*. Armonk, N.Y.: M. E. Sharpe, 1990.

Goldman, Merle. *Modern Chinese Literature in the May Fourth Era*. Cambridge, Mass.: Harvard University Press, 1977.

Gonzalez, Roberto E. *Alejo Carpentier, The Pilgrim at Home*. Ithaca, N.Y.: Cornell University Press, 1977.

Goodwin, K. L. *Understanding Poetry: A Study of Ten Poets*. London, England: Heinemann, 1982.

Gordon, Haim, ed. *The Dictionary of Existentialism*. Westport, Conn.: Greenwood Press, 1999.

Gordon, Haim. *Naguib Mahfouz's Egypt: Existential Themes in his Writings*. Westport, Conn.: Greenwood Press, 1990.

———. *Sartre's Philosophy and the Challenge of Education*. Lewiston, N.Y.: Edwin Mellen Press, 2001.

Gordon, Lois. *The World of Samuel Beckett*. New Haven, Conn.: Yale University Press, 1996.

Gotlieb, Vera, and Paul Allain, eds. *The Cambridge Companion to Chekhov*. Cambridge: Cambridge University Press, 2000.

Gracia, Jorge. *Literary Philosophers: Borges, Calvino, Eco*. London: Routledge, 2002.

Graham, Robb. *Balzac: A Biography*. New York: Norton, 1994.

Grant, Judith S. *Robertson Davies: Man of Myth*. New York: Viking, 1994.

Gray, Nancy. *Language Unbound: On Experimental Writing by Women*. Urbana: University of Illinois Press, 1992.

Grayson, Jane, et al., eds. *Nabokov's World* (2 vols). London: Palgrave MacMillan, 2002.

Green, Mary Jean, ed. *Postcolonial Subjects: Francophone Women Writers*. Minneapolis: University of Minnesota Press, 1996.

Greider, Jerome B. *Hu Shih and the Chinese Renaissance: Liberalism in the Chinese Revolution, 1917–1937*. Cambridge, Mass.: Harvard University Press, 1970.

Gross, John, ed. *The Modern Movement*. London: Harvill, 1992.

Grossman, Joan. *Valery Bryusov and the Riddle of Russian Decadence*. Berkeley: University of California Press, 1985.

Guibert, Rita. *Seven Voices: Seven Latin American Writers Talk of Rita Guibert*. Translated by Frances Partridge. New York: Knopf, 1972.

Guicharnaud, Jacques. *Raymond Queneau*. Translated by June Guicharnaud. New York: Columbia University Press, 1965.

Guignon, Charles and Derk Pereboom, eds. *Existentialism: Basic Writings*. Indianapolis, Ind.: Hackett, 2001.

Guillen, Jorge. *Guillen on Guillen: The Poetry and the Poet*. Translated by Reginald Gibbons. Princeton, N.J.: Princeton University Press, 1979.

Gupla, Suman. *V. S. Naipaul*. Plymouth, New Zealand: Northcote House in Association with the British Council, 1999.

Haberly, David. *Three Sad Races: Racial Identity and National Consciousness in Brazilian Literature*. New York: Cambridge University Press, 1983.

Hadda, Janet. *Issaac Bashevis Singer: A Life*. New York: Oxford University Press, 1997.

Haines, Brigid, ed. *Herta Müller*. Cardiff: University of Wales, 1998.

Hale, Thomas, ed. *Critical Perspectives on Aimé Césaire*. Washington, D.C.: Three Continents Press, 1992.

Hanrahan, Gene Z. *Heavensent*. London: J. M. Dent and Sons, 1951.

Harris, Jane G. *Osip Mandelstam*. Boston: Twayne, 1988.

Harris, Wilson. *Selected Essays of Wilson Harris: The Unfinished Genesis of the Imagination*. New York: Routledge, 1999.

Harss, Luis, and Barbara Dohmann. *Into the Mainstream: Conversations with Latin-American Writers*. New York: Harper & Row, 1969.

Hasan, Mushirul, and Asmin Roy. *Living Together Separately: Cultural India in History and Politics*. New Delhi: Oxford University Press, 2005.

Hasek, Jaroslav. *The Bachura Scandal and Other Stories and Sketches*. Translated by Alan Menhennet. London, England: Angel, 1991.

Hasluck, Nicholas. *Anchor and Other Poems*. Fremantle, Australia: Fremantle Arts Center Press, 1976.

Hassall, Anthony J. *Dancing on Hot MacAdam: Peter Carey's Fiction*. St. Lucia, B.W.I.: University of Queensland Press, 1998.

Hawley, John C., ed. *Writing the Nation: Self and Country in the Postcolonial Imagination*. The Netherlands: Rodopi, 1996.

Havel, Václav. *The Garden Party and Other Plays*. New York: Grove Press, 1993.

Hayman, Ronald. *Eugène Ionesco*. New York: Frederick Ungar, 1976.

Head, Bessie. *A Woman Alone: Autobiographical Writings*. Oxford: Heinemann, 1990.

Heilbut, Anthony. *Thomas Mann: Eros and Literature*. Riverside: University of California Press, 1997.

Hemingway, Maurice. *Emilia Pardo Bazan: The Making of a Novelist*. Cambridge: Cambridge University Press, 1983.

Herdan, Innes. *The Pen and the Sword: Literature and Revolution in Modern China*. London: Zed Books Ltd., 1992.

Hermond, Joest. *Heinrich Heine's Contested Identities: Politics, Religion, and Nationalism in Nineteenth Century Germany*. New York: Peter Lang, 1999.

Heron, G. A. *The Poetry of Okot p'Bitek*. London: Heinemann, 1976.

Hettinga, Donald. *The Brothers Grimm: Two Lives, One Legacy*. London: Clarion Books, 2001.

Hewitt, Nicholas. *The Life of Celine: A Critical Biography*. Malden, U.K.: Blackwell, 1999.

Heywood, Christopher, ed. *Aspects of South African Literature*. New York: Africana, 1976.

Higgonnet, Margaret R., and Joan Templeton, eds. *Feminist Explorations of Literary Space*. Amherst: University of Massachusetts Press, 1994.

Hintz, Suzanne S. *Rosario Ferre, A Search for Identity*. New York: Peter Lang, 1995.

Hsia, C. T. *A History of Modern Chinese Literature*. New Haven, Conn.: Yale University Press, 1961.

Hofmannsthal, Hugo von. *The Lyrical Poems of Hugo von Hofmannsthal*. Translated by Charles Wharton Stark. New Haven, Conn.: Yale University Press, 1918.

———. *Selected Plays and Libretti*. Edited by Michael Hamburger. New York: Oxford University Press, 2000.

Hogsett, Charlotte. *The Literary Existence of Germain de Stael*. Carbondale: Southern Illinois University Press, 1987.

Holman, Martin. *The Book of Masks*. London: Readers International, 1976.

Holub, Robert. *Friedrich Nietzche*. Boston: Twayne, 1995.

Hopwood, Mererid, and David Basker, eds. *Sarah Kirsch*. Cardiff: University of Wales Press, 1997.

Horn, Pierre L. *Marguerite Yourcenar*. Boston: Twayne, 1985.

Howells, Christina, ed. *The Cambridge Companion to Margaret Atwood*. Cambridge: Cambridge University Press, 2006.

———. *The Cambridge Companion to Sartre*. New York: Cambridge University Press, 1992.

Howells, Coral A. *Alice Munro*. New York: St. Martin's Press, 1998.

Huggan, Graham. *Peter Carey*. Oxford, England: Oxford University Press, 1997.

Hulme, Peter, and William H. Sherman. *The Tempest and Its Travels*. Philadelphia: University of Pennsylvania Press, 2000.

Hyslop, Lois B. *Charles Baudelaire Revisited*. Boston: Twayne, 1992.

Idema, Wilt L., and Lloyd L. Haft. *A Guide to Chinese Literature*. Ann Arbor, Mich.: Center for Chinese Studies, 1997.

Ilie, Paul. *Unamuno; An Existential View of Self and Society*. Madison: University of Wisconsin Press, 1967.

Indyk, Ivor. *David Malouf*. New York: Oxford University Press, 1993.

Innes, C. L. *Chinua Achebe*. New York: Cambridge University Press, 1992.

Ito, Ken K. *Vision of Desire: Tanizaki's Fictional Worlds*. Stanford: Stanford University Press, 1991.

Ivask, Ivar. *The Perpetual Present: The Poetry and Prose of Octavio Paz*. Norman: University of Oklahoma Press, 1973.

Jack, Belinda E. *George Sand: A Woman's Life Writ Large*. London: Chatto and Windus, 1999.

Janecek, Gerald. *Andrey Bely: A Critical Review*. Lexington: Kentucky University Press, 1978.

Jeannet, Angela M., and Giuliana Sanguinetti Katz, eds. *Natalia Ginzburg: A Voice of the Twentieth Century*. Toronto: University of Toronto Press, 2000.

Ji-Moon, Suh, and Julie Pickering. *The Descendants of Cain*. Armonk, N.Y.: M. E. Sharpe, Inc., 1997.

Jolly, Rosemary. *Colonization, Violence, and Narration in White South African Writing: André Brink, Breyten Breytenbach, and J. M. Coetzee*. Athens: Ohio University Press, 1996.

Jonsson, Stephen. *Subject Without a Nation: Robert Musil and the History of Modern Identity*. Durham, N.C.: Duke University Press, 2001.

Jrade, Cathy. *Rubén Dario and the Romantic Search for Unity: The Modernist Recourse to Esoteric Tradition*. Austin: University of Texas Press, 1983.

Kain, Geoffrey R., ed. *R. K. Narayan: Contemporary Critical Perspectives*. East Lansing: Michigan State University Press, 1993.

Kalb, Jonathon. *The Theater of Heiner Muller*. Munich, Germany: C. H. Beck, 1984.

Kamber, Richard. *On Sartre*. Belmont, Calif.: Wadsworth, 1999.

Kanes, Martin. *Père Goriot: Anatomy of a Troubled World*. Boston: Twayne, 1993.

Kanes, Martin, ed. *Critical Essays on Honoré de Balzac*. Boston: G. K. Hall, 1990.

Kanik, Orhan V. *I, Orhan Veli: Poems by Orhan Veli*. Translated by Murat Nemet-Nejat. Brooklyn, N.Y.: Hanging Loose Press, 1989.

Karsen, Sonja. *Jaime Torres Bodet; A Poet in a Changing World*. Saratoga Springs, N.Y.: Skidmore College, 1963.

Kaschnitz, Marie L. *Selected Later Poems of Marie Luise Kashnitz*. Translated by Lisel Mueller. Princeton, N.J.: Princeton University Press, 1980.

———. *Circe's Mountain: Stories by Marie Luise Kaschnitz*. Translated by Lisel Mueller. Minneapolis: Milkweed Editions, 1990.

Katrak, Ketu. *Wole Soyinka and Modern Tragedy: A Study of Dramatic Theory and Practice*. Westport, Conn.: Greenwood Press, 1986.

Keats, Jonathan. *Stendhal*. London: Sinclair-Stevenson, 1994.

Keeley, Edmund. *Cavafy's Alexandria*. Princeton, N.J.: Princeton University Press, 1995.

Keene, Donald. *Dawn to the West: Japanese Literature of the Modern Era: Fiction*. New York: Columbia University Press, 1998.

Keene, Donald, ed. *Modern Japanese Literature*. New York: Grove Press, 1956.

Kemp-Welch, A. *Stalin and the Literary Intelligentsia, 1928–1939*. New York: St. Martin's Press, 1991.

Ketchian, Sonia I. *The Poetic Craft of Bella Akhmadulina*. University Park: Pennsylvania State University Press, 1993.

Keys, Roger. *The Reluctant Modernist: Andrei Belyi and the Development of Russian Fiction*. Oxford: Clarendon Press, 1996.

Khan, Md. Akhtar Jamal. *V. S. Naipaul: A Critical Study*. New Delhi: Creative Books, 1998.

Killam, G. D. *An Introduction to the Writings of Ngugi*. London: Heinemann, 1980.

King, Bruce. *Derek Walcott, a Caribbean Life*. New York: Oxford University Press, 2000.

———. *V. S. Naipaul*. London: Macmillan, 1993.

King, Michael. *Wrestling with the Angel: A Life of Janet Frame*. Washington, D.C.: Counterpoint Press, 2000.

Kipalani, Krishan. *Rabindranath Tagore: A Biography*. London: Oxford University Press, 1962.

Kirsner, Robert. *The Novels and Travels of Camilo Jose Cela*. Chapel Hill: University of North Carolina Press, 1964.

Klein, Leonard S. *Latin American Literature in the 20th Century*. New York: Frederick Ungar, 1986.

Kluback, William. *Paul Valery: A Philosopher for Philosophers: The Sage*. New York: Peter Lang, 2000.

Knapp, Bettina L. *Jean Cocteau*. Boston: Twayne, 1989.

———. *Maurice Maeterlinck*. Boston: Twayne, 1975.

———. *Nathalie Sarraute*. Atlanta, Ga.: Rodopi, 1994.

———. *Paul Claudel*. New York: Frederick Ungar, 1982.

Knight, Kelton W. *Anne Hebert: In Search of the First Garden*. New York: Peter Lang, 1998.

Knowles, Anthony V. *Ivan Turgenev*. Boston: Twayne, 1988.

Knowlson, James. *Damned to Fame: The Life of Samuel Beckett*. New York: Simon & Schuster, 1996.

Knox, Bernard. *Backing into the Future: The Classical Tradition and Its Renewal*. New York: Norton, 1994.

Kobler, J. F. *Katherine Mansfield: A Study of the Short Fiction*. Boston: Twayne, 1990.

Koepke, Wulf. *Understanding Max Frisch*. Columbia: University of South Carolina Press, 1991.

Kolbert, Jack. *The Worlds of Elie Wiesel: An Overview of His Career and Major Themes*. Selinsgrove, Pa.: Susquehanna University Press, 2001.

Kolinsky, Eva, and Wilfried van der Will, eds. *The Cambridge Companion to Modern German Culture*. New York: Cambridge University Press, 1998.

Kossoff, Philip. *Valiant Heart: A Biography of Heinrich Heine*. London: Cornwall Books, 1983.

Kostalevsky, Marina. *Dostoevsky and Soloviev: The Art of Integral Vision*. New Haven, Conn.: Yale University Press, 1997.

Kourilsky, Francoise, and Catherine Temerson. *Plays by Women: An International Anthology*. New York: Ubu Repertory Theatre Publications, 1989.

Kramer, Reinhold. *Mordecai Richler: Leaving St. Urbain*. Montreal: McGill-Queens University Press, 2008.

Kremer, Roberta S., ed. *Memory and Mastery: Primo Levi as Writer and Witness*. Albany: State University of New York Press, 2001.

Kriseova, Eda. *Václav Havel: The Authorized Biography*. New York: St. Martin's Press, 1993.

Krispyn, Egbert. *Gunter Eich*. Boston: Twayne, 1971.

Kunene, Mazisi. *The Ancestors and the Sacred Mountain*. London: Heinemann, 1982.

Kuo, Helena. *The Quest for Love of Lao Lee*. New York: Reynal and Hitchcock, 1948.

Kurahashi Yumiko. *The Woman with the Flying Head and Other Stories of Kurahashi Yumiko*. Translated by Atsuko Sakaki. Armonk, N.Y.: M. E. Sharpe, 1998.

Kurpershoek, P. M. *The Short Stories of Yusuf Idris: A Modern Egyptian Author*. Leiden, The Netherlands: Brill, 1981.

Lacoue-Labarthe, Philippe, ed. *The Literary Absolute: The Theory of Literature in German Romanticism*. Albany: State University of New York Press, 1988.

Lagercrantz, Olaf. *August Strindberg*. New York: Farrar, Straus & Giroux, 1984.

Lahusen, Thomas. *How Life Writes the Book: Real Socialism and Socialist Realism in Stalin's Russia*. Ithaca, N.Y.: Cornell University Press, 1997.

Larson, Wendy. *Women and Writing in Modern China*. Stanford, Calif.: Stanford University Press, 1998.

Last, Rex W. *German Dadaist Literature: Kurt Schitters, Hugo Ball, Hans Arp*. Boston: Twayne, 1973.

Lau, Joseph S. M., and Howard Goldblatt, eds. *The Columbia Anthology of Modern Chinese Literature*. New York: Columbia University Press, 1995.

Lawrie, Steven W. *Erich Fried: A Writer Without a Country*. New York: Peter Lang, 1996.

Leatherborrow, William J. *Feodor Dostoevsky: A Reference Guide*. Boston: G. K. Hall, 1990.

Lederer, Wolfgang. *The Kiss of the Snow Queen: Hans Christian Andersen and Man's Redemption by Woman*. Berkeley: University of California Press, 1990.

Lednicki, Waclaw. *Adam Mickiewicz in World Literature*. Berkeley: University of California Press, 1956.

Lee, Leo Ou-fan. *Voices from the Iron House: A Study of Lu Xun*. Bloomington: Indiana University Press, 1987.

Lee, Mabel. *Soul Mountain*. New York: HarperCollins, 1999.

Lee, Peter H., ed. *The Silence of Love: Twentieth-Century Korean Poetry*. Honolulu: University of Hawaii Press, 1980.

Le Gassick, Trevor, ed. *Critical Perspectives on Naguib Mahfouz.* Washington, D.C.: Three Continents Press, 1991.

Lennon, Nigey. *Alfred Jarry: The Man with the Axe.* Los Angeles: Panjandrm Books, 1984.

Lerner, Michael G. *Maupassant.* New York: G. Braziller, 1975.

Lindfors, Bernth. *Conversations with Chinua Achebe.* Jackson: University Press of Mississippi, 1997.

———. *Dem-Say: Interviews with Eight Nigerian Authors.* Austin, Tex.: African and Afro-American Studies and Research Center, 1974.

———. *Early Achebe.* Trenton, N.J.: Africa World Press, 2009.

Linn, Rolf N. *Heinrich Mann.* Boston: Twayne, 1967.

Lippit, Noriko, and Kyoko Selden, eds. *Stories by Contemporary Japanese Women Writers.* New York: M. E. Sharpe, 1982.

Lloyd, Rosemary. *Mallarmé: The Poet and His Circle.* Ithaca, N.Y.: Cornell University Press, 1999.

Lokke, Kari. *Gerard de Nerval: The Poet as Social Visionary.* Lexington, Ky.: French Forum, 1987.

Lombard, Charles M. *Lamartine.* Boston: Twayne, 1973.

Long, J. J. *The Novels of Thomas Bernhard: Form and Its Function.* Rochester, N.Y.: Camden House, 2001.

Loose, Gerhard. *Ernst Junger.* Boston: Twayne, 1974.

Luce, Jacqui, and Don Luce. *Quiet Courage: Poems from Viet Nam.* Washington, D.C.: Indochina Mobile Education Project, 1974.

Lukacs, Georg. *The Theory of the Novel.* Translated by Anna Bostock. Cambridge, Mass.: MIT Press, 1974.

Lutzeler, Paul M. *Hermann Broch: A Biography.* Translated by Janice Fureness. London: Quarter, 1987.

Lyell, William A. *Cat Country: A Satirical Novel of China in the 1930s.* Columbus: Ohio State University Press, 1970.

———. *Lu Hsun's Vision of Reality.* Berkeley: University of California Press, 1976.

Lykiard, Alexis. *Jean Rhys Revisited.* Exeter, U.K.: Stride Publications, 2000.

MacDonald, Paul S., ed. *The Existentialist Reader: An Anthology of Key Texts.* New York: Routledge, 2001.

Magidoff, Robert, ed. *Russian Science Fiction: An Anthology.* Translated by Doris Johnson. New York: New York University Press, 1964.

Magill, Frank N. *Masterpieces of Latino Literature.* New York: HarperCollins, 1994.

Magnarelli, Sharon. *Understanding Jose Donoso.* Columbia: University of South Carolina, 1993.

Makward, Edris, et al. *The Growth of African Literature.* Lawrenceville, N.J.: Africa World Press, 1998.

Malcolm, Janet. *Reading Chekhov: A Critical Journey.* New York: Random House, 2002.

Malik, Hafeez, ed. *Iqbal, Poet-Philosopher of Pakistan.* New York: Columbia University Press, 1971.

Malti-Douglas, Fedwa. *Men, Women, and God: Nawal El Saadawi and Arab Feminist Poetics.* Berkeley: University of California Press, 1995.

Mandel, Siegfried. *Group 47: The Reflected Intellect.* Edwardsville: Southern Illinois University Press, 1973.

Mann, Heinrich. *Henry, King of France.* Translated by Eric Sutton. New York: Knopf, 1939.

Mao, Chen. *Between Tradition and Change: The Hermeneutics of May Fourth Literature.* Lanham, Md.: University Press of America, 1997.

Marable, Manning, ed. *Dispatches from the Ebony Tower.* New York: Columbia University Press, 2000.

Marcus, Marvin. *Paragons of the Ordinary: The Biographical Literature of Mori Ogai.* Honolulu: University of Hawaii Press, 1993.

Marinetti, F. T. *The Futurist Cookbook.* Translated by Suzanne Brill, edited and introduction by Lesley Chamberlain. San Fransico: Bedford Arts, 1989.

Maron, Monika. *Silent Close No. 6.* Translated by David Newton Marinelli. Columbia, La.: Reader's International, 1993.

Marr, David. *Patrick White: A Life.* New York: Knopf, 1991.

Martin, Gerald. *Gabriel García Márquez: A Life.* New York: Knopf, 2009.

Martin, Helmut, and Jeffrey Kinkley, eds. *Modern Chinese Writers: Self-Portrayals*. Armonk, N.Y.: M. E. Sharpe, 1992.

Masaoka Shiki. *Masaoka Shiki: Selected Poems*. Translated by Burton Watson. New York: Columbia University Press, 1997.

Massardier-Kenney, Françoise. *Gender in the Fiction of George Sand*. Atlanta: Rodopi, 2000.

Mathy, Frances. *Shiga Naoya*. Boston: Twayne, 1974.

Matthews, J. H. *Theatre in Dada and Surrealism*. Syracuse, N.Y.: Syracuse University Press, 1974.

McBride, William. *Sartre's Life, Times and Vision-du-Monde*. New York: Garland, 1997.

McDougall, Bonnie S., and Kam Louie. *The Literature of China in the Twentieth Century*. New York: Columbia University Press, 1997.

McGlathery, James. *E. T. A. Hoffmann*. Boston: Twayne, 1997.

McGuinness, Patrick, ed. *Symbolism, Decadence and the Fin de Siècle: French and European Perspectives*. Exeter, U.K.: University of Exeter Press, 2000.

McLaughlin, Martin. *Italo Calvino*. Edinburgh: Edinburgh University Press, 1998.

McRae, Robert. *Resistance and Revolution*. Ottawa: Carleton University Press, 1997.

Meeks, Brian. *Voiceprint: An Anthology of Oral and Related Poetry from the Caribbean*. Essex, England: Longman Group UK Limited, 1989.

Mellown, Elgin W. *Jean Rhys: A Descriptive and Annotated Bibliography of Works and Criticism*. New York: Garland, 1984.

Merini, Rafika. *Two Major Francophone Women Writers: Assia Djebar and Leila Sebbar: A Thematic Study of Their Works*. New York: Peter Lang, 1999.

Metzger, Michael M., and Erika A Metzger. *Stefan George*. Boston: Twayne, 1972.

Meyer, Michael. *Strindberg: A Biography*. Oxford: Oxford University Press, 1987.

Mileck, Joseph. *Hermann Hesse: Life and Art*. Riverside: University of California Press, 1981.

Miller, Yvette E., and Charles Rossman. *Gabriel García Márquez*. Pittsburgh, Pa.: University of Pittsburgh, 1985.

Milosz, Czeslaw. *The History of Polish Literature*. Berkeley: University of California Press, 1983.

Mistral, Gabriela. *Selected Poems*. Translated Doris Dana. Baltimore: Johns Hopkins University Press, 1971.

Misurella, Fred. *Understanding Milan Kundera: Public Events, Private Affairs*. Columbia: University of South Carolina Press, 1993.

Mitchell, Stephen. *Freud and Beyond: A History of Modern Psychoanalytical Thought*. New York: Basic Books, 1996.

Mitler, Louis. *Contemporary Turkish Writers: A Critical Bio-Bibliography*. Bloomington: Indiana University Press, 1988.

Moi, Toril. *Simone de Beauvoir: The Making of an Intellectual Woman*. New York: Oxford University Press, 2009.

Moon, Vasant. *Growing up Untouchable in India: A Dalit Autobiography*. Translated by Gail Omvedt. New Delhi: Vistaar Publishing, 2002.

Moore, Gerald. *Twelve African Writers*. London: Hutchinson University Library for Africa, 1980.

Moosa, Matti. *The Early Novels of Naguib Mahfouz: Images of Modern Egypt*. Gainesville: University Press of Florida, 1994.

Moran, Dominic. *Questions of the Liminal in the Fiction of Julio Cortázar*. Oxford: Oxford University Press, 2001.

Mortimer, Armine K. *Writing Realism: Representations in French Fiction*. Baltimore: Johns Hopkins University Press, 2000.

Mortimer, Mildred P. *Journeys Through the French African Novel*. Westport, Conn.: Heinemann, 1990.

Mortimer, Mildred P., ed. *Maghrebian Mosaic: A Literature in Transition*. Boulder, Colo.: Lynne Rienner Publishers, 2001.

Moses, Claire G. *Feminism, Socialism and French Romanticism*. Bloomington: Indiana University Press, 1993.

Mueller, Heiner. *A Heiner Muller Reader: Plays, Poetry, Prose*. Translated by Carl Weber. Baltimore: Johns Hopkins University Press, 2001.

Mulhern, Chieko I., ed. *Japanese Women Writers: A Bio-critical Sourcebook*. Westport, Conn.: Greenwood Press, 1994.

Mullaney, Julie. *Arundhati Roy's* The God of Small Things: *A Reader's Guide.* London: Continuum International Publishing Group, 2002.

Munsterer, Hanns Otto. *The Young Brecht.* Concord, Mass.: Paul and Company Publishers Consortium, 1992.

Naess, Harald. *Knut Hamsun.* Boston: Twayne, 1984.

Naipaul, V. S. *Between Father and Son: Family Letters.* New York: Vintage Books, 2001.

———. *Half a Life.* New York: Knopf, 2001.

Nantell, Judith. *Rafael Alberti's Poetry of the Thirties: The Poet's Public Voice.* Athens: University of Georgia Press, 1986.

Napier, Susan. *Escape from the Wasteland: Romanticism and Realism in the Fiction of Mishima Yukio and Ōe Kenzaburō.* Cambridge, Mass.: Harvard University Press, 1991.

Naughton, John. *The Poetics of Yves Bonnefoy.* Chicago: University of Chicago Press, 1984.

Naravane, Vishwanath S. *Sarojini Naidu: An Introduction to Her Life, Work, and Poetry.* New Delhi: Orient Longman Ltd., 1996.

Nasta, Sheila, ed. *Motherlands: Black Women's Writing from Africa.* New Brunswick, N.J.: Rutgers University Press, 1992.

Nathan, John. *Mishima: A Biography.* New York: Da Capo Press, 2000.

Nathan, Leonard, and Arthur Quinn. *The Poet's Work: An Introduction to Czeslaw Milosz.* Cambridge, Mass.: Harvard University Press, 1991.

Nathan, Robert L. *The Dreamtime.* Woodstock, N.Y.: Overlook Press, 1975.

Nelson, Emmanuel S., ed. *Contemporary African American Novelists: A Bio-Bibliographical Critical Sourcebook.* Westport, Conn.: Greenwood Press, 1999.

Nevin, Thomas. *Ernst Junger and Germany: Into the Abyss, 1914–1945.* Durham, N.C.: Duke University Press, 1997.

Ngũgĩ wa Thiong'o. *Dreams in a Time of War: A Childhood Memoir.* New York: Pantheon, 2010.

Niebylski, Dianna C. *The Poem on the Edge of the Word: The Limits of Language and the Uses of Silence in the Poetry of Mallarmé, Rilke and Vallejo.* New York: Peter Lang, 1993.

Nieh, Hauling. *Literature of the Hundred Flowers.* New York: Columbia University Press, 1981.

Nugent, Robert. *Paul Éluard.* Boston: Twayne, 1974.

Oba Minako. *Stories by Contemporary Japanese Women Writers.* Translated by Noriko Mizuta Lippit and Kyoko Irye Selden. Armonk, N.Y.: M. E. Sharpe, 1982.

O'Ceallachain, Eanna. *Eugenio Montale: The Poetry of Later Years.* Oxford: Legenda, 2001.

O'Healey, Aine. *Cesare Pavese.* Boston: Twayne, 1988.

O'Neil, Patrick. *Günter Grass Revisited.* Boston: Twayne, 1999.

Osbourne, John. *Gerhart Hauptmann and the Naturalist Drama.* London: Routledge, 1999.

Painter, George D. *Chateaubriand: A Biography.* New York: Knopf, 1978.

Pandurang, Mala. *Vikram Seth: Multiple Locations, Multiple Affiliation.* New Delhi: Rawat, 2001.

Panny, Judith D. *I Have What I Gave: The Fiction of Janet Frame.* New York: George Braziller, 1993.

Paperno, Irina. *Chernyshevsky and the Age of Realism.* Stanford, Calif.: Stanford University Press, 1988.

Paravisini-Gerbert, Lizabeth. *Jamaica Kincaid: A Critical Companion.* Westport, Conn.: Greenwood Press, 1999.

Parrot, Cecil. *The Bad Bohemian: The Life of Jaroslav Hašek, Creator of the Good Soldier Svejk.* London, England: Bodley Head, 1978.

Partridge, Monica. *Alexander Herzen.* Paris: Unesco, 1984.

Patt, Beatrice P. *Pío Baroja y Nessi.* Boston: Twayne, 1971.

Paul, Georgina, and Helmut Schmitz, eds. *Entgegenkommen: Dialogues with Barbara Kohler.* Atlanta, Ga.: Rodopi, 2000.

Peixoto, Marta. *Passionate Fictions: Gender, Narrative, and Violence in Clarice Lispector.* Minneapolis: University of Minnesota Press, 1994.

Peled, Mattityahu. *Religion My Own: The Literary Works of Najib Mahfuz.* New Brunswick, N.J.: Transaction Books, 1983.

Pelensky, Olga A. *Isak Dinesen: Critical Views .* Athens: Ohio University Press, 1993.

Penrod, Lynn. *Hélène Cixous.* Boston: Twayne, 1996.

Peretz, Isaac L. *Selected Stories*. Translated by Eli Katz. New York: Zhitlowsky Foundation for Jewish Culture, 1991.

Peterman, Michael. *Robertson Davies*. Boston: Twayne, 1986.

Peterson, Thomas E. *Alberto Moravia*. Boston: Twayne, 1996.

Petro, Peter, ed. *Critical Essays on Milan Kundera*. New York: G. K. Hall, 1999.

Pfaff, Francoise. *The Cinema of Ousmane Sembene, a Pioneer of African Film*. Westport, Conn.: Greenwood Press, 1984.

Pilarde, Jo-Ann. *Simone de Beauvoir Writing the Self: Philosophy Becomes Autobiography*. Westport, Conn.: Praeger, 1999.

Piore, Nance K. *Lightning: The Poetry of René Char*. Boston: Northeastern University Press, 1981.

Plunka, Gene A., ed. *Antonin Artaud and the Modern Theatre*. Madison, N.J.: Fairleigh Dickinson University Press, 1994.

Polcari, Stephanie. *Abstract Expressionism and the Modern Experience*. Cambridge: Cambridge University Press, 1993.

Popkin, Michael, ed. *Modern Black Writers*. New York: Frederick Ungar, 1978.

Porter, Laurence M. *Victor Hugo*. Boston: Twayne, 1999.

Powers, Lyall. *Alien Heart: The Life and Work of Margaret Laurence*. East Lansing: Michigan State University Press, 2004.

Preston, Paul. *Salvador de Madariaga and the Quest for Liberty in Spain*. Oxford: Clarendon Press, 1987.

Proffer, Ellendea. *A Pictorial Biography of Mikhail Bulgakov*. Ann Arbor, Mich.: Ardis, 1984.

Prokushev, Yuri. *Sergei Yesenin: The Man, the Verse, the Age*. Moscow: Progress Publishers, 1979.

Pulver, Elsbeth. *Marie Luise Kaschnitz*. Munich, Germany: C. H. Beck, 1984.

Putnam, Walter. *Paul Valéry Revisited*. Boston: Twayne, 1995.

Rabson, Steve. *Righteous Cause or Tragic Folly: Changing Views of War in Modern Japanese Poetry*. Ann Arbor: University of Michigan, Center for Japanese Studies, 1998.

Rai, Amrit. *Premchand: His Life and Times*. New York: Oxford University Press, 2002.

Rayfield, Donal. *Anton Chekhov: A Life*. Chicago: Northwestern University Press, 2000.

Reddick, John. *Georg Büchner: The Shattered Whole*. Oxford: Clarendon Press, 1994.

Redwitz, Eckenbert. *The Image of the Woman in the Works of Ingeborg Bachmann*. New York: Peter Lang, 1993.

Reeder, Roberta. *Anna Akhmatova: Poet and Prophet*. New York: Picador, 1995.

Reid, J. H. *Narration and Description in the French Realist Novel: The Temporality of Lying and Forgetting*. Cambridge: Cambridge University Press, 1993.

Reiss, Timothy J. *For the Geography of a Soul: Emerging Perspectives on Kamau Brathwaite*. Lawrenceville, N.J.: Africa World Press, 2001.

Resch, Margit. *Understanding Christa Wolf: Retuning Home to a Foreign Land*. Columbia: University of South Carolina Press, 1997.

Rhys, Jean. *The Collected Short Stories*. New York: Norton, 1978.

Ribbans, Geoffrey. *History and Fiction in Galdós's Narratives*. London, England: Oxford University Press, 1993.

Rice, Martin P. *Valery Bruisov and the Rise of Russian Symbolism*. Ann Arbor, Mich: Ardis, 1975.

Richardson, Angelique, and Chris Willis, eds. *The New Woman in Fiction and in Fact: Fin de Siècle Feminisms*. New York: Palgrave, 2001.

Richardson, Joanna. *Baudelaire*. New York: St. Martin's Press, 1994.

Ridge, George R. *Joris-Karl Huysmans*. Boston: Twayne, 1968.

Rimer, John T. *Mori Ōgai*. Boston: Twayne, 1975.

Ritchie, J. M. *Gottfried Benn: The Unreconstructed Expressionist*. London: Oswald Wolff, 1972.

Robb, Graham. *Arthur Rimbaud*. New York: Norton, 2000.

Robbe-Grillet, Alain. *For a New Novel: Essays on Fiction*. Translated by Richard Howard. New York: Grove Press, 1966.

Robin, Regine. *Socialist Realism: An Impossible Aesthetic*. Translated by Catherine Porter. Stanford, Calif.: Stanford University Press, 1991.

Robinson, Roger, and Nelson Wattie, eds. *The Oxford Companion to New Zealand Literature.* Oxford: Oxford University Press, 1998.

Robson, Clifford. *Ngugi wa Thiong'o.* London: Macmillan, 1979.

Rojas, Sonia R., and Edna Aguirre Rehbeim, eds. *Critical Approaches to Isabel Allende's Novels.* New York: Peter Lang, 1991.

Rose, Henry. *Henrik Ibsen: Poet, Mystic, and Moralist.* New York: Haskell, 1972.

Roumani, Judith. *Albert Memmi.* Philadelphia: Celfan, 1987.

Rowley, Hazel. *Christina Stead: A Biography.* New York: Henry Holt & Company, 1995.

Rubin, Jay, ed. *Modern Japanese Writers.* New York: Charles Scribner's Sons, 2001.

Russell, Ralph. *Ghālib.* Cambridge, Mass.: Harvard University Press, 1969.

Sachs, Nelly. *The Seeker, and Other Poems.* Translated by Ruth Mead, Matthew Mead, and Michael Hamburger. New York: Farrar, Straus & Giroux, 1970.

Safransky, Rudiger. *Nietzsche: A Philosophical Biography.* New York: Norton, 2001.

Saint, Nigel. *Marguerite Yourcenar: Reading the Visual.* Oxford: Legenda, 2000.

Salma, Jayyusi. *Trends and Movements in Modern Arabic Poetry.* Leiden, The Netherlands: Brill, 1977.

Samson, Earl. *Nikolai Gumilev.* Boston: Twayne, 1979.

Samuel, Maurice. *The World of Sholom Aleichem.* New York: Dramatists Play Series, 1948.

San Juan, E. *Aimé Césaire: Surrealism and Revolution.* Bowling Green, Ohio: Bowling Green State University Press, 2000.

———. *From the Masses, to the Masses: Third World Literature and Revolution.* Minneapolis: MEP Publications, 1994.

Savory, Elaine. *Jean Rhys.* New York: Cambridge University Press, 1999.

Scammell, Michael. *Solzhenitsyn: A Biography.* New York: Norton, 1984.

Schalow, Paul G., and Janet A. Walker, eds. *The Woman's Hand: Gender and Theory in Japanese Women's Writing.* Stanford, Calif.: Stanford University Press, 1996.

Schierbeck, Sachiko. *Japanese Women Novelists in the Twentieth Century: 104 Biographies 1900–1993.* Copenhagen: Museum Tusculanum Press, 1994.

Schiff, Stacy. *Saint-Exupéry: A Biography.* New York: Knopf, 1995.

Schoolfield, George C. *Edith Sodergran: Modernist Poet in Finland.* Westport, Conn.: Greenwood Press, 1984.

Scholtz, Sally. *On de Beauvoir.* Belmont, Calif.: Wadsworth/Thomson Learning, 2000.

Schulte-Sasse, Jochen, ed. *Theory as Practice: An Anthology of Early German Romantic Writings.* Indianapolis: University of Minnesota Press, 1997.

Schulze, Julia. *Rigoberta Menchu Tum: Champion of Human Rights.* New York: Burke, John Gordon Publisher, Inc., 1997.

Schwarz, Roberto. *Misplaced Ideas: Essays on Brazilian Culture.* New York: Verso, 1992.

Schwartz, Ronald. *Spain's New Wave Novelists, 1950–1974.* Lanham, Md.: Scarecrow Press, 1976.

Schwartz-Bart, Simone. *Between Two Worlds.* Translated by Barbara Bray. New York: Harper & Row, 1981.

———. *The Bridge and Beyond.* Translated by Barbara Bray. New York: Atheneum, 1974.

Schweitzer, Victoria. *Tsvetaeva.* New York: Farrar, Straus & Giroux, 1993.

Schwertfeger, Ruth. *Else Lasker-Schuler: Inside This Deathly Solitude.* Oxford: Berg Publishers, Ltd., 1991.

Scott-Stokes, Henry. *The Life and Death of Yukio Mishima.* New York: Farrar, Straus & Giroux, 1974.

Seifert, Jaroslav. *The Early Poetry of Jaroslav Seifert.* Translated by Dana Loewy. Evanston, Ill.: Hydra Books, 1997.

Sergio, Pacifici, ed. *From Verismo to Experimentalism: Essays on the Modern Italian Novel.* Bloomington: Indiana University Press, 1970.

Shaked, Gershon. *Shmuel Yosef Agnon: A Revolutionary Traditionalist.* Translated by Jeffery M. Green. New York: New York University Press, 1989.

Shapiro, Gavriel. *Nabokov at Cornell.* Ithaca, N.Y.: Cornell University Press, 2003.

Sharma, A. P. *The Mind and Art of Arundhati Roy.* London: Minerva Press, 2003.

Sharman, Adam, ed. *The Poetry and Poetics of César Vallejo: The Fourth Angle of the Circle.* Lewiston, N.Y.: Edwin Mellen Press, 1997.

Sharpe, Lesley. *Friedrich Schiller: Drama, Thought, and Politics.* Cambridge: Cambridge University Press, 1991.

Shava, Piniel. *A People's Voice: Black South African Writing in the Twentieth Century.* London: Zed Books, 1989.

Sheridan, Susan. *Christina Stead.* Bloomington: Indiana University Press, 1988.

Sherman, Joseph. *Writers in Yiddish.* Detroit: Thomson Gale, 2007.

Silva, A. J. Simoes da. *The Luxury of Nationalist Despair: George Lamming's Fiction as Decolonizing Project.* Atlanta, Ga.: Rodopi, 2000.

Simms, Norman. *Silence and Invisibility: A Study of the New Literature from the Pacific.* Washington, D.C.: Three Continents Press, 1986.

Simons, Margaret. A *Beauvoir and the Second Sex: Feminism, Race and the Origins of Existentialism.* Boston: Lanham, Rowman and Littlefield, 1999.

Simpson, Michael, and John Untfrecker. *Dreams of the Rainbow: Poems by Kauraka Kauraka.* Honolulu: University of Hawaii at Manoa, East-West Center, 1986.

Singh, Amritjit, Joseph T. Skerrett, Jr., and Robert E. Hogan, eds. *Memory and Cultural Politics: New Approaches to American Ethnic Literatures.* Ann Arbor, Mich.: Edwards Brothers, 1996.

Singh, G. *Leopardi and the Theory of Poetry.* Lexington: University of Kentucky Press, 1964.

Smart, Ian I. *Nicolas Guillen, Popular Poet of the Caribbean.* Columbia: University of Missouri Press, 1990.

Smethurst, Colin. *Chateaubriand, Atala and René.* London: Grant and Cutler, 1995.

Smith, Roch C. *Understanding Alain Robbe-Grillet.* Columbia: University of South Carolina Press, 2000.

Snyder, Stephen, and Philip Gabriel, eds. *Ōe and Beyond: Fiction in Contemporary Japan.* Honolulu: University of Hawaii Press, 1999.

Sodergran, Edith. *Love and Solitude: Selected Poems, 1916–1923.* Translated by Stina Katchadourian. Seattle: Fjord Press, 1985.

Sole, Carlos A. *Latin American Writers.* New York: Charles Scribner's Sons, 1989.

Solecki, Sam. *Prague Blues: The Fiction of Josef Skvorecky.* New York: Ecco Press, 1990.

Soto, Francisco. *Reinaldo Arenas.* Boston: Twayne, 1998.

Spector, Robert D. *Pär Lagerkvist.* Boston: Twayne, 1973.

Spivak, Gayatri. *In Other Worlds: Essays in Cultural Politics.* New York: Routledge, 1987.

Stafford, Helene. *Mallarmé and the Poetics of Everyday Life: A Study of the Concept of the Ordinary in His Verse and Prose.* Atlanta, Ga.: Rodopi, 2000.

Standish, Peter. *Understanding Julio Cortázar.* Columbia: University of South Carolina Press, 2001.

Stavans, Ilan. *Julio Cortázar: A Study of the Short Fiction.* Boston: Twayne, 1996.

Stead, C. K. *In the Glass Case: Essays on New Zealand Literature.* Auckland, N.Z.: Auckland University Press, 1981.

———. *Kin of Place: Essays on New Zealand Writers.* Auckland, N.Z.: Auckland University Press, 2002.

Stephan, Halina. *Translating the Absurd: Drama and Prose of Slawomir Mrozek.* The Netherlands: Rodopi, 1997.

Sterling, Richard L. *The Prose Works of Saint-John Perse: Towards an Understanding of His Poetry.* New York: Peter Lang, 1994.

Stevens, Shelley. *Rosalia de Castro and the Galician Revival.* London: Tamesis Books Ltd., 1986.

Stilman, Leon. *Gogol.* New York: Columbia University Press, 1990.

Stratton, Florence. *Contemporary African Literature and the Politics of Gender.* New York: Routledge, 1994.

Strauss, J. *Judith Wright.* Melbourne: Oxford University Press, 1995.

Strong-Boag, Veronica J., and Carole Gerson. *Paddling Her Own Canoe: The Times and Texts of E. Pauline Johnson.* Toronto: University of Toronto Press, 2000.

Stuhr, Rebecca. *Reading Khaled Hosseini.* Santa Barbara, Calif.: Greenwood Publishing Group, 2009.

Sucher, Laurie. *The Fiction of Ruth Prawer Jhabvala: The Politics of Passion.* New York: St. Martin's Press, 1989.

Suk, Jeannie. *Postcolonial Paradoxes in French Caribbean Writing: Césaire, Glissant, Condé.* Oxford: Clarendon Press, 2001.

Szymborska, Wislawa. *Miracle Fair: Selected Poems of Wislawa Szymborska.* Translated by Joanna Trzeciak. New York: Norton, 2001.

Talbot, Emile J. *Stendhal Revisited.* Boston: Twayne, 1993.

Tam Kwok-kan. *Soul of Chaos: Critical Perspectives on Gao Xingjian.* Hong Kong: The Chinese University Press, 2001.

Tanaka, Yukiko, ed. *To Love and to Write: Selections by Japanese Women Writers 1913–1938.* Seattle: Seal Press, 1987.

Tapia, John R. *The Indian in the Spanish-American Novel.* Durango, Colo.: University Press of America, 1981.

Tarabishi, George. *Woman Against Her Sex: A Critique of Nawal El-Saadawi, with a Reply by Nawal ElSaadawi.* London: Al-Saqi Books, 1988.

Terras, Victor. *Vladimir Mayakovsky.* Boston: Twayne, 1983.

Thomas, H. *Elias Canetti.* Boston: Twayne, 1993.

Thurman, Judith. *Isak Dinesen: The Life of a Storyteller.* New York: St. Martin's Press, 1982.

———. *Secrets of the Flesh: A Life of Colette.* New York: Knopf, 1999.

Tisdall, Caroline, and Angela Bozolla. *Futurism.* Oxford, England: Oxford University Press, 1978.

Tollerson, Marie. *Mythology and Cosmology in the Narratives of Bernard Dadie and Birago Diop.* Washington, D.C.: Three Continents Press, 1984.

Tomalin, Claire. *Katherine Mansfield: A Secret Life.* New York: Knopf, 1988.

Tong-gyu Hwang. *Strong Winds at Mishi Pass.* Groveport, Ohio: White Pines Press, 2001.

———. *Wind Burial: Selected Poems of Hwang Tong-gyu.* Laurenberg, N.C.: St. Andrew's Press, 1990.

Treat, John W., ed. *Contemporary Japan and Popular Culture.* Honolulu: University of Hawaii Press, 1996.

Treece, David. *Exiles, Allies, Rebels: Brazil's Indianist Movement, Indigenist Politics, and the Imperial Nation-State.* Westport, Conn.: Greenwood Press, 2000.

Trump, Martin. *Rendering Things Visible: Essays on South African Literary Culture.* Athens: Ohio University Press, 1990.

Tsatsos, Ioanna. *My Brother George Seferis.* Translated by Jean Demos. St. Paul, Minn.: North Central, 1982.

Tuwim, Julian. *The Dancing Socrates, and Other Poems.* Translated by Adam Gillon. Boston: Twayne, 1968.

Ueda Makoto. *Modern Japanese Writers.* Stanford, Calif.: Stanford University Press, 1976.

Umeh, Marie, ed. *Emerging Perspectives on Flora Nwapa.* Lawrenceville, N.J.: Africa World Press, 1998.

Unger, Richard. *Friedrich Holderlin.* Boston: Twayne, 1984.

Uraizee, Joya F. *This Is No Place for a Woman: Nadine Gordimer, Nayantara Sahgal, Buchi Emecheta, and the Politics of Gender.* Lawrenceville, N.J.: Africa World Press, 2000.

Vassanji, M. G., and John Ralston Saul. *Mordecai Richler* (Extraordinary Canadians). Toronto: Penguin Canada, 2009.

Vernon, Victoria V. *Daughters of the Moon: Wish, Will and Social Constraint in Fiction by Modern Japanese Women.* Berkeley: University of California Press, Institute of East Asian Studies, 1988.

Viain, Robert. *The Poetry of Hugo von Hofmannsthal and French Symbolism.* New York: Oxford University Press, 2000.

Vohra, Ranbir. *Lao She and the Chinese Revolution.* Cambridge, Mass.: Harvard University Press, East Asian Research Center, 1974.

Vucinich, Wayne, ed. *Ivo Andric Revisited: The Bridge Still Stands.* Berkeley: University of California Regents, 1996.

Wade, Michael. *Peter Abrahams.* London: Evans Bros., 1972.

Wagner, Irmagard. *Goethe.* Boston: Twayne, 1999.

Wagner, Rudolf G. *Inside a Service Trade: Studies in Contemporary Chinese Prose.* Cambridge, Mass.: Council on East Asian Studies, Harvard University, 1992.

Wall, Cheryl, ed. *Changing Our Own Words: Essays on Criticism, Theory, and Writing by Black Women.* Piscataway, N.J.: Rutgers University Press, 1989.

Watts, Jane. *Black Writers from South Africa: Towards a Discourse of Liberation.* New York: St. Martin's Press, 1989.

Weimar, Karl S., ed. *German Language and Literature: Seven Essays.* Englewood Cliffs, N.J.: Prentice Hall, 1974.

Weiss, Beno. *Italo Svevo.* Boston: Twayne, 1987.

———. *Understanding Italo Calvino.* Columbia: University of South Carolina Press, 1995.

Weiss, Timothy F. *On the Margins: The Art of Exile in V. S. Naipaul.* Boston: University of Massachusetts Press, 1992.

Wellington, Beth. *Reflections on Lorca's Private Mythology: Once Five Years Pass and the Rural Plays.* New York: Peter Lang, 1993.

Welsh, David J. *Adam Mickiewicz.* Boston: Twayne, 1966.

White, Clement A. *Decoding the Word: Nicolas Guillen as Maker and Debunker of Myth.* Miami, Fla.: Universal, 1993.

Whitford, Frank. *Oskar Kokoschka: A Life.* New York: Atheneum, 1986.

Whitmore, Katherine P. R. *The Generation of 1898 in Spain as Seen Through Its Fictional Hero.* Northampton, Mass.: Smith College, 1936.

Willbanks, Ray. *Australian Voices: Writers and Their Work.* Austin: University of Texas Press, 1991.

Williams, Eric, ed. *The Dark Flutes of Fall: Critical Essays on Georg Trakl.* Rochester, N.Y.: Camden House, 1991.

Williams, John. *Goethe: A Critical Biography.* Oxford, England: Blackwell Publishers, 2001.

Williams, Raymond L. *The Writings of Carlos Fuentes.* Austin: University of Texas Press, 1996.

Wilson, Machiko N. *The Marginal World of Ōe Kenzaburō: A Study in Themes and Techniques.* Armonk, N.Y.: M. E. Sharpe, 1986.

Wisse, Ruth R. *I. L. Peretz and the Making of Modern Jewish Culture.* Seattle: University of Washington Press, 1991.

Wolf, Christa. *Cassandra: A Novel and Four Essays.* Translated by Jan van Heurck. New York: Farrar, Straus & Giroux, 1984.

Wolfe, Peter, ed. *Critical Essays on Patrick White.* Boston: G. K. Hall, 1990.

Wolpert, Stanley. *Gandhi's Passion: The Life and Legacy of Gandhi.* New York: Oxford University Press, 2001.

Wright, Derek. *Wole Soyinka Revisited.* Boston: Twayne, 1993.

Wright, Edgar, ed. *The Critical Evaluation of African Literature.* London: Heinemann, 1973.

Wullschlager, Jackie. *Hans Christian Andersen: The Life of a Storyteller.* New York: Knopf, 2001.

Yamada Eimi. *Monkey Brain Sushi: New Tastes in Japanese Fiction.* Translated by Terry Gallagher. New York: Kodansha International, 1991.

Yang, Winston L. Y., and Nathan K. Mao, eds. *Modern Chinese Fiction: A Guide to Its Study and Appreciation; Essays and Bibliographies.* Boston: G. K. Hall, 1981.

Yip Wai-Lim, ed. *Modern Chinese Poetry: Twenty Poets from the Republic of China, 1955–1965.* Iowa City: University of Iowa Press, 1970.

Yourcenar, Marguerite. *Mishima: A Vision of the Void.* Translated by Alberto Manguel. New York: Farrar, Straus & Giroux, 1986.

Yu Beongsheon. *Akutagawa: An Introduction.* Detroit: Wayne State University Press, 1972.

———. *Han Yong-un and Yi Kwang-su: Two Pioneers of Modern Korean Literature.* Detroit: Wayne State University Press, 1992.

Zeidan, Joseph. *Arab Women Novelists.* Binghamton: State University of New York Press, 1995.

Zhao, Henry Y. H. *Towards a Modern Zen Theatre: Gao Xingian and Chinese Theatre Experimentalism.* London, England: School of Oriental and African Studies, 2000.

Ziolkowski, Theodore. *Herman Broch.* New York: Columbia University Press, 1964.

INDEX